Colorado's Territorial Masons:

An Annotated Index of the *Proceedings of the Grand Lodge of Colorado*, 1861-1876

Compiled by Dina C. Carson

Colorado's Territorial Masons:

An Annotated Index of the *Proceedings of the Grand Lodge of Colorado*, 1861-1876

Compiled by Dina C. Carson

Published by:
Iron Gate Publishing
P.O. Box 999
Niwot, CO 80544

All rights reserved. No part of this book may be reproduced or transmitted in any form or by any means, electronic or mechanical, including photocopying, recording or any information storage and retrieval system without written permission from the author, except for the inclusion of brief quotations in a review.

The Publisher of this directory makes no representation that it is absolutely accurate or complete. Errors and omissions, whether typographical, clerical or otherwise do sometimes occur and may occur anywhere within the body of this publication. The Publisher does not assume and hereby disclaims any liability to any party for loss or damage by errors or omissions in this publication, whether such errors or omissions result from negligence, accident or any other cause.

Iron Gate Publishing has used its best efforts in collecting and preparing material for inclusion in the *Colorado's Territorial Masons: An Annotated Index of the Proceedings of the Grand Lodge of Colorado, 1861-1876*, but does not warrant that the information herein is complete or accurate, and does not assume, and hereby disclaims, any liability to any person for any loss or damage caused by errors or ommissions in the *Colorado's Territorial Masons: An Annotated Index of the Proceedings of the Grand Lodge of Colorado, 1861-1876*, whether such errors or omissions result from negligence, accident or any other cause.

Copyright © 2013 by Dina C. Carson
Printed in the United States of America

ISBN   1-879579-85-5   978-1-879579-85-9

Introduction

The Masons have a history in Colorado longer than the state or territory itself. The first Masonic lodges formed in the area were done so under the auspices of the Kansas and Nebraska Grand Lodges. The territory now known as Colorado was split along the 40th parallel (the baseline), with the northern area belonging to Nebraska Territory and the southern area belonging to Kansas Territory. There were probably some gold seekers in the area west of the continental divide belonging to Utah Territory before 1861, although there were no Masonic lodges formed in that area until much later.

The Kansas Grand Lodge allowed lodges to form at Auraria and Nevadaville, and granted a charter to the Golden City lodge as Golden City Lodge No. 34. That lodge would become Golden City Lodge No. 1 under the Colorado Grand Lodge a few years later. The lodge at Auraria would become Denver Lodge No. 5, and the lodge at Nevadaville would become Nevada Lodge No. 4.

The Nebraska Grand Lodge granted charters to Summit Lodge No. 7 in Parkville, and Rocky Mountain Lodge No. 8 in Gold Hill. These lodges would become the second and third lodges to form under the Colorado Grand Lodge. Unfortunately, neither of these lodges survived very long. They were established in early mining camps that did not meet the test of ore or time.

During the Territorial period, the following lodges were established:

- Golden City Lodge No. 1, Golden City
- Summit Lodge No. 2, Parkville (dispensation surrendered)
- Rocky Mountain Lodge No. 3, Gold Hill (extinct)
- Nevada Lodge No. 4, Nevadaville
- Denver Lodge No. 5, Denver
- Chivington Lodge No. 6, Central City (name changed to Central No. 6 in 1868)
- Union Lodge No. 7, Denver
- Empire Lodge NO. 8, Empire City
- Montana Lodge No. 9, Virginia City, Montana Terr (to Grand Lodge of Montana)
- Helena Lodge No. 10, Helena City, Montana Terr (to Grand Lodge of Montana)
- Black Hawk Lodge No. 11, Black Hawk
- Washington Lodge No. 12, Georgetown
- El Paso Lodge No. 13, Colorado City
- Columbia Lodge No. 14, Boulder City
- Mount Moriah Lodge No. 15, Canon City
- Cheyenne Lodge No. 16, Cheyenne, Dakota Terr (Wyoming Territory) (to Grand Lodge of Wyoming)
- Pueblo Lodge No. 17, Pueblo
- Laramie Lodge No. 18, Laramie, Wyoming Territory (to Grand Lodge of Wyoming)
- Collins Lodge No. 19, Fort Collins
- Occidental Lodge No. 20, Greeley
- Argenta Lodge No. 21, Salt Lake City (to Grand Lodge of Utah)
- Weston Lodge No. 22, Littleton
- St Vrain Lodge No. 23, Longmont
- Evanston Lodge No. 24, Evanston, Wyoming Territory (to Grand Lodge of Wyoming)
- Doric Lodge No. 25, Fairplay
- Idaho Springs No. 26, Idaho Springs

Colorado's Territorial Masons

    Huerfano Lodge No. 27, Walsenburg
    Las Animas Lodge No. 28, Trinidad
    Del Norte Lodge No. 29, Del Norte
    King Solomon Lodge No. 30, West Las Animas
    South Pueblo Lodge No. 31, South Pueblo

There were also a few lodges that formed under dispensation but did not become full lodges including the Valmont Lodge, U. D., at Valmont (dispensation surrendered), the Germania Lodge U. D. at Denver (dispensation surrendered), and the Grand Island Lodge U. D., at Middle Boulder (now Nederland). There was no clear indication from the Proceedings what became of the Grand Island Lodge U. D. except that it was not granted a charter. Nearing the end of the Territorial period, the Olive Branch Lodge U. D., at Saguache was formed and would become Olive Branch Lodge No. 32.

The Proceedings

The annotated listings are taken from the annual Proceedings of the Colorado Grand Lodge, A. F. and A. M. The full titles of each of these publications are as follows with the abbreviation used in the listing:

Proceedings of the Grand Lodge of Colorado of the Most Ancient and Honorable Fraternity of Free and Accepted Masons, and its Several Communications from A L 4861 to A L 5899 Inclusive (Proceedings 1861-1869).

Proceedings of the M. W. Grand Lodge of A. F. and A. M. of Colorado at its Tenth Annual Communication Held at Central, September 27 and 28, A. D. 1870, A. L. 5870 (Proceedings 1870).

Proceedings of the M. W. Grand Lodge of A. F. and A. M. of Colorado at its Eleventh Annual Communication Held at Central, September 26 and 27, A. D. 1871, A. L. 5871 (Proceedings 1871).

Proceedings of the M. W. Grand Lodge of A. F. and A. M. of Colorado at its Twelth Annual Communication Held at Central, September 24th, 1872, A. L. 5872 (Proceedings 1872).

Proceedings of the M. W. Grand Lodge of A. F. and A. M. of Colorado at its 13th Annual Communication Held at Denver, Sept. 30 and Oct. 1, 1873, A. L. 5873 (Proceedings 1873).

Proceedings of the M. W. Grand Lodge of A. F. and A. M. of Colorado at its 14th Annual Communication Held at Denver, Sept. 29 and 30, 1874, A. L. 5874 (Proceedings 1874).

Proceedings of the M. W. Grand Lodge A. F. and A. M. of Colorado, at an Emergent Communication Held Sept 20, A. L. 5875, at Boulder, to Lay the Corner Stone of the Territorial University, at its Fifteenth Annual Communication Held at Denver, September 21 and 22, 1875, A. L. 5875 (Colorado University Cornerstone Laying).

Proceedings of the Grand Lodge of Colorado Held at Denver, September 21st and 22nd, A. D. 1875, A. L. 5875. Fifteenth Annual Communication (Proceedings 1875).

Proceedings of the M. W. Grand Lodge of A. F. and A. M of Colorado at its Sixteenth Annual Communication Held at Denver, September 19 and 20, A. D. 1876, A. L. 5876 (Proceedings 1876).

Names

Names are listed exactly as they are given in the *Proceedings*. On occasion where known mistakes were found, a correction to the correct name will appear in brackets.

There are a few listings with common names that are a combined listing for more than one individual. Masons did not join more than one lodge simultaneously. They obtained a demit from their original lodge before joining a lodge in a new place of residence.

Terms

Some of the following terms are used to indicate what each person's role was when mentioned in the *Proceedings*:

Introduction

Title: Each of the men who attended the Grand Lodge had a title. The following titles belonged to elected offices: Grand Master, Deputy Grand Master, Senior Grand Warden, Junior Grand Warden, Grand Treasurer and Grand Secretary.

These positions were appointed: Grand Chaplain, Grand Orator, Grand Lecturer, Grand Marshal, Senior Grand Deacon, Junior Grand Deacon, Grand Steward and Grand Tiler.

Committee: The individual was a member of one of the Grand Lodge committees. The designation "committee" followed by a city indicates the individual's place of residence.

Motion or Resolution: The member was offering a motion or a resolution.

Apprentice and Fellowcraft: Masons earn degrees in stages. An individual with either of these terms in his listing was a new member earning his degrees.

Demitted: The individual had requested to leave his lodge usually to join a lodge in a different area.

Dropped from the rolls: Members who were not current with dues could be dropped from the rolls.

Lodge Name: When individuals appear in the returns for each lodge, the name of the lodge will appear after the date, indicating membership. Many lodge names are followed by the city where the lodge meets. Where the location of the lodge is not apparent from the name, the city where the lodge met has been included. Some lodges met in more than one location during the period covered by this index.

Grand Lodge of [another state]: Members of the Colorado Grand Lodge served as representatives of the Grand Lodges of other states to the Colorado Grand Lodge, and members of other Grand Lodges served as representatives of the Grand Lodge of Colorado in their home states. Communications were received from other lodges around the country and around the world. If names were mentioned within those communications, they have been included in this index with an indication of where the individual lived or belonged to a Masonic lodge.

U D: Under dispensation. When new lodges were formed they were granted dispensation to form and meet, but were only given a charter if they met certain requirements.

Every effort has been made to assure that these listings are correct, however, we can only be as accurate as the *Proceedings* themselves were, so some listings may contain inaccuracies. We hope you enjoy as much as we have the discoveries we have made about Colorado's Territorial Masons.

— The Boulder Pioneers Project

A

Abbot, E H
Proceedings 1872, pg 33 (1872 Sept 24), Occidental Lodge No. 20, Greeley

Abbott, Alex G
Proceedings 1874, pg 46 (1874 Sept 30) Grand Lodge of California

Abbott, C S
Proceedings 1861-1869, pg 166 (1866 Oct 2), Nevada Lodge No. 4, Nevadaville
Proceedings 1861-1869, pg 170 (1866 Oct 2), Black Hawk Lodge U D, Black Hawk
Proceedings 1871, pg 23 (1871 Sept 27), Black Hawk Lodge No. 11, Black Hawk

Abbott, Charles S
Proceedings 1861-1869, pg 192 (1867 Oct 8), Nevada Lodge No. 4, Nevadaville, Dimitted
Proceedings 1861-1869, pg 196 (1867 Oct 8), Black Hawk Lodge No. 11, Black Hawk
Proceedings 1870, pg 25 (1870 Sept 28), Black Hawk Lodge No. 11, Black Hawk
Proceedings 1872, pg 25 (1872 Sept 24), Black Hawk Lodge No. 11, Black Hawk, Dropped from the Rolls

Abbott, Chas S
Proceedings 1861-1869, pg 111 (1863 Nov 3), Nevada Lodge No. 4, Nevadaville
Proceedings 1861-1869, pg 132 (1864 Nov 8), Nevada Lodge No. 4, Nevadaville
Proceedings 1861-1869, pg 148 (1865 Nov 7), Nevada Lodge No. 4, Nevadaville
Proceedings 1861-1869, pg 227 (1868 Oct 7), Black Hawk Lodge No. 11, Black Hawk
Proceedings 1861-1869, pg 309 (1869 Sept 29), Black Hawk Lodge No. 11, Black Hawk

Abbott, E H
Proceedings 1871, pg 30 (1871 Sept 27), Occidental Lodge U D, Greeley
Proceedings 1873, pg 49 (1873 Oct 1), Occidental Lodge No. 20, Greeley
Proceedings 1874, pg 225 (1874 Sept 30), Occidental Lodge No. 20, Greeley
Proceedings 1875, pg 87 (1875 Sept 22), Occidental Lodge No. 20, Greeley

Abbott, Eugene H
Proceedings 1876, pg 40 (1876 Sept 20), Occidental Lodge No. 20, Greeley

Abel, Alex G
Proceedings 1872, pg 56 (1872 Sept 24) Grand Lodge of California

Abell, A G
Proceedings 1861-1869, pg 240 (1867 Oct 8) Grand Secretary of California

Abell, Alex G
Proceedings 1861-1869, pg 316 (1869 Sept 29) Grand Lodge of California
Proceedings 1870, pg 34 (1870 Sept 28) Grand Secretary, Grand Lodge of California
Proceedings 1870, pg 45 (1869 Oct 12) Grand Secretary, Grand Lodge of California
Proceedings 1870, pg 48 (1869 Oct 12) Grand Secretary, Grand Lodge of California
Proceedings 1871, pg 35 (1871 Sept 27) Grand Secretary, Grand Lodge of California
Proceedings 1872, pg 43 (1872 Sept 24) San Francisco, Grand Lodge of California
Proceedings 1873, pg 60 (1873 Oct 1) Grand Lodge of California, San Francisco
Proceedings 1874, pg 204 (1874 Sept 30) Grand Lodge of California, San Francisco
Proceedings 1875, pg 24 (1875 Sept 21) Grand Lodge of California
Proceedings 1875, pg 96 (1875 Sept 22) Grand Lodge of California, San Francisco
Proceedings 1876, pg 54 (1876 Sept 20) Grand Lodge of California, San Francisco

Abell, Alexander G
Proceedings 1861-1869, pg 240 (1867 Oct 8) Grand Secretary of California
Proceedings 1861-1869, pg 324 (1868 Oct 18) Grand Secretary, Grand Lodge of California

Abney, Jackson
Proceedings 1874, pg 221 (1874 Sept 30), Cheyenne Lodge No. 16, Cheyenne, Wyoming Territory

Abrams, Moses
Proceedings 1872, pg 19 (1872 Sept 24), Denver Lodge No. 5, Denver
Proceedings 1873, pg 37 (1873 Oct 1), Denver Lodge No. 5, Denver, Dimitted

Ackerman, Jas
Proceedings 1874, pg 227 (1874 Sept 30), St Vrain No. 23, Longmont

Adams, B C
Proceedings 1873, pg 50 (1873 Oct 1), Occidental Lodge No. 20, Greeley
Proceedings 1874, pg 225 (1874 Sept 30), Occidental Lodge No. 20, Greeley
Proceedings 1875, pg 87 (1875 Sept 22), Occidental Lodge No. 20, Greeley
Proceedings 1876, pg 40 (1876 Sept 20), Occidental Lodge No. 20, Greeley

Adams, Charles B
Proceedings 1861-1869, pg 312 (1869 Sept 29), Pueblo Lodge No. 17, Pueblo, Fellowcraft
Proceedings 1870, pg 30 (1870 Sept 28), Pueblo Lodge No. 17, Pueblo
Proceedings 1871, pg 28 (1871 Sept 27), Pueblo Lodge No. 17, Pueblo
Proceedings 1873, pg 47 (1873 Oct 1), Pueblo Lodge No. 17, Pueblo
Proceedings 1874, pg 222 (1874 Sept 30), Pueblo Lodge No. 17, Pueblo, Pueblo County
Proceedings 1876, pg 38 (1876 Sept 20) Pueblo Lodge No. 17

Colorado's Territorial Masons

Adams, Chas
Proceedings 1876, pg 36 (1876 Sept 20), El Paso Lodge No. 13, Colorado City, Apprentice

Adams, Chas B
Proceedings 1875, pg 85 (1875 Sept 22) Pueblo Lodge No. 17

Adams, F E
Proceedings 1873, pg 46 (1873 Oct 1), Cheyenne Lodge No. 16, Cheyenne, Wyoming Territory

Adams, G H
Proceedings 1861-1869, pg 306 (1869 Sept 29), Central Lodge No. 6, Central City

Adams, G S
Proceedings 1873, pg cover (1873 Oct 1), Pueblo Chapter No. 3, Pueblo

Adams, Geo H
Proceedings 1861-1869, pg 224 (1868 Oct 7), Chivington Lodge No. 6, Central City
Proceedings 1870, pg 22 (1870 Sept 28), Central Lodge No. 6, Central City
Proceedings 1871, pg 20 (1871 Sept 27), Central Lodge No. 6, Central
Proceedings 1872, pg 21 (1872 Sept 24), Denver Lodge No. 5, Denver
Proceedings 1873, pg 3 (1873 Sept 30) Grand Chaplain
Proceedings 1873, pg 4 (1873 Sept 30) pall bearer for George M Randall
Proceedings 1873, pg 16 (1873 Oct 1) Grand Chaplain
Proceedings 1874, pg 212 (1874 Sept 30), Central Lodge No. 6, Central

Adams, Geo S
Proceedings 1875, pg 85 (1875 Sept 22) Pueblo Lodge No. 17

Adams, George H
Proceedings 1873, pg 38 (1873 Oct 1), Central Lodge No. 6, Central City
Proceedings 1875, pg 77 (1875 Sept 22), Central Lodge No. 6, Central City, Stricken from the rolls

Adams, George S
Proceedings 1874, pg 222 (1874 Sept 30), Pueblo Lodge No. 17, Pueblo, Pueblo County
Proceedings 1876, pg 38 (1876 Sept 20) Pueblo Lodge No. 17

Adams, J N
Proceedings 1861-1869, pg 113 (1863 Nov 3), Chivington Lodge No. 6, Central City
Proceedings 1861-1869, pg 134 (1864 Nov 8), Chivington Lodge No. 6, Central City
Proceedings 1861-1869, pg 150 (1865 Nov 7), Chivington Lodge No. 6, Central City
Proceedings 1861-1869, pg 168 (1866 Oct 2), Chivington Lodge No. 6, Central City
Proceedings 1861-1869, pg 193 (1867 Oct 8), Chivington Lodge No. 6, Central City
Proceedings 1861-1869, pg 224 (1868 Oct 7), Chivington Lodge No. 6, Central City
Proceedings 1861-1869, pg 306 (1869 Sept 29), Central Lodge No. 6, Central City
Proceedings 1870, pg 22 (1870 Sept 28), Central Lodge No. 6, Central City
Proceedings 1871, pg 20 (1871 Sept 27), Central Lodge No. 6, Central
Proceedings 1872, pg 22 (1872 Sept 24), Denver Lodge No. 5, Denver, Stricken from the Roll

Adams, M S
Proceedings 1861-1869, pg 253 (1867 Oct 15), Grand Master, Grand Lodge of Kansas
Proceedings 1861-1869, pg 330 (1868 Oct 20) Grand Master, Grand Lodge of Kansas

Adams, W H
Proceedings 1861-1869, pg 157 (1866 Oct 1), deceased, Grand Secretary, Grand Lodge of Pennsylvania

Addleman, J S
Proceedings 1861-1869, pg 167 (1866 Oct 2) Denver Lodge No. 5
Proceedings 1861-1869, pg 192 (1867 Oct 8) Denver Lodge No. 5
Proceedings 1861-1869, pg 223 (1868 Oct 7) Denver Lodge No. 5
Proceedings 1861-1869, pg 305 (1869 Sept 29) Denver Lodge No. 5
Proceedings 1870, pg 21 (1870 Sept 28), Denver Lodge No. 5, Denver
Proceedings 1872, pg 20 (1872 Sept 24), Denver Lodge No. 5, Denver

Addome, F E
Proceedings 1861-1869, pg 312 (1869 Sept 29), Cheyenne Lodge No. 16, Cheyenne

Addoms, F C
Proceedings 1870, pg 28 (1870 Sept 28), Cheyenne Lodge No. 16, Cheyenne, Wyoming Territory

Addoms, F E
Proceedings 1871, pg 27 (1871 Sept 27), Cheyenne Lodge No. 16, Cheyenne, Wyoming Territory
Proceedings 1872, pg 29 (1872 Sept 24), Cheyenne Lodge No. 16, Cheyenne, Wyoming Territory
Proceedings 1874, pg 6 (1874 Sept 29), Cheyenne Lodge No. 16, Cheyenne, Wyoming Territory
Proceedings 1874, pg 6 (1874 Sept 29) committee
Proceedings 1874, pg 21 (1874 Sept 29) committee
Proceedings 1874, pg 32 (1874 Sept 30) Senior Grand Steward, Cheyenne
Proceedings 1874, pg 32 (1874 Sept 30) committee
Proceedings 1874, pg 36 (1874 Sept 30) committee
Proceedings 1874, pg 36 (1874 Sept 30) per diem
Proceedings 1874, pg 220 (1874 Sept 30), Cheyenne Lodge No. 16, Cheyenne, Wyoming Territory

African Lodge No. 459
Proceedings 1870, pg 73 (1784 Sept 29) City of Boston

Aicheson, W
Proceedings 1861-1869, pg 224 (1868 Oct 7), Chivington Lodge No. 6, Central City

Aicheson, William
Proceedings 1872, pg 21 (1872 Sept 24), Denver Lodge No. 5, Denver
Proceedings 1874, pg 212 (1874 Sept 30), Central Lodge No. 6, Central

Aicheson, Wm
Proceedings 1861-1869, pg 193 (1867 Oct 8), Chivington Lodge No. 6, Central City
Proceedings 1861-1869, pg 306 (1869 Sept 29), Central Lodge No. 6, Central City
Proceedings 1870, pg 22 (1870 Sept 28), Central Lodge No. 6, Central City

Aitcheson, William
Proceedings 1873, pg 38 (1873 Oct 1), Central Lodge No. 6, Central City
Proceedings 1875, pg 76 (1875 Sept 22), Central Lodge No. 6, Central City
Proceedings 1876, pg 32 (1876 Sept 20), Central Lodge No. 6, Central City

Aitcheson, Wm
Proceedings 1861-1869, pg 168 (1866 Oct 2), Chivington Lodge No. 6, Central City
Proceedings 1871, pg 20 (1871 Sept 27), Central Lodge No. 6, Central

Alane, Andrew
Proceedings 1861-1869, pg 223 (1868 Oct 7) Denver Lodge No. 5

Alber, Charles
Proceedings 1861-1869, pg 77 (1862 Nov 4), Nevada Lodge No. 4, Nevadaville, Apprentice
Proceedings 1861-1869, pg 111 (1863 Nov 3), Nevada Lodge No. 4, Nevadaville, Fellowcraft
Proceedings 1861-1869, pg 192 (1867 Oct 8), Nevada Lodge No. 4, Nevadaville, Fellowcraft

Alber, Chas
Proceedings 1861-1869, pg 132 (1864 Nov 8), Nevada Lodge No. 4, Nevadaville, Fellowcraft
Proceedings 1861-1869, pg 148 (1865 Nov 7), Nevada Lodge No. 4, Nevadaville, Fellowcraft
Proceedings 1861-1869, pg 166 (1866 Oct 2), Nevada Lodge No. 4, Nevadaville, Fellowcraft
Proceedings 1861-1869, pg 222 (1868 Oct 7), Nevada Lodge No. 4, Nevadaville, Fellowcraft

Alcorn, John A
Proceedings 1876, pg 40 (1876 Sept 20), Occidental Lodge No. 20, Greeley

Alden, A B
Proceedings 1873, pg 61 (1873 Oct 1) Grand Lodge of Wisconsin, Portage City

Aldrich, J M
Proceedings 1861-1869, pg 166 (1866 Oct 2), Nevada Lodge No. 4, Nevadaville, Fellowcraft
Proceedings 1861-1869, pg 192 (1867 Oct 8), Nevada Lodge No. 4, Nevadaville
Proceedings 1861-1869, pg 304 (1869 Sept 29), Nevada Lodge No. 4, Nevadaville

Aldrich, John M
Proceedings 1861-1869, pg 222 (1868 Oct 7), Nevada Lodge No. 4, Nevadaville
Proceedings 1870, pg 20 (1870 Sept 28), Nevada Lodge No. 4, Nevadaville
Proceedings 1871, pg 18 (1871 Sept 27), Nevada Lodge No. 4, Bald Mountain
Proceedings 1872, pg 18 (1872 Sept 24), Nevada Lodge No. 4, Bald Mountain
Proceedings 1873, pg 36 (1873 Oct 1), Nevada Lodge No. 4, Nevada
Proceedings 1874, pg 211 (1874 Sept 30), Nevada Lodge No. 4, Bald Mountain, Gilpin County, Stricken from the rolls

Alexander, John M
Proceedings 1875, pg 90 (1875 Sept 22), Huerfano Lodge U D, Walsenburg
Proceedings 1876, pg 43 (1876 Sept 20), Huerfano Lodge No. 27, Walsenburg

Alkins, Alex W
Proceedings 1875, pg 79 (1875 Sept 22), Union Lodge No. 7, Denver, Apprentice

Allason, W J
Proceedings 1872, pg 30 (1872 Sept 24), Cheyenne Lodge No. 16, Cheyenne, Wyoming Territory, Fellowcraft

Allen, A P
Proceedings 1861-1869, pg 77 (1862 Nov 4) Denver Lodge No. 5
Proceedings 1861-1869, pg 112 (1863 Nov 3) Denver Lodge No. 5
Proceedings 1861-1869, pg 133 (1864 Nov 8) Denver Lodge No. 5
Proceedings 1861-1869, pg 149 (1865 Nov 7), Nevada Lodge No. 4, Nevadaville
Proceedings 1861-1869, pg 167 (1866 Oct 2) Denver Lodge No. 5
Proceedings 1861-1869, pg 192 (1867 Oct 8) Denver Lodge No. 5
Proceedings 1861-1869, pg 224 (1868 Oct 7) Denver Lodge No. 5, Dimitted
Proceedings 1861-1869, pg 230 (1868 Oct 7), Valmont Lodge U D, Valmont

Allen, Chas B
Proceedings 1872, pg 31 (1872 Sept 24), Pueblo Lodge No. 17, Pueblo

Allen, H E
Proceedings 1873, pg 6 (1873 Sept 30), Weston Lodge No. 22, Littleton
Proceedings 1873, pg 32 (1873 Oct 1) mileage and per diem
Proceedings 1874, pg 226 (1874 Sept 30), Weston Lodge No. 22, Littleton
Proceedings 1876, pg 41 (1876 Sept 20), Weston Lodge No. 22, Littleton

Allen, H W
Proceedings 1861-1869, pg 168 (1866 Oct 2), Chivington Lodge No. 6, Central City

Colorado's Territorial Masons

Allen, H W, cont.
    Proceedings 1861-1869, pg 194 (1867 Oct 8), Chivington Lodge No. 6, Central City, Dimitted
    Proceedings 1861-1869, pg 230 (1868 Oct 7), Valmont Lodge U D, Valmont

Allen, Henry
    Proceedings 1872, pg 74 (1872 Sept 24) Grand Lodge of Montana, deceased

Allen, Henry E
    Proceedings 1872, pg 7 (1872 Sept 24), [Weston] Lodge U D, Littleton
    Proceedings 1872, pg 34 (1872 Sept 24), Weston Lodge No. 22, Littleton
    Proceedings 1873, pg 17 (1873 Oct 1) Junior Grand Warden
    Proceedings 1873, pg 51 (1873 Oct 1), Weston Lodge No. 22, Littleton
    Proceedings 1874, pg 4 (1874 Sept 29) Junior Grand Steward
    Proceedings 1875, pg 88 (1875 Sept 22), Weston Lodge No. 22, Littleton
    Proceedings 1876, pg 41 (1876 Sept 20), Weston Lodge No. 22, Littleton

Allen, J L
    Proceedings 1871, pg 29 (1871 Sept 27), Laramie Lodge No. 18, Laramie, Wyoming Territory, Apprentice
    Proceedings 1873, pg 48 (1873 Oct 1), Laramie Lodge No. 18, Laramie, Wyoming Territory, Apprentice
    Proceedings 1874, pg 224 (1874 Sept 30), Laramie Lodge No. 18, Laramie City,, permission granted to take degrees in Lebanon Lodge No. 32, Laconia, NH

Allen, J S
    Proceedings 1870, pg 31 (1870 Sept 28), Laramie Lodge No. 18, Laramie, Wyoming Territory, Apprentice

Allen, J T
    Proceedings 1872, pg 32 (1872 Sept 24), Laramie Lodge No. 18, Laramie, Wyoming Territory, Apprentice

Allen, James D
    Proceedings 1861-1869, pg 309 (1869 Sept 29), Washington Lodge No. 12, Georgetown
    Proceedings 1870, pg 26 (1870 Sept 28), Washington Lodge No. 12, Georgetown
    Proceedings 1871, pg 24 (1871 Sept 27), Washington Lodge No. 12, Georgetown
    Proceedings 1872, pg 25 (1872 Sept 24), Washington Lodge No. 12, Georgetown
    Proceedings 1873, pg 42 (1873 Oct 1), Washington Lodge No. 12, Georgetown
    Proceedings 1874, pg 218 (1874 Sept 30), Washington Lodge No. 12, Georgetown, Stricken from the rolls

Allen, Jas D
    Proceedings 1861-1869, pg 227 (1868 Oct 7), Washington Lodge No. 12, Georgetown

Allen, Jno
    Proceedings 1861-1869, pg 77 (1862 Nov 4), Nevada Lodge No. 4, Nevadaville

Allen, John
    Proceedings 1861-1869, pg 111 (1863 Nov 3), Nevada Lodge No. 4, Nevadaville
    Proceedings 1861-1869, pg 132 (1864 Nov 8), Nevada Lodge No. 4, Nevadaville, dimitted

Allen, L A
    Proceedings 1870, pg 30 (1870 Sept 28), Pueblo Lodge No. 17, Pueblo, Apprentice
    Proceedings 1871, pg 28 (1871 Sept 27), Pueblo Lodge No. 17, Pueblo, Apprentice
    Proceedings 1872, pg 31 (1872 Sept 24), Pueblo Lodge No. 17, Pueblo
    Proceedings 1873, pg 47 (1873 Oct 1), Pueblo Lodge No. 17, Pueblo
    Proceedings 1874, pg 222 (1874 Sept 30), Pueblo Lodge No. 17, Pueblo, Pueblo County
    Proceedings 1875, pg 85 (1875 Sept 22) Pueblo Lodge No. 17, Demitted

Allen, S P
    Proceedings 1861-1869, pg 226 (1868 Oct 7), Empire Lodge No. 8, Empire City

Allen, Saml P
    Proceedings 1861-1869, pg 308 (1869 Sept 29), Empire Lodge No. 8, Empire City

Allen, Samuel P
    Proceedings 1861-1869, pg 170 (1866 Oct 2), Empire Lodge No. 8, Empire City
    Proceedings 1861-1869, pg 195 (1867 Oct 8), Empire Lodge No. 8, Empire City
    Proceedings 1870, pg 24 (1870 Sept 28), Empire Lodge No. 8, Empire
    Proceedings 1872, pg 23 (1872 Sept 24), Empire Lodge No. 8, Empire
    Proceedings 1873, pg 40 (1873 Oct 1), Empire Lodge No. 8, Empire
    Proceedings 1874, pg 215 (1874 Sept 30), Empire Lodge No. 8, Empire

Allen, W F
    Proceedings 1874, pg 223 (1874 Sept 30), Laramie Lodge No. 18, Laramie City

Allen, W H
    Proceedings 1861-1869, pg 150 (1865 Nov 7), Chivington Lodge No. 6, Central City

Allen, W W
    Proceedings 1872, pg 36 (1872 Sept 24), Ashlar Lodge U D, Colorado Springs

Allen, Wm A
    Proceedings 1872, pg 44 (1872 Sept 24), Grand Lodge of Pennsylvania

Allen, Wm F
    Proceedings 1861-1869, pg 193 (1867 Oct 8), Chivington Lodge No. 6, Central City
    Proceedings 1861-1869, pg 224 (1868 Oct 7), Chivington Lodge No. 6, Central City
    Proceedings 1861-1869, pg 306 (1869 Sept 29), Central Lodge No. 6, Central City

Proceedings 1870, pg 23 (1870 Sept 28), Central Lodge No. 6, Central City, Dimitted

Allen, Z G
Proceedings 1861-1869, pg 312 (1869 Sept 29), Pueblo Lodge No. 17, Pueblo
Proceedings 1870, pg 29 (1870 Sept 28), Pueblo Lodge No. 17, Pueblo
Proceedings 1871, pg 28 (1871 Sept 27), Pueblo Lodge No. 17, Pueblo
Proceedings 1872, pg 30 (1872 Sept 24), Pueblo Lodge No. 17, Pueblo
Proceedings 1873, pg 47 (1873 Oct 1), Pueblo Lodge No. 17, Pueblo
Proceedings 1874, pg 222 (1874 Sept 30), Pueblo Lodge No. 17, Pueblo, Pueblo County
Proceedings 1875, pg 85 (1875 Sept 22) Pueblo Lodge No. 17, died
Proceedings 1875, pg 94 (1875 Sept 22) Pueblo Lodge No. 17

Allison, John B
Proceedings 1876, pg 50 (1876 Sept 20), Las Animas Lodge No. 28, Trinidad

Allison, W J
Proceedings 1873, pg 46 (1873 Oct 1), Cheyenne Lodge No. 16, Cheyenne, Wyoming Territory, Fellowcraft
Proceedings 1874, pg 221 (1874 Sept 30), Cheyenne Lodge No. 16, Cheyenne, Wyoming Territory, Fellowcraft

Allisson, John B
Proceedings 1876, pg 44 (1876 Sept 20), Las Animas Lodge No. 28, Trinidad

Alliston, John B
Proceedings 1875, pg 91 (1875 Sept 22), Las Animas Lodge U D, Trinidad

Allmond, J P
Proceedings 1861-1869, pg 327 (1868 June 27) Grand Secretary, Grand Lodge of Delaware
Proceedings 1870, pg 52 (1869 June 28) Grand Secretary, Grand Lodge of Delaware
Proceedings 1872, pg 43 (1872 Sept 24) Wilmington, Grand Lodge of Delaware
Proceedings 1873, pg 60 (1873 Oct 1) Grand Lodge of Delaware, Wilmington
Proceedings 1874, pg 51 (1874 Sept 30) Grand Lodge of Delaware

Allmond, John P
Proceedings 1861-1869, pg 316 (1869 Sept 29) Grand Lodge of Delaware
Proceedings 1870, pg 34 (1870 Sept 28) Grand Secretary, Grand Lodge of Delaware
Proceedings 1871, pg 35 (1871 Sept 27) Grand Secretary, Grand Lodge of Delaware
Proceedings 1874, pg 204 (1874 Sept 30) Grand Lodge of Delaware, Wilmington

Almond, J P
Proceedings 1872, pg 58 (1872 Sept 24) Grand Lodge of Delaware

Alpina Grand Lodge
Proceedings 1872, pg 47 (1872 Sept 24), Berne, Switzerland

American Freemason
Proceedings 1861-1869, pg 291 (1869 Sept 28) of Cincinnati
Proceedings 1870, pg 11 (1870 Sept 27), Cincinnati, OH

Ames, L B
Proceedings 1873, pg 51 (1873 Oct 1), Weston Lodge No. 22, Littleton
Proceedings 1874, pg 226 (1874 Sept 30), Weston Lodge No. 22, Littleton

Ames, Lewis B
Proceedings 1872, pg 34 (1872 Sept 24), Weston Lodge No. 22, Littleton
Proceedings 1875, pg 88 (1875 Sept 22), Weston Lodge No. 22, Littleton
Proceedings 1876, pg 41 (1876 Sept 20), Weston Lodge No. 22, Littleton

Ames, T P
Proceedings 1861-1869, pg 80 (1863 May 6) Denver Lodge No. 5
Proceedings 1861-1869, pg 98 (1863 Nov 2) Denver Lodge No. 5
Proceedings 1861-1869, pg 99 (1863 Nov 2) Denver Lodge No. 5, Grand Orator
Proceedings 1861-1869, pg 100 (1863 Nov 2) committee
Proceedings 1861-1869, pg 100 (1863 Nov 3) Grand Orator
Proceedings 1861-1869, pg 103 (1863 Nov 3) Denver Lodge No. 5
Proceedings 1861-1869, pg 112 (1863 Nov 3) Denver Lodge No. 5
Proceedings 1861-1869, pg 305 (1869 Sept 29) Denver Lodge No. 5

Ames, Thomas P
Proceedings 1861-1869, pg 192 (1867 Oct 8) Denver Lodge No. 5
Proceedings 1870, pg 21 (1870 Sept 28), Denver Lodge No. 5, Denver
Proceedings 1872, pg 20 (1872 Sept 24), Denver Lodge No. 5, Denver

Ames, Thos P
Proceedings 1861-1869, pg 116 (1864 Nov 7) Denver Lodge No. 5
Proceedings 1861-1869, pg 223 (1868 Oct 7) Denver Lodge No. 5

Amos, W D
Proceedings 1861-1869, pg 147 (1865 Nov 7) Golden City Lodge No. 1

Amsbarry, Wm N
Proceedings 1872, pg 22 (1872 Sept 24), Denver Lodge No. 5, Denver

Amsbary, W A
Proceedings 1861-1869, pg 224 (1868 Oct 7), Chivington Lodge No. 6, Central City

11

Colorado's Territorial Masons

Amsbary, W A, cont.
Proceedings 1870, pg 15 (1870 Sept 28) now living at Georgetown, Central Lodge No. 6, Central City

Amsbary, Wm A
Proceedings 1861-1869, pg 299 (1869 Sept 29) Grand Chaplain

Amsbury
Proceedings 1876, pg 14 (1874 Nov 6) funeral held by 6 Nov 1874

Amsbury, L
Proceedings 1876, pg 14 (1874 Oct 6) receipt for money advanced by E T Stone

Amsbury, Lewis
Proceedings 1875, pg 33 (1875 Sept 22), St Paul Lodge No. 124, Auburn, NY

Amsbury, W A
Proceedings 1871, pg 20 (1871 Sept 27), Central Lodge No. 6, Central

Amsbury, Wm A
Proceedings 1861-1869, pg 193 (1867 Oct 8), Chivington Lodge No. 6, Central City
Proceedings 1861-1869, pg 306 (1869 Sept 29), Central Lodge No. 6, Central City
Proceedings 1870, pg 22 (1870 Sept 28), Central Lodge No. 6, Central City

Anderson, J C
Proceedings 1861-1869, pg 151 (1865 Nov 7), Chivington Lodge No. 6, Central City
Proceedings 1861-1869, pg 169 (1866 Oct 2), Union Lodge No. 7, Denver
Proceedings 1861-1869, pg 225 (1868 Oct 7), Union Lodge No. 7, Denver

Anderson, James
Proceedings 1874, pg 224 (1874 Sept 30), Laramie Lodge No. 18, Laramie City, Fellowcraft

Anderson, Jno C
Proceedings 1861-1869, pg 102 (1863 Nov 3) petition for formation of a new lodge in Denver
Proceedings 1871, pg 21 (1871 Sept 27), Union Lodge No. 7, Denver

Anderson, John C
Proceedings 1861-1869, pg 134 (1864 Nov 8), Union Lodge No. 7, Denver
Proceedings 1861-1869, pg 195 (1867 Oct 8), Union Lodge No. 7, Denver
Proceedings 1861-1869, pg 307 (1869 Sept 29), Union Lodge No. 7, Denver
Proceedings 1870, pg 23 (1870 Sept 28), Union Lodge No. 7, Denver
Proceedings 1872, pg 22 (1872 Sept 24), Union Lodge No. 7, Denver
Proceedings 1873, pg 39 (1873 Oct 1), Union Lodge No. 7, Denver
Proceedings 1874, pg 214 (1874 Sept 30), Union Lodge No. 7, Denver
Proceedings 1875, pg 78 (1875 Sept 22), Union Lodge No. 7, Denver
Proceedings 1876, pg 33 (1876 Sept 20), Union Lodge No. 7, Denver

Anderson, Joseph
Proceedings 1876, pg 29 (1876 Sept 20) Golden City Lodge No. 1

Anderson, Joseph M
Proceedings 1861-1869, pg 282 (1867 Oct 7), Grand Master, Grand Lodge of Tennessee
Proceedings 1861-1869, pg 346 (1868 Oct 4) Grand Master, Grand Lodge of Tennessee

Anderson, L C
Proceedings 1870, pg 30 (1870 Sept 28), Laramie Lodge No. 18, Laramie, Wyoming Territory

Anderson, O A
Proceedings 1876, pg 37 (1876 Sept 20), Columbia Lodge No. 14, Boulder, Apprentice

Anderson, P
Proceedings 1861-1869, pg 166 (1866 Oct 2), Nevada Lodge No. 4, Nevadaville
Proceedings 1861-1869, pg 222 (1868 Oct 7), Nevada Lodge No. 4, Nevadaville
Proceedings 1871, pg 29 (1871 Sept 27), Collins Lodge No. 19, Fort Collins
Proceedings 1876, pg 5 (1876 Sept 19), Collins Lodge No. 19, Fort Collins

Anderson, Peter
Proceedings 1872, pg 32 (1872 Sept 24), Collins Lodge No. 19, Fort Collins
Proceedings 1873, pg 49 (1873 Oct 1), Collins Lodge No. 19, Fort Collins
Proceedings 1874, pg 224 (1874 Sept 30), Collins Lodge No. 19, Fort Collins, Larimer County
Proceedings 1875, pg 86 (1875 Sept 22), Collins Lodge No. 19, Fort Collins
Proceedings 1876, pg 39 (1876 Sept 20), Collins Lodge No. 19, Fort Collins

Anderson, Pres
Proceedings 1861-1869, pg 148 (1865 Nov 7), Nevada Lodge No. 4, Nevadaville

Anderson, Preston
Proceedings 1861-1869, pg 77 (1862 Nov 4), Nevada Lodge No. 4, Nevadaville
Proceedings 1861-1869, pg 111 (1863 Nov 3), Nevada Lodge No. 4, Nevadaville
Proceedings 1861-1869, pg 132 (1864 Nov 8), Nevada Lodge No. 4, Nevadaville
Proceedings 1861-1869, pg 192 (1867 Oct 8), Nevada Lodge No. 4, Nevadaville
Proceedings 1861-1869, pg 304 (1869 Sept 29), Nevada Lodge No. 4, Nevadaville
Proceedings 1870, pg 20 (1870 Sept 28), Nevada Lodge No. 4, Nevadaville
Proceedings 1871, pg 18 (1871 Sept 27), Nevada Lodge No. 4, Bald Mountain

Proceedings 1872, pg 18 (1872 Sept 24), Nevada Lodge No. 4, Bald Mountain

Proceedings 1873, pg 36 (1873 Oct 1), Nevada Lodge No. 4, Nevada

Proceedings 1874, pg 211 (1874 Sept 30), Nevada Lodge No. 4, Bald Mountain, Gilpin County, Stricken from the rolls

Anderson, Rufus E

Proceedings 1874, pg 204 (1874 Sept 30) Grand Lodge of Missouri, Palmyra

Anderson, T J H

Proceedings 1872, pg 88 (1872 Sept 24) Grand Lodge of Texas, deceased

Andre, F L

Proceedings 1861-1869, pg 226 (1868 Oct 7), Empire Lodge No. 8, Empire City

Proceedings 1873, pg 51 (1873 Oct 1), Weston Lodge No. 22, Littleton

Proceedings 1874, pg 226 (1874 Sept 30), Weston Lodge No. 22, Littleton

Andre, Francis L

Proceedings 1861-1869, pg 195 (1867 Oct 8), Empire Lodge No. 8, Empire City

Proceedings 1861-1869, pg 308 (1869 Sept 29), Empire Lodge No. 8, Empire City

Proceedings 1870, pg 24 (1870 Sept 28), Empire Lodge No. 8, Empire

Proceedings 1872, pg 23 (1872 Sept 24), Empire Lodge No. 8, Empire

Proceedings 1873, pg 41 (1873 Oct 1), Empire Lodge No. 8, Empire

Proceedings 1874, pg 215 (1874 Sept 30), Empire Lodge No. 8, Empire, Demitted

Andre, Frank L

Proceedings 1872, pg 34 (1872 Sept 24), Weston Lodge No. 22, Littleton

Proceedings 1875, pg 88 (1875 Sept 22), Weston Lodge No. 22, Littleton

Proceedings 1876, pg 41 (1876 Sept 20), Weston Lodge No. 22, Littleton

Andrew, E H

Proceedings 1873, pg 51 (1873 Oct 1), St Vrain Lodge No. 23, Longmont

Proceedings 1874, pg 227 (1874 Sept 30), St Vrain No. 23, Longmont

Andrew, Francis L

Proceedings 1861-1869, pg 170 (1866 Oct 2), Empire Lodge No. 8, Empire City

Andrews, E H

Proceedings 1861-1869, pg 197 (1867 Oct 8), Columbia Lodge U D, Boulder, Apprentice

Proceedings 1861-1869, pg 228 (1868 Oct 7), Columbia Lodge No. 14, Columbia City

Proceedings 1870, pg 27 (1870 Sept 28), Columbia Lodge No. 14, Boulder City

Proceedings 1871, pg 25 (1871 Sept 27), Columbia Lodge No. 14, Boulder City

Proceedings 1872, pg 14 (1872 Sept 24), St Vrain Lodge No. 23, Longmont

Proceedings 1872, pg 27 (1872 Sept 24), Columbia Lodge No. 14, Boulder

Proceedings 1872, pg 35 (1872 Sept 24), St Vrain Lodge No. 23, Longmont

Proceedings 1861-1869, pg 310 (1869 Sept 29), Columbia Lodge No. 14, Boulder City

Andrews, Elijah H

Proceedings 1873, pg 45 (1873 Oct 1), Columbia Lodge No. 14, Boulder, Dimitted

Proceedings 1876, pg 48 (1876 Sept 20), St Vrain Lodge No. 23, Longmont, 1875 Dec

Proceedings 1876, pg 37 (1876 Sept 20), Columbia Lodge No. 14, Boulder

Anfenger, Louis

Proceedings 1875, pg 75 (1875 Sept 22) Denver Lodge No. 5

Proceedings 1876, pg 31 (1876 Sept 20) Denver Lodge No. 5

Anker, M

Proceedings 1861-1869, pg 229 (1868 Oct 7), Pueblo Lodge U D, Pueblo

Anker, Moses

Proceedings 1861-1869, pg 167 (1866 Oct 2) Denver Lodge No. 5

Proceedings 1861-1869, pg 192 (1867 Oct 8) Denver Lodge No. 5

Proceedings 1861-1869, pg 223 (1868 Oct 7) Denver Lodge No. 5

Proceedings 1861-1869, pg 294 (1869 Sept 28) Denver Lodge No 5

Proceedings 1861-1869, pg 305 (1869 Sept 29) Denver Lodge No. 5, Dimitted

Proceedings 1870, pg 21 (1870 Sept 28), Denver Lodge No. 5, Denver

Proceedings 1872, pg 20 (1872 Sept 24), Denver Lodge No. 5, Denver

Proceedings 1874, pg 211 (1874 Sept 30), Denver Lodge No. 5, Denver

Proceedings 1874, pg 212 (1874 Sept 30), Denver Lodge No. 5, Denver, Reinstated

Proceedings 1875, pg 75 (1875 Sept 22) Denver Lodge No. 5

Proceedings 1876, pg 49 (1876 Sept 20) Denver Lodge No. 5, 1876 Aug 19

Annis, E B

Proceedings 1871, pg 30 (1871 Sept 27), Occidental Lodge U D, Greeley

Proceedings 1872, pg 33 (1872 Sept 24), Occidental Lodge No. 20, Greeley

Proceedings 1873, pg 50 (1873 Oct 1), Occidental Lodge No. 20, Greeley

Proceedings 1874, pg 225 (1874 Sept 30), Occidental Lodge No. 20, Greeley

Proceedings 1875, pg 87 (1875 Sept 22), Occidental Lodge No. 20, Greeley

Colorado's Territorial Masons

Annis, Emmet B
    Proceedings 1876, pg 40 (1876 Sept 20), Occidental Lodge No. 20, Greeley

Annis, W D
    Proceedings 1861-1869, pg 110 (1863 Nov 3) Golden City Lodge No. 1, Apprentice
    Proceedings 1861-1869, pg 131 (1864 Nov 8) Golden City Lodge No. 1

Antes, Wm
    Proceedings 1861-1869, pg 149 (1865 Nov 7), Nevada Lodge No. 4, Nevadaville
    Proceedings 1861-1869, pg 167 (1866 Oct 2) Denver Lodge No. 5, dimitted

Anthon, John H
    Proceedings 1870, pg 94 (1870 June 7) Grand Master, Grand Lodge of New York
    Proceedings 1872, pg 75 (1872 Sept 24) Grand Lodge of New York

Anthony
    Proceedings 1861-1869, pg 177 (1867 Oct 7) committee
    Proceedings 1861-1869, pg 188 (1867 Oct 8) motion
    Proceedings 1861-1869, pg 202 (1868 Oct 6) committee
    Proceedings 1861-1869, pg 211 (1868 May 11), Union Lodge No. 7, Denver
    Proceedings 1861-1869, pg 216 (1868 Oct 7) resolution
    Proceedings 1861-1869, pg 217 (1868 Oct 7) motion
    Proceedings 1861-1869, pg 217 (1868 Oct 7) resolution
    Proceedings 1861-1869, pg 218 (1868 Oct 7) resolution
    Proceedings 1861-1869, pg 297 (1869 Sept 28) motion
    Proceedings 1861-1869, pg 301 (1869 Sept 29) resolution
    Proceedings 1861-1869, pg 302 (1869 Sept 29) committee
    Proceedings 1872, pg 8 (1872 Aug 24) laid the cornerstone at a Denver public school
    Proceedings 1872, pg 13 (1872 Sept 24) resolution
    Proceedings 1872, pg 14 (1872 Sept 24) motion
    Proceedings 1872, pg 15 (1872 Sept 24) motion
    Proceedings 1872, pg 95 (1872 Sept 24) Grand Lodge of Colorado
    Proceedings 1873, pg 5 (1873 Sept 30) Deputy Grand Master
    Proceedings 1873, pg 12 (1873 Sept 30) motion
    Proceedings 1874, pg 29 (1874 Sept 29) Grand Master
    Proceedings 1874, pg 31 (1874 Sept 30) Grand Master
    Proceedings 1874, pg 35 (1874 Sept 30) Grand Master
    Proceedings 1875, pg 31 (1875 Sept 22) Grand Master
    Proceedings 1876, pg 14 (1876 Sept 19) committee
    Proceedings 1876, pg 25 (1876 Sept 20) amendment

Anthony, Jesse B
    Proceedings 1861-1869, pg 291 (1869 Sept 28), of Troy, NY

Anthony, Scott J
    Proceedings 1876, pg 33 (1876 Sept 20), Union Lodge No. 7, Denver

Anthony, W D
    Proceedings 1861-1869, pg 135 (1864 Nov 8), Union Lodge No. 7, Denver, Apprentice
    Proceedings 1861-1869, pg 151 (1865 Nov 7), Chivington Lodge No. 6, Central City
    Proceedings 1861-1869, pg 154 (1866 Oct 1), Union Lodge No. 7, Denver
    Proceedings 1861-1869, pg 169 (1866 Oct 2), Union Lodge No. 7, Denver
    Proceedings 1861-1869, pg 176 (1867 Oct 7), Union Lodge No. 7, Denver
    Proceedings 1861-1869, pg 182 (1867 Oct 7) warrant paid
    Proceedings 1861-1869, pg 185 (1867 Oct 7) Junior Grand Warden
    Proceedings 1861-1869, pg 186 (1867 Oct 8) per diem
    Proceedings 1861-1869, pg 195 (1867 Oct 8), Union Lodge No. 7, Denver
    Proceedings 1861-1869, pg 201 (1868 Oct 6) Junior Grand Warden
    Proceedings 1861-1869, pg 202 (1868 Oct 6) Junior Grand Warden
    Proceedings 1861-1869, pg 202 (1868 Oct 6), Union Lodge No. 7, Denver
    Proceedings 1861-1869, pg 212 (1868 Oct 6) warrant paid
    Proceedings 1861-1869, pg 219 (1868 Oct 7) committee
    Proceedings 1861-1869, pg 219 (1868 Oct 7) mileage allowed
    Proceedings 1861-1869, pg 220 (1868 Oct 7) committee
    Proceedings 1861-1869, pg 225 (1868 Oct 7), Union Lodge No. 7, Denver
    Proceedings 1861-1869, pg 289 (1869 Sept 28) Junior Grand Warden
    Proceedings 1861-1869, pg 300 (1869 Sept 29) Junior Grand Warden
    Proceedings 1861-1869, pg 307 (1869 Sept 29), Union Lodge No. 7, Denver
    Proceedings 1861-1869, pg 315 (1869 Sept 29) Junior Grand Warden, 1867
    Proceedings 1861-1869, pg 315 (1869 Sept 29) Junior Grand Warden, 1868
    Proceedings 1870, pg cover (1870 Sept 28) Past Senior Grand Warden, Denver
    Proceedings 1870, pg 13 (1870 Sept 27) committee
    Proceedings 1870, pg 17 (1870 Sept 28) committee
    Proceedings 1870, pg 32 (1870 Sept 28) Senior Grand Warden, 1869
    Proceedings 1870, pg 32 (1870 Sept 28) Junior Grand Warden, 1867
    Proceedings 1870, pg 32 (1870 Sept 28) Junior Grand Warden, 1868
    Proceedings 1871, pg 3 (1871 Sept 26) Junior Grand Deacon
    Proceedings 1871, pg 4 (1871 Sept 26), Union Lodge No. 7, Denver
    Proceedings 1871, pg 4 (1871 Sept 26) Committee
    Proceedings 1871, pg 5 (1871 Sept 26) Committee
    Proceedings 1871, pg 12 (1871 Sept 26) Committee
    Proceedings 1871, pg 12 (1871 Sept 26) Committee
    Proceedings 1871, pg 14 (1871 Sept 27), Union Lodge No. 7, Denver
    Proceedings 1871, pg 21 (1871 Sept 27), Union Lodge No. 7, Denver

Anthony, W D, cont.
- Proceedings 1871, pg 34 (1871 Sept 27) Senior Grand Warden, 1869
- Proceedings 1871, pg 34 (1871 Sept 27) Deputy Grand Master, 1871
- Proceedings 1871, pg 34 (1871 Sept 27) Junior Grand Warden, 1867
- Proceedings 1871, pg 34 (1871 Sept 27) Junior Grand Warden, 1868
- Proceedings 1872, pg 4 (1872 Sept 24) Deputy Grand Master
- Proceedings 1872, pg 16 (1872 Sept 24) Deputy Grand Master
- Proceedings 1872, pg 42 (1872 Sept 24) Junior Grand Warden, 1868
- Proceedings 1872, pg 42 (1872 Sept 24) Junior Grand Warden, 1867
- Proceedings 1872, pg 42 (1872 Sept 24) Deputy Grand Master, 1871-1872
- Proceedings 1872, pg 42 (1872 Sept 24) Senior Grand Warden, 1869
- Proceedings 1873, pg 5 (1873 Sept 30) Deputy Grand Master
- Proceedings 1873, pg 6 (1873 Sept 30) committee
- Proceedings 1873, pg 31 (1873 Oct 1) mileage and per diem
- Proceedings 1873, pg 39 (1873 Oct 1), Union Lodge No. 7, Denver
- Proceedings 1873, pg 58 (1873 Oct 1) Junior Grand Warden, 1868
- Proceedings 1873, pg 58 (1873 Oct 1) Junior Grand Warden, 1867
- Proceedings 1873, pg 58 (1873 Oct 1) Senior Grand Warden, 1869
- Proceedings 1873, pg 58 (1873 Oct 1) Deputy Grand Master, 1871-1872
- Proceedings 1874, pg 5 (1874 Sept 29) Grand Master
- Proceedings 1874, pg 32 (1874 Sept 30) Grand Master
- Proceedings 1874, pg 34 (1874 Sept 30) committee
- Proceedings 1874, pg 36 (1874 Sept 30) per diem
- Proceedings 1874, pg 213 (1874 Sept 30), Union Lodge No. 7, Denver
- Proceedings 1875, pg 16 (1875 Sept 21) Grand Master
- Proceedings 1875, pg 24 (1875 Sept 21) donation to the library fund
- Proceedings 1875, pg 33 (1875 Sept 22) Grand Master
- Proceedings 1875, pg 35 (1875 Sept 22) committee
- Proceedings 1875, pg 35 (1875 Sept 22) motion
- Proceedings 1875, pg 36 (1875 Sept 22) resolution
- Proceedings 1875, pg 37 (1875 Sept 22) per diem
- Proceedings 1875, pg 78 (1875 Sept 22), Union Lodge No. 7, Denver
- Proceedings 1876, pg 6 (1876 Sept 19) Golden City Lodge No. 1
- Proceedings 1876, pg 12 (1876 Sept 19) donation to the library fund
- Proceedings 1876, pg 17 (1876 Sept 19) committee
- Proceedings 1876, pg 21 (1876 Sept 20) Grand Lodge of Wisconsin, Grand Representative
- Proceedings 1876, pg 22 (1876 Sept 20) committee
- Proceedings 1876, pg 32 (1876 Sept 20), Union Lodge No. 7, Denver

Anthony, Webster
- Proceedings 1874, pg cover (1874 Sept 30) Grand Master, Denver

Anthony, Webster D
- Colorado University Cornerstone Laying, pg 3 (1875 Sept 20) Grand Master
- Proceedings 1861-1869, pg 298 (1869 Sept 28) Senior Grand Warden
- Proceedings 1870, pg 23 (1870 Sept 28), Union Lodge No. 7, Denver
- Proceedings 1871, pg cover (1871 Sept 27) Deputy Grand Master, Denver
- Proceedings 1871, pg 13 (1871 Sept 26) Deputy Grand Master
- Proceedings 1872, pg cover (1872 Sept 24), Colorado Commandery No. 1, Denver
- Proceedings 1872, pg cover (1872 Sept 24) Deputy Grand Master, Denver
- Proceedings 1872, pg 3 (1872 Sept 24) Deputy Grand Master
- Proceedings 1872, pg 4 (1872 Sept 24) Deputy Grand Master
- Proceedings 1872, pg 12 (1872 Sept 24) Deputy Grand Master
- Proceedings 1872, pg 22 (1872 Sept 24), Union Lodge No. 7, Denver
- Proceedings 1873, pg cover (1873 Oct 1) Grand Master, Denver
- Proceedings 1873, pg cover (1873 Sept 30) Grand Master, Denver, Arapahoe County
- Proceedings 1873, pg 3 (1873 Sept 30) Deputy Grand Master
- Proceedings 1873, pg 4 (1873 Sept 30) Deputy Grand Master
- Proceedings 1873, pg 14 (1873 Sept 30) Grand Master
- Proceedings 1873, pg 28 (1873 Oct 1) resolution
- Proceedings 1873, pg 29 (1873 Oct 1) resolution
- Proceedings 1873, pg 59 (1873 Oct 1) Grand Master, 1873
- Proceedings 1873, pg 60 (1873 Oct 1) Grand Lodge of Colorado, Denver
- Proceedings 1874, pg cover (1874 Sept 29) Grand Master, Denver, Arapahoe County
- Proceedings 1874, pg cover (1874 Sept 30) committee, Denver
- Proceedings 1874, pg 3 (1874 Sept 29) Grand Master
- Proceedings 1874, pg 6 (1874 Sept 29), Grand Representative, Grand Lodge of Kansas
- Proceedings 1874, pg 17 (1874 Sept 29) Grand Master
- Proceedings 1874, pg 29 (1874 Sept 29) Grand Master
- Proceedings 1874, pg 204 (1874 Sept 30) Grand Lodge of Colorado, Denver
- Proceedings 1874, pg 206 (1874 Sept 30) Junior Grand Warden, 1868
- Proceedings 1874, pg 206 (1874 Sept 30) Senior Grand Warden, 1869

Anthony, Webster D, cont.
- Proceedings 1874, pg 206 (1874 Sept 30) Junior Grand Warden, 1867
- Proceedings 1874, pg 206 (1874 Sept 30) Grand Master, 1874
- Proceedings 1874, pg 206 (1874 Sept 30) Grand Master, 1873
- Proceedings 1874, pg 206 (1874 Sept 30) Deputy Grand Master, 1871
- Proceedings 1874, pg 206 (1874 Sept 30) Deputy Grand Master, 1872
- Proceedings 1874, pg 207 (1874 Sept 30) Grand Lodge of Kansas, Denver
- Proceedings 1875, pg cover (1875 Sept 22) committee, Denver
- Proceedings 1875, pg 15 (1875 Sept 21) Grand Master
- Proceedings 1875, pg 21 (1875 Sept 21) Grand Master
- Proceedings 1875, pg 37 (1875 Sept 22) committee, Denver
- Proceedings 1875, pg 93 (1875 Sept 22) Deputy Grand Master, 1871
- Proceedings 1875, pg 93 (1875 Sept 22) Senior Grand Warden, 1869
- Proceedings 1875, pg 93 (1875 Sept 22) Grand Master, 1873
- Proceedings 1875, pg 93 (1875 Sept 22) Deputy Grand Master, 1872
- Proceedings 1875, pg 93 (1875 Sept 22) Junior Grand Warden, 1868
- Proceedings 1875, pg 93 (1875 Sept 22) Grand Master, 1874
- Proceedings 1875, pg 93 (1875 Sept 22) Junior Grand Warden, 1867
- Proceedings 1875, pg 95 (1875 Sept 22) Grand Lodge of Kansas, Denver, CO
- Proceedings 1876, pg cover (1876 Sept 20) committee, Denver
- Proceedings 1876, pg 8 (1875 Dec 5) special duty to convene an emergency communication
- Proceedings 1876, pg 8 (1875 Dec 9) dispensation to lay the corner stone of the building of the Ladies Relief Society of Denver
- Proceedings 1876, pg 26 (1876 Sept 20) committee
- Proceedings 1876, pg 53 (1876 Sept 20) Grand Lodge of Wisconsin, of Denver, CO
- Proceedings 1876, pg 53 (1876 Sept 20) Grand Lodge of Kansas, of Denver, CO,

Appel, A M
- Proceedings 1861-1869, pg 312 (1869 Sept 29), Cheyenne Lodge No. 16, Cheyenne
- Proceedings 1870, pg 28 (1870 Sept 28), Cheyenne Lodge No. 16, Cheyenne, Wyoming Territory
- Proceedings 1871, pg cover (1871 Sept 27) Grand Marshal, Cheyenne
- Proceedings 1871, pg 4 (1871 Sept 26), Cheyenne Lodge No. 16, Cheyenne, Wyoming Territory
- Proceedings 1871, pg 5 (1871 Sept 26) Committee
- Proceedings 1871, pg 12 (1871 Sept 26) Committee
- Proceedings 1871, pg 14 (1871 Sept 27) Grand Marshal
- Proceedings 1871, pg 14 (1871 Sept 27), Cheyenne Lodge No. 16, Cheyenne, Wyoming Territory
- Proceedings 1871, pg 15 (1871 Sept 27) Committee
- Proceedings 1871, pg 27 (1871 Sept 27), Cheyenne Lodge No. 16, Cheyenne, Wyoming Territory
- Proceedings 1872, pg 29 (1872 Sept 24), Cheyenne Lodge No. 16, Cheyenne, Wyoming Territory
- Proceedings 1873, pg 3 (1873 Sept 30) Senior Grand Steward
- Proceedings 1873, pg 46 (1873 Oct 1), Cheyenne Lodge No. 16, Cheyenne, Wyoming Territory, Dimitted
- Proceedings 1874, pg 214 (1874 Sept 30), Union Lodge No. 7, Denver
- Proceedings 1875, pg 78 (1875 Sept 22), Union Lodge No. 7, Denver
- Proceedings 1876, pg 33 (1876 Sept 20), Union Lodge No. 7, Denver
- Proceedings 1876, pg 50 (1876 Sept 20), Union Lodge No. 7, Denver

Appel, Morris
- Proceedings 1871, pg 29 (1871 Sept 27), Laramie Lodge No. 18, Laramie, Wyoming Territory
- Proceedings 1872, pg 29 (1872 Sept 24), Cheyenne Lodge No. 16, Cheyenne, Wyoming Territory
- Proceedings 1872, pg 32 (1872 Sept 24), Laramie Lodge No. 18, Laramie, Wyoming Territory, Dimitted
- Proceedings 1873, pg 46 (1873 Oct 1), Cheyenne Lodge No. 16, Cheyenne, Wyoming Territory
- Proceedings 1874, pg 221 (1874 Sept 30), Cheyenne Lodge No. 16, Cheyenne, Wyoming Territory

Argenta Lodge
- Proceedings 1871, pg 8 (1871 Apr 8) established in Salt Lake City

Argenta Lodge No. 21
- Proceedings 1875, pg 20 (1875 Sept 21) Grand Lodge of Utah
- Proceedings 1876, pg 47 (1876 Sept 20), Argenta Lodge No. 3, Grand Lodge of Utah

Argenta Lodge No. 21, Salt Lake City
- Proceedings 1871, pg 12 (1871 Sept 26)
- Proceedings 1872, pg 7 (1872 Sept 24) dispensation given
- Proceedings 1872, pg 8 (1872 Sept 24) has taken a Charter from the Grand Lodge of Utah
- Proceedings 1872, pg 11 (1872 Sept 24), now Argenta Lodge No. 3, Utah Register
- Proceedings 1872, pg 34 (1872 Sept 24) Grand Lodge of Utah
- Proceedings 1874, pg 226 (1874 Sept 30), now Argenta Lodge No. 3, Grand Lodge of Utah

Argenta Lodge No. 21, Salt Lake City, Utah Territory
- Proceedings 1872, pg 89 (1872 Sept 24), chartered by the Grand Lodge of Colorado, 26 Sept 1871
- Proceedings 1873, pg 50 (1873 Oct 1), now Argenta Lodge No. 3, Grand Lodge of Utah

Argenta Lodge No. 3
- Proceedings 1875, pg 88 (1875 Sept 22) Grand Lodge of Utah

Colorado's Territorial Masons

Argenta Lodge U D, Salt Lake City
Proceedings 1871, pg 10 (1871 Sept 26)
Proceedings 1871, pg 12 (1871 Sept 26)

Armstrong, Andrew
Proceedings 1875, pg 86 (1875 Sept 22), Collins Lodge No. 19, Fort Collins
Proceedings 1876, pg 39 (1876 Sept 20), Collins Lodge No. 19, Fort Collins

Armstrong, James J
Proceedings 1871, pg 30 (1871 Sept 27), Occidental Lodge U D, Greeley

Armstrong, Robert
Proceedings 1873, pg 50 (1873 Oct 1), Occidental Lodge No. 20, Greeley
Proceedings 1874, pg 225 (1874 Sept 30), Occidental Lodge No. 20, Greeley
Proceedings 1875, pg 87 (1875 Sept 22), Occidental Lodge No. 20, Greeley
Proceedings 1876, pg 38 (1876 Sept 20) Pueblo Lodge No. 17
Proceedings 1876, pg 40 (1876 Sept 20), Occidental Lodge No. 20, Greeley

Armstrong, W S
Proceedings 1874, pg 223 (1874 Sept 30), Laramie Lodge No. 18, Laramie City

Arnedt, W D
Proceedings 1861-1869, pg 305 (1869 Sept 29) Denver Lodge No. 5

Arnett, W D
Proceedings 1861-1869, pg 149 (1865 Nov 7), Nevada Lodge No. 4, Nevadaville
Proceedings 1861-1869, pg 167 (1866 Oct 2) Denver Lodge No. 5
Proceedings 1870, pg 21 (1870 Sept 28), Denver Lodge No. 5, Denver

Arnett, William D
Proceedings 1876, pg 31 (1876 Sept 20) Denver Lodge No. 5

Arnett, Wm D
Proceedings 1861-1869, pg 192 (1867 Oct 8) Denver Lodge No. 5
Proceedings 1861-1869, pg 223 (1868 Oct 7) Denver Lodge No. 5
Proceedings 1871, pg 19 (1871 Sept 27) Denver Lodge No. 5
Proceedings 1872, pg 19 (1872 Sept 24), Denver Lodge No. 5, Denver
Proceedings 1873, pg 37 (1873 Oct 1), Denver Lodge No. 5, Denver
Proceedings 1874, pg 211 (1874 Sept 30), Denver Lodge No. 5, Denver
Proceedings 1875, pg 75 (1875 Sept 22) Denver Lodge No. 5

Arthur, George W
Proceedings 1875, pg 80 (1875 Sept 22) Black Hawk Lodge No. 11
Proceedings 1876, pg 34 (1876 Sept 20) Black Hawk Lodge No. 11

Arthur, J B
Proceedings 1873, pg 6 (1873 Sept 30), Collins Lodge No. 19, Fort Collins
Proceedings 1876, pg 5 (1876 Sept 19), Collins Lodge No. 19, Fort Collins
Proceedings 1876, pg 6 (1876 Sept 19) committee
Proceedings 1876, pg 22 (1876 Sept 20), Collins Lodge No. 19, Fort Collins

Arthur, James B
Proceedings 1871, pg 30 (1871 Sept 27), Collins Lodge No. 19, Fort Collins
Proceedings 1872, pg 32 (1872 Sept 24), Collins Lodge No. 19, Fort Collins
Proceedings 1873, pg 49 (1873 Oct 1), Collins Lodge No. 19, Fort Collins
Proceedings 1874, pg 224 (1874 Sept 30), Collins Lodge No. 19, Fort Collins, Larimer County
Proceedings 1875, pg 86 (1875 Sept 22), Collins Lodge No. 19, Fort Collins
Proceedings 1876, pg cover (1876 Sept 20) committee, Fort Collins
Proceedings 1876, pg 23 (1876 Sept 20) committee
Proceedings 1876, pg 26 (1876 Sept 20) committee
Proceedings 1876, pg 39 (1876 Sept 20), Collins Lodge No. 19, Fort Collins

Arthur, James S
Proceedings 1874, pg 224 (1874 Sept 30), Collins Lodge No. 19, Fort Collins, Larimer County
Proceedings 1875, pg 86 (1875 Sept 22), Collins Lodge No. 19, Fort Collins
Proceedings 1876, pg 39 (1876 Sept 20), Collins Lodge No. 19, Fort Collins

Arthur, Jas B
Proceedings 1876, pg 16 (1876 Sept 19) committee

Arthur, John
Proceedings 1874, pg 224 (1874 Sept 30), Collins Lodge No. 19, Fort Collins, Larimer County, Fellowcraft
Proceedings 1875, pg 86 (1875 Sept 22), Collins Lodge No. 19, Fort Collins
Proceedings 1876, pg 39 (1876 Sept 20), Collins Lodge No. 19, Fort Collins

Artist, A S
Proceedings 1871, pg 29 (1871 Sept 27), Laramie Lodge No. 18, Laramie, Wyoming Territory
Proceedings 1872, pg 32 (1872 Sept 24), Laramie Lodge No. 18, Laramie, Wyoming Territory
Proceedings 1874, pg 223 (1874 Sept 30), Laramie Lodge No. 18, Laramie City

Artist, Andrew
Proceedings 1870, pg 31 (1870 Sept 28), Laramie Lodge No. 18, Laramie, Wyoming Territory, Fellowcraft
Proceedings 1873, pg 48 (1873 Oct 1), Laramie Lodge No. 18, Laramie, Wyoming Territory

Colorado's Territorial Masons

Asbury, P
    Proceedings 1861-1869, pg 42 (1861 Dec 10), Summit Lodge No. 2, Parkville
    Proceedings 1861-1869, pg 76 (1862 Nov 4), Summit Lodge No. 2, Parkville
    Proceedings 1861-1869, pg 110 (1863 Nov 3), Summit Lodge No. 2, Parkville
    Proceedings 1861-1869, pg 132 (1864 Nov 8) Golden City Lodge No. 1

Ashby, J T
    Proceedings 1875, pg 84 (1875 Sept 22), Mount Moriah Lodge No. 15, Canon City
    Proceedings 1876, pg 37 (1876 Sept 20), Mount Moriah Lodge No. 15, Canon City

Ashlar Lodge U D, Colorado Springs
    Proceedings 1872, pg 35 (1872 Sept 24) dispensation granted 24 Sept 1872
    Proceedings 1873, pg 12 (1873 Sept 30)
    Proceedings 1873, pg 15 (1873 Oct 1)
    Proceedings 1873, pg 19 (1873 Oct 1)
    Proceedings 1873, pg 19 (1873 Oct 1) denied a charter
    Proceedings 1873, pg 52 (1873 Oct 1) Dispensation recalled
    Proceedings 1874, pg 13 (1874 Sept 29) communication received
    Proceedings 1872, pg 5 (1872 Sept 24) petition

Ashler
    Proceedings 1861-1869, pg 317 (1869 Sept 29), Masonic Magazine of Chicago, IL

Ashley
    Proceedings 1861-1869, pg 143 (1865 Nov 7) resolution

Ashley, A O
    Proceedings 1861-1869, pg 167 (1866 Oct 2) Denver Lodge No. 5
    Proceedings 1861-1869, pg 192 (1867 Oct 8) Denver Lodge No. 5
    Proceedings 1861-1869, pg 223 (1868 Oct 7) Denver Lodge No. 5
    Proceedings 1861-1869, pg 305 (1869 Sept 29) Denver Lodge No. 5
    Proceedings 1870, pg 21 (1870 Sept 28), Denver Lodge No. 5, Denver, Dimitted

Ashley, E M
    Proceedings 1861-1869, pg 116 (1864 Nov 7), Union Lodge No. 7, Denver
    Proceedings 1861-1869, pg 134 (1864 Nov 8), Union Lodge No. 7, Denver
    Proceedings 1861-1869, pg 137 (1865 Nov 6), Union Lodge No. 7, Denver
    Proceedings 1861-1869, pg 138 (1865 Nov 6) committee
    Proceedings 1861-1869, pg 138 (1865 Nov 6) committee
    Proceedings 1861-1869, pg 141 (1865 Nov 7) committee
    Proceedings 1861-1869, pg 142 (1865 Nov 7) committee
    Proceedings 1861-1869, pg 144 (1865 Nov 7), Union Lodge No. 7, Denver
    Proceedings 1861-1869, pg 159 (1866 Oct 1) warrant

Ashley, Eli M
    Proceedings 1861-1869, pg 102 (1863 Nov 3) petition for formation of a new lodge in Denver
    Proceedings 1861-1869, pg 141 (1865 Nov 7) Teller
    Proceedings 1861-1869, pg 151 (1865 Nov 7), Chivington Lodge No. 6, Central City
    Proceedings 1861-1869, pg 169 (1866 Oct 2), Union Lodge No. 7, Denver
    Proceedings 1861-1869, pg 195 (1867 Oct 8), Union Lodge No. 7, Denver
    Proceedings 1861-1869, pg 225 (1868 Oct 7), Union Lodge No. 7, Denver
    Proceedings 1861-1869, pg 307 (1869 Sept 29), Union Lodge No. 7, Denver
    Proceedings 1870, pg 23 (1870 Sept 28), Union Lodge No. 7, Denver
    Proceedings 1871, pg 21 (1871 Sept 27), Union Lodge No. 7, Denver
    Proceedings 1872, pg 22 (1872 Sept 24), Union Lodge No. 7, Denver
    Proceedings 1873, pg 39 (1873 Oct 1), Union Lodge No. 7, Denver
    Proceedings 1874, pg 213 (1874 Sept 30), Union Lodge No. 7, Denver
    Proceedings 1875, pg 78 (1875 Sept 22), Union Lodge No. 7, Denver
    Proceedings 1876, pg 32 (1876 Sept 20), Union Lodge No. 7, Denver

Ashley, O A
    Proceedings 1861-1869, pg 148 (1865 Nov 7), Nevada Lodge No. 4, Nevadaville

Ashley, W
    Proceedings 1875, pg 74 (1875 Sept 22) Golden City Lodge No. 1, Stricken from the rolls

Ashley, William
    Proceedings 1861-1869, pg 221 (1868 Oct 7) Golden City Lodge No. 1
    Proceedings 1870, pg 19 (1870 Sept 28), Golden City Lodge No. 1, Golden City
    Proceedings 1872, pg 17 (1872 Sept 24), Golden City Lodge No. 1, Golden City
    Proceedings 1873, pg 35 (1873 Oct 1), Golden City Lodge No. 1, Golden City
    Proceedings 1874, pg 209 (1874 Sept 30), Golden City Lodge No. 1, Golden City

Ashley, Wm
    Proceedings 1861-1869, pg 147 (1865 Nov 7) Golden City Lodge No. 1
    Proceedings 1861-1869, pg 165 (1866 Oct 2) Golden City Lodge No. 1
    Proceedings 1861-1869, pg 191 (1867 Oct 8) Golden City Lodge No. 1
    Proceedings 1861-1869, pg 303 (1869 Sept 29) Golden City Lodge No. 1
    Proceedings 1871, pg 17 (1871 Sept 27), Golden City Lodge No. 1, Golden City

Ashton, Thomas J
Proceedings 1870, pg 20 (1870 Sept 28), Nevada Lodge No. 4, Nevadaville, Dimitted

Ashton, Thos J
Proceedings 1861-1869, pg 222 (1868 Oct 7), Nevada Lodge No. 4, Nevadaville, Fellowcraft
Proceedings 1861-1869, pg 304 (1869 Sept 29), Nevada Lodge No. 4, Nevadaville

Asker, Milton
Proceedings 1870, pg 29 (1870 Sept 28), Cheyenne Lodge No. 16, Cheyenne, Wyoming Territory, Fellowcraft
Proceedings 1861-1869, pg 312 (1869 Sept 29), Cheyenne Lodge No. 16, Cheyenne, Fellowcraft
Proceedings 1871, pg 27 (1871 Sept 27), Cheyenne Lodge No. 16, Cheyenne, Wyoming Territory, Fellowcraft
Proceedings 1872, pg 30 (1872 Sept 24), Cheyenne Lodge No. 16, Cheyenne, Wyoming Territory, Fellowcraft

Atkins, A W
Proceedings 1861-1869, pg 169 (1866 Oct 2), Union Lodge No. 7, Denver, Apprentice
Proceedings 1861-1869, pg 195 (1867 Oct 8), Union Lodge No. 7, Denver, Apprentice

Atkins, Alex W
Proceedings 1861-1869, pg 226 (1868 Oct 7), Union Lodge No. 7, Denver, Apprentice
Proceedings 1861-1869, pg 308 (1869 Sept 29), Union Lodge No. 7, Denver, Apprentice
Proceedings 1871, pg 22 (1871 Sept 27), Union Lodge No. 7, Denver, Apprentice
Proceedings 1872, pg 23 (1872 Sept 24), Union Lodge No. 7, Denver, Apprentice
Proceedings 1873, pg 40 (1873 Oct 1), Union Lodge No. 7, Denver, Apprentice
Proceedings 1874, pg 214 (1874 Sept 30), Union Lodge No. 7, Denver, Apprentice
Proceedings 1876, pg 33 (1876 Sept 20), Union Lodge No. 7, Denver, Apprentice

Atkins, Alexander W
Proceedings 1870, pg 24 (1870 Sept 28), Union Lodge No. 7, Denver, Apprentice

Atkins, H A
Proceedings 1861-1869, pg 284 (1867 Sept 18) Grand Lodge of Washington

Atkinson, James
Proceedings 1871, pg 30 (1871 Sept 27), Occidental Lodge U D, Greeley
Proceedings 1872, pg 33 (1872 Sept 24), Occidental Lodge No. 20, Greeley
Proceedings 1873, pg 50 (1873 Oct 1), Occidental Lodge No. 20, Greeley
Proceedings 1874, pg 225 (1874 Sept 30), Occidental Lodge No. 20, Greeley
Proceedings 1875, pg 87 (1875 Sept 22), Occidental Lodge No. 20, Greeley
Proceedings 1876, pg 49 (1876 Sept 20), Occidental Lodge No. 20, Greeley, 1875 Nov 1

Atwood, W J
Proceedings 1873, pg 52 (1873 Oct 1), St Vrain Lodge No. 23, Longmont, Apprentice
Proceedings 1874, pg 227 (1874 Sept 30), St Vrain No. 23, Longmont, Apprentice
Proceedings 1876, pg 41 (1876 Sept 20), St Vrain Lodge No. 23, Longmont, Apprentice

Austen, H E
Proceedings 1876, pg 33 (1876 Sept 20), Union Lodge No. 7, Denver

Austin
Proceedings 1875, pg 81 (1875 Sept 22), Washington Lodge No. 12, Georgetown, Reinstated

Austin, Eugene
Proceedings 1870, pg 26 (1870 Sept 28), Washington Lodge No. 12, Georgetown
Proceedings 1871, pg 24 (1871 Sept 27), Washington Lodge No. 12, Georgetown
Proceedings 1872, pg 25 (1872 Sept 24), Washington Lodge No. 12, Georgetown
Proceedings 1873, pg 42 (1873 Oct 1), Washington Lodge No. 12, Georgetown
Proceedings 1874, pg 218 (1874 Sept 30), Washington Lodge No. 12, Georgetown, Stricken from the rolls

Austin, H E
Proceedings 1871, pg 21 (1871 Sept 27), Union Lodge No. 7, Denver
Proceedings 1872, pg 22 (1872 Sept 24), Union Lodge No. 7, Denver
Proceedings 1873, pg 39 (1873 Oct 1), Union Lodge No. 7, Denver
Proceedings 1874, pg 214 (1874 Sept 30), Union Lodge No. 7, Denver
Proceedings 1875, pg 78 (1875 Sept 22), Union Lodge No. 7, Denver

Austin, J D
Proceedings 1874, pg 211 (1874 Sept 30), Denver Lodge No. 5, Denver
Proceedings 1875, pg 75 (1875 Sept 22) Denver Lodge No. 5
Proceedings 1876, pg 48 (1876 Sept 20) Denver Lodge No. 5, 1876 Jan 1

Austin, James M
Proceedings 1861-1869, pg 316 (1869 Sept 29) Grand Lodge of New York
Proceedings 1861-1869, pg 341 (1868 June 2) Grand Secretary, Grand Lodge of New York
Proceedings 1870, pg 34 (1870 Sept 28) Grand Secretary, Grand Lodge of New York
Proceedings 1870, pg 94 (1870 June 7) Grand Secretary, Grand Lodge of New York
Proceedings 1871, pg 35 (1871 Sept 27) Grand Secretary, Grand Lodge of New York
Proceedings 1872, pg 44 (1872 Sept 24) New York, Grand Lodge of New York
Proceedings 1872, pg 75 (1872 Sept 24) Grand Lodge of New York

Colorado's Territorial Masons

Austin, James M, cont.
    Proceedings 1873, pg 61 (1873 Oct 1) Grand Lodge of New York, New York
    Proceedings 1874, pg 204 (1874 Sept 30) Grand Lodge of New York, New York
    Proceedings 1875, pg 96 (1875 Sept 22) Grand Lodge of New York, New York
    Proceedings 1876, pg 54 (1876 Sept 20) Grand Lodge of New York, New York

Austin, Jas M
    Proceedings 1874, pg 109 (1874 Sept 30) Grand Lodge of New York

Austin, S D
    Proceedings 1871, pg 24 (1871 Sept 27), Washington Lodge No. 12, Georgetown
    Proceedings 1875, pg 81 (1875 Sept 22), Washington Lodge No. 12, Georgetown, Demitted

Austin, Schuyler D
    Proceedings 1861-1869, pg 309 (1869 Sept 29), Washington Lodge No. 12, Georgetown
    Proceedings 1870, pg 26 (1870 Sept 28), Washington Lodge No. 12, Georgetown
    Proceedings 1872, pg 25 (1872 Sept 24), Washington Lodge No. 12, Georgetown
    Proceedings 1873, pg 42 (1873 Oct 1), Washington Lodge No. 12, Georgetown
    Proceedings 1874, pg 218 (1874 Sept 30), Washington Lodge No. 12, Georgetown, Stricken from the rolls
    Proceedings 1876, pg 37 (1876 Sept 20), Columbia Lodge No. 14, Boulder

Avery, W F
    Proceedings 1861-1869, pg 192 (1867 Oct 8), Nevada Lodge No. 4, Nevadaville
    Proceedings 1861-1869, pg 304 (1869 Sept 29), Nevada Lodge No. 4, Nevadaville
    Proceedings 1871, pg 18 (1871 Sept 27), Nevada Lodge No. 4, Bald Mountain, died
    Proceedings 1871, pg 32 (1871 Sept 27), Nevada Lodge No. 4, Bald Mountain

Avery, W H
    Proceedings 1861-1869, pg 132 (1864 Nov 8), Nevada Lodge No. 4, Nevadaville

Avery, William F
    Proceedings 1870, pg 20 (1870 Sept 28), Nevada Lodge No. 4, Nevadaville

Avery, Wm F
    Proceedings 1861-1869, pg 77 (1862 Nov 4), Nevada Lodge No. 4, Nevadaville
    Proceedings 1861-1869, pg 111 (1863 Nov 3), Nevada Lodge No. 4, Nevadaville
    Proceedings 1861-1869, pg 148 (1865 Nov 7), Nevada Lodge No. 4, Nevadaville
    Proceedings 1861-1869, pg 166 (1866 Oct 2), Nevada Lodge No. 4, Nevadaville
    Proceedings 1861-1869, pg 222 (1868 Oct 7), Nevada Lodge No. 4, Nevadaville

Aylesworth, C H
    Proceedings 1861-1869, pg 226 (1868 Oct 7), Empire Lodge No. 8, Empire City

Aylesworth, Charles H
    Proceedings 1874, pg 215 (1874 Sept 30), Empire Lodge No. 8, Empire

Aylesworth, Chas
    Proceedings 1873, pg 6 (1873 Sept 30), Empire Lodge No. 8, Empire

Aylesworth, Chas H
    Proceedings 1861-1869, pg 170 (1866 Oct 2), Empire Lodge No. 8, Empire City
    Proceedings 1861-1869, pg 308 (1869 Sept 29), Empire Lodge No. 8, Empire City
    Proceedings 1870, pg 24 (1870 Sept 28), Empire Lodge No. 8, Empire
    Proceedings 1872, pg 23 (1872 Sept 24), Empire Lodge No. 8, Empire

Aylsworth, Charles H
    Proceedings 1873, pg 40 (1873 Oct 1), Empire Lodge No. 8, Empire

Aylsworth, Chas H
    Proceedings 1861-1869, pg 195 (1867 Oct 8), Empire Lodge No. 8, Empire City
    Proceedings 1875, pg 81 (1875 Sept 22), Washington Lodge No. 12, Georgetown
    Proceedings 1876, pg 35 (1876 Sept 20), Washington Lodge No. 12, Georgetown

B

Babcock, F M
    Proceedings 1871, pg 30 (1871 Sept 27), Occidental Lodge U D, Greeley
    Proceedings 1872, pg 33 (1872 Sept 24), Occidental Lodge No. 20, Greeley

Babcock, Frank M
    Proceedings 1873, pg 50 (1873 Oct 1), Occidental Lodge No. 20, Greeley, died
    Proceedings 1873, pg 57 (1873 Oct 1), Occidental Lodge No. 20, Greeley

Bache, A B
    Proceedings 1870, pg 29 (1870 Sept 28), Cheyenne Lodge No. 16, Cheyenne, Wyoming Territory, Apprentice
    Proceedings 1871, pg 27 (1871 Sept 27), Cheyenne Lodge No. 16, Cheyenne, Wyoming Territory, Apprentice
    Proceedings 1872, pg 30 (1872 Sept 24), Cheyenne Lodge No. 16, Cheyenne, Wyoming Territory, Apprentice
    Proceedings 1873, pg 46 (1873 Oct 1), Cheyenne Lodge No. 16, Cheyenne, Wyoming Territory, Apprentice
    Proceedings 1874, pg 221 (1874 Sept 30), Cheyenne Lodge No. 16, Cheyenne, Wyoming Territory, Apprentice

Bachell, B R S
    Proceedings 1861-1869, pg 194 (1867 Oct 8), Chivington Lodge No. 6, Central City

Bachelor, James C
Proceedings 1872, pg 67 (1872 Sept 24) Grand Lodge of Louisiana

Bachtel, B R S
Proceedings 1871, pg 20 (1871 Sept 27), Central Lodge No. 6, Central

Bachtel, Benton R S
Proceedings 1872, pg 22 (1872 Sept 24), Denver Lodge No. 5, Denver

Bachtell, B R S
Proceedings 1870, pg 22 (1870 Sept 28), Central Lodge No. 6, Central City

Backus, W R
Proceedings 1876, pg 34 (1876 Sept 20) Black Hawk Lodge No. 11

Backus, William R
Proceedings 1874, pg 216 (1874 Sept 30), Black Hawk Lodge No. 11, Black Hawk

Backus, Wm R
Proceedings 1873, pg 42 (1873 Oct 1), Black Hawk Lodge No. 11, Black Hawk, Apprentice
Proceedings 1875, pg 80 (1875 Sept 22) Black Hawk Lodge No. 11

Baer, Frederick
Proceedings 1861-1869, pg 111 (1863 Nov 3), Summit Lodge No. 2, Parkville

Bagby, Robert F
Proceedings 1861-1869, pg 313 (1869 Sept 29), Pueblo Lodge No. 17, Pueblo, Apprentice
Proceedings 1870, pg 30 (1870 Sept 28), Pueblo Lodge No. 17, Pueblo, Apprentice
Proceedings 1871, pg 28 (1871 Sept 27), Pueblo Lodge No. 17, Pueblo, Apprentice
Proceedings 1872, pg 31 (1872 Sept 24), Pueblo Lodge No. 17, Pueblo, Apprentice
Proceedings 1874, pg 222 (1874 Sept 30), Pueblo Lodge No. 17, Pueblo, Pueblo County, Apprentice
Proceedings 1875, pg 85 (1875 Sept 22) Pueblo Lodge No. 17, Apprentice
Proceedings 1876, pg 39 (1876 Sept 20) Pueblo Lodge No. 17, Apprentice

Bagley, Robert F
Proceedings 1873, pg 47 (1873 Oct 1), Pueblo Lodge No. 17, Pueblo, Apprentice

Bailey, Aldvin
Proceedings 1876, pg 34 (1876 Sept 20) Black Hawk Lodge No. 11

Bailey, G
Proceedings 1861-1869, pg 110 (1863 Nov 3) Golden City Lodge No. 1

Bailey, H L
Proceedings 1861-1869, pg 225 (1868 Oct 7), Union Lodge No. 7, Denver
Proceedings 1861-1869, pg 307 (1869 Sept 29), Union Lodge No. 7, Denver
Proceedings 1871, pg 21 (1871 Sept 27), Union Lodge No. 7, Denver
Proceedings 1872, pg 22 (1872 Sept 24), Union Lodge No. 7, Denver
Proceedings 1873, pg 39 (1873 Oct 1), Union Lodge No. 7, Denver
Proceedings 1874, pg 214 (1874 Sept 30), Union Lodge No. 7, Denver
Proceedings 1875, pg 78 (1875 Sept 22), Union Lodge No. 7, Denver
Proceedings 1876, pg 33 (1876 Sept 20), Union Lodge No. 7, Denver

Bailey, Hiram L
Proceedings 1870, pg 23 (1870 Sept 28), Union Lodge No. 7, Denver

Bailey, J C
Proceedings 1872, pg 33 (1872 Sept 24), Occidental Lodge No. 20, Greeley
Proceedings 1873, pg 50 (1873 Oct 1), Occidental Lodge No. 20, Greeley, Dimitted

Bailey, J L
Proceedings 1861-1869, pg 135 (1864 Nov 8), Union Lodge No. 7, Denver, Apprentice
Proceedings 1861-1869, pg 151 (1865 Nov 7), Chivington Lodge No. 6, Central City
Proceedings 1861-1869, pg 169 (1866 Oct 2), Union Lodge No. 7, Denver
Proceedings 1861-1869, pg 195 (1867 Oct 8), Union Lodge No. 7, Denver
Proceedings 1861-1869, pg 220 (1868 Oct 7) Grand Tyler
Proceedings 1861-1869, pg 225 (1868 Oct 7), Union Lodge No. 7, Denver
Proceedings 1871, pg 21 (1871 Sept 27), Union Lodge No. 7, Denver

Bailey, J M
Proceedings 1872, pg 33 (1872 Sept 24), Occidental Lodge No. 20, Greeley
Proceedings 1873, pg 50 (1873 Oct 1), Occidental Lodge No. 20, Greeley
Proceedings 1874, pg 225 (1874 Sept 30), Occidental Lodge No. 20, Greeley
Proceedings 1875, pg 87 (1875 Sept 22), Occidental Lodge No. 20, Greeley

Bailey, James M
Proceedings 1871, pg 30 (1871 Sept 27), Occidental Lodge U D, Greeley
Proceedings 1876, pg 40 (1876 Sept 20), Occidental Lodge No. 20, Greeley

Bailey, Joel D
Proceedings 1871, pg 30 (1871 Sept 27), Collins Lodge No. 19, Fort Collins, Fellowcraft
Proceedings 1873, pg 49 (1873 Oct 1), Collins Lodge No. 19, Fort Collins, died

Bailey, Joel S
Proceedings 1873, pg 57 (1873 Oct 1), Collins Lodge No. 19, Fort Collins

Colorado's Territorial Masons

Bailey, Joseph D
　Proceedings 1872, pg 33 (1872 Sept 24), Collins Lodge No. 19, Fort Collins

Bailey, Joseph L
　Proceedings 1861-1869, pg 307 (1869 Sept 29), Union Lodge No. 7, Denver
　Proceedings 1870, pg 23 (1870 Sept 28), Union Lodge No. 7, Denver
　Proceedings 1872, pg 22 (1872 Sept 24), Union Lodge No. 7, Denver
　Proceedings 1873, pg 39 (1873 Oct 1), Union Lodge No. 7, Denver
　Proceedings 1874, pg 214 (1874 Sept 30), Union Lodge No. 7, Denver
　Proceedings 1875, pg 78 (1875 Sept 22), Union Lodge No. 7, Denver
　Proceedings 1876, pg 33 (1876 Sept 20), Union Lodge No. 7, Denver

Bailey, L M
　Proceedings 1876, pg 38 (1876 Sept 20) Pueblo Lodge No. 17

Bailey, Levi M
　Proceedings 1876, pg 45 (1876 Sept 20) South Pueblo Lodge U D

Bailey, Mark W
　Proceedings 1876, pg 54 (1876 Sept 20) Grand Lodge of Dakota, Canton

Bailey, Melvin
　Proceedings 1873, pg 42 (1873 Oct 1), Black Hawk Lodge No. 11, Black Hawk
　Proceedings 1874, pg 216 (1874 Sept 30), Black Hawk Lodge No. 11, Black Hawk

Bailey, S
　Proceedings 1861-1869, pg 131 (1864 Nov 8) Golden City Lodge No. 1

Bailey, Stephen
　Proceedings 1861-1869, pg 147 (1865 Nov 7) Golden City Lodge No. 1
　Proceedings 1861-1869, pg 191 (1867 Oct 8) Golden City Lodge No. 1
　Proceedings 1861-1869, pg 221 (1868 Oct 7) Golden City Lodge No. 1
　Proceedings 1861-1869, pg 303 (1869 Sept 29) Golden City Lodge No. 1
　Proceedings 1870, pg 19 (1870 Sept 28), Golden City Lodge No. 1, Golden City
　Proceedings 1871, pg 17 (1871 Sept 27), Golden City Lodge No. 1, Golden City
　Proceedings 1872, pg 17 (1872 Sept 24), Golden City Lodge No. 1, Golden City
　Proceedings 1873, pg 35 (1873 Oct 1), Golden City Lodge No. 1, Golden City
　Proceedings 1874, pg 209 (1874 Sept 30), Golden City Lodge No. 1, Golden City
　Proceedings 1875, pg 73 (1875 Sept 22) Golden City Lodge No. 1
　Proceedings 1876, pg 29 (1876 Sept 20) Golden City Lodge No. 1

Baily & Brown
　Proceedings 1874, pg 19 (1874 Sept 29), of Chicago, IL

Baily, Melvin
　Proceedings 1872, pg 24 (1872 Sept 24), Black Hawk Lodge No. 11, Black Hawk
　Proceedings 1875, pg 80 (1875 Sept 22) Black Hawk Lodge No. 11

Bain, D W
　Proceedings 1861-1869, pg 316 (1869 Sept 29) Grand Lodge of North Carolina
　Proceedings 1870, pg 34 (1870 Sept 28) Grand Secretary, Grand Lodge of North Carolina
　Proceedings 1871, pg 35 (1871 Sept 27) Grand Secretary, Grand Lodge of North Carolina

Bain, Donald W
　Proceedings 1861-1869, pg 343 (1868 Dec 7) Grand Secretary, Grand Lodge of North Carolina
　Proceedings 1870, pg 95 (1869 Dec 6) Grand Secretary, Grand Lodge of North Carolina
　Proceedings 1872, pg 44 (1872 Sept 24) Raleigh, Grand Lodge of North Carolina
　Proceedings 1872, pg 82 (1872 Sept 24) Grand Lodge of North Carolina
　Proceedings 1873, pg 61 (1873 Oct 1) Grand Lodge of North Carolina, Raleigh
　Proceedings 1874, pg 113 (1874 Sept 30) Grand Lodge of North Carolina
　Proceedings 1874, pg 204 (1874 Sept 30) Grand Lodge of North Carolina, Raleigh
　Proceedings 1875, pg 96 (1875 Sept 22) Grand Lodge of North Carolina, Raleigh
　Proceedings 1876, pg 54 (1876 Sept 20) Grand Lodge of North Carolina, Raleigh

Bain, William F
　Proceedings 1861-1869, pg 277 (1867 Dec 2), Grand Secretary, Grand Lodge of North Carolina, deceased

Baker, E K
　Proceedings 1861-1869, pg 170 (1866 Oct 2), Black Hawk Lodge U D, Black Hawk
　Proceedings 1861-1869, pg 196 (1867 Oct 8), Black Hawk Lodge No. 11, Black Hawk
　Proceedings 1861-1869, pg 227 (1868 Oct 7), Black Hawk Lodge No. 11, Black Hawk
　Proceedings 1870, pg 25 (1870 Sept 28), Black Hawk Lodge No. 11, Black Hawk
　Proceedings 1871, pg 23 (1871 Sept 27), Black Hawk Lodge No. 11, Black Hawk, Stricken from roll

Baker, Ed K
　Proceedings 1861-1869, pg 309 (1869 Sept 29), Black Hawk Lodge No. 11, Black Hawk

Baker, Edwin
　Proceedings 1872, pg 44 (1872 Sept 24) Providence, Grand Lodge of Rhode Island
　Proceedings 1873, pg 61 (1873 Oct 1) Grand Lodge of Rhode Island, Providence
　Proceedings 1874, pg 121 (1874 Sept 30) Grand Lodge of Rhode Island

Proceedings 1874, pg 205 (1874 Sept 30) Grand Lodge of Rhode Island, Providence

Proceedings 1875, pg 96 (1875 Sept 22) Grand Lodge of Rhode Island, Providence

Proceedings 1876, pg 54 (1876 Sept 20) Grand Lodge of Rhode Island, Providence

Baker, James L

Proceedings 1875, pg 91 (1875 Sept 22), Las Animas Lodge U D, Trinidad

Proceedings 1876, pg 44 (1876 Sept 20), Las Animas Lodge No. 28, Trinidad

Baker, N A

Proceedings 1861-1869, pg 167 (1866 Oct 2) Denver Lodge No. 5

Proceedings 1861-1869, pg 193 (1867 Oct 8) Denver Lodge No. 5

Proceedings 1861-1869, pg 230 (1868 Oct 7), Cheyenne Lodge U D, Cheyenne, Dakota Territory

Proceedings 1861-1869, pg 305 (1869 Sept 29) Denver Lodge No. 5, Dimitted

Proceedings 1861-1869, pg 312 (1869 Sept 29), Cheyenne Lodge No. 16, Cheyenne

Proceedings 1870, pg 29 (1870 Sept 28), Cheyenne Lodge No. 16, Cheyenne, Wyoming Territory

Proceedings 1871, pg 4 (1871 Sept 26), Cheyenne Lodge No. 16, Cheyenne, Wyoming Territory

Proceedings 1871, pg 27 (1871 Sept 27), Cheyenne Lodge No. 16, Cheyenne, Wyoming Territory

Proceedings 1872, pg 29 (1872 Sept 24), Cheyenne Lodge No. 16, Cheyenne, Wyoming Territory

Proceedings 1873, pg 46 (1873 Oct 1), Cheyenne Lodge No. 16, Cheyenne, Wyoming Territory, Dimitted

Baker, V

Proceedings 1870, pg 30 (1870 Sept 28), Laramie Lodge No. 18, Laramie, Wyoming Territory

Proceedings 1871, pg 29 (1871 Sept 27), Laramie Lodge No. 18, Laramie, Wyoming Territory

Proceedings 1872, pg 32 (1872 Sept 24), Laramie Lodge No. 18, Laramie, Wyoming Territory

Proceedings 1873, pg 48 (1873 Oct 1), Laramie Lodge No. 18, Laramie, Wyoming Territory

Proceedings 1874, pg 223 (1874 Sept 30), Laramie Lodge No. 18, Laramie City

Balck, W H

Proceedings 1870, pg 29 (1870 Sept 28), Cheyenne Lodge No. 16, Cheyenne, Wyoming Territory

Baldauf, F H

Proceedings 1875, pg 89 (1875 Sept 22), Doric Lodge No. 25, Fairplay

Proceedings 1876, pg 42 (1876 Sept 20), Doric Lodge No. 25, Fairplay

Baldwin, D

Proceedings 1873, pg 45 (1873 Oct 1), Mount Moriah Lodge No. 15, Canon City

Proceedings 1876, pg 38 (1876 Sept 20), Mount Moriah Lodge No. 15, Canon City

Baldwin, D W

Proceedings 1875, pg 84 (1875 Sept 22), Mount Moriah Lodge No. 15, Canon City, Demitted

Baldwin, Daniel W

Proceedings 1874, pg 220 (1874 Sept 30), Mount Moriah Lodge No. 15, Canon City

Baldwin, David

Proceedings 1872, pg 29 (1872 Sept 24), Mount Moriah Lodge No. 15, Canon City

Baldwin, Geo W

Proceedings 1874, pg 227 (1874 Sept 30), St Vrain No. 23, Longmont, Apprentice

Proceedings 1876, pg 41 (1876 Sept 20), St Vrain Lodge No. 23, Longmont, Apprentice

Baldwin, W W

Proceedings 1861-1869, pg 230 (1868 Oct 7), Valmont Lodge U D, Valmont

Ball, D J

Proceedings 1861-1869, pg 111 (1863 Nov 3), Nevada Lodge No. 4, Nevadaville

Proceedings 1861-1869, pg 132 (1864 Nov 8), Nevada Lodge No. 4, Nevadaville

Proceedings 1861-1869, pg 148 (1865 Nov 7), Nevada Lodge No. 4, Nevadaville

Proceedings 1870, pg 24 (1870 Sept 28), Empire Lodge No. 8, Empire

Proceedings 1875, pg 25 (1875 Sept 21), Empire Lodge No. 8, Empire

Ball, David J

Proceedings 1861-1869, pg 151 (1865 Nov 7), Empire Lodge U D, Empire City

Proceedings 1861-1869, pg 170 (1866 Oct 2), Empire Lodge No. 8, Empire City

Proceedings 1861-1869, pg 195 (1867 Oct 8), Empire Lodge No. 8, Empire City

Proceedings 1861-1869, pg 226 (1868 Oct 7), Empire Lodge No. 8, Empire City

Proceedings 1861-1869, pg 308 (1869 Sept 29), Empire Lodge No. 8, Empire City

Proceedings 1872, pg 23 (1872 Sept 24), Empire Lodge No. 8, Empire

Proceedings 1873, pg 40 (1873 Oct 1), Empire Lodge No. 8, Empire

Proceedings 1874, pg 215 (1874 Sept 30), Empire Lodge No. 8, Empire

Proceedings 1875, pg 23 (1874 Dec 5), Empire Lodge No. 8, Empire

Ball, Doric S

Proceedings 1870, pg 39 (1869 Dec 6) Grand Lodge of Alabama, deceased

Ball, J D

Proceedings 1861-1869, pg 166 (1866 Oct 2), Nevada Lodge No. 4, Nevadaville, dimitted

Ballard, J B

Proceedings 1871, pg 23 (1871 Sept 27), Black Hawk Lodge No. 11, Black Hawk

Colorado's Territorial Masons

Ballard, J B, cont.
Proceedings 1870, pg 25 (1870 Sept 28), Black Hawk Lodge No. 11, Black Hawk

Ballard, John B
Proceedings 1861-1869, pg 309 (1869 Sept 29), Black Hawk Lodge No. 11, Black Hawk
Proceedings 1872, pg 24 (1872 Sept 24), Black Hawk Lodge No. 11, Black Hawk
Proceedings 1873, pg 41 (1873 Oct 1), Black Hawk Lodge No. 11, Black Hawk
Proceedings 1874, pg 216 (1874 Sept 30), Black Hawk Lodge No. 11, Black Hawk
Proceedings 1875, pg 17 (1875 Sept 21) Black Hawk Lodge No. 11
Proceedings 1875, pg 80 (1875 Sept 22) Black Hawk Lodge No. 11
Proceedings 1876, pg 34 (1876 Sept 20) Black Hawk Lodge No. 11

Baning, John A
Proceedings 1872, pg 17 (1872 Sept 24), Golden City Lodge No. 1, Golden City

Banker, A H
Proceedings 1873, pg 37 (1873 Oct 1), Denver Lodge No. 5, Denver

Banks, Henry C
Proceedings 1876, pg 38 (1876 Sept 20) Pueblo Lodge No. 17
Proceedings 1876, pg 45 (1876 Sept 20) South Pueblo Lodge U D

Banks, Horace N
Proceedings 1876, pg 5 (1876 Sept 19) Pueblo Lodge No. 17
Proceedings 1876, pg 7 (1876 Mar 17), South Pueblo Lodge U D, South Pueblo
Proceedings 1876, pg 24 (1876 Sept 20), South Pueblo Lodge No. 31, South Pueblo
Proceedings 1876, pg 38 (1876 Sept 20) Pueblo Lodge No. 17
Proceedings 1876, pg 45 (1876 Sept 20) South Pueblo Lodge U D

Banks, N P
Proceedings 1861-1869, pg 260 (1868 June)

Banning, John A
Proceedings 1873, pg 35 (1873 Oct 1), Golden City Lodge No. 1, Golden City
Proceedings 1874, pg 209 (1874 Sept 30), Golden City Lodge No. 1, Golden City
Proceedings 1875, pg 73 (1875 Sept 22) Golden City Lodge No. 1
Proceedings 1876, pg 29 (1876 Sept 20) Golden City Lodge No. 1
Proceedings 1876, pg 50 (1876 Sept 20) Golden City Lodge No. 1

Banning, R F
Proceedings 1874, pg 223 (1874 Sept 30), Laramie Lodge No. 18, Laramie City

Banta, Daniel
Proceedings 1874, pg 212 (1874 Sept 30), Central Lodge No. 6, Central
Proceedings 1875, pg 76 (1875 Sept 22), Central Lodge No. 6, Central City
Proceedings 1876, pg 32 (1876 Sept 20), Central Lodge No. 6, Central City

Banta, J H
Proceedings 1874, pg 220 (1874 Sept 30), Mount Moriah Lodge No. 15, Canon City
Proceedings 1875, pg 84 (1875 Sept 22), Mount Moriah Lodge No. 15, Canon City
Proceedings 1876, pg 38 (1876 Sept 20), Mount Moriah Lodge No. 15, Canon City

Baraclough, Henry A
Proceedings 1876, pg 44 (1876 Sept 20), Las Animas Lodge No. 28, Trinidad

Barber, Luke E
Proceedings 1870, pg 34 (1870 Sept 28) Grand Secretary, Grand Lodge of Arkansas
Proceedings 1870, pg 45 (1869 Nov 1) Grand Secretary, Grand Lodge of Arkansas
Proceedings 1871, pg 35 (1871 Sept 27) Grand Secretary, Grand Lodge of Arkansas
Proceedings 1872, pg 43 (1872 Sept 24) Little Rock, Grand Lodge of Arkansas
Proceedings 1872, pg 54 (1872 Sept 24) Grand Lodge of Arkansas
Proceedings 1873, pg 60 (1873 Oct 1) Grand Lodge of Arkansas, Little Rock
Proceedings 1874, pg 44 (1874 Sept 30) Grand Lodge of Arkansas
Proceedings 1875, pg 24 (1875 Sept 21) Grand Lodge of Arkansas
Proceedings 1875, pg 96 (1875 Sept 22) Grand Lodge of Arkansas, Little Rock
Proceedings 1876, pg 54 (1876 Sept 20) Grand Lodge of Arkansas, Little Rock

Barbour, Chauncy
Proceedings 1861-1869, pg 135 (1864 Nov 8), Union Lodge No. 7, Denver, Fellowcraft

Bardeen, C V
Proceedings 1873, pg 52 (1873 Oct 1), Ashlar Lodge U D, Colorado Springs

Bardill, C
Proceedings 1876, pg 41 (1876 Sept 20), St Vrain Lodge No. 23, Longmont

Bardin, C
Proceedings 1874, pg 227 (1874 Sept 30), St Vrain No. 23, Longmont

Barhight, Alonzo J
Proceedings 1875, pg 76 (1875 Sept 22), Central Lodge No. 6, Central City
Proceedings 1876, pg 31 (1876 Sept 20), Central Lodge No. 6, Central City

Barker, A H
 Proceedings 1861-1869, pg 77 (1862 Nov 4) Denver Lodge No. 5
 Proceedings 1861-1869, pg 112 (1863 Nov 3) Denver Lodge No. 5
 Proceedings 1861-1869, pg 133 (1864 Nov 8) Denver Lodge No. 5
 Proceedings 1861-1869, pg 149 (1865 Nov 7), Nevada Lodge No. 4, Nevadaville
 Proceedings 1861-1869, pg 192 (1867 Oct 8) Denver Lodge No. 5
 Proceedings 1861-1869, pg 223 (1868 Oct 7) Denver Lodge No. 5
 Proceedings 1861-1869, pg 305 (1869 Sept 29) Denver Lodge No. 5
 Proceedings 1870, pg 21 (1870 Sept 28), Denver Lodge No. 5, Denver
 Proceedings 1871, pg 19 (1871 Sept 27) Denver Lodge No. 5
 Proceedings 1872, pg 19 (1872 Sept 24), Denver Lodge No. 5, Denver
 Proceedings 1874, pg 211 (1874 Sept 30), Denver Lodge No. 5, Denver
 Proceedings 1875, pg 75 (1875 Sept 22) Denver Lodge No. 5
 Proceedings 1876, pg 31 (1876 Sept 20) Denver Lodge No. 5

Barker, Alfred H
 Proceedings 1871, pg 30 (1871 Sept 27), Occidental Lodge U D, Greeley

Barker, Luke E
 Proceedings 1874, pg 204 (1874 Sept 30) Grand Lodge of Arkansas, Little Rock

Barker, W J
 Proceedings 1861-1869, pg 309 (1869 Sept 29), Black Hawk Lodge No. 11, Black Hawk
 Proceedings 1870, pg 25 (1870 Sept 28), Black Hawk Lodge No. 11, Black Hawk
 Proceedings 1871, pg 23 (1871 Sept 27), Black Hawk Lodge No. 11, Black Hawk
 Proceedings 1872, pg 25 (1872 Sept 24), Black Hawk Lodge No. 11, Black Hawk, Dimitted

Barker, William J
 Proceedings 1876, pg 33 (1876 Sept 20), Union Lodge No. 7, Denver

Barkhurst, Ira C
 Proceedings 1861-1869, pg 170 (1866 Oct 2), Black Hawk Lodge U D, Black Hawk
 Proceedings 1861-1869, pg 196 (1867 Oct 8), Black Hawk Lodge No. 11, Black Hawk
 Proceedings 1861-1869, pg 227 (1868 Oct 7), Black Hawk Lodge No. 11, Black Hawk
 Proceedings 1861-1869, pg 309 (1869 Sept 29), Black Hawk Lodge No. 11, Black Hawk
 Proceedings 1870, pg 25 (1870 Sept 28), Black Hawk Lodge No. 11, Black Hawk
 Proceedings 1871, pg 23 (1871 Sept 27), Black Hawk Lodge No. 11, Black Hawk
 Proceedings 1872, pg 24 (1872 Sept 24), Black Hawk Lodge No. 11, Black Hawk
 Proceedings 1873, pg 41 (1873 Oct 1), Black Hawk Lodge No. 11, Black Hawk
 Proceedings 1874, pg 216 (1874 Sept 30), Black Hawk Lodge No. 11, Black Hawk
 Proceedings 1875, pg 80 (1875 Sept 22) Black Hawk Lodge No. 11
 Proceedings 1876, pg 34 (1876 Sept 20) Black Hawk Lodge No. 11

Barkley, A H
 Proceedings 1872, pg 43 (1872 Sept 24) Crawfordville, Grand Lodge of Mississippi
 Proceedings 1872, pg 71 (1872 Sept 24) Grand Lodge of Mississippi
 Proceedings 1873, pg 60 (1873 Oct 1) Grand Lodge of Mississippi, Crawfordville
 Proceedings 1874, pg 90 (1874 Sept 30) Grand Lodge of Mississippi
 Proceedings 1874, pg 204 (1874 Sept 30) Grand Lodge of Mississippi, Crawfordville

Barlight, A Joseph
 Proceedings 1874, pg 213 (1874 Sept 30), Central Lodge No. 6, Central, Apprentice

Barlow, E L
 Proceedings 1873, pg 43 (1873 Oct 1), El Paso Lodge No. 13, Colorado City

Barlow, G S
 Proceedings 1861-1869, pg 310 (1869 Sept 29), El Paso Lodge No. 13, Colorado City
 Proceedings 1872, pg 26 (1872 Sept 24), El Paso Lodge No. 13, Colorado City
 Proceedings 1874, pg 218 (1874 Sept 30), El Paso Lodge No. 13, Colorado Springs
 Proceedings 1875, pg 82 (1875 Sept 22), El Paso Lodge No. 13, Colorado Springs
 Proceedings 1876, pg 36 (1876 Sept 20), El Paso Lodge No. 13, Colorado City

Barlow, Geo S
 Proceedings 1870, pg 27 (1870 Sept 28), El Paso Lodge No. 13, Colorado City

Barlow, George L
 Proceedings 1871, pg 25 (1871 Sept 27), El Paso Lodge No. 13, Colorado City

Barnard, A M
 Proceedings 1873, pg 39 (1873 Oct 1), Union Lodge No. 7, Denver
 Proceedings 1874, pg 214 (1874 Sept 30), Union Lodge No. 7, Denver
 Proceedings 1875, pg 79 (1875 Sept 22), Union Lodge No. 7, Denver, Stricken from the rolls

Barnard, Albert M
 Proceedings 1870, pg 23 (1870 Sept 28), Union Lodge No. 7, Denver
 Proceedings 1871, pg 21 (1871 Sept 27), Union Lodge No. 7, Denver

Barnard, Albert M, cont.
    Proceedings 1872, pg 22 (1872 Sept 24), Union Lodge No. 7, Denver

Barnard, L C
    Proceedings 1876, pg 38 (1876 Sept 20), Mount Moriah Lodge No. 15, Canon City

Barnard, O C
    Proceedings 1861-1869, pg 312 (1869 Sept 29), Cheyenne Lodge No. 16, Cheyenne, Fellowcraft
    Proceedings 1870, pg 29 (1870 Sept 28), Cheyenne Lodge No. 16, Cheyenne, Wyoming Territory
    Proceedings 1871, pg 27 (1871 Sept 27), Cheyenne Lodge No. 16, Cheyenne, Wyoming Territory
    Proceedings 1872, pg 29 (1872 Sept 24), Cheyenne Lodge No. 16, Cheyenne, Wyoming Territory

Barndollar, Ferd
    Proceedings 1871, pg 28 (1871 Sept 27), Pueblo Lodge No. 17, Pueblo
    Proceedings 1872, pg 31 (1872 Sept 24), Pueblo Lodge No. 17, Pueblo
    Proceedings 1873, pg 47 (1873 Oct 1), Pueblo Lodge No. 17, Pueblo
    Proceedings 1874, pg 222 (1874 Sept 30), Pueblo Lodge No. 17, Pueblo, Pueblo County

Barndollar, Ferd W
    Proceedings 1861-1869, pg 312 (1869 Sept 29), Pueblo Lodge No. 17, Pueblo
    Proceedings 1875, pg 85 (1875 Sept 22) Pueblo Lodge No. 17

Barndollar, Ferdinand
    Proceedings 1876, pg 38 (1876 Sept 20) Pueblo Lodge No. 17

Barndollar, George
    Proceedings 1876, pg 38 (1876 Sept 20) Pueblo Lodge No. 17

Barnes, David
    Colorado University Cornerstone Laying, pg 3 (1875 Sept 20) Grand Tiler

Barnes, George W
    Proceedings 1876, pg 40 (1876 Sept 20), Occidental Lodge No. 20, Greeley

Barnes, T
    Proceedings 1861-1869, pg 168 (1866 Oct 2), Chivington Lodge No. 6, Central City

Barnes, Thomas
    Proceedings 1861-1869, pg 134 (1864 Nov 8), Chivington Lodge No. 6, Central City
    Proceedings 1861-1869, pg 150 (1865 Nov 7), Chivington Lodge No. 6, Central City
    Proceedings 1861-1869, pg 194 (1867 Oct 8), Chivington Lodge No. 6, Central City
    Proceedings 1872, pg 21 (1872 Sept 24), Denver Lodge No. 5, Denver
    Proceedings 1873, pg 38 (1873 Oct 1), Central Lodge No. 6, Central City
    Proceedings 1874, pg 212 (1874 Sept 30), Central Lodge No. 6, Central
    Proceedings 1875, pg 76 (1875 Sept 22), Central Lodge No. 6, Central City
    Proceedings 1876, pg 32 (1876 Sept 20), Central Lodge No. 6, Central City

Barnes, Thos
    Proceedings 1861-1869, pg 78 (1862 Nov 4), Chivington Lodge No. 6, Central City, Fellowcraft
    Proceedings 1861-1869, pg 112 (1863 Nov 3), Chivington Lodge No. 6, Central City
    Proceedings 1861-1869, pg 224 (1868 Oct 7), Chivington Lodge No. 6, Central City
    Proceedings 1861-1869, pg 306 (1869 Sept 29), Central Lodge No. 6, Central City
    Proceedings 1870, pg 22 (1870 Sept 28), Central Lodge No. 6, Central City
    Proceedings 1871, pg 20 (1871 Sept 27), Central Lodge No. 6, Central

Barnett, W W
    Proceedings 1861-1869, pg 312 (1869 Sept 29), Cheyenne Lodge No. 16, Cheyenne
    Proceedings 1870, pg 29 (1870 Sept 28), Cheyenne Lodge No. 16, Cheyenne, Wyoming Territory, Dimitted,

Barney
    Proceedings 1861-1869, pg 43 (1861 Dec 10), Rocky Mountain Lodge No. 3, Gold Hill

Barney, J P
    Proceedings 1875, pg 91 (1875 Sept 22), Las Animas Lodge U D, Trinidad
    Proceedings 1876, pg 43 (1876 Sept 20), Las Animas Lodge No. 28, Trinidad

Barney, Royal S
    Proceedings 1876, pg 36 (1876 Sept 20), Columbia Lodge No. 14, Boulder

Barney, William A
    Proceedings 1875, pg 83 (1875 Sept 22), Columbia Lodge No. 14, Boulder

Barney, William M
    Proceedings 1871, pg 25 (1871 Sept 27), Columbia Lodge No. 14, Boulder City
    Proceedings 1874, pg 219 (1874 Sept 30), Columbia Lodge No. 14, Boulder, Boulder County
    Proceedings 1876, pg 37 (1876 Sept 20), Columbia Lodge No. 14, Boulder

Barney, Wm M
    Proceedings 1861-1869, pg 230 (1868 Oct 7), Valmont Lodge U D, Valmont
    Proceedings 1861-1869, pg 310 (1869 Sept 29), Columbia Lodge No. 14, Boulder City
    Proceedings 1870, pg 27 (1870 Sept 28), Columbia Lodge No. 14, Boulder City
    Proceedings 1872, pg 28 (1872 Sept 24), Columbia Lodge No. 14, Boulder
    Proceedings 1873, pg 44 (1873 Oct 1), Columbia Lodge No. 14, Boulder

Barnum, L
Proceedings 1875, pg 85 (1875 Sept 22) Pueblo Lodge No. 17

Barnum, Lew
Proceedings 1874, pg 222 (1874 Sept 30), Pueblo Lodge No. 17, Pueblo, Pueblo County

Barnum, Lewis
Proceedings 1861-1869, pg 312 (1869 Sept 29), Pueblo Lodge No. 17, Pueblo
Proceedings 1870, pg 30 (1870 Sept 28), Pueblo Lodge No. 17, Pueblo
Proceedings 1871, pg 28 (1871 Sept 27), Pueblo Lodge No. 17, Pueblo
Proceedings 1872, pg 31 (1872 Sept 24), Pueblo Lodge No. 17, Pueblo
Proceedings 1873, pg 47 (1873 Oct 1), Pueblo Lodge No. 17, Pueblo

Barnum, Thomas
Proceedings 1861-1869, pg 135 (1864 Nov 8), Union Lodge No. 7, Denver, Apprentice

Barondollar [Barndollar], Ferd
Proceedings 1870, pg 30 (1870 Sept 28), Pueblo Lodge No. 17, Pueblo

Barr, Frederick
Proceedings 1861-1869, pg 132 (1864 Nov 8) Golden City Lodge No. 1

Barr, James
Proceedings 1871, pg 30 (1871 Sept 27), Collins Lodge No. 19, Fort Collins, Apprentice
Proceedings 1872, pg 33 (1872 Sept 24), Collins Lodge No. 19, Fort Collins, Apprentice
Proceedings 1873, pg 49 (1873 Oct 1), Collins Lodge No. 19, Fort Collins, Apprentice
Proceedings 1874, pg 225 (1874 Sept 30), Collins Lodge No. 19, Fort Collins, Larimer County, Apprentice
Proceedings 1875, pg 86 (1875 Sept 22), Collins Lodge No. 19, Fort Collins, Fellowcraft
Proceedings 1876, pg 40 (1876 Sept 20), Collins Lodge No. 19, Fort Collins, Fellow Craft

Barrelle, A
Proceedings 1861-1869, pg 134 (1864 Nov 8), Chivington Lodge No. 6, Central City
Proceedings 1861-1869, pg 150 (1865 Nov 7), Chivington Lodge No. 6, Central City, reverend
Proceedings 1861-1869, pg 168 (1866 Oct 2), Chivington Lodge No. 6, Central City, dimitted

Barrelle, Almond
Proceedings 1861-1869, pg 115 (1864 Nov 7) Grand Chaplain
Proceedings 1861-1869, pg 116 (1864 Nov 7) Grand Chaplain

Barrett, Geo H
Proceedings 1861-1869, pg 222 (1868 Oct 7), Nevada Lodge No. 4, Nevadaville
Proceedings 1861-1869, pg 304 (1869 Sept 29), Nevada Lodge No. 4, Nevadaville
Proceedings 1872, pg 26 (1872 Sept 24), Washington Lodge No. 12, Georgetown
Proceedings 1873, pg 43 (1873 Oct 1), Washington Lodge No. 12, Georgetown
Proceedings 1875, pg 81 (1875 Sept 22), Washington Lodge No. 12, Georgetown
Proceedings 1871, pg 20 (1871 Sept 27), Central Lodge No. 6, Central
Proceedings 1875, pg 76 (1875 Sept 22), Central Lodge No. 6, Central City

Barrett, George H
Proceedings 1861-1869, pg 192 (1867 Oct 8), Nevada Lodge No. 4, Nevadaville
Proceedings 1870, pg 20 (1870 Sept 28), Nevada Lodge No. 4, Nevadaville, Dimitted
Proceedings 1870, pg 26 (1870 Sept 28), Washington Lodge No. 12, Georgetown
Proceedings 1874, pg 217 (1874 Sept 30), Washington Lodge No. 12, Georgetown
Proceedings 1876, pg 35 (1876 Sept 20), Washington Lodge No. 12, Georgetown

Barrett, George W
Proceedings 1872, pg 21 (1872 Sept 24), Denver Lodge No. 5, Denver
Proceedings 1873, pg 38 (1873 Oct 1), Central Lodge No. 6, Central City
Proceedings 1876, pg 32 (1876 Sept 20), Central Lodge No. 6, Central City
Proceedings 1876, pg 50 (1876 Sept 20), Central Lodge No. 6, Central City

Barrett, John L
Proceedings 1876, pg 40 (1876 Sept 20), Occidental Lodge No. 20, Greeley

Barriclough, Henry A
Proceedings 1875, pg 91 (1875 Sept 22), Las Animas Lodge U D, Trinidad

Barroll, F H
Proceedings 1861-1869, pg 312 (1869 Sept 29), Cheyenne Lodge No. 16, Cheyenne
Proceedings 1870, pg 29 (1870 Sept 28), Cheyenne Lodge No. 16, Cheyenne, Wyoming Territory
Proceedings 1871, pg 28 (1871 Sept 27), Cheyenne Lodge No. 16, Cheyenne, Wyoming Territory, Apprentice

Barron, James
Proceedings 1871, pg 29 (1871 Sept 27), Laramie Lodge No. 18, Laramie, Wyoming Territory
Proceedings 1872, pg 32 (1872 Sept 24), Laramie Lodge No. 18, Laramie, Wyoming Territory
Proceedings 1873, pg 48 (1873 Oct 1), Laramie Lodge No. 18, Laramie, Wyoming Territory
Proceedings 1874, pg 223 (1874 Sept 30), Laramie Lodge No. 18, Laramie City

Barry, Alexander
Proceedings 1873, pg 49 (1873 Oct 1), Collins Lodge No. 19, Fort Collins
Proceedings 1875, pg 86 (1875 Sept 22), Collins Lodge No. 19, Fort Collins

Colorado's Territorial Masons

Barry, Alexander, cont.
Proceedings 1876, pg 39 (1876 Sept 20), Collins Lodge No. 19, Fort Collins

Barry, Geo L
Proceedings 1861-1869, pg 245 (1867 Nov 7) Grand Lodge of Georgia

Barry, George L
Proceedings 1870, pg 55 (1869 Oct 26) Grand Lodge of Georgia, deceased

Bartells, J L
Proceedings 1861-1869, pg 305 (1869 Sept 29) Denver Lodge No. 5

Bartels, J L
Proceedings 1861-1869, pg 167 (1866 Oct 2) Denver Lodge No. 5
Proceedings 1861-1869, pg 192 (1867 Oct 8) Denver Lodge No. 5
Proceedings 1861-1869, pg 223 (1868 Oct 7) Denver Lodge No. 5
Proceedings 1871, pg 19 (1871 Sept 27) Denver Lodge No. 5
Proceedings 1872, pg 19 (1872 Sept 24), Denver Lodge No. 5, Denver

Bartels, Julius L
Proceedings 1861-1869, pg 230 (1868 Oct 7), Germania Lodge U D, Denver
Proceedings 1870, pg 21 (1870 Sept 28), Denver Lodge No. 5, Denver
Proceedings 1873, pg 37 (1873 Oct 1), Denver Lodge No. 5, Denver, Dimitted

Bartels, L F
Proceedings 1861-1869, pg 307 (1869 Sept 29), Union Lodge No. 7, Denver
Proceedings 1874, pg 215 (1874 Sept 30), Union Lodge No. 7, Denver, died

Bartels, Louis F
Proceedings 1870, pg 23 (1870 Sept 28), Union Lodge No. 7, Denver
Proceedings 1871, pg 21 (1871 Sept 27), Union Lodge No. 7, Denver
Proceedings 1872, pg 22 (1872 Sept 24), Union Lodge No. 7, Denver
Proceedings 1873, pg 39 (1873 Oct 1), Union Lodge No. 7, Denver

Barter, William
Proceedings 1873, pg 35 (1873 Oct 1), Golden City Lodge No. 1, Golden City

Barter, Wm
Proceedings 1871, pg 17 (1871 Sept 27), Golden City Lodge No. 1, Golden City, Apprentice

Barth, Wm
Proceedings 1861-1869, pg 230 (1868 Oct 7), Germania Lodge U D, Denver

Bartholomew, J A
Proceedings 1861-1869, pg 191 (1867 Oct 8) Golden City Lodge No. 1, Apprentice
Proceedings 1861-1869, pg 221 (1868 Oct 7) Golden City Lodge No. 1, Apprentice
Proceedings 1861-1869, pg 303 (1869 Sept 29) Golden City Lodge No. 1, Apprentice

Bartholomew, J W
Proceedings 1861-1869, pg 131 (1864 Nov 8) Golden City Lodge No. 1, Apprentice
Proceedings 1861-1869, pg 147 (1865 Nov 7) Golden City Lodge No. 1, Apprentice
Proceedings 1861-1869, pg 165 (1866 Oct 2) Golden City Lodge No. 1, Apprentice

Bartholomew, Joseph
Proceedings 1861-1869, pg 110 (1863 Nov 3) Golden City Lodge No. 1, Apprentice

Bartlett, A
Proceedings 1861-1869, pg 167 (1866 Oct 2) Denver Lodge No. 5
Proceedings 1861-1869, pg 192 (1867 Oct 8) Denver Lodge No. 5
Proceedings 1861-1869, pg 224 (1868 Oct 7) Denver Lodge No. 5, Dimitted
Proceedings 1861-1869, pg 229 (1868 Oct 7), Pueblo Lodge U D, Pueblo
Proceedings 1861-1869, pg 288 (1869 Sept 28), Pueblo Lodge No. 17, Pueblo
Proceedings 1861-1869, pg 312 (1869 Sept 29), Pueblo Lodge No. 17, Pueblo

Bartlett, Aug
Proceedings 1874, pg 223 (1874 Sept 30), Pueblo Lodge No. 17, Pueblo, Pueblo County, Stricken from the rolls

Bartlett, Augustus
Proceedings 1861-1869, pg 133 (1864 Nov 8) Denver Lodge No. 5, Apprentice
Proceedings 1861-1869, pg 138 (1864 Dec 14) Denver Lodge No. 5
Proceedings 1861-1869, pg 149 (1865 Nov 7), Nevada Lodge No. 4, Nevadaville
Proceedings 1870, pg 30 (1870 Sept 28), Pueblo Lodge No. 17, Pueblo
Proceedings 1871, pg 28 (1871 Sept 27), Pueblo Lodge No. 17, Pueblo
Proceedings 1872, pg 31 (1872 Sept 24), Pueblo Lodge No. 17, Pueblo
Proceedings 1873, pg 47 (1873 Oct 1), Pueblo Lodge No. 17, Pueblo

Bartlett, C L
Proceedings 1861-1869, pg 51 (1862 Nov 4) Grand Steward
Proceedings 1861-1869, pg 77 (1862 Nov 4) Denver Lodge No. 5
Proceedings 1861-1869, pg 149 (1865 Nov 7), Nevada Lodge No. 4, Nevadaville
Proceedings 1861-1869, pg 167 (1866 Oct 2) Denver Lodge No. 5
Proceedings 1861-1869, pg 192 (1867 Oct 8) Denver Lodge No. 5
Proceedings 1861-1869, pg 224 (1868 Oct 7) Denver Lodge No. 5, Dimitted

Bartlett, Charles L
Proceedings 1861-1869, pg 112 (1863 Nov 3) Denver Lodge No. 5

Bartlett, Chas L
Proceedings 1861-1869, pg 133 (1864 Nov 8) Denver Lodge No. 5

Barton
Proceedings 1861-1869, pg 317 (1869 Sept 29), Judge of Worcester, MA

Barton, Reuben
Proceedings 1861-1869, pg 165 (1866 Oct 2) Golden City Lodge No. 1
Proceedings 1861-1869, pg 191 (1867 Oct 8) Golden City Lodge No. 1

Barton, William
Proceedings 1871, pg 24 (1871 Sept 27), Washington Lodge No. 12, Georgetown, Dimitted
Proceedings 1875, pg 73 (1875 Sept 22) Golden City Lodge No. 1
Proceedings 1876, pg 29 (1876 Sept 20) Golden City Lodge No. 1

Barton, Wm
Proceedings 1861-1869, pg 179 (1867 Oct 7), Washington Lodge No. 12, Georgetown
Proceedings 1861-1869, pg 227 (1868 Oct 7), Washington Lodge No. 12, Georgetown
Proceedings 1861-1869, pg 309 (1869 Sept 29), Washington Lodge No. 12, Georgetown
Proceedings 1870, pg 26 (1870 Sept 28), Washington Lodge No. 12, Georgetown

Bartor, William
Proceedings 1874, pg 209 (1874 Sept 30), Golden City Lodge No. 1, Golden City

Basford, H O
Proceedings 1861-1869, pg 150 (1865 Nov 7), Chivington Lodge No. 6, Central City
Proceedings 1861-1869, pg 168 (1866 Oct 2), Chivington Lodge No. 6, Central City
Proceedings 1861-1869, pg 194 (1867 Oct 8), Chivington Lodge No. 6, Central City
Proceedings 1861-1869, pg 225 (1868 Oct 7), Chivington Lodge No. 6, Central City, Dimitted

Bason, Seth
Proceedings 1870, pg 27 (1870 Sept 28), El Paso Lodge No. 13, Colorado City

Bass, C T P
Proceedings 1875, pg 91 (1875 Sept 22), Las Animas Lodge U D, Trinidad
Proceedings 1876, pg 44 (1876 Sept 20), Las Animas Lodge No. 28, Trinidad

Basset, Isaac C
Proceedings 1876, pg 7 (1876 Mar 15), Olive Branch Lodge U D, Saguache

Bassett, Alden
Proceedings 1870, pg 27 (1870 Sept 28), El Paso Lodge No. 13, Colorado City
Proceedings 1871, pg 25 (1871 Sept 27), El Paso Lodge No. 13, Colorado City
Proceedings 1872, pg 26 (1872 Sept 24), El Paso Lodge No. 13, Colorado City
Proceedings 1873, pg 43 (1873 Oct 1), El Paso Lodge No. 13, Colorado City
Proceedings 1874, pg 218 (1874 Sept 30), El Paso Lodge No. 13, Colorado Springs
Proceedings 1875, pg 82 (1875 Sept 22), El Paso Lodge No. 13, Colorado Springs
Proceedings 1876, pg 36 (1876 Sept 20), El Paso Lodge No. 13, Colorado City

Bassett, Beach
Proceedings 1871, pg 30 (1871 Sept 27), Occidental Lodge U D, Greeley
Proceedings 1872, pg 33 (1872 Sept 24), Occidental Lodge No. 20, Greeley
Proceedings 1873, pg 50 (1873 Oct 1), Occidental Lodge No. 20, Greeley, died
Proceedings 1873, pg 57 (1873 Oct 1), Occidental Lodge No. 20, Greeley

Bassett, Geo W
Proceedings 1874, pg 212 (1874 Sept 30), Central Lodge No. 6, Central

Bassett, Isaac C
Proceedings 1876, pg 46 (1876 Sept 20), Olive Branch Lodge U D, Saguache

Bassett, Owen A
Proceedings 1874, pg 11 (1874 Sept 3), of Lawrence, Grand Representative to the Grand East of Kansas
Proceedings 1874, pg 204 (1874 Sept 30) Grand Lodge of Kansas, Lawrence
Proceedings 1874, pg 207 (1874 Sept 30) Grand Lodge of Kansas, Lawrence
Proceedings 1875, pg 95 (1875 Sept 22) Grand Lodge of Kansas, Lawrence, KS
Proceedings 1876, pg 53 (1876 Sept 20) Grand Lodge of Kansas, of Lawrence, KS

Batchelder, J C
Proceedings 1874, pg 204 (1874 Sept 30) Grand Lodge of Louisiana, New Orleans

Batchell, B R S
Proceedings 1861-1869, pg 168 (1866 Oct 2), Chivington Lodge No. 6, Central City

Batchelor, J C
Proceedings 1861-1869, pg 255 (1868 Feb 10), Grand Secretary, Grand Lodge of Louisiana
Proceedings 1870, pg 62 (1870 Feb 14) Grand Secretary, Grand Lodge of Louisiana

Batchelor, James C
Proceedings 1861-1869, pg 316 (1869 Sept 29) Grand Lodge of Louisiana
Proceedings 1861-1869, pg 331 (1868 Feb 8) Grand Secretary, Grand Lodge of Louisiana
Proceedings 1870, pg 34 (1870 Sept 28) Grand Secretary, Grand Lodge of Louisiana

Colorado's Territorial Masons

Batchelor, James C, cont.
    Proceedings 1871, pg 35 (1871 Sept 27) Grand Secretary, Grand Lodge of Louisiana
    Proceedings 1872, pg 43 (1872 Sept 24) New Orleans, Grand Lodge of Louisiana
    Proceedings 1873, pg 60 (1873 Oct 1) Grand Lodge of Louisiana, New Orleans
    Proceedings 1874, pg 73 (1874 Sept 30) Grand Lodge of Louisiana
    Proceedings 1875, pg 96 (1875 Sept 22) Grand Lodge of Louisiana, New Orleans
    Proceedings 1876, pg 54 (1876 Sept 20) Grand Lodge of Louisiana, New Orleans

Batchelor, Joseph B
    Proceedings 1872, pg 44 (1872 Sept 24) Raleigh, Grand Lodge of North Carolina

Batchtel, B R S
    Proceedings 1861-1869, pg 306 (1869 Sept 29), Central Lodge No. 6, Central City
    Proceedings 1861-1869, pg 224 (1868 Oct 7), Chivington Lodge No. 6, Central City

Bates, A C
    Proceedings 1871, pg 30 (1871 Sept 27), Occidental Lodge U D, Greeley
    Proceedings 1872, pg 33 (1872 Sept 24), Occidental Lodge No. 20, Greeley
    Proceedings 1873, pg 50 (1873 Oct 1), Occidental Lodge No. 20, Greeley
    Proceedings 1874, pg 225 (1874 Sept 30), Occidental Lodge No. 20, Greeley
    Proceedings 1875, pg 87 (1875 Sept 22), Occidental Lodge No. 20, Greeley

Bates, Alvah C
    Proceedings 1876, pg 40 (1876 Sept 20), Occidental Lodge No. 20, Greeley

Bates, Henry C
    Proceedings 1873, pg 43 (1873 Oct 1), Washington Lodge No. 12, Georgetown, Apprentice
    Proceedings 1874, pg 217 (1874 Sept 30), Washington Lodge No. 12, Georgetown
    Proceedings 1875, pg 81 (1875 Sept 22), Washington Lodge No. 12, Georgetown
    Proceedings 1876, pg 35 (1876 Sept 20), Washington Lodge No. 12, Georgetown

Bates, Thomas H
    Proceedings 1871, pg 31 (1871 Sept 27), Argenta Lodge U D, Salt Lake City, Utah

Bates, W J
    Proceedings 1872, pg 93 (1872 Sept 24) Grand Lodge of West Virginia

Bates, Walter
    Proceedings 1872, pg 23 (1872 Sept 24), Union Lodge No. 7, Denver, Fellowcraft
    Proceedings 1873, pg 39 (1873 Oct 1), Union Lodge No. 7, Denver
    Proceedings 1874, pg 214 (1874 Sept 30), Union Lodge No. 7, Denver
    Proceedings 1875, pg 78 (1875 Sept 22), Union Lodge No. 7, Denver
    Proceedings 1876, pg 33 (1876 Sept 20), Union Lodge No. 7, Denver

Bates, William J
    Proceedings 1870, pg 105 (1869 Nov 9) Grand Master, Grand Lodge of West Virginia

Bates, Wm J
    Proceedings 1861-1869, pg 349 (1868 Nov 10) Grand Master, Grand Lodge of West Virginia

Batlin, Asa H
    Proceedings 1873, pg 61 (1873 Oct 1) Grand Lodge of Ohio, Steubenville

Battin, Asa H
    Proceedings 1874, pg 117 (1874 Sept 30) Grand Lodge of Ohio
    Proceedings 1874, pg 204 (1874 Sept 30) Grand Lodge of Ohio, Steubenville

Baulfauf, Frank H
    Proceedings 1874, pg 228 (1874 Sept 30), Doric Lodge U D, Fairplay

Baum, H M
    Proceedings 1873, pg 48 (1873 Oct 1), Laramie Lodge No. 18, Laramie, Wyoming Territory

Baum, Henry M
    Proceedings 1874, pg 219 (1874 Sept 30), Columbia Lodge No. 14, Boulder, Boulder County
    Proceedings 1875, pg 83 (1875 Sept 22), Columbia Lodge No. 14, Boulder
    Proceedings 1876, pg 37 (1876 Sept 20), Columbia Lodge No. 14, Boulder
    Proceedings 1876, pg 50 (1876 Sept 20), Columbia Lodge No. 14, Boulder

Baxter, James
    Proceedings 1861-1869, pg 148 (1865 Nov 7), Nevada Lodge No. 4, Nevadaville
    Proceedings 1861-1869, pg 166 (1866 Oct 2), Nevada Lodge No. 4, Nevadaville
    Proceedings 1861-1869, pg 192 (1867 Oct 8), Nevada Lodge No. 4, Nevadaville
    Proceedings 1861-1869, pg 304 (1869 Sept 29), Nevada Lodge No. 4, Nevadaville
    Proceedings 1870, pg 20 (1870 Sept 28), Nevada Lodge No. 4, Nevadaville
    Proceedings 1871, pg 18 (1871 Sept 27), Nevada Lodge No. 4, Bald Mountain
    Proceedings 1872, pg 19 (1872 Sept 24), Nevada Lodge No. 4, Bald Mountain, Dimitted

Baxter, Jas
    Proceedings 1861-1869, pg 222 (1868 Oct 7), Nevada Lodge No. 4, Nevadaville

Baxter, William
    Proceedings 1872, pg 17 (1872 Sept 24), Golden City Lodge No. 1, Golden City, Fellowcraft

Bayles, B H
　Proceedings 1876, pg 31 (1876 Sept 20) Denver Lodge No. 5

Beach, A
　Proceedings 1870, pg 29 (1870 Sept 28), Pueblo Lodge No. 17, Pueblo

Beach, Aug
　Proceedings 1871, pg 28 (1871 Sept 27), Pueblo Lodge No. 17, Pueblo
　Proceedings 1872, pg 30 (1872 Sept 24), Pueblo Lodge No. 17, Pueblo
　Proceedings 1873, pg 47 (1873 Oct 1), Pueblo Lodge No. 17, Pueblo
　Proceedings 1874, pg 222 (1874 Sept 30), Pueblo Lodge No. 17, Pueblo, Pueblo County
　Proceedings 1875, pg 85 (1875 Sept 22) Pueblo Lodge No. 17

Beach, Augustus
　Proceedings 1861-1869, pg 312 (1869 Sept 29), Pueblo Lodge No. 17, Pueblo

Beach, E C
　Proceedings 1861-1869, pg 168 (1866 Oct 2), Chivington Lodge No. 6, Central City
　Proceedings 1861-1869, pg 193 (1867 Oct 8), Chivington Lodge No. 6, Central City
　Proceedings 1861-1869, pg 202 (1868 Oct 6), Chivington Lodge No. 6, Central City
　Proceedings 1861-1869, pg 224 (1868 Oct 7), Chivington Lodge No. 6, Central City
　Proceedings 1870, pg 4 (1870 Sept 27), Central Lodge No. 6, Central City
　Proceedings 1870, pg 16 (1870 Sept 28), Central Lodge No. 6, Central City
　Proceedings 1870, pg 22 (1870 Sept 28), Central Lodge No. 6, Central City
　Proceedings 1871, pg 4 (1871 Sept 26), Central Lodge No. 6, Central City
　Proceedings 1871, pg 5 (1871 Sept 26) Committee
　Proceedings 1871, pg 12 (1871 Sept 26) Committee
　Proceedings 1871, pg 14 (1871 Sept 27), Central Lodge No. 6, Central City

Beach, Elam C
　Proceedings 1861-1869, pg 306 (1869 Sept 29), Central Lodge No. 6, Central City
　Proceedings 1871, pg 20 (1871 Sept 27), Central Lodge No. 6, Central
　Proceedings 1871, pg 20 (1871 Sept 27), Central Lodge No. 6, Central
　Proceedings 1872, pg 21 (1872 Sept 24), Denver Lodge No. 5, Denver
　Proceedings 1873, pg 38 (1873 Oct 1), Central Lodge No. 6, Central City
　Proceedings 1874, pg 212 (1874 Sept 30), Central Lodge No. 6, Central
　Proceedings 1876, pg 31 (1876 Sept 20), Central Lodge No. 6, Central City

Beach, Elame B
　Proceedings 1875, pg 76 (1875 Sept 22), Central Lodge No. 6, Central City

Beach, M S
　Proceedings 1861-1869, pg 102 (1863 Nov 3) petition for formation of a new lodge in Denver

Beale, Geo E
　Proceedings 1873, pg 43 (1873 Oct 1), Washington Lodge No. 12, Georgetown
　Proceedings 1875, pg 81 (1875 Sept 22), Washington Lodge No. 12, Georgetown, Demitted

Beale, George E
　Proceedings 1874, pg 217 (1874 Sept 30), Washington Lodge No. 12, Georgetown

Beall, John H
　Proceedings 1874, pg 218 (1874 Sept 30), El Paso Lodge No. 13, Colorado Springs
　Proceedings 1875, pg 82 (1875 Sept 22), El Paso Lodge No. 13, Colorado Springs

Beall, John N
　Proceedings 1876, pg 35 (1876 Sept 20), El Paso Lodge No. 13, Colorado City

Beals, D T
　Proceedings 1861-1869, pg 113 (1863 Nov 3), Chivington Lodge No. 6, Central City, Apprentice
　Proceedings 1861-1869, pg 134 (1864 Nov 8), Chivington Lodge No. 6, Central City, Apprentice
　Proceedings 1861-1869, pg 150 (1865 Nov 7), Chivington Lodge No. 6, Central City, Apprentice
　Proceedings 1861-1869, pg 169 (1866 Oct 2), Chivington Lodge No. 6, Central City, Apprentice
　Proceedings 1861-1869, pg 194 (1867 Oct 8), Chivington Lodge No. 6, Central City, Apprentice
　Proceedings 1861-1869, pg 225 (1868 Oct 7), Chivington Lodge No. 6, Central City, Apprentice
　Proceedings 1861-1869, pg 307 (1869 Sept 29), Central Lodge No. 6, Central City, Apprentice

Beals, David T
　Proceedings 1870, pg 22 (1870 Sept 28), Central Lodge No. 6, Central City, Apprentice
　Proceedings 1871, pg 21 (1871 Sept 27), Central Lodge No. 6, Central, Apprentice
　Proceedings 1872, pg 21 (1872 Sept 24), Denver Lodge No. 5, Denver, Apprentice
　Proceedings 1873, pg 39 (1873 Oct 1), Central Lodge No. 6, Central City, Apprentice
　Proceedings 1874, pg 213 (1874 Sept 30), Central Lodge No. 6, Central, Apprentice
　Proceedings 1875, pg 77 (1875 Sept 22), Central Lodge No. 6, Central City, Apprentice
　Proceedings 1876, pg 32 (1876 Sept 20), Central Lodge No. 6, Central City, Apprentice

Beals, E H
　Proceedings 1861-1869, pg 78 (1862 Nov 4), Chivington Lodge No. 6, Central City
　Proceedings 1861-1869, pg 113 (1863 Nov 3), Chivington Lodge No. 6, Central City

Colorado's Territorial Masons

Beals, E H, cont.
- Proceedings 1861-1869, pg 134 (1864 Nov 8), Chivington Lodge No. 6, Central City
- Proceedings 1861-1869, pg 150 (1865 Nov 7), Chivington Lodge No. 6, Central City
- Proceedings 1861-1869, pg 168 (1866 Oct 2), Chivington Lodge No. 6, Central City
- Proceedings 1861-1869, pg 193 (1867 Oct 8), Chivington Lodge No. 6, Central City
- Proceedings 1861-1869, pg 224 (1868 Oct 7), Chivington Lodge No. 6, Central City
- Proceedings 1861-1869, pg 306 (1869 Sept 29), Central Lodge No. 6, Central City
- Proceedings 1870, pg 22 (1870 Sept 28), Central Lodge No. 6, Central City
- Proceedings 1871, pg 20 (1871 Sept 27), Central Lodge No. 6, Central
- Proceedings 1872, pg 22 (1872 Sept 24), Denver Lodge No. 5, Denver

Bean, A J
- Proceedings 1875, pg 78 (1875 Sept 22), Union Lodge No. 7, Denver
- Proceedings 1876, pg 33 (1876 Sept 20), Union Lodge No. 7, Denver

Beardsley, I H
- Proceedings 1871, pg 24 (1871 Sept 27), Washington Lodge No. 12, Georgetown, Fellowcraft
- Proceedings 1875, pg 81 (1875 Sept 22), Washington Lodge No. 12, Georgetown

Beardsley, Isaac H
- Proceedings 1872, pg 26 (1872 Sept 24), Washington Lodge No. 12, Georgetown
- Proceedings 1873, pg 43 (1873 Oct 1), Washington Lodge No. 12, Georgetown
- Proceedings 1874, pg 217 (1874 Sept 30), Washington Lodge No. 12, Georgetown
- Proceedings 1876, pg 35 (1876 Sept 20), Washington Lodge No. 12, Georgetown

Beary, L D
- Proceedings 1874, pg 221 (1874 Sept 30), Cheyenne Lodge No. 16, Cheyenne, Wyoming Territory

Bearzy, John B
- Proceedings 1874, pg 229 (1874 Sept 30), Idaho Springs Lodge U D, Idaho Springs

Beason, Seth
- Proceedings 1861-1869, pg 310 (1869 Sept 29), El Paso Lodge No. 13, Colorado City

Beauzy, J B
- Proceedings 1875, pg 89 (1875 Sept 22) Idaho Springs Lodge U D

Beauzy, John B
- Proceedings 1876, pg 43 (1876 Sept 20) Idaho Springs Lodge No. 26

Beckelman, Frederick
- Proceedings 1861-1869, pg 312 (1869 Sept 29), Cheyenne Lodge No. 16, Cheyenne, Apprentice

Becker, P
- Proceedings 1876, pg 36 (1876 Sept 20), El Paso Lodge No. 13, Colorado City

Becker, Peter
- Proceedings 1873, pg 13 (1873 Sept 30), Ashlar Lodge U D, Colorado Springs
- Proceedings 1873, pg 52 (1873 Oct 1), Ashlar Lodge U D, Colorado Springs
- Proceedings 1874, pg 218 (1874 Sept 30), El Paso Lodge No. 13, Colorado Springs
- Proceedings 1875, pg 82 (1875 Sept 22), El Paso Lodge No. 13, Colorado Springs

Beckner, S W E
- Proceedings 1874, pg 19 (1874 Sept 29), of New York City, NY

Beckwith, A C
- Proceedings 1861-1869, pg 230 (1868 Oct 7), Cheyenne Lodge U D, Cheyenne, Dakota Territory
- Proceedings 1861-1869, pg 312 (1869 Sept 29), Cheyenne Lodge No. 16, Cheyenne
- Proceedings 1870, pg 29 (1870 Sept 28), Cheyenne Lodge No. 16, Cheyenne, Wyoming Territory
- Proceedings 1871, pg 27 (1871 Sept 27), Cheyenne Lodge No. 16, Cheyenne, Wyoming Territory
- Proceedings 1872, pg 29 (1872 Sept 24), Cheyenne Lodge No. 16, Cheyenne, Wyoming Territory
- Proceedings 1873, pg 46 (1873 Oct 1), Cheyenne Lodge No. 16, Cheyenne, Wyoming Territory
- Proceedings 1874, pg 221 (1874 Sept 30), Cheyenne Lodge No. 16, Cheyenne, Wyoming Territory

Beean, Samevel
- Proceedings 1870, pg 76 (1789 June 4) a Blackeman

Beebee, F W
- Proceedings 1874, pg 229 (1874 Sept 30), Idaho Springs Lodge U D, Idaho Springs

Beers, E F
- Proceedings 1875, pg 89 (1875 Sept 22), Doric Lodge No. 25, Fairplay
- Proceedings 1876, pg 42 (1876 Sept 20), Doric Lodge No. 25, Fairplay

Beers, Eli F
- Proceedings 1874, pg 228 (1874 Sept 30), Doric Lodge U D, Fairplay

Beers, Guy
- Proceedings 1873, pg 48 (1873 Oct 1), Laramie Lodge No. 18, Laramie, Wyoming Territory, Fellowcraft
- Proceedings 1874, pg 223 (1874 Sept 30), Laramie Lodge No. 18, Laramie City

Beery, N
- Proceedings 1861-1869, pg 76 (1862 Nov 4), Summit Lodge No. 2, Parkville
- Proceedings 1861-1869, pg 111 (1863 Nov 3), Summit Lodge No. 2, Parkville, dimitted

Beery, R W
- Proceedings 1861-1869, pg 100 (1863 Aug 13), Summit Lodge No. 2, Parkville

Beeson, Seth
Proceedings 1871, pg 25 (1871 Sept 27), El Paso Lodge No. 13, Colorado City
Proceedings 1872, pg 27 (1872 Sept 24), El Paso Lodge No. 13, Colorado City
Proceedings 1873, pg 43 (1873 Oct 1), El Paso Lodge No. 13, Colorado City
Proceedings 1874, pg 218 (1874 Sept 30), El Paso Lodge No. 13, Colorado Springs
Proceedings 1875, pg 82 (1875 Sept 22), El Paso Lodge No. 13, Colorado Springs, Stricken from the rolls

Behm, Lewis
Proceedings 1861-1869, pg 42 (1861 Dec 10), Summit Lodge No. 2, Parkville

Behm, Louis
Proceedings 1861-1869, pg 77 (1862 Nov 4) Denver Lodge No. 5
Proceedings 1861-1869, pg 112 (1863 Nov 3) Denver Lodge No. 5
Proceedings 1861-1869, pg 133 (1864 Nov 8) Denver Lodge No. 5, dimitted
Proceedings 1861-1869, pg 152 (1865 Nov 7), Helena City Lodge U D, Helena City, Montana Territory

Behrung, Emile
Proceedings 1871, pg 25 (1871 Sept 27), El Paso Lodge No. 13, Colorado City

Beighley, H B
Proceedings 1875, pg 89 (1875 Sept 22) Idaho Springs Lodge U D

Beighley, Henry B
Proceedings 1876, pg 42 (1876 Sept 20) Idaho Springs Lodge No. 26

Belcher, Charles T
Proceedings 1876, pg 29 (1876 Sept 20) Golden City Lodge No. 1

Belcher, Chas
Proceedings 1874, pg 226 (1874 Sept 30), Weston Lodge No. 22, Littleton
Proceedings 1875, pg 88 (1875 Sept 22), Weston Lodge No. 22, Littleton, Demitted

Belcher, Chas T
Proceedings 1875, pg 73 (1875 Sept 22) Golden City Lodge No. 1

Belcher, Freeman
Proceedings 1861-1869, pg 230 (1868 Oct 7), Valmont Lodge U D, Valmont
Proceedings 1861-1869, pg 310 (1869 Sept 29), Columbia Lodge No. 14, Boulder City
Proceedings 1870, pg 27 (1870 Sept 28), Columbia Lodge No. 14, Boulder City
Proceedings 1871, pg 25 (1871 Sept 27), Columbia Lodge No. 14, Boulder City
Proceedings 1872, pg 28 (1872 Sept 24), Columbia Lodge No. 14, Boulder
Proceedings 1873, pg 45 (1873 Oct 1), Columbia Lodge No. 14, Boulder, Dimitted
Proceedings 1876, pg 41 (1876 Sept 20), St Vrain Lodge No. 23, Longmont

Belcher, G N
Proceedings 1861-1869, pg 131 (1864 Nov 8) Golden City Lodge No. 1
Proceedings 1861-1869, pg 147 (1865 Nov 7) Golden City Lodge No. 1
Proceedings 1861-1869, pg 160 (1866 Oct 2) Golden City Lodge No. 1
Proceedings 1861-1869, pg 165 (1866 Oct 2) Golden City Lodge No. 1
Proceedings 1861-1869, pg 176 (1867 Oct 7) Golden City Lodge No. 1
Proceedings 1861-1869, pg 191 (1867 Oct 8) Golden City Lodge No. 1
Proceedings 1861-1869, pg 203 (1868 Oct 6) Senior Warden
Proceedings 1861-1869, pg 221 (1868 Oct 7) Golden City Lodge No. 1
Proceedings 1861-1869, pg 303 (1869 Sept 29) Golden City Lodge No. 1
Proceedings 1870, pg 19 (1870 Sept 28), Golden City Lodge No. 1, Golden City
Proceedings 1871, pg 17 (1871 Sept 27), Golden City Lodge No. 1, Golden City
Proceedings 1874, pg 5 (1874 Sept 29), Golden City Lodge No. 1, Golden City

Belcher, Geo W
Proceedings 1873, pg 51 (1873 Oct 1), Weston Lodge No. 22, Littleton
Proceedings 1875, pg 88 (1875 Sept 22), Weston Lodge No. 22, Littleton
Proceedings 1876, pg 5 (1876 Sept 19), Weston Lodge No. 22, Littleton

Belcher, George
Proceedings 1874, pg 226 (1874 Sept 30), Weston Lodge No. 22, Littleton

Belcher, George W
Proceedings 1872, pg 35 (1872 Sept 24), Weston Lodge No. 22, Littleton
Proceedings 1876, pg 41 (1876 Sept 20), Weston Lodge No. 22, Littleton

Belcher, Gilbert N
Proceedings 1872, pg 17 (1872 Sept 24), Golden City Lodge No. 1, Golden City
Proceedings 1873, pg 35 (1873 Oct 1), Golden City Lodge No. 1, Golden City
Proceedings 1874, pg 209 (1874 Sept 30), Golden City Lodge No. 1, Golden City
Proceedings 1875, pg 73 (1875 Sept 22) Golden City Lodge No. 1
Proceedings 1876, pg 29 (1876 Sept 20) Golden City Lodge No. 1

Belcher, W H
Proceedings 1861-1869, pg 111 (1863 Nov 3), Nevada Lodge No. 4, Nevadaville
Proceedings 1861-1869, pg 148 (1865 Nov 7), Nevada Lodge No. 4, Nevadaville

Colorado's Territorial Masons

Belcher, W H, cont.
Proceedings 1861-1869, pg 166 (1866 Oct 2), Nevada Lodge No. 4, Nevadaville
Proceedings 1861-1869, pg 192 (1867 Oct 8), Nevada Lodge No. 4, Nevadaville
Proceedings 1861-1869, pg 304 (1869 Sept 29), Nevada Lodge No. 4, Nevadaville
Proceedings 1871, pg 18 (1871 Sept 27), Nevada Lodge No. 4, Bald Mountain, Dimitted

Belcher, W N
Proceedings 1861-1869, pg 132 (1864 Nov 8), Nevada Lodge No. 4, Nevadaville

Belcher, William H
Proceedings 1870, pg 20 (1870 Sept 28), Nevada Lodge No. 4, Nevadaville

Belcher, Wm H
Proceedings 1861-1869, pg 77 (1862 Nov 4), Nevada Lodge No. 4, Nevadaville
Proceedings 1861-1869, pg 222 (1868 Oct 7), Nevada Lodge No. 4, Nevadaville

Belford, James B
Colorado University Cornerstone Laying, pg 6 (1875 Sept 20) gave an address

Bell, Francis R
Proceedings 1861-1869, pg 308 (1869 Sept 29), Union Lodge No. 7, Denver, Stricken from the rolls

Bell, John H
Proceedings 1876, pg 54 (1876 Sept 20) Grand Lodge of Manitoba, Winnipeg

Bell, John J
Proceedings 1861-1869, pg 271 (1867 June 12) Grand Lodge of New Hampshire
Proceedings 1872, pg 44 (1872 Sept 24) Exeter, Grand Lodge of New Hampshire
Proceedings 1872, pg 77 (1872 Sept 24) Grand Lodge of New Hampshire
Proceedings 1873, pg 61 (1873 Oct 1) Grand Lodge of New Hampshire, Exeter
Proceedings 1874, pg 105 (1874 Sept 30) Grand Lodge of New Hampshire
Proceedings 1874, pg 204 (1874 Sept 30) Grand Lodge of New Hampshire, Exeter

Bellamy, Charles T
Proceedings 1874, pg 217 (1874 Sept 30), Washington Lodge No. 12, Georgetown

Bellamy, Chas T
Proceedings 1861-1869, pg 309 (1869 Sept 29), Washington Lodge No. 12, Georgetown
Proceedings 1870, pg 26 (1870 Sept 28), Washington Lodge No. 12, Georgetown
Proceedings 1871, pg 24 (1871 Sept 27), Washington Lodge No. 12, Georgetown
Proceedings 1872, pg 26 (1872 Sept 24), Washington Lodge No. 12, Georgetown
Proceedings 1873, pg 42 (1873 Oct 1), Washington Lodge No. 12, Georgetown
Proceedings 1875, pg 81 (1875 Sept 22), Washington Lodge No. 12, Georgetown
Proceedings 1876, pg 35 (1876 Sept 20), Washington Lodge No. 12, Georgetown

Belliman, John
Proceedings 1874, pg 6 (1874 Sept 29), St Vrain Lodge No. 23, Longmont

Bellman, John
Proceedings 1874, pg 227 (1874 Sept 30), St Vrain No. 23, Longmont
Proceedings 1876, pg 18 (1876 Sept 20), St Vrain Lodge No. 23, Longmont
Proceedings 1876, pg 41 (1876 Sept 20), St Vrain Lodge No. 23, Longmont

Benbage, E L
Proceedings 1873, pg 41 (1873 Oct 1), Black Hawk Lodge No. 11, Black Hawk
Proceedings 1874, pg 216 (1874 Sept 30), Black Hawk Lodge No. 11, Black Hawk
Proceedings 1875, pg 80 (1875 Sept 22) Black Hawk Lodge No. 11

Benckley, John A
Proceedings 1870, pg 28 (1870 Sept 28), Mount Moriah Lodge No. 15, Canon City

Benjamin, J E
Proceedings 1875, pg 73 (1875 Sept 22) Golden City Lodge No. 1
Proceedings 1876, pg 29 (1876 Sept 20) Golden City Lodge No. 1

Bennet, Joseph P
Proceedings 1876, pg 41 (1876 Sept 20), Weston Lodge No. 22, Littleton

Bennett, A D
Proceedings 1873, pg 50 (1873 Oct 1), Occidental Lodge No. 20, Greeley
Proceedings 1874, pg 225 (1874 Sept 30), Occidental Lodge No. 20, Greeley
Proceedings 1875, pg 87 (1875 Sept 22), Occidental Lodge No. 20, Greeley
Proceedings 1876, pg 40 (1876 Sept 20), Occidental Lodge No. 20, Greeley

Bennett, A S
Proceedings 1872, pg 18 (1872 Sept 24), Nevada Lodge No. 4, Bald Mountain
Proceedings 1875, pg 74 (1875 Sept 22), Nevada Lodge No. 4, Nevada
Proceedings 1876, pg 30 (1876 Sept 20) Nevada Lodge No. 4

Bennett, Agariah S
Proceedings 1873, pg 36 (1873 Oct 1), Nevada Lodge No. 4, Nevada

Bennett, Azariah S
Proceedings 1874, pg 210 (1874 Sept 30), Nevada Lodge No. 4, Bald Mountain, Gilpin County

Bennett, B F
Proceedings 1861-1869, pg 149 (1865 Nov 7), Nevada Lodge No. 4, Nevadaville, Apprentice

Bennett, F R
Proceedings 1861-1869, pg 167 (1866 Oct 2) Denver Lodge No. 5
Proceedings 1861-1869, pg 193 (1867 Oct 8) Denver Lodge No. 5
Proceedings 1861-1869, pg 223 (1868 Oct 7) Denver Lodge No. 5
Proceedings 1861-1869, pg 305 (1869 Sept 29) Denver Lodge No. 5
Proceedings 1870, pg 21 (1870 Sept 28), Denver Lodge No. 5, Denver
Proceedings 1872, pg 20 (1872 Sept 24), Denver Lodge No. 5, Denver

Bennett, Jos P
Proceedings 1874, pg 226 (1874 Sept 30), Weston Lodge No. 22, Littleton
Proceedings 1875, pg 88 (1875 Sept 22), Weston Lodge No. 22, Littleton

Benson, A S
Proceedings 1875, pg 73 (1875 Sept 22) Golden City Lodge No. 1
Proceedings 1876, pg 29 (1876 Sept 20) Golden City Lodge No. 1

Bent, G C
Proceedings 1875, pg 85 (1875 Sept 22) Pueblo Lodge No. 17

Bentley, Elijah
Proceedings 1861-1869, pg 195 (1867 Oct 8), Empire Lodge No. 8, Empire City

Bentley, W G
Proceedings 1872, pg 33 (1872 Sept 24), Occidental Lodge No. 20, Greeley
Proceedings 1874, pg 225 (1874 Sept 30), Occidental Lodge No. 20, Greeley
Proceedings 1875, pg 17 (1875 Sept 21), Collins Lodge No. 19, Fort Collins
Proceedings 1875, pg 17 (1875 Sept 21) committee
Proceedings 1875, pg 33 (1875 Sept 22) committee
Proceedings 1875, pg 34 (1875 Sept 22) committee
Proceedings 1875, pg 38 (1875 Sept 22), Occidental Lodge No. 20, Greeley
Proceedings 1875, pg 87 (1875 Sept 22), Occidental Lodge No. 20, Greeley
Proceedings 1876, pg 5 (1876 Sept 19), Occidental Lodge No. 20, Greeley
Proceedings 1876, pg 6 (1876 Sept 19) committee
Proceedings 1876, pg 13 (1876 Mar 20), Occidental Lodge No. 20, Greeley
Proceedings 1876, pg 22 (1876 Sept 20), Occidental Lodge No. 20, Greeley
Proceedings 1876, pg 22 (1876 Sept 20) committee
Proceedings 1876, pg 40 (1876 Sept 20), Occidental Lodge No. 20, Greeley

Bentley, Wyllys G
Proceedings 1876, pg 24 (1876 Sept 20) committee

Bently, Elijah
Proceedings 1861-1869, pg 170 (1866 Oct 2), Empire Lodge No. 8, Empire City
Proceedings 1861-1869, pg 226 (1868 Oct 7), Empire Lodge No. 8, Empire City
Proceedings 1861-1869, pg 308 (1869 Sept 29), Empire Lodge No. 8, Empire City
Proceedings 1870, pg 24 (1870 Sept 28), Empire Lodge No. 8, Empire
Proceedings 1872, pg 23 (1872 Sept 24), Empire Lodge No. 8, Empire
Proceedings 1873, pg 41 (1873 Oct 1), Empire Lodge No. 8, Empire
Proceedings 1874, pg 215 (1874 Sept 30), Empire Lodge No. 8, Empire

Bently, W G
Proceedings 1873, pg 50 (1873 Oct 1), Occidental Lodge No. 20, Greeley
Proceedings 1875, pg 31 (1875 Sept 21) committee

Benton, Canon
Proceedings 1875, pg 90 (1875 Sept 22), Huerfano Lodge U D, Walsenburg

Berg, Abraham
Proceedings 1874, pg 8 (1874 Jan 1), Doric Lodge U D, Fairplay

Berger, A E
Proceedings 1861-1869, pg 197 (1867 Oct 8), Columbia Lodge U D, Boulder
Proceedings 1861-1869, pg 228 (1868 Oct 7), Columbia Lodge No. 14, Columbia City

Berger, Andrew
Proceedings 1861-1869, pg 310 (1869 Sept 29), Columbia Lodge No. 14, Boulder City
Proceedings 1870, pg 27 (1870 Sept 28), Columbia Lodge No. 14, Boulder City
Proceedings 1871, pg 25 (1871 Sept 27), Columbia Lodge No. 14, Boulder City
Proceedings 1872, pg 27 (1872 Sept 24), Columbia Lodge No. 14, Boulder
Proceedings 1873, pg 44 (1873 Oct 1), Columbia Lodge No. 14, Boulder
Proceedings 1874, pg 219 (1874 Sept 30), Columbia Lodge No. 14, Boulder, Boulder County
Proceedings 1875, pg 83 (1875 Sept 22), Columbia Lodge No. 14, Boulder, Stricken from the rolls

Bergh, A
Proceedings 1874, pg 220 (1874 Sept 30), Mount Moriah Lodge No. 15, Canon City, Demitted
Proceedings 1875, pg 89 (1875 Sept 22), Doric Lodge No. 25, Fairplay
Proceedings 1876, pg 5 (1876 Sept 19), Doric Lodge No. 25, Fairplay
Proceedings 1876, pg 5 (1876 Sept 19) committee
Proceedings 1876, pg 22 (1876 Sept 20), Doric Lodge No. 25, Fairplay

Bergh, Abraham
    Proceedings 1873, pg 45 (1873 Oct 1), Mount Moriah Lodge No. 15, Canon City
    Proceedings 1874, pg 35 (1874 Sept 30), Doric Lodge No. 25, Fairplay
    Proceedings 1874, pg 228 (1874 Sept 30), Doric Lodge U D, Fairplay
    Proceedings 1876, pg cover (1876 Sept 20) Junior Grand Warden, Fairplay
    Proceedings 1876, pg 42 (1876 Sept 20), Doric Lodge No. 25, Fairplay

Bergman, Isaac
    Proceedings 1874, pg 221 (1874 Sept 30), Cheyenne Lodge No. 16, Cheyenne, Wyoming Territory

Bernard, O C
    Proceedings 1873, pg 46 (1873 Oct 1), Cheyenne Lodge No. 16, Cheyenne, Wyoming Territory
    Proceedings 1874, pg 221 (1874 Sept 30), Cheyenne Lodge No. 16, Cheyenne, Wyoming Territory

Berry
    Proceedings 1870, pg 11 (1870 Sept 27), of Portland, ME,, Editor, The Masonic Token

Berry, Barnard
    Proceedings 1861-1869, pg 193 (1867 Oct 8) Denver Lodge No. 5
    Proceedings 1870, pg 21 (1870 Sept 28), Denver Lodge No. 5, Denver
    Proceedings 1871, pg 19 (1871 Sept 27) Denver Lodge No. 5
    Proceedings 1873, pg 37 (1873 Oct 1), Denver Lodge No. 5, Denver
    Proceedings 1874, pg 211 (1874 Sept 30), Denver Lodge No. 5, Denver
    Proceedings 1861-1869, pg 149 (1865 Nov 7), Nevada Lodge No. 4, Nevadaville
    Proceedings 1861-1869, pg 167 (1866 Oct 2) Denver Lodge No. 5
    Proceedings 1861-1869, pg 223 (1868 Oct 7) Denver Lodge No. 5
    Proceedings 1861-1869, pg 305 (1869 Sept 29) Denver Lodge No. 5
    Proceedings 1872, pg 19 (1872 Sept 24), Denver Lodge No. 5, Denver
    Proceedings 1875, pg 75 (1875 Sept 22) Denver Lodge No. 5
    Proceedings 1876, pg 31 (1876 Sept 20) Denver Lodge No. 5

Berry, D B
    Proceedings 1861-1869, pg 229 (1868 Oct 7), Pueblo Lodge U D, Pueblo
    Proceedings 1861-1869, pg 312 (1869 Sept 29), Pueblo Lodge No. 17, Pueblo
    Proceedings 1874, pg 222 (1874 Sept 30), Pueblo Lodge No. 17, Pueblo, Pueblo County
    Proceedings 1875, pg 85 (1875 Sept 22) Pueblo Lodge No. 17
    Proceedings 1876, pg 38 (1876 Sept 20) Pueblo Lodge No. 17

Berry, David B
    Proceedings 1870, pg 30 (1870 Sept 28), Pueblo Lodge No. 17, Pueblo
    Proceedings 1871, pg 28 (1871 Sept 27), Pueblo Lodge No. 17, Pueblo
    Proceedings 1872, pg 31 (1872 Sept 24), Pueblo Lodge No. 17, Pueblo
    Proceedings 1873, pg 47 (1873 Oct 1), Pueblo Lodge No. 17, Pueblo

Berry, Ira
    Proceedings 1861-1869, pg 259 (1868 May 5), Grand Master, Grand Lodge of Maine
    Proceedings 1861-1869, pg 332 (1869 May 4) Grand Secretary, Grand Lodge of Maine
    Proceedings 1870, pg 34 (1870 Sept 28) Grand Secretary, Grand Lodge of Maine
    Proceedings 1870, pg 64 (1870 May 3) Grand Secretary, Grand Lodge of Maine
    Proceedings 1871, pg 35 (1871 Sept 27) Grand Secretary, Grand Lodge of Maine
    Proceedings 1872, pg 43 (1872 Sept 24) Portland, Grand Lodge of Maine
    Proceedings 1872, pg 70 (1872 Sept 24) Grand Lodge of Maine
    Proceedings 1873, pg 60 (1873 Oct 1) Grand Lodge of Maine, Portland
    Proceedings 1874, pg 19 (1874 Sept 29), of Portland, ME
    Proceedings 1874, pg 77 (1874 Sept 30) Grand Lodge of Maine
    Proceedings 1874, pg 78 (1874 Sept 30) Grand Lodge of Maine
    Proceedings 1874, pg 204 (1874 Sept 30) Grand Lodge of Maine, Portland
    Proceedings 1875, pg 96 (1875 Sept 22) Grand Lodge of Maine, Portland
    Proceedings 1876, pg 54 (1876 Sept 20) Grand Lodge of Maine, Portland

Berry, John S
    Proceedings 1870, pg 66 (1869 Nov 15) Grand Master, Grand Lodge of Maryland

Berry, Julius
    Proceedings 1861-1869, pg 193 (1867 Oct 8) Denver Lodge No. 5
    Proceedings 1861-1869, pg 223 (1868 Oct 7) Denver Lodge No. 5
    Proceedings 1861-1869, pg 305 (1869 Sept 29) Denver Lodge No. 5
    Proceedings 1870, pg 21 (1870 Sept 28), Denver Lodge No. 5, Denver
    Proceedings 1871, pg 19 (1871 Sept 27) Denver Lodge No. 5
    Proceedings 1872, pg 20 (1872 Sept 24), Denver Lodge No. 5, Denver, Dimitted
    Proceedings 1872, pg 31 (1872 Sept 24), Pueblo Lodge No. 17, Pueblo
    Proceedings 1873, pg 47 (1873 Oct 1), Pueblo Lodge No. 17, Pueblo
    Proceedings 1874, pg 222 (1874 Sept 30), Pueblo Lodge No. 17, Pueblo, Pueblo County

Proceedings 1875, pg 85 (1875 Sept 22) Pueblo Lodge No. 17

Proceedings 1876, pg 38 (1876 Sept 20) Pueblo Lodge No. 17

Berry, N

Proceedings 1861-1869, pg 42 (1861 Dec 10), Summit Lodge No. 2, Parkville

Berry, R W

Proceedings 1861-1869, pg 111 (1863 Nov 3), Summit Lodge No. 2, Parkville, dimitted

Bertolette, John C

Proceedings 1873, pg 39 (1873 Oct 1), Union Lodge No. 7, Denver

Proceedings 1874, pg 214 (1874 Sept 30), Union Lodge No. 7, Denver

Proceedings 1875, pg 78 (1875 Sept 22), Union Lodge No. 7, Denver

Proceedings 1876, pg 41 (1876 Sept 20), Weston Lodge No. 22, Littleton

Proceedings 1876, pg 48 (1876 Sept 20), Union Lodge No. 7, Denver, 1876 Feb 12

Beshoar, M

Proceedings 1861-1869, pg 229 (1868 Oct 7), Pueblo Lodge U D, Pueblo

Proceedings 1874, pg 222 (1874 Sept 30), Pueblo Lodge No. 17, Pueblo, Pueblo County

Proceedings 1875, pg 85 (1875 Sept 22) Pueblo Lodge No. 17

Proceedings 1876, pg 6 (1876 Sept 19), Las Animas Lodge No. 28, Trinidad

Proceedings 1876, pg 22 (1876 Sept 20), Las Animas Lodge No. 28, Trinidad

Beshoar, Michael

Proceedings 1861-1869, pg 312 (1869 Sept 29), Pueblo Lodge No. 17, Pueblo

Proceedings 1870, pg 30 (1870 Sept 28), Pueblo Lodge No. 17, Pueblo

Proceedings 1871, pg 28 (1871 Sept 27), Pueblo Lodge No. 17, Pueblo

Proceedings 1873, pg 47 (1873 Oct 1), Pueblo Lodge No. 17, Pueblo

Proceedings 1875, pg 91 (1875 Sept 22), Las Animas Lodge U D, Trinidad

Proceedings 1876, pg 43 (1876 Sept 20), Las Animas Lodge No. 28, Trinidad

Proceedings 1876, pg 48 (1876 Sept 20) Pueblo Lodge No. 17, 1876 Feb 12

Beshore, Michael

Proceedings 1872, pg 31 (1872 Sept 24), Pueblo Lodge No. 17, Pueblo

Best, John

Proceedings 1861-1869, pg 168 (1866 Oct 2), Chivington Lodge No. 6, Central City

Proceedings 1861-1869, pg 224 (1868 Oct 7), Chivington Lodge No. 6, Central City

Proceedings 1861-1869, pg 306 (1869 Sept 29), Central Lodge No. 6, Central City

Proceedings 1870, pg 22 (1870 Sept 28), Central Lodge No. 6, Central City

Proceedings 1871, pg 20 (1871 Sept 27), Central Lodge No. 6, Central

Proceedings 1872, pg 21 (1872 Sept 24), Denver Lodge No. 5, Denver

Proceedings 1873, pg 38 (1873 Oct 1), Central Lodge No. 6, Central City

Proceedings 1874, pg 212 (1874 Sept 30), Central Lodge No. 6, Central

Proceedings 1875, pg 76 (1875 Sept 22), Central Lodge No. 6, Central City

Proceedings 1876, pg 32 (1876 Sept 20), Central Lodge No. 6, Central City

Best, John A

Proceedings 1861-1869, pg 194 (1867 Oct 8), Chivington Lodge No. 6, Central City

Best, R W

Proceedings 1861-1869, pg 343 (1868 Dec 7) Grand Master, Grand Lodge of North Carolina

Betts, George C

Proceedings 1861-1869, pg 135 (1864 Nov 8), Union Lodge No. 7, Denver, dimitted

Beverage, James

Proceedings 1874, pg 219 (1874 Sept 30), Columbia Lodge No. 14, Boulder, Boulder County

Proceedings 1876, pg 37 (1876 Sept 20), Columbia Lodge No. 14, Boulder

Proceedings 1875, pg 83 (1875 Sept 22), Columbia Lodge No. 14, Boulder

Beverly, James C

Proceedings 1861-1869, pg 111 (1863 Nov 3), Nevada Lodge No. 4, Nevadaville

Bichelman, Fred'k

Proceedings 1870, pg 29 (1870 Sept 28), Cheyenne Lodge No. 16, Cheyenne, Wyoming Territory, Apprentice

Bickleman, Frederick

Proceedings 1871, pg 27 (1871 Sept 27), Cheyenne Lodge No. 16, Cheyenne, Wyoming Territory, Apprentice

Bicklman, Fred K

Proceedings 1872, pg 49 (1872 Sept 24), Cheyenne Lodge No. 16, Cheyenne, Wyoming Territory

Bidle, E

Proceedings 1861-1869, pg 76 (1862 Nov 4), Summit Lodge No. 2, Parkville

Proceedings 1861-1869, pg 111 (1863 Nov 3), Summit Lodge No. 2, Parkville, deceased

Biggs, A J

Proceedings 1861-1869, pg 148 (1865 Nov 7), Nevada Lodge No. 4, Nevadaville

Proceedings 1861-1869, pg 166 (1866 Oct 2), Nevada Lodge No. 4, Nevadaville

Proceedings 1861-1869, pg 192 (1867 Oct 8), Nevada Lodge No. 4, Nevadaville

Proceedings 1861-1869, pg 222 (1868 Oct 7), Nevada Lodge No. 4, Nevadaville

Colorado's Territorial Masons

Biggs, A J, cont.
Proceedings 1861-1869, pg 304 (1869 Sept 29), Nevada Lodge No. 4, Nevadaville
Proceedings 1871, pg 18 (1871 Sept 27), Nevada Lodge No. 4, Bald Mountain

Biggs, Andrew J
Proceedings 1861-1869, pg 132 (1864 Nov 8), Nevada Lodge No. 4, Nevadaville, Apprentice
Proceedings 1872, pg 18 (1872 Sept 24), Nevada Lodge No. 4, Bald Mountain
Proceedings 1873, pg 36 (1873 Oct 1), Nevada Lodge No. 4, Nevada
Proceedings 1874, pg 211 (1874 Sept 30), Nevada Lodge No. 4, Bald Mountain, Gilpin County, Stricken from the rolls

Biggs, H
Proceedings 1861-1869, pg 303 (1869 Sept 29) Golden City Lodge No. 1, Apprentice

Biggs, Hezekiah
Proceedings 1870, pg 19 (1870 Sept 28), Golden City Lodge No. 1, Golden City
Proceedings 1871, pg 17 (1871 Sept 27), Golden City Lodge No. 1, Golden City
Proceedings 1872, pg 18 (1872 Sept 24), Golden City Lodge No. 1, Golden City, Dimitted
Proceedings 1872, pg 27 (1872 Sept 24), El Paso Lodge No. 13, Colorado City
Proceedings 1873, pg 43 (1873 Oct 1), El Paso Lodge No. 13, Colorado City
Proceedings 1874, pg 218 (1874 Sept 30), El Paso Lodge No. 13, Colorado Springs, Demitted
Proceedings 1875, pg 88 (1875 Sept 22), Weston Lodge No. 22, Littleton
Proceedings 1876, pg 41 (1876 Sept 20), Weston Lodge No. 22, Littleton
Proceedings 1874, pg 226 (1874 Sept 30), Weston Lodge No. 22, Littleton

Biggt, Andrew J
Proceedings 1870, pg 20 (1870 Sept 28), Nevada Lodge No. 4, Nevadaville

Bigham, J
Proceedings 1871, pg 26 (1871 Sept 27), Mount Moriah Lodge No. 15, Canon City

Bigham, John
Proceedings 1872, pg 29 (1872 Sept 24), Mount Moriah Lodge No. 15, Canon City
Proceedings 1873, pg 45 (1873 Oct 1), Mount Moriah Lodge No. 15, Canon City
Proceedings 1876, pg 38 (1876 Sept 20), Mount Moriah Lodge No. 15, Canon City

Bigler
Proceedings 1875, pg 28 (1875 Sept 21) motion
Proceedings 1876, pg 17 (1876 Sept 19) motion

Bigler, J A J
Proceedings 1871, pg 19 (1871 Sept 27) Denver Lodge No. 5

Proceedings 1872, pg 19 (1872 Sept 24), Denver Lodge No. 5, Denver
Proceedings 1873, pg 6 (1873 Sept 30), Denver Lodge No. 5, Denver
Proceedings 1873, pg 37 (1873 Oct 1), Denver Lodge No. 5, Denver
Proceedings 1874, pg 3 (1874 Sept 29) Junior Grand Deacon
Proceedings 1874, pg 5 (1874 Sept 29), Denver Lodge No. 5, Denver
Proceedings 1874, pg 37 (1874 Sept 30) resolution
Proceedings 1874, pg 211 (1874 Sept 30), Denver Lodge No. 5, Denver
Proceedings 1875, pg cover (1875 Sept 22) Junior Grand Warden, Denver
Proceedings 1875, pg 16 (1875 Sept 21) Denver Lodge No. 5
Proceedings 1875, pg 17 (1875 Sept 21) committee
Proceedings 1875, pg 38 (1875 Sept 22) per diem
Proceedings 1876, pg 4 (1876 Sept 19) Denver Lodge No. 5
Proceedings 1876, pg 30 (1876 Sept 20) Denver Lodge No. 5

Bigler, Jacob A
Proceedings 1876, pg cover (1876 Sept 20) Grand Treasurer, Denver

Bigler, Jacob A J
Colorado University Cornerstone Laying, pg 3 (1875 Sept 20) Senior Grand Deacon
Proceedings 1870, pg 21 (1870 Sept 28), Denver Lodge No. 5, Denver
Proceedings 1875, pg 33 (1875 Sept 22) Junior Grand Warden, Denver
Proceedings 1875, pg 75 (1875 Sept 22) Denver Lodge No. 5
Proceedings 1876, pg 3 (1876 Sept 19) Junior Grand Deacon
Proceedings 1876, pg 18 (1876 Sept 19) Grand Treasurer

Biles, James
Proceedings 1861-1869, pg 284 (1867 Sept 18), Grand Master, Grand Lodge of Washington

Bill, F R
Proceedings 1861-1869, pg 151 (1865 Nov 7), Chivington Lodge No. 6, Central City

Bill, Francis R
Proceedings 1861-1869, pg 102 (1863 Nov 3) petition for formation of a new lodge in Denver
Proceedings 1861-1869, pg 134 (1864 Nov 8), Union Lodge No. 7, Denver
Proceedings 1861-1869, pg 169 (1866 Oct 2), Union Lodge No. 7, Denver
Proceedings 1861-1869, pg 195 (1867 Oct 8), Union Lodge No. 7, Denver
Proceedings 1861-1869, pg 225 (1868 Oct 7), Union Lodge No. 7, Denver

Billings
Proceedings 1870, pg 11 (1870 Sept 27), of Chicago, IL,, Editor, The Mystic Star

Billings, Geo N
  Proceedings 1861-1869, pg 169 (1866 Oct 2), Union Lodge No. 7, Denver
  Proceedings 1861-1869, pg 225 (1868 Oct 7), Union Lodge No. 7, Denver
  Proceedings 1861-1869, pg 307 (1869 Sept 29), Union Lodge No. 7, Denver
  Proceedings 1870, pg 23 (1870 Sept 28), Union Lodge No. 7, Denver
  Proceedings 1871, pg 21 (1871 Sept 27), Union Lodge No. 7, Denver
  Proceedings 1872, pg 22 (1872 Sept 24), Union Lodge No. 7, Denver
  Proceedings 1874, pg 214 (1874 Sept 30), Union Lodge No. 7, Denver
  Proceedings 1875, pg 78 (1875 Sept 22), Union Lodge No. 7, Denver

Billings, George N
  Proceedings 1873, pg 39 (1873 Oct 1), Union Lodge No. 7, Denver
  Proceedings 1876, pg 33 (1876 Sept 20), Union Lodge No. 7, Denver

Binckley, John A
  Proceedings 1861-1869, pg 311 (1869 Sept 29), Mount Moriah Lodge No. 15, Canon City

Bingham, Jno R
  Proceedings 1870, pg 56 (1869 Oct 4) Binghampton Lodge No. 177, Grand Lodge of New York

Bingham, John
  Proceedings 1874, pg 220 (1874 Sept 30), Mount Moriah Lodge No. 15, Canon City
  Proceedings 1875, pg 84 (1875 Sept 22), Mount Moriah Lodge No. 15, Canon City
  Proceedings 1876, pg 50 (1876 Sept 20), Mount Moriah Lodge No. 15, Canon City

Binghurst, Geo H
  Proceedings 1874, pg 205 (1874 Sept 30) Grand Lodge of Texas, Houston

Binkley, John A
  Proceedings 1871, pg 26 (1871 Sept 27), Mount Moriah Lodge No. 15, Canon City
  Proceedings 1873, pg 45 (1873 Oct 1), Mount Moriah Lodge No. 15, Canon City
  Proceedings 1874, pg 220 (1874 Sept 30), Mount Moriah Lodge No. 15, Canon City
  Proceedings 1875, pg 84 (1875 Sept 22), Mount Moriah Lodge No. 15, Canon City
  Proceedings 1876, pg 38 (1876 Sept 20), Mount Moriah Lodge No. 15, Canon City

Bird, James
  Proceedings 1873, pg 48 (1873 Oct 1), Laramie Lodge No. 18, Laramie, Wyoming Territory, Apprentice
  Proceedings 1874, pg 224 (1874 Sept 30), Laramie Lodge No. 18, Laramie City, Apprentice

Birdsall, C S
  Proceedings 1861-1869, pg 131 (1864 Nov 8) Golden City Lodge No. 1, Apprentice

Birdsell, C S
  Proceedings 1861-1869, pg 110 (1863 Nov 3) Golden City Lodge No. 1, Apprentice,

Bishop
  Proceedings 1870, pg 11 (1870 Sept 27), of San Francisco, CA,, Editor, The Masonic Mirror

Bishop, Alex G
  Proceedings 1876, pg 34 (1876 Sept 20) Black Hawk Lodge No. 11

Bishop, William
  Proceedings 1875, pg 89 (1875 Sept 22) Idaho Springs Lodge U D
  Proceedings 1876, pg 43 (1876 Sept 20) Idaho Springs Lodge No. 26

Bissell, Charles R
  Proceedings 1874, pg 218 (1874 Sept 30), El Paso Lodge No. 13, Colorado Springs
  Proceedings 1875, pg 82 (1875 Sept 22), El Paso Lodge No. 13, Colorado Springs
  Proceedings 1876, pg 36 (1876 Sept 20), El Paso Lodge No. 13, Colorado City

Bixby, Amos
  Proceedings 1861-1869, pg 197 (1867 Oct 8), Columbia Lodge U D, Boulder, Apprentice
  Proceedings 1861-1869, pg 228 (1868 Oct 7), Columbia Lodge No. 14, Columbia City, Apprentice
  Proceedings 1870, pg 28 (1870 Sept 28), Columbia Lodge No. 14, Boulder City, Apprentice
  Proceedings 1871, pg 26 (1871 Sept 27), Columbia Lodge No. 14, Boulder City, Apprentice
  Proceedings 1872, pg 28 (1872 Sept 24), Columbia Lodge No. 14, Boulder, Apprentice
  Proceedings 1873, pg 45 (1873 Oct 1), Columbia Lodge No. 14, Boulder, Apprentice
  Proceedings 1874, pg 219 (1874 Sept 30), Columbia Lodge No. 14, Boulder, Boulder County, Apprentice
  Proceedings 1875, pg 83 (1875 Sept 22), Columbia Lodge No. 14, Boulder, Apprentice
  Proceedings 1876, pg 37 (1876 Sept 20), Columbia Lodge No. 14, Boulder, Apprentice

Blachley, A T
  Proceedings 1873, pg 43 (1873 Oct 1), El Paso Lodge No. 13, Colorado City
  Proceedings 1874, pg 218 (1874 Sept 30), El Paso Lodge No. 13, Colorado Springs
  Proceedings 1875, pg 82 (1875 Sept 22), El Paso Lodge No. 13, Colorado Springs
  Proceedings 1876, pg 49 (1876 Sept 20), El Paso Lodge No. 13, Colorado City, 1876 July 22

Blachley, H F
  Proceedings 1872, pg 27 (1872 Sept 24), El Paso Lodge No. 13, Colorado City

Blachly, F C
  Proceedings 1875, pg 85 (1875 Sept 22) Pueblo Lodge No. 17
  Proceedings 1876, pg 38 (1876 Sept 20) Pueblo Lodge No. 17

Black Hawk Lodge No. 11
    Proceedings 1875, pg 23 (1875 Sept 21) has not provided annual returns
    Proceedings 1875, pg 25 (1875 Sept 21) dues paid
    Proceedings 1875, pg 92 (1875 Sept 22)
    Proceedings 1876, pg 52 (1876 Sept 20)

Black Hawk Lodge No. 11, Black Hawk
    Proceedings 1861-1869, pg 156 (1866 Oct 1) charter granted
    Proceedings 1861-1869, pg 181 (1867 Oct 7) dues paid
    Proceedings 1861-1869, pg 292 (1869 Sept 28) paid dues after report was submitted
    Proceedings 1874, pg 208 (1874 Sept 30)
    Proceedings 1876, pg 13 (1876 Sept 19) dues paid
    Proceedings 1876, pg 24 (1876 Sept 20) correction to returns

Black Hawk Lodge U D, Black Hawk
    Proceedings 1861-1869, pg 155 (1866 Feb 1) dispensation
    Proceedings 1861-1869, pg 158 (1866 Feb 16) dispensation

Black, W H
    Proceedings 1871, pg 27 (1871 Sept 27), Cheyenne Lodge No. 16, Cheyenne, Wyoming Territory
    Proceedings 1872, pg 29 (1872 Sept 24), Cheyenne Lodge No. 16, Cheyenne, Wyoming Territory
    Proceedings 1873, pg 46 (1873 Oct 1), Cheyenne Lodge No. 16, Cheyenne, Wyoming Territory
    Proceedings 1874, pg 221 (1874 Sept 30), Cheyenne Lodge No. 16, Cheyenne, Wyoming Territory

Blackie
    Proceedings 1872, pg 88 (1872 Sept 24) Grand Lodge of Tennessee

Blackie, Geo L
    Proceedings 1872, pg 86 (1872 Sept 24) Grand Lodge of Tennessee

Blackie, Geo S
    Proceedings 1872, pg 44 (1872 Sept 24) Nashville, Grand Lodge of Tennessee
    Proceedings 1872, pg 87 (1872 Sept 24) Grand Lodge of Tennessee
    Proceedings 1873, pg 61 (1873 Oct 1) Grand Lodge of Tennessee, Nashville,

Blackshear
    Proceedings 1874, pg 58 (1874 Sept 30) Grand Lodge of Georgia

Blackshear, J E
    Proceedings 1861-1869, pg 316 (1869 Sept 29) Grand Lodge of Georgia
    Proceedings 1870, pg 34 (1870 Sept 28) Grand Secretary, Grand Lodge of Georgia
    Proceedings 1870, pg 53 (1869 Oct 26) Grand Secretary, Grand Lodge of Georgia
    Proceedings 1871, pg 35 (1871 Sept 27) Grand Secretary, Grand Lodge of Georgia
    Proceedings 1872, pg 43 (1872 Sept 24) Macon, Grand Lodge of Georgia
    Proceedings 1872, pg 59 (1872 Sept 24) Grand Lodge of Georgia
    Proceedings 1872, pg 61 (1872 Sept 24) Grand Lodge of Georgia
    Proceedings 1873, pg 60 (1873 Oct 1) Grand Lodge of Georgia, Macon

Blackshear, J Emmet
    Proceedings 1870, pg 55 (1869 Oct 26) Grand Lodge of Georgia
    Proceedings 1874, pg 57 (1874 Sept 30) Grand Lodge of Georgia
    Proceedings 1874, pg 204 (1874 Sept 30) Grand Lodge of Georgia, Macon
    Proceedings 1875, pg 96 (1875 Sept 22) Grand Lodge of Georgia, Macon
    Proceedings 1876, pg 54 (1876 Sept 20) Grand Lodge of Georgia, Macon,

Blair
    Proceedings 1861-1869, pg 80 (1863 May 6) committee
    Proceedings 1861-1869, pg 106 (1863 Nov 3) motion

Blair, C H
    Proceedings 1861-1869, pg 76 (1862 Nov 4), Summit Lodge No. 2, Parkville
    Proceedings 1861-1869, pg 80 (1863 May 6) committee
    Proceedings 1861-1869, pg 80 (1863 May 6), Summit Lodge No. 2, Parkville
    Proceedings 1861-1869, pg 92 (1863 Apr 17) committee
    Proceedings 1861-1869, pg 97 (1863 Nov 2) Grand Junior Deacon
    Proceedings 1861-1869, pg 100 (1863 Nov 2) committee
    Proceedings 1861-1869, pg 110 (1863 Nov 3), Summit Lodge No. 2, Parkville
    Proceedings 1861-1869, pg 131 (1864 Nov 8) Golden City Lodge No. 1
    Proceedings 1861-1869, pg 180 (1867 Oct 7) dues received
    Proceedings 1861-1869, pg 181 (1867 May 11) dues paid

Blair, Charles H
    Proceedings 1861-1869, pg 98 (1863 Nov 2) committee
    Proceedings 1861-1869, pg 98 (1863 Nov 2), Summit Lodge No. 2, Parkville
    Proceedings 1861-1869, pg 99 (1863 Nov 2), Summit Lodge No. 2, Parkville, Grand Junior Deacon
    Proceedings 1874, pg 214 (1874 Sept 30), Union Lodge No. 7, Denver
    Proceedings 1875, pg 78 (1875 Sept 22), Union Lodge No. 7, Denver
    Proceedings 1876, pg 33 (1876 Sept 20), Union Lodge No. 7, Denver

Blair, Chas H
    Proceedings 1861-1869, pg 94 (1863 Apr 17) committee
    Proceedings 1861-1869, pg 98 (1863 Nov 2) committee
    Proceedings 1861-1869, pg 100 (1863 Nov 3) Grand Junior Deacon

Blair, F M
    Proceedings 1870, pg 58 (1870 May 24), Honorary Member, Grand Lodge of Indiana, deceased

Blair, John
    Proceedings 1872, pg 36 (1872 Sept 24), Ashlar Lodge U D, Colorado Springs

Blake
    Proceedings 1861-1869, pg 34 (1861 Dec 10) old Auraria Lodge U D organized under the Grand Lodge of Kansas
    Proceedings 1861-1869, pg 37 (1861 Dec 12) motion

Blake, C H
    Proceedings 1861-1869, pg 38 (1861 Dec 12) Senior Grand Deacon
    Proceedings 1861-1869, pg 112 (1863 Nov 3) Denver Lodge No. 5
    Proceedings 1861-1869, pg 149 (1865 Nov 7), Nevada Lodge No. 4, Nevadaville
    Proceedings 1861-1869, pg 167 (1866 Oct 2) Denver Lodge No. 5

Blake, Charles
    Proceedings 1861-1869, pg 224 (1868 Oct 7) Denver Lodge No. 5, Dimitted

Blake, Charles H
    Proceedings 1861-1869, pg 192 (1867 Oct 8) Denver Lodge No. 5
    Proceedings 1861-1869, pg 312 (1869 Sept 29), Pueblo Lodge No. 17, Pueblo
    Proceedings 1870, pg 30 (1870 Sept 28), Pueblo Lodge No. 17, Pueblo
    Proceedings 1871, pg 28 (1871 Sept 27), Pueblo Lodge No. 17, Pueblo
    Proceedings 1872, pg 31 (1872 Sept 24), Pueblo Lodge No. 17, Pueblo
    Proceedings 1873, pg 47 (1873 Oct 1), Pueblo Lodge No. 17, Pueblo
    Proceedings 1874, pg 222 (1874 Sept 30), Pueblo Lodge No. 17, Pueblo, Pueblo County
    Proceedings 1876, pg 38 (1876 Sept 20) Pueblo Lodge No. 17

Blake, Chas H
    Proceedings 1861-1869, pg 77 (1862 Nov 4) Denver Lodge No. 5
    Proceedings 1861-1869, pg 133 (1864 Nov 8) Denver Lodge No. 5
    Proceedings 1875, pg 85 (1875 Sept 22) Pueblo Lodge No. 17

Blake, E S
    Proceedings 1871, pg 23 (1871 Sept 27), Black Hawk Lodge No. 11, Black Hawk
    Proceedings 1873, pg 41 (1873 Oct 1), Black Hawk Lodge No. 11, Black Hawk
    Proceedings 1874, pg 216 (1874 Sept 30), Black Hawk Lodge No. 11, Black Hawk
    Proceedings 1875, pg 80 (1875 Sept 22) Black Hawk Lodge No. 11

Blake, E T
    Proceedings 1872, pg 24 (1872 Sept 24), Black Hawk Lodge No. 11, Black Hawk

Blake, Edward S
    Proceedings 1876, pg 34 (1876 Sept 20) Black Hawk Lodge No. 11

Blake, Henry
    Proceedings 1861-1869, pg 43 (1861 Dec 10), Rocky Mountain Lodge No. 3, Gold Hill

Blake, Wm K
    Proceedings 1872, pg 85 (1872 Sept 24) Grand Lodge of South Carolina

Blankenship, C T
    Proceedings 1871, pg 19 (1871 Sept 27) Denver Lodge No. 5
    Proceedings 1872, pg 19 (1872 Sept 24), Denver Lodge No. 5, Denver
    Proceedings 1873, pg 37 (1873 Oct 1), Denver Lodge No. 5, Denver
    Proceedings 1874, pg 211 (1874 Sept 30), Denver Lodge No. 5, Denver
    Proceedings 1875, pg 76 (1875 Sept 22) Denver Lodge No. 5, Stricken from the rolls

Blatchley, F C
    Proceedings 1874, pg 222 (1874 Sept 30), Pueblo Lodge No. 17, Pueblo, Pueblo County

Bleim, A K
    Proceedings 1861-1869, pg 35 (1861 Oct 23), Summit Lodge No. 2, Parkville

Blett, Absalom
    Proceedings 1871, pg 23 (1871 Sept 27), Black Hawk Lodge No. 11, Black Hawk
    Proceedings 1872, pg 24 (1872 Sept 24), Black Hawk Lodge No. 11, Black Hawk
    Proceedings 1873, pg 41 (1873 Oct 1), Black Hawk Lodge No. 11, Black Hawk
    Proceedings 1874, pg 216 (1874 Sept 30), Black Hawk Lodge No. 11, Black Hawk
    Proceedings 1875, pg 80 (1875 Sept 22) Black Hawk Lodge No. 11
    Proceedings 1876, pg 34 (1876 Sept 20) Black Hawk Lodge No. 11

Blinn, A K
    Proceedings 1861-1869, pg 42 (1861 Dec 10), Summit Lodge No. 2, Parkville
    Proceedings 1861-1869, pg 76 (1862 Nov 4), Summit Lodge No. 2, Parkville
    Proceedings 1861-1869, pg 111 (1863 Nov 3), Summit Lodge No. 2, Parkville, dimitted

Blinn, Henry H
    Proceedings 1874, pg 227 (1874 Sept 30), St Vrain No. 23, Longmont, died

Blocher, W D
    Proceedings 1861-1869, pg 236 (1867 Nov 4) Grand Secretary of Arkansas
    Proceedings 1870, pg 40 (1869 Nov 1) Grand Secretary, Grand Lodge of Arkansas
    Proceedings 1870, pg 45 (1869 Nov 1) Grand Master, Grand Lodge of Arkansas

Blocher, William D
    Proceedings 1861-1869, pg 316 (1869 Sept 29) Grand Lodge of Arkansas

Colorado's Territorial Masons

Blocher, William D, cont.
Proceedings 1861-1869, pg 324 (1868 Nov 16) Grand Secretary, Grand Lodge of Arkansas,

Block Emanuel
Proceedings 1876, pg 31 (1876 Sept 20) Denver Lodge No. 5
Proceedings 1874, pg 211 (1874 Sept 30), Denver Lodge No. 5, Denver
Proceedings 1875, pg 75 (1875 Sept 22) Denver Lodge No. 5

Blodgett, Samuel
Proceedings 1871, pg 30 (1871 Sept 27), Occidental Lodge U D, Greeley
Proceedings 1872, pg 33 (1872 Sept 24), Occidental Lodge No. 20, Greeley
Proceedings 1873, pg 50 (1873 Oct 1), Occidental Lodge No. 20, Greeley
Proceedings 1874, pg 225 (1874 Sept 30), Occidental Lodge No. 20, Greeley
Proceedings 1875, pg 87 (1875 Sept 22), Occidental Lodge No. 20, Greeley
Proceedings 1876, pg 40 (1876 Sept 20), Occidental Lodge No. 20, Greeley

Blon [Blore], W R
Proceedings 1872, pg 7 (1872 June 22), [St Vrain] Lodge U D, Longmont
Proceedings 1873, pg 51 (1873 Oct 1), St Vrain Lodge No. 23, Longmont

Blon [Blore], Wm R
Proceedings 1872, pg 35 (1872 Sept 24), St Vrain Lodge No. 23, Longmont

Bloom, John W
Proceedings 1875, pg 91 (1875 Sept 22), Las Animas Lodge U D, Trinidad
Proceedings 1876, pg 44 (1876 Sept 20), Las Animas Lodge No. 28, Trinidad

Blore, W R
Proceedings 1861-1869, pg 197 (1867 Oct 8), Columbia Lodge U D, Boulder, Fellowcraft
Proceedings 1861-1869, pg 228 (1868 Oct 7), Columbia Lodge No. 14, Columbia City
Proceedings 1871, pg 5 (1871 Sept 26), Columbia Lodge No. 14, Boulder City
Proceedings 1874, pg 227 (1874 Sept 30), St Vrain No. 23, Longmont

Blore, Wm R
Proceedings 1861-1869, pg 310 (1869 Sept 29), Columbia Lodge No. 14, Boulder City
Proceedings 1870, pg 27 (1870 Sept 28), Columbia Lodge No. 14, Boulder City
Proceedings 1871, pg 25 (1871 Sept 27), Columbia Lodge No. 14, Boulder City
Proceedings 1872, pg 48 (1872 Sept 24), Columbia Lodge No. 14, Boulder
Proceedings 1873, pg 45 (1873 Oct 1), Columbia Lodge No. 14, Boulder, Dimitted

Blose [Blore], W R
Proceedings 1876, pg 41 (1876 Sept 20), St Vrain Lodge No. 23, Longmont

Blundell, Henry
Proceedings 1874, pg 225 (1874 Sept 30), Occidental Lodge No. 20, Greeley
Proceedings 1875, pg 87 (1875 Sept 22), Occidental Lodge No. 20, Greeley
Proceedings 1876, pg 40 (1876 Sept 20), Occidental Lodge No. 20, Greeley

Boax, J J
Proceedings 1874, pg 224 (1874 Sept 30), Laramie Lodge No. 18, Laramie City, Fellowcraft

Bock, David
Proceedings 1861-1869, pg 310 (1869 Sept 29), Columbia Lodge No. 14, Boulder City
Proceedings 1870, pg 27 (1870 Sept 28), Columbia Lodge No. 14, Boulder City
Proceedings 1871, pg 25 (1871 Sept 27), Columbia Lodge No. 14, Boulder City
Proceedings 1872, pg 27 (1872 Sept 24), Columbia Lodge No. 14, Boulder
Proceedings 1872, pg 28 (1872 Sept 24), Columbia Lodge No. 14, Boulder
Proceedings 1872, pg 48 (1872 Sept 24), Columbia Lodge No. 14, Boulder
Proceedings 1873, pg 44 (1873 Oct 1), Columbia Lodge No. 14, Boulder
Proceedings 1874, pg 219 (1874 Sept 30), Columbia Lodge No. 14, Boulder, Boulder County
Proceedings 1875, pg 83 (1875 Sept 22), Columbia Lodge No. 14, Boulder
Proceedings 1876, pg 36 (1876 Sept 20), Columbia Lodge No. 14, Boulder

Boehler, Adolf
Proceedings 1873, pg 43 (1873 Oct 1), Washington Lodge No. 12, Georgetown
Proceedings 1874, pg 217 (1874 Sept 30), Washington Lodge No. 12, Georgetown
Proceedings 1875, pg 81 (1875 Sept 22), Washington Lodge No. 12, Georgetown

Boehler, Adolph
Proceedings 1876, pg 35 (1876 Sept 20), Washington Lodge No. 12, Georgetown

Bogue, F Newton
Proceedings 1861-1869, pg 308 (1869 Sept 29), Empire Lodge No. 8, Empire City, Apprentice

Boles, Jackson
Proceedings 1873, pg 37 (1873 Oct 1), Denver Lodge No. 5, Denver
Proceedings 1874, pg 211 (1874 Sept 30), Denver Lodge No. 5, Denver
Proceedings 1875, pg 75 (1875 Sept 22) Denver Lodge No. 5
Proceedings 1876, pg 30 (1876 Sept 20) Denver Lodge No. 5

Bonner, Thos R
Proceedings 1874, pg 205 (1874 Sept 30) Grand Lodge of Texas, Tyler

Borst, W W
Proceedings 1872, pg 23 (1872 Sept 24), Union Lodge No. 7, Denver, Apprentice
Proceedings 1873, pg 40 (1873 Oct 1), Union Lodge No. 7, Denver, Apprentice
Proceedings 1874, pg 214 (1874 Sept 30), Union Lodge No. 7, Denver, Apprentice
Proceedings 1875, pg 79 (1875 Sept 22), Union Lodge No. 7, Denver, Apprentice
Proceedings 1876, pg 33 (1876 Sept 20), Union Lodge No. 7, Denver, Apprentice

Borton, Reuben
Proceedings 1861-1869, pg 42 (1861 Dec 10) Golden City Lodge No. 1
Proceedings 1861-1869, pg 110 (1863 Nov 3) Golden City Lodge No. 1
Proceedings 1861-1869, pg 131 (1864 Nov 8) Golden City Lodge No. 1
Proceedings 1861-1869, pg 147 (1865 Nov 7) Golden City Lodge No. 1
Proceedings 1861-1869, pg 221 (1868 Oct 7) Golden City Lodge No. 1
Proceedings 1861-1869, pg 303 (1869 Sept 29) Golden City Lodge No. 1
Proceedings 1870, pg 19 (1870 Sept 28), Golden City Lodge No. 1, Golden City
Proceedings 1871, pg 17 (1871 Sept 27), Golden City Lodge No. 1, Golden City
Proceedings 1872, pg 18 (1872 Sept 24), Golden City Lodge No. 1, Golden City, Stricken from the Roll

Borwles [Bowles], J W
Proceedings 1861-1869, pg 148 (1865 Nov 7), Nevada Lodge No. 4, Nevadaville

Boswell, N K
Proceedings 1861-1869, pg 230 (1868 Oct 7), Cheyenne Lodge U D, Cheyenne, Dakota Territory
Proceedings 1861-1869, pg 312 (1869 Sept 29), Cheyenne Lodge No. 16, Cheyenne
Proceedings 1870, pg 29 (1870 Sept 28), Cheyenne Lodge No. 16, Cheyenne, Wyoming Territory
Proceedings 1871, pg 27 (1871 Sept 27), Cheyenne Lodge No. 16, Cheyenne, Wyoming Territory
Proceedings 1872, pg 29 (1872 Sept 24), Cheyenne Lodge No. 16, Cheyenne, Wyoming Territory
Proceedings 1873, pg 46 (1873 Oct 1), Cheyenne Lodge No. 16, Cheyenne, Wyoming Territory
Proceedings 1874, pg 221 (1874 Sept 30), Cheyenne Lodge No. 16, Cheyenne, Wyoming Territory

Boswell, N R
Proceedings 1870, pg 30 (1870 Sept 28), Laramie Lodge No. 18, Laramie, Wyoming Territory

Bosworth, J O
Proceedings 1876, pg 33 (1876 Sept 20), Union Lodge No. 7, Denver

Bosworth, R W
Proceedings 1875, pg 86 (1875 Sept 22), Collins Lodge No. 19, Fort Collins
Proceedings 1876, pg 39 (1876 Sept 20), Collins Lodge No. 19, Fort Collins

Botsford, A J
Proceedings 1861-1869, pg 312 (1869 Sept 29), Cheyenne Lodge No. 16, Cheyenne
Proceedings 1870, pg 29 (1870 Sept 28), Cheyenne Lodge No. 16, Cheyenne, Wyoming Territory
Proceedings 1871, pg 27 (1871 Sept 27), Cheyenne Lodge No. 16, Cheyenne, Wyoming Territory
Proceedings 1872, pg 29 (1872 Sept 24), Cheyenne Lodge No. 16, Cheyenne, Wyoming Territory
Proceedings 1874, pg 221 (1874 Sept 30), Cheyenne Lodge No. 16, Cheyenne, Wyoming Territory

Bott, A
Proceedings 1861-1869, pg 228 (1868 Oct 7), El Paso Lodge No. 13, Colorado City
Proceedings 1861-1869, pg 310 (1869 Sept 29), El Paso Lodge No. 13, Colorado City
Proceedings 1872, pg 26 (1872 Sept 24), El Paso Lodge No. 13, Colorado City

Bott, Anthony
Proceedings 1870, pg 26 (1870 Sept 28), El Paso Lodge No. 13, Colorado City
Proceedings 1871, pg 24 (1871 Sept 27), El Paso Lodge No. 13, Colorado City
Proceedings 1873, pg 43 (1873 Oct 1), El Paso Lodge No. 13, Colorado City
Proceedings 1874, pg 218 (1874 Sept 30), El Paso Lodge No. 13, Colorado Springs
Proceedings 1875, pg 82 (1875 Sept 22), El Paso Lodge No. 13, Colorado Springs
Proceedings 1876, pg 36 (1876 Sept 20), El Paso Lodge No. 13, Colorado City
Proceedings 1861-1869, pg 196 (1867 Oct 8), El Paso Lodge U D, Colorado City

Botts, A
Proceedings 1861-1869, pg 171 (1866 Oct 2), El Paso U D, Colorado City, Apprentice

Bottsford, A J
Proceedings 1873, pg 46 (1873 Oct 1), Cheyenne Lodge No. 16, Cheyenne, Wyoming Territory

Bouck, Gabriel
Proceedings 1870, pg 106 (1870 June 14) Grand Master, Grand Lodge of Wisconsin

Boughton, Clark
Proceedings 1874, pg 225 (1874 Sept 30), Collins Lodge No. 19, Fort Collins, Larimer County, Apprentice
Proceedings 1875, pg 94 (1875 Sept 22), Collins Lodge No. 19, Fort Collins

Boughton, J H
Proceedings 1875, pg 86 (1875 Sept 22), Collins Lodge No. 19, Fort Collins

Colorado's Territorial Masons

Boughton, Jay H
Proceedings 1874, pg 224 (1874 Sept 30), Collins Lodge No. 19, Fort Collins, Larimer County
Proceedings 1876, pg 39 (1876 Sept 20), Collins Lodge No. 19, Fort Collins

Boulder County News
Colorado University Cornerstone Laying, pg 4 (1875 Sept 20) cornerstone contents

Boulder Valley Railroad
Proceedings 1874, pg 13 (1874 Aug 27) reduced rates for Masons attending the Grand Lodge

Bowen, R P
Proceedings 1873, pg 60 (1873 Oct 1) Grand Lodge of Mississippi, Chulahoma
Proceedings 1874, pg 89 (1874 Sept 30) Grand Lodge of Mississippi

Bowen, Thomas M
Proceedings 1876, pg 7 (1875 Sept 24) Del Norte Lodge U D
Proceedings 1876, pg 44 (1876 Sept 20) Del Norte Lodge U D
Proceedings 1876, pg 44 (1876 Sept 20) Del Norte Lodge U D

Bowen, Wm R
Proceedings 1872, pg 43 (1872 Sept 24) Omaha, Grand Lodge of Nebraska
Proceedings 1873, pg 60 (1873 Oct 1) Grand Lodge of Nebraska, Omaha
Proceedings 1874, pg 96 (1874 Sept 30) Grand Lodge of Nebraska
Proceedings 1874, pg 204 (1874 Sept 30) Grand Lodge of Nebraska, Omaha
Proceedings 1875, pg 96 (1875 Sept 22) Grand Lodge of Nebraska, Omaha
Proceedings 1876, pg 54 (1876 Sept 20) Grand Lodge of Nebraska, Omaha

Bowler, J C
Proceedings 1861-1869, pg 165 (1866 Oct 2) Golden City Lodge No. 1

Bowler, Jno C
Proceedings 1876, pg 50 (1876 Sept 20) Golden City Lodge No. 1

Bowles, J C
Proceedings 1861-1869, pg 131 (1864 Nov 8) Golden City Lodge No. 1
Proceedings 1861-1869, pg 147 (1865 Nov 7) Golden City Lodge No. 1
Proceedings 1861-1869, pg 191 (1867 Oct 8) Golden City Lodge No. 1
Proceedings 1861-1869, pg 221 (1868 Oct 7) Golden City Lodge No. 1
Proceedings 1861-1869, pg 303 (1869 Sept 29) Golden City Lodge No. 1
Proceedings 1870, pg 19 (1870 Sept 28), Golden City Lodge No. 1, Golden City
Proceedings 1871, pg 17 (1871 Sept 27), Golden City Lodge No. 1, Golden City

Bowles, J W
Proceedings 1861-1869, pg 111 (1863 Nov 3), Nevada Lodge No. 4, Nevadaville
Proceedings 1861-1869, pg 116 (1864 Nov 7) Golden City Lodge No. 1
Proceedings 1861-1869, pg 132 (1864 Nov 8), Nevada Lodge No. 4, Nevadaville
Proceedings 1861-1869, pg 166 (1866 Oct 2), Nevada Lodge No. 4, Nevadaville, dimitted
Proceedings 1873, pg 51 (1873 Oct 1), Weston Lodge No. 22, Littleton
Proceedings 1874, pg 6 (1874 Sept 29), Weston Lodge No. 22, Littleton
Proceedings 1874, pg 226 (1874 Sept 30), Weston Lodge No. 22, Littleton
Proceedings 1876, pg 41 (1876 Sept 20), Weston Lodge No. 22, Littleton

Bowles, Jno C
Proceedings 1875, pg 73 (1875 Sept 22) Golden City Lodge No. 1

Bowles, John C
Proceedings 1876, pg 29 (1876 Sept 20) Golden City Lodge No. 1

Bowles, Jonathan C
Proceedings 1861-1869, pg 110 (1863 Nov 3) Golden City Lodge No. 1
Proceedings 1872, pg 17 (1872 Sept 24), Golden City Lodge No. 1, Golden City
Proceedings 1873, pg 35 (1873 Oct 1), Golden City Lodge No. 1, Golden City
Proceedings 1874, pg 209 (1874 Sept 30), Golden City Lodge No. 1, Golden City

Bowles, Jos W
Proceedings 1861-1869, pg 77 (1862 Nov 4), Nevada Lodge No. 4, Nevadaville
Proceedings 1875, pg 88 (1875 Sept 22), Weston Lodge No. 22, Littleton

Bowles, Joseph
Proceedings 1872, pg 34 (1872 Sept 24), Weston Lodge No. 22, Littleton

Bowles, Joseph W
Proceedings 1872, pg 7 (1872 Sept 24), [Weston] Lodge U D, Littleton

Bowman, A H
Proceedings 1870, pg 29 (1870 Sept 28), Cheyenne Lodge No. 16, Cheyenne, Wyoming Territory, Apprentice

Bowman, Charles W
Proceedings 1876, pg 45 (1876 Sept 20), King Solomon Lodge U D, West Las Animas

Bowman, Nathan P
Proceedings 1874, pg 205 (1874 Sept 30) Grand Lodge of Vermont, St Johnsbury

Bowman, S H
Proceedings 1861-1869, pg 167 (1866 Oct 2) Denver Lodge No. 5

Proceedings 1861-1869, pg 193 (1867 Oct 8) Denver Lodge No. 5

Proceedings 1861-1869, pg 223 (1868 Oct 7) Denver Lodge No. 5

Proceedings 1861-1869, pg 304 (1869 Sept 29) Denver Lodge No. 5

Proceedings 1874, pg 6 (1874 Sept 29) committee

Proceedings 1874, pg 6 (1874 Sept 29), Pueblo Lodge No. 17, Pueblo

Proceedings 1874, pg 36 (1874 Sept 30) per diem

Proceedings 1874, pg 38 (1874 Sept 30) resolution

Proceedings 1874, pg 222 (1874 Sept 30), Pueblo Lodge No. 17, Pueblo, Pueblo County

Proceedings 1875, pg 85 (1875 Sept 22) Pueblo Lodge No. 17

Proceedings 1876, pg 38 (1876 Sept 20) Pueblo Lodge No. 17

Bowman, Sam H

Proceedings 1872, pg cover (1872 Sept 24), Pueblo Chapter No. 3, Pueblo

Proceedings 1873, pg cover (1873 Oct 1), Pueblo Chapter No. 3, Pueblo

Proceedings 1873, pg 47 (1873 Oct 1), Pueblo Lodge No. 17, Pueblo

Proceedings 1876, pg 45 (1876 Sept 20), King Solomon Lodge U D, West Las Animas

Bowman, Saml H

Proceedings 1870, pg 20 (1870 Sept 28), Denver Lodge No. 5, Denver

Proceedings 1871, pg 20 (1871 Sept 27) Denver Lodge No. 5, Dimitted

Bowman, Samuel

Proceedings 1861-1869, pg 288 (1869 Sept 28) Denver Lodge No 5

Bowman, Samuel H

Proceedings 1871, pg 28 (1871 Sept 27), Pueblo Lodge No. 17, Pueblo

Proceedings 1872, pg 31 (1872 Sept 24), Pueblo Lodge No. 17, Pueblo

Proceedings 1876, pg 7 (1875 Sept 28) dispensation to dedicate Huerfano Lodge No. 27

Proceedings 1876, pg 7 (1877 Feb 7), King Solomon Lodge U D, West Las Animas

Proceedings 1876, pg 8 (1875 Sept 28) dispensation to dedicate Las Animas Lodge No. 28

Bowman, W Samuel H

Proceedings 1874, pg 3 (1874 Sept 29) Senior Grand Deacon

Boyce, J R

Proceedings 1861-1869, pg 102 (1863 Nov 3) petition for formation of a new lodge in Denver

Proceedings 1861-1869, pg 134 (1864 Nov 8), Union Lodge No. 7, Denver

Proceedings 1861-1869, pg 151 (1865 Nov 7), Chivington Lodge No. 6, Central City

Proceedings 1861-1869, pg 169 (1866 Oct 2), Union Lodge No. 7, Denver, demitted

Boyce, James R

Proceedings 1872, pg 43 (1872 Sept 24) Helena, Grand Lodge of Montana

Proceedings 1873, pg 60 (1873 Oct 1) Grand Lodge of Montana, Helena

Boyd, Alex H

Proceedings 1861-1869, pg 307 (1869 Sept 29), Union Lodge No. 7, Denver

Proceedings 1871, pg 21 (1871 Sept 27), Union Lodge No. 7, Denver

Proceedings 1872, pg 22 (1872 Sept 24), Union Lodge No. 7, Denver

Proceedings 1872, pg 36 (1872 Sept 24), Ashlar Lodge U D, Colorado Springs

Proceedings 1873, pg 40 (1873 Oct 1), Union Lodge No. 7, Denver, Stricken from the rolls

Boyd, Alexander H

Proceedings 1870, pg 23 (1870 Sept 28), Union Lodge No. 7, Denver

Boyd, T P

Proceedings 1861-1869, pg 131 (1864 Nov 8) Golden City Lodge No. 1

Proceedings 1861-1869, pg 147 (1865 Nov 7) Golden City Lodge No. 1

Proceedings 1861-1869, pg 165 (1866 Oct 2) Golden City Lodge No. 1, deceased

Boyd, W J

Proceedings 1870, pg 30 (1870 Sept 28), Laramie Lodge No. 18, Laramie, Wyoming Territory

Proceedings 1871, pg 29 (1871 Sept 27), Laramie Lodge No. 18, Laramie, Wyoming Territory

Proceedings 1872, pg 32 (1872 Sept 24), Laramie Lodge No. 18, Laramie, Wyoming Territory, Dimitted,

Boyer Lodge No. 1

Proceedings 1870, pg 70 (1869 Sept 8) New York City

Boyer, Henry

Proceedings 1861-1869, pg 309 (1869 Sept 29), Washington Lodge No. 12, Georgetown

Proceedings 1870, pg 26 (1870 Sept 28), Washington Lodge No. 12, Georgetown

Proceedings 1871, pg 24 (1871 Sept 27), Washington Lodge No. 12, Georgetown

Proceedings 1872, pg 25 (1872 Sept 24), Washington Lodge No. 12, Georgetown

Proceedings 1873, pg 42 (1873 Oct 1), Washington Lodge No. 12, Georgetown

Proceedings 1874, pg 217 (1874 Sept 30), Washington Lodge No. 12, Georgetown

Proceedings 1875, pg 81 (1875 Sept 22), Washington Lodge No. 12, Georgetown

Proceedings 1876, pg 35 (1876 Sept 20), Washington Lodge No. 12, Georgetown

Boylam, John

Proceedings 1872, pg 24 (1872 Sept 24), Black Hawk Lodge No. 11, Black Hawk

Colorado's Territorial Masons

Boylan, J
    Proceedings 1861-1869, pg 168 (1866 Oct 2), Chivington Lodge No. 6, Central City

Boylan, John
    Proceedings 1861-1869, pg 150 (1865 Nov 7), Chivington Lodge No. 6, Central City
    Proceedings 1861-1869, pg 170 (1866 Oct 2), Black Hawk Lodge U D, Black Hawk
    Proceedings 1861-1869, pg 194 (1867 Oct 8), Chivington Lodge No. 6, Central City, Dimitted
    Proceedings 1861-1869, pg 196 (1867 Oct 8), Black Hawk Lodge No. 11, Black Hawk
    Proceedings 1861-1869, pg 226 (1868 Oct 7), Black Hawk Lodge No. 11, Black Hawk
    Proceedings 1861-1869, pg 297 (1869 Sept 28), Black Hawk Lodge No. 11, Black Hawk
    Proceedings 1861-1869, pg 309 (1869 Sept 29), Black Hawk Lodge No. 11, Black Hawk
    Proceedings 1870, pg 4 (1870 Sept 27), Black Hawk Lodge No. 11, Black Hawk
    Proceedings 1870, pg 25 (1870 Sept 28), Black Hawk Lodge No. 11, Black Hawk
    Proceedings 1871, pg 23 (1871 Sept 27), Black Hawk Lodge No. 11, Black Hawk
    Proceedings 1873, pg 41 (1873 Oct 1), Black Hawk Lodge No. 11, Black Hawk
    Proceedings 1874, pg 216 (1874 Sept 30), Black Hawk Lodge No. 11, Black Hawk
    Proceedings 1875, pg 80 (1875 Sept 22) Black Hawk Lodge No. 11
    Proceedings 1876, pg 34 (1876 Sept 20) Black Hawk Lodge No. 11

Braden, Samuel
    Proceedings 1870, pg 26 (1870 Sept 28), Washington Lodge No. 12, Georgetown
    Proceedings 1871, pg 24 (1871 Sept 27), Washington Lodge No. 12, Georgetown
    Proceedings 1872, pg 26 (1872 Sept 24), Washington Lodge No. 12, Georgetown
    Proceedings 1873, pg 42 (1873 Oct 1), Washington Lodge No. 12, Georgetown
    Proceedings 1874, pg 217 (1874 Sept 30), Washington Lodge No. 12, Georgetown, Demitted

Braden, William
    Proceedings 1876, pg 42 (1876 Sept 20), Doric Lodge No. 25, Fairplay

Braden, Wm
    Proceedings 1875, pg 89 (1875 Sept 22), Doric Lodge No. 25, Fairplay

Bradfield, William
    Proceedings 1876, pg 38 (1876 Sept 20) Pueblo Lodge No. 17

Bradley, J C
    Proceedings 1861-1869, pg 166 (1866 Oct 2), Nevada Lodge No. 4, Nevadaville
    Proceedings 1861-1869, pg 192 (1867 Oct 8), Nevada Lodge No. 4, Nevadaville

Bradley, James C
    Proceedings 1861-1869, pg 132 (1864 Nov 8), Nevada Lodge No. 4, Nevadaville

Bradley, Jas C
    Proceedings 1861-1869, pg 77 (1862 Nov 4), Nevada Lodge No. 4, Nevadaville
    Proceedings 1861-1869, pg 148 (1865 Nov 7), Nevada Lodge No. 4, Nevadaville
    Proceedings 1861-1869, pg 222 (1868 Oct 7), Nevada Lodge No. 4, Nevadaville, Dimitted

Bradley, S H
    Proceedings 1861-1869, pg 227 (1868 Oct 7), Black Hawk Lodge No. 11, Black Hawk
    Proceedings 1861-1869, pg 309 (1869 Sept 29), Black Hawk Lodge No. 11, Black Hawk
    Proceedings 1870, pg 25 (1870 Sept 28), Black Hawk Lodge No. 11, Black Hawk
    Proceedings 1871, pg 23 (1871 Sept 27), Black Hawk Lodge No. 11, Black Hawk
    Proceedings 1872, pg 24 (1872 Sept 24), Black Hawk Lodge No. 11, Black Hawk
    Proceedings 1873, pg 41 (1873 Oct 1), Black Hawk Lodge No. 11, Black Hawk
    Proceedings 1875, pg 80 (1875 Sept 22) Black Hawk Lodge No. 11
    Proceedings 1876, pg 34 (1876 Sept 20) Black Hawk Lodge No. 11

Bradstreet, J H
    Proceedings 1871, pg 29 (1871 Sept 27), Collins Lodge No. 19, Fort Collins
    Proceedings 1876, pg 51 (1876 Sept 20), Collins Lodge No. 19, Fort Collins, 1876 Mar 4

Bradstreet, Jos H
    Proceedings 1870, pg 31 (1870 Sept 28), Collins Lodge No. 19, Fort Collins

Bradstreet, Joseph H
    Proceedings 1872, pg 33 (1872 Sept 24), Collins Lodge No. 19, Fort Collins
    Proceedings 1873, pg 49 (1873 Oct 1), Collins Lodge No. 19, Fort Collins
    Proceedings 1874, pg 224 (1874 Sept 30), Collins Lodge No. 19, Fort Collins, Larimer County
    Proceedings 1875, pg 86 (1875 Sept 22), Collins Lodge No. 19, Fort Collins

Brainard, Thomas C
    Proceedings 1875, pg 83 (1875 Sept 22), Columbia Lodge No. 14, Boulder, Apprentice

Brainard, Thos C
    Proceedings 1876, pg 37 (1876 Sept 20), Columbia Lodge No. 14, Boulder, Apprentice

Bramel, C W
    Proceedings 1861-1869, pg 227 (1868 Oct 7), Washington Lodge No. 12, Georgetown
    Proceedings 1861-1869, pg 309 (1869 Sept 29), Washington Lodge No. 12, Georgetown
    Proceedings 1875, pg 81 (1875 Sept 22), Washington Lodge No. 12, Georgetown, Demitted

Bramel, Charles W
- Proceedings 1871, pg 24 (1871 Sept 27), Washington Lodge No. 12, Georgetown
- Proceedings 1874, pg 217 (1874 Sept 30), Washington Lodge No. 12, Georgetown

Bramel, Chas W
- Proceedings 1870, pg 26 (1870 Sept 28), Washington Lodge No. 12, Georgetown
- Proceedings 1872, pg 26 (1872 Sept 24), Washington Lodge No. 12, Georgetown
- Proceedings 1873, pg 42 (1873 Oct 1), Washington Lodge No. 12, Georgetown

Bramel, S W
- Proceedings 1873, pg 48 (1873 Oct 1), Laramie Lodge No. 18, Laramie, Wyoming Territory

Bramel, W S
- Proceedings 1870, pg 31 (1870 Sept 28), Laramie Lodge No. 18, Laramie, Wyoming Territory
- Proceedings 1871, pg 29 (1871 Sept 27), Laramie Lodge No. 18, Laramie, Wyoming Territory
- Proceedings 1872, pg 32 (1872 Sept 24), Laramie Lodge No. 18, Laramie, Wyoming Territory
- Proceedings 1874, pg 223 (1874 Sept 30), Laramie Lodge No. 18, Laramie City

Bramlette, Wm
- Proceedings 1872, pg 44 (1872 Sept 24) Paris, Grand Lodge of Texas,

Bramwell
- Proceedings 1873, pg 27 (1873 Oct 1) committee

Bramwell, John M
- Proceedings 1861-1869, pg 316 (1869 Sept 29) Grand Lodge of Indiana
- Proceedings 1861-1869, pg 330 (1869 May 25) Grand Secretary, Grand Lodge of Indiana
- Proceedings 1870, pg 34 (1870 Sept 28) Grand Secretary, Grand Lodge of Indiana
- Proceedings 1870, pg 57 (1870 May 24) Grand Secretary, Grand Lodge of Indiana
- Proceedings 1871, pg 35 (1871 Sept 27) Grand Secretary, Grand Lodge of Indiana
- Proceedings 1872, pg 64 (1872 Sept 24) Grand Lodge of Indiana
- Proceedings 1873, pg 26 (1873 Oct 1) to publish his memorial
- Proceedings 1873, pg 60 (1873 Oct 1) Grand Lodge of Indiana, Indianapolis
- Proceedings 1874, pg 64 (1874 Sept 30) Grand Lodge of Indiana
- Proceedings 1874, pg 204 (1874 Sept 30) Grand Lodge of Indiana, Indianapolis
- Proceedings 1875, pg 96 (1875 Sept 22) Grand Lodge of Indiana, Indianapolis
- Proceedings 1876, pg 54 (1876 Sept 20) Grand Lodge of Indiana, Indianapolis

Brandis, William
- Proceedings 1871, pg 29 (1871 Sept 27), Laramie Lodge No. 18, Laramie, Wyoming Territory
- Proceedings 1873, pg 48 (1873 Oct 1), Laramie Lodge No. 18, Laramie, Wyoming Territory
- Proceedings 1874, pg 223 (1874 Sept 30), Laramie Lodge No. 18, Laramie City

Brandis, Wm
- Proceedings 1872, pg 31 (1872 Sept 24), Laramie Lodge No. 18, Laramie, Wyoming Territory

Brandley
- Proceedings 1874, pg 16 (1874 Sept 29) gift of $105 to the Masons as his dying wish

Brandley, John G
- Proceedings 1861-1869, pg 122 (1864 Nov 8), Soldier, Co C 1st Colorado Cav, killed in battle with the Indians in May or June last (1864).
- Proceedings 1861-1869, pg 125 (1864 Nov 8) deceased
- Proceedings 1861-1869, pg 129 (1864 Nov 8) tribute
- Proceedings 1874, pg 15 (1874 Sept 29), deceased, Co C, 1st Colorado Cavalry, mortally wounded in a fight with Indians during the summer of 1864

Brandley, S H
- Proceedings 1874, pg 216 (1874 Sept 30), Black Hawk Lodge No. 11, Black Hawk

Brassler, C L
- Proceedings 1861-1869, pg 167 (1866 Oct 2) Denver Lodge No. 5, Apprentice

Brassler, Chas A
- Proceedings 1861-1869, pg 78 (1862 Nov 4) Denver Lodge No. 5, Apprentice

Brassler, Chas L
- Proceedings 1861-1869, pg 133 (1864 Nov 8) Denver Lodge No. 5, Apprentice

Braum, Nicholas
- Proceedings 1873, pg 47 (1873 Oct 1), Pueblo Lodge No. 17, Pueblo, Apprentice

Braun, Michael
- Proceedings 1871, pg 18 (1871 Sept 27), Nevada Lodge No. 4, Bald Mountain
- Proceedings 1872, pg 18 (1872 Sept 24), Nevada Lodge No. 4, Bald Mountain
- Proceedings 1873, pg 36 (1873 Oct 1), Nevada Lodge No. 4, Nevada
- Proceedings 1874, pg 210 (1874 Sept 30), Nevada Lodge No. 4, Bald Mountain, Gilpin County
- Proceedings 1875, pg 74 (1875 Sept 22), Nevada Lodge No. 4, Nevada
- Proceedings 1876, pg 30 (1876 Sept 20) Nevada Lodge No. 4

Braun, N
- Proceedings 1874, pg 222 (1874 Sept 30), Pueblo Lodge No. 17, Pueblo, Pueblo County
- Proceedings 1876, pg 38 (1876 Sept 20) Pueblo Lodge No. 17

Braun, Nic
- Proceedings 1875, pg 85 (1875 Sept 22) Pueblo Lodge No. 17

Colorado's Territorial Masons

Braun, Theo F
    Proceedings 1875, pg 85 (1875 Sept 22) Pueblo Lodge No. 17

Braun, Theodore F
    Proceedings 1871, pg 28 (1871 Sept 27), Pueblo Lodge No. 17, Pueblo, Fellowcraft
    Proceedings 1872, pg 31 (1872 Sept 24), Pueblo Lodge No. 17, Pueblo
    Proceedings 1873, pg 47 (1873 Oct 1), Pueblo Lodge No. 17, Pueblo
    Proceedings 1874, pg 222 (1874 Sept 30), Pueblo Lodge No. 17, Pueblo, Pueblo County
    Proceedings 1876, pg 38 (1876 Sept 20) Pueblo Lodge No. 17

Brchenell [Burchineel], W K
    Proceedings 1875, pg 89 (1875 Sept 22), Doric Lodge No. 25, Fairplay

Breath, S M
    Proceedings 1861-1869, pg 42 (1861 Dec 10) Golden City Lodge No. 1
    Proceedings 1861-1869, pg 110 (1863 Nov 3) Golden City Lodge No. 1
    Proceedings 1861-1869, pg 131 (1864 Nov 8) Golden City Lodge No. 1
    Proceedings 1861-1869, pg 147 (1865 Nov 7) Golden City Lodge No. 1
    Proceedings 1861-1869, pg 165 (1866 Oct 2) Golden City Lodge No. 1
    Proceedings 1861-1869, pg 191 (1867 Oct 8) Golden City Lodge No. 1
    Proceedings 1861-1869, pg 221 (1868 Oct 7) Golden City Lodge No. 1
    Proceedings 1861-1869, pg 303 (1869 Sept 29) Golden City Lodge No. 1
    Proceedings 1870, pg 19 (1870 Sept 28), Golden City Lodge No. 1, Golden City
    Proceedings 1871, pg 17 (1871 Sept 27), Golden City Lodge No. 1, Golden City
    Proceedings 1872, pg 18 (1872 Sept 24), Golden City Lodge No. 1, Golden City, Stricken from the Roll

Breed, Enoch P
    Proceedings 1872, pg 75 (1872 Sept 24) Grand Lodge of New York

Breen, Michael
    Proceedings 1871, pg 28 (1871 Sept 27), Pueblo Lodge No. 17, Pueblo, Fellowcraft
    Proceedings 1872, pg 31 (1872 Sept 24), Pueblo Lodge No. 17, Pueblo
    Proceedings 1873, pg 47 (1873 Oct 1), Pueblo Lodge No. 17, Pueblo
    Proceedings 1874, pg 222 (1874 Sept 30), Pueblo Lodge No. 17, Pueblo, Pueblo County
    Proceedings 1875, pg 85 (1875 Sept 22) Pueblo Lodge No. 17
    Proceedings 1876, pg 38 (1876 Sept 20) Pueblo Lodge No. 17
    Proceedings 1876, pg 44 (1876 Sept 20) Del Norte Lodge U D

Breese, Robert
    Proceedings 1874, pg 211 (1874 Sept 30), Denver Lodge No. 5, Denver
    Proceedings 1875, pg 75 (1875 Sept 22) Denver Lodge No. 5
    Proceedings 1876, pg 31 (1876 Sept 20) Denver Lodge No. 5

Brennan
    Proceedings 1870, pg 11 (1870 Sept 27), of Cincinnati, OH,, Editor, The American Freemason

Brent, Frederick J
    Proceedings 1876, pg 33 (1876 Sept 20), Union Lodge No. 7, Denver

Brent, Thomas L
    Proceedings 1861-1869, pg 312 (1869 Sept 29), Cheyenne Lodge No. 16, Cheyenne, Apprentice
    Proceedings 1870, pg 29 (1870 Sept 28), Cheyenne Lodge No. 16, Cheyenne, Wyoming Territory, Apprentice
    Proceedings 1871, pg 27 (1871 Sept 27), Cheyenne Lodge No. 16, Cheyenne, Wyoming Territory, Apprentice
    Proceedings 1872, pg 30 (1872 Sept 24), Cheyenne Lodge No. 16, Cheyenne, Wyoming Territory, Apprentice
    Proceedings 1874, pg 221 (1874 Sept 30), Cheyenne Lodge No. 16, Cheyenne, Wyoming Territory

Brent, Thos L
    Proceedings 1873, pg 46 (1873 Oct 1), Cheyenne Lodge No. 16, Cheyenne, Wyoming Territory

Bresler, C L
    Proceedings 1861-1869, pg 149 (1865 Nov 7), Nevada Lodge No. 4, Nevadaville, Apprentice

Brewer, G C
    Proceedings 1874, pg 211 (1874 Sept 30), Denver Lodge No. 5, Denver

Brewer, G G
    Proceedings 1861-1869, pg 149 (1865 Nov 7), Nevada Lodge No. 4, Nevadaville
    Proceedings 1861-1869, pg 166 (1866 Oct 2) Denver Lodge No. 5
    Proceedings 1861-1869, pg 192 (1867 Oct 8) Denver Lodge No. 5
    Proceedings 1861-1869, pg 223 (1868 Oct 7) Denver Lodge No. 5
    Proceedings 1861-1869, pg 305 (1869 Sept 29) Denver Lodge No. 5
    Proceedings 1870, pg 17 (1870 Sept 28) Committee, Denver
    Proceedings 1870, pg 17 (1870 Sept 28) committee
    Proceedings 1870, pg 20 (1870 Sept 28), Denver Lodge No. 5, Denver
    Proceedings 1871, pg cover (1871 Sept 27) committee, Denver
    Proceedings 1871, pg 4 (1871 Sept 26) Committee
    Proceedings 1871, pg 4 (1871 Sept 26) Denver Lodge No. 5
    Proceedings 1871, pg 5 (1871 Sept 26) Committee
    Proceedings 1871, pg 12 (1871 Sept 26) Committee

Proceedings 1871, pg 14 (1871 Sept 27) Denver Lodge No. 5

Proceedings 1871, pg 16 (1871 Sept 27) Committee

Proceedings 1871, pg 19 (1871 Sept 27) Denver Lodge No. 5

Proceedings 1871, pg 19 (1871 Sept 27) Denver Lodge No. 5

Proceedings 1872, pg cover (1872 Sept 24) committee, Denver

Proceedings 1872, pg 4 (1872 Sept 24), Denver Lodge No. 5, Denver

Proceedings 1872, pg 4 (1872 Sept 24) gave the opening prayer

Proceedings 1872, pg 5 (1872 Sept 24) committee

Proceedings 1872, pg 5 (1872 Sept 24) committee

Proceedings 1872, pg 14 (1872 Sept 24) committee

Proceedings 1872, pg 16 (1872 Sept 24) committee

Proceedings 1872, pg 16 (1872 Sept 24), Denver Lodge No. 5, Denver

Proceedings 1872, pg 19 (1872 Sept 24), Denver Lodge No. 5, Denver

Proceedings 1873, pg 37 (1873 Oct 1), Denver Lodge No. 5, Denver

Proceedings 1875, pg 75 (1875 Sept 22) Denver Lodge No. 5

Proceedings 1876, pg 30 (1876 Sept 20) Denver Lodge No. 5

Brewer, G W

Proceedings 1861-1869, pg 168 (1866 Oct 2), Chivington Lodge No. 6, Central City

Proceedings 1861-1869, pg 194 (1867 Oct 8), Chivington Lodge No. 6, Central City

Brewer, Gardner G

Proceedings 1861-1869, pg 133 (1864 Nov 8) Denver Lodge No. 5

Brewer, Geo W

Proceedings 1861-1869, pg 224 (1868 Oct 7), Chivington Lodge No. 6, Central City

Proceedings 1861-1869, pg 306 (1869 Sept 29), Central Lodge No. 6, Central City

Proceedings 1870, pg 22 (1870 Sept 28), Central Lodge No. 6, Central City

Proceedings 1871, pg 20 (1871 Sept 27), Central Lodge No. 6, Central

Proceedings 1873, pg 39 (1873 Oct 1), Central Lodge No. 6, Central City, died

Brewer, George W

Proceedings 1873, pg 57 (1873 Oct 1), Central Lodge No. 6, Central City

Bridwell, W T

Proceedings 1875, pg 84 (1875 Sept 22), Mount Moriah Lodge No. 15, Canon City

Proceedings 1876, pg 37 (1876 Sept 20), Mount Moriah Lodge No. 15, Canon City

Briggs, Andrew J

Proceedings 1861-1869, pg 138 (1864 Dec 14), Nevada Lodge No. 4, Nevadaville

Bringharst, Geo H

Proceedings 1873, pg 61 (1873 Oct 1) Grand Lodge of Texas, Houston

Bringhurst

Proceedings 1870, pg 11 (1870 Sept 27) Grand Secretary

Bringhurst, Geo H

Proceedings 1861-1869, pg 316 (1869 Sept 29) Grand Lodge of Texas

Proceedings 1861-1869, pg 348 (1869 June 14) Grand Secretary, Grand Lodge of Texas

Proceedings 1870, pg 34 (1870 Sept 28) Grand Secretary, Grand Lodge of Texas

Proceedings 1870, pg 102 (1870 June 13) Grand Secretary, Grand Lodge of Texas

Proceedings 1872, pg 44 (1872 Sept 24) Houston, Grand Lodge of Texas

Proceedings 1872, pg 88 (1872 Sept 24) Grand Lodge of Texas

Proceedings 1874, pg 124 (1874 Sept 30) Grand Lodge of Texas

Proceedings 1875, pg 96 (1875 Sept 22) Grand Lodge of Texas, Houston

Proceedings 1876, pg 54 (1876 Sept 20) Grand Lodge of Texas, Houston

Bringhurst, George H

Proceedings 1861-1869, pg 283 (1867 Oct 7), Grand Secretary, Grand Lodge of Texas

Proceedings 1871, pg 35 (1871 Sept 27) Grand Secretary, Grand Lodge of Texas

Brinkley, John A

Proceedings 1872, pg 29 (1872 Sept 24), Mount Moriah Lodge No. 15, Canon City

Brinsmaide, Allan T

Proceedings 1872, pg 44 (1872 Sept 24) , Grand Lodge of Ohio

Bristol, B J

Proceedings 1871, pg 29 (1871 Sept 27), Laramie Lodge No. 18, Laramie, Wyoming Territory, Apprentice

Proceedings 1872, pg 32 (1872 Sept 24), Laramie Lodge No. 18, Laramie, Wyoming Territory

Proceedings 1873, pg 48 (1873 Oct 1), Laramie Lodge No. 18, Laramie, Wyoming Territory

Proceedings 1874, pg 223 (1874 Sept 30), Laramie Lodge No. 18, Laramie City

Broadie, John

Proceedings 1873, pg 44 (1873 Oct 1), Columbia Lodge No. 14, Boulder

Proceedings 1874, pg 219 (1874 Sept 30), Columbia Lodge No. 14, Boulder, Boulder County

Proceedings 1875, pg 83 (1875 Sept 22), Columbia Lodge No. 14, Boulder

Proceedings 1876, pg 37 (1876 Sept 20), Columbia Lodge No. 14, Boulder

Broadwell, J M

Proceedings 1861-1869, pg 45 (1862 Nov 3) Denver Lodge No. 5

Broadwell, J M, cont.
   Proceedings 1861-1869, pg 46 (1862 Nov 3) Teller
   Proceedings 1861-1869, pg 46 (1862 Nov 3) committee
   Proceedings 1861-1869, pg 77 (1862 Nov 4) Denver Lodge No. 5
   Proceedings 1861-1869, pg 112 (1863 Nov 3) Denver Lodge No. 5
   Proceedings 1861-1869, pg 133 (1864 Nov 8) Denver Lodge No. 5
   Proceedings 1861-1869, pg 167 (1866 Oct 2) Denver Lodge No. 5
   Proceedings 1861-1869, pg 193 (1867 Oct 8) Denver Lodge No. 5
   Proceedings 1861-1869, pg 305 (1869 Sept 29) Denver Lodge No. 5
   Proceedings 1870, pg 21 (1870 Sept 28), Denver Lodge No. 5, Denver
   Proceedings 1871, pg 19 (1871 Sept 27) Denver Lodge No. 5
   Proceedings 1872, pg 19 (1872 Sept 24), Denver Lodge No. 5, Denver
   Proceedings 1875, pg 75 (1875 Sept 22) Denver Lodge No. 5
   Proceedings 1876, pg 49 (1876 Sept 20) Denver Lodge No. 5, 1876 Aug 19

Broadwell, James M
   Proceedings 1874, pg 211 (1874 Sept 30), Denver Lodge No. 5, Denver

Broadwell, Jas M
   Proceedings 1873, pg 37 (1873 Oct 1), Denver Lodge No. 5, Denver

Brock, Geo W
   Proceedings 1861-1869, pg 132 (1864 Nov 8), Nevada Lodge No. 4, Nevadaville, Apprentice
   Proceedings 1861-1869, pg 148 (1865 Nov 7), Nevada Lodge No. 4, Nevadaville, Apprentice
   Proceedings 1861-1869, pg 166 (1866 Oct 2), Nevada Lodge No. 4, Nevadaville, Apprentice
   Proceedings 1861-1869, pg 192 (1867 Oct 8), Nevada Lodge No. 4, Nevadaville, Apprentice
   Proceedings 1861-1869, pg 222 (1868 Oct 7), Nevada Lodge No. 4, Nevadaville, Apprentice

Brock, George W
   Proceedings 1861-1869, pg 112 (1863 Nov 3), Nevada Lodge No. 4, Nevadaville, Apprentice

Brocker, F A
   Proceedings 1861-1869, pg 230 (1868 Oct 7), Germania Lodge U D, Denver
   Proceedings 1861-1869, pg 307 (1869 Sept 29), Union Lodge No. 7, Denver

Brocker, Franz A
   Proceedings 1870, pg 24 (1870 Sept 28), Union Lodge No. 7, Denver, Died

Brodwell, J M
   Proceedings 1861-1869, pg 223 (1868 Oct 7) Denver Lodge No. 5

Bromwell
   Proceedings 1871, pg 4 (1871 Sept 26) Past Grand Master, Illinois
   Proceedings 1874, pg 71 (1874 Sept 30) eulogy given for Past Grand Master Randall
   Proceedings 1874, pg 77 (1874 Sept 30) Past Grand Master
   Proceedings 1874, pg 111 (1874 Sept 30) Past Grand Master

Bromwell, H P H
   Proceedings 1871, pg 13 (1871 Sept 26) Past Grand Master, Grand Lodge of Illinois
   Proceedings 1871, pg 14 (1871 Sept 27) Past Grand Master, Grand Lodge of Illinois
   Proceedings 1873, pg 4 (1873 Sept 30) pall bearer for George M Randall
   Proceedings 1873, pg 4 (1873 Sept 30) Past Grand Master, Grand Lodge of Illinois
   Proceedings 1873, pg 14 (1873 Sept 30) Grand Orator
   Proceedings 1873, pg 14 (1873 Sept 30) committee
   Proceedings 1873, pg 16 (1873 Oct 1) Grand Orator
   Proceedings 1873, pg 20 (1873 Oct 1) delivered George M Randall's Memorial Address
   Proceedings 1874, pg 3 (1874 Sept 29) Grand Orator
   Proceedings 1874, pg 21 (1874 Sept 29) Grand Orator
   Proceedings 1874, pg 28 (1874 Sept 29) Grand Orator
   Proceedings 1874, pg 211 (1874 Sept 30), Denver Lodge No. 5, Denver
   Proceedings 1875, pg 75 (1875 Sept 22) Denver Lodge No. 5
   Proceedings 1876, pg 31 (1876 Sept 20) Denver Lodge No. 5

Brookfield, A A
   Proceedings 1873, pg 45 (1873 Oct 1), Columbia Lodge No. 14, Boulder, Apprentice
   Proceedings 1874, pg 219 (1874 Sept 30), Columbia Lodge No. 14, Boulder, Boulder County, Apprentice
   Proceedings 1875, pg 83 (1875 Sept 22), Columbia Lodge No. 14, Boulder, Apprentice
   Proceedings 1876, pg 37 (1876 Sept 20), Columbia Lodge No. 14, Boulder, Apprentice

Brookins, S B
   Proceedings 1870, pg 30 (1870 Sept 28), Laramie Lodge No. 18, Laramie, Wyoming Territory
   Proceedings 1872, pg 32 (1872 Sept 24), Laramie Lodge No. 18, Laramie, Wyoming Territory, Dimitted

Brookins, Silas B
   Proceedings 1871, pg 29 (1871 Sept 27), Laramie Lodge No. 18, Laramie, Wyoming Territory

Brooks, O
   Proceedings 1861-1869, pg 305 (1869 Sept 29) Denver Lodge No. 5

Brooks, Orson
   Proceedings 1870, pg 21 (1870 Sept 28), Denver Lodge No. 5, Denver
   Proceedings 1871, pg 19 (1871 Sept 27) Denver Lodge No. 5
   Proceedings 1872, pg 19 (1872 Sept 24), Denver Lodge No. 5, Denver

Proceedings 1873, pg 37 (1873 Oct 1), Denver Lodge No. 5, Denver

Proceedings 1874, pg 5 (1874 Sept 29), Denver Lodge No. 5, Denver

Proceedings 1874, pg 211 (1874 Sept 30), Denver Lodge No. 5, Denver

Proceedings 1875, pg 75 (1875 Sept 22) Denver Lodge No. 5

Proceedings 1876, pg 31 (1876 Sept 20) Denver Lodge No. 5

Brosius, W L

Proceedings 1875, pg 82 (1875 Sept 22), El Paso Lodge No. 13, Colorado Springs

Proceedings 1876, pg 35 (1876 Sept 20), El Paso Lodge No. 13, Colorado City

Brower, T J

Proceedings 1861-1869, pg 78 (1862 Nov 4), Chivington Lodge No. 6, Central City

Proceedings 1861-1869, pg 113 (1863 Nov 3), Chivington Lodge No. 6, Central City

Proceedings 1861-1869, pg 150 (1865 Nov 7), Chivington Lodge No. 6, Central City

Proceedings 1861-1869, pg 168 (1866 Oct 2), Chivington Lodge No. 6, Central City

Proceedings 1861-1869, pg 194 (1867 Oct 8), Chivington Lodge No. 6, Central City, Dimitted

Brower, Thomas J

Proceedings 1861-1869, pg 134 (1864 Nov 8), Chivington Lodge No. 6, Central City

Brown

Proceedings 1861-1869, pg 37 (1861 Dec 12) motion

Proceedings 1861-1869, pg 122 (1864 Nov 8) committee

Proceedings 1861-1869, pg 127 (1864 Nov 8) Deputy Grand Master

Proceedings 1861-1869, pg 144 (1865 Nov 7) motion

Proceedings 1874, pg 76 (1874 Sept 30) Grand Lodge of Kansas

Brown (Baily & Brown)

Proceedings 1874, pg 19 (1874 Sept 29), of Chicago, IL

Brown, D H

Proceedings 1871, pg 20 (1871 Sept 27), Central Lodge No. 6, Central

Brown, E A

Proceedings 1861-1869, pg 113 (1863 Nov 3), Montana Lodge U D, Central City

Brown, E H

Proceedings 1861-1869, pg 78 (1862 Nov 4), Chivington Lodge No. 6, Central City

Proceedings 1861-1869, pg 113 (1863 Nov 3), Chivington Lodge No. 6, Central City

Proceedings 1861-1869, pg 134 (1864 Nov 8), Chivington Lodge No. 6, Central City

Proceedings 1861-1869, pg 150 (1865 Nov 7), Chivington Lodge No. 6, Central City

Proceedings 1861-1869, pg 168 (1866 Oct 2), Chivington Lodge No. 6, Central City

Proceedings 1861-1869, pg 193 (1867 Oct 8), Chivington Lodge No. 6, Central City

Proceedings 1861-1869, pg 224 (1868 Oct 7), Chivington Lodge No. 6, Central City

Proceedings 1861-1869, pg 306 (1869 Sept 29), Central Lodge No. 6, Central City

Proceedings 1870, pg 22 (1870 Sept 28), Central Lodge No. 6, Central City

Brown, Edwin H

Proceedings 1872, pg 22 (1872 Sept 24), Denver Lodge No. 5, Denver

Brown, G G

Proceedings 1874, pg 127 (1874 Sept 30) Grand Secretary

Brown, J C

Proceedings 1861-1869, pg 196 (1867 Oct 8), El Paso Lodge U D, Colorado City

Proceedings 1861-1869, pg 228 (1868 Oct 7), El Paso Lodge No. 13, Colorado City

Proceedings 1861-1869, pg 310 (1869 Sept 29), El Paso Lodge No. 13, Colorado City

Brown, J H

Proceedings 1861-1869, pg 331 (1868 Oct 20) Grand Master, Grand Lodge of Kansas

Brown, J S

Proceedings 1861-1869, pg 195 (1867 Oct 8), Union Lodge No. 7, Denver

Proceedings 1861-1869, pg 307 (1869 Sept 29), Union Lodge No. 7, Denver

Proceedings 1875, pg 78 (1875 Sept 22), Union Lodge No. 7, Denver

Proceedings 1876, pg 33 (1876 Sept 20), Union Lodge No. 7, Denver

Brown, J Sidney

Proceedings 1861-1869, pg 169 (1866 Oct 2), Union Lodge No. 7, Denver

Proceedings 1861-1869, pg 225 (1868 Oct 7), Union Lodge No. 7, Denver

Proceedings 1870, pg 23 (1870 Sept 28), Union Lodge No. 7, Denver

Proceedings 1871, pg 21 (1871 Sept 27), Union Lodge No. 7, Denver

Proceedings 1872, pg 22 (1872 Sept 24), Union Lodge No. 7, Denver

Proceedings 1873, pg 39 (1873 Oct 1), Union Lodge No. 7, Denver

Proceedings 1874, pg 214 (1874 Sept 30), Union Lodge No. 7, Denver

Brown, J W

Proceedings 1873, pg 60 (1873 Oct 1) Grand Lodge of Idaho, Idaho City

Brown, James A

Proceedings 1876, pg 39 (1876 Sept 20), Collins Lodge No. 19, Fort Collins

Brown, John

Proceedings 1875, pg 86 (1875 Sept 22), Collins Lodge No. 19, Fort Collins

Colorado's Territorial Masons

Brown, John C
   Proceedings 1870, pg 27 (1870 Sept 28), El Paso Lodge No. 13, Colorado City, Died
   Proceedings 1872, pg 87 (1872 Sept 24) Grand Lodge of Tennessee

Brown, John H
   Proceedings 1870, pg 60 (1869 Oct 20) Grand Master, Grand Lodge of Kansas
   Proceedings 1871, pg 35 (1871 Sept 27) Grand Secretary, Grand Lodge of Kansas
   Proceedings 1872, pg 43 (1872 Sept 24) Leavenworth, Grand Lodge of Kansas
   Proceedings 1872, pg 67 (1872 Sept 24) Grand Lodge of Kansas
   Proceedings 1873, pg 60 (1873 Oct 1) Grand Lodge of Kansas, Leavenworth
   Proceedings 1874, pg 71 (1874 Sept 30) Grand Lodge of Kansas
   Proceedings 1874, pg 72 (1874 Sept 30) Grand Lodge of Kansas
   Proceedings 1874, pg 204 (1874 Sept 30) Grand Lodge of Kansas, Leavenworth

Brown, John M
   Proceedings 1875, pg 96 (1875 Sept 22) Grand Lodge of Kansas, Leavenworth
   Proceedings 1876, pg 54 (1876 Sept 20) Grand Lodge of Kansas, Wyandot

Brown, John N
   Proceedings 1861-1869, pg 312 (1869 Sept 29), Pueblo Lodge No. 17, Pueblo
   Proceedings 1870, pg 30 (1870 Sept 28), Pueblo Lodge No. 17, Pueblo
   Proceedings 1871, pg 28 (1871 Sept 27), Pueblo Lodge No. 17, Pueblo
   Proceedings 1872, pg 31 (1872 Sept 24), Pueblo Lodge No. 17, Pueblo
   Proceedings 1873, pg 47 (1873 Oct 1), Pueblo Lodge No. 17, Pueblo
   Proceedings 1874, pg 223 (1874 Sept 30), Pueblo Lodge No. 17, Pueblo, Pueblo County, Stricken from the rolls

Brown, John R
   Proceedings 1871, pg 30 (1871 Sept 27), Collins Lodge No. 19, Fort Collins
   Proceedings 1872, pg 33 (1872 Sept 24), Collins Lodge No. 19, Fort Collins
   Proceedings 1873, pg 49 (1873 Oct 1), Collins Lodge No. 19, Fort Collins
   Proceedings 1874, pg 224 (1874 Sept 30), Collins Lodge No. 19, Fort Collins, Larimer County
   Proceedings 1876, pg 39 (1876 Sept 20), Collins Lodge No. 19, Fort Collins

Brown, Jonas W
   Proceedings 1870, pg 57 (1869 Oct 4) Grand Master, Grand Lodge of Idaho
   Proceedings 1872, pg 43 (1872 Sept 24) Idaho City, Grand Lodge of Idaho

Brown, M C
   Proceedings 1870, pg 30 (1870 Sept 28), Laramie Lodge No. 18, Laramie, Wyoming Territory
   Proceedings 1871, pg 29 (1871 Sept 27), Laramie Lodge No. 18, Laramie, Wyoming Territory
   Proceedings 1872, pg 32 (1872 Sept 24), Laramie Lodge No. 18, Laramie, Wyoming Territory
   Proceedings 1873, pg 48 (1873 Oct 1), Laramie Lodge No. 18, Laramie, Wyoming Territory
   Proceedings 1874, pg 223 (1874 Sept 30), Laramie Lodge No. 18, Laramie City

Brown, Michael
   Proceedings 1870, pg 20 (1870 Sept 28), Nevada Lodge No. 4, Nevadaville

Brown, O B
   Proceedings 1861-1869, pg 31 (1861 Dec 10) Junior Grand Warden
   Proceedings 1861-1869, pg 32 (1861 Dec 10), Summit Lodge No 7, Parkville
   Proceedings 1861-1869, pg 34 (1861 Dec 10) committee
   Proceedings 1861-1869, pg 36 (1861 Dec 12) Grand Treasurer
   Proceedings 1861-1869, pg 42 (1861 Dec 10), Summit Lodge No. 2, Parkville
   Proceedings 1861-1869, pg 44 (1862 Nov 3) Grand Treasurer
   Proceedings 1861-1869, pg 45 (1862 Nov 3), Summit Lodge No. 2, Parkville
   Proceedings 1861-1869, pg 45 (1862 Nov 3) committee
   Proceedings 1861-1869, pg 46 (1862 Nov 3) Grand Treasurer
   Proceedings 1861-1869, pg 47 (1862 Nov 3) committee
   Proceedings 1861-1869, pg 51 (1862 Nov 4) Grand Treasurer
   Proceedings 1861-1869, pg 52 (1862 Nov 4) Grand Treasurer
   Proceedings 1861-1869, pg 53 (1862 Nov 4) committee
   Proceedings 1861-1869, pg 54 (1862 Nov 4) committee
   Proceedings 1861-1869, pg 76 (1862 Nov 4), Summit Lodge No. 2, Parkville
   Proceedings 1861-1869, pg 79 (1863 May 6) Grand Treasurer
   Proceedings 1861-1869, pg 80 (1863 May 6) Grand Treasurer
   Proceedings 1861-1869, pg 80 (1863 May 6), Summit Lodge No. 2, Parkville
   Proceedings 1861-1869, pg 91 (1863 Apr 17) committee
   Proceedings 1861-1869, pg 93 (1863 Apr 17) committee
   Proceedings 1861-1869, pg 94 (1863 Apr 17) Grand Treasurer
   Proceedings 1861-1869, pg 94 (1863 Apr 17), Summit Lodge No. 2, Parkville
   Proceedings 1861-1869, pg 97 (1863 Nov 2) Grand Treasurer
   Proceedings 1861-1869, pg 98 (1863 Nov 2), Summit Lodge No. 2, Parkville
   Proceedings 1861-1869, pg 98 (1863 Nov 2) Grand Treasurer

Brown, O B, cont.
- Proceedings 1861-1869, pg 99 (1863 Nov 2), Summit Lodge No. 2, Parkville, Grand Senior Warden
- Proceedings 1861-1869, pg 100 (1863 Nov 2) committee
- Proceedings 1861-1869, pg 100 (1863 Nov 3) Grand Senior Warden
- Proceedings 1861-1869, pg 101 (1862 Nov 4) Grand Treasurer
- Proceedings 1861-1869, pg 101 (1863 Nov 3) Grand Secretary
- Proceedings 1861-1869, pg 102 (1863 Nov 3) Grand Treasurer
- Proceedings 1861-1869, pg 103 (1863 Nov 3) committee
- Proceedings 1861-1869, pg 103 (1863 Nov 3), Summit Lodge No. 2, Parkville
- Proceedings 1861-1869, pg 110 (1863 Nov 3), Summit Lodge No. 2, Parkville
- Proceedings 1861-1869, pg 115 (1864 Nov 7) Senior Grand Warden
- Proceedings 1861-1869, pg 115 (1864 Nov 7) committee
- Proceedings 1861-1869, pg 116 (1864 Nov 7) Senior Grand Warden
- Proceedings 1861-1869, pg 116 (1864 Nov 7) Senior Grand Warden
- Proceedings 1861-1869, pg 116 (1864 Nov 7) committee
- Proceedings 1861-1869, pg 117 (1864 Nov 7) committee
- Proceedings 1861-1869, pg 118 (1864 Nov 8) Denver Lodge No. 5, Deputy Grand Master
- Proceedings 1861-1869, pg 119 (1863 Nov 3) warrant drawn
- Proceedings 1861-1869, pg 119 (1863 Nov 3) warrant drawn
- Proceedings 1861-1869, pg 119 (1864 Nov 8) committee
- Proceedings 1861-1869, pg 119 (1864 Nov 8) Grand Treasurer
- Proceedings 1861-1869, pg 123 (1864 Nov 8) committee
- Proceedings 1861-1869, pg 124 (1864 Nov 8) committee
- Proceedings 1861-1869, pg 125 (1864 Nov 8) committee
- Proceedings 1861-1869, pg 126 (1864 Nov 8) Grand Senior Warden
- Proceedings 1861-1869, pg 126 (1864 Nov 8) committee
- Proceedings 1861-1869, pg 132 (1864 Nov 8) Golden City Lodge No. 1
- Proceedings 1861-1869, pg 136 (1865 Nov 6) Deputy Grand Master
- Proceedings 1861-1869, pg 137 (1865 Nov 6) committee
- Proceedings 1861-1869, pg 137 (1865 Nov 6) committee
- Proceedings 1861-1869, pg 137 (1865 Nov 6) Deputy Grand Master
- Proceedings 1861-1869, pg 138 (1865 Nov 6) committee
- Proceedings 1861-1869, pg 138 (1865 Nov 6) committee
- Proceedings 1861-1869, pg 138 (1865 Nov 6) Deputy Grand Master
- Proceedings 1861-1869, pg 139 (1864 Dec 14) library fund
- Proceedings 1861-1869, pg 139 (1864 Dec 17) library fund
- Proceedings 1861-1869, pg 139 (1865 Feb 23) library fund
- Proceedings 1861-1869, pg 139 (1865 Jan 13) library fund
- Proceedings 1861-1869, pg 139 (1865 July 8) library fund
- Proceedings 1861-1869, pg 139 (1865 May 1) library fund
- Proceedings 1861-1869, pg 139 (1865 Nov 6) Deputy Grand Master
- Proceedings 1861-1869, pg 140 (1864 Nov 8) warrant
- Proceedings 1861-1869, pg 141 (1865 Nov 7), Union Lodge No. 7, Denver
- Proceedings 1861-1869, pg 143 (1865 Nov 7) committee
- Proceedings 1861-1869, pg 144 (1865 Nov 7) Deputy Grand Master
- Proceedings 1861-1869, pg 144 (1865 Nov 7) committee
- Proceedings 1861-1869, pg 151 (1865 Nov 7), Chivington Lodge No. 6, Central City
- Proceedings 1861-1869, pg 169 (1866 Oct 2), Union Lodge No. 7, Denver, demitted
- Proceedings 1861-1869, pg 315 (1869 Sept 29) Grand Treasurer, 1862, Dimitted
- Proceedings 1861-1869, pg 315 (1869 Sept 29) Deputy Grand Master, 1865, Dimitted
- Proceedings 1861-1869, pg 315 (1869 Sept 29) Grand Treasurer, December 1861, Dimitted
- Proceedings 1861-1869, pg 315 (1869 Sept 29) Deputy Grand Master, 1864, Dimitted
- Proceedings 1861-1869, pg 315 (1869 Sept 29) Senior Grand Warden, 1863, Dimitted
- Proceedings 1870, pg 32 (1870 Sept 28) Deputy Grand Master, 1865, Dimitted
- Proceedings 1870, pg 32 (1870 Sept 28) Deputy Grand Master, 1864, Dimitted
- Proceedings 1870, pg 32 (1870 Sept 28) Senior Grand Warden, 1863, Dimitted
- Proceedings 1870, pg 32 (1870 Sept 28) Grand Treasurer, December 1861, Dimitted
- Proceedings 1870, pg 32 (1870 Sept 28) Grand Treasurer, 1862, Dimitted
- Proceedings 1871, pg 34 (1871 Sept 27) Grand Treasurer, Dec 1861, Dimitted
- Proceedings 1871, pg 34 (1871 Sept 27) Grand Treasurer, 1862, Dimitted
- Proceedings 1871, pg 34 (1871 Sept 27) Deputy Grand Master, 1865, Dimitted
- Proceedings 1871, pg 34 (1871 Sept 27) Senior Grand Warden, 1863, Dimitted
- Proceedings 1871, pg 34 (1871 Sept 27) Deputy Grand Master, 1864, Dimitted
- Proceedings 1872, pg 42 (1872 Sept 24) Grand Treasurer, December 1861, Dimitted
- Proceedings 1872, pg 42 (1872 Sept 24) Senior Grand Warden, 1863, Dimitted
- Proceedings 1872, pg 42 (1872 Sept 24) Deputy Grand Master, 1864, Dimitted
- Proceedings 1872, pg 42 (1872 Sept 24) Deputy Grand Master, 1865, Dimitted
- Proceedings 1872, pg 42 (1872 Sept 24) Grand Treasurer, 1862, Dimitted
- Proceedings 1873, pg 58 (1873 Oct 1) Deputy Grand Master, 1864, Dimitted
- Proceedings 1873, pg 58 (1873 Oct 1) Deputy Grand Master, 1865
- Proceedings 1873, pg 58 (1873 Oct 1) Senior Grand Warden, 1863, Dimitted

Brown, O B, cont.
Proceedings 1873, pg 58 (1873 Oct 1) Grand Treasurer, 1862, Dimitted
Proceedings 1873, pg 58 (1873 Oct 1) Grand Treasurer, Dec 1861, Dimitted
Proceedings 1874, pg 15 (1874 Sept 29) committee Brown, O B
Proceedings 1874, pg 206 (1874 Sept 30) Deputy Grand Master, 1865, demitted
Proceedings 1874, pg 206 (1874 Sept 30) Deputy Grand Master, 1864, demitted
Proceedings 1874, pg 206 (1874 Sept 30) Senior Grand Warden, 1863, demitted
Proceedings 1874, pg 206 (1874 Sept 30) Grand Treasurer, 1862, demitted
Proceedings 1874, pg 206 (1874 Sept 30) Grand Treasurer, Dec 1861, demitted

Brown, Oliphant B
Proceedings 1875, pg 93 (1875 Sept 22) Deputy Grand Master, 1864, Demitted
Proceedings 1875, pg 93 (1875 Sept 22) Grand Treasurer, Dec 1861, Demitted
Proceedings 1875, pg 93 (1875 Sept 22) Deputy Grand Master, 1865, Demitted
Proceedings 1875, pg 93 (1875 Sept 22) Grand Treasurer, 1862, Demitted
Proceedings 1875, pg 93 (1875 Sept 22) Senior Grand Warden, 1863, Demitted

Brown, S G
Proceedings 1861-1869, pg 145 (1865 Nov 7) , Grand Tyler
Proceedings 1861-1869, pg 166 (1866 Oct 2), Nevada Lodge No. 4, Nevadaville
Proceedings 1861-1869, pg 192 (1867 Oct 8), Nevada Lodge No. 4, Nevadaville
Proceedings 1861-1869, pg 304 (1869 Sept 29), Nevada Lodge No. 4, Nevadaville
Proceedings 1875, pg 74 (1875 Sept 22), Nevada Lodge No. 4, Nevada

Brown, Silas G
Proceedings 1861-1869, pg 77 (1862 Nov 4), Nevada Lodge No. 4, Nevadaville
Proceedings 1861-1869, pg 111 (1863 Nov 3), Nevada Lodge No. 4, Nevadaville
Proceedings 1861-1869, pg 132 (1864 Nov 8), Nevada Lodge No. 4, Nevadaville
Proceedings 1861-1869, pg 147 (1865 Nov 7), Nevada Lodge No. 4, Nevadaville
Proceedings 1861-1869, pg 222 (1868 Oct 7), Nevada Lodge No. 4, Nevadaville
Proceedings 1870, pg 20 (1870 Sept 28), Nevada Lodge No. 4, Nevadaville
Proceedings 1871, pg 18 (1871 Sept 27), Nevada Lodge No. 4, Bald Mountain
Proceedings 1872, pg 18 (1872 Sept 24), Nevada Lodge No. 4, Bald Mountain
Proceedings 1873, pg 36 (1873 Oct 1), Nevada Lodge No. 4, Nevada
Proceedings 1874, pg 210 (1874 Sept 30), Nevada Lodge No. 4, Bald Mountain, Gilpin County
Proceedings 1876, pg 30 (1876 Sept 20) Nevada Lodge No. 4

Brown, W C
Proceedings 1874, pg 221 (1874 Sept 30), Cheyenne Lodge No. 16, Cheyenne, Wyoming Territory

Brown, W G
Proceedings 1875, pg 75 (1875 Sept 22) Denver Lodge No. 5

Brown, W H
Proceedings 1870, pg 29 (1870 Sept 28), Cheyenne Lodge No. 16, Cheyenne, Wyoming Territory, Apprentice
Proceedings 1871, pg 27 (1871 Sept 27), Cheyenne Lodge No. 16, Cheyenne, Wyoming Territory, Apprentice
Proceedings 1872, pg 30 (1872 Sept 24), Cheyenne Lodge No. 16, Cheyenne, Wyoming Territory, Apprentice
Proceedings 1873, pg 46 (1873 Oct 1), Cheyenne Lodge No. 16, Cheyenne, Wyoming Territory, Apprentice
Proceedings 1874, pg 221 (1874 Sept 30), Cheyenne Lodge No. 16, Cheyenne, Wyoming Territory, Apprentice

Brown, Wm G
Proceedings 1876, pg 30 (1876 Sept 20) Denver Lodge No. 5

Brownell, A W
Proceedings 1861-1869, pg 227 (1868 Oct 7), Washington Lodge No. 12, Georgetown
Proceedings 1861-1869, pg 288 (1869 Sept 28), Washington Lodge No. 12, Georgetown
Proceedings 1861-1869, pg 309 (1869 Sept 29), Washington Lodge No. 12, Georgetown
Proceedings 1870, pg 26 (1870 Sept 28), Washington Lodge No. 12, Georgetown
Proceedings 1871, pg 24 (1871 Sept 27), Washington Lodge No. 12, Georgetown
Proceedings 1874, pg 217 (1874 Sept 30), Washington Lodge No. 12, Georgetown
Proceedings 1876, pg 35 (1876 Sept 20), Washington Lodge No. 12, Georgetown

Brownell, Ai W
Proceedings 1873, pg 42 (1873 Oct 1), Washington Lodge No. 12, Georgetown
Proceedings 1875, pg 81 (1875 Sept 22), Washington Lodge No. 12, Georgetown

Brownell, Ali W
Proceedings 1872, pg 26 (1872 Sept 24), Washington Lodge No. 12, Georgetown

Brownville Band
Proceedings 1873, pg 18 (1873 Oct 1) bill paid

Brubaker, William
Proceedings 1876, pg 42 (1876 Sept 20), Doric Lodge No. 25, Fairplay

Bruce, J C
Proceedings 1861-1869, pg 113 (1863 Nov 3), Chivington Lodge No. 6, Central City, Apprentice

Proceedings 1861-1869, pg 150 (1865 Nov 7), Chivington Lodge No. 6, Central City, Apprentice

Proceedings 1861-1869, pg 169 (1866 Oct 2), Chivington Lodge No. 6, Central City, Apprentice

Proceedings 1861-1869, pg 194 (1867 Oct 8), Chivington Lodge No. 6, Central City, Apprentice

Proceedings 1861-1869, pg 225 (1868 Oct 7), Chivington Lodge No. 6, Central City, Apprentice

Bruce, Jno C

Proceedings 1871, pg 21 (1871 Sept 27), Central Lodge No. 6, Central, Apprentice

Proceedings 1872, pg 21 (1872 Sept 24), Denver Lodge No. 5, Denver, Apprentice

Bruce, John C

Proceedings 1861-1869, pg 134 (1864 Nov 8), Chivington Lodge No. 6, Central City, Apprentice

Proceedings 1861-1869, pg 307 (1869 Sept 29), Central Lodge No. 6, Central City, Apprentice

Proceedings 1870, pg 22 (1870 Sept 28), Central Lodge No. 6, Central City, Apprentice

Proceedings 1873, pg 39 (1873 Oct 1), Central Lodge No. 6, Central City, Apprentice

Proceedings 1874, pg 213 (1874 Sept 30), Central Lodge No. 6, Central, Apprentice

Proceedings 1875, pg 77 (1875 Sept 22), Central Lodge No. 6, Central City, Apprentice

Proceedings 1876, pg 32 (1876 Sept 20), Central Lodge No. 6, Central City, Apprentice

Bruderlin, Emile

Proceedings 1876, pg 31 (1876 Sept 20) Denver Lodge No. 5

Brune, F F

Proceedings 1861-1869, pg 179 (1867 Oct 7), Washington Lodge No. 12, Georgetown

Proceedings 1861-1869, pg 227 (1868 Oct 7), Washington Lodge No. 12, Georgetown

Brunel, I B

Proceedings 1861-1869, pg 150 (1865 Nov 7), Chivington Lodge No. 6, Central City

Proceedings 1861-1869, pg 132 (1864 Nov 8), Nevada Lodge No. 4, Nevadaville, dimitted

Proceedings 1861-1869, pg 168 (1866 Oct 2), Chivington Lodge No. 6, Central City

Proceedings 1861-1869, pg 194 (1867 Oct 8), Chivington Lodge No. 6, Central City

Proceedings 1861-1869, pg 306 (1869 Sept 29), Central Lodge No. 6, Central City

Brunell, Isaac B

Proceedings 1861-1869, pg 111 (1863 Nov 3), Nevada Lodge No. 4, Nevadaville

Proceedings 1861-1869, pg 134 (1864 Nov 8), Chivington Lodge No. 6, Central City

Proceedings 1861-1869, pg 224 (1868 Oct 7), Chivington Lodge No. 6, Central City

Proceedings 1870, pg 23 (1870 Sept 28), Central Lodge No. 6, Central City, Dimitted,

Bruns

Proceedings 1874, pg 122 (1874 Sept 30) Grand Lodge of South Carolina

Bruns, R S

Proceedings 1861-1869, pg 280 (1867 Nov 19), Grand Secretary, Grand Lodge of South Carolina

Proceedings 1870, pg 101 (1869 Nov 16) Grand Secretary, Grand Lodge of South Carolina

Proceedings 1874, pg 121 (1874 Sept 30) Grand Lodge of South Carolina

Proceedings 1874, pg 123 (1874 Sept 30) Grand Lodge of South Carolina, deceased

Bruns, Robert S

Proceedings 1861-1869, pg 316 (1869 Sept 29) Grand Lodge of South Carolina

Brush, David L

Proceedings 1872, pg 33 (1872 Sept 24), Collins Lodge No. 19, Fort Collins

Brush, J L

Proceedings 1873, pg 50 (1873 Oct 1), Occidental Lodge No. 20, Greeley

Proceedings 1874, pg 225 (1874 Sept 30), Occidental Lodge No. 20, Greeley

Proceedings 1875, pg 87 (1875 Sept 22), Occidental Lodge No. 20, Greeley

Brush, Jared L

Proceedings 1873, pg 49 (1873 Oct 1), Collins Lodge No. 19, Fort Collins, Dimitted

Proceedings 1876, pg 40 (1876 Sept 20), Occidental Lodge No. 20, Greeley

Brush, Jurard L

Proceedings 1871, pg 30 (1871 Sept 27), Collins Lodge No. 19, Fort Collins, Fellowcraft

Bryan, G H

Proceedings 1861-1869, pg 196 (1867 Oct 8), El Paso Lodge U D, Colorado City

Bryant, C M

Proceedings 1861-1869, pg 196 (1867 Oct 8), El Paso Lodge U D, Colorado City

Proceedings 1861-1869, pg 310 (1869 Sept 29), El Paso Lodge No. 13, Colorado City

Proceedings 1870, pg 27 (1870 Sept 28), El Paso Lodge No. 13, Colorado City

Proceedings 1873, pg 43 (1873 Oct 1), El Paso Lodge No. 13, Colorado City

Proceedings 1874, pg 218 (1874 Sept 30), El Paso Lodge No. 13, Colorado Springs

Proceedings 1875, pg 82 (1875 Sept 22), El Paso Lodge No. 13, Colorado Springs

Bryant, Charles M

Proceedings 1871, pg 25 (1871 Sept 27), El Paso Lodge No. 13, Colorado City

Bryant, Chas M

Proceedings 1872, pg 27 (1872 Sept 24), El Paso Lodge No. 13, Colorado City

Colorado's Territorial Masons

Bryant, Chas M, cont.
Proceedings 1876, pg 49 (1876 Sept 20), El Paso Lodge No. 13, Colorado City, 1876 July 22

Bryant, G A
Proceedings 1861-1869, pg 228 (1868 Oct 7), El Paso Lodge No. 13, Colorado City

Bryant, G H
Proceedings 1861-1869, pg 149 (1865 Nov 7), Nevada Lodge No. 4, Nevadaville
Proceedings 1861-1869, pg 167 (1866 Oct 2) Denver Lodge No. 5
Proceedings 1861-1869, pg 305 (1869 Sept 29) Denver Lodge No. 5

Bryant, Geo H
Proceedings 1861-1869, pg 133 (1864 Nov 8) Denver Lodge No. 5
Proceedings 1861-1869, pg 193 (1867 Oct 8) Denver Lodge No. 5
Proceedings 1861-1869, pg 223 (1868 Oct 7) Denver Lodge No. 5
Proceedings 1861-1869, pg 310 (1869 Sept 29), El Paso Lodge No. 13, Colorado City
Proceedings 1870, pg 21 (1870 Sept 28), Denver Lodge No. 5, Denver
Proceedings 1870, pg 27 (1870 Sept 28), El Paso Lodge No. 13, Colorado City
Proceedings 1872, pg 20 (1872 Sept 24), Denver Lodge No. 5, Denver
Proceedings 1874, pg 226 (1874 Sept 30), Weston Lodge No. 22, Littleton
Proceedings 1875, pg 88 (1875 Sept 22), Weston Lodge No. 22, Littleton

Bryant, George
Proceedings 1872, pg 27 (1872 Sept 24), El Paso Lodge No. 13, Colorado City, Dimitted

Bryant, George H
Proceedings 1871, pg 25 (1871 Sept 27), El Paso Lodge No. 13, Colorado City
Proceedings 1876, pg 41 (1876 Sept 20), Weston Lodge No. 22, Littleton

Bryant, O M
Proceedings 1861-1869, pg 228 (1868 Oct 7), El Paso Lodge No. 13, Colorado City

Bryce, J R
Proceedings 1861-1869, pg 152 (1865 Nov 7), Montana Lodge U D, Virginia City, Montana Territory

Buchanan, G W
Proceedings 1861-1869, pg 150 (1865 Nov 7), Chivington Lodge No. 6, Central City
Proceedings 1861-1869, pg 168 (1866 Oct 2), Chivington Lodge No. 6, Central City
Proceedings 1861-1869, pg 194 (1867 Oct 8), Chivington Lodge No. 6, Central City
Proceedings 1861-1869, pg 225 (1868 Oct 7), Chivington Lodge No. 6, Central City, Dimitted
Proceedings 1861-1869, pg 227 (1868 Oct 7), Washington Lodge No. 12, Georgetown
Proceedings 1861-1869, pg 309 (1869 Sept 29), Washington Lodge No. 12, Georgetown
Proceedings 1870, pg 26 (1870 Sept 28), Washington Lodge No. 12, Georgetown

Buchanan, Geo W
Proceedings 1872, pg 26 (1872 Sept 24), Washington Lodge No. 12, Georgetown

Buchanan, George W
Proceedings 1861-1869, pg 134 (1864 Nov 8), Chivington Lodge No. 6, Central City
Proceedings 1871, pg 24 (1871 Sept 27), Washington Lodge No. 12, Georgetown
Proceedings 1873, pg 43 (1873 Oct 1), Washington Lodge No. 12, Georgetown
Proceedings 1874, pg 218 (1874 Sept 30), Washington Lodge No. 12, Georgetown, Stricken from the rolls

Buchanan, T J
Proceedings 1861-1869, pg 151 (1865 Nov 7), Empire Lodge U D, Empire City
Proceedings 1861-1869, pg 195 (1867 Oct 8), Empire Lodge No. 8, Empire City

Buchanan, Thos J
Proceedings 1861-1869, pg 170 (1866 Oct 2), Empire Lodge No. 8, Empire City

Buchtel, John T
Proceedings 1875, pg 87 (1875 Sept 22), Occidental Lodge No. 20, Greeley
Proceedings 1876, pg 40 (1876 Sept 20), Occidental Lodge No. 20, Greeley

Buck, J L
Proceedings 1861-1869, pg 111 (1863 Nov 3), Nevada Lodge No. 4, Nevadaville, dimitted

Buckley, John A
Proceedings 1872, pg 35 (1872 Sept 24), St Vrain Lodge No. 23, Longmont
Proceedings 1873, pg 51 (1873 Oct 1), St Vrain Lodge No. 23, Longmont
Proceedings 1874, pg 227 (1874 Sept 30), St Vrain No. 23, Longmont
Proceedings 1876, pg 41 (1876 Sept 20), St Vrain Lodge No. 23, Longmont

Buckmiller, A E
Proceedings 1861-1869, pg 113 (1863 Nov 3), Chivington Lodge No. 6, Central City
Proceedings 1861-1869, pg 134 (1864 Nov 8), Chivington Lodge No. 6, Central City
Proceedings 1861-1869, pg 150 (1865 Nov 7), Chivington Lodge No. 6, Central City
Proceedings 1861-1869, pg 168 (1866 Oct 2), Chivington Lodge No. 6, Central City
Proceedings 1861-1869, pg 194 (1867 Oct 8), Chivington Lodge No. 6, Central City
Proceedings 1861-1869, pg 225 (1868 Oct 7), Chivington Lodge No. 6, Central City, Dimitted,

Budd
Proceedings 1874, pg 52 (1874 Sept 30) Grand Lodge of Delaware

Budd, J Thomas
Proceedings 1872, pg 59 (1872 Sept 24) Grand Lodge of Delaware

Budd, J Thos
Proceedings 1873, pg 60 (1873 Oct 1) Grand Lodge of Delaware, Middleton

Budd, Sylramus [Sylvanus]
Proceedings 1861-1869, pg 311 (1869 Sept 29), Columbia Lodge No. 14, Boulder City, Apprentice

Budd, Sylvanus
Proceedings 1870, pg 27 (1870 Sept 28), Columbia Lodge No. 14, Boulder City
Proceedings 1871, pg 25 (1871 Sept 27), Columbia Lodge No. 14, Boulder City
Proceedings 1872, pg 28 (1872 Sept 24), Columbia Lodge No. 14, Boulder
Proceedings 1873, pg 44 (1873 Oct 1), Columbia Lodge No. 14, Boulder
Proceedings 1874, pg 219 (1874 Sept 30), Columbia Lodge No. 14, Boulder, Boulder County
Proceedings 1875, pg 83 (1875 Sept 22), Columbia Lodge No. 14, Boulder
Proceedings 1876, pg 37 (1876 Sept 20), Columbia Lodge No. 14, Boulder

Buel, Bela S
Proceedings 1861-1869, pg 150 (1865 Nov 7), Chivington Lodge No. 6, Central City

Buell, B S
Proceedings 1861-1869, pg 134 (1864 Nov 8), Chivington Lodge No. 6, Central City, Fellowcraft
Proceedings 1861-1869, pg 168 (1866 Oct 2), Chivington Lodge No. 6, Central City
Proceedings 1861-1869, pg 194 (1867 Oct 8), Chivington Lodge No. 6, Central City

Buell, Bela S
Proceedings 1861-1869, pg 225 (1868 Oct 7), Chivington Lodge No. 6, Central City, Dimitted

Buell, S A
Proceedings 1861-1869, pg 168 (1866 Oct 2), Chivington Lodge No. 6, Central City
Proceedings 1861-1869, pg 194 (1867 Oct 8), Chivington Lodge No. 6, Central City
Proceedings 1861-1869, pg 224 (1868 Oct 7), Chivington Lodge No. 6, Central City

Buell, Sam A
Proceedings 1861-1869, pg 306 (1869 Sept 29), Central Lodge No. 6, Central City
Proceedings 1870, pg 22 (1870 Sept 28), Central Lodge No. 6, Central City

Buell, Sam'l A
Proceedings 1871, pg 21 (1871 Sept 27), Central Lodge No. 6, Central, died

Buell, Samuel A
Proceedings 1871, pg 32 (1871 Sept 27), Central Lodge No. 6, Central

Bull, H P
Proceedings 1872, pg 32 (1872 Sept 24), Laramie Lodge No. 18, Laramie, Wyoming Territory, Apprentice
Proceedings 1873, pg 48 (1873 Oct 1), Laramie Lodge No. 18, Laramie, Wyoming Territory, permission granted to take degrees elsewhere

Bull, Henry P
Proceedings 1871, pg 29 (1871 Sept 27), Laramie Lodge No. 18, Laramie, Wyoming Territory, Apprentice

Bulletin of the Grand Orient of France
Proceedings 1861-1869, pg 291 (1869 Sept 28)
Proceedings 1876, pg 12 (1876 Sept 19) published at Paris

Bullock, T J
Proceedings 1871, pg 24 (1871 Sept 27), Washington Lodge No. 12, Georgetown

Bullock, Talbot J
Proceedings 1870, pg 26 (1870 Sept 28), Washington Lodge No. 12, Georgetown
Proceedings 1872, pg 26 (1872 Sept 24), Washington Lodge No. 12, Georgetown, Dimitted

Bunn, David
Proceedings 1873, pg 44 (1873 Oct 1), Columbia Lodge No. 14, Boulder
Proceedings 1874, pg 219 (1874 Sept 30), Columbia Lodge No. 14, Boulder, Boulder County
Proceedings 1875, pg 83 (1875 Sept 22), Columbia Lodge No. 14, Boulder
Proceedings 1876, pg 36 (1876 Sept 20), Columbia Lodge No. 14, Boulder

Bunting, Wm F
Proceedings 1861-1869, pg 316 (1869 Sept 29) Grand Lodge of New Brunswick
Proceedings 1861-1869, pg 342 (1868 Sept 23) Grand Secretary, Grand Lodge of New Brunswick
Proceedings 1870, pg 34 (1870 Sept 28) Grand Secretary, Grand Lodge of New Brunswick
Proceedings 1870, pg 95 (1869 Sept 22) Grand Secretary, Grand Lodge of New Brunswick
Proceedings 1871, pg 35 (1871 Sept 27) Grand Secretary, Grand Lodge of New Brunswick
Proceedings 1872, pg 43 (1872 Sept 24) Saint John, Grand Lodge of New Brunswick
Proceedings 1872, pg 76 (1872 Sept 24) Grand Lodge of New Brunswick
Proceedings 1873, pg 61 (1873 Oct 1) Grand Lodge of New Brunswick, Saint John
Proceedings 1874, pg 103 (1874 Sept 30) Grand Lodge of New Brunswick
Proceedings 1874, pg 104 (1874 Sept 30) Grand Lodge of New Brunswick
Proceedings 1874, pg 204 (1874 Sept 30) Grand Lodge of New Brunswick, St John
Proceedings 1875, pg 96 (1875 Sept 22) Grand Lodge of New Brunswick, St John
Proceedings 1876, pg 54 (1876 Sept 20) Grand Lodge of New Brunswick, St John

Colorado's Territorial Masons

Burbage, E I
Proceedings 1872, pg 24 (1872 Sept 24), Black Hawk Lodge No. 11, Black Hawk

Burbage, E L
Proceedings 1871, pg 23 (1871 Sept 27), Black Hawk Lodge No. 11, Black Hawk
Proceedings 1876, pg 48 (1876 Sept 20) Black Hawk Lodge No. 11, 1875 Dec 23

Burchineel, Wm K
Proceedings 1876, pg 42 (1876 Sept 20), Doric Lodge No. 25, Fairplay

Burdick
Proceedings 1872, pg 13 (1872 Sept 24) resolution

Burdick, J A
Proceedings 1861-1869, pg 166 (1866 Oct 2), Nevada Lodge No. 4, Nevadaville
Proceedings 1861-1869, pg 192 (1867 Oct 8), Nevada Lodge No. 4, Nevadaville
Proceedings 1861-1869, pg 222 (1868 Oct 7), Nevada Lodge No. 4, Nevadaville, Dimitted
Proceedings 1861-1869, pg 287 (1869 Sept 28) Junior Grand Warden
Proceedings 1861-1869, pg 299 (1869 Sept 29) Junior Grand Steward
Proceedings 1870, pg 4 (1870 Sept 27), Washington Lodge No. 12, Georgetown
Proceedings 1870, pg 15 (1870 Sept 28) committee
Proceedings 1870, pg 16 (1870 Sept 28), Washington Lodge No. 12, Georgetown
Proceedings 1871, pg 3 (1871 Sept 26) Grand Lecturer
Proceedings 1871, pg 4 (1871 Sept 26), Washington Lodge No. 12, Georgetown
Proceedings 1871, pg 14 (1871 Sept 27), Washington Lodge No. 12, Georgetown
Proceedings 1871, pg 24 (1871 Sept 27), Washington Lodge No. 12, Georgetown
Proceedings 1872, pg 4 (1872 Sept 24) visiting
Proceedings 1872, pg 5 (1872 Sept 24) committee
Proceedings 1872, pg 15 (1872 Sept 24) Grand Marshal
Proceedings 1872, pg 16 (1872 Sept 24), Washington Lodge No. 12, Georgetown

Burdick, James A
Proceedings 1861-1869, pg 132 (1864 Nov 8), Nevada Lodge No. 4, Nevadaville
Proceedings 1861-1869, pg 179 (1867 Oct 7), Washington Lodge No. 12, Georgetown
Proceedings 1861-1869, pg 288 (1869 Sept 28), Washington Lodge No. 12, Georgetown
Proceedings 1870, pg cover (1870 Sept 28) Grand Lecturer, Georgetown
Proceedings 1872, pg 16 (1872 Sept 24) committee
Proceedings 1872, pg 25 (1872 Sept 24), Washington Lodge No. 12, Georgetown
Proceedings 1872, pg 25 (1872 Sept 24), Washington Lodge No. 12, Georgetown
Proceedings 1873, pg 42 (1873 Oct 1), Washington Lodge No. 12, Georgetown
Proceedings 1874, pg 217 (1874 Sept 30), Washington Lodge No. 12, Georgetown
Proceedings 1876, pg 34 (1876 Sept 20), Washington Lodge No. 12, Georgetown

Burdick, Jas A
Proceedings 1861-1869, pg 111 (1863 Nov 3), Nevada Lodge No. 4, Nevadaville
Proceedings 1861-1869, pg 148 (1865 Nov 7), Nevada Lodge No. 4, Nevadaville
Proceedings 1861-1869, pg 227 (1868 Oct 7), Washington Lodge No. 12, Georgetown
Proceedings 1861-1869, pg 309 (1869 Sept 29), Washington Lodge No. 12, Georgetown
Proceedings 1870, pg 13 (1870 Sept 27) Grand Lecturer
Proceedings 1870, pg 26 (1870 Sept 28), Washington Lodge No. 12, Georgetown
Proceedings 1875, pg 81 (1875 Sept 22), Washington Lodge No. 12, Georgetown

Burdlick, J A
Proceedings 1861-1869, pg 77 (1862 Nov 4), Nevada Lodge No. 4, Nevadaville

Burdsall, C S
Proceedings 1861-1869, pg 147 (1865 Nov 7) Golden City Lodge No. 1, Apprentice
Proceedings 1861-1869, pg 165 (1866 Oct 2) Golden City Lodge No. 1, Apprentice

Burk, S
Proceedings 1861-1869, pg 111 (1863 Nov 3), Summit Lodge No. 2, Parkville, dimitted

Burk, Samuel
Proceedings 1861-1869, pg 76 (1862 Nov 4), Summit Lodge No. 2, Parkville, Apprentice

Burke, R A
Proceedings 1873, pg 50 (1873 Oct 1), Occidental Lodge No. 20, Greeley

Burke, Richard
Proceedings 1871, pg 30 (1871 Sept 27), Occidental Lodge U D, Greeley
Proceedings 1872, pg 33 (1872 Sept 24), Occidental Lodge No. 20, Greeley
Proceedings 1874, pg 225 (1874 Sept 30), Occidental Lodge No. 20, Greeley
Proceedings 1875, pg 87 (1875 Sept 22), Occidental Lodge No. 20, Greeley
Proceedings 1876, pg 40 (1876 Sept 20), Occidental Lodge No. 20, Greeley

Burleigh, R A
Proceedings 1870, pg 31 (1870 Sept 28), Laramie Lodge No. 18, Laramie, Wyoming Territory
Proceedings 1871, pg 29 (1871 Sept 27), Laramie Lodge No. 18, Laramie, Wyoming Territory
Proceedings 1872, pg 32 (1872 Sept 24), Laramie Lodge No. 18, Laramie, Wyoming Territory
Proceedings 1873, pg 48 (1873 Oct 1), Laramie Lodge No. 18, Laramie, Wyoming Territory
Proceedings 1874, pg 223 (1874 Sept 30), Laramie Lodge No. 18, Laramie City

Burlingame, E E
Proceedings 1861-1869, pg 227 (1868 Oct 7), Washington Lodge No. 12, Georgetown
Proceedings 1861-1869, pg 309 (1869 Sept 29), Washington Lodge No. 12, Georgetown
Proceedings 1870, pg 26 (1870 Sept 28), Washington Lodge No. 12, Georgetown
Proceedings 1871, pg 24 (1871 Sept 27), Washington Lodge No. 12, Georgetown
Proceedings 1874, pg 218 (1874 Sept 30), Washington Lodge No. 12, Georgetown, Stricken from the rolls
Proceedings 1875, pg 81 (1875 Sept 22), Washington Lodge No. 12, Georgetown, Reinstated
Proceedings 1875, pg 81 (1875 Sept 22), Washington Lodge No. 12, Georgetown, Demitted

Burlingame, Eugene E
Proceedings 1872, pg 26 (1872 Sept 24), Washington Lodge No. 12, Georgetown
Proceedings 1873, pg 42 (1873 Oct 1), Washington Lodge No. 12, Georgetown

Burnill, John F
Proceedings 1875, pg 96 (1875 Sept 22) Grand Lodge of Illinois, Springfield

Burns, Francis
Proceedings 1872, pg 69 (1872 Sept 24) Grand Lodge of Maryland

Burns, R S
Proceedings 1861-1869, pg 346 (1868 Nov 17) Grand Secretary, Grand Lodge of South Carolina
Proceedings 1872, pg 44 (1872 Sept 24) Charleston, Grand Lodge of South Carolina
Proceedings 1873, pg 61 (1873 Oct 1) Grand Lodge of South Carolina, Charleston

Burns, William
Proceedings 1870, pg 31 (1870 Sept 28), Laramie Lodge No. 18, Laramie, Wyoming Territory
Proceedings 1871, pg 29 (1871 Sept 27), Laramie Lodge No. 18, Laramie, Wyoming Territory
Proceedings 1873, pg 48 (1873 Oct 1), Laramie Lodge No. 18, Laramie, Wyoming Territory
Proceedings 1874, pg 223 (1874 Sept 30), Laramie Lodge No. 18, Laramie City

Burns, Wm
Proceedings 1872, pg 31 (1872 Sept 24), Laramie Lodge No. 18, Laramie, Wyoming Territory

Burr, Henry
Proceedings 1874, pg 218 (1874 Sept 30), El Paso Lodge No. 13, Colorado Springs
Proceedings 1875, pg 82 (1875 Sept 22), El Paso Lodge No. 13, Colorado Springs
Proceedings 1876, pg 36 (1876 Sept 20), El Paso Lodge No. 13, Colorado City

Burrell, Harvey M
Proceedings 1876, pg 32 (1876 Sept 20), Central Lodge No. 6, Central City

Burrill
Proceedings 1874, pg 62 (1874 Sept 30) Grand Lodge of Illinois

Burrill, John F
Proceedings 1876, pg 54 (1876 Sept 20) Grand Lodge of Illinois, Springfield

Burrill, John T
Proceedings 1873, pg 60 (1873 Oct 1) Grand Lodge of Illinois, Springfield

Burris, William
Proceedings 1870, pg 26 (1870 Sept 28), Washington Lodge No. 12, Georgetown
Proceedings 1871, pg 24 (1871 Sept 27), Washington Lodge No. 12, Georgetown
Proceedings 1873, pg 42 (1873 Oct 1), Washington Lodge No. 12, Georgetown
Proceedings 1874, pg 217 (1874 Sept 30), Washington Lodge No. 12, Georgetown
Proceedings 1875, pg 81 (1875 Sept 22), Washington Lodge No. 12, Georgetown, Demitted

Burris, Wm
Proceedings 1861-1869, pg 227 (1868 Oct 7), Washington Lodge No. 12, Georgetown, Fellowcraft

Burris, Wm
Proceedings 1861-1869, pg 309 (1869 Sept 29), Washington Lodge No. 12, Georgetown
Proceedings 1872, pg 26 (1872 Sept 24), Washington Lodge No. 12, Georgetown

Burritt, John F
Proceedings 1874, pg 204 (1874 Sept 30) Grand Lodge of Illinois, Springfield

Burroughs, H M
Proceedings 1861-1869, pg 311 (1869 Sept 29), Mount Moriah Lodge No. 15, Canon City
Proceedings 1870, pg 28 (1870 Sept 28), Mount Moriah Lodge No. 15, Canon City
Proceedings 1872, pg 29 (1872 Sept 24), Mount Moriah Lodge No. 15, Canon City
Proceedings 1874, pg 220 (1874 Sept 30), Mount Moriah Lodge No. 15, Canon City
Proceedings 1875, pg 84 (1875 Sept 22), Mount Moriah Lodge No. 15, Canon City
Proceedings 1876, pg 38 (1876 Sept 20), Mount Moriah Lodge No. 15, Canon City

Burroughs, Henry M
Proceedings 1871, pg 26 (1871 Sept 27), Mount Moriah Lodge No. 15, Canon City

Burroughs, N M
Proceedings 1861-1869, pg 229 (1868 Oct 7), Canon Lodge U D, Canon City

Burrows, H M
Proceedings 1873, pg 45 (1873 Oct 1), Mount Moriah Lodge No. 15, Canon City

Burrows, John S
Proceedings 1876, pg 53 (1876 Sept 20) Grand Lodge of Wisconsin, of Fond du Lac, WI

Colorado's Territorial Masons

Bursell, L C
Proceedings 1870, pg 21 (1870 Sept 28), Denver Lodge No. 5, Denver
Proceedings 1871, pg 19 (1871 Sept 27) Denver Lodge No. 5
Proceedings 1872, pg 20 (1872 Sept 24), Denver Lodge No. 5, Denver, died
Proceedings 1872, pg 39 (1872 Sept 24), Denver Lodge No. 5, Denver

Bursell, S C
Proceedings 1872, pg 14 (1872 Sept 24), Denver Lodge No. 5, Denver, deceased on 2 July 1870

Burt, A S
Proceedings 1870, pg 29 (1870 Sept 28), Cheyenne Lodge No. 16, Cheyenne, Wyoming Territory, Fellowcraft
Proceedings 1871, pg 27 (1871 Sept 27), Cheyenne Lodge No. 16, Cheyenne, Wyoming Territory, Fellowcraft
Proceedings 1872, pg 49 (1872 Sept 24), Cheyenne Lodge No. 16, Cheyenne, Wyoming Territory

Burt, C C
Proceedings 1861-1869, pg 196 (1867 Oct 8), El Paso Lodge U D, Colorado City
Proceedings 1861-1869, pg 228 (1868 Oct 7), El Paso Lodge No. 13, Colorado City
Proceedings 1861-1869, pg 229 (1868 Oct 7), Pueblo Lodge U D, Pueblo
Proceedings 1874, pg 222 (1874 Sept 30), Pueblo Lodge No. 17, Pueblo, Pueblo County
Proceedings 1876, pg 38 (1876 Sept 20) Pueblo Lodge No. 17

Burt, Chauncey C
Proceedings 1861-1869, pg 312 (1869 Sept 29), Pueblo Lodge No. 17, Pueblo
Proceedings 1870, pg 30 (1870 Sept 28), Pueblo Lodge No. 17, Pueblo
Proceedings 1871, pg 28 (1871 Sept 27), Pueblo Lodge No. 17, Pueblo
Proceedings 1873, pg 47 (1873 Oct 1), Pueblo Lodge No. 17, Pueblo
Proceedings 1872, pg 31 (1872 Sept 24), Pueblo Lodge No. 17, Pueblo

Burtis, J J
Proceedings 1870, pg 59 (1870 June 7) Grand Lodge of Iowa, owner, Opera House at Davenport, IA

Burton, A A
Proceedings 1871, pg 29 (1871 Sept 27), Laramie Lodge No. 18, Laramie, Wyoming Territory
Proceedings 1872, pg 32 (1872 Sept 24), Laramie Lodge No. 18, Laramie, Wyoming Territory
Proceedings 1873, pg 48 (1873 Oct 1), Laramie Lodge No. 18, Laramie, Wyoming Territory
Proceedings 1874, pg 223 (1874 Sept 30), Laramie Lodge No. 18, Laramie City

Burton, C Myers
Proceedings 1871, pg 24 (1871 Sept 27), El Paso Lodge No. 13, Colorado City

Burwell, Samuel M
Proceedings 1876, pg 7 (1876 Mar 17), South Pueblo Lodge U D, South Pueblo, suspended from a lodge in Indiana

Busby, R
Proceedings 1861-1869, pg 309 (1869 Sept 29), Black Hawk Lodge No. 11, Black Hawk

Busby, Robert
Proceedings 1861-1869, pg 196 (1867 Oct 8), Black Hawk Lodge No. 11, Black Hawk
Proceedings 1861-1869, pg 227 (1868 Oct 7), Black Hawk Lodge No. 11, Black Hawk
Proceedings 1871, pg 23 (1871 Sept 27), Black Hawk Lodge No. 11, Black Hawk
Proceedings 1872, pg 24 (1872 Sept 24), Black Hawk Lodge No. 11, Black Hawk
Proceedings 1873, pg 41 (1873 Oct 1), Black Hawk Lodge No. 11, Black Hawk
Proceedings 1874, pg 216 (1874 Sept 30), Black Hawk Lodge No. 11, Black Hawk
Proceedings 1875, pg 80 (1875 Sept 22) Black Hawk Lodge No. 11
Proceedings 1876, pg 34 (1876 Sept 20) Black Hawk Lodge No. 11

Busby, Robt
Proceedings 1870, pg 25 (1870 Sept 28), Black Hawk Lodge No. 11, Black Hawk

Bush, Arthur W
Proceedings 1875, pg 83 (1875 Sept 22), Columbia Lodge No. 14, Boulder
Proceedings 1876, pg 37 (1876 Sept 20), Columbia Lodge No. 14, Boulder

Bush, J E
Proceedings 1861-1869, pg 305 (1869 Sept 29) Denver Lodge No. 5, Fellowcraft
Proceedings 1870, pg 21 (1870 Sept 28), Denver Lodge No. 5, Denver, given permission to receive degrees elsewhere
Proceedings 1874, pg 223 (1874 Sept 30), Laramie Lodge No. 18, Laramie City

Bush, John E
Proceedings 1861-1869, pg 223 (1868 Oct 7) Denver Lodge No. 5, Apprentice

Bussell, H M
Proceedings 1861-1869, pg 147 (1865 Nov 7) Golden City Lodge No. 1
Proceedings 1861-1869, pg 165 (1866 Oct 2) Golden City Lodge No. 1
Proceedings 1861-1869, pg 221 (1868 Oct 7) Golden City Lodge No. 1
Proceedings 1861-1869, pg 303 (1869 Sept 29) Golden City Lodge No. 1
Proceedings 1870, pg 19 (1870 Sept 28), Golden City Lodge No. 1, Golden City
Proceedings 1872, pg 18 (1872 Sept 24), Golden City Lodge No. 1, Golden City, Stricken from the Roll

Colorado's Territorial Masons

Bussell, L E
Proceedings 1861-1869, pg 305 (1869 Sept 29) Denver Lodge No. 5

Butler
Proceedings 1861-1869, pg 87 (1863 Apr 17) Golden City Lodge No. 1

Butler, A J
Proceedings 1861-1869, pg 85 (1863 Apr 7) Golden City Lodge No. 1
Proceedings 1861-1869, pg 110 (1863 Nov 3) Golden City Lodge No. 1
Proceedings 1861-1869, pg 131 (1864 Nov 8) Golden City Lodge No. 1
Proceedings 1861-1869, pg 147 (1865 Nov 7) Golden City Lodge No. 1
Proceedings 1861-1869, pg 165 (1866 Oct 2) Golden City Lodge No. 1
Proceedings 1861-1869, pg 191 (1867 Oct 8) Golden City Lodge No. 1, Dimitted

Butler, H A
Proceedings 1861-1869, pg 43 (1861 Dec 10), Rocky Mountain Lodge No. 3, Gold Hill

Butler, Hugh
Proceedings 1861-1869, pg 194 (1867 Oct 8), Chivington Lodge No. 6, Central City
Proceedings 1861-1869, pg 224 (1868 Oct 7), Chivington Lodge No. 6, Central City
Proceedings 1861-1869, pg 306 (1869 Sept 29), Central Lodge No. 6, Central City
Proceedings 1870, pg 22 (1870 Sept 28), Central Lodge No. 6, Central City
Proceedings 1871, pg 20 (1871 Sept 27), Central Lodge No. 6, Central
Proceedings 1872, pg 21 (1872 Sept 24), Denver Lodge No. 5, Denver
Proceedings 1873, pg 38 (1873 Oct 1), Central Lodge No. 6, Central City
Proceedings 1874, pg 212 (1874 Sept 30), Central Lodge No. 6, Central
Proceedings 1875, pg 76 (1875 Sept 22), Central Lodge No. 6, Central City
Proceedings 1876, pg 32 (1876 Sept 20), Central Lodge No. 6, Central City

Butler, N T
Proceedings 1861-1869, pg 152 (1865 Nov 7), Montana Lodge U D, Virginia City, Montana Territory

Butler, Samuel
Proceedings 1861-1869, pg 192 (1867 Oct 8), Nevada Lodge No. 4, Nevadaville
Proceedings 1861-1869, pg 222 (1868 Oct 7), Nevada Lodge No. 4, Nevadaville, Dimitted

Buttles, J F
Proceedings 1871, pg 25 (1871 Sept 27), Columbia Lodge No. 14, Boulder City
Proceedings 1872, pg 28 (1872 Sept 24), Columbia Lodge No. 14, Boulder
Proceedings 1873, pg 44 (1873 Oct 1), Columbia Lodge No. 14, Boulder
Proceedings 1874, pg 219 (1874 Sept 30), Columbia Lodge No. 14, Boulder, Boulder County
Proceedings 1875, pg 83 (1875 Sept 22), Columbia Lodge No. 14, Boulder
Proceedings 1876, pg 37 (1876 Sept 20), Columbia Lodge No. 14, Boulder

Butts, Chas O
Proceedings 1876, pg 45 (1876 Sept 20) South Pueblo Lodge U D

Buyaze, Julius
Proceedings 1876, pg 37 (1876 Sept 20), Columbia Lodge No. 14, Boulder, Apprentice

Buzzard, S M
Proceedings 1861-1869, pg 196 (1867 Oct 8), El Paso Lodge U D, Colorado City
Proceedings 1861-1869, pg 228 (1868 Oct 7), El Paso Lodge No. 13, Colorado City
Proceedings 1861-1869, pg 310 (1869 Sept 29), El Paso Lodge No. 13, Colorado City
Proceedings 1870, pg 26 (1870 Sept 28), El Paso Lodge No. 13, Colorado City
Proceedings 1871, pg 4 (1871 Sept 26), El Paso Lodge No. 13, Colorado City
Proceedings 1871, pg 14 (1871 Sept 27), El Paso Lodge No. 13, Colorado City
Proceedings 1871, pg 24 (1871 Sept 27), El Paso Lodge No. 13, Colorado City
Proceedings 1872, pg 26 (1872 Sept 24), El Paso Lodge No. 13, Colorado City
Proceedings 1873, pg 43 (1873 Oct 1), El Paso Lodge No. 13, Colorado City
Proceedings 1874, pg 218 (1874 Sept 30), El Paso Lodge No. 13, Colorado Springs
Proceedings 1875, pg 82 (1875 Sept 22), El Paso Lodge No. 13, Colorado Springs

Buzzard, Sylvester M
Proceedings 1876, pg 36 (1876 Sept 20), El Paso Lodge No. 13, Colorado City

Byan, G H
Proceedings 1861-1869, pg 171 (1866 Oct 2), El Paso U D, Colorado City, Fellowcraft,

Byers
Proceedings 1873, pg 30 (1873 Oct 1) resolution
Proceedings 1873, pg 30 (1873 Oct 1) resolution
Proceedings 1874, pg 39 (1874 Sept 30) motion
Proceedings 1876, pg 14 (1876 Sept 19) committee
Proceedings 1876, pg 14 (1876 Sept 19) Grand Lodge of New York, Grand Representative
Proceedings 1876, pg 22 (1876 Sept 20) motion
Proceedings 1876, pg 25 (1876 Sept 20) motion
Proceedings 1876, pg 26 (1876 Sept 20) resolution

Byers & Dailey
Proceedings 1861-1869, pg 119 (1864 Mar 1) warrant drawn
Proceedings 1861-1869, pg 159 (1866 Oct 1) warrant

Byers, W N
- Proceedings 1861-1869, pg 167 (1866 Oct 2) Denver Lodge No. 5
- Proceedings 1861-1869, pg 305 (1869 Sept 29) Denver Lodge No. 5
- Proceedings 1873, pg 6 (1873 Sept 30), Denver Lodge No. 5, Denver
- Proceedings 1873, pg 32 (1873 Oct 1) bill for printing
- Proceedings 1876, pg 22 (1876 Sept 20) Denver Lodge No. 5

Byers, Wm N
- Proceedings 1861-1869, pg 77 (1862 Nov 4) Denver Lodge No. 5
- Proceedings 1861-1869, pg 112 (1863 Nov 3) Denver Lodge No. 5
- Proceedings 1861-1869, pg 133 (1864 Nov 8) Denver Lodge No. 5
- Proceedings 1861-1869, pg 149 (1865 Nov 7), Nevada Lodge No. 4, Nevadaville
- Proceedings 1861-1869, pg 192 (1867 Oct 8) Denver Lodge No. 5
- Proceedings 1861-1869, pg 223 (1868 Oct 7) Denver Lodge No. 5
- Proceedings 1870, pg 21 (1870 Sept 28), Denver Lodge No. 5, Denver
- Proceedings 1871, pg 19 (1871 Sept 27) Denver Lodge No. 5
- Proceedings 1872, pg 19 (1872 Sept 24), Denver Lodge No. 5, Denver
- Proceedings 1873, pg cover (1873 Oct 1) committee, Denver
- Proceedings 1873, pg cover (1873 Oct 1), Colorado Commandery No. 1, Denver
- Proceedings 1873, pg 4 (1873 Sept 30) pall bearer for George M Randall
- Proceedings 1873, pg 14 (1873 Sept 30) committee
- Proceedings 1873, pg 32 (1873 Oct 1) committee
- Proceedings 1873, pg 37 (1873 Oct 1), Denver Lodge No. 5, Denver
- Proceedings 1874, pg 5 (1874 Sept 29), Denver Lodge No. 5, Denver
- Proceedings 1874, pg 19 (1874 Sept 29) bill paid
- Proceedings 1874, pg 21 (1874 Sept 29) committee
- Proceedings 1874, pg 29 (1874 Sept 29) committee
- Proceedings 1874, pg 32 (1874 Sept 30) committee
- Proceedings 1874, pg 36 (1874 Sept 30) per diem
- Proceedings 1874, pg 211 (1874 Sept 30), Denver Lodge No. 5, Denver
- Proceedings 1875, pg 24 (1875 Sept 21) donation to the library fund
- Proceedings 1875, pg 28 (1875 Sept 21) committee
- Proceedings 1875, pg 30 (1875 Sept 21) Grand Lodge of New York, Grand Representative
- Proceedings 1875, pg 36 (1875 Sept 22) Grand Lodge of New York, Grand Representative
- Proceedings 1875, pg 75 (1875 Sept 22) Denver Lodge No. 5
- Proceedings 1875, pg 95 (1875 Sept 22) Grand Lodge of New York, Denver, CO
- Proceedings 1876, pg 4 (1876 Sept 19) Denver Lodge No. 5
- Proceedings 1876, pg 15 (1876 Sept 8) Grand Lodge of New York, Grand Representative
- Proceedings 1876, pg 17 (1876 Sept 19) committee
- Proceedings 1876, pg 30 (1876 Sept 20) Denver Lodge No. 5
- Proceedings 1876, pg 53 (1876 Sept 20) Grand Lodge of New York, of Denver, CO

Byles, Charles
- Proceedings 1870, pg 107 (1869 Sept 16) Grand Lodge of Washington Territory, deceased

Caigre, Henry
- Proceedings 1874, pg 222 (1874 Sept 30), Pueblo Lodge No. 17, Pueblo, Pueblo County

Cain, Robert
- Proceedings 1874, pg 228 (1874 Sept 30), Doric Lodge U D, Fairplay, Fellowcraft
- Proceedings 1875, pg 89 (1875 Sept 22), Doric Lodge No. 25, Fairplay, Fellowcraft
- Proceedings 1876, pg 42 (1876 Sept 20), Doric Lodge No. 25, Fairplay, Fellow Craft

Cairns, J D
- Proceedings 1876, pg 29 (1876 Sept 20) Golden City Lodge No. 1

Cairns, Jacob D
- Proceedings 1875, pg 73 (1875 Sept 22) Golden City Lodge No. 1

Caldwell, John D
- Proceedings 1861-1869, pg 316 (1869 Sept 29) Grand Lodge of Ohio
- Proceedings 1861-1869, pg 344 (1868 Oct 20) Grand Secretary, Grand Lodge of Ohio
- Proceedings 1870, pg 34 (1870 Sept 28) Grand Secretary, Grand Lodge of Ohio
- Proceedings 1871, pg 35 (1871 Sept 27) Grand Secretary, Grand Lodge of Ohio
- Proceedings 1872, pg 44 (1872 Sept 24) Cincinnati, Grand Lodge of Ohio
- Proceedings 1872, pg 84 (1872 Sept 24) Grand Lodge of Ohio
- Proceedings 1873, pg 61 (1873 Oct 1) Grand Lodge of Ohio, Cincinnati
- Proceedings 1874, pg 117 (1874 Sept 30) Grand Lodge of Ohio
- Proceedings 1874, pg 204 (1874 Sept 30) Grand Lodge of Ohio, Cincinnati
- Proceedings 1875, pg 96 (1875 Sept 22) Grand Lodge of Ohio, Cincinnati
- Proceedings 1876, pg 54 (1876 Sept 20) Grand Lodge of Ohio, Cincinnati

Caldwell, W P
   Proceedings 1861-1869, pg 116 (1864 Nov 7) Grand Tyler
   Proceedings 1861-1869, pg 134 (1864 Nov 8), Chivington Lodge No. 6, Central City
   Proceedings 1861-1869, pg 140 (1864 Nov 8) warrant
   Proceedings 1861-1869, pg 150 (1865 Nov 7), Chivington Lodge No. 6, Central City
   Proceedings 1861-1869, pg 168 (1866 Oct 2), Chivington Lodge No. 6, Central City
   Proceedings 1861-1869, pg 194 (1867 Oct 8), Chivington Lodge No. 6, Central City
   Proceedings 1861-1869, pg 224 (1868 Oct 7), Chivington Lodge No. 6, Central City
   Proceedings 1861-1869, pg 306 (1869 Sept 29), Central Lodge No. 6, Central City
   Proceedings 1870, pg 22 (1870 Sept 28), Central Lodge No. 6, Central City

Caldwell, Wm P
   Proceedings 1871, pg 21 (1871 Sept 27), Central Lodge No. 6, Central, Dimitted

Callaha, James
   Proceedings 1872, pg 30 (1872 Sept 24), Cheyenne Lodge No. 16, Cheyenne, Wyoming Territory, Fellowcraft

Callahan, James
   Proceedings 1874, pg 221 (1874 Sept 30), Cheyenne Lodge No. 16, Cheyenne, Wyoming Territory

Callahan, Jas
   Proceedings 1873, pg 46 (1873 Oct 1), Cheyenne Lodge No. 16, Cheyenne, Wyoming Territory

Callaway, John M
   Proceedings 1876, pg 39 (1876 Sept 20), Collins Lodge No. 19, Fort Collins
   Proceedings 1874, pg 224 (1874 Sept 30), Collins Lodge No. 19, Fort Collins, Larimer County
   Proceedings 1875, pg 86 (1875 Sept 22), Collins Lodge No. 19, Fort Collins

Camblin, N
   Proceedings 1875, pg 91 (1875 Sept 22), Las Animas Lodge U D, Trinidad
   Proceedings 1876, pg 44 (1876 Sept 20), Las Animas Lodge No. 28, Trinidad

Cameron, R A
   Proceedings 1871, pg 30 (1871 Sept 27), Occidental Lodge U D, Greeley
   Proceedings 1873, pg 50 (1873 Oct 1), Occidental Lodge No. 20, Greeley
   Proceedings 1874, pg 225 (1874 Sept 30), Occidental Lodge No. 20, Greeley

Cameron, Robert
   Proceedings 1861-1869, pg 196 (1867 Oct 8), Black Hawk Lodge No. 11, Black Hawk
   Proceedings 1861-1869, pg 227 (1868 Oct 7), Black Hawk Lodge No. 11, Black Hawk
   Proceedings 1861-1869, pg 309 (1869 Sept 29), Black Hawk Lodge No. 11, Black Hawk
   Proceedings 1870, pg 25 (1870 Sept 28), Black Hawk Lodge No. 11, Black Hawk
   Proceedings 1871, pg 23 (1871 Sept 27), Black Hawk Lodge No. 11, Black Hawk
   Proceedings 1872, pg 24 (1872 Sept 24), Black Hawk Lodge No. 11, Black Hawk
   Proceedings 1873, pg 42 (1873 Oct 1), Black Hawk Lodge No. 11, Black Hawk
   Proceedings 1874, pg 216 (1874 Sept 30), Black Hawk Lodge No. 11, Black Hawk, Demitted
   Proceedings 1875, pg 77 (1875 Sept 22), Central Lodge No. 6, Central City
   Proceedings 1876, pg 32 (1876 Sept 20), Central Lodge No. 6, Central City

Cameron, Robert A
   Proceedings 1875, pg 87 (1875 Sept 22), Occidental Lodge No. 20, Greeley
   Proceedings 1876, pg 40 (1876 Sept 20), Occidental Lodge No. 20, Greeley

Campbell, Alex R
   Proceedings 1875, pg 90 (1875 Sept 22), Huerfano Lodge U D, Walsenburg, Apprentice

Campbell, Alexander R
   Proceedings 1876, pg 43 (1876 Sept 20), Huerfano Lodge No. 27, Walsenburg, Apprentice

Campbell, B Rush
   Proceedings 1870, pg 34 (1870 Sept 28) Grand Secretary, Grand Lodge of South Carolina
   Proceedings 1870, pg 102 (1869 Nov 16) Grand Secretary, Grand Lodge of South Carolina
   Proceedings 1871, pg 35 (1871 Sept 27) Grand Secretary, Grand Lodge of South Carolina
   Proceedings 1872, pg 44 (1872 Sept 24) Charleston, Grand Lodge of South Carolina
   Proceedings 1872, pg 85 (1872 Sept 24) Grand Lodge of South Carolina
   Proceedings 1873, pg 61 (1873 Oct 1) Grand Lodge of South Carolina, Charleston
   Proceedings 1874, pg 205 (1874 Sept 30) Grand Lodge of South Carolina, Charleston

Campbell, Charles A
   Proceedings 1874, pg 224 (1874 Sept 30), Collins Lodge No. 19, Fort Collins, Larimer County
   Proceedings 1875, pg 86 (1875 Sept 22), Collins Lodge No. 19, Fort Collins
   Proceedings 1876, pg 39 (1876 Sept 20), Collins Lodge No. 19, Fort Collins

Campbell, John L
   Proceedings 1876, pg 37 (1876 Sept 20), Columbia Lodge No. 14, Boulder

Campbell, Matthew
   Proceedings 1874, pg 225 (1874 Sept 30), Collins Lodge No. 19, Fort Collins, Larimer County, Demitted

Campbell, Neel
   Proceedings 1872, pg 32 (1872 Sept 24), Laramie Lodge No. 18, Laramie, Wyoming Territory, Apprentice

Colorado's Territorial Masons

Campbell, Neil
    Proceedings 1871, pg 29 (1871 Sept 27), Laramie Lodge No. 18, Laramie, Wyoming Territory, Apprentice
    Proceedings 1873, pg 48 (1873 Oct 1), Laramie Lodge No. 18, Laramie, Wyoming Territory, died

Campbell, R M
    Proceedings 1861-1869, pg 152 (1865 Nov 7), Montana Lodge U D, Virginia City, Montana Territory

Campbell, Rush
    Proceedings 1874, pg 121 (1874 Sept 30) Grand Lodge of South Carolina

Campbell, Sanford B
    Proceedings 1875, pg 83 (1875 Sept 22), Columbia Lodge No. 14, Boulder
    Proceedings 1876, pg 37 (1876 Sept 20), Columbia Lodge No. 14, Boulder

Campbell, T F
    Proceedings 1874, pg 119 (1874 Sept 30) Grand Lodge of Oregon

Campbell, T J
    Proceedings 1870, pg 22 (1870 Sept 28), Central Lodge No. 6, Central City
    Proceedings 1871, pg 20 (1871 Sept 27), Central Lodge No. 6, Central

Campbell, Thomas J
    Proceedings 1873, pg 38 (1873 Oct 1), Central Lodge No. 6, Central City
    Proceedings 1875, pg 77 (1875 Sept 22), Central Lodge No. 6, Central City, Stricken from the rolls

Campbell, Thos J
    Proceedings 1861-1869, pg 306 (1869 Sept 29), Central Lodge No. 6, Central City
    Proceedings 1872, pg 21 (1872 Sept 24), Denver Lodge No. 5, Denver
    Proceedings 1874, pg 213 (1874 Sept 30), Central Lodge No. 6, Central

Campbell, W E
    Proceedings 1861-1869, pg 312 (1869 Sept 29), Cheyenne Lodge No. 16, Cheyenne
    Proceedings 1870, pg 29 (1870 Sept 28), Cheyenne Lodge No. 16, Cheyenne, Wyoming Territory
    Proceedings 1871, pg 28 (1871 Sept 27), Cheyenne Lodge No. 16, Cheyenne, Wyoming Territory, Apprentice

Campbell, W M
    Proceedings 1861-1869, pg 42 (1861 Dec 10), Summit Lodge No. 2, Parkville

Canadian Freemason
    Proceedings 1874, pg 50 (1874 Sept 30), published in Toronto, Ontario

Canadian Masonic News
    Proceedings 1876, pg 12 (1876 Sept 19) published at Montreal

Canfield, Isaac
    Proceedings 1872, pg 33 (1872 Sept 24), Occidental Lodge No. 20, Greeley
    Proceedings 1873, pg 49 (1873 Oct 1), Occidental Lodge No. 20, Greeley
    Proceedings 1874, pg 225 (1874 Sept 30), Occidental Lodge No. 20, Greeley
    Proceedings 1875, pg 87 (1875 Sept 22), Occidental Lodge No. 20, Greeley
    Proceedings 1876, pg 40 (1876 Sept 20), Occidental Lodge No. 20, Greeley

Cannon, Henry R
    Proceedings 1861-1869, pg 342 (1869 Jan 20) Grand Master, Grand Lodge of New Jersey
    Proceedings 1870, pg 92 (1870 Jan 19) Grand Master, Grand Lodge of New Jersey

Canon City
    Proceedings 1861-1869, pg 178 (1867 July 25) petition to form a lodge
    Proceedings 1861-1869, pg 207 (1867 Dec 11) granted a lodge

Canon City Lodge U D
    Proceedings 1861-1869, pg 35 (1861 Dec 10)
    Proceedings 1861-1869, pg 208 (1868 Apr) not visited because of Indian troubles
    Proceedings 1861-1869, pg 211 (1868 Aug) arranged for a visit

Canon Lodge U D, Canon City
    Proceedings 1861-1869, pg 180 (1867 Oct 7) dispensation granted

Canon, Benton
    Proceedings 1876, pg 43 (1876 Sept 20), Huerfano Lodge No. 27, Walsenburg

Capps, Samuel J
    Proceedings 1875, pg 90 (1875 Sept 22), Huerfano Lodge U D, Walsenburg, Apprentice
    Proceedings 1876, pg 43 (1876 Sept 20), Huerfano Lodge No. 27, Walsenburg

Cargill, David
    Proceedings 1872, pg 43 (1872 Sept 24) Augusta, Grand Lodge of Maine
    Proceedings 1873, pg 60 (1873 Oct 1) Grand Lodge of Maine, Augusta
    Proceedings 1874, pg 77 (1874 Sept 30) Grand Lodge of Maine
    Proceedings 1874, pg 204 (1874 Sept 30) Grand Lodge of Maine, Augusta

Carlile, J N
    Proceedings 1876, pg 39 (1876 Sept 20) Pueblo Lodge No. 17, Apprentice

Carlile, James N
    Proceedings 1871, pg 28 (1871 Sept 27), Pueblo Lodge No. 17, Pueblo, Apprentice
    Proceedings 1873, pg 47 (1873 Oct 1), Pueblo Lodge No. 17, Pueblo, Apprentice
    Proceedings 1874, pg 222 (1874 Sept 30), Pueblo Lodge No. 17, Pueblo, Pueblo County, Apprentice
    Proceedings 1875, pg 85 (1875 Sept 22) Pueblo Lodge No. 17, Apprentice

Carlile, Jas N
 Proceedings 1872, pg 31 (1872 Sept 24), Pueblo Lodge No. 17, Pueblo, Apprentice

Carlile, W K
 Proceedings 1872, pg 31 (1872 Sept 24), Pueblo Lodge No. 17, Pueblo, Apprentice
 Proceedings 1873, pg 47 (1873 Oct 1), Pueblo Lodge No. 17, Pueblo, Apprentice
 Proceedings 1874, pg 222 (1874 Sept 30), Pueblo Lodge No. 17, Pueblo, Pueblo County, Apprentice
 Proceedings 1875, pg 85 (1875 Sept 22) Pueblo Lodge No. 17, Apprentice
 Proceedings 1876, pg 39 (1876 Sept 20) Pueblo Lodge No. 17, Apprentice

Carlile, William K
 Proceedings 1861-1869, pg 313 (1869 Sept 29), Pueblo Lodge No. 17, Pueblo, Apprentice
 Proceedings 1871, pg 28 (1871 Sept 27), Pueblo Lodge No. 17, Pueblo, Apprentice

Carlile, Wm K
 Proceedings 1870, pg 30 (1870 Sept 28), Pueblo Lodge No. 17, Pueblo, Apprentice

Carling, E B
 Proceedings 1861-1869, pg 216 (1868 Oct 7) Senior Warden of Cheyenne
 Proceedings 1861-1869, pg 230 (1868 Oct 7), Cheyenne Lodge U D, Cheyenne, Dakota Territory
 Proceedings 1861-1869, pg 288 (1869 Sept 28), Cheyenne Lodge No. 16, Cheyenne
 Proceedings 1861-1869, pg 301 (1869 Sept 29), Cheyenne Lodge No. 16, Cheyenne
 Proceedings 1861-1869, pg 311 (1869 Sept 29), Cheyenne Lodge No. 16, Cheyenne
 Proceedings 1870, pg 28 (1870 Sept 28), Cheyenne Lodge No. 16, Cheyenne, Wyoming Territory
 Proceedings 1871, pg 27 (1871 Sept 27), Cheyenne Lodge No. 16, Cheyenne, Wyoming Territory
 Proceedings 1872, pg 29 (1872 Sept 24), Cheyenne Lodge No. 16, Cheyenne, Wyoming Territory
 Proceedings 1873, pg 46 (1873 Oct 1), Cheyenne Lodge No. 16, Cheyenne, Wyoming Territory
 Proceedings 1874, pg 221 (1874 Sept 30), Cheyenne Lodge No. 16, Cheyenne, Wyoming Territory

Carmack, Thomas K
 Proceedings 1876, pg 37 (1876 Sept 20), Columbia Lodge No. 14, Boulder

Carmeron, R A
 Proceedings 1872, pg 33 (1872 Sept 24), Occidental Lodge No. 20, Greeley

Carnes, J C
 Proceedings 1861-1869, pg 131 (1864 Nov 8) Golden City Lodge No. 1
 Proceedings 1861-1869, pg 147 (1865 Nov 7) Golden City Lodge No. 1
 Proceedings 1861-1869, pg 165 (1866 Oct 2) Golden City Lodge No. 1
 Proceedings 1861-1869, pg 221 (1868 Oct 7) Golden City Lodge No. 1
 Proceedings 1870, pg 19 (1870 Sept 28), Golden City Lodge No. 1, Golden City
 Proceedings 1871, pg 17 (1871 Sept 27), Golden City Lodge No. 1, Golden City
 Proceedings 1872, pg 17 (1872 Sept 24), Golden City Lodge No. 1, Golden City

Carnes, Jacob D
 Proceedings 1873, pg 35 (1873 Oct 1), Golden City Lodge No. 1, Golden City
 Proceedings 1874, pg 209 (1874 Sept 30), Golden City Lodge No. 1, Golden City

Carns, J D
 Proceedings 1861-1869, pg 191 (1867 Oct 8) Golden City Lodge No. 1
 Proceedings 1861-1869, pg 303 (1869 Sept 29) Golden City Lodge No. 1

Carothers, W T
 Proceedings 1861-1869, pg 132 (1864 Nov 8), Nevada Lodge No. 4, Nevadaville
 Proceedings 1861-1869, pg 147 (1865 Nov 7), Nevada Lodge No. 4, Nevadaville
 Proceedings 1861-1869, pg 166 (1866 Oct 2), Nevada Lodge No. 4, Nevadaville, dimitted

Carpenter, A S
 Proceedings 1861-1869, pg 226 (1868 Oct 7), Empire Lodge No. 8, Empire City
 Proceedings 1861-1869, pg 308 (1869 Sept 29), Empire Lodge No. 8, Empire City
 Proceedings 1870, pg 24 (1870 Sept 28), Empire Lodge No. 8, Empire
 Proceedings 1872, pg 4 (1872 Sept 24), Empire Lodge No. 8, Empire
 Proceedings 1872, pg 23 (1872 Sept 24), Empire Lodge No. 8, Empire
 Proceedings 1873, pg 6 (1873 Sept 30), Empire Lodge No. 8, Empire
 Proceedings 1873, pg 7 (1873 Sept 30) committee
 Proceedings 1873, pg 7 (1873 Sept 30), Empire Lodge No. 8, Empire
 Proceedings 1873, pg 18 (1873 Oct 1) committee
 Proceedings 1873, pg 31 (1873 Oct 1) mileage and per diem

Carpenter, Albert
 Proceedings 1861-1869, pg 264 (1868 Oct 22) found to be an imposter

Carpenter, Alvin S
 Proceedings 1873, pg 40 (1873 Oct 1), Empire Lodge No. 8, Empire
 Proceedings 1874, pg 215 (1874 Sept 30), Empire Lodge No. 8, Empire

Carpenter, C C
 Proceedings 1861-1869, pg 42 (1861 Dec 10), Summit Lodge No. 2, Parkville
 Proceedings 1861-1869, pg 76 (1862 Nov 4), Summit Lodge No. 2, Parkville, dimitted
 Proceedings 1861-1869, pg 165 (1866 Oct 2) Golden City Lodge No. 1

Carpenter, C C, cont.
    Proceedings 1861-1869, pg 191 (1867 Oct 8) Golden City Lodge No. 1
    Proceedings 1861-1869, pg 221 (1868 Oct 7) Golden City Lodge No. 1
    Proceedings 1861-1869, pg 303 (1869 Sept 29) Golden City Lodge No. 1
    Proceedings 1870, pg 19 (1870 Sept 28), Golden City Lodge No. 1, Golden City
    Proceedings 1871, pg cover (1871 Sept 27) committee, Golden City
    Proceedings 1871, pg 5 (1871 Sept 26), Golden City Lodge No. 1, Golden City
    Proceedings 1871, pg 14 (1871 Sept 27), Golden City Lodge No. 1, Golden City
    Proceedings 1871, pg 16 (1871 Sept 27) Committee
    Proceedings 1871, pg 17 (1871 Sept 27), Golden City Lodge No. 1, Golden City
    Proceedings 1872, pg 17 (1872 Sept 24), Golden City Lodge No. 1, Golden City
    Proceedings 1873, pg 35 (1873 Oct 1), Golden City Lodge No. 1, Golden City
    Proceedings 1874, pg 209 (1874 Sept 30), Golden City Lodge No. 1, Golden City
    Proceedings 1875, pg 73 (1875 Sept 22) Golden City Lodge No. 1
    Proceedings 1876, pg 29 (1876 Sept 20) Golden City Lodge No. 1

Carpenter, Chester C
    Proceedings 1861-1869, pg 160 (1866 Oct 2) Golden City Lodge No. 1
    Proceedings 1873, pg 35 (1873 Oct 1), Golden City Lodge No. 1, Golden City

Carpenter, Frank
    Proceedings 1874, pg 229 (1874 Sept 30), Idaho Springs Lodge U D, Idaho Springs

Carpenter, Isaac
    Proceedings 1872, pg 27 (1872 Sept 24), El Paso Lodge No. 13, Colorado City, Apprentice
    Proceedings 1873, pg 44 (1873 Oct 1), El Paso Lodge No. 13, Colorado City, Apprentice

Carpenter, J M
    Proceedings 1861-1869, pg 100 (1863 Aug 13), Summit Lodge No. 2, Parkville
    Proceedings 1861-1869, pg 111 (1863 Nov 3), Summit Lodge No. 2, Parkville, dimitted

Carpenter, Peter A
    Proceedings 1871, pg 30 (1871 Sept 27), Collins Lodge No. 19, Fort Collins

Carpenter, Peter N
    Proceedings 1871, pg 30 (1871 Sept 27), Collins Lodge No. 19, Fort Collins, died
    Proceedings 1871, pg 32 (1871 Sept 27), Collins Lodge No. 19, Fort Collins

Carr, B L
    Proceedings 1872, pg 35 (1872 Sept 24), St Vrain Lodge No. 23, Longmont
    Proceedings 1873, pg 51 (1873 Oct 1), St Vrain Lodge No. 23, Longmont
    Proceedings 1874, pg 6 (1874 Sept 29), St Vrain Lodge No. 23, Longmont
    Proceedings 1874, pg 34 (1874 Sept 30) resolution
    Proceedings 1874, pg 227 (1874 Sept 30), St Vrain No. 23, Longmont
    Proceedings 1876, pg 22 (1876 Sept 20), St Vrain Lodge No. 23, Longmont

Carr, Byron L
    Proceedings 1876, pg cover (1876 Sept 20) Grand Orator, Longmont
    Proceedings 1876, pg 18 (1876 Sept 20), St Vrain Lodge No. 23, Longmont
    Proceedings 1876, pg 41 (1876 Sept 20), St Vrain Lodge No. 23, Longmont

Carr, E T
    Proceedings 1861-1869, pg 253 (1867 Oct 15), Grand Secretary, Grand Lodge of Kansas
    Proceedings 1861-1869, pg 316 (1869 Sept 29) Grand Lodge of Kansas
    Proceedings 1861-1869, pg 331 (1868 Oct 20) Grand Secretary, Grand Lodge of Kansas
    Proceedings 1870, pg 34 (1870 Sept 28) Grand Secretary, Grand Lodge of Kansas
    Proceedings 1870, pg 60 (1869 Oct 20) Grand Secretary, Grand Lodge of Kansas
    Proceedings 1872, pg 67 (1872 Sept 24) Grand Lodge of Kansas
    Proceedings 1875, pg 74 (1875 Sept 22), Nevada Lodge No. 4, Nevada

Carr, Ezra T
    Proceedings 1871, pg 18 (1871 Sept 27), Nevada Lodge No. 4, Bald Mountain
    Proceedings 1872, pg 18 (1872 Sept 24), Nevada Lodge No. 4, Bald Mountain
    Proceedings 1873, pg 36 (1873 Oct 1), Nevada Lodge No. 4, Nevada
    Proceedings 1876, pg 30 (1876 Sept 20) Nevada Lodge No. 4
    Proceedings 1874, pg 210 (1874 Sept 30), Nevada Lodge No. 4, Bald Mountain, Gilpin County

Carroll, C N
    Proceedings 1876, pg 43 (1876 Sept 20), Huerfano Lodge No. 27, Walsenburg

Carrothers, Wm T
    Proceedings 1861-1869, pg 111 (1863 Nov 3), Nevada Lodge No. 4, Nevadaville

Carson [Corson]
    Proceedings 1861-1869, pg 215 (1868 Oct 6) Teller Carson [Corson]
    Proceedings 1872, pg 14 (1872 Sept 24) resolution

Carson [Corson], W A
    Proceedings 1861-1869, pg 228 (1868 Oct 7), Columbia Lodge No. 14, Columbia City
    Proceedings 1871, pg 5 (1871 Sept 26), Columbia Lodge No. 14, Boulder City

Proceedings 1872, pg 27 (1872 Sept 24), Columbia Lodge No. 14, Boulder

Carson Lodge No. 1, Nevada

Proceedings 1874, pg 14 (1874 Feb 6) Grand Lodge of Nevada

Carson, Enoch T

Proceedings 1861-1869, pg 279 (1867 Oct 15) Grand Lodge of Ohio

Cartee, L F

Proceedings 1872, pg 43 (1872 Sept 24) Boise City, Grand Lodge of Idaho

Proceedings 1873, pg 60 (1873 Oct 1) Grand Lodge of Idaho, Boise City

Proceedings 1874, pg 60 (1874 Sept 30) Grand Lodge of Idaho

Carter

Proceedings 1861-1869, pg 5 (1861 Aug 2) teller

Carter, E

Proceedings 1861-1869, pg 111 (1863 Nov 3), Summit Lodge No. 2, Parkville

Carter, Edwin

Proceedings 1861-1869, pg 132 (1864 Nov 8) Golden City Lodge No. 1

Carter, Eli

Proceedings 1861-1869, pg 3 (1861 Aug 2) Golden City Lodge No. 1

Proceedings 1861-1869, pg 4 (1861 Aug 2) Golden City Lodge No. 1

Proceedings 1861-1869, pg 4 (1861 Aug 2) Golden City Lodge No. 1

Proceedings 1861-1869, pg 5 (1861 Aug 2) Grand Treasurer, Golden City

Proceedings 1861-1869, pg 5 (1861 Aug 2) committee

Proceedings 1861-1869, pg 42 (1861 Dec 10) Golden City Lodge No. 1

Proceedings 1861-1869, pg 110 (1863 Nov 3) Golden City Lodge No. 1

Proceedings 1861-1869, pg 131 (1864 Nov 8) Golden City Lodge No. 1

Proceedings 1861-1869, pg 147 (1865 Nov 7) Golden City Lodge No. 1

Proceedings 1861-1869, pg 165 (1866 Oct 2) Golden City Lodge No. 1

Proceedings 1861-1869, pg 191 (1867 Oct 8) Golden City Lodge No. 1

Proceedings 1861-1869, pg 221 (1868 Oct 7) Golden City Lodge No. 1, Dimitted

Proceedings 1861-1869, pg 315 (1869 Sept 29) Grand Treasurer, August 1861, Dimitted

Proceedings 1870, pg 32 (1870 Sept 28) Grand Treasurer, August 1861, Dimitted

Proceedings 1871, pg 34 (1871 Sept 27) Grand Treasurer, Aug 1861, Dimitted

Proceedings 1872, pg 42 (1872 Sept 24) Grand Treasurer, August 1861, Dimitted

Proceedings 1873, pg 58 (1873 Oct 1) Grand Treasurer, Aug 1861, Dimitted

Proceedings 1874, pg 206 (1874 Sept 30) Grand Treasurer, Aug 1861, demitted

Proceedings 1875, pg 93 (1875 Sept 22) Grand Treasurer, Aug 1861, Demitted

Carter, Geo W

Proceedings 1861-1869, pg 228 (1868 Oct 7), Columbia Lodge No. 14, Columbia City

Proceedings 1861-1869, pg 311 (1869 Sept 29), Columbia Lodge No. 14, Boulder City

Proceedings 1870, pg 27 (1870 Sept 28), Columbia Lodge No. 14, Boulder City

Proceedings 1872, pg 28 (1872 Sept 24), Columbia Lodge No. 14, Boulder

Proceedings 1873, pg 44 (1873 Oct 1), Columbia Lodge No. 14, Boulder

Proceedings 1875, pg 83 (1875 Sept 22), Columbia Lodge No. 14, Boulder

Carter, George A

Proceedings 1871, pg 25 (1871 Sept 27), Columbia Lodge No. 14, Boulder City

Carter, George W

Proceedings 1861-1869, pg 196 (1867 Oct 8), Columbia Lodge U D, Boulder

Proceedings 1874, pg 219 (1874 Sept 30), Columbia Lodge No. 14, Boulder, Boulder County

Proceedings 1876, pg 37 (1876 Sept 20), Columbia Lodge No. 14, Boulder

Carter, J C

Proceedings 1861-1869, pg 167 (1866 Oct 2) Denver Lodge No. 5

Proceedings 1861-1869, pg 193 (1867 Oct 8) Denver Lodge No. 5

Proceedings 1861-1869, pg 223 (1868 Oct 7) Denver Lodge No. 5

Proceedings 1861-1869, pg 305 (1869 Sept 29) Denver Lodge No. 5, Dimitted

Carter, John C

Proceedings 1861-1869, pg 133 (1864 Nov 8) Denver Lodge No. 5, Apprentice

Carter, John M

Proceedings 1874, pg 204 (1874 Sept 30) Grand Lodge of Maryland, Baltimore

Carter, L F

Proceedings 1872, pg 66 (1872 Sept 24) Grand Lodge of Idaho

Casels, Geo

Proceedings 1861-1869, pg 309 (1869 Sept 29), Black Hawk Lodge No. 11, Black Hawk

Casey, J C

Proceedings 1861-1869, pg 223 (1868 Oct 7) Denver Lodge No. 5

Proceedings 1871, pg 19 (1871 Sept 27) Denver Lodge No. 5

Casey, J G

Proceedings 1861-1869, pg 193 (1867 Oct 8) Denver Lodge No. 5

Colorado's Territorial Masons

Casey, J G, cont.
    Proceedings 1861-1869, pg 305 (1869 Sept 29) Denver Lodge No. 5
    Proceedings 1870, pg 21 (1870 Sept 28), Denver Lodge No. 5, Denver
    Proceedings 1872, pg 20 (1872 Sept 24), Denver Lodge No. 5, Denver
    Proceedings 1873, pg 37 (1873 Oct 1), Denver Lodge No. 5, Denver
    Proceedings 1874, pg 212 (1874 Sept 30), Denver Lodge No. 5, Denver, Demitted
    Proceedings 1875, pg 88 (1875 Sept 22), Weston Lodge No. 22, Littleton
    Proceedings 1876, pg 41 (1876 Sept 20), Weston Lodge No. 22, Littleton

Casler, J C
    Proceedings 1861-1869, pg 149 (1865 Nov 7), Nevada Lodge No. 4, Nevadaville, Fellowcraft

Cassel, Geo
    Proceedings 1870, pg 25 (1870 Sept 28), Black Hawk Lodge No. 11, Black Hawk, Dimitted

Cassell, A
    Proceedings 1861-1869, pg 148 (1865 Nov 7), Nevada Lodge No. 4, Nevadaville, dimitted

Cassell, A W
    Proceedings 1861-1869, pg 112 (1863 Nov 3), Nevada Lodge No. 4, Nevadaville, Apprentice

Cassell, Asahel
    Proceedings 1861-1869, pg 132 (1864 Nov 8), Nevada Lodge No. 4, Nevadaville

Cassell, Ashel
    Proceedings 1861-1869, pg 77 (1862 Nov 4), Nevada Lodge No. 4, Nevadaville, Apprentice

Cassell, Charles W
    Proceedings 1861-1869, pg 111 (1863 Nov 3), Nevada Lodge No. 4, Nevadaville

Cassell, Chas W
    Proceedings 1861-1869, pg 77 (1862 Nov 4), Nevada Lodge No. 4, Nevadaville, Apprentice
    Proceedings 1861-1869, pg 132 (1864 Nov 8), Nevada Lodge No. 4, Nevadaville, deceased

Cassells, Geo
    Proceedings 1861-1869, pg 170 (1866 Oct 2), Black Hawk Lodge U D, Black Hawk
    Proceedings 1861-1869, pg 227 (1868 Oct 7), Black Hawk Lodge No. 11, Black Hawk
    Proceedings 1873, pg 46 (1873 Oct 1), Cheyenne Lodge No. 16, Cheyenne, Wyoming Territory

Cassels, George
    Proceedings 1861-1869, pg 150 (1865 Nov 7), Chivington Lodge No. 6, Central City, Fellowcraft
    Proceedings 1861-1869, pg 196 (1867 Oct 8), Black Hawk Lodge No. 11, Black Hawk
    Proceedings 1872, pg 29 (1872 Sept 24), Cheyenne Lodge No. 16, Cheyenne, Wyoming Territory
    Proceedings 1874, pg 221 (1874 Sept 30), Cheyenne Lodge No. 16, Cheyenne, Wyoming Territory

Cassiday, Charles
    Proceedings 1876, pg 30 (1876 Sept 20) Nevada Lodge No. 4

Cassidy, James
    Proceedings 1876, pg 45 (1876 Sept 20), King Solomon Lodge U D, West Las Animas

Casto, Joseph
    Proceedings 1861-1869, pg 110 (1863 Nov 3) Golden City Lodge No. 1
    Proceedings 1861-1869, pg 131 (1864 Nov 8) Golden City Lodge No. 1
    Proceedings 1861-1869, pg 147 (1865 Nov 7) Golden City Lodge No. 1
    Proceedings 1861-1869, pg 165 (1866 Oct 2) Golden City Lodge No. 1

Cathcart, Thomas L
    Proceedings 1876, pg 33 (1876 Sept 20), Union Lodge No. 7, Denver

Cathcart, Thos L
    Proceedings 1875, pg 79 (1875 Sept 22), Union Lodge No. 7, Denver, Fellowcraft

Cayly, Peter H
    Proceedings 1876, pg 39 (1876 Sept 20), Collins Lodge No. 19, Fort Collins

Cazarnowsky, Henry
    Proceedings 1876, pg 34 (1876 Sept 20), Washington Lodge No. 12, Georgetown

Central City Chapter No. 1
    Proceedings 1871, pg cover (1871 Sept 27) Central

Central City Chapter No. 1, Royal Arch Masons
    Proceedings 1861-1869, pg 161 (1866 Oct 2) host of Grand Lodge Meeting

Central City Commandery No. 2
    Proceedings 1871, pg cover (1871 Sept 27) Central

Central Lodge No. 6
    Proceedings 1861-1869, pg 317 (1869 Sept 29), Central City, Colorado Territory
    Proceedings 1875, pg 25 (1875 Sept 21) dues paid
    Proceedings 1875, pg 34 (1875 Sept 22) work and statistics do not agree
    Proceedings 1875, pg 92 (1875 Sept 22)
    Proceedings 1876, pg 52 (1876 Sept 20)

Central Lodge No. 6, Central
    Proceedings 1872, pg 11 (1872 Sept 24) failed to make timely returns
    Proceedings 1876, pg 8 (1876 June 26), dispensation granted to appear in a public proccession for the centennial celebration on July 4, 1876
    Proceedings 1876, pg 13 (1876 Sept 16) dues paid
    Proceedings 1874, pg 19 (1874 Sept 29) returns late
    Proceedings 1874, pg 208 (1874 Sept 30)

Cerperon, J R
    Proceedings 1876, pg 48 (1876 Sept 20), Mount Moriah Lodge No. 15, Canon City, 1876 May 6,

Colorado's Territorial Masons

Chadwick
Proceedings 1870, pg 98 (1869 June 21) Past Grand Master, Grand Lodge of Oregon

Chadwick, S F
Proceedings 1870, pg 98 (1870 June 20) Past Grand Master, Grand Lodge of Oregon
Proceedings 1872, pg 44 (1872 Sept 24) Salem, Grand Lodge of Oregon
Proceedings 1872, pg 84 (1872 Sept 24) Grand Lodge of Oregon
Proceedings 1873, pg 61 (1873 Oct 1) Grand Lodge of Oregon, Salem
Proceedings 1874, pg 119 (1874 Sept 30) Grand Lodge of Oregon
Proceedings 1874, pg 205 (1874 Sept 30) Grand Lodge of Oregon, Salem

Chaffin, J T
Proceedings 1873, pg 46 (1873 Oct 1), Cheyenne Lodge No. 16, Cheyenne, Wyoming Territory
Proceedings 1874, pg 221 (1874 Sept 30), Cheyenne Lodge No. 16, Cheyenne, Wyoming Territory

Chamard, John
Proceedings 1861-1869, pg 151 (1865 Nov 7), Chivington Lodge No. 6, Central City
Proceedings 1861-1869, pg 169 (1866 Oct 2), Union Lodge No. 7, Denver
Proceedings 1861-1869, pg 195 (1867 Oct 8), Union Lodge No. 7, Denver
Proceedings 1861-1869, pg 225 (1868 Oct 7), Union Lodge No. 7, Denver
Proceedings 1861-1869, pg 307 (1869 Sept 29), Union Lodge No. 7, Denver
Proceedings 1870, pg 24 (1870 Sept 28), Union Lodge No. 7, Denver, Died

Chamberlain, H B
Proceedings 1861-1869, pg 149 (1865 Nov 7), Nevada Lodge No. 4, Nevadaville, Apprentice
Proceedings 1861-1869, pg 167 (1866 Oct 2) Denver Lodge No. 5, Apprentice
Proceedings 1861-1869, pg 193 (1867 Oct 8) Denver Lodge No. 5, Apprentice
Proceedings 1861-1869, pg 223 (1868 Oct 7) Denver Lodge No. 5, Apprentice
Proceedings 1861-1869, pg 305 (1869 Sept 29) Denver Lodge No. 5, Apprentice

Chamberlin, Henry
Proceedings 1872, pg 43 (1872 Sept 24) Three Oaks, Grand Lodge of Michigan

Chambers, Coote M
Proceedings 1875, pg 96 (1875 Sept 22) Grand Lodge of British Columbia, Victoria
Proceedings 1876, pg 54 (1876 Sept 20) Grand Lodge of British Columbia, Victoria

Champney, William J
Proceedings 1870, pg 77 (1824 Jan 5) African Lodge at Boston

Chandler, I H
Proceedings 1861-1869, pg 226 (1868 Oct 7), Union Lodge No. 7, Denver, Apprentice

Chandler, Isaac
Proceedings 1861-1869, pg 135 (1864 Nov 8), Union Lodge No. 7, Denver, Apprentice
Proceedings 1861-1869, pg 151 (1865 Nov 7), Chivington Lodge No. 6, Central City, Apprentice

Chandler, Isaac H
Proceedings 1861-1869, pg 169 (1866 Oct 2), Union Lodge No. 7, Denver, Apprentice

Chandler, J H
Proceedings 1861-1869, pg 195 (1867 Oct 8), Union Lodge No. 7, Denver, Apprentice

Chapin, H C
Proceedings 1861-1869, pg 227 (1868 Oct 7), Washington Lodge No. 12, Georgetown
Proceedings 1861-1869, pg 309 (1869 Sept 29), Washington Lodge No. 12, Georgetown
Proceedings 1871, pg 24 (1871 Sept 27), Washington Lodge No. 12, Georgetown
Proceedings 1875, pg 81 (1875 Sept 22), Washington Lodge No. 12, Georgetown

Chapin, Howard C
Proceedings 1870, pg 26 (1870 Sept 28), Washington Lodge No. 12, Georgetown
Proceedings 1872, pg 26 (1872 Sept 24), Washington Lodge No. 12, Georgetown
Proceedings 1873, pg 43 (1873 Oct 1), Washington Lodge No. 12, Georgetown
Proceedings 1874, pg 217 (1874 Sept 30), Washington Lodge No. 12, Georgetown
Proceedings 1876, pg 35 (1876 Sept 20), Washington Lodge No. 12, Georgetown

Chaplain, John W
Proceedings 1872, pg 71 (1872 Sept 24) Grand Lodge of Michigan

Chaplin
Proceedings 1870, pg 11 (1870 Sept 27), of Kalamazoo, MI,, Editor, The Michigan Freemason

Chapman, J E
Proceedings 1872, pg 35 (1872 Sept 24), St Vrain Lodge No. 23, Longmont
Proceedings 1873, pg 6 (1873 Sept 30), St Vrain Lodge No. 23, Longmont
Proceedings 1873, pg 51 (1873 Oct 1), St Vrain Lodge No. 23, Longmont
Proceedings 1876, pg 41 (1876 Sept 20), St Vrain Lodge No. 23, Longmont

Chapman, Joseph
Proceedings 1874, pg 68 (1874 Sept 30) Grand Lodge of Iowa
Proceedings 1874, pg 204 (1874 Sept 30) Grand Lodge of Iowa, Dubuque

Colorado's Territorial Masons

Chapman, Joshua E
   Proceedings 1861-1869, pg 311 (1869 Sept 29), Columbia Lodge No. 14, Boulder City, Fellowcraft
   Proceedings 1870, pg 27 (1870 Sept 28), Columbia Lodge No. 14, Boulder City
   Proceedings 1871, pg 25 (1871 Sept 27), Columbia Lodge No. 14, Boulder City
   Proceedings 1872, pg 28 (1872 Sept 24), Columbia Lodge No. 14, Boulder
   Proceedings 1873, pg 45 (1873 Oct 1), Columbia Lodge No. 14, Boulder, Dimitted
   Proceedings 1874, pg 227 (1874 Sept 30), St Vrain No. 23, Longmont

Chapman, W H
   Proceedings 1875, pg 89 (1875 Sept 22), Doric Lodge No. 25, Fairplay, Demitted
   Proceedings 1876, pg 42 (1876 Sept 20), Doric Lodge No. 25, Fairplay

Chapman, Wilmot H
   Proceedings 1874, pg 228 (1874 Sept 30), Doric Lodge U D, Fairplay

Chapman, Wm H
   Proceedings 1861-1869, pg 294 (1869 Sept 28) expelled from Pueblo Lodge No. 17
   Proceedings 1861-1869, pg 296 (1869 Sept 28), Pueblo Lodge No. 17, Pueblo
   Proceedings 1861-1869, pg 313 (1869 Sept 29), Pueblo Lodge No. 17, Pueblo, Expelled

Chappel, R B
   Proceedings 1875, pg 89 (1875 Sept 22), Doric Lodge No. 25, Fairplay

Chappel, Robert B
   Proceedings 1874, pg 228 (1874 Sept 30), Doric Lodge U D, Fairplay
   Proceedings 1876, pg 42 (1876 Sept 20), Doric Lodge No. 25, Fairplay

Charles, J Q
   Proceedings 1861-1869, pg 230 (1868 Oct 7), Germania Lodge U D, Denver
   Proceedings 1861-1869, pg 307 (1869 Sept 29), Union Lodge No. 7, Denver
   Proceedings 1876, pg 33 (1876 Sept 20), Union Lodge No. 7, Denver

Charles, James M
   Proceedings 1872, pg 26 (1872 Sept 24), Washington Lodge No. 12, Georgetown
   Proceedings 1873, pg 43 (1873 Oct 1), Washington Lodge No. 12, Georgetown
   Proceedings 1874, pg 217 (1874 Sept 30), Washington Lodge No. 12, Georgetown
   Proceedings 1876, pg 35 (1876 Sept 20), Washington Lodge No. 12, Georgetown

Charles, Jas M
   Proceedings 1875, pg 81 (1875 Sept 22), Washington Lodge No. 12, Georgetown

Charles, John Q
   Proceedings 1870, pg 23 (1870 Sept 28), Union Lodge No. 7, Denver
   Proceedings 1871, pg 21 (1871 Sept 27), Union Lodge No. 7, Denver
   Proceedings 1872, pg 22 (1872 Sept 24), Union Lodge No. 7, Denver
   Proceedings 1873, pg 40 (1873 Oct 1), Union Lodge No. 7, Denver
   Proceedings 1874, pg 214 (1874 Sept 30), Union Lodge No. 7, Denver
   Proceedings 1875, pg 78 (1875 Sept 22), Union Lodge No. 7, Denver

Charles, Thomas J
   Proceedings 1876, pg 35 (1876 Sept 20), Washington Lodge No. 12, Georgetown

Charmard, John
   Proceedings 1861-1869, pg 134 (1864 Nov 8), Union Lodge No. 7, Denver

Chase
   Proceedings 1861-1869, pg 37 (1861 Dec 12) motion
   Proceedings 1861-1869, pg 117 (1864 Nov 7) committee

Chase, Geo F
   Proceedings 1861-1869, pg 311 (1869 Sept 29), Columbia Lodge No. 14, Boulder City
   Proceedings 1872, pg 27 (1872 Sept 24), Columbia Lodge No. 14, Boulder
   Proceedings 1873, pg 44 (1873 Oct 1), Columbia Lodge No. 14, Boulder
   Proceedings 1873, pg 46 (1873 Oct 1), Cheyenne Lodge No. 16, Cheyenne, Wyoming Territory, Apprentice

Chase, Geo T
   Proceedings 1870, pg 27 (1870 Sept 28), Columbia Lodge No. 14, Boulder City

Chase, George F
   Proceedings 1871, pg 25 (1871 Sept 27), Columbia Lodge No. 14, Boulder City
   Proceedings 1874, pg 219 (1874 Sept 30), Columbia Lodge No. 14, Boulder, Boulder County
   Proceedings 1874, pg 221 (1874 Sept 30), Cheyenne Lodge No. 16, Cheyenne, Wyoming Territory
   Proceedings 1875, pg 83 (1875 Sept 22), Columbia Lodge No. 14, Boulder
   Proceedings 1876, pg 36 (1876 Sept 20), Columbia Lodge No. 14, Boulder

Chase, Horace
   Proceedings 1861-1869, pg 316 (1869 Sept 29) Grand Lodge of New Hampshire
   Proceedings 1861-1869, pg 342 (1868 June 10) Grand Secretary, Grand Lodge of New Hampshire

Chase, L B
   Proceedings 1870, pg 31 (1870 Sept 28), Laramie Lodge No. 18, Laramie, Wyoming Territory

Chase, L W
   Proceedings 1861-1869, pg 33 (1861 Dec 10) committee
   Proceedings 1861-1869, pg 33 (1861 Dec 10), Nevada Lodge No. 4, Nevadaville

Proceedings 1861-1869, pg 38 (1861 Dec 12) Junior Grand Warden
Proceedings 1861-1869, pg 39 (1861 Dec 12) chairman
Proceedings 1861-1869, pg 44 (1862 Nov 3) Grand Junior Deacon
Proceedings 1861-1869, pg 45 (1862 Nov 3), Nevada Lodge No. 4, Nevadaville
Proceedings 1861-1869, pg 51 (1862 Nov 4) Senior Grand Deacon
Proceedings 1861-1869, pg 76 (1862 Nov 4), Nevada Lodge No. 4, Nevadaville
Proceedings 1861-1869, pg 79 (1863 May 6) Senior Grand Deacon
Proceedings 1861-1869, pg 94 (1863 Apr 17) Grand Deacon
Proceedings 1861-1869, pg 116 (1864 Nov 7), Chivington Lodge No. 6, Central City
Proceedings 1861-1869, pg 116 (1864 Nov 7) Junior Grand Deacon
Proceedings 1861-1869, pg 118 (1864 Nov 8), Chivington Lodge No. 6, Central City, Grand Treasurer
Proceedings 1861-1869, pg 126 (1864 Nov 8), Chivington Lodge No. 6, Central City
Proceedings 1861-1869, pg 126 (1864 Nov 8) committee
Proceedings 1861-1869, pg 127 (1864 Nov 8) committee
Proceedings 1861-1869, pg 127 (1864 Nov 8), Chivington Lodge No. 6, Central City
Proceedings 1861-1869, pg 140 (1864 Nov 8) warrant
Proceedings 1861-1869, pg 140 (1865 Nov 6) Grand Treasurer
Proceedings 1861-1869, pg 140 (1865 Nov 6) Grand Treasurer
Proceedings 1861-1869, pg 150 (1865 Nov 7), Chivington Lodge No. 6, Central City
Proceedings 1861-1869, pg 168 (1866 Oct 2), Chivington Lodge No. 6, Central City
Proceedings 1861-1869, pg 194 (1867 Oct 8), Chivington Lodge No. 6, Central City
Proceedings 1861-1869, pg 224 (1868 Oct 7), Chivington Lodge No. 6, Central City
Proceedings 1861-1869, pg 306 (1869 Sept 29), Central Lodge No. 6, Central City
Proceedings 1861-1869, pg 315 (1869 Sept 29) Grand Treasurer, 1864
Proceedings 1870, pg 22 (1870 Sept 28), Central Lodge No. 6, Central City
Proceedings 1870, pg 32 (1870 Sept 28) Grand Treasurer, 1864
Proceedings 1871, pg 34 (1871 Sept 27) Grand Treasurer, 1864
Proceedings 1872, pg 42 (1872 Sept 24) Grand Treasurer, 1864
Proceedings 1873, pg 58 (1873 Oct 1) Grand Treasurer, 1864

Chase, Lyman
Proceedings 1874, pg 206 (1874 Sept 30) Grand Treasurer, 1864

Chase, Lyman W
Proceedings 1861-1869, pg 111 (1863 Nov 3), Nevada Lodge No. 4, Nevadaville
Proceedings 1861-1869, pg 113 (1863 Nov 3), Montana Lodge U D, Central City
Proceedings 1861-1869, pg 132 (1864 Nov 8), Nevada Lodge No. 4, Nevadaville, dimitted
Proceedings 1861-1869, pg 133 (1864 Nov 8), Chivington Lodge No. 6, Central City
Proceedings 1871, pg 20 (1871 Sept 27), Central Lodge No. 6, Central
Proceedings 1872, pg 21 (1872 Sept 24), Denver Lodge No. 5, Denver
Proceedings 1873, pg 38 (1873 Oct 1), Central Lodge No. 6, Central City
Proceedings 1874, pg 212 (1874 Sept 30), Central Lodge No. 6, Central
Proceedings 1875, pg 76 (1875 Sept 22), Central Lodge No. 6, Central City
Proceedings 1875, pg 93 (1875 Sept 22) Grand Treasurer, 1864
Proceedings 1876, pg 31 (1876 Sept 20), Central Lodge No. 6, Central City

Chaytor, Geo W
Proceedings 1874, pg 204 (1874 Sept 30) Grand Lodge of Delaware

Chaytor, George W
Proceedings 1874, pg 52 (1874 Sept 30) Grand Lodge of Delaware
Proceedings 1874, pg 112 (1874 Sept 30) Grand Lodge of Delaware

Cheeseman, W S
Proceedings 1861-1869, pg 193 (1867 Oct 8) Denver Lodge No. 5

Cheesman, N F
Proceedings 1861-1869, pg 191 (1867 Oct 8) Golden City Lodge No. 1
Proceedings 1861-1869, pg 221 (1868 Oct 7) Golden City Lodge No. 1
Proceedings 1861-1869, pg 303 (1869 Sept 29) Golden City Lodge No. 1
Proceedings 1870, pg 19 (1870 Sept 28), Golden City Lodge No. 1, Golden City, Dimitted

Cheesman, W S
Proceedings 1861-1869, pg 112 (1863 Nov 3) Denver Lodge No. 5
Proceedings 1861-1869, pg 133 (1864 Nov 8) Denver Lodge No. 5
Proceedings 1861-1869, pg 149 (1865 Nov 7), Nevada Lodge No. 4, Nevadaville
Proceedings 1861-1869, pg 167 (1866 Oct 2) Denver Lodge No. 5
Proceedings 1861-1869, pg 223 (1868 Oct 7) Denver Lodge No. 5
Proceedings 1861-1869, pg 305 (1869 Sept 29) Denver Lodge No. 5
Proceedings 1870, pg 21 (1870 Sept 28), Denver Lodge No. 5, Denver

Colorado's Territorial Masons

Cheesman, W S, cont.
Proceedings 1871, pg 19 (1871 Sept 27) Denver Lodge No. 5
Proceedings 1872, pg 20 (1872 Sept 24), Denver Lodge No. 5, Denver
Proceedings 1873, pg 37 (1873 Oct 1), Denver Lodge No. 5, Denver
Proceedings 1874, pg 211 (1874 Sept 30), Denver Lodge No. 5, Denver
Proceedings 1875, pg 75 (1875 Sept 22) Denver Lodge No. 5
Proceedings 1876, pg 31 (1876 Sept 20) Denver Lodge No. 5

Cheever, B W
Proceedings 1871, pg 24 (1871 Sept 27), Washington Lodge No. 12, Georgetown

Cheever, Byron W
Proceedings 1872, pg 26 (1872 Sept 24), Washington Lodge No. 12, Georgetown
Proceedings 1873, pg 43 (1873 Oct 1), Washington Lodge No. 12, Georgetown, Dimitted

Chestnut, Matthew T
Proceedings 1876, pg 44 (1876 Sept 20) Del Norte Lodge U D

Chever, D A
Proceedings 1861-1869, pg 151 (1865 Nov 7), Chivington Lodge No. 6, Central City, Apprentice
Proceedings 1861-1869, pg 169 (1866 Oct 2), Union Lodge No. 7, Denver, Apprentice
Proceedings 1861-1869, pg 195 (1867 Oct 8), Union Lodge No. 7, Denver
Proceedings 1861-1869, pg 225 (1868 Oct 7), Union Lodge No. 7, Denver
Proceedings 1861-1869, pg 307 (1869 Sept 29), Union Lodge No. 7, Denver

Chever, David A
Proceedings 1861-1869, pg 135 (1864 Nov 8), Union Lodge No. 7, Denver, Apprentice
Proceedings 1870, pg 23 (1870 Sept 28), Union Lodge No. 7, Denver
Proceedings 1871, pg 21 (1871 Sept 27), Union Lodge No. 7, Denver
Proceedings 1872, pg 22 (1872 Sept 24), Union Lodge No. 7, Denver
Proceedings 1873, pg 40 (1873 Oct 1), Union Lodge No. 7, Denver
Proceedings 1874, pg 214 (1874 Sept 30), Union Lodge No. 7, Denver
Proceedings 1875, pg 78 (1875 Sept 22), Union Lodge No. 7, Denver
Proceedings 1876, pg 33 (1876 Sept 20), Union Lodge No. 7, Denver

Cheyenne Lodge No. 1
Proceedings 1875, pg 28 (1875 Mar 1) Grand Lodge of Wyoming
Proceedings 1875, pg 84 (1875 Sept 22) Grand Lodge of Wyoming

Cheyenne Lodge No. 16
Proceedings 1875, pg 20 (1875 Mar 15) Grand Lodge of Wyoming
Proceedings 1875, pg 23 (1875 Sept 21) Grand Lodge of Wyoming
Proceedings 1875, pg 24 (1875 Sept 21) returned charter
Proceedings 1876, pg 46 (1876 Sept 20), Cheyenne Lodge No. 1, Grand Lodge of Wyoming Territory

Cheyenne Lodge No. 16, Cheyenne
Proceedings 1872, pg 8 (1872 June 6) dispensation given
Proceedings 1872, pg 16 (1872 Sept 24) allowed mileage and per diem

Cheyenne Lodge No. 16, Cheyenne, Dakota Terr
Proceedings 1861-1869, pg 216 (1868 Oct 7) granted charter

Cheyenne Lodge No. 16, Cheyenne, Wyoming Territory
Proceedings 1874, pg 11 (1874 Jan 22) new Masonic Lodge dedicated
Proceedings 1874, pg 208 (1874 Sept 30)

Cheyenne Lodge, U D, Cheyenne, Dakota Territory
Proceedings 1861-1869, pg 207 (1868 Apr) granted a lodge
Proceedings 1861-1869, pg 207 (1868 Apr 1) in working order
Proceedings 1861-1869, pg 210 (1868 Jan 28), Visited, found it safe and convenient
Proceedings 1861-1869, pg 211 (1868 May 30) visited

Chilcott, G M
Proceedings 1861-1869, pg 131 (1864 Nov 8) Golden City Lodge No. 1
Proceedings 1861-1869, pg 147 (1865 Nov 7) Golden City Lodge No. 1
Proceedings 1861-1869, pg 165 (1866 Oct 2) Golden City Lodge No. 1
Proceedings 1861-1869, pg 303 (1869 Sept 29) Golden City Lodge No. 1, Dimitted
Proceedings 1874, pg 222 (1874 Sept 30), Pueblo Lodge No. 17, Pueblo, Pueblo County
Proceedings 1875, pg 85 (1875 Sept 22) Pueblo Lodge No. 17
Proceedings 1876, pg 38 (1876 Sept 20) Pueblo Lodge No. 17

Chilcott, Geo M
Proceedings 1861-1869, pg 191 (1867 Oct 8) Golden City Lodge No. 1
Proceedings 1861-1869, pg 221 (1868 Oct 7) Golden City Lodge No. 1
Proceedings 1870, pg 30 (1870 Sept 28), Pueblo Lodge No. 17, Pueblo
Proceedings 1872, pg 31 (1872 Sept 24), Pueblo Lodge No. 17, Pueblo

Chilcott, George M
Proceedings 1871, pg 28 (1871 Sept 27), Pueblo Lodge No. 17, Pueblo
Proceedings 1873, pg 47 (1873 Oct 1), Pueblo Lodge No. 17, Pueblo

Childs
Proceedings 1874, pg 12 (1874 Jan 30) of Greeley
Proceedings 1876, pg 20 (1876 Sept 20) motion

Childs, F K
Proceedings 1871, pg 7 (1870 Nov 29), Occidental Lodge U D, Greeley

Childs, F L
Colorado University Cornerstone Laying, pg 3 (1875 Sept 20) Junior Grand Warden
Proceedings 1871, pg 30 (1871 Sept 27), Occidental Lodge U D, Greeley
Proceedings 1872, pg 3 (1872 Sept 24) Senior Grand Deacon
Proceedings 1872, pg 4 (1872 Sept 24), Occidental Lodge No. 20, Greeley
Proceedings 1872, pg 5 (1872 Sept 24) committee
Proceedings 1872, pg 5 (1872 Sept 24) committee
Proceedings 1872, pg 14 (1872 Sept 24) committee
Proceedings 1872, pg 15 (1872 Sept 24) committee
Proceedings 1872, pg 15 (1872 Sept 24) Senior Grand Deacon
Proceedings 1872, pg 16 (1872 Sept 24), Occidental Lodge No. 20, Greeley
Proceedings 1872, pg 33 (1872 Sept 24), Occidental Lodge No. 20, Greeley
Proceedings 1873, pg cover (1873 Oct 1) committee, Greeley
Proceedings 1873, pg 6 (1873 Sept 30), Occidental Lodge No. 20, Greeley
Proceedings 1873, pg 31 (1873 Oct 1) mileage and per diem
Proceedings 1873, pg 32 (1873 Oct 1) committee
Proceedings 1873, pg 49 (1873 Oct 1), Occidental Lodge No. 20, Greeley
Proceedings 1874, pg cover (1874 Sept 30) Junior Grand Warden, Greeley
Proceedings 1874, pg 3 (1874 Sept 29) Junior Grand Warden
Proceedings 1874, pg 4 (1874 Sept 29) committee
Proceedings 1874, pg 6 (1874 Sept 29), Occidental Lodge No. 20, Greeley
Proceedings 1874, pg 6 (1874 Sept 29) committee
Proceedings 1874, pg 29 (1874 Sept 29) Junior Grand Warden
Proceedings 1874, pg 36 (1874 Sept 30) per diem
Proceedings 1874, pg 37 (1874 Sept 30) resolution
Proceedings 1874, pg 206 (1874 Sept 30) Junior Grand Warden, 1874
Proceedings 1874, pg 225 (1874 Sept 30), Occidental Lodge No. 20, Greeley
Proceedings 1875, pg 16 (1875 Sept 21) Junior Grand Warden
Proceedings 1875, pg 37 (1875 Sept 22) per diem
Proceedings 1875, pg 87 (1875 Sept 22), Occidental Lodge No. 20, Greeley
Proceedings 1876, pg 4 (1876 Sept 19) Senior Grand Warden
Proceedings 1876, pg 22 (1876 Sept 20) Senior Grand Warden
Proceedings 1876, pg 40 (1876 Sept 20), Occidental Lodge No. 20, Greeley

Childs, Francis L
Proceedings 1875, pg cover (1875 Sept 22) Senior Grand Warden, Greeley
Proceedings 1875, pg 15 (1875 Sept 21) Junior Grand Warden
Proceedings 1875, pg 30 (1875 Sept 21) Senior Grand Warden
Proceedings 1875, pg 33 (1875 Sept 22) motion
Proceedings 1875, pg 93 (1875 Sept 22) Senior Grand Warden, 1875
Proceedings 1875, pg 93 (1875 Sept 22) Junior Grand Warden, 1874
Proceedings 1876, pg cover (1876 Sept 20) Deputy Grand Master, Greeley
Proceedings 1876, pg 3 (1876 Sept 19) Senior Grand Warden
Proceedings 1876, pg 18 (1876 Sept 19) Deputy Grand Master

Childs, L
Proceedings 1873, pg 3 (1873 Sept 30) Senior Grand Deacon

Chilton, William P
Proceedings 1870, pg 40 (1869 Dec 6) Grand Master, Grand Lodge of Alabama
Proceedings 1872, pg 54 (1872 Sept 24) Grand Lodge of Alabama, died 20 Jan 1871

Chinn, R W
Proceedings 1871, pg 17 (1871 Sept 27), Golden City Lodge No. 1, Golden City

Chinn, Robt W
Proceedings 1872, pg 17 (1872 Sept 24), Golden City Lodge No. 1, Golden City

Chinn, Rolla W
Proceedings 1873, pg 35 (1873 Oct 1), Golden City Lodge No. 1, Golden City
Proceedings 1874, pg 209 (1874 Sept 30), Golden City Lodge No. 1, Golden City
Proceedings 1875, pg 73 (1875 Sept 22) Golden City Lodge No. 1
Proceedings 1876, pg 29 (1876 Sept 20) Golden City Lodge No. 1

Chivington
Proceedings 1861-1869, pg 5 (1861 Aug 2) teller
Proceedings 1861-1869, pg 95 (1863 Apr 17) Past Grand Master
Proceedings 1861-1869, pg 105 (1863 Nov 3) motion
Proceedings 1861-1869, pg 107 (1863 Nov 3) motion
Proceedings 1861-1869, pg 140 (1865 Nov 6) motion

Chivington Lodge No. 6
Proceedings 1861-1869, pg 49 (1862 Nov 3) Central City
Proceedings 1861-1869, pg 139 (1865 Nov 6) dues paid
Proceedings 1861-1869, pg 158 (1866 Oct 1) dues paid
Proceedings 1861-1869, pg 181 (1867 Oct 7) dues paid
Proceedings 1861-1869, pg 187 (1867 Oct 8) motion

Colorado's Territorial Masons

Chivington Lodge No. 6, cont.
Proceedings 1861-1869, pg 217 (1868 Oct 7) requesting a name change to Central Lodge No. 6
Proceedings 1861-1869, pg 317 (1869 Sept 29), Central City, Colorado Territory
Proceedings 1871, pg 6 (1861 Sept 19) established at Central

Chivington Lodge U D
Proceedings 1861-1869, pg 33 (1861 Dec 10) charter granted 19 Sept 1861

Chivington, J M
Proceedings 1861-1869, pg 4 (1861 Aug 2), Rocky Mountain Lodge No 8, Gold Hill
Proceedings 1861-1869, pg 4 (1861 Aug 2) Reverend
Proceedings 1861-1869, pg 5 (1861 Aug 2) Grand Master, Gold Hill
Proceedings 1861-1869, pg 7 (1861 Aug 3) Grand Master
Proceedings 1861-1869, pg 31 (1861 Dec 10) Grand Master
Proceedings 1861-1869, pg 35 (1861 Dec 10)
Proceedings 1861-1869, pg 36 (1861 Dec 12) Grand Master
Proceedings 1861-1869, pg 37 (1861 Dec 12) Grand Master
Proceedings 1861-1869, pg 41 (1861 Dec 12) Grand Master
Proceedings 1861-1869, pg 43 (1861 Dec 10), Rocky Mountain Lodge No. 3, Gold Hill
Proceedings 1861-1869, pg 79 (1863 May 6) Permanent Member
Proceedings 1861-1869, pg 80 (1863 May 6) Past Grand Master
Proceedings 1861-1869, pg 92 (1863 Apr 17) committee
Proceedings 1861-1869, pg 93 (1863 Apr 17) committee
Proceedings 1861-1869, pg 93 (1863 Apr 17) motion
Proceedings 1861-1869, pg 94 (1863 Apr 17) Past Grand Master
Proceedings 1861-1869, pg 97 (1863 Nov 2) Past Grand Master
Proceedings 1861-1869, pg 98 (1863 Nov 2) Past Grand Master
Proceedings 1861-1869, pg 99 (1863 Nov 2) Grand Marshal
Proceedings 1861-1869, pg 100 (1863 Nov 2) committee
Proceedings 1861-1869, pg 100 (1863 Nov 3) Past Grand Master
Proceedings 1861-1869, pg 101 (1863 Jan 5), dispensation, King Solomon's Lodge
Proceedings 1861-1869, pg 102 (1863 Nov 3) committee
Proceedings 1861-1869, pg 102 (1863 Nov 3) petition for formation of a new lodge in Denver
Proceedings 1861-1869, pg 103 (1863 Nov 3) Past Grand Master
Proceedings 1861-1869, pg 103 (1863 Nov 3) donated per diem to the Grand Lodge
Proceedings 1861-1869, pg 107 (1863 Nov 3) committee
Proceedings 1861-1869, pg 113 (1863 Nov 3), Chivington Lodge No. 6, Central City
Proceedings 1861-1869, pg 127 (1864 Nov 8) committee
Proceedings 1861-1869, pg 134 (1864 Nov 8), Union Lodge No. 7, Denver
Proceedings 1861-1869, pg 134 (1864 Nov 8), Chivington Lodge No. 6, Central City, dimitted
Proceedings 1861-1869, pg 136 (1865 Nov 6) Past Grand Master
Proceedings 1861-1869, pg 138 (1865 Nov 6) Past Grand Master
Proceedings 1861-1869, pg 144 (1865 Nov 7) Past Grand Master
Proceedings 1861-1869, pg 145 (1865 Nov 7), Union Lodge No. 7, Denver, Grand Marshal
Proceedings 1861-1869, pg 145 (1865 Nov 7) committee
Proceedings 1861-1869, pg 151 (1865 Nov 7), Chivington Lodge No. 6, Central City
Proceedings 1861-1869, pg 157 (1866 Oct 1) absent from the Territory
Proceedings 1861-1869, pg 159 (1866 Oct 1) warrant
Proceedings 1861-1869, pg 169 (1866 Oct 2), Union Lodge No. 7, Denver
Proceedings 1861-1869, pg 195 (1867 Oct 8), Union Lodge No. 7, Denver
Proceedings 1861-1869, pg 225 (1868 Oct 7), Union Lodge No. 7, Denver
Proceedings 1861-1869, pg 307 (1869 Sept 29), Union Lodge No. 7, Denver
Proceedings 1861-1869, pg 315 (1869 Sept 29) Grand Master, August 1861
Proceedings 1861-1869, pg 315 (1869 Sept 29) Grand Master, December 1861
Proceedings 1870, pg 23 (1870 Sept 28), Union Lodge No. 7, Denver
Proceedings 1870, pg 32 (1870 Sept 28) Grand Master, August 1861, Dimitted
Proceedings 1870, pg 32 (1870 Sept 28) Grand Master, December 1861
Proceedings 1871, pg 6 (1861 Aug 2) Grand Master
Proceedings 1871, pg 6 (1861 Dec 10) Grand Master
Proceedings 1871, pg 34 (1871 Sept 27) Grand Master, Dec 1861
Proceedings 1871, pg 34 (1871 Sept 27) Grand Master, Aug 1861
Proceedings 1872, pg 42 (1872 Sept 24) Grand Master, August 1861
Proceedings 1872, pg 42 (1872 Sept 24) Grand Master, December 1861
Proceedings 1873, pg 58 (1873 Oct 1) Grand Master, Dec 1861, Dropped from the Rolls
Proceedings 1873, pg 58 (1873 Oct 1) Grand Master, Aug 1861, Dropped from the Rolls

Chivington, Jno M
Proceedings 1871, pg 21 (1871 Sept 27), Union Lodge No. 7, Denver

Chivington, John M
Proceedings 1872, pg 23 (1872 Sept 24), Union Lodge No. 7, Denver
Proceedings 1873, pg 40 (1873 Oct 1), Union Lodge No. 7, Denver, Stricken from the rolls

Proceedings 1874, pg 206 (1874 Sept 30) Grand Master, Aug 1861

Proceedings 1874, pg 206 (1874 Sept 30) Grand Master, Dec 1861

Proceedings 1875, pg 93 (1875 Sept 22) Grand Master, Dec 1861, Stricken from the roll

Proceedings 1875, pg 93 (1875 Sept 22) Grand Master, Aug 1861, Stricken from the roll

Christeson, Wilburn

Proceedings 1876, pg 42 (1876 Sept 20), Doric Lodge No. 25, Fairplay

Christian, William A

Proceedings 1876, pg 31 (1876 Sept 20) Denver Lodge No. 5

Christian, Wm A

Proceedings 1872, pg 20 (1872 Sept 24), Denver Lodge No. 5, Denver

Proceedings 1873, pg 37 (1873 Oct 1), Denver Lodge No. 5, Denver

Proceedings 1874, pg 211 (1874 Sept 30), Denver Lodge No. 5, Denver

Proceedings 1875, pg 75 (1875 Sept 22) Denver Lodge No. 5

Proceedings 1875, pg 76 (1875 Sept 22) Denver Lodge No. 5, Reinstated

Proceedings 1875, pg 76 (1875 Sept 22) Denver Lodge No. 5, Suspended

Christie, Wm S

Proceedings 1875, pg 81 (1875 Sept 22), Washington Lodge No. 12, Georgetown

Christison, W

Proceedings 1875, pg 89 (1875 Sept 22), Doric Lodge No. 25, Fairplay

Christoe, Fred J

Proceedings 1874, pg 229 (1874 Sept 30), Idaho Springs Lodge U D, Idaho Springs

Chubbuck, Sam'l W

Proceedings 1874, pg 204 (1874 Sept 30) Grand Lodge of Nevada, Gold Hill

Chubbuck, Samuel W

Proceedings 1875, pg 96 (1875 Sept 22) Grand Lodge of Nevada, Gold Hill

Proceedings 1876, pg 54 (1876 Sept 20) Grand Lodge of Nevada, Gold Hill

Church, Frank

Proceedings 1876, pg 31 (1876 Sept 20) Denver Lodge No. 5

Churches, John

Proceedings 1861-1869, pg 191 (1867 Oct 8) Golden City Lodge No. 1, Apprentice

Proceedings 1861-1869, pg 221 (1868 Oct 7) Golden City Lodge No. 1

Proceedings 1861-1869, pg 303 (1869 Sept 29) Golden City Lodge No. 1

Proceedings 1870, pg 19 (1870 Sept 28), Golden City Lodge No. 1, Golden City

Proceedings 1871, pg 17 (1871 Sept 27), Golden City Lodge No. 1, Golden City

Proceedings 1872, pg 17 (1872 Sept 24), Golden City Lodge No. 1, Golden City

Proceedings 1873, pg 35 (1873 Oct 1), Golden City Lodge No. 1, Golden City

Proceedings 1874, pg 209 (1874 Sept 30), Golden City Lodge No. 1, Golden City

Proceedings 1875, pg 73 (1875 Sept 22) Golden City Lodge No. 1

Proceedings 1876, pg 29 (1876 Sept 20) Golden City Lodge No. 1

Cinnamond, Daniel

Proceedings 1874, pg 221 (1874 Sept 30), Cheyenne Lodge No. 16, Cheyenne, Wyoming Territory

Claffin, J T

Proceedings 1872, pg 29 (1872 Sept 24), Cheyenne Lodge No. 16, Cheyenne, Wyoming Territory

Claiborne, Gilbert G

Proceedings 1861-1869, pg 239 (1867 Oct 8) Grand Master of California

Proceedings 1861-1869, pg 240 (1867 Oct 8) Grand Master of California

Clapp, George A

Proceedings 1870, pg 29 (1870 Sept 28), Cheyenne Lodge No. 16, Cheyenne, Wyoming Territory, Apprentice

Clapp, George H

Proceedings 1871, pg 27 (1871 Sept 27), Cheyenne Lodge No. 16, Cheyenne, Wyoming Territory, Apprentice

Proceedings 1872, pg 30 (1872 Sept 24), Cheyenne Lodge No. 16, Cheyenne, Wyoming Territory, Apprentice

Proceedings 1873, pg 46 (1873 Oct 1), Cheyenne Lodge No. 16, Cheyenne, Wyoming Territory, Apprentice

Proceedings 1874, pg 221 (1874 Sept 30), Cheyenne Lodge No. 16, Cheyenne, Wyoming Territory, Apprentice,

Clark

Proceedings 1861-1869, pg 177 (1867 Oct 7) committee

Proceedings 1861-1869, pg 177 (1867 Oct 7) committee

Proceedings 1861-1869, pg 179 (1867 Oct 7) motion

Proceedings 1861-1869, pg 213 (1868 Oct 6) Grand Secretary of Vermont

Proceedings 1874, pg 129 (1874 Sept 30) Grand Lodge of Vermont

Clark, A

Proceedings 1861-1869, pg 305 (1869 Sept 29) Denver Lodge No. 5

Clark, A B

Proceedings 1870, pg 25 (1870 Sept 28), Black Hawk Lodge No. 11, Black Hawk

Proceedings 1872, pg 24 (1872 Sept 24), Black Hawk Lodge No. 11, Black Hawk

Proceedings 1876, pg 34 (1876 Sept 20) Black Hawk Lodge No. 11

Clark, Ambrose B

Proceedings 1861-1869, pg 309 (1869 Sept 29), Black Hawk Lodge No. 11, Black Hawk

Colorado's Territorial Masons

Clark, Ambrose B, cont.
    Proceedings 1871, pg 23 (1871 Sept 27), Black Hawk Lodge No. 11, Black Hawk
    Proceedings 1873, pg 41 (1873 Oct 1), Black Hawk Lodge No. 11, Black Hawk
    Proceedings 1874, pg 216 (1874 Sept 30), Black Hawk Lodge No. 11, Black Hawk
    Proceedings 1875, pg 80 (1875 Sept 22) Black Hawk Lodge No. 11

Clark, Andrew
    Proceedings 1876, pg 35 (1876 Sept 20), Washington Lodge No. 12, Georgetown, Fellow Craft

Clark, Boughton
    Proceedings 1875, pg 86 (1875 Sept 22), Collins Lodge No. 19, Fort Collins, died

Clark, C A
    Proceedings 1873, pg 48 (1873 Oct 1), Laramie Lodge No. 18, Laramie, Wyoming Territory

Clark, C E
    Proceedings 1861-1869, pg 148 (1865 Nov 7), Nevada Lodge No. 4, Nevadaville, dimitted

Clark, C H
    Proceedings 1872, pg 32 (1872 Sept 24), Laramie Lodge No. 18, Laramie, Wyoming Territory
    Proceedings 1874, pg 223 (1874 Sept 30), Laramie Lodge No. 18, Laramie City

Clark, C J
    Proceedings 1861-1869, pg 151 (1865 Nov 7), Chivington Lodge No. 6, Central City

Clark, C W
    Proceedings 1871, pg 29 (1871 Sept 27), Laramie Lodge No. 18, Laramie, Wyoming Territory

Clark, Charles C
    Proceedings 1872, pg 82 (1872 Sept 24) Grand Lodge of North Carolina

Clark, Chas C
    Proceedings 1872, pg 44 (1872 Sept 24) Newburn, Grand Lodge of North Carolina

Clark, D G
    Proceedings 1870, pg 98 (1869 June 21) Grand Master, Grand Lodge of Oregon
    Proceedings 1870, pg 98 (1870 June 20) Grand Master, Grand Lodge of Oregon
    Proceedings 1872, pg 83 (1872 Sept 24) Grand Lodge of Oregon

Clark, E P
    Proceedings 1871, pg 19 (1871 Sept 27) Denver Lodge No. 5
    Proceedings 1872, pg 20 (1872 Sept 24), Denver Lodge No. 5, Denver
    Proceedings 1873, pg 37 (1873 Oct 1), Denver Lodge No. 5, Denver
    Proceedings 1874, pg 211 (1874 Sept 30), Denver Lodge No. 5, Denver
    Proceedings 1875, pg 75 (1875 Sept 22) Denver Lodge No. 5
    Proceedings 1876, pg 31 (1876 Sept 20) Denver Lodge No. 5

Clark, F A
    Proceedings 1861-1869, pg 148 (1865 Nov 7), Nevada Lodge No. 4, Nevadaville
    Proceedings 1861-1869, pg 154 (1866 Oct 1) Denver Lodge No. 5
    Proceedings 1861-1869, pg 155 (1866 Oct 1) committee
    Proceedings 1861-1869, pg 160 (1866 Oct 2) Grand Teller
    Proceedings 1861-1869, pg 166 (1866 Oct 2) Denver Lodge No. 5
    Proceedings 1861-1869, pg 176 (1867 Oct 7) Denver Lodge No. 5
    Proceedings 1861-1869, pg 186 (1867 Oct 8) per diem
    Proceedings 1861-1869, pg 192 (1867 Oct 8) Denver Lodge No. 5
    Proceedings 1861-1869, pg 223 (1868 Oct 7) Denver Lodge No. 5
    Proceedings 1873, pg 37 (1873 Oct 1), Denver Lodge No. 5, Denver

Clark, Fred A
    Proceedings 1861-1869, pg 133 (1864 Nov 8) Denver Lodge No. 5
    Proceedings 1870, pg 21 (1870 Sept 28), Denver Lodge No. 5, Denver
    Proceedings 1872, pg 19 (1872 Sept 24), Denver Lodge No. 5, Denver
    Proceedings 1874, pg 212 (1874 Sept 30), Denver Lodge No. 5, Denver, died

Clark, Fred'k A
    Proceedings 1871, pg 19 (1871 Sept 27) Denver Lodge No. 5

Clark, G T
    Proceedings 1861-1869, pg 149 (1865 Nov 7), Nevada Lodge No. 4, Nevadaville
    Proceedings 1861-1869, pg 167 (1866 Oct 2) Denver Lodge No. 5
    Proceedings 1861-1869, pg 305 (1869 Sept 29) Denver Lodge No. 5

Clark, Gaylor J
    Proceedings 1870, pg 91 (1868 June 24) Grand Orator, Grand Lodge of Nebraska

Clark, Geo T
    Proceedings 1861-1869, pg 112 (1863 Nov 3) Denver Lodge No. 5
    Proceedings 1861-1869, pg 133 (1864 Nov 8) Denver Lodge No. 5
    Proceedings 1861-1869, pg 193 (1867 Oct 8) Denver Lodge No. 5
    Proceedings 1861-1869, pg 223 (1868 Oct 7) Denver Lodge No. 5
    Proceedings 1870, pg 21 (1870 Sept 28), Denver Lodge No. 5, Denver
    Proceedings 1872, pg 20 (1872 Sept 24), Denver Lodge No. 5, Denver
    Proceedings 1873, pg 37 (1873 Oct 1), Denver Lodge No. 5, Denver

Proceedings 1874, pg 211 (1874 Sept 30), Denver Lodge No. 5, Denver

Proceedings 1875, pg 75 (1875 Sept 22) Denver Lodge No. 5

Proceedings 1876, pg 49 (1876 Sept 20) Denver Lodge No. 5, 1876 Aug 19

Clark, George T

Proceedings 1871, pg 19 (1871 Sept 27) Denver Lodge No. 5

Clark, H C

Proceedings 1870, pg 31 (1870 Sept 28), Laramie Lodge No. 18, Laramie, Wyoming Territory

Proceedings 1861-1869, pg 167 (1866 Oct 2) Denver Lodge No. 5

Proceedings 1861-1869, pg 193 (1867 Oct 8) Denver Lodge No. 5

Proceedings 1861-1869, pg 223 (1868 Oct 7) Denver Lodge No. 5

Proceedings 1870, pg 21 (1870 Sept 28), Denver Lodge No. 5, Denver

Proceedings 1872, pg 20 (1872 Sept 24), Denver Lodge No. 5, Denver, Dimitted

Clark, Henry

Proceedings 1861-1869, pg 316 (1869 Sept 29) Grand Lodge of Vermont

Proceedings 1861-1869, pg 348 (1868 June 10) Grand Secretary, Grand Lodge of Vermont

Proceedings 1870, pg 34 (1870 Sept 28) Grand Secretary, Grand Lodge of Vermont

Proceedings 1870, pg 104 (1869 June 9) Grand Secretary, Grand Lodge of Vermont

Proceedings 1871, pg 35 (1871 Sept 27) Grand Secretary, Grand Lodge of Vermont

Proceedings 1872, pg 44 (1872 Sept 24) Ruthland, Grand Lodge of Vermont

Proceedings 1873, pg 61 (1873 Oct 1) Grand Lodge of Vermont, Ruthland

Proceedings 1874, pg 128 (1874 Sept 30) Grand Lodge of Vermont

Proceedings 1874, pg 205 (1874 Sept 30) Grand Lodge of Vermont, Rutland

Proceedings 1875, pg 96 (1875 Sept 22) Grand Lodge of Vermont, Rutland

Proceedings 1876, pg 54 (1876 Sept 20) Grand Lodge of Vermont, Rutland

Clark, J J

Proceedings 1870, pg 31 (1870 Sept 28), Laramie Lodge No. 18, Laramie, Wyoming Territory

Proceedings 1871, pg 29 (1871 Sept 27), Laramie Lodge No. 18, Laramie, Wyoming Territory

Proceedings 1872, pg 32 (1872 Sept 24), Laramie Lodge No. 18, Laramie, Wyoming Territory

Proceedings 1873, pg 48 (1873 Oct 1), Laramie Lodge No. 18, Laramie, Wyoming Territory, Dimitted

Clark, James

Proceedings 1861-1869, pg 78 (1862 Nov 4), Chivington Lodge No. 6, Central City

Proceedings 1861-1869, pg 134 (1864 Nov 8), Chivington Lodge No. 6, Central City

Proceedings 1861-1869, pg 150 (1865 Nov 7), Chivington Lodge No. 6, Central City

Proceedings 1861-1869, pg 168 (1866 Oct 2), Chivington Lodge No. 6, Central City

Proceedings 1861-1869, pg 194 (1867 Oct 8), Chivington Lodge No. 6, Central City

Proceedings 1861-1869, pg 224 (1868 Oct 7), Chivington Lodge No. 6, Central City

Proceedings 1861-1869, pg 306 (1869 Sept 29), Central Lodge No. 6, Central City

Proceedings 1870, pg 22 (1870 Sept 28), Central Lodge No. 6, Central City

Proceedings 1871, pg 20 (1871 Sept 27), Central Lodge No. 6, Central

Proceedings 1872, pg 21 (1872 Sept 24), Denver Lodge No. 5, Denver

Proceedings 1873, pg 38 (1873 Oct 1), Central Lodge No. 6, Central City

Proceedings 1874, pg 212 (1874 Sept 30), Central Lodge No. 6, Central

Proceedings 1875, pg 76 (1875 Sept 22), Central Lodge No. 6, Central City

Proceedings 1876, pg 32 (1876 Sept 20), Central Lodge No. 6, Central City

Clark, Jas

Proceedings 1861-1869, pg 113 (1863 Nov 3), Chivington Lodge No. 6, Central City

Clark, John J

Proceedings 1873, pg 49 (1873 Oct 1), Collins Lodge No. 19, Fort Collins

Proceedings 1874, pg 224 (1874 Sept 30), Collins Lodge No. 19, Fort Collins, Larimer County

Proceedings 1875, pg 86 (1875 Sept 22), Collins Lodge No. 19, Fort Collins

Proceedings 1876, pg 39 (1876 Sept 20), Collins Lodge No. 19, Fort Collins

Clark, John M

Proceedings 1861-1869, pg 112 (1863 Nov 3) Denver Lodge No. 5, dimitted

Clark, L C

Proceedings 1861-1869, pg 151 (1865 Nov 7), Chivington Lodge No. 6, Central City

Clark, Langdom

Proceedings 1861-1869, pg 308 (1869 Sept 29), Union Lodge No. 7, Denver, Stricken from the rolls

Proceedings 1861-1869, pg 134 (1864 Nov 8), Union Lodge No. 7, Denver

Clark, Langdon

Proceedings 1861-1869, pg 169 (1866 Oct 2), Union Lodge No. 7, Denver

Proceedings 1861-1869, pg 195 (1867 Oct 8), Union Lodge No. 7, Denver

Proceedings 1861-1869, pg 225 (1868 Oct 7), Union Lodge No. 7, Denver

Colorado's Territorial Masons

Clark, R A
    Proceedings 1861-1869, pg 150 (1865 Nov 7), Chivington Lodge No. 6, Central City
    Proceedings 1861-1869, pg 168 (1866 Oct 2), Chivington Lodge No. 6, Central City
    Proceedings 1861-1869, pg 170 (1866 Oct 2), Black Hawk Lodge U D, Black Hawk
    Proceedings 1861-1869, pg 194 (1867 Oct 8), Chivington Lodge No. 6, Central City, Dimitted
    Proceedings 1861-1869, pg 227 (1868 Oct 7), Black Hawk Lodge No. 11, Black Hawk

Clark, Robert A
    Proceedings 1861-1869, pg 196 (1867 Oct 8), Black Hawk Lodge No. 11, Black Hawk
    Proceedings 1861-1869, pg 309 (1869 Sept 29), Black Hawk Lodge No. 11, Black Hawk, died

Clark, T O
    Proceedings 1861-1869, pg 150 (1865 Nov 7), Chivington Lodge No. 6, Central City
    Proceedings 1861-1869, pg 168 (1866 Oct 2), Chivington Lodge No. 6, Central City

Clark, Thomas O
    Proceedings 1861-1869, pg 194 (1867 Oct 8), Chivington Lodge No. 6, Central City, Dimitted

Clark, W M
    Proceedings 1875, pg 33 (1875 Sept 22) committee

Clark, William M
    Proceedings 1874, pg 217 (1874 Sept 30), Washington Lodge No. 12, Georgetown
    Proceedings 1875, pg 17 (1875 Sept 21), Washington Lodge No. 12, Georgetown
    Proceedings 1875, pg 31 (1875 Sept 21) committee

Clark, Wm M
    Proceedings 1875, pg 81 (1875 Sept 22), Washington Lodge No. 12, Georgetown
    Proceedings 1876, pg 34 (1876 Sept 20), Washington Lodge No. 12, Georgetown

Clarke
    Proceedings 1861-1869, pg 177 (1867 Oct 7) committee
    Proceedings 1861-1869, pg 185 (1867 Oct 7) Teller

Clarke, C J
    Proceedings 1861-1869, pg 169 (1866 Oct 2), Union Lodge No. 7, Denver
    Proceedings 1861-1869, pg 176 (1867 Oct 7), Union Lodge No. 7, Denver
    Proceedings 1861-1869, pg 187 (1867 Oct 8) committee
    Proceedings 1861-1869, pg 195 (1867 Oct 8), Union Lodge No. 7, Denver
    Proceedings 1861-1869, pg 202 (1868 Oct 6), Union Lodge No. 7, Denver
    Proceedings 1861-1869, pg 225 (1868 Oct 7), Union Lodge No. 7, Denver

Clarke, Chas E
    Proceedings 1861-1869, pg 132 (1864 Nov 8), Nevada Lodge No. 4, Nevadaville

Clarke, Clarance J
    Proceedings 1861-1869, pg 307 (1869 Sept 29), Union Lodge No. 7, Denver
    Proceedings 1861-1869, pg 134 (1864 Nov 8), Union Lodge No. 7, Denver
    Proceedings 1870, pg 23 (1870 Sept 28), Union Lodge No. 7, Denver
    Proceedings 1871, pg 21 (1871 Sept 27), Union Lodge No. 7, Denver
    Proceedings 1872, pg 22 (1872 Sept 24), Union Lodge No. 7, Denver
    Proceedings 1873, pg 39 (1873 Oct 1), Union Lodge No. 7, Denver
    Proceedings 1874, pg 214 (1874 Sept 30), Union Lodge No. 7, Denver
    Proceedings 1875, pg 78 (1875 Sept 22), Union Lodge No. 7, Denver
    Proceedings 1876, pg 33 (1876 Sept 20), Union Lodge No. 7, Denver

Clarke, F A
    Proceedings 1861-1869, pg 212 (1868 Oct 6) warrant paid

Clarke, H T
    Proceedings 1861-1869, pg 305 (1869 Sept 29) Denver Lodge No. 5

Clarkson, J
    Proceedings 1861-1869, pg 113 (1863 Nov 3), Chivington Lodge No. 6, Central City

Clarkson, James
    Proceedings 1861-1869, pg 134 (1864 Nov 8), Chivington Lodge No. 6, Central City, dimitted

Clay, Charles E
    Proceedings 1874, pg 221 (1874 Sept 30), Cheyenne Lodge No. 16, Cheyenne, Wyoming Territory, Fellowcraft

Clayton, G W
    Proceedings 1861-1869, pg 149 (1865 Nov 7), Nevada Lodge No. 4, Nevadaville
    Proceedings 1861-1869, pg 167 (1866 Oct 2) Denver Lodge No. 5

Clayton, Geo W
    Proceedings 1861-1869, pg 112 (1863 Nov 3) Denver Lodge No. 5

Clayton, George W
    Proceedings 1861-1869, pg 77 (1862 Nov 4) Denver Lodge No. 5
    Proceedings 1861-1869, pg 133 (1864 Nov 8) Denver Lodge No. 5
    Proceedings 1861-1869, pg 193 (1867 Oct 8) Denver Lodge No. 5, Dimitted

Clayton, Thos S
    Proceedings 1873, pg 4 (1873 Sept 30) pall bearer for George M Randall

Cleaveland, J R
    Proceedings 1861-1869, pg 168 (1866 Oct 2), Chivington Lodge No. 6, Central City
    Proceedings 1861-1869, pg 194 (1867 Oct 8), Chivington Lodge No. 6, Central City

Proceedings 1861-1869, pg 224 (1868 Oct 7), Chivington Lodge No. 6, Central City

Proceedings 1861-1869, pg 306 (1869 Sept 29), Central Lodge No. 6, Central City

Proceedings 1870, pg 22 (1870 Sept 28), Central Lodge No. 6, Central City

Proceedings 1871, pg 20 (1871 Sept 27), Central Lodge No. 6, Central

Cleaveland, Jno R

Proceedings 1872, pg 21 (1872 Sept 24), Denver Lodge No. 5, Denver

Proceedings 1873, pg 38 (1873 Oct 1), Central Lodge No. 6, Central City

Proceedings 1874, pg 213 (1874 Sept 30), Central Lodge No. 6, Central

Cleaveland, John R

Proceedings 1875, pg 77 (1875 Sept 22), Central Lodge No. 6, Central City

Proceedings 1876, pg 32 (1876 Sept 20), Central Lodge No. 6, Central City

Proceedings 1876, pg 50 (1876 Sept 20), Central Lodge No. 6, Central City

Clellan, James

Proceedings 1861-1869, pg 193 (1867 Oct 8) Denver Lodge No. 5

Proceedings 1861-1869, pg 305 (1869 Sept 29) Denver Lodge No. 5

Proceedings 1870, pg 21 (1870 Sept 28), Denver Lodge No. 5, Denver

Clellan, Jas

Proceedings 1861-1869, pg 223 (1868 Oct 7) Denver Lodge No. 5

Clelland, J

Proceedings 1871, pg 19 (1871 Sept 27) Denver Lodge No. 5

Clelland, James

Proceedings 1872, pg 20 (1872 Sept 24), Denver Lodge No. 5, Denver

Proceedings 1873, pg 37 (1873 Oct 1), Denver Lodge No. 5, Denver, Dimitted

Proceedings 1873, pg 45 (1873 Oct 1), Mount Moriah Lodge No. 15, Canon City

Proceedings 1874, pg 220 (1874 Sept 30), Mount Moriah Lodge No. 15, Canon City

Proceedings 1875, pg 84 (1875 Sept 22), Mount Moriah Lodge No. 15, Canon City

Proceedings 1876, pg 38 (1876 Sept 20), Mount Moriah Lodge No. 15, Canon City

Clements, C C

Proceedings 1861-1869, pg 169 (1866 Oct 2), Union Lodge No. 7, Denver, Apprentice

Proceedings 1861-1869, pg 195 (1867 Oct 8), Union Lodge No. 7, Denver

Proceedings 1861-1869, pg 225 (1868 Oct 7), Union Lodge No. 7, Denver

Proceedings 1861-1869, pg 307 (1869 Sept 29), Union Lodge No. 7, Denver

Proceedings 1875, pg 79 (1875 Sept 22), Union Lodge No. 7, Denver, Demitted

Clements, Court C

Proceedings 1871, pg 21 (1871 Sept 27), Union Lodge No. 7, Denver

Proceedings 1873, pg 40 (1873 Oct 1), Union Lodge No. 7, Denver

Proceedings 1874, pg 214 (1874 Sept 30), Union Lodge No. 7, Denver

Clements, Courtland C

Proceedings 1870, pg 23 (1870 Sept 28), Union Lodge No. 7, Denver

Proceedings 1872, pg 22 (1872 Sept 24), Union Lodge No. 7, Denver

Clendenning, Ebenezer D

Proceedings 1874, pg 224 (1874 Sept 30), Collins Lodge No. 19, Fort Collins, Larimer County

Proceedings 1875, pg 86 (1875 Sept 22), Collins Lodge No. 19, Fort Collins

Clendenning, Ebenezer D
Lodge No. 19, Fort Collins

Clery, Thomas E

Proceedings 1872, pg 18 (1872 Sept 24), Nevada Lodge No. 4, Bald Mountain

Proceedings 1873, pg 36 (1873 Oct 1), Nevada Lodge No. 4, Nevada

Proceedings 1874, pg 210 (1874 Sept 30), Nevada Lodge No. 4, Bald Mountain, Gilpin County

Proceedings 1876, pg 30 (1876 Sept 20) Nevada Lodge No. 4

Clery, Thos E

Proceedings 1871, pg 18 (1871 Sept 27), Nevada Lodge No. 4, Bald Mountain

Proceedings 1875, pg 74 (1875 Sept 22), Nevada Lodge No. 4, Nevada

Cleveland, R

Proceedings 1861-1869, pg 305 (1869 Sept 29) Denver Lodge No. 5

Proceedings 1872, pg 20 (1872 Sept 24), Denver Lodge No. 5, Denver

Cleveland, Robert

Proceedings 1861-1869, pg 149 (1865 Nov 7), Nevada Lodge No. 4, Nevadaville

Proceedings 1861-1869, pg 167 (1866 Oct 2) Denver Lodge No. 5

Proceedings 1861-1869, pg 193 (1867 Oct 8) Denver Lodge No. 5

Proceedings 1870, pg 21 (1870 Sept 28), Denver Lodge No. 5, Denver

Cleveland, Robt

Proceedings 1861-1869, pg 223 (1868 Oct 7) Denver Lodge No. 5

Clewell, T H

Proceedings 1861-1869, pg 111 (1863 Nov 3), Nevada Lodge No. 4, Nevadaville

Proceedings 1861-1869, pg 132 (1864 Nov 8), Nevada Lodge No. 4, Nevadaville

Colorado's Territorial Masons

Clewell, T H, cont.
    Proceedings 1861-1869, pg 148 (1865 Nov 7), Nevada Lodge No. 4, Nevadaville
    Proceedings 1861-1869, pg 166 (1866 Oct 2), Nevada Lodge No. 4, Nevadaville
    Proceedings 1861-1869, pg 192 (1867 Oct 8), Nevada Lodge No. 4, Nevadaville
    Proceedings 1861-1869, pg 222 (1868 Oct 7), Nevada Lodge No. 4, Nevadaville, Dimitted

Clinton, DeWitt
    Proceedings 1870, pg 42 (1869 Nov 1) Grand Lodge of Arkansas

Clinton, S C
    Proceedings 1861-1869, pg 147 (1865 Nov 7) Golden City Lodge No. 1
    Proceedings 1861-1869, pg 165 (1866 Oct 2) Golden City Lodge No. 1
    Proceedings 1861-1869, pg 191 (1867 Oct 8) Golden City Lodge No. 1
    Proceedings 1861-1869, pg 221 (1868 Oct 7) Golden City Lodge No. 1
    Proceedings 1861-1869, pg 303 (1869 Sept 29) Golden City Lodge No. 1
    Proceedings 1870, pg 19 (1870 Sept 28), Golden City Lodge No. 1, Golden City
    Proceedings 1871, pg 17 (1871 Sept 27), Golden City Lodge No. 1, Golden City
    Proceedings 1872, pg 18 (1872 Sept 24), Golden City Lodge No. 1, Golden City, Stricken from the Roll

Clough, H A
    Proceedings 1861-1869, pg 168 (1866 Oct 2), Chivington Lodge No. 6, Central City
    Proceedings 1861-1869, pg 194 (1867 Oct 8), Chivington Lodge No. 6, Central City
    Proceedings 1861-1869, pg 224 (1868 Oct 7), Chivington Lodge No. 6, Central City
    Proceedings 1861-1869, pg 305 (1869 Sept 29) Denver Lodge No. 5
    Proceedings 1861-1869, pg 306 (1869 Sept 29), Central Lodge No. 6, Central City
    Proceedings 1872, pg 20 (1872 Sept 24), Denver Lodge No. 5, Denver
    Proceedings 1872, pg 48 (1872 Sept 24), Denver Lodge No. 5, Denver
    Proceedings 1873, pg 46 (1873 Oct 1), Cheyenne Lodge No. 16, Cheyenne, Wyoming Territory
    Proceedings 1876, pg 49 (1876 Sept 20) Denver Lodge No. 5, 1876 Aug 19

Clough, Henry A
    Proceedings 1870, pg 20 (1870 Sept 28), Denver Lodge No. 5, Denver
    Proceedings 1870, pg 23 (1870 Sept 28), Central Lodge No. 6, Central City, Dimitted
    Proceedings 1871, pg 27 (1871 Sept 27), Cheyenne Lodge No. 16, Cheyenne, Wyoming Territory
    Proceedings 1872, pg 29 (1872 Sept 24), Cheyenne Lodge No. 16, Cheyenne, Wyoming Territory
    Proceedings 1873, pg 37 (1873 Oct 1), Denver Lodge No. 5, Denver
    Proceedings 1874, pg 211 (1874 Sept 30), Denver Lodge No. 5, Denver
    Proceedings 1874, pg 221 (1874 Sept 30), Cheyenne Lodge No. 16, Cheyenne, Wyoming Territory
    Proceedings 1875, pg 75 (1875 Sept 22) Denver Lodge No. 5

Clough, W
    Proceedings 1874, pg 222 (1874 Sept 30), Pueblo Lodge No. 17, Pueblo, Pueblo County, Fellowcraft
    Proceedings 1875, pg 85 (1875 Sept 22) Pueblo Lodge No. 17, Fellowcraft
    Proceedings 1876, pg 39 (1876 Sept 20) Pueblo Lodge No. 17, Fellow Craft

Clough, Worsnop
    Proceedings 1873, pg 47 (1873 Oct 1), Pueblo Lodge No. 17, Pueblo, Fellowcraft

Clow, David
    Proceedings 1871, pg 25 (1871 Sept 27), Columbia Lodge No. 14, Boulder City
    Proceedings 1872, pg 28 (1872 Sept 24), Columbia Lodge No. 14, Boulder
    Proceedings 1873, pg 44 (1873 Oct 1), Columbia Lodge No. 14, Boulder
    Proceedings 1874, pg 219 (1874 Sept 30), Columbia Lodge No. 14, Boulder, Boulder County
    Proceedings 1875, pg 83 (1875 Sept 22), Columbia Lodge No. 14, Boulder
    Proceedings 1876, pg 37 (1876 Sept 20), Columbia Lodge No. 14, Boulder

Clow, Richard
    Proceedings 1875, pg 83 (1875 Sept 22), Columbia Lodge No. 14, Boulder
    Proceedings 1876, pg 37 (1876 Sept 20), Columbia Lodge No. 14, Boulder

Clucas, William
    Proceedings 1872, pg 22 (1872 Sept 24), Union Lodge No. 7, Denver
    Proceedings 1873, pg 39 (1873 Oct 1), Union Lodge No. 7, Denver
    Proceedings 1874, pg 214 (1874 Sept 30), Union Lodge No. 7, Denver
    Proceedings 1875, pg 79 (1875 Sept 22), Union Lodge No. 7, Denver, Stricken from the rolls

Cluff, Chester P
    Proceedings 1876, pg 37 (1876 Sept 20), Columbia Lodge No. 14, Boulder

Clutter, J E
    Proceedings 1873, pg 52 (1873 Oct 1), Ashlar Lodge U D, Colorado Springs, Apprentice

Coakley, W L
    Proceedings 1874, pg 221 (1874 Sept 30), Cheyenne Lodge No. 16, Cheyenne, Wyoming Territory

Coates, John
    Proceedings 1861-1869, pg 261 (1868 Oct 7), Grand Master, Grand Lodge of Maryland
    Proceedings 1861-1869, pg 332 (1868 Nov 16) Grand Master, Grand Lodge of Maryland

Proceedings 1870, pg 65 (1869 Nov 15) Grand Master, Grand Lodge of Maryland

Cobb, A S
Proceedings 1861-1869, pg 168 (1866 Oct 2), Chivington Lodge No. 6, Central City
Proceedings 1861-1869, pg 194 (1867 Oct 8), Chivington Lodge No. 6, Central City
Proceedings 1861-1869, pg 224 (1868 Oct 7), Chivington Lodge No. 6, Central City
Proceedings 1861-1869, pg 306 (1869 Sept 29), Central Lodge No. 6, Central City
Proceedings 1870, pg 22 (1870 Sept 28), Central Lodge No. 6, Central City
Proceedings 1871, pg 20 (1871 Sept 27), Central Lodge No. 6, Central

Cobb, Alfred S
Proceedings 1861-1869, pg 77 (1862 Nov 4) Denver Lodge No. 5
Proceedings 1861-1869, pg 112 (1863 Nov 3) Denver Lodge No. 5, dimitted
Proceedings 1872, pg 22 (1872 Sept 24), Denver Lodge No. 5, Denver

Cobb, Amos E
Proceedings 1861-1869, pg 325 (1869 May 12) Grand Master, Grand Lodge of Connecticut
Proceedings 1870, pg 50 (1870 May 11) Grand Master, Grand Lodge of Connecticut

Cobb, C D
Proceedings 1870, pg 21 (1870 Sept 28), Denver Lodge No. 5, Denver, Apprentice

Cobb, E W
Proceedings 1861-1869, pg 77 (1862 Nov 4) Denver Lodge No. 5
Proceedings 1861-1869, pg 112 (1863 Nov 3) Denver Lodge No. 5
Proceedings 1861-1869, pg 133 (1864 Nov 8) Denver Lodge No. 5
Proceedings 1861-1869, pg 149 (1865 Nov 7), Nevada Lodge No. 4, Nevadaville
Proceedings 1861-1869, pg 167 (1866 Oct 2) Denver Lodge No. 5
Proceedings 1861-1869, pg 193 (1867 Oct 8) Denver Lodge No. 5
Proceedings 1861-1869, pg 223 (1868 Oct 7) Denver Lodge No. 5
Proceedings 1861-1869, pg 305 (1869 Sept 29) Denver Lodge No. 5
Proceedings 1870, pg 21 (1870 Sept 28), Denver Lodge No. 5, Denver
Proceedings 1871, pg 19 (1871 Sept 27) Denver Lodge No. 5
Proceedings 1872, pg 19 (1872 Sept 24), Denver Lodge No. 5, Denver
Proceedings 1873, pg 37 (1873 Oct 1), Denver Lodge No. 5, Denver
Proceedings 1874, pg 211 (1874 Sept 30), Denver Lodge No. 5, Denver
Proceedings 1875, pg 75 (1875 Sept 22) Denver Lodge No. 5

Cobb, E Winslow
Proceedings 1876, pg 31 (1876 Sept 20) Denver Lodge No. 5

Cobb, G W
Proceedings 1870, pg 28 (1870 Sept 28), Mount Moriah Lodge No. 15, Canon City, Fellowcraft
Proceedings 1873, pg 45 (1873 Oct 1), Mount Moriah Lodge No. 15, Canon City
Proceedings 1874, pg 220 (1874 Sept 30), Mount Moriah Lodge No. 15, Canon City
Proceedings 1875, pg 84 (1875 Sept 22), Mount Moriah Lodge No. 15, Canon City

Cobb, Geo W
Proceedings 1872, pg 29 (1872 Sept 24), Mount Moriah Lodge No. 15, Canon City

Cobb, George W
Proceedings 1871, pg 26 (1871 Sept 27), Mount Moriah Lodge No. 15, Canon City
Proceedings 1876, pg 37 (1876 Sept 20), Mount Moriah Lodge No. 15, Canon City

Codling, Joseph
Proceedings 1861-1869, pg 191 (1867 Oct 8), Nevada Lodge No. 4, Nevadaville
Proceedings 1861-1869, pg 222 (1868 Oct 7), Nevada Lodge No. 4, Nevadaville
Proceedings 1861-1869, pg 304 (1869 Sept 29), Nevada Lodge No. 4, Nevadaville
Proceedings 1870, pg 20 (1870 Sept 28), Nevada Lodge No. 4, Nevadaville
Proceedings 1871, pg 18 (1871 Sept 27), Nevada Lodge No. 4, Bald Mountain, Dimitted

Coe, Geo H
Proceedings 1861-1869, pg 330 (1868 June 22) Grand Master, Grand Lodge of Idaho Territory
Proceedings 1870, pg 56 (1869 Oct 4) Grand Master, Grand Lodge of Idaho

Coe, George H
Proceedings 1861-1869, pg 250 (1867 Dec 16), Grand Master, Grand Lodge of Idaho
Proceedings 1861-1869, pg 251 (1867 Dec 16), Grand Master, Grand Lodge of Idaho

Coffinbury, S C
Proceedings 1861-1869, pg 332 (1869 Jan 13) Grand Master, Grand Lodge of Michigan

Coffman, A W
Proceedings 1874, pg 227 (1874 Sept 30), St Vrain No. 23, Longmont
Proceedings 1876, pg 41 (1876 Sept 20), St Vrain Lodge No. 23, Longmont

Coffman, E J
Proceedings 1861-1869, pg 230 (1868 Oct 7), Valmont Lodge U D, Valmont
Proceedings 1870, pg 27 (1870 Sept 28), Columbia Lodge No. 14, Boulder City
Proceedings 1871, pg 25 (1871 Sept 27), Columbia Lodge No. 14, Boulder City

Colorado's Territorial Masons

Coffman, E J, cont.
Proceedings 1872, pg 7 (1872 June 22), [St Vrain] Lodge U D, Longmont
Proceedings 1872, pg 28 (1872 Sept 24), Columbia Lodge No. 14, Boulder
Proceedings 1872, pg 35 (1872 Sept 24), St Vrain Lodge No. 23, Longmont
Proceedings 1873, pg 6 (1873 Sept 30), St Vrain Lodge No. 23, Longmont
Proceedings 1873, pg 45 (1873 Oct 1), Columbia Lodge No. 14, Boulder, Dimitted
Proceedings 1873, pg 51 (1873 Oct 1), St Vrain Lodge No. 23, Longmont
Proceedings 1874, pg 227 (1874 Sept 30), St Vrain No. 23, Longmont
Proceedings 1876, pg 41 (1876 Sept 20), St Vrain Lodge No. 23, Longmont

Coffman, Geo F
Proceedings 1874, pg 227 (1874 Sept 30), St Vrain No. 23, Longmont

Coffman, George F
Proceedings 1876, pg 41 (1876 Sept 20), St Vrain Lodge No. 23, Longmont

Coffman, J D
Proceedings 1874, pg 227 (1874 Sept 30), St Vrain No. 23, Longmont

Coffman, Jesse D
Proceedings 1873, pg 51 (1873 Oct 1), St Vrain Lodge No. 23, Longmont, Fellowcraft

Cofield, J B
Proceedings 1861-1869, pg 51 (1862 Nov 4) Grand Standard Bearer
Proceedings 1861-1869, pg 113 (1863 Nov 3), Chivington Lodge No. 6, Central City
Proceedings 1861-1869, pg 134 (1864 Nov 8), Chivington Lodge No. 6, Central City
Proceedings 1861-1869, pg 150 (1865 Nov 7), Chivington Lodge No. 6, Central City
Proceedings 1861-1869, pg 168 (1866 Oct 2), Chivington Lodge No. 6, Central City
Proceedings 1861-1869, pg 194 (1867 Oct 8), Chivington Lodge No. 6, Central City
Proceedings 1861-1869, pg 224 (1868 Oct 7), Chivington Lodge No. 6, Central City
Proceedings 1861-1869, pg 306 (1869 Sept 29), Central Lodge No. 6, Central City

Cofield, Joseph B
Proceedings 1861-1869, pg 78 (1862 Nov 4), Chivington Lodge No. 6, Central City
Proceedings 1870, pg 23 (1870 Sept 28), Central Lodge No. 6, Central City, Dimitted

Cofman, J D
Proceedings 1876, pg 41 (1876 Sept 20), St Vrain Lodge No. 23, Longmont

Cohn, Louis
Proceedings 1874, pg 205 (1874 Sept 30) Grand Lodge of Utah, Salt Lake

Proceedings 1875, pg 90 (1875 Sept 22), Huerfano Lodge U D, Walsenburg, Apprentice
Proceedings 1876, pg 43 (1876 Sept 20), Huerfano Lodge No. 27, Walsenburg, Apprentice

Colburn, Joseph
Proceedings 1874, pg 219 (1874 Sept 30), Columbia Lodge No. 14, Boulder, Boulder County, Fellowcraft
Proceedings 1875, pg 83 (1875 Sept 22), Columbia Lodge No. 14, Boulder, Fellowcraft
Proceedings 1876, pg 37 (1876 Sept 20), Columbia Lodge No. 14, Boulder, Fellow Craft

Cole, J F
Proceedings 1872, pg 34 (1872 Sept 24), Occidental Lodge No. 20, Greeley, Apprentice
Proceedings 1873, pg 50 (1873 Oct 1), Occidental Lodge No. 20, Greeley, Apprentice
Proceedings 1874, pg 226 (1874 Sept 30), Occidental Lodge No. 20, Greeley, Apprentice
Proceedings 1875, pg 87 (1875 Sept 22), Occidental Lodge No. 20, Greeley, Apprentice
Proceedings 1876, pg 40 (1876 Sept 20), Occidental Lodge No. 20, Greeley, Apprentice

Cole, J M
Proceedings 1875, pg 89 (1875 Sept 22), Doric Lodge No. 25, Fairplay

Cole, James M
Proceedings 1874, pg 228 (1874 Sept 30), Doric Lodge U D, Fairplay
Proceedings 1876, pg 42 (1876 Sept 20), Doric Lodge No. 25, Fairplay

Coleman, D
Proceedings 1861-1869, pg 312 (1869 Sept 29), Pueblo Lodge No. 17, Pueblo
Proceedings 1870, pg 30 (1870 Sept 28), Pueblo Lodge No. 17, Pueblo
Proceedings 1871, pg 28 (1871 Sept 27), Pueblo Lodge No. 17, Pueblo
Proceedings 1872, pg 31 (1872 Sept 24), Pueblo Lodge No. 17, Pueblo
Proceedings 1873, pg 47 (1873 Oct 1), Pueblo Lodge No. 17, Pueblo
Proceedings 1874, pg 223 (1874 Sept 30), Pueblo Lodge No. 17, Pueblo, Pueblo County, Stricken from the rolls

Coleman, Geo C
Proceedings 1876, pg 50 (1876 Sept 20) Golden City Lodge No. 1

Coleman, Geo W
Proceedings 1875, pg 73 (1875 Sept 22) Golden City Lodge No. 1

Coleman, George C
Proceedings 1874, pg 209 (1874 Sept 30), Golden City Lodge No. 1, Golden City
Proceedings 1876, pg 29 (1876 Sept 20) Golden City Lodge No. 1

Coleman, J
Proceedings 1861-1869, pg 113 (1863 Nov 3), Chivington Lodge No. 6, Central City

Proceedings 1861-1869, pg 168 (1866 Oct 2), Chivington Lodge No. 6, Central City

Coleman, Jos
Proceedings 1861-1869, pg 134 (1864 Nov 8), Chivington Lodge No. 6, Central City
Proceedings 1861-1869, pg 224 (1868 Oct 7), Chivington Lodge No. 6, Central City

Coleman, Joseph
Proceedings 1861-1869, pg 150 (1865 Nov 7), Chivington Lodge No. 6, Central City
Proceedings 1861-1869, pg 194 (1867 Oct 8), Chivington Lodge No. 6, Central City
Proceedings 1861-1869, pg 306 (1869 Sept 29), Central Lodge No. 6, Central City
Proceedings 1870, pg 22 (1870 Sept 28), Central Lodge No. 6, Central City
Proceedings 1871, pg 20 (1871 Sept 27), Central Lodge No. 6, Central
Proceedings 1872, pg 21 (1872 Sept 24), Denver Lodge No. 5, Denver
Proceedings 1873, pg 38 (1873 Oct 1), Central Lodge No. 6, Central City
Proceedings 1874, pg 212 (1874 Sept 30), Central Lodge No. 6, Central
Proceedings 1875, pg 77 (1875 Sept 22), Central Lodge No. 6, Central City
Proceedings 1876, pg 32 (1876 Sept 20), Central Lodge No. 6, Central City
Proceedings 1876, pg 50 (1876 Sept 20), Central Lodge No. 6, Central City

Collam, John
Proceedings 1870, pg 24 (1870 Sept 28), Empire Lodge No. 8, Empire

Collier
Proceedings 1876, pg 5 (1876 Sept 19) motion
Proceedings 1876, pg 14 (1876 Sept 19) committee
Proceedings 1876, pg 23 (1876 Sept 20) motion
Proceedings 1876, pg 24 (1876 Sept 20) resolution

Collier & Hall
Proceedings 1861-1869, pg 182 (1867 Oct 7) warrant paid
Proceedings 1861-1869, pg 212 (1868 Oct 6) warrant paid

Collier & Wells
Proceedings 1861-1869, pg 140 (1864 Nov 8) warrant

Collier, D C
Proceedings 1861-1869, pg 113 (1863 Nov 3), Chivington Lodge No. 6, Central City
Proceedings 1861-1869, pg 150 (1865 Nov 7), Chivington Lodge No. 6, Central City
Proceedings 1861-1869, pg 168 (1866 Oct 2), Chivington Lodge No. 6, Central City
Proceedings 1861-1869, pg 194 (1867 Oct 8), Chivington Lodge No. 6, Central City
Proceedings 1861-1869, pg 224 (1868 Oct 7), Chivington Lodge No. 6, Central City
Proceedings 1861-1869, pg 306 (1869 Sept 29), Central Lodge No. 6, Central City
Proceedings 1870, pg 22 (1870 Sept 28), Central Lodge No. 6, Central City
Proceedings 1871, pg 20 (1871 Sept 27), Central Lodge No. 6, Central
Proceedings 1876, pg 4 (1876 Sept 19), Central Lodge No. 6, Central City
Proceedings 1876, pg 4 (1876 Sept 19) committee
Proceedings 1876, pg 5 (1876 Sept 19) committee
Proceedings 1876, pg 18 (1876 Sept 20) committee

Collier, David C
Proceedings 1861-1869, pg 133 (1864 Nov 8), Chivington Lodge No. 6, Central City
Proceedings 1872, pg 21 (1872 Sept 24), Denver Lodge No. 5, Denver
Proceedings 1873, pg 38 (1873 Oct 1), Central Lodge No. 6, Central City
Proceedings 1874, pg 213 (1874 Sept 30), Central Lodge No. 6, Central
Proceedings 1876, pg cover (1876 Sept 20) committee, Central
Proceedings 1876, pg 26 (1876 Sept 20) committee
Proceedings 1876, pg 31 (1876 Sept 20), Central Lodge No. 6, Central City

Collins
Proceedings 1861-1869, pg 143 (1865 Nov 7) motion
Proceedings 1875, pg 29 (1875 Sept 21), Washington Lodge No. 12, Georgetown
Proceedings 1876, pg 15 (1876 Sept 19) resolution
Proceedings 1876, pg 18 (1876 Sept 19) Grand Teller
Proceedings 1876, pg 22 (1876 Sept 20) motion

Collins Lodge No. 19
Proceedings 1875, pg 23 (1875 Sept 21) has not provided annual returns
Proceedings 1875, pg 25 (1875 Sept 21) dues paid
Proceedings 1875, pg 92 (1875 Sept 22)
Proceedings 1876, pg 52 (1876 Sept 20)

Collins Lodge No. 19, Fort Collins
Proceedings 1870, pg 31 (1870 Sept 28) dispensation granted 9 May 1870
Proceedings 1871, pg 7 (1870 Nov 29) recommended the formation of the Greeley Lodge
Proceedings 1872, pg 14 (1872 Sept 24) returns not complete
Proceedings 1874, pg 12 (1874 Jan 30) communication received
Proceedings 1874, pg 19 (1874 Sept 29) returns late
Proceedings 1874, pg 208 (1874 Sept 30)
Proceedings 1876, pg 13 (1876 Sept 19) dues paid

Collins, C H
Proceedings 1861-1869, pg 230 (1868 Oct 7), Cheyenne Lodge U D, Cheyenne, Dakota Territory
Proceedings 1861-1869, pg 312 (1869 Sept 29), Cheyenne Lodge No. 16, Cheyenne
Proceedings 1870, pg 29 (1870 Sept 28), Cheyenne Lodge No. 16, Cheyenne, Wyoming Territory
Proceedings 1871, pg 27 (1871 Sept 27), Cheyenne Lodge No. 16, Cheyenne, Wyoming Territory
Proceedings 1872, pg 29 (1872 Sept 24), Cheyenne Lodge No. 16, Cheyenne, Wyoming Territory
Proceedings 1873, pg 46 (1873 Oct 1), Cheyenne Lodge No. 16, Cheyenne, Wyoming Territory

Colorado's Territorial Masons

Collins, C H, cont.
Proceedings 1874, pg 221 (1874 Sept 30), Cheyenne Lodge No. 16, Cheyenne, Wyoming Territory

Collins, David C
Proceedings 1875, pg 77 (1875 Sept 22), Central Lodge No. 6, Central City

Collins, E H
Proceedings 1861-1869, pg 102 (1863 Nov 3) petition for formation of a new lodge in Denver
Proceedings 1861-1869, pg 124 (1864 Nov 8), Union Lodge No. 7, Denver, Junior Grand Deacon
Proceedings 1861-1869, pg 134 (1864 Nov 8), Union Lodge No. 7, Denver
Proceedings 1861-1869, pg 137 (1865 Nov 6), Union Lodge No. 7, Denver
Proceedings 1861-1869, pg 138 (1865 Nov 6) committee
Proceedings 1861-1869, pg 151 (1865 Nov 7), Chivington Lodge No. 6, Central City
Proceedings 1861-1869, pg 169 (1866 Oct 2), Union Lodge No. 7, Denver
Proceedings 1861-1869, pg 195 (1867 Oct 8), Union Lodge No. 7, Denver
Proceedings 1861-1869, pg 225 (1868 Oct 7), Union Lodge No. 7, Denver
Proceedings 1861-1869, pg 307 (1869 Sept 29), Union Lodge No. 7, Denver
Proceedings 1873, pg 39 (1873 Oct 1), Union Lodge No. 7, Denver
Proceedings 1874, pg 5 (1874 Sept 29), Union Lodge No. 7, Denver
Proceedings 1874, pg 6 (1874 Sept 29) committee
Proceedings 1874, pg 36 (1874 Sept 30) committee
Proceedings 1874, pg 36 (1874 Sept 30) per diem
Proceedings 1874, pg 213 (1874 Sept 30), Union Lodge No. 7, Denver
Proceedings 1875, pg 17 (1875 Sept 21) committee
Proceedings 1875, pg 17 (1875 Sept 21), Union Lodge No. 7, Denver
Proceedings 1875, pg 30 (1875 Sept 21) motion
Proceedings 1875, pg 32 (1875 Sept 22) committee
Proceedings 1875, pg 37 (1875 Sept 22) committee, Denver
Proceedings 1875, pg 38 (1875 Sept 22) per diem
Proceedings 1875, pg 78 (1875 Sept 22), Union Lodge No. 7, Denver
Proceedings 1876, pg 5 (1876 Sept 19), Union Lodge No. 7, Denver
Proceedings 1876, pg 22 (1876 Sept 20) committee
Proceedings 1876, pg 26 (1876 Sept 20) committee
Proceedings 1876, pg 32 (1876 Sept 20), Union Lodge No. 7, Denver

Collins, Ed H
Proceedings 1871, pg 21 (1871 Sept 27), Union Lodge No. 7, Denver
Proceedings 1872, pg 22 (1872 Sept 24), Union Lodge No. 7, Denver
Proceedings 1875, pg cover (1875 Sept 22) committee, Denver
Proceedings 1876, pg cover (1876 Sept 20) Grand Steward, Denver

Collins, Edward H
Proceedings 1870, pg 23 (1870 Sept 28), Union Lodge No. 7, Denver

Collins, R J
Proceedings 1875, pg 81 (1875 Sept 22), Washington Lodge No. 12, Georgetown

Collins, Russell J
Proceedings 1873, pg 43 (1873 Oct 1), Washington Lodge No. 12, Georgetown
Proceedings 1874, pg 217 (1874 Sept 30), Washington Lodge No. 12, Georgetown
Proceedings 1876, pg 35 (1876 Sept 20), Washington Lodge No. 12, Georgetown

Collins, W S
Proceedings 1861-1869, pg 169 (1866 Oct 2), Union Lodge No. 7, Denver
Proceedings 1861-1869, pg 195 (1867 Oct 8), Union Lodge No. 7, Denver
Proceedings 1861-1869, pg 225 (1868 Oct 7), Union Lodge No. 7, Denver

Collins, William S
Proceedings 1871, pg 22 (1871 Sept 27), Union Lodge No. 7, Denver, Dimitted

Collins, Wm S
Proceedings 1861-1869, pg 307 (1869 Sept 29), Union Lodge No. 7, Denver
Proceedings 1870, pg 23 (1870 Sept 28), Union Lodge No. 7, Denver

Collom, John
Proceedings 1861-1869, pg 170 (1866 Oct 2), Empire Lodge No. 8, Empire City
Proceedings 1861-1869, pg 195 (1867 Oct 8), Empire Lodge No. 8, Empire City
Proceedings 1861-1869, pg 226 (1868 Oct 7), Empire Lodge No. 8, Empire City
Proceedings 1861-1869, pg 308 (1869 Sept 29), Empire Lodge No. 8, Empire City
Proceedings 1872, pg 23 (1872 Sept 24), Empire Lodge No. 8, Empire
Proceedings 1873, pg 41 (1873 Oct 1), Empire Lodge No. 8, Empire
Proceedings 1874, pg 215 (1874 Sept 30), Empire Lodge No. 8, Empire
Proceedings 1874, pg 229 (1874 Sept 30), Idaho Springs Lodge U D, Idaho Springs
Proceedings 1875, pg 89 (1875 Sept 22) Idaho Springs Lodge U D
Proceedings 1876, pg 43 (1876 Sept 20) Idaho Springs Lodge No. 26

Collum, Henry
Proceedings 1872, pg 36 (1872 Sept 24), Ashlar Lodge U D, Colorado Springs

Colony, O E
    Proceedings 1861-1869, pg 113 (1863 Nov 3), Montana Lodge U D, Central City
    Proceedings 1861-1869, pg 134 (1864 Nov 8), Chivington Lodge No. 6, Central City
    Proceedings 1861-1869, pg 150 (1865 Nov 7), Chivington Lodge No. 6, Central City, dimitted,

Colorado Central Railroad
    Proceedings 1874, pg 13 (1874 Aug 27) reduced rates for Masons attending the Grand Lodge

Colorado Commandery No. 1
    Proceedings 1871, pg cover (1871 Sept 27) Denver
    Proceedings 1871, pg 11 (1871 Sept 19) Asylum held at Denver

Colorado Miner
    Colorado University Cornerstone Laying, pg 4 (1875 Sept 20) cornerstone contents

Colorado Transcript
    Colorado University Cornerstone Laying, pg 4 (1875 Sept 20) cornerstone contents

Columbia City
    Proceedings 1861-1869, pg 177 (1866 Nov 17) petition to form a lodge

Columbia Lodge No. 14
    Proceedings 1875, pg 23 (1875 Sept 21) has not provided a list of officers
    Proceedings 1875, pg 25 (1875 Sept 21) dues paid Columbia Lodge No. 14
    Proceedings 1875, pg 92 (1875 Sept 22) Columbia Lodge No. 14
    Proceedings 1876, pg 52 (1876 Sept 20)

Columbia Lodge No. 14, Boulder
    Proceedings 1861-1869, pg 292 (1869 Sept 28) grand dispensation
    Proceedings 1872, pg 11 (1872 Sept 24) failed to make timely returns
    Proceedings 1872, pg 14 (1872 Sept 24) returns not complete
    Proceedings 1874, pg 208 (1874 Sept 30)
    Proceedings 1876, pg 12 (1876 Sept 19) returns received only 15 days before annual communication
    Proceedings 1876, pg 13 (1876 Sept 19) dues paid
    Proceedings 1876, pg 24 (1876 Sept 20) correction to returns

Columbia Lodge No. 14, Columbia
    Proceedings 1861-1869, pg 189 (1867 Oct 8) charter granted
    Proceedings 1861-1869, pg 208 (1868 Apr) requesting a move to Boulder City
    Proceedings 1861-1869, pg 214 (1868 Oct 6) Petition from Columbia Lodge No. 14 to move from Columbia City to Boulder City

Columbia Lodge U D
    Proceedings 1861-1869, pg 181 (1866 Dec 16) dispensation granted
    Proceedings 1861-1869, pg 181 (1867 Oct 7) paid dues
    Proceedings 1861-1869, pg 181 (1867 Oct 7) dues paid
    Proceedings 1861-1869, pg 188 (1867 Oct 8) communication received

Combs, W S
    Proceedings 1870, pg 79 (1870 Jan 11) Grand Secretary, Grand Lodge of Minnesota

Combs, William S
    Proceedings 1861-1869, pg 316 (1869 Sept 29) Grand Lodge of Minnesota
    Proceedings 1870, pg 34 (1870 Sept 28) Grand Secretary, Grand Lodge of Minnesota
    Proceedings 1871, pg 35 (1871 Sept 27) Grand Secretary, Grand Lodge of Minnesota

Combs, Wm S
    Proceedings 1872, pg 43 (1872 Sept 24) St Paul, Grand Lodge of Minnesota

Compton, Amos
    Proceedings 1870, pg 22 (1870 Sept 28), Central Lodge No. 6, Central City
    Proceedings 1871, pg 20 (1871 Sept 27), Central Lodge No. 6, Central
    Proceedings 1872, pg 21 (1872 Sept 24), Denver Lodge No. 5, Denver
    Proceedings 1873, pg 38 (1873 Oct 1), Central Lodge No. 6, Central City
    Proceedings 1874, pg 213 (1874 Sept 30), Central Lodge No. 6, Central
    Proceedings 1875, pg 77 (1875 Sept 22), Central Lodge No. 6, Central City
    Proceedings 1876, pg 32 (1876 Sept 20), Central Lodge No. 6, Central City
    Proceedings 1876, pg 50 (1876 Sept 20), Central Lodge No. 6, Central City

Comstock, Chas
    Proceedings 1874, pg 226 (1874 Sept 30), Weston Lodge No. 22, Littleton
    Proceedings 1875, pg 88 (1875 Sept 22), Weston Lodge No. 22, Littleton
    Proceedings 1876, pg 48 (1876 Sept 20), Weston Lodge No. 22, Littleton, 1875 Oct 1

Comstock, Fred
    Proceedings 1874, pg 226 (1874 Sept 30), Weston Lodge No. 22, Littleton
    Proceedings 1875, pg 88 (1875 Sept 22), Weston Lodge No. 22, Littleton

Comstock, Frederick
    Proceedings 1876, pg 41 (1876 Sept 20), Weston Lodge No. 22, Littleton

Congdon, G E
    Proceedings 1871, pg 4 (1871 Sept 26), Black Hawk Lodge No. 11, Black Hawk
    Proceedings 1871, pg 14 (1871 Sept 27), Black Hawk Lodge No. 11, Black Hawk
    Proceedings 1871, pg 23 (1871 Sept 27), Black Hawk Lodge No. 11, Black Hawk

Colorado's Territorial Masons

Congdon, G W
Proceedings 1870, pg 4 (1870 Sept 27), Black Hawk Lodge No. 11, Black Hawk

Congdon, Geo E
Proceedings 1861-1869, pg 227 (1868 Oct 7), Black Hawk Lodge No. 11, Black Hawk
Proceedings 1861-1869, pg 309 (1869 Sept 29), Black Hawk Lodge No. 11, Black Hawk
Proceedings 1870, pg 25 (1870 Sept 28), Black Hawk Lodge No. 11, Black Hawk

Congdon, George
Proceedings 1873, pg 41 (1873 Oct 1), Black Hawk Lodge No. 11, Black Hawk
Proceedings 1874, pg 216 (1874 Sept 30), Black Hawk Lodge No. 11, Black Hawk

Congdon, George E
Proceedings 1872, pg 24 (1872 Sept 24), Black Hawk Lodge No. 11, Black Hawk
Proceedings 1875, pg 80 (1875 Sept 22) Black Hawk Lodge No. 11, Demitted

Congle, J B
Proceedings 1874, pg 205 (1874 Sept 30) Grand Lodge of Oregon

Conley, Harry
Proceedings 1870, pg 31 (1870 Sept 28), Collins Lodge No. 19, Fort Collins, Apprentice

Conley, W H
Proceedings 1871, pg 29 (1871 Sept 27), Collins Lodge No. 19, Fort Collins

Conley, Walter
Proceedings 1876, pg 7 (1875 Sept 24) Del Norte Lodge U D

Conley, William H
Proceedings 1873, pg 49 (1873 Oct 1), Collins Lodge No. 19, Fort Collins
Proceedings 1874, pg 225 (1874 Sept 30), Collins Lodge No. 19, Fort Collins, Larimer County, Demitted

Conley, Wm H
Proceedings 1872, pg 33 (1872 Sept 24), Collins Lodge No. 19, Fort Collins

Conly, Walter
Proceedings 1876, pg 44 (1876 Sept 20) Del Norte Lodge U D

Connelly, Chas
Proceedings 1861-1869, pg 225 (1868 Oct 7), Union Lodge No. 7, Denver

Connelly, J C
Proceedings 1861-1869, pg 304 (1869 Sept 29), Nevada Lodge No. 4, Nevadaville

Connelly, Samuel B
Proceedings 1872, pg 66 (1872 Sept 24) Grand Lodge of Idaho

Conner, A M
Proceedings 1875, pg 91 (1875 Sept 22), Las Animas Lodge U D, Trinidad, Apprentice

Conner, James
Proceedings 1870, pg 101 (1869 Nov 16) Grand Master, Grand Lodge of South Carolina

Conner, W S
Proceedings 1870, pg 29 (1870 Sept 28), Cheyenne Lodge No. 16, Cheyenne, Wyoming Territory, Apprentice

Conner, William G
Proceedings 1871, pg 27 (1871 Sept 27), Cheyenne Lodge No. 16, Cheyenne, Wyoming Territory

Connor, A M
Proceedings 1876, pg 44 (1876 Sept 20), Las Animas Lodge No. 28, Trinidad

Connor, James
Proceedings 1861-1869, pg 346 (1868 Nov 17) Grand Master, Grand Lodge of South Carolina

Connor, W G
Proceedings 1873, pg 46 (1873 Oct 1), Cheyenne Lodge No. 16, Cheyenne, Wyoming Territory

Connor, William G
Proceedings 1872, pg 29 (1872 Sept 24), Cheyenne Lodge No. 16, Cheyenne, Wyoming Territory

Connors, W G
Proceedings 1874, pg 221 (1874 Sept 30), Cheyenne Lodge No. 16, Cheyenne, Wyoming Territory

Conroy, Pierre
Proceedings 1876, pg 37 (1876 Sept 20), Columbia Lodge No. 14, Boulder, Apprentice

Conroy, Thomas
Proceedings 1861-1869, pg 312 (1869 Sept 29), Cheyenne Lodge No. 16, Cheyenne
Proceedings 1870, pg 29 (1870 Sept 28), Cheyenne Lodge No. 16, Cheyenne, Wyoming Territory
Proceedings 1871, pg 27 (1871 Sept 27), Cheyenne Lodge No. 16, Cheyenne, Wyoming Territory
Proceedings 1872, pg 29 (1872 Sept 24), Cheyenne Lodge No. 16, Cheyenne, Wyoming Territory
Proceedings 1874, pg 221 (1874 Sept 30), Cheyenne Lodge No. 16, Cheyenne, Wyoming Territory

Conroy, Thos
Proceedings 1873, pg 46 (1873 Oct 1), Cheyenne Lodge No. 16, Cheyenne, Wyoming Territory

Cook
Proceedings 1861-1869, pg 52 (1862 Nov 4) committee

Cook, C A
Proceedings 1861-1869, pg 99 (1863 Nov 2) Denver Lodge No. 5, Grand Sword Bearer
Proceedings 1861-1869, pg 149 (1865 Nov 7), Nevada Lodge No. 4, Nevadaville
Proceedings 1861-1869, pg 167 (1866 Oct 2) Denver Lodge No. 5
Proceedings 1861-1869, pg 305 (1869 Sept 29) Denver Lodge No. 5

Cook, Charles
Proceedings 1872, pg 29 (1872 Sept 24), Cheyenne Lodge No. 16, Cheyenne, Wyoming Territory

Proceedings 1874, pg 221 (1874 Sept 30), Cheyenne Lodge No. 16, Cheyenne, Wyoming Territory

Cook, Charles A
Proceedings 1872, pg 48 (1872 Sept 24), Denver Lodge No. 5, Denver

Cook, Chas
Proceedings 1873, pg 46 (1873 Oct 1), Cheyenne Lodge No. 16, Cheyenne, Wyoming Territory

Cook, Chas A
Proceedings 1861-1869, pg 77 (1862 Nov 4) Denver Lodge No. 5
Proceedings 1861-1869, pg 112 (1863 Nov 3) Denver Lodge No. 5
Proceedings 1861-1869, pg 193 (1867 Oct 8) Denver Lodge No. 5
Proceedings 1861-1869, pg 223 (1868 Oct 7) Denver Lodge No. 5
Proceedings 1872, pg 20 (1872 Sept 24), Denver Lodge No. 5, Denver
Proceedings 1873, pg 37 (1873 Oct 1), Denver Lodge No. 5, Denver
Proceedings 1874, pg 211 (1874 Sept 30), Denver Lodge No. 5, Denver
Proceedings 1875, pg 75 (1875 Sept 22) Denver Lodge No. 5
Proceedings 1876, pg 49 (1876 Sept 20) Denver Lodge No. 5, 1876 Aug 19

Cook, Chas H
Proceedings 1861-1869, pg 133 (1864 Nov 8) Denver Lodge No. 5

Cook, D J
Proceedings 1861-1869, pg 307 (1869 Sept 29), Union Lodge No. 7, Denver
Proceedings 1876, pg 33 (1876 Sept 20), Union Lodge No. 7, Denver

Cook, David
Proceedings 1873, pg 5 (1873 Sept 30) Grand Marshal

Cook, David I
Proceedings 1872, pg 22 (1872 Sept 24), Union Lodge No. 7, Denver

Cook, David J
Proceedings 1861-1869, pg 225 (1868 Oct 7), Union Lodge No. 7, Denver
Proceedings 1870, pg 23 (1870 Sept 28), Union Lodge No. 7, Denver
Proceedings 1871, pg 21 (1871 Sept 27), Union Lodge No. 7, Denver
Proceedings 1873, pg 40 (1873 Oct 1), Union Lodge No. 7, Denver
Proceedings 1874, pg 214 (1874 Sept 30), Union Lodge No. 7, Denver
Proceedings 1875, pg 78 (1875 Sept 22), Union Lodge No. 7, Denver

Cook, G D
Proceedings 1870, pg 25 (1870 Sept 28), Black Hawk Lodge No. 11, Black Hawk

Cook, Geo D
Proceedings 1861-1869, pg 197 (1867 Oct 8), Columbia Lodge U D, Boulder, Apprentice
Proceedings 1861-1869, pg 228 (1868 Oct 7), Columbia Lodge No. 14, Columbia City
Proceedings 1872, pg 25 (1872 Sept 24), Black Hawk Lodge No. 11, Black Hawk

Cook, George D
Proceedings 1861-1869, pg 311 (1869 Sept 29), Columbia Lodge No. 14, Boulder City, Dimitted
Proceedings 1871, pg 23 (1871 Sept 27), Black Hawk Lodge No. 11, Black Hawk
Proceedings 1873, pg 41 (1873 Oct 1), Black Hawk Lodge No. 11, Black Hawk
Proceedings 1874, pg 216 (1874 Sept 30), Black Hawk Lodge No. 11, Black Hawk
Proceedings 1875, pg 80 (1875 Sept 22) Black Hawk Lodge No. 11
Proceedings 1876, pg 34 (1876 Sept 20) Black Hawk Lodge No. 11

Cook, J W
Proceedings 1870, pg 29 (1870 Sept 28), Cheyenne Lodge No. 16, Cheyenne, Wyoming Territory

Cook, Joseph W
Proceedings 1871, pg 27 (1871 Sept 27), Cheyenne Lodge No. 16, Cheyenne, Wyoming Territory
Proceedings 1872, pg 30 (1872 Sept 24), Cheyenne Lodge No. 16, Cheyenne, Wyoming Territory, Dimitted

Cook, Mariner
Proceedings 1874, pg 209 (1874 Sept 30), Golden City Lodge No. 1, Golden City
Proceedings 1875, pg 73 (1875 Sept 22) Golden City Lodge No. 1
Proceedings 1876, pg 29 (1876 Sept 20) Golden City Lodge No. 1

Cook, R E
Proceedings 1861-1869, pg 149 (1865 Nov 7), Nevada Lodge No. 4, Nevadaville, dimitted
Proceedings 1861-1869, pg 152 (1865 Nov 7), Montana Lodge U D, Virginia City, Montana Territory

Cook, S H
Proceedings 1861-1869, pg 149 (1865 Nov 7), Nevada Lodge No. 4, Nevadaville
Proceedings 1861-1869, pg 167 (1866 Oct 2) Denver Lodge No. 5, deceased

Cook, Sam H
Proceedings 1861-1869, pg 77 (1862 Nov 4) Denver Lodge No. 5
Proceedings 1861-1869, pg 112 (1863 Nov 3) Denver Lodge No. 5
Proceedings 1861-1869, pg 133 (1864 Nov 8) Denver Lodge No. 5

Cooke, C E
Proceedings 1861-1869, pg 77 (1862 Nov 4) Denver Lodge No. 5
Proceedings 1861-1869, pg 112 (1863 Nov 3) Denver Lodge No. 5, deceased

Colorado's Territorial Masons

Cooke, Joseph W
Proceedings 1861-1869, pg 312 (1869 Sept 29), Cheyenne Lodge No. 16, Cheyenne, Apprentice

Cooke, R E
Proceedings 1861-1869, pg 51 (1862 Nov 4) Grand Marshal
Proceedings 1861-1869, pg 112 (1863 Nov 3) Denver Lodge No. 5

Cooke, Richard E
Proceedings 1861-1869, pg 45 (1862 Nov 3) Denver Lodge No. 5
Proceedings 1861-1869, pg 77 (1862 Nov 4) Denver Lodge No. 5
Proceedings 1861-1869, pg 133 (1864 Nov 8) Denver Lodge No. 5

Cooley, G B
Proceedings 1872, pg 43 (1872 Sept 24) Mantorville, Grand Lodge of Minnesota

Cooling, Jos
Proceedings 1861-1869, pg 166 (1866 Oct 2), Nevada Lodge No. 4, Nevadaville, Apprentice

Coon, John
Proceedings 1861-1869, pg 42 (1861 Dec 10), Summit Lodge No. 2, Parkville
Proceedings 1861-1869, pg 76 (1862 Nov 4), Summit Lodge No. 2, Parkville
Proceedings 1861-1869, pg 110 (1863 Nov 3), Summit Lodge No. 2, Parkville
Proceedings 1861-1869, pg 132 (1864 Nov 8) Golden City Lodge No. 1

Cooper, A D
Proceedings 1871, pg 24 (1871 Sept 27), Washington Lodge No. 12, Georgetown
Proceedings 1874, pg 220 (1874 Sept 30), Mount Moriah Lodge No. 15, Canon City
Proceedings 1875, pg 84 (1875 Sept 22), Mount Moriah Lodge No. 15, Canon City
Proceedings 1876, pg 38 (1876 Sept 20), Mount Moriah Lodge No. 15, Canon City

Cooper, Adam D
Proceedings 1861-1869, pg 227 (1868 Oct 7), Washington Lodge No. 12, Georgetown
Proceedings 1861-1869, pg 309 (1869 Sept 29), Washington Lodge No. 12, Georgetown
Proceedings 1870, pg 26 (1870 Sept 28), Washington Lodge No. 12, Georgetown
Proceedings 1872, pg 26 (1872 Sept 24), Washington Lodge No. 12, Georgetown, Dimitted

Cooper, E H
Proceedings 1873, pg 47 (1873 Oct 1), Pueblo Lodge No. 17, Pueblo
Proceedings 1874, pg 223 (1874 Sept 30), Pueblo Lodge No. 17, Pueblo, Pueblo County, Stricken from the rolls

Cooper, J A
Proceedings 1876, pg 31 (1876 Sept 20) Denver Lodge No. 5

Cooper, J G
Proceedings 1872, pg 34 (1872 Sept 24), Occidental Lodge No. 20, Greeley

Cooper, J W
Proceedings 1861-1869, pg 169 (1866 Oct 2), Chivington Lodge No. 6, Central City, Apprentice
Proceedings 1861-1869, pg 194 (1867 Oct 8), Chivington Lodge No. 6, Central City, Apprentice
Proceedings 1861-1869, pg 225 (1868 Oct 7), Chivington Lodge No. 6, Central City, Apprentice
Proceedings 1861-1869, pg 307 (1869 Sept 29), Central Lodge No. 6, Central City, Apprentice
Proceedings 1870, pg 22 (1870 Sept 28), Central Lodge No. 6, Central City, Apprentice

Cooper, James G
Proceedings 1873, pg 50 (1873 Oct 1), Occidental Lodge No. 20, Greeley
Proceedings 1874, pg 225 (1874 Sept 30), Occidental Lodge No. 20, Greeley
Proceedings 1875, pg 87 (1875 Sept 22), Occidental Lodge No. 20, Greeley
Proceedings 1876, pg 40 (1876 Sept 20), Occidental Lodge No. 20, Greeley

Cooper, Jno W
Proceedings 1871, pg 21 (1871 Sept 27), Central Lodge No. 6, Central, Apprentice
Proceedings 1872, pg 21 (1872 Sept 24), Denver Lodge No. 5, Denver, Apprentice

Cooper, John W
Proceedings 1873, pg 39 (1873 Oct 1), Central Lodge No. 6, Central City, Apprentice
Proceedings 1874, pg 213 (1874 Sept 30), Central Lodge No. 6, Central, Apprentice
Proceedings 1875, pg 77 (1875 Sept 22), Central Lodge No. 6, Central City, Apprentice
Proceedings 1876, pg 32 (1876 Sept 20), Central Lodge No. 6, Central City, Apprentice

Cooper, R C
Proceedings 1874, pg 222 (1874 Sept 30), Pueblo Lodge No. 17, Pueblo, Pueblo County
Proceedings 1875, pg 85 (1875 Sept 22) Pueblo Lodge No. 17
Proceedings 1876, pg 38 (1876 Sept 20) Pueblo Lodge No. 17

Cooper, Rollin C
Proceedings 1872, pg 31 (1872 Sept 24), Pueblo Lodge No. 17, Pueblo, Fellowcraft
Proceedings 1873, pg 47 (1873 Oct 1), Pueblo Lodge No. 17, Pueblo

Coots, M J
Proceedings 1875, pg 90 (1875 Sept 22), Huerfano Lodge U D, Walsenburg
Proceedings 1876, pg 43 (1876 Sept 20), Huerfano Lodge No. 27, Walsenburg

Corbett, W F
Proceedings 1861-1869, pg 312 (1869 Sept 29), Cheyenne Lodge No. 16, Cheyenne

Proceedings 1870, pg 28 (1870 Sept 28), Cheyenne Lodge No. 16, Cheyenne, Wyoming Territory

Proceedings 1872, pg 29 (1872 Sept 24), Cheyenne Lodge No. 16, Cheyenne, Wyoming Territory

Proceedings 1873, pg 46 (1873 Oct 1), Cheyenne Lodge No. 16, Cheyenne, Wyoming Territory

Corbett, Wm W

Proceedings 1872, pg 30 (1872 Sept 24), Cheyenne Lodge No. 16, Cheyenne, Wyoming Territory

Corbin, D C

Proceedings 1861-1869, pg 134 (1864 Nov 8), Union Lodge No. 7, Denver

Proceedings 1861-1869, pg 151 (1865 Nov 7), Chivington Lodge No. 6, Central City

Proceedings 1861-1869, pg 169 (1866 Oct 2), Union Lodge No. 7, Denver

Proceedings 1861-1869, pg 195 (1867 Oct 8), Union Lodge No. 7, Denver

Proceedings 1861-1869, pg 225 (1868 Oct 7), Union Lodge No. 7, Denver

Proceedings 1861-1869, pg 307 (1869 Sept 29), Union Lodge No. 7, Denver

Corbin, Daniel C

Proceedings 1870, pg 24 (1870 Sept 28), Union Lodge No. 7, Denver, Dimitted

Corbitt, W F

Proceedings 1874, pg 221 (1874 Sept 30), Cheyenne Lodge No. 16, Cheyenne, Wyoming Territory

Corlett, A T

Proceedings 1874, pg 221 (1874 Sept 30), Cheyenne Lodge No. 16, Cheyenne, Wyoming Territory

Corlett, W W

Proceedings 1873, pg 46 (1873 Oct 1), Cheyenne Lodge No. 16, Cheyenne, Wyoming Territory

Proceedings 1874, pg 220 (1874 Sept 30), Cheyenne Lodge No. 16, Cheyenne, Wyoming Territory

Corley, Hugh A

Proceedings 1861-1869, pg 328 (1868 Jan 13) Grand Secretary, Grand Lodge of Florida

Cornell, G B

Proceedings 1861-1869, pg 134 (1864 Nov 8), Chivington Lodge No. 6, Central City

Proceedings 1861-1869, pg 150 (1865 Nov 7), Chivington Lodge No. 6, Central City

Proceedings 1861-1869, pg 168 (1866 Oct 2), Chivington Lodge No. 6, Central City

Proceedings 1861-1869, pg 194 (1867 Oct 8), Chivington Lodge No. 6, Central City

Proceedings 1861-1869, pg 224 (1868 Oct 7), Chivington Lodge No. 6, Central City

Proceedings 1861-1869, pg 306 (1869 Sept 29), Central Lodge No. 6, Central City

Proceedings 1870, pg 22 (1870 Sept 28), Central Lodge No. 6, Central City

Proceedings 1871, pg 20 (1871 Sept 27), Central Lodge No. 6, Central

Cornell, Gideon

Proceedings 1875, pg 91 (1875 Sept 22), Las Animas Lodge U D, Trinidad

Cornell, Gideon B

Proceedings 1872, pg 21 (1872 Sept 24), Denver Lodge No. 5, Denver

Proceedings 1873, pg 38 (1873 Oct 1), Central Lodge No. 6, Central City

Proceedings 1874, pg 213 (1874 Sept 30), Central Lodge No. 6, Central

Proceedings 1875, pg 19 (1875 Mar 15), Las Animas Lodge U D, Trinidad

Proceedings 1875, pg 77 (1875 Sept 22), Central Lodge No. 6, Central City, Demitted

Proceedings 1876, pg 43 (1876 Sept 20), Las Animas Lodge No. 28, Trinidad

Proceedings 1875, pg 34 (1875 Sept 22), Las Animas Lodge No. 28, Trinidad

Cornell, S B

Proceedings 1876, pg 44 (1876 Sept 20), Las Animas Lodge No. 28, Trinidad

Cornell, Stephen B

Proceedings 1875, pg 91 (1875 Sept 22), Las Animas Lodge U D, Trinidad

Corner Stone

Proceedings 1874, pg 19 (1874 Sept 29), published at New York City, NY

Proceedings 1875, pg 23 (1875 Sept 21) published at NY

Proceedings 1876, pg 12 (1876 Sept 19) published at New York City

Corning, Geo C

Proceedings 1872, pg 28 (1872 Sept 24), Columbia Lodge No. 14, Boulder, Apprentice

Proceedings 1873, pg 44 (1873 Oct 1), Columbia Lodge No. 14, Boulder

Corning, George C

Proceedings 1874, pg 219 (1874 Sept 30), Columbia Lodge No. 14, Boulder, Boulder County

Proceedings 1875, pg 83 (1875 Sept 22), Columbia Lodge No. 14, Boulder

Proceedings 1876, pg 37 (1876 Sept 20), Columbia Lodge No. 14, Boulder

Cornish, N D

Proceedings 1875, pg 81 (1875 Sept 22), Washington Lodge No. 12, Georgetown

Cornish, Nicholas D

Proceedings 1874, pg 217 (1874 Sept 30), Washington Lodge No. 12, Georgetown

Proceedings 1876, pg 35 (1876 Sept 20), Washington Lodge No. 12, Georgetown

Cornish, Norman

Proceedings 1874, pg 217 (1874 Sept 30), Washington Lodge No. 12, Georgetown

Cornish, Thomas

Proceedings 1871, pg 24 (1871 Sept 27), Washington Lodge No. 12, Georgetown

Colorado's Territorial Masons

Cornish, Thomas, cont.
Proceedings 1872, pg 25 (1872 Sept 24), Washington Lodge No. 12, Georgetown
Proceedings 1873, pg 42 (1873 Oct 1), Washington Lodge No. 12, Georgetown
Proceedings 1875, pg 81 (1875 Sept 22), Washington Lodge No. 12, Georgetown
Proceedings 1876, pg 34 (1876 Sept 20), Washington Lodge No. 12, Georgetown

Corporan, J R
Proceedings 1875, pg 84 (1875 Sept 22), Mount Moriah Lodge No. 15, Canon City

Corporon, J R
Proceedings 1874, pg 220 (1874 Sept 30), Mount Moriah Lodge No. 15, Canon City

Corson
Proceedings 1870, pg 5 (1870 Sept 27) committee

Corson, W A
Proceedings 1861-1869, pg 197 (1867 Oct 8), Columbia Lodge U D, Boulder
Proceedings 1861-1869, pg 202 (1868 Oct 6), Columbia Lodge No. 14, Columbia
Proceedings 1870, pg 4 (1870 Sept 27), Columbia Lodge No. 14, Boulder
Proceedings 1870, pg 16 (1870 Sept 28) committee
Proceedings 1870, pg 27 (1870 Sept 28), Columbia Lodge No. 14, Boulder City
Proceedings 1872, pg 4 (1872 Sept 24), Columbia Lodge No. 14, Boulder City
Proceedings 1872, pg 16 (1872 Sept 24), Columbia Lodge No. 14, Boulder City

Corson, William A
Proceedings 1873, pg 44 (1873 Oct 1), Columbia Lodge No. 14, Boulder
Proceedings 1874, pg 219 (1874 Sept 30), Columbia Lodge No. 14, Boulder, Boulder County
Proceedings 1875, pg 83 (1875 Sept 22), Columbia Lodge No. 14, Boulder
Proceedings 1876, pg 36 (1876 Sept 20), Columbia Lodge No. 14, Boulder

Corson, Wm A
Proceedings 1861-1869, pg 311 (1869 Sept 29), Columbia Lodge No. 14, Boulder City
Proceedings 1870, pg cover (1870 Sept 28) Junior Grand Steward, Boulder
Proceedings 1870, pg 13 (1870 Sept 27) Junior Grand Steward
Proceedings 1871, pg 25 (1871 Sept 27), Columbia Lodge No. 14, Boulder City

Cottrill, Jedd P C
Proceedings 1874, pg 205 (1874 Sept 30) Grand Lodge of Wisconsin, Milwaukee

Coulson, W W
Proceedings 1876, pg 41 (1876 Sept 20), St Vrain Lodge No. 23, Longmont

Coultier, John
Proceedings 1875, pg 82 (1875 Sept 22), El Paso Lodge No. 13, Colorado Springs

Courier
Proceedings 1861-1869, pg 291 (1869 Sept 28) of New York

Courter, John
Proceedings 1874, pg 218 (1874 Sept 30), El Paso Lodge No. 13, Colorado Springs
Proceedings 1876, pg 36 (1876 Sept 20), El Paso Lodge No. 13, Colorado City

Covington, Philip
Proceedings 1876, pg 40 (1876 Sept 20), Occidental Lodge No. 20, Greeley

Cowan, James
Proceedings 1874, pg 216 (1874 Sept 30), Black Hawk Lodge No. 11, Black Hawk, Fellowcraft

Cowanhoven, H P
Proceedings 1872, pg 24 (1872 Sept 24), Black Hawk Lodge No. 11, Black Hawk

Cowen, James
Proceedings 1876, pg 34 (1876 Sept 20) Black Hawk Lodge No. 11, Fellow Craft

Cowen, Miles
Proceedings 1874, pg 209 (1874 Sept 30), Golden City Lodge No. 1, Golden City
Proceedings 1875, pg 73 (1875 Sept 22) Golden City Lodge No. 1

Cowenhoven, H P
Proceedings 1861-1869, pg 227 (1868 Oct 7), Black Hawk Lodge No. 11, Black Hawk
Proceedings 1861-1869, pg 309 (1869 Sept 29), Black Hawk Lodge No. 11, Black Hawk
Proceedings 1870, pg 25 (1870 Sept 28), Black Hawk Lodge No. 11, Black Hawk
Proceedings 1871, pg 23 (1871 Sept 27), Black Hawk Lodge No. 11, Black Hawk
Proceedings 1873, pg 42 (1873 Oct 1), Black Hawk Lodge No. 11, Black Hawk
Proceedings 1874, pg 216 (1874 Sept 30), Black Hawk Lodge No. 11, Black Hawk

Cowenhoven, Henry P
Proceedings 1875, pg 80 (1875 Sept 22) Black Hawk Lodge No. 11
Proceedings 1876, pg 34 (1876 Sept 20) Black Hawk Lodge No. 11

Cowin, James
Proceedings 1875, pg 80 (1875 Sept 22) Black Hawk Lodge No. 11, Fellowcraft

Cowles, W S
Proceedings 1861-1869, pg 341 (1869 Jan 12) Grand Secretary, Grand Lodge of Minnesota

Cox, G W
Proceedings 1874, pg 226 (1874 Sept 30), Weston Lodge No. 22, Littleton

Proceedings 1875, pg 88 (1875 Sept 22), Weston Lodge No. 22, Littleton, Demitted

Cox, Lemuel
Proceedings 1870, pg 51 (1870 May 11) Grand Lodge of Connecticut, age 93

Cox, S M
Proceedings 1861-1869, pg 229 (1868 Oct 7), Canon Lodge U D, Canon City
Proceedings 1861-1869, pg 311 (1869 Sept 29), Mount Moriah Lodge No. 15, Canon City
Proceedings 1870, pg 28 (1870 Sept 28), Mount Moriah Lodge No. 15, Canon City
Proceedings 1871, pg 26 (1871 Sept 27), Mount Moriah Lodge No. 15, Canon City
Proceedings 1872, pg 29 (1872 Sept 24), Mount Moriah Lodge No. 15, Canon City
Proceedings 1873, pg 45 (1873 Oct 1), Mount Moriah Lodge No. 15, Canon City, Suspended

Cox, William
Proceedings 1861-1869, pg 111 (1863 Nov 3), Summit Lodge No. 2, Parkville, dimitted

Cox, Wm
Proceedings 1861-1869, pg 42 (1861 Dec 10), Summit Lodge No. 2, Parkville
Proceedings 1861-1869, pg 76 (1862 Nov 4), Summit Lodge No. 2, Parkville

Cozens, N Z
Proceedings 1861-1869, pg 138 (1865 Nov 6) committee
Proceedings 1861-1869, pg 150 (1865 Nov 7), Chivington Lodge No. 6, Central City
Proceedings 1861-1869, pg 154 (1866 Oct 1), Chivington Lodge No. 6, Central City
Proceedings 1861-1869, pg 168 (1866 Oct 2), Chivington Lodge No. 6, Central City
Proceedings 1861-1869, pg 194 (1867 Oct 8), Chivington Lodge No. 6, Central City
Proceedings 1861-1869, pg 224 (1868 Oct 7), Chivington Lodge No. 6, Central City
Proceedings 1861-1869, pg 306 (1869 Sept 29), Central Lodge No. 6, Central City
Proceedings 1870, pg 22 (1870 Sept 28), Central Lodge No. 6, Central City
Proceedings 1871, pg 20 (1871 Sept 27), Central Lodge No. 6, Central

Cozens, Nelson Z
Proceedings 1861-1869, pg 137 (1865 Nov 6), Chivington Lodge No. 6, Central City
Proceedings 1872, pg 21 (1872 Sept 24), Denver Lodge No. 5, Denver
Proceedings 1873, pg 38 (1873 Oct 1), Central Lodge No. 6, Central City
Proceedings 1874, pg 213 (1874 Sept 30), Central Lodge No. 6, Central
Proceedings 1875, pg 77 (1875 Sept 22), Central Lodge No. 6, Central City, Stricken from the rolls

Cozens, W Z
Proceedings 1861-1869, pg 168 (1866 Oct 2), Chivington Lodge No. 6, Central City
Proceedings 1861-1869, pg 194 (1867 Oct 8), Chivington Lodge No. 6, Central City
Proceedings 1861-1869, pg 224 (1868 Oct 7), Chivington Lodge No. 6, Central City
Proceedings 1861-1869, pg 306 (1869 Sept 29), Central Lodge No. 6, Central City
Proceedings 1870, pg 22 (1870 Sept 28), Central Lodge No. 6, Central City
Proceedings 1871, pg 20 (1871 Sept 27), Central Lodge No. 6, Central

Cozens, William Z
Proceedings 1873, pg 38 (1873 Oct 1), Central Lodge No. 6, Central City
Proceedings 1874, pg 213 (1874 Sept 30), Central Lodge No. 6, Central
Proceedings 1875, pg 77 (1875 Sept 22), Central Lodge No. 6, Central City
Proceedings 1876, pg 32 (1876 Sept 20), Central Lodge No. 6, Central City

Cozens, Wm Z
Proceedings 1861-1869, pg 113 (1863 Nov 3), Montana Lodge U D, Central City
Proceedings 1872, pg 21 (1872 Sept 24), Denver Lodge No. 5, Denver

Craft, I L
Proceedings 1861-1869, pg 226 (1868 Oct 7), Union Lodge No. 7, Denver, Apprentice

Craft, J L
Proceedings 1861-1869, pg 308 (1869 Sept 29), Union Lodge No. 7, Denver, Apprentice

Craig, M M
Proceedings 1861-1869, pg 196 (1867 Oct 8), El Paso Lodge U D, Colorado City
Proceedings 1861-1869, pg 228 (1868 Oct 7), El Paso Lodge No. 13, Colorado City
Proceedings 1870, pg 28 (1870 Sept 28), Mount Moriah Lodge No. 15, Canon City
Proceedings 1871, pg 26 (1871 Sept 27), Mount Moriah Lodge No. 15, Canon City
Proceedings 1872, pg 28 (1872 Sept 24), Mount Moriah Lodge No. 15, Canon City
Proceedings 1873, pg 45 (1873 Oct 1), Mount Moriah Lodge No. 15, Canon City
Proceedings 1875, pg 84 (1875 Sept 22), Mount Moriah Lodge No. 15, Canon City
Proceedings 1876, pg 38 (1876 Sept 20), Mount Moriah Lodge No. 15, Canon City

Craig, M Mills
Proceedings 1861-1869, pg 229 (1868 Oct 7), Canon Lodge U D, Canon City
Proceedings 1861-1869, pg 311 (1869 Sept 29), Mount Moriah Lodge No. 15, Canon City

Colorado's Territorial Masons

Craig, P
Proceedings 1861-1869, pg 229 (1868 Oct 7), Pueblo Lodge U D, Pueblo

Craig, P
Proceedings 1861-1869, pg 312 (1869 Sept 29), Pueblo Lodge No. 17, Pueblo
Proceedings 1875, pg 85 (1875 Sept 22) Pueblo Lodge No. 17
Proceedings 1876, pg 38 (1876 Sept 20) Pueblo Lodge No. 17

Craig, Philander
Proceedings 1870, pg 30 (1870 Sept 28), Pueblo Lodge No. 17, Pueblo
Proceedings 1871, pg 28 (1871 Sept 27), Pueblo Lodge No. 17, Pueblo
Proceedings 1872, pg 31 (1872 Sept 24), Pueblo Lodge No. 17, Pueblo
Proceedings 1873, pg 47 (1873 Oct 1), Pueblo Lodge No. 17, Pueblo
Proceedings 1874, pg 222 (1874 Sept 30), Pueblo Lodge No. 17, Pueblo, Pueblo County

Craine, Geo
Proceedings 1861-1869, pg 166 (1866 Oct 2), Nevada Lodge No. 4, Nevadaville, dimitted

Craine, George
Proceedings 1861-1869, pg 132 (1864 Nov 8), Nevada Lodge No. 4, Nevadaville
Proceedings 1861-1869, pg 148 (1865 Nov 7), Nevada Lodge No. 4, Nevadaville

Craine, J E
Proceedings 1861-1869, pg 148 (1865 Nov 7), Nevada Lodge No. 4, Nevadaville
Proceedings 1861-1869, pg 166 (1866 Oct 2), Nevada Lodge No. 4, Nevadaville
Proceedings 1861-1869, pg 192 (1867 Oct 8), Nevada Lodge No. 4, Nevadaville
Proceedings 1861-1869, pg 304 (1869 Sept 29), Nevada Lodge No. 4, Nevadaville

Craine, Jno E
Proceedings 1875, pg 74 (1875 Sept 22), Nevada Lodge No. 4, Nevada

Craine, John E
Proceedings 1861-1869, pg 132 (1864 Nov 8), Nevada Lodge No. 4, Nevadaville
Proceedings 1861-1869, pg 222 (1868 Oct 7), Nevada Lodge No. 4, Nevadaville
Proceedings 1870, pg 20 (1870 Sept 28), Nevada Lodge No. 4, Nevadaville
Proceedings 1871, pg 18 (1871 Sept 27), Nevada Lodge No. 4, Bald Mountain
Proceedings 1872, pg 18 (1872 Sept 24), Nevada Lodge No. 4, Bald Mountain
Proceedings 1873, pg 36 (1873 Oct 1), Nevada Lodge No. 4, Nevada
Proceedings 1874, pg 211 (1874 Sept 30), Nevada Lodge No. 4, Bald Mountain, Gilpin County, Stricken from the rolls

Proceedings 1875, pg 75 (1875 Sept 22), Nevada Lodge No. 4, Nevada, Reinstated
Proceedings 1876, pg 48 (1876 Sept 20) Nevada Lodge No. 4, 1876 Feb 22

Cram, W J
Proceedings 1861-1869, pg 221 (1868 Oct 7) Golden City Lodge No. 1
Proceedings 1861-1869, pg 303 (1869 Sept 29) Golden City Lodge No. 1

Crane, Henry
Proceedings 1872, pg 30 (1872 Sept 24), Cheyenne Lodge No. 16, Cheyenne, Wyoming Territory

Cranmer, W H H
Proceedings 1876, pg 33 (1876 Sept 20), Union Lodge No. 7, Denver, Apprentice

Crater, G E
Proceedings 1861-1869, pg 151 (1865 Nov 7), Chivington Lodge No. 6, Central City

Crater, Geo E
Proceedings 1861-1869, pg 169 (1866 Oct 2), Union Lodge No. 7, Denver
Proceedings 1861-1869, pg 225 (1868 Oct 7), Union Lodge No. 7, Denver
Proceedings 1861-1869, pg 307 (1869 Sept 29), Union Lodge No. 7, Denver
Proceedings 1871, pg 21 (1871 Sept 27), Union Lodge No. 7, Denver
Proceedings 1872, pg 22 (1872 Sept 24), Union Lodge No. 7, Denver
Proceedings 1873, pg 39 (1873 Oct 1), Union Lodge No. 7, Denver
Proceedings 1874, pg 214 (1874 Sept 30), Union Lodge No. 7, Denver

Crater, George E
Proceedings 1861-1869, pg 135 (1864 Nov 8), Union Lodge No. 7, Denver, Apprentice
Proceedings 1861-1869, pg 195 (1867 Oct 8), Union Lodge No. 7, Denver
Proceedings 1870, pg 23 (1870 Sept 28), Union Lodge No. 7, Denver
Proceedings 1875, pg 78 (1875 Sept 22), Union Lodge No. 7, Denver
Proceedings 1876, pg 33 (1876 Sept 20), Union Lodge No. 7, Denver

Craven, John
Proceedings 1872, pg 64 (1872 Sept 24) Grand Lodge of Indiana

Craven, T H
Proceedings 1861-1869, pg 148 (1865 Nov 7), Nevada Lodge No. 4, Nevadaville
Proceedings 1861-1869, pg 166 (1866 Oct 2), Nevada Lodge No. 4, Nevadaville
Proceedings 1861-1869, pg 202 (1868 Oct 6), Nevada Lodge No. 4, Nevadaville
Proceedings 1861-1869, pg 304 (1869 Sept 29), Nevada Lodge No. 4, Nevadaville

Proceedings 1871, pg 4 (1871 Sept 26), Mount Moriah Lodge No. 15, Canon City
Proceedings 1871, pg 4 (1871 Sept 26) Committee
Proceedings 1871, pg 5 (1871 Sept 26) Committee
Proceedings 1871, pg 14 (1871 Sept 27), Mount Moriah Lodge No. 15, Canon City
Proceedings 1871, pg 14 (1871 Sept 27) Senior Grand Deacon
Proceedings 1871, pg 26 (1871 Sept 27), Mount Moriah Lodge No. 15, Canon City

Craven, Thomas H
Proceedings 1870, pg 20 (1870 Sept 28), Nevada Lodge No. 4, Nevadaville, Dimitted
Proceedings 1871, pg 5 (1871 Sept 26) Committee
Proceedings 1874, pg 220 (1874 Sept 30), Mount Moriah Lodge No. 15, Canon City
Proceedings 1875, pg 84 (1875 Sept 22), Mount Moriah Lodge No. 15, Canon City
Proceedings 1876, pg 37 (1876 Sept 20), Mount Moriah Lodge No. 15, Canon City

Craven, Thos H
Proceedings 1861-1869, pg 191 (1867 Oct 8), Nevada Lodge No. 4, Nevadaville
Proceedings 1861-1869, pg 222 (1868 Oct 7), Nevada Lodge No. 4, Nevadaville
Proceedings 1871, pg cover (1871 Sept 27) Senior Grand Deacon, Canon City
Proceedings 1872, pg 28 (1872 Sept 24), Mount Moriah Lodge No. 15, Canon City
Proceedings 1873, pg 45 (1873 Oct 1), Mount Moriah Lodge No. 15, Canon City

Crawford, J N
Proceedings 1861-1869, pg 196 (1867 Oct 8), Black Hawk Lodge No. 11, Black Hawk
Proceedings 1861-1869, pg 226 (1868 Oct 7), Black Hawk Lodge No. 11, Black Hawk
Proceedings 1861-1869, pg 309 (1869 Sept 29), Black Hawk Lodge No. 11, Black Hawk, Dimitted

Crawford, R R
Proceedings 1874, pg 218 (1874 Sept 30), El Paso Lodge No. 13, Colorado Springs
Proceedings 1875, pg 82 (1875 Sept 22), El Paso Lodge No. 13, Colorado Springs
Proceedings 1876, pg 36 (1876 Sept 20), El Paso Lodge No. 13, Colorado City

Creason, B F
Proceedings 1874, pg 220 (1874 Sept 30), Mount Moriah Lodge No. 15, Canon City, Demitted

Creason, Benj F
Proceedings 1873, pg 45 (1873 Oct 1), Mount Moriah Lodge No. 15, Canon City

Cree, Alex
Proceedings 1872, pg 26 (1872 Sept 24), Washington Lodge No. 12, Georgetown
Proceedings 1873, pg 43 (1873 Oct 1), Washington Lodge No. 12, Georgetown
Proceedings 1875, pg 81 (1875 Sept 22), Washington Lodge No. 12, Georgetown

Cree, Alexander
Proceedings 1861-1869, pg 227 (1868 Oct 7), Washington Lodge No. 12, Georgetown
Proceedings 1861-1869, pg 309 (1869 Sept 29), Washington Lodge No. 12, Georgetown
Proceedings 1874, pg 217 (1874 Sept 30), Washington Lodge No. 12, Georgetown
Proceedings 1876, pg 35 (1876 Sept 20), Washington Lodge No. 12, Georgetown

Cree, James
Proceedings 1861-1869, pg 150 (1865 Nov 7), Chivington Lodge No. 6, Central City, Apprentice
Proceedings 1861-1869, pg 169 (1866 Oct 2), Chivington Lodge No. 6, Central City, Apprentice

Creek, Alex
Proceedings 1871, pg 24 (1871 Sept 27), Washington Lodge No. 12, Georgetown

Cregier, Dewitt C
Proceedings 1872, pg 62 (1872 Sept 24) Grand Lodge of Illinois
Proceedings 1874, pg 62 (1874 Sept 30) Grand Lodge of Illinois

Creig, M Mills
Proceedings 1874, pg 220 (1874 Sept 30), Mount Moriah Lodge No. 15, Canon City

Crocker, Felix
Proceedings 1861-1869, pg 110 (1863 Nov 3) Golden City Lodge No. 1, Apprentice
Proceedings 1861-1869, pg 131 (1864 Nov 8) Golden City Lodge No. 1
Proceedings 1861-1869, pg 147 (1865 Nov 7) Golden City Lodge No. 1
Proceedings 1861-1869, pg 165 (1866 Oct 2) Golden City Lodge No. 1
Proceedings 1861-1869, pg 191 (1867 Oct 8) Golden City Lodge No. 1
Proceedings 1861-1869, pg 221 (1868 Oct 7) Golden City Lodge No. 1
Proceedings 1861-1869, pg 303 (1869 Sept 29) Golden City Lodge No. 1

Crockett, E
Proceedings 1861-1869, pg 166 (1866 Oct 2), Nevada Lodge No. 4, Nevadaville

Crockett, Ed
Proceedings 1861-1869, pg 192 (1867 Oct 8), Nevada Lodge No. 4, Nevadaville

Crockett, Edward
Proceedings 1861-1869, pg 111 (1863 Nov 3), Nevada Lodge No. 4, Nevadaville
Proceedings 1861-1869, pg 132 (1864 Nov 8), Nevada Lodge No. 4, Nevadaville
Proceedings 1861-1869, pg 148 (1865 Nov 7), Nevada Lodge No. 4, Nevadaville
Proceedings 1861-1869, pg 222 (1868 Oct 7), Nevada Lodge No. 4, Nevadaville
Proceedings 1861-1869, pg 304 (1869 Sept 29), Nevada Lodge No. 4, Nevadaville

Crockett, Edward, cont.
  Proceedings 1870, pg 20 (1870 Sept 28), Nevada Lodge No. 4, Nevadaville
  Proceedings 1871, pg 18 (1871 Sept 27), Nevada Lodge No. 4, Bald Mountain
  Proceedings 1872, pg 19 (1872 Sept 24), Nevada Lodge No. 4, Bald Mountain
  Proceedings 1873, pg 36 (1873 Oct 1), Nevada Lodge No. 4, Nevada
  Proceedings 1874, pg 211 (1874 Sept 30), Nevada Lodge No. 4, Bald Mountain, Gilpin County, Stricken from the rolls

Croft, J Loring
  Proceedings 1870, pg 24 (1870 Sept 28), Union Lodge No. 7, Denver, Died

Crohn, Marcus
  Proceedings 1861-1869, pg 306 (1869 Sept 29), Central Lodge No. 6, Central City
  Proceedings 1870, pg 22 (1870 Sept 28), Central Lodge No. 6, Central City
  Proceedings 1871, pg 20 (1871 Sept 27), Central Lodge No. 6, Central
  Proceedings 1872, pg 21 (1872 Sept 24), Denver Lodge No. 5, Denver
  Proceedings 1873, pg 38 (1873 Oct 1), Central Lodge No. 6, Central City
  Proceedings 1874, pg 213 (1874 Sept 30), Central Lodge No. 6, Central
  Proceedings 1875, pg 77 (1875 Sept 22), Central Lodge No. 6, Central City
  Proceedings 1876, pg 32 (1876 Sept 20), Central Lodge No. 6, Central City
  Proceedings 1876, pg 50 (1876 Sept 20), Central Lodge No. 6, Central City

Crohn, Theodore
  Proceedings 1873, pg 38 (1873 Oct 1), Central Lodge No. 6, Central City
  Proceedings 1874, pg 213 (1874 Sept 30), Central Lodge No. 6, Central
  Proceedings 1875, pg 77 (1875 Sept 22), Central Lodge No. 6, Central City, Demitted

Crome, Frederick
  Proceedings 1876, pg 42 (1876 Sept 20), Doric Lodge No. 25, Fairplay

Crook, A J M
  Proceedings 1861-1869, pg 149 (1865 Nov 7), Nevada Lodge No. 4, Nevadaville, dimitted

Crook, T D
  Proceedings 1875, pg 91 (1875 Sept 22), Las Animas Lodge U D, Trinidad
  Proceedings 1876, pg 44 (1876 Sept 20), Las Animas Lodge No. 28, Trinidad
  Proceedings 1876, pg 50 (1876 Sept 20), Las Animas Lodge No. 28, Trinidad

Crooks, C E
  Proceedings 1876, pg 31 (1876 Sept 20) Denver Lodge No. 5

Crooks, Cyrus E
  Proceedings 1875, pg 75 (1875 Sept 22) Denver Lodge No. 5

Crosier, E
  Proceedings 1861-1869, pg 113 (1863 Nov 3), Chivington Lodge No. 6, Central City

Crosier, E R
  Proceedings 1861-1869, pg 134 (1864 Nov 8), Chivington Lodge No. 6, Central City, dimitted

Cross, Jeremy L
  Proceedings 1870, pg 50 (1870 May 11) Grand Lodge of Connecticut

Cross, Thomas
  Proceedings 1873, pg 49 (1873 Oct 1), Collins Lodge No. 19, Fort Collins
  Proceedings 1874, pg 224 (1874 Sept 30), Collins Lodge No. 19, Fort Collins, Larimer County
  Proceedings 1875, pg 86 (1875 Sept 22), Collins Lodge No. 19, Fort Collins
  Proceedings 1876, pg 39 (1876 Sept 20), Collins Lodge No. 19, Fort Collins

Cross, William H
  Proceedings 1873, pg 36 (1873 Oct 1), Nevada Lodge No. 4, Nevada

Cross, Wm H
  Proceedings 1871, pg 18 (1871 Sept 27), Nevada Lodge No. 4, Bald Mountain
  Proceedings 1872, pg 19 (1872 Sept 24), Nevada Lodge No. 4, Bald Mountain, Dimitted
  Proceedings 1874, pg 211 (1874 Sept 30), Nevada Lodge No. 4, Bald Mountain, Gilpin County, Stricken from the rolls

Crow, Henry
  Proceedings 1870, pg 26 (1870 Sept 28), Washington Lodge No. 12, Georgetown
  Proceedings 1871, pg 24 (1871 Sept 27), Washington Lodge No. 12, Georgetown
  Proceedings 1872, pg 26 (1872 Sept 24), Washington Lodge No. 12, Georgetown
  Proceedings 1873, pg 43 (1873 Oct 1), Washington Lodge No. 12, Georgetown
  Proceedings 1874, pg 217 (1874 Sept 30), Washington Lodge No. 12, Georgetown
  Proceedings 1875, pg 81 (1875 Sept 22), Washington Lodge No. 12, Georgetown
  Proceedings 1876, pg 48 (1876 Sept 20), Washington Lodge No. 12, Georgetown, 1875 Sept 11

Crow, Richard
  Proceedings 1873, pg 44 (1873 Oct 1), Columbia Lodge No. 14, Boulder
  Proceedings 1874, pg 219 (1874 Sept 30), Columbia Lodge No. 14, Boulder, Boulder County
  Proceedings 1875, pg 83 (1875 Sept 22), Columbia Lodge No. 14, Boulder
  Proceedings 1876, pg 37 (1876 Sept 20), Columbia Lodge No. 14, Boulder

Crowell, A N
Proceedings 1874, pg 211 (1874 Sept 30), Denver Lodge No. 5, Denver
Proceedings 1875, pg 75 (1875 Sept 22) Denver Lodge No. 5
Proceedings 1876, pg 30 (1876 Sept 20) Denver Lodge No. 5

Crowell, B C
Proceedings 1861-1869, pg 228 (1868 Oct 7), El Paso Lodge No. 13, Colorado City

Crowell, B F
Proceedings 1861-1869, pg 310 (1869 Sept 29), El Paso Lodge No. 13, Colorado City
Proceedings 1870, pg 26 (1870 Sept 28), El Paso Lodge No. 13, Colorado City
Proceedings 1872, pg 27 (1872 Sept 24), El Paso Lodge No. 13, Colorado City
Proceedings 1873, pg 6 (1873 Sept 30), El Paso Lodge No. 13, Colorado City
Proceedings 1873, pg 7 (1873 Sept 30) committee
Proceedings 1873, pg 43 (1873 Oct 1), El Paso Lodge No. 13, Colorado City
Proceedings 1874, pg 218 (1874 Sept 30), El Paso Lodge No. 13, Colorado Springs
Proceedings 1875, pg 82 (1875 Sept 22), El Paso Lodge No. 13, Colorado Springs
Proceedings 1876, pg 5 (1876 Sept 19), El Paso Lodge No. 13, Colorado Springs
Proceedings 1876, pg 36 (1876 Sept 20), El Paso Lodge No. 13, Colorado City

Crowell, Benj F
Proceedings 1876, pg 18 (1876 Sept 19) Junior Grand Warden

Crowell, Benjamin F
Proceedings 1861-1869, pg 196 (1867 Oct 8), El Paso Lodge U D, Colorado City
Proceedings 1876, pg cover (1876 Sept 20) Junior Grand Warden, Colorado Springs
Proceedings 1871, pg 25 (1871 Sept 27), El Paso Lodge No. 13, Colorado City

Cru, Alexander
Proceedings 1870, pg 26 (1870 Sept 28), Washington Lodge No. 12, Georgetown

Crum, Adelbert
Proceedings 1861-1869, pg 309 (1869 Sept 29), Black Hawk Lodge No. 11, Black Hawk
Proceedings 1870, pg 25 (1870 Sept 28), Black Hawk Lodge No. 11, Black Hawk, Dimitted

Culbertson, A J
Proceedings 1861-1869, pg 78 (1862 Nov 4), Chivington Lodge No. 6, Central City, Apprentice
Proceedings 1861-1869, pg 113 (1863 Nov 3), Chivington Lodge No. 6, Central City
Proceedings 1861-1869, pg 134 (1864 Nov 8), Chivington Lodge No. 6, Central City, dimitted

Culver, William E
Proceedings 1876, pg 45 (1876 Sept 20), King Solomon Lodge U D, West Las Animas

Culver, Wm E
Proceedings 1876, pg 24 (1876 Sept 20), King Solomon Lodge No. 30, West Las Animas

Cummigs, T
Proceedings 1861-1869, pg 131 (1864 Nov 8) Golden City Lodge No. 1, dimitted

Cummins, Theodore
Proceedings 1861-1869, pg 110 (1863 Nov 3) Golden City Lodge No. 1, Fellowcraft

Cumner, Nathanial W
Proceedings 1874, pg 104 (1874 Sept 30) Grand Lodge of New Hampshire
Proceedings 1874, pg 106 (1874 Sept 30) Grand Lodge of New Hampshire
Proceedings 1872, pg 44 (1872 Sept 24) Manchester, Grand Lodge of New Hampshire
Proceedings 1874, pg 204 (1874 Sept 30) Grand Lodge of New Hampshire, Manchester

Cunningham, A
Proceedings 1861-1869, pg 151 (1865 Nov 7), Chivington Lodge No. 6, Central City
Proceedings 1861-1869, pg 195 (1867 Oct 8), Union Lodge No. 7, Denver
Proceedings 1861-1869, pg 225 (1868 Oct 7), Union Lodge No. 7, Denver

Cunningham, Austin
Proceedings 1861-1869, pg 169 (1866 Oct 2), Union Lodge No. 7, Denver
Proceedings 1861-1869, pg 307 (1869 Sept 29), Union Lodge No. 7, Denver
Proceedings 1870, pg 23 (1870 Sept 28), Union Lodge No. 7, Denver
Proceedings 1871, pg 21 (1871 Sept 27), Union Lodge No. 7, Denver
Proceedings 1872, pg 22 (1872 Sept 24), Union Lodge No. 7, Denver
Proceedings 1873, pg 40 (1873 Oct 1), Union Lodge No. 7, Denver, Stricken from the rolls

Curran, Benj
Proceedings 1872, pg 77 (1872 Sept 24) Grand Lodge of Nova Scotia
Proceedings 1874, pg 204 (1874 Sept 30) Grand Lodge of Nova Scotia, Halifax
Proceedings 1876, pg 54 (1876 Sept 20) Grand Lodge of Nova Scotia, Halifax
Proceedings 1872, pg 44 (1872 Sept 24) Halifax, Grand Lodge of Nova Scotia
Proceedings 1873, pg 61 (1873 Oct 1) Grand Lodge of Nova Scotia, Halifax

Curren, Benjamin
Proceedings 1874, pg 116 (1874 Sept 30) Grand Lodge of Nova Scotia

Colorado's Territorial Masons

Currie
Proceedings 1861-1869, pg 269 (1867 Sept 17), Grand Master, Grand Lodge of Nevada

Currie, John C
Proceedings 1861-1869, pg 269 (1867 Sept 17), Grand Master, Grand Lodge of Nevada
Proceedings 1861-1869, pg 342 (1868 Sept 15) Grand Master, Grand Lodge of Nevada
Proceedings 1871, pg 35 (1871 Sept 27) Grand Secretary, Grand Lodge of Nevada

Currier, G W
Proceedings 1861-1869, pg 170 (1866 Oct 2), Black Hawk Lodge U D, Black Hawk

Currier, S A
Proceedings 1873, pg 37 (1873 Oct 1), Denver Lodge No. 5, Denver
Proceedings 1874, pg 211 (1874 Sept 30), Denver Lodge No. 5, Denver
Proceedings 1875, pg 75 (1875 Sept 22) Denver Lodge No. 5
Proceedings 1876, pg 31 (1876 Sept 20) Denver Lodge No. 5

Curry, W H
Proceedings 1861-1869, pg 303 (1869 Sept 29) Golden City Lodge No. 1, Apprentice

Curry, William H
Proceedings 1876, pg 29 (1876 Sept 20) Golden City Lodge No. 1

Curry, Wm H
Proceedings 1873, pg 35 (1873 Oct 1), Golden City Lodge No. 1, Golden City
Proceedings 1874, pg 209 (1874 Sept 30), Golden City Lodge No. 1, Golden City
Proceedings 1875, pg 73 (1875 Sept 22) Golden City Lodge No. 1

Curtice H A
Proceedings 1876, pg 41 (1876 Sept 20), Weston Lodge No. 22, Littleton
Proceedings 1873, pg 51 (1873 Oct 1), Weston Lodge No. 22, Littleton
Proceedings 1874, pg 226 (1874 Sept 30), Weston Lodge No. 22, Littleton
Proceedings 1875, pg 88 (1875 Sept 22), Weston Lodge No. 22, Littleton

Curtice, Henry A
Proceedings 1872, pg 34 (1872 Sept 24), Weston Lodge No. 22, Littleton

Curtis, A F
Proceedings 1861-1869, pg 227 (1868 Oct 7), Washington Lodge No. 12, Georgetown
Proceedings 1861-1869, pg 309 (1869 Sept 29), Washington Lodge No. 12, Georgetown
Proceedings 1871, pg 24 (1871 Sept 27), Washington Lodge No. 12, Georgetown
Proceedings 1875, pg 81 (1875 Sept 22), Washington Lodge No. 12, Georgetown

Curtis, Andrew F
Proceedings 1870, pg 26 (1870 Sept 28), Washington Lodge No. 12, Georgetown
Proceedings 1872, pg 26 (1872 Sept 24), Washington Lodge No. 12, Georgetown
Proceedings 1873, pg 43 (1873 Oct 1), Washington Lodge No. 12, Georgetown
Proceedings 1874, pg 217 (1874 Sept 30), Washington Lodge No. 12, Georgetown
Proceedings 1876, pg 35 (1876 Sept 20), Washington Lodge No. 12, Georgetown

Curtis, E G
Proceedings 1872, pg 36 (1872 Sept 24), Ashlar Lodge U D, Colorado Springs

Curtis, H H
Proceedings 1876, pg 41 (1876 Sept 20), Weston Lodge No. 22, Littleton

Curtis, John
Proceedings 1876, pg 9 (1876 Oct 21) Grand Lodge of Pennsylvania, Grand Representative, of Philadelphia, PA"
Proceedings 1876, pg 53 (1876 Sept 20) Grand Lodge of Pennsylvania, of Philadelphia, PA

Curtis, Rodney
Proceedings 1861-1869, pg 151 (1865 Nov 7), Chivington Lodge No. 6, Central City
Proceedings 1861-1869, pg 169 (1866 Oct 2), Union Lodge No. 7, Denver
Proceedings 1861-1869, pg 195 (1867 Oct 8), Union Lodge No. 7, Denver
Proceedings 1861-1869, pg 225 (1868 Oct 7), Union Lodge No. 7, Denver
Proceedings 1861-1869, pg 307 (1869 Sept 29), Union Lodge No. 7, Denver
Proceedings 1870, pg 23 (1870 Sept 28), Union Lodge No. 7, Denver
Proceedings 1871, pg 21 (1871 Sept 27), Union Lodge No. 7, Denver
Proceedings 1872, pg 23 (1872 Sept 24), Union Lodge No. 7, Denver
Proceedings 1873, pg 40 (1873 Oct 1), Union Lodge No. 7, Denver
Proceedings 1874, pg 214 (1874 Sept 30), Union Lodge No. 7, Denver
Proceedings 1875, pg 78 (1875 Sept 22), Union Lodge No. 7, Denver
Proceedings 1876, pg 33 (1876 Sept 20), Union Lodge No. 7, Denver

Cushing
Proceedings 1874, pg 48 (1874 Sept 30) of Texas

Cushing, E H
Proceedings 1873, pg 61 (1873 Oct 1) Grand Lodge of Texas, Houston
Proceedings 1874, pg 124 (1874 Sept 30) Grand Lodge of Texas

Cushman, Madora
Proceedings 1861-1869, pg 102 (1863 Nov 3) Montana Lodge U D

Proceedings 1861-1869, pg 113 (1863 Nov 3), Montana Lodge U D, Central City, Apprentice

Cushman, William H
Proceedings 1876, pg 35 (1876 Sept 20), Washington Lodge No. 12, Georgetown

Cushman, Wm H
Proceedings 1875, pg 81 (1875 Sept 22), Washington Lodge No. 12, Georgetown

Cuthbert, N
Proceedings 1872, pg 36 (1872 Sept 24), Ashlar Lodge U D, Colorado Springs

Cutting, Walter
Proceedings 1871, pg 19 (1871 Sept 27) Denver Lodge No. 5
Proceedings 1872, pg 20 (1872 Sept 24), Denver Lodge No. 5, Denver
Proceedings 1873, pg 37 (1873 Oct 1), Denver Lodge No. 5, Denver
Proceedings 1874, pg 212 (1874 Sept 30), Denver Lodge No. 5, Denver, Stricken from the rolls

Czarnowsky, Henry
Proceedings 1875, pg 81 (1875 Sept 22), Washington Lodge No. 12, Georgetown

Dahlberg, Alfred
Proceedings 1876, pg 44 (1876 Sept 20) Del Norte Lodge U D

Daigre, Henry
Proceedings 1870, pg 30 (1870 Sept 28), Pueblo Lodge No. 17, Pueblo
Proceedings 1871, pg 28 (1871 Sept 27), Pueblo Lodge No. 17, Pueblo
Proceedings 1872, pg 31 (1872 Sept 24), Pueblo Lodge No. 17, Pueblo
Proceedings 1873, pg 47 (1873 Oct 1), Pueblo Lodge No. 17, Pueblo
Proceedings 1875, pg 85 (1875 Sept 22) Pueblo Lodge No. 17
Proceedings 1875, pg 90 (1875 Sept 22), Huerfano Lodge U D, Walsenburg
Proceedings 1876, pg 43 (1876 Sept 20), Huerfano Lodge No. 27, Walsenburg
Proceedings 1876, pg 48 (1876 Sept 20) Pueblo Lodge No. 17, 1876 Feb 10,

Dailey (Byers & Dailey)
Proceedings 1861-1869, pg 119 (1864 Mar 1) warrant drawn

Dailey, Baker & Smart
Proceedings 1871, pg cover (1871 Sept 26) Printers, Denver

Dailey, Don C
Proceedings 1861-1869, pg 226 (1868 Oct 7), Empire Lodge No. 8, Empire City

Proceedings 1872, pg 23 (1872 Sept 24), Empire Lodge No. 8, Empire

Dailey, Isaac
Proceedings 1876, pg 43 (1876 Sept 20), Huerfano Lodge No. 27, Walsenburg, Apprentice

Dailey, J L
Proceedings 1861-1869, pg 133 (1864 Nov 8) Denver Lodge No. 5

Dailey, James M
Proceedings 1873, pg 42 (1873 Oct 1), Washington Lodge No. 12, Georgetown

Dailey, Jas M
Proceedings 1875, pg 81 (1875 Sept 22), Washington Lodge No. 12, Georgetown

Dailey, John L
Proceedings 1861-1869, pg 112 (1863 Nov 3) Denver Lodge No. 5
Proceedings 1861-1869, pg 149 (1865 Nov 7), Nevada Lodge No. 4, Nevadaville
Proceedings 1861-1869, pg 223 (1868 Oct 7) Denver Lodge No. 5
Proceedings 1861-1869, pg 299 (1869 Sept 29) Grand Marshal
Proceedings 1870, pg 21 (1870 Sept 28), Denver Lodge No. 5, Denver
Proceedings 1871, pg 19 (1871 Sept 27) Denver Lodge No. 5
Proceedings 1872, pg 20 (1872 Sept 24), Denver Lodge No. 5, Denver
Proceedings 1873, pg 37 (1873 Oct 1), Denver Lodge No. 5, Denver
Proceedings 1874, pg 211 (1874 Sept 30), Denver Lodge No. 5, Denver
Proceedings 1875, pg 75 (1875 Sept 22) Denver Lodge No. 5
Proceedings 1876, pg 31 (1876 Sept 20) Denver Lodge No. 5

Dailey, Peter H
Proceedings 1874, pg 224 (1874 Sept 30), Collins Lodge No. 19, Fort Collins, Larimer County

Dailey, W M
Proceedings 1861-1869, pg 149 (1865 Nov 7), Nevada Lodge No. 4, Nevadaville
Proceedings 1861-1869, pg 167 (1866 Oct 2) Denver Lodge No. 5

Dailey, William M
Proceedings 1876, pg 31 (1876 Sept 20) Denver Lodge No. 5

Dailey, Wm
Proceedings 1874, pg 228 (1874 Sept 30), Evanston Lodge U D, Evanston, Uintah County, Wyoming Territory

Dailey, Wm M
Proceedings 1861-1869, pg 112 (1863 Nov 3) Denver Lodge No. 5
Proceedings 1861-1869, pg 133 (1864 Nov 8) Denver Lodge No. 5

Colorado's Territorial Masons

Dailey, Wm M, cont.
Proceedings 1870, pg 21 (1870 Sept 28), Denver Lodge No. 5, Denver
Proceedings 1871, pg 19 (1871 Sept 27) Denver Lodge No. 5
Proceedings 1872, pg 20 (1872 Sept 24), Denver Lodge No. 5, Denver
Proceedings 1873, pg 37 (1873 Oct 1), Denver Lodge No. 5, Denver
Proceedings 1874, pg 211 (1874 Sept 30), Denver Lodge No. 5, Denver
Proceedings 1875, pg 75 (1875 Sept 22) Denver Lodge No. 5
Proceedings 1861-1869, pg 223 (1868 Oct 7) Denver Lodge No. 5

Daily (Byers & Dailey)
Proceedings 1861-1869, pg 159 (1866 Oct 1) warrant

Daily Advertiser
Proceedings 1861-1869, pg 317 (1869 Sept 29), of Detroit, MI

Daily Colorado Sentinel
Colorado University Cornerstone Laying, pg 4 (1875 Sept 20) cornerstone contents

Daily Rocky Mountain News
Colorado University Cornerstone Laying, pg 4 (1875 Sept 20) cornerstone contents

Daily Times
Colorado University Cornerstone Laying, pg 4 (1875 Sept 20) cornerstone contents, Denver

Daily, D C
Proceedings 1870, pg 24 (1870 Sept 28), Empire Lodge No. 8, Empire

Daily, Don C
Proceedings 1861-1869, pg 308 (1869 Sept 29), Empire Lodge No. 8, Empire City
Proceedings 1873, pg 41 (1873 Oct 1), Empire Lodge No. 8, Empire
Proceedings 1874, pg 215 (1874 Sept 30), Empire Lodge No. 8, Empire

Daily, J L
Proceedings 1861-1869, pg 305 (1869 Sept 29) Denver Lodge No. 5

Daily, James M
Proceedings 1872, pg 25 (1872 Sept 24), Washington Lodge No. 12, Georgetown
Proceedings 1874, pg 217 (1874 Sept 30), Washington Lodge No. 12, Georgetown
Proceedings 1876, pg 35 (1876 Sept 20), Washington Lodge No. 12, Georgetown

Daily, John L
Proceedings 1861-1869, pg 193 (1867 Oct 8) Denver Lodge No. 5

Daily, Wm M
Proceedings 1861-1869, pg 193 (1867 Oct 8) Denver Lodge No. 5

Proceedings 1861-1869, pg 305 (1869 Sept 29) Denver Lodge No. 5

Daley, Richard
Proceedings 1874, pg 224 (1874 Sept 30), Laramie Lodge No. 18, Laramie City, Apprentice

Dalliba, J E
Proceedings 1861-1869, pg 81 (1863 Apr 18) Denver Lodge No. 5

Dalton, Thomas
Proceedings 1870, pg 74 (1827 June 18) United Grand Lodge of England

Dame, Charles C
Proceedings 1861-1869, pg 260 (1868 June), Grand Master, Grand Lodge of Massachusetts
Proceedings 1870, pg 68 (1869 Sept 8) Grand Lodge of Massachusetts

Dana, Charles C
Proceedings 1861-1869, pg 331 (1868 Dec 9) Grand Master, Grand Lodge of Massachusetts

Dane, Geo
Proceedings 1872, pg 23 (1872 Sept 24), Union Lodge No. 7, Denver

Dane, George
Proceedings 1870, pg 23 (1870 Sept 28), Union Lodge No. 7, Denver
Proceedings 1871, pg 21 (1871 Sept 27), Union Lodge No. 7, Denver
Proceedings 1873, pg 40 (1873 Oct 1), Union Lodge No. 7, Denver
Proceedings 1874, pg 214 (1874 Sept 30), Union Lodge No. 7, Denver
Proceedings 1875, pg 78 (1875 Sept 22), Union Lodge No. 7, Denver
Proceedings 1876, pg 33 (1876 Sept 20), Union Lodge No. 7, Denver

Daniel, R N
Proceedings 1871, pg 28 (1871 Sept 27), Pueblo Lodge No. 17, Pueblo
Proceedings 1861-1869, pg 229 (1868 Oct 7), Pueblo Lodge U D, Pueblo
Proceedings 1861-1869, pg 312 (1869 Sept 29), Pueblo Lodge No. 17, Pueblo
Proceedings 1872, pg 30 (1872 Sept 24), Pueblo Lodge No. 17, Pueblo
Proceedings 1875, pg 85 (1875 Sept 22) Pueblo Lodge No. 17
Proceedings 1876, pg 38 (1876 Sept 20) Pueblo Lodge No. 17
Proceedings 1874, pg 222 (1874 Sept 30), Pueblo Lodge No. 17, Pueblo, Pueblo County

Daniels, Robert N
Proceedings 1870, pg 30 (1870 Sept 28), Pueblo Lodge No. 17, Pueblo
Proceedings 1873, pg 47 (1873 Oct 1), Pueblo Lodge No. 17, Pueblo

Danielson, F M
   Proceedings 1861-1869, pg 168 (1866 Oct 2), Chivington Lodge No. 6, Central City
   Proceedings 1861-1869, pg 194 (1867 Oct 8), Chivington Lodge No. 6, Central City
   Proceedings 1861-1869, pg 224 (1868 Oct 7), Chivington Lodge No. 6, Central City
   Proceedings 1861-1869, pg 306 (1869 Sept 29), Central Lodge No. 6, Central City
   Proceedings 1871, pg 13 (1871 Sept 26) Denver Lodge No. 5
   Proceedings 1871, pg 19 (1871 Sept 27) Denver Lodge No. 5
   Proceedings 1873, pg 37 (1873 Oct 1), Denver Lodge No. 5, Denver
   Proceedings 1874, pg 211 (1874 Sept 30), Denver Lodge No. 5, Denver

Danielson, Frank M
   Proceedings 1870, pg 23 (1870 Sept 28), Central Lodge No. 6, Central City, Dimitted
   Proceedings 1875, pg 75 (1875 Sept 22) Denver Lodge No. 5

Dargen, D G
   Proceedings 1861-1869, pg 303 (1869 Sept 29) Golden City Lodge No. 1
   Proceedings 1870, pg 19 (1870 Sept 28), Golden City Lodge No. 1, Golden City
   Proceedings 1871, pg 17 (1871 Sept 27), Golden City Lodge No. 1, Golden City
   Proceedings 1872, pg 17 (1872 Sept 24), Golden City Lodge No. 1, Golden City
   Proceedings 1861-1869, pg 131 (1864 Nov 8) Golden City Lodge No. 1
   Proceedings 1861-1869, pg 165 (1866 Oct 2) Golden City Lodge No. 1
   Proceedings 1861-1869, pg 191 (1867 Oct 8) Golden City Lodge No. 1
   Proceedings 1861-1869, pg 221 (1868 Oct 7) Golden City Lodge No. 1

Dargin, David G
   Proceedings 1861-1869, pg 110 (1863 Nov 3) Golden City Lodge No. 1

Darnell, D O
   Proceedings 1861-1869, pg 179 (1867 Oct 7), Washington Lodge No. 12, Georgetown
   Proceedings 1861-1869, pg 227 (1868 Oct 7), Washington Lodge No. 12, Georgetown

Darnell, J K
   Proceedings 1875, pg 89 (1875 Sept 22), Doric Lodge No. 25, Fairplay
   Proceedings 1876, pg 42 (1876 Sept 20), Doric Lodge No. 25, Fairplay

Darnell, J M
   Proceedings 1875, pg 73 (1875 Sept 22) Golden City Lodge No. 1

Darnell, John
   Proceedings 1876, pg 29 (1876 Sept 20) Golden City Lodge No. 1

Darrah, B F
   Proceedings 1861-1869, pg 227 (1868 Oct 7), Washington Lodge No. 12, Georgetown
   Proceedings 1871, pg 24 (1871 Sept 27), Washington Lodge No. 12, Georgetown

Darrah, Ben F
   Proceedings 1875, pg 81 (1875 Sept 22), Washington Lodge No. 12, Georgetown

Darrah, Benj F
   Proceedings 1861-1869, pg 309 (1869 Sept 29), Washington Lodge No. 12, Georgetown
   Proceedings 1870, pg 26 (1870 Sept 28), Washington Lodge No. 12, Georgetown
   Proceedings 1872, pg 26 (1872 Sept 24), Washington Lodge No. 12, Georgetown
   Proceedings 1873, pg 43 (1873 Oct 1), Washington Lodge No. 12, Georgetown
   Proceedings 1876, pg 50 (1876 Sept 20), Washington Lodge No. 12, Georgetown

Darrah, Benjamin F
   Proceedings 1874, pg 217 (1874 Sept 30), Washington Lodge No. 12, Georgetown
   Proceedings 1876, pg 35 (1876 Sept 20), Washington Lodge No. 12, Georgetown

Dassler, George W
   Proceedings 1861-1869, pg 145 (1865 Nov 7) Denver Lodge No. 5, Senior Grand Deacon

Daugherty, Thomas C
   Proceedings 1871, pg 27 (1871 Sept 27), Cheyenne Lodge No. 16, Cheyenne, Wyoming Territory

Davidson, A
   Proceedings 1861-1869, pg 124 (1864 Nov 8) Denver Lodge No. 5, Grand Tyler
   Proceedings 1861-1869, pg 133 (1864 Nov 8) Denver Lodge No. 5
   Proceedings 1861-1869, pg 136 (1865 Nov 6) Grand Tyler
   Proceedings 1861-1869, pg 159 (1866 Oct 1) warrant
   Proceedings 1861-1869, pg 223 (1868 Oct 7) Denver Lodge No. 5
   Proceedings 1861-1869, pg 305 (1869 Sept 29) Denver Lodge No. 5

Davidson, Alex
   Proceedings 1861-1869, pg 148 (1865 Nov 7), Nevada Lodge No. 4, Nevadaville
   Proceedings 1861-1869, pg 160 (1866 Oct 2) Denver Lodge No. 5, Grand Tyler
   Proceedings 1861-1869, pg 161 (1866 Oct 2) Grand Tyler
   Proceedings 1861-1869, pg 166 (1866 Oct 2) Denver Lodge No. 5
   Proceedings 1861-1869, pg 193 (1867 Oct 8) Denver Lodge No. 5
   Proceedings 1870, pg 21 (1870 Sept 28), Denver Lodge No. 5, Denver
   Proceedings 1872, pg 20 (1872 Sept 24), Denver Lodge No. 5, Denver
   Proceedings 1873, pg 37 (1873 Oct 1), Denver Lodge No. 5, Denver

Colorado's Territorial Masons

Davidson, Alex, cont.
Proceedings 1874, pg 211 (1874 Sept 30), Denver Lodge No. 5, Denver
Proceedings 1875, pg 75 (1875 Sept 22) Denver Lodge No. 5

Davidson, Alexander
Proceedings 1871, pg 19 (1871 Sept 27) Denver Lodge No. 5
Proceedings 1876, pg 31 (1876 Sept 20) Denver Lodge No. 5

Davidson, David
Proceedings 1876, pg 33 (1876 Sept 20), Union Lodge No. 7, Denver

Davidson, F M
Proceedings 1872, pg 15 (1872 Sept 24) Junior Grand Steward
Proceedings 1872, pg 19 (1872 Sept 24), Denver Lodge No. 5, Denver
Proceedings 1876, pg 31 (1876 Sept 20) Denver Lodge No. 5

Davidson, J C
Proceedings 1861-1869, pg 112 (1863 Nov 3) Denver Lodge No. 5
Proceedings 1861-1869, pg 133 (1864 Nov 8) Denver Lodge No. 5
Proceedings 1861-1869, pg 193 (1867 Oct 8) Denver Lodge No. 5
Proceedings 1861-1869, pg 223 (1868 Oct 7) Denver Lodge No. 5
Proceedings 1861-1869, pg 305 (1869 Sept 29) Denver Lodge No. 5
Proceedings 1870, pg 21 (1870 Sept 28), Denver Lodge No. 5, Denver
Proceedings 1873, pg 37 (1873 Oct 1), Denver Lodge No. 5, Denver

Davidson, Jere C
Proceedings 1872, pg 20 (1872 Sept 24), Denver Lodge No. 5, Denver

Davidson, Jeremiah C
Proceedings 1874, pg 212 (1874 Sept 30), Denver Lodge No. 5, Denver, died

Davidson, Joe C
Proceedings 1871, pg 19 (1871 Sept 27) Denver Lodge No. 5

Davidson, Joseph C
Proceedings 1871, pg 20 (1871 Sept 27) Denver Lodge No. 5, died
Proceedings 1871, pg 32 (1871 Sept 27), Denver Lodge No. 5, Denver

Davies, William Abraham
Proceedings 1861-1869, pg 240 (1867 Oct 8) Grand Master of California

Davis, A A J
Proceedings 1870, pg 31 (1870 Sept 28), Collins Lodge No. 19, Fort Collins
Proceedings 1876, pg 39 (1876 Sept 20), Collins Lodge No. 19, Fort Collins

Davis, A B
Proceedings 1861-1869, pg 112 (1863 Nov 3), Chivington Lodge No. 6, Central City
Proceedings 1861-1869, pg 134 (1864 Nov 8), Chivington Lodge No. 6, Central City
Proceedings 1861-1869, pg 150 (1865 Nov 7), Chivington Lodge No. 6, Central City
Proceedings 1861-1869, pg 168 (1866 Oct 2), Chivington Lodge No. 6, Central City
Proceedings 1861-1869, pg 194 (1867 Oct 8), Chivington Lodge No. 6, Central City
Proceedings 1861-1869, pg 224 (1868 Oct 7), Chivington Lodge No. 6, Central City
Proceedings 1861-1869, pg 306 (1869 Sept 29), Central Lodge No. 6, Central City
Proceedings 1870, pg 22 (1870 Sept 28), Central Lodge No. 6, Central City
Proceedings 1871, pg 20 (1871 Sept 27), Central Lodge No. 6, Central
Proceedings 1872, pg 22 (1872 Sept 24), Denver Lodge No. 5, Denver

Davis, Adriel B
Proceedings 1861-1869, pg 78 (1862 Nov 4), Chivington Lodge No. 6, Central City, Fellowcraft

Davis, Albert A J
Proceedings 1874, pg 224 (1874 Sept 30), Collins Lodge No. 19, Fort Collins, Larimer County
Proceedings 1875, pg 86 (1875 Sept 22), Collins Lodge No. 19, Fort Collins
Proceedings 1871, pg 30 (1871 Sept 27), Collins Lodge No. 19, Fort Collins
Proceedings 1872, pg 33 (1872 Sept 24), Collins Lodge No. 19, Fort Collins
Proceedings 1873, pg 49 (1873 Oct 1), Collins Lodge No. 19, Fort Collins

Davis, C C
Proceedings 1861-1869, pg 151 (1865 Nov 7), Chivington Lodge No. 6, Central City, Fellowcraft
Proceedings 1861-1869, pg 169 (1866 Oct 2), Union Lodge No. 7, Denver
Proceedings 1861-1869, pg 195 (1867 Oct 8), Union Lodge No. 7, Denver
Proceedings 1861-1869, pg 225 (1868 Oct 7), Union Lodge No. 7, Denver
Proceedings 1861-1869, pg 307 (1869 Sept 29), Union Lodge No. 7, Denver
Proceedings 1876, pg 33 (1876 Sept 20), Union Lodge No. 7, Denver
Proceedings 1876, pg 50 (1876 Sept 20), Union Lodge No. 7, Denver

Davis, Chamber C
Proceedings 1873, pg 40 (1873 Oct 1), Union Lodge No. 7, Denver
Proceedings 1871, pg 21 (1871 Sept 27), Union Lodge No. 7, Denver
Proceedings 1872, pg 23 (1872 Sept 24), Union Lodge No. 7, Denver
Proceedings 1874, pg 214 (1874 Sept 30), Union Lodge No. 7, Denver

Proceedings 1875, pg 78 (1875 Sept 22), Union Lodge No. 7, Denver

Proceedings 1870, pg 23 (1870 Sept 28), Union Lodge No. 7, Denver

Davis, David

Proceedings 1874, pg 219 (1874 Sept 30), Columbia Lodge No. 14, Boulder, Boulder County

Proceedings 1875, pg 83 (1875 Sept 22), Columbia Lodge No. 14, Boulder

Proceedings 1876, pg 37 (1876 Sept 20), Columbia Lodge No. 14, Boulder

Davis, F N

Proceedings 1876, pg 31 (1876 Sept 20) Denver Lodge No. 5

Davis, Flavius N

Proceedings 1875, pg 75 (1875 Sept 22) Denver Lodge No. 5

Davis, Ira W

Proceedings 1872, pg 19 (1872 Sept 24), Nevada Lodge No. 4, Bald Mountain, Fellowcraft

Proceedings 1873, pg 36 (1873 Oct 1), Nevada Lodge No. 4, Nevada

Proceedings 1874, pg 210 (1874 Sept 30), Nevada Lodge No. 4, Bald Mountain, Gilpin County

Proceedings 1875, pg 74 (1875 Sept 22), Nevada Lodge No. 4, Nevada

Proceedings 1876, pg 30 (1876 Sept 20) Nevada Lodge No. 4

Proceedings 1876, pg 50 (1876 Sept 20) Nevada Lodge No. 4

Davis, J E

Proceedings 1874, pg 225 (1874 Sept 30), Occidental Lodge No. 20, Greeley

Proceedings 1875, pg 87 (1875 Sept 22), Occidental Lodge No. 20, Greeley

Proceedings 1876, pg 40 (1876 Sept 20), Occidental Lodge No. 20, Greeley

Davis, J P

Proceedings 1870, pg 24 (1870 Sept 28), Empire Lodge No. 8, Empire

Davis, James P

Proceedings 1861-1869, pg 308 (1869 Sept 29), Empire Lodge No. 8, Empire City

Proceedings 1872, pg 24 (1872 Sept 24), Empire Lodge No. 8, Empire, died

Proceedings 1872, pg 39 (1872 Sept 24), Empire Lodge No. 8, Empire

Davis, Jas P

Proceedings 1861-1869, pg 226 (1868 Oct 7), Empire Lodge No. 8, Empire City

Davis, John

Proceedings 1861-1869, pg 228 (1868 Oct 7), Columbia Lodge No. 14, Columbia City, Fellowcraft

Proceedings 1861-1869, pg 311 (1869 Sept 29), Columbia Lodge No. 14, Boulder City

Proceedings 1870, pg 27 (1870 Sept 28), Columbia Lodge No. 14, Boulder City

Proceedings 1871, pg 25 (1871 Sept 27), Columbia Lodge No. 14, Boulder City

Proceedings 1872, pg 28 (1872 Sept 24), Columbia Lodge No. 14, Boulder

Proceedings 1873, pg 44 (1873 Oct 1), Columbia Lodge No. 14, Boulder

Proceedings 1874, pg 219 (1874 Sept 30), Columbia Lodge No. 14, Boulder, Boulder County

Proceedings 1875, pg 83 (1875 Sept 22), Columbia Lodge No. 14, Boulder

Proceedings 1876, pg 37 (1876 Sept 20), Columbia Lodge No. 14, Boulder

Davis, Joseph

Proceedings 1861-1869, pg 167 (1866 Oct 2) Denver Lodge No. 5, Fellowcraft

Proceedings 1861-1869, pg 193 (1867 Oct 8) Denver Lodge No. 5

Proceedings 1861-1869, pg 223 (1868 Oct 7) Denver Lodge No. 5

Proceedings 1870, pg 21 (1870 Sept 28), Denver Lodge No. 5, Denver

Proceedings 1871, pg 19 (1871 Sept 27) Denver Lodge No. 5

Proceedings 1872, pg 20 (1872 Sept 24), Denver Lodge No. 5, Denver

Proceedings 1873, pg 37 (1873 Oct 1), Denver Lodge No. 5, Denver

Proceedings 1874, pg 211 (1874 Sept 30), Denver Lodge No. 5, Denver

Proceedings 1875, pg 76 (1875 Sept 22) Denver Lodge No. 5, Stricken from the rolls

Proceedings 1875, pg 91 (1875 Sept 22), Las Animas Lodge U D, Trinidad

Proceedings 1876, pg 9 (1875 Oct 17), granted demit from Denver Lodge No. 5, charter member Las Animas Lodge No. 28

Proceedings 1876, pg 44 (1876 Sept 20), Las Animas Lodge No. 28, Trinidad

Proceedings 1876, pg 48 (1876 Sept 20) Denver Lodge No. 5, 1876 Nov 6

Proceedings 1876, pg 51 (1876 Sept 20) Denver Lodge No. 5, 1875 Mar 6

Davis, Lewis

Proceedings 1861-1869, pg 110 (1863 Nov 3) Golden City Lodge No. 1

Proceedings 1861-1869, pg 131 (1864 Nov 8) Golden City Lodge No. 1

Proceedings 1861-1869, pg 147 (1865 Nov 7) Golden City Lodge No. 1

Proceedings 1861-1869, pg 165 (1866 Oct 2) Golden City Lodge No. 1

Proceedings 1861-1869, pg 191 (1867 Oct 8) Golden City Lodge No. 1

Proceedings 1861-1869, pg 221 (1868 Oct 7) Golden City Lodge No. 1

Proceedings 1861-1869, pg 303 (1869 Sept 29) Golden City Lodge No. 1

Proceedings 1870, pg 19 (1870 Sept 28), Golden City Lodge No. 1, Golden City

Davis, Lewis, cont.
    Proceedings 1871, pg 17 (1871 Sept 27), Golden City Lodge No. 1, Golden City
    Proceedings 1872, pg 17 (1872 Sept 24), Golden City Lodge No. 1, Golden City
    Proceedings 1873, pg 35 (1873 Oct 1), Golden City Lodge No. 1, Golden City
    Proceedings 1874, pg 209 (1874 Sept 30), Golden City Lodge No. 1, Golden City
    Proceedings 1875, pg 74 (1875 Sept 22) Golden City Lodge No. 1, Stricken from the rolls

Davis, N R
    Proceedings 1872, pg 30 (1872 Sept 24), Cheyenne Lodge No. 16, Cheyenne, Wyoming Territory
    Proceedings 1873, pg 46 (1873 Oct 1), Cheyenne Lodge No. 16, Cheyenne, Wyoming Territory
    Proceedings 1874, pg 221 (1874 Sept 30), Cheyenne Lodge No. 16, Cheyenne, Wyoming Territory

Davis, Park
    Proceedings 1872, pg 44 (1872 Sept 24) St Albans, Grand Lodge of Vermont
    Proceedings 1873, pg 61 (1873 Oct 1) Grand Lodge of Vermont, St Albans
    Proceedings 1874, pg 128 (1874 Sept 30) Grand Lodge of Vermont

Davis, T A
    Proceedings 1872, pg 32 (1872 Sept 24), Laramie Lodge No. 18, Laramie, Wyoming Territory
    Proceedings 1873, pg 48 (1873 Oct 1), Laramie Lodge No. 18, Laramie, Wyoming Territory
    Proceedings 1874, pg 223 (1874 Sept 30), Laramie Lodge No. 18, Laramie City
    Proceedings 1876, pg 45 (1876 Sept 20), King Solomon Lodge U D, West Las Animas

Davis, T B
    Proceedings 1861-1869, pg 308 (1869 Sept 29), Union Lodge No. 7, Denver, received permission to receive degrees in Canada

Davis, W P
    Proceedings 1871, pg 27 (1871 Sept 27), Cheyenne Lodge No. 16, Cheyenne, Wyoming Territory
    Proceedings 1873, pg 46 (1873 Oct 1), Cheyenne Lodge No. 16, Cheyenne, Wyoming Territory
    Proceedings 1874, pg 221 (1874 Sept 30), Cheyenne Lodge No. 16, Cheyenne, Wyoming Territory

Davis, W T
    Proceedings 1874, pg 222 (1874 Sept 30), Pueblo Lodge No. 17, Pueblo, Pueblo County
    Proceedings 1875, pg 85 (1875 Sept 22) Pueblo Lodge No. 17
    Proceedings 1876, pg 38 (1876 Sept 20) Pueblo Lodge No. 17

Davis, Weston T
    Proceedings 1876, pg 45 (1876 Sept 20) South Pueblo Lodge U D

Davis, William A
    Proceedings 1861-1869, pg 324 (1868 Oct 18) Grand Master, Grand Lodge of California

Davis, Wm B
    Proceedings 1870, pg 29 (1870 Sept 28), Cheyenne Lodge No. 16, Cheyenne, Wyoming Territory

Davis, Wm P
    Proceedings 1861-1869, pg 312 (1869 Sept 29), Cheyenne Lodge No. 16, Cheyenne, Fellowcraft
    Proceedings 1872, pg 30 (1872 Sept 24), Cheyenne Lodge No. 16, Cheyenne, Wyoming Territory

Dawkins
    Proceedings 1874, pg 56 (1874 Sept 30) Grand Lodge of Florida
    Proceedings 1874, pg 107 (1874 Sept 30)

Dawkins, D C
    Proceedings 1870, pg 52 (1870 Jan 12) Grand Secretary, Grand Lodge of Florida
    Proceedings 1870, pg 53 (1870 Jan 12) Grand Secretary, Grand Lodge of Florida
    Proceedings 1872, pg 43 (1872 Sept 24) Jacksonville, Grand Lodge of Florida
    Proceedings 1872, pg 59 (1872 Sept 24) Grand Lodge of Florida
    Proceedings 1873, pg 60 (1873 Oct 1) Grand Lodge of Florida, Jacksonville

Dawkins, Dewitt C
    Proceedings 1861-1869, pg 316 (1869 Sept 29) Grand Lodge of Florida
    Proceedings 1861-1869, pg 328 (1868 Jan 13) Grand Master, Grand Lodge of Florida
    Proceedings 1870, pg 34 (1870 Sept 28) Grand Secretary, Grand Lodge of Florida
    Proceedings 1871, pg 35 (1871 Sept 27) Grand Secretary, Grand Lodge of Florida
    Proceedings 1874, pg 55 (1874 Sept 30) Grand Lodge of Florida
    Proceedings 1874, pg 204 (1874 Sept 30) Grand Lodge of Florida, Jacksonville
    Proceedings 1875, pg 96 (1875 Sept 22) Grand Lodge of Florida, Jacksonville
    Proceedings 1876, pg 54 (1876 Sept 20) Grand Lodge of Florida, Jacksonville

Dawley, James M
    Proceedings 1874, pg 219 (1874 Sept 30), Columbia Lodge No. 14, Boulder, Boulder County
    Proceedings 1875, pg 83 (1875 Sept 22), Columbia Lodge No. 14, Boulder
    Proceedings 1876, pg 37 (1876 Sept 20), Columbia Lodge No. 14, Boulder
    Proceedings 1876, pg 50 (1876 Sept 20), Columbia Lodge No. 14, Boulder

Dawon, J E
    Proceedings 1861-1869, pg 54 (1862 Nov 4) Golden City Lodge No. 1
    Proceedings 1861-1869, pg 31 (1861 Dec 10) committee
    Proceedings 1861-1869, pg 31 (1861 Dec 10) Senior Grand Deacon

Proceedings 1861-1869, pg 32 (1861 Dec 10) Golden City Lodge No. 1
Proceedings 1861-1869, pg 33 (1861 Dec 10) committee
Proceedings 1861-1869, pg 33 (1861 Dec 10) committee
Proceedings 1861-1869, pg 38 (1861 Dec 12) Grand Marshal

Dawson, James E
Proceedings 1861-1869, pg 42 (1861 Dec 10) Golden City Lodge No. 1

Dawson, Jonathan S
Proceedings 1861-1869, pg 348 (1868 Oct 4) Grand Master, Grand Lodge of Tennessee

Day, William J
Proceedings 1876, pg 44 (1876 Sept 20) Del Norte Lodge U D, Apprentice

Dayly, Peter H
Proceedings 1875, pg 86 (1875 Sept 22), Collins Lodge No. 19, Fort Collins

Dayton
Proceedings 1861-1869, pg 178 (1867 Aug 26) petition to form a lodge

Dayton, T J
Proceedings 1870, pg 6 (1870 Jan 31) Laramie City Lodge U D
Proceedings 1870, pg 30 (1870 Sept 28), Laramie Lodge No. 18, Laramie, Wyoming Territory
Proceedings 1871, pg 29 (1871 Sept 27), Laramie Lodge No. 18, Laramie, Wyoming Territory
Proceedings 1872, pg 32 (1872 Sept 24), Laramie Lodge No. 18, Laramie, Wyoming Territory
Proceedings 1873, pg 6 (1873 Sept 30), Laramie Lodge No. 18, Laramie, Wyoming Territory
Proceedings 1873, pg 48 (1873 Oct 1), Laramie Lodge No. 18, Laramie, Wyoming Territory
Proceedings 1873, pg 48 (1873 Oct 1), Laramie Lodge No. 18, Laramie, Wyoming Territory
Proceedings 1874, pg 223 (1874 Sept 30), Laramie Lodge No. 18, Laramie City

Dcurran, Benj
Proceedings 1875, pg 96 (1875 Sept 22) Grand Lodge of Nova Scotia, Halifax

De Grasse, John V
Proceedings 1870, pg 73 (1858 June 30) Prince Hall Grand Lodge

Deal, William
Proceedings 1876, pg 43 (1876 Sept 20), Huerfano Lodge No. 27, Walsenburg

Dean, Thos J
Proceedings 1874, pg 229 (1874 Sept 30), Idaho Springs Lodge U D, Idaho Springs

DeBotie, H M
Proceedings 1875, pg 81 (1875 Sept 22), Washington Lodge No. 12, Georgetown, Demitted

Dechert, Henry M
Proceedings 1873, pg 61 (1873 Oct 1) Grand Lodge of Pennsylvania, Providence

Dechest, Henry M
Proceedings 1874, pg 120 (1874 Sept 30) Grand Lodge of Pennsylvania

Defferbacker, J W
Proceedings 1874, pg 221 (1874 Sept 30), Cheyenne Lodge No. 16, Cheyenne, Wyoming Territory

Deitch, Jonas
Proceedings 1861-1869, pg 134 (1864 Nov 8), Union Lodge No. 7, Denver
Proceedings 1861-1869, pg 151 (1865 Nov 7), Chivington Lodge No. 6, Central City

Deitsch, Isador
Proceedings 1871, pg 21 (1871 Sept 27), Union Lodge No. 7, Denver
Proceedings 1873, pg 40 (1873 Oct 1), Union Lodge No. 7, Denver
Proceedings 1874, pg 214 (1874 Sept 30), Union Lodge No. 7, Denver, Demitted

Deitsch, Isadore
Proceedings 1861-1869, pg 169 (1866 Oct 2), Union Lodge No. 7, Denver
Proceedings 1861-1869, pg 195 (1867 Oct 8), Union Lodge No. 7, Denver
Proceedings 1861-1869, pg 225 (1868 Oct 7), Union Lodge No. 7, Denver
Proceedings 1861-1869, pg 307 (1869 Sept 29), Union Lodge No. 7, Denver
Proceedings 1870, pg 23 (1870 Sept 28), Union Lodge No. 7, Denver
Proceedings 1872, pg 23 (1872 Sept 24), Union Lodge No. 7, Denver

Deitsch, Jonas
Proceedings 1861-1869, pg 169 (1866 Oct 2), Union Lodge No. 7, Denver
Proceedings 1861-1869, pg 195 (1867 Oct 8), Union Lodge No. 7, Denver
Proceedings 1861-1869, pg 225 (1868 Oct 7), Union Lodge No. 7, Denver
Proceedings 1861-1869, pg 307 (1869 Sept 29), Union Lodge No. 7, Denver
Proceedings 1870, pg 23 (1870 Sept 28), Union Lodge No. 7, Denver
Proceedings 1871, pg 21 (1871 Sept 27), Union Lodge No. 7, Denver
Proceedings 1872, pg 23 (1872 Sept 24), Union Lodge No. 7, Denver, Dimitted

Deitsch, M
Proceedings 1861-1869, pg 223 (1868 Oct 7) Denver Lodge No. 5
Proceedings 1861-1869, pg 305 (1869 Sept 29) Denver Lodge No. 5
Proceedings 1870, pg 21 (1870 Sept 28), Denver Lodge No. 5, Denver

Del Norte Lodge No. 29
Proceedings 1876, pg 52 (1876 Sept 20)

Del Norte Lodge No. 29, Del Norte
Proceedings 1876, pg 24 (1876 Sept 20) charter granted

Del Norte Lodge U D
    Proceedings 1876, pg 7 (1875 Sept 24) dispensation granted
    Proceedings 1876, pg 12 (1876 Sept 19) dues paid and petition for a charter received
    Proceedings 1876, pg 13 (1876 Aug 20) dispensation fee paid

Del Norte Lodge U D, Del Norte
    Proceedings 1876, pg 13 (1876 Sept 16) dues paid
    Proceedings 1876, pg 24 (1876 Sept 20) returns correct

Demars, Paul
    Proceedings 1874, pg 224 (1874 Sept 30), Laramie Lodge No. 18, Laramie City, Fellowcraft,

Denis, Joseph
    Proceedings 1872, pg 21 (1872 Sept 24), Denver Lodge No. 5, Denver, Apprentice
    Proceedings 1873, pg 38 (1873 Oct 1), Central Lodge No. 6, Central City
    Proceedings 1875, pg 77 (1875 Sept 22), Central Lodge No. 6, Central City
    Proceedings 1875, pg 89 (1875 Sept 22) Idaho Springs Lodge U D
    Proceedings 1876, pg 48 (1876 Sept 20), Central Lodge No. 6, Central City, 1875 Sept 22

Denison, Charles W
    Proceedings 1871, pg 24 (1871 Sept 27), Washington Lodge No. 12, Georgetown
    Proceedings 1874, pg 218 (1874 Sept 30), Washington Lodge No. 12, Georgetown, Stricken from the rolls

Denison, Chas W
    Proceedings 1861-1869, pg 309 (1869 Sept 29), Washington Lodge No. 12, Georgetown
    Proceedings 1872, pg 25 (1872 Sept 24), Washington Lodge No. 12, Georgetown
    Proceedings 1873, pg 42 (1873 Oct 1), Washington Lodge No. 12, Georgetown

Deniston, W W
    Proceedings 1873, pg 3 (1873 Sept 30) Junior Grand Warden
    Proceedings 1875, pg 79 (1875 Sept 22), Union Lodge No. 7, Denver, Stricken from the rolls

Deniston, Ward W
    Proceedings 1870, pg 23 (1870 Sept 28), Union Lodge No. 7, Denver
    Proceedings 1871, pg 21 (1871 Sept 27), Union Lodge No. 7, Denver
    Proceedings 1872, pg 23 (1872 Sept 24), Union Lodge No. 7, Denver
    Proceedings 1873, pg 40 (1873 Oct 1), Union Lodge No. 7, Denver

Dennis, B C
    Proceedings 1861-1869, pg 99 (1863 Nov 2) Grand Chaplain
    Proceedings 1861-1869, pg 131 (1864 Nov 8) Golden City Lodge No. 1, dimitted

Dennis, Joseph
    Proceedings 1874, pg 213 (1874 Sept 30), Central Lodge No. 6, Central
    Proceedings 1874, pg 229 (1874 Sept 30), Idaho Springs Lodge U D, Idaho Springs
    Proceedings 1876, pg 43 (1876 Sept 20) Idaho Springs Lodge No. 26
    Proceedings 1876, pg 50 (1876 Sept 20) Idaho Springs Lodge No. 26

Dennison, C W
    Proceedings 1861-1869, pg 227 (1868 Oct 7), Washington Lodge No. 12, Georgetown, Fellowcraft

Dennison, Chas W
    Proceedings 1870, pg 26 (1870 Sept 28), Washington Lodge No. 12, Georgetown

Denniston, W W
    Proceedings 1861-1869, pg 307 (1869 Sept 29), Union Lodge No. 7, Denver

Denniston, Ward W
    Proceedings 1874, pg 214 (1874 Sept 30), Union Lodge No. 7, Denver

Densmore, George
    Proceedings 1874, pg 217 (1874 Sept 30), Washington Lodge No. 12, Georgetown
    Proceedings 1875, pg 81 (1875 Sept 22), Washington Lodge No. 12, Georgetown
    Proceedings 1876, pg 35 (1876 Sept 20), Washington Lodge No. 12, Georgetown

Denver and Rio Grand Railroad
    Proceedings 1874, pg 13 (1874 Aug 27) reduced rates for Masons attending the Grand Lodge

Denver and South Park Railroad
    Proceedings 1874, pg 13 (1874 Aug 27) reduced rates for Masons attending the Grand Lodge

Denver Chapter No. 2
    Proceedings 1871, pg cover (1871 Sept 27) Denver

Denver City Band
    Proceedings 1874, pg 49 (1874 Sept 30) bill for Northrup funeral

Denver Lodge
    Proceedings 1871, pg 6 (1861 Oct 24) established at Denver

Denver Lodge No. 5
    Proceedings 1861-1869, pg 36 (1861 Dec 10) admitted
    Proceedings 1861-1869, pg 138 (1864 Dec 14) communication
    Proceedings 1861-1869, pg 139 (1865 Nov 6) dues paid
    Proceedings 1861-1869, pg 158 (1866 Oct 1) dues paid
    Proceedings 1861-1869, pg 178 (1867 Feb 19) permission to spread the ballot
    Proceedings 1861-1869, pg 181 (1867 Oct 7) dues paid
    Proceedings 1861-1869, pg 211 (1868 Oct 3) visited
    Proceedings 1875, pg 25 (1875 Sept 21) dues paid
    Proceedings 1875, pg 92 (1875 Sept 22)
    Proceedings 1876, pg 52 (1876 Sept 20)

Denver Lodge No. 5, Denver
Proceedings 1872, pg 11 (1872 Sept 24) failed to make timely returns
Proceedings 1872, pg 14 (1872 Sept 24) returns not complete
Proceedings 1874, pg 208 (1874 Sept 30)
Proceedings 1876, pg 13 (1876 Sept 18) dues paid

Denver Lodge U D
Proceedings 1861-1869, pg 33 (1861 Dec 10) charter granted 24 Oct 1861
Proceedings 1861-1869, pg 95 (1863 Apr 17) petition for formation

Denver Pacific Railroad
Proceedings 1874, pg 13 (1874 Aug 27) reduced rates for Masons attending the Grand Lodge

Denver Tribune
Colorado University Cornerstone Laying, pg 4 (1875 Sept 20) cornerstone contents

DeOlevara, John
Proceedings 1876, pg 43 (1876 Sept 20), Huerfano Lodge No. 27, Walsenburg
Proceedings 1875, pg 90 (1875 Sept 22), Huerfano Lodge U D, Walsenburg

Depp, G W
Proceedings 1861-1869, pg 229 (1868 Oct 7), Canon Lodge U D, Canon City
Proceedings 1861-1869, pg 311 (1869 Sept 29), Mount Moriah Lodge No. 15, Canon City
Proceedings 1870, pg 28 (1870 Sept 28), Mount Moriah Lodge No. 15, Canon City
Proceedings 1871, pg 26 (1871 Sept 27), Mount Moriah Lodge No. 15, Canon City
Proceedings 1872, pg 29 (1872 Sept 24), Mount Moriah Lodge No. 15, Canon City
Proceedings 1873, pg 45 (1873 Oct 1), Mount Moriah Lodge No. 15, Canon City, Dimitted

Depp, H E
Proceedings 1861-1869, pg 42 (1861 Dec 10), Summit Lodge No. 2, Parkville
Proceedings 1861-1869, pg 76 (1862 Nov 4), Summit Lodge No. 2, Parkville, dimitted

Depp, J H
Proceedings 1861-1869, pg 42 (1861 Dec 10), Summit Lodge No. 2, Parkville
Proceedings 1861-1869, pg 76 (1862 Nov 4), Summit Lodge No. 2, Parkville, dimitted
Proceedings 1861-1869, pg 229 (1868 Oct 7), Canon Lodge U D, Canon City
Proceedings 1861-1869, pg 311 (1869 Sept 29), Mount Moriah Lodge No. 15, Canon City
Proceedings 1870, pg 28 (1870 Sept 28), Mount Moriah Lodge No. 15, Canon City
Proceedings 1871, pg 26 (1871 Sept 27), Mount Moriah Lodge No. 15, Canon City
Proceedings 1872, pg 29 (1872 Sept 24), Mount Moriah Lodge No. 15, Canon City
Proceedings 1873, pg 45 (1873 Oct 1), Mount Moriah Lodge No. 15, Canon City, Dimitted

Depp, Joseph H
Proceedings 1874, pg 222 (1874 Sept 30), Pueblo Lodge No. 17, Pueblo, Pueblo County
Proceedings 1876, pg 38 (1876 Sept 20) Pueblo Lodge No. 17

Depps, Jos H
Proceedings 1875, pg 85 (1875 Sept 22) Pueblo Lodge No. 17

DeRandamie, Abraham C
Proceedings 1870, pg 77 (1824 Jan 5) African Lodge at Boston

DeReamer, J R
Proceedings 1876, pg 38 (1876 Sept 20) Pueblo Lodge No. 17

DeRemer, J R
Proceedings 1874, pg 222 (1874 Sept 30), Pueblo Lodge No. 17, Pueblo, Pueblo County
Proceedings 1875, pg 85 (1875 Sept 22) Pueblo Lodge No. 17

Deren, A J
Proceedings 1870, pg 4 (1870 Sept 27) Past Grand Master

Derr, James P
Proceedings 1874, pg 225 (1874 Sept 30), Collins Lodge No. 19, Fort Collins, Larimer County, Demitted

Desellem, Samuel
Proceedings 1875, pg 78 (1875 Sept 22), Union Lodge No. 7, Denver
Proceedings 1876, pg 33 (1876 Sept 20), Union Lodge No. 7, Denver

Deuel, H P
Proceedings 1870, pg 91 (1869 Oct 26) Grand Master, Grand Lodge of Nebraska

Deuel, Harry P
Proceedings 1870, pg 91 (1869 Oct 26) Grand Master, Grand Lodge of Nebraska

Devor, J R
Proceedings 1861-1869, pg 133 (1864 Nov 8) Denver Lodge No. 5
Proceedings 1861-1869, pg 149 (1865 Nov 7), Nevada Lodge No. 4, Nevadaville
Proceedings 1861-1869, pg 167 (1866 Oct 2) Denver Lodge No. 5, dimitted

DeVotie, H M
Proceedings 1871, pg 24 (1871 Sept 27), Washington Lodge No. 12, Georgetown
Proceedings 1875, pg 87 (1875 Sept 22), Occidental Lodge No. 20, Greeley

DeVotie, Henry M
Proceedings 1870, pg 26 (1870 Sept 28), Washington Lodge No. 12, Georgetown
Proceedings 1872, pg 25 (1872 Sept 24), Washington Lodge No. 12, Georgetown
Proceedings 1873, pg 42 (1873 Oct 1), Washington Lodge No. 12, Georgetown
Proceedings 1874, pg 217 (1874 Sept 30), Washington Lodge No. 12, Georgetown

Colorado's Territorial Masons

DeVotie, Henry M, cont.
  Proceedings 1876, pg 40 (1876 Sept 20), Occidental Lodge No. 20, Greeley

Dew, J P
  Proceedings 1874, pg 211 (1874 Sept 30), Denver Lodge No. 5, Denver
  Proceedings 1875, pg 76 (1875 Sept 22) Denver Lodge No. 5, Demitted

Dew, John
  Proceedings 1874, pg 211 (1874 Sept 30), Denver Lodge No. 5, Denver
  Proceedings 1875, pg 75 (1875 Sept 22) Denver Lodge No. 5
  Proceedings 1876, pg 49 (1876 Sept 20) Denver Lodge No. 5, 1876 Aug 19

Dexter, J V
  Proceedings 1861-1869, pg 306 (1869 Sept 29), Central Lodge No. 6, Central City
  Proceedings 1870, pg 22 (1870 Sept 28), Central Lodge No. 6, Central City
  Proceedings 1872, pg 4 (1872 Sept 24), Central Lodge No. 6, Central

Dexter, James
  Proceedings 1874, pg 228 (1874 Sept 30), Doric Lodge U D, Fairplay

Dexter, James V
  Proceedings 1871, pg 20 (1871 Sept 27), Central Lodge No. 6, Central
  Proceedings 1872, pg cover (1872 Sept 24), Central City Council, U D, Central
  Proceedings 1872, pg 21 (1872 Sept 24), Denver Lodge No. 5, Denver
  Proceedings 1873, pg 38 (1873 Oct 1), Central Lodge No. 6, Central City
  Proceedings 1874, pg 8 (1874 Jan 1), Doric Lodge U D, Fairplay
  Proceedings 1874, pg 212 (1874 Sept 30), Central Lodge No. 6, Central
  Proceedings 1875, pg 32 (1875 Sept 22) Doric Lodge No. 25, also a member of Oriental Lodge No. 33, Illinois
  Proceedings 1875, pg 76 (1875 Sept 22), Central Lodge No. 6, Central City
  Proceedings 1876, pg 48 (1876 Sept 20), Central Lodge No. 6, Central City, 1875 Jan 13

Dexter, Jas V
  Proceedings 1874, pg 35 (1874 Sept 30), Central Lodge No. 6, Central City

Deyo, R H
  Proceedings 1876, pg 48 (1876 Sept 20), Columbia Lodge No. 14, Boulder, 1876 May 13,

Dick David
  Proceedings 1861-1869, pg 77 (1862 Nov 4), Nevada Lodge No. 4, Nevadaville, dimitted

Dick, D
  Proceedings 1861-1869, pg 111 (1863 Nov 3), Nevada Lodge No. 4, Nevadaville, dimitted

Dickenson, R E
  Proceedings 1873, pg 50 (1873 Oct 1), Occidental Lodge No. 20, Greeley

Dickenson, W H
  Proceedings 1876, pg 12 (1876 Sept 19) died

Dickenson, W N
  Proceedings 1874, pg 216 (1874 Sept 30), Black Hawk Lodge No. 11, Black Hawk, Apprentice

Dickerson, R E
  Proceedings 1874, pg 225 (1874 Sept 30), Occidental Lodge No. 20, Greeley
  Proceedings 1875, pg 87 (1875 Sept 22), Occidental Lodge No. 20, Greeley
  Proceedings 1876, pg 49 (1876 Sept 20), Occidental Lodge No. 20, Greeley, 1875 Nov 1

Dickerson, W N
  Proceedings 1861-1869, pg 170 (1866 Oct 2), Black Hawk Lodge U D, Black Hawk, Apprentice
  Proceedings 1861-1869, pg 196 (1867 Oct 8), Black Hawk Lodge No. 11, Black Hawk, Apprentice
  Proceedings 1871, pg 23 (1871 Sept 27), Black Hawk Lodge No. 11, Black Hawk, Apprentice
  Proceedings 1872, pg 25 (1872 Sept 24), Black Hawk Lodge No. 11, Black Hawk, Apprentice
  Proceedings 1876, pg 34 (1876 Sept 20) Black Hawk Lodge No. 11, Apprentice

Dickerson, William N
  Proceedings 1875, pg 80 (1875 Sept 22) Black Hawk Lodge No. 11, Apprentice

Dickerson, Wm N
  Proceedings 1861-1869, pg 227 (1868 Oct 7), Black Hawk Lodge No. 11, Black Hawk, Apprentice
  Proceedings 1873, pg 42 (1873 Oct 1), Black Hawk Lodge No. 11, Black Hawk, Apprentice

Dickey, Joseph P
  Proceedings 1872, pg 22 (1872 Sept 24), Union Lodge No. 7, Denver
  Proceedings 1873, pg 40 (1873 Oct 1), Union Lodge No. 7, Denver
  Proceedings 1874, pg 214 (1874 Sept 30), Union Lodge No. 7, Denver
  Proceedings 1875, pg 78 (1875 Sept 22), Union Lodge No. 7, Denver
  Proceedings 1876, pg 48 (1876 Sept 20), Union Lodge No. 7, Denver, 1876 Aug 12

Dickinson, Dr
  Proceedings 1861-1869, pg 210 (1867 Nov), of Michigan, residing at Colorado City

Dickinson, Wm H
  Proceedings 1875, pg 31 (1875 Sept 22) charges against
  Proceedings 1875, pg 32 (1875 Sept 22), of Colorado Springs, has presented himself as a Grand Lecturer to newly formed lodged and has charged money for his lectures. He is not a member of any lodge in this jurisdiction.

Dickson, L H
   Proceedings 1876, pg 41 (1876 Sept 20), St Vrain Lodge No. 23, Longmont

Diedenbach, J M
   Proceedings 1861-1869, pg 167 (1866 Oct 2) Denver Lodge No. 5
   Proceedings 1861-1869, pg 193 (1867 Oct 8) Denver Lodge No. 5
   Proceedings 1861-1869, pg 224 (1868 Oct 7) Denver Lodge No. 5, Dimitted

Diefendorf, Fox
   Proceedings 1861-1869, pg 42 (1861 Dec 10) Golden City Lodge No. 1
   Proceedings 1861-1869, pg 131 (1864 Nov 8) Golden City Lodge No. 1
   Proceedings 1861-1869, pg 147 (1865 Nov 7) Golden City Lodge No. 1
   Proceedings 1861-1869, pg 165 (1866 Oct 2) Golden City Lodge No. 1
   Proceedings 1861-1869, pg 191 (1867 Oct 8) Golden City Lodge No. 1
   Proceedings 1861-1869, pg 221 (1868 Oct 7) Golden City Lodge No. 1
   Proceedings 1861-1869, pg 303 (1869 Sept 29) Golden City Lodge No. 1
   Proceedings 1861-1869, pg 110 (1863 Nov 3) Golden City Lodge No. 1

Diehl, Charles
   Proceedings 1874, pg 205 (1874 Sept 30) Grand Lodge of Utah, Salt Lake

Diehl, Christopher
   Proceedings 1872, pg 44 (1872 Sept 24) Salt Lake, Grand Lodge of Utah
   Proceedings 1873, pg 61 (1873 Oct 1) Grand Lodge of Utah, Salt Lake
   Proceedings 1874, pg 126 (1874 Sept 30) Grand Lodge of Utah
   Proceedings 1875, pg 96 (1875 Sept 22) Grand Lodge of Utah, Salt Lake
   Proceedings 1876, pg 54 (1876 Sept 20) Grand Lodge of Utah, Salt Lake

Dier, W A
   Proceedings 1875, pg 73 (1875 Sept 22) Golden City Lodge No. 1

Dier, William A
   Proceedings 1876, pg 29 (1876 Sept 20) Golden City Lodge No. 1

Diffenbacher, J W
   Proceedings 1871, pg 27 (1871 Sept 27), Cheyenne Lodge No. 16, Cheyenne, Wyoming Territory
   Proceedings 1872, pg 30 (1872 Sept 24), Cheyenne Lodge No. 16, Cheyenne, Wyoming Territory
   Proceedings 1873, pg 46 (1873 Oct 1), Cheyenne Lodge No. 16, Cheyenne, Wyoming Territory

Dimick, Erastus H
   Proceedings 1876, pg 37 (1876 Sept 20), Columbia Lodge No. 14, Boulder

Dimsdall, J
   Proceedings 1861-1869, pg 152 (1865 Nov 7), Montana Lodge U D, Virginia City, Montana Territory

Dinsmore, Thomas H
   Proceedings 1874, pg 225 (1874 Sept 30), Occidental Lodge No. 20, Greeley
   Proceedings 1875, pg 87 (1875 Sept 22), Occidental Lodge No. 20, Greeley
   Proceedings 1876, pg 40 (1876 Sept 20), Occidental Lodge No. 20, Greeley

Disbrow, Park
   Proceedings 1861-1869, pg 170 (1866 Oct 2), Empire Lodge No. 8, Empire City, Fellowcraft

Disbrow, Tyler
   Proceedings 1861-1869, pg 170 (1866 Oct 2), Empire Lodge No. 8, Empire City
   Proceedings 1861-1869, pg 195 (1867 Oct 8), Empire Lodge No. 8, Empire City
   Proceedings 1861-1869, pg 226 (1868 Oct 7), Empire Lodge No. 8, Empire City
   Proceedings 1861-1869, pg 308 (1869 Sept 29), Empire Lodge No. 8, Empire City, died

Divelbiss, James H
   Proceedings 1876, pg 24 (1876 Sept 20), South Pueblo Lodge No. 31, South Pueblo
   Proceedings 1876, pg 45 (1876 Sept 20) South Pueblo Lodge U D

Divelbiss, Jas H
   Proceedings 1876, pg 7 (1876 Mar 17), South Pueblo Lodge U D, South Pueblo

Dixon, S H
   Proceedings 1870, pg 39 (1869 Dec 6) Grand Lodge of Alabama, deceased

Dockery
   Proceedings 1870, pg 85 (1869 Oct 11), Warren Lodge No. 74, at Ketesville

Dodds, John F
   Proceedings 1876, pg 38 (1876 Sept 20), Mount Moriah Lodge No. 15, Canon City

Dodge, G E
   Proceedings 1872, pg 43 (1872 Sept 24), Grand Lodge of Arkansas
   Proceedings 1873, pg 60 (1873 Oct 1) Grand Lodge of Arkansas

Dodge, Geo E
   Proceedings 1874, pg 45 (1874 Sept 30) Grand Lodge of Arkansas

Doll (Smith & Doll)
   Proceedings 1874, pg 49 (1874 Sept 30) bill for coffin and hearse

Dollisen, George W
   Proceedings 1874, pg 209 (1874 Sept 30), Golden City Lodge No. 1, Golden City

Colorado's Territorial Masons

Dollison, G W
    Proceedings 1870, pg 19 (1870 Sept 28), Golden City Lodge No. 1, Golden City
    Proceedings 1871, pg 17 (1871 Sept 27), Golden City Lodge No. 1, Golden City

Dollison, Geo W
    Proceedings 1872, pg 17 (1872 Sept 24), Golden City Lodge No. 1, Golden City
    Proceedings 1875, pg 73 (1875 Sept 22) Golden City Lodge No. 1

Dollison, George W
    Proceedings 1873, pg 35 (1873 Oct 1), Golden City Lodge No. 1, Golden City
    Proceedings 1876, pg 29 (1876 Sept 20) Golden City Lodge No. 1

Donahue, J T
    Proceedings 1872, pg 32 (1872 Sept 24), Laramie Lodge No. 18, Laramie, Wyoming Territory

Donald, William
    Proceedings 1872, pg 25 (1872 Sept 24), Black Hawk Lodge No. 11, Black Hawk
    Proceedings 1873, pg 42 (1873 Oct 1), Black Hawk Lodge No. 11, Black Hawk
    Proceedings 1874, pg 216 (1874 Sept 30), Black Hawk Lodge No. 11, Black Hawk
    Proceedings 1875, pg 80 (1875 Sept 22) Black Hawk Lodge No. 11
    Proceedings 1876, pg 34 (1876 Sept 20) Black Hawk Lodge No. 11

Donaldson
    Proceedings 1870, pg 14 (1870 Sept 27) Grand Master, Grand Lodge of the District of Columbia

Donaldson, R B
    Proceedings 1861-1869, pg 244 (1867 Nov 7), Grand Master, Grand Lodge of District of Columbia
    Proceedings 1861-1869, pg 326 (1868 Nov 8) Grand Master, Grand Lodge of District of Columbia
    Proceedings 1870, pg 9 (1870 Sept 27) Grand Master of the District of Columbia

Donley, Robert
    Proceedings 1870, pg 27 (1870 Sept 28), El Paso Lodge No. 13, Colorado City, Apprentice
    Proceedings 1871, pg 25 (1871 Sept 27), El Paso Lodge No. 13, Colorado City, Apprentice

Donnelly, C
    Proceedings 1861-1869, pg 151 (1865 Nov 7), Chivington Lodge No. 6, Central City

Donnelly, Charles
    Proceedings 1861-1869, pg 134 (1864 Nov 8), Union Lodge No. 7, Denver
    Proceedings 1861-1869, pg 195 (1867 Oct 8), Union Lodge No. 7, Denver
    Proceedings 1861-1869, pg 307 (1869 Sept 29), Union Lodge No. 7, Denver
    Proceedings 1870, pg 23 (1870 Sept 28), Union Lodge No. 7, Denver
    Proceedings 1872, pg 23 (1872 Sept 24), Union Lodge No. 7, Denver
    Proceedings 1873, pg 39 (1873 Oct 1), Union Lodge No. 7, Denver
    Proceedings 1874, pg 214 (1874 Sept 30), Union Lodge No. 7, Denver
    Proceedings 1875, pg 78 (1875 Sept 22), Union Lodge No. 7, Denver
    Proceedings 1876, pg 33 (1876 Sept 20), Union Lodge No. 7, Denver

Donnelly, Chas
    Proceedings 1861-1869, pg 169 (1866 Oct 2), Union Lodge No. 7, Denver
    Proceedings 1871, pg 21 (1871 Sept 27), Union Lodge No. 7, Denver

Donnelly, F R
    Proceedings 1861-1869, pg 229 (1868 Oct 7), Pueblo Lodge U D, Pueblo

Donnelly, Geo A
    Proceedings 1874, pg 204 (1874 Sept 30) Grand Lodge of Arkansas, Searcy

Donnelly, J C
    Proceedings 1861-1869, pg 148 (1865 Nov 7), Nevada Lodge No. 4, Nevadaville
    Proceedings 1861-1869, pg 166 (1866 Oct 2), Nevada Lodge No. 4, Nevadaville
    Proceedings 1861-1869, pg 192 (1867 Oct 8), Nevada Lodge No. 4, Nevadaville

Donnelly, James C
    Proceedings 1870, pg 20 (1870 Sept 28), Nevada Lodge No. 4, Nevadaville
    Proceedings 1872, pg 19 (1872 Sept 24), Nevada Lodge No. 4, Bald Mountain
    Proceedings 1873, pg 36 (1873 Oct 1), Nevada Lodge No. 4, Nevada

Donnelly, Jas C
    Proceedings 1861-1869, pg 222 (1868 Oct 7), Nevada Lodge No. 4, Nevadaville
    Proceedings 1871, pg 18 (1871 Sept 27), Nevada Lodge No. 4, Bald Mountain
    Proceedings 1874, pg 211 (1874 Sept 30), Nevada Lodge No. 4, Bald Mountain, Gilpin County, Stricken from the rolls

Donnelly, Robert
    Proceedings 1873, pg 44 (1873 Oct 1), El Paso Lodge No. 13, Colorado City, Fellowcraft

Donnelly, Robt
    Proceedings 1876, pg 36 (1876 Sept 20), El Paso Lodge No. 13, Colorado City, Fellow Craft

Donnely, Robert
    Proceedings 1872, pg 27 (1872 Sept 24), El Paso Lodge No. 13, Colorado City, Apprentice

Donohue, J F
    Proceedings 1874, pg 223 (1874 Sept 30), Laramie Lodge No. 18, Laramie City

Colorado's Territorial Masons

Donohue, J T
Proceedings 1871, pg 29 (1871 Sept 27), Laramie Lodge No. 18, Laramie, Wyoming Territory
Proceedings 1873, pg 48 (1873 Oct 1), Laramie Lodge No. 18, Laramie, Wyoming Territory

Dore, John
Proceedings 1872, pg 44 (1872 Sept 24) Richmond, Grand Lodge of Virginia
Proceedings 1872, pg 90 (1872 Sept 24) Grand Lodge of Virginia
Proceedings 1874, pg 205 (1874 Sept 30) Grand Lodge of Virginia, Richmond,

Doric Lodge [No. 25]
Proceedings 1875, pg 25 (1875 Sept 21) payment for charter

Doric Lodge No. 25
Proceedings 1875, pg 23 (1875 Sept 21) has not provided annual returns
Proceedings 1875, pg 25 (1875 Sept 21) dues paid
Proceedings 1875, pg 34 (1875 Sept 22) work and statistics do not agree
Proceedings 1875, pg 38 (1875 Sept 22) 90 miles allowed for per diem
Proceedings 1875, pg 92 (1875 Sept 22)
Proceedings 1876, pg 52 (1876 Sept 20)

Doric Lodge No. 25, Fairplay
Proceedings 1874, pg 35 (1874 Sept 30) charter granted
Proceedings 1876, pg 8 (1876 Aug 26) dispensation granted to confer a degree to James Lewis
Proceedings 1876, pg 12 (1876 Sept 19) returns received only 15 days before annual communication
Proceedings 1876, pg 13 (1876 Sept 6) dues paid

Doric Lodge U D, Fairplay
Proceedings 1874, pg 8 (1874 Jan 1) dispensation granted
Proceedings 1874, pg 19 (1874 Sept 29) dues paid
Proceedings 1874, pg 19 (1874 Sept 29) returns late
Proceedings 1874, pg 208 (1874 Sept 30)

Dorsy, Abram
Proceedings 1872, pg 48 (1872 Sept 24), Golden City Lodge No. 1, Golden City

Dory, John A
Proceedings 1874, pg 229 (1874 Sept 30), Idaho Springs Lodge U D, Idaho Springs
Proceedings 1875, pg 89 (1875 Sept 22) Idaho Springs Lodge U D
Proceedings 1876, pg 42 (1876 Sept 20) Idaho Springs Lodge No. 26

Dosey, Abram
Proceedings 1871, pg 17 (1871 Sept 27), Golden City Lodge No. 1, Golden City, Apprentice

Dost, G W
Proceedings 1874, pg 223 (1874 Sept 30), Laramie Lodge No. 18, Laramie City

Doston, Peter K
Proceedings 1873, pg 47 (1873 Oct 1), Pueblo Lodge No. 17, Pueblo, Apprentice

Dotsen, P K
Proceedings 1874, pg 9 (1874 Feb 18) dispensation denied
Proceedings 1872, pg 31 (1872 Sept 24), Pueblo Lodge No. 17, Pueblo, Apprentice

Dotson, Peter K
Proceedings 1861-1869, pg 313 (1869 Sept 29), Pueblo Lodge No. 17, Pueblo, Apprentice
Proceedings 1870, pg 30 (1870 Sept 28), Pueblo Lodge No. 17, Pueblo, Apprentice
Proceedings 1871, pg 28 (1871 Sept 27), Pueblo Lodge No. 17, Pueblo, Apprentice
Proceedings 1874, pg 222 (1874 Sept 30), Pueblo Lodge No. 17, Pueblo, Pueblo County
Proceedings 1875, pg 85 (1875 Sept 22) Pueblo Lodge No. 17
Proceedings 1876, pg 38 (1876 Sept 20) Pueblo Lodge No. 17

Doty, Silas
Proceedings 1873, pg 49 (1873 Oct 1), Collins Lodge No. 19, Fort Collins, Apprentice
Proceedings 1874, pg 224 (1874 Sept 30), Collins Lodge No. 19, Fort Collins, Larimer County
Proceedings 1875, pg 86 (1875 Sept 22), Collins Lodge No. 19, Fort Collins
Proceedings 1876, pg 39 (1876 Sept 20), Collins Lodge No. 19, Fort Collins

Dougherty, M J
Proceedings 1861-1869, pg 77 (1862 Nov 4) Denver Lodge No. 5
Proceedings 1861-1869, pg 112 (1863 Nov 3) Denver Lodge No. 5
Proceedings 1861-1869, pg 133 (1864 Nov 8) Denver Lodge No. 5
Proceedings 1861-1869, pg 149 (1865 Nov 7), Nevada Lodge No. 4, Nevadaville, deceased

Dougherty, T C
Proceedings 1873, pg 46 (1873 Oct 1), Cheyenne Lodge No. 16, Cheyenne, Wyoming Territory

Dougherty, Thomas C
Proceedings 1870, pg 29 (1870 Sept 28), Cheyenne Lodge No. 16, Cheyenne, Wyoming Territory
Proceedings 1874, pg 221 (1874 Sept 30), Cheyenne Lodge No. 16, Cheyenne, Wyoming Territory

Dougherty, Thos C
Proceedings 1872, pg 30 (1872 Sept 24), Cheyenne Lodge No. 16, Cheyenne, Wyoming Territory, Dimitted

Douglas, James
Proceedings 1873, pg 38 (1873 Oct 1), Denver Lodge No. 5, Denver, died
Proceedings 1873, pg 57 (1873 Oct 1), Denver Lodge No. 5, Denver

Douglas, Jas W
Proceedings 1870, pg 21 (1870 Sept 28), Denver Lodge No. 5, Denver
Proceedings 1871, pg 19 (1871 Sept 27) Denver Lodge No. 5

Colorado's Territorial Masons

Douglas, Jas W, cont.
   Proceedings 1872, pg 20 (1872 Sept 24), Denver Lodge No. 5, Denver

Douglass, J H
   Proceedings 1861-1869, pg 167 (1866 Oct 2) Denver Lodge No. 5

Douglass, J W
   Proceedings 1861-1869, pg 149 (1865 Nov 7), Nevada Lodge No. 4, Nevadaville, Fellowcraft
   Proceedings 1861-1869, pg 193 (1867 Oct 8) Denver Lodge No. 5
   Proceedings 1861-1869, pg 223 (1868 Oct 7) Denver Lodge No. 5
   Proceedings 1861-1869, pg 305 (1869 Sept 29) Denver Lodge No. 5

Dove, John
   Proceedings 1861-1869, pg 291 (1869 Sept 28), Grand Secretary, Grand Lodge of Virginia
   Proceedings 1861-1869, pg 316 (1869 Sept 29) Grand Lodge of Virginia
   Proceedings 1861-1869, pg 349 (1868 Dec 14) Grand Secretary, Grand Lodge of Virginia
   Proceedings 1870, pg 34 (1870 Sept 28) Grand Secretary, Grand Lodge of Virginia
   Proceedings 1871, pg 35 (1871 Sept 27) Grand Secretary, Grand Lodge of Virginia
   Proceedings 1873, pg 61 (1873 Oct 1) Grand Lodge of Virginia, Richmond
   Proceedings 1874, pg 129 (1874 Sept 30) Grand Lodge of Virginia
   Proceedings 1875, pg 96 (1875 Sept 22) Grand Lodge of Virginia, Richmond
   Proceedings 1876, pg 54 (1876 Sept 20) Grand Lodge of Virginia, Richmond

Dover, John
   Proceedings 1870, pg 104 (1869 Dec 13) Grand Secretary, Grand Lodge of Virginia

Dow, F E
   Proceedings 1875, pg 82 (1875 Sept 22), El Paso Lodge No. 13, Colorado Springs
   Proceedings 1876, pg 36 (1876 Sept 20), El Paso Lodge No. 13, Colorado City

Dowdell, J N
   Proceedings 1875, pg 87 (1875 Sept 22), Occidental Lodge No. 20, Greeley
   Proceedings 1876, pg 40 (1876 Sept 20), Occidental Lodge No. 20, Greeley

Dowden, J N
   Proceedings 1874, pg 225 (1874 Sept 30), Occidental Lodge No. 20, Greeley

Dowey, S W
   Proceedings 1874, pg 223 (1874 Sept 30), Laramie Lodge No. 18, Laramie City

Downen, B F
   Proceedings 1861-1869, pg 193 (1867 Oct 8) Denver Lodge No. 5

Proceedings 1861-1869, pg 223 (1868 Oct 7) Denver Lodge No. 5
Proceedings 1861-1869, pg 305 (1869 Sept 29) Denver Lodge No. 5, Dimitted
Proceedings 1872, pg 35 (1872 Sept 24), St Vrain Lodge No. 23, Longmont
Proceedings 1873, pg 51 (1873 Oct 1), St Vrain Lodge No. 23, Longmont
Proceedings 1874, pg 227 (1874 Sept 30), St Vrain No. 23, Longmont
Proceedings 1876, pg 41 (1876 Sept 20), St Vrain Lodge No. 23, Longmont
Proceedings 1861-1869, pg 149 (1865 Nov 7), Nevada Lodge No. 4, Nevadaville, Apprentice
Proceedings 1861-1869, pg 167 (1866 Oct 2) Denver Lodge No. 5, Fellowcraft

Downey, S W
   Proceedings 1870, pg 31 (1870 Sept 28), Laramie Lodge No. 18, Laramie, Wyoming Territory
   Proceedings 1871, pg 29 (1871 Sept 27), Laramie Lodge No. 18, Laramie, Wyoming Territory
   Proceedings 1872, pg 32 (1872 Sept 24), Laramie Lodge No. 18, Laramie, Wyoming Territory
   Proceedings 1873, pg 48 (1873 Oct 1), Laramie Lodge No. 18, Laramie, Wyoming Territory

Downey, W O
   Proceedings 1871, pg 29 (1871 Sept 27), Laramie Lodge No. 18, Laramie, Wyoming Territory
   Proceedings 1872, pg 32 (1872 Sept 24), Laramie Lodge No. 18, Laramie, Wyoming Territory
   Proceedings 1873, pg 48 (1873 Oct 1), Laramie Lodge No. 18, Laramie, Wyoming Territory
   Proceedings 1874, pg 223 (1874 Sept 30), Laramie Lodge No. 18, Laramie City

Downing, C P
   Proceedings 1871, pg 29 (1871 Sept 27), Collins Lodge No. 19, Fort Collins
   Proceedings 1872, pg 36 (1872 Sept 24), Ashlar Lodge U D, Colorado Springs
   Proceedings 1873, pg 13 (1873 Sept 30), Ashlar Lodge U D, Colorado Springs
   Proceedings 1874, pg 218 (1874 Sept 30), El Paso Lodge No. 13, Colorado Springs
   Proceedings 1875, pg 82 (1875 Sept 22), El Paso Lodge No. 13, Colorado Springs
   Proceedings 1876, pg 36 (1876 Sept 20), El Paso Lodge No. 13, Colorado City

Downing, C Perry
   Proceedings 1872, pg 33 (1872 Sept 24), Collins Lodge No. 19, Fort Collins
   Proceedings 1873, pg 49 (1873 Oct 1), Collins Lodge No. 19, Fort Collins
   Proceedings 1874, pg 225 (1874 Sept 30), Collins Lodge No. 19, Fort Collins, Larimer County, Demitted

Downing, Jacob
   Proceedings 1861-1869, pg 134 (1864 Nov 8), Union Lodge No. 7, Denver
   Proceedings 1861-1869, pg 151 (1865 Nov 7), Chivington Lodge No. 6, Central City

Proceedings 1861-1869, pg 169 (1866 Oct 2), Union Lodge No. 7, Denver

Proceedings 1861-1869, pg 195 (1867 Oct 8), Union Lodge No. 7, Denver

Proceedings 1861-1869, pg 225 (1868 Oct 7), Union Lodge No. 7, Denver

Proceedings 1861-1869, pg 307 (1869 Sept 29), Union Lodge No. 7, Denver

Proceedings 1870, pg 23 (1870 Sept 28), Union Lodge No. 7, Denver

Proceedings 1871, pg 21 (1871 Sept 27), Union Lodge No. 7, Denver

Proceedings 1872, pg 23 (1872 Sept 24), Union Lodge No. 7, Denver

Proceedings 1873, pg 40 (1873 Oct 1), Union Lodge No. 7, Denver

Proceedings 1874, pg 214 (1874 Sept 30), Union Lodge No. 7, Denver

Proceedings 1875, pg 78 (1875 Sept 22), Union Lodge No. 7, Denver

Proceedings 1876, pg 33 (1876 Sept 20), Union Lodge No. 7, Denver

Downing, W S

Proceedings 1861-1869, pg 227 (1868 Oct 7), Washington Lodge No. 12, Georgetown

Proceedings 1871, pg 24 (1871 Sept 27), Washington Lodge No. 12, Georgetown

Downing, William S

Proceedings 1872, pg 25 (1872 Sept 24), Washington Lodge No. 12, Georgetown

Proceedings 1874, pg 217 (1874 Sept 30), Washington Lodge No. 12, Georgetown

Proceedings 1876, pg 35 (1876 Sept 20), Washington Lodge No. 12, Georgetown

Downing, Wm S

Proceedings 1861-1869, pg 192 (1867 Oct 8), Nevada Lodge No. 4, Nevadaville, Apprentice

Proceedings 1861-1869, pg 309 (1869 Sept 29), Washington Lodge No. 12, Georgetown

Proceedings 1870, pg 26 (1870 Sept 28), Washington Lodge No. 12, Georgetown

Proceedings 1873, pg 43 (1873 Oct 1), Washington Lodge No. 12, Georgetown

Proceedings 1875, pg 81 (1875 Sept 22), Washington Lodge No. 12, Georgetown

Doyle, J B

Proceedings 1861-1869, pg 78 (1862 Nov 4) Denver Lodge No. 5, Apprentice

Proceedings 1861-1869, pg 133 (1864 Nov 8) Denver Lodge No. 5, deceased

Doyle, Thomas A

Proceedings 1861-1869, pg 280 (1867 Oct 7), Grand Master, Grand Lodge of Rhode Island

Proceedings 1861-1869, pg 346 (1868 Aug 6) Grand Master, Grand Lodge of Rhode Island

Proceedings 1870, pg 100 (1869 Nov 15) Grand Master, Grand Lodge of Rhode Island

Proceedings 1873, pg 61 (1873 Oct 1) Grand Lodge of Rhode Island, Providence

Draper, G A

Proceedings 1873, pg 46 (1873 Oct 1), Cheyenne Lodge No. 16, Cheyenne, Wyoming Territory

Proceedings 1874, pg 221 (1874 Sept 30), Cheyenne Lodge No. 16, Cheyenne, Wyoming Territory

Drew, Milo A

Proceedings 1870, pg 21 (1870 Sept 28), Denver Lodge No. 5, Denver

Proceedings 1871, pg 19 (1871 Sept 27) Denver Lodge No. 5

Proceedings 1872, pg 20 (1872 Sept 24), Denver Lodge No. 5, Denver

Proceedings 1873, pg 37 (1873 Oct 1), Denver Lodge No. 5, Denver

Proceedings 1874, pg 212 (1874 Sept 30), Denver Lodge No. 5, Denver, Stricken from the rolls

Drips, J W

Proceedings 1861-1869, pg 151 (1865 Nov 7), Empire Lodge U D, Empire City

Proceedings 1861-1869, pg 226 (1868 Oct 7), Empire Lodge No. 8, Empire City

Proceedings 1870, pg 24 (1870 Sept 28), Empire Lodge No. 8, Empire

Drips, James W

Proceedings 1861-1869, pg 195 (1867 Oct 8), Empire Lodge No. 8, Empire City

Proceedings 1861-1869, pg 308 (1869 Sept 29), Empire Lodge No. 8, Empire City

Proceedings 1872, pg 23 (1872 Sept 24), Empire Lodge No. 8, Empire

Proceedings 1873, pg 41 (1873 Oct 1), Empire Lodge No. 8, Empire

Proceedings 1874, pg 215 (1874 Sept 30), Empire Lodge No. 8, Empire

Drips, Jas W

Proceedings 1861-1869, pg 170 (1866 Oct 2), Empire Lodge No. 8, Empire City

Drummond

Proceedings 1861-1869, pg 257 (1868 May 5) Grand Lodge of Maine

Proceedings 1861-1869, pg 258 (1868 May 5) Grand Lodge of Maine

Proceedings 1861-1869, pg 259 (1868 May 5) Grand Lodge of Maine

Proceedings 1872, pg 71 (1872 Sept 24) Grand Lodge of Maine

Proceedings 1874, pg 43 (1874 Sept 30) committee

Proceedings 1874, pg 47 (1874 Sept 30)

Proceedings 1874, pg 115 (1874 Sept 30) Grand Lodge of Maine

Drummond, Josiah H

Proceedings 1861-1869, pg 104 (1863 Nov 3) Grand Master of Maine

Proceedings 1870, pg 65 (1870 May 3) Grand Lodge of Maine

Proceedings 1872, pg 43 (1872 Sept 24) Portland, Grand Lodge of Maine

Colorado's Territorial Masons

Drummond, Josiah H, cont.
Proceedings 1872, pg 70 (1872 Sept 24) Grand Lodge of Maine
Proceedings 1873, pg 60 (1873 Oct 1) Grand Lodge of Maine, Portland
Proceedings 1874, pg 79 (1874 Sept 30) Grand Lodge of Maine
Proceedings 1874, pg 204 (1874 Sept 30) Grand Lodge of Maine, Portland

Drummond, M
Proceedings 1875, pg 88 (1875 Sept 22), Weston Lodge No. 22, Littleton, Demitted

Drummond, Mark
Proceedings 1872, pg 34 (1872 Sept 24), Weston Lodge No. 22, Littleton
Proceedings 1873, pg 51 (1873 Oct 1), Weston Lodge No. 22, Littleton
Proceedings 1874, pg 226 (1874 Sept 30), Weston Lodge No. 22, Littleton

Druse, H J
Proceedings 1861-1869, pg 194 (1867 Oct 8), Chivington Lodge No. 6, Central City

Dryden, William C
Proceedings 1876, pg 44 (1876 Sept 20) Del Norte Lodge U D

Dubal, E R
Proceedings 1873, pg 60 (1873 Oct 1) Grand Lodge of Arkansas, Fort Smith

Dubois, R
Proceedings 1875, pg 89 (1875 Sept 22), Doric Lodge No. 25, Fairplay

Dubois, Rufus
Proceedings 1876, pg 42 (1876 Sept 20), Doric Lodge No. 25, Fairplay

Ducket, J A
Proceedings 1873, pg 45 (1873 Oct 1), Mount Moriah Lodge No. 15, Canon City
Proceedings 1875, pg 84 (1875 Sept 22), Mount Moriah Lodge No. 15, Canon City
Proceedings 1874, pg 220 (1874 Sept 30), Mount Moriah Lodge No. 15, Canon City
Proceedings 1876, pg 38 (1876 Sept 20), Mount Moriah Lodge No. 15, Canon City

Dudley, C E
Proceedings 1875, pg 89 (1875 Sept 22), Doric Lodge No. 25, Fairplay

Dudley, C F
Proceedings 1876, pg 50 (1876 Sept 20), Doric Lodge No. 25, Fairplay

Dudley, Chas E
Proceedings 1874, pg 228 (1874 Sept 30), Doric Lodge U D, Fairplay

Dudley, J H
Proceedings 1861-1869, pg 133 (1864 Nov 8) Denver Lodge No. 5
Proceedings 1861-1869, pg 149 (1865 Nov 7), Nevada Lodge No. 4, Nevadaville
Proceedings 1861-1869, pg 167 (1866 Oct 2) Denver Lodge No. 5
Proceedings 1861-1869, pg 193 (1867 Oct 8) Denver Lodge No. 5
Proceedings 1861-1869, pg 223 (1868 Oct 7) Denver Lodge No. 5
Proceedings 1861-1869, pg 305 (1869 Sept 29) Denver Lodge No. 5
Proceedings 1870, pg 21 (1870 Sept 28), Denver Lodge No. 5, Denver
Proceedings 1871, pg 20 (1871 Sept 27) Denver Lodge No. 5, Dimitted

Duell, Harry P
Proceedings 1872, pg 75 (1872 Sept 24) Grand Lodge of Nebraska

Duggan, George
Proceedings 1876, pg 33 (1876 Sept 20), Union Lodge No. 7, Denver

Duhme, Herman
Proceedings 1875, pg 90 (1875 Sept 22), Huerfano Lodge U D, Walsenburg, Fellowcraft
Proceedings 1876, pg 43 (1876 Sept 20), Huerfano Lodge No. 27, Walsenburg, Fellow Craft

Duke, J B
Proceedings 1875, pg 85 (1875 Sept 22) Pueblo Lodge No. 17
Proceedings 1876, pg 38 (1876 Sept 20) Pueblo Lodge No. 17

Dumner, Nathaniel W
Proceedings 1873, pg 61 (1873 Oct 1) Grand Lodge of New Hampshire, Manchester

Dunagan, J J
Proceedings 1861-1869, pg 168 (1866 Oct 2), Chivington Lodge No. 6, Central City
Proceedings 1875, pg 77 (1875 Sept 22), Central Lodge No. 6, Central City
Proceedings 1876, pg 32 (1876 Sept 20), Central Lodge No. 6, Central City
Proceedings 1876, pg 50 (1876 Sept 20), Central Lodge No. 6, Central City

Dunagan, P H
Proceedings 1861-1869, pg 168 (1866 Oct 2), Chivington Lodge No. 6, Central City

Dunagan, Park H
Proceedings 1876, pg 32 (1876 Sept 20), Central Lodge No. 6, Central City

Dunagan, Patrick H
Proceedings 1875, pg 77 (1875 Sept 22), Central Lodge No. 6, Central City

Dunaway, Wm M
Proceedings 1872, pg 88 (1872 Sept 24) Grand Lodge of Tennessee, died 22 Aug 1872

Duncan, Harmon
Proceedings 1861-1869, pg 43 (1861 Dec 10), Summit Lodge No. 2, Parkville
Proceedings 1861-1869, pg 76 (1862 Nov 4), Summit Lodge No. 2, Parkville, Apprentice

Duncan, Hugh
Proceedings 1861-1869, pg 152 (1865 Nov 7), Montana Lodge U D, Virginia City, Montana Territory

Duncan, John
Proceedings 1873, pg 40 (1873 Oct 1), Union Lodge No. 7, Denver, Apprentice
Proceedings 1874, pg 214 (1874 Sept 30), Union Lodge No. 7, Denver
Proceedings 1875, pg 78 (1875 Sept 22), Union Lodge No. 7, Denver
Proceedings 1876, pg 33 (1876 Sept 20), Union Lodge No. 7, Denver
Proceedings 1876, pg 50 (1876 Sept 20), Union Lodge No. 7, Denver

Duneway, Wm M
Proceedings 1872, pg 44 (1872 Sept 24) Jackson (died 22 Aug 1872), Grand Lodge of Tennessee

Dunhan, Martin
Proceedings 1873, pg 60 (1873 Oct 1) Grand Lodge of Nebraska, Omaha

Dunkin, Nicholas
Proceedings 1875, pg 77 (1875 Sept 22), Central Lodge No. 6, Central City
Proceedings 1876, pg 32 (1876 Sept 20), Central Lodge No. 6, Central City
Proceedings 1876, pg 50 (1876 Sept 20), Central Lodge No. 6, Central City

Dunn, Henry
Proceedings 1861-1869, pg 229 (1868 Oct 7), Canon Lodge U D, Canon City
Proceedings 1861-1869, pg 311 (1869 Sept 29), Mount Moriah Lodge No. 15, Canon City
Proceedings 1870, pg 28 (1870 Sept 28), Mount Moriah Lodge No. 15, Canon City, Dimitted
Proceedings 1871, pg 12 (1871 Sept 26), Mount Moriah Lodge No. 15, Canon City, listed as dimitted on 4 Mar 1871 and in Feb 1870
Proceedings 1871, pg 27 (1871 Sept 27), Mount Moriah Lodge No. 15, Canon City, Dimitted

Dunn, James
Proceedings 1873, pg 44 (1873 Oct 1), Columbia Lodge No. 14, Boulder
Proceedings 1874, pg 219 (1874 Sept 30), Columbia Lodge No. 14, Boulder, Boulder County
Proceedings 1875, pg 83 (1875 Sept 22), Columbia Lodge No. 14, Boulder
Proceedings 1876, pg 37 (1876 Sept 20), Columbia Lodge No. 14, Boulder

Dunn, Wm
Proceedings 1861-1869, pg 77 (1862 Nov 4) Denver Lodge No. 5
Proceedings 1861-1869, pg 112 (1863 Nov 3) Denver Lodge No. 5, deceased

Dunnegan, J J
Proceedings 1861-1869, pg 113 (1863 Nov 3), Chivington Lodge No. 6, Central City, Fellowcraft
Proceedings 1861-1869, pg 134 (1864 Nov 8), Chivington Lodge No. 6, Central City
Proceedings 1861-1869, pg 150 (1865 Nov 7), Chivington Lodge No. 6, Central City
Proceedings 1861-1869, pg 194 (1867 Oct 8), Chivington Lodge No. 6, Central City
Proceedings 1861-1869, pg 224 (1868 Oct 7), Chivington Lodge No. 6, Central City
Proceedings 1861-1869, pg 306 (1869 Sept 29), Central Lodge No. 6, Central City
Proceedings 1870, pg 22 (1870 Sept 28), Central Lodge No. 6, Central City
Proceedings 1871, pg 20 (1871 Sept 27), Central Lodge No. 6, Central
Proceedings 1872, pg 21 (1872 Sept 24), Denver Lodge No. 5, Denver
Proceedings 1873, pg 38 (1873 Oct 1), Central Lodge No. 6, Central City
Proceedings 1874, pg 213 (1874 Sept 30), Central Lodge No. 6, Central

Dunnegan, P H
Proceedings 1861-1869, pg 134 (1864 Nov 8), Chivington Lodge No. 6, Central City
Proceedings 1861-1869, pg 150 (1865 Nov 7), Chivington Lodge No. 6, Central City
Proceedings 1861-1869, pg 194 (1867 Oct 8), Chivington Lodge No. 6, Central City
Proceedings 1861-1869, pg 224 (1868 Oct 7), Chivington Lodge No. 6, Central City
Proceedings 1861-1869, pg 306 (1869 Sept 29), Central Lodge No. 6, Central City
Proceedings 1870, pg 22 (1870 Sept 28), Central Lodge No. 6, Central City
Proceedings 1871, pg 20 (1871 Sept 27), Central Lodge No. 6, Central
Proceedings 1872, pg 21 (1872 Sept 24), Denver Lodge No. 5, Denver

Dunnegan, Patrick H
Proceedings 1873, pg 38 (1873 Oct 1), Central Lodge No. 6, Central City
Proceedings 1874, pg 213 (1874 Sept 30), Central Lodge No. 6, Central

Dunscomb, Wm E
Proceedings 1861-1869, pg 335 (1868 Oct 12) Grand Master, Grand Lodge of Missouri

Dunton, Robert F
Proceedings 1875, pg 91 (1875 Sept 22), Las Animas Lodge U D, Trinidad
Proceedings 1876, pg 43 (1876 Sept 20), Las Animas Lodge No. 28, Trinidad

Durbin, J H
Proceedings 1873, pg 46 (1873 Oct 1), Cheyenne Lodge No. 16, Cheyenne, Wyoming Territory

Colorado's Territorial Masons

Durbin, J H, cont.
Proceedings 1874, pg 221 (1874 Sept 30), Cheyenne Lodge No. 16, Cheyenne, Wyoming Territory

Durbin, John H
Proceedings 1870, pg 29 (1870 Sept 28), Cheyenne Lodge No. 16, Cheyenne, Wyoming Territory
Proceedings 1871, pg 27 (1871 Sept 27), Cheyenne Lodge No. 16, Cheyenne, Wyoming Territory
Proceedings 1872, pg 30 (1872 Sept 24), Cheyenne Lodge No. 16, Cheyenne, Wyoming Territory

Durell, Jesse
Proceedings 1873, pg 40 (1873 Oct 1), Union Lodge No. 7, Denver, Apprentice
Proceedings 1874, pg 214 (1874 Sept 30), Union Lodge No. 7, Denver, Apprentice

Durfee, Deloss
Proceedings 1873, pg 52 (1873 Oct 1), Ashlar Lodge U D, Colorado Springs, Apprentice

Durgan, D C
Proceedings 1875, pg 74 (1875 Sept 22) Golden City Lodge No. 1, Stricken from the rolls

Durgen, David G
Proceedings 1873, pg 35 (1873 Oct 1), Golden City Lodge No. 1, Golden City
Proceedings 1874, pg 209 (1874 Sept 30), Golden City Lodge No. 1, Golden City

Durgin, D G
Proceedings 1861-1869, pg 147 (1865 Nov 7) Golden City Lodge No. 1

Durham, J H
Proceedings 1861-1869, pg 131 (1864 Nov 8) Golden City Lodge No. 1
Proceedings 1861-1869, pg 147 (1865 Nov 7) Golden City Lodge No. 1
Proceedings 1861-1869, pg 165 (1866 Oct 2) Golden City Lodge No. 1
Proceedings 1870, pg 19 (1870 Sept 28), Golden City Lodge No. 1, Golden City
Proceedings 1871, pg 17 (1871 Sept 27), Golden City Lodge No. 1, Golden City, Dimitted

Durham, John H
Proceedings 1861-1869, pg 191 (1867 Oct 8) Golden City Lodge No. 1
Proceedings 1861-1869, pg 221 (1868 Oct 7) Golden City Lodge No. 1
Proceedings 1861-1869, pg 303 (1869 Sept 29) Golden City Lodge No. 1

Durkee, F M
Proceedings 1861-1869, pg 77 (1862 Nov 4) Denver Lodge No. 5
Proceedings 1861-1869, pg 112 (1863 Nov 3) Denver Lodge No. 5
Proceedings 1861-1869, pg 133 (1864 Nov 8) Denver Lodge No. 5
Proceedings 1861-1869, pg 149 (1865 Nov 7), Nevada Lodge No. 4, Nevadaville
Proceedings 1861-1869, pg 167 (1866 Oct 2) Denver Lodge No. 5
Proceedings 1861-1869, pg 193 (1867 Oct 8) Denver Lodge No. 5
Proceedings 1861-1869, pg 223 (1868 Oct 7) Denver Lodge No. 5
Proceedings 1861-1869, pg 305 (1869 Sept 29) Denver Lodge No. 5
Proceedings 1870, pg 21 (1870 Sept 28), Denver Lodge No. 5, Denver
Proceedings 1872, pg 20 (1872 Sept 24), Denver Lodge No. 5, Denver

Durlucher, Simon
Proceedings 1870, pg 6 (1870 Jan 31) Laramie City Lodge U D
Proceedings 1870, pg 30 (1870 Sept 28), Laramie Lodge No. 18, Laramie, Wyoming Territory

Durrell, Jesse
Proceedings 1875, pg 79 (1875 Sept 22), Union Lodge No. 7, Denver, Apprentice
Proceedings 1876, pg 33 (1876 Sept 20), Union Lodge No. 7, Denver, Apprentice

Dustin, G W
Proceedings 1874, pg 223 (1874 Sept 30), Laramie Lodge No. 18, Laramie City

DuVal, E R
Proceedings 1874, pg 44 (1874 Sept 30) Grand Lodge of Arkansas
Proceedings 1874, pg 45 (1874 Sept 30) Grand Lodge of Arkansas

Dwe, James P
Proceedings 1873, pg 49 (1873 Oct 1), Collins Lodge No. 19, Fort Collins

Dyer, B L
Proceedings 1876, pg 43 (1876 Sept 20), Huerfano Lodge No. 27, Walsenburg

Dyer, J G
Proceedings 1876, pg 43 (1876 Sept 20), Huerfano Lodge No. 27, Walsenburg

Dyer, John L
Proceedings 1861-1869, pg 110 (1863 Nov 3), Summit Lodge No. 2, Parkville
Proceedings 1861-1869, pg 132 (1864 Nov 8) Golden City Lodge No. 1

Eacker, John
  Proceedings 1872, pg 34 (1872 Sept 24), Occidental Lodge No. 20, Greeley
  Proceedings 1873, pg 49 (1873 Oct 1), Occidental Lodge No. 20, Greeley
  Proceedings 1874, pg 225 (1874 Sept 30), Occidental Lodge No. 20, Greeley
  Proceedings 1875, pg 87 (1875 Sept 22), Occidental Lodge No. 20, Greeley
  Proceedings 1876, pg 40 (1876 Sept 20), Occidental Lodge No. 20, Greeley

Eames, J H
  Proceedings 1861-1869, pg 223 (1868 Oct 7) Denver Lodge No. 5
  Proceedings 1861-1869, pg 305 (1869 Sept 29) Denver Lodge No. 5
  Proceedings 1870, pg 21 (1870 Sept 28), Denver Lodge No. 5, Denver
  Proceedings 1872, pg 20 (1872 Sept 24), Denver Lodge No. 5, Denver

Eames, James H
  Proceedings 1861-1869, pg 192 (1867 Oct 8) Denver Lodge No. 5

Earhart, R P
  Proceedings 1872, pg 44 (1872 Sept 24) Salem, Grand Lodge of Oregon
  Proceedings 1873, pg 61 (1873 Oct 1) Grand Lodge of Oregon, Salem
  Proceedings 1874, pg 205 (1874 Sept 30) Grand Lodge of Oregon, Salem

Earhart, Rocky P
  Proceedings 1875, pg 96 (1875 Sept 22) Grand Lodge of Oregon, Portland
  Proceedings 1876, pg 54 (1876 Sept 20) Grand Lodge of Oregon, Portland,

Earl de Grey and Ripon
  Proceedings 1872, pg 58 (1872 Sept 24) Grand Master of Masons in England

Eashart, R P
  Proceedings 1874, pg 118 (1874 Sept 30) Grand Lodge of Oregon

Easley, John
  Proceedings 1874, pg 229 (1874 Sept 30), Idaho Springs Lodge U D, Idaho Springs

Eason
  Proceedings 1870, pg 42 (1869 Nov 1) Provincial Grand Lecturer, of England,

Eaton
  Proceedings 1873, pg 13 (1873 Sept 30) motion

Eaton, B H
  Proceedings 1870, pg 6 (1870 May 9), Fidelity Lodge U D, Fort Collins
  Proceedings 1871, pg 29 (1871 Sept 27), Collins Lodge No. 19, Fort Collins

Eaton, Benj H
  Proceedings 1870, pg 31 (1870 Sept 28), Collins Lodge No. 19, Fort Collins
  Proceedings 1872, pg 33 (1872 Sept 24), Collins Lodge No. 19, Fort Collins

Eaton, Benjamin H
  Proceedings 1873, pg 49 (1873 Oct 1), Collins Lodge No. 19, Fort Collins
  Proceedings 1874, pg 224 (1874 Sept 30), Collins Lodge No. 19, Fort Collins, Larimer County
  Proceedings 1875, pg 86 (1875 Sept 22), Collins Lodge No. 19, Fort Collins
  Proceedings 1876, pg 39 (1876 Sept 20), Collins Lodge No. 19, Fort Collins

Eaton, E I
  Proceedings 1875, pg 82 (1875 Sept 22), El Paso Lodge No. 13, Colorado Springs

Eaton, E J
  Proceedings 1876, pg 35 (1876 Sept 20), El Paso Lodge No. 13, Colorado City

Eaton, O
  Proceedings 1871, pg 30 (1871 Sept 27), Occidental Lodge U D, Greeley

Eaton, Oscar
  Proceedings 1872, pg 33 (1872 Sept 24), Occidental Lodge No. 20, Greeley
  Proceedings 1873, pg 6 (1873 Sept 30), Occidental Lodge No. 20, Greeley
  Proceedings 1873, pg 49 (1873 Oct 1), Occidental Lodge No. 20, Greeley
  Proceedings 1874, pg 225 (1874 Sept 30), Occidental Lodge No. 20, Greeley
  Proceedings 1875, pg 87 (1875 Sept 22), Occidental Lodge No. 20, Greeley, Demitted

Ebbets, Geo
  Proceedings 1861-1869, pg 312 (1869 Sept 29), Pueblo Lodge No. 17, Pueblo
  Proceedings 1870, pg 29 (1870 Sept 28), Pueblo Lodge No. 17, Pueblo
  Proceedings 1872, pg 31 (1872 Sept 24), Pueblo Lodge No. 17, Pueblo

Ebbetts, George
  Proceedings 1871, pg 28 (1871 Sept 27), Pueblo Lodge No. 17, Pueblo
  Proceedings 1873, pg 47 (1873 Oct 1), Pueblo Lodge No. 17, Pueblo
  Proceedings 1874, pg 222 (1874 Sept 30), Pueblo Lodge No. 17, Pueblo, Pueblo County
  Proceedings 1875, pg 85 (1875 Sept 22) Pueblo Lodge No. 17
  Proceedings 1876, pg 38 (1876 Sept 20) Pueblo Lodge No. 17

Ebbitts, George
  Proceedings 1876, pg 50 (1876 Sept 20) Pueblo Lodge No. 17

Eberlein, W F
 Proceedings 1861-1869, pg 196 (1867 Oct 8), Black Hawk Lodge No. 11, Black Hawk

Eberlin, W F
 Proceedings 1861-1869, pg 170 (1866 Oct 2), Black Hawk Lodge U D, Black Hawk
 Proceedings 1861-1869, pg 309 (1869 Sept 29), Black Hawk Lodge No. 11, Black Hawk
 Proceedings 1870, pg 25 (1870 Sept 28), Black Hawk Lodge No. 11, Black Hawk
 Proceedings 1872, pg 25 (1872 Sept 24), Black Hawk Lodge No. 11, Black Hawk
 Proceedings 1861-1869, pg 227 (1868 Oct 7), Black Hawk Lodge No. 11, Black Hawk

Eberlin, Wm Frederick
 Proceedings 1873, pg 42 (1873 Oct 1), Black Hawk Lodge No. 11, Black Hawk, Dimitted

Eberline, W F
 Proceedings 1871, pg 23 (1871 Sept 27), Black Hawk Lodge No. 11, Black Hawk

Eckhardt, Otto
 Proceedings 1861-1869, pg 304 (1869 Sept 29), Nevada Lodge No. 4, Nevadaville
 Proceedings 1870, pg 20 (1870 Sept 28), Nevada Lodge No. 4, Nevadaville
 Proceedings 1871, pg 18 (1871 Sept 27), Nevada Lodge No. 4, Bald Mountain
 Proceedings 1872, pg 4 (1872 Sept 24), Nevada Lodge No. 4, Bald Mountain
 Proceedings 1872, pg 18 (1872 Sept 24), Nevada Lodge No. 4, Bald Mountain
 Proceedings 1873, pg 36 (1873 Oct 1), Nevada Lodge No. 4, Nevada
 Proceedings 1874, pg 210 (1874 Sept 30), Nevada Lodge No. 4, Bald Mountain, Gilpin County
 Proceedings 1875, pg 74 (1875 Sept 22), Nevada Lodge No. 4, Nevada
 Proceedings 1876, pg 30 (1876 Sept 20) Nevada Lodge No. 4

Eckhart, Otto
 Proceedings 1861-1869, pg 192 (1867 Oct 8), Nevada Lodge No. 4, Nevadaville
 Proceedings 1861-1869, pg 222 (1868 Oct 7), Nevada Lodge No. 4, Nevadaville

Eckstein, Sam
 Proceedings 1875, pg 85 (1875 Sept 22) Pueblo Lodge No. 17
 Proceedings 1876, pg 50 (1876 Sept 20) Pueblo Lodge No. 17
 Proceedings 1861-1869, pg 313 (1869 Sept 29), Pueblo Lodge No. 17, Pueblo, Apprentice

Eckstein, Samuel
 Proceedings 1870, pg 30 (1870 Sept 28), Pueblo Lodge No. 17, Pueblo
 Proceedings 1871, pg 28 (1871 Sept 27), Pueblo Lodge No. 17, Pueblo
 Proceedings 1872, pg 31 (1872 Sept 24), Pueblo Lodge No. 17, Pueblo
 Proceedings 1873, pg 47 (1873 Oct 1), Pueblo Lodge No. 17, Pueblo
 Proceedings 1874, pg 222 (1874 Sept 30), Pueblo Lodge No. 17, Pueblo, Pueblo County
 Proceedings 1876, pg 38 (1876 Sept 20) Pueblo Lodge No. 17

Eclectic Grand Lodge of Frankfort-on-Main
 Proceedings 1872, pg 47 (1872 Sept 24), Frankfort, [Germany]

Eddy, Edward
 Proceedings 1875, pg 81 (1875 Sept 22), Washington Lodge No. 12, Georgetown
 Proceedings 1876, pg 35 (1876 Sept 20), Washington Lodge No. 12, Georgetown

Edger, John
 Proceedings 1876, pg 45 (1876 Sept 20) South Pueblo Lodge U D, Fellow Craft,

Edmondson
 Proceedings 1870, pg 57 (1869 Oct 4) Grand Secretary, Grand Lodge of Idaho

Edmondson, P E
 Proceedings 1861-1869, pg 316 (1869 Sept 29) Grand Lodge of Idaho Territory
 Proceedings 1861-1869, pg 330 (1868 June 22) Grand Secretary, Grand Lodge of Idaho Territory
 Proceedings 1861-1869, pg 250 (1867 Dec 16), Grand Secretary, Grand Lodge of Idaho
 Proceedings 1861-1869, pg 251 (1867 Dec 16), Grand Secretary, Grand Lodge of Idaho
 Proceedings 1870, pg 56 (1869 Oct 4) Grand Secretary, Grand Lodge of Idaho

Edson, M W
 Proceedings 1861-1869, pg 149 (1865 Nov 7), Nevada Lodge No. 4, Nevadaville
 Proceedings 1861-1869, pg 167 (1866 Oct 2) Denver Lodge No. 5, dimitted

Edwards, J
 Proceedings 1876, pg 29 (1876 Sept 20) Golden City Lodge No. 1

Edwards, James W
 Proceedings 1872, pg 19 (1872 Sept 24), Nevada Lodge No. 4, Bald Mountain, Fellowcraft
 Proceedings 1873, pg 36 (1873 Oct 1), Nevada Lodge No. 4, Nevada
 Proceedings 1874, pg 210 (1874 Sept 30), Nevada Lodge No. 4, Bald Mountain, Gilpin County
 Proceedings 1876, pg 30 (1876 Sept 20) Nevada Lodge No. 4

Edwards, Jas W
 Proceedings 1875, pg 74 (1875 Sept 22), Nevada Lodge No. 4, Nevada

Edwards, Jenkins
 Proceedings 1875, pg 73 (1875 Sept 22) Golden City Lodge No. 1

Edwards, John
Proceedings 1874, pg 229 (1874 Sept 30), Idaho Springs Lodge U D, Idaho Springs

Edwards, John W
Proceedings 1875, pg 90 (1875 Sept 22) Idaho Springs Lodge U D, Wisconsin Lodge No. 37, Wisconsin, Suspended

Effingham, A
Proceedings 1870, pg 72 (1784 Sept 29) Grand Master, Grand Lodge of Masons, London

Eggen, C L
Proceedings 1872, pg 17 (1872 Sept 24), Golden City Lodge No. 1, Golden City
Proceedings 1861-1869, pg 147 (1865 Nov 7) Golden City Lodge No. 1, Apprentice
Proceedings 1861-1869, pg 165 (1866 Oct 2) Golden City Lodge No. 1
Proceedings 1870, pg 19 (1870 Sept 28), Golden City Lodge No. 1, Golden City
Proceedings 1871, pg 17 (1871 Sept 27), Golden City Lodge No. 1, Golden City
Proceedings 1873, pg 35 (1873 Oct 1), Golden City Lodge No. 1, Golden City
Proceedings 1874, pg 209 (1874 Sept 30), Golden City Lodge No. 1, Golden City, died

Eggers, Chas L
Proceedings 1861-1869, pg 191 (1867 Oct 8) Golden City Lodge No. 1

Eggers, E L
Proceedings 1861-1869, pg 221 (1868 Oct 7) Golden City Lodge No. 1
Proceedings 1861-1869, pg 303 (1869 Sept 29) Golden City Lodge No. 1

Eginton, Chas
Proceedings 1870, pg 62 (1869 Oct 18) Grand Master, Grand Lodge of Kentucky

Ehle, Joseph
Proceedings 1861-1869, pg 77 (1862 Nov 4) Denver Lodge No. 5
Proceedings 1861-1869, pg 112 (1863 Nov 3) Denver Lodge No. 5
Proceedings 1861-1869, pg 133 (1864 Nov 8) Denver Lodge No. 5
Proceedings 1861-1869, pg 149 (1865 Nov 7), Nevada Lodge No. 4, Nevadaville, dimitted,

El Paso Lodge No. 13
Proceedings 1873, pg 30 (1873 Oct 1) removed from Colorado City to Colorado Springs
Proceedings 1875, pg 23 (1875 Sept 21) has not provided a list of officers
Proceedings 1875, pg 23 (1875 Sept 21) has not provided annual returns
Proceedings 1875, pg 25 (1875 Sept 21) dues paid
Proceedings 1875, pg 92 (1875 Sept 22)
Proceedings 1876, pg 52 (1876 Sept 20)

El Paso Lodge No. 13, Colorado City
Proceedings 1861-1869, pg 189 (1867 Oct 8) charter granted
Proceedings 1861-1869, pg 210 (1867 Nov) dedicated
Proceedings 1861-1869, pg 211 (1868 Aug) arranged for a visit
Proceedings 1874, pg 19 (1874 Sept 29) returns incomplete
Proceedings 1874, pg 208 (1874 Sept 30)

El Paso Lodge No. 13, Colorado Springs
Proceedings 1876, pg 13 (1876 Sept 19) dues paid

El Paso Lodge U D, Colorado City
Proceedings 1861-1869, pg 154 (1866 Jan 27) dispensation
Proceedings 1861-1869, pg 156 (1866 Oct 1) dispensation
Proceedings 1861-1869, pg 158 (1865 Dec 1) dispensation
Proceedings 1861-1869, pg 181 (1867 Oct 7) paid dues
Proceedings 1861-1869, pg 181 (1867 Oct 7) dues paid
Proceedings 1861-1869, pg 188 (1867 Oct 8) communication received
Proceedings 1861-1869, pg 206 (1867 Nov 7), El Paso Lodge No. 13, Colorado City

Elbert
Proceedings 1861-1869, pg 117 (1864 Nov 7) committee
Proceedings 1861-1869, pg 289 (1869 Sept 28) committee

Elbert, S H
Proceedings 1861-1869, pg 102 (1863 Nov 3) petition for formation of a new lodge in Denver
Proceedings 1861-1869, pg 116 (1864 Nov 7), Union Lodge No. 7, Denver
Proceedings 1861-1869, pg 140 (1864 Nov 8) warrant
Proceedings 1861-1869, pg 144 (1865 Nov 7) Committee
Proceedings 1861-1869, pg 169 (1866 Oct 2), Union Lodge No. 7, Denver
Proceedings 1861-1869, pg 195 (1867 Oct 8), Union Lodge No. 7, Denver
Proceedings 1861-1869, pg 225 (1868 Oct 7), Union Lodge No. 7, Denver
Proceedings 1861-1869, pg 301 (1869 Sept 29), Union Lodge No. 7, Denver

Elbert, Sam H
Proceedings 1861-1869, pg 115 (1864 Nov 7) committee
Proceedings 1861-1869, pg 115 (1864 Nov 7) Junior Grand Deacon
Proceedings 1861-1869, pg 116 (1864 Nov 7) committee
Proceedings 1861-1869, pg 117 (1864 Nov 7) committee
Proceedings 1861-1869, pg 119 (1864 Nov 8) committee
Proceedings 1861-1869, pg 122 (1864 Nov 8) committee
Proceedings 1861-1869, pg 123 (1864 Nov 8) committee
Proceedings 1861-1869, pg 124 (1864 Nov 8) committee
Proceedings 1861-1869, pg 125 (1864 Nov 8) committee
Proceedings 1861-1869, pg 126 (1864 Nov 8) committee
Proceedings 1861-1869, pg 126 (1864 Nov 8), Union Lodge No. 7, Denver
Proceedings 1861-1869, pg 127 (1864 Nov 8) committee
Proceedings 1861-1869, pg 134 (1864 Nov 8), Union Lodge No. 7, Denver
Proceedings 1861-1869, pg 230 (1868 Oct 7), Germania Lodge U D, Denver

Colorado's Territorial Masons

Elbert, Sam H, cont.
  Proceedings 1861-1869, pg 288 (1869 Sept 28), Union Lodge No. 7, Denver
  Proceedings 1861-1869, pg 307 (1869 Sept 29), Union Lodge No. 7, Denver
  Proceedings 1871, pg 21 (1871 Sept 27), Union Lodge No. 7, Denver
  Proceedings 1874, pg 15 (1874 Sept 29) committee

Elbert, Sam'l H
  Proceedings 1876, pg 32 (1876 Sept 20), Union Lodge No. 7, Denver

Elbert, Samuel
  Proceedings 1875, pg 78 (1875 Sept 22), Union Lodge No. 7, Denver

Elbert, Samuel H
  Proceedings 1861-1869, pg 151 (1865 Nov 7), Chivington Lodge No. 6, Central City
  Proceedings 1870, pg 23 (1870 Sept 28), Union Lodge No. 7, Denver
  Proceedings 1872, pg 22 (1872 Sept 24), Union Lodge No. 7, Denver
  Proceedings 1873, pg 4 (1873 Sept 30) pall bearer for George M Randall
  Proceedings 1873, pg 39 (1873 Oct 1), Union Lodge No. 7, Denver
  Proceedings 1874, pg 213 (1874 Sept 30), Union Lodge No. 7, Denver

Elder, H G
  Proceedings 1876, pg 33 (1876 Sept 20), Union Lodge No. 7, Denver
  Proceedings 1876, pg 50 (1876 Sept 20), Union Lodge No. 7, Denver

Elder, Harry G
  Proceedings 1861-1869, pg 226 (1868 Oct 7), Union Lodge No. 7, Denver, Apprentice
  Proceedings 1861-1869, pg 308 (1869 Sept 29), Union Lodge No. 7, Denver, Fellowcraft
  Proceedings 1873, pg 40 (1873 Oct 1), Union Lodge No. 7, Denver

Elder, Henry
  Proceedings 1870, pg 23 (1870 Sept 28), Union Lodge No. 7, Denver

Elder, Henry G
  Proceedings 1871, pg 21 (1871 Sept 27), Union Lodge No. 7, Denver
  Proceedings 1872, pg 23 (1872 Sept 24), Union Lodge No. 7, Denver
  Proceedings 1874, pg 214 (1874 Sept 30), Union Lodge No. 7, Denver
  Proceedings 1875, pg 78 (1875 Sept 22), Union Lodge No. 7, Denver

Elderkin, W A
  Proceedings 1871, pg 19 (1871 Sept 27) Denver Lodge No. 5
  Proceedings 1872, pg 20 (1872 Sept 24), Denver Lodge No. 5, Denver
  Proceedings 1873, pg 37 (1873 Oct 1), Denver Lodge No. 5, Denver
  Proceedings 1874, pg 212 (1874 Sept 30), Denver Lodge No. 5, Denver
  Proceedings 1875, pg 76 (1875 Sept 22) Denver Lodge No. 5
  Proceedings 1876, pg 31 (1876 Sept 20) Denver Lodge No. 5

Elderkin, Wm A
  Proceedings 1876, pg 50 (1876 Sept 20) Denver Lodge No. 5

Eldred, H R
  Proceedings 1861-1869, pg 134 (1864 Nov 8), Chivington Lodge No. 6, Central City
  Proceedings 1861-1869, pg 150 (1865 Nov 7), Chivington Lodge No. 6, Central City
  Proceedings 1861-1869, pg 168 (1866 Oct 2), Chivington Lodge No. 6, Central City
  Proceedings 1861-1869, pg 194 (1867 Oct 8), Chivington Lodge No. 6, Central City
  Proceedings 1861-1869, pg 224 (1868 Oct 7), Chivington Lodge No. 6, Central City
  Proceedings 1861-1869, pg 230 (1868 Oct 7), Valmont Lodge U D, Valmont
  Proceedings 1861-1869, pg 306 (1869 Sept 29), Central Lodge No. 6, Central City
  Proceedings 1870, pg 15 (1870 Sept 28) now living at Boulder, Central Lodge No. 6, Central City
  Proceedings 1870, pg 22 (1870 Sept 28), Central Lodge No. 6, Central City
  Proceedings 1871, pg 11 (1871 Sept 26), Central Lodge No. 6, Central City, Living in Boulder
  Proceedings 1871, pg 20 (1871 Sept 27), Central Lodge No. 6, Central

Eldred, Holden R
  Proceedings 1872, pg 21 (1872 Sept 24), Denver Lodge No. 5, Denver
  Proceedings 1873, pg 38 (1873 Oct 1), Central Lodge No. 6, Central City
  Proceedings 1874, pg 213 (1874 Sept 30), Central Lodge No. 6, Central
  Proceedings 1875, pg 77 (1875 Sept 22), Central Lodge No. 6, Central City, Stricken from the rolls

Eldridge, Z
  Proceedings 1873, pg 50 (1873 Oct 1), Occidental Lodge No. 20, Greeley
  Proceedings 1874, pg 225 (1874 Sept 30), Occidental Lodge No. 20, Greeley
  Proceedings 1875, pg 87 (1875 Sept 22), Occidental Lodge No. 20, Greeley
  Proceedings 1876, pg 40 (1876 Sept 20), Occidental Lodge No. 20, Greeley

Elgin, Robert M
  Proceedings 1872, pg 88 (1872 Sept 24) Grand Lodge of Texas

Ellingham, John J
  Proceedings 1872, pg 28 (1872 Sept 24), Columbia Lodge No. 14, Boulder, Fellowcraft

Proceedings 1873, pg 44 (1873 Oct 1), Columbia Lodge No. 14, Boulder

Proceedings 1874, pg 219 (1874 Sept 30), Columbia Lodge No. 14, Boulder, Boulder County

Proceedings 1875, pg 83 (1875 Sept 22), Columbia Lodge No. 14, Boulder

Proceedings 1876, pg 37 (1876 Sept 20), Columbia Lodge No. 14, Boulder

Ellingham, R

Proceedings 1871, pg 25 (1871 Sept 27), Columbia Lodge No. 14, Boulder City

Ellingham, Robert

Proceedings 1870, pg 27 (1870 Sept 28), Columbia Lodge No. 14, Boulder City

Proceedings 1872, pg 27 (1872 Sept 24), Columbia Lodge No. 14, Boulder

Proceedings 1873, pg 44 (1873 Oct 1), Columbia Lodge No. 14, Boulder

Proceedings 1874, pg 219 (1874 Sept 30), Columbia Lodge No. 14, Boulder, Boulder County

Proceedings 1875, pg 83 (1875 Sept 22), Columbia Lodge No. 14, Boulder

Proceedings 1876, pg 37 (1876 Sept 20), Columbia Lodge No. 14, Boulder

Elliott, Ezra T

Proceedings 1876, pg 24 (1876 Sept 20), Del Norte Lodge No. 29, Del Norte

Proceedings 1876, pg 44 (1876 Sept 20) Del Norte Lodge U D

Elliott, James

Proceedings 1871, pg 23 (1871 Sept 27), Black Hawk Lodge No. 11, Black Hawk

Proceedings 1872, pg 24 (1872 Sept 24), Black Hawk Lodge No. 11, Black Hawk

Proceedings 1873, pg 42 (1873 Oct 1), Black Hawk Lodge No. 11, Black Hawk

Proceedings 1874, pg 216 (1874 Sept 30), Black Hawk Lodge No. 11, Black Hawk

Proceedings 1875, pg 80 (1875 Sept 22) Black Hawk Lodge No. 11

Proceedings 1876, pg 34 (1876 Sept 20) Black Hawk Lodge No. 11

Elliott, S A

Proceedings 1875, pg 87 (1875 Sept 22), Occidental Lodge No. 20, Greeley

Proceedings 1876, pg 40 (1876 Sept 20), Occidental Lodge No. 20, Greeley

Ellis, A L

Proceedings 1875, pg 83 (1875 Sept 22), Columbia Lodge No. 14, Boulder

Proceedings 1876, pg 37 (1876 Sept 20), Columbia Lodge No. 14, Boulder

Ellis, Abe R

Proceedings 1874, pg 222 (1874 Sept 30), Pueblo Lodge No. 17, Pueblo, Pueblo County

Proceedings 1875, pg 85 (1875 Sept 22) Pueblo Lodge No. 17

Proceedings 1876, pg 38 (1876 Sept 20) Pueblo Lodge No. 17

Ellis, Abram R

Proceedings 1876, pg 45 (1876 Sept 20) South Pueblo Lodge U D

Ellis, H H

Proceedings 1861-1869, pg 223 (1868 Oct 7) Denver Lodge No. 5, Fellowcraft

Proceedings 1861-1869, pg 305 (1869 Sept 29) Denver Lodge No. 5, received permission to receive degrees in another lodge

Ellis, Henry

Proceedings 1870, pg 29 (1870 Sept 28), Cheyenne Lodge No. 16, Cheyenne, Wyoming Territory

Ellis, Henry H

Proceedings 1871, pg 27 (1871 Sept 27), Cheyenne Lodge No. 16, Cheyenne, Wyoming Territory

Proceedings 1872, pg 29 (1872 Sept 24), Cheyenne Lodge No. 16, Cheyenne, Wyoming Territory

Proceedings 1873, pg 46 (1873 Oct 1), Cheyenne Lodge No. 16, Cheyenne, Wyoming Territory

Proceedings 1874, pg 221 (1874 Sept 30), Cheyenne Lodge No. 16, Cheyenne, Wyoming Territory

Ellis, J M

Proceedings 1861-1869, pg 177 (1866 Nov 17), Mount Moriah Lodge U D, Great Salt Lake City

Ellis, John V

Proceedings 1870, pg 94 (1869 Sept 22) Grand Secretary, Grand Lodge of New Brunswick

Proceedings 1872, pg 43 (1872 Sept 24) Carleton, Grand Lodge of New Brunswick

Proceedings 1873, pg 61 (1873 Oct 1) Grand Lodge of New Brunswick, Carleton

Proceedings 1874, pg 103 (1874 Sept 30) Grand Lodge of New Brunswick

Proceedings 1874, pg 204 (1874 Sept 30) Grand Lodge of New Brunswick, St John

Ellis, Robert

Proceedings 1874, pg 8 (1874 July 14), Idaho Springs Lodge U D, Idaho Springs

Proceedings 1875, pg 90 (1875 Sept 22) Idaho Springs Lodge U D, died

Proceedings 1875, pg 94 (1875 Sept 22) Idaho Springs Lodge U D

Ellis, Robt

Proceedings 1874, pg 229 (1874 Sept 30), Idaho Springs Lodge U D, Idaho Springs

Ellis, W T

Proceedings 1861-1869, pg 150 (1865 Nov 7), Chivington Lodge No. 6, Central City

Proceedings 1861-1869, pg 168 (1866 Oct 2), Chivington Lodge No. 6, Central City

Ellis, William

Proceedings 1873, pg 50 (1873 Oct 1), Occidental Lodge No. 20, Greeley

Colorado's Territorial Masons

Ellis, William, cont.
Proceedings 1874, pg 225 (1874 Sept 30), Occidental Lodge No. 20, Greeley
Proceedings 1876, pg 40 (1876 Sept 20), Occidental Lodge No. 20, Greeley

Ellis, William T
Proceedings 1872, pg 22 (1872 Sept 24), Denver Lodge No. 5, Denver, died

Ellis, Wm
Proceedings 1875, pg 87 (1875 Sept 22), Occidental Lodge No. 20, Greeley

Ellis, Wm T
Proceedings 1861-1869, pg 134 (1864 Nov 8), Chivington Lodge No. 6, Central City
Proceedings 1861-1869, pg 194 (1867 Oct 8), Chivington Lodge No. 6, Central City
Proceedings 1861-1869, pg 224 (1868 Oct 7), Chivington Lodge No. 6, Central City
Proceedings 1861-1869, pg 306 (1869 Sept 29), Central Lodge No. 6, Central City
Proceedings 1870, pg 22 (1870 Sept 28), Central Lodge No. 6, Central City
Proceedings 1871, pg 20 (1871 Sept 27), Central Lodge No. 6, Central
Proceedings 1872, pg 39 (1872 Sept 24), Central Lodge No. 6, Central

Ellison, Jas M
Proceedings 1872, pg 36 (1872 Sept 24), Ashlar Lodge U D, Colorado Springs

Elm Street Publishing Company
Proceedings 1861-1869, pg 290 (1869 Sept 28), of Cincinnati, OH

Elmire, George
Proceedings 1876, pg 43 (1876 Sept 20), Huerfano Lodge No. 27, Walsenburg, Fellow Craft

Emperor, W M
Proceedings 1876, pg 41 (1876 Sept 20), Weston Lodge No. 22, Littleton

Emperor, William
Proceedings 1870, pg 20 (1870 Sept 28), Nevada Lodge No. 4, Nevadaville
Proceedings 1872, pg 19 (1872 Sept 24), Nevada Lodge No. 4, Bald Mountain
Proceedings 1873, pg 36 (1873 Oct 1), Nevada Lodge No. 4, Nevada, Dimitted

Emperor, Wm
Proceedings 1861-1869, pg 192 (1867 Oct 8), Nevada Lodge No. 4, Nevadaville
Proceedings 1861-1869, pg 222 (1868 Oct 7), Nevada Lodge No. 4, Nevadaville
Proceedings 1861-1869, pg 304 (1869 Sept 29), Nevada Lodge No. 4, Nevadaville
Proceedings 1870, pg 4 (1870 Sept 27), Nevada Lodge No. 4, Nevadaville
Proceedings 1871, pg 18 (1871 Sept 27), Nevada Lodge No. 4, Bald Mountain
Proceedings 1874, pg 226 (1874 Sept 30), Weston Lodge No. 22, Littleton
Proceedings 1875, pg 88 (1875 Sept 22), Weston Lodge No. 22, Littleton

Empire City Lodge No. 8
Proceedings 1861-1869, pg 140 (1865 Nov 6) charter granted

Empire City Lodge U D
Proceedings 1861-1869, pg 95 (1863 Apr 17) petition for formation
Proceedings 1861-1869, pg 137 (1865 Nov 6), Empire City Lodge U D, Clear Creek County
Proceedings 1861-1869, pg 139 (1864 Nov 17) dispensation
Proceedings 1861-1869, pg 139 (1865 Nov 6) requesting charter

Empire Lodge No. 8
Proceedings 1875, pg 20 (1874 Dec 5) surrendered its charter to the Grand Lodge
Proceedings 1876, pg 46 (1876 Sept 20) charter surrendered

Empire Lodge No. 8, Empire
Proceedings 1871, pg 22 (1871 Sept 27) no return
Proceedings 1872, pg 6 (1872 Sept 24) dispensation given
Proceedings 1872, pg 11 (1872 Sept 24) has made returns and paid dues
Proceedings 1872, pg 11 (1872 Sept 24) failed to make timely returns

Empire Lodge No. 8, Empire City
Proceedings 1861-1869, pg 158 (1865 Nov 7) dues paid
Proceedings 1861-1869, pg 158 (1866 Oct 1) dues paid
Proceedings 1861-1869, pg 181 (1867 Oct 7) dues paid
Proceedings 1874, pg 19 (1874 Sept 29) returns late
Proceedings 1874, pg 208 (1874 Sept 30)
Proceedings 1875, pg 79 (1875 Sept 22) charter surrendered
Proceedings 1876, pg 13 (1875 Oct 6) dues from members paid

Empire Lodge No. 8, Empire, Clear Creek County
Proceedings 1875, pg 23 (1874 Dec 5) communication

Enberger, Lipman Schwartz
Proceedings 1873, pg 45 (1873 Oct 1), Columbia Lodge No. 14, Boulder, died

England, G A
Proceedings 1874, pg 221 (1874 Sept 30), Cheyenne Lodge No. 16, Cheyenne, Wyoming Territory

Englesby, Leverett B
Proceedings 1861-1869, pg 348 (1868 June 10) Grand Master, Grand Lodge of Vermont
Proceedings 1870, pg 104 (1869 June 9) Past Grand Master, Grand Lodge of Vermont,

English
Proceedings 1861-1869, pg 236 (1867 Nov 4) communication
Proceedings 1870, pg 43 (1869 Nov 1) Grand Lodge of Arkansas

English, E H
　Proceedings 1861-1869, pg 235 (1867 Nov 4) Grand Master of Arkansas
　Proceedings 1861-1869, pg 322 (1868 Nov 16) Grand Master, Grand Lodge of Arkansas
　Proceedings 1870, pg 40 (1869 Nov 1) Grand Master, Grand Lodge of Arkansas

English, Elbert H
　Proceedings 1861-1869, pg 324 (1868 Nov 16) Grand Master, Grand Lodge of Arkansas

Engstrom, A G
　Proceedings 1870, pg 31 (1870 Sept 28), Laramie Lodge No. 18, Laramie, Wyoming Territory
　Proceedings 1871, pg 29 (1871 Sept 27), Laramie Lodge No. 18, Laramie, Wyoming Territory
　Proceedings 1872, pg 32 (1872 Sept 24), Laramie Lodge No. 18, Laramie, Wyoming Territory
　Proceedings 1873, pg 48 (1873 Oct 1), Laramie Lodge No. 18, Laramie, Wyoming Territory
　Proceedings 1874, pg 223 (1874 Sept 30), Laramie Lodge No. 18, Laramie City

Entwistle, Thomas
　Proceedings 1861-1869, pg 196 (1867 Oct 8), Black Hawk Lodge No. 11, Black Hawk
　Proceedings 1861-1869, pg 227 (1868 Oct 7), Black Hawk Lodge No. 11, Black Hawk
　Proceedings 1871, pg 23 (1871 Sept 27), Black Hawk Lodge No. 11, Black Hawk
　Proceedings 1874, pg 216 (1874 Sept 30), Black Hawk Lodge No. 11, Black Hawk
　Proceedings 1875, pg 80 (1875 Sept 22) Black Hawk Lodge No. 11
　Proceedings 1876, pg 34 (1876 Sept 20) Black Hawk Lodge No. 11

Entwistle, Thos
　Proceedings 1861-1869, pg 309 (1869 Sept 29), Black Hawk Lodge No. 11, Black Hawk
　Proceedings 1870, pg 25 (1870 Sept 28), Black Hawk Lodge No. 11, Black Hawk
　Proceedings 1872, pg 25 (1872 Sept 24), Black Hawk Lodge No. 11, Black Hawk
　Proceedings 1873, pg 42 (1873 Oct 1), Black Hawk Lodge No. 11, Black Hawk

Epperson, H P
　Proceedings 1875, pg 89 (1875 Sept 22), Doric Lodge No. 25, Fairplay, Fellowcraft

Epperson, Hiram P
　Proceedings 1876, pg 42 (1876 Sept 20), Doric Lodge No. 25, Fairplay

Eppstein, Isaac
　Proceedings 1876, pg 44 (1876 Sept 20), Las Animas Lodge No. 28, Trinidad

Eppstein, M
　Proceedings 1874, pg 222 (1874 Sept 30), Pueblo Lodge No. 17, Pueblo, Pueblo County
　Proceedings 1875, pg 85 (1875 Sept 22) Pueblo Lodge No. 17
　Proceedings 1876, pg 38 (1876 Sept 20) Pueblo Lodge No. 17

Epstein, Isaac
　Proceedings 1875, pg 91 (1875 Sept 22), Las Animas Lodge U D, Trinidad

Erans, John
　Proceedings 1870, pg 23 (1870 Sept 28), Union Lodge No. 7, Denver

Erskins, Peter
　Proceedings 1861-1869, pg 191 (1867 Oct 8) Golden City Lodge No. 1, Fellowcraft

Escranbrack, Thomas R
　Proceedings 1874, pg 67 (1874 Sept 30) Grand Lodge of Iowa

Escranbrack, Thos R
　Proceedings 1874, pg 71 (1874 Sept 30) Grand Lodge of Iowa

Eskens, Peter
　Proceedings 1871, pg 17 (1871 Sept 27), Golden City Lodge No. 1, Golden City

Eskin, Peter
　Proceedings 1875, pg 73 (1875 Sept 22) Golden City Lodge No. 1
　Proceedings 1876, pg 29 (1876 Sept 20) Golden City Lodge No. 1
　Proceedings 1876, pg 50 (1876 Sept 20) Golden City Lodge No. 1

Eskins, Peter
　Proceedings 1861-1869, pg 221 (1868 Oct 7) Golden City Lodge No. 1
　Proceedings 1861-1869, pg 303 (1869 Sept 29) Golden City Lodge No. 1
　Proceedings 1870, pg 19 (1870 Sept 28), Golden City Lodge No. 1, Golden City
　Proceedings 1872, pg 17 (1872 Sept 24), Golden City Lodge No. 1, Golden City
　Proceedings 1873, pg 35 (1873 Oct 1), Golden City Lodge No. 1, Golden City
　Proceedings 1874, pg 209 (1874 Sept 30), Golden City Lodge No. 1, Golden City

Esmond, Bart
　Proceedings 1861-1869, pg 197 (1867 Oct 8), Columbia Lodge U D, Boulder

Estabrook, Geo W
　Proceedings 1873, pg 36 (1873 Oct 1), Nevada Lodge No. 4, Nevada

Estabrooks, Geo W
　Proceedings 1874, pg 210 (1874 Sept 30), Nevada Lodge No. 4, Bald Mountain, Gilpin County
　Proceedings 1875, pg 74 (1875 Sept 22), Nevada Lodge No. 4, Nevada

Estabrooks, George W
　Proceedings 1876, pg 30 (1876 Sept 20) Nevada Lodge No. 4

Estelle, James M
   Proceedings 1876, pg 35 (1876 Sept 20), Washington Lodge No. 12, Georgetown

Ettien, David
   Proceedings 1861-1869, pg 150 (1865 Nov 7), Chivington Lodge No. 6, Central City, Apprentice
   Proceedings 1861-1869, pg 169 (1866 Oct 2), Chivington Lodge No. 6, Central City, Apprentice
   Proceedings 1861-1869, pg 194 (1867 Oct 8), Chivington Lodge No. 6, Central City, Apprentice
   Proceedings 1861-1869, pg 225 (1868 Oct 7), Chivington Lodge No. 6, Central City, Apprentice
   Proceedings 1861-1869, pg 307 (1869 Sept 29), Central Lodge No. 6, Central City, Apprentice
   Proceedings 1870, pg 22 (1870 Sept 28), Central Lodge No. 6, Central City, Apprentice
   Proceedings 1871, pg 21 (1871 Sept 27), Central Lodge No. 6, Central, Apprentice
   Proceedings 1872, pg 21 (1872 Sept 24), Denver Lodge No. 5, Denver, Apprentice
   Proceedings 1874, pg 213 (1874 Sept 30), Central Lodge No. 6, Central, Apprentice
   Proceedings 1875, pg 77 (1875 Sept 22), Central Lodge No. 6, Central City, Apprentice
   Proceedings 1876, pg 32 (1876 Sept 20), Central Lodge No. 6, Central City, Apprentice

Ettien, David T
   Proceedings 1873, pg 39 (1873 Oct 1), Central Lodge No. 6, Central City, Apprentice

Eurgens, A
   Proceedings 1874, pg 223 (1874 Sept 30), Laramie Lodge No. 18, Laramie City
   Proceedings 1873, pg 48 (1873 Oct 1), Laramie Lodge No. 18, Laramie, Wyoming Territory, Fellowcraft

Eussen, B W
   Proceedings 1861-1869, pg 77 (1862 Nov 4), Nevada Lodge No. 4, Nevadaville
   Proceedings 1861-1869, pg 111 (1863 Nov 3), Nevada Lodge No. 4, Nevadaville
   Proceedings 1861-1869, pg 132 (1864 Nov 8), Nevada Lodge No. 4, Nevadaville
   Proceedings 1861-1869, pg 148 (1865 Nov 7), Nevada Lodge No. 4, Nevadaville
   Proceedings 1861-1869, pg 166 (1866 Oct 2), Nevada Lodge No. 4, Nevadaville
   Proceedings 1861-1869, pg 192 (1867 Oct 8), Nevada Lodge No. 4, Nevadaville
   Proceedings 1861-1869, pg 222 (1868 Oct 7), Nevada Lodge No. 4, Nevadaville
   Proceedings 1861-1869, pg 304 (1869 Sept 29), Nevada Lodge No. 4, Nevadaville
   Proceedings 1875, pg 74 (1875 Sept 22), Nevada Lodge No. 4, Nevada
   Proceedings 1876, pg 30 (1876 Sept 20) Nevada Lodge No. 4

Eussen, Baltis W
   Proceedings 1870, pg 20 (1870 Sept 28), Nevada Lodge No. 4, Nevadaville

Eussen, Baltus W
   Proceedings 1871, pg 18 (1871 Sept 27), Nevada Lodge No. 4, Bald Mountain
   Proceedings 1872, pg 19 (1872 Sept 24), Nevada Lodge No. 4, Bald Mountain
   Proceedings 1873, pg 36 (1873 Oct 1), Nevada Lodge No. 4, Nevada
   Proceedings 1874, pg 210 (1874 Sept 30), Nevada Lodge No. 4, Bald Mountain, Gilpin County

Evans
   Proceedings 1870, pg 7 (1870 June 24), President, Denver Pacific Railway Company

Evans, E R
   Proceedings 1861-1869, pg 227 (1868 Oct 7), Washington Lodge No. 12, Georgetown
   Proceedings 1871, pg 24 (1871 Sept 27), Washington Lodge No. 12, Georgetown

Evans, Elias R
   Proceedings 1861-1869, pg 309 (1869 Sept 29), Washington Lodge No. 12, Georgetown
   Proceedings 1870, pg 26 (1870 Sept 28), Washington Lodge No. 12, Georgetown
   Proceedings 1872, pg 26 (1872 Sept 24), Washington Lodge No. 12, Georgetown, Dimitted

Evans, Erastus C
   Proceedings 1876, pg 34 (1876 Sept 20), Washington Lodge No. 12, Georgetown

Evans, Evan
   Proceedings 1876, pg 42 (1876 Sept 20), Doric Lodge No. 25, Fairplay

Evans, Jno
   Proceedings 1861-1869, pg 102 (1863 Nov 3) petition for formation of a new lodge in Denver
   Proceedings 1871, pg 21 (1871 Sept 27), Union Lodge No. 7, Denver

Evans, John
   Proceedings 1861-1869, pg 134 (1864 Nov 8), Union Lodge No. 7, Denver
   Proceedings 1861-1869, pg 151 (1865 Nov 7), Chivington Lodge No. 6, Central City
   Proceedings 1861-1869, pg 169 (1866 Oct 2), Union Lodge No. 7, Denver
   Proceedings 1861-1869, pg 195 (1867 Oct 8), Union Lodge No. 7, Denver
   Proceedings 1861-1869, pg 225 (1868 Oct 7), Union Lodge No. 7, Denver
   Proceedings 1861-1869, pg 307 (1869 Sept 29), Union Lodge No. 7, Denver
   Proceedings 1872, pg 23 (1872 Sept 24), Union Lodge No. 7, Denver
   Proceedings 1873, pg 40 (1873 Oct 1), Union Lodge No. 7, Denver
   Proceedings 1874, pg 214 (1874 Sept 30), Union Lodge No. 7, Denver
   Proceedings 1875, pg 78 (1875 Sept 22), Union Lodge No. 7, Denver
   Proceedings 1876, pg 33 (1876 Sept 20), Union Lodge No. 7, Denver

Evans, Samuel
Proceedings 1872, pg 69 (1872 Sept 24) Grand Lodge of Massachusetts

Evans, W H
Proceedings 1861-1869, pg 167 (1866 Oct 2) Denver Lodge No. 5, Apprentice
Proceedings 1861-1869, pg 193 (1867 Oct 8) Denver Lodge No. 5, Apprentice
Proceedings 1861-1869, pg 223 (1868 Oct 7) Denver Lodge No. 5, Apprentice
Proceedings 1861-1869, pg 305 (1869 Sept 29) Denver Lodge No. 5, Apprentice

Evans, W N
Proceedings 1861-1869, pg 149 (1865 Nov 7), Nevada Lodge No. 4, Nevadaville, Apprentice,

Evanston Lodge [No. 24]
Proceedings 1875, pg 25 (1875 Sept 21) payment for charter

Evanston Lodge No. 24
Proceedings 1875, pg 20 (1875 Sept 21) Grand Lodge of Wyoming
Proceedings 1875, pg 23 (1875 Sept 21) Grand Lodge of Wyoming
Proceedings 1875, pg 24 (1875 Sept 21) has not returned charter

Evanston Lodge No. 24, Evanston, Wyoming Territory
Proceedings 1874, pg 35 (1874 Sept 30) charter granted

Evanston Lodge No. 4
Proceedings 1875, pg 88 (1875 Sept 22) Grand Lodge of Wyoming
Proceedings 1876, pg 47 (1876 Sept 20), Evanston Lodge No. 4, Grant Lodge of Wyoming Territory

Evanston Lodge U D, Evanston, WY
Proceedings 1875, pg 19 (1874 Nov 14) communication

Evanston Lodge U D, Evanston, Wyoming Territory
Proceedings 1873, pg 10 (1873 Sept 30) dispensation granted 8 Sept 1873
Proceedings 1873, pg 12 (1873 Sept 30)
Proceedings 1873, pg 19 (1873 Oct 1) dispensation continued
Proceedings 1874, pg 8 (1874 Sept 29) dispensation granted
Proceedings 1874, pg 19 (1874 Sept 29) dues paid
Proceedings 1874, pg 208 (1874 Sept 30)
Everett, Francis E
Proceedings 1875, pg 73 (1875 Sept 22) Golden City Lodge No. 1

Everett, Francis E
Proceedings 1876, pg 29 (1876 Sept 20) Golden City Lodge No. 1

Evergreen
Proceedings 1870, pg 11 (1870 Sept 27), Dubuque, IA
Proceedings 1871, pg 10 (1871 Sept 26) masonic magazine
Proceedings 1872, pg 11 (1872 Sept 24), published at Davenport, IA

Ewers, J S
Proceedings 1861-1869, pg 169 (1866 Oct 2), Chivington Lodge No. 6, Central City, Apprentice
Proceedings 1861-1869, pg 194 (1867 Oct 8), Chivington Lodge No. 6, Central City, Apprentice
Proceedings 1861-1869, pg 225 (1868 Oct 7), Chivington Lodge No. 6, Central City, Apprentice
Proceedings 1861-1869, pg 307 (1869 Sept 29), Central Lodge No. 6, Central City, Apprentice

Ewers, James S
Proceedings 1870, pg 22 (1870 Sept 28), Central Lodge No. 6, Central City, Apprentice
Proceedings 1871, pg 21 (1871 Sept 27), Central Lodge No. 6, Central, Apprentice
Proceedings 1872, pg 21 (1872 Sept 24), Denver Lodge No. 5, Denver, Apprentice
Proceedings 1873, pg 39 (1873 Oct 1), Central Lodge No. 6, Central City, Apprentice
Proceedings 1874, pg 213 (1874 Sept 30), Central Lodge No. 6, Central, Apprentice
Proceedings 1875, pg 77 (1875 Sept 22), Central Lodge No. 6, Central City, Apprentice
Proceedings 1876, pg 32 (1876 Sept 20), Central Lodge No. 6, Central City, Apprentice

Ewing, James
Proceedings 1861-1869, pg 4 (1861 Aug 2), Summit Lodge No 7, Parkville
Proceedings 1861-1869, pg 4 (1861 Aug 2), Summit Lodge No 7, Parkville
Proceedings 1861-1869, pg 5 (1861 Aug 2) Senior Grand Warden, Parkville
Proceedings 1861-1869, pg 5 (1861 Aug 2) WM
Proceedings 1861-1869, pg 42 (1861 Dec 10), Summit Lodge No. 2, Parkville
Proceedings 1861-1869, pg 76 (1862 Nov 4), Summit Lodge No. 2, Parkville, dimitted
Proceedings 1871, pg 34 (1871 Sept 27) Senior Grand Warden, Aug 1861, Dimitted
Proceedings 1872, pg 42 (1872 Sept 24) Senior Grand Warden, August 1861, Dimitted
Proceedings 1873, pg 58 (1873 Oct 1) Senior Grand Warden, Aug 1861, Dimitted
Proceedings 1874, pg 206 (1874 Sept 30) Senior Grand Warden, Aug 1861, demitted
Proceedings 1875, pg 93 (1875 Sept 22) Senior Grand Warden, Aug 1861, Demitted

Ewing, Jas
Proceedings 1861-1869, pg 315 (1869 Sept 29) Senior Grand Warden, August 1861, Dimitted
Proceedings 1870, pg 32 (1870 Sept 28) Senior Grand Warden, August 1861, Dimitted

Eyster, George S
Proceedings 1876, pg 9 (1876 Jan 5) Grand Lodge of West Virginia, Grand Representative, of Halltown, WV"
Proceedings 1876, pg 53 (1876 Sept 20) Grand Lodge of West Virginia, of Halltown, WV

Fabian, S J
Proceedings 1875, pg 89 (1875 Sept 22) Idaho Springs Lodge U D

Fabian, Samuel J
Proceedings 1876, pg 43 (1876 Sept 20) Idaho Springs Lodge No. 26

Fahringer, A M
Proceedings 1874, pg 214 (1874 Sept 30), Union Lodge No. 7, Denver
Proceedings 1875, pg 78 (1875 Sept 22), Union Lodge No. 7, Denver
Proceedings 1876, pg 33 (1876 Sept 20), Union Lodge No. 7, Denver

Fahringer, Adam M
Proceedings 1870, pg 23 (1870 Sept 28), Union Lodge No. 7, Denver, Fellowcraft
Proceedings 1872, pg 22 (1872 Sept 24), Union Lodge No. 7, Denver
Proceedings 1873, pg 40 (1873 Oct 1), Union Lodge No. 7, Denver

Failing, H H
Proceedings 1861-1869, pg 192 (1867 Oct 8) Denver Lodge No. 5
Proceedings 1874, pg 212 (1874 Sept 30), Denver Lodge No. 5, Denver
Proceedings 1875, pg 76 (1875 Sept 22) Denver Lodge No. 5
Proceedings 1876, pg 31 (1876 Sept 20) Denver Lodge No. 5

Failing, Henry H
Proceedings 1870, pg 21 (1870 Sept 28), Denver Lodge No. 5, Denver
Proceedings 1871, pg 19 (1871 Sept 27) Denver Lodge No. 5
Proceedings 1872, pg 19 (1872 Sept 24), Denver Lodge No. 5, Denver
Proceedings 1873, pg 37 (1873 Oct 1), Denver Lodge No. 5, Denver

Failling, H H
Proceedings 1861-1869, pg 223 (1868 Oct 7) Denver Lodge No. 5

Fairbank, R V
Proceedings 1861-1869, pg 307 (1869 Sept 29), Union Lodge No. 7, Denver

Fairbanks, R V
Proceedings 1861-1869, pg 111 (1863 Nov 3), Summit Lodge No. 2, Parkville, Apprentice
Proceedings 1861-1869, pg 134 (1864 Nov 8), Union Lodge No. 7, Denver
Proceedings 1861-1869, pg 151 (1865 Nov 7), Chivington Lodge No. 6, Central City
Proceedings 1861-1869, pg 169 (1866 Oct 2), Union Lodge No. 7, Denver
Proceedings 1861-1869, pg 195 (1867 Oct 8), Union Lodge No. 7, Denver
Proceedings 1873, pg 40 (1873 Oct 1), Union Lodge No. 7, Denver
Proceedings 1874, pg 214 (1874 Sept 30), Union Lodge No. 7, Denver
Proceedings 1875, pg 79 (1875 Sept 22), Union Lodge No. 7, Denver, died
Proceedings 1875, pg 94 (1875 Sept 22), Union Lodge No. 7, Denver

Fairbanks, R Virgil
Proceedings 1870, pg 23 (1870 Sept 28), Union Lodge No. 7, Denver
Proceedings 1871, pg 21 (1871 Sept 27), Union Lodge No. 7, Denver
Proceedings 1872, pg 23 (1872 Sept 24), Union Lodge No. 7, Denver

Fairbanks, R W
Proceedings 1861-1869, pg 225 (1868 Oct 7), Union Lodge No. 7, Denver

Fairchild
Proceedings 1861-1869, pg 34 (1861 Dec 10), Grand Master at Atchison, KS

Fairchild, D L
Proceedings 1861-1869, pg 77 (1862 Nov 4), Nevada Lodge No. 4, Nevadaville
Proceedings 1861-1869, pg 111 (1863 Nov 3), Nevada Lodge No. 4, Nevadaville
Proceedings 1861-1869, pg 132 (1864 Nov 8), Nevada Lodge No. 4, Nevadaville
Proceedings 1861-1869, pg 148 (1865 Nov 7), Nevada Lodge No. 4, Nevadaville
Proceedings 1861-1869, pg 166 (1866 Oct 2), Nevada Lodge No. 4, Nevadaville
Proceedings 1861-1869, pg 192 (1867 Oct 8), Nevada Lodge No. 4, Nevadaville
Proceedings 1861-1869, pg 304 (1869 Sept 29), Nevada Lodge No. 4, Nevadaville

Fairchild, David L
Proceedings 1870, pg 20 (1870 Sept 28), Nevada Lodge No. 4, Nevadaville, Dimitted

Fairchilds, D L
Proceedings 1861-1869, pg 222 (1868 Oct 7), Nevada Lodge No. 4, Nevadaville

Faires, E G
Proceedings 1874, pg 218 (1874 Sept 30), El Paso Lodge No. 13, Colorado Springs

Fairhurst, G W
Proceedings 1861-1869, pg 196 (1867 Oct 8), Black Hawk Lodge No. 11, Black Hawk

Fairhurst, W G
Proceedings 1861-1869, pg 150 (1865 Nov 7), Chivington Lodge No. 6, Central City
Proceedings 1861-1869, pg 168 (1866 Oct 2), Chivington Lodge No. 6, Central City
Proceedings 1861-1869, pg 170 (1866 Oct 2), Black Hawk Lodge U D, Black Hawk

Proceedings 1861-1869, pg 194 (1867 Oct 8), Chivington Lodge No. 6, Central City, Dimitted
Proceedings 1861-1869, pg 226 (1868 Oct 7), Black Hawk Lodge No. 11, Black Hawk
Proceedings 1861-1869, pg 309 (1869 Sept 29), Black Hawk Lodge No. 11, Black Hawk
Proceedings 1870, pg 25 (1870 Sept 28), Black Hawk Lodge No. 11, Black Hawk
Proceedings 1871, pg 23 (1871 Sept 27), Black Hawk Lodge No. 11, Black Hawk
Proceedings 1872, pg 25 (1872 Sept 24), Black Hawk Lodge No. 11, Black Hawk
Proceedings 1873, pg 42 (1873 Oct 1), Black Hawk Lodge No. 11, Black Hawk
Proceedings 1874, pg 216 (1874 Sept 30), Black Hawk Lodge No. 11, Black Hawk
Proceedings 1876, pg 34 (1876 Sept 20) Black Hawk Lodge No. 11

Fairhurst, Wm G
Proceedings 1875, pg 80 (1875 Sept 22) Black Hawk Lodge No. 11

Faiver, Joseph
Proceedings 1861-1869, pg 149 (1865 Nov 7), Nevada Lodge No. 4, Nevadaville, dimitted

Faivre, D
Proceedings 1875, pg 89 (1875 Sept 22) Idaho Springs Lodge U D

Faivre, Denis
Proceedings 1872, pg 26 (1872 Sept 24), Washington Lodge No. 12, Georgetown

Faivre, Dennis
Proceedings 1861-1869, pg 227 (1868 Oct 7), Washington Lodge No. 12, Georgetown
Proceedings 1861-1869, pg 309 (1869 Sept 29), Washington Lodge No. 12, Georgetown
Proceedings 1870, pg 26 (1870 Sept 28), Washington Lodge No. 12, Georgetown
Proceedings 1871, pg 24 (1871 Sept 27), Washington Lodge No. 12, Georgetown
Proceedings 1873, pg 42 (1873 Oct 1), Washington Lodge No. 12, Georgetown
Proceedings 1874, pg 217 (1874 Sept 30), Washington Lodge No. 12, Georgetown
Proceedings 1874, pg 229 (1874 Sept 30), Idaho Springs Lodge U D, Idaho Springs
Proceedings 1875, pg 81 (1875 Sept 22), Washington Lodge No. 12, Georgetown, Demitted
Proceedings 1876, pg 42 (1876 Sept 20) Idaho Springs Lodge No. 26

Faivre, Joseph
Proceedings 1861-1869, pg 77 (1862 Nov 4) Denver Lodge No. 5
Proceedings 1861-1869, pg 112 (1863 Nov 3) Denver Lodge No. 5
Proceedings 1861-1869, pg 133 (1864 Nov 8) Denver Lodge No. 5

Falkner, C W
Proceedings 1874, pg 209 (1874 Sept 30), Golden City Lodge No. 1, Golden City

Fall, A
Proceedings 1861-1869, pg 152 (1865 Nov 7), Helena City Lodge U D, Helena City, Montana Territory, Fellowcraft

Fallett, M V
Proceedings 1874, pg 223 (1874 Sept 30), Laramie Lodge No. 18, Laramie City

Fanham, H H Jr
Proceedings 1872, pg 25 (1872 Sept 24), Black Hawk Lodge No. 11, Black Hawk

Fanuin, H P
Proceedings 1873, pg 48 (1873 Oct 1), Laramie Lodge No. 18, Laramie, Wyoming Territory
Proceedings 1874, pg 223 (1874 Sept 30), Laramie Lodge No. 18, Laramie City

Farewell, C B
Proceedings 1871, pg 31 (1871 Sept 27), Occidental Lodge U D, Greeley, Apprentice

Farewell, C D
Proceedings 1871, pg 30 (1871 Sept 27), Occidental Lodge U D, Greeley

Faringer, Adam M
Proceedings 1871, pg 21 (1871 Sept 27), Union Lodge No. 7, Denver

Farley, Alfred
Proceedings 1870, pg 31 (1870 Sept 28), Laramie Lodge No. 18, Laramie, Wyoming Territory, Apprentice
Proceedings 1871, pg 29 (1871 Sept 27), Laramie Lodge No. 18, Laramie, Wyoming Territory
Proceedings 1872, pg 32 (1872 Sept 24), Laramie Lodge No. 18, Laramie, Wyoming Territory
Proceedings 1873, pg 48 (1873 Oct 1), Laramie Lodge No. 18, Laramie, Wyoming Territory
Proceedings 1874, pg 223 (1874 Sept 30), Laramie Lodge No. 18, Laramie City

Farling, H H
Proceedings 1861-1869, pg 305 (1869 Sept 29) Denver Lodge No. 5

Farmer, B F
Proceedings 1874, pg 218 (1874 Sept 30), El Paso Lodge No. 13, Colorado Springs
Proceedings 1875, pg 82 (1875 Sept 22), El Paso Lodge No. 13, Colorado Springs
Proceedings 1876, pg 49 (1876 Sept 20), El Paso Lodge No. 13, Colorado City, 1876 July 22

Farmer, C C
Proceedings 1861-1869, pg 152 (1865 Nov 7), Helena City Lodge U D, Helena City, Montana Territory

Farmer, Fred C
Proceedings 1873, pg 40 (1873 Oct 1), Union Lodge No. 7, Denver

Colorado's Territorial Masons

Farmer, Fred C, cont.
Proceedings 1874, pg 214 (1874 Sept 30), Union Lodge No. 7, Denver
Proceedings 1875, pg 78 (1875 Sept 22), Union Lodge No. 7, Denver

Farmer, Frederick C
Proceedings 1876, pg 33 (1876 Sept 20), Union Lodge No. 7, Denver

Farmer, John W
Proceedings 1875, pg 90 (1875 Sept 22), Huerfano Lodge U D, Walsenburg
Proceedings 1876, pg 43 (1876 Sept 20), Huerfano Lodge No. 27, Walsenburg

Farmer, T B
Proceedings 1861-1869, pg 305 (1869 Sept 29) Denver Lodge No. 5, Apprentice

Farmer, Thomas B
Proceedings 1871, pg 19 (1871 Sept 27) Denver Lodge No. 5
Proceedings 1872, pg 20 (1872 Sept 24), Denver Lodge No. 5, Denver, died

Farmer, Thos B
Proceedings 1872, pg 39 (1872 Sept 24), Denver Lodge No. 5, Denver

Farnham, H H Jr
Proceedings 1870, pg 25 (1870 Sept 28), Black Hawk Lodge No. 11, Black Hawk
Proceedings 1871, pg 23 (1871 Sept 27), Black Hawk Lodge No. 11, Black Hawk

Farnum, H H
Proceedings 1861-1869, pg 309 (1869 Sept 29), Black Hawk Lodge No. 11, Black Hawk

Farnum, H H Jr
Proceedings 1861-1869, pg 227 (1868 Oct 7), Black Hawk Lodge No. 11, Black Hawk
Proceedings 1873, pg 42 (1873 Oct 1), Black Hawk Lodge No. 11, Black Hawk
Proceedings 1874, pg 216 (1874 Sept 30), Black Hawk Lodge No. 11, Black Hawk
Proceedings 1875, pg 80 (1875 Sept 22) Black Hawk Lodge No. 11
Proceedings 1876, pg 34 (1876 Sept 20) Black Hawk Lodge No. 11
Proceedings 1876, pg 50 (1876 Sept 20) Black Hawk Lodge No. 11

Farran, John
Proceedings 1874, pg 130 (1874 Sept 30) Grand Lodge of Michigan

Farrel, Edward
Proceedings 1870, pg 30 (1870 Sept 28), Laramie Lodge No. 18, Laramie, Wyoming Territory
Proceedings 1873, pg 48 (1873 Oct 1), Laramie Lodge No. 18, Laramie, Wyoming Territory
Proceedings 1871, pg 29 (1871 Sept 27), Laramie Lodge No. 18, Laramie, Wyoming Territory
Proceedings 1872, pg 31 (1872 Sept 24), Laramie Lodge No. 18, Laramie, Wyoming Territory
Proceedings 1874, pg 223 (1874 Sept 30), Laramie Lodge No. 18, Laramie City

Farrer, Samuel
Proceedings 1861-1869, pg 309 (1869 Sept 29), Black Hawk Lodge No. 11, Black Hawk

Farris, E G
Proceedings 1875, pg 82 (1875 Sept 22), El Paso Lodge No. 13, Colorado Springs, Demitted

Farsett, J W
Proceedings 1872, pg 23 (1872 Sept 24), Union Lodge No. 7, Denver, Apprentice

Farver, Samuel
Proceedings 1861-1869, pg 227 (1868 Oct 7), Black Hawk Lodge No. 11, Black Hawk
Proceedings 1870, pg 25 (1870 Sept 28), Black Hawk Lodge No. 11, Black Hawk
Proceedings 1871, pg 23 (1871 Sept 27), Black Hawk Lodge No. 11, Black Hawk
Proceedings 1872, pg 25 (1872 Sept 24), Black Hawk Lodge No. 11, Black Hawk
Proceedings 1873, pg 42 (1873 Oct 1), Black Hawk Lodge No. 11, Black Hawk
Proceedings 1874, pg 216 (1874 Sept 30), Black Hawk Lodge No. 11, Black Hawk
Proceedings 1875, pg 80 (1875 Sept 22) Black Hawk Lodge No. 11
Proceedings 1876, pg 50 (1876 Sept 20) Black Hawk Lodge No. 11

Farwell, C B
Proceedings 1873, pg 50 (1873 Oct 1), Occidental Lodge No. 20, Greeley, Apprentice
Proceedings 1874, pg 226 (1874 Sept 30), Occidental Lodge No. 20, Greeley, Apprentice
Proceedings 1875, pg 87 (1875 Sept 22), Occidental Lodge No. 20, Greeley, Apprentice
Proceedings 1876, pg 40 (1876 Sept 20), Occidental Lodge No. 20, Greeley, Granted permission to take degrees elsewhere

Farwell, C D
Proceedings 1872, pg 33 (1872 Sept 24), Occidental Lodge No. 20, Greeley
Proceedings 1873, pg 50 (1873 Oct 1), Occidental Lodge No. 20, Greeley
Proceedings 1875, pg 87 (1875 Sept 22), Occidental Lodge No. 20, Greeley

Farwell, Cyrus D
Proceedings 1874, pg 225 (1874 Sept 30), Occidental Lodge No. 20, Greeley
Proceedings 1876, pg 40 (1876 Sept 20), Occidental Lodge No. 20, Greeley

Fassett, J W
Proceedings 1873, pg 40 (1873 Oct 1), Union Lodge No. 7, Denver, Apprentice
Proceedings 1874, pg 214 (1874 Sept 30), Union Lodge No. 7, Denver, Apprentice

Proceedings 1875, pg 79 (1875 Sept 22), Union Lodge No. 7, Denver, Apprentice

Proceedings 1876, pg 33 (1876 Sept 20), Union Lodge No. 7, Denver

Fatheree, John

Proceedings 1870, pg 84 (1870 Jan 17) Grand Lodge of Mississippi, deceased

Faulkner, C W

Proceedings 1875, pg 73 (1875 Sept 22) Golden City Lodge No. 1

Proceedings 1876, pg 29 (1876 Sept 20) Golden City Lodge No. 1

Proceedings 1876, pg 50 (1876 Sept 20) Golden City Lodge No. 1

Faulkner, Chas W

Proceedings 1873, pg 35 (1873 Oct 1), Golden City Lodge No. 1, Golden City

Faulkner, Clarence W

Proceedings 1872, pg 17 (1872 Sept 24), Golden City Lodge No. 1, Golden City, Apprentice

Faver, Samuel

Proceedings 1876, pg 34 (1876 Sept 20) Black Hawk Lodge No. 11

Favere, Samuel

Proceedings 1861-1869, pg 196 (1867 Oct 8), Black Hawk Lodge No. 11, Black Hawk

Favinger, George

Proceedings 1870, pg 29 (1870 Sept 28), Cheyenne Lodge No. 16, Cheyenne, Wyoming Territory, Dimitted

Fearn, Geo R

Proceedings 1872, pg 71 (1872 Sept 24) Grand Lodge of Mississippi

Febles, John C

Proceedings 1874, pg 214 (1874 Sept 30), Union Lodge No. 7, Denver

Proceedings 1875, pg 78 (1875 Sept 22), Union Lodge No. 7, Denver

Fee, Geo D

Proceedings 1870, pg 84 (1870 Jan 17) Grand Lodge of Mississippi, deceased

Feebles, John C

Proceedings 1876, pg 49 (1876 Sept 20), Union Lodge No. 7, Denver, 1876 Aug 26

Felch, G W

Proceedings 1876, pg 50 (1876 Sept 20) Pueblo Lodge No. 17

Felch, H H

Proceedings 1875, pg 84 (1875 Sept 22), Mount Moriah Lodge No. 15, Canon City

Proceedings 1876, pg 38 (1876 Sept 20), Mount Moriah Lodge No. 15, Canon City

Felch, J W

Proceedings 1875, pg 85 (1875 Sept 22) Pueblo Lodge No. 17

Proceedings 1876, pg 38 (1876 Sept 20) Pueblo Lodge No. 17

Felch, Jno W

Proceedings 1875, pg 85 (1875 Sept 22) Pueblo Lodge No. 17, Reinstated

Felch, John W

Proceedings 1861-1869, pg 312 (1869 Sept 29), Pueblo Lodge No. 17, Pueblo

Proceedings 1870, pg 30 (1870 Sept 28), Pueblo Lodge No. 17, Pueblo

Proceedings 1871, pg 28 (1871 Sept 27), Pueblo Lodge No. 17, Pueblo

Proceedings 1872, pg 31 (1872 Sept 24), Pueblo Lodge No. 17, Pueblo

Proceedings 1873, pg 47 (1873 Oct 1), Pueblo Lodge No. 17, Pueblo

Proceedings 1874, pg 223 (1874 Sept 30), Pueblo Lodge No. 17, Pueblo, Pueblo County, Stricken from the rolls

Fellow, Ephraim

Proceedings 1875, pg 73 (1875 Sept 22) Golden City Lodge No. 1

Fellows, A C

Proceedings 1861-1869, pg 227 (1868 Oct 7), Washington Lodge No. 12, Georgetown

Proceedings 1870, pg 4 (1870 Sept 27), Washington Lodge No. 12, Georgetown

Proceedings 1870, pg 16 (1870 Sept 28) committee

Proceedings 1871, pg 24 (1871 Sept 27), Washington Lodge No. 12, Georgetown

Fellows, Al C

Proceedings 1875, pg 81 (1875 Sept 22), Washington Lodge No. 12, Georgetown

Proceedings 1876, pg 35 (1876 Sept 20), Washington Lodge No. 12, Georgetown

Fellows, Almon C

Proceedings 1870, pg 26 (1870 Sept 28), Washington Lodge No. 12, Georgetown

Proceedings 1872, pg 26 (1872 Sept 24), Washington Lodge No. 12, Georgetown

Proceedings 1873, pg 42 (1873 Oct 1), Washington Lodge No. 12, Georgetown

Proceedings 1874, pg 217 (1874 Sept 30), Washington Lodge No. 12, Georgetown

Fellows, Almond C

Proceedings 1861-1869, pg 309 (1869 Sept 29), Washington Lodge No. 12, Georgetown

Fellows, E

Proceedings 1861-1869, pg 131 (1864 Nov 8) Golden City Lodge No. 1

Proceedings 1861-1869, pg 147 (1865 Nov 7) Golden City Lodge No. 1

Proceedings 1861-1869, pg 154 (1866 Oct 1) Golden City Lodge No. 1

Proceedings 1861-1869, pg 160 (1866 Oct 2) Golden City Lodge No. 1, Grand Sword Bearer

Proceedings 1861-1869, pg 161 (1866 Oct 2) Grand Marshal

Fellows, E, cont.
  Proceedings 1861-1869, pg 162 (1866 Oct 2) Golden City Lodge No. 1
  Proceedings 1861-1869, pg 165 (1866 Oct 2) Golden City Lodge No. 1
  Proceedings 1861-1869, pg 191 (1867 Oct 8) Golden City Lodge No. 1
  Proceedings 1870, pg 19 (1870 Sept 28), Golden City Lodge No. 1, Golden City
  Proceedings 1871, pg 17 (1871 Sept 27), Golden City Lodge No. 1, Golden City
  Proceedings 1872, pg 17 (1872 Sept 24), Golden City Lodge No. 1, Golden City

Fellows, Ephraim
  Proceedings 1873, pg 35 (1873 Oct 1), Golden City Lodge No. 1, Golden City
  Proceedings 1874, pg 209 (1874 Sept 30), Golden City Lodge No. 1, Golden City
  Proceedings 1876, pg 29 (1876 Sept 20) Golden City Lodge No. 1
  Proceedings 1876, pg 50 (1876 Sept 20) Golden City Lodge No. 1
  Proceedings 1861-1869, pg 221 (1868 Oct 7) Golden City Lodge No. 1
  Proceedings 1861-1869, pg 303 (1869 Sept 29) Golden City Lodge No. 1

Fenton
  Proceedings 1861-1869, pg 263 (1868 Oct 7), Grand Secretary, Grand Lodge of Michigan

Fenton, James
  Proceedings 1861-1869, pg 316 (1869 Sept 29) Grand Lodge of Michigan
  Proceedings 1861-1869, pg 332 (1868 Nov 16) Grand Secretary, Grand Lodge of Maryland
  Proceedings 1861-1869, pg 333 (1869 Jan 13) Grand Secretary, Grand Lodge of Michigan
  Proceedings 1870, pg 34 (1870 Sept 28) Grand Secretary, Grand Lodge of Michigan
  Proceedings 1870, pg 77 (1870 Jan 12) Grand Secretary, Grand Lodge of Michigan
  Proceedings 1871, pg 35 (1871 Sept 27) Grand Secretary, Grand Lodge of Michigan
  Proceedings 1872, pg 71 (1872 Sept 24) Grand Lodge of Michigan
  Proceedings 1872, pg 72 (1872 Sept 24) Grand Lodge of Michigan

Fenwick, John
  Proceedings 1870, pg 30 (1870 Sept 28), Laramie Lodge No. 18, Laramie, Wyoming Territory

Ferguson, George
  Proceedings 1875, pg 81 (1875 Sept 22), Washington Lodge No. 12, Georgetown
  Proceedings 1876, pg 35 (1876 Sept 20), Washington Lodge No. 12, Georgetown

Ferguson, H W
  Proceedings 1875, pg 86 (1875 Sept 22), Collins Lodge No. 19, Fort Collins
  Proceedings 1876, pg 39 (1876 Sept 20), Collins Lodge No. 19, Fort Collins

Ferrell, J M
  Proceedings 1861-1869, pg 5 (1861 Aug 2) Grand Marshal, Golden City
  Proceedings 1861-1869, pg 110 (1863 Nov 3) Golden City Lodge No. 1
  Proceedings 1861-1869, pg 221 (1868 Oct 7) Golden City Lodge No. 1
  Proceedings 1861-1869, pg 303 (1869 Sept 29) Golden City Lodge No. 1

Ferrill, J M
  Proceedings 1861-1869, pg 165 (1866 Oct 2) Golden City Lodge No. 1

Ferrill, John M
  Proceedings 1861-1869, pg 42 (1861 Dec 10) Golden City Lodge No. 1
  Proceedings 1861-1869, pg 131 (1864 Nov 8) Golden City Lodge No. 1
  Proceedings 1861-1869, pg 147 (1865 Nov 7) Golden City Lodge No. 1
  Proceedings 1861-1869, pg 191 (1867 Oct 8) Golden City Lodge No. 1

Ferris & Hammond
  Proceedings 1874, pg 19 (1874 Sept 29), of Providence, RI

Fetta, Christian
  Proceedings 1873, pg 60 (1873 Oct 1) Grand Lodge of Indiana, Richmond

Fetter, Christian
  Proceedings 1874, pg 64 (1874 Sept 30) Grand Lodge of Indiana

Feuerstein, H
  Proceedings 1861-1869, pg 192 (1867 Oct 8) Denver Lodge No. 5
  Proceedings 1861-1869, pg 223 (1868 Oct 7) Denver Lodge No. 5

Feuerstein, Henry
  Proceedings 1861-1869, pg 133 (1864 Nov 8) Denver Lodge No. 5
  Proceedings 1871, pg 19 (1871 Sept 27) Denver Lodge No. 5
  Proceedings 1873, pg 37 (1873 Oct 1), Denver Lodge No. 5, Denver
  Proceedings 1874, pg 212 (1874 Sept 30), Denver Lodge No. 5, Denver

Feuerstine, H
  Proceedings 1861-1869, pg 230 (1868 Oct 7), Germania Lodge U D, Denver

Feurestein, Henry
  Proceedings 1876, pg 49 (1876 Sept 20) Denver Lodge No. 5, 1876 Aug 19

Feurstein, H
  Proceedings 1861-1869, pg 305 (1869 Sept 29) Denver Lodge No. 5

Feurstein, Henry
　Proceedings 1861-1869, pg 149 (1865 Nov 7), Nevada Lodge No. 4, Nevadaville
　Proceedings 1861-1869, pg 167 (1866 Oct 2) Denver Lodge No. 5
　Proceedings 1870, pg 21 (1870 Sept 28), Denver Lodge No. 5, Denver
　Proceedings 1872, pg 19 (1872 Sept 24), Denver Lodge No. 5, Denver

Fidelity Lodge U D
　Proceedings 1870, pg 11 (1870 Sept 27)
　Proceedings 1870, pg 15 (1870 Sept 28) chartered as Collins Lodge No. 19

Field, William
　Proceedings 1870, pg 101 (1869 Dec 31) Grand Lodge of Rhode Island, deceased, Special Communication paying the last tribute of respect

Fillins, John
　Proceedings 1861-1869, pg 227 (1868 Oct 7), Washington Lodge No. 12, Georgetown, Apprentice
　Proceedings 1861-1869, pg 309 (1869 Sept 29), Washington Lodge No. 12, Georgetown

Fillium, Phillip
　Proceedings 1873, pg 42 (1873 Oct 1), Washington Lodge No. 12, Georgetown

Fillius, John
　Proceedings 1870, pg 26 (1870 Sept 28), Washington Lodge No. 12, Georgetown
　Proceedings 1871, pg 24 (1871 Sept 27), Washington Lodge No. 12, Georgetown
　Proceedings 1872, pg 26 (1872 Sept 24), Washington Lodge No. 12, Georgetown
　Proceedings 1873, pg 42 (1873 Oct 1), Washington Lodge No. 12, Georgetown
　Proceedings 1874, pg 217 (1874 Sept 30), Washington Lodge No. 12, Georgetown
　Proceedings 1875, pg 81 (1875 Sept 22), Washington Lodge No. 12, Georgetown
　Proceedings 1876, pg 35 (1876 Sept 20), Washington Lodge No. 12, Georgetown

Fillius, Philip
　Proceedings 1875, pg 81 (1875 Sept 22), Washington Lodge No. 12, Georgetown
　Proceedings 1876, pg 35 (1876 Sept 20), Washington Lodge No. 12, Georgetown
　Proceedings 1871, pg 24 (1871 Sept 27), Washington Lodge No. 12, Georgetown
　Proceedings 1872, pg 26 (1872 Sept 24), Washington Lodge No. 12, Georgetown
　Proceedings 1874, pg 217 (1874 Sept 30), Washington Lodge No. 12, Georgetown

Fillmore, John S
　Proceedings 1861-1869, pg 135 (1864 Nov 8), Union Lodge No. 7, Denver, Fellowcraft
　Proceedings 1861-1869, pg 151 (1865 Nov 7), Chivington Lodge No. 6, Central City, deceased

Finch, E V
　Proceedings 1874, pg 32 (1874 Sept 30) Grand Chaplain, Denver

Finch, P V
　Colorado University Cornerstone Laying, pg 3 (1875 Sept 20) Grand Chaplain
　Proceedings 1875, pg cover (1875 Sept 22) Grand Chaplain, Denver
　Proceedings 1875, pg 15 (1875 Sept 21) Grand Chaplain
　Proceedings 1875, pg 33 (1875 Sept 22) Grand Chaplain, Denver
　Proceedings 1876, pg cover (1876 Sept 20) Grand Chaplain, Denver
　Proceedings 1876, pg 3 (1876 Sept 19) Grand Chaplain

Finch, P Voorhies
　Proceedings 1876, pg 33 (1876 Sept 20), Union Lodge No. 7, Denver

Finehart, Matt E
　Proceedings 1876, pg 33 (1876 Sept 20), Union Lodge No. 7, Denver, Apprentice

Finfrock, J H
　Proceedings 1870, pg 30 (1870 Sept 28), Laramie Lodge No. 18, Laramie, Wyoming Territory
　Proceedings 1871, pg 29 (1871 Sept 27), Laramie Lodge No. 18, Laramie, Wyoming Territory
　Proceedings 1872, pg 32 (1872 Sept 24), Laramie Lodge No. 18, Laramie, Wyoming Territory
　Proceedings 1873, pg 48 (1873 Oct 1), Laramie Lodge No. 18, Laramie, Wyoming Territory
　Proceedings 1874, pg 223 (1874 Sept 30), Laramie Lodge No. 18, Laramie City

Finks, D E
　Proceedings 1875, pg 89 (1875 Sept 22), Doric Lodge No. 25, Fairplay, Apprentice
　Proceedings 1876, pg 42 (1876 Sept 20), Doric Lodge No. 25, Fairplay, Apprentice,

Finlay
　Proceedings 1876, pg 5 (1876 Sept 19) Nevada Lodge No. 4

Finlay, W M
　Proceedings 1876, pg 22 (1876 Sept 20) Nevada Lodge No. 4

Finlay, William
　Proceedings 1870, pg 20 (1870 Sept 28), Nevada Lodge No. 4, Nevadaville

Finlay, Wm M
　Proceedings 1871, pg 18 (1871 Sept 27), Nevada Lodge No. 4, Bald Mountain
　Proceedings 1875, pg 74 (1875 Sept 22), Nevada Lodge No. 4, Nevada
　Proceedings 1876, pg 6 (1876 Sept 19) committee
　Proceedings 1876, pg 16 (1876 Sept 19) committee
　Proceedings 1876, pg 23 (1876 Sept 20) committee
　Proceedings 1876, pg 30 (1876 Sept 20) Nevada Lodge No. 4

Finlay, Wm N
 Proceedings 1876, pg 4 (1876 Sept 19) Nevada Lodge No. 4

Finley, Fobert
 Proceedings 1872, pg 27 (1872 Sept 24), El Paso Lodge No. 13, Colorado City

Finley, Jos
 Proceedings 1861-1869, pg 169 (1866 Oct 2), Union Lodge No. 7, Denver

Finley, Joseph
 Proceedings 1861-1869, pg 135 (1864 Nov 8), Union Lodge No. 7, Denver, Apprentice
 Proceedings 1861-1869, pg 151 (1865 Nov 7), Chivington Lodge No. 6, Central City

Finley, Robert
 Proceedings 1861-1869, pg 310 (1869 Sept 29), El Paso Lodge No. 13, Colorado City
 Proceedings 1870, pg 26 (1870 Sept 28), El Paso Lodge No. 13, Colorado City
 Proceedings 1871, pg 24 (1871 Sept 27), El Paso Lodge No. 13, Colorado City
 Proceedings 1873, pg 43 (1873 Oct 1), El Paso Lodge No. 13, Colorado City
 Proceedings 1874, pg 218 (1874 Sept 30), El Paso Lodge No. 13, Colorado Springs
 Proceedings 1875, pg 82 (1875 Sept 22), El Paso Lodge No. 13, Colorado Springs
 Proceedings 1876, pg 36 (1876 Sept 20), El Paso Lodge No. 13, Colorado City

Finley, W M
 Proceedings 1873, pg 5 (1873 Sept 30), Nevada Lodge No. 4, Bald Mountain
 Proceedings 1873, pg 31 (1873 Oct 1) mileage and per diem

Finley, William M
 Proceedings 1872, pg 18 (1872 Sept 24), Nevada Lodge No. 4, Bald Mountain
 Proceedings 1873, pg 36 (1873 Oct 1), Nevada Lodge No. 4, Nevada

Finley, Wm
 Proceedings 1861-1869, pg 304 (1869 Sept 29), Nevada Lodge No. 4, Nevadaville

Finley, Wm M
 Proceedings 1872, pg 4 (1872 Sept 24) visiting
 Proceedings 1874, pg 210 (1874 Sept 30), Nevada Lodge No. 4, Bald Mountain, Gilpin County

Finley, Wm N
 Proceedings 1872, pg 4 (1872 Sept 24), Nevada Lodge No. 4, Bald Mountain

Finly, Joseph
 Proceedings 1861-1869, pg 169 (1866 Oct 2), Union Lodge No. 7, Denver, deceased

Firtz Simmons, Geo H
 Proceedings 1872, pg 25 (1872 Sept 24), Black Hawk Lodge No. 11, Black Hawk

Fischer, Peter
 Proceedings 1861-1869, pg 230 (1868 Oct 7), Germania Lodge U D, Denver
 Proceedings 1874, pg 215 (1874 Sept 30), Union Lodge No. 7, Denver, Stricken from the rolls,

Fisher
 Proceedings 1861-1869, pg 52 (1862 Nov 4) committee

Fisher, James
 Proceedings 1861-1869, pg 170 (1866 Oct 2), Black Hawk Lodge U D, Black Hawk
 Proceedings 1861-1869, pg 196 (1867 Oct 8), Black Hawk Lodge No. 11, Black Hawk
 Proceedings 1861-1869, pg 227 (1868 Oct 7), Black Hawk Lodge No. 11, Black Hawk
 Proceedings 1861-1869, pg 309 (1869 Sept 29), Black Hawk Lodge No. 11, Black Hawk
 Proceedings 1870, pg 25 (1870 Sept 28), Black Hawk Lodge No. 11, Black Hawk
 Proceedings 1871, pg 23 (1871 Sept 27), Black Hawk Lodge No. 11, Black Hawk
 Proceedings 1872, pg 25 (1872 Sept 24), Black Hawk Lodge No. 11, Black Hawk
 Proceedings 1873, pg 42 (1873 Oct 1), Black Hawk Lodge No. 11, Black Hawk
 Proceedings 1874, pg 216 (1874 Sept 30), Black Hawk Lodge No. 11, Black Hawk
 Proceedings 1875, pg 80 (1875 Sept 22) Black Hawk Lodge No. 11
 Proceedings 1876, pg 34 (1876 Sept 20) Black Hawk Lodge No. 11

Fisher, Paul A
 Proceedings 1876, pg 33 (1876 Sept 20), Union Lodge No. 7, Denver, Apprentice

Fisher, Peter
 Proceedings 1870, pg 23 (1870 Sept 28), Union Lodge No. 7, Denver
 Proceedings 1871, pg 21 (1871 Sept 27), Union Lodge No. 7, Denver
 Proceedings 1872, pg 22 (1872 Sept 24), Union Lodge No. 7, Denver
 Proceedings 1873, pg 40 (1873 Oct 1), Union Lodge No. 7, Denver

Fisher, Redwood
 Proceedings 1861-1869, pg 135 (1864 Nov 8), Union Lodge No. 7, Denver, Apprentice
 Proceedings 1861-1869, pg 139 (1865 May 1), Union Lodge No. 7, Denver
 Proceedings 1861-1869, pg 151 (1865 Nov 7), Chivington Lodge No. 6, Central City
 Proceedings 1861-1869, pg 169 (1866 Oct 2), Union Lodge No. 7, Denver
 Proceedings 1861-1869, pg 184 (1867 Oct 5), Union Lodge No. 7, Denver
 Proceedings 1861-1869, pg 195 (1867 Oct 8), Union Lodge No. 7, Denver
 Proceedings 1861-1869, pg 225 (1868 Oct 7), Union Lodge No. 7, Denver

Proceedings 1861-1869, pg 307 (1869 Sept 29), Union Lodge No. 7, Denver

Proceedings 1870, pg 24 (1870 Sept 28), Union Lodge No. 7, Denver, Died

Fisher, Robert J

Proceedings 1872, pg 85 (1872 Sept 24) Grand Lodge of Pennsylvania

Fisher, T M

Proceedings 1873, pg 46 (1873 Oct 1), Cheyenne Lodge No. 16, Cheyenne, Wyoming Territory

Proceedings 1874, pg 221 (1874 Sept 30), Cheyenne Lodge No. 16, Cheyenne, Wyoming Territory

Fisher, W G

Proceedings 1872, pg 36 (1872 Sept 24), Ashlar Lodge U D, Colorado Springs

Proceedings 1873, pg 39 (1873 Oct 1), Union Lodge No. 7, Denver

Proceedings 1875, pg 78 (1875 Sept 22), Union Lodge No. 7, Denver

Fisher, W H

Proceedings 1861-1869, pg 44 (1862 Nov 3) Grand Chaplain

Proceedings 1861-1869, pg 51 (1862 Nov 4) Grand Chaplain

Proceedings 1861-1869, pg 79 (1863 May 6) Grand Chaplain

Proceedings 1861-1869, pg 94 (1863 Apr 17) Grand Chaplain

Proceedings 1861-1869, pg 113 (1863 Nov 3), Chivington Lodge No. 6, Central City

Fisher, William G

Proceedings 1876, pg 33 (1876 Sept 20), Union Lodge No. 7, Denver

Fisher, William H

Proceedings 1861-1869, pg 134 (1864 Nov 8), Chivington Lodge No. 6, Central City, dimitted

Fisher, Wm G

Proceedings 1874, pg 214 (1874 Sept 30), Union Lodge No. 7, Denver

Fisher, Wm H

Proceedings 1861-1869, pg 45 (1862 Nov 3), Chivington Lodge No. 6, Central City

Proceedings 1861-1869, pg 54 (1862 Nov 4) committee

Proceedings 1861-1869, pg 78 (1862 Nov 4), Chivington Lodge No. 6, Central City

Fisk, J M

Proceedings 1871, pg 30 (1871 Sept 27), Occidental Lodge U D, Greeley

Proceedings 1872, pg 33 (1872 Sept 24), Occidental Lodge No. 20, Greeley

Proceedings 1873, pg 50 (1873 Oct 1), Occidental Lodge No. 20, Greeley

Fisk, Jeremiah

Proceedings 1874, pg 225 (1874 Sept 30), Occidental Lodge No. 20, Greeley

Fisk, Jeremiah M

Proceedings 1875, pg 87 (1875 Sept 22), Occidental Lodge No. 20, Greeley

Proceedings 1876, pg 40 (1876 Sept 20), Occidental Lodge No. 20, Greeley

Fitch, Elisha S

Proceedings 1861-1869, pg 331 (1868 Oct 19) Grand Master, Grand Lodge of Kentucky

Proceedings 1870, pg 61 (1869 Oct 18) Grand Master, Grand Lodge of Kentucky

Fitch, M H

Proceedings 1875, pg 85 (1875 Sept 22) Pueblo Lodge No. 17

Proceedings 1876, pg 38 (1876 Sept 20) Pueblo Lodge No. 17

Fitch, William

Proceedings 1870, pg 49 (1869 July 14) Grand Lodge of Canada, deceased

Fitz Simmons, ___

Proceedings 1861-1869, pg 309 (1869 Sept 29), Black Hawk Lodge No. 11, Black Hawk

Fitzsimmons, G H

Proceedings 1870, pg 25 (1870 Sept 28), Black Hawk Lodge No. 11, Black Hawk

Proceedings 1871, pg 23 (1871 Sept 27), Black Hawk Lodge No. 11, Black Hawk

Fitzsimmons, Geo H

Proceedings 1873, pg 42 (1873 Oct 1), Black Hawk Lodge No. 11, Black Hawk

Proceedings 1876, pg 34 (1876 Sept 20) Black Hawk Lodge No. 11

Fitzsimmons, George H

Proceedings 1874, pg 216 (1874 Sept 30), Black Hawk Lodge No. 11, Black Hawk

Proceedings 1875, pg 80 (1875 Sept 22) Black Hawk Lodge No. 11

Flanagan, James F

Proceedings 1876, pg 42 (1876 Sept 20), Doric Lodge No. 25, Fairplay, Apprentice

Flanagan, Patrick

Proceedings 1870, pg 25 (1870 Sept 28), Black Hawk Lodge No. 11, Black Hawk

Proceedings 1871, pg 23 (1871 Sept 27), Black Hawk Lodge No. 11, Black Hawk

Proceedings 1872, pg 25 (1872 Sept 24), Black Hawk Lodge No. 11, Black Hawk

Proceedings 1874, pg 216 (1874 Sept 30), Black Hawk Lodge No. 11, Black Hawk

Proceedings 1861-1869, pg 309 (1869 Sept 29), Black Hawk Lodge No. 11, Black Hawk

Proceedings 1875, pg 80 (1875 Sept 22) Black Hawk Lodge No. 11

Proceedings 1876, pg 34 (1876 Sept 20) Black Hawk Lodge No. 11

Proceedings 1876, pg 50 (1876 Sept 20) Black Hawk Lodge No. 11

Colorado's Territorial Masons

Flanagan, Patrick, cont.
    Proceedings 1873, pg 42 (1873 Oct 1), Black Hawk Lodge No. 11, Black Hawk

Fleeman, Thomas H
    Proceedings 1876, pg 7 (1877 Feb 7), King Solomon Lodge U D, West Las Animas

Fleeman, Thos J
    Proceedings 1876, pg 45 (1876 Sept 20), King Solomon Lodge U D, West Las Animas

Flinn, O
    Proceedings 1861-1869, pg 76 (1862 Nov 4), Summit Lodge No. 2, Parkville, dimitted

Florman, Robert
    Proceedings 1861-1869, pg 230 (1868 Oct 7), Valmont Lodge U D, Valmont

Flower, H F
    Proceedings 1872, pg 33 (1872 Sept 24), Occidental Lodge No. 20, Greeley
    Proceedings 1873, pg 49 (1873 Oct 1), Occidental Lodge No. 20, Greeley
    Proceedings 1874, pg 225 (1874 Sept 30), Occidental Lodge No. 20, Greeley
    Proceedings 1875, pg 87 (1875 Sept 22), Occidental Lodge No. 20, Greeley
    Proceedings 1876, pg 40 (1876 Sept 20), Occidental Lodge No. 20, Greeley

Flower, J B
    Proceedings 1872, pg 33 (1872 Sept 24), Occidental Lodge No. 20, Greeley
    Proceedings 1873, pg 50 (1873 Oct 1), Occidental Lodge No. 20, Greeley

Flower, James B
    Proceedings 1874, pg 225 (1874 Sept 30), Occidental Lodge No. 20, Greeley
    Proceedings 1875, pg 17 (1875 Sept 21), Collins Lodge No. 19, Fort Collins
    Proceedings 1876, pg 40 (1876 Sept 20), Occidental Lodge No. 20, Greeley

Flower, Jas B
    Proceedings 1875, pg 87 (1875 Sept 22), Occidental Lodge No. 20, Greeley

Floyd, M H
    Proceedings 1861-1869, pg 131 (1864 Nov 8) Golden City Lodge No. 1
    Proceedings 1861-1869, pg 147 (1865 Nov 7) Golden City Lodge No. 1, dimitted

Floyd, S F
    Proceedings 1875, pg 73 (1875 Sept 22) Golden City Lodge No. 1

Floyd, S T
    Proceedings 1874, pg 209 (1874 Sept 30), Golden City Lodge No. 1, Golden City
    Proceedings 1876, pg 29 (1876 Sept 20) Golden City Lodge No. 1

Follet, M V
    Proceedings 1870, pg 30 (1870 Sept 28), Laramie Lodge No. 18, Laramie, Wyoming Territory
    Proceedings 1871, pg 29 (1871 Sept 27), Laramie Lodge No. 18, Laramie, Wyoming Territory
    Proceedings 1872, pg 32 (1872 Sept 24), Laramie Lodge No. 18, Laramie, Wyoming Territory
    Proceedings 1873, pg 48 (1873 Oct 1), Laramie Lodge No. 18, Laramie, Wyoming Territory

Folley, J P
    Proceedings 1861-1869, pg 150 (1865 Nov 7), Chivington Lodge No. 6, Central City, Fellowcraft
    Proceedings 1861-1869, pg 168 (1866 Oct 2), Chivington Lodge No. 6, Central City
    Proceedings 1861-1869, pg 170 (1866 Oct 2), Black Hawk Lodge U D, Black Hawk
    Proceedings 1861-1869, pg 194 (1867 Oct 8), Chivington Lodge No. 6, Central City, Dimitted

Folley, John P
    Proceedings 1861-1869, pg 195 (1867 Oct 8), Black Hawk Lodge No. 11, Black Hawk
    Proceedings 1861-1869, pg 227 (1868 Oct 7), Black Hawk Lodge No. 11, Black Hawk
    Proceedings 1861-1869, pg 309 (1869 Sept 29), Black Hawk Lodge No. 11, Black Hawk, Dimitted

Foot, Smith
    Proceedings 1871, pg 27 (1871 Sept 27), Cheyenne Lodge No. 16, Cheyenne, Wyoming Territory

Foote, F M
    Proceedings 1874, pg 228 (1874 Sept 30), Evanston Lodge U D, Evanston, Uintah County, Wyoming Territory

Foote, Lucien A
    Proceedings 1874, pg 204 (1874 Sept 30) Grand Lodge of Indiana, Crawfordsville

Foote, Smith C
    Proceedings 1872, pg 30 (1872 Sept 24), Cheyenne Lodge No. 16, Cheyenne, Wyoming Territory, Dimitted
    Proceedings 1872, pg 36 (1872 Sept 24), Ashlar Lodge U D, Colorado Springs

Forberg, Charles
    Proceedings 1876, pg 30 (1876 Sept 20) Nevada Lodge No. 4

Forbes, A R
    Proceedings 1875, pg 81 (1875 Sept 22), Washington Lodge No. 12, Georgetown

Forbes, Albert R
    Proceedings 1876, pg 35 (1876 Sept 20), Washington Lodge No. 12, Georgetown

Forbess, S A
    Proceedings 1874, pg 227 (1874 Sept 30), St Vrain No. 23, Longmont
    Proceedings 1876, pg 41 (1876 Sept 20), St Vrain Lodge No. 23, Longmont

Ford, A F
    Proceedings 1870, pg 21 (1870 Sept 28), Denver Lodge No. 5, Denver

Ford, Frank
    Proceedings 1873, pg 40 (1873 Oct 1), Union Lodge No. 7, Denver
    Proceedings 1874, pg 213 (1874 Sept 30), Union Lodge No. 7, Denver
    Proceedings 1875, pg 78 (1875 Sept 22), Union Lodge No. 7, Denver
    Proceedings 1876, pg 33 (1876 Sept 20), Union Lodge No. 7, Denver

Ford, H F
    Proceedings 1861-1869, pg 77 (1862 Nov 4) Denver Lodge No. 5
    Proceedings 1861-1869, pg 112 (1863 Nov 3) Denver Lodge No. 5
    Proceedings 1861-1869, pg 149 (1865 Nov 7), Nevada Lodge No. 4, Nevadaville
    Proceedings 1861-1869, pg 167 (1866 Oct 2) Denver Lodge No. 5
    Proceedings 1861-1869, pg 223 (1868 Oct 7) Denver Lodge No. 5
    Proceedings 1871, pg 19 (1871 Sept 27) Denver Lodge No. 5
    Proceedings 1872, pg 19 (1872 Sept 24), Denver Lodge No. 5, Denver

Ford, H T
    Proceedings 1861-1869, pg 305 (1869 Sept 29) Denver Lodge No. 5

Ford, Hi F
    Proceedings 1861-1869, pg 133 (1864 Nov 8) Denver Lodge No. 5
    Proceedings 1873, pg 37 (1873 Oct 1), Denver Lodge No. 5, Denver
    Proceedings 1875, pg 76 (1875 Sept 22) Denver Lodge No. 5
    Proceedings 1876, pg 49 (1876 Sept 20) Denver Lodge No. 5, 1876 Aug 19

Ford, Hiram F
    Proceedings 1861-1869, pg 42 (1861 Dec 10) Golden City Lodge No. 1
    Proceedings 1874, pg 212 (1874 Sept 30), Denver Lodge No. 5, Denver

Ford, Sam'l J
    Proceedings 1876, pg 35 (1876 Sept 20), Washington Lodge No. 12, Georgetown, Fellow Craft

Ford, W R
    Proceedings 1861-1869, pg 77 (1862 Nov 4) Denver Lodge No. 5
    Proceedings 1861-1869, pg 112 (1863 Nov 3) Denver Lodge No. 5
    Proceedings 1861-1869, pg 149 (1865 Nov 7), Nevada Lodge No. 4, Nevadaville
    Proceedings 1861-1869, pg 167 (1866 Oct 2) Denver Lodge No. 5
    Proceedings 1861-1869, pg 305 (1869 Sept 29) Denver Lodge No. 5

Ford, Wm R
    Proceedings 1861-1869, pg 133 (1864 Nov 8) Denver Lodge No. 5
    Proceedings 1861-1869, pg 192 (1867 Oct 8) Denver Lodge No. 5
    Proceedings 1861-1869, pg 223 (1868 Oct 7) Denver Lodge No. 5
    Proceedings 1870, pg 21 (1870 Sept 28), Denver Lodge No. 5, Denver
    Proceedings 1871, pg 19 (1871 Sept 27) Denver Lodge No. 5
    Proceedings 1872, pg 20 (1872 Sept 24), Denver Lodge No. 5, Denver
    Proceedings 1873, pg 37 (1873 Oct 1), Denver Lodge No. 5, Denver
    Proceedings 1874, pg 212 (1874 Sept 30), Denver Lodge No. 5, Denver
    Proceedings 1875, pg 76 (1875 Sept 22) Denver Lodge No. 5
    Proceedings 1876, pg 49 (1876 Sept 20) Denver Lodge No. 5, 1876 Aug 19

Forgy, C E
    Proceedings 1861-1869, pg 132 (1864 Nov 8), Nevada Lodge No. 4, Nevadaville
    Proceedings 1861-1869, pg 148 (1865 Nov 7), Nevada Lodge No. 4, Nevadaville
    Proceedings 1861-1869, pg 166 (1866 Oct 2), Nevada Lodge No. 4, Nevadaville, dimitted,

Fort Collins Standard
    Colorado University Cornerstone Laying, pg 4 (1875 Sept 20) cornerstone contents

Foster, E L N
    Proceedings 1875, pg 81 (1875 Sept 22), Washington Lodge No. 12, Georgetown

Foster, Ernest L
    Proceedings 1874, pg 217 (1874 Sept 30), Washington Lodge No. 12, Georgetown

Foster, Ernest L N
    Proceedings 1876, pg 34 (1876 Sept 20), Washington Lodge No. 12, Georgetown

Foster, R M
    Proceedings 1861-1869, pg 132 (1864 Nov 8), Nevada Lodge No. 4, Nevadaville
    Proceedings 1861-1869, pg 148 (1865 Nov 7), Nevada Lodge No. 4, Nevadaville
    Proceedings 1861-1869, pg 166 (1866 Oct 2), Nevada Lodge No. 4, Nevadaville
    Proceedings 1861-1869, pg 192 (1867 Oct 8), Nevada Lodge No. 4, Nevadaville, Dimitted

Fouch, Albert
    Proceedings 1875, pg 90 (1875 Sept 22), Huerfano Lodge U D, Walsenburg
    Proceedings 1876, pg 48 (1876 Sept 20), Huerfano Lodge No. 27, Walsenburg, 1875 Nov 6

Foushe, A S
    Proceedings 1874, pg 211 (1874 Sept 30), Denver Lodge No. 5, Denver

Foushee, A S
    Proceedings 1872, pg 19 (1872 Sept 24), Denver Lodge No. 5, Denver

Colorado's Territorial Masons

Foushee, A S, cont.
    Proceedings 1876, pg 49 (1876 Sept 20) Denver Lodge No. 5, 1876 Aug 19

Foushee, Arthur S
    Proceedings 1873, pg 37 (1873 Oct 1), Denver Lodge No. 5, Denver
    Proceedings 1875, pg 76 (1875 Sept 22) Denver Lodge No. 5

Fowler, W R
    Proceedings 1861-1869, pg 229 (1868 Oct 7), Canon Lodge U D, Canon City
    Proceedings 1861-1869, pg 311 (1869 Sept 29), Mount Moriah Lodge No. 15, Canon City
    Proceedings 1870, pg 28 (1870 Sept 28), Mount Moriah Lodge No. 15, Canon City
    Proceedings 1871, pg 26 (1871 Sept 27), Mount Moriah Lodge No. 15, Canon City
    Proceedings 1872, pg 29 (1872 Sept 24), Mount Moriah Lodge No. 15, Canon City
    Proceedings 1873, pg 45 (1873 Oct 1), Mount Moriah Lodge No. 15, Canon City, Suspended

Fox, Christopher G
    Proceedings 1872, pg 44 (1872 Sept 24) Buffalo, Grand Lodge of New York
    Proceedings 1873, pg 61 (1873 Oct 1) Grand Lodge of New York, Buffalo
    Proceedings 1874, pg 109 (1874 Sept 30) Grand Lodge of New York

Fox, J M
    Proceedings 1861-1869, pg 77 (1862 Nov 4) Denver Lodge No. 5
    Proceedings 1861-1869, pg 112 (1863 Nov 3) Denver Lodge No. 5, dimitted
    Proceedings 1873, pg 6 (1873 Sept 30), Weston Lodge No. 22, Littleton
    Proceedings 1873, pg 51 (1873 Oct 1), Weston Lodge No. 22, Littleton
    Proceedings 1874, pg 6 (1874 Sept 29), Weston Lodge No. 22, Littleton
    Proceedings 1874, pg 36 (1874 Sept 30) per diem
    Proceedings 1874, pg 226 (1874 Sept 30), Weston Lodge No. 22, Littleton
    Proceedings 1875, pg 18 (1875 Sept 21), Weston Lodge No. 22, Littleton
    Proceedings 1875, pg 38 (1875 Sept 22) per diem
    Proceedings 1875, pg 88 (1875 Sept 22), Weston Lodge No. 22, Littleton
    Proceedings 1876, pg 41 (1876 Sept 20), Weston Lodge No. 22, Littleton

France
    Proceedings 1861-1869, pg 202 (1868 Oct 6) committee
    Proceedings 1873, pg 9 (1873 Sept 30), Ashlar Lodge U D, Colorado Springs
    Proceedings 1873, pg 10 (1873 Sept 30), Ashlar Lodge U D, Colorado Springs

France, L B
    Proceedings 1861-1869, pg 169 (1866 Oct 2), Union Lodge No. 7, Denver
    Proceedings 1861-1869, pg 195 (1867 Oct 8), Union Lodge No. 7, Denver
    Proceedings 1861-1869, pg 225 (1868 Oct 7), Union Lodge No. 7, Denver
    Proceedings 1861-1869, pg 288 (1869 Sept 28), Union Lodge No. 7, Denver
    Proceedings 1861-1869, pg 307 (1869 Sept 29), Union Lodge No. 7, Denver
    Proceedings 1870, pg cover (1870 Sept 28) Grand Orator, Denver
    Proceedings 1870, pg 13 (1870 Sept 27) Grant Orator
    Proceedings 1871, pg 3 (1871 Sept 26) Grand Orator
    Proceedings 1871, pg 21 (1871 Sept 27), Union Lodge No. 7, Denver
    Proceedings 1872, pg 22 (1872 Sept 24), Union Lodge No. 7, Denver
    Proceedings 1874, pg 213 (1874 Sept 30), Union Lodge No. 7, Denver
    Proceedings 1875, pg 78 (1875 Sept 22), Union Lodge No. 7, Denver
    Proceedings 1876, pg 32 (1876 Sept 20), Union Lodge No. 7, Denver
    Proceedings 1873, pg 39 (1873 Oct 1), Union Lodge No. 7, Denver

France, Lewis B
    Proceedings 1870, pg 23 (1870 Sept 28), Union Lodge No. 7, Denver

France, M
    Proceedings 1861-1869, pg 168 (1866 Oct 2), Chivington Lodge No. 6, Central City

France, Matt
    Proceedings 1861-1869, pg 150 (1865 Nov 7), Chivington Lodge No. 6, Central City
    Proceedings 1861-1869, pg 179 (1867 Oct 7), Washington Lodge No. 12, Georgetown
    Proceedings 1861-1869, pg 194 (1867 Oct 8), Chivington Lodge No. 6, Central City
    Proceedings 1861-1869, pg 202 (1868 Oct 6), Washington Lodge No. 12, Georgetown
    Proceedings 1861-1869, pg 219 (1868 Oct 7), Washington Lodge No. 12, Georgetown
    Proceedings 1861-1869, pg 219 (1868 Oct 7) committee
    Proceedings 1861-1869, pg 225 (1868 Oct 7), Chivington Lodge No. 6, Central City, Dimitted
    Proceedings 1861-1869, pg 227 (1868 Oct 7), Washington Lodge No. 12, Georgetown
    Proceedings 1861-1869, pg 309 (1869 Sept 29), Washington Lodge No. 12, Georgetown
    Proceedings 1870, pg 26 (1870 Sept 28), Washington Lodge No. 12, Georgetown
    Proceedings 1871, pg 24 (1871 Sept 27), Washington Lodge No. 12, Georgetown
    Proceedings 1872, pg 13 (1872 Sept 24), Ashlar Lodge U D, Colorado Springs
    Proceedings 1872, pg 26 (1872 Sept 24), Washington Lodge No. 12, Georgetown
    Proceedings 1872, pg 35 (1872 Sept 24), Ashlar Lodge U D, Colorado Springs

Proceedings 1873, pg 8 (1873 Jan 23), Ashlar Lodge U D, Colorado Springs

Proceedings 1873, pg 13 (1873 Sept 30), Ashlar Lodge U D, Colorado Springs

Proceedings 1873, pg 42 (1873 Oct 1), Washington Lodge No. 12, Georgetown

Proceedings 1874, pg 217 (1874 Sept 30), Washington Lodge No. 12, Georgetown, Demitted

Proceedings 1875, pg 30 (1875 Sept 21), El Paso Lodge No. 13, Colorado Springs

Proceedings 1875, pg 38 (1875 Sept 22) per diem

Proceedings 1875, pg 82 (1875 Sept 22), El Paso Lodge No. 13, Colorado Springs

Proceedings 1876, pg 36 (1876 Sept 20), El Paso Lodge No. 13, Colorado City

Frank, Hiram

Proceedings 1872, pg 29 (1872 Sept 24), Cheyenne Lodge No. 16, Cheyenne, Wyoming Territory

Proceedings 1873, pg 46 (1873 Oct 1), Cheyenne Lodge No. 16, Cheyenne, Wyoming Territory

Frary

Proceedings 1861-1869, pg 87 (1863 Apr 17) Golden City Lodge No. 1

Proceedings 1861-1869, pg 99 (1863 Nov 2) teller

Proceedings 1874, pg 96 (1874 Sept 30) Grand Lodge of Montana

Frary, D W

Proceedings 1861-1869, pg 119 (1863 Nov 3) warrant drawn

Frary, L M

Proceedings 1861-1869, pg 303 (1869 Sept 29) Golden City Lodge No. 1

Proceedings 1861-1869, pg 42 (1861 Dec 10) Golden City Lodge No. 1

Frary, L W

Proceedings 1861-1869, pg 51 (1862 Nov 4) Grand Sword Bearer

Proceedings 1861-1869, pg 79 (1863 May 6) Grand Sword Bearer

Proceedings 1861-1869, pg 80 (1863 May 6) Golden City Lodge No. 1

Proceedings 1861-1869, pg 86 (1863 Feb 22) Golden City Lodge No. 1

Proceedings 1861-1869, pg 94 (1863 Apr 17) Grand Sword Bearer

Proceedings 1861-1869, pg 94 (1863 Apr 17) Golden City Lodge No. 1

Proceedings 1861-1869, pg 98 (1863 Nov 2) Golden City Lodge No. 1

Proceedings 1861-1869, pg 98 (1863 Nov 2) Grand Sword Bearer

Proceedings 1861-1869, pg 99 (1863 Nov 2) Golden City Lodge No. 1, Grand Treasurer

Proceedings 1861-1869, pg 100 (1863 Nov 2) committee

Proceedings 1861-1869, pg 100 (1863 Nov 3) Grand Treasurer

Proceedings 1861-1869, pg 101 (1863 Nov 3) Grand Treasurer

Proceedings 1861-1869, pg 103 (1863 Nov 3) Golden City Lodge No. 1

Proceedings 1861-1869, pg 110 (1863 Nov 3) Golden City Lodge No. 1

Proceedings 1861-1869, pg 118 (1864 Mar 1) Grand Treasurer

Proceedings 1861-1869, pg 119 (1863 Nov 3) warrant drawn

Proceedings 1861-1869, pg 119 (1864 Nov 8) Grand Treasurer

Proceedings 1861-1869, pg 127 (1864 Nov 8) Grand Treasurer

Proceedings 1861-1869, pg 131 (1864 Nov 8) Golden City Lodge No. 1

Proceedings 1861-1869, pg 139 (1865 Nov 6), Montana Lodge U D, Virginia City, Montana Territory

Proceedings 1861-1869, pg 147 (1865 Nov 7) Golden City Lodge No. 1

Proceedings 1861-1869, pg 152 (1865 Nov 7), Montana Lodge U D, Virginia City, Montana Territory

Proceedings 1861-1869, pg 165 (1866 Oct 2) Golden City Lodge No. 1

Proceedings 1861-1869, pg 191 (1867 Oct 8) Golden City Lodge No. 1

Proceedings 1861-1869, pg 221 (1868 Oct 7) Golden City Lodge No. 1

Proceedings 1861-1869, pg 315 (1869 Sept 29) Grand Treasurer, 1863, Dimitted

Proceedings 1870, pg 19 (1870 Sept 28), Golden City Lodge No. 1, Golden City

Proceedings 1870, pg 32 (1870 Sept 28) Grand Treasurer, 1863, Dimitted

Proceedings 1871, pg 17 (1871 Sept 27), Golden City Lodge No. 1, Golden City

Proceedings 1871, pg 34 (1871 Sept 27) Grand Treasurer, 1863, Dimitted

Proceedings 1872, pg 17 (1872 Sept 24), Golden City Lodge No. 1, Golden City

Proceedings 1872, pg 42 (1872 Sept 24) Grand Treasurer, 1863, Dimitted

Proceedings 1873, pg 58 (1873 Oct 1) Grand Treasurer, 1863

Frary, Leander

Proceedings 1874, pg 206 (1874 Sept 30) Grand Treasurer, 1863

Frary, Leander W

Proceedings 1861-1869, pg 267 (1867 Jan 20), Grand Master, Grand Lodge of Montana

Proceedings 1870, pg 88 (1868 Oct 5) Grand Master, Grand Lodge of Montana

Proceedings 1873, pg 35 (1873 Oct 1), Golden City Lodge No. 1, Golden City, dimitted in 1865

Proceedings 1875, pg 93 (1875 Sept 22) Grand Treasurer, 1863, Demitted

Fraternal Publishing Company

Proceedings 1861-1869, pg 290 (1869 Sept 28), of Cincinnati, OH

Frazer, G B
   Proceedings 1874, pg 36 (1874 Sept 30) per diem

Frazer, R
   Proceedings 1861-1869, pg 168 (1866 Oct 2), Chivington Lodge No. 6, Central City

Frazer, Robert
   Proceedings 1861-1869, pg 150 (1865 Nov 7), Chivington Lodge No. 6, Central City
   Proceedings 1861-1869, pg 170 (1866 Oct 2), Black Hawk Lodge U D, Black Hawk
   Proceedings 1861-1869, pg 195 (1867 Oct 8), Black Hawk Lodge No. 11, Black Hawk
   Proceedings 1861-1869, pg 226 (1868 Oct 7), Black Hawk Lodge No. 11, Black Hawk
   Proceedings 1861-1869, pg 297 (1869 Sept 28), Black Hawk Lodge No. 11, Black Hawk
   Proceedings 1871, pg 23 (1871 Sept 27), Black Hawk Lodge No. 11, Black Hawk
   Proceedings 1872, pg 25 (1872 Sept 24), Black Hawk Lodge No. 11, Black Hawk
   Proceedings 1873, pg 42 (1873 Oct 1), Black Hawk Lodge No. 11, Black Hawk
   Proceedings 1874, pg 216 (1874 Sept 30), Black Hawk Lodge No. 11, Black Hawk
   Proceedings 1875, pg 80 (1875 Sept 22) Black Hawk Lodge No. 11

Frazer, Robt
   Proceedings 1861-1869, pg 78 (1862 Nov 4), Chivington Lodge No. 6, Central City
   Proceedings 1861-1869, pg 309 (1869 Sept 29), Black Hawk Lodge No. 11, Black Hawk

Frazier
   Proceedings 1861-1869, pg 210 (1867 Nov) to post with Dr Dickinson
   Proceedings 1861-1869, pg 289 (1869 Sept 28) committee
   Proceedings 1872, pg 7 (1872 Sept 24), El Paso Lodge No. 13, Colorado City

Frazier, G B
   Proceedings 1861-1869, pg 171 (1866 Oct 2), El Paso U D, Colorado City
   Proceedings 1861-1869, pg 180 (1867 Oct 7) petition to form a lodge
   Proceedings 1861-1869, pg 196 (1867 Oct 8), El Paso Lodge U D, Colorado City
   Proceedings 1861-1869, pg 206 (1868 Oct 6) petition
   Proceedings 1861-1869, pg 207 (1867 Dec 11), Canon City Lodge U D, Canon City, Worshipful Master
   Proceedings 1861-1869, pg 228 (1868 Oct 7), El Paso Lodge No. 13, Colorado City, Dimitted
   Proceedings 1861-1869, pg 229 (1868 Oct 7), Canon Lodge U D, Canon City
   Proceedings 1861-1869, pg 299 (1869 Sept 29) Grand Sword Bearer
   Proceedings 1861-1869, pg 301 (1869 Sept 29), Mount Moriah Lodge No. 15, Canon City
   Proceedings 1861-1869, pg 301 (1869 Sept 29) committee
   Proceedings 1861-1869, pg 311 (1869 Sept 29), Mount Moriah Lodge No. 15, Canon City
   Proceedings 1870, pg 28 (1870 Sept 28), Mount Moriah Lodge No. 15, Canon City
   Proceedings 1871, pg 26 (1871 Sept 27), Mount Moriah Lodge No. 15, Canon City
   Proceedings 1871, pg 26 (1871 Sept 27), Mount Moriah Lodge No. 15, Canon City
   Proceedings 1872, pg 28 (1872 Sept 24), Mount Moriah Lodge No. 15, Canon City
   Proceedings 1873, pg 45 (1873 Oct 1), Mount Moriah Lodge No. 15, Canon City
   Proceedings 1874, pg 6 (1874 Sept 29), Mount Moriah Lodge No. 15, Canon City
   Proceedings 1874, pg 32 (1874 Sept 30) Junior Grand Deacon, Canon City
   Proceedings 1874, pg 220 (1874 Sept 30), Mount Moriah Lodge No. 15, Canon City
   Proceedings 1875, pg 84 (1875 Sept 22), Mount Moriah Lodge No. 15, Canon City
   Proceedings 1876, pg 8 (1875 Dec 15), dispensation to consecrate Mount Moriah Lodge No. 15, Canon City
   Proceedings 1876, pg 38 (1876 Sept 20), Mount Moriah Lodge No. 15, Canon City

Frazier, Gideon B
   Proceedings 1861-1869, pg 288 (1869 Sept 28), Mount Moriah Lodge No. 15, Canon City

Frazier, H J
   Proceedings 1861-1869, pg 229 (1868 Oct 7), Canon Lodge U D, Canon City
   Proceedings 1861-1869, pg 311 (1869 Sept 29), Mount Moriah Lodge No. 15, Canon City
   Proceedings 1870, pg 28 (1870 Sept 28), Mount Moriah Lodge No. 15, Canon City
   Proceedings 1871, pg 26 (1871 Sept 27), Mount Moriah Lodge No. 15, Canon City

Frazier, Henry J
   Proceedings 1872, pg 29 (1872 Sept 24), Mount Moriah Lodge No. 15, Canon City, died
   Proceedings 1872, pg 39 (1872 Sept 24), Mount Moriah Lodge No. 15, Canon City

Frazier, R
   Proceedings 1861-1869, pg 113 (1863 Nov 3), Chivington Lodge No. 6, Central City
   Proceedings 1871, pg 4 (1871 Sept 26), Mount Moriah Lodge No. 15, Canon City

Frazier, R J
   Proceedings 1861-1869, pg 171 (1866 Oct 2), El Paso U D, Colorado City
   Proceedings 1861-1869, pg 196 (1867 Oct 8), El Paso Lodge U D, Colorado City
   Proceedings 1861-1869, pg 228 (1868 Oct 7), El Paso Lodge No. 13, Colorado City, Dimitted
   Proceedings 1861-1869, pg 229 (1868 Oct 7), Canon Lodge U D, Canon City
   Proceedings 1861-1869, pg 311 (1869 Sept 29), Mount Moriah Lodge No. 15, Canon City
   Proceedings 1870, pg 28 (1870 Sept 28), Mount Moriah Lodge No. 15, Canon City
   Proceedings 1871, pg 26 (1871 Sept 27), Mount Moriah Lodge No. 15, Canon City

Proceedings 1872, pg 29 (1872 Sept 24), Mount Moriah Lodge No. 15, Canon City

Proceedings 1873, pg 45 (1873 Oct 1), Mount Moriah Lodge No. 15, Canon City

Proceedings 1874, pg 220 (1874 Sept 30), Mount Moriah Lodge No. 15, Canon City

Proceedings 1875, pg 84 (1875 Sept 22), Mount Moriah Lodge No. 15, Canon City

Proceedings 1876, pg 38 (1876 Sept 20), Mount Moriah Lodge No. 15, Canon City

Frazier, Robert
Proceedings 1861-1869, pg 134 (1864 Nov 8), Chivington Lodge No. 6, Central City

Proceedings 1861-1869, pg 194 (1867 Oct 8), Chivington Lodge No. 6, Central City, Dimitted

Proceedings 1870, pg 25 (1870 Sept 28), Black Hawk Lodge No. 11, Black Hawk

Proceedings 1876, pg 34 (1876 Sept 20) Black Hawk Lodge No. 11

Frazier, S
Proceedings 1861-1869, pg 311 (1869 Sept 29), Mount Moriah Lodge No. 15, Canon City

Frazier, Stephen
Proceedings 1861-1869, pg 171 (1866 Oct 2), El Paso U D, Colorado City

Proceedings 1861-1869, pg 196 (1867 Oct 8), El Paso Lodge U D, Colorado City

Proceedings 1861-1869, pg 207 (1867 Dec 11) Junior Warden

Proceedings 1861-1869, pg 229 (1868 Oct 7), Canon Lodge U D, Canon City

Proceedings 1870, pg 28 (1870 Sept 28), Mount Moriah Lodge No. 15, Canon City

Proceedings 1871, pg 27 (1871 Sept 27), Mount Moriah Lodge No. 15, Canon City, died

Proceedings 1871, pg 32 (1871 Sept 27), Mount Moriah Lodge No. 15, Canon City

Frazier, Thomas
Proceedings 1871, pg 26 (1871 Sept 27), Mount Moriah Lodge No. 15, Canon City

Proceedings 1872, pg 29 (1872 Sept 24), Mount Moriah Lodge No. 15, Canon City

Proceedings 1874, pg 220 (1874 Sept 30), Mount Moriah Lodge No. 15, Canon City

Proceedings 1875, pg 84 (1875 Sept 22), Mount Moriah Lodge No. 15, Canon City

Proceedings 1876, pg 38 (1876 Sept 20), Mount Moriah Lodge No. 15, Canon City

Frazier, Thos
Proceedings 1873, pg 45 (1873 Oct 1), Mount Moriah Lodge No. 15, Canon City

Frazier, W Gideon B
Proceedings 1874, pg 3 (1874 Sept 29) Senior Grand Steward

Fredendall, Ira L
Proceedings 1870, pg 29 (1870 Sept 28), Cheyenne Lodge No. 16, Cheyenne, Wyoming Territory

Proceedings 1872, pg 29 (1872 Sept 24), Cheyenne Lodge No. 16, Cheyenne, Wyoming Territory

Frederick, Henry
Proceedings 1870, pg 73 (1784 Sept 29) Duke of Cumberland

Proceedings 1870, pg 77 (1784 Sept 29) Duke of Cumberland

Frederick, Wm
Proceedings 1861-1869, pg 165 (1866 Oct 2) Golden City Lodge No. 1

Proceedings 1861-1869, pg 131 (1864 Nov 8) Golden City Lodge No. 1

Proceedings 1861-1869, pg 191 (1867 Oct 8) Golden City Lodge No. 1, Dimitted

Fredrick, Wm
Proceedings 1861-1869, pg 147 (1865 Nov 7) Golden City Lodge No. 1

Freeman, C F
Proceedings 1876, pg 31 (1876 Sept 20) Denver Lodge No. 5

Freeman, Edgar
Proceedings 1861-1869, pg 226 (1868 Oct 7), Empire Lodge No. 8, Empire City

Proceedings 1861-1869, pg 308 (1869 Sept 29), Empire Lodge No. 8, Empire City

Proceedings 1870, pg 24 (1870 Sept 28), Empire Lodge No. 8, Empire

Proceedings 1872, pg 23 (1872 Sept 24), Empire Lodge No. 8, Empire

Proceedings 1874, pg 215 (1874 Sept 30), Empire Lodge No. 8, Empire

Freeman, James H
Proceedings 1875, pg 87 (1875 Sept 22), Occidental Lodge No. 20, Greeley

Proceedings 1874, pg 225 (1874 Sept 30), Occidental Lodge No. 20, Greeley

Proceedings 1876, pg 40 (1876 Sept 20), Occidental Lodge No. 20, Greeley

Freemason
Proceedings 1861-1869, pg 291 (1869 Sept 28) of St Louis
Proceedings 1870, pg 11 (1870 Sept 27), St Louis, MO
Proceedings 1871, pg 10 (1871 Sept 26) masonic magazine
Proceedings 1872, pg 11 (1872 Sept 24), published at St Louis, MO
Proceedings 1873, pg 15 (1873 Oct 1), published at St Louis, MO
Proceedings 1874, pg 19 (1874 Sept 29), published at St Louis, MO
Proceedings 1875, pg 23 (1875 Sept 21), published at St Louis, MO

Freemasons Repository
Proceedings 1874, pg 19 (1874 Sept 29), published at Providence, RI
Proceedings 1872, pg 11 (1872 Sept 24), published at Providence, RI
Proceedings 1875, pg 23 (1875 Sept 21), published at Providence, RI

Colorado's Territorial Masons

Freemason's Repository
    Proceedings 1876, pg 11 (1876 Sept 19), published at Providence, RI

French, B B
    Proceedings 1861-1869, pg 244 (1867 Sept 4), Past Grand Master, Grand Lodge of District of Columbia
    Proceedings 1861-1869, pg 245 (1867 Nov 7), Past Grand Master, Grand Lodge of District of Columbia

French, Benj Brown
    Proceedings 1872, pg 58 (1872 Sept 24) Grand Lodge of the District of Columbia, deceased

French, M H
    Proceedings 1876, pg 33 (1876 Sept 20), Union Lodge No. 7, Denver

French, S M
    Proceedings 1874, pg 5 (1874 Sept 29), Golden City Lodge No. 1, Golden City
    Proceedings 1874, pg 209 (1874 Sept 30), Golden City Lodge No. 1, Golden City
    Proceedings 1875, pg 73 (1875 Sept 22) Golden City Lodge No. 1
    Proceedings 1876, pg 48 (1876 Sept 20) Denver Lodge No. 5, 1876 July 1
    Proceedings 1876, pg 48 (1876 Sept 20) Golden City Lodge No. 1, 1875 Nov 20

French, S T
    Proceedings 1875, pg 82 (1875 Sept 22), El Paso Lodge No. 13, Colorado Springs
    Proceedings 1876, pg 36 (1876 Sept 20), El Paso Lodge No. 13, Colorado City

French, Z
    Proceedings 1861-1869, pg 152 (1865 Nov 7), Helena City Lodge U D, Helena City, Montana Territory, Apprentice

Freund, F W
    Proceedings 1874, pg 212 (1874 Sept 30), Denver Lodge No. 5, Denver
    Proceedings 1876, pg 31 (1876 Sept 20) Denver Lodge No. 5

Freund, Frank W
    Proceedings 1871, pg 19 (1871 Sept 27) Denver Lodge No. 5
    Proceedings 1872, pg 19 (1872 Sept 24), Denver Lodge No. 5, Denver
    Proceedings 1873, pg 37 (1873 Oct 1), Denver Lodge No. 5, Denver
    Proceedings 1875, pg 76 (1875 Sept 22) Denver Lodge No. 5

Freund, Isaac
    Proceedings 1861-1869, pg 223 (1868 Oct 7) Denver Lodge No. 5
    Proceedings 1870, pg 21 (1870 Sept 28), Denver Lodge No. 5, Denver
    Proceedings 1871, pg 19 (1871 Sept 27) Denver Lodge No. 5
    Proceedings 1872, pg 19 (1872 Sept 24), Denver Lodge No. 5, Denver
    Proceedings 1873, pg 37 (1873 Oct 1), Denver Lodge No. 5, Denver
    Proceedings 1874, pg 212 (1874 Sept 30), Denver Lodge No. 5, Denver
    Proceedings 1875, pg 76 (1875 Sept 22) Denver Lodge No. 5
    Proceedings 1876, pg 31 (1876 Sept 20) Denver Lodge No. 5

Fridendall, Ira L
    Proceedings 1871, pg 27 (1871 Sept 27), Cheyenne Lodge No. 16, Cheyenne, Wyoming Territory

Friedenhall, Ira
    Proceedings 1873, pg 46 (1873 Oct 1), Cheyenne Lodge No. 16, Cheyenne, Wyoming Territory
    Proceedings 1874, pg 221 (1874 Sept 30), Cheyenne Lodge No. 16, Cheyenne, Wyoming Territory

Friend, I
    Proceedings 1861-1869, pg 305 (1869 Sept 29) Denver Lodge No. 5

Fries, F F
    Proceedings 1861-1869, pg 76 (1862 Nov 4), Summit Lodge No. 2, Parkville, dimitted

Frisbee, R K
    Proceedings 1861-1869, pg 192 (1867 Oct 8) Denver Lodge No. 5
    Proceedings 1861-1869, pg 195 (1867 Oct 8), Union Lodge No. 7, Denver

Frisbie, S S
    Proceedings 1871, pg 30 (1871 Sept 27), Occidental Lodge U D, Greeley

Frizzell
    Proceedings 1872, pg 88 (1872 Sept 24) Grand Lodge of Tennessee

Frizzell, John
    Proceedings 1861-1869, pg 316 (1869 Sept 29) Grand Lodge of Tennessee
    Proceedings 1861-1869, pg 348 (1868 Oct 4) Grand Secretary, Grand Lodge of Tennessee
    Proceedings 1870, pg 34 (1870 Sept 28) Grand Secretary, Grand Lodge of Tennessee
    Proceedings 1871, pg 35 (1871 Sept 27) Grand Secretary, Grand Lodge of Tennessee
    Proceedings 1872, pg 44 (1872 Sept 24) Nashville, Grand Lodge of Tennessee
    Proceedings 1872, pg 86 (1872 Sept 24) Grand Lodge of Tennessee
    Proceedings 1872, pg 87 (1872 Sept 24) Grand Lodge of Tennessee
    Proceedings 1873, pg 61 (1873 Oct 1) Grand Lodge of Tennessee, Nashville
    Proceedings 1874, pg 123 (1874 Sept 30) Grand Lodge of Tennessee
    Proceedings 1874, pg 124 (1874 Sept 30) Grand Lodge of Tennessee

Proceedings 1874, pg 205 (1874 Sept 30) Grand Lodge of Tennessee, Nashville
Proceedings 1875, pg 96 (1875 Sept 22) Grand Lodge of Tennessee, Nashville
Proceedings 1876, pg 54 (1876 Sept 20) Grand Lodge of Tennessee, Nashville

Fry, Israel
Proceedings 1873, pg 44 (1873 Oct 1), El Paso Lodge No. 13, Colorado City, Apprentice

Fuerstine, Henry
Proceedings 1875, pg 76 (1875 Sept 22) Denver Lodge No. 5

Fuller, Charles A
Proceedings 1861-1869, pg 213 (1868 Oct 6) Past Grand Master of Tennessee has died

Fuller, Chas A
Proceedings 1861-1869, pg 282 (1867 Oct 7), Grand Secretary, Grand Lodge of Tennessee

Fuller, J L
Proceedings 1876, pg 42 (1876 Sept 20), Doric Lodge No. 25, Fairplay

Fuller, Samuel G
Proceedings 1875, pg 87 (1875 Sept 22), Occidental Lodge No. 20, Greeley
Proceedings 1876, pg 40 (1876 Sept 20), Occidental Lodge No. 20, Greeley

Fuller, Wm A
Proceedings 1861-1869, pg 153 (1866 Oct 1) Grand Chaplain

Fullerton, James
Proceedings 1876, pg 44 (1876 Sept 20) Del Norte Lodge U D, Apprentice

Fullerton, W
Proceedings 1870, pg 25 (1870 Sept 28), Black Hawk Lodge No. 11, Black Hawk

Fullerton, William
Proceedings 1873, pg 42 (1873 Oct 1), Black Hawk Lodge No. 11, Black Hawk
Proceedings 1874, pg 216 (1874 Sept 30), Black Hawk Lodge No. 11, Black Hawk
Proceedings 1875, pg 17 (1875 Sept 21) Black Hawk Lodge No. 11
Proceedings 1875, pg 30 (1875 Sept 21) Black Hawk Lodge No. 11
Proceedings 1875, pg 80 (1875 Sept 22) Black Hawk Lodge No. 11
Proceedings 1876, pg 6 (1876 Sept 19) committee
Proceedings 1876, pg 24 (1876 Sept 20) committee

Fullerton, William C
Proceedings 1876, pg 30 (1876 Sept 20) Nevada Lodge No. 4

Fullerton, Wm
Proceedings 1871, pg cover (1871 Sept 27) Junior Grand Steward, Black Hawk
Proceedings 1871, pg 4 (1871 Sept 26), Black Hawk Lodge No. 11, Black Hawk
Proceedings 1871, pg 14 (1871 Sept 27) Junior Grand Steward
Proceedings 1871, pg 23 (1871 Sept 27), Black Hawk Lodge No. 11, Black Hawk
Proceedings 1872, pg 3 (1872 Sept 24) Junior Grand Steward
Proceedings 1872, pg 15 (1872 Sept 24) Senior Grand Steward
Proceedings 1872, pg 24 (1872 Sept 24), Black Hawk Lodge No. 11, Black Hawk
Proceedings 1874, pg 5 (1874 Sept 29), Black Hawk Lodge No. 11, Black Hawk
Proceedings 1875, pg 17 (1875 Sept 21) committee
Proceedings 1875, pg 17 (1875 Sept 21) Black Hawk Lodge No. 11
Proceedings 1875, pg 34 (1875 Sept 22) committee
Proceedings 1875, pg 38 (1875 Sept 22) per diem
Proceedings 1876, pg 5 (1876 Sept 19) Black Hawk Lodge No. 11
Proceedings 1876, pg 22 (1876 Sept 20) Black Hawk Lodge No. 11
Proceedings 1876, pg 34 (1876 Sept 20) Black Hawk Lodge No. 11

Fulton, R L
Proceedings 1870, pg 30 (1870 Sept 28), Laramie Lodge No. 18, Laramie, Wyoming Territory

Fulton, Robert L
Proceedings 1871, pg 29 (1871 Sept 27), Laramie Lodge No. 18, Laramie, Wyoming Territory, Dimitted

Furnas, R W
Proceedings 1870, pg 34 (1870 Sept 28) Grand Secretary, Grand Lodge of Nebraska
Proceedings 1870, pg 91 (1869 Oct 26) Grand Secretary, Grand Lodge of Nebraska
Proceedings 1870, pg 91 (1869 Oct 26) Grand Secretary, Grand Lodge of Nebraska
Proceedings 1871, pg 35 (1871 Sept 27) Grand Secretary, Grand Lodge of Nebraska

Furnass, Robert W
Proceedings 1872, pg 75 (1872 Sept 24) Grand Lodge of Nebraska

Furniss, John G
Proceedings 1874, pg 221 (1874 Sept 30), Cheyenne Lodge No. 16, Cheyenne, Wyoming Territory

Furst, Joseph
Proceedings 1876, pg 31 (1876 Sept 20) Denver Lodge No. 5

G

Gaines, Richard
 Proceedings 1874, pg 218 (1874 Sept 30), El Paso Lodge No. 13, Colorado Springs
 Proceedings 1875, pg 82 (1875 Sept 22), El Paso Lodge No. 13, Colorado Springs
 Proceedings 1876, pg 36 (1876 Sept 20), El Paso Lodge No. 13, Colorado City

Galbraith, R
 Proceedings 1870, pg 31 (1870 Sept 28), Laramie Lodge No. 18, Laramie, Wyoming Territory

Galbraith, R M
 Proceedings 1870, pg 30 (1870 Sept 28), Laramie Lodge No. 18, Laramie, Wyoming Territory

Gallahar, Daniel J
 Proceedings 1875, pg 73 (1875 Sept 22) Golden City Lodge No. 1

Gallaher, D J
 Proceedings 1876, pg 29 (1876 Sept 20) Golden City Lodge No. 1
 Proceedings 1876, pg 50 (1876 Sept 20) Golden City Lodge No. 1

Gallatin, D G
 Proceedings 1861-1869, pg 229 (1868 Oct 7), Pueblo Lodge U D, Pueblo

Gallop, S C
 Proceedings 1874, pg 6 (1874 Sept 29), Pueblo Lodge No. 17, Pueblo

Gallup, Francis
 Proceedings 1872, pg cover (1872 Sept 24), Denver Chapter No. 2, Denver

Gallup, I C
 Proceedings 1874, pg 222 (1874 Sept 30), Pueblo Lodge No. 17, Pueblo, Pueblo County

Gallup, S C
 Proceedings 1871, pg 28 (1871 Sept 27), Pueblo Lodge No. 17, Pueblo
 Proceedings 1872, pg 30 (1872 Sept 24), Pueblo Lodge No. 17, Pueblo
 Proceedings 1875, pg 85 (1875 Sept 22) Pueblo Lodge No. 17
 Proceedings 1876, pg 38 (1876 Sept 20) Pueblo Lodge No. 17

Gallup, Samuel C
 Proceedings 1873, pg 47 (1873 Oct 1), Pueblo Lodge No. 17, Pueblo

Gardner
 Proceedings 1872, pg 68 (1872 Sept 24) Grand Lodge of Massachusetts

Gardner, C H
 Proceedings 1861-1869, pg 230 (1868 Oct 7), Valmont Lodge U D, Valmont

 Proceedings 1872, pg 35 (1872 Sept 24), St Vrain Lodge No. 23, Longmont
 Proceedings 1873, pg 51 (1873 Oct 1), St Vrain Lodge No. 23, Longmont
 Proceedings 1874, pg 227 (1874 Sept 30), St Vrain No. 23, Longmont
 Proceedings 1876, pg 24 (1876 Sept 20), St Vrain Lodge No. 23, Longmont
 Proceedings 1876, pg 41 (1876 Sept 20), St Vrain Lodge No. 23, Longmont

Gardner, E I
 Proceedings 1876, pg 31 (1876 Sept 20) Denver Lodge No. 5

Gardner, E L
 Proceedings 1861-1869, pg 78 (1862 Nov 4), Chivington Lodge No. 6, Central City
 Proceedings 1861-1869, pg 113 (1863 Nov 3), Chivington Lodge No. 6, Central City
 Proceedings 1861-1869, pg 134 (1864 Nov 8), Chivington Lodge No. 6, Central City
 Proceedings 1861-1869, pg 150 (1865 Nov 7), Chivington Lodge No. 6, Central City
 Proceedings 1861-1869, pg 165 (1866 Oct 2) Golden City Lodge No. 1
 Proceedings 1861-1869, pg 168 (1866 Oct 2), Chivington Lodge No. 6, Central City
 Proceedings 1861-1869, pg 191 (1867 Oct 8) Golden City Lodge No. 1
 Proceedings 1861-1869, pg 194 (1867 Oct 8), Chivington Lodge No. 6, Central City
 Proceedings 1861-1869, pg 224 (1868 Oct 7), Chivington Lodge No. 6, Central City
 Proceedings 1861-1869, pg 300 (1869 Sept 29), Central Lodge No. 6, living in Denver
 Proceedings 1861-1869, pg 306 (1869 Sept 29), Central Lodge No. 6, Central City
 Proceedings 1870, pg 23 (1870 Sept 28), Central Lodge No. 6, Central City, Dimitted
 Proceedings 1874, pg 211 (1874 Sept 30), Denver Lodge No. 5, Denver
 Proceedings 1875, pg 75 (1875 Sept 22) Denver Lodge No. 5

Gardner, J D
 Proceedings 1873, pg 48 (1873 Oct 1), Laramie Lodge No. 18, Laramie, Wyoming Territory
 Proceedings 1874, pg 223 (1874 Sept 30), Laramie Lodge No. 18, Laramie City

Gardner, Samuel G
 Proceedings 1870, pg 77 (1824 Jan 5) African Lodge at Boston

Gardner, T B
 Proceedings 1861-1869, pg 221 (1868 Oct 7) Golden City Lodge No. 1
 Proceedings 1861-1869, pg 303 (1869 Sept 29) Golden City Lodge No. 1
 Proceedings 1870, pg 19 (1870 Sept 28), Golden City Lodge No. 1, Golden City

Proceedings 1871, pg 17 (1871 Sept 27), Golden City Lodge No. 1, Golden City

Gardner, Thomas B
Proceedings 1872, pg 18 (1872 Sept 24), Golden City Lodge No. 1, Golden City, Stricken from the Roll

Gardner, William Sewall
Proceedings 1861-1869, pg 331 (1868 Dec 9) Grand Master, Grand Lodge of Massachusetts
Proceedings 1870, pg 67 (1869 Sept 8) Grand Master, Grand Lodge of Massachusetts
Proceedings 1870, pg 75 (1870 May 5) Grand Master, Grand Lodge of Massachusetts

Gardner, Wm T
Proceedings 1872, pg 68 (1872 Sept 24) Grand Lodge of Massachusetts

Garfield, Ellery I
Proceedings 1876, pg 54 (1876 Sept 20) Grand Lodge of Michigan, Kalamazoo

Garrett, Erasmus
Proceedings 1872, pg 21 (1872 Sept 24), Denver Lodge No. 5, Denver

Garrett, Thomas E
Proceedings 1872, pg 72 (1872 Sept 24) Grand Lodge of Missouri

Garrett, Thos E
Proceedings 1872, pg 43 (1872 Sept 24) St Louis, Grand Lodge of Missouri

Garrish, J H
Proceedings 1861-1869, pg 305 (1869 Sept 29) Denver Lodge No. 5

Garrott, E
Proceedings 1861-1869, pg 168 (1866 Oct 2), Chivington Lodge No. 6, Central City
Proceedings 1861-1869, pg 194 (1867 Oct 8), Chivington Lodge No. 6, Central City
Proceedings 1861-1869, pg 224 (1868 Oct 7), Chivington Lodge No. 6, Central City
Proceedings 1861-1869, pg 306 (1869 Sept 29), Central Lodge No. 6, Central City
Proceedings 1870, pg 22 (1870 Sept 28), Central Lodge No. 6, Central City
Proceedings 1871, pg 20 (1871 Sept 27), Central Lodge No. 6, Central

Garrott, Erasmus
Proceedings 1873, pg 39 (1873 Oct 1), Central Lodge No. 6, Central City, Dimitted

Garrott, Erastus
Proceedings 1861-1869, pg 150 (1865 Nov 7), Chivington Lodge No. 6, Central City

Garson, M J
Proceedings 1876, pg 31 (1876 Sept 20) Denver Lodge No. 5

Garson, Moe J
Proceedings 1875, pg 75 (1875 Sept 22) Denver Lodge No. 5

Garvin, W H
Proceedings 1861-1869, pg 112 (1863 Nov 3) Denver Lodge No. 5, Fellowcraft
Proceedings 1861-1869, pg 133 (1864 Nov 8) Denver Lodge No. 5
Proceedings 1861-1869, pg 149 (1865 Nov 7), Nevada Lodge No. 4, Nevadaville
Proceedings 1861-1869, pg 167 (1866 Oct 2) Denver Lodge No. 5, dimitted

Gassels, G
Proceedings 1861-1869, pg 168 (1866 Oct 2), Chivington Lodge No. 6, Central City

Gatchell, Henry T F
Proceedings 1872, pg 36 (1872 Sept 24), Ashlar Lodge U D, Colorado Springs

Gates, J E
Proceedings 1861-1869, pg 133 (1864 Nov 8) Denver Lodge No. 5
Proceedings 1861-1869, pg 148 (1865 Nov 7), Nevada Lodge No. 4, Nevadaville
Proceedings 1861-1869, pg 166 (1866 Oct 2) Denver Lodge No. 5
Proceedings 1861-1869, pg 192 (1867 Oct 8) Denver Lodge No. 5
Proceedings 1861-1869, pg 216 (1868 Oct 7) Worshipful Master of Cheyenne
Proceedings 1861-1869, pg 216 (1868 Oct 7) removed as Senior Warden of Cheyenne
Proceedings 1861-1869, pg 223 (1868 Oct 7) Denver Lodge No. 5
Proceedings 1861-1869, pg 229 (1868 Oct 7), Cheyenne Lodge U D, Cheyenne, Dakota Territory
Proceedings 1861-1869, pg 305 (1869 Sept 29) Denver Lodge No. 5, Dimitted
Proceedings 1861-1869, pg 311 (1869 Sept 29), Cheyenne Lodge No. 16, Cheyenne
Proceedings 1870, pg 28 (1870 Sept 28), Cheyenne Lodge No. 16, Cheyenne, Wyoming Territory
Proceedings 1870, pg 30 (1870 Sept 28), Laramie Lodge No. 18, Laramie, Wyoming Territory
Proceedings 1871, pg 29 (1871 Sept 27), Laramie Lodge No. 18, Laramie, Wyoming Territory
Proceedings 1871, pg 29 (1871 Sept 27), Laramie Lodge No. 18, Laramie, Wyoming Territory
Proceedings 1872, pg cover (1872 Sept 24) committee, Laramie City, Wyoming
Proceedings 1872, pg 4 (1872 Sept 24), Laramie Lodge No. 18, Laramie, Wyoming Territory
Proceedings 1872, pg 16 (1872 Sept 24) committee
Proceedings 1872, pg 16 (1872 Sept 24), Laramie Lodge No. 18, Laramie, Wyoming Territory
Proceedings 1872, pg 31 (1872 Sept 24), Laramie Lodge No. 18, Laramie, Wyoming Territory
Proceedings 1873, pg 7 (1873 Sept 30), Laramie Lodge No. 18, Laramie, Wyoming Territory
Proceedings 1873, pg 7 (1873 Sept 30) committee
Proceedings 1873, pg 17 (1873 Oct 1) Junior Grand Warden

Colorado's Territorial Masons

Gates, J E, cont.
Proceedings 1873, pg 18 (1873 Oct 1) committee
Proceedings 1873, pg 27 (1873 Oct 1) committee
Proceedings 1873, pg 31 (1873 Oct 1) mileage and per diem
Proceedings 1873, pg 48 (1873 Oct 1), Laramie Lodge No. 18, Laramie, Wyoming Territory
Proceedings 1874, pg 223 (1874 Sept 30), Laramie Lodge No. 18, Laramie City

Gates, J G
Proceedings 1873, pg 48 (1873 Oct 1), Laramie Lodge No. 18, Laramie, Wyoming Territory

Gates, John
Proceedings 1871, pg 31 (1871 Sept 27), Occidental Lodge U D, Greeley
Proceedings 1873, pg 50 (1873 Oct 1), Occidental Lodge No. 20, Greeley, Apprentice
Proceedings 1874, pg 226 (1874 Sept 30), Occidental Lodge No. 20, Greeley, Apprentice
Proceedings 1875, pg 87 (1875 Sept 22), Occidental Lodge No. 20, Greeley, Apprentice
Proceedings 1876, pg 40 (1876 Sept 20), Occidental Lodge No. 20, Greeley, Apprentice

Gathright, Thomas S
Proceedings 1861-1869, pg 266 (1867 Jan 20), Grand Master, Grand Lodge of Mississippi

Gathright, Thos S
Proceedings 1861-1869, pg 333 (1869 Jan 18) Grand Master, Grand Lodge of Mississippi
Proceedings 1861-1869, pg 335 (1869 Jan 18) Grand Master, Grand Lodge of Mississippi
Proceedings 1870, pg 81 (1870 Jan 17) Grand Master, Grand Lodge of Mississippi
Proceedings 1874, pg 204 (1874 Sept 30) Grand Lodge of Mississippi, Gholson

Gehrung, E C
Proceedings 1861-1869, pg 196 (1867 Oct 8), El Paso Lodge U D, Colorado City
Proceedings 1861-1869, pg 310 (1869 Sept 29), El Paso Lodge No. 13, Colorado City
Proceedings 1870, pg 27 (1870 Sept 28), El Paso Lodge No. 13, Colorado City
Proceedings 1871, pg 25 (1871 Sept 27), El Paso Lodge No. 13, Colorado City, Dimitted
Proceedings 1874, pg 211 (1874 Sept 30), Denver Lodge No. 5, Denver

Gehrung, Emile
Proceedings 1861-1869, pg 196 (1867 Oct 8), El Paso Lodge U D, Colorado City
Proceedings 1861-1869, pg 310 (1869 Sept 29), El Paso Lodge No. 13, Colorado City
Proceedings 1870, pg 27 (1870 Sept 28), El Paso Lodge No. 13, Colorado City
Proceedings 1872, pg 26 (1872 Sept 24), El Paso Lodge No. 13, Colorado City
Proceedings 1873, pg 43 (1873 Oct 1), El Paso Lodge No. 13, Colorado City
Proceedings 1874, pg 218 (1874 Sept 30), El Paso Lodge No. 13, Colorado Springs
Proceedings 1875, pg 82 (1875 Sept 22), El Paso Lodge No. 13, Colorado Springs
Proceedings 1876, pg 36 (1876 Sept 20), El Paso Lodge No. 13, Colorado City

Gehrung, Eug C
Proceedings 1872, pg 19 (1872 Sept 24), Denver Lodge No. 5, Denver
Proceedings 1873, pg 37 (1873 Oct 1), Denver Lodge No. 5, Denver
Proceedings 1875, pg 75 (1875 Sept 22) Denver Lodge No. 5

Gehrung, Eugene C
Proceedings 1876, pg 31 (1876 Sept 20) Denver Lodge No. 5

Geier, David C
Proceedings 1872, pg 27 (1872 Sept 24), El Paso Lodge No. 13, Colorado City

Geiger, David
Proceedings 1875, pg 78 (1875 Sept 22), Union Lodge No. 7, Denver

Georgetown
Proceedings 1861-1869, pg 178 (1867 Aug 7) petition to form a lodge

Gerham, Thomas L
Proceedings 1861-1869, pg 152 (1865 Nov 7), Montana Lodge U D, Virginia City, Montana Territory, Fellowcraft

Germania Lodge No. 18, Denver
Proceedings 1861-1869, pg 216 (1868 Oct 7) resolution to grant charter lost

Germania Lodge U D
Proceedings 1861-1869, pg 207 (1868 Apr) requesting another lodge in Denver

Gerrish, J H
Proceedings 1861-1869, pg 112 (1863 Nov 3) Denver Lodge No. 5
Proceedings 1861-1869, pg 149 (1865 Nov 7), Nevada Lodge No. 4, Nevadaville
Proceedings 1861-1869, pg 167 (1866 Oct 2) Denver Lodge No. 5

Gerrish, John H
Proceedings 1861-1869, pg 77 (1862 Nov 4) Denver Lodge No. 5
Proceedings 1861-1869, pg 192 (1867 Oct 8) Denver Lodge No. 5
Proceedings 1861-1869, pg 223 (1868 Oct 7) Denver Lodge No. 5
Proceedings 1870, pg 21 (1870 Sept 28), Denver Lodge No. 5, Denver
Proceedings 1871, pg 19 (1871 Sept 27) Denver Lodge No. 5
Proceedings 1872, pg 19 (1872 Sept 24), Denver Lodge No. 5, Denver

Proceedings 1873, pg 37 (1873 Oct 1), Denver Lodge No. 5, Denver

Proceedings 1874, pg 212 (1874 Sept 30), Denver Lodge No. 5, Denver, Stricken from the rolls

Proceedings 1861-1869, pg 133 (1864 Nov 8) Denver Lodge No. 5

Gerry, L A C

Proceedings 1872, pg 69 (1872 Sept 24) Grand Lodge of Maryland

Gerry, M B

Proceedings 1874, pg 214 (1874 Sept 30), Union Lodge No. 7, Denver

Proceedings 1875, pg 79 (1875 Sept 22), Union Lodge No. 7, Denver, Demitted

Proceedings 1876, pg 39 (1876 Sept 20) Pueblo Lodge No. 17

Gertisen, John

Proceedings 1876, pg 44 (1876 Sept 20) Del Norte Lodge U D

Gerton, S

Proceedings 1861-1869, pg 196 (1867 Oct 8), El Paso Lodge U D, Colorado City

Gerton, T

Proceedings 1861-1869, pg 228 (1868 Oct 7), El Paso Lodge No. 13, Colorado City

Gertue, T

Proceedings 1861-1869, pg 170 (1866 Oct 2), El Paso U D, Colorado City

Gest

Proceedings 1861-1869, pg 117 (1864 Nov 7) committee

Proceedings 1861-1869, pg 128 (1864 Nov 8) motion

Gest, J H

Proceedings 1861-1869, pg 77 (1862 Nov 4), Nevada Lodge No. 4, Nevadaville

Proceedings 1861-1869, pg 99 (1863 Nov 2), Nevada Lodge No. 4, Nevadaville, Grand Junior Warden

Proceedings 1861-1869, pg 111 (1863 Nov 3), Nevada Lodge No. 4, Nevadaville

Proceedings 1861-1869, pg 115 (1864 Nov 7) Junior Grand Warden

Proceedings 1861-1869, pg 116 (1864 Nov 7) Junior Grand Warden

Proceedings 1861-1869, pg 116 (1864 Nov 7) Junior Grand Warden

Proceedings 1861-1869, pg 122 (1864 Nov 8) committee

Proceedings 1861-1869, pg 125 (1864 Nov 8) committee

Proceedings 1861-1869, pg 126 (1864 Nov 8) committee

Proceedings 1861-1869, pg 126 (1864 Nov 8) Grand Junior Warden

Proceedings 1861-1869, pg 127 (1864 Nov 8) committee

Proceedings 1861-1869, pg 132 (1864 Nov 8), Nevada Lodge No. 4, Nevadaville

Proceedings 1861-1869, pg 140 (1864 Nov 8) warrant

Proceedings 1861-1869, pg 148 (1865 Nov 7), Nevada Lodge No. 4, Nevadaville

Proceedings 1861-1869, pg 166 (1866 Oct 2), Nevada Lodge No. 4, Nevadaville, dimitted

Proceedings 1861-1869, pg 315 (1869 Sept 29) Junior Grand Warden, 1863, Dimitted

Proceedings 1870, pg 32 (1870 Sept 28) Junior Grand Warden, 1863, Dimitted

Proceedings 1871, pg 34 (1871 Sept 27) Junior Grand Warden, 1863, Dimitted

Proceedings 1872, pg 42 (1872 Sept 24) Junior Grand Warden, 1863, Dimitted

Proceedings 1873, pg 58 (1873 Oct 1) Junior Grand Warden, 1863

Gest, Joshua H

Proceedings 1874, pg 206 (1874 Sept 30) Junior Grand Warden, 1863, demitted

Proceedings 1875, pg 93 (1875 Sept 22) Junior Grand Warden, 1863, Demitted

Gherung, E C

Proceedings 1861-1869, pg 228 (1868 Oct 7), El Paso Lodge No. 13, Colorado City

Gherung, Emile

Proceedings 1861-1869, pg 228 (1868 Oct 7), El Paso Lodge No. 13, Colorado City

Giardi, Pascal

Proceedings 1876, pg 9 (1875 Dec 28) grante demit from Grand Orient of France to apply for membership in Pueblo Lodge No. 17

Gibson

Proceedings 1874, pg 113 (1874 Sept 30) Grand Lodge of New York

Gibson, James

Proceedings 1861-1869, pg 341 (1868 June 2) Grand Master, Grand Lodge of New York

Proceedings 1870, pg 94 (1870 June 7) Grand Master, Grand Lodge of New York

Proceedings 1872, pg 44 (1872 Sept 24) New York, Grand Lodge of New York

Proceedings 1873, pg 61 (1873 Oct 1) Grand Lodge of New York, New York

Proceedings 1874, pg 111 (1874 Sept 30) Grand Lodge of New York

Gilbert, Clark

Proceedings 1875, pg 83 (1875 Sept 22), Columbia Lodge No. 14, Boulder

Proceedings 1876, pg 36 (1876 Sept 20), Columbia Lodge No. 14, Boulder

Gilbert, Clark W

Proceedings 1874, pg 219 (1874 Sept 30), Columbia Lodge No. 14, Boulder, Boulder County, Apprentice

Gilbert, George

Proceedings 1861-1869, pg 313 (1869 Sept 29), Pueblo Lodge No. 17, Pueblo, Apprentice

Proceedings 1870, pg 30 (1870 Sept 28), Pueblo Lodge No. 17, Pueblo, Fellowcraft

Proceedings 1871, pg 28 (1871 Sept 27), Pueblo Lodge No. 17, Pueblo, Fellowcraft

Proceedings 1872, pg 31 (1872 Sept 24), Pueblo Lodge No. 17, Pueblo

Colorado's Territorial Masons

Gilbert, George, cont.
Proceedings 1873, pg 47 (1873 Oct 1), Pueblo Lodge No. 17, Pueblo
Proceedings 1874, pg 222 (1874 Sept 30), Pueblo Lodge No. 17, Pueblo, Pueblo County
Proceedings 1875, pg 85 (1875 Sept 22) Pueblo Lodge No. 17
Proceedings 1876, pg 38 (1876 Sept 20) Pueblo Lodge No. 17

Gilbert, J R
Proceedings 1861-1869, pg 99 (1863 Nov 2) Golden City Lodge No. 1, Grand Marshal
Proceedings 1861-1869, pg 147 (1865 Nov 7) Golden City Lodge No. 1
Proceedings 1861-1869, pg 152 (1865 Nov 7), Montana Lodge U D, Virginia City, Montana Territory
Proceedings 1861-1869, pg 165 (1866 Oct 2) Golden City Lodge No. 1
Proceedings 1861-1869, pg 221 (1868 Oct 7) Golden City Lodge No. 1
Proceedings 1861-1869, pg 303 (1869 Sept 29) Golden City Lodge No. 1
Proceedings 1870, pg 19 (1870 Sept 28), Golden City Lodge No. 1, Golden City
Proceedings 1871, pg 17 (1871 Sept 27), Golden City Lodge No. 1, Golden City

Gilbert, John H
Proceedings 1861-1869, pg 110 (1863 Nov 3) Golden City Lodge No. 1

Gilbert, John R
Proceedings 1861-1869, pg 131 (1864 Nov 8) Golden City Lodge No. 1
Proceedings 1861-1869, pg 191 (1867 Oct 8) Golden City Lodge No. 1
Proceedings 1872, pg 17 (1872 Sept 24), Golden City Lodge No. 1, Golden City
Proceedings 1873, pg 35 (1873 Oct 1), Golden City Lodge No. 1, Golden City
Proceedings 1874, pg 209 (1874 Sept 30), Golden City Lodge No. 1, Golden City
Proceedings 1875, pg 73 (1875 Sept 22) Golden City Lodge No. 1
Proceedings 1876, pg 29 (1876 Sept 20) Golden City Lodge No. 1
Proceedings 1876, pg 50 (1876 Sept 20) Golden City Lodge No. 1

Gilbert, Richard
Proceedings 1876, pg 34 (1876 Sept 20) Black Hawk Lodge No. 11

Gilchrist, William J
Proceedings 1872, pg 26 (1872 Sept 24), Washington Lodge No. 12, Georgetown, Fellowcraft
Proceedings 1874, pg 217 (1874 Sept 30), Washington Lodge No. 12, Georgetown, Fellowcraft
Proceedings 1876, pg 35 (1876 Sept 20), Washington Lodge No. 12, Georgetown

Gilchrist, Wm J
Proceedings 1873, pg 43 (1873 Oct 1), Washington Lodge No. 12, Georgetown, Fellowcraft
Proceedings 1875, pg 81 (1875 Sept 22), Washington Lodge No. 12, Georgetown

Gill, J G
Proceedings 1861-1869, pg 111 (1863 Nov 3), Summit Lodge No. 2, Parkville, dimitted

Gill, Jacob
Proceedings 1861-1869, pg 310 (1869 Sept 29), El Paso Lodge No. 13, Colorado City
Proceedings 1870, pg 27 (1870 Sept 28), El Paso Lodge No. 13, Colorado City
Proceedings 1871, pg 25 (1871 Sept 27), El Paso Lodge No. 13, Colorado City, died
Proceedings 1871, pg 32 (1871 Sept 27), El Paso Lodge No. 13, Colorado City

Gill, John G
Proceedings 1861-1869, pg 76 (1862 Nov 4), Summit Lodge No. 2, Parkville

Gill, William
Proceedings 1876, pg 43 (1876 Sept 20) Idaho Springs Lodge No. 26

Gill, Z
Proceedings 1861-1869, pg 228 (1868 Oct 7), El Paso Lodge No. 13, Colorado City

Gilleland, A J
Proceedings 1874, pg 220 (1874 Sept 30), Mount Moriah Lodge No. 15, Canon City

Gillett, Geo
Proceedings 1861-1869, pg 167 (1866 Oct 2) Denver Lodge No. 5
Proceedings 1861-1869, pg 224 (1868 Oct 7) Denver Lodge No. 5, Dimitted

Gillett, George
Proceedings 1861-1869, pg 192 (1867 Oct 8) Denver Lodge No. 5

Gillett, H H
Proceedings 1861-1869, pg 149 (1865 Nov 7), Nevada Lodge No. 4, Nevadaville
Proceedings 1861-1869, pg 166 (1866 Oct 2) Denver Lodge No. 5
Proceedings 1861-1869, pg 192 (1867 Oct 8) Denver Lodge No. 5
Proceedings 1861-1869, pg 224 (1868 Oct 7) Denver Lodge No. 5, Dimitted

Gillette, Geo A
Proceedings 1875, pg 78 (1875 Sept 22), Union Lodge No. 7, Denver

Gillette, George A
Proceedings 1874, pg 214 (1874 Sept 30), Union Lodge No. 7, Denver
Proceedings 1876, pg 33 (1876 Sept 20), Union Lodge No. 7, Denver

Gilliland, A J
Proceedings 1875, pg 84 (1875 Sept 22), Mount Moriah Lodge No. 15, Canon City
Proceedings 1876, pg 38 (1876 Sept 20), Mount Moriah Lodge No. 15, Canon City

Gillson, G W
Proceedings 1861-1869, pg 42 (1861 Dec 10), Summit Lodge No. 2, Parkville

Gilman Band
Proceedings 1875, pg 36 (1875 Sept 22) paid for band services

Gilmore, John
Proceedings 1861-1869, pg 110 (1863 Nov 3) Golden City Lodge No. 1
Proceedings 1861-1869, pg 131 (1864 Nov 8) Golden City Lodge No. 1
Proceedings 1861-1869, pg 147 (1865 Nov 7) Golden City Lodge No. 1, dimitted

Gilpin, Wm (Hon)
Colorado University Cornerstone Laying, pg 14 (1875 Sept 20) gave an address

Gilson, S H
Proceedings 1871, pg 21 (1871 Sept 27), Union Lodge No. 7, Denver
Proceedings 1876, pg 49 (1876 Sept 20), Union Lodge No. 7, Denver, 1876 Aug 26

Gilson, Sam H
Proceedings 1874, pg 214 (1874 Sept 30), Union Lodge No. 7, Denver

Gilson, Samuel H
Proceedings 1872, pg 22 (1872 Sept 24), Union Lodge No. 7, Denver
Proceedings 1873, pg 39 (1873 Oct 1), Union Lodge No. 7, Denver
Proceedings 1875, pg 78 (1875 Sept 22), Union Lodge No. 7, Denver

Girard, M Elvi
Proceedings 1873, pg 60 (1873 Oct 1) Grand Lodge of Louisiana, New Orleans

Girard, Michael Elvi
Proceedings 1874, pg 73 (1874 Sept 30) Grand Lodge of Louisiana

Girard, Michel Eloi
Proceedings 1874, pg 204 (1874 Sept 30) Grand Lodge of Louisiana, New Orleans

Gird, C C
Proceedings 1873, pg 39 (1873 Oct 1), Union Lodge No. 7, Denver
Proceedings 1874, pg 214 (1874 Sept 30), Union Lodge No. 7, Denver
Proceedings 1876, pg 33 (1876 Sept 20), Union Lodge No. 7, Denver

Gird, Chris C
Proceedings 1870, pg 23 (1870 Sept 28), Union Lodge No. 7, Denver
Proceedings 1871, pg 21 (1871 Sept 27), Union Lodge No. 7, Denver
Proceedings 1872, pg 22 (1872 Sept 24), Union Lodge No. 7, Denver

Gird, Christ C
Proceedings 1875, pg 78 (1875 Sept 22), Union Lodge No. 7, Denver
Proceedings 1861-1869, pg 307 (1869 Sept 29), Union Lodge No. 7, Denver

Glaze, D W
Proceedings 1861-1869, pg 227 (1868 Oct 7), Washington Lodge No. 12, Georgetown
Proceedings 1861-1869, pg 309 (1869 Sept 29), Washington Lodge No. 12, Georgetown

Glaze, Daniel W
Proceedings 1870, pg 26 (1870 Sept 28), Washington Lodge No. 12, Georgetown
Proceedings 1871, pg 24 (1871 Sept 27), Washington Lodge No. 12, Georgetown
Proceedings 1872, pg 26 (1872 Sept 24), Washington Lodge No. 12, Georgetown
Proceedings 1873, pg 42 (1873 Oct 1), Washington Lodge No. 12, Georgetown
Proceedings 1874, pg 217 (1874 Sept 30), Washington Lodge No. 12, Georgetown
Proceedings 1875, pg 81 (1875 Sept 22), Washington Lodge No. 12, Georgetown
Proceedings 1876, pg 35 (1876 Sept 20), Washington Lodge No. 12, Georgetown

Gleed, James
Proceedings 1876, pg 45 (1876 Sept 20) South Pueblo Lodge U D

Glendenin, J Y
Proceedings 1875, pg 19 (1874 Nov 14), Evanston Lodge U D, Evanston, Uintah County, Wyoming Territory, deceased shortly after 14 Nov 1874

Glendenin, John Y
Proceedings 1874, pg 212 (1874 Sept 30), Central Lodge No. 6, Central

Glendinen, J Y
Proceedings 1861-1869, pg 150 (1865 Nov 7), Chivington Lodge No. 6, Central City
Proceedings 1861-1869, pg 154 (1866 Oct 1), Chivington Lodge No. 6, Central City
Proceedings 1861-1869, pg 168 (1866 Oct 2), Chivington Lodge No. 6, Central City
Proceedings 1861-1869, pg 193 (1867 Oct 8), Chivington Lodge No. 6, Central City
Proceedings 1861-1869, pg 224 (1868 Oct 7), Chivington Lodge No. 6, Central City
Proceedings 1861-1869, pg 306 (1869 Sept 29), Central Lodge No. 6, Central City
Proceedings 1870, pg 22 (1870 Sept 28), Central Lodge No. 6, Central City

Glendinen, Jno Y
Proceedings 1871, pg 20 (1871 Sept 27), Central Lodge No. 6, Central

Colorado's Territorial Masons

Glendinen, John Y
   Proceedings 1861-1869, pg 134 (1864 Nov 8), Chivington Lodge No. 6, Central City, Fellowcraft
   Proceedings 1872, pg 21 (1872 Sept 24), Denver Lodge No. 5, Denver
   Proceedings 1873, pg 38 (1873 Oct 1), Central Lodge No. 6, Central City
   Proceedings 1875, pg 77 (1875 Sept 22), Central Lodge No. 6, Central City, died
   Proceedings 1875, pg 94 (1875 Sept 22), Central Lodge No. 6, Central City

Glenn, Thos M
   Proceedings 1874, pg 227 (1874 Sept 30), St Vrain No. 23, Longmont
   Proceedings 1876, pg 48 (1876 Sept 20), St Vrain Lodge No. 23, Longmont, no date

Glotfelter, E S
   Proceedings 1861-1869, pg 5 (1861 Aug 2) Grand Steward, Gold Hill
   Proceedings 1861-1869, pg 38 (1861 Dec 12) Grand Steward
   Proceedings 1861-1869, pg 43 (1861 Dec 10), Rocky Mountain Lodge No. 3, Gold Hill

Goddard, John L
   Proceedings 1861-1869, pg 253 (1867 Oct 15), Grand Master, Grand Lodge of Pennsylvania, deceased
   Proceedings 1861-1869, pg 264 (1868 Oct 22), Grand Master, Grand Lodge of Pennsylvania, deceased

Golden City Lodge
   Proceedings 1871, pg 6 (1860 Oct 17) Grand Lodge of Kansas

Golden City Lodge No. 1
   Proceedings 1861-1869, pg 4 (1861 Aug 2) organized 17 Oct 1860 by the M W Grand Lodge of Kansas
   Proceedings 1861-1869, pg 6 (1861 Aug 3) Golden City
   Proceedings 1861-1869, pg 138 (1864 Dec 17) communication
   Proceedings 1861-1869, pg 139 (1865 Nov 6) dues paid
   Proceedings 1861-1869, pg 158 (1866 Oct 1) dues paid
   Proceedings 1861-1869, pg 178 (1866 Dec 22) officers installed
   Proceedings 1861-1869, pg 181 (1867 Oct 7) dues paid
   Proceedings 1875, pg 23 (1875 Sept 21) has not provided a list of officers
   Proceedings 1875, pg 23 (1875 Sept 21) has not provided annual returns
   Proceedings 1875, pg 25 (1875 Sept 21) dues paid
   Proceedings 1875, pg 92 (1875 Sept 22)
   Proceedings 1876, pg 13 (1876 Sept 7) dues paid
   Proceedings 1876, pg 24 (1876 Sept 20) correction to returns
   Proceedings 1876, pg 52 (1876 Sept 20)

Golden City Lodge No. 1, Golden City
   Proceedings 1872, pg 11 (1872 Sept 24) failed to make timely returns
   Proceedings 1872, pg 14 (1872 Sept 24) returns not complete
   Proceedings 1874, pg 208 (1874 Sept 30)

Golden Lodge No. 1
   Proceedings 1861-1869, pg 210 (1868 Feb 20) visited
   Proceedings 1861-1869, pg 210 (1868 Feb 5) visited

Golding, W A
   Proceedings 1874, pg 221 (1874 Sept 30), Cheyenne Lodge No. 16, Cheyenne, Wyoming Territory

Goldring, W A
   Proceedings 1870, pg 29 (1870 Sept 28), Cheyenne Lodge No. 16, Cheyenne, Wyoming Territory
   Proceedings 1871, pg 27 (1871 Sept 27), Cheyenne Lodge No. 16, Cheyenne, Wyoming Territory
   Proceedings 1872, pg 29 (1872 Sept 24), Cheyenne Lodge No. 16, Cheyenne, Wyoming Territory
   Proceedings 1873, pg 46 (1873 Oct 1), Cheyenne Lodge No. 16, Cheyenne, Wyoming Territory

Goldsmith, A
   Proceedings 1861-1869, pg 133 (1864 Nov 8) Denver Lodge No. 5
   Proceedings 1861-1869, pg 149 (1865 Nov 7), Nevada Lodge No. 4, Nevadaville
   Proceedings 1861-1869, pg 167 (1866 Oct 2) Denver Lodge No. 5
   Proceedings 1861-1869, pg 192 (1867 Oct 8) Denver Lodge No. 5
   Proceedings 1861-1869, pg 223 (1868 Oct 7) Denver Lodge No. 5
   Proceedings 1861-1869, pg 305 (1869 Sept 29) Denver Lodge No. 5
   Proceedings 1870, pg 21 (1870 Sept 28), Denver Lodge No. 5, Denver
   Proceedings 1871, pg 19 (1871 Sept 27) Denver Lodge No. 5
   Proceedings 1872, pg 20 (1872 Sept 24), Denver Lodge No. 5, Denver
   Proceedings 1873, pg 37 (1873 Oct 1), Denver Lodge No. 5, Denver, Dimitted
   Proceedings 1873, pg 37 (1873 Oct 1), Denver Lodge No. 5, Denver, reinstated
   Proceedings 1874, pg 222 (1874 Sept 30), Pueblo Lodge No. 17, Pueblo, Pueblo County
   Proceedings 1875, pg 85 (1875 Sept 22) Pueblo Lodge No. 17
   Proceedings 1876, pg 38 (1876 Sept 20) Pueblo Lodge No. 17

Goldsmith, Abraham
   Proceedings 1873, pg 47 (1873 Oct 1), Pueblo Lodge No. 17, Pueblo

Goldsmith, Abram
   Proceedings 1873, pg 19 (1873 Oct 1), Denver Lodge No. 5, Denver

Goldsmith, Jacob
   Proceedings 1861-1869, pg 167 (1866 Oct 2) Denver Lodge No. 5
   Proceedings 1861-1869, pg 193 (1867 Oct 8) Denver Lodge No. 5, Dimitted

Goldsworthy, James
　Proceedings 1873, pg 52 (1873 Oct 1), St Vrain Lodge No. 23, Longmont, Apprentice
　Proceedings 1874, pg 209 (1874 Sept 30), Golden City Lodge No. 1, Golden City
　Proceedings 1876, pg 29 (1876 Sept 20) Golden City Lodge No. 1

Goldsworthy, Jas
　Proceedings 1875, pg 73 (1875 Sept 22) Golden City Lodge No. 1

Good, John
　Proceedings 1861-1869, pg 133 (1864 Nov 8) Denver Lodge No. 5, Apprentice
　Proceedings 1861-1869, pg 149 (1865 Nov 7), Nevada Lodge No. 4, Nevadaville, Apprentice
　Proceedings 1861-1869, pg 167 (1866 Oct 2) Denver Lodge No. 5, Apprentice
　Proceedings 1861-1869, pg 193 (1867 Oct 8) Denver Lodge No. 5, Apprentice
　Proceedings 1861-1869, pg 223 (1868 Oct 7) Denver Lodge No. 5, Apprentice
　Proceedings 1861-1869, pg 305 (1869 Sept 29) Denver Lodge No. 5, Apprentice

Goodhue, Justin A
　Proceedings 1861-1869, pg 307 (1869 Sept 29), Union Lodge No. 7, Denver
　Proceedings 1870, pg 24 (1870 Sept 28), Union Lodge No. 7, Denver, Dimitted

Goodnight, Charles
　Proceedings 1861-1869, pg 312 (1869 Sept 29), Pueblo Lodge No. 17, Pueblo
　Proceedings 1870, pg 30 (1870 Sept 28), Pueblo Lodge No. 17, Pueblo
　Proceedings 1871, pg 28 (1871 Sept 27), Pueblo Lodge No. 17, Pueblo
　Proceedings 1873, pg 47 (1873 Oct 1), Pueblo Lodge No. 17, Pueblo
　Proceedings 1874, pg 222 (1874 Sept 30), Pueblo Lodge No. 17, Pueblo, Pueblo County
　Proceedings 1875, pg 85 (1875 Sept 22) Pueblo Lodge No. 17
　Proceedings 1876, pg 38 (1876 Sept 20) Pueblo Lodge No. 17

Goodnight, Chas
　Proceedings 1872, pg 31 (1872 Sept 24), Pueblo Lodge No. 17, Pueblo

Goodrich, A F
　Proceedings 1875, pg 82 (1875 Sept 22), El Paso Lodge No. 13, Colorado Springs, Fellowcraft
　Proceedings 1876, pg 36 (1876 Sept 20), El Paso Lodge No. 13, Colorado City, Apprentice

Goodspeed, J H
　Proceedings 1861-1869, pg 169 (1866 Oct 2), Union Lodge No. 7, Denver
　Proceedings 1861-1869, pg 195 (1867 Oct 8), Union Lodge No. 7, Denver
　Proceedings 1861-1869, pg 225 (1868 Oct 7), Union Lodge No. 7, Denver
　Proceedings 1861-1869, pg 307 (1869 Sept 29), Union Lodge No. 7, Denver
　Proceedings 1871, pg 22 (1871 Sept 27), Union Lodge No. 7, Denver, Dimitted

Goodspeed, Joseph H
　Proceedings 1870, pg 23 (1870 Sept 28), Union Lodge No. 7, Denver

Goodwin, D H
　Proceedings 1873, pg 51 (1873 Oct 1), Weston Lodge No. 22, Littleton
　Proceedings 1874, pg 226 (1874 Sept 30), Weston Lodge No. 22, Littleton
　Proceedings 1875, pg 88 (1875 Sept 22), Weston Lodge No. 22, Littleton
　Proceedings 1876, pg 41 (1876 Sept 20), Weston Lodge No. 22, Littleton

Goodwin, H
　Proceedings 1872, pg 35 (1872 Sept 24), St Vrain Lodge No. 23, Longmont
　Proceedings 1873, pg 51 (1873 Oct 1), St Vrain Lodge No. 23, Longmont
　Proceedings 1874, pg 227 (1874 Sept 30), St Vrain No. 23, Longmont
　Proceedings 1876, pg 41 (1876 Sept 20), St Vrain Lodge No. 23, Longmont

Goodwin, H S
　Proceedings 1876, pg 33 (1876 Sept 20), Union Lodge No. 7, Denver

Goodwin, P S
　Proceedings 1876, pg 38 (1876 Sept 20), Mount Moriah Lodge No. 15, Canon City

Gordy, J C
　Proceedings 1861-1869, pg 254 (1868 Feb 10), Grand Lecturer, Grand Lodge of Louisiana

Gore, Aaron
　Proceedings 1876, pg 33 (1876 Sept 20), Union Lodge No. 7, Denver

Gorin, Jerome B
　Proceedings 1861-1869, pg 248 (1867 Nov 7), Grand Master, Grand Lodge of Illinois

Gorin, Jerome R
　Proceedings 1861-1869, pg 328 (1868 Oct 6) Grand Master, Grand Lodge of Illinois

Goss, Abel
　Proceedings 1874, pg 219 (1874 Sept 30), Columbia Lodge No. 14, Boulder, Boulder County
　Proceedings 1875, pg 83 (1875 Sept 22), Columbia Lodge No. 14, Boulder
　Proceedings 1876, pg 37 (1876 Sept 20), Columbia Lodge No. 14, Boulder

Goss, C J
　Proceedings 1861-1869, pg 43 (1861 Dec 10), Rocky Mountain Lodge No. 3, Gold Hill
　Proceedings 1861-1869, pg 133 (1864 Nov 8) Denver Lodge No. 5

Colorado's Territorial Masons

Goss, C J, cont.
- Proceedings 1861-1869, pg 133 (1864 Nov 8) Denver Lodge No. 5
- Proceedings 1861-1869, pg 149 (1865 Nov 7), Nevada Lodge No. 4, Nevadaville
- Proceedings 1861-1869, pg 167 (1866 Oct 2) Denver Lodge No. 5
- Proceedings 1861-1869, pg 192 (1867 Oct 8) Denver Lodge No. 5
- Proceedings 1861-1869, pg 223 (1868 Oct 7) Denver Lodge No. 5
- Proceedings 1861-1869, pg 305 (1869 Sept 29) Denver Lodge No. 5
- Proceedings 1870, pg 21 (1870 Sept 28), Denver Lodge No. 5, Denver
- Proceedings 1871, pg 19 (1871 Sept 27) Denver Lodge No. 5
- Proceedings 1872, pg 19 (1872 Sept 24), Denver Lodge No. 5, Denver
- Proceedings 1873, pg 37 (1873 Oct 1), Denver Lodge No. 5, Denver
- Proceedings 1874, pg 212 (1874 Sept 30), Denver Lodge No. 5, Denver
- Proceedings 1875, pg 75 (1875 Sept 22) Denver Lodge No. 5
- Proceedings 1876, pg 31 (1876 Sept 20) Denver Lodge No. 5

Goss, D P
- Proceedings 1872, pg 35 (1872 Sept 24), St Vrain Lodge No. 23, Longmont

Goss, P D
- Proceedings 1861-1869, pg 230 (1868 Oct 7), Valmont Lodge U D, Valmont
- Proceedings 1873, pg 51 (1873 Oct 1), St Vrain Lodge No. 23, Longmont
- Proceedings 1874, pg 227 (1874 Sept 30), St Vrain No. 23, Longmont, Demitted

Gotcher, J N
- Proceedings 1874, pg 220 (1874 Sept 30), Mount Moriah Lodge No. 15, Canon City
- Proceedings 1875, pg 84 (1875 Sept 22), Mount Moriah Lodge No. 15, Canon City
- Proceedings 1876, pg 48 (1876 Sept 20), Mount Moriah Lodge No. 15, Canon City, 1876 May 6

Gottesleben, P
- Proceedings 1874, pg 214 (1874 Sept 30), Union Lodge No. 7, Denver
- Proceedings 1875, pg 78 (1875 Sept 22), Union Lodge No. 7, Denver
- Proceedings 1876, pg 33 (1876 Sept 20), Union Lodge No. 7, Denver

Gottesleben, Peter
- Proceedings 1861-1869, pg 230 (1868 Oct 7), Germania Lodge U D, Denver
- Proceedings 1870, pg 23 (1870 Sept 28), Union Lodge No. 7, Denver
- Proceedings 1871, pg 21 (1871 Sept 27), Union Lodge No. 7, Denver
- Proceedings 1873, pg 39 (1873 Oct 1), Union Lodge No. 7, Denver

Gottesleben, Peter A
- Proceedings 1872, pg 22 (1872 Sept 24), Union Lodge No. 7, Denver

Gottlesleben, P A
- Proceedings 1861-1869, pg 307 (1869 Sept 29), Union Lodge No. 7, Denver

Gould, A S
- Proceedings 1871, pg 31 (1871 Sept 27), Argenta Lodge U D, Salt Lake City, Utah

Gould, James L
- Proceedings 1872, pg 57 (1872 Sept 24) Grand Lodge of Connecticut

Gouley
- Proceedings 1861-1869, pg 266 (1868 Oct 7) Grand Lodge of Missouri
- Proceedings 1870, pg 11 (1870 Sept 27), of St Louis, MO,, Editor, The Freemason
- Proceedings 1874, pg 94 (1874 Sept 30) Grand Lodge of Missouri

Gouley, Frank
- Proceedings 1872, pg 72 (1872 Sept 24) Grand Lodge of Missouri

Gouley, Geo F
- Proceedings 1875, pg 96 (1875 Sept 22) Grand Lodge of Missouri, St Louis
- Proceedings 1876, pg 54 (1876 Sept 20) Grand Lodge of Missouri, St Louis

Gouley, Geo Frank
- Proceedings 1861-1869, pg 316 (1869 Sept 29) Grand Lodge of Missouri
- Proceedings 1861-1869, pg 335 (1868 Oct 12) Grand Secretary, Grand Lodge of Missouri
- Proceedings 1870, pg 34 (1870 Sept 28) Grand Secretary, Grand Lodge of Missouri
- Proceedings 1870, pg 84 (1869 Oct 11) Grand Secretary, Grand Lodge of Missouri
- Proceedings 1873, pg 60 (1873 Oct 1) Grand Lodge of Missouri, St Louis
- Proceedings 1874, pg 90 (1874 Sept 30) Grand Lodge of Missouri
- Proceedings 1874, pg 204 (1874 Sept 30) Grand Lodge of Missouri, St Louis

Gouley, George F
- Proceedings 1874, pg 19 (1874 Sept 29), of St Louis, MO

Gouley, George Frank
- Proceedings 1861-1869, pg 265 (1868 Oct 7), Grand Secretary, Grand Lodge of Missouri
- Proceedings 1871, pg 35 (1871 Sept 27) Grand Secretary, Grand Lodge of Missouri

Gourley, Geo Frank
- Proceedings 1870, pg 88 (1869 Oct 11) Grand Secretary, Grand Lodge of Missouri
- Proceedings 1870, pg 88 (1869 Oct 11) Grand Lodge of Missouri

Gove, Aaron
Proceedings 1875, pg 78 (1875 Sept 22), Union Lodge No. 7, Denver

Gove, Carlos
Proceedings 1871, pg 19 (1871 Sept 27) Denver Lodge No. 5, Apprentice
Proceedings 1872, pg 19 (1872 Sept 24), Denver Lodge No. 5, Denver
Proceedings 1873, pg 37 (1873 Oct 1), Denver Lodge No. 5, Denver
Proceedings 1874, pg 211 (1874 Sept 30), Denver Lodge No. 5, Denver
Proceedings 1875, pg 75 (1875 Sept 22) Denver Lodge No. 5
Proceedings 1876, pg 31 (1876 Sept 20) Denver Lodge No. 5

Gowley, Geo Frank
Proceedings 1872, pg 43 (1872 Sept 24) St Louis, Grand Lodge of Missouri

Goyce, J R
Proceedings 1874, pg 94 (1874 Sept 30) Grand Lodgeof Montana

Grace, Henry
Proceedings 1861-1869, pg 230 (1868 Oct 7), Valmont Lodge U D, Valmont

Grace, Wm P
Proceedings 1861-1869, pg 77 (1862 Nov 4), Nevada Lodge No. 4, Nevadaville
Proceedings 1861-1869, pg 111 (1863 Nov 3), Nevada Lodge No. 4, Nevadaville, expelled

Graeff, Michael B
Proceedings 1875, pg 89 (1875 Sept 22) Idaho Springs Lodge U D
Proceedings 1876, pg 42 (1876 Sept 20) Idaho Springs Lodge No. 26

Grafton, D R
Proceedings 1873, pg 61 (1873 Oct 1) Grand Lodge of Tennessee, Chattanooga
Proceedings 1874, pg 123 (1874 Sept 30) Grand Lodge of Tennessee

Grafton, W H
Proceedings 1861-1869, pg 77 (1862 Nov 4), Nevada Lodge No. 4, Nevadaville
Proceedings 1861-1869, pg 111 (1863 Nov 3), Nevada Lodge No. 4, Nevadaville, dimitted
Proceedings 1861-1869, pg 112 (1863 Nov 3) Denver Lodge No. 5
Proceedings 1861-1869, pg 149 (1865 Nov 7), Nevada Lodge No. 4, Nevadaville
Proceedings 1861-1869, pg 167 (1866 Oct 2) Denver Lodge No. 5
Proceedings 1861-1869, pg 192 (1867 Oct 8) Denver Lodge No. 5
Proceedings 1861-1869, pg 224 (1868 Oct 7) Denver Lodge No. 5, Dimitted

Grafton, Wm H
Proceedings 1861-1869, pg 133 (1864 Nov 8) Denver Lodge No. 5

Graham, I T
Proceedings 1876, pg 34 (1876 Sept 20) Black Hawk Lodge No. 11

Graham, James A
Proceedings 1872, pg 55 (1872 Sept 24) Grand Lodge of British Columbia

Graham, James M
Proceedings 1876, pg 43 (1876 Sept 20) Idaho Springs Lodge No. 26

Graham, John H
Proceedings 1872, pg 44 (1872 Sept 24) Richmond, Grand Lodge of Quebec
Proceedings 1872, pg 95 (1872 Sept 24) Grand Lodge of Quebec
Proceedings 1874, pg 120 (1874 Sept 30) Grand Lodge of Quebec
Proceedings 1874, pg 205 (1874 Sept 30) Grand Lodge of Quebec, Richmond

Graham, L K
Proceedings 1871, pg 29 (1871 Sept 27), Laramie Lodge No. 18, Laramie, Wyoming Territory
Proceedings 1872, pg 32 (1872 Sept 24), Laramie Lodge No. 18, Laramie, Wyoming Territory
Proceedings 1873, pg 48 (1873 Oct 1), Laramie Lodge No. 18, Laramie, Wyoming Territory
Proceedings 1874, pg 223 (1874 Sept 30), Laramie Lodge No. 18, Laramie City

Grain, Otto
Proceedings 1873, pg 48 (1873 Oct 1), Laramie Lodge No. 18, Laramie, Wyoming Territory, Fellowcraft,

Grand Council of Luxembourg
Proceedings 1872, pg 47 (1872 Sept 24) Luxembourg

Grand Island Lodge U D
Proceedings 1873, pg 17 (1873 Oct 1), at Middle Boulder, Boulder, County

Grand Lodge of Alabama
Proceedings 1861-1869, pg 234 (1867 Dec 2) communication
Proceedings 1861-1869, pg 236 (1867 Dec 2) communication
Proceedings 1861-1869, pg 238 (1867 Dec 2) many indigent orphans of deceased Masons are being educated at the expense of the lodges
Proceedings 1861-1869, pg 316 (1869 Sept 29) esta 14 June 1821, Montgomery, AL
Proceedings 1870, pg 34 (1870 Sept 28) esta 14 June 1821, Montgomery
Proceedings 1870, pg 37 (1870 Sept 28) correspondence received, 1869
Proceedings 1870, pg 38 (1869 Dec 6) supports the Masonic Orphans' Home
Proceedings 1871, pg 35 (1871 Sept 27) Montgomery, esta 14 June 1821

Grand Lodge of Alabama, cont.
Proceedings 1872, pg 45 (1872 Sept 24) Montgomery
Proceedings 1872, pg 53 (1872 Sept 24)
Proceedings 1874, pg 43 (1874 Sept 30) Proceedings received
Proceedings 1874, pg 44 (1874 Sept 30) report 1873
Proceedings 1874, pg 202 (1874 Sept 30)
Proceedings 1874, pg 204 (1874 Sept 30)

Grand Lodge of Arkansas
Proceedings 1861-1869, pg 234 (1867 Nov 4) communication
Proceedings 1861-1869, pg 316 (1869 Sept 29) esta 22 Feb 1832, Little Rock, AR
Proceedings 1870, pg 34 (1870 Sept 28) esta 22 Feb 1832, Little Rock
Proceedings 1870, pg 37 (1870 Sept 28) correspondence received, 1869
Proceedings 1871, pg 35 (1871 Sept 27) Little Rock, esta 22 Feb 1832
Proceedings 1872, pg 45 (1872 Sept 24) Little Rock
Proceedings 1872, pg 53 (1872 Sept 24)
Proceedings 1874, pg 43 (1874 Sept 30) Proceedings received
Proceedings 1874, pg 44 (1874 Sept 30) report 1873
Proceedings 1874, pg 202 (1874 Sept 30)
Proceedings 1874, pg 204 (1874 Sept 30)

Grand Lodge of British Columbia
Proceedings 1872, pg 45 (1872 Sept 24) Victoria
Proceedings 1872, pg 53 (1872 Sept 24)
Proceedings 1874, pg 83 (1874 Sept 30)
Proceedings 1874, pg 96 (1874 Sept 30)
Proceedings 1874, pg 104 (1874 Sept 30)
Proceedings 1874, pg 133 (1874 Sept 30)
Proceedings 1874, pg 202 (1874 Sept 30)
Proceedings 1874, pg 204 (1874 Sept 30)
Proceedings 1876, pg 11 (1876 Sept 19) full record of Proceedings in the Grand Library

Grand Lodge of California
Proceedings 1861-1869, pg 103 (1863 Nov 3) communication
Proceedings 1861-1869, pg 234 (1867 Oct 8) communication
Proceedings 1861-1869, pg 240 (1867 Oct 8) believed to have the finest library of Masonic materials on the continent
Proceedings 1861-1869, pg 316 (1869 Sept 29) esta 18 Apr 1850, San Francisco, CA
Proceedings 1870, pg 34 (1870 Sept 28) esta 18 Apr 1850, San Francisco
Proceedings 1870, pg 37 (1870 Sept 28) correspondence received, 1869
Proceedings 1871, pg 35 (1871 Sept 27) San Francisco, esta 18 Apr 1850
Proceedings 1872, pg 45 (1872 Sept 24) San Francisco
Proceedings 1872, pg 53 (1872 Sept 24)
Proceedings 1874, pg 43 (1874 Sept 30) Proceedings received
Proceedings 1874, pg 46 (1874 Sept 30) report 1873
Proceedings 1874, pg 202 (1874 Sept 30)
Proceedings 1874, pg 204 (1874 Sept 30)
Proceedings 1876, pg 11 (1876 Sept 19) full record of Proceedings in the Grand Library

Grand Lodge of Canada
Proceedings 1861-1869, pg 234 (1867 July 10) communication
Proceedings 1861-1869, pg 316 (1869 Sept 29) esta 10 Oct 1855, Hamilton, Ontario
Proceedings 1870, pg 34 (1870 Sept 28) esta 10 Oct 1855, Hamilton
Proceedings 1870, pg 37 (1870 Sept 28) correspondence received, 1869
Proceedings 1871, pg 35 (1871 Sept 27), Hamilton, Ontario, esta 10 Oct 1855
Proceedings 1872, pg 45 (1872 Sept 24)
Grand Lodge of Canada
Proceedings 1872, pg 47 (1872 Sept 24), Hamilton, [Ontario] Canada
Proceedings 1874, pg 43 (1874 Sept 30) Proceedings received
Proceedings 1874, pg 47 (1874 Sept 30) report 1873
Proceedings 1874, pg 49 (1874 Sept 30) receipt of The Official Protocols
Proceedings 1874, pg 202 (1874 Sept 30)
Proceedings 1874, pg 204 (1874 Sept 30)
Proceedings 1876, pg 11 (1876 Sept 19) full record of Proceedings in the Grand Library
Proceedings 1876, pg 11 (1876 Sept 19) issues received for the Grand Library

Grand Lodge of Chile
Proceedings 1870, pg 34 (1870 Sept 28) Valparaiso

Grand Lodge of Chili [Chile]
Proceedings 1872, pg 47 (1872 Sept 24), Valparaiso, Chili [Chile]

Grand Lodge of Colorado
Proceedings 1871, pg 6 (1861 Aug 2) established at Golden City

Grand Lodge of Connecticut
Proceedings 1861-1869, pg 234 (1867 May 8) communication
Proceedings 1861-1869, pg 316 (1869 Sept 29) esta 8 July 1789, Hartford, CT
Proceedings 1870, pg 34 (1870 Sept 28) esta 8 July 1789, Hartford
Proceedings 1870, pg 37 (1870 Sept 28) correspondence received, 1870
Proceedings 1871, pg 35 (1871 Sept 27) Hartford, esta 8 July 1789
Proceedings 1872, pg 45 (1872 Sept 24) Hartford
Proceedings 1872, pg 53 (1872 Sept 24)
Proceedings 1874, pg 43 (1874 Sept 30) Proceedings received
Proceedings 1874, pg 50 (1874 Sept 30) report 1873
Proceedings 1874, pg 125 (1874 Sept 30)
Proceedings 1874, pg 202 (1874 Sept 30)
Proceedings 1874, pg 204 (1874 Sept 30)
Proceedings 1874, pg 207 (1874 Sept 30)

Grand Lodge of Dakota
Proceedings 1876, pg 26 (1876 Sept 20) recognition

Grand Lodge of Delaware
Proceedings 1861-1869, pg 234 (1867 June 27) communication
Proceedings 1861-1869, pg 316 (1869 Sept 29) esta 6 June 1806, Wilmington, DE
Proceedings 1870, pg 34 (1870 Sept 28) esta 6 June 1806, Wilmington
Proceedings 1870, pg 37 (1870 Sept 28) correspondence received, 1869
Proceedings 1871, pg 35 (1871 Sept 27) Wilmington, esta 6 June 1806
Proceedings 1872, pg 45 (1872 Sept 24) Wilmington
Proceedings 1872, pg 53 (1872 Sept 24)
Proceedings 1874, pg 43 (1874 Sept 30) Proceedings received
Proceedings 1874, pg 51 (1874 Sept 30) report 1873
Proceedings 1874, pg 202 (1874 Sept 30)
Proceedings 1874, pg 204 (1874 Sept 30)

Grand Lodge of Denmark
Proceedings 1872, pg 47 (1872 Sept 24), Copenhagen, Denmark

Grand Lodge of District of Columbia
Proceedings 1861-1869, pg 316 (1869 Sept 29) esta 11 Dec 1810, Washington, DC,

Grand Lodge of Florida
Proceedings 1861-1869, pg 316 (1869 Sept 29) esta 5 July 1830, Jacksonville, FL
Proceedings 1870, pg 34 (1870 Sept 28) esta 5 July 1830, Jacksonville
Proceedings 1870, pg 37 (1870 Sept 28) correspondence received, 1870
Proceedings 1871, pg 35 (1871 Sept 27) Jacksonville, esta 5 July 1830
Proceedings 1872, pg 45 (1872 Sept 24) Jacksonville
Proceedings 1872, pg 53 (1872 Sept 24)
Proceedings 1874, pg 43 (1874 Sept 30) Proceedings received
Proceedings 1874, pg 55 (1874 Sept 30) report 1874
Proceedings 1874, pg 202 (1874 Sept 30)
Proceedings 1874, pg 204 (1874 Sept 30)
Proceedings 1876, pg 11 (1876 Sept 19) issues received for the Grand Library
Proceedings 1876, pg 11 (1876 Sept 19) full record of Proceedings in the Grand Library

Grand Lodge of Georgia
Proceedings 1861-1869, pg 234 (1867 Oct 30) communication
Proceedings 1861-1869, pg 316 (1869 Sept 29) esta 16 Dec 1796, Macon, GA
Proceedings 1870, pg 34 (1870 Sept 28) esta 16 Dec 1786, Macon
Proceedings 1870, pg 37 (1870 Sept 28) correspondence received, 1869
Proceedings 1871, pg 35 (1871 Sept 27) Macon, esta 16 Dec 1786
Proceedings 1872, pg 45 (1872 Sept 24) Macon
Proceedings 1872, pg 53 (1872 Sept 24)
Proceedings 1874, pg 43 (1874 Sept 30) Proceedings received
Proceedings 1874, pg 56 (1874 Sept 30) report 1873
Proceedings 1874, pg 125 (1874 Sept 30)
Proceedings 1874, pg 202 (1874 Sept 30)
Proceedings 1874, pg 204 (1874 Sept 30)

Grand Lodge of Gera
Proceedings 1872, pg 47 (1872 Sept 24), Gera, [Germany]

Grand Lodge of Hamburg
Proceedings 1872, pg 14 (1872 Sept 24) not to be recognized by members
Proceedings 1872, pg 47 (1872 Sept 24), Hamburg, [Germany]

Grand Lodge of Hanover
Proceedings 1872, pg 47 (1872 Sept 24) extinct

Grand Lodge of Idaho
Proceedings 1861-1869, pg 234 (1867 Dec 16) communication
Proceedings 1870, pg 37 (1870 Sept 28) correspondence received, 1869
Proceedings 1872, pg 45 (1872 Sept 24) Silver City
Proceedings 1872, pg 53 (1872 Sept 24)
Proceedings 1874, pg 43 (1874 Sept 30) Proceedings received
Proceedings 1874, pg 60 (1874 Sept 30) report 1873
Proceedings 1874, pg 202 (1874 Sept 30)
Proceedings 1874, pg 204 (1874 Sept 30)
Proceedings 1876, pg 11 (1876 Sept 19) full record of Proceedings in the Grand Library

Grand Lodge of Idaho Territory
Proceedings 1861-1869, pg 316 (1869 Sept 29) esta 16 Dec 1867, Idaho City, ID
Proceedings 1870, pg 34 (1870 Sept 28) esta 16 Dec 1867, Idaho City
Proceedings 1871, pg 35 (1871 Sept 27) Boise City, esta 16 Dec 1867,

Grand Lodge of Illinois
Proceedings 1861-1869, pg 103 (1863 Nov 3) communication
Proceedings 1861-1869, pg 234 (1867 Oct 1) communication
Proceedings 1861-1869, pg 316 (1869 Sept 29) esta 6 Apr 1840, Springfield, IL
Proceedings 1870, pg 34 (1870 Sept 28) esta 6 Apr 1840, Springfield
Proceedings 1871, pg 35 (1871 Sept 27) Springfield, esta 6 Apr 1840
Proceedings 1872, pg 45 (1872 Sept 24) Chicago
Proceedings 1872, pg 53 (1872 Sept 24)
Proceedings 1874, pg 43 (1874 Sept 30) Proceedings received
Proceedings 1874, pg 61 (1874 Sept 30) report 1873
Proceedings 1874, pg 126 (1874 Sept 30)
Proceedings 1874, pg 202 (1874 Sept 30)
Proceedings 1874, pg 204 (1874 Sept 30)
Proceedings 1874, pg 207 (1874 Sept 30)

Colorado's Territorial Masons

Grand Lodge of Illinois, cont.
    Proceedings 1874, pg 207 (1874 Sept 30)
    Proceedings 1875, pg 22 (1875 Sept 21) Proceedings received

Grand Lodge of Indian Territory
    Proceedings 1875, pg 24 (1875 Sept 21) asking recognition

Grand Lodge of Indiana
    Proceedings 1861-1869, pg 103 (1863 Nov 3) communication
    Proceedings 1861-1869, pg 290 (1869 Sept 28) correpondence
    Proceedings 1861-1869, pg 316 (1869 Sept 29) esta 12 Jan 1818, Indianapolis, IN
    Proceedings 1870, pg 34 (1870 Sept 28) esta 12 Jan 1818, Indianapolis
    Proceedings 1870, pg 37 (1870 Sept 28) correspondence received, 1870
    Proceedings 1871, pg 35 (1871 Sept 27) Indianapolis, esta 12 Jan 1818
    Proceedings 1872, pg 45 (1872 Sept 24) Indianapolis
    Proceedings 1872, pg 53 (1872 Sept 24)
    Proceedings 1874, pg 43 (1874 Sept 30) Proceedings received
    Proceedings 1874, pg 64 (1874 Sept 30) report 1874
    Proceedings 1874, pg 202 (1874 Sept 30)
    Proceedings 1874, pg 204 (1874 Sept 30)

Grand Lodge of Iowa
    Proceedings 1861-1869, pg 103 (1863 Nov 3) communication
    Proceedings 1861-1869, pg 234 (1867 June 4) communication
    Proceedings 1861-1869, pg 250 (1867 June 4) supports the Soldiers' Orphans' Home
    Proceedings 1861-1869, pg 290 (1869 Sept 28) correpondence
    Proceedings 1861-1869, pg 316 (1869 Sept 29) esta 8 Jan 1844, Iowa City, IA
    Proceedings 1870, pg 34 (1870 Sept 28) esta 8 Jan 1844, Iowa City
    Proceedings 1870, pg 37 (1870 Sept 28) correspondence received, 1870
    Proceedings 1871, pg 35 (1871 Sept 27) Iowa City, esta 8 Jan 1844
    Proceedings 1872, pg 45 (1872 Sept 24) Davenport
    Proceedings 1872, pg 53 (1872 Sept 24)
    Proceedings 1874, pg 43 (1874 Sept 30) Proceedings received
    Proceedings 1874, pg 66 (1874 Sept 30) report 1873
    Proceedings 1874, pg 68 (1874 Sept 30) report 1874
    Proceedings 1874, pg 202 (1874 Sept 30)
    Proceedings 1874, pg 204 (1874 Sept 30)
    Proceedings 1876, pg 11 (1876 Sept 19) full record of Proceedings in the Grand Library

Grand Lodge of Ireland
    Proceedings 1872, pg 47 (1872 Sept 24), Dublin, Ireland

Grand Lodge of Kansas
    Proceedings 1861-1869, pg 103 (1863 Nov 3) communication
    Proceedings 1861-1869, pg 234 (1867 Oct 15) communication
    Proceedings 1861-1869, pg 316 (1869 Sept 29) esta 17 Mar 1856, Fort Leavenworth, KS
    Proceedings 1870, pg 34 (1870 Sept 28) esta 17 Mar 1856, Leavenworth
    Proceedings 1871, pg 10 (1871 Sept 26)
    Proceedings 1871, pg 35 (1871 Sept 27) Leavenworth, esta 17 Mar 1856
    Proceedings 1872, pg 53 (1872 Sept 24)
    Proceedings 1874, pg 43 (1874 Sept 30) Proceedings received
    Proceedings 1874, pg 71 (1874 Sept 30) report 1873
    Proceedings 1874, pg 202 (1874 Sept 30)
    Proceedings 1874, pg 204 (1874 Sept 30)
    Proceedings 1874, pg 207 (1874 Sept 30)

Grand Lodge of Kentucky
    Proceedings 1861-1869, pg 316 (1869 Sept 29) esta 13 Oct 1800, Greensburg, KY
    Proceedings 1870, pg 34 (1870 Sept 28) esta 13 Oct 1800, Louisville
    Proceedings 1870, pg 37 (1870 Sept 28) correspondence received, 1869
    Proceedings 1870, pg 62 (1869 Oct 18) supports the Masonic Widows' and Orphans' Home
    Proceedings 1872, pg 45 (1872 Sept 24)
    Proceedings 1874, pg 43 (1874 Sept 30) Proceedings received
    Proceedings 1874, pg 73 (1874 Sept 30) report 1873
    Proceedings 1874, pg 202 (1874 Sept 30)
    Proceedings 1874, pg 204 (1874 Sept 30)

Grand Lodge of Louisiana
    Proceedings 1861-1869, pg 103 (1863 Nov 3) communication
    Proceedings 1861-1869, pg 234 (1868 Feb 10) communication
    Proceedings 1861-1869, pg 316 (1869 Sept 29) esta 11 July 1812, New Orleans, LA
    Proceedings 1870, pg 34 (1870 Sept 28) esta 11 July 1812, New Orleans
    Proceedings 1870, pg 37 (1870 Sept 28) correspondence received, 1870
    Proceedings 1870, pg 102 (1869 Nov 16)
    Proceedings 1871, pg 35 (1871 Sept 27) New Orleans, esta 11 July 1812
    Proceedings 1872, pg 45 (1872 Sept 24) New Orleans
    Proceedings 1872, pg 53 (1872 Sept 24)
    Proceedings 1874, pg 43 (1874 Sept 30) Proceedings received
    Proceedings 1874, pg 73 (1874 Sept 30) report 1874
    Proceedings 1874, pg 202 (1874 Sept 30)
    Proceedings 1874, pg 204 (1874 Sept 30)
    Proceedings 1874, pg 207 (1874 Sept 30)

Grand Lodge of Maine
    Proceedings 1861-1869, pg 103 (1863 Nov 3) communication
    Proceedings 1861-1869, pg 234 (1868 May 5) communication

Proceedings 1861-1869, pg 316 (1869 Sept 29) esta 1 June 1820, Portland, ME
Proceedings 1870, pg 34 (1870 Sept 28) esta 1 June 1820, Portland
Proceedings 1870, pg 37 (1870 Sept 28) correspondence received, 1870
Proceedings 1871, pg 11 (1871 Sept 26)
Proceedings 1871, pg 35 (1871 Sept 27) Portland, esta 1 June 1820
Proceedings 1872, pg 45 (1872 Sept 24) Portland
Proceedings 1872, pg 53 (1872 Sept 24)
Proceedings 1873, pg 15 (1873 Oct 1)
Proceedings 1874, pg 43 (1874 Sept 30) Proceedings received
Proceedings 1874, pg 77 (1874 Sept 30) report 1874
Proceedings 1874, pg 78 (1874 Sept 30) there were 28 lodges chartered in Massachusetts before the grand lodge existed
Proceedings 1874, pg 202 (1874 Sept 30)
Proceedings 1874, pg 204 (1874 Sept 30)
Proceedings 1874, pg 207 (1874 Sept 30)

Grand Lodge of Manitoba
Proceedings 1875, pg 24 (1875 Sept 21) asking recognition
Proceedings 1876, pg 11 (1876 Sept 19) full record of Proceedings in the Grand Library
Proceedings 1876, pg 26 (1876 Sept 20) recognition

Grand Lodge of Maryland
Proceedings 1861-1869, pg 234 (1867 Nov 18) communication
Proceedings 1861-1869, pg 316 (1869 Sept 29) esta 17 Apr 1787, Baltimore, MD
Proceedings 1870, pg 34 (1870 Sept 28) esta 17 Apr 1787, Baltimore
Proceedings 1870, pg 37 (1870 Sept 28) correspondence received, 1869
Proceedings 1871, pg 35 (1871 Sept 27) Baltimore, esta 17 Apr 1787
Proceedings 1872, pg 45 (1872 Sept 24) Baltimore
Proceedings 1872, pg 53 (1872 Sept 24)
Proceedings 1874, pg 43 (1874 Sept 30) Proceedings received
Proceedings 1874, pg 79 (1874 Sept 30) report 1873
Proceedings 1874, pg 204 (1874 Sept 30)

Grand Lodge of Massachusetts
Proceedings 1861-1869, pg 103 (1863 Nov 3) communication
Proceedings 1861-1869, pg 234 (1867 Dec 11) communication
Proceedings 1861-1869, pg 316 (1869 Sept 29) esta 30 Apr 1733, Boston, MA
Proceedings 1870, pg 34 (1870 Sept 28) esta 30 Apr 1733, Boston
Proceedings 1870, pg 37 (1870 Sept 28) correspondence received, 1869
Proceedings 1871, pg 35 (1871 Sept 27) Boston, esta 30 Apr 1733
Proceedings 1872, pg 45 (1872 Sept 24) Boston
Proceedings 1872, pg 53 (1872 Sept 24)
Proceedings 1873, pg 15 (1873 Oct 1)
Proceedings 1874, pg 43 (1874 Sept 30) Proceedings received
Proceedings 1874, pg 80 (1874 Sept 30) report 1873
Proceedings 1874, pg 202 (1874 Sept 30)
Proceedings 1874, pg 204 (1874 Sept 30)

Grand Lodge of Michigan
Proceedings 1861-1869, pg 103 (1863 Nov 3) communication
Proceedings 1861-1869, pg 234 (1868 Jan 9) communication
Proceedings 1861-1869, pg 316 (1869 Sept 29) esta 28 June 1826, Detroit, MI
Proceedings 1870, pg 34 (1870 Sept 28) esta 28 June 1826, Detroit
Proceedings 1870, pg 37 (1870 Sept 28) correspondence received, 1870
Proceedings 1871, pg 35 (1871 Sept 27) Detroit, esta 28 June 1826
Proceedings 1872, pg 45 (1872 Sept 24) Detroit
Proceedings 1872, pg 53 (1872 Sept 24)
Proceedings 1874, pg 43 (1874 Sept 30) Proceedings received
Proceedings 1874, pg 83 (1874 Sept 30) report 1874
Proceedings 1874, pg 202 (1874 Sept 30)

Grand Lodge of Minesota
Proceedings 1861-1869, pg 234 (1867 Oct 22) communication
Proceedings 1861-1869, pg 316 (1869 Sept 29) esta 23 Feb 1853, St Paul, MN
Proceedings 1870, pg 10 (1870 Sept 27)
Proceedings 1870, pg 34 (1870 Sept 28) esta 23 Feb 1853, St Paul
Proceedings 1870, pg 37 (1870 Sept 28) correspondence received, 1870
Proceedings 1871, pg 35 (1871 Sept 27) St Paul, esta 23 Feb 1853
Proceedings 1872, pg 45 (1872 Sept 24) St Paul
Proceedings 1872, pg 53 (1872 Sept 24)
Proceedings 1874, pg 43 (1874 Sept 30) Proceedings received
Proceedings 1874, pg 85 (1874 Sept 30) report 1874
Proceedings 1874, pg 202 (1874 Sept 30)
Proceedings 1874, pg 204 (1874 Sept 30)
Proceedings 1874, pg 207 (1874 Sept 30)

Grand Lodge of Mississippi
Proceedings 1861-1869, pg 234 (1868 Jan 20) communication
Proceedings 1861-1869, pg 316 (1869 Sept 29) esta 27 July 1818, Jackson, MS
Proceedings 1870, pg 34 (1870 Sept 28) esta 27 July 1818, Jackson
Proceedings 1870, pg 37 (1870 Sept 28) correspondence received, 1870
Proceedings 1870, pg 82 (1870 Jan 17) supports the Orphans' Home
Proceedings 1871, pg 35 (1871 Sept 27) Jackson, esta 27 July 1818
Proceedings 1872, pg 45 (1872 Sept 24) Holly Springs
Proceedings 1872, pg 53 (1872 Sept 24)

Colorado's Territorial Masons

Grand Lodge of Mississippi, cont.
    Proceedings 1874, pg 43 (1874 Sept 30) Proceedings received
    Proceedings 1874, pg 89 (1874 Sept 30) report 1874
    Proceedings 1874, pg 202 (1874 Sept 30)
    Proceedings 1874, pg 204 (1874 Sept 30)

Grand Lodge of Missouri
    Proceedings 1861-1869, pg 103 (1863 Nov 3) communication
    Proceedings 1861-1869, pg 234 (1867 Oct 14) communication
    Proceedings 1861-1869, pg 316 (1869 Sept 29) esta 23 Apr 1821, St Louis, MO
    Proceedings 1870, pg 11 (1870 Sept 27)
    Proceedings 1870, pg 34 (1870 Sept 28) esta 23 Apr 1821, St Louis
    Proceedings 1870, pg 37 (1870 Sept 28) correspondence received, 1869
    Proceedings 1871, pg 10 (1871 Sept 26)
    Proceedings 1871, pg 35 (1871 Sept 27) St Louis, esta 23 Apr 1821
    Proceedings 1872, pg 45 (1872 Sept 24) St Louis
    Proceedings 1872, pg 53 (1872 Sept 24)
    Proceedings 1874, pg 43 (1874 Sept 30) Proceedings received
    Proceedings 1874, pg 90 (1874 Sept 30) report 1873
    Proceedings 1874, pg 202 (1874 Sept 30)
    Proceedings 1874, pg 204 (1874 Sept 30)
    Proceedings 1874, pg 207 (1874 Sept 30)

Grand Lodge of Montana
    Proceedings 1861-1869, pg 234 (1867 Oct 7) communication
    Proceedings 1861-1869, pg 316 (1869 Sept 29) esta 24 Jan 1866, Helena, MT
    Proceedings 1870, pg 34 (1870 Sept 28) esta 24 Jan 1866, Helena
    Proceedings 1870, pg 37 (1870 Sept 28) correspondence received, 1868-1869
    Proceedings 1871, pg 7 (1871 Sept 26)
    Proceedings 1871, pg 35 (1871 Sept 27) Virginia City, esta 24 Jan 1866
    Proceedings 1872, pg 45 (1872 Sept 24) Deer Lodge City
    Proceedings 1872, pg 53 (1872 Sept 24)
    Proceedings 1874, pg 43 (1874 Sept 30) Proceedings received
    Proceedings 1874, pg 94 (1874 Sept 30) report 1873
    Proceedings 1874, pg 202 (1874 Sept 30)
    Proceedings 1874, pg 204 (1874 Sept 30)
    Proceedings 1876, pg 11 (1876 Sept 19) full record of Proceedings in the Grand Library
    Proceedings 1876, pg 11 (1876 Sept 19) issues received for the Grand Library

Grand Lodge of Montana Territory
    Proceedings 1861-1869, pg 239 (1867 Oct 8) formed

Grand Lodge of Nebraska
    Proceedings 1861-1869, pg 234 (1867 June 19) communication
    Proceedings 1861-1869, pg 267 (1867 June 19) celebrating its 10th anniversary
    Proceedings 1861-1869, pg 268 (1867 June 19) supporting a Masonic Orphan Asylum
    Proceedings 1861-1869, pg 316 (1869 Sept 29) esta 23 Sept 1857, Plattsmouth, NE
    Proceedings 1870, pg 34 (1870 Sept 28) esta 23 Sept 1857, Brownville
    Proceedings 1870, pg 37 (1870 Sept 28) correspondence received, 1868-1869
    Proceedings 1871, pg 35 (1871 Sept 27) Brownville, esta 23 Sept 1857
    Proceedings 1872, pg 46 (1872 Sept 24) Lincoln
    Proceedings 1872, pg 53 (1872 Sept 24)
    Proceedings 1874, pg 43 (1874 Sept 30) Proceedings received
    Proceedings 1874, pg 96 (1874 Sept 30) report 1873
    Proceedings 1874, pg 202 (1874 Sept 30)
    Proceedings 1874, pg 204 (1874 Sept 30)
    Proceedings 1874, pg 207 (1874 Sept 30)
    Proceedings 1876, pg 11 (1876 Sept 19) full record of Proceedings in the Grand Library

Grand Lodge of Nevada
    Proceedings 1861-1869, pg 234 (1867 Sept 17) communication
    Proceedings 1861-1869, pg 316 (1869 Sept 29) esta 16 Jan 1865, Virginia City, NV
    Proceedings 1870, pg 34 (1870 Sept 28) esta 16 Jan 1865, Virginia City
    Proceedings 1870, pg 37 (1870 Sept 28) correspondence received, 1869
    Proceedings 1871, pg 35 (1871 Sept 27) Virginia, esta 16 Jan 1865
    Proceedings 1872, pg 46 (1872 Sept 24) Virginia
    Proceedings 1872, pg 53 (1872 Sept 24)
    Proceedings 1874, pg 43 (1874 Sept 30) Proceedings received
    Proceedings 1874, pg 99 (1874 Sept 30) report 1873
    Proceedings 1874, pg 202 (1874 Sept 30)
    Proceedings 1874, pg 204 (1874 Sept 30)
    Proceedings 1876, pg 11 (1876 Sept 19) full record of Proceedings in the Grand Library

Grand Lodge of New Brunswick
    Proceedings 1861-1869, pg 234 (1868 Jan 22) communication
    Proceedings 1861-1869, pg 270 (1868 Jan 22) established
    Proceedings 1861-1869, pg 316 (1869 Sept 29) esta 9 Oct 1867, St Johns, New Brunswick
    Proceedings 1870, pg 34 (1870 Sept 28) esta 9 Oct 1867, St Johns
    Proceedings 1870, pg 37 (1870 Sept 28) correspondence received, 1869
    Proceedings 1871, pg 35 (1871 Sept 27) St Johns, esta 9 Oct 1867
    Proceedings 1872, pg 45 (1872 Sept 24) Saint John
    Proceedings 1872, pg 47 (1872 Sept 24), St Johns, New Brunswick
    Proceedings 1872, pg 53 (1872 Sept 24)
    Proceedings 1874, pg 43 (1874 Sept 30) Proceedings received
    Proceedings 1874, pg 103 (1874 Sept 30) report 1873
    Proceedings 1874, pg 202 (1874 Sept 30)

Proceedings 1874, pg 204 (1874 Sept 30)
Proceedings 1876, pg 11 (1876 Sept 19) full record of Proceedings in the Grand Library

Grand Lodge of New Hampshire
Proceedings 1861-1869, pg 234 (1866 Dec 27) communication
Proceedings 1861-1869, pg 291 (1869 Sept 28) correpondence
Proceedings 1861-1869, pg 316 (1869 Sept 29) esta 8 July 1789, Hopkinton, NH
Proceedings 1870, pg 34 (1870 Sept 28) esta 8 July 1789, Concord
Proceedings 1871, pg 35 (1871 Sept 27) Concord, esta 8 July 1789
Proceedings 1872, pg 45 (1872 Sept 24) Concord
Proceedings 1872, pg 53 (1872 Sept 24)
Proceedings 1874, pg 43 (1874 Sept 30) Proceedings received
Proceedings 1874, pg 104 (1874 Sept 30) report 1873
Proceedings 1874, pg 106 (1874 Sept 30) report 1874
Proceedings 1874, pg 202 (1874 Sept 30)
Proceedings 1874, pg 204 (1874 Sept 30)

Grand Lodge of New Jersey
Proceedings 1861-1869, pg 103 (1863 Nov 3) communication
Proceedings 1861-1869, pg 234 (1867 Jan 16) communication
Proceedings 1861-1869, pg 316 (1869 Sept 29) esta 18 Dec 1786, Trenton, NJ
Proceedings 1870, pg 34 (1870 Sept 28) esta 18 Dec 1786, Trenton
Proceedings 1870, pg 37 (1870 Sept 28) correspondence received, 1870
Proceedings 1871, pg 35 (1871 Sept 27) Trenton, esta 18 Dec 1786
Proceedings 1872, pg 45 (1872 Sept 24) Trenton
Proceedings 1872, pg 53 (1872 Sept 24)
Proceedings 1874, pg 43 (1874 Sept 30) Proceedings received
Proceedings 1874, pg 108 (1874 Sept 30) report 1874
Proceedings 1874, pg 203 (1874 Sept 30)
Proceedings 1874, pg 204 (1874 Sept 30)

Grand Lodge of New York
Proceedings 1861-1869, pg 103 (1863 Nov 3) communication
Proceedings 1861-1869, pg 234 (1867 June 4) communication
Proceedings 1861-1869, pg 235 (1867 Nov 4) sent $5000 for the relief of southern families
Proceedings 1861-1869, pg 291 (1869 Sept 28) correpondence
Proceedings 1861-1869, pg 316 (1869 Sept 29) esta 5 Sept 1781, New York, NY
Proceedings 1870, pg 34 (1870 Sept 28) esta 5 Sept 1781, New York
Proceedings 1870, pg 37 (1870 Sept 28) correspondence received, 1870
Proceedings 1871, pg 35 (1871 Sept 27) New York, esta 5 Sept 1781
Proceedings 1872, pg 45 (1872 Sept 24) New York
Proceedings 1872, pg 53 (1872 Sept 24)
Proceedings 1874, pg 43 (1874 Sept 30) Proceedings received
Proceedings 1874, pg 109 (1874 Sept 30) report 1874
Proceedings 1874, pg 203 (1874 Sept 30)
Proceedings 1874, pg 204 (1874 Sept 30)
Proceedings 1875, pg 26 (1875 Sept 21) communication

Grand Lodge of North Carolina
Proceedings 1861-1869, pg 234 (1867 Dec 2) communication
Proceedings 1861-1869, pg 316 (1869 Sept 29) esta 14 Jan 1771, Raleigh, NC
Proceedings 1870, pg 34 (1870 Sept 28) esta 14 Jan 1771, Raleigh
Proceedings 1870, pg 37 (1870 Sept 28) correspondence received, 1869
Proceedings 1871, pg 35 (1871 Sept 27) Raleigh, esta 14 Jan 1771
Proceedings 1872, pg 45 (1872 Sept 24) Raleigh
Proceedings 1872, pg 53 (1872 Sept 24)
Proceedings 1874, pg 43 (1874 Sept 30) Proceedings received
Proceedings 1874, pg 113 (1874 Sept 30) report 1873
Proceedings 1874, pg 203 (1874 Sept 30)
Proceedings 1874, pg 204 (1874 Sept 30)

Grand Lodge of Nova Scotia
Proceedings 1861-1869, pg 234 (1867 June 21) communication
Proceedings 1861-1869, pg 239 (1867 Oct 8) formed
Proceedings 1861-1869, pg 278 (1866 Nov 30) established
Proceedings 1861-1869, pg 316 (1869 Sept 29) esta 21 June 1866, Halifax, Nova Scotia
Proceedings 1870, pg 34 (1870 Sept 28) esta 21 June 1806, Halifax
Proceedings 1871, pg 35 (1871 Sept 27) Halifax, esta 21 June 1806
Proceedings 1872, pg 46 (1872 Sept 24) Halifax
Proceedings 1872, pg 47 (1872 Sept 24), Halifax, Nova Scotia
Proceedings 1872, pg 53 (1872 Sept 24)
Proceedings 1874, pg 43 (1874 Sept 30) Proceedings received
Proceedings 1874, pg 116 (1874 Sept 30) report 1873
Proceedings 1874, pg 203 (1874 Sept 30)
Proceedings 1874, pg 204 (1874 Sept 30)

Grand Lodge of Ohio
Proceedings 1861-1869, pg 234 (1867 Oct 15) communication
Proceedings 1861-1869, pg 316 (1869 Sept 29) esta 7 Jan 1808, Cincinnati, OH
Proceedings 1870, pg 34 (1870 Sept 28) esta 7 Jan 1808, Cincinnati
Proceedings 1871, pg 35 (1871 Sept 27) Cincinnati, esta 7 Jan 1808
Proceedings 1872, pg 46 (1872 Sept 24) Mansfield
Proceedings 1872, pg 53 (1872 Sept 24)
Proceedings 1874, pg 43 (1874 Sept 30) Proceedings received

Colorado's Territorial Masons

Grand Lodge of Ohio, cont.
    Proceedings 1874, pg 117 (1874 Sept 30) report 1873
    Proceedings 1874, pg 203 (1874 Sept 30)
    Proceedings 1874, pg 204 (1874 Sept 30)

Grand Lodge of Oregon
    Proceedings 1861-1869, pg 103 (1863 Nov 3) communication
    Proceedings 1861-1869, pg 103 (1863 Nov 3) communication
    Proceedings 1861-1869, pg 234 (1867 June 24) communication
    Proceedings 1861-1869, pg 279 (1867 June 24)
    Proceedings 1861-1869, pg 316 (1869 Sept 29) esta 16 Aug 1851, Portland, OR
    Proceedings 1870, pg 34 (1870 Sept 28) esta 16 Aug 1851, Portland
    Proceedings 1870, pg 37 (1870 Sept 28) correspondence received, 1869-1870
    Proceedings 1871, pg 35 (1871 Sept 27) Portland, esta 16 Aug 1851
    Proceedings 1872, pg 46 (1872 Sept 24) Salem
    Proceedings 1872, pg 53 (1872 Sept 24)
    Proceedings 1874, pg 43 (1874 Sept 30) Proceedings received
    Proceedings 1874, pg 118 (1874 Sept 30) report 1873
    Proceedings 1874, pg 203 (1874 Sept 30)
    Proceedings 1874, pg 205 (1874 Sept 30)
    Proceedings 1874, pg 207 (1874 Sept 30)

Grand Lodge of Pennsylvania
    Proceedings 1861-1869, pg 316 (1869 Sept 29) esta 20 June 1764, Philadelphia, PA
    Proceedings 1870, pg 34 (1870 Sept 28) esta 20 June 1764, Philadelphia
    Proceedings 1870, pg 37 (1870 Sept 28) correspondence received, 1869
    Proceedings 1871, pg 35 (1871 Sept 27) Philadelphia, esta 20 June 1764
    Proceedings 1872, pg 46 (1872 Sept 24) Philadelphia
    Proceedings 1872, pg 53 (1872 Sept 24)
    Proceedings 1874, pg 43 (1874 Sept 30) Proceedings received
    Proceedings 1874, pg 119 (1874 Sept 30) report 1873
    Proceedings 1874, pg 203 (1874 Sept 30)
    Proceedings 1874, pg 205 (1874 Sept 30)

Grand Lodge of Prince Edward Island
    Proceedings 1875, pg 24 (1875 Sept 21) asking recognition
    Proceedings 1876, pg 11 (1876 Sept 19) full record of Proceedings in the Grand Library
    Proceedings 1876, pg 26 (1876 Sept 20) recognition

Grand Lodge of Quebec
    Proceedings 1870, pg 93 (1870 Jan 19)
    Proceedings 1870, pg 103 (1870 June 13)
    Proceedings 1871, pg 16 (1871 Sept 27)
    Proceedings 1872, pg 46 (1872 Sept 24) Montreal
    Proceedings 1872, pg 53 (1872 Sept 24)
    Proceedings 1874, pg 13 (1874 Sept 29)
    Proceedings 1874, pg 33 (1874 Sept 30) recognized
    Proceedings 1874, pg 43 (1874 Sept 30) Proceedings received
    Proceedings 1874, pg 49 (1874 Sept 30) receipt of The Official Protocols
    Proceedings 1874, pg 120 (1874 Sept 30) report 1873
    Proceedings 1874, pg 203 (1874 Sept 30)
    Proceedings 1874, pg 205 (1874 Sept 30)
    Proceedings 1876, pg 11 (1876 Sept 19) full record of Proceedings in the Grand Library

Grand Lodge of Rhode Island
    Proceedings 1861-1869, pg 234 (1867 June 25) communication
    Proceedings 1861-1869, pg 316 (1869 Sept 29) esta 25 June 1791, Providence, RI
    Proceedings 1870, pg 34 (1870 Sept 28) esta 25 June 1791, Providence
    Proceedings 1870, pg 37 (1870 Sept 28) correspondence received, 1870
    Proceedings 1871, pg 35 (1871 Sept 27) Providence, esta 25 June 1791
    Proceedings 1872, pg 46 (1872 Sept 24) Providence
    Proceedings 1873, pg 15 (1873 Oct 1)
    Proceedings 1874, pg 43 (1874 Sept 30) Proceedings received
    Proceedings 1874, pg 121 (1874 Sept 30) report 1873
    Proceedings 1874, pg 203 (1874 Sept 30)
    Proceedings 1874, pg 205 (1874 Sept 30)

Grand Lodge of Saxony
    Proceedings 1872, pg 47 (1872 Sept 24), Dresden, Saxony [Germany]

Grand Lodge of Scotland
    Proceedings 1870, pg 95 (1869 Sept 22)
    Proceedings 1872, pg 47 (1872 Sept 24), Edinburgh, Scotland

Grand Lodge of South Carolina
    Proceedings 1861-1869, pg 234 (1867 Nov 19) communication
    Proceedings 1861-1869, pg 316 (1869 Sept 29) esta 24 Mar 1787, Charleston, SC
    Proceedings 1870, pg 34 (1870 Sept 28) esta 24 Mar 1787, Lawrence
    Proceedings 1870, pg 37 (1870 Sept 28) correspondence received, 1869
    Proceedings 1871, pg 35 (1871 Sept 27) Charleston, esta 24 Mar 1787
    Proceedings 1872, pg 46 (1872 Sept 24) Charleston
    Proceedings 1872, pg 53 (1872 Sept 24)
    Proceedings 1874, pg 43 (1874 Sept 30) Proceedings received
    Proceedings 1874, pg 121 (1874 Sept 30) report 1873
    Proceedings 1874, pg 203 (1874 Sept 30)
    Proceedings 1874, pg 205 (1874 Sept 30)

Grand Lodge of Sweden and Norway
    Proceedings 1872, pg 47 (1872 Sept 24), Stockholm, Sweden

Grand Lodge of Tennessee
    Proceedings 1861-1869, pg 234 (1867 Oct 7) communication

Proceedings 1861-1869, pg 316 (1869 Sept 29) esta 14 Oct 1794, Nashville, TN
Proceedings 1870, pg 34 (1870 Sept 28) esta 14 Oct 1794, Nashville
Proceedings 1871, pg 35 (1871 Sept 27) Nashville, esta 14 Oct 1794
Proceedings 1872, pg 46 (1872 Sept 24) Nashville
Proceedings 1872, pg 53 (1872 Sept 24)
Proceedings 1874, pg 43 (1874 Sept 30) Proceedings received
Proceedings 1874, pg 123 (1874 Sept 30) report 1873
Proceedings 1874, pg 203 (1874 Sept 30)
Proceedings 1874, pg 205 (1874 Sept 30)

Grand Lodge of Texas
Proceedings 1861-1869, pg 234 (1867 June 8) communication
Proceedings 1861-1869, pg 316 (1869 Sept 29) esta 20 Dec 1837, Houston, TX
Proceedings 1870, pg 10 (1870 Sept 27)
Proceedings 1870, pg 34 (1870 Sept 28) esta 20 Dec 1837, Houston
Proceedings 1870, pg 37 (1870 Sept 28) correspondence received, 1870
Proceedings 1871, pg 35 (1871 Sept 27) Houston, esta 20 Dec 1837
Proceedings 1872, pg 46 (1872 Sept 24) Houston
Proceedings 1872, pg 53 (1872 Sept 24)
Proceedings 1874, pg 43 (1874 Sept 30) Proceedings received
Proceedings 1874, pg 124 (1874 Sept 30) report 1874
Proceedings 1874, pg 203 (1874 Sept 30)
Proceedings 1874, pg 205 (1874 Sept 30)
Proceedings 1876, pg 11 (1876 Sept 19) full record of Proceedings in the Grand Library

Grand Lodge of the District of Columbia
Proceedings 1861-1869, pg 103 (1863 Nov 3) communication
Proceedings 1861-1869, pg 234 (1867 Oct 30) communication
Proceedings 1870, pg 34 (1870 Sept 28) esta 11 Dec 1810, Washington
Proceedings 1871, pg 35 (1871 Sept 27) Washington, esta 11 Dec 1810
Proceedings 1872, pg 45 (1872 Sept 24) Washington
Proceedings 1872, pg 53 (1872 Sept 24)
Proceedings 1874, pg 43 (1874 Sept 30) Proceedings received
Proceedings 1874, pg 52 (1874 Sept 30) report 1873
Proceedings 1874, pg 202 (1874 Sept 30)
Proceedings 1874, pg 204 (1874 Sept 30)

Grand Lodge of the Indian Territory
Proceedings 1876, pg 11 (1876 Sept 19) full record of Proceedings in the Grand Library
Proceedings 1876, pg 26 (1876 Sept 20) recognition

Grand Lodge of Utah
Proceedings 1872, pg 46 (1872 Sept 24) Salt Lake
Proceedings 1872, pg 53 (1872 Sept 24)
Proceedings 1874, pg 43 (1874 Sept 30) Proceedings received

Proceedings 1874, pg 83 (1874 Sept 30)
Proceedings 1874, pg 96 (1874 Sept 30)
Proceedings 1874, pg 104 (1874 Sept 30)
Proceedings 1874, pg 126 (1874 Sept 30) report 1873
Proceedings 1874, pg 203 (1874 Sept 30)
Proceedings 1874, pg 205 (1874 Sept 30)
Proceedings 1876, pg 11 (1876 Sept 19) full record of Proceedings in the Grand Library

Grand Lodge of Vermont
Proceedings 1861-1869, pg 103 (1863 Nov 3) communication
Proceedings 1861-1869, pg 316 (1869 Sept 29) esta 14 Oct 1794, Poultney, VT
Proceedings 1870, pg 34 (1870 Sept 28) esta 14 Oct 1794, Rutland
Proceedings 1870, pg 37 (1870 Sept 28) correspondence received, 1869
Proceedings 1871, pg 35 (1871 Sept 27) Rutland, esta 14 Oct 1794
Proceedings 1872, pg 46 (1872 Sept 24) Burlington
Proceedings 1872, pg 53 (1872 Sept 24)
Proceedings 1874, pg 43 (1874 Sept 30) Proceedings received
Proceedings 1874, pg 50 (1874 Sept 30)
Proceedings 1874, pg 128 (1874 Sept 30) report 1873
Proceedings 1874, pg 203 (1874 Sept 30)
Proceedings 1874, pg 205 (1874 Sept 30)

Grand Lodge of Virginia
Proceedings 1861-1869, pg 234 (1867 Dec 9) communication
Proceedings 1861-1869, pg 283 (1867 Dec 9)
Proceedings 1861-1869, pg 316 (1869 Sept 29) esta 6 May 1777, Richmond, VA
Proceedings 1870, pg 34 (1870 Sept 28) esta 6 May 1777, Richmond
Proceedings 1870, pg 37 (1870 Sept 28) correspondence received, 1869
Proceedings 1870, pg 106 (1869 Nov 9)
Proceedings 1871, pg 35 (1871 Sept 27) Richmond, esta 6 May 1777
Proceedings 1872, pg 46 (1872 Sept 24) Richmond
Proceedings 1872, pg 53 (1872 Sept 24)
Proceedings 1874, pg 43 (1874 Sept 30) Proceedings received
Proceedings 1874, pg 129 (1874 Sept 30) report 1873
Proceedings 1874, pg 203 (1874 Sept 30)
Proceedings 1874, pg 205 (1874 Sept 30)
Proceedings 1875, pg 22 (1875 Sept 21) Proceedings received

Grand Lodge of Washington
Proceedings 1861-1869, pg 234 (1867 Sept 18) communication
Proceedings 1861-1869, pg 283 (1867 Sept 18)
Proceedings 1861-1869, pg 316 (1869 Sept 29) esta 9 Dec 1858, Olympia, WA
Proceedings 1870, pg 34 (1870 Sept 28) esta 9 Dec 1858, Olympia
Proceedings 1870, pg 37 (1870 Sept 28) correspondence received, 1869

Colorado's Territorial Masons

Grand Lodge of Washington, cont.
Proceedings 1871, pg 35 (1871 Sept 27) Olympia, esta 9 Dec 1858
Proceedings 1872, pg 46 (1872 Sept 24) Olympia
Proceedings 1872, pg 53 (1872 Sept 24)
Proceedings 1874, pg 43 (1874 Sept 30) Proceedings received
Proceedings 1874, pg 131 (1874 Sept 30) report 1873
Proceedings 1874, pg 203 (1874 Sept 30)
Proceedings 1874, pg 205 (1874 Sept 30)
Proceedings 1876, pg 11 (1876 Sept 19) issues received for the Grand Library

Grand Lodge of Washington Territory
Proceedings 1861-1869, pg 103 (1863 Nov 3) communication

Grand Lodge of West Virginia
Proceedings 1861-1869, pg 239 (1867 Oct 8) formed
Proceedings 1861-1869, pg 316 (1869 Sept 29) esta 12 Apr 1865, Wheeling, WV
Proceedings 1870, pg 34 (1870 Sept 28) esta 12 Apr 1865, Wheeling
Proceedings 1870, pg 37 (1870 Sept 28) correspondence received, 1869
Proceedings 1871, pg 35 (1871 Sept 27) Wheeling, esta 12 Apr 1865
Proceedings 1872, pg 46 (1872 Sept 24) Wheeling
Proceedings 1872, pg 53 (1872 Sept 24)
Proceedings 1874, pg 43 (1874 Sept 30) Proceedings received
Proceedings 1874, pg 133 (1874 Sept 30) report 1873
Proceedings 1874, pg 203 (1874 Sept 30)
Proceedings 1874, pg 205 (1874 Sept 30)

Grand Lodge of Wisconsin
Proceedings 1861-1869, pg 103 (1863 Nov 3) communication
Proceedings 1861-1869, pg 234 (1867 June 11) communication
Proceedings 1861-1869, pg 316 (1869 Sept 29) esta 18 Dec 1843, Milwaukee, WI
Proceedings 1870, pg 34 (1870 Sept 28) esta 18 Dec 1843, Milwaukee
Proceedings 1870, pg 37 (1870 Sept 28) correspondence received, 1870
Proceedings 1871, pg 35 (1871 Sept 27) Milwaukee, esta 18 Dec 1843
Proceedings 1872, pg 46 (1872 Sept 24) Milwaukee
Proceedings 1872, pg 53 (1872 Sept 24)
Proceedings 1874, pg 203 (1874 Sept 30)
Proceedings 1874, pg 205 (1874 Sept 30)

Grand Lodge of Wyoming
Proceedings 1876, pg 11 (1876 Sept 19) full record of Proceedings in the Grand Library

Grand Lodge of Wyoming Territory
Proceedings 1875, pg 24 (1875 Sept 21) asking recognition
Proceedings 1875, pg 36 (1875 Sept 22) recognized

Grand Lodge Zur Eintracht
Proceedings 1872, pg 47 (1872 Sept 24), Hesse Darmstadt, [Germany]

Grand Lodge Zur Sonne
Proceedings 1872, pg 47 (1872 Sept 24), Bayreuth, Bavaria

Grand Orient and Supreme Council of Hungary
Proceedings 1875, pg 24 (1875 Sept 21) asking recognition

Grand Orient of Belgium
Proceedings 1872, pg 47 (1872 Sept 24), Brussels, Belgium

Grand Orient of Brazil
Proceedings 1872, pg 47 (1872 Sept 24), Rio Janeiro, Brazil

Grand Orient of Buenos Ayres [Aries]
Proceedings 1872, pg 47 (1872 Sept 24), Buenos Ayres [Aires], [Argengina]

Grand Orient of Cuba
Proceedings 1872, pg 47 (1872 Sept 24) Cuba

Grand Orient of Egypt
Proceedings 1875, pg 24 (1875 Sept 21) asking recognition

Grand Orient of France
Proceedings 1861-1869, pg 235 (1868 Oct 7)
Proceedings 1870, pg 34 (1870 Sept 28) Paris
Proceedings 1870, pg 95 (1869 Dec 6)
Proceedings 1870, pg 98 (1870 June 20)
Proceedings 1870, pg 104 (1869 June 9)
Proceedings 1872, pg 14 (1872 Sept 24) not to be recognized by members
Proceedings 1872, pg 47 (1872 Sept 24), Paris, France

Grand Orient of Hayti [Haiti]
Proceedings 1872, pg 47 (1872 Sept 24), Port au Prince, Hayti [Haiti]

Grand Orient of Hellas
Proceedings 1872, pg 47 (1872 Sept 24), Athens, Greece

Grand Orient of Holland
Proceedings 1872, pg 47 (1872 Sept 24), The Hague, Holland

Grand Orient of Italy
Proceedings 1870, pg 93 (1870 Jan 19)
Proceedings 1872, pg 47 (1872 Sept 24), Florence, Italy

Grand Orient of Lusitania
Proceedings 1872, pg 47 (1872 Sept 24), Lisbon, Portugal

Grand Orient of Mexico
Proceedings 1872, pg 47 (1872 Sept 24) Mexico

Grand Orient of New Granada
Proceedings 1872, pg 47 (1872 Sept 24), Carthagenia, New Granada

Grand Orient of Peru
Proceedings 1872, pg 47 (1872 Sept 24), Lima, Peru

Grand Orient of St Domingo
Proceedings 1872, pg 47 (1872 Sept 24) St Domingo

Grand Orient of Uruguay
Proceedings 1872, pg 47 (1872 Sept 24), Montevideo, Uruguay

Grand Secretary of Alabama
Proceedings 1861-1869, pg 238 (1867 Dec 2) proposed to gather photographs of all living Past Grand Masters

Granite, Lake County
Proceedings 1861-1869, pg 293 (1869 Sept 28) not granted a dispensation to open a lodge

Grant, A A
Proceedings 1875, pg 85 (1875 Sept 22) Pueblo Lodge No. 17
Proceedings 1876, pg 39 (1876 Sept 20) Pueblo Lodge No. 17

Graunn, Otto
Proceedings 1874, pg 223 (1874 Sept 30), Laramie Lodge No. 18, Laramie City

Graver, L R
Proceedings 1874, pg 221 (1874 Sept 30), Cheyenne Lodge No. 16, Cheyenne, Wyoming Territory

Graves, E S
Proceedings 1861-1869, pg 167 (1866 Oct 2) Denver Lodge No. 5

Graves, Elijah S
Proceedings 1861-1869, pg 193 (1867 Oct 8) Denver Lodge No. 5, Died

Graves, L R
Proceedings 1861-1869, pg 229 (1868 Oct 7), Pueblo Lodge U D, Pueblo

Graves, Wm
Proceedings 1870, pg 52 (1869 June 28) Grand Lodge of Delaware, deceased

Gravestock, John
Proceedings 1873, pg 45 (1873 Oct 1), Mount Moriah Lodge No. 15, Canon City, Apprentice
Proceedings 1874, pg 220 (1874 Sept 30), Mount Moriah Lodge No. 15, Canon City
Proceedings 1876, pg 37 (1876 Sept 20), Mount Moriah Lodge No. 15, Canon City

Gray, Charles F
Proceedings 1874, pg 222 (1874 Sept 30), Pueblo Lodge No. 17, Pueblo, Pueblo County, Apprentice
Proceedings 1875, pg 85 (1875 Sept 22) Pueblo Lodge No. 17, Apprentice
Proceedings 1876, pg 39 (1876 Sept 20) Pueblo Lodge No. 17, Apprentice

Gray, Geo H Jr
Proceedings 1872, pg 71 (1872 Sept 24) Grand Lodge of Mississippi, deceased

Gray, John
Proceedings 1875, pg 85 (1875 Sept 22) Pueblo Lodge No. 17
Proceedings 1876, pg 39 (1876 Sept 20) Pueblo Lodge No. 17
Proceedings 1876, pg 45 (1876 Sept 20) South Pueblo Lodge U D

Gray, Peter
Proceedings 1861-1869, pg 283 (1867 Oct 7), Grand Master, Grand Lodge of Texas

Gray, Peter W
Proceedings 1861-1869, pg 348 (1869 June 14) Grand Master, Grand Lodge of Texas

Gray, William
Proceedings 1861-1869, pg 77 (1862 Nov 4) Denver Lodge No. 5
Proceedings 1861-1869, pg 112 (1863 Nov 3) Denver Lodge No. 5
Proceedings 1861-1869, pg 133 (1864 Nov 8) Denver Lodge No. 5
Proceedings 1861-1869, pg 139 (1865 Nov 6), Montana Lodge U D, Virginia City, Montana Territory
Proceedings 1861-1869, pg 149 (1865 Nov 7), Nevada Lodge No. 4, Nevadaville
Proceedings 1861-1869, pg 152 (1865 Nov 7), Montana Lodge U D, Virginia City, Montana Territory

Gray, Wm
Proceedings 1861-1869, pg 167 (1866 Oct 2) Denver Lodge No. 5, dimitted,

Greeley Tribune
Colorado University Cornerstone Laying, pg 4 (1875 Sept 20) cornerstone contents

Green, B
Proceedings 1861-1869, pg 168 (1866 Oct 2), Chivington Lodge No. 6, Central City

Green, Basil
Proceedings 1861-1869, pg 133 (1864 Nov 8), Chivington Lodge No. 6, Central City
Proceedings 1861-1869, pg 150 (1865 Nov 7), Chivington Lodge No. 6, Central City
Proceedings 1861-1869, pg 194 (1867 Oct 8), Chivington Lodge No. 6, Central City
Proceedings 1861-1869, pg 224 (1868 Oct 7), Chivington Lodge No. 6, Central City
Proceedings 1861-1869, pg 306 (1869 Sept 29), Central Lodge No. 6, Central City
Proceedings 1870, pg 22 (1870 Sept 28), Central Lodge No. 6, Central City
Proceedings 1871, pg 20 (1871 Sept 27), Central Lodge No. 6, Central

Green, Bazil
Proceedings 1872, pg 22 (1872 Sept 24), Denver Lodge No. 5, Denver

Green, Charles D
Proceedings 1870, pg 100 (1869 Nov 15) Grand Secretary, Grand Lodge of Rhode Island

Green, D S
Proceedings 1861-1869, pg 150 (1865 Nov 7), Chivington Lodge No. 6, Central City
Proceedings 1861-1869, pg 168 (1866 Oct 2), Chivington Lodge No. 6, Central City
Proceedings 1861-1869, pg 194 (1867 Oct 8), Chivington Lodge No. 6, Central City
Proceedings 1861-1869, pg 224 (1868 Oct 7), Chivington Lodge No. 6, Central City
Proceedings 1870, pg 22 (1870 Sept 28), Central Lodge No. 6, Central City

Colorado's Territorial Masons

Green, D S, cont.
    Proceedings 1871, pg 20 (1871 Sept 27), Central Lodge No. 6, Central

Green, David S
    Proceedings 1861-1869, pg 134 (1864 Nov 8), Chivington Lodge No. 6, Central City
    Proceedings 1861-1869, pg 306 (1869 Sept 29), Central Lodge No. 6, Central City
    Proceedings 1872, pg 21 (1872 Sept 24), Denver Lodge No. 5, Denver
    Proceedings 1873, pg 38 (1873 Oct 1), Central Lodge No. 6, Central City
    Proceedings 1874, pg 213 (1874 Sept 30), Central Lodge No. 6, Central
    Proceedings 1875, pg 77 (1875 Sept 22), Central Lodge No. 6, Central City, Stricken from the rolls

Green, Henry
    Proceedings 1861-1869, pg 197 (1867 Oct 8), Columbia Lodge U D, Boulder
    Proceedings 1861-1869, pg 228 (1868 Oct 7), Columbia Lodge No. 14, Columbia City
    Proceedings 1861-1869, pg 310 (1869 Sept 29), Columbia Lodge No. 14, Boulder City
    Proceedings 1870, pg 27 (1870 Sept 28), Columbia Lodge No. 14, Boulder City
    Proceedings 1871, pg 25 (1871 Sept 27), Columbia Lodge No. 14, Boulder City
    Proceedings 1872, pg 27 (1872 Sept 24), Columbia Lodge No. 14, Boulder
    Proceedings 1873, pg 44 (1873 Oct 1), Columbia Lodge No. 14, Boulder
    Proceedings 1874, pg 219 (1874 Sept 30), Columbia Lodge No. 14, Boulder, Boulder County
    Proceedings 1875, pg 83 (1875 Sept 22), Columbia Lodge No. 14, Boulder, Stricken from the rolls
    Proceedings 1876, pg 37 (1876 Sept 20), Columbia Lodge No. 14, Boulder
    Proceedings 1876, pg 51 (1876 Sept 20), Columbia Lodge No. 14, Boulder, 1876 June 24

Green, L G H
    Proceedings 1861-1869, pg 113 (1863 Nov 3), Chivington Lodge No. 6, Central City

Green, M
    Proceedings 1875, pg 82 (1875 Sept 22), El Paso Lodge No. 13, Colorado Springs
    Proceedings 1876, pg 36 (1876 Sept 20), El Paso Lodge No. 13, Colorado City

Green, Marmaduke
    Proceedings 1872, pg 36 (1872 Sept 24), Ashlar Lodge U D, Colorado Springs

Green, Spencer
    Proceedings 1872, pg 25 (1872 Sept 24), Black Hawk Lodge No. 11, Black Hawk

Greene, B
    Proceedings 1861-1869, pg 78 (1862 Nov 4), Chivington Lodge No. 6, Central City
    Proceedings 1861-1869, pg 113 (1863 Nov 3), Chivington Lodge No. 6, Central City

Greene, Bengmen
    Proceedings 1870, pg 76 (1789 Nov 9)

Greene, Charles D
    Proceedings 1861-1869, pg 280 (1867 Oct 7), Grand Secretary, Grand Lodge of Rhode Island
    Proceedings 1861-1869, pg 316 (1869 Sept 29) Grand Lodge of Rhode Island
    Proceedings 1861-1869, pg 346 (1868 Aug 6) Grand Secretary, Grand Lodge of Rhode Island
    Proceedings 1870, pg 34 (1870 Sept 28) Grand Secretary, Grand Lodge of Rhode Island
    Proceedings 1871, pg 35 (1871 Sept 27) Grand Secretary, Grand Lodge of Rhode Island

Greene, D S
    Proceedings 1861-1869, pg 78 (1862 Nov 4), Chivington Lodge No. 6, Central City, Apprentice
    Proceedings 1861-1869, pg 113 (1863 Nov 3), Chivington Lodge No. 6, Central City

Greene, L G H
    Proceedings 1861-1869, pg 134 (1864 Nov 8), Chivington Lodge No. 6, Central City
    Proceedings 1861-1869, pg 150 (1865 Nov 7), Chivington Lodge No. 6, Central City
    Proceedings 1861-1869, pg 168 (1866 Oct 2), Chivington Lodge No. 6, Central City, dimitted

Greene, Luther G H
    Proceedings 1861-1869, pg 78 (1862 Nov 4), Chivington Lodge No. 6, Central City

Greenfell, Geo E
    Proceedings 1874, pg 227 (1874 Sept 30), St Vrain No. 23, Longmont, Apprentice

Greenfield, E
    Proceedings 1876, pg 49 (1876 Sept 20) Denver Lodge No. 5, 1876 Aug 19

Greenfield, Enos
    Proceedings 1871, pg 19 (1871 Sept 27) Denver Lodge No. 5
    Proceedings 1872, pg 19 (1872 Sept 24), Denver Lodge No. 5, Denver
    Proceedings 1873, pg 37 (1873 Oct 1), Denver Lodge No. 5, Denver
    Proceedings 1874, pg 211 (1874 Sept 30), Denver Lodge No. 5, Denver
    Proceedings 1875, pg 75 (1875 Sept 22) Denver Lodge No. 5

Greenleaf
    Proceedings 1861-1869, pg 177 (1867 Oct 7) committee
    Proceedings 1861-1869, pg 185 (1867 Oct 7) committee
    Proceedings 1861-1869, pg 190 (1867 Oct 8) committee
    Proceedings 1861-1869, pg 202 (1868 Oct 6) committee
    Proceedings 1861-1869, pg 289 (1869 Sept 28) committee
    Proceedings 1861-1869, pg 296 (1869 Sept 28) resolution

Greenleaf, L M
    Proceedings 1873, pg 4 (1873 Sept 30) pall bearer for George M Randall

Greenleaf, L N
   Proceedings 1861-1869, pg 133 (1864 Nov 8) Denver Lodge No. 5
   Proceedings 1861-1869, pg 137 (1865 Nov 6) committee
   Proceedings 1861-1869, pg 137 (1865 Nov 6) Denver Lodge No. 5
   Proceedings 1861-1869, pg 137 (1865 Nov 6) committee
   Proceedings 1861-1869, pg 138 (1865 Nov 6) committee
   Proceedings 1861-1869, pg 144 (1865 Nov 7) Denver Lodge No. 5
   Proceedings 1861-1869, pg 148 (1865 Nov 7), Nevada Lodge No. 4, Nevadaville
   Proceedings 1861-1869, pg 153 (1866 Oct 1) Senior Grand Deacon
   Proceedings 1861-1869, pg 154 (1866 Oct 1) Denver Lodge No. 5
   Proceedings 1861-1869, pg 155 (1866 Oct 1) committee
   Proceedings 1861-1869, pg 156 (1866 Oct 1) committee
   Proceedings 1861-1869, pg 159 (1866 Oct 1) warrant
   Proceedings 1861-1869, pg 160 (1866 Oct 2) Denver Lodge No. 5
   Proceedings 1861-1869, pg 161 (1866 Oct 2) Junior Grand Warden
   Proceedings 1861-1869, pg 162 (1866 Oct 2) Denver Lodge No. 5
   Proceedings 1861-1869, pg 166 (1866 Oct 2) Denver Lodge No. 5
   Proceedings 1861-1869, pg 175 (1867 Oct 7) Junior Grand Warden
   Proceedings 1861-1869, pg 176 (1867 Oct 7) Junior Grand Warden
   Proceedings 1861-1869, pg 182 (1867 Oct 7) warrant paid
   Proceedings 1861-1869, pg 186 (1867 Oct 8) Junior Green Warden
   Proceedings 1861-1869, pg 186 (1867 Oct 8) committee
   Proceedings 1861-1869, pg 187 (1867 Oct 8) committee
   Proceedings 1861-1869, pg 192 (1867 Oct 8) Denver Lodge No. 5
   Proceedings 1861-1869, pg 202 (1868 Oct 6) Denver Lodge No. 5
   Proceedings 1861-1869, pg 212 (1868 Oct 6) warrant paid
   Proceedings 1861-1869, pg 219 (1868 Oct 7) Grand Orator
   Proceedings 1861-1869, pg 219 (1868 Oct 7) Denver Lodge No. 5
   Proceedings 1861-1869, pg 223 (1868 Oct 7) Denver Lodge No. 5
   Proceedings 1861-1869, pg 287 (1869 Sept 28) Grand Orator
   Proceedings 1861-1869, pg 288 (1869 Sept 28) Denver Lodge No 5
   Proceedings 1861-1869, pg 300 (1869 Sept 29) Denver Lodge No. 5
   Proceedings 1861-1869, pg 302 (1869 Sept 29) committee
   Proceedings 1861-1869, pg 304 (1869 Sept 29) Denver Lodge No. 5
   Proceedings 1861-1869, pg 315 (1869 Sept 29) Junior Grand Warden, 1866
   Proceedings 1870, pg 12 (1870 Sept 27) committee
   Proceedings 1870, pg 21 (1870 Sept 28), Denver Lodge No. 5, Denver
   Proceedings 1870, pg 32 (1870 Sept 28) Junior Grand Warden, 1866
   Proceedings 1870, pg 107 (1869 Sept 16) Grand Lodge of Colorado
   Proceedings 1871, pg 19 (1871 Sept 27) Denver Lodge No. 5
   Proceedings 1871, pg 34 (1871 Sept 27) Junior Grand Warden, 1866
   Proceedings 1872, pg 19 (1872 Sept 24), Denver Lodge No. 5, Denver
   Proceedings 1872, pg 42 (1872 Sept 24) Junior Grand Warden, 1866
   Proceedings 1873, pg 37 (1873 Oct 1), Denver Lodge No. 5, Denver
   Proceedings 1873, pg 58 (1873 Oct 1) Junior Grand Warden, 1866
   Proceedings 1874, pg 211 (1874 Sept 30), Denver Lodge No. 5, Denver
   Proceedings 1875, pg 75 (1875 Sept 22) Denver Lodge No. 5
   Proceedings 1876, pg 30 (1876 Sept 20) Denver Lodge No. 5

Greenleaf, Lawrence N
   Proceedings 1874, pg 206 (1874 Sept 30) Junior Grand Warden, 1866
   Proceedings 1875, pg 93 (1875 Sept 22) Junior Grand Warden, 1866

Greenslip, G H
   Proceedings 1861-1869, pg 305 (1869 Sept 29) Denver Lodge No. 5

Greenslit, G H
   Proceedings 1861-1869, pg 149 (1865 Nov 7), Nevada Lodge No. 4, Nevadaville
   Proceedings 1861-1869, pg 167 (1866 Oct 2) Denver Lodge No. 5

Greenslit, Geo H
   Proceedings 1861-1869, pg 192 (1867 Oct 8) Denver Lodge No. 5
   Proceedings 1861-1869, pg 223 (1868 Oct 7) Denver Lodge No. 5
   Proceedings 1870, pg 21 (1870 Sept 28), Denver Lodge No. 5, Denver
   Proceedings 1871, pg 19 (1871 Sept 27) Denver Lodge No. 5
   Proceedings 1872, pg 19 (1872 Sept 24), Denver Lodge No. 5, Denver
   Proceedings 1873, pg 38 (1873 Oct 1), Denver Lodge No. 5, Denver, Striken from the rolls

Gregg, D C
   Proceedings 1873, pg 48 (1873 Oct 1), Laramie Lodge No. 18, Laramie, Wyoming Territory, Apprentice
   Proceedings 1874, pg 224 (1874 Sept 30), Laramie Lodge No. 18, Laramie City, Apprentice

Gregg, J E
   Proceedings 1861-1869, pg 77 (1862 Nov 4), Nevada Lodge No. 4, Nevadaville
   Proceedings 1861-1869, pg 148 (1865 Nov 7), Nevada Lodge No. 4, Nevadaville

Gregg, J E, cont.
    Proceedings 1861-1869, pg 166 (1866 Oct 2), Nevada Lodge No. 4, Nevadaville
    Proceedings 1861-1869, pg 192 (1867 Oct 8), Nevada Lodge No. 4, Nevadaville
    Proceedings 1861-1869, pg 304 (1869 Sept 29), Nevada Lodge No. 4, Nevadaville
    Proceedings 1871, pg 18 (1871 Sept 27), Nevada Lodge No. 4, Bald Mountain

Gregg, John E
    Proceedings 1861-1869, pg 111 (1863 Nov 3), Nevada Lodge No. 4, Nevadaville
    Proceedings 1861-1869, pg 132 (1864 Nov 8), Nevada Lodge No. 4, Nevadaville
    Proceedings 1861-1869, pg 222 (1868 Oct 7), Nevada Lodge No. 4, Nevadaville
    Proceedings 1870, pg 20 (1870 Sept 28), Nevada Lodge No. 4, Nevadaville
    Proceedings 1872, pg 19 (1872 Sept 24), Nevada Lodge No. 4, Bald Mountain
    Proceedings 1873, pg 36 (1873 Oct 1), Nevada Lodge No. 4, Nevada, Dimitted

Gregory, Jackson
    Proceedings 1876, pg 44 (1876 Sept 20), Las Animas Lodge No. 28, Trinidad

Gregory, James
    Proceedings 1875, pg 91 (1875 Sept 22), Las Animas Lodge U D, Trinidad

Grench, B B
    Proceedings 1861-1869, pg 325 (1868 Nov 8) Grand Master, Grand Lodge of District of Columbia

Grenfell, Geo E
    Proceedings 1876, pg 41 (1876 Sept 20), St Vrain Lodge No. 23, Longmont, Apprentice

Grey, O C
    Proceedings 1870, pg 43 (1869 Nov 1) Grand Lodge of Arkansas

Griffin, Fred F
    Proceedings 1873, pg 39 (1873 Oct 1), Union Lodge No. 7, Denver
    Proceedings 1874, pg 214 (1874 Sept 30), Union Lodge No. 7, Denver
    Proceedings 1875, pg 78 (1875 Sept 22), Union Lodge No. 7, Denver

Griffin, Frederick F
    Proceedings 1876, pg 33 (1876 Sept 20), Union Lodge No. 7, Denver

Griffith, Charles W
    Proceedings 1874, pg 214 (1874 Sept 30), Union Lodge No. 7, Denver
    Proceedings 1876, pg 33 (1876 Sept 20), Union Lodge No. 7, Denver

Griffith, Chas W
    Proceedings 1875, pg 78 (1875 Sept 22), Union Lodge No. 7, Denver

Griffith, G E
    Proceedings 1876, pg 41 (1876 Sept 20), Weston Lodge No. 22, Littleton

Griffith, George
    Proceedings 1873, pg 51 (1873 Oct 1), Weston Lodge No. 22, Littleton
    Proceedings 1874, pg 226 (1874 Sept 30), Weston Lodge No. 22, Littleton
    Proceedings 1875, pg 88 (1875 Sept 22), Weston Lodge No. 22, Littleton

Griger, David
    Proceedings 1876, pg 32 (1876 Sept 20), Union Lodge No. 7, Denver

Griggs, Albert O
    Proceedings 1861-1869, pg 226 (1868 Oct 7), Empire Lodge No. 8, Empire City
    Proceedings 1861-1869, pg 308 (1869 Sept 29), Empire Lodge No. 8, Empire City
    Proceedings 1870, pg 24 (1870 Sept 28), Empire Lodge No. 8, Empire
    Proceedings 1873, pg 41 (1873 Oct 1), Empire Lodge No. 8, Empire
    Proceedings 1874, pg 215 (1874 Sept 30), Empire Lodge No. 8, Empire
    Proceedings 1872, pg 23 (1872 Sept 24), Empire Lodge No. 8, Empire

Grill, H H T
    Proceedings 1861-1869, pg 230 (1868 Oct 7), Germania Lodge U D, Denver

Griswold, Charles
    Proceedings 1874, pg 85 (1874 Sept 30) Grand Lodge of Minnesota

Griswold, Chas
    Proceedings 1873, pg 60 (1873 Oct 1) Grand Lodge of Minnesota, Red Wing
    Proceedings 1874, pg 204 (1874 Sept 30) Grand Lodge of Minnesota, Red Wing

Griswold, L D
    Proceedings 1871, pg 26 (1871 Sept 27), Mount Moriah Lodge No. 15, Canon City
    Proceedings 1872, pg 28 (1872 Sept 24), Mount Moriah Lodge No. 15, Canon City
    Proceedings 1873, pg 45 (1873 Oct 1), Mount Moriah Lodge No. 15, Canon City
    Proceedings 1874, pg 220 (1874 Sept 30), Mount Moriah Lodge No. 15, Canon City
    Proceedings 1875, pg 84 (1875 Sept 22), Mount Moriah Lodge No. 15, Canon City
    Proceedings 1876, pg 37 (1876 Sept 20), Mount Moriah Lodge No. 15, Canon City

Grocer, J A
    Proceedings 1873, pg 48 (1873 Oct 1), Laramie Lodge No. 18, Laramie, Wyoming Territory

Groesbeck, J B
    Proceedings 1872, pg 28 (1872 Sept 24), Columbia Lodge No. 14, Boulder, Dimitted

Proceedings 1874, pg 219 (1874 Sept 30), Columbia Lodge No. 14, Boulder, Boulder County

Groesbeck, James B
Proceedings 1875, pg 83 (1875 Sept 22), Columbia Lodge No. 14, Boulder
Proceedings 1871, pg 26 (1871 Sept 27), Columbia Lodge No. 14, Boulder City, Apprentice
Proceedings 1876, pg 36 (1876 Sept 20), Columbia Lodge No. 14, Boulder

Grover, J A
Proceedings 1872, pg 32 (1872 Sept 24), Laramie Lodge No. 18, Laramie, Wyoming Territory
Proceedings 1874, pg 223 (1874 Sept 30), Laramie Lodge No. 18, Laramie City

Groves, James R
Proceedings 1871, pg 19 (1871 Sept 27) Denver Lodge No. 5, Apprentice
Proceedings 1874, pg 212 (1874 Sept 30), Denver Lodge No. 5, Denver
Proceedings 1875, pg 76 (1875 Sept 22) Denver Lodge No. 5, Stricken from the rolls

Groves, Jas R
Proceedings 1872, pg 19 (1872 Sept 24), Denver Lodge No. 5, Denver
Proceedings 1873, pg 37 (1873 Oct 1), Denver Lodge No. 5, Denver

Grovestock, John
Proceedings 1875, pg 84 (1875 Sept 22), Mount Moriah Lodge No. 15, Canon City

Guier, D C
Proceedings 1861-1869, pg 310 (1869 Sept 29), El Paso Lodge No. 13, Colorado City

Guilbert
Proceedings 1861-1869, pg 250 (1867 June 4) Grand Lodge of Iowa
Proceedings 1870, pg 11 (1870 Sept 27), of Dubuque, IA,, Editor, The Evergreen
Proceedings 1861-1869, pg 245 (1867 Nov 7) of Iowa

Guin, John T
Proceedings 1872, pg 28 (1872 Sept 24), Columbia Lodge No. 14, Boulder

Guin, Thomas J
Proceedings 1873, pg 45 (1873 Oct 1), Columbia Lodge No. 14, Boulder, Dimitted

Guinn, John T
Proceedings 1870, pg 28 (1870 Sept 28), Columbia Lodge No. 14, Boulder City, Fellowcraft
Proceedings 1871, pg 25 (1871 Sept 27), Columbia Lodge No. 14, Boulder City

Guire, D C
Proceedings 1861-1869, pg 228 (1868 Oct 7), El Paso Lodge No. 13, Colorado City, Apprentice
Proceedings 1873, pg 43 (1873 Oct 1), El Paso Lodge No. 13, Colorado City
Proceedings 1876, pg 36 (1876 Sept 20), El Paso Lodge No. 13, Colorado City

Guire, David C
Proceedings 1870, pg 27 (1870 Sept 28), El Paso Lodge No. 13, Colorado City
Proceedings 1871, pg 25 (1871 Sept 27), El Paso Lodge No. 13, Colorado City
Proceedings 1874, pg 218 (1874 Sept 30), El Paso Lodge No. 13, Colorado Springs
Proceedings 1875, pg 82 (1875 Sept 22), El Paso Lodge No. 13, Colorado Springs

Gunn, Spencer
Proceedings 1873, pg 17 (1873 Oct 1), petition for a Lodge at Middle Boulder, Boulder County to be called Grand Island Lodge
Proceedings 1873, pg 42 (1873 Oct 1), Black Hawk Lodge No. 11, Black Hawk
Proceedings 1874, pg 7 (1874 Sept 29) petition for a lodge at Middle Boulder refused
Proceedings 1874, pg 216 (1874 Sept 30), Black Hawk Lodge No. 11, Black Hawk
Proceedings 1875, pg 80 (1875 Sept 22) Black Hawk Lodge No. 11
Proceedings 1876, pg 34 (1876 Sept 20) Black Hawk Lodge No. 11

Gurley, Charles D
Proceedings 1876, pg 33 (1876 Sept 20), Union Lodge No. 7, Denver

Gurley, Chas D
Proceedings 1875, pg 78 (1875 Sept 22), Union Lodge No. 7, Denver

Gurley, E W
Proceedings 1871, pg 15 (1871 Sept 27) Senior Grand Warden
Proceedings 1871, pg 30 (1871 Sept 27), Occidental Lodge U D, Greeley
Proceedings 1872, pg 34 (1872 Sept 24), Occidental Lodge No. 20, Greeley, Suspended
Proceedings 1874, pg 226 (1874 Sept 30), Occidental Lodge No. 20, Greeley, Demitted
Proceedings 1874, pg 226 (1874 Sept 30), Occidental Lodge No. 20, Greeley, Reinstated

Gurley, G W
Proceedings 1871, pg 7 (1870 Nov 29), Occidental Lodge U D, Greeley

Gutshall, S P
Proceedings 1870, pg 27 (1870 Sept 28), El Paso Lodge No. 13, Colorado City, Fellowcraft
Proceedings 1873, pg 43 (1873 Oct 1), El Paso Lodge No. 13, Colorado City
Proceedings 1876, pg 36 (1876 Sept 20), El Paso Lodge No. 13, Colorado City

Gutshall, Sam'l P
Proceedings 1874, pg 218 (1874 Sept 30), El Paso Lodge No. 13, Colorado Springs

Gutshall, Samuel F
Proceedings 1872, pg 27 (1872 Sept 24), El Paso Lodge No. 13, Colorado City

Gutshall, Samuel P
   Proceedings 1871, pg 25 (1871 Sept 27), El Paso Lodge No. 13, Colorado City
   Proceedings 1875, pg 82 (1875 Sept 22), El Paso Lodge No. 13, Colorado Springs

Gutterson, Charles L
   Proceedings 1876, pg 37 (1876 Sept 20), Columbia Lodge No. 14, Boulder

Guy, J C
   Proceedings 1861-1869, pg 112 (1863 Nov 3) Denver Lodge No. 5, dimitted

Guyaze, Julius
   Proceedings 1875, pg 83 (1875 Sept 22), Columbia Lodge No. 14, Boulder, Apprentice

Haas, Herman
   Proceedings 1871, pg 27 (1871 Sept 27), Cheyenne Lodge No. 16, Cheyenne, Wyoming Territory, Apprentice
   Proceedings 1872, pg 29 (1872 Sept 24), Cheyenne Lodge No. 16, Cheyenne, Wyoming Territory
   Proceedings 1873, pg 46 (1873 Oct 1), Cheyenne Lodge No. 16, Cheyenne, Wyoming Territory
   Proceedings 1874, pg 220 (1874 Sept 30), Cheyenne Lodge No. 16, Cheyenne, Wyoming Territory

Hacker
   Proceedings 1861-1869, pg 213 (1868 Oct 6) Grand Secretary of Indiana

Hadden, George
   Proceedings 1874, pg 220 (1874 Sept 30), Mount Moriah Lodge No. 15, Canon City
   Proceedings 1875, pg 84 (1875 Sept 22), Mount Moriah Lodge No. 15, Canon City
   Proceedings 1876, pg 38 (1876 Sept 20), Mount Moriah Lodge No. 15, Canon City

Haff, Jacob
   Proceedings 1873, pg 37 (1873 Oct 1), Denver Lodge No. 5, Denver
   Proceedings 1874, pg 211 (1874 Sept 30), Denver Lodge No. 5, Denver
   Proceedings 1875, pg 76 (1875 Sept 22) Denver Lodge No. 5, Stricken from the rolls

Haffy, John B
   Proceedings 1876, pg 44 (1876 Sept 20) Del Norte Lodge U D

Hafner, O
   Proceedings 1876, pg 36 (1876 Sept 20), El Paso Lodge No. 13, Colorado City

Haines, J H
   Proceedings 1861-1869, pg 77 (1862 Nov 4), Nevada Lodge No. 4, Nevadaville
   Proceedings 1861-1869, pg 111 (1863 Nov 3), Nevada Lodge No. 4, Nevadaville
   Proceedings 1861-1869, pg 132 (1864 Nov 8), Nevada Lodge No. 4, Nevadaville, dimitted

Haines, W B
   Proceedings 1875, pg 84 (1875 Sept 22), Mount Moriah Lodge No. 15, Canon City
   Proceedings 1876, pg 38 (1876 Sept 20), Mount Moriah Lodge No. 15, Canon City

Hains, J T
   Proceedings 1874, pg 220 (1874 Sept 30), Mount Moriah Lodge No. 15, Canon City

Hains, Robert
   Proceedings 1871, pg 23 (1871 Sept 27), Black Hawk Lodge No. 11, Black Hawk

Hair, John A
   Proceedings 1874, pg 211 (1874 Sept 30), Denver Lodge No. 5, Denver
   Proceedings 1875, pg 75 (1875 Sept 22) Denver Lodge No. 5
   Proceedings 1876, pg 31 (1876 Sept 20) Denver Lodge No. 5

Haires, Jesse
   Proceedings 1874, pg 225 (1874 Sept 30), Occidental Lodge No. 20, Greeley

Hale, N M
   Proceedings 1861-1869, pg 76 (1862 Nov 4), Summit Lodge No. 2, Parkville, Apprentice

Haley, Ora
   Proceedings 1870, pg 31 (1870 Sept 28), Laramie Lodge No. 18, Laramie, Wyoming Territory
   Proceedings 1871, pg 29 (1871 Sept 27), Laramie Lodge No. 18, Laramie, Wyoming Territory
   Proceedings 1872, pg 31 (1872 Sept 24), Laramie Lodge No. 18, Laramie, Wyoming Territory
   Proceedings 1873, pg 48 (1873 Oct 1), Laramie Lodge No. 18, Laramie, Wyoming Territory
   Proceedings 1874, pg 223 (1874 Sept 30), Laramie Lodge No. 18, Laramie City

Hall
   Proceedings 1861-1869, pg 186 (1867 Oct 8) motion
   Proceedings 1870, pg 60 (1869 Oct 20) Grand Lodge of Kansas
   Proceedings 1870, pg 90 (1869 Oct 4) Grand Lodge of Colorado

Hall (Collier & Hall)
   Proceedings 1861-1869, pg 182 (1867 Oct 7) warrant paid
   Proceedings 1861-1869, pg 212 (1868 Oct 6) warrant paid

Hall, Assyria
   Proceedings 1874, pg 228 (1874 Sept 30), Doric Lodge U D, Fairplay, Apprentice

Hall, Asyria
   Proceedings 1875, pg 89 (1875 Sept 22), Doric Lodge No. 25, Fairplay
   Proceedings 1876, pg 42 (1876 Sept 20), Doric Lodge No. 25, Fairplay

Hall, B S
    Proceedings 1861-1869, pg 171 (1866 Oct 2), El Paso U D, Colorado City, Apprentice
    Proceedings 1861-1869, pg 196 (1867 Oct 8), El Paso Lodge U D, Colorado City
    Proceedings 1861-1869, pg 228 (1868 Oct 7), El Paso Lodge No. 13, Colorado City
    Proceedings 1861-1869, pg 310 (1869 Sept 29), El Paso Lodge No. 13, Colorado City
    Proceedings 1870, pg 27 (1870 Sept 28), El Paso Lodge No. 13, Colorado City
    Proceedings 1873, pg 43 (1873 Oct 1), El Paso Lodge No. 13, Colorado City

Hall, Benj F
    Proceedings 1872, pg 27 (1872 Sept 24), El Paso Lodge No. 13, Colorado City

Hall, Benj S
    Proceedings 1874, pg 218 (1874 Sept 30), El Paso Lodge No. 13, Colorado Springs

Hall, Benjamin F
    Proceedings 1871, pg 25 (1871 Sept 27), El Paso Lodge No. 13, Colorado City

Hall, Benjamin S
    Proceedings 1875, pg 82 (1875 Sept 22), El Paso Lodge No. 13, Colorado Springs, Stricken from the rolls

Hall, C L
    Proceedings 1861-1869, pg 305 (1869 Sept 29) Denver Lodge No. 5
    Proceedings 1870, pg 21 (1870 Sept 28), Denver Lodge No. 5, Denver
    Proceedings 1872, pg 20 (1872 Sept 24), Denver Lodge No. 5, Denver

Hall, Charles L
    Proceedings 1861-1869, pg 193 (1867 Oct 8) Denver Lodge No. 5

Hall, Chas L
    Proceedings 1861-1869, pg 223 (1868 Oct 7) Denver Lodge No. 5

Hall, Frank
    Proceedings 1861-1869, pg 134 (1864 Nov 8), Chivington Lodge No. 6, Central City, Fellowcraft
    Proceedings 1861-1869, pg 150 (1865 Nov 7), Chivington Lodge No. 6, Central City
    Proceedings 1861-1869, pg 168 (1866 Oct 2), Chivington Lodge No. 6, Central City
    Proceedings 1861-1869, pg 175 (1867 Oct 7) Senior Grand Deacon
    Proceedings 1861-1869, pg 176 (1867 Oct 7), Chivington Lodge No. 6, Central City
    Proceedings 1861-1869, pg 190 (1867 Oct 8) committee
    Proceedings 1861-1869, pg 193 (1867 Oct 8), Chivington Lodge No. 6, Central City
    Proceedings 1861-1869, pg 212 (1868 Oct 6) warrant paid
    Proceedings 1861-1869, pg 219 (1868 Oct 7) Grand Marshal
    Proceedings 1861-1869, pg 224 (1868 Oct 7), Chivington Lodge No. 6, Central City
    Proceedings 1861-1869, pg 286 (1867 Oct 7) Grand Lodge of Colorado
    Proceedings 1861-1869, pg 306 (1869 Sept 29), Central Lodge No. 6, Central City
    Proceedings 1870, pg 22 (1870 Sept 28), Central Lodge No. 6, Central City
    Proceedings 1871, pg 20 (1871 Sept 27), Central Lodge No. 6, Central
    Proceedings 1872, pg 21 (1872 Sept 24), Denver Lodge No. 5, Denver
    Proceedings 1873, pg 4 (1873 Sept 30) pall bearer for George M Randall
    Proceedings 1873, pg 38 (1873 Oct 1), Central Lodge No. 6, Central City
    Proceedings 1874, pg 213 (1874 Sept 30), Central Lodge No. 6, Central
    Proceedings 1875, pg 77 (1875 Sept 22), Central Lodge No. 6, Central City
    Proceedings 1876, pg 32 (1876 Sept 20), Central Lodge No. 6, Central City

Hall, G F
    Proceedings 1861-1869, pg 312 (1869 Sept 29), Pueblo Lodge No. 17, Pueblo

Hall, G W
    Proceedings 1861-1869, pg 112 (1863 Nov 3), Nevada Lodge No. 4, Nevadaville, Apprentice
    Proceedings 1861-1869, pg 132 (1864 Nov 8), Nevada Lodge No. 4, Nevadaville, Apprentice
    Proceedings 1861-1869, pg 151 (1865 Nov 7), Empire Lodge U D, Empire City, Fellowcraft

Hall, Geo F
    Proceedings 1870, pg 30 (1870 Sept 28), Pueblo Lodge No. 17, Pueblo
    Proceedings 1872, pg 31 (1872 Sept 24), Pueblo Lodge No. 17, Pueblo

Hall, Geo M
    Proceedings 1870, pg 104 (1869 June 9) Grand Master, Grand Lodge of Vermont
    Proceedings 1872, pg 90 (1872 Sept 24) Grand Lodge of Vermont
    Proceedings 1872, pg 23 (1872 Sept 24), Empire Lodge No. 8, Empire

Hall, George F
    Proceedings 1871, pg 28 (1871 Sept 27), Pueblo Lodge No. 17, Pueblo
    Proceedings 1873, pg 47 (1873 Oct 1), Pueblo Lodge No. 17, Pueblo
    Proceedings 1874, pg 223 (1874 Sept 30), Pueblo Lodge No. 17, Pueblo, Pueblo County, Stricken from the rolls

Hall, George M
    Proceedings 1861-1869, pg 348 (1868 June 10) Grand Master, Grand Lodge of Vermont

Hall, George W
    Proceedings 1873, pg 41 (1873 Oct 1), Empire Lodge No. 8, Empire
    Proceedings 1874, pg 215 (1874 Sept 30), Empire Lodge No. 8, Empire

Colorado's Territorial Masons

Hall, Hairus W
    Proceedings 1875, pg 81 (1875 Sept 22), Washington Lodge No. 12, Georgetown

Hall, J W
    Proceedings 1871, pg 24 (1871 Sept 27), Washington Lodge No. 12, Georgetown

Hall, Jairus W
    Proceedings 1861-1869, pg 227 (1868 Oct 7), Washington Lodge No. 12, Georgetown
    Proceedings 1861-1869, pg 309 (1869 Sept 29), Washington Lodge No. 12, Georgetown
    Proceedings 1870, pg 26 (1870 Sept 28), Washington Lodge No. 12, Georgetown
    Proceedings 1872, pg 25 (1872 Sept 24), Washington Lodge No. 12, Georgetown
    Proceedings 1876, pg 35 (1876 Sept 20), Washington Lodge No. 12, Georgetown
    Proceedings 1861-1869, pg 179 (1867 Oct 7), Washington Lodge No. 12, Georgetown
    Proceedings 1873, pg 42 (1873 Oct 1), Washington Lodge No. 12, Georgetown
    Proceedings 1874, pg 217 (1874 Sept 30), Washington Lodge No. 12, Georgetown

Hall, Joseph F
    Proceedings 1876, pg 32 (1876 Sept 20), Central Lodge No. 6, Central City

Hall, M E
    Proceedings 1861-1869, pg 112 (1863 Nov 3) Denver Lodge No. 5
    Proceedings 1861-1869, pg 149 (1865 Nov 7), Nevada Lodge No. 4, Nevadaville, dimitted

Hall, Moses
    Proceedings 1861-1869, pg 307 (1869 Sept 29), Central Lodge No. 6, Central City, Apprentice
    Proceedings 1870, pg 22 (1870 Sept 28), Central Lodge No. 6, Central City
    Proceedings 1871, pg 20 (1871 Sept 27), Central Lodge No. 6, Central
    Proceedings 1872, pg 21 (1872 Sept 24), Denver Lodge No. 5, Denver
    Proceedings 1873, pg 39 (1873 Oct 1), Central Lodge No. 6, Central City
    Proceedings 1874, pg 213 (1874 Sept 30), Central Lodge No. 6, Central
    Proceedings 1875, pg 77 (1875 Sept 22), Central Lodge No. 6, Central City
    Proceedings 1876, pg 32 (1876 Sept 20), Central Lodge No. 6, Central City

Hall, N W
    Proceedings 1873, pg 50 (1873 Oct 1), Occidental Lodge No. 20, Greeley

Hall, Niagara W
    Proceedings 1874, pg 225 (1874 Sept 30), Occidental Lodge No. 20, Greeley
    Proceedings 1875, pg 87 (1875 Sept 22), Occidental Lodge No. 20, Greeley
    Proceedings 1876, pg 40 (1876 Sept 20), Occidental Lodge No. 20, Greeley

Hall, Prince
    Proceedings 1861-1869, pg 334 (1784 Sept 29) African Lodge No. 459
    Proceedings 1870, pg 69 (1787 Apr 29) African Lodge at Boston
    Proceedings 1870, pg 72 (1784 Sept 29) African Lodge at Boston
    Proceedings 1870, pg 73 (1784 Sept 29) African Lodge at Boston
    Proceedings 1870, pg 75 (1813) African Lodge at Boston
    Proceedings 1870, pg 76 (1789 June 4) African Lodge at Boston
    Proceedings 1870, pg 76 (1789 Nov 9) African Lodge at Boston
    Proceedings 1870, pg 77 (1784 Sept 29)

Hall, Robert D
    Proceedings 1873, pg 35 (1873 Oct 1), Golden City Lodge No. 1, Golden City
    Proceedings 1876, pg 29 (1876 Sept 20) Golden City Lodge No. 1

Hall, Robt D
    Proceedings 1875, pg 73 (1875 Sept 22) Golden City Lodge No. 1

Hall, Rob't D
    Proceedings 1874, pg 209 (1874 Sept 30), Golden City Lodge No. 1, Golden City

Hall, S C
    Proceedings 1861-1869, pg 311 (1869 Sept 29), Mount Moriah Lodge No. 15, Canon City
    Proceedings 1870, pg 28 (1870 Sept 28), Mount Moriah Lodge No. 15, Canon City
    Proceedings 1871, pg 26 (1871 Sept 27), Mount Moriah Lodge No. 15, Canon City
    Proceedings 1872, pg 29 (1872 Sept 24), Mount Moriah Lodge No. 15, Canon City
    Proceedings 1873, pg 45 (1873 Oct 1), Mount Moriah Lodge No. 15, Canon City
    Proceedings 1875, pg 89 (1875 Sept 22), Doric Lodge No. 25, Fairplay, Demitted

Hall, Sebastian C
    Proceedings 1874, pg 228 (1874 Sept 30), Doric Lodge U D, Fairplay

Hall, W J
    Proceedings 1876, pg 34 (1876 Sept 20) Black Hawk Lodge No. 11, Fellow Craft

Hall, Wm E
    Proceedings 1861-1869, pg 133 (1864 Nov 8) Denver Lodge No. 5

Haller, Granville O
    Proceedings 1874, pg 131 (1874 Sept 30) Grand Lodge of Washington

Hallet, Moses
    Proceedings 1861-1869, pg 149 (1865 Nov 7), Nevada Lodge No. 4, Nevadaville, Apprentice

Proceedings 1861-1869, pg 193 (1867 Oct 8) Denver Lodge No. 5

Proceedings 1861-1869, pg 223 (1868 Oct 7) Denver Lodge No. 5

Proceedings 1870, pg 21 (1870 Sept 28), Denver Lodge No. 5, Denver

Proceedings 1872, pg 20 (1872 Sept 24), Denver Lodge No. 5, Denver

Hallett, M

Proceedings 1861-1869, pg 305 (1869 Sept 29) Denver Lodge No. 5

Hallett, Moses

Proceedings 1861-1869, pg 133 (1864 Nov 8) Denver Lodge No. 5, Apprentice

Proceedings 1861-1869, pg 167 (1866 Oct 2) Denver Lodge No. 5, Apprentice

Proceedings 1871, pg 19 (1871 Sept 27) Denver Lodge No. 5

Proceedings 1873, pg 37 (1873 Oct 1), Denver Lodge No. 5, Denver

Proceedings 1874, pg 211 (1874 Sept 30), Denver Lodge No. 5, Denver

Proceedings 1875, pg 75 (1875 Sept 22) Denver Lodge No. 5

Proceedings 1876, pg 31 (1876 Sept 20) Denver Lodge No. 5

Halverson, Christian

Proceedings 1873, pg 44 (1873 Oct 1), Columbia Lodge No. 14, Boulder

Proceedings 1874, pg 219 (1874 Sept 30), Columbia Lodge No. 14, Boulder, Boulder County

Halvorsen, Christopher

Proceedings 1875, pg 83 (1875 Sept 22), Columbia Lodge No. 14, Boulder

Halvorson, Christen

Proceedings 1872, pg 28 (1872 Sept 24), Columbia Lodge No. 14, Boulder

Proceedings 1876, pg 37 (1876 Sept 20), Columbia Lodge No. 14, Boulder

Hamar, D A

Proceedings 1861-1869, pg 111 (1863 Nov 3), Nevada Lodge No. 4, Nevadaville, Fellowcraft,

Hambel

Proceedings 1875, pg 29 (1875 Sept 21) presented the case of George A Smith

Proceedings 1876, pg 20 (1876 Sept 20) committee

Proceedings 1876, pg 25 (1876 Sept 20) resolution

Proceedings 1876, pg 26 (1876 Sept 20) motion

Hambel, J R

Proceedings 1861-1869, pg 227 (1868 Oct 7), Washington Lodge No. 12, Georgetown

Proceedings 1871, pg 4 (1871 Sept 26), Washington Lodge No. 12, Georgetown

Proceedings 1871, pg 24 (1871 Sept 27), Washington Lodge No. 12, Georgetown

Proceedings 1872, pg 4 (1872 Sept 24), Black Hawk Lodge No. 11, Black Hawk

Proceedings 1873, pg 6 (1873 Sept 30), Washington Lodge No. 12, Georgetown

Proceedings 1874, pg 6 (1874 Sept 29) committee

Proceedings 1874, pg 36 (1874 Sept 30) per diem

Proceedings 1876, pg 6 (1876 Sept 19) committee

Proceedings 1876, pg 23 (1876 Sept 20) committee

Hambel, John R

Proceedings 1870, pg 26 (1870 Sept 28), Washington Lodge No. 12, Georgetown

Proceedings 1872, pg 25 (1872 Sept 24), Washington Lodge No. 12, Georgetown

Proceedings 1873, pg 14 (1873 Sept 30) Grand Teller

Proceedings 1873, pg 42 (1873 Oct 1), Washington Lodge No. 12, Georgetown

Proceedings 1874, pg 6 (1874 Sept 29), Washington Lodge No. 12, Georgetown

Proceedings 1874, pg 217 (1874 Sept 30), Washington Lodge No. 12, Georgetown

Proceedings 1875, pg 17 (1875 Sept 21), Washington Lodge No. 12, Georgetown

Proceedings 1875, pg 17 (1875 Sept 21) committee

Proceedings 1875, pg 24 (1875 Sept 21) donation to the library fund

Proceedings 1875, pg 34 (1875 Sept 22) committee

Proceedings 1875, pg 38 (1875 Sept 22) per diem

Proceedings 1875, pg 81 (1875 Sept 22), Washington Lodge No. 12, Georgetown

Proceedings 1876, pg cover (1876 Sept 20) committee, Georgetown

Proceedings 1876, pg 5 (1876 Sept 19), Washington Lodge No. 12, Georgetown

Proceedings 1876, pg 22 (1876 Sept 20) committee

Proceedings 1876, pg 22 (1876 Sept 20), Washington Lodge No. 12, Georgetown

Proceedings 1876, pg 24 (1876 Sept 20) committee

Proceedings 1876, pg 26 (1876 Sept 20) committee

Proceedings 1876, pg 34 (1876 Sept 20), Washington Lodge No. 12, Georgetown

Proceedings 1876, pg 35 (1876 Sept 20), Washington Lodge No. 12, Georgetown

Hamberger, Ben

Proceedings 1861-1869, pg 312 (1869 Sept 29), Cheyenne Lodge No. 16, Cheyenne

Hamberger, Benj

Proceedings 1870, pg 29 (1870 Sept 28), Cheyenne Lodge No. 16, Cheyenne, Wyoming Territory

Proceedings 1872, pg 29 (1872 Sept 24), Cheyenne Lodge No. 16, Cheyenne, Wyoming Territory

Hamble, John R

Proceedings 1861-1869, pg 309 (1869 Sept 29), Washington Lodge No. 12, Georgetown

Hamblin, Oliver T

Proceedings 1873, pg 45 (1873 Oct 1), Columbia Lodge No. 14, Boulder, Dimitted

Hamburger, Benj

Proceedings 1873, pg 46 (1873 Oct 1), Cheyenne Lodge No. 16, Cheyenne, Wyoming Territory

Colorado's Territorial Masons

Hamburger, Benjamin
Proceedings 1871, pg 27 (1871 Sept 27), Cheyenne Lodge No. 16, Cheyenne, Wyoming Territory
Proceedings 1874, pg 221 (1874 Sept 30), Cheyenne Lodge No. 16, Cheyenne, Wyoming Territory

Hamer, D A
Proceedings 1861-1869, pg 132 (1864 Nov 8), Nevada Lodge No. 4, Nevadaville
Proceedings 1861-1869, pg 148 (1865 Nov 7), Nevada Lodge No. 4, Nevadaville
Proceedings 1861-1869, pg 166 (1866 Oct 2), Nevada Lodge No. 4, Nevadaville

Hamilton, J F
Proceedings 1861-1869, pg 102 (1863 Nov 3) petition for formation of a new lodge in Denver

Hamilton, W E
Proceedings 1875, pg 80 (1875 Sept 22) Black Hawk Lodge No. 11
Proceedings 1876, pg 34 (1876 Sept 20) Black Hawk Lodge No. 11

Hamilton, William E
Proceedings 1874, pg 216 (1874 Sept 30), Black Hawk Lodge No. 11, Black Hawk

Hamilton, Wm B
Proceedings 1875, pg 90 (1875 Sept 22), Huerfano Lodge U D, Walsenburg
Proceedings 1876, pg 43 (1876 Sept 20), Huerfano Lodge No. 27, Walsenburg

Hamilton, Wm E
Proceedings 1872, pg 24 (1872 Sept 24), Black Hawk Lodge No. 11, Black Hawk
Proceedings 1873, pg 42 (1873 Oct 1), Black Hawk Lodge No. 11, Black Hawk

Hamlin, A D
Proceedings 1872, pg 31 (1872 Sept 24), Pueblo Lodge No. 17, Pueblo
Proceedings 1873, pg 47 (1873 Oct 1), Pueblo Lodge No. 17, Pueblo
Proceedings 1874, pg 222 (1874 Sept 30), Pueblo Lodge No. 17, Pueblo, Pueblo County
Proceedings 1875, pg 85 (1875 Sept 22) Pueblo Lodge No. 17, died
Proceedings 1875, pg 94 (1875 Sept 22) Pueblo Lodge No. 17

Hamlin, O T
Proceedings 1870, pg 27 (1870 Sept 28), Columbia Lodge No. 14, Boulder City
Proceedings 1871, pg 25 (1871 Sept 27), Columbia Lodge No. 14, Boulder City
Proceedings 1872, pg 28 (1872 Sept 24), Columbia Lodge No. 14, Boulder
Proceedings 1872, pg 35 (1872 Sept 24), St Vrain Lodge No. 23, Longmont
Proceedings 1873, pg 51 (1873 Oct 1), St Vrain Lodge No. 23, Longmont
Proceedings 1874, pg 227 (1874 Sept 30), St Vrain No. 23, Longmont
Proceedings 1876, pg 41 (1876 Sept 20), St Vrain Lodge No. 23, Longmont

Hamlin, Oliver T
Proceedings 1861-1869, pg 311 (1869 Sept 29), Columbia Lodge No. 14, Boulder City

Hammond (Ferris & Hammond)
Proceedings 1874, pg 19 (1874 Sept 29), of Providence, RI

Hammond, H J
Proceedings 1861-1869, pg 134 (1864 Nov 8), Chivington Lodge No. 6, Central City
Proceedings 1861-1869, pg 150 (1865 Nov 7), Chivington Lodge No. 6, Central City
Proceedings 1861-1869, pg 168 (1866 Oct 2), Chivington Lodge No. 6, Central City
Proceedings 1861-1869, pg 194 (1867 Oct 8), Chivington Lodge No. 6, Central City, Dimitted,

Hamor
Proceedings 1870, pg 5 (1870 Sept 27) committee

Hamor, A
Proceedings 1861-1869, pg 288 (1869 Sept 28), Nevada Lodge No. 4, Nevadaville

Hamor, D A
Proceedings 1861-1869, pg 222 (1868 Oct 7), Nevada Lodge No. 4, Nevadaville
Proceedings 1861-1869, pg 299 (1869 Sept 29) Senior Grand Steward
Proceedings 1861-1869, pg 304 (1869 Sept 29), Nevada Lodge No. 4, Nevadaville
Proceedings 1870, pg 4 (1870 Sept 27), Nevada Lodge No. 4, Nevadaville
Proceedings 1870, pg 12 (1870 Sept 27) committee
Proceedings 1870, pg 16 (1870 Sept 28), Nevada Lodge No. 4, Nevadaville
Proceedings 1871, pg 18 (1871 Sept 27), Nevada Lodge No. 4, Bald Mountain
Proceedings 1875, pg 74 (1875 Sept 22), Nevada Lodge No. 4, Nevada

Hamor, David A
Proceedings 1861-1869, pg 191 (1867 Oct 8), Nevada Lodge No. 4, Nevadaville
Proceedings 1870, pg cover (1870 Sept 28) Grand Sword Bearer, Bald Mountain
Proceedings 1870, pg 13 (1870 Sept 27) Grand Sword Bearer
Proceedings 1870, pg 20 (1870 Sept 28), Nevada Lodge No. 4, Nevadaville
Proceedings 1872, pg 18 (1872 Sept 24), Nevada Lodge No. 4, Bald Mountain
Proceedings 1873, pg 36 (1873 Oct 1), Nevada Lodge No. 4, Nevada
Proceedings 1874, pg 210 (1874 Sept 30), Nevada Lodge No. 4, Bald Mountain, Gilpin County
Proceedings 1876, pg 30 (1876 Sept 20) Nevada Lodge No. 4

Hamor, Jas A
Proceedings 1870, pg 3 (1870 Sept 27) Junior Grand Steward

Colorado's Territorial Masons

Hamson, Conrad
Proceedings 1874, pg 217 (1874 Sept 30), Washington Lodge No. 12, Georgetown

Hanaeur, A
Proceedings 1861-1869, pg 77 (1862 Nov 4) Denver Lodge No. 5

Hananer, A
Proceedings 1861-1869, pg 223 (1868 Oct 7) Denver Lodge No. 5

Hanauer, A
Proceedings 1861-1869, pg 112 (1863 Nov 3) Denver Lodge No. 5
Proceedings 1861-1869, pg 124 (1864 Nov 8) Denver Lodge No. 5, Grand Steward
Proceedings 1861-1869, pg 133 (1864 Nov 8) Denver Lodge No. 5
Proceedings 1861-1869, pg 149 (1865 Nov 7), Nevada Lodge No. 4, Nevadaville
Proceedings 1861-1869, pg 167 (1866 Oct 2) Denver Lodge No. 5
Proceedings 1861-1869, pg 193 (1867 Oct 8) Denver Lodge No. 5
Proceedings 1861-1869, pg 305 (1869 Sept 29) Denver Lodge No. 5
Proceedings 1870, pg 21 (1870 Sept 28), Denver Lodge No. 5, Denver
Proceedings 1871, pg 19 (1871 Sept 27) Denver Lodge No. 5
Proceedings 1872, pg 19 (1872 Sept 24), Denver Lodge No. 5, Denver
Proceedings 1874, pg 211 (1874 Sept 30), Denver Lodge No. 5, Denver
Proceedings 1875, pg 75 (1875 Sept 22) Denver Lodge No. 5
Proceedings 1876, pg 31 (1876 Sept 20) Denver Lodge No. 5

Hanchet, E E
Proceedings 1861-1869, pg 226 (1868 Oct 7), Black Hawk Lodge No. 11, Black Hawk

Hanchet, Ed E
Proceedings 1861-1869, pg 196 (1867 Oct 8), Black Hawk Lodge No. 11, Black Hawk
Proceedings 1861-1869, pg 309 (1869 Sept 29), Black Hawk Lodge No. 11, Black Hawk, Dimitted

Hancock, C W
Proceedings 1872, pg 43 (1872 Sept 24) Washington, Grand Lodge of the District of Columbia

Hanenstine, W I
Proceedings 1871, pg 23 (1871 Sept 27), Black Hawk Lodge No. 11, Black Hawk, Apprentice

Hannauer, A
Proceedings 1873, pg 37 (1873 Oct 1), Denver Lodge No. 5, Denver

Hanschka, Richard
Proceedings 1875, pg 74 (1875 Sept 22), Nevada Lodge No. 4, Nevada

Hanschke, Richard
Proceedings 1876, pg 30 (1876 Sept 20) Nevada Lodge No. 4

Hansen, A J
Proceedings 1876, pg 41 (1876 Sept 20), St Vrain Lodge No. 23, Longmont

Hansen, Conrad
Proceedings 1861-1869, pg 227 (1868 Oct 7), Washington Lodge No. 12, Georgetown, Apprentice
Proceedings 1861-1869, pg 309 (1869 Sept 29), Washington Lodge No. 12, Georgetown
Proceedings 1870, pg 26 (1870 Sept 28), Washington Lodge No. 12, Georgetown
Proceedings 1871, pg 24 (1871 Sept 27), Washington Lodge No. 12, Georgetown
Proceedings 1872, pg 26 (1872 Sept 24), Washington Lodge No. 12, Georgetown
Proceedings 1873, pg 42 (1873 Oct 1), Washington Lodge No. 12, Georgetown
Proceedings 1875, pg 81 (1875 Sept 22), Washington Lodge No. 12, Georgetown
Proceedings 1876, pg 35 (1876 Sept 20), Washington Lodge No. 12, Georgetown

Hanson, Snyder
Proceedings 1873, pg 45 (1873 Oct 1), Columbia Lodge No. 14, Boulder, Apprentice

Happersett, J C G
Proceedings 1876, pg 45 (1876 Sept 20), King Solomon Lodge U D, West Las Animas

Harby, James
Proceedings 1861-1869, pg 78 (1862 Nov 4), Chivington Lodge No. 6, Central City, dimitted
Proceedings 1861-1869, pg 78 (1862 Nov 4), Chivington Lodge No. 6, Central City

Harder, John N
Proceedings 1875, pg 81 (1875 Sept 22), Washington Lodge No. 12, Georgetown
Proceedings 1876, pg 35 (1876 Sept 20), Washington Lodge No. 12, Georgetown

Hardesty, John F
Proceedings 1871, pg 18 (1871 Sept 27), Nevada Lodge No. 4, Bald Mountain
Proceedings 1872, pg 19 (1872 Sept 24), Nevada Lodge No. 4, Bald Mountain
Proceedings 1873, pg 36 (1873 Oct 1), Nevada Lodge No. 4, Nevada
Proceedings 1874, pg 210 (1874 Sept 30), Nevada Lodge No. 4, Bald Mountain, Gilpin County, Demitted

Hardin, M R
Proceedings 1875, pg 90 (1875 Sept 22), Huerfano Lodge U D, Walsenburg
Proceedings 1876, pg 48 (1876 Sept 20), Huerfano Lodge No. 27, Walsenburg, 1875 Oct 16

Hardy, I E
Proceedings 1861-1869, pg 3 (1861 Aug 2) Golden City Lodge No. 1

Colorado's Territorial Masons

Hardy, I E, cont.
Proceedings 1861-1869, pg 4 (1861 Aug 2) committee
Proceedings 1861-1869, pg 4 (1861 Aug 2) Golden City Lodge No. 1
Proceedings 1861-1869, pg 5 (1861 Aug 2) Grand Lecturer, Golden City

Hardy, Isaac E
Proceedings 1861-1869, pg 42 (1861 Dec 10) Golden City Lodge No. 1

Hardy, W H
Proceedings 1872, pg 43 (1872 Sept 24) Paulding, Grand Lodge of Mississippi

Hare, O T
Proceedings 1861-1869, pg 152 (1865 Nov 7), Helena City Lodge U D, Helena City, Montana Territory

Hare, W D
Proceedings 1870, pg 98 (1870 June 20) oration, Grand Lodge of Oregon

Harker, O H
Proceedings 1861-1869, pg 134 (1864 Nov 8), Chivington Lodge No. 6, Central City
Proceedings 1861-1869, pg 150 (1865 Nov 7), Chivington Lodge No. 6, Central City
Proceedings 1861-1869, pg 168 (1866 Oct 2), Chivington Lodge No. 6, Central City
Proceedings 1861-1869, pg 193 (1867 Oct 8), Chivington Lodge No. 6, Central City
Proceedings 1861-1869, pg 224 (1868 Oct 7), Chivington Lodge No. 6, Central City
Proceedings 1861-1869, pg 307 (1869 Sept 29), Central Lodge No. 6, Central City, Dimitted

Harker, Oliver H
Proceedings 1874, pg 219 (1874 Sept 30), Columbia Lodge No. 14, Boulder, Boulder County
Proceedings 1875, pg 83 (1875 Sept 22), Columbia Lodge No. 14, Boulder
Proceedings 1876, pg 37 (1876 Sept 20), Columbia Lodge No. 14, Boulder

Harkness, M K
Proceedings 1871, pg 8 (1871 Apr 8), Argenta Lodge U D, Salt Lake City
Proceedings 1871, pg 31 (1871 Sept 27), Argenta Lodge U D, Salt Lake City, Utah

Harlan, John
Proceedings 1873, pg 41 (1873 Oct 1), Black Hawk Lodge No. 11, Black Hawk
Proceedings 1874, pg 216 (1874 Sept 30), Black Hawk Lodge No. 11, Black Hawk
Proceedings 1875, pg 80 (1875 Sept 22) Black Hawk Lodge No. 11
Proceedings 1876, pg 34 (1876 Sept 20) Black Hawk Lodge No. 11

Harlan, Thomas
Proceedings 1870, pg 29 (1870 Sept 28), Cheyenne Lodge No. 16, Cheyenne, Wyoming Territory, Apprentice
Proceedings 1871, pg 27 (1871 Sept 27), Cheyenne Lodge No. 16, Cheyenne, Wyoming Territory
Proceedings 1872, pg 29 (1872 Sept 24), Cheyenne Lodge No. 16, Cheyenne, Wyoming Territory
Proceedings 1874, pg 221 (1874 Sept 30), Cheyenne Lodge No. 16, Cheyenne, Wyoming Territory, Demitted

Harlan, Thos
Proceedings 1873, pg 46 (1873 Oct 1), Cheyenne Lodge No. 16, Cheyenne, Wyoming Territory

Harlow, R G
Proceedings 1861-1869, pg 312 (1869 Sept 29), Cheyenne Lodge No. 16, Cheyenne
Proceedings 1870, pg 29 (1870 Sept 28), Cheyenne Lodge No. 16, Cheyenne, Wyoming Territory, Dimitted

Harlow, S C
Proceedings 1870, pg 29 (1870 Sept 28), Cheyenne Lodge No. 16, Cheyenne, Wyoming Territory
Proceedings 1871, pg 28 (1871 Sept 27), Cheyenne Lodge No. 16, Cheyenne, Wyoming Territory, Apprentice

Harlow, W H
Proceedings 1861-1869, pg 312 (1869 Sept 29), Cheyenne Lodge No. 16, Cheyenne
Proceedings 1870, pg 29 (1870 Sept 28), Cheyenne Lodge No. 16, Cheyenne, Wyoming Territory
Proceedings 1871, pg 28 (1871 Sept 27), Cheyenne Lodge No. 16, Cheyenne, Wyoming Territory, Apprentice

Harmer, William L
Proceedings 1876, pg 43 (1876 Sept 20), Huerfano Lodge No. 27, Walsenburg

Harmes, Wm L
Proceedings 1875, pg 90 (1875 Sept 22), Huerfano Lodge U D, Walsenburg, Fellowcraft

Harmon, G D
Proceedings 1872, pg 28 (1872 Sept 24), Columbia Lodge No. 14, Boulder, Apprentice

Harmon, Geo D
Proceedings 1870, pg 28 (1870 Sept 28), Columbia Lodge No. 14, Boulder City, Apprentice
Proceedings 1873, pg 44 (1873 Oct 1), Columbia Lodge No. 14, Boulder
Proceedings 1861-1869, pg 311 (1869 Sept 29), Columbia Lodge No. 14, Boulder City, Apprentice
Proceedings 1871, pg 26 (1871 Sept 27), Columbia Lodge No. 14, Boulder City, Apprentice
Proceedings 1874, pg 219 (1874 Sept 30), Columbia Lodge No. 14, Boulder, Boulder County
Proceedings 1875, pg 83 (1875 Sept 22), Columbia Lodge No. 14, Boulder
Proceedings 1876, pg 37 (1876 Sept 20), Columbia Lodge No. 14, Boulder

Harney, Geo
Proceedings 1872, pg 22 (1872 Sept 24), Union Lodge No. 7, Denver

Harney, George
Proceedings 1870, pg 23 (1870 Sept 28), Union Lodge No. 7, Denver
Proceedings 1871, pg 22 (1871 Sept 27), Union Lodge No. 7, Denver

Proceedings 1873, pg 39 (1873 Oct 1), Union Lodge No. 7, Denver

Proceedings 1874, pg 214 (1874 Sept 30), Union Lodge No. 7, Denver

Proceedings 1876, pg 33 (1876 Sept 20), Union Lodge No. 7, Denver

Harper, J C

Proceedings 1870, pg 26 (1870 Sept 28), Washington Lodge No. 12, Georgetown, Dimitted

Harper, Jno

Proceedings 1871, pg 22 (1871 Sept 27), Union Lodge No. 7, Denver

Harper, John

Proceedings 1861-1869, pg 230 (1868 Oct 7), Cheyenne Lodge U D, Cheyenne, Dakota Territory

Proceedings 1861-1869, pg 312 (1869 Sept 29), Cheyenne Lodge No. 16, Cheyenne

Proceedings 1870, pg 29 (1870 Sept 28), Cheyenne Lodge No. 16, Cheyenne, Wyoming Territory

Proceedings 1871, pg 28 (1871 Sept 27), Cheyenne Lodge No. 16, Cheyenne, Wyoming Territory, Apprentice

Proceedings 1872, pg 22 (1872 Sept 24), Union Lodge No. 7, Denver

Proceedings 1873, pg 39 (1873 Oct 1), Union Lodge No. 7, Denver

Proceedings 1874, pg 214 (1874 Sept 30), Union Lodge No. 7, Denver

Proceedings 1875, pg 79 (1875 Sept 22), Union Lodge No. 7, Denver, died

Proceedings 1875, pg 94 (1875 Sept 22), Union Lodge No. 7, Denver

Harrington, H M

Proceedings 1861-1869, pg 225 (1868 Oct 7), Union Lodge No. 7, Denver

Harrington, Horace

Proceedings 1870, pg 31 (1870 Sept 28), Laramie Lodge No. 18, Laramie, Wyoming Territory

Harris

Proceedings 1861-1869, pg 246 (1867 Nov 7) Grand Master of Georgia

Harris, A C

Proceedings 1871, pg 17 (1871 Sept 27), Golden City Lodge No. 1, Golden City

Proceedings 1872, pg 17 (1872 Sept 24), Golden City Lodge No. 1, Golden City

Proceedings 1875, pg 29 (1875 Sept 21), Union Lodge No. 7, Denver, money refunded for that expended on a Master Mason's widow

Proceedings 1875, pg 31 (1875 Sept 21) committee

Proceedings 1875, pg 34 (1875 Sept 22) motion

Harris, A W

Proceedings 1861-1869, pg 288 (1869 Sept 28), Columbia Lodge No. 14, Columbia City

Proceedings 1861-1869, pg 311 (1869 Sept 29), Columbia Lodge No. 14, Boulder City

Proceedings 1875, pg 83 (1875 Sept 22), Columbia Lodge No. 14, Boulder

Proceedings 1876, pg 48 (1876 Sept 20), Columbia Lodge No. 14, Boulder, 1876 Jan 8

Harris, Addison W

Proceedings 1870, pg 27 (1870 Sept 28), Columbia Lodge No. 14, Boulder City

Proceedings 1871, pg 25 (1871 Sept 27), Columbia Lodge No. 14, Boulder City

Proceedings 1872, pg 28 (1872 Sept 24), Columbia Lodge No. 14, Boulder

Proceedings 1873, pg 44 (1873 Oct 1), Columbia Lodge No. 14, Boulder

Harris, Anson W

Proceedings 1874, pg 219 (1874 Sept 30), Columbia Lodge No. 14, Boulder, Boulder County

Harris, Arther C

Proceedings 1876, pg 48 (1876 Sept 20) Golden City Lodge No. 1, 1876 Feb 5

Proceedings 1861-1869, pg 221 (1868 Oct 7) Golden City Lodge No. 1

Proceedings 1861-1869, pg 303 (1869 Sept 29) Golden City Lodge No. 1

Proceedings 1870, pg 19 (1870 Sept 28), Golden City Lodge No. 1, Golden City

Proceedings 1873, pg 35 (1873 Oct 1), Golden City Lodge No. 1, Golden City

Proceedings 1874, pg 209 (1874 Sept 30), Golden City Lodge No. 1, Golden City

Proceedings 1875, pg 16 (1875 Sept 21) Golden City Lodge No. 1

Proceedings 1875, pg 33 (1875 Sept 22) committee

Proceedings 1875, pg 73 (1875 Sept 22) Golden City Lodge No. 1

Proceedings 1876, pg 44 (1876 Sept 20), Las Animas Lodge No. 28, Trinidad

Harris, Ezekiel

Proceedings 1871, pg 18 (1871 Sept 27), Nevada Lodge No. 4, Bald Mountain, Dimitted

Harris, Franklin

Proceedings 1876, pg 34 (1876 Sept 20) Black Hawk Lodge No. 11

Harris, Franklin M

Proceedings 1874, pg 216 (1874 Sept 30), Black Hawk Lodge No. 11, Black Hawk

Proceedings 1875, pg 80 (1875 Sept 22) Black Hawk Lodge No. 11, Demitted

Harris, G M

Proceedings 1871, pg 24 (1871 Sept 27), Washington Lodge No. 12, Georgetown

Harris, Geo M

Proceedings 1870, pg 26 (1870 Sept 28), Washington Lodge No. 12, Georgetown, Fellowcraft

Proceedings 1872, pg 26 (1872 Sept 24), Washington Lodge No. 12, Georgetown

Proceedings 1874, pg 6 (1874 Sept 29), Washington Lodge No. 12, Georgetown

Proceedings 1875, pg 81 (1875 Sept 22), Washington Lodge No. 12, Georgetown

Colorado's Territorial Masons

Harris, George M
Proceedings 1873, pg 43 (1873 Oct 1), Washington Lodge No. 12, Georgetown
Proceedings 1874, pg 217 (1874 Sept 30), Washington Lodge No. 12, Georgetown
Proceedings 1876, pg 35 (1876 Sept 20), Washington Lodge No. 12, Georgetown

Harris, John
Proceedings 1861-1869, pg 328 (1868 Oct 27) Grand Master, Grand Lodge of Georgia
Proceedings 1876, pg 43 (1876 Sept 20), Huerfano Lodge No. 27, Walsenburg

Harris, John A
Proceedings 1873, pg 61 (1873 Oct 1) Grand Lodge of New Hampshire, Concord
Proceedings 1874, pg 106 (1874 Sept 30) Grand Lodge of New Hampshire
Proceedings 1874, pg 204 (1874 Sept 30) Grand Lodge of New Hampshire, Concord
Proceedings 1875, pg 96 (1875 Sept 22) Grand Lodge of New Hampshire, Concord
Proceedings 1876, pg 29 (1876 Sept 20) Golden City Lodge No. 1
Proceedings 1876, pg 54 (1876 Sept 20) Grand Lodge of New Hampshire, Concord

Harris, John C
Proceedings 1876, pg 45 (1876 Sept 20) South Pueblo Lodge U D

Harris, Myers
Proceedings 1871, pg 25 (1871 Sept 27), Columbia Lodge No. 14, Boulder City
Proceedings 1872, pg 28 (1872 Sept 24), Columbia Lodge No. 14, Boulder
Proceedings 1873, pg 44 (1873 Oct 1), Columbia Lodge No. 14, Boulder
Proceedings 1874, pg 219 (1874 Sept 30), Columbia Lodge No. 14, Boulder, Boulder County
Proceedings 1875, pg 83 (1875 Sept 22), Columbia Lodge No. 14, Boulder
Proceedings 1876, pg 37 (1876 Sept 20), Columbia Lodge No. 14, Boulder

Harris, Robert
Proceedings 1872, pg 24 (1872 Sept 24), Black Hawk Lodge No. 11, Black Hawk
Proceedings 1873, pg 41 (1873 Oct 1), Black Hawk Lodge No. 11, Black Hawk
Proceedings 1874, pg 216 (1874 Sept 30), Black Hawk Lodge No. 11, Black Hawk
Proceedings 1875, pg 80 (1875 Sept 22) Black Hawk Lodge No. 11, Stricken from the rolls
Proceedings 1876, pg 34 (1876 Sept 20) Black Hawk Lodge No. 11
Proceedings 1876, pg 51 (1876 Sept 20) Black Hawk Lodge No. 11, 1876 July 27

Harris, Thomas B
Proceedings 1861-1869, pg 316 (1869 Sept 29) Grand Lodge of Canada
Proceedings 1861-1869, pg 325 (1868 July 8) Grand Secretary, Grand Lodge of Canada
Proceedings 1870, pg 34 (1870 Sept 28) Grand Secretary, Grand Lodge of Canada
Proceedings 1870, pg 48 (1869 July 14) Grand Secretary, Grand Lodge of Canada
Proceedings 1871, pg 35 (1871 Sept 27) Grand Secretary, Grand Lodge of Canada
Proceedings 1872, pg 43 (1872 Sept 24) Hamilton, Grand Lodge of Canada
Proceedings 1873, pg 60 (1873 Oct 1) Grand Lodge of Canada, Hamilton

Harris, Thos Bird
Proceedings 1874, pg 47 (1874 Sept 30) Grand Lodge of Canada
Proceedings 1874, pg 50 (1874 Sept 30)

Harrison
Proceedings 1861-1869, pg 87 (1863 Apr 17) Golden City Lodge No. 1
Proceedings 1861-1869, pg 88 (1863 Apr 17) Golden City Lodge No. 1
Proceedings 1861-1869, pg 89 (1863 Apr 17) Golden City Lodge No. 1

Harrison, D E
Proceedings 1861-1869, pg 86 (1863 Feb 22) Golden City Lodge No. 1
Proceedings 1861-1869, pg 99 (1863 Nov 2) Golden City Lodge No. 1, Grand Standard Bearer
Proceedings 1861-1869, pg 116 (1864 Nov 7) Golden City Lodge No. 1
Proceedings 1861-1869, pg 131 (1864 Nov 8) Golden City Lodge No. 1
Proceedings 1861-1869, pg 147 (1865 Nov 7) Golden City Lodge No. 1
Proceedings 1861-1869, pg 165 (1866 Oct 2) Golden City Lodge No. 1
Proceedings 1861-1869, pg 191 (1867 Oct 8) Golden City Lodge No. 1
Proceedings 1861-1869, pg 221 (1868 Oct 7) Golden City Lodge No. 1
Proceedings 1861-1869, pg 303 (1869 Sept 29) Golden City Lodge No. 1
Proceedings 1870, pg 19 (1870 Sept 28), Golden City Lodge No. 1, Golden City
Proceedings 1871, pg 17 (1871 Sept 27), Golden City Lodge No. 1, Golden City
Proceedings 1872, pg 17 (1872 Sept 24), Golden City Lodge No. 1, Golden City
Proceedings 1873, pg 5 (1873 Sept 30), Golden City Lodge No. 1, Golden City
Proceedings 1876, pg 29 (1876 Sept 20) Golden City Lodge No. 1

Harrison, Duncan E
Proceedings 1861-1869, pg 110 (1863 Nov 3) Golden City Lodge No. 1
Proceedings 1873, pg 35 (1873 Oct 1), Golden City Lodge No. 1, Golden City
Proceedings 1874, pg 209 (1874 Sept 30), Golden City Lodge No. 1, Golden City

Proceedings 1875, pg 73 (1875 Sept 22) Golden City Lodge No. 1

Harrison, E
Proceedings 1861-1869, pg 86 (1863 Feb 14) Golden City Lodge No. 1

Harrison, R M
Proceedings 1875, pg 89 (1875 Sept 22), Doric Lodge No. 25, Fairplay
Proceedings 1876, pg 48 (1876 Sept 20), Doric Lodge No. 25, Fairplay, 1876 Jan 1

Harrison, Robert M
Proceedings 1874, pg 228 (1874 Sept 30), Doric Lodge U D, Fairplay

Hart
Proceedings 1861-1869, pg 289 (1869 Sept 28) committee
Proceedings 1861-1869, pg 297 (1869 Sept 28) Teller
Proceedings 1870, pg 5 (1870 Sept 27) motion
Proceedings 1870, pg 9 (1870 Sept 27) committee
Proceedings 1871, pg 4 (1871 Sept 26) Committee
Proceedings 1871, pg 4 (1871 Sept 26) Deputy Grand Master
Proceedings 1871, pg 13 (1871 Sept 26) motion
Proceedings 1871, pg 15 (1871 Sept 27) Committee
Proceedings 1871, pg 15 (1871 Sept 27) resolution
Proceedings 1871, pg 16 (1871 Sept 27) motion
Proceedings 1873, pg 29 (1873 Oct 1) resolution
Proceedings 1873, pg 30 (1873 Oct 1) resolution
Proceedings 1876, pg 20 (1876 Sept 20) committee

Hart, C J
Proceedings 1861-1869, pg 193 (1867 Oct 8) Denver Lodge No. 5
Proceedings 1861-1869, pg 223 (1868 Oct 7) Denver Lodge No. 5
Proceedings 1861-1869, pg 229 (1868 Oct 7), Pueblo Lodge U D, Pueblo
Proceedings 1861-1869, pg 288 (1869 Sept 28), Pueblo Lodge No. 17, Pueblo
Proceedings 1861-1869, pg 299 (1869 Sept 29) Senior Grand Warden
Proceedings 1861-1869, pg 301 (1869 Sept 29), Pueblo Lodge No. 17, Pueblo
Proceedings 1861-1869, pg 305 (1869 Sept 29) Denver Lodge No. 5, Dimitted
Proceedings 1861-1869, pg 312 (1869 Sept 29), Pueblo Lodge No. 17, Pueblo
Proceedings 1870, pg cover (1870 Sept 28) Deputy Grand Master, Pueblo
Proceedings 1870, pg 3 (1870 Sept 27) Senior Grand Deacon
Proceedings 1870, pg 4 (1870 Sept 27), Pueblo Lodge No. 17, Pueblo
Proceedings 1870, pg 13 (1870 Sept 27) Deputy Grand Master
Proceedings 1870, pg 16 (1870 Sept 28), Pueblo Lodge No. 17, Pueblo
Proceedings 1870, pg 17 (1870 Sept 28) committee
Proceedings 1870, pg 29 (1870 Sept 28), Pueblo Lodge No. 17, Pueblo
Proceedings 1870, pg 32 (1870 Sept 28) Deputy Grand Master, 1870
Proceedings 1871, pg cover (1871 Sept 27) Past Deuty Grand Master, Pueblo
Proceedings 1871, pg cover (1871 Sept 27) Grand Orator, Pueblo
Proceedings 1871, pg 3 (1871 Sept 26) Deputy Grand Master
Proceedings 1871, pg 4 (1871 Sept 26) Deputy Grand Master
Proceedings 1871, pg 5 (1871 Sept 26), Pueblo Lodge No. 17, Pueblo
Proceedings 1871, pg 5 (1871 Sept 26) Committee
Proceedings 1871, pg 5 (1871 Sept 26) Committee
Proceedings 1871, pg 14 (1871 Sept 27) Grand Orator
Proceedings 1871, pg 14 (1871 Sept 27) Deputy Grand Master
Proceedings 1871, pg 16 (1871 Sept 27) Committee
Proceedings 1871, pg 28 (1871 Sept 27), Pueblo Lodge No. 17, Pueblo
Proceedings 1871, pg 34 (1871 Sept 27) Deputy Grand Master, 1870
Proceedings 1872, pg 30 (1872 Sept 24), Pueblo Lodge No. 17, Pueblo
Proceedings 1872, pg 42 (1872 Sept 24) Deputy Grand Master, 1870
Proceedings 1873, pg 4 (1873 Sept 30) pall bearer for George M Randall
Proceedings 1873, pg 5 (1873 Sept 30) Past Deputy Grand Master
Proceedings 1873, pg 6 (1873 Sept 30), Pueblo Chapter No. 3, Pueblo
Proceedings 1873, pg 7 (1873 Sept 30) committee
Proceedings 1873, pg 14 (1873 Sept 30) motion
Proceedings 1873, pg 17 (1873 Oct 1) Grand Marshal
Proceedings 1873, pg 19 (1873 Oct 1) committee
Proceedings 1873, pg 31 (1873 Oct 1) mileage and per diem
Proceedings 1873, pg 58 (1873 Oct 1) Deputy Grand Master, 1870
Proceedings 1874, pg 4 (1874 Sept 29) Past Deputy Grand Master
Proceedings 1874, pg 4 (1874 Sept 29) committee
Proceedings 1874, pg 5 (1874 Sept 29) Past Deputy Grand Master
Proceedings 1874, pg 6 (1874 Sept 29) committee
Proceedings 1874, pg 11 (1874 June 24) to lay the cornerstone for the public water works building in Pueblo
Proceedings 1874, pg 17 (1874 Sept 29) committee
Proceedings 1874, pg 21 (1874 Sept 29) committee
Proceedings 1874, pg 29 (1874 Sept 29) committee
Proceedings 1874, pg 32 (1874 Sept 30) Grand Orator, Pueblo
Proceedings 1874, pg 32 (1874 Sept 30) Grand Marshal
Proceedings 1874, pg 36 (1874 Sept 30) per diem
Proceedings 1874, pg 38 (1874 Sept 30) resolution
Proceedings 1875, pg cover (1875 Sept 22) Grand Orator, Pueblo
Proceedings 1875, pg 16 (1875 Sept 21) Past Deputy Grand Master

Hart, C J, cont.
   Proceedings 1875, pg 17 (1875 Sept 21) Pueblo Lodge No. 17
   Proceedings 1875, pg 28 (1875 Sept 21) committee
   Proceedings 1875, pg 30 (1875 Sept 21) motion
   Proceedings 1875, pg 31 (1875 Sept 22) case of Wm H Dickinson
   Proceedings 1875, pg 33 (1875 Sept 22) Grand Orator, Pueblo
   Proceedings 1875, pg 36 (1875 Sept 22) resolution
   Proceedings 1875, pg 37 (1875 Sept 22) per diem
   Proceedings 1876, pg cover (1876 Sept 20) Grand Marshal, Pueblo
   Proceedings 1876, pg 6 (1876 Sept 19) committee
   Proceedings 1876, pg 18 (1876 Sept 19) Pueblo Lodge No. 17
   Proceedings 1876, pg 21 (1876 Sept 20) Grand Lodge of Georgia, Grand Representative
   Proceedings 1876, pg 22 (1876 Sept 20) Pueblo Lodge No. 17
   Proceedings 1876, pg 23 (1876 Sept 20) committee

Hart, Clarence J
   Colorado University Cornerstone Laying, pg 3 (1875 Sept 20) Grand Orator
   Proceedings 1875, pg 15 (1875 Sept 21) Grand Orator
   Proceedings 1876, pg 53 (1876 Sept 20) Grand Lodge of Georgia, of Pueblo, CO
   Proceedings 1873, pg 4 (1873 Sept 30) Past Deputy Grand Master
   Proceedings 1873, pg 47 (1873 Oct 1), Pueblo Lodge No. 17, Pueblo
   Proceedings 1874, pg 3 (1874 Sept 29) Past Deputy Grand Master
   Proceedings 1874, pg 206 (1874 Sept 30) Deputy Grand Master, 1870
   Proceedings 1874, pg 222 (1874 Sept 30), Pueblo Lodge No. 17, Pueblo, Pueblo County
   Proceedings 1875, pg 85 (1875 Sept 22) Pueblo Lodge No. 17
   Proceedings 1875, pg 93 (1875 Sept 22) Deputy Grand Master, 1870
   Proceedings 1876, pg 38 (1876 Sept 20) Pueblo Lodge No. 17

Hart, Elick
   Proceedings 1876, pg 45 (1876 Sept 20), King Solomon Lodge U D, West Las Animas

Hart, J C
   Proceedings 1861-1869, pg 296 (1869 Sept 28), Pueblo Lodge No. 17, Pueblo

Hart, James W
   Proceedings 1876, pg 48 (1876 Sept 20) Denver Lodge No. 5, 1876 Jan 1
   Proceedings 1873, pg 37 (1873 Oct 1), Denver Lodge No. 5, Denver
   Proceedings 1874, pg 211 (1874 Sept 30), Denver Lodge No. 5, Denver
   Proceedings 1875, pg 75 (1875 Sept 22) Denver Lodge No. 5

Hart, Thos J
   Proceedings 1861-1869, pg 307 (1869 Sept 29), Central Lodge No. 6, Central City, died

Hartman, H
   Proceedings 1861-1869, pg 306 (1869 Sept 29), Central Lodge No. 6, Central City
   Proceedings 1870, pg 22 (1870 Sept 28), Central Lodge No. 6, Central City

Hartman, Henry
   Proceedings 1861-1869, pg 193 (1867 Oct 8), Chivington Lodge No. 6, Central City
   Proceedings 1861-1869, pg 224 (1868 Oct 7), Chivington Lodge No. 6, Central City
   Proceedings 1871, pg 20 (1871 Sept 27), Central Lodge No. 6, Central
   Proceedings 1872, pg 21 (1872 Sept 24), Denver Lodge No. 5, Denver
   Proceedings 1873, pg 39 (1873 Oct 1), Central Lodge No. 6, Central City
   Proceedings 1874, pg 213 (1874 Sept 30), Central Lodge No. 6, Central
   Proceedings 1875, pg 77 (1875 Sept 22), Central Lodge No. 6, Central City
   Proceedings 1876, pg 32 (1876 Sept 20), Central Lodge No. 6, Central City

Harvey, Christopher
   Proceedings 1876, pg 37 (1876 Sept 20), Columbia Lodge No. 14, Boulder
   Proceedings 1876, pg 50 (1876 Sept 20), Columbia Lodge No. 14, Boulder

Harvey, F L
   Proceedings 1876, pg 16 (1876 Sept 19), General Agent, Washington National Monument Society

Harvey, R
   Proceedings 1861-1869, pg 306 (1869 Sept 29), Central Lodge No. 6, Central City
   Proceedings 1870, pg 4 (1870 Sept 27), Central Lodge No. 6, Central City

Harvey, Richard
   Proceedings 1861-1869, pg 193 (1867 Oct 8), Chivington Lodge No. 6, Central City
   Proceedings 1861-1869, pg 224 (1868 Oct 7), Chivington Lodge No. 6, Central City
   Proceedings 1870, pg 22 (1870 Sept 28), Central Lodge No. 6, Central City
   Proceedings 1872, pg 21 (1872 Sept 24), Denver Lodge No. 5, Denver
   Proceedings 1873, pg 39 (1873 Oct 1), Central Lodge No. 6, Central City
   Proceedings 1874, pg 213 (1874 Sept 30), Central Lodge No. 6, Central
   Proceedings 1875, pg 77 (1875 Sept 22), Central Lodge No. 6, Central City
   Proceedings 1876, pg 32 (1876 Sept 20), Central Lodge No. 6, Central City

Harvey, Rich'd
   Proceedings 1871, pg 20 (1871 Sept 27), Central Lodge No. 6, Central

Hasford, W F
    Proceedings 1873, pg 46 (1873 Oct 1), Cheyenne Lodge No. 16, Cheyenne, Wyoming Territory

Haskell
    Proceedings 1861-1869, pg 92 (1863 Apr 17) committee

Haskell, H B
    Proceedings 1861-1869, pg 42 (1861 Dec 10), Summit Lodge No. 2, Parkville
    Proceedings 1861-1869, pg 45 (1862 Nov 3), Summit Lodge No. 2, Parkville
    Proceedings 1861-1869, pg 76 (1862 Nov 4), Summit Lodge No. 2, Parkville
    Proceedings 1861-1869, pg 80 (1863 May 6), Summit Lodge No. 2, Parkville
    Proceedings 1861-1869, pg 93 (1863 Apr 17) committee
    Proceedings 1861-1869, pg 94 (1863 Apr 17), Summit Lodge No. 2, Parkville
    Proceedings 1861-1869, pg 94 (1863 Apr 17), Summit Lodge No. 2, Parkville
    Proceedings 1861-1869, pg 99 (1863 Nov 2), Summit Lodge No. 2, Parkville, Grand Steward
    Proceedings 1861-1869, pg 110 (1863 Nov 3), Summit Lodge No. 2, Parkville
    Proceedings 1861-1869, pg 132 (1864 Nov 8) Golden City Lodge No. 1
    Proceedings 1861-1869, pg 169 (1866 Oct 2), Union Lodge No. 7, Denver
    Proceedings 1861-1869, pg 195 (1867 Oct 8), Union Lodge No. 7, Denver
    Proceedings 1861-1869, pg 202 (1868 Oct 6), Union Lodge No. 7, Denver
    Proceedings 1861-1869, pg 225 (1868 Oct 7), Union Lodge No. 7, Denver
    Proceedings 1861-1869, pg 307 (1869 Sept 29), Union Lodge No. 7, Denver

Haskell, Hubbard
    Proceedings 1870, pg 12 (1870 Sept 27) expelled, Union Lodge No. 7, Denver

Haskell, Hubbard B
    Proceedings 1870, pg 24 (1870 Sept 28), Union Lodge No. 7, Denver, Expelled

Haskell, N D
    Proceedings 1861-1869, pg 110 (1863 Nov 3), Summit Lodge No. 2, Parkville
    Proceedings 1861-1869, pg 201 (1868 Oct 6) Grand Tyler
    Proceedings 1861-1869, pg 219 (1868 Oct 7) Tyler
    Proceedings 1861-1869, pg 224 (1868 Oct 7), Chivington Lodge No. 6, Central City
    Proceedings 1870, pg 15 (1870 Sept 28) Grand Tyler
    Proceedings 1870, pg 22 (1870 Sept 28), Central Lodge No. 6, Central City, Not a Member

Haskell, Noah D
    Proceedings 1861-1869, pg 124 (1864 Nov 8), Summit Lodge No. 2, Parkville, Grand Sword Bearer
    Proceedings 1861-1869, pg 132 (1864 Nov 8) Golden City Lodge No. 1
    Proceedings 1861-1869, pg 299 (1869 Sept 29) Grand Tyler
    Proceedings 1861-1869, pg 306 (1869 Sept 29), Central Lodge No. 6, Central City, Not a Member
    Proceedings 1870, pg 3 (1870 Sept 27) Grand Tyler
    Proceedings 1874, pg 131 (1874 Sept 30) Grand Lodge of Colorado, made a Mason in 1819, is the oldest Mason in this jurisdiction,

Haskin
    Proceedings 1861-1869, pg 177 (1867 Oct 7) committee

Haskin, H A
    Proceedings 1861-1869, pg 77 (1862 Nov 4), Nevada Lodge No. 4, Nevadaville
    Proceedings 1861-1869, pg 111 (1863 Nov 3), Nevada Lodge No. 4, Nevadaville
    Proceedings 1861-1869, pg 132 (1864 Nov 8), Nevada Lodge No. 4, Nevadaville
    Proceedings 1861-1869, pg 148 (1865 Nov 7), Nevada Lodge No. 4, Nevadaville
    Proceedings 1861-1869, pg 151 (1865 Nov 7), Empire Lodge U D, Empire City
    Proceedings 1861-1869, pg 153 (1866 Oct 1) Grand Steward
    Proceedings 1861-1869, pg 154 (1866 Oct 1), Empire Lodge No. 8, Empire City
    Proceedings 1861-1869, pg 155 (1866 Oct 1) committee
    Proceedings 1861-1869, pg 160 (1866 Oct 2), Empire Lodge No. 8, Empire City, Junior Grand Deacon
    Proceedings 1861-1869, pg 161 (1866 Oct 2) Junior Grand Deacon
    Proceedings 1861-1869, pg 162 (1866 Oct 2), Empire Lodge No. 8, Empire City
    Proceedings 1861-1869, pg 166 (1866 Oct 2), Nevada Lodge No. 4, Nevadaville, dimitted
    Proceedings 1861-1869, pg 175 (1867 Oct 7) Junior Grand Deacon
    Proceedings 1861-1869, pg 176 (1867 Oct 7), Empire Lodge No. 8, Empire City
    Proceedings 1861-1869, pg 182 (1867 Oct 7) warrant paid
    Proceedings 1861-1869, pg 186 (1867 Oct 8) per diem
    Proceedings 1861-1869, pg 190 (1867 Oct 8) Senior Grand Deacon
    Proceedings 1861-1869, pg 195 (1867 Oct 8), Empire Lodge No. 8, Empire City
    Proceedings 1861-1869, pg 212 (1868 Oct 6) warrant paid
    Proceedings 1861-1869, pg 226 (1868 Oct 7), Empire Lodge No. 8, Empire City
    Proceedings 1870, pg 24 (1870 Sept 28), Empire Lodge No. 8, Empire

Haskin, Hiram A
    Proceedings 1861-1869, pg 170 (1866 Oct 2), Empire Lodge No. 8, Empire City
    Proceedings 1861-1869, pg 308 (1869 Sept 29), Empire Lodge No. 8, Empire City
    Proceedings 1872, pg 23 (1872 Sept 24), Empire Lodge No. 8, Empire
    Proceedings 1873, pg 40 (1873 Oct 1), Empire Lodge No. 8, Empire
    Proceedings 1874, pg 215 (1874 Sept 30), Empire Lodge No. 8, Empire

Colorado's Territorial Masons

Haskins, H A
    Proceedings 1861-1869, pg 140 (1865 Nov 6), Empire Lodge No. 8, Empire City

Haskins, J P
    Proceedings 1861-1869, pg 170 (1866 Oct 2), Empire Lodge No. 8, Empire City
    Proceedings 1861-1869, pg 195 (1867 Oct 8), Empire Lodge No. 8, Empire City
    Proceedings 1861-1869, pg 226 (1868 Oct 7), Empire Lodge No. 8, Empire City
    Proceedings 1861-1869, pg 308 (1869 Sept 29), Empire Lodge No. 8, Empire City
    Proceedings 1870, pg 24 (1870 Sept 28), Empire Lodge No. 8, Empire

Haskins, Jeremiah P
    Proceedings 1872, pg 23 (1872 Sept 24), Empire Lodge No. 8, Empire
    Proceedings 1873, pg 41 (1873 Oct 1), Empire Lodge No. 8, Empire
    Proceedings 1874, pg 215 (1874 Sept 30), Empire Lodge No. 8, Empire

Hastie, Robert
    Proceedings 1873, pg 39 (1873 Oct 1), Central Lodge No. 6, Central City
    Proceedings 1874, pg 212 (1874 Sept 30), Central Lodge No. 6, Central
    Proceedings 1875, pg 76 (1875 Sept 22), Central Lodge No. 6, Central City
    Proceedings 1876, pg 4 (1876 Sept 19), Central Lodge No. 6, Central City
    Proceedings 1876, pg 31 (1876 Sept 20), Central Lodge No. 6, Central City

Haswell, T
    Proceedings 1861-1869, pg 228 (1868 Oct 7), Columbia Lodge No. 14, Columbia City

Haswell, Theo
    Proceedings 1861-1869, pg 148 (1865 Nov 7), Nevada Lodge No. 4, Nevadaville
    Proceedings 1861-1869, pg 166 (1866 Oct 2), Nevada Lodge No. 4, Nevadaville
    Proceedings 1861-1869, pg 192 (1867 Oct 8), Nevada Lodge No. 4, Nevadaville
    Proceedings 1861-1869, pg 222 (1868 Oct 7), Nevada Lodge No. 4, Nevadaville, Dimitted

Haswell, Theodore
    Proceedings 1861-1869, pg 132 (1864 Nov 8), Nevada Lodge No. 4, Nevadaville
    Proceedings 1861-1869, pg 178 (1866 Nov 17) Columbia City Lodge U D
    Proceedings 1861-1869, pg 189 (1867 Oct 8), Columbia Lodge No. 14, Columbia
    Proceedings 1861-1869, pg 196 (1867 Oct 8), Columbia Lodge U D, Boulder
    Proceedings 1861-1869, pg 310 (1869 Sept 29), Columbia Lodge No. 14, Boulder City
    Proceedings 1870, pg 27 (1870 Sept 28), Columbia Lodge No. 14, Boulder City
    Proceedings 1871, pg 25 (1871 Sept 27), Columbia Lodge No. 14, Boulder City
    Proceedings 1872, pg 27 (1872 Sept 24), Columbia Lodge No. 14, Boulder
    Proceedings 1873, pg 44 (1873 Oct 1), Columbia Lodge No. 14, Boulder
    Proceedings 1874, pg 219 (1874 Sept 30), Columbia Lodge No. 14, Boulder, Boulder County
    Proceedings 1875, pg 83 (1875 Sept 22), Columbia Lodge No. 14, Boulder
    Proceedings 1876, pg 36 (1876 Sept 20), Columbia Lodge No. 14, Boulder

Haswell, W S
    Proceedings 1861-1869, pg 304 (1869 Sept 29), Nevada Lodge No. 4, Nevadaville
    Proceedings 1871, pg 4 (1871 Sept 26), Nevada Lodge No. 4, Nevadaville
    Proceedings 1871, pg 14 (1871 Sept 27), Nevada Lodge No. 4, Nevadaville
    Proceedings 1871, pg 14 (1871 Sept 27) Grand Sword Bearer
    Proceedings 1872, pg 6 (1872 Sept 24), Nevada Lodge No. 4, Bald Mountain
    Proceedings 1872, pg 15 (1872 Sept 24) Grand Sword Bearer
    Proceedings 1875, pg 81 (1875 Sept 22), Washington Lodge No. 12, Georgetown

Haswell, W T
    Proceedings 1872, pg 16 (1872 Sept 24), Nevada Lodge No. 4, Bald Mountain

Haswell, William S
    Proceedings 1872, pg 18 (1872 Sept 24), Nevada Lodge No. 4, Bald Mountain
    Proceedings 1874, pg 217 (1874 Sept 30), Washington Lodge No. 12, Georgetown

Haswell, Wm S
    Proceedings 1870, pg 20 (1870 Sept 28), Nevada Lodge No. 4, Nevadaville
    Proceedings 1871, pg cover (1871 Sept 27) Grand Sword Bearer, Bald Mountain
    Proceedings 1871, pg 18 (1871 Sept 27), Nevada Lodge No. 4, Bald Mountain
    Proceedings 1873, pg 36 (1873 Oct 1), Nevada Lodge No. 4, Nevada, Dimitted
    Proceedings 1873, pg 43 (1873 Oct 1), Washington Lodge No. 12, Georgetown
    Proceedings 1876, pg 35 (1876 Sept 20), Washington Lodge No. 12, Georgetown

Hathaway, C G
    Proceedings 1875, pg 89 (1875 Sept 22), Doric Lodge No. 25, Fairplay
    Proceedings 1876, pg 42 (1876 Sept 20), Doric Lodge No. 25, Fairplay

Hathaway, Curtis G
    Proceedings 1874, pg 8 (1874 Jan 1), Doric Lodge U D, Fairplay
    Proceedings 1874, pg 228 (1874 Sept 30), Doric Lodge U D, Fairplay

Hathaway, Mark
Proceedings 1875, pg 83 (1875 Sept 22), Columbia Lodge No. 14, Boulder
Proceedings 1876, pg 37 (1876 Sept 20), Columbia Lodge No. 14, Boulder

Hatswell, John
Proceedings 1861-1869, pg 222 (1868 Oct 7), Nevada Lodge No. 4, Nevadaville
Proceedings 1861-1869, pg 304 (1869 Sept 29), Nevada Lodge No. 4, Nevadaville
Proceedings 1870, pg 20 (1870 Sept 28), Nevada Lodge No. 4, Nevadaville
Proceedings 1871, pg 18 (1871 Sept 27), Nevada Lodge No. 4, Bald Mountain
Proceedings 1872, pg 19 (1872 Sept 24), Nevada Lodge No. 4, Bald Mountain
Proceedings 1873, pg 36 (1873 Oct 1), Nevada Lodge No. 4, Nevada
Proceedings 1874, pg 211 (1874 Sept 30), Nevada Lodge No. 4, Bald Mountain, Gilpin County, Stricken from the rolls

Hattan, R L
Proceedings 1861-1869, pg 305 (1869 Sept 29) Denver Lodge No. 5

Hatten, R I
Proceedings 1872, pg 20 (1872 Sept 24), Denver Lodge No. 5, Denver

Hatten, R L
Proceedings 1861-1869, pg 193 (1867 Oct 8) Denver Lodge No. 5
Proceedings 1861-1869, pg 223 (1868 Oct 7) Denver Lodge No. 5
Proceedings 1870, pg 21 (1870 Sept 28), Denver Lodge No. 5, Denver
Proceedings 1871, pg 19 (1871 Sept 27) Denver Lodge No. 5
Proceedings 1873, pg 38 (1873 Oct 1), Denver Lodge No. 5, Denver, Striken from the rolls
Proceedings 1874, pg 211 (1874 Sept 30), Denver Lodge No. 5, Denver
Proceedings 1874, pg 212 (1874 Sept 30), Denver Lodge No. 5, Denver, Reinstated
Proceedings 1875, pg 75 (1875 Sept 22) Denver Lodge No. 5
Proceedings 1876, pg 49 (1876 Sept 20) Denver Lodge No. 5, 1876 Aug 19

Hattenbach, Isaac
Proceedings 1873, pg 36 (1873 Oct 1), Nevada Lodge No. 4, Nevada
Proceedings 1874, pg 210 (1874 Sept 30), Nevada Lodge No. 4, Bald Mountain, Gilpin County
Proceedings 1875, pg 74 (1875 Sept 22), Nevada Lodge No. 4, Nevada
Proceedings 1876, pg 30 (1876 Sept 20) Nevada Lodge No. 4

Hattenbach, M
Proceedings 1876, pg 33 (1876 Sept 20), Union Lodge No. 7, Denver

Hattenbach, Michael
Proceedings 1861-1869, pg 304 (1869 Sept 29), Nevada Lodge No. 4, Nevadaville
Proceedings 1870, pg 20 (1870 Sept 28), Nevada Lodge No. 4, Nevadaville
Proceedings 1871, pg 18 (1871 Sept 27), Nevada Lodge No. 4, Bald Mountain
Proceedings 1872, pg 19 (1872 Sept 24), Nevada Lodge No. 4, Bald Mountain
Proceedings 1873, pg 36 (1873 Oct 1), Nevada Lodge No. 4, Nevada
Proceedings 1874, pg 210 (1874 Sept 30), Nevada Lodge No. 4, Bald Mountain, Gilpin County
Proceedings 1875, pg 74 (1875 Sept 22), Nevada Lodge No. 4, Nevada
Proceedings 1876, pg 48 (1876 Sept 20) Nevada Lodge No. 4, 1876 Jan 22

Hatzdorf, Herman
Proceedings 1874, pg 222 (1874 Sept 30), Pueblo Lodge No. 17, Pueblo, Pueblo County, Demitted

Hauck, C C
Proceedings 1873, pg 39 (1873 Oct 1), Union Lodge No. 7, Denver
Proceedings 1874, pg 214 (1874 Sept 30), Union Lodge No. 7, Denver
Proceedings 1875, pg 78 (1875 Sept 22), Union Lodge No. 7, Denver
Proceedings 1876, pg 33 (1876 Sept 20), Union Lodge No. 7, Denver

Hauenstein, W J
Proceedings 1876, pg 34 (1876 Sept 20) Black Hawk Lodge No. 11

Hauenstine, Wolf J
Proceedings 1873, pg 41 (1873 Oct 1), Black Hawk Lodge No. 11, Black Hawk
Proceedings 1874, pg 216 (1874 Sept 30), Black Hawk Lodge No. 11, Black Hawk
Proceedings 1875, pg 80 (1875 Sept 22) Black Hawk Lodge No. 11

Haux, Benjamin F
Proceedings 1870, pg 24 (1870 Sept 28), Union Lodge No. 7, Denver, Dimitted

Hawes, Jesse
Proceedings 1872, pg 33 (1872 Sept 24), Occidental Lodge No. 20, Greeley
Proceedings 1873, pg 50 (1873 Oct 1), Occidental Lodge No. 20, Greeley
Proceedings 1875, pg 87 (1875 Sept 22), Occidental Lodge No. 20, Greeley
Proceedings 1876, pg 40 (1876 Sept 20), Occidental Lodge No. 20, Greeley

Hawley, H J
Proceedings 1861-1869, pg 225 (1868 Oct 7), Chivington Lodge No. 6, Central City, Apprentice
Proceedings 1861-1869, pg 306 (1869 Sept 29), Central Lodge No. 6, Central City
Proceedings 1870, pg 22 (1870 Sept 28), Central Lodge No. 6, Central City

Hawley, H J, cont.
    Proceedings 1871, pg 20 (1871 Sept 27), Central Lodge No. 6, Central

Hawley, Henry J
    Proceedings 1872, pg 21 (1872 Sept 24), Denver Lodge No. 5, Denver
    Proceedings 1873, pg 39 (1873 Oct 1), Central Lodge No. 6, Central City
    Proceedings 1874, pg 213 (1874 Sept 30), Central Lodge No. 6, Central
    Proceedings 1875, pg 77 (1875 Sept 22), Central Lodge No. 6, Central City
    Proceedings 1876, pg 32 (1876 Sept 20), Central Lodge No. 6, Central City

Hawley, James A
    Proceedings 1872, pg 43 (1872 Sept 24) Dixon, Grand Lodge of Illinois
    Proceedings 1873, pg 15 (1873 Oct 1), of Dixon, IL
    Proceedings 1873, pg 60 (1873 Oct 1) Grand Lodge of Illinois, Dixon
    Proceedings 1874, pg 61 (1874 Sept 30) Grand Lodge of Illinois
    Proceedings 1874, pg 204 (1874 Sept 30) Grand Lodge of Illinois, Dixon
    Proceedings 1874, pg 207 (1874 Sept 30) Grand Lodge of Illinois, Dixon
    Proceedings 1875, pg 95 (1875 Sept 22) Grand Lodge of Illinois, Dixon, IL
    Proceedings 1876, pg 53 (1876 Sept 20) Grand Lodge of Illinois, of Dixon, IL

Haws, Geo W
    Proceedings 1873, pg 46 (1873 Oct 1), Cheyenne Lodge No. 16, Cheyenne, Wyoming Territory

Haws, George W
    Proceedings 1872, pg 29 (1872 Sept 24), Cheyenne Lodge No. 16, Cheyenne, Wyoming Territory
    Proceedings 1874, pg 220 (1874 Sept 30), Cheyenne Lodge No. 16, Cheyenne, Wyoming Territory

Hay, H G
    Proceedings 1874, pg 221 (1874 Sept 30), Cheyenne Lodge No. 16, Cheyenne, Wyoming Territory

Hayden, Lewis
    Proceedings 1870, pg 67 (1869 Sept 8) Grand Lodge of Massachusetts
    Proceedings 1870, pg 70 (1869 Sept 8) petitioner

Hayes, Ransom A
    Proceedings 1876, pg 39 (1876 Sept 20) Pueblo Lodge No. 17

Hayes, Stokely D
    Proceedings 1875, pg 91 (1875 Sept 22), Las Animas Lodge U D, Trinidad

Hayes, Wm S
    Proceedings 1874, pg 204 (1874 Sept 30) Grand Lodge of Delaware, Wilmington
    Proceedings 1875, pg 96 (1875 Sept 22) Grand Lodge of Delaware, Wilmington
    Proceedings 1876, pg 54 (1876 Sept 20) Grand Lodge of Delaware, Wilmington

Hayford, J H
    Proceedings 1861-1869, pg 229 (1868 Oct 7), Cheyenne Lodge U D, Cheyenne, Dakota Territory
    Proceedings 1861-1869, pg 311 (1869 Sept 29), Cheyenne Lodge No. 16, Cheyenne
    Proceedings 1870, pg 6 (1870 Jan 31) Laramie City Lodge U D
    Proceedings 1870, pg 29 (1870 Sept 28), Cheyenne Lodge No. 16, Cheyenne, Wyoming Territory, Dimitted
    Proceedings 1870, pg 30 (1870 Sept 28), Laramie Lodge No. 18, Laramie, Wyoming Territory
    Proceedings 1871, pg 5 (1871 Sept 26), Laramie Lodge No. 18, Laramie, Wyoming Territory
    Proceedings 1871, pg 5 (1871 Sept 26) Committee
    Proceedings 1871, pg 12 (1871 Sept 26) Committee
    Proceedings 1871, pg 15 (1871 Sept 27), Laramie Lodge No. 18, Laramie, Wyoming Territory
    Proceedings 1871, pg 15 (1871 Sept 27) Committee
    Proceedings 1871, pg 29 (1871 Sept 27), Laramie Lodge No. 18, Laramie, Wyoming Territory
    Proceedings 1871, pg 29 (1871 Sept 27), Laramie Lodge No. 18, Laramie, Wyoming Territory
    Proceedings 1872, pg 31 (1872 Sept 24), Laramie Lodge No. 18, Laramie, Wyoming Territory
    Proceedings 1873, pg 48 (1873 Oct 1), Laramie Lodge No. 18, Laramie, Wyoming Territory
    Proceedings 1873, pg 48 (1873 Oct 1), Laramie Lodge No. 18, Laramie, Wyoming Territory
    Proceedings 1874, pg 223 (1874 Sept 30), Laramie Lodge No. 18, Laramie City

Hayman
    Proceedings 1861-1869, pg 48 (1862 Nov 3) motion

Hayman, B C
    Proceedings 1861-1869, pg 45 (1862 Nov 3) committee
    Proceedings 1861-1869, pg 45 (1862 Nov 3) Denver Lodge No. 5
    Proceedings 1861-1869, pg 47 (1862 Nov 3) committee
    Proceedings 1861-1869, pg 51 (1862 Nov 4) Junior Grand Warden
    Proceedings 1861-1869, pg 54 (1862 Nov 4) installed
    Proceedings 1861-1869, pg 79 (1863 May 6) Junior Grand Deacon
    Proceedings 1861-1869, pg 112 (1863 Nov 3) Denver Lodge No. 5
    Proceedings 1861-1869, pg 133 (1864 Nov 8) Denver Lodge No. 5
    Proceedings 1861-1869, pg 149 (1865 Nov 7), Nevada Lodge No. 4, Nevadaville
    Proceedings 1861-1869, pg 167 (1866 Oct 2) Denver Lodge No. 5
    Proceedings 1861-1869, pg 193 (1867 Oct 8) Denver Lodge No. 5
    Proceedings 1861-1869, pg 223 (1868 Oct 7) Denver Lodge No. 5
    Proceedings 1861-1869, pg 305 (1869 Sept 29) Denver Lodge No. 5

Proceedings 1870, pg 21 (1870 Sept 28), Denver Lodge No. 5, Denver

Proceedings 1872, pg 20 (1872 Sept 24), Denver Lodge No. 5, Denver

Hayman, Benj C

Proceedings 1861-1869, pg 77 (1862 Nov 4) Denver Lodge No. 5

Hays, Ransom A

Proceedings 1875, pg 85 (1875 Sept 22) Pueblo Lodge No. 17

Hays, Stokely D

Proceedings 1876, pg 43 (1876 Sept 20), Las Animas Lodge No. 28, Trinidad

Hayslip, G P

Proceedings 1874, pg 222 (1874 Sept 30), Pueblo Lodge No. 17, Pueblo, Pueblo County

Proceedings 1875, pg 85 (1875 Sept 22) Pueblo Lodge No. 17

Proceedings 1876, pg 38 (1876 Sept 20) Pueblo Lodge No. 17

Hayslip, Geo P

Proceedings 1872, pg 31 (1872 Sept 24), Pueblo Lodge No. 17, Pueblo

Hayslip, George P

Proceedings 1871, pg 28 (1871 Sept 27), Pueblo Lodge No. 17, Pueblo

Proceedings 1873, pg 47 (1873 Oct 1), Pueblo Lodge No. 17, Pueblo

Hazen, N F

Proceedings 1875, pg 87 (1875 Sept 22), Occidental Lodge No. 20, Greeley

Hazen, Norman F

Proceedings 1873, pg 50 (1873 Oct 1), Occidental Lodge No. 20, Greeley

Proceedings 1874, pg 225 (1874 Sept 30), Occidental Lodge No. 20, Greeley

Proceedings 1876, pg 40 (1876 Sept 20), Occidental Lodge No. 20, Greeley

Heard, John T

Proceedings 1874, pg 82 (1874 Sept 30) Grand Lodge of Massachusetts

Heath, A

Proceedings 1861-1869, pg 111 (1863 Nov 3), Summit Lodge No. 2, Parkville, Apprentice

Proceedings 1861-1869, pg 132 (1864 Nov 8) Golden City Lodge No. 1, Apprentice,

Hedge[s]

Proceedings 1874, pg 95 (1874 Sept 30) Grand Lodge of Montana

Hedge[s], Cornelius

Proceedings 1874, pg 94 (1874 Sept 30) Grand Lodgeof Montana

Hedges

Proceedings 1870, pg 90 (1869 Oct 4) Grand Lodge of Montana

Hedges, Cornelius

Proceedings 1861-1869, pg 152 (1865 Nov 7), Helena City Lodge U D, Helena City, Montana Territory

Proceedings 1861-1869, pg 155 (1866 Oct 1), Helena City Lodge No. 10, Helena City, Montana Territory

Proceedings 1870, pg 89 (1869 Oct 4) Grand Lodge of Montana

Proceedings 1872, pg 73 (1872 Sept 24) Grand Lodge of Montana

Proceedings 1874, pg 96 (1874 Sept 30) Grand Lodge of Montana

Proceedings 1874, pg 204 (1874 Sept 30) Grand Lodge of Montana, Helena

Proceedings 1875, pg 96 (1875 Sept 22) Grand Lodge of Montana, Helena

Proceedings 1876, pg 54 (1876 Sept 20) Grand Lodge of Montana, Helena

Heinebaugh, C

Proceedings 1861-1869, pg 193 (1867 Oct 8) Denver Lodge No. 5

Heiser, H H

Proceedings 1861-1869, pg 170 (1866 Oct 2), Black Hawk Lodge U D, Black Hawk

Proceedings 1861-1869, pg 196 (1867 Oct 8), Black Hawk Lodge No. 11, Black Hawk

Proceedings 1861-1869, pg 227 (1868 Oct 7), Black Hawk Lodge No. 11, Black Hawk

Proceedings 1861-1869, pg 309 (1869 Sept 29), Black Hawk Lodge No. 11, Black Hawk

Proceedings 1870, pg 25 (1870 Sept 28), Black Hawk Lodge No. 11, Black Hawk

Proceedings 1871, pg 23 (1871 Sept 27), Black Hawk Lodge No. 11, Black Hawk

Proceedings 1872, pg 24 (1872 Sept 24), Black Hawk Lodge No. 11, Black Hawk

Proceedings 1873, pg 41 (1873 Oct 1), Black Hawk Lodge No. 11, Black Hawk

Proceedings 1874, pg 216 (1874 Sept 30), Black Hawk Lodge No. 11, Black Hawk, Demitted

Proceedings 1875, pg 75 (1875 Sept 22) Denver Lodge No. 5

Proceedings 1876, pg 31 (1876 Sept 20) Denver Lodge No. 5

Heiskell, Tyler D

Proceedings 1875, pg 87 (1875 Sept 22), Occidental Lodge No. 20, Greeley

Heisterman

Proceedings 1874, pg 133 (1874 Sept 30) Grand Lodge of British Columbia

Heisterman, H F

Proceedings 1874, pg 204 (1874 Sept 30) Grand Lodge of British Columbia, Victoria

Heisterman, Henry F

Proceedings 1872, pg 43 (1872 Sept 24) Victoria, Grand Lodge of British Columbia

Proceedings 1872, pg 56 (1872 Sept 24) Grand Lodge of British Columbia

Colorado's Territorial Masons

Heisterman, Henry F, cont.
Proceedings 1873, pg 60 (1873 Oct 1) Grand Lodge of British Columbia, Victoria

Helena City Lodge No. 10
Proceedings 1861-1869, pg 141 (1865 Nov 7) granted charter
Proceedings 1861-1869, pg 308 (1869 Sept 29) Under the jurisdiction of the Grand Lodge of Montana
Proceedings 1875, pg 79 (1875 Sept 22) Grand Lodge of Montana
Proceedings 1876, pg 46 (1876 Sept 20), Helena Lodge No. 3, Grand Lodge of Montana

Helena City Lodge No. 10, Helena City
Proceedings 1871, pg 22 (1871 Sept 27) Grand Lodge of Montana
Helena City Lodge No. 10, Helena City
Proceedings 1872, pg 24 (1872 Sept 24) Grand Lodge of Montana
Proceedings 1873, pg 41 (1873 Oct 1), now Helena Lodge No. 3, Grand Lodge of Montana

Helena City Lodge No. 10, Helena City, Montana Territory
Proceedings 1861-1869, pg 226 (1868 Oct 7) Under the jurisdiction of the Grand Lodge of Montana
Proceedings 1874, pg 215 (1874 Sept 30), now Helena Lodge No. 3, Grand Lodge of Montana

Helena City Lodge No. 21
Proceedings 1875, pg 20 (1875 Sept 21) Grand Lodge of Montana

Helena City Lodge U D
Proceedings 1861-1869, pg 137 (1865 Nov 6), Helena Lodge U D, Helena, Adgerton County, Montana Territory
Proceedings 1861-1869, pg 139 (1865 July 10) dispensation
Proceedings 1861-1869, pg 139 (1865 Nov 6) requesting charter
Proceedings 1861-1869, pg 139 (1865 Oct 25) petition for charter
Proceedings 1861-1869, pg 181 (1867 Oct 7) charter returned

Helena Lodge No. 3, Helena City
Proceedings 1870, pg 25 (1870 Sept 28) under the jurisdiction of the Grand Lodge of Montana

Hellman, Benjamin
Proceedings 1874, pg 221 (1874 Sept 30), Cheyenne Lodge No. 16, Cheyenne, Wyoming Territory

Helson, J
Proceedings 1870, pg 28 (1870 Sept 28), Mount Moriah Lodge No. 15, Canon City

Helstrom, J N
Proceedings 1861-1869, pg 42 (1861 Dec 10), Summit Lodge No. 2, Parkville

Henderson, E W
Proceedings 1861-1869, pg 77 (1862 Nov 4), Nevada Lodge No. 4, Nevadaville
Proceedings 1861-1869, pg 111 (1863 Nov 3), Nevada Lodge No. 4, Nevadaville
Proceedings 1861-1869, pg 132 (1864 Nov 8), Nevada Lodge No. 4, Nevadaville
Proceedings 1861-1869, pg 148 (1865 Nov 7), Nevada Lodge No. 4, Nevadaville
Proceedings 1861-1869, pg 166 (1866 Oct 2), Nevada Lodge No. 4, Nevadaville
Proceedings 1861-1869, pg 192 (1867 Oct 8), Nevada Lodge No. 4, Nevadaville, Dimitted

Henderson, J P
Proceedings 1875, pg 75 (1875 Sept 22) Denver Lodge No. 5

Henderson, J T
Proceedings 1876, pg 31 (1876 Sept 20) Denver Lodge No. 5

Henderson, John T
Proceedings 1861-1869, pg 77 (1862 Nov 4) Denver Lodge No. 5
Proceedings 1861-1869, pg 112 (1863 Nov 3) Denver Lodge No. 5
Proceedings 1861-1869, pg 133 (1864 Nov 8) Denver Lodge No. 5, dimitted

Henderson, Joseph W
Proceedings 1874, pg 211 (1874 Sept 30), Denver Lodge No. 5, Denver

Henderson, M P
Proceedings 1872, pg 34 (1872 Sept 24), Occidental Lodge No. 20, Greeley, Apprentice
Proceedings 1873, pg 50 (1873 Oct 1), Occidental Lodge No. 20, Greeley
Proceedings 1874, pg 225 (1874 Sept 30), Occidental Lodge No. 20, Greeley
Proceedings 1875, pg 87 (1875 Sept 22), Occidental Lodge No. 20, Greeley

Henderson, Milton P
Proceedings 1876, pg 40 (1876 Sept 20), Occidental Lodge No. 20, Greeley

Henderson, W H
Proceedings 1861-1869, pg 227 (1868 Oct 7), Washington Lodge No. 12, Georgetown

Henderson, W S
Proceedings 1874, pg 227 (1874 Sept 30), St Vrain No. 23, Longmont
Proceedings 1876, pg 41 (1876 Sept 20), St Vrain Lodge No. 23, Longmont

Henderson, Wm H
Proceedings 1861-1869, pg 310 (1869 Sept 29), Washington Lodge No. 12, Georgetown, Suspended
Proceedings 1870, pg 12 (1870 Sept 27) expelled, Washington Lodge No. 12, Georgetown
Proceedings 1870, pg 26 (1870 Sept 28), Washington Lodge No. 12, Georgetown, Expelled

Hendren, C D
Proceedings 1875, pg 90 (1875 Sept 22), Huerfano Lodge U D, Walsenburg

Proceedings 1876, pg 43 (1876 Sept 20), Huerfano Lodge No. 27, Walsenburg

Hendricks, G W
Proceedings 1874, pg 214 (1874 Sept 30), Union Lodge No. 7, Denver, Fellowcraft
Proceedings 1875, pg 78 (1875 Sept 22), Union Lodge No. 7, Denver
Proceedings 1876, pg 33 (1876 Sept 20), Union Lodge No. 7, Denver
Proceedings 1876, pg 50 (1876 Sept 20), Union Lodge No. 7, Denver

Hendry, J B
Proceedings 1861-1869, pg 42 (1861 Dec 10) Golden City Lodge No. 1
Proceedings 1861-1869, pg 110 (1863 Nov 3) Golden City Lodge No. 1
Proceedings 1861-1869, pg 131 (1864 Nov 8) Golden City Lodge No. 1
Proceedings 1861-1869, pg 147 (1865 Nov 7) Golden City Lodge No. 1
Proceedings 1861-1869, pg 165 (1866 Oct 2) Golden City Lodge No. 1
Proceedings 1872, pg 17 (1872 Sept 24), Golden City Lodge No. 1, Golden City
Proceedings 1874, pg 209 (1874 Sept 30), Golden City Lodge No. 1, Golden City
Proceedings 1875, pg 73 (1875 Sept 22) Golden City Lodge No. 1

Hendry, John B
Proceedings 1861-1869, pg 221 (1868 Oct 7) Golden City Lodge No. 1
Proceedings 1861-1869, pg 303 (1869 Sept 29) Golden City Lodge No. 1

Henley, Michael J
Proceedings 1874, pg 99 (1874 Sept 30) Grand Lodge of Nevada

Henry
Proceedings 1871, pg 13 (1871 Sept 26) Grand Teller
Proceedings 1871, pg 15 (1871 Sept 27) resolution
Proceedings 1872, pg 12 (1872 Sept 24) teller
Proceedings 1872, pg 12 (1872 Sept 24) resolution
Proceedings 1873, pg 29 (1873 Oct 1) committee
Proceedings 1873, pg 29 (1873 Oct 1) motion
Proceedings 1875, pg 35 (1875 Sept 22) Grand Master
Proceedings 1876, pg 6 (1876 Sept 19) Grand Master
Proceedings 1876, pg 15 (1876 Sept 19) Grand Master
Proceedings 1876, pg 18 (1876 Sept 20) Grand Master
Proceedings 1876, pg 22 (1876 Sept 20) motion
Proceedings 1876, pg 23 (1876 Sept 20) motion
Proceedings 1876, pg 25 (1876 Sept 20) resolution
Proceedings 1876, pg 25 (1876 Sept 20) motion

Henry, I N
Proceedings 1861-1869, pg 222 (1868 Oct 7), Nevada Lodge No. 4, Nevadaville
Proceedings 1861-1869, pg 304 (1869 Sept 29), Nevada Lodge No. 4, Nevadaville

Henry, Isaac N
Proceedings 1870, pg 5 (1870 Sept 27), Nevada Lodge No. 4, Nevadaville
Proceedings 1870, pg 20 (1870 Sept 28), Nevada Lodge No. 4, Nevadaville
Proceedings 1871, pg 18 (1871 Sept 27), Nevada Lodge No. 4, Bald Mountain
Proceedings 1872, pg 18 (1872 Sept 24), Nevada Lodge No. 4, Bald Mountain
Proceedings 1873, pg 36 (1873 Oct 1), Nevada Lodge No. 4, Nevada
Proceedings 1874, pg 210 (1874 Sept 30), Nevada Lodge No. 4, Bald Mountain, Gilpin County
Proceedings 1875, pg 74 (1875 Sept 22), Nevada Lodge No. 4, Nevada
Proceedings 1876, pg 30 (1876 Sept 20) Nevada Lodge No. 4

Henry, L N
Proceedings 1861-1869, pg 192 (1867 Oct 8), Nevada Lodge No. 4, Nevadaville

Henry, O E
Proceedings 1872, pg 27 (1872 Sept 24), Columbia Lodge No. 14, Boulder
Proceedings 1874, pg 219 (1874 Sept 30), Columbia Lodge No. 14, Boulder, Boulder County
Proceedings 1875, pg 83 (1875 Sept 22), Columbia Lodge No. 14, Boulder

Henry, O H
Proceedings 1861-1869, pg 148 (1865 Nov 7), Nevada Lodge No. 4, Nevadaville
Proceedings 1861-1869, pg 166 (1866 Oct 2), Nevada Lodge No. 4, Nevadaville
Proceedings 1861-1869, pg 192 (1867 Oct 8), Nevada Lodge No. 4, Nevadaville
Proceedings 1861-1869, pg 196 (1867 Oct 8), Columbia Lodge U D, Boulder
Proceedings 1861-1869, pg 222 (1868 Oct 7), Nevada Lodge No. 4, Nevadaville, Dimitted
Proceedings 1861-1869, pg 228 (1868 Oct 7), Columbia Lodge No. 14, Columbia City
Proceedings 1870, pg 4 (1870 Sept 27), Columbia Lodge No. 14, Boulder
Proceedings 1870, pg 13 (1870 Sept 27) Grand Teller
Proceedings 1870, pg 15 (1870 Sept 28) committee
Proceedings 1870, pg 16 (1870 Sept 28), Columbia Lodge No. 14, Boulder
Proceedings 1870, pg 27 (1870 Sept 28), Columbia Lodge No. 14, Boulder City
Proceedings 1871, pg 3 (1871 Sept 26) Grand Marshal
Proceedings 1871, pg 4 (1871 Sept 26) Committee
Proceedings 1871, pg 4 (1871 Sept 26), Columbia Lodge No. 14, Boulder City
Proceedings 1871, pg 5 (1871 Sept 26) Committee
Proceedings 1871, pg 12 (1871 Sept 26) Committee
Proceedings 1871, pg 14 (1871 Sept 27) Grand Lecturer
Proceedings 1871, pg 14 (1871 Sept 27), Columbia Lodge No. 14, Boulder City
Proceedings 1871, pg 15 (1871 Sept 27) Committee

Henry, O H, cont.
- Proceedings 1872, pg 4 (1872 Sept 24), Columbia Lodge No. 14, Boulder City
- Proceedings 1872, pg 5 (1872 Sept 24) committee
- Proceedings 1873, pg 18 (1873 Oct 1) motion
- Proceedings 1874, pg 5 (1874 Sept 29) Junior Grand Warden
- Proceedings 1874, pg 6 (1874 Sept 29) committee
- Proceedings 1874, pg 36 (1874 Sept 30) per diem
- Proceedings 1875, pg 16 (1875 Sept 21) committee
- Proceedings 1875, pg 16 (1875 Sept 21) Senior Grand Warden
- Proceedings 1875, pg 17 (1875 Sept 21) committee
- Proceedings 1875, pg 18 (1875 Sept 21) committee
- Proceedings 1875, pg 30 (1875 Sept 21) committee
- Proceedings 1875, pg 37 (1875 Sept 22) per diem
- Proceedings 1876, pg 4 (1876 Sept 19) Grand Master
- Proceedings 1876, pg 22 (1876 Sept 20) Grand Master

Henry, Oramel E
- Proceedings 1870, pg 28 (1870 Sept 28), Columbia Lodge No. 14, Boulder City, Fellowcraft
- Proceedings 1871, pg 25 (1871 Sept 27), Columbia Lodge No. 14, Boulder City
- Proceedings 1876, pg 37 (1876 Sept 20), Columbia Lodge No. 14, Boulder

Henry, Oren H
- Colorado University Cornerstone Laying, pg cover (1875 Sept 20) Grand Master, Boulder
- Colorado University Cornerstone Laying, pg 3 (1875 Sept 20) Senior Grand Warden
- Proceedings 1861-1869, pg 310 (1869 Sept 29), Columbia Lodge No. 14, Boulder City
- Proceedings 1871, pg 25 (1871 Sept 27), Columbia Lodge No. 14, Boulder City
- Proceedings 1872, pg 3 (1872 Sept 24) Grand Lecturer
- Proceedings 1872, pg 15 (1872 Sept 24) Grand Lecturer
- Proceedings 1872, pg 27 (1872 Sept 24), Columbia Lodge No. 14, Boulder
- Proceedings 1873, pg cover (1873 Oct 1) Junior Grand Warden, Boulder
- Proceedings 1873, pg 3 (1873 Sept 30) Grand Lecturer
- Proceedings 1873, pg 14 (1873 Sept 30) Junior Grand Warden
- Proceedings 1873, pg 44 (1873 Oct 1), Columbia Lodge No. 14, Boulder
- Proceedings 1873, pg 59 (1873 Oct 1) Junior Grand Warden, 1873
- Proceedings 1874, pg cover (1874 Sept 30) Senior Grand Warden, Boulder
- Proceedings 1874, pg 4 (1874 Sept 29) Junior Grand Warden
- Proceedings 1874, pg 29 (1874 Sept 29) Senior Grand Warden
- Proceedings 1874, pg 206 (1874 Sept 30) Junior Grand Warden, 1873
- Proceedings 1874, pg 206 (1874 Sept 30) Senior Grand Warden, 1874
- Proceedings 1874, pg 219 (1874 Sept 30), Columbia Lodge No. 14, Boulder, Boulder County
- Proceedings 1875, pg cover (1875 Sept 22) Grand Master, Boulder
- Proceedings 1875, pg 15 (1875 Sept 21) Senior Grand Warden
- Proceedings 1875, pg 30 (1875 Sept 21) Grand Master
- Proceedings 1875, pg 33 (1875 Sept 22) Grand Master
- Proceedings 1875, pg 83 (1875 Sept 22), Columbia Lodge No. 14, Boulder
- Proceedings 1875, pg 93 (1875 Sept 22) Senior Grand Warden, 1874
- Proceedings 1875, pg 93 (1875 Sept 22) Grand Master, 1875
- Proceedings 1875, pg 93 (1875 Sept 22) Junior Grand Warden, 1873
- Proceedings 1876, pg cover (1876 Sept 20) committee, Boulder
- Proceedings 1876, pg 3 (1876 Sept 19) Grand Master
- Proceedings 1876, pg 10 (1876 Sept 19) Grand Master
- Proceedings 1876, pg 26 (1876 Sept 20) committee
- Proceedings 1876, pg 36 (1876 Sept 20), Columbia Lodge No. 14, Boulder

Henry, Orin H
- Proceedings 1861-1869, pg 288 (1869 Sept 28), Columbia Lodge No. 14, Columbia City
- Proceedings 1870, pg cover (1870 Sept 28) Grand Marshal, Boulder
- Proceedings 1871, pg cover (1871 Sept 27) Grand Lecturer, Boulder

Henry, Ormal E
- Proceedings 1873, pg 44 (1873 Oct 1), Columbia Lodge No. 14, Boulder

Henry, Thomas Y
- Proceedings 1870, pg 52 (1870 Jan 12) Grand Lodge of Florida, deceased

Hensi, Martin
- Proceedings 1861-1869, pg 309 (1869 Sept 29), Washington Lodge No. 12, Georgetown
- Proceedings 1870, pg 26 (1870 Sept 28), Washington Lodge No. 12, Georgetown
- Proceedings 1871, pg 24 (1871 Sept 27), Washington Lodge No. 12, Georgetown
- Proceedings 1874, pg 222 (1874 Sept 30), Pueblo Lodge No. 17, Pueblo, Pueblo County
- Proceedings 1875, pg 85 (1875 Sept 22) Pueblo Lodge No. 17
- Proceedings 1876, pg 39 (1876 Sept 20) Pueblo Lodge No. 17

Henson, Henry
- Proceedings 1861-1869, pg 134 (1864 Nov 8), Union Lodge No. 7, Denver
- Proceedings 1861-1869, pg 151 (1865 Nov 7), Chivington Lodge No. 6, Central City
- Proceedings 1861-1869, pg 169 (1866 Oct 2), Union Lodge No. 7, Denver
- Proceedings 1861-1869, pg 195 (1867 Oct 8), Union Lodge No. 7, Denver
- Proceedings 1861-1869, pg 225 (1868 Oct 7), Union Lodge No. 7, Denver

Proceedings 1861-1869, pg 307 (1869 Sept 29), Union Lodge No. 7, Denver

Proceedings 1870, pg 23 (1870 Sept 28), Union Lodge No. 7, Denver

Proceedings 1871, pg 22 (1871 Sept 27), Union Lodge No. 7, Denver

Proceedings 1872, pg 22 (1872 Sept 24), Union Lodge No. 7, Denver

Proceedings 1873, pg 40 (1873 Oct 1), Union Lodge No. 7, Denver, Dimitted

Proceedings 1876, pg 44 (1876 Sept 20) Del Norte Lodge U D

Herbert, H P
Proceedings 1861-1869, pg 149 (1865 Nov 7), Nevada Lodge No. 4, Nevadaville, Fellowcraft

Herring, James
Proceedings 1870, pg 70 (1846) Grand Secretary, Grand Lodge of Massachusetts

Herrington, H M
Proceedings 1861-1869, pg 307 (1869 Sept 29), Union Lodge No. 7, Denver

Proceedings 1871, pg 22 (1871 Sept 27), Union Lodge No. 7, Denver, Dimitted

Herrington, Henry M
Proceedings 1870, pg 23 (1870 Sept 28), Union Lodge No. 7, Denver

Herron, O F
Proceedings 1872, pg 35 (1872 Sept 24), St Vrain Lodge No. 23, Longmont, Apprentice

Proceedings 1873, pg 51 (1873 Oct 1), St Vrain Lodge No. 23, Longmont

Proceedings 1874, pg 227 (1874 Sept 30), St Vrain No. 23, Longmont

Proceedings 1876, pg 41 (1876 Sept 20), St Vrain Lodge No. 23, Longmont

Hertel, G W
Proceedings 1875, pg 75 (1875 Sept 22) Denver Lodge No. 5

Proceedings 1875, pg 76 (1875 Sept 22) Denver Lodge No. 5, Reinstated

Hertel, Geo W
Proceedings 1861-1869, pg 112 (1863 Nov 3) Denver Lodge No. 5

Proceedings 1861-1869, pg 223 (1868 Oct 7) Denver Lodge No. 5

Proceedings 1870, pg 21 (1870 Sept 28), Denver Lodge No. 5, Denver

Proceedings 1871, pg 19 (1871 Sept 27) Denver Lodge No. 5

Proceedings 1872, pg 20 (1872 Sept 24), Denver Lodge No. 5, Denver

Hertel, George W
Proceedings 1861-1869, pg 77 (1862 Nov 4) Denver Lodge No. 5

Proceedings 1861-1869, pg 193 (1867 Oct 8) Denver Lodge No. 5

Proceedings 1876, pg 31 (1876 Sept 20) Denver Lodge No. 5

Hertell, G W
Proceedings 1861-1869, pg 305 (1869 Sept 29) Denver Lodge No. 5

Proceedings 1874, pg 212 (1874 Sept 30), Denver Lodge No. 5, Denver, Stricken from the rolls

Hertell, Geo W
Proceedings 1861-1869, pg 133 (1864 Nov 8) Denver Lodge No. 5

Proceedings 1873, pg 37 (1873 Oct 1), Denver Lodge No. 5, Denver

Hervey, John
Proceedings 1870, pg 74 (1868 Nov 11) United Grand Lodge of England

Proceedings 1870, pg 75 (1868 Nov 11) Grand Secretary, United Grand Lodge of England

Proceedings 1870, pg 76 (1870 May 5) Grand Secretary, United Grand Lodge of England

Hervey, S O
Proceedings 1875, pg 75 (1875 Sept 22) Denver Lodge No. 5

Proceedings 1876, pg 30 (1876 Sept 20) Denver Lodge No. 5

Hetrich
Proceedings 1874, pg 14 (1874 Feb 6), formerly of Union Lodge No. 7, Denver

Hetrich, F D
Proceedings 1861-1869, pg 226 (1868 Oct 7), Union Lodge No. 7, Denver, Apprentice

Hetrich, Frank D
Proceedings 1874, pg 13 (1874 Feb 6), formerly of Union Lodge No. 7, Denver

Hetrick, Frank
Proceedings 1861-1869, pg 308 (1869 Sept 29), Union Lodge No. 7, Denver, Fellowcraft

Hetrick, Frank D
Proceedings 1870, pg 23 (1870 Sept 28), Union Lodge No. 7, Denver, Fellowcraft

Proceedings 1871, pg 22 (1871 Sept 27), Union Lodge No. 7, Denver, Fellowcraft

Proceedings 1872, pg 23 (1872 Sept 24), Union Lodge No. 7, Denver, Fellowcraft

Proceedings 1873, pg 40 (1873 Oct 1), Union Lodge No. 7, Denver, Fellowcraft

Proceedings 1874, pg 214 (1874 Sept 30), Union Lodge No. 7, Denver, Fellowcraft

Proceedings 1875, pg 79 (1875 Sept 22), Union Lodge No. 7, Denver, Fellowcraft

Proceedings 1876, pg 33 (1876 Sept 20), Union Lodge No. 7, Denver, Fellow Craft

Heuenstine, Wolf J
Proceedings 1872, pg 24 (1872 Sept 24), Black Hawk Lodge No. 11, Black Hawk

Colorado's Territorial Masons

Heusi, Martin
Proceedings 1872, pg 26 (1872 Sept 24), Washington Lodge No. 12, Georgetown, Dimitted

Hevefend, R
Proceedings 1861-1869, pg 152 (1865 Nov 7), Helena City Lodge U D, Helena City, Montana Territory

Hewett, Frank
Proceedings 1874, pg 228 (1874 Sept 30), Evanston Lodge U D, Evanston, Uintah County, Wyoming Territory, Apprentice

Hewitt, O B
Proceedings 1870, pg 91 (1869 Oct 26) Grand Orator, Grand Lodge of Nebraska

Hexter, E
Proceedings 1861-1869, pg 223 (1868 Oct 7) Denver Lodge No. 5
Proceedings 1861-1869, pg 305 (1869 Sept 29) Denver Lodge No. 5, Dimitted

Heyser, Josiah
Proceedings 1861-1869, pg 312 (1869 Sept 29), Cheyenne Lodge No. 16, Cheyenne, Apprentice

Hibbard, F I
Proceedings 1861-1869, pg 192 (1867 Oct 8), Nevada Lodge No. 4, Nevadaville
Proceedings 1861-1869, pg 304 (1869 Sept 29), Nevada Lodge No. 4, Nevadaville

Hibbard, F J
Proceedings 1861-1869, pg 166 (1866 Oct 2), Nevada Lodge No. 4, Nevadaville

Hibbard, Fred J
Proceedings 1861-1869, pg 222 (1868 Oct 7), Nevada Lodge No. 4, Nevadaville

Hibbard, Frederic J
Proceedings 1870, pg 20 (1870 Sept 28), Nevada Lodge No. 4, Nevadaville, Dimitted

Hickey, J S
Proceedings 1874, pg 223 (1874 Sept 30), Laramie Lodge No. 18, Laramie City

Hicks, S H
Proceedings 1875, pg 73 (1875 Sept 22) Golden City Lodge No. 1

Hicks, William
Proceedings 1870, pg 43 (1869 Nov 1) Grand Lodge of Arkansas, deceased

Hicks, Wm
Proceedings 1870, pg 41 (1869 Nov 1) Grand Lodge of Arkansas, deceased

Hieskell, Tyler D
Proceedings 1876, pg 40 (1876 Sept 20), Occidental Lodge No. 20, Greeley

Hiesterman, Henry F
Proceedings 1872, pg 55 (1872 Sept 24) Grand Lodge of British Columbia

Higenbotam, John
Proceedings 1872, pg 33 (1872 Sept 24), Occidental Lodge No. 20, Greeley
Proceedings 1873, pg 50 (1873 Oct 1), Occidental Lodge No. 20, Greeley

Higenbottom, J
Proceedings 1871, pg 30 (1871 Sept 27), Occidental Lodge U D, Greeley

Higginbottam, John
Proceedings 1874, pg 225 (1874 Sept 30), Occidental Lodge No. 20, Greeley

Higgins, George W
Proceedings 1876, pg 45 (1876 Sept 20), King Solomon Lodge U D, West Las Animas

Higgins, J A
Proceedings 1871, pg 24 (1871 Sept 27), Washington Lodge No. 12, Georgetown
Proceedings 1875, pg 81 (1875 Sept 22), Washington Lodge No. 12, Georgetown, Demitted

Higgins, John A
Proceedings 1861-1869, pg 310 (1869 Sept 29), Washington Lodge No. 12, Georgetown, Fellowcraft
Proceedings 1870, pg 26 (1870 Sept 28), Washington Lodge No. 12, Georgetown
Proceedings 1872, pg 26 (1872 Sept 24), Washington Lodge No. 12, Georgetown
Proceedings 1873, pg 43 (1873 Oct 1), Washington Lodge No. 12, Georgetown
Proceedings 1874, pg 217 (1874 Sept 30), Washington Lodge No. 12, Georgetown
Proceedings 1875, pg 73 (1875 Sept 22) Golden City Lodge No. 1
Proceedings 1876, pg 29 (1876 Sept 20) Golden City Lodge No. 1

Higgs, B Wilson
Proceedings 1876, pg 54 (1876 Sept 20) Grand Lodge of Prince Edward Island, Charlottetown

Higinbotam, J
Proceedings 1875, pg 87 (1875 Sept 22), Occidental Lodge No. 20, Greeley, Demitted

Higley, J C
Proceedings 1872, pg 33 (1872 Sept 24), Occidental Lodge No. 20, Greeley
Proceedings 1873, pg 50 (1873 Oct 1), Occidental Lodge No. 20, Greeley

Higley, Jonas C
Proceedings 1861-1869, pg 226 (1868 Oct 7), Union Lodge No. 7, Denver, Apprentice
Proceedings 1861-1869, pg 307 (1869 Sept 29), Union Lodge No. 7, Denver
Proceedings 1870, pg 23 (1870 Sept 28), Union Lodge No. 7, Denver
Proceedings 1871, pg 22 (1871 Sept 27), Union Lodge No. 7, Denver
Proceedings 1872, pg 23 (1872 Sept 24), Union Lodge No. 7, Denver, Dimitted

Proceedings 1874, pg 225 (1874 Sept 30), Occidental Lodge No. 20, Greeley

Proceedings 1875, pg 87 (1875 Sept 22), Occidental Lodge No. 20, Greeley

Proceedings 1876, pg 40 (1876 Sept 20), Occidental Lodge No. 20, Greeley

Hildrech, John L

Proceedings 1873, pg 47 (1873 Oct 1), Pueblo Lodge No. 17, Pueblo

Hildreth, John L

Proceedings 1874, pg 222 (1874 Sept 30), Pueblo Lodge No. 17, Pueblo, Pueblo County

Proceedings 1875, pg 85 (1875 Sept 22) Pueblo Lodge No. 17

Proceedings 1876, pg 39 (1876 Sept 20) Pueblo Lodge No. 17

Hill, C L

Proceedings 1861-1869, pg 113 (1863 Nov 3), Chivington Lodge No. 6, Central City, Fellowcraft

Proceedings 1861-1869, pg 168 (1866 Oct 2), Chivington Lodge No. 6, Central City

Hill, Charles I

Proceedings 1876, pg 32 (1876 Sept 20), Central Lodge No. 6, Central City

Hill, Charles L

Proceedings 1861-1869, pg 134 (1864 Nov 8), Chivington Lodge No. 6, Central City

Proceedings 1861-1869, pg 150 (1865 Nov 7), Chivington Lodge No. 6, Central City

Proceedings 1861-1869, pg 193 (1867 Oct 8), Chivington Lodge No. 6, Central City

Proceedings 1861-1869, pg 306 (1869 Sept 29), Central Lodge No. 6, Central City

Proceedings 1873, pg 38 (1873 Oct 1), Central Lodge No. 6, Central City

Proceedings 1874, pg 213 (1874 Sept 30), Central Lodge No. 6, Central

Proceedings 1875, pg 77 (1875 Sept 22), Central Lodge No. 6, Central City

Proceedings 1876, pg 50 (1876 Sept 20), Central Lodge No. 6, Central City

Hill, Chas L

Proceedings 1861-1869, pg 224 (1868 Oct 7), Chivington Lodge No. 6, Central City

Proceedings 1870, pg 22 (1870 Sept 28), Central Lodge No. 6, Central City

Proceedings 1871, pg 20 (1871 Sept 27), Central Lodge No. 6, Central

Proceedings 1872, pg 21 (1872 Sept 24), Denver Lodge No. 5, Denver

Hill, Demetrius

Proceedings 1861-1869, pg 227 (1868 Oct 7), Washington Lodge No. 12, Georgetown

Proceedings 1861-1869, pg 309 (1869 Sept 29), Washington Lodge No. 12, Georgetown

Proceedings 1870, pg 26 (1870 Sept 28), Washington Lodge No. 12, Georgetown

Proceedings 1871, pg 24 (1871 Sept 27), Washington Lodge No. 12, Georgetown

Proceedings 1872, pg 25 (1872 Sept 24), Washington Lodge No. 12, Georgetown

Proceedings 1873, pg 43 (1873 Oct 1), Washington Lodge No. 12, Georgetown

Proceedings 1874, pg 217 (1874 Sept 30), Washington Lodge No. 12, Georgetown

Proceedings 1875, pg 81 (1875 Sept 22), Washington Lodge No. 12, Georgetown

Proceedings 1876, pg 35 (1876 Sept 20), Washington Lodge No. 12, Georgetown

Hill, E P

Proceedings 1871, pg 24 (1871 Sept 27), Washington Lodge No. 12, Georgetown

Hill, Ezra P

Proceedings 1870, pg 26 (1870 Sept 28), Washington Lodge No. 12, Georgetown

Proceedings 1872, pg 26 (1872 Sept 24), Washington Lodge No. 12, Georgetown

Proceedings 1873, pg 43 (1873 Oct 1), Washington Lodge No. 12, Georgetown

Proceedings 1874, pg 217 (1874 Sept 30), Washington Lodge No. 12, Georgetown

Proceedings 1875, pg 81 (1875 Sept 22), Washington Lodge No. 12, Georgetown

Proceedings 1876, pg 35 (1876 Sept 20), Washington Lodge No. 12, Georgetown

Hill, John

Proceedings 1870, pg 30 (1870 Sept 28), Laramie Lodge No. 18, Laramie, Wyoming Territory

Hill, Noah

Proceedings 1861-1869, pg 77 (1862 Nov 4) Denver Lodge No. 5

Proceedings 1861-1869, pg 133 (1864 Nov 8) Denver Lodge No. 5

Proceedings 1861-1869, pg 149 (1865 Nov 7), Nevada Lodge No. 4, Nevadaville

Proceedings 1861-1869, pg 167 (1866 Oct 2) Denver Lodge No. 5

Hill, S C

Proceedings 1874, pg 220 (1874 Sept 30), Mount Moriah Lodge No. 15, Canon City, Demitted

Hill, Thomas J

Proceedings 1870, pg 27 (1870 Sept 28), Columbia Lodge No. 14, Boulder City

Proceedings 1871, pg 25 (1871 Sept 27), Columbia Lodge No. 14, Boulder City

Proceedings 1872, pg 27 (1872 Sept 24), Columbia Lodge No. 14, Boulder

Proceedings 1873, pg 45 (1873 Oct 1), Columbia Lodge No. 14, Boulder, died

Proceedings 1873, pg 57 (1873 Oct 1), Columbia Lodge No. 14, Boulder

Hill, Thos J

Proceedings 1861-1869, pg 310 (1869 Sept 29), Columbia Lodge No. 14, Boulder City

Hill, W C
Proceedings 1873, pg 39 (1873 Oct 1), Union Lodge No. 7, Denver
Proceedings 1875, pg 79 (1875 Sept 22), Union Lodge No. 7, Denver, Stricken from the rolls

Hill, William H
Proceedings 1870, pg 48 (1869 Oct 12) Grand Lodge of California

Hill, Wm C
Proceedings 1874, pg 214 (1874 Sept 30), Union Lodge No. 7, Denver

Hill, Wm E
Proceedings 1872, pg 43 (1872 Sept 24) Nebraska City, Grand Lodge of Nebraska
Proceedings 1874, pg 96 (1874 Sept 30) Grand Lodge of Nebraska

Hill, Wm H
Proceedings 1872, pg 43 (1872 Sept 24) Sacramento, Grand Lodge of California
Proceedings 1872, pg 57 (1872 Sept 24) Grand Lodge of California
Proceedings 1873, pg 60 (1873 Oct 1) Grand Lodge of California, Sacramento
Proceedings 1874, pg 47 (1874 Sept 30) Grand Lodge of California

Hillard, J B
Proceedings 1873, pg 43 (1873 Oct 1), El Paso Lodge No. 13, Colorado City
Proceedings 1871, pg 25 (1871 Sept 27), El Paso Lodge No. 13, Colorado City
Proceedings 1872, pg 27 (1872 Sept 24), El Paso Lodge No. 13, Colorado City
Proceedings 1876, pg 36 (1876 Sept 20), El Paso Lodge No. 13, Colorado City

Hilliard, John B
Proceedings 1874, pg 218 (1874 Sept 30), El Paso Lodge No. 13, Colorado Springs
Proceedings 1875, pg 82 (1875 Sept 22), El Paso Lodge No. 13, Colorado Springs

Hilliard, R T
Proceedings 1874, pg 228 (1874 Sept 30), Evanston Lodge U D, Evanston, Uintah County, Wyoming Territory

Hilliker, C W
Proceedings 1870, pg 30 (1870 Sept 28), Laramie Lodge No. 18, Laramie, Wyoming Territory

Hilliker, Charles M
Proceedings 1876, pg 24 (1876 Sept 20), Del Norte Lodge No. 29, Del Norte
Proceedings 1876, pg 44 (1876 Sept 20) Del Norte Lodge U D

Hillyer, Giles M
Proceedings 1872, pg 71 (1872 Sept 24) Grand Lodge of Mississippi, deceased

Hilton, B A
Proceedings 1874, pg 226 (1874 Sept 30), Weston Lodge No. 22, Littleton, Suspended
Proceedings 1876, pg 48 (1876 Sept 20), Weston Lodge No. 22, Littleton, 1876 Mar 18
Proceedings 1876, pg 51 (1876 Sept 20), Weston Lodge No. 22, Littleton, 1876 Mar 18

Hilton, B W
Proceedings 1872, pg 33 (1872 Sept 24), Occidental Lodge No. 20, Greeley
Proceedings 1873, pg 50 (1873 Oct 1), Occidental Lodge No. 20, Greeley
Proceedings 1874, pg 225 (1874 Sept 30), Occidental Lodge No. 20, Greeley
Proceedings 1875, pg 87 (1875 Sept 22), Occidental Lodge No. 20, Greeley

Hilton, Benj W
Proceedings 1876, pg 48 (1876 Sept 20), Occidental Lodge No. 20, Greeley, 1876 Jan 28
Proceedings 1876, pg 49 (1876 Sept 20), Occidental Lodge No. 20, Greeley, 1875 Nov 1
Proceedings 1876, pg 51 (1876 Sept 20), Occidental Lodge No. 20, Greeley, 1876 Jan 28

Hilton, Benjamin W
Proceedings 1871, pg 30 (1871 Sept 27), Occidental Lodge U D, Greeley

Hilton, G F
Proceedings 1870, pg 31 (1870 Sept 28), Laramie Lodge No. 18, Laramie, Wyoming Territory
Proceedings 1872, pg 32 (1872 Sept 24), Laramie Lodge No. 18, Laramie, Wyoming Territory
Proceedings 1872, pg 32 (1872 Sept 24), Laramie Lodge No. 18, Laramie, Wyoming Territory, Reinstated
Proceedings 1873, pg 48 (1873 Oct 1), Laramie Lodge No. 18, Laramie, Wyoming Territory, Dimitted

Hilton, George F
Proceedings 1871, pg 29 (1871 Sept 27), Laramie Lodge No. 18, Laramie, Wyoming Territory, Suspended

Hilton, John I
Proceedings 1870, pg 77 (1824 Jan 5) African Lodge at Boston

Hilton, John T
Proceedings 1861-1869, pg 334 (1784 Sept 29) Grand Master, Prince Hall Grand Lodge of Ancient York Masonry
Proceedings 1861-1869, pg 335 (1827) Grand Master, Prince Hall Grand Lodge of Ancient York Masonry
Proceedings 1870, pg 74 (1827 June 18) United Grand Lodge of England

Himebaugh, C
Proceedings 1870, pg 21 (1870 Sept 28), Denver Lodge No. 5, Denver

Himelaugh, Clinton
Proceedings 1861-1869, pg 223 (1868 Oct 7) Denver Lodge No. 5

Himrod, C
Proceedings 1874, pg 61 (1874 Sept 30) Grand Lodge of Idaho

Hindry, J B
Proceedings 1870, pg 19 (1870 Sept 28), Golden City Lodge No. 1, Golden City
Proceedings 1871, pg 17 (1871 Sept 27), Golden City Lodge No. 1, Golden City

Hindry, John B
Proceedings 1861-1869, pg 191 (1867 Oct 8) Golden City Lodge No. 1
Proceedings 1873, pg 35 (1873 Oct 1), Golden City Lodge No. 1, Golden City
Proceedings 1876, pg 29 (1876 Sept 20) Golden City Lodge No. 1

Hinebaugh, C
Proceedings 1861-1869, pg 305 (1869 Sept 29) Denver Lodge No. 5

Hinkle, D S
Proceedings 1861-1869, pg 111 (1863 Nov 3), Summit Lodge No. 2, Parkville, Fellowcraft

Hinkle, Geo W
Proceedings 1874, pg 225 (1874 Sept 30), Occidental Lodge No. 20, Greeley
Proceedings 1875, pg 87 (1875 Sept 22), Occidental Lodge No. 20, Greeley

Hinkle, George W
Proceedings 1876, pg 40 (1876 Sept 20), Occidental Lodge No. 20, Greeley

Hinsdale, Geo A
Proceedings 1870, pg 30 (1870 Sept 28), Pueblo Lodge No. 17, Pueblo, Fellowcraft
Proceedings 1872, pg 31 (1872 Sept 24), Pueblo Lodge No. 17, Pueblo, Fellowcraft

Hinsdale, George A
Proceedings 1871, pg 28 (1871 Sept 27), Pueblo Lodge No. 17, Pueblo, Fellowcraft
Proceedings 1873, pg 47 (1873 Oct 1), Pueblo Lodge No. 17, Pueblo, Fellowcraft
Proceedings 1874, pg 223 (1874 Sept 30), Pueblo Lodge No. 17, Pueblo, Pueblo County, died

Hitchings, H B
Proceedings 1861-1869, pg 102 (1863 Nov 3) petition for formation of a new lodge in Denver
Proceedings 1861-1869, pg 134 (1864 Nov 8), Union Lodge No. 7, Denver
Proceedings 1861-1869, pg 151 (1865 Nov 7), Chivington Lodge No. 6, Central City, reverend
Proceedings 1861-1869, pg 160 (1866 Oct 2), Union Lodge No. 7, Denver, Grand Chaplain
Proceedings 1861-1869, pg 161 (1866 Oct 2) Grand Chaplain
Proceedings 1861-1869, pg 169 (1866 Oct 2), Union Lodge No. 7, Denver
Proceedings 1861-1869, pg 175 (1867 Oct 7) Grand Chaplain
Proceedings 1861-1869, pg 190 (1867 Oct 8) Grand Chaplain
Proceedings 1861-1869, pg 219 (1868 Oct 7) Grand Chaplain
Proceedings 1861-1869, pg 225 (1868 Oct 7), Union Lodge No. 7, Denver
Proceedings 1861-1869, pg 308 (1869 Sept 29), Union Lodge No. 7, Denver, Dimitted

Hitchings, Henry
Proceedings 1861-1869, pg 149 (1865 Nov 7), Nevada Lodge No. 4, Nevadaville
Proceedings 1861-1869, pg 167 (1866 Oct 2) Denver Lodge No. 5

Hitchins, H
Proceedings 1861-1869, pg 112 (1863 Nov 3) Denver Lodge No. 5, Fellowcraft
Proceedings 1861-1869, pg 193 (1867 Oct 8) Denver Lodge No. 5
Proceedings 1861-1869, pg 223 (1868 Oct 7) Denver Lodge No. 5
Proceedings 1861-1869, pg 305 (1869 Sept 29) Denver Lodge No. 5

Hitchins, H B
Proceedings 1861-1869, pg 195 (1867 Oct 8), Union Lodge No. 7, Denver

Hitchins, Henry
Proceedings 1861-1869, pg 133 (1864 Nov 8) Denver Lodge No. 5
Proceedings 1870, pg 21 (1870 Sept 28), Denver Lodge No. 5, Denver
Proceedings 1872, pg 20 (1872 Sept 24), Denver Lodge No. 5, Denver

Hoag, A N
Proceedings 1871, pg 30 (1871 Sept 27), Occidental Lodge U D, Greeley, Fellowcraft
Proceedings 1872, pg 33 (1872 Sept 24), Occidental Lodge No. 20, Greeley
Proceedings 1874, pg 226 (1874 Sept 30), Occidental Lodge No. 20, Greeley, Demitted

Hoag, Addison N
Proceedings 1873, pg 50 (1873 Oct 1), Occidental Lodge No. 20, Greeley
Proceedings 1874, pg 224 (1874 Sept 30), Collins Lodge No. 19, Fort Collins, Larimer County
Proceedings 1875, pg 86 (1875 Sept 22), Collins Lodge No. 19, Fort Collins
Proceedings 1876, pg 39 (1876 Sept 20), Collins Lodge No. 19, Fort Collins

Hoagland, John A
Proceedings 1875, pg 73 (1875 Sept 22) Golden City Lodge No. 1
Proceedings 1876, pg 29 (1876 Sept 20) Golden City Lodge No. 1

Hoblin, Wm J
Proceedings 1861-1869, pg 194 (1867 Oct 8), Chivington Lodge No. 6, Central City

Hockaday, C N
Proceedings 1872, pg 27 (1872 Sept 24), Columbia Lodge No. 14, Boulder
Proceedings 1875, pg 83 (1875 Sept 22), Columbia Lodge No. 14, Boulder

Hockaday, C N, cont.
Proceedings 1876, pg 37 (1876 Sept 20), Columbia Lodge No. 14, Boulder

Hockaday, Charles M
Proceedings 1873, pg 44 (1873 Oct 1), Columbia Lodge No. 14, Boulder

Hockaday, Charles N
Proceedings 1871, pg 25 (1871 Sept 27), Columbia Lodge No. 14, Boulder City
Proceedings 1874, pg 219 (1874 Sept 30), Columbia Lodge No. 14, Boulder, Boulder County

Hockaday, Chas M
Proceedings 1870, pg 27 (1870 Sept 28), Columbia Lodge No. 14, Boulder City

Hockaday, Chas N
Proceedings 1861-1869, pg 311 (1869 Sept 29), Columbia Lodge No. 14, Boulder City, Apprentice

Hodges, Cornelius
Proceedings 1872, pg 43 (1872 Sept 24) Helena, Grand Lodge of Montana
Proceedings 1873, pg 60 (1873 Oct 1) Grand Lodge of Montana, Helena

Hodges, J H
Proceedings 1861-1869, pg 149 (1865 Nov 7), Nevada Lodge No. 4, Nevadaville
Proceedings 1861-1869, pg 167 (1866 Oct 2) Denver Lodge No. 5
Proceedings 1861-1869, pg 305 (1869 Sept 29) Denver Lodge No. 5
Proceedings 1876, pg 31 (1876 Sept 20) Denver Lodge No. 5

Hodges, James H
Proceedings 1870, pg 21 (1870 Sept 28), Denver Lodge No. 5, Denver
Proceedings 1871, pg 19 (1871 Sept 27) Denver Lodge No. 5
Proceedings 1873, pg 37 (1873 Oct 1), Denver Lodge No. 5, Denver
Proceedings 1874, pg 211 (1874 Sept 30), Denver Lodge No. 5, Denver
Proceedings 1875, pg 75 (1875 Sept 22) Denver Lodge No. 5

Hodges, Jas H
Proceedings 1861-1869, pg 133 (1864 Nov 8) Denver Lodge No. 5
Proceedings 1861-1869, pg 193 (1867 Oct 8) Denver Lodge No. 5
Proceedings 1861-1869, pg 223 (1868 Oct 7) Denver Lodge No. 5
Proceedings 1872, pg 20 (1872 Sept 24), Denver Lodge No. 5, Denver

Hodgman, H
Proceedings 1870, pg 31 (1870 Sept 28), Laramie Lodge No. 18, Laramie, Wyoming Territory

Hodgman, Henry
Proceedings 1871, pg 29 (1871 Sept 27), Laramie Lodge No. 18, Laramie, Wyoming Territory
Proceedings 1872, pg 32 (1872 Sept 24), Laramie Lodge No. 18, Laramie, Wyoming Territory
Proceedings 1873, pg 48 (1873 Oct 1), Laramie Lodge No. 18, Laramie, Wyoming Territory
Proceedings 1874, pg 223 (1874 Sept 30), Laramie Lodge No. 18, Laramie City

Hodgson, J H
Proceedings 1873, pg 39 (1873 Oct 1), Union Lodge No. 7, Denver
Proceedings 1874, pg 214 (1874 Sept 30), Union Lodge No. 7, Denver
Proceedings 1876, pg 33 (1876 Sept 20), Union Lodge No. 7, Denver

Hodgson, Jas H
Proceedings 1871, pg 22 (1871 Sept 27), Union Lodge No. 7, Denver

Hodgson, Joseph H
Proceedings 1870, pg 24 (1870 Sept 28), Union Lodge No. 7, Denver, Apprentice
Proceedings 1872, pg 22 (1872 Sept 24), Union Lodge No. 7, Denver
Proceedings 1875, pg 78 (1875 Sept 22), Union Lodge No. 7, Denver

Hoffman, Joseph
Proceedings 1875, pg 90 (1875 Sept 22), Huerfano Lodge U D, Walsenburg, Apprentice
Proceedings 1876, pg 43 (1876 Sept 20), Huerfano Lodge No. 27, Walsenburg, Apprentice

Hoffman, L I
Proceedings 1875, pg 85 (1875 Sept 22) Pueblo Lodge No. 17, Demitted

Hogarty, J M
Proceedings 1875, pg 87 (1875 Sept 22), Occidental Lodge No. 20, Greeley

Hogarty, Michael J
Proceedings 1876, pg 40 (1876 Sept 20), Occidental Lodge No. 20, Greeley

Holbrook, John R
Proceedings 1872, pg 76 (1872 Sept 24) Grand Lodge of New Hampshire

Holland, J M
Proceedings 1861-1869, pg 193 (1867 Oct 8) Denver Lodge No. 5
Proceedings 1861-1869, pg 223 (1868 Oct 7) Denver Lodge No. 5
Proceedings 1861-1869, pg 305 (1869 Sept 29) Denver Lodge No. 5

Holland, Joseph S
Proceedings 1875, pg 91 (1875 Sept 22), Las Animas Lodge U D, Trinidad

Holland, Samuel P
Proceedings 1870, pg 31 (1870 Sept 28), Collins Lodge No. 19, Fort Collins

Proceedings 1871, pg 30 (1871 Sept 27), Collins Lodge No. 19, Fort Collins

Proceedings 1872, pg 32 (1872 Sept 24), Collins Lodge No. 19, Fort Collins

Proceedings 1873, pg 49 (1873 Oct 1), Collins Lodge No. 19, Fort Collins

Proceedings 1874, pg 224 (1874 Sept 30), Collins Lodge No. 19, Fort Collins, Larimer County

Proceedings 1875, pg 86 (1875 Sept 22), Collins Lodge No. 19, Fort Collins

Proceedings 1876, pg 39 (1876 Sept 20), Collins Lodge No. 19, Fort Collins

Holliday, W H

Proceedings 1874, pg 223 (1874 Sept 30), Laramie Lodge No. 18, Laramie City

Hollingsworth, L F

Proceedings 1874, pg 218 (1874 Sept 30), El Paso Lodge No. 13, Colorado Springs

Proceedings 1875, pg 82 (1875 Sept 22), El Paso Lodge No. 13, Colorado Springs

Proceedings 1876, pg 49 (1876 Sept 20), El Paso Lodge No. 13, Colorado City, 1876 July 22

Hollom, Joseph S

Proceedings 1876, pg 50 (1876 Sept 20), Las Animas Lodge No. 28, Trinidad

Proceedings 1876, pg 44 (1876 Sept 20), Las Animas Lodge No. 28, Trinidad

Holloway, N B

Proceedings 1861-1869, pg 224 (1868 Oct 7), Chivington Lodge No. 6, Central City

Holloway, U B

Proceedings 1861-1869, pg 78 (1862 Nov 4), Chivington Lodge No. 6, Central City, Apprentice

Proceedings 1861-1869, pg 113 (1863 Nov 3), Chivington Lodge No. 6, Central City

Proceedings 1861-1869, pg 134 (1864 Nov 8), Chivington Lodge No. 6, Central City

Proceedings 1861-1869, pg 150 (1865 Nov 7), Chivington Lodge No. 6, Central City

Proceedings 1861-1869, pg 168 (1866 Oct 2), Chivington Lodge No. 6, Central City

Proceedings 1861-1869, pg 194 (1867 Oct 8), Chivington Lodge No. 6, Central City

Proceedings 1861-1869, pg 306 (1869 Sept 29), Central Lodge No. 6, Central City

Proceedings 1870, pg 22 (1870 Sept 28), Central Lodge No. 6, Central City

Proceedings 1871, pg 20 (1871 Sept 27), Central Lodge No. 6, Central

Holloway, Uriah B

Proceedings 1872, pg 22 (1872 Sept 24), Denver Lodge No. 5, Denver

Holly

Proceedings 1861-1869, pg 35 (1861 Dec 10) motion

Proceedings 1861-1869, pg 37 (1861 Dec 12) motion

Proceedings 1861-1869, pg 41 (1861 Dec 12) motion

Holly, C F

Proceedings 1861-1869, pg 3 (1861 Aug 2), Rocky Mountain Lodge No 8, Gold Hill

Proceedings 1861-1869, pg 4 (1861 Aug 2) committee

Proceedings 1861-1869, pg 4 (1861 Aug 2), Rocky Mountain Lodge No 8, Gold Hill

Proceedings 1861-1869, pg 5 (1861 Aug 2) Grand Orator, Gold Hill

Proceedings 1861-1869, pg 5 (1861 Aug 2) committee

Proceedings 1861-1869, pg 6 (1861 Aug 2) committee

Proceedings 1861-1869, pg 32 (1861 Dec 10) committee

Proceedings 1861-1869, pg 33 (1861 Dec 10) committee

Proceedings 1861-1869, pg 34 (1861 Dec 10) committee

Proceedings 1861-1869, pg 43 (1861 Dec 10), Rocky Mountain Lodge No. 3, Gold Hill

Holly, Chas F

Proceedings 1861-1869, pg 32 (1861 Dec 10), Rocky Mountain Lodge No 8, Gold Hill

Proceedings 1861-1869, pg 33 (1861 Dec 10) committee

Proceedings 1861-1869, pg 54 (1862 Nov 4), Rocky Mountain Lodge No. 3, Gold Hill

Holly, Hiram S

Proceedings 1876, pg 45 (1876 Sept 20), King Solomon Lodge U D, West Las Animas

Holmes

Proceedings 1861-1869, pg 276 (1867 June 4), Grand Master, Grand Lodge of New York

Proceedings 1873, pg 9 (1873 Sept 30), Ashlar Lodge U D, Colorado Springs

Holmes, Charles

Proceedings 1861-1869, pg 312 (1869 Sept 29), Pueblo Lodge No. 17, Pueblo

Proceedings 1870, pg 30 (1870 Sept 28), Pueblo Lodge No. 17, Pueblo

Proceedings 1871, pg 28 (1871 Sept 27), Pueblo Lodge No. 17, Pueblo

Proceedings 1872, pg 13 (1872 Sept 24), Ashlar Lodge U D, Colorado Springs

Proceedings 1872, pg 35 (1872 Sept 24), Ashlar Lodge U D, Colorado Springs

Proceedings 1873, pg 8 (1873 Jan 23), Ashlar Lodge U D, Colorado Springs

Proceedings 1873, pg 47 (1873 Oct 1), Pueblo Lodge No. 17, Pueblo

Proceedings 1874, pg 222 (1874 Sept 30), Pueblo Lodge No. 17, Pueblo, Pueblo County

Proceedings 1874, pg 223 (1874 Sept 30), Pueblo Lodge No. 17, Pueblo, Pueblo County, Reinstated

Proceedings 1875, pg 85 (1875 Sept 22) Pueblo Lodge No. 17

Proceedings 1876, pg 39 (1876 Sept 20) Pueblo Lodge No. 17

Holmes, Chas

Proceedings 1872, pg 31 (1872 Sept 24), Pueblo Lodge No. 17, Pueblo

Proceedings 1873, pg 13 (1873 Sept 30), Ashlar Lodge U D, Colorado Springs

Colorado's Territorial Masons

Holmes, N
Proceedings 1871, pg 31 (1871 Sept 27), Occidental Lodge U D, Greeley
Proceedings 1872, pg 34 (1872 Sept 24), Occidental Lodge No. 20, Greeley, Fellowcraft

Holmes, Nelson
Proceedings 1873, pg 50 (1873 Oct 1), Occidental Lodge No. 20, Greeley, Fellowcraft
Proceedings 1874, pg 225 (1874 Sept 30), Occidental Lodge No. 20, Greeley, Fellowcraft
Proceedings 1875, pg 87 (1875 Sept 22), Occidental Lodge No. 20, Greeley, Fellowcraft
Proceedings 1876, pg 40 (1876 Sept 20), Occidental Lodge No. 20, Greeley, Fellow Craft

Holmes, Robert D
Proceedings 1861-1869, pg 274 (1867 June 4), Grand Master, Grand Lodge of New York
Proceedings 1870, pg 94 (1870 June 7) Grand Lodge of New York, deceased

Holt, J M
Proceedings 1861-1869, pg 5 (1861 Aug 2) Junior Grand Warden, Gold Hill
Proceedings 1861-1869, pg 43 (1861 Dec 10), Rocky Mountain Lodge No. 3, Gold Hill
Proceedings 1861-1869, pg 315 (1869 Sept 29) Junior Grand Warden, August 1861, Dimitted
Proceedings 1870, pg 32 (1870 Sept 28) Junior Grand Warden, August 1861, Dimitted
Proceedings 1871, pg 34 (1871 Sept 27) Junior Grand Warden, Aug 1861, Dimitted
Proceedings 1872, pg 42 (1872 Sept 24) Junior Grand Warden, August 1861, Dimitted
Proceedings 1873, pg 58 (1873 Oct 1) Junior Grand Warden, Aug 1861, Dimitted
Proceedings 1874, pg 206 (1874 Sept 30) Junior Grand Warden, Aug 1861, deceased
Proceedings 1875, pg 93 (1875 Sept 22) Junior Grand Warden, Aug 1861, Deceased

Holt, Rowland
Proceedings 1870, pg 73 (1784 Sept 29) Deputy Grand Master, Grand Lodge of Massachusetts
Proceedings 1870, pg 76 (1789 Nov 9)

Hood, D W C
Proceedings 1875, pg 75 (1875 Sept 22) Denver Lodge No. 5
Proceedings 1876, pg 31 (1876 Sept 20) Denver Lodge No. 5

Hooper, H N
Proceedings 1861-1869, pg 196 (1867 Oct 8), El Paso Lodge U D, Colorado City

Hooper, Henry N
Proceedings 1861-1869, pg 171 (1866 Oct 2), El Paso U D, Colorado City

Hopkins, Abel
Proceedings 1870, pg 34 (1870 Sept 28) Grand Secretary, Grand Lodge of New Hampshire
Proceedings 1871, pg 35 (1871 Sept 27) Grand Secretary, Grand Lodge of New Hampshire

Hopkins, D L
Proceedings 1876, pg 36 (1876 Sept 20), Columbia Lodge No. 14, Boulder

Hopkins, Geo M
Proceedings 1870, pg 21 (1870 Sept 28), Denver Lodge No. 5, Denver
Proceedings 1871, pg 19 (1871 Sept 27) Denver Lodge No. 5
Proceedings 1872, pg 20 (1872 Sept 24), Denver Lodge No. 5, Denver
Proceedings 1873, pg 37 (1873 Oct 1), Denver Lodge No. 5, Denver
Proceedings 1874, pg 211 (1874 Sept 30), Denver Lodge No. 5, Denver
Proceedings 1875, pg 76 (1875 Sept 22) Denver Lodge No. 5, Stricken from the rolls
Proceedings 1861-1869, pg 342 (1868 Sept 15) Grand Master, Grand Lodge of Nevada
Proceedings 1870, pg 92 (1869 Sept 21) Grand Master, Grand Lodge of Nevada

Hoppe, A F
Proceedings 1861-1869, pg 196 (1867 Oct 8), Black Hawk Lodge No. 11, Black Hawk
Proceedings 1861-1869, pg 227 (1868 Oct 7), Black Hawk Lodge No. 11, Black Hawk
Proceedings 1861-1869, pg 309 (1869 Sept 29), Black Hawk Lodge No. 11, Black Hawk
Proceedings 1871, pg 23 (1871 Sept 27), Black Hawk Lodge No. 11, Black Hawk
Proceedings 1872, pg 24 (1872 Sept 24), Black Hawk Lodge No. 11, Black Hawk
Proceedings 1873, pg 42 (1873 Oct 1), Black Hawk Lodge No. 11, Black Hawk
Proceedings 1874, pg 216 (1874 Sept 30), Black Hawk Lodge No. 11, Black Hawk
Proceedings 1875, pg 80 (1875 Sept 22) Black Hawk Lodge No. 11
Proceedings 1876, pg 34 (1876 Sept 20) Black Hawk Lodge No. 11

Hoppee, A F
Proceedings 1870, pg 25 (1870 Sept 28), Black Hawk Lodge No. 11, Black Hawk

Hoppy, A F
Proceedings 1861-1869, pg 170 (1866 Oct 2), Black Hawk Lodge U D, Black Hawk

Horen, Ed
Proceedings 1876, pg 34 (1876 Sept 20) Black Hawk Lodge No. 11

Horn, T G
Proceedings 1876, pg 36 (1876 Sept 20), El Paso Lodge No. 13, Colorado City

Hornbeck, E D
Proceedings 1874, pg 209 (1874 Sept 30), Golden City Lodge No. 1, Golden City, Apprentice

Proceedings 1875, pg 73 (1875 Sept 22) Golden City Lodge No. 1, Apprentice

Proceedings 1876, pg 29 (1876 Sept 20) Golden City Lodge No. 1, Apprentice

Hornbeck, Elliot D
Proceedings 1872, pg 17 (1872 Sept 24), Golden City Lodge No. 1, Golden City, Apprentice

Horner, E J
Proceedings 1861-1869, pg 327 (1868 June 27) Grand Master, Grand Lodge of Delaware

Horner, Edwin J
Proceedings 1870, pg 52 (1869 June 28) Grand Master, Grand Lodge of Delaware

Horner, J W
Proceedings 1861-1869, pg 197 (1867 Oct 8), Columbia Lodge U D, Boulder

Horr, M L
Proceedings 1861-1869, pg 225 (1868 Oct 7), Union Lodge No. 7, Denver

Proceedings 1861-1869, pg 307 (1869 Sept 29), Union Lodge No. 7, Denver

Proceedings 1876, pg 33 (1876 Sept 20), Union Lodge No. 7, Denver

Horr, Monroe L
Proceedings 1870, pg 23 (1870 Sept 28), Union Lodge No. 7, Denver

Proceedings 1871, pg 22 (1871 Sept 27), Union Lodge No. 7, Denver

Proceedings 1872, pg 22 (1872 Sept 24), Union Lodge No. 7, Denver

Proceedings 1873, pg 39 (1873 Oct 1), Union Lodge No. 7, Denver

Proceedings 1874, pg 214 (1874 Sept 30), Union Lodge No. 7, Denver

Proceedings 1875, pg 78 (1875 Sept 22), Union Lodge No. 7, Denver

Hosford, W F
Proceedings 1874, pg 220 (1874 Sept 30), Cheyenne Lodge No. 16, Cheyenne, Wyoming Territory

Hoskinson, G E
Proceedings 1874, pg 205 (1874 Sept 30) Grand Lodge of Wisconsin, Green Bay

Hoskinson, Geo E
Proceedings 1872, pg 44 (1872 Sept 24) Green Bay, Grand Lodge of Wisconsin

Proceedings 1873, pg 61 (1873 Oct 1) Grand Lodge of Wisconsin, Green Bay

Hosmer, H L
Proceedings 1861-1869, pg 139 (1865 Nov 6), Montana Lodge U D, Virginia City, Montana Territory

Proceedings 1861-1869, pg 152 (1865 Nov 7), Montana Lodge U D, Virginia City, Montana Territory

Proceedings 1871, pg 35 (1871 Sept 27) Grand Secretary, Grand Lodge of Montana

Hosmer, Henry L
Proceedings 1872, pg 73 (1872 Sept 24) Grand Lodge of Montana

Hotchkiss, Arthur
Proceedings 1871, pg 30 (1871 Sept 27), Occidental Lodge U D, Greeley

Hough
Proceedings 1870, pg 94 (1870 Jan 19) Grand Lodge of New Jersey

Hough, J J
Proceedings 1871, pg 24 (1871 Sept 27), Washington Lodge No. 12, Georgetown

Hough, Jos H
Proceedings 1874, pg 108 (1874 Sept 30) Grand Lodge of New Jersey

Proceedings 1875, pg 96 (1875 Sept 22) Grand Lodge of New Jersey, Trenton

Proceedings 1876, pg 54 (1876 Sept 20) Grand Lodge of New Jersey, Trenton

Hough, Joseph
Proceedings 1861-1869, pg 309 (1869 Sept 29), Washington Lodge No. 12, Georgetown

Hough, Joseph H
Proceedings 1861-1869, pg 274 (1867 Jan 16), Grand Secretary, Grand Lodge of New Jersey

Proceedings 1861-1869, pg 291 (1869 Sept 28), Grand Secretary, Grand Lodge of New Jersey

Proceedings 1861-1869, pg 316 (1869 Sept 29) Grand Lodge of New Jersey

Proceedings 1861-1869, pg 342 (1869 Jan 20) Grand Secretary, Grand Lodge of New Jersey

Proceedings 1870, pg 34 (1870 Sept 28) Grand Secretary, Grand Lodge of New Jersey

Proceedings 1870, pg 92 (1870 Jan 19) Grand Secretary, Grand Lodge of New Jersey

Proceedings 1870, pg 93 (1870 Jan 19) Grand Secretary, Grand Lodge of New Jersey

Proceedings 1871, pg 35 (1871 Sept 27) Grand Secretary, Grand Lodge of New Jersey

Proceedings 1872, pg 44 (1872 Sept 24) Trenton, Grand Lodge of New Jersey

Proceedings 1872, pg 77 (1872 Sept 24) Grand Lodge of New Jersey

Proceedings 1872, pg 78 (1872 Sept 24) Grand Lodge of New Jersey

Proceedings 1873, pg 61 (1873 Oct 1) Grand Lodge of New Jersey, Trenton

Proceedings 1874, pg 204 (1874 Sept 30) Grand Lodge of New Jersey, Trenton

Hough, Joseph J
Proceedings 1870, pg 26 (1870 Sept 28), Washington Lodge No. 12, Georgetown

Proceedings 1872, pg 25 (1872 Sept 24), Washington Lodge No. 12, Georgetown

Proceedings 1873, pg 42 (1873 Oct 1), Washington Lodge No. 12, Georgetown

Proceedings 1874, pg 218 (1874 Sept 30), Washington Lodge No. 12, Georgetown, died

Colorado's Territorial Masons

Houghton, Giles E
  Proceedings 1874, pg 221 (1874 Sept 30), Cheyenne Lodge No. 16, Cheyenne, Wyoming Territory

Householder, W S
  Proceedings 1874, pg 216 (1874 Sept 30), Black Hawk Lodge No. 11, Black Hawk
  Proceedings 1875, pg 80 (1875 Sept 22) Black Hawk Lodge No. 11

Housholder, W L
  Proceedings 1876, pg 34 (1876 Sept 20) Black Hawk Lodge No. 11

Houx, B F
  Proceedings 1861-1869, pg 151 (1865 Nov 7), Chivington Lodge No. 6, Central City
  Proceedings 1861-1869, pg 169 (1866 Oct 2), Union Lodge No. 7, Denver
  Proceedings 1861-1869, pg 195 (1867 Oct 8), Union Lodge No. 7, Denver
  Proceedings 1861-1869, pg 225 (1868 Oct 7), Union Lodge No. 7, Denver
  Proceedings 1861-1869, pg 307 (1869 Sept 29), Union Lodge No. 7, Denver

Howard, B C
  Proceedings 1870, pg 31 (1870 Sept 28), Laramie Lodge No. 18, Laramie, Wyoming Territory
  Proceedings 1871, pg 29 (1871 Sept 27), Laramie Lodge No. 18, Laramie, Wyoming Territory
  Proceedings 1872, pg 32 (1872 Sept 24), Laramie Lodge No. 18, Laramie, Wyoming Territory
  Proceedings 1873, pg 48 (1873 Oct 1), Laramie Lodge No. 18, Laramie, Wyoming Territory
  Proceedings 1874, pg 224 (1874 Sept 30), Laramie Lodge No. 18, Laramie City, Demitted

Howard, Michael
  Proceedings 1873, pg 43 (1873 Oct 1), Washington Lodge No. 12, Georgetown
  Proceedings 1874, pg 217 (1874 Sept 30), Washington Lodge No. 12, Georgetown
  Proceedings 1875, pg 81 (1875 Sept 22), Washington Lodge No. 12, Georgetown
  Proceedings 1876, pg 35 (1876 Sept 20), Washington Lodge No. 12, Georgetown

Howard, N R
  Proceedings 1870, pg 28 (1870 Sept 28), Columbia Lodge No. 14, Boulder City, Apprentice
  Proceedings 1871, pg 26 (1871 Sept 27), Columbia Lodge No. 14, Boulder City, Apprentice
  Proceedings 1872, pg 28 (1872 Sept 24), Columbia Lodge No. 14, Boulder, Apprentice
  Proceedings 1873, pg 45 (1873 Oct 1), Columbia Lodge No. 14, Boulder, Apprentice
  Proceedings 1874, pg 219 (1874 Sept 30), Columbia Lodge No. 14, Boulder, Boulder County, Apprentice
  Proceedings 1875, pg 83 (1875 Sept 22), Columbia Lodge No. 14, Boulder, Apprentice
  Proceedings 1876, pg 37 (1876 Sept 20), Columbia Lodge No. 14, Boulder, Apprentice

Howard, Nelson
  Proceedings 1871, pg 30 (1871 Sept 27), Collins Lodge No. 19, Fort Collins, Apprentice
  Proceedings 1872, pg 33 (1872 Sept 24), Collins Lodge No. 19, Fort Collins, Apprentice
  Proceedings 1873, pg 49 (1873 Oct 1), Collins Lodge No. 19, Fort Collins, Apprentice
  Proceedings 1874, pg 225 (1874 Sept 30), Collins Lodge No. 19, Fort Collins, Larimer County, Apprentice

Howard, Peter
  Proceedings 1870, pg 77 (1824 Jan 5) African Lodge at Boston

Howard, Thomas
  Proceedings 1870, pg 73 (1784 Sept 29) Earl of Effingham
  Proceedings 1870, pg 77 (1784 Sept 29) Earl of Effingham

Howard, Thomas F
  Proceedings 1876, pg 35 (1876 Sept 20), Washington Lodge No. 12, Georgetown

Howard, Thos F
  Proceedings 1875, pg 81 (1875 Sept 22), Washington Lodge No. 12, Georgetown

Howard, Thos G
  Proceedings 1876, pg 50 (1876 Sept 20), Washington Lodge No. 12, Georgetown

Howard, W R
  Proceedings 1870, pg 4 (1870 Sept 27), Columbia Lodge No. 14, Boulder

Howard, William H
  Proceedings 1870, pg 64 (1870 Feb 14) Grand Lodge of Louisiana, deceased

Howbert, I
  Proceedings 1871, pg 24 (1871 Sept 27), El Paso Lodge No. 13, Colorado City
  Proceedings 1873, pg 6 (1873 Sept 30), El Paso Lodge No. 13, Colorado City

Howbert, Irving
  Proceedings 1872, pg 26 (1872 Sept 24), El Paso Lodge No. 13, Colorado City
  Proceedings 1873, pg 43 (1873 Oct 1), El Paso Lodge No. 13, Colorado City
  Proceedings 1874, pg 218 (1874 Sept 30), El Paso Lodge No. 13, Colorado Springs
  Proceedings 1875, pg 82 (1875 Sept 22), El Paso Lodge No. 13, Colorado Springs
  Proceedings 1876, pg 36 (1876 Sept 20), El Paso Lodge No. 13, Colorado City

Howe, Geo M
  Proceedings 1870, pg 20 (1870 Sept 28), Denver Lodge No. 5, Denver, Not a Member
  Proceedings 1871, pg 11 (1871 Sept 26) Recorder, Colorado Commandery, No. 1
  Proceedings 1873, pg cover (1873 Oct 1), Denver Chapter No. 2, Denver
  Proceedings 1873, pg cover (1873 Oct 1), Colorado Commandery No. 1, Denver
  Proceedings 1873, pg 17 (1873 Oct 1) Grand Organist

Proceedings 1874, pg 3 (1874 Sept 29) Grand Organist

Proceedings 1874, pg 32 (1874 Sept 30) Grand Organist, Denver

Proceedings 1875, pg cover (1875 Sept 22) Grand Lecturer, Denver

Proceedings 1875, pg 33 (1875 Sept 22) Grand Lecturer, Denver

Proceedings 1875, pg 75 (1875 Sept 22) Denver Lodge No. 5

Proceedings 1876, pg 5 (1876 Sept 19) Denver Lodge No. 5

Proceedings 1876, pg 14 (1876 Mar 20) Grand Lecturer

Howe, George M

Proceedings 1875, pg 15 (1875 Sept 21) Grand Organist

Proceedings 1875, pg 24 (1875 Sept 21) Assistant Librarian

Proceedings 1876, pg cover (1876 Sept 20) Grand Lecturer, Denver

Proceedings 1876, pg 3 (1876 Sept 19) Grand Lecturer

Proceedings 1876, pg 30 (1876 Sept 20) Denver Lodge No. 5

Howe, O B

Proceedings 1861-1869, pg 152 (1865 Nov 7), Helena City Lodge U D, Helena City, Montana Territory

Howe, Samuel

Proceedings 1876, pg 31 (1876 Sept 20) Denver Lodge No. 5

Howell, C S

Proceedings 1870, pg 29 (1870 Sept 28), Cheyenne Lodge No. 16, Cheyenne, Wyoming Territory, Fellowcraft

Howell, Charles L

Proceedings 1871, pg 27 (1871 Sept 27), Cheyenne Lodge No. 16, Cheyenne, Wyoming Territory, Fellowcraft

Proceedings 1872, pg 30 (1872 Sept 24), Cheyenne Lodge No. 16, Cheyenne, Wyoming Territory, Fellowcraft

Proceedings 1874, pg 221 (1874 Sept 30), Cheyenne Lodge No. 16, Cheyenne, Wyoming Territory, Fellowcraft

Howell, Chas L

Proceedings 1861-1869, pg 312 (1869 Sept 29), Cheyenne Lodge No. 16, Cheyenne, Fellowcraft

Proceedings 1873, pg 46 (1873 Oct 1), Cheyenne Lodge No. 16, Cheyenne, Wyoming Territory, Fellowcraft

Howell, J S

Proceedings 1861-1869, pg 112 (1863 Nov 3) Denver Lodge No. 5

Proceedings 1861-1869, pg 133 (1864 Nov 8) Denver Lodge No. 5

Proceedings 1861-1869, pg 149 (1865 Nov 7), Nevada Lodge No. 4, Nevadaville

Proceedings 1861-1869, pg 167 (1866 Oct 2) Denver Lodge No. 5

Proceedings 1861-1869, pg 193 (1867 Oct 8) Denver Lodge No. 5

Proceedings 1861-1869, pg 223 (1868 Oct 7) Denver Lodge No. 5

Proceedings 1861-1869, pg 305 (1869 Sept 29) Denver Lodge No. 5

Proceedings 1870, pg 21 (1870 Sept 28), Denver Lodge No. 5, Denver

Proceedings 1872, pg 20 (1872 Sept 24), Denver Lodge No. 5, Denver

Howell, W R

Proceedings 1873, pg 6 (1873 Sept 30), Columbia Lodge No. 14, Boulder

Proceedings 1873, pg 7 (1873 Sept 30) committee

Proceedings 1873, pg 31 (1873 Oct 1) mileage and per diem

Proceedings 1873, pg 32 (1873 Oct 1) committee

Howell, William

Proceedings 1861-1869, pg 303 (1869 Sept 29) Golden City Lodge No. 1

Howell, William R

Proceedings 1873, pg 44 (1873 Oct 1), Columbia Lodge No. 14, Boulder

Proceedings 1874, pg 219 (1874 Sept 30), Columbia Lodge No. 14, Boulder, Boulder County

Proceedings 1875, pg 83 (1875 Sept 22), Columbia Lodge No. 14, Boulder

Proceedings 1876, pg 36 (1876 Sept 20), Columbia Lodge No. 14, Boulder

Howell, Wm

Proceedings 1861-1869, pg 221 (1868 Oct 7) Golden City Lodge No. 1

Proceedings 1861-1869, pg 230 (1868 Oct 7), Valmont Lodge U D, Valmont

Howell, Wm R

Proceedings 1861-1869, pg 165 (1866 Oct 2) Golden City Lodge No. 1

Proceedings 1861-1869, pg 191 (1867 Oct 8) Golden City Lodge No. 1

Proceedings 1870, pg 19 (1870 Sept 28), Golden City Lodge No. 1, Golden City, Dimitted

Proceedings 1870, pg 27 (1870 Sept 28), Columbia Lodge No. 14, Boulder City

Proceedings 1871, pg 25 (1871 Sept 27), Columbia Lodge No. 14, Boulder City

Proceedings 1872, pg 27 (1872 Sept 24), Columbia Lodge No. 14, Boulder

Proceedings 1873, pg 14 (1873 Sept 30) Grand Teller

Proceedings 1873, pg 16 (1873 Oct 1) Grand Lecturer

Howes, W J L

Proceedings 1876, pg 48 (1876 Sept 20), Columbia Lodge No. 14, Boulder, 1876 Jan 8

Howland, S W

Proceedings 1871, pg 31 (1871 Sept 27), Argenta Lodge U D, Salt Lake City, Utah, Apprentice

Howlert, Irvine

Proceedings 1870, pg 27 (1870 Sept 28), El Paso Lodge No. 13, Colorado City

Hows, Geo W

Proceedings 1872, pg 8 (1872 June 6), Cheyenne Lodge No. 16, Cheyenne, Wyoming Territory

Howse, W J L
  Proceedings 1873, pg 44 (1873 Oct 1), Columbia Lodge No. 14, Boulder
  Proceedings 1875, pg 83 (1875 Sept 22), Columbia Lodge No. 14, Boulder

Howse, W L
  Proceedings 1874, pg 219 (1874 Sept 30), Columbia Lodge No. 14, Boulder, Boulder County

Hoyle, S Z
  Proceedings 1875, pg 73 (1875 Sept 22) Golden City Lodge No. 1

Hoyle, Stephen Z
  Proceedings 1874, pg 209 (1874 Sept 30), Golden City Lodge No. 1, Golden City
  Proceedings 1876, pg 29 (1876 Sept 20) Golden City Lodge No. 1

Hoyt, C A
  Proceedings 1861-1869, pg 224 (1868 Oct 7), Chivington Lodge No. 6, Central City
  Proceedings 1861-1869, pg 306 (1869 Sept 29), Central Lodge No. 6, Central City

Hoyt, Charles A
  Proceedings 1861-1869, pg 194 (1867 Oct 8), Chivington Lodge No. 6, Central City
  Proceedings 1875, pg 77 (1875 Sept 22), Central Lodge No. 6, Central City
  Proceedings 1876, pg 32 (1876 Sept 20), Central Lodge No. 6, Central City

Hoyt, Chas A
  Proceedings 1870, pg 22 (1870 Sept 28), Central Lodge No. 6, Central City
  Proceedings 1871, pg 20 (1871 Sept 27), Central Lodge No. 6, Central
  Proceedings 1872, pg 21 (1872 Sept 24), Denver Lodge No. 5, Denver
  Proceedings 1873, pg 39 (1873 Oct 1), Central Lodge No. 6, Central City
  Proceedings 1874, pg 213 (1874 Sept 30), Central Lodge No. 6, Central
  Proceedings 1876, pg 50 (1876 Sept 20), Central Lodge No. 6, Central City

Hoyt, James A
  Proceedings 1874, pg 123 (1874 Sept 30) Grand Lodge of South Carolina

Hoyt, S N
  Proceedings 1875, pg 79 (1875 Sept 22), Union Lodge No. 7, Denver, Stricken from the rolls

Hoyt, Sam'l N
  Proceedings 1871, pg 22 (1871 Sept 27), Union Lodge No. 7, Denver

Hoyt, Samuel N
  Proceedings 1861-1869, pg 307 (1869 Sept 29), Union Lodge No. 7, Denver
  Proceedings 1870, pg 23 (1870 Sept 28), Union Lodge No. 7, Denver
  Proceedings 1872, pg 22 (1872 Sept 24), Union Lodge No. 7, Denver
  Proceedings 1873, pg 39 (1873 Oct 1), Union Lodge No. 7, Denver
  Proceedings 1874, pg 214 (1874 Sept 30), Union Lodge No. 7, Denver

Hubbell, R M
  Proceedings 1876, pg 41 (1876 Sept 20), St Vrain Lodge No. 23, Longmont

Hudd, J Thos
  Proceedings 1872, pg 43 (1872 Sept 24) Middletown, Grand Lodge of Delaware

Hudgens, J W
  Proceedings 1861-1869, pg 152 (1865 Nov 7), Montana Lodge U D, Virginia City, Montana Territory

Huerfano Lodge No. 27
  Proceedings 1876, pg 52 (1876 Sept 20)

Huerfano Lodge No. 27, Walsenburg
  Proceedings 1875, pg 90 (1875 Sept 22), dispensation granted 25 Aug 1874, charter granted 22 Sept 1875
  Proceedings 1876, pg 8 (1875 Oct 6) lodge dedicated and officers installed
  Proceedings 1876, pg 13 (1875 Sept 22) charter fees paid
  Proceedings 1876, pg 24 (1876 Sept 20) correction to returns

Huerfano Lodge U D
  Proceedings 1875, pg 25 (1875 Sept 21) dues paid
  Proceedings 1875, pg 34 (1875 Sept 22) chartered as Huerfano Lodge No. 27
  Proceedings 1875, pg 92 (1875 Sept 22)

Huerfano Lodge U D, Walsenburg
  Proceedings 1874, pg 8 (1874 Aug 27) dispensation granted
  Proceedings 1874, pg 19 (1874 Sept 29) returns late
  Proceedings 1874, pg 19 (1874 Sept 29) failed to make a return
  Proceedings 1874, pg 35 (1874 Sept 30) charter not granted
  Proceedings 1874, pg 208 (1874 Sept 30)
  Proceedings 1875, pg 19 (1874 Apr) communication

Huerfano Lodge U D, Walsenburg
  Proceedings 1875, pg 24 (1875 Sept 21) returns

Huff, James
  Proceedings 1861-1869, pg 112 (1863 Nov 3), Nevada Lodge No. 4, Nevadaville, Apprentice
  Proceedings 1861-1869, pg 132 (1864 Nov 8), Nevada Lodge No. 4, Nevadaville, Apprentice
  Proceedings 1861-1869, pg 148 (1865 Nov 7), Nevada Lodge No. 4, Nevadaville, Apprentice
  Proceedings 1861-1869, pg 166 (1866 Oct 2), Nevada Lodge No. 4, Nevadaville, Apprentice
  Proceedings 1861-1869, pg 192 (1867 Oct 8), Nevada Lodge No. 4, Nevadaville, Apprentice
  Proceedings 1861-1869, pg 222 (1868 Oct 7), Nevada Lodge No. 4, Nevadaville, Apprentice

Huffman, L J
  Proceedings 1874, pg 222 (1874 Sept 30), Pueblo Lodge No. 17, Pueblo, Pueblo County

Colorado's Territorial Masons

Huges, Robert
Proceedings 1861-1869, pg 148 (1865 Nov 7), Nevada Lodge No. 4, Nevadaville

Hughan, James
Proceedings 1874, pg 62 (1874 Sept 30) Grand Lodge of England

Hughes, Ed C
Proceedings 1861-1869, pg 227 (1868 Oct 7), Black Hawk Lodge No. 11, Black Hawk
Proceedings 1861-1869, pg 309 (1869 Sept 29), Black Hawk Lodge No. 11, Black Hawk
Proceedings 1870, pg 25 (1870 Sept 28), Black Hawk Lodge No. 11, Black Hawk
Proceedings 1871, pg 23 (1871 Sept 27), Black Hawk Lodge No. 11, Black Hawk
Proceedings 1872, pg 24 (1872 Sept 24), Black Hawk Lodge No. 11, Black Hawk
Proceedings 1873, pg 41 (1873 Oct 1), Black Hawk Lodge No. 11, Black Hawk
Proceedings 1875, pg 80 (1875 Sept 22) Black Hawk Lodge No. 11
Proceedings 1876, pg 34 (1876 Sept 20) Black Hawk Lodge No. 11

Hughes, Edward C
Proceedings 1874, pg 216 (1874 Sept 30), Black Hawk Lodge No. 11, Black Hawk

Hughes, Hugh
Proceedings 1861-1869, pg 312 (1869 Sept 29), Cheyenne Lodge No. 16, Cheyenne, Apprentice
Proceedings 1871, pg 28 (1871 Sept 27), Cheyenne Lodge No. 16, Cheyenne, Wyoming Territory, Apprentice
Proceedings 1872, pg 30 (1872 Sept 24), Cheyenne Lodge No. 16, Cheyenne, Wyoming Territory, Apprentice
Proceedings 1873, pg 46 (1873 Oct 1), Cheyenne Lodge No. 16, Cheyenne, Wyoming Territory, Apprentice
Proceedings 1874, pg 221 (1874 Sept 30), Cheyenne Lodge No. 16, Cheyenne, Wyoming Territory, Apprentice

Hughes, Robert
Proceedings 1861-1869, pg 166 (1866 Oct 2), Nevada Lodge No. 4, Nevadaville
Proceedings 1861-1869, pg 222 (1868 Oct 7), Nevada Lodge No. 4, Nevadaville
Proceedings 1861-1869, pg 304 (1869 Sept 29), Nevada Lodge No. 4, Nevadaville
Proceedings 1870, pg 20 (1870 Sept 28), Nevada Lodge No. 4, Nevadaville
Proceedings 1872, pg 18 (1872 Sept 24), Nevada Lodge No. 4, Bald Mountain
Proceedings 1873, pg 36 (1873 Oct 1), Nevada Lodge No. 4, Nevada
Proceedings 1874, pg 211 (1874 Sept 30), Nevada Lodge No. 4, Bald Mountain, Gilpin County, Stricken from the rolls

Hughes, Robt
Proceedings 1861-1869, pg 191 (1867 Oct 8), Nevada Lodge No. 4, Nevadaville
Proceedings 1871, pg 18 (1871 Sept 27), Nevada Lodge No. 4, Bald Mountain

Hughes, Thos
Proceedings 1872, pg 36 (1872 Sept 24), Ashlar Lodge U D, Colorado Springs

Hughs, Hugh
Proceedings 1870, pg 29 (1870 Sept 28), Cheyenne Lodge No. 16, Cheyenne, Wyoming Territory, Apprentice

Hugman, B C
Proceedings 1861-1869, pg 94 (1863 Apr 17) Grand Deacon

Hull
Proceedings 1861-1869, pg 267 (1867 Jan 20), Grand Master, Grand Lodge of Montana

Hultman, August
Proceedings 1876, pg 29 (1876 Sept 20) Golden City Lodge No. 1, Fellow Craft

Humphrey, J F
Proceedings 1872, pg 36 (1872 Sept 24), Ashlar Lodge U D, Colorado Springs

Humphrey, William
Proceedings 1861-1869, pg 134 (1864 Nov 8), Chivington Lodge No. 6, Central City, Apprentice
Proceedings 1873, pg 39 (1873 Oct 1), Central Lodge No. 6, Central City, Apprentice
Proceedings 1874, pg 213 (1874 Sept 30), Central Lodge No. 6, Central, Apprentice
Proceedings 1875, pg 77 (1875 Sept 22), granted permittion to earn degrees at Wasatch Lodge No. 1, Utah

Humphrey, Wm
Proceedings 1861-1869, pg 113 (1863 Nov 3), Chivington Lodge No. 6, Central City, Apprentice
Proceedings 1861-1869, pg 150 (1865 Nov 7), Chivington Lodge No. 6, Central City, Apprentice
Proceedings 1861-1869, pg 169 (1866 Oct 2), Chivington Lodge No. 6, Central City, Apprentice
Proceedings 1861-1869, pg 194 (1867 Oct 8), Chivington Lodge No. 6, Central City, Apprentice
Proceedings 1861-1869, pg 225 (1868 Oct 7), Chivington Lodge No. 6, Central City, Apprentice
Proceedings 1861-1869, pg 307 (1869 Sept 29), Central Lodge No. 6, Central City, Apprentice
Proceedings 1870, pg 22 (1870 Sept 28), Central Lodge No. 6, Central City, Apprentice
Proceedings 1871, pg 21 (1871 Sept 27), Central Lodge No. 6, Central, Apprentice
Proceedings 1872, pg 21 (1872 Sept 24), Denver Lodge No. 5, Denver, Apprentice

Hunt, Frederick A
Proceedings 1876, pg 37 (1876 Sept 20), Columbia Lodge No. 14, Boulder

Hunt, J S
Proceedings 1870, pg 28 (1870 Sept 28), Cheyenne Lodge No. 16, Cheyenne, Wyoming Territory, Not a Member
Proceedings 1871, pg 27 (1871 Sept 27), Cheyenne Lodge No. 16, Cheyenne, Wyoming Territory
Proceedings 1872, pg 49 (1872 Sept 24), Cheyenne Lodge No. 16, Cheyenne, Wyoming Territory

Hunt, J S, cont.
Proceedings 1874, pg 221 (1874 Sept 30), Cheyenne Lodge No. 16, Cheyenne, Wyoming Territory

Hunt, James S
Proceedings 1861-1869, pg 312 (1869 Sept 29), Pueblo Lodge No. 17, Pueblo
Proceedings 1870, pg 30 (1870 Sept 28), Pueblo Lodge No. 17, Pueblo

Hunt, William K
Proceedings 1875, pg 83 (1875 Sept 22), Columbia Lodge No. 14, Boulder

Hunt, William L
Proceedings 1876, pg 37 (1876 Sept 20), Columbia Lodge No. 14, Boulder

Hunt, William R
Proceedings 1874, pg 219 (1874 Sept 30), Columbia Lodge No. 14, Boulder, Boulder County

Hunter, H W
Proceedings 1872, pg 36 (1872 Sept 24), Ashlar Lodge U D, Colorado Springs

Hunter, John
Proceedings 1874, pg 228 (1874 Sept 30), Evanston Lodge U D, Evanston, Uintah County, Wyoming Territory, Apprentice

Huntington, A J
Proceedings 1875, pg 88 (1875 Sept 22), Weston Lodge No. 22, Littleton
Proceedings 1876, pg 41 (1876 Sept 20), Weston Lodge No. 22, Littleton

Huntington, J W
Proceedings 1861-1869, pg 149 (1865 Nov 7), Nevada Lodge No. 4, Nevadaville
Proceedings 1861-1869, pg 166 (1866 Oct 2) Denver Lodge No. 5
Proceedings 1861-1869, pg 193 (1867 Oct 8) Denver Lodge No. 5
Proceedings 1861-1869, pg 224 (1868 Oct 7) Denver Lodge No. 5, Dimitted

Huntsman, C R
Proceedings 1861-1869, pg 110 (1863 Nov 3) Golden City Lodge No. 1
Proceedings 1861-1869, pg 131 (1864 Nov 8) Golden City Lodge No. 1, dimitted

Hupper, E A
Proceedings 1861-1869, pg 196 (1867 Oct 8), Columbia Lodge U D, Boulder

Hurd, Nathan S
Proceedings 1873, pg 43 (1873 Oct 1), Washington Lodge No. 12, Georgetown
Proceedings 1874, pg 217 (1874 Sept 30), Washington Lodge No. 12, Georgetown
Proceedings 1875, pg 81 (1875 Sept 22), Washington Lodge No. 12, Georgetown
Proceedings 1876, pg 34 (1876 Sept 20), Washington Lodge No. 12, Georgetown

Hurford
Proceedings 1861-1869, pg 345 (1868 June 22) Grand Secretary, Grand Lodge of Oregon

Hurford, J E
Proceedings 1861-1869, pg 316 (1869 Sept 29) Grand Lodge of Oregon
Proceedings 1870, pg 34 (1870 Sept 28) Grand Secretary, Grand Lodge of Oregon
Proceedings 1870, pg 97 (1869 June 21) Grand Secretary, Grand Lodge of Oregon
Proceedings 1870, pg 98 (1870 June 20) Grand Master, Grand Lodge of Oregon
Proceedings 1871, pg 35 (1871 Sept 27) Grand Secretary, Grand Lodge of Oregon
Proceedings 1872, pg 83 (1872 Sept 24) Grand Lodge of Oregon

Hurlburt, Frank B
Proceedings 1874, pg 216 (1874 Sept 30), Black Hawk Lodge No. 11, Black Hawk

Hurlbut, F B
Proceedings 1861-1869, pg 170 (1866 Oct 2), Black Hawk Lodge U D, Black Hawk
Proceedings 1861-1869, pg 195 (1867 Oct 8), Black Hawk Lodge No. 11, Black Hawk
Proceedings 1861-1869, pg 227 (1868 Oct 7), Black Hawk Lodge No. 11, Black Hawk
Proceedings 1876, pg 48 (1876 Sept 20) Black Hawk Lodge No. 11, 1876 Feb 24

Hurlbut, Frank B
Proceedings 1861-1869, pg 309 (1869 Sept 29), Black Hawk Lodge No. 11, Black Hawk
Proceedings 1875, pg 80 (1875 Sept 22) Black Hawk Lodge No. 11

Hurlbut, H E
Proceedings 1861-1869, pg 170 (1866 Oct 2), Black Hawk Lodge U D, Black Hawk
Proceedings 1861-1869, pg 230 (1868 Oct 7), Valmont Lodge U D, Valmont

Hurlbut, T B
Proceedings 1870, pg 25 (1870 Sept 28), Black Hawk Lodge No. 11, Black Hawk, Dimitted

Hurney, George
Proceedings 1861-1869, pg 307 (1869 Sept 29), Union Lodge No. 7, Denver

Hurst, R B
Proceedings 1875, pg 89 (1875 Sept 22), Doric Lodge No. 25, Fairplay, Apprentice
Proceedings 1876, pg 51 (1876 Sept 20), Doric Lodge No. 25, Fairplay, 1875 Nov 6

Hurst, Robert B
Proceedings 1874, pg 228 (1874 Sept 30), Doric Lodge U D, Fairplay, Apprentice

Hurtel, G W
Proceedings 1861-1869, pg 167 (1866 Oct 2) Denver Lodge No. 5

Hussey, Warren
- Proceedings 1861-1869, pg 149 (1865 Nov 7), Nevada Lodge No. 4, Nevadaville, Apprentice
- Proceedings 1861-1869, pg 167 (1866 Oct 2) Denver Lodge No. 5
- Proceedings 1861-1869, pg 193 (1867 Oct 8) Denver Lodge No. 5
- Proceedings 1861-1869, pg 223 (1868 Oct 7) Denver Lodge No. 5
- Proceedings 1861-1869, pg 305 (1869 Sept 29) Denver Lodge No. 5
- Proceedings 1870, pg 21 (1870 Sept 28), Denver Lodge No. 5, Denver
- Proceedings 1871, pg 31 (1871 Sept 27), Argenta Lodge U D, Salt Lake City, Utah
- Proceedings 1872, pg 20 (1872 Sept 24), Denver Lodge No. 5, Denver, Dimitted

Hutchenson, Joseph
- Proceedings 1874, pg 220 (1874 Sept 30), Mount Moriah Lodge No. 15, Canon City
- Proceedings 1875, pg 84 (1875 Sept 22), Mount Moriah Lodge No. 15, Canon City
- Proceedings 1876, pg 38 (1876 Sept 20), Mount Moriah Lodge No. 15, Canon City

Hutchins, Abel
- Proceedings 1872, pg 44 (1872 Sept 24) Concord, Grand Lodge of New Hampshire
- Proceedings 1874, pg 104 (1874 Sept 30) Grand Lodge of New Hampshire

Hutchins, R
- Proceedings 1861-1869, pg 134 (1864 Nov 8), Chivington Lodge No. 6, Central City
- Proceedings 1861-1869, pg 150 (1865 Nov 7), Chivington Lodge No. 6, Central City
- Proceedings 1861-1869, pg 168 (1866 Oct 2), Chivington Lodge No. 6, Central City
- Proceedings 1861-1869, pg 193 (1867 Oct 8), Chivington Lodge No. 6, Central City
- Proceedings 1861-1869, pg 224 (1868 Oct 7), Chivington Lodge No. 6, Central City
- Proceedings 1861-1869, pg 306 (1869 Sept 29), Central Lodge No. 6, Central City
- Proceedings 1870, pg 22 (1870 Sept 28), Central Lodge No. 6, Central City
- Proceedings 1871, pg 20 (1871 Sept 27), Central Lodge No. 6, Central

Hutchins, Roswell
- Proceedings 1872, pg 22 (1872 Sept 24), Denver Lodge No. 5, Denver

Hutchins, S A
- Proceedings 1875, pg 78 (1875 Sept 22), Union Lodge No. 7, Denver

Hutchins, S H
- Proceedings 1874, pg 214 (1874 Sept 30), Union Lodge No. 7, Denver
- Proceedings 1876, pg 33 (1876 Sept 20), Union Lodge No. 7, Denver

Hutchins, Sam'l A
- Proceedings 1871, pg 22 (1871 Sept 27), Union Lodge No. 7, Denver

Hutchins, Sam'l H
- Proceedings 1873, pg 39 (1873 Oct 1), Union Lodge No. 7, Denver

Hutchins, Samuel A
- Proceedings 1870, pg 23 (1870 Sept 28), Union Lodge No. 7, Denver
- Proceedings 1872, pg 22 (1872 Sept 24), Union Lodge No. 7, Denver

Hutchinson, J
- Proceedings 1861-1869, pg 168 (1866 Oct 2), Chivington Lodge No. 6, Central City
- Proceedings 1861-1869, pg 193 (1867 Oct 8), Chivington Lodge No. 6, Central City

Hutchinson, J C
- Proceedings 1861-1869, pg 152 (1865 Nov 7), Helena City Lodge U D, Helena City, Montana Territory

Hutchinson, J W
- Proceedings 1871, pg 27 (1871 Sept 27), Cheyenne Lodge No. 16, Cheyenne, Wyoming Territory
- Proceedings 1872, pg 29 (1872 Sept 24), Cheyenne Lodge No. 16, Cheyenne, Wyoming Territory
- Proceedings 1873, pg 46 (1873 Oct 1), Cheyenne Lodge No. 16, Cheyenne, Wyoming Territory, Dimitted

Hutchinson, James
- Proceedings 1861-1869, pg 306 (1869 Sept 29), Central Lodge No. 6, Central City
- Proceedings 1872, pg 21 (1872 Sept 24), Denver Lodge No. 5, Denver
- Proceedings 1873, pg 38 (1873 Oct 1), Central Lodge No. 6, Central City
- Proceedings 1874, pg 213 (1874 Sept 30), Central Lodge No. 6, Central
- Proceedings 1875, pg 77 (1875 Sept 22), Central Lodge No. 6, Central City
- Proceedings 1876, pg 32 (1876 Sept 20), Central Lodge No. 6, Central City

Hutchinson, Jas
- Proceedings 1861-1869, pg 224 (1868 Oct 7), Chivington Lodge No. 6, Central City
- Proceedings 1861-1869, pg 288 (1869 Sept 28), Central Lodge No. 6, Central City
- Proceedings 1870, pg 22 (1870 Sept 28), Central Lodge No. 6, Central City
- Proceedings 1871, pg 20 (1871 Sept 27), Central Lodge No. 6, Central

Hutchinson, S
- Proceedings 1861-1869, pg 196 (1867 Oct 8), Black Hawk Lodge No. 11, Black Hawk
- Proceedings 1861-1869, pg 227 (1868 Oct 7), Black Hawk Lodge No. 11, Black Hawk

Hutchinson, Spence
- Proceedings 1861-1869, pg 309 (1869 Sept 29), Black Hawk Lodge No. 11, Black Hawk

Hutchinson, Spence, cont.
Proceedings 1870, pg 25 (1870 Sept 28), Black Hawk Lodge No. 11, Black Hawk

Hutchinson, Spencely
Proceedings 1871, pg 23 (1871 Sept 27), Black Hawk Lodge No. 11, Black Hawk, Dimitted

Hutchinson, W N
Proceedings 1861-1869, pg 227 (1868 Oct 7), Washington Lodge No. 12, Georgetown
Proceedings 1861-1869, pg 309 (1869 Sept 29), Washington Lodge No. 12, Georgetown
Proceedings 1871, pg 24 (1871 Sept 27), Washington Lodge No. 12, Georgetown

Hutchinson, William N
Proceedings 1874, pg 217 (1874 Sept 30), Washington Lodge No. 12, Georgetown

Hutchinson, Wm N
Proceedings 1870, pg 26 (1870 Sept 28), Washington Lodge No. 12, Georgetown
Proceedings 1872, pg cover (1872 Sept 24), Georgetown Chapter U D, Georgetown
Proceedings 1872, pg 25 (1872 Sept 24), Washington Lodge No. 12, Georgetown
Proceedings 1873, pg cover (1873 Oct 1), Georgetown Chapter U D, Georgetown
Proceedings 1873, pg 43 (1873 Oct 1), Washington Lodge No. 12, Georgetown
Proceedings 1875, pg 81 (1875 Sept 22), Washington Lodge No. 12, Georgetown
Proceedings 1876, pg 35 (1876 Sept 20), Washington Lodge No. 12, Georgetown

Hutel, G W
Proceedings 1861-1869, pg 149 (1865 Nov 7), Nevada Lodge No. 4, Nevadaville

Hymman
Proceedings 1874, pg 19 (1874 Sept 29) of Philadelphia

Hyndman, M B
Proceedings 1871, pg 18 (1871 Sept 27), Nevada Lodge No. 4, Bald Mountain
Proceedings 1875, pg 74 (1875 Sept 22), Nevada Lodge No. 4, Nevada
Proceedings 1876, pg 30 (1876 Sept 20) Nevada Lodge No. 4

Hyndman, Mark B
Proceedings 1872, pg 18 (1872 Sept 24), Nevada Lodge No. 4, Bald Mountain
Proceedings 1873, pg 36 (1873 Oct 1), Nevada Lodge No. 4, Nevada
Proceedings 1874, pg 210 (1874 Sept 30), Nevada Lodge No. 4, Bald Mountain, Gilpin County

Hyndman, William
Proceedings 1870, pg 20 (1870 Sept 28), Nevada Lodge No. 4, Nevadaville, Dimitted

Hyndman, Wm
Proceedings 1861-1869, pg 192 (1867 Oct 8), Nevada Lodge No. 4, Nevadaville

Proceedings 1861-1869, pg 222 (1868 Oct 7), Nevada Lodge No. 4, Nevadaville
Proceedings 1861-1869, pg 304 (1869 Sept 29), Nevada Lodge No. 4, Nevadaville

Hyneman
Proceedings 1870, pg 11 (1870 Sept 27), of Philadelphia, PA,, Editor, The Mason's Home Book

Hyneman, Leon
Proceedings 1861-1869, pg 213 (1868 Oct 6) of Philadelphia

Hyneman's Review of Freemasonry in England 1567 to 1813
Proceedings 1872, pg 10 (1872 Sept 24)

Idaho Springs Lodge No. 26
Proceedings 1876, pg 52 (1876 Sept 20)

Idaho Springs Lodge No. 26, Idaho Springs
Proceedings 1875, pg 89 (1875 Sept 22), dispensation granted 16 July 1874, charter granted 22 Sept 1875
Proceedings 1876, pg 7 (1875 Oct 9) lodge dedicated and officers installed
Proceedings 1876, pg 13 (1875 Sept 22) charter fees paid
Proceedings 1876, pg 13 (1875 Sept 5) dues paid

Idaho Springs Lodge U D
Proceedings 1875, pg 24 (1875 Sept 21) returns and petition for a charter
Proceedings 1875, pg 25 (1875 Sept 21) dues paid
Proceedings 1875, pg 34 (1875 Sept 22) chartered as Idaho Springs Lodge No. 26
Proceedings 1875, pg 92 (1875 Sept 22)

Idaho Springs Lodge U D, Idaho Springs
Proceedings 1874, pg 8 (1874 July 14) dispensation granted
Proceedings 1874, pg 19 (1874 Sept 29) returned its dispensation and work
Proceedings 1874, pg 19 (1874 Sept 29) returns late
Proceedings 1874, pg 35 (1874 Sept 30) charter not granted
Proceedings 1874, pg 208 (1874 Sept 30)

Idaho, Clear Creek
Proceedings 1861-1869, pg 293 (1869 Sept 28) not granted dispensation to open a lodge

Iliff, William H
Proceedings 1876, pg 33 (1876 Sept 20), Union Lodge No. 7, Denver

Inglefield, S J
Proceedings 1876, pg 41 (1876 Sept 20), St Vrain Lodge No. 23, Longmont

Inglesby, Charles
Proceedings 1875, pg 96 (1875 Sept 22) Grand Lodge of South Carolina, Charleston
Proceedings 1876, pg 54 (1876 Sept 20) Grand Lodge of South Carolina, Charleston

Inman, Geo F
   Proceedings 1875, pg 87 (1875 Sept 22), Occidental Lodge No. 20, Greeley

Inman, George F
   Proceedings 1874, pg 225 (1874 Sept 30), Occidental Lodge No. 20, Greeley
   Proceedings 1876, pg 40 (1876 Sept 20), Occidental Lodge No. 20, Greeley

Innes, E W
   Proceedings 1861-1869, pg 171 (1866 Oct 2), El Paso U D, Colorado City, Apprentice
   Proceedings 1861-1869, pg 196 (1867 Oct 8), El Paso Lodge U D, Colorado City

Inskeep, V F
   Proceedings 1861-1869, pg 224 (1868 Oct 7), Chivington Lodge No. 6, Central City
   Proceedings 1870, pg 22 (1870 Sept 28), Central Lodge No. 6, Central City
   Proceedings 1871, pg 20 (1871 Sept 27), Central Lodge No. 6, Central
   Proceedings 1873, pg 47 (1873 Oct 1), Pueblo Lodge No. 17, Pueblo
   Proceedings 1861-1869, pg 306 (1869 Sept 29), Central Lodge No. 6, Central City

Inskeep, Vans F
   Proceedings 1861-1869, pg 102 (1863 Nov 3) Montana Lodge U D
   Proceedings 1861-1869, pg 113 (1863 Nov 3), Montana Lodge U D, Central City

Inskeep, Vaus F
   Proceedings 1861-1869, pg 194 (1867 Oct 8), Chivington Lodge No. 6, Central City
   Proceedings 1872, pg 21 (1872 Sept 24), Denver Lodge No. 5, Denver, Dimitted
   Proceedings 1874, pg 223 (1874 Sept 30), Pueblo Lodge No. 17, Pueblo, Pueblo County, Stricken from the rolls,

Ira Berry
   Proceedings 1861-1869, pg 316 (1869 Sept 29) Grand Lodge of Maine

Ireland, S L
   Proceedings 1861-1869, pg 149 (1865 Nov 7), Nevada Lodge No. 4, Nevadaville
   Proceedings 1861-1869, pg 167 (1866 Oct 2) Denver Lodge No. 5, deceased
   Proceedings 1861-1869, pg 132 (1864 Nov 8), Nevada Lodge No. 4, Nevadaville, Apprentice
   Proceedings 1861-1869, pg 148 (1865 Nov 7), Nevada Lodge No. 4, Nevadaville, Apprentice
   Proceedings 1861-1869, pg 166 (1866 Oct 2), Nevada Lodge No. 4, Nevadaville, Apprentice
   Proceedings 1861-1869, pg 192 (1867 Oct 8), Nevada Lodge No. 4, Nevadaville, Apprentice
   Proceedings 1861-1869, pg 112 (1863 Nov 3), Nevada Lodge No. 4, Nevadaville, Apprentice
   Proceedings 1861-1869, pg 222 (1868 Oct 7), Nevada Lodge No. 4, Nevadaville, Apprentice

Irion, J W
   Proceedings 1861-1869, pg 171 (1866 Oct 2), El Paso U D, Colorado City
   Proceedings 1861-1869, pg 196 (1867 Oct 8), El Paso Lodge U D, Colorado City
   Proceedings 1861-1869, pg 310 (1869 Sept 29), El Paso Lodge No. 13, Colorado City
   Proceedings 1871, pg 25 (1871 Sept 27), El Paso Lodge No. 13, Colorado City
   Proceedings 1874, pg 218 (1874 Sept 30), El Paso Lodge No. 13, Colorado Springs
   Proceedings 1875, pg 82 (1875 Sept 22), El Paso Lodge No. 13, Colorado Springs, Stricken from the rolls

Irish, O H
   Proceedings 1870, pg 90 (1868 June 24) Grand Master, Grand Lodge of Nebraska

Iron, J W
   Proceedings 1861-1869, pg 228 (1868 Oct 7), El Paso Lodge No. 13, Colorado City

Irvin, D A
   Proceedings 1876, pg 34 (1876 Sept 20) Black Hawk Lodge No. 11

Irvin, Samuel D
   Proceedings 1873, pg 60 (1873 Oct 1) Grand Lodge of Georgia, Macon
   Proceedings 1874, pg 56 (1874 Sept 30) Grand Lodge of Georgia
   Proceedings 1874, pg 204 (1874 Sept 30) Grand Lodge of Georgia, Macon

Irvine, D A
   Proceedings 1870, pg 25 (1870 Sept 28), Black Hawk Lodge No. 11, Black Hawk

Irvine, David A
   Proceedings 1861-1869, pg 309 (1869 Sept 29), Black Hawk Lodge No. 11, Black Hawk

Irwin, David A
   Proceedings 1871, pg 23 (1871 Sept 27), Black Hawk Lodge No. 11, Black Hawk
   Proceedings 1872, pg 24 (1872 Sept 24), Black Hawk Lodge No. 11, Black Hawk

Irwin, David A
   Proceedings 1873, pg 42 (1873 Oct 1), Black Hawk Lodge No. 11, Black Hawk
   Proceedings 1874, pg 216 (1874 Sept 30), Black Hawk Lodge No. 11, Black Hawk
   Proceedings 1875, pg 80 (1875 Sept 22) Black Hawk Lodge No. 11

Irwin, J W
   Proceedings 1870, pg 27 (1870 Sept 28), El Paso Lodge No. 13, Colorado City
   Proceedings 1872, pg 27 (1872 Sept 24), El Paso Lodge No. 13, Colorado City
   Proceedings 1873, pg 43 (1873 Oct 1), El Paso Lodge No. 13, Colorado City

Colorado's Territorial Masons

Irwin, Joseph
Proceedings 1876, pg 37 (1876 Sept 20), Columbia Lodge No. 14, Boulder, Fellow Craft

Irwin, S M
Proceedings 1861-1869, pg 82 (1863 May 6) Denver Lodge No. 5, Rejected

Irwin, W R
Proceedings 1861-1869, pg 139 (1865 Feb 23), Union Lodge No. 7, Denver

Irwin, William H
Proceedings 1876, pg 29 (1876 Sept 20) Golden City Lodge No. 1

Isaacson, J H
Proceedings 1874, pg 205 (1874 Sept 30) Grand Lodge of Quebec, Montreal

Isaacson, John H
Proceedings 1872, pg 44 (1872 Sept 24) Montreal, Grand Lodge of Quebec
Proceedings 1874, pg 120 (1874 Sept 30) Grand Lodge of Quebec

Isacson, John H
Proceedings 1875, pg 96 (1875 Sept 22) Grand Lodge of Quebec, Montreal
Proceedings 1876, pg 54 (1876 Sept 20) Grand Lodge of Quebec, Montreal

Israel, James H
Proceedings 1873, pg 49 (1873 Oct 1), Collins Lodge No. 19, Fort Collins, Fellowcraft
Proceedings 1874, pg 225 (1874 Sept 30), Collins Lodge No. 19, Fort Collins, Larimer County, Expelled

J

Jackson, G W
Proceedings 1875, pg 83 (1875 Sept 22), Columbia Lodge No. 14, Boulder

Jackson, George W
Proceedings 1876, pg 37 (1876 Sept 20), Columbia Lodge No. 14, Boulder

Jackson, James
Proceedings 1870, pg 77 (1824 Jan 5) African Lodge at Boston

Jackson, John
Proceedings 1861-1869, pg 111 (1863 Nov 3), Nevada Lodge No. 4, Nevadaville
Proceedings 1861-1869, pg 132 (1864 Nov 8), Nevada Lodge No. 4, Nevadaville, deceased

Jackson, Pearley
Proceedings 1870, pg 60 (1870 June 7) Grand Lodge of Iowa, deceased

Jackson, Wm S
Proceedings 1872, pg 36 (1872 Sept 24), Ashlar Lodge U D, Colorado Springs

Jacobs
Proceedings 1874, pg 67 (1874 Sept 30) Grand Lodge of Louisiana
Proceedings 1874, pg 77 (1874 Sept 30) Grand Lodge of Louisiana

Jacobs, A
Proceedings 1861-1869, pg 78 (1862 Nov 4), Chivington Lodge No. 6, Central City
Proceedings 1861-1869, pg 78 (1862 Nov 4) Denver Lodge No. 5, dimitted
Proceedings 1861-1869, pg 113 (1863 Nov 3), Chivington Lodge No. 6, Central City
Proceedings 1861-1869, pg 134 (1864 Nov 8), Chivington Lodge No. 6, Central City
Proceedings 1861-1869, pg 150 (1865 Nov 7), Chivington Lodge No. 6, Central City
Proceedings 1861-1869, pg 168 (1866 Oct 2), Chivington Lodge No. 6, Central City
Proceedings 1861-1869, pg 194 (1867 Oct 8), Chivington Lodge No. 6, Central City
Proceedings 1861-1869, pg 224 (1868 Oct 7), Chivington Lodge No. 6, Central City
Proceedings 1861-1869, pg 306 (1869 Sept 29), Central Lodge No. 6, Central City
Proceedings 1870, pg 22 (1870 Sept 28), Central Lodge No. 6, Central City
Proceedings 1871, pg 20 (1871 Sept 27), Central Lodge No. 6, Central
Proceedings 1872, pg 21 (1872 Sept 24), Denver Lodge No. 5, Denver

Jacobs, Abraham
Proceedings 1873, pg 39 (1873 Oct 1), Central Lodge No. 6, Central City
Proceedings 1874, pg 213 (1874 Sept 30), Central Lodge No. 6, Central
Proceedings 1875, pg 77 (1875 Sept 22), Central Lodge No. 6, Central City
Proceedings 1876, pg 32 (1876 Sept 20), Central Lodge No. 6, Central City

Jacobs, G W
Proceedings 1861-1869, pg 150 (1865 Nov 7), Chivington Lodge No. 6, Central City
Proceedings 1861-1869, pg 168 (1866 Oct 2), Chivington Lodge No. 6, Central City
Proceedings 1861-1869, pg 194 (1867 Oct 8), Chivington Lodge No. 6, Central City

Jacobs, Geo W
Proceedings 1861-1869, pg 225 (1868 Oct 7), Chivington Lodge No. 6, Central City, Dimitted

Jacobs, George W
Proceedings 1861-1869, pg 134 (1864 Nov 8), Chivington Lodge No. 6, Central City, Apprentice

Jacobs, H H
Proceedings 1861-1869, pg 230 (1868 Oct 7), Valmont Lodge U D, Valmont

Jacobs, H S
Proceedings 1873, pg 60 (1873 Oct 1) Grand Lodge of Louisiana, New Orleans

Proceedings 1874, pg 204 (1874 Sept 30) Grand Lodge of Louisiana, New Orleans

Jacobs, Henry S
Proceedings 1874, pg 74 (1874 Sept 30) Grand Lodge of Louisiana

Jaffa, Samuel
Proceedings 1875, pg 91 (1875 Sept 22), Las Animas Lodge U D, Trinidad
Proceedings 1876, pg 43 (1876 Sept 20), Las Animas Lodge No. 28, Trinidad

Jaffa, Solomon H
Proceedings 1876, pg 44 (1876 Sept 20), Las Animas Lodge No. 28, Trinidad

James, Edward
Proceedings 1861-1869, pg 151 (1865 Nov 7), Empire Lodge U D, Empire City
Proceedings 1861-1869, pg 170 (1866 Oct 2), Empire Lodge No. 8, Empire City
Proceedings 1861-1869, pg 195 (1867 Oct 8), Empire Lodge No. 8, Empire City
Proceedings 1861-1869, pg 226 (1868 Oct 7), Empire Lodge No. 8, Empire City

James, Thos
Proceedings 1861-1869, pg 133 (1864 Nov 8) Denver Lodge No. 5

James, W H
Proceedings 1861-1869, pg 111 (1863 Nov 3), Nevada Lodge No. 4, Nevadaville
Proceedings 1861-1869, pg 166 (1866 Oct 2), Nevada Lodge No. 4, Nevadaville
Proceedings 1861-1869, pg 304 (1869 Sept 29), Nevada Lodge No. 4, Nevadaville

James, William H
Proceedings 1861-1869, pg 132 (1864 Nov 8), Nevada Lodge No. 4, Nevadaville
Proceedings 1870, pg 20 (1870 Sept 28), Nevada Lodge No. 4, Nevadaville
Proceedings 1871, pg 18 (1871 Sept 27), Nevada Lodge No. 4, Bald Mountain
Proceedings 1872, pg 18 (1872 Sept 24), Nevada Lodge No. 4, Bald Mountain
Proceedings 1873, pg 36 (1873 Oct 1), Nevada Lodge No. 4, Nevada
Proceedings 1874, pg 210 (1874 Sept 30), Nevada Lodge No. 4, Bald Mountain, Gilpin County
Proceedings 1876, pg 30 (1876 Sept 20) Nevada Lodge No. 4

James, Wm H
Proceedings 1861-1869, pg 77 (1862 Nov 4), Nevada Lodge No. 4, Nevadaville
Proceedings 1861-1869, pg 148 (1865 Nov 7), Nevada Lodge No. 4, Nevadaville
Proceedings 1861-1869, pg 192 (1867 Oct 8), Nevada Lodge No. 4, Nevadaville
Proceedings 1861-1869, pg 222 (1868 Oct 7), Nevada Lodge No. 4, Nevadaville

Proceedings 1875, pg 74 (1875 Sept 22), Nevada Lodge No. 4, Nevada

Jamison, W E
Proceedings 1870, pg 29 (1870 Sept 28), Cheyenne Lodge No. 16, Cheyenne, Wyoming Territory, Fellowcraft

Jamison, W G
Proceedings 1861-1869, pg 312 (1869 Sept 29), Cheyenne Lodge No. 16, Cheyenne, Fellowcraft
Proceedings 1871, pg 27 (1871 Sept 27), Cheyenne Lodge No. 16, Cheyenne, Wyoming Territory, Fellowcraft
Proceedings 1872, pg 30 (1872 Sept 24), Cheyenne Lodge No. 16, Cheyenne, Wyoming Territory, Fellowcraft
Proceedings 1874, pg 221 (1874 Sept 30), Cheyenne Lodge No. 16, Cheyenne, Wyoming Territory, Fellowcraft

Jannison, W J
Proceedings 1873, pg 46 (1873 Oct 1), Cheyenne Lodge No. 16, Cheyenne, Wyoming Territory, Fellowcraft

January, Wm A
Proceedings 1874, pg 204 (1874 Sept 30) Grand Lodge of California

Jarvis, Frank
Proceedings 1876, pg 45 (1876 Sept 20) South Pueblo Lodge U D

Jawson, J E
Proceedings 1861-1869, pg 32 (1861 Dec 10) committee

Jeff Davis Lodge No. 7
Proceedings 1874, pg 55 (1874 Sept 30) Grand Lodge of Florida

Jeffrey, Francis
Proceedings 1861-1869, pg 222 (1868 Oct 7), Nevada Lodge No. 4, Nevadaville, Fellowcraft
Proceedings 1861-1869, pg 304 (1869 Sept 29), Nevada Lodge No. 4, Nevadaville
Proceedings 1870, pg 20 (1870 Sept 28), Nevada Lodge No. 4, Nevadaville
Proceedings 1871, pg 18 (1871 Sept 27), Nevada Lodge No. 4, Bald Mountain
Proceedings 1872, pg 18 (1872 Sept 24), Nevada Lodge No. 4, Bald Mountain
Proceedings 1873, pg 36 (1873 Oct 1), Nevada Lodge No. 4, Nevada
Proceedings 1874, pg 210 (1874 Sept 30), Nevada Lodge No. 4, Bald Mountain, Gilpin County
Proceedings 1875, pg 74 (1875 Sept 22), Nevada Lodge No. 4, Nevada
Proceedings 1876, pg 30 (1876 Sept 20) Nevada Lodge No. 4

Jeffrey, J K
Proceedings 1871, pg 27 (1871 Sept 27), Cheyenne Lodge No. 16, Cheyenne, Wyoming Territory
Proceedings 1872, pg cover (1872 Sept 24) committee, Cheyenne
Proceedings 1872, pg 12 (1872 Sept 24), Cheyenne Lodge No. 16, Cheyenne, Wyoming Territory
Proceedings 1872, pg 16 (1872 Sept 24) committee
Proceedings 1872, pg 29 (1872 Sept 24), Cheyenne Lodge No. 16, Cheyenne, Wyoming Territory

Colorado's Territorial Masons

Jeffrey, J K, cont.
Proceedings 1874, pg 6 (1874 Sept 29), Cheyenne Lodge No. 16, Cheyenne, Wyoming Territory
Proceedings 1874, pg 220 (1874 Sept 30), Cheyenne Lodge No. 16, Cheyenne, Wyoming Territory
Proceedings 1875, pg 24 (1875 Sept 21), Wyoming Lodge No. 28, South Pass City, member of Cheyenne Lodge No. 16
Proceedings 1875, pg 96 (1875 Sept 22) Grand Lodge of Wyoming, Cheyenne
Proceedings 1876, pg 54 (1876 Sept 20) Grand Lodge of Wyoming, Cheyenne

Jenkins, Jacob
Proceedings 1861-1869, pg 335 (1827) candidate for National Grand Master, Prince Hall Grand Lodge of Ancient York Masonry

Jenkins, Wm S
Proceedings 1873, pg 52 (1873 Oct 1), Ashlar Lodge U D, Colorado Springs, Apprentice

Jenning, J F
Proceedings 1873, pg 48 (1873 Oct 1), Laramie Lodge No. 18, Laramie, Wyoming Territory, Apprentice

Jennings, G F
Proceedings 1874, pg 224 (1874 Sept 30), Laramie Lodge No. 18, Laramie City, Fellowcraft

Jennings, J
Proceedings 1861-1869, pg 166 (1866 Oct 2), Nevada Lodge No. 4, Nevadaville

Jennings, Joshua
Proceedings 1861-1869, pg 111 (1863 Nov 3), Nevada Lodge No. 4, Nevadaville
Proceedings 1861-1869, pg 132 (1864 Nov 8), Nevada Lodge No. 4, Nevadaville
Proceedings 1861-1869, pg 148 (1865 Nov 7), Nevada Lodge No. 4, Nevadaville
Proceedings 1861-1869, pg 192 (1867 Oct 8), Nevada Lodge No. 4, Nevadaville
Proceedings 1861-1869, pg 222 (1868 Oct 7), Nevada Lodge No. 4, Nevadaville, Dimitted

Jensen, H C F
Proceedings 1876, pg 33 (1876 Sept 20), Union Lodge No. 7, Denver

Jensen, H P
Proceedings 1870, pg 29 (1870 Sept 28), Cheyenne Lodge No. 16, Cheyenne, Wyoming Territory, Dimitted

Jensen, Henry C F
Proceedings 1874, pg 214 (1874 Sept 30), Union Lodge No. 7, Denver
Proceedings 1875, pg 78 (1875 Sept 22), Union Lodge No. 7, Denver

Jenson, H P
Proceedings 1861-1869, pg 311 (1869 Sept 29), Cheyenne Lodge No. 16, Cheyenne

Jester, W H
Proceedings 1861-1869, pg 147 (1865 Nov 7), Nevada Lodge No. 4, Nevadaville
Proceedings 1861-1869, pg 166 (1866 Oct 2), Nevada Lodge No. 4, Nevadaville
Proceedings 1861-1869, pg 304 (1869 Sept 29), Nevada Lodge No. 4, Nevadaville

Jester, William H
Proceedings 1861-1869, pg 132 (1864 Nov 8), Nevada Lodge No. 4, Nevadaville
Proceedings 1870, pg 20 (1870 Sept 28), Nevada Lodge No. 4, Nevadaville
Proceedings 1872, pg 18 (1872 Sept 24), Nevada Lodge No. 4, Bald Mountain
Proceedings 1873, pg 36 (1873 Oct 1), Nevada Lodge No. 4, Nevada
Proceedings 1874, pg 210 (1874 Sept 30), Nevada Lodge No. 4, Bald Mountain, Gilpin County
Proceedings 1876, pg 30 (1876 Sept 20) Nevada Lodge No. 4

Jester, Wm H
Proceedings 1861-1869, pg 77 (1862 Nov 4), Nevada Lodge No. 4, Nevadaville
Proceedings 1861-1869, pg 111 (1863 Nov 3), Nevada Lodge No. 4, Nevadaville
Proceedings 1861-1869, pg 192 (1867 Oct 8), Nevada Lodge No. 4, Nevadaville
Proceedings 1861-1869, pg 222 (1868 Oct 7), Nevada Lodge No. 4, Nevadaville
Proceedings 1871, pg 18 (1871 Sept 27), Nevada Lodge No. 4, Bald Mountain
Proceedings 1875, pg 74 (1875 Sept 22), Nevada Lodge No. 4, Nevada

Jewell, Henry
Proceedings 1861-1869, pg 306 (1869 Sept 29), Central Lodge No. 6, Central City, Fellowcraft
Proceedings 1870, pg 22 (1870 Sept 28), Central Lodge No. 6, Central City
Proceedings 1871, pg 20 (1871 Sept 27), Central Lodge No. 6, Central
Proceedings 1871, pg 21 (1871 Sept 27), Central Lodge No. 6, Central, Dimitted

Jewett, E H
Proceedings 1861-1869, pg 77 (1862 Nov 4) Denver Lodge No. 5
Proceedings 1861-1869, pg 112 (1863 Nov 3) Denver Lodge No. 5
Proceedings 1861-1869, pg 133 (1864 Nov 8) Denver Lodge No. 5
Proceedings 1861-1869, pg 149 (1865 Nov 7), Nevada Lodge No. 4, Nevadaville
Proceedings 1861-1869, pg 167 (1866 Oct 2) Denver Lodge No. 5
Proceedings 1861-1869, pg 193 (1867 Oct 8) Denver Lodge No. 5
Proceedings 1861-1869, pg 223 (1868 Oct 7) Denver Lodge No. 5
Proceedings 1861-1869, pg 305 (1869 Sept 29) Denver Lodge No. 5
Proceedings 1870, pg 21 (1870 Sept 28), Denver Lodge No. 5, Denver

Proceedings 1871, pg 19 (1871 Sept 27) Denver Lodge No. 5

Proceedings 1872, pg 20 (1872 Sept 24), Denver Lodge No. 5, Denver

Jineson, William A

Proceedings 1876, pg 45 (1876 Sept 20), King Solomon Lodge U D, West Las Animas

Joblin, W J

Proceedings 1861-1869, pg 168 (1866 Oct 2), Chivington Lodge No. 6, Central City

Proceedings 1861-1869, pg 306 (1869 Sept 29), Central Lodge No. 6, Central City

Proceedings 1870, pg 22 (1870 Sept 28), Central Lodge No. 6, Central City

Joblin, William J

Proceedings 1873, pg 38 (1873 Oct 1), Central Lodge No. 6, Central City

Proceedings 1874, pg 212 (1874 Sept 30), Central Lodge No. 6, Central

Proceedings 1875, pg 76 (1875 Sept 22), Central Lodge No. 6, Central City

Proceedings 1876, pg 32 (1876 Sept 20), Central Lodge No. 6, Central City

Joblin, Wm J

Proceedings 1861-1869, pg 224 (1868 Oct 7), Chivington Lodge No. 6, Central City

Proceedings 1861-1869, pg 288 (1869 Sept 28), Central Lodge No. 6, Central City

Proceedings 1871, pg 20 (1871 Sept 27), Central Lodge No. 6, Central

Proceedings 1872, pg 21 (1872 Sept 24), Denver Lodge No. 5, Denver

Johns, Henry

Proceedings 1874, pg 212 (1874 Sept 30), Central Lodge No. 6, Central

Proceedings 1875, pg 77 (1875 Sept 22), Central Lodge No. 6, Central City, died

Proceedings 1875, pg 94 (1875 Sept 22), Central Lodge No. 6, Central City

Johns, John

Proceedings 1861-1869, pg 196 (1867 Oct 8), Black Hawk Lodge No. 11, Black Hawk, Died

Johns, R H

Proceedings 1873, pg 48 (1873 Oct 1), Laramie Lodge No. 18, Laramie, Wyoming Territory

Proceedings 1874, pg 223 (1874 Sept 30), Laramie Lodge No. 18, Laramie City

Proceedings 1875, pg 87 (1875 Sept 22), Occidental Lodge No. 20, Greeley

Proceedings 1876, pg 40 (1876 Sept 20), Occidental Lodge No. 20, Greeley

Johns, Stephen

Proceedings 1861-1869, pg 170 (1866 Oct 2), Black Hawk Lodge U D, Black Hawk

Proceedings 1861-1869, pg 196 (1867 Oct 8), Black Hawk Lodge No. 11, Black Hawk

Proceedings 1861-1869, pg 227 (1868 Oct 7), Black Hawk Lodge No. 11, Black Hawk

Proceedings 1861-1869, pg 309 (1869 Sept 29), Black Hawk Lodge No. 11, Black Hawk

Proceedings 1870, pg 25 (1870 Sept 28), Black Hawk Lodge No. 11, Black Hawk

Proceedings 1871, pg 23 (1871 Sept 27), Black Hawk Lodge No. 11, Black Hawk

Proceedings 1871, pg 23 (1871 Sept 27), Black Hawk Lodge No. 11, Black Hawk

Proceedings 1873, pg 42 (1873 Oct 1), Black Hawk Lodge No. 11, Black Hawk

Proceedings 1874, pg 216 (1874 Sept 30), Black Hawk Lodge No. 11, Black Hawk

Proceedings 1875, pg 80 (1875 Sept 22) Black Hawk Lodge No. 11

Proceedings 1876, pg 34 (1876 Sept 20) Black Hawk Lodge No. 11

Proceedings 1872, pg 24 (1872 Sept 24), Black Hawk Lodge No. 11, Black Hawk

Johns, T J

Proceedings 1861-1869, pg 148 (1865 Nov 7), Nevada Lodge No. 4, Nevadaville, Fellowcraft

Proceedings 1861-1869, pg 178 (1866 Nov 17) Columbia City Lodge U D

Proceedings 1861-1869, pg 192 (1867 Oct 8), Nevada Lodge No. 4, Nevadaville

Proceedings 1861-1869, pg 222 (1868 Oct 7), Nevada Lodge No. 4, Nevadaville, Dimitted

Proceedings 1861-1869, pg 228 (1868 Oct 7), Columbia Lodge No. 14, Columbia City

Proceedings 1861-1869, pg 230 (1868 Oct 7), Cheyenne Lodge U D, Cheyenne, Dakota Territory

Proceedings 1861-1869, pg 312 (1869 Sept 29), Cheyenne Lodge No. 16, Cheyenne

Johns, Thomas J

Proceedings 1861-1869, pg 196 (1867 Oct 8), Columbia Lodge U D, Boulder

Proceedings 1870, pg 27 (1870 Sept 28), Columbia Lodge No. 14, Boulder City

Proceedings 1871, pg 26 (1871 Sept 27), Columbia Lodge No. 14, Boulder City, Dimitted

Johns, Thos J

Proceedings 1861-1869, pg 166 (1866 Oct 2), Nevada Lodge No. 4, Nevadaville

Proceedings 1861-1869, pg 310 (1869 Sept 29), Columbia Lodge No. 14, Boulder City

Johnson, A A

Proceedings 1874, pg 222 (1874 Sept 30), Pueblo Lodge No. 17, Pueblo, Pueblo County

Proceedings 1875, pg 85 (1875 Sept 22) Pueblo Lodge No. 17

Proceedings 1876, pg 39 (1876 Sept 20) Pueblo Lodge No. 17

Proceedings 1876, pg 50 (1876 Sept 20) Pueblo Lodge No. 17

Colorado's Territorial Masons

Johnson, A W
    Proceedings 1875, pg 90 (1875 Sept 22), Huerfano Lodge U D, Walsenburg
    Proceedings 1876, pg 43 (1876 Sept 20), Huerfano Lodge No. 27, Walsenburg

Johnson, Albert
    Proceedings 1861-1869, pg 179 (1867 Oct 7), Washington Lodge No. 12, Georgetown
    Proceedings 1861-1869, pg 227 (1868 Oct 7), Washington Lodge No. 12, Georgetown
    Proceedings 1861-1869, pg 309 (1869 Sept 29), Washington Lodge No. 12, Georgetown
    Proceedings 1870, pg 26 (1870 Sept 28), Washington Lodge No. 12, Georgetown
    Proceedings 1871, pg 24 (1871 Sept 27), Washington Lodge No. 12, Georgetown
    Proceedings 1872, pg 26 (1872 Sept 24), Washington Lodge No. 12, Georgetown
    Proceedings 1873, pg 43 (1873 Oct 1), Washington Lodge No. 12, Georgetown
    Proceedings 1874, pg 217 (1874 Sept 30), Washington Lodge No. 12, Georgetown
    Proceedings 1875, pg 81 (1875 Sept 22), Washington Lodge No. 12, Georgetown
    Proceedings 1876, pg 35 (1876 Sept 20), Washington Lodge No. 12, Georgetown

Johnson, Amasa A
    Proceedings 1861-1869, pg 312 (1869 Sept 29), Pueblo Lodge No. 17, Pueblo
    Proceedings 1870, pg 30 (1870 Sept 28), Pueblo Lodge No. 17, Pueblo, Dimitted
    Proceedings 1871, pg 28 (1871 Sept 27), Pueblo Lodge No. 17, Pueblo
    Proceedings 1872, pg 31 (1872 Sept 24), Pueblo Lodge No. 17, Pueblo
    Proceedings 1873, pg 47 (1873 Oct 1), Pueblo Lodge No. 17, Pueblo

Johnson, Andrew
    Proceedings 1861-1869, pg 260 (1868 June) President of the United States

Johnson, B F
    Proceedings 1873, pg 50 (1873 Oct 1), Occidental Lodge No. 20, Greeley
    Proceedings 1874, pg 225 (1874 Sept 30), Occidental Lodge No. 20, Greeley
    Proceedings 1875, pg 87 (1875 Sept 22), Occidental Lodge No. 20, Greeley
    Proceedings 1876, pg 40 (1876 Sept 20), Occidental Lodge No. 20, Greeley

Johnson, B S
    Proceedings 1872, pg 54 (1872 Sept 24) Grand Lodge of Arkansas

Johnson, C W
    Proceedings 1861-1869, pg 78 (1862 Nov 4), Chivington Lodge No. 6, Central City
    Proceedings 1861-1869, pg 113 (1863 Nov 3), Chivington Lodge No. 6, Central City
    Proceedings 1861-1869, pg 134 (1864 Nov 8), Chivington Lodge No. 6, Central City
    Proceedings 1861-1869, pg 150 (1865 Nov 7), Chivington Lodge No. 6, Central City, dimitted
    Proceedings 1861-1869, pg 194 (1867 Oct 8), Chivington Lodge No. 6, Central City
    Proceedings 1861-1869, pg 224 (1868 Oct 7), Chivington Lodge No. 6, Central City

Johnson, Charles
    Proceedings 1872, pg 21 (1872 Sept 24), Denver Lodge No. 5, Denver
    Proceedings 1873, pg 38 (1873 Oct 1), Central Lodge No. 6, Central City
    Proceedings 1874, pg 212 (1874 Sept 30), Central Lodge No. 6, Central
    Proceedings 1875, pg 76 (1875 Sept 22), Central Lodge No. 6, Central City
    Proceedings 1876, pg 48 (1876 Sept 20), Central Lodge No. 6, Central City, 1875 Dec 22

Johnson, Charles W
    Proceedings 1875, pg 77 (1875 Sept 22), Central Lodge No. 6, Central City, Stricken from the rolls

Johnson, Chas
    Proceedings 1861-1869, pg 306 (1869 Sept 29), Central Lodge No. 6, Central City
    Proceedings 1870, pg 22 (1870 Sept 28), Central Lodge No. 6, Central City
    Proceedings 1871, pg 20 (1871 Sept 27), Central Lodge No. 6, Central

Johnson, Chas W
    Proceedings 1861-1869, pg 306 (1869 Sept 29), Central Lodge No. 6, Central City
    Proceedings 1870, pg 22 (1870 Sept 28), Central Lodge No. 6, Central City
    Proceedings 1871, pg 20 (1871 Sept 27), Central Lodge No. 6, Central
    Proceedings 1872, pg 21 (1872 Sept 24), Denver Lodge No. 5, Denver
    Proceedings 1873, pg 38 (1873 Oct 1), Central Lodge No. 6, Central City
    Proceedings 1874, pg 212 (1874 Sept 30), Central Lodge No. 6, Central

Johnson, D W
    Proceedings 1861-1869, pg 111 (1863 Nov 3), Summit Lodge No. 2, Parkville
    Proceedings 1861-1869, pg 131 (1864 Nov 8) Golden City Lodge No. 1

Johnson, E P
    Proceedings 1861-1869, pg 312 (1869 Sept 29), Cheyenne Lodge No. 16, Cheyenne
    Proceedings 1870, pg 29 (1870 Sept 28), Cheyenne Lodge No. 16, Cheyenne, Wyoming Territory
    Proceedings 1871, pg 27 (1871 Sept 27), Cheyenne Lodge No. 16, Cheyenne, Wyoming Territory
    Proceedings 1872, pg 29 (1872 Sept 24), Cheyenne Lodge No. 16, Cheyenne, Wyoming Territory
    Proceedings 1873, pg 46 (1873 Oct 1), Cheyenne Lodge No. 16, Cheyenne, Wyoming Territory

Proceedings 1874, pg 221 (1874 Sept 30), Cheyenne Lodge No. 16, Cheyenne, Wyoming Territory

Johnson, F C
Proceedings 1861-1869, pg 179 (1867 Oct 7), Washington Lodge No. 12, Georgetown
Proceedings 1861-1869, pg 227 (1868 Oct 7), Washington Lodge No. 12, Georgetown

Johnson, H A
Proceedings 1861-1869, pg 77 (1862 Nov 4), Nevada Lodge No. 4, Nevadaville
Proceedings 1861-1869, pg 78 (1862 Nov 4), Chivington Lodge No. 6, Central City
Proceedings 1861-1869, pg 113 (1863 Nov 3), Chivington Lodge No. 6, Central City
Proceedings 1861-1869, pg 134 (1864 Nov 8), Chivington Lodge No. 6, Central City
Proceedings 1861-1869, pg 150 (1865 Nov 7), Chivington Lodge No. 6, Central City
Proceedings 1861-1869, pg 168 (1866 Oct 2), Chivington Lodge No. 6, Central City
Proceedings 1861-1869, pg 194 (1867 Oct 8), Chivington Lodge No. 6, Central City
Proceedings 1861-1869, pg 224 (1868 Oct 7), Chivington Lodge No. 6, Central City
Proceedings 1861-1869, pg 306 (1869 Sept 29), Central Lodge No. 6, Central City
Proceedings 1870, pg 22 (1870 Sept 28), Central Lodge No. 6, Central City
Proceedings 1871, pg 20 (1871 Sept 27), Central Lodge No. 6, Central

Johnson, Hiram A
Proceedings 1872, pg 21 (1872 Sept 24), Denver Lodge No. 5, Denver
Proceedings 1873, pg 39 (1873 Oct 1), Central Lodge No. 6, Central City
Proceedings 1874, pg 213 (1874 Sept 30), Central Lodge No. 6, Central
Proceedings 1875, pg 77 (1875 Sept 22), Central Lodge No. 6, Central City
Proceedings 1876, pg 32 (1876 Sept 20), Central Lodge No. 6, Central City
Proceedings 1876, pg 50 (1876 Sept 20), Central Lodge No. 6, Central City

Johnson, I M
Proceedings 1871, pg 30 (1871 Sept 27), Occidental Lodge U D, Greeley
Proceedings 1872, pg 33 (1872 Sept 24), Occidental Lodge No. 20, Greeley
Proceedings 1875, pg 87 (1875 Sept 22), Occidental Lodge No. 20, Greeley
Proceedings 1876, pg 49 (1876 Sept 20), Occidental Lodge No. 20, Greeley, 1875 Nov 1

Johnson, J A
Proceedings 1876, pg 41 (1876 Sept 20), Weston Lodge No. 22, Littleton

Johnson, J H
Proceedings 1872, pg 33 (1872 Sept 24), Occidental Lodge No. 20, Greeley
Proceedings 1873, pg 50 (1873 Oct 1), Occidental Lodge No. 20, Greeley
Proceedings 1874, pg 225 (1874 Sept 30), Occidental Lodge No. 20, Greeley
Proceedings 1875, pg 87 (1875 Sept 22), Occidental Lodge No. 20, Greeley
Proceedings 1876, pg 40 (1876 Sept 20), Occidental Lodge No. 20, Greeley

Johnson, J J
Proceedings 1861-1869, pg 151 (1865 Nov 7), Chivington Lodge No. 6, Central City
Proceedings 1861-1869, pg 312 (1869 Sept 29), Cheyenne Lodge No. 16, Cheyenne
Proceedings 1871, pg 27 (1871 Sept 27), Cheyenne Lodge No. 16, Cheyenne, Wyoming Territory
Proceedings 1872, pg 30 (1872 Sept 24), Cheyenne Lodge No. 16, Cheyenne, Wyoming Territory, Dimitted

Johnson, J M
Proceedings 1873, pg 50 (1873 Oct 1), Occidental Lodge No. 20, Greeley
Proceedings 1874, pg 225 (1874 Sept 30), Occidental Lodge No. 20, Greeley

Johnson, J P
Proceedings 1861-1869, pg 311 (1869 Sept 29), Cheyenne Lodge No. 16, Cheyenne
Proceedings 1870, pg 29 (1870 Sept 28), Cheyenne Lodge No. 16, Cheyenne, Wyoming Territory
Proceedings 1871, pg 27 (1871 Sept 27), Cheyenne Lodge No. 16, Cheyenne, Wyoming Territory
Proceedings 1872, pg 30 (1872 Sept 24), Cheyenne Lodge No. 16, Cheyenne, Wyoming Territory, Dimitted

Johnson, James H
Proceedings 1871, pg 30 (1871 Sept 27), Occidental Lodge U D, Greeley

Johnson, Jay J
Proceedings 1861-1869, pg 102 (1863 Nov 3) petition for formation of a new lodge in Denver
Proceedings 1861-1869, pg 119 (1863 Dec 3) warrant drawn
Proceedings 1861-1869, pg 134 (1864 Nov 8), Union Lodge No. 7, Denver
Proceedings 1861-1869, pg 169 (1866 Oct 2), Union Lodge No. 7, Denver
Proceedings 1861-1869, pg 195 (1867 Oct 8), Union Lodge No. 7, Denver
Proceedings 1861-1869, pg 225 (1868 Oct 7), Union Lodge No. 7, Denver
Proceedings 1861-1869, pg 229 (1868 Oct 7), Cheyenne Lodge U D, Cheyenne, Dakota Territory
Proceedings 1861-1869, pg 308 (1869 Sept 29), Union Lodge No. 7, Denver, Dimitted
Proceedings 1870, pg 29 (1870 Sept 28), Cheyenne Lodge No. 16, Cheyenne, Wyoming Territory, Dimitted

Johnson, John E
Proceedings 1872, pg 26 (1872 Sept 24), Washington Lodge No. 12, Georgetown
Proceedings 1873, pg 43 (1873 Oct 1), Washington Lodge No. 12, Georgetown

Colorado's Territorial Masons

Johnson, John E, cont.
    Proceedings 1874, pg 217 (1874 Sept 30), Washington Lodge No. 12, Georgetown
    Proceedings 1875, pg 81 (1875 Sept 22), Washington Lodge No. 12, Georgetown
    Proceedings 1876, pg 35 (1876 Sept 20), Washington Lodge No. 12, Georgetown

Johnson, Joseph H
    Proceedings 1872, pg 43 (1872 Sept 24) Talladega, Grand Lodge of Alabama
    Proceedings 1872, pg 53 (1872 Sept 24) Grand Lodge of Alabama
    Proceedings 1873, pg 60 (1873 Oct 1) Grand Lodge of Alabama, Talladega
    Proceedings 1874, pg 43 (1874 Sept 30) Grand Lodge of Alabama

Johnson, M V
    Proceedings 1874, pg 209 (1874 Sept 30), Golden City Lodge No. 1, Golden City
    Proceedings 1875, pg 73 (1875 Sept 22) Golden City Lodge No. 1
    Proceedings 1876, pg 29 (1876 Sept 20) Golden City Lodge No. 1

Johnson, P C
    Proceedings 1876, pg 33 (1876 Sept 20), Union Lodge No. 7, Denver

Johnson, Stephen H
    Proceedings 1861-1869, pg 341 (1868 June 2) Grand Master, Grand Lodge of New York

Johnson, T W
    Proceedings 1861-1869, pg 305 (1869 Sept 29) Denver Lodge No. 5
    Proceedings 1872, pg 19 (1872 Sept 24), Denver Lodge No. 5, Denver

Johnson, Theron
    Proceedings 1861-1869, pg 193 (1867 Oct 8) Denver Lodge No. 5
    Proceedings 1861-1869, pg 223 (1868 Oct 7) Denver Lodge No. 5

Johnson, Theron W
    Proceedings 1861-1869, pg 167 (1866 Oct 2) Denver Lodge No. 5
    Proceedings 1870, pg 21 (1870 Sept 28), Denver Lodge No. 5, Denver
    Proceedings 1871, pg 19 (1871 Sept 27) Denver Lodge No. 5
    Proceedings 1873, pg 37 (1873 Oct 1), Denver Lodge No. 5, Denver
    Proceedings 1874, pg 212 (1874 Sept 30), Denver Lodge No. 5, Denver, Stricken from the rolls

Johnston, J A
    Proceedings 1873, pg 51 (1873 Oct 1), Weston Lodge No. 22, Littleton
    Proceedings 1874, pg 226 (1874 Sept 30), Weston Lodge No. 22, Littleton
    Proceedings 1875, pg 18 (1875 Sept 21), Weston Lodge No. 22, Littleton
    Proceedings 1875, pg 88 (1875 Sept 22), Weston Lodge No. 22, Littleton

Johnston, James A
    Proceedings 1872, pg 34 (1872 Sept 24), Weston Lodge No. 22, Littleton

Johnston, Robert A
    Proceedings 1875, pg 88 (1875 Sept 22), Weston Lodge No. 22, Littleton
    Proceedings 1875, pg 88 (1875 Sept 22), Weston Lodge No. 22, Littleton
    Proceedings 1876, pg 41 (1876 Sept 20), Weston Lodge No. 22, Littleton

Johnstone, E W
    Proceedings 1873, pg 40 (1873 Oct 1), Union Lodge No. 7, Denver, Apprentice
    Proceedings 1874, pg 213 (1874 Sept 30), Union Lodge No. 7, Denver
    Proceedings 1875, pg 78 (1875 Sept 22), Union Lodge No. 7, Denver
    Proceedings 1876, pg 33 (1876 Sept 20), Union Lodge No. 7, Denver

Jones
    Proceedings 1861-1869, pg 177 (1867 Oct 7) committee
    Proceedings 1861-1869, pg 212 (1868 Oct 6) committee
    Proceedings 1870, pg 50 (1870 May 11) Grand Lodge of Connecticut, age 80

Jones, A E
    Proceedings 1875, pg 89 (1875 Sept 22), Doric Lodge No. 25, Fairplay
    Proceedings 1876, pg 42 (1876 Sept 20), Doric Lodge No. 25, Fairplay

Jones, A M
    Proceedings 1861-1869, pg 111 (1863 Nov 3), Nevada Lodge No. 4, Nevadaville
    Proceedings 1861-1869, pg 115 (1864 Nov 7) Grand Tyler
    Proceedings 1861-1869, pg 116 (1864 Nov 7), Nevada Lodge No. 4, Nevadaville
    Proceedings 1861-1869, pg 132 (1864 Nov 8), Nevada Lodge No. 4, Nevadaville
    Proceedings 1861-1869, pg 147 (1865 Nov 7), Nevada Lodge No. 4, Nevadaville
    Proceedings 1861-1869, pg 153 (1866 Oct 1) Grand Steward
    Proceedings 1861-1869, pg 154 (1866 Oct 1), Nevada Lodge No. 4, Nevadaville
    Proceedings 1861-1869, pg 155 (1866 Oct 1) committee
    Proceedings 1861-1869, pg 156 (1866 Oct 1) committee
    Proceedings 1861-1869, pg 161 (1866 Oct 2) Senior Grand Warden
    Proceedings 1861-1869, pg 162 (1866 Oct 2), Nevada Lodge No. 4, Nevadaville
    Proceedings 1861-1869, pg 166 (1866 Oct 2), Nevada Lodge No. 4, Nevadaville
    Proceedings 1861-1869, pg 176 (1867 Oct 7) Senior Grand Warden
    Proceedings 1861-1869, pg 178 (1866 Dec 28), Nevada Lodge No. 4, Nevadaville

Proceedings 1861-1869, pg 180 (1867 Oct 7) committee
Proceedings 1861-1869, pg 182 (1867 Oct 7) warrant paid
Proceedings 1861-1869, pg 186 (1867 Oct 8) Senior Grand Warden
Proceedings 1861-1869, pg 189 (1867 Oct 8) committee
Proceedings 1861-1869, pg 192 (1867 Oct 8), Nevada Lodge No. 4, Nevadaville
Proceedings 1861-1869, pg 201 (1868 Oct 6) Senior Grand Warden
Proceedings 1861-1869, pg 202 (1868 Oct 6) Senior Grand Warden
Proceedings 1861-1869, pg 212 (1868 Oct 6) warrant paid
Proceedings 1861-1869, pg 218 (1868 Oct 7) committee
Proceedings 1861-1869, pg 219 (1868 Oct 7) mileage allowed
Proceedings 1861-1869, pg 222 (1868 Oct 7), Nevada Lodge No. 4, Nevadaville
Proceedings 1861-1869, pg 304 (1869 Sept 29), Nevada Lodge No. 4, Nevadaville
Proceedings 1871, pg 18 (1871 Sept 27), Nevada Lodge No. 4, Bald Mountain

Jones, Aaron M
Proceedings 1861-1869, pg 160 (1866 Oct 2), Nevada Lodge No. 4, Nevadaville
Proceedings 1861-1869, pg 175 (1867 Oct 7) Senior Grand Warden
Proceedings 1861-1869, pg 185 (1867 Oct 7) Senior Grand Warden
Proceedings 1861-1869, pg 315 (1869 Sept 29) Senior Grand Warden, 1866
Proceedings 1861-1869, pg 315 (1869 Sept 29) Senior Grand Warden, 1867
Proceedings 1870, pg 20 (1870 Sept 28), Nevada Lodge No. 4, Nevadaville
Proceedings 1870, pg 32 (1870 Sept 28) Senior Grand Warden, 1867
Proceedings 1870, pg 32 (1870 Sept 28) Senior Grand Warden, 1866
Proceedings 1871, pg 34 (1871 Sept 27) Senior Grand Warden, 1867
Proceedings 1871, pg 34 (1871 Sept 27) Senior Grand Warden, 1866
Proceedings 1872, pg 18 (1872 Sept 24), Nevada Lodge No. 4, Bald Mountain
Proceedings 1872, pg 42 (1872 Sept 24) Senior Grand Warden, 1866
Proceedings 1872, pg 42 (1872 Sept 24) Senior Grand Warden, 1867
Proceedings 1873, pg 36 (1873 Oct 1), Nevada Lodge No. 4, Nevada
Proceedings 1873, pg 36 (1873 Oct 1), Nevada Lodge No. 4, Nevada
Proceedings 1873, pg 58 (1873 Oct 1) Senior Grand Warden, 1867
Proceedings 1873, pg 58 (1873 Oct 1) Senior Grand Warden, 1866
Proceedings 1874, pg 206 (1874 Sept 30) Senior Grand Warden, 1867
Proceedings 1874, pg 206 (1874 Sept 30) Senior Grand Warden, 1866
Proceedings 1874, pg 210 (1874 Sept 30), Nevada Lodge No. 4, Bald Mountain, Gilpin County
Proceedings 1875, pg 74 (1875 Sept 22), Nevada Lodge No. 4, Nevada
Proceedings 1875, pg 93 (1875 Sept 22) Senior Grand Warden, 1866
Proceedings 1875, pg 93 (1875 Sept 22) Senior Grand Warden, 1867
Proceedings 1876, pg 30 (1876 Sept 20) Nevada Lodge No. 4

Jones, Albert E
Proceedings 1874, pg 228 (1874 Sept 30), Doric Lodge U D, Fairplay

Jones, Charles P
Proceedings 1876, pg 7 (1877 Feb 7), King Solomon Lodge U D, West Las Animas
Proceedings 1876, pg 45 (1876 Sept 20), King Solomon Lodge U D, West Las Animas

Jones, D W
Proceedings 1874, pg 220 (1874 Sept 30), Mount Moriah Lodge No. 15, Canon City
Proceedings 1875, pg 84 (1875 Sept 22), Mount Moriah Lodge No. 15, Canon City

Jones, David
Proceedings 1876, pg 38 (1876 Sept 20), Mount Moriah Lodge No. 15, Canon City

Jones, E Paul
Proceedings 1861-1869, pg 169 (1866 Oct 2), Chivington Lodge No. 6, Central City, Fellowcraft
Proceedings 1861-1869, pg 194 (1867 Oct 8), Chivington Lodge No. 6, Central City
Proceedings 1861-1869, pg 224 (1868 Oct 7), Chivington Lodge No. 6, Central City
Proceedings 1861-1869, pg 306 (1869 Sept 29), Central Lodge No. 6, Central City
Proceedings 1870, pg 22 (1870 Sept 28), Central Lodge No. 6, Central City
Proceedings 1871, pg 20 (1871 Sept 27), Central Lodge No. 6, Central
Proceedings 1872, pg 21 (1872 Sept 24), Denver Lodge No. 5, Denver
Proceedings 1873, pg 38 (1873 Oct 1), Central Lodge No. 6, Central City
Proceedings 1874, pg 212 (1874 Sept 30), Central Lodge No. 6, Central
Proceedings 1875, pg 77 (1875 Sept 22), Central Lodge No. 6, Central City, Stricken from the rolls

Jones, Edward B
Proceedings 1872, pg 43 (1872 Sept 24) Paducah, Grand Lodge of Kentucky

Jones, G W
Proceedings 1861-1869, pg 303 (1869 Sept 29) Golden City Lodge No. 1, Apprentice

Jones, I W
Proceedings 1876, pg 41 (1876 Sept 20), St Vrain Lodge No. 23, Longmont

Colorado's Territorial Masons

Jones, J H
    Proceedings 1872, pg 34 (1872 Sept 24), Occidental Lodge No. 20, Greeley
    Proceedings 1873, pg 49 (1873 Oct 1), Occidental Lodge No. 20, Greeley
    Proceedings 1874, pg 225 (1874 Sept 30), Occidental Lodge No. 20, Greeley
    Proceedings 1875, pg 87 (1875 Sept 22), Occidental Lodge No. 20, Greeley

Jones, James
    Proceedings 1861-1869, pg 148 (1865 Nov 7), Nevada Lodge No. 4, Nevadaville
    Proceedings 1861-1869, pg 166 (1866 Oct 2), Nevada Lodge No. 4, Nevadaville
    Proceedings 1861-1869, pg 192 (1867 Oct 8), Nevada Lodge No. 4, Nevadaville
    Proceedings 1861-1869, pg 222 (1868 Oct 7), Nevada Lodge No. 4, Nevadaville
    Proceedings 1861-1869, pg 304 (1869 Sept 29), Nevada Lodge No. 4, Nevadaville
    Proceedings 1870, pg 20 (1870 Sept 28), Nevada Lodge No. 4, Nevadaville

Jones, James H
    Proceedings 1876, pg 40 (1876 Sept 20), Occidental Lodge No. 20, Greeley

Jones, James K
    Proceedings 1871, pg 18 (1871 Sept 27), Nevada Lodge No. 4, Bald Mountain
    Proceedings 1872, pg 18 (1872 Sept 24), Nevada Lodge No. 4, Bald Mountain
    Proceedings 1873, pg 36 (1873 Oct 1), Nevada Lodge No. 4, Nevada
    Proceedings 1874, pg 210 (1874 Sept 30), Nevada Lodge No. 4, Bald Mountain, Gilpin County
    Proceedings 1875, pg 74 (1875 Sept 22), Nevada Lodge No. 4, Nevada
    Proceedings 1876, pg 48 (1876 Sept 20) Nevada Lodge No. 4, 1875 Nov 13

Jones, John S
    Proceedings 1861-1869, pg 140 (1865 Nov 6), Empire Lodge No. 8, Empire City
    Proceedings 1861-1869, pg 151 (1865 Nov 7), Empire Lodge U D, Empire City
    Proceedings 1861-1869, pg 170 (1866 Oct 2), Empire Lodge No. 8, Empire City
    Proceedings 1861-1869, pg 195 (1867 Oct 8), Empire Lodge No. 8, Empire City
    Proceedings 1861-1869, pg 226 (1868 Oct 7), Empire Lodge No. 8, Empire City, Dimitted

Jones, Lewis
    Proceedings 1861-1869, pg 229 (1868 Oct 7), Canon Lodge U D, Canon City
    Proceedings 1861-1869, pg 311 (1869 Sept 29), Mount Moriah Lodge No. 15, Canon City
    Proceedings 1870, pg 28 (1870 Sept 28), Mount Moriah Lodge No. 15, Canon City
    Proceedings 1871, pg 26 (1871 Sept 27), Mount Moriah Lodge No. 15, Canon City
    Proceedings 1872, pg 29 (1872 Sept 24), Mount Moriah Lodge No. 15, Canon City
    Proceedings 1873, pg 45 (1873 Oct 1), Mount Moriah Lodge No. 15, Canon City
    Proceedings 1874, pg 220 (1874 Sept 30), Mount Moriah Lodge No. 15, Canon City
    Proceedings 1875, pg 84 (1875 Sept 22), Mount Moriah Lodge No. 15, Canon City

Jones, O W
    Proceedings 1861-1869, pg 311 (1869 Sept 29), Mount Moriah Lodge No. 15, Canon City
    Proceedings 1870, pg 28 (1870 Sept 28), Mount Moriah Lodge No. 15, Canon City
    Proceedings 1873, pg 45 (1873 Oct 1), Mount Moriah Lodge No. 15, Canon City
    Proceedings 1874, pg 220 (1874 Sept 30), Mount Moriah Lodge No. 15, Canon City
    Proceedings 1875, pg 84 (1875 Sept 22), Mount Moriah Lodge No. 15, Canon City
    Proceedings 1876, pg 38 (1876 Sept 20), Mount Moriah Lodge No. 15, Canon City

Jones, Orville W
    Proceedings 1871, pg 26 (1871 Sept 27), Mount Moriah Lodge No. 15, Canon City
    Proceedings 1872, pg 29 (1872 Sept 24), Mount Moriah Lodge No. 15, Canon City

Jones, Perry
    Proceedings 1876, pg 39 (1876 Sept 20), Collins Lodge No. 19, Fort Collins

Jones, Robert H
    Proceedings 1870, pg 20 (1870 Sept 28), Nevada Lodge No. 4, Nevadaville
    Proceedings 1872, pg 18 (1872 Sept 24), Nevada Lodge No. 4, Bald Mountain
    Proceedings 1873, pg 36 (1873 Oct 1), Nevada Lodge No. 4, Nevada, Dimitted

Jones, Robt H
    Proceedings 1871, pg 18 (1871 Sept 27), Nevada Lodge No. 4, Bald Mountain

Jones, Rufus P
    Proceedings 1876, pg 54 (1876 Sept 20) Grand Lodge of Indian Territory, Caddo

Jones, Stephen F
    Proceedings 1876, pg 45 (1876 Sept 20), King Solomon Lodge U D, West Las Animas

Jones, T J
    Proceedings 1861-1869, pg 230 (1868 Oct 7), Valmont Lodge U D, Valmont
    Proceedings 1872, pg 28 (1872 Sept 24), Columbia Lodge No. 14, Boulder

Jones, Theodore R
    Proceedings 1876, pg 43 (1876 Sept 20), Huerfano Lodge No. 27, Walsenburg, Apprentice

Jones, Thomas
    Proceedings 1875, pg 83 (1875 Sept 22), Columbia Lodge No. 14, Boulder

Proceedings 1876, pg 37 (1876 Sept 20), Columbia Lodge No. 14, Boulder

Jones, Thomas J
Proceedings 1870, pg 27 (1870 Sept 28), Columbia Lodge No. 14, Boulder City
Proceedings 1871, pg 25 (1871 Sept 27), Columbia Lodge No. 14, Boulder City
Proceedings 1873, pg 44 (1873 Oct 1), Columbia Lodge No. 14, Boulder
Proceedings 1874, pg 219 (1874 Sept 30), Columbia Lodge No. 14, Boulder, Boulder County
Proceedings 1875, pg 83 (1875 Sept 22), Columbia Lodge No. 14, Boulder, Stricken from the rolls
Proceedings 1876, pg 37 (1876 Sept 20), Columbia Lodge No. 14, Boulder
Proceedings 1876, pg 51 (1876 Sept 20), Columbia Lodge No. 14, Boulder, 1876 Apr 10

Jones, Thos J
Proceedings 1861-1869, pg 310 (1869 Sept 29), Columbia Lodge No. 14, Boulder City

Jones, W
Proceedings 1861-1869, pg 168 (1866 Oct 2), Chivington Lodge No. 6, Central City

Jones, W C M
Proceedings 1861-1869, pg 113 (1863 Nov 3), Chivington Lodge No. 6, Central City, Apprentice
Proceedings 1861-1869, pg 134 (1864 Nov 8), Chivington Lodge No. 6, Central City
Proceedings 1861-1869, pg 150 (1865 Nov 7), Chivington Lodge No. 6, Central City
Proceedings 1861-1869, pg 168 (1866 Oct 2), Chivington Lodge No. 6, Central City
Proceedings 1861-1869, pg 194 (1867 Oct 8), Chivington Lodge No. 6, Central City
Proceedings 1861-1869, pg 224 (1868 Oct 7), Chivington Lodge No. 6, Central City
Proceedings 1861-1869, pg 306 (1869 Sept 29), Central Lodge No. 6, Central City
Proceedings 1870, pg 22 (1870 Sept 28), Central Lodge No. 6, Central City
Proceedings 1871, pg 20 (1871 Sept 27), Central Lodge No. 6, Central

Jones, Washington
Proceedings 1861-1869, pg 110 (1863 Nov 3) Golden City Lodge No. 1, Apprentice
Proceedings 1861-1869, pg 191 (1867 Oct 8) Golden City Lodge No. 1, Apprentice
Proceedings 1861-1869, pg 221 (1868 Oct 7) Golden City Lodge No. 1, Apprentice

Jones, William
Proceedings 1861-1869, pg 133 (1864 Nov 8), Chivington Lodge No. 6, Central City
Proceedings 1861-1869, pg 150 (1865 Nov 7), Chivington Lodge No. 6, Central City
Proceedings 1861-1869, pg 306 (1869 Sept 29), Central Lodge No. 6, Central City
Proceedings 1872, pg 21 (1872 Sept 24), Denver Lodge No. 5, Denver
Proceedings 1873, pg 38 (1873 Oct 1), Central Lodge No. 6, Central City
Proceedings 1874, pg 212 (1874 Sept 30), Central Lodge No. 6, Central
Proceedings 1875, pg 77 (1875 Sept 22), Central Lodge No. 6, Central City
Proceedings 1876, pg 32 (1876 Sept 20), Central Lodge No. 6, Central City

Jones, William C M
Proceedings 1873, pg 38 (1873 Oct 1), Central Lodge No. 6, Central City
Proceedings 1874, pg 212 (1874 Sept 30), Central Lodge No. 6, Central
Proceedings 1875, pg 77 (1875 Sept 22), Central Lodge No. 6, Central City
Proceedings 1876, pg 32 (1876 Sept 20), Central Lodge No. 6, Central City

Jones, Wm
Proceedings 1861-1869, pg 113 (1863 Nov 3), Montana Lodge U D, Central City
Proceedings 1861-1869, pg 194 (1867 Oct 8), Chivington Lodge No. 6, Central City
Proceedings 1861-1869, pg 224 (1868 Oct 7), Chivington Lodge No. 6, Central City
Proceedings 1870, pg 22 (1870 Sept 28), Central Lodge No. 6, Central City
Proceedings 1871, pg 20 (1871 Sept 27), Central Lodge No. 6, Central

Jones, Wm C M
Proceedings 1872, pg 21 (1872 Sept 24), Denver Lodge No. 5, Denver
Proceedings 1876, pg 50 (1876 Sept 20), Central Lodge No. 6, Central City

Joolin, Wm J
Proceedings 1876, pg 50 (1876 Sept 20), Central Lodge No. 6, Central City

Jordan
Proceedings 1870, pg 96 (1865 Mar), of Boston, Massachusetts

Jordan, John
Proceedings 1872, pg 21 (1872 Sept 24), Denver Lodge No. 5, Denver
Proceedings 1874, pg 212 (1874 Sept 30), Central Lodge No. 6, Central
Proceedings 1876, pg 31 (1876 Sept 20), Central Lodge No. 6, Central City

Jordan, John T
Proceedings 1872, pg 91 (1872 Sept 24) Grand Lodge of Washington
Proceedings 1873, pg 38 (1873 Oct 1), Central Lodge No. 6, Central City

Jordan, M L
Proceedings 1875, pg 85 (1875 Sept 22) Pueblo Lodge No. 17

Jordon, John
Proceedings 1875, pg 76 (1875 Sept 22), Central Lodge No. 6, Central City

Jordon, M L
Proceedings 1874, pg 222 (1874 Sept 30), Pueblo Lodge No. 17, Pueblo, Pueblo County
Proceedings 1876, pg 39 (1876 Sept 20) Pueblo Lodge No. 17

Joseph, Adolph
Proceedings 1874, pg 60 (1874 Sept 30) Grand Lodge of Georgia

Joy, Henry L
Proceedings 1874, pg 223 (1874 Sept 30), Laramie Lodge No. 18, Laramie City

Judd, C T
Proceedings 1861-1869, pg 154 (1866 Jan 27), El Paso Lodge U D, Colorado City
Proceedings 1861-1869, pg 170 (1866 Oct 2), El Paso U D, Colorado City
Proceedings 1861-1869, pg 196 (1867 Oct 8), El Paso Lodge U D, Colorado City
Proceedings 1861-1869, pg 228 (1868 Oct 7), El Paso Lodge No. 13, Colorado City
Proceedings 1861-1869, pg 310 (1869 Sept 29), El Paso Lodge No. 13, Colorado City
Proceedings 1870, pg 27 (1870 Sept 28), El Paso Lodge No. 13, Colorado City, Expelled

Judd, Cyrus T
Proceedings 1870, pg 12 (1870 Sept 27) expelled, El Paso Lodge No. 13, Colorado City

Juneman, F W
Proceedings 1874, pg 219 (1874 Sept 30), Columbia Lodge No. 14, Boulder, Boulder County
Proceedings 1875, pg 83 (1875 Sept 22), Columbia Lodge No. 14, Boulder
Proceedings 1876, pg 37 (1876 Sept 20), Columbia Lodge No. 14, Boulder

Jussen, H P
Proceedings 1861-1869, pg 230 (1868 Oct 7), Cheyenne Lodge U D, Cheyenne, Dakota Territory

K

Kafka, Louis
Proceedings 1875, pg 77 (1875 Sept 22), Central Lodge No. 6, Central City, Fellowcraft
Proceedings 1876, pg 32 (1876 Sept 20), Central Lodge No. 6, Central City, Fellow Craft,

Kansas Pacific Railroad
Proceedings 1874, pg 13 (1874 Aug 27) reduced rates for Masons attending the Grand Lodge

Kassler, G W
Proceedings 1861-1869, pg 305 (1869 Sept 29) Denver Lodge No. 5
Proceedings 1876, pg 31 (1876 Sept 20) Denver Lodge No. 5

Kassler, Geo W
Proceedings 1861-1869, pg 77 (1862 Nov 4) Denver Lodge No. 5
Proceedings 1861-1869, pg 112 (1863 Nov 3) Denver Lodge No. 5
Proceedings 1861-1869, pg 123 (1864 Nov 8) Denver Lodge No. 5, Senior Grand Deacon
Proceedings 1861-1869, pg 133 (1864 Nov 8) Denver Lodge No. 5
Proceedings 1861-1869, pg 136 (1865 Nov 6) Senior Grand Deacon
Proceedings 1861-1869, pg 138 (1865 Nov 6) committee
Proceedings 1861-1869, pg 223 (1868 Oct 7) Denver Lodge No. 5
Proceedings 1870, pg 21 (1870 Sept 28), Denver Lodge No. 5, Denver
Proceedings 1871, pg 19 (1871 Sept 27) Denver Lodge No. 5
Proceedings 1872, pg 20 (1872 Sept 24), Denver Lodge No. 5, Denver
Proceedings 1873, pg 37 (1873 Oct 1), Denver Lodge No. 5, Denver
Proceedings 1874, pg 211 (1874 Sept 30), Denver Lodge No. 5, Denver
Proceedings 1875, pg 75 (1875 Sept 22) Denver Lodge No. 5

Kassler, George W
Proceedings 1861-1869, pg 193 (1867 Oct 8) Denver Lodge No. 5

Kaster, I H
Proceedings 1861-1869, pg 224 (1868 Oct 7) Denver Lodge No. 5, Dimitted

Kastner, Joseph
Proceedings 1872, pg 34 (1872 Sept 24), Occidental Lodge No. 20, Greeley
Proceedings 1873, pg 50 (1873 Oct 1), Occidental Lodge No. 20, Greeley
Proceedings 1874, pg 226 (1874 Sept 30), Occidental Lodge No. 20, Greeley, Demitted

Kastor, I H
  Proceedings 1861-1869, pg 149 (1865 Nov 7), Nevada Lodge No. 4, Nevadaville
  Proceedings 1861-1869, pg 167 (1866 Oct 2) Denver Lodge No. 5
  Proceedings 1861-1869, pg 193 (1867 Oct 8) Denver Lodge No. 5
  Proceedings 1871, pg 19 (1871 Sept 27) Denver Lodge No. 5
  Proceedings 1872, pg 20 (1872 Sept 24), Denver Lodge No. 5, Denver
  Proceedings 1873, pg 37 (1873 Oct 1), Denver Lodge No. 5, Denver
  Proceedings 1874, pg 211 (1874 Sept 30), Denver Lodge No. 5, Denver
  Proceedings 1875, pg 75 (1875 Sept 22) Denver Lodge No. 5
  Proceedings 1876, pg 31 (1876 Sept 20) Denver Lodge No. 5

Kaufmann, John C
  Proceedings 1861-1869, pg 230 (1868 Oct 7), Germania Lodge U D, Denver, Apprentice

Kean, John
  Proceedings 1861-1869, pg 110 (1863 Nov 3) Golden City Lodge No. 1
  Proceedings 1861-1869, pg 131 (1864 Nov 8) Golden City Lodge No. 1
  Proceedings 1861-1869, pg 191 (1867 Oct 8) Golden City Lodge No. 1
  Proceedings 1861-1869, pg 221 (1868 Oct 7) Golden City Lodge No. 1
  Proceedings 1861-1869, pg 303 (1869 Sept 29) Golden City Lodge No. 1
  Proceedings 1870, pg 19 (1870 Sept 28), Golden City Lodge No. 1, Golden City
  Proceedings 1871, pg 17 (1871 Sept 27), Golden City Lodge No. 1, Golden City
  Proceedings 1872, pg 17 (1872 Sept 24), Golden City Lodge No. 1, Golden City
  Proceedings 1873, pg 35 (1873 Oct 1), Golden City Lodge No. 1, Golden City
  Proceedings 1874, pg 209 (1874 Sept 30), Golden City Lodge No. 1, Golden City
  Proceedings 1875, pg 74 (1875 Sept 22) Golden City Lodge No. 1, Stricken from the rolls

Keane, John
  Proceedings 1861-1869, pg 85 (1863 Apr 7) Golden City Lodge No. 1
  Proceedings 1861-1869, pg 147 (1865 Nov 7) Golden City Lodge No. 1
  Proceedings 1861-1869, pg 165 (1866 Oct 2) Golden City Lodge No. 1

Keck, Rudolph
  Proceedings 1873, pg 43 (1873 Oct 1), Washington Lodge No. 12, Georgetown, Apprentice
  Proceedings 1874, pg 9 (1874 Jan 10) dispensation granted
  Proceedings 1874, pg 217 (1874 Sept 30), Washington Lodge No. 12, Georgetown
  Proceedings 1875, pg 81 (1875 Sept 22), Washington Lodge No. 12, Georgetown
  Proceedings 1876, pg 35 (1876 Sept 20), Washington Lodge No. 12, Georgetown

Keeling, W
  Proceedings 1861-1869, pg 229 (1868 Oct 7), Pueblo Lodge U D, Pueblo, Fellowcraft
  Proceedings 1874, pg 222 (1874 Sept 30), Pueblo Lodge No. 17, Pueblo, Pueblo County
  Proceedings 1875, pg 85 (1875 Sept 22) Pueblo Lodge No. 17
  Proceedings 1876, pg 39 (1876 Sept 20) Pueblo Lodge No. 17

Keeling, Weldon
  Proceedings 1861-1869, pg 312 (1869 Sept 29), Pueblo Lodge No. 17, Pueblo
  Proceedings 1870, pg 30 (1870 Sept 28), Pueblo Lodge No. 17, Pueblo
  Proceedings 1871, pg 28 (1871 Sept 27), Pueblo Lodge No. 17, Pueblo
  Proceedings 1872, pg 31 (1872 Sept 24), Pueblo Lodge No. 17, Pueblo
  Proceedings 1873, pg 47 (1873 Oct 1), Pueblo Lodge No. 17, Pueblo

Keene
  Proceedings 1861-1869, pg 87 (1863 Apr 17) Golden City Lodge No. 1

Keene, H B
  Proceedings 1861-1869, pg 76 (1862 Nov 4), Summit Lodge No. 2, Parkville, dimitted

Keer, David
  Proceedings 1871, pg 26 (1871 Sept 27), Columbia Lodge No. 14, Boulder City, Apprentice

Keil, Otto
  Proceedings 1873, pg 48 (1873 Oct 1), Laramie Lodge No. 18, Laramie, Wyoming Territory, Fellowcraft

Keith, Alex
  Proceedings 1872, pg 44 (1872 Sept 24) Halifax, Grand Lodge of Nova Scotia
  Proceedings 1873, pg 61 (1873 Oct 1) Grand Lodge of Nova Scotia, Halifax

Keith, Alexander
  Proceedings 1872, pg 77 (1872 Sept 24) Grand Lodge of Nova Scotia
  Proceedings 1874, pg 116 (1874 Sept 30) Grand Lodge of Nova Scotia
  Proceedings 1874, pg 117 (1874 Sept 30) Grand Lodge of Nova Scotia, died 14 Dec 1873

Keith, W M
  Proceedings 1861-1869, pg 148 (1865 Nov 7), Nevada Lodge No. 4, Nevadaville
  Proceedings 1861-1869, pg 167 (1866 Oct 2) Denver Lodge No. 5

Colorado's Territorial Masons

Keith, W N
    Proceedings 1861-1869, pg 305 (1869 Sept 29) Denver Lodge No. 5

Keith, Wm M
    Proceedings 1861-1869, pg 78 (1862 Nov 4) Denver Lodge No. 5, Fellowcraft
    Proceedings 1861-1869, pg 112 (1863 Nov 3) Denver Lodge No. 5
    Proceedings 1861-1869, pg 133 (1864 Nov 8) Denver Lodge No. 5
    Proceedings 1861-1869, pg 193 (1867 Oct 8) Denver Lodge No. 5
    Proceedings 1861-1869, pg 223 (1868 Oct 7) Denver Lodge No. 5
    Proceedings 1870, pg 21 (1870 Sept 28), Denver Lodge No. 5, Denver
    Proceedings 1871, pg 19 (1871 Sept 27) Denver Lodge No. 5
    Proceedings 1872, pg 20 (1872 Sept 24), Denver Lodge No. 5, Denver

Keithley, Daniel S
    Proceedings 1875, pg 81 (1875 Sept 22), Washington Lodge No. 12, Georgetown
    Proceedings 1876, pg 35 (1876 Sept 20), Washington Lodge No. 12, Georgetown
    Proceedings 1876, pg 50 (1876 Sept 20), Washington Lodge No. 12, Georgetown

Kelley, J
    Proceedings 1861-1869, pg 159 (1866 Oct 1) warrant

Kelley, James
    Proceedings 1861-1869, pg 131 (1864 Nov 8) Golden City Lodge No. 1
    Proceedings 1861-1869, pg 203 (1868 Oct 6) Worshipful Master

Kelly
    Proceedings 1861-1869, pg 177 (1867 Oct 7) committee
    Proceedings 1861-1869, pg 212 (1868 Oct 6) committee
    Proceedings 1861-1869, pg 216 (1868 Oct 7) resolution
    Proceedings 1861-1869, pg 289 (1869 Sept 28) committee

Kelly, J
    Proceedings 1861-1869, pg 138 (1865 Nov 6) committee
    Proceedings 1861-1869, pg 219 (1868 Oct 7) Golden City Lodge No. 1
    Proceedings 1871, pg 17 (1871 Sept 27), Golden City Lodge No. 1, Golden City

Kelly, James
    Proceedings 1861-1869, pg 110 (1863 Nov 3) Golden City Lodge No. 1
    Proceedings 1861-1869, pg 137 (1865 Nov 6) Golden City Lodge No. 1
    Proceedings 1861-1869, pg 144 (1865 Nov 7) Golden City Lodge No. 1
    Proceedings 1861-1869, pg 145 (1865 Nov 7) Golden City Lodge No. 1, Junior Grand Deacon
    Proceedings 1861-1869, pg 147 (1865 Nov 7) Golden City Lodge No. 1
    Proceedings 1861-1869, pg 160 (1866 Oct 2) Golden City Lodge No. 1
    Proceedings 1861-1869, pg 175 (1867 Oct 7) Swand Sword Bearer
    Proceedings 1861-1869, pg 176 (1867 Oct 7) Golden City Lodge No. 1
    Proceedings 1861-1869, pg 186 (1867 Oct 8) per diem
    Proceedings 1861-1869, pg 189 (1867 Oct 8) committee
    Proceedings 1861-1869, pg 190 (1867 Oct 8) Junior Grand Deacon
    Proceedings 1861-1869, pg 191 (1867 Oct 8) Golden City Lodge No. 1
    Proceedings 1861-1869, pg 218 (1868 Oct 7) committee
    Proceedings 1861-1869, pg 219 (1868 Oct 7) Senior Grand Deacon
    Proceedings 1861-1869, pg 221 (1868 Oct 7) Golden City Lodge No. 1
    Proceedings 1861-1869, pg 287 (1869 Sept 28) Grand Deacon
    Proceedings 1861-1869, pg 288 (1869 Sept 28) Golden City Lodge No. 1
    Proceedings 1861-1869, pg 300 (1869 Sept 29) Golden City Lodge No. 1
    Proceedings 1861-1869, pg 300 (1869 Sept 29) committee
    Proceedings 1861-1869, pg 302 (1869 Sept 29) committee
    Proceedings 1861-1869, pg 303 (1869 Sept 29) Golden City Lodge No. 1
    Proceedings 1871, pg 17 (1871 Sept 27), Golden City Lodge No. 1, Golden City
    Proceedings 1872, pg 17 (1872 Sept 24), Golden City Lodge No. 1, Golden City
    Proceedings 1873, pg 35 (1873 Oct 1), Golden City Lodge No. 1, Golden City
    Proceedings 1873, pg 35 (1873 Oct 1), Golden City Lodge No. 1, Golden City
    Proceedings 1874, pg 209 (1874 Sept 30), Golden City Lodge No. 1, Golden City
    Proceedings 1874, pg 209 (1874 Sept 30), Golden City Lodge No. 1, Golden City
    Proceedings 1875, pg 73 (1875 Sept 22) Golden City Lodge No. 1
    Proceedings 1876, pg 4 (1876 Sept 19) Golden City Lodge No. 1
    Proceedings 1876, pg 22 (1876 Sept 20) Golden City Lodge No. 1
    Proceedings 1876, pg 29 (1876 Sept 20) Golden City Lodge No. 1

Kelly, Jas
    Proceedings 1861-1869, pg 161 (1866 Oct 2) Grand Sword Bearer
    Proceedings 1861-1869, pg 165 (1866 Oct 2) Golden City Lodge No. 1
    Proceedings 1861-1869, pg 212 (1868 Oct 6) warrant paid
    Proceedings 1870, pg 19 (1870 Sept 28), Golden City Lodge No. 1, Golden City

Kempton, L S
    Proceedings 1873, pg 50 (1873 Oct 1), Occidental Lodge No. 20, Greeley

Kempton, S S
   Proceedings 1871, pg 31 (1871 Sept 27), Occidental Lodge U D, Greeley
   Proceedings 1872, pg 34 (1872 Sept 24), Occidental Lodge No. 20, Greeley
   Proceedings 1874, pg 225 (1874 Sept 30), Occidental Lodge No. 20, Greeley
   Proceedings 1875, pg 87 (1875 Sept 22), Occidental Lodge No. 20, Greeley
   Proceedings 1876, pg 40 (1876 Sept 20), Occidental Lodge No. 20, Greeley

Kendall, Alpheus
   Proceedings 1871, pg 30 (1871 Sept 27), Occidental Lodge U D, Greeley

Kendall, H W
   Proceedings 1871, pg 25 (1871 Sept 27), El Paso Lodge No. 13, Colorado City
   Proceedings 1872, pg 27 (1872 Sept 24), El Paso Lodge No. 13, Colorado City
   Proceedings 1876, pg 36 (1876 Sept 20), El Paso Lodge No. 13, Colorado City

Kendall, Homer
   Proceedings 1875, pg 82 (1875 Sept 22), El Paso Lodge No. 13, Colorado Springs

Kennaly, John
   Proceedings 1873, pg 60 (1873 Oct 1) Grand Lodge of Idaho, Idaho City
   Proceedings 1874, pg 60 (1874 Sept 30) Grand Lodge of Idaho

Kennedy, L
   Proceedings 1861-1869, pg 134 (1864 Nov 8), Chivington Lodge No. 6, Central City, Apprentice
   Proceedings 1861-1869, pg 150 (1865 Nov 7), Chivington Lodge No. 6, Central City, Apprentice
   Proceedings 1861-1869, pg 169 (1866 Oct 2), Chivington Lodge No. 6, Central City, Apprentice
   Proceedings 1861-1869, pg 194 (1867 Oct 8), Chivington Lodge No. 6, Central City, Apprentice

Kennedy, Lawrence
   Proceedings 1861-1869, pg 78 (1862 Nov 4), Chivington Lodge No. 6, Central City, Apprentice
   Proceedings 1861-1869, pg 113 (1863 Nov 3), Chivington Lodge No. 6, Central City, Apprentice

Kennedy, Silas S
   Proceedings 1876, pg 40 (1876 Sept 20), Occidental Lodge No. 20, Greeley

Kennely, John
   Proceedings 1874, pg 204 (1874 Sept 30) Grand Lodge of Idaho, Idaho City

Kenney, W A
   Proceedings 1861-1869, pg 52 (1862 Nov 4) decesed
   Proceedings 1861-1869, pg 53 (1862 Nov 4) deceased
   Proceedings 1861-1869, pg 54 (1862 Nov 4) deceased
   Proceedings 1861-1869, pg 38 (1861 Dec 12) Grand Chaplain

Kenyon, Joseph
   Proceedings 1874, pg 220 (1874 Sept 30), Mount Moriah Lodge No. 15, Canon City, Fellowcraft
   Proceedings 1875, pg 84 (1875 Sept 22), Mount Moriah Lodge No. 15, Canon City
   Proceedings 1876, pg 38 (1876 Sept 20), Mount Moriah Lodge No. 15, Canon City

Kerfoot, Leigh
   Proceedings 1873, pg 48 (1873 Oct 1), Laramie Lodge No. 18, Laramie, Wyoming Territory
   Proceedings 1874, pg 223 (1874 Sept 30), Laramie Lodge No. 18, Laramie City

Kerr, A L
   Proceedings 1861-1869, pg 152 (1865 Nov 7), Montana Lodge U D, Virginia City, Montana Territory

Kerr, Benj
   Proceedings 1861-1869, pg 170 (1866 Oct 2), Empire Lodge No. 8, Empire City
   Proceedings 1861-1869, pg 226 (1868 Oct 7), Empire Lodge No. 8, Empire City

Kerr, Benjamin
   Proceedings 1861-1869, pg 195 (1867 Oct 8), Empire Lodge No. 8, Empire City
   Proceedings 1861-1869, pg 308 (1869 Sept 29), Empire Lodge No. 8, Empire City
   Proceedings 1870, pg 24 (1870 Sept 28), Empire Lodge No. 8, Empire
   Proceedings 1872, pg 23 (1872 Sept 24), Empire Lodge No. 8, Empire
   Proceedings 1873, pg 41 (1873 Oct 1), Empire Lodge No. 8, Empire
   Proceedings 1874, pg 215 (1874 Sept 30), Empire Lodge No. 8, Empire

Kerr, David
   Proceedings 1872, pg 28 (1872 Sept 24), Columbia Lodge No. 14, Boulder
   Proceedings 1873, pg 44 (1873 Oct 1), Columbia Lodge No. 14, Boulder
   Proceedings 1874, pg 219 (1874 Sept 30), Columbia Lodge No. 14, Boulder, Boulder County
   Proceedings 1875, pg 83 (1875 Sept 22), Columbia Lodge No. 14, Boulder
   Proceedings 1876, pg 37 (1876 Sept 20), Columbia Lodge No. 14, Boulder

Kerr, J W
   Proceedings 1861-1869, pg 149 (1865 Nov 7), Nevada Lodge No. 4, Nevadaville, Apprentice
   Proceedings 1861-1869, pg 167 (1866 Oct 2) Denver Lodge No. 5, Apprentice
   Proceedings 1861-1869, pg 193 (1867 Oct 8) Denver Lodge No. 5, Apprentice
   Proceedings 1861-1869, pg 223 (1868 Oct 7) Denver Lodge No. 5, Apprentice
   Proceedings 1861-1869, pg 305 (1869 Sept 29) Denver Lodge No. 5, Apprentice

Colorado's Territorial Masons

Kerr, John W
  Proceedings 1861-1869, pg 112 (1863 Nov 3) Denver Lodge No. 5, Apprentice
  Proceedings 1861-1869, pg 133 (1864 Nov 8) Denver Lodge No. 5, Apprentice

Kerr, R H
  Proceedings 1876, pg 33 (1876 Sept 20), Union Lodge No. 7, Denver

Kerrigan, T W
  Proceedings 1876, pg 48 (1876 Sept 20), Central Lodge No. 6, Central City, 1875 Oct 13

Kerrigan, Thos W
  Proceedings 1875, pg 77 (1875 Sept 22), Central Lodge No. 6, Central City

Kershaw
  Proceedings 1874, pg 123 (1874 Sept 30) Grand Lodge of South Carolina

Kershaw, J
  Proceedings 1861-1869, pg 193 (1867 Oct 8) Denver Lodge No. 5
  Proceedings 1861-1869, pg 223 (1868 Oct 7) Denver Lodge No. 5
  Proceedings 1861-1869, pg 305 (1869 Sept 29) Denver Lodge No. 5

Kershaw, J B
  Proceedings 1874, pg 121 (1874 Sept 30) Grand Lodge of South Carolina

Kershaw, Jere
  Proceedings 1873, pg 37 (1873 Oct 1), Denver Lodge No. 5, Denver
  Proceedings 1874, pg 211 (1874 Sept 30), Denver Lodge No. 5, Denver

Kershaw, Jerry
  Proceedings 1861-1869, pg 149 (1865 Nov 7), Nevada Lodge No. 4, Nevadaville
  Proceedings 1861-1869, pg 167 (1866 Oct 2) Denver Lodge No. 5

Kershaw, Joseph B
  Proceedings 1874, pg 205 (1874 Sept 30) Grand Lodge of South Carolina, Camden

Kershew, Jere
  Proceedings 1870, pg 21 (1870 Sept 28), Denver Lodge No. 5, Denver

Kershow, J
  Proceedings 1861-1869, pg 112 (1863 Nov 3) Denver Lodge No. 5

Kershow, Jere
  Proceedings 1872, pg 20 (1872 Sept 24), Denver Lodge No. 5, Denver
  Proceedings 1875, pg 75 (1875 Sept 22) Denver Lodge No. 5
  Proceedings 1876, pg 49 (1876 Sept 20) Denver Lodge No. 5, 1876 Aug 19

Kershow, Jeremiah
  Proceedings 1861-1869, pg 77 (1862 Nov 4) Denver Lodge No. 5

Kershow, Jerry
  Proceedings 1861-1869, pg 133 (1864 Nov 8) Denver Lodge No. 5

Kessler, Marion
  Proceedings 1876, pg 37 (1876 Sept 20), Columbia Lodge No. 14, Boulder

Kettle, G E
  Proceedings 1861-1869, pg 76 (1862 Nov 4), Summit Lodge No. 2, Parkville, Apprentice

Keyser, Josiah
  Proceedings 1870, pg 29 (1870 Sept 28), Cheyenne Lodge No. 16, Cheyenne, Wyoming Territory, Apprentice
  Proceedings 1871, pg 28 (1871 Sept 27), Cheyenne Lodge No. 16, Cheyenne, Wyoming Territory, Apprentice
  Proceedings 1872, pg 30 (1872 Sept 24), Cheyenne Lodge No. 16, Cheyenne, Wyoming Territory, Apprentice
  Proceedings 1873, pg 46 (1873 Oct 1), Cheyenne Lodge No. 16, Cheyenne, Wyoming Territory, Apprentice
  Proceedings 1874, pg 221 (1874 Sept 30), Cheyenne Lodge No. 16, Cheyenne, Wyoming Territory, Apprentice

Kibler, James
  Proceedings 1871, pg 30 (1871 Sept 27), Occidental Lodge U D, Greeley
  Proceedings 1872, pg 33 (1872 Sept 24), Occidental Lodge No. 20, Greeley
  Proceedings 1873, pg 50 (1873 Oct 1), Occidental Lodge No. 20, Greeley
  Proceedings 1874, pg 225 (1874 Sept 30), Occidental Lodge No. 20, Greeley
  Proceedings 1875, pg 87 (1875 Sept 22), Occidental Lodge No. 20, Greeley
  Proceedings 1876, pg 48 (1876 Sept 20), Occidental Lodge No. 20, Greeley, 1875 Nov 12

Kiel, Otto
  Proceedings 1874, pg 224 (1874 Sept 30), Laramie Lodge No. 18, Laramie City, Fellowcraft,

Kimball
  Proceedings 1861-1869, pg 82 (1863 Apr 18) Denver Lodge No. 5, Accepted
  Proceedings 1861-1869, pg 83 (1863 May 6) Denver Lodge No. 5

Kimball, E C
  Proceedings 1872, pg 36 (1872 Sept 24), Ashlar Lodge U D, Colorado Springs

Kimball, G K
  Proceedings 1861-1869, pg 92 (1863 Apr 17) Denver Lodge No. 5
  Proceedings 1861-1869, pg 149 (1865 Nov 7), Nevada Lodge No. 4, Nevadaville
  Proceedings 1861-1869, pg 167 (1866 Oct 2) Denver Lodge No. 5
  Proceedings 1861-1869, pg 193 (1867 Oct 8) Denver Lodge No. 5

Proceedings 1861-1869, pg 223 (1868 Oct 7) Denver Lodge No. 5

Proceedings 1861-1869, pg 305 (1869 Sept 29) Denver Lodge No. 5

Proceedings 1870, pg 21 (1870 Sept 28), Denver Lodge No. 5, Denver

Proceedings 1871, pg 19 (1871 Sept 27) Denver Lodge No. 5

Proceedings 1872, pg 20 (1872 Sept 24), Denver Lodge No. 5, Denver

Proceedings 1874, pg 212 (1874 Sept 30), Denver Lodge No. 5, Denver, Reinstated

Kimball, G R
Proceedings 1873, pg 38 (1873 Oct 1), Denver Lodge No. 5, Denver, Striken from the rolls

Proceedings 1875, pg 73 (1875 Sept 22) Golden City Lodge No. 1

Kimball, G W
Proceedings 1874, pg 212 (1874 Sept 30), Denver Lodge No. 5, Denver, Demitted

Kimball, Geo K
Proceedings 1861-1869, pg 112 (1863 Nov 3) Denver Lodge No. 5

Proceedings 1861-1869, pg 133 (1864 Nov 8) Denver Lodge No. 5

Kimball, George K
Proceedings 1861-1869, pg 81 (1863 Apr 18) Denver Lodge No. 5, Rejected

Proceedings 1876, pg 4 (1876 Sept 19) Golden City Lodge No. 1

Proceedings 1876, pg 29 (1876 Sept 20) Golden City Lodge No. 1

Kime, James
Proceedings 1861-1869, pg 310 (1869 Sept 29), El Paso Lodge No. 13, Colorado City

Proceedings 1861-1869, pg 311 (1869 Sept 29), Cheyenne Lodge No. 16, Cheyenne, Not a member

Proceedings 1870, pg 27 (1870 Sept 28), El Paso Lodge No. 13, Colorado City

Proceedings 1871, pg 25 (1871 Sept 27), El Paso Lodge No. 13, Colorado City, died

Proceedings 1871, pg 32 (1871 Sept 27), El Paso Lodge No. 13, Colorado City

Proceedings 1872, pg 27 (1872 Sept 24), El Paso Lodge No. 13, Colorado City

Proceedings 1872, pg 27 (1872 Sept 24), El Paso Lodge No. 13, Colorado City, heretofore erroneously reported dead

Proceedings 1873, pg 43 (1873 Oct 1), El Paso Lodge No. 13, Colorado City

Proceedings 1874, pg 218 (1874 Sept 30), El Paso Lodge No. 13, Colorado Springs

Proceedings 1875, pg 82 (1875 Sept 22), El Paso Lodge No. 13, Colorado Springs, died

Proceedings 1875, pg 94 (1875 Sept 22), El Paso Lodge No. 13, Colorado Springs

Kincaid, Joseph K
Proceedings 1876, pg 43 (1876 Sept 20), Huerfano Lodge No. 27, Walsenburg

Kindall, H W
Proceedings 1873, pg 43 (1873 Oct 1), El Paso Lodge No. 13, Colorado City

Kindall, Homer W
Proceedings 1874, pg 218 (1874 Sept 30), El Paso Lodge No. 13, Colorado Springs

King Solomon Lodge No. 30
Proceedings 1876, pg 52 (1876 Sept 20)

King Solomon Lodge No. 30, West Las Animas
Proceedings 1876, pg 24 (1876 Sept 20) charter granted

King Solomon Lodge U D, West Las Animas
Proceedings 1876, pg 7 (1877 Feb 7) dispensation granted

Proceedings 1876, pg 12 (1876 Sept 19) dues paid and petition for a charter received

Proceedings 1876, pg 13 (1876 Aug 20) dispensation fee paid

Proceedings 1876, pg 13 (1876 Sept 10) dues paid

Proceedings 1876, pg 24 (1876 Sept 20) returns correct

King, Charles
Proceedings 1861-1869, pg 151 (1865 Nov 7), Empire Lodge U D, Empire City, Fellowcraft

Proceedings 1861-1869, pg 170 (1866 Oct 2), Empire Lodge No. 8, Empire City

Proceedings 1861-1869, pg 195 (1867 Oct 8), Empire Lodge No. 8, Empire City

Proceedings 1861-1869, pg 226 (1868 Oct 7), Empire Lodge No. 8, Empire City

Proceedings 1861-1869, pg 308 (1869 Sept 29), Empire Lodge No. 8, Empire City

Proceedings 1872, pg 23 (1872 Sept 24), Empire Lodge No. 8, Empire

Proceedings 1873, pg 41 (1873 Oct 1), Empire Lodge No. 8, Empire

Proceedings 1874, pg 215 (1874 Sept 30), Empire Lodge No. 8, Empire

King, Francis L
Proceedings 1861-1869, pg 157 (1866 Oct 1), deceased, Grand Secretary, Grand Lodge of Indiana

King, James
Proceedings 1870, pg 31 (1870 Sept 28), Laramie Lodge No. 18, Laramie, Wyoming Territory

Proceedings 1871, pg 29 (1871 Sept 27), Laramie Lodge No. 18, Laramie, Wyoming Territory

Proceedings 1872, pg 32 (1872 Sept 24), Laramie Lodge No. 18, Laramie, Wyoming Territory

Proceedings 1873, pg 48 (1873 Oct 1), Laramie Lodge No. 18, Laramie, Wyoming Territory

Proceedings 1874, pg 223 (1874 Sept 30), Laramie Lodge No. 18, Laramie City

King, Robert
Proceedings 1875, pg 83 (1875 Sept 22), Columbia Lodge No. 14, Boulder

Proceedings 1876, pg 37 (1876 Sept 20), Columbia Lodge No. 14, Boulder

Kings, Charles
Proceedings 1870, pg 24 (1870 Sept 28), Empire Lodge No. 8, Empire

Kingsbury, E W
Proceedings 1861-1869, pg 77 (1862 Nov 4) Denver Lodge No. 5
Proceedings 1861-1869, pg 149 (1865 Nov 7), Nevada Lodge No. 4, Nevadaville
Proceedings 1861-1869, pg 167 (1866 Oct 2) Denver Lodge No. 5
Proceedings 1861-1869, pg 193 (1867 Oct 8) Denver Lodge No. 5
Proceedings 1861-1869, pg 223 (1868 Oct 7) Denver Lodge No. 5
Proceedings 1861-1869, pg 305 (1869 Sept 29) Denver Lodge No. 5
Proceedings 1870, pg 21 (1870 Sept 28), Denver Lodge No. 5, Denver

Kingsbury, Ed W
Proceedings 1861-1869, pg 112 (1863 Nov 3) Denver Lodge No. 5
Proceedings 1861-1869, pg 133 (1864 Nov 8) Denver Lodge No. 5

Kinney, J H
Proceedings 1861-1869, pg 150 (1865 Nov 7), Chivington Lodge No. 6, Central City
Proceedings 1861-1869, pg 168 (1866 Oct 2), Chivington Lodge No. 6, Central City
Proceedings 1861-1869, pg 170 (1866 Oct 2), Black Hawk Lodge U D, Black Hawk
Proceedings 1861-1869, pg 224 (1868 Oct 7), Chivington Lodge No. 6, Central City
Proceedings 1870, pg 22 (1870 Sept 28), Central Lodge No. 6, Central City

Kinney, J W
Proceedings 1874, pg 209 (1874 Sept 30), Golden City Lodge No. 1, Golden City

Kinney, Jno H
Proceedings 1872, pg 22 (1872 Sept 24), Denver Lodge No. 5, Denver

Kinney, John H
Proceedings 1861-1869, pg 194 (1867 Oct 8), Chivington Lodge No. 6, Central City
Proceedings 1861-1869, pg 306 (1869 Sept 29), Central Lodge No. 6, Central City
Proceedings 1871, pg 20 (1871 Sept 27), Central Lodge No. 6, Central

Kinny, John
Proceedings 1876, pg 29 (1876 Sept 20) Golden City Lodge No. 1
Proceedings 1876, pg 50 (1876 Sept 20) Golden City Lodge No. 1

Kip, John
Proceedings 1861-1869, pg 134 (1864 Nov 8), Chivington Lodge No. 6, Central City, Fellowcraft
Proceedings 1861-1869, pg 150 (1865 Nov 7), Chivington Lodge No. 6, Central City
Proceedings 1861-1869, pg 168 (1866 Oct 2), Chivington Lodge No. 6, Central City
Proceedings 1861-1869, pg 194 (1867 Oct 8), Chivington Lodge No. 6, Central City
Proceedings 1861-1869, pg 224 (1868 Oct 7), Chivington Lodge No. 6, Central City
Proceedings 1861-1869, pg 306 (1869 Sept 29), Central Lodge No. 6, Central City
Proceedings 1870, pg 22 (1870 Sept 28), Central Lodge No. 6, Central City
Proceedings 1871, pg 20 (1871 Sept 27), Central Lodge No. 6, Central
Proceedings 1872, pg 21 (1872 Sept 24), Denver Lodge No. 5, Denver
Proceedings 1873, pg 38 (1873 Oct 1), Central Lodge No. 6, Central City
Proceedings 1874, pg 213 (1874 Sept 30), Central Lodge No. 6, Central
Proceedings 1875, pg 76 (1875 Sept 22), Central Lodge No. 6, Central City
Proceedings 1876, pg 32 (1876 Sept 20), Central Lodge No. 6, Central City
Proceedings 1876, pg 50 (1876 Sept 20), Central Lodge No. 6, Central City

Kirby
Proceedings 1876, pg 25 (1876 Sept 20) motion

Kirby, John F
Proceedings 1861-1869, pg 86 (1863 Feb 14) Golden City Lodge No. 1
Proceedings 1861-1869, pg 86 (1863 Feb 22) Golden City Lodge No. 1
Proceedings 1861-1869, pg 110 (1863 Nov 3) Golden City Lodge No. 1
Proceedings 1861-1869, pg 131 (1864 Nov 8) Golden City Lodge No. 1
Proceedings 1861-1869, pg 147 (1865 Nov 7) Golden City Lodge No. 1
Proceedings 1861-1869, pg 165 (1866 Oct 2) Golden City Lodge No. 1
Proceedings 1861-1869, pg 191 (1867 Oct 8) Golden City Lodge No. 1
Proceedings 1861-1869, pg 221 (1868 Oct 7) Golden City Lodge No. 1
Proceedings 1861-1869, pg 303 (1869 Sept 29) Golden City Lodge No. 1, Dimitted

Kirby, M C
Proceedings 1861-1869, pg 191 (1867 Oct 8) Golden City Lodge No. 1
Proceedings 1861-1869, pg 221 (1868 Oct 7) Golden City Lodge No. 1
Proceedings 1861-1869, pg 303 (1869 Sept 29) Golden City Lodge No. 1
Proceedings 1870, pg cover (1870 Sept 28) Senior Grand Steward, Golden City
Proceedings 1870, pg 12 (1870 Sept 27) Senior Warden, Golden City Lodge No. 1, Golden City
Proceedings 1870, pg 13 (1870 Sept 27) Senior Grand Steward

Proceedings 1870, pg 19 (1870 Sept 28), Golden City Lodge No. 1, Golden City

Proceedings 1871, pg 3 (1871 Sept 26) Senior Grand Steward

Proceedings 1871, pg 4 (1871 Sept 26), Golden City Lodge No. 1, Golden City

Proceedings 1871, pg 17 (1871 Sept 27), Golden City Lodge No. 1, Golden City

Proceedings 1872, pg cover (1872 Sept 24) committee, Golden

Proceedings 1872, pg 12 (1872 Sept 24), Golden City Lodge No. 1, Golden City

Proceedings 1872, pg 16 (1872 Sept 24), Golden City Lodge No. 1, Golden City

Proceedings 1872, pg 16 (1872 Sept 24) committee

Proceedings 1872, pg 17 (1872 Sept 24), Golden City Lodge No. 1, Golden City

Proceedings 1873, pg 5 (1873 Sept 30), Golden City Lodge No. 1, Golden City

Proceedings 1873, pg 31 (1873 Oct 1) mileage and per diem

Proceedings 1874, pg 5 (1874 Sept 29), Golden City Lodge No. 1, Golden City

Proceedings 1874, pg 6 (1874 Sept 29) committee

Proceedings 1874, pg 36 (1874 Sept 30) committee

Proceedings 1874, pg 36 (1874 Sept 30) per diem

Proceedings 1875, pg 16 (1875 Sept 21) Golden City Lodge No. 1

Proceedings 1875, pg 17 (1875 Sept 21) committee

Proceedings 1875, pg 34 (1875 Sept 22) Junior Grand Warden

Proceedings 1875, pg 37 (1875 Sept 22) per diem

Proceedings 1876, pg 6 (1876 Sept 19) Junior Grand Warden

Proceedings 1876, pg 22 (1876 Sept 20) Junior Grand Warden

Kirby, Marcellus C

Proceedings 1873, pg 16 (1873 Oct 1) Senior Grand Deacon

Proceedings 1873, pg 35 (1873 Oct 1), Golden City Lodge No. 1, Golden City

Proceedings 1874, pg 4 (1874 Sept 29) Senior Grand Deacon

Proceedings 1874, pg 209 (1874 Sept 30), Golden City Lodge No. 1, Golden City

Proceedings 1875, pg 15 (1875 Sept 21) Junior Grand Deacon

Proceedings 1875, pg 30 (1875 Sept 21) Junior Grand Warden

Proceedings 1875, pg 73 (1875 Sept 22) Golden City Lodge No. 1

Proceedings 1875, pg cover (1875 Sept 22) Junior Grand Warden, Golden

Proceedings 1875, pg 93 (1875 Sept 22) Junior Grand Warden, 1875

Proceedings 1876, pg 29 (1876 Sept 20) Golden City Lodge No. 1

Kirkandal, D

Proceedings 1876, pg 38 (1876 Sept 20), Mount Moriah Lodge No. 15, Canon City, Apprentice

Kirker, R A

Proceedings 1875, pg 89 (1875 Sept 22), Doric Lodge No. 25, Fairplay

Proceedings 1876, pg 42 (1876 Sept 20), Doric Lodge No. 25, Fairplay

Kirker, Robert A

Proceedings 1874, pg 228 (1874 Sept 30), Doric Lodge U D, Fairplay

Kirkland, James

Proceedings 1861-1869, pg 308 (1869 Sept 29), Empire Lodge No. 8, Empire City

Proceedings 1870, pg 24 (1870 Sept 28), Empire Lodge No. 8, Empire

Kittle, G E

Proceedings 1861-1869, pg 43 (1861 Dec 10), Summit Lodge No. 2, Parkville

Klein, Jos

Proceedings 1861-1869, pg 230 (1868 Oct 7), Germania Lodge U D, Denver

Klershow, Jere

Proceedings 1871, pg 19 (1871 Sept 27) Denver Lodge No. 5

Kline, D

Proceedings 1861-1869, pg 113 (1863 Nov 3), Chivington Lodge No. 6, Central City

Proceedings 1861-1869, pg 168 (1866 Oct 2), Chivington Lodge No. 6, Central City

Kline, David

Proceedings 1861-1869, pg 134 (1864 Nov 8), Chivington Lodge No. 6, Central City

Proceedings 1861-1869, pg 150 (1865 Nov 7), Chivington Lodge No. 6, Central City

Proceedings 1861-1869, pg 194 (1867 Oct 8), Chivington Lodge No. 6, Central City

Proceedings 1861-1869, pg 224 (1868 Oct 7), Chivington Lodge No. 6, Central City

Proceedings 1861-1869, pg 306 (1869 Sept 29), Central Lodge No. 6, Central City

Proceedings 1870, pg 22 (1870 Sept 28), Central Lodge No. 6, Central City

Proceedings 1871, pg 20 (1871 Sept 27), Central Lodge No. 6, Central

Proceedings 1872, pg 21 (1872 Sept 24), Denver Lodge No. 5, Denver

Proceedings 1873, pg 38 (1873 Oct 1), Central Lodge No. 6, Central City

Proceedings 1874, pg 213 (1874 Sept 30), Central Lodge No. 6, Central

Proceedings 1875, pg 76 (1875 Sept 22), Central Lodge No. 6, Central City

Proceedings 1876, pg 32 (1876 Sept 20), Central Lodge No. 6, Central City

Colorado's Territorial Masons

Kline, H
    Proceedings 1861-1869, pg 113 (1863 Nov 3), Chivington Lodge No. 6, Central City, dimitted
    Proceedings 1861-1869, pg 305 (1869 Sept 29) Denver Lodge No. 5

Kline, Henry
    Proceedings 1861-1869, pg 133 (1864 Nov 8) Denver Lodge No. 5
    Proceedings 1861-1869, pg 149 (1865 Nov 7), Nevada Lodge No. 4, Nevadaville
    Proceedings 1861-1869, pg 167 (1866 Oct 2) Denver Lodge No. 5
    Proceedings 1861-1869, pg 193 (1867 Oct 8) Denver Lodge No. 5
    Proceedings 1861-1869, pg 223 (1868 Oct 7) Denver Lodge No. 5
    Proceedings 1870, pg 21 (1870 Sept 28), Denver Lodge No. 5, Denver
    Proceedings 1871, pg 19 (1871 Sept 27) Denver Lodge No. 5
    Proceedings 1873, pg 38 (1873 Oct 1), Denver Lodge No. 5, Denver, Striken from the rolls

Kline, James
    Proceedings 1861-1869, pg 196 (1867 Oct 8), El Paso Lodge U D, Colorado City, Fellowcraft

Kline, Jos
    Proceedings 1861-1869, pg 148 (1865 Nov 7), Nevada Lodge No. 4, Nevadaville

Kline, Joseph
    Proceedings 1861-1869, pg 167 (1866 Oct 2) Denver Lodge No. 5
    Proceedings 1861-1869, pg 193 (1867 Oct 8) Denver Lodge No. 5
    Proceedings 1861-1869, pg 223 (1868 Oct 7) Denver Lodge No. 5
    Proceedings 1861-1869, pg 305 (1869 Sept 29) Denver Lodge No. 5
    Proceedings 1870, pg 21 (1870 Sept 28), Denver Lodge No. 5, Denver
    Proceedings 1871, pg 19 (1871 Sept 27) Denver Lodge No. 5
    Proceedings 1873, pg 38 (1873 Oct 1), Denver Lodge No. 5, Denver, Striken from the rolls

Kline, P A
    Proceedings 1875, pg 74 (1875 Sept 22), Nevada Lodge No. 4, Nevada

Kline, Perry A
    Proceedings 1861-1869, pg 166 (1866 Oct 2), Nevada Lodge No. 4, Nevadaville
    Proceedings 1861-1869, pg 192 (1867 Oct 8), Nevada Lodge No. 4, Nevadaville
    Proceedings 1861-1869, pg 222 (1868 Oct 7), Nevada Lodge No. 4, Nevadaville
    Proceedings 1861-1869, pg 304 (1869 Sept 29), Nevada Lodge No. 4, Nevadaville
    Proceedings 1870, pg 20 (1870 Sept 28), Nevada Lodge No. 4, Nevadaville
    Proceedings 1871, pg 18 (1871 Sept 27), Nevada Lodge No. 4, Bald Mountain
    Proceedings 1873, pg 36 (1873 Oct 1), Nevada Lodge No. 4, Nevada
    Proceedings 1874, pg 210 (1874 Sept 30), Nevada Lodge No. 4, Bald Mountain, Gilpin County
    Proceedings 1876, pg 30 (1876 Sept 20) Nevada Lodge No. 4

Klock, J I
    Proceedings 1875, pg 75 (1875 Sept 22) Denver Lodge No. 5
    Proceedings 1876, pg 31 (1876 Sept 20) Denver Lodge No. 5

Klock, John I
    Proceedings 1874, pg 211 (1874 Sept 30), Denver Lodge No. 5, Denver

Knap, Grosvenor
    Proceedings 1874, pg 223 (1874 Sept 30), Laramie Lodge No. 18, Laramie City
    Proceedings 1871, pg 29 (1871 Sept 27), Laramie Lodge No. 18, Laramie, Wyoming Territory
    Proceedings 1873, pg 48 (1873 Oct 1), Laramie Lodge No. 18, Laramie, Wyoming Territory
    Proceedings 1872, pg 32 (1872 Sept 24), Laramie Lodge No. 18, Laramie, Wyoming Territory

Knapp, M H
    Proceedings 1861-1869, pg 147 (1865 Nov 7) Golden City Lodge No. 1, Apprentice
    Proceedings 1861-1869, pg 165 (1866 Oct 2) Golden City Lodge No. 1, Apprentice
    Proceedings 1861-1869, pg 191 (1867 Oct 8) Golden City Lodge No. 1, Apprentice
    Proceedings 1861-1869, pg 221 (1868 Oct 7) Golden City Lodge No. 1, Apprentice
    Proceedings 1861-1869, pg 303 (1869 Sept 29) Golden City Lodge No. 1, Apprentice

Knapp, Richard F
    Proceedings 1873, pg 60 (1873 Oct 1) Grand Lodge of Alabama, Mobile

Knopp, Richard F
    Proceedings 1872, pg 43 (1872 Sept 24) Mobile, Grand Lodge of Alabama

Knoth, C W
    Proceedings 1873, pg 52 (1873 Oct 1), St Vrain Lodge No. 23, Longmont, Apprentice
    Proceedings 1874, pg 227 (1874 Sept 30), St Vrain No. 23, Longmont
    Proceedings 1876, pg 41 (1876 Sept 20), St Vrain Lodge No. 23, Longmont

Knott, Edward
    Proceedings 1876, pg 43 (1876 Sept 20), Huerfano Lodge No. 27, Walsenburg

Knott, Edwin
    Proceedings 1875, pg 90 (1875 Sept 22), Huerfano Lodge U D, Walsenburg, Fellowcraft

Knott, R F
Proceedings 1872, pg 54 (1872 Sept 24) Grand Lodge of Alabama

Knott, Richard F
Proceedings 1874, pg 44 (1874 Sept 30) Grand Lodge of Alabama, died on 22 Nov 1873

Knowlton, W F
Proceedings 1873, pg 40 (1873 Oct 1), Union Lodge No. 7, Denver

Knowlton, William F
Proceedings 1876, pg 33 (1876 Sept 20), Union Lodge No. 7, Denver

Knowlton, Wm F
Proceedings 1861-1869, pg 307 (1869 Sept 29), Union Lodge No. 7, Denver
Proceedings 1870, pg 23 (1870 Sept 28), Union Lodge No. 7, Denver
Proceedings 1871, pg 22 (1871 Sept 27), Union Lodge No. 7, Denver
Proceedings 1872, pg 22 (1872 Sept 24), Union Lodge No. 7, Denver
Proceedings 1874, pg 214 (1874 Sept 30), Union Lodge No. 7, Denver
Proceedings 1875, pg 78 (1875 Sept 22), Union Lodge No. 7, Denver

Knox, John
Proceedings 1873, pg 44 (1873 Oct 1), Columbia Lodge No. 14, Boulder
Proceedings 1874, pg 219 (1874 Sept 30), Columbia Lodge No. 14, Boulder, Boulder County
Proceedings 1875, pg 83 (1875 Sept 22), Columbia Lodge No. 14, Boulder
Proceedings 1876, pg 37 (1876 Sept 20), Columbia Lodge No. 14, Boulder

Knox, Solomon
Proceedings 1861-1869, pg 170 (1866 Oct 2), Empire Lodge No. 8, Empire City, demitted

Kohler, F W
Proceedings 1872, pg 28 (1872 Sept 24), Columbia Lodge No. 14, Boulder

Kohler, Fred W
Proceedings 1873, pg 44 (1873 Oct 1), Columbia Lodge No. 14, Boulder
Proceedings 1874, pg 219 (1874 Sept 30), Columbia Lodge No. 14, Boulder, Boulder County
Proceedings 1875, pg 83 (1875 Sept 22), Columbia Lodge No. 14, Boulder

Kohler, Frederick W
Proceedings 1870, pg 28 (1870 Sept 28), Columbia Lodge No. 14, Boulder City, Apprentice
Proceedings 1871, pg 25 (1871 Sept 27), Columbia Lodge No. 14, Boulder City
Proceedings 1876, pg 37 (1876 Sept 20), Columbia Lodge No. 14, Boulder

Kort, L H
Proceedings 1873, pg 48 (1873 Oct 1), Laramie Lodge No. 18, Laramie, Wyoming Territory, permission granted to take degrees elsewhere

Korty, L H
Proceedings 1871, pg 29 (1871 Sept 27), Laramie Lodge No. 18, Laramie, Wyoming Territory, Apprentice

Kortz, L H
Proceedings 1872, pg 32 (1872 Sept 24), Laramie Lodge No. 18, Laramie, Wyoming Territory, Apprentice

Kountz, Charles B
Proceedings 1870, pg 23 (1870 Sept 28), Union Lodge No. 7, Denver

Kountze, C B
Proceedings 1861-1869, pg 169 (1866 Oct 2), Union Lodge No. 7, Denver
Proceedings 1861-1869, pg 195 (1867 Oct 8), Union Lodge No. 7, Denver
Proceedings 1873, pg 39 (1873 Oct 1), Union Lodge No. 7, Denver
Proceedings 1874, pg 213 (1874 Sept 30), Union Lodge No. 7, Denver
Proceedings 1875, pg 78 (1875 Sept 22), Union Lodge No. 7, Denver
Proceedings 1876, pg 33 (1876 Sept 20), Union Lodge No. 7, Denver

Kountze, Charles B
Proceedings 1872, pg 22 (1872 Sept 24), Union Lodge No. 7, Denver

Kountze, Chas B
Proceedings 1861-1869, pg 225 (1868 Oct 7), Union Lodge No. 7, Denver
Proceedings 1861-1869, pg 307 (1869 Sept 29), Union Lodge No. 7, Denver
Proceedings 1871, pg 22 (1871 Sept 27), Union Lodge No. 7, Denver

Kountze, Luther
Proceedings 1861-1869, pg 134 (1864 Nov 8), Union Lodge No. 7, Denver
Proceedings 1861-1869, pg 151 (1865 Nov 7), Chivington Lodge No. 6, Central City
Proceedings 1861-1869, pg 169 (1866 Oct 2), Union Lodge No. 7, Denver
Proceedings 1861-1869, pg 195 (1867 Oct 8), Union Lodge No. 7, Denver
Proceedings 1861-1869, pg 225 (1868 Oct 7), Union Lodge No. 7, Denver
Proceedings 1861-1869, pg 308 (1869 Sept 29), Union Lodge No. 7, Denver, Dimitted

Krack, G
Proceedings 1861-1869, pg 76 (1862 Nov 4), Summit Lodge No. 2, Parkville
Proceedings 1861-1869, pg 111 (1863 Nov 3), Summit Lodge No. 2, Parkville
Proceedings 1861-1869, pg 132 (1864 Nov 8) Golden City Lodge No. 1, dimitted

Kram, W J
- Proceedings 1861-1869, pg 191 (1867 Oct 8) Golden City Lodge No. 1
- Proceedings 1870, pg 19 (1870 Sept 28), Golden City Lodge No. 1, Golden City
- Proceedings 1871, pg 17 (1871 Sept 27), Golden City Lodge No. 1, Golden City
- Proceedings 1871, pg 30 (1871 Sept 27), Occidental Lodge U D, Greeley
- Proceedings 1872, pg 18 (1872 Sept 24), Golden City Lodge No. 1, Golden City, Stricken from the Roll
- Proceedings 1873, pg 50 (1873 Oct 1), Occidental Lodge No. 20, Greeley
- Proceedings 1874, pg 225 (1874 Sept 30), Occidental Lodge No. 20, Greeley
- Proceedings 1875, pg 87 (1875 Sept 22), Occidental Lodge No. 20, Greeley
- Proceedings 1876, pg 49 (1876 Sept 20), Occidental Lodge No. 20, Greeley, 1875 Nov 1

Kribs, W H
- Proceedings 1874, pg 214 (1874 Sept 30), Union Lodge No. 7, Denver
- Proceedings 1875, pg 78 (1875 Sept 22), Union Lodge No. 7, Denver
- Proceedings 1876, pg 33 (1876 Sept 20), Union Lodge No. 7, Denver

Krone, J L
- Proceedings 1874, pg 223 (1874 Sept 30), Laramie Lodge No. 18, Laramie City

Kruse, Gustave
- Proceedings 1875, pg 76 (1875 Sept 22), Central Lodge No. 6, Central City
- Proceedings 1876, pg 32 (1876 Sept 20), Central Lodge No. 6, Central City

Kruse, H J
- Proceedings 1861-1869, pg 113 (1863 Nov 3), Chivington Lodge No. 6, Central City
- Proceedings 1861-1869, pg 133 (1864 Nov 8), Chivington Lodge No. 6, Central City
- Proceedings 1861-1869, pg 150 (1865 Nov 7), Chivington Lodge No. 6, Central City
- Proceedings 1861-1869, pg 168 (1866 Oct 2), Chivington Lodge No. 6, Central City
- Proceedings 1861-1869, pg 224 (1868 Oct 7), Chivington Lodge No. 6, Central City
- Proceedings 1861-1869, pg 306 (1869 Sept 29), Central Lodge No. 6, Central City
- Proceedings 1870, pg 22 (1870 Sept 28), Central Lodge No. 6, Central City
- Proceedings 1871, pg 20 (1871 Sept 27), Central Lodge No. 6, Central

Kruse, H Jacob
- Proceedings 1872, pg 21 (1872 Sept 24), Denver Lodge No. 5, Denver
- Proceedings 1873, pg 38 (1873 Oct 1), Central Lodge No. 6, Central City
- Proceedings 1874, pg 213 (1874 Sept 30), Central Lodge No. 6, Central
- Proceedings 1875, pg 76 (1875 Sept 22), Central Lodge No. 6, Central City
- Proceedings 1876, pg 32 (1876 Sept 20), Central Lodge No. 6, Central City

L

Lagre, P F
- Proceedings 1874, pg 211 (1874 Sept 30), Denver Lodge No. 5, Denver

Lake
- Proceedings 1871, pg 13 (1871 Sept 26) Grand Teller

Lake, Benj
- Proceedings 1861-1869, pg 134 (1864 Nov 8), Chivington Lodge No. 6, Central City, Apprentice
- Proceedings 1861-1869, pg 168 (1866 Oct 2), Chivington Lodge No. 6, Central City
- Proceedings 1861-1869, pg 194 (1867 Oct 8), Chivington Lodge No. 6, Central City
- Proceedings 1861-1869, pg 224 (1868 Oct 7), Chivington Lodge No. 6, Central City
- Proceedings 1861-1869, pg 306 (1869 Sept 29), Central Lodge No. 6, Central City
- Proceedings 1870, pg 22 (1870 Sept 28), Central Lodge No. 6, Central City
- Proceedings 1871, pg 4 (1871 Sept 26), Central Lodge No. 6, Central City
- Proceedings 1872, pg 21 (1872 Sept 24), Denver Lodge No. 5, Denver

Lake, Benjamin
- Proceedings 1861-1869, pg 150 (1865 Nov 7), Chivington Lodge No. 6, Central City
- Proceedings 1871, pg 20 (1871 Sept 27), Central Lodge No. 6, Central
- Proceedings 1873, pg 38 (1873 Oct 1), Central Lodge No. 6, Central City
- Proceedings 1874, pg 213 (1874 Sept 30), Central Lodge No. 6, Central
- Proceedings 1875, pg 77 (1875 Sept 22), Central Lodge No. 6, Central City
- Proceedings 1876, pg 48 (1876 Sept 20), Central Lodge No. 6, Central City, 1876 Jan 13

Lake, C O
- Proceedings 1874, pg 227 (1874 Sept 30), St Vrain No. 23, Longmont
- Proceedings 1876, pg 41 (1876 Sept 20), St Vrain Lodge No. 23, Longmont

Lake, D D
- Proceedings 1870, pg 22 (1870 Sept 28), Central Lodge No. 6, Central City
- Proceedings 1871, pg 20 (1871 Sept 27), Central Lodge No. 6, Central

Lake, David D
- Proceedings 1861-1869, pg 225 (1868 Oct 7), Chivington Lodge No. 6, Central City, Fellowcraft
- Proceedings 1861-1869, pg 306 (1869 Sept 29), Central Lodge No. 6, Central City

Proceedings 1872, pg 21 (1872 Sept 24), Denver Lodge No. 5, Denver

Proceedings 1873, pg 38 (1873 Oct 1), Central Lodge No. 6, Central City

Proceedings 1874, pg 213 (1874 Sept 30), Central Lodge No. 6, Central

Proceedings 1875, pg 77 (1875 Sept 22), Central Lodge No. 6, Central City

Proceedings 1876, pg 32 (1876 Sept 20), Central Lodge No. 6, Central City

Lake, R C
Proceedings 1861-1869, pg 224 (1868 Oct 7), Chivington Lodge No. 6, Central City

Proceedings 1870, pg 22 (1870 Sept 28), Central Lodge No. 6, Central City

Lake, Richard C
Proceedings 1861-1869, pg 306 (1869 Sept 29), Central Lodge No. 6, Central City

Proceedings 1872, pg 21 (1872 Sept 24), Denver Lodge No. 5, Denver

Proceedings 1873, pg 38 (1873 Oct 1), Central Lodge No. 6, Central City

Proceedings 1874, pg 213 (1874 Sept 30), Central Lodge No. 6, Central

Proceedings 1875, pg 76 (1875 Sept 22), Central Lodge No. 6, Central City

Proceedings 1876, pg 31 (1876 Sept 20), Central Lodge No. 6, Central City

Lake, Rich'd C
Proceedings 1871, pg 20 (1871 Sept 27), Central Lodge No. 6, Central

Lamb, H W
Proceedings 1876, pg 36 (1876 Sept 20), El Paso Lodge No. 13, Colorado City

Lamb, Henry W
Proceedings 1874, pg 218 (1874 Sept 30), El Paso Lodge No. 13, Colorado Springs

Proceedings 1875, pg 82 (1875 Sept 22), El Paso Lodge No. 13, Colorado Springs

Lamb, Reuben P
Proceedings 1861-1869, pg 192 (1867 Oct 8) Denver Lodge No. 5

Proceedings 1861-1869, pg 223 (1868 Oct 7) Denver Lodge No. 5

Lamber, J B
Proceedings 1861-1869, pg 149 (1865 Nov 7), Nevada Lodge No. 4, Nevadaville

Proceedings 1861-1869, pg 167 (1866 Oct 2) Denver Lodge No. 5

Proceedings 1861-1869, pg 305 (1869 Sept 29) Denver Lodge No. 5

Lamber, John B
Proceedings 1861-1869, pg 77 (1862 Nov 4) Denver Lodge No. 5

Proceedings 1861-1869, pg 112 (1863 Nov 3) Denver Lodge No. 5

Proceedings 1861-1869, pg 133 (1864 Nov 8) Denver Lodge No. 5

Proceedings 1861-1869, pg 193 (1867 Oct 8) Denver Lodge No. 5

Proceedings 1861-1869, pg 223 (1868 Oct 7) Denver Lodge No. 5

Lamber, Joseph
Proceedings 1861-1869, pg 223 (1868 Oct 7) Denver Lodge No. 5

Lambers, John B
Proceedings 1870, pg 21 (1870 Sept 28), Denver Lodge No. 5, Denver

Proceedings 1872, pg 20 (1872 Sept 24), Denver Lodge No. 5, Denver

Lambert, J
Proceedings 1861-1869, pg 305 (1869 Sept 29) Denver Lodge No. 5

Lambert, Jos
Proceedings 1871, pg cover (1871 Sept 27) Junior Grand Deacon, Denver

Proceedings 1871, pg 14 (1871 Sept 27) Junior Grand Deacon

Proceedings 1871, pg 19 (1871 Sept 27) Denver Lodge No. 5

Proceedings 1875, pg 16 (1875 Sept 21) Denver Lodge No. 5

Lambert, Joseph
Proceedings 1861-1869, pg 167 (1866 Oct 2) Denver Lodge No. 5, Apprentice

Proceedings 1861-1869, pg 193 (1867 Oct 8) Denver Lodge No. 5

Proceedings 1870, pg 21 (1870 Sept 28), Denver Lodge No. 5, Denver

Proceedings 1871, pg 4 (1871 Sept 26) Denver Lodge No. 5

Proceedings 1872, pg 19 (1872 Sept 24), Denver Lodge No. 5, Denver

Proceedings 1873, pg 37 (1873 Oct 1), Denver Lodge No. 5, Denver

Proceedings 1874, pg 211 (1874 Sept 30), Denver Lodge No. 5, Denver

Proceedings 1875, pg 75 (1875 Sept 22) Denver Lodge No. 5

Proceedings 1876, pg 4 (1876 Sept 19) Denver Lodge No. 5

Proceedings 1876, pg 26 (1876 Sept 20) committee

Proceedings 1876, pg 31 (1876 Sept 20) Denver Lodge No. 5

Lambert, R L
Proceedings 1871, pg 28 (1871 Sept 27), Pueblo Lodge No. 17, Pueblo, Apprentice

Proceedings 1872, pg 31 (1872 Sept 24), Pueblo Lodge No. 17, Pueblo, Apprentice

Lambert, Robert
Proceedings 1876, pg 39 (1876 Sept 20) Pueblo Lodge No. 17, Permission granted to take degrees elsewhere

Lambert, Robert L
    Proceedings 1873, pg 47 (1873 Oct 1), Pueblo Lodge No. 17, Pueblo, Apprentice
    Proceedings 1874, pg 222 (1874 Sept 30), Pueblo Lodge No. 17, Pueblo, Pueblo County, Apprentice
    Proceedings 1875, pg 85 (1875 Sept 22) Pueblo Lodge No. 17, Apprentice

Lambert, W H
    Proceedings 1874, pg 205 (1874 Sept 30) Grand Lodge of Virginia, Alexandria

Lamberton, Robert A
    Proceedings 1870, pg 100 (1869 Dec 27) Grand Master, Grand Lodge of Pennsylvania
    Proceedings 1872, pg 85 (1872 Sept 24) Grand Lodge of Pennsylvania

Lander, M H
    Proceedings 1871, pg 24 (1871 Sept 27), Washington Lodge No. 12, Georgetown

Landers, Milton H
    Proceedings 1870, pg 26 (1870 Sept 28), Washington Lodge No. 12, Georgetown
    Proceedings 1872, pg 26 (1872 Sept 24), Washington Lodge No. 12, Georgetown
    Proceedings 1873, pg 43 (1873 Oct 1), Washington Lodge No. 12, Georgetown
    Proceedings 1874, pg 217 (1874 Sept 30), Washington Lodge No. 12, Georgetown
    Proceedings 1875, pg 81 (1875 Sept 22), Washington Lodge No. 12, Georgetown
    Proceedings 1876, pg 35 (1876 Sept 20), Washington Lodge No. 12, Georgetown
    Proceedings 1876, pg 50 (1876 Sept 20), Washington Lodge No. 12, Georgetown

Landesloge
    Proceedings 1872, pg 47 (1872 Sept 24), Berlin, Prussia

Landmark
    Proceedings 1871, pg 10 (1871 Sept 26) masonic magazine

Langdon, J B
    Proceedings 1861-1869, pg 110 (1863 Nov 3) Golden City Lodge No. 1, Apprentice
    Proceedings 1861-1869, pg 131 (1864 Nov 8) Golden City Lodge No. 1
    Proceedings 1861-1869, pg 221 (1868 Oct 7) Golden City Lodge No. 1
    Proceedings 1861-1869, pg 303 (1869 Sept 29) Golden City Lodge No. 1

Lange, Charles
    Proceedings 1861-1869, pg 152 (1865 Nov 7), Montana Lodge U D, Virginia City, Montana Territory

Langeman, Chas
    Proceedings 1873, pg 52 (1873 Oct 1), Ashlar Lodge U D, Colorado Springs

Langerin, Charles
    Proceedings 1874, pg 218 (1874 Sept 30), El Paso Lodge No. 13, Colorado Springs

Langevin, C
    Proceedings 1873, pg 13 (1873 Sept 30), Ashlar Lodge U D, Colorado Springs

Langevin, Charles
    Proceedings 1875, pg 82 (1875 Sept 22), El Paso Lodge No. 13, Colorado Springs
    Proceedings 1876, pg 36 (1876 Sept 20), El Paso Lodge No. 13, Colorado City

Langford, N P
    Proceedings 1861-1869, pg 267 (1867 Jan 20), Grand Historian, Grand Lodge of Montana
    Proceedings 1870, pg 90 (1869 Oct 4) Grand Master, Grand Lodge of Montana

Langram, Jas J
    Proceedings 1872, pg 25 (1872 Sept 24), Black Hawk Lodge No. 11, Black Hawk

Lansingh, K V R
    Proceedings 1876, pg 32 (1876 Sept 20), Union Lodge No. 7, Denver

Lapoint, Geo
    Proceedings 1872, pg 28 (1872 Sept 24), Columbia Lodge No. 14, Boulder, Dimitted

LaPoint, George
    Proceedings 1861-1869, pg 310 (1869 Sept 29), Columbia Lodge No. 14, Boulder City
    Proceedings 1870, pg 27 (1870 Sept 28), Columbia Lodge No. 14, Boulder City
    Proceedings 1871, pg 25 (1871 Sept 27), Columbia Lodge No. 14, Boulder City

Laramie Lodge No. 18
    Proceedings 1875, pg 20 (1875 Mar 15) Grand Lodge of Wyoming
    Proceedings 1875, pg 23 (1875 Sept 21) Grand Lodge of Wyoming
    Proceedings 1875, pg 24 (1875 Sept 21) returned charter
    Proceedings 1876, pg 47 (1876 Sept 20), Laramie Lodge No. 2, Grand Lodge of Wyoming Territory
    Proceedings 1870, pg 30 (1870 Sept 28) dispensation granted 31 Jan 1870

Laramie Lodge No. 18, Laramie, Wyoming Territory
    Proceedings 1873, pg 10 (1873 Sept 30)
    Proceedings 1874, pg 208 (1874 Sept 30)

Laramie Lodge No. 3
    Proceedings 1875, pg 86 (1875 Sept 22) Grand Lodge of Wyoming

Laramie Lodge U D
    Proceedings 1870, pg 11 (1870 Sept 27)
    Proceedings 1870, pg 15 (1870 Sept 28) chartered as Laramie Lodge No. 18

Larkin, F J
    Proceedings 1875, pg 73 (1875 Sept 22) Golden City Lodge No. 1

Larkin, John T
    Proceedings 1876, pg 29 (1876 Sept 20) Golden City Lodge No. 1

Larner
Proceedings 1872, pg 58 (1872 Sept 24) Grand Lodge of the District of Columbia

Larner, Noble D
Proceedings 1861-1869, pg 316 (1869 Sept 29) Grand Lodge of District of Columbia
Proceedings 1861-1869, pg 326 (1868 Nov 8) Grand Secretary, Grand Lodge of District of Columbia
Proceedings 1870, pg 34 (1870 Sept 28) Grand Secretary, Grand Lodge of the District of Columbia
Proceedings 1871, pg 35 (1871 Sept 27) Grand Secretary, Grand Lodge of the District of Columbia
Proceedings 1872, pg 58 (1872 Sept 24) Grand Lodge of the District of Columbia

Las Animas Lodge [U D]
Proceedings 1875, pg 25 (1875 Sept 21) payment for dispensation

Las Animas Lodge No. 28
Proceedings 1875, pg 91 (1875 Sept 22), dispensation granted 17 Mar 1875, charter granted 22 Sept 1875
Proceedings 1876, pg 52 (1876 Sept 20)

Las Animas Lodge No. 28, Walsenburg
Proceedings 1876, pg 8 (1875 Oct 7) lodge dedicated and officers installed
Proceedings 1876, pg 13 (1875 Sept 22) charter fees paid
Proceedings 1876, pg 13 (1876 Sept 8) dues paid

Las Animas Lodge U D
Proceedings 1875, pg 25 (1875 Sept 21) dues paid
Proceedings 1875, pg 34 (1875 Sept 22), chartered as Las Animas Lodge No. 28, Trinidad
Proceedings 1875, pg 92 (1875 Sept 22)

Las Animas Lodge U D, Trinidad
Proceedings 1875, pg 19 (1875 Mar 15) dispensation granted
Proceedings 1875, pg 20 (1875 Sept 21) communication
Proceedings 1875, pg 24 (1875 Sept 21) returns

Lassiter, R W
Proceedings 1861-1869, pg 277 (1867 Dec 2) Grand Lodge of North Carolina

Lathrop, S P
Proceedings 1861-1869, pg 170 (1866 Oct 2), Black Hawk Lodge U D, Black Hawk

Latrobe, John H B
Proceedings 1872, pg 43 (1872 Sept 24) Baltimore, Grand Lodge of Maryland
Proceedings 1873, pg 60 (1873 Oct 1) Grand Lodge of Maryland, Baltimore
Proceedings 1874, pg 79 (1874 Sept 30) Grand Lodge of Maryland
Proceedings 1874, pg 204 (1874 Sept 30) Grand Lodge of Maryland, Baltimore

Laub, R P
Proceedings 1861-1869, pg 305 (1869 Sept 29) Denver Lodge No. 5, Dimitted

Laughram, James
Proceedings 1870, pg 25 (1870 Sept 28), Black Hawk Lodge No. 11, Black Hawk

Laughram, James J
Proceedings 1873, pg 42 (1873 Oct 1), Black Hawk Lodge No. 11, Black Hawk

Laughran, James
Proceedings 1861-1869, pg 196 (1867 Oct 8), Black Hawk Lodge No. 11, Black Hawk
Proceedings 1861-1869, pg 309 (1869 Sept 29), Black Hawk Lodge No. 11, Black Hawk
Proceedings 1871, pg 23 (1871 Sept 27), Black Hawk Lodge No. 11, Black Hawk

Laughran, James J
Proceedings 1874, pg 216 (1874 Sept 30), Black Hawk Lodge No. 11, Black Hawk
Proceedings 1875, pg 80 (1875 Sept 22) Black Hawk Lodge No. 11, Stricken from the rolls

Laurie, J Wimburn
Proceedings 1874, pg 204 (1874 Sept 30) Grand Lodge of Nova Scotia, Halifax

Lavalle, John
Proceedings 1875, pg 79 (1875 Sept 22), Union Lodge No. 7, Denver, Apprentice

Lavelle, John
Proceedings 1870, pg 24 (1870 Sept 28), Union Lodge No. 7, Denver, Apprentice
Proceedings 1871, pg 22 (1871 Sept 27), Union Lodge No. 7, Denver, Apprentice
Proceedings 1872, pg 23 (1872 Sept 24), Union Lodge No. 7, Denver, Apprentice
Proceedings 1873, pg 40 (1873 Oct 1), Union Lodge No. 7, Denver, Apprentice
Proceedings 1874, pg 214 (1874 Sept 30), Union Lodge No. 7, Denver, Apprentice
Proceedings 1876, pg 33 (1876 Sept 20), Union Lodge No. 7, Denver, Apprentice

Lavin, T W
Proceedings 1861-1869, pg 149 (1865 Nov 7), Nevada Lodge No. 4, Nevadaville
Proceedings 1861-1869, pg 167 (1866 Oct 2) Denver Lodge No. 5, deceased

Lavin, Thos W
Proceedings 1861-1869, pg 77 (1862 Nov 4) Denver Lodge No. 5
Proceedings 1861-1869, pg 112 (1863 Nov 3) Denver Lodge No. 5
Proceedings 1861-1869, pg 133 (1864 Nov 8) Denver Lodge No. 5

Law, G
Proceedings 1871, pg 30 (1871 Sept 27), Occidental Lodge U D, Greeley
Proceedings 1872, pg 33 (1872 Sept 24), Occidental Lodge No. 20, Greeley
Proceedings 1873, pg 50 (1873 Oct 1), Occidental Lodge No. 20, Greeley

Colorado's Territorial Masons

Law, Guilelmus
Proceedings 1874, pg 225 (1874 Sept 30), Occidental Lodge No. 20, Greeley
Proceedings 1875, pg 87 (1875 Sept 22), Occidental Lodge No. 20, Greeley
Proceedings 1876, pg 40 (1876 Sept 20), Occidental Lodge No. 20, Greeley

Law, Harvey M
Proceedings 1876, pg 40 (1876 Sept 20), Occidental Lodge No. 20, Greeley, Fellow Craft,

Lawrence
Proceedings 1870, pg 43 (1869 Nov 1) Grand Lodge of Arkansas
Proceedings 1870, pg 44 (1869 Nov 1) Grand Lodge of Arkansas

Lawrence, John
Proceedings 1876, pg 46 (1876 Sept 20), Olive Branch Lodge U D, Saguache

Lawrence, Robert
Proceedings 1861-1869, pg 152 (1865 Nov 7), Helena City Lodge U D, Helena City, Montana Territory

Lawrence, Samuel
Proceedings 1861-1869, pg 328 (1868 Oct 27) Grand Master, Grand Lodge of Georgia
Proceedings 1870, pg 53 (1869 Oct 26) Grand Master, Grand Lodge of Georgia
Proceedings 1872, pg 43 (1872 Sept 24) Atlanta, Grand Lodge of Georgia
Proceedings 1872, pg 59 (1872 Sept 24) Grand Lodge of Georgia
Proceedings 1873, pg 60 (1873 Oct 1) Grand Lodge of Georgia, Atlanta
Proceedings 1874, pg 56 (1874 Sept 30) Grand Lodge of Georgia

Lawton, A L
Proceedings 1876, pg 36 (1876 Sept 20), El Paso Lodge No. 13, Colorado City

Laxton, Thos
Proceedings 1876, pg 42 (1876 Sept 20), Doric Lodge No. 25, Fairplay, Apprentice

Laycook, W J
Proceedings 1874, pg 227 (1874 Sept 30), St Vrain No. 23, Longmont

Laycook, William I
Proceedings 1876, pg 41 (1876 Sept 20), St Vrain Lodge No. 23, Longmont

Lea, Alfred E
Proceedings 1873, pg 44 (1873 Oct 1), Columbia Lodge No. 14, Boulder
Proceedings 1874, pg 219 (1874 Sept 30), Columbia Lodge No. 14, Boulder, Boulder County
Proceedings 1875, pg 83 (1875 Sept 22), Columbia Lodge No. 14, Boulder
Proceedings 1876, pg 37 (1876 Sept 20), Columbia Lodge No. 14, Boulder

Leach, D D
Proceedings 1861-1869, pg 196 (1867 Oct 8), Black Hawk Lodge No. 11, Black Hawk
Proceedings 1861-1869, pg 226 (1868 Oct 7), Black Hawk Lodge No. 11, Black Hawk
Proceedings 1861-1869, pg 309 (1869 Sept 29), Black Hawk Lodge No. 11, Black Hawk
Proceedings 1870, pg 25 (1870 Sept 28), Black Hawk Lodge No. 11, Black Hawk
Proceedings 1871, pg 23 (1871 Sept 27), Black Hawk Lodge No. 11, Black Hawk
Proceedings 1871, pg 23 (1871 Sept 27), Black Hawk Lodge No. 11, Black Hawk

Leach, H C
Proceedings 1861-1869, pg 151 (1865 Nov 7), Chivington Lodge No. 6, Central City
Proceedings 1861-1869, pg 169 (1866 Oct 2), Union Lodge No. 7, Denver

Leach, H S
Proceedings 1874, pg 226 (1874 Sept 30), Weston Lodge No. 22, Littleton
Proceedings 1875, pg 88 (1875 Sept 22), Weston Lodge No. 22, Littleton
Proceedings 1876, pg 41 (1876 Sept 20), Weston Lodge No. 22, Littleton

Leach, Henry C
Proceedings 1861-1869, pg 135 (1864 Nov 8), Union Lodge No. 7, Denver, Apprentice
Proceedings 1861-1869, pg 195 (1867 Oct 8), Union Lodge No. 7, Denver
Proceedings 1861-1869, pg 225 (1868 Oct 7), Union Lodge No. 7, Denver
Proceedings 1861-1869, pg 307 (1869 Sept 29), Union Lodge No. 7, Denver
Proceedings 1870, pg 23 (1870 Sept 28), Union Lodge No. 7, Denver
Proceedings 1871, pg 22 (1871 Sept 27), Union Lodge No. 7, Denver
Proceedings 1872, pg 22 (1872 Sept 24), Union Lodge No. 7, Denver
Proceedings 1873, pg 40 (1873 Oct 1), Union Lodge No. 7, Denver, Dimitted

Leach, Richard
Proceedings 1861-1869, pg 134 (1864 Nov 8), Union Lodge No. 7, Denver
Proceedings 1861-1869, pg 151 (1865 Nov 7), Chivington Lodge No. 6, Central City
Proceedings 1861-1869, pg 169 (1866 Oct 2), Union Lodge No. 7, Denver, demitted

Lead, H S
Proceedings 1873, pg 51 (1873 Oct 1), Weston Lodge No. 22, Littleton

Leasley, R C
Proceedings 1875, pg 82 (1875 Sept 22), El Paso Lodge No. 13, Colorado Springs

Lecavalier, J A
Proceedings 1870, pg 21 (1870 Sept 28), Denver Lodge No. 5, Denver

LeCavalier, J E
Proceedings 1861-1869, pg 192 (1867 Oct 8) Denver Lodge No. 5
Proceedings 1861-1869, pg 223 (1868 Oct 7) Denver Lodge No. 5
Proceedings 1872, pg 20 (1872 Sept 24), Denver Lodge No. 5, Denver
Proceedings 1873, pg 37 (1873 Oct 1), Denver Lodge No. 5, Denver, Dimitted
Proceedings 1861-1869, pg 304 (1869 Sept 29) Denver Lodge No. 5

LeCavlier, J A
Proceedings 1871, pg 19 (1871 Sept 27) Denver Lodge No. 5

Lee, D K
Proceedings 1873, pg 13 (1873 Sept 30), Ashlar Lodge U D, Colorado Springs
Proceedings 1873, pg 52 (1873 Oct 1), Ashlar Lodge U D, Colorado Springs
Proceedings 1874, pg 218 (1874 Sept 30), El Paso Lodge No. 13, Colorado Springs
Proceedings 1875, pg 82 (1875 Sept 22), El Paso Lodge No. 13, Colorado Springs
Proceedings 1876, pg 36 (1876 Sept 20), El Paso Lodge No. 13, Colorado City

Lee, H W
Proceedings 1871, pg 30 (1871 Sept 27), Occidental Lodge U D, Greeley

Lee, Jesse M
Proceedings 1872, pg 30 (1872 Sept 24), Cheyenne Lodge No. 16, Cheyenne, Wyoming Territory, Apprentice
Proceedings 1873, pg 46 (1873 Oct 1), Cheyenne Lodge No. 16, Cheyenne, Wyoming Territory, Apprentice
Proceedings 1874, pg 221 (1874 Sept 30), Cheyenne Lodge No. 16, Cheyenne, Wyoming Territory, Apprentice

Lee, L C
Proceedings 1861-1869, pg 152 (1865 Nov 7), Montana Lodge U D, Virginia City, Montana Territory

Lee, R M
Proceedings 1876, pg 41 (1876 Sept 20), Weston Lodge No. 22, Littleton

Lee, W H
Proceedings 1871, pg 7 (1870 Nov 29), Occidental Lodge U D, Greeley
Proceedings 1871, pg 15 (1871 Sept 27), Occidental Lodge No. 20, Greeley

Lee, Wm Wallace
Proceedings 1874, pg 204 (1874 Sept 30) Grand Lodge of Connecticut, West Meridian

Leech, D D
Proceedings 1872, pg 25 (1872 Sept 24), Black Hawk Lodge No. 11, Black Hawk, Dimitted

Lees, David
Proceedings 1861-1869, pg 77 (1862 Nov 4), Nevada Lodge No. 4, Nevadaville
Proceedings 1861-1869, pg 111 (1863 Nov 3), Nevada Lodge No. 4, Nevadaville
Proceedings 1861-1869, pg 132 (1864 Nov 8), Nevada Lodge No. 4, Nevadaville
Proceedings 1861-1869, pg 148 (1865 Nov 7), Nevada Lodge No. 4, Nevadaville
Proceedings 1861-1869, pg 166 (1866 Oct 2), Nevada Lodge No. 4, Nevadaville
Proceedings 1861-1869, pg 179 (1867 Oct 7), Washington Lodge No. 12, Georgetown
Proceedings 1861-1869, pg 192 (1867 Oct 8), Nevada Lodge No. 4, Nevadaville
Proceedings 1861-1869, pg 202 (1868 Oct 6), Washington Lodge No. 12, Georgetown
Proceedings 1861-1869, pg 222 (1868 Oct 7), Nevada Lodge No. 4, Nevadaville, Dimitted
Proceedings 1861-1869, pg 227 (1868 Oct 7), Washington Lodge No. 12, Georgetown
Proceedings 1861-1869, pg 309 (1869 Sept 29), Washington Lodge No. 12, Georgetown
Proceedings 1870, pg 26 (1870 Sept 28), Washington Lodge No. 12, Georgetown
Proceedings 1871, pg 24 (1871 Sept 27), Washington Lodge No. 12, Georgetown
Proceedings 1872, pg 26 (1872 Sept 24), Washington Lodge No. 12, Georgetown
Proceedings 1873, pg 43 (1873 Oct 1), Washington Lodge No. 12, Georgetown
Proceedings 1875, pg 73 (1875 Sept 22) Golden City Lodge No. 1
Proceedings 1875, pg 81 (1875 Sept 22), Washington Lodge No. 12, Georgetown, Demitted
Proceedings 1876, pg 6 (1876 Sept 19) Golden City Lodge No. 1
Proceedings 1876, pg 29 (1876 Sept 20) Golden City Lodge No. 1

Lees, James
Proceedings 1861-1869, pg 77 (1862 Nov 4), Nevada Lodge No. 4, Nevadaville
Proceedings 1861-1869, pg 111 (1863 Nov 3), Nevada Lodge No. 4, Nevadaville
Proceedings 1861-1869, pg 132 (1864 Nov 8), Nevada Lodge No. 4, Nevadaville, dimitted
Proceedings 1870, pg 26 (1870 Sept 28), Washington Lodge No. 12, Georgetown
Proceedings 1871, pg 24 (1871 Sept 27), Washington Lodge No. 12, Georgetown
Proceedings 1872, pg 25 (1872 Sept 24), Washington Lodge No. 12, Georgetown
Proceedings 1873, pg 42 (1873 Oct 1), Washington Lodge No. 12, Georgetown
Proceedings 1874, pg 217 (1874 Sept 30), Washington Lodge No. 12, Georgetown
Proceedings 1875, pg 81 (1875 Sept 22), Washington Lodge No. 12, Georgetown

Lees, Thomas
Proceedings 1876, pg 31 (1876 Sept 20) Denver Lodge No. 5

Colorado's Territorial Masons

Leet, Arthur J
  Proceedings 1876, pg 9 (1876 Nov 20) Grand Lodge of Georgia, Grand Representative, of Ringold, GA"
  Proceedings 1876, pg 53 (1876 Sept 20) Grand Lodge of Georgia, of Ringgold, GA

Legere, P F
  Proceedings 1875, pg 75 (1875 Sept 22) Denver Lodge No. 5

Legree, P F
  Proceedings 1876, pg 49 (1876 Sept 20) Denver Lodge No. 5, 1876 Aug 19

Leighton, Hampton W
  Proceedings 1876, pg 44 (1876 Sept 20), Las Animas Lodge No. 28, Trinidad

Leighton, Harry C
  Proceedings 1876, pg 9 (1876 May 5) Grand Lodge of Iowa, Grand Representative, of Oscaloosa, IA"

Leighton, Henry C
  Proceedings 1876, pg 53 (1876 Sept 20) Grand Lodge of Iowa, of Oscaloosa, IA

Leimer, C F
  Proceedings 1861-1869, pg 230 (1868 Oct 7), Germania Lodge U D, Denver

Leimer, Charles F
  Proceedings 1874, pg 214 (1874 Sept 30), Union Lodge No. 7, Denver
  Proceedings 1876, pg 33 (1876 Sept 20), Union Lodge No. 7, Denver

Leimer, Charles Fred
  Proceedings 1870, pg 23 (1870 Sept 28), Union Lodge No. 7, Denver

Leimer, Chas F
  Proceedings 1861-1869, pg 307 (1869 Sept 29), Union Lodge No. 7, Denver
  Proceedings 1871, pg 22 (1871 Sept 27), Union Lodge No. 7, Denver
  Proceedings 1873, pg 40 (1873 Oct 1), Union Lodge No. 7, Denver

Leimer, Chas Fred
  Proceedings 1872, pg 22 (1872 Sept 24), Union Lodge No. 7, Denver
  Proceedings 1875, pg 78 (1875 Sept 22), Union Lodge No. 7, Denver

Leiner [Leyner], P A
  Proceedings 1861-1869, pg 305 (1869 Sept 29) Denver Lodge No. 5, received permission to receive degrees in another lodge

Leis, James
  Proceedings 1876, pg 35 (1876 Sept 20), Washington Lodge No. 12, Georgetown

Leissert, L B
  Proceedings 1871, pg 29 (1871 Sept 27), Collins Lodge No. 19, Fort Collins

Leitzman, Charles
  Proceedings 1870, pg 25 (1870 Sept 28), Black Hawk Lodge No. 11, Black Hawk
  Proceedings 1871, pg 23 (1871 Sept 27), Black Hawk Lodge No. 11, Black Hawk
  Proceedings 1872, pg 25 (1872 Sept 24), Black Hawk Lodge No. 11, Black Hawk
  Proceedings 1873, pg 42 (1873 Oct 1), Black Hawk Lodge No. 11, Black Hawk
  Proceedings 1874, pg 216 (1874 Sept 30), Black Hawk Lodge No. 11, Black Hawk
  Proceedings 1876, pg 34 (1876 Sept 20) Black Hawk Lodge No. 11

Leitzman, Chas
  Proceedings 1861-1869, pg 309 (1869 Sept 29), Black Hawk Lodge No. 11, Black Hawk

Leland, Theodore
  Proceedings 1874, pg 211 (1874 Sept 30), Denver Lodge No. 5, Denver
  Proceedings 1875, pg 16 (1875 Sept 21) Denver Lodge No. 5
  Proceedings 1875, pg 75 (1875 Sept 22) Denver Lodge No. 5
  Proceedings 1876, pg 31 (1876 Sept 20) Denver Lodge No. 5

Lemmex, Abram
  Proceedings 1861-1869, pg 230 (1868 Oct 7), Valmont Lodge U D, Valmont

Lemont, Levi P
  Proceedings 1874, pg 19 (1874 Sept 29) of Maine

Lennon, J A
  Proceedings 1876, pg 33 (1876 Sept 20), Union Lodge No. 7, Denver

Lennon, John A
  Proceedings 1873, pg 40 (1873 Oct 1), Union Lodge No. 7, Denver
  Proceedings 1874, pg 214 (1874 Sept 30), Union Lodge No. 7, Denver
  Proceedings 1875, pg 78 (1875 Sept 22), Union Lodge No. 7, Denver

Leonard, B C
  Proceedings 1874, pg 222 (1874 Sept 30), Pueblo Lodge No. 17, Pueblo, Pueblo County
  Proceedings 1875, pg 85 (1875 Sept 22) Pueblo Lodge No. 17
  Proceedings 1876, pg 39 (1876 Sept 20) Pueblo Lodge No. 17

Leonard, Bolivar C
  Proceedings 1870, pg 30 (1870 Sept 28), Pueblo Lodge No. 17, Pueblo
  Proceedings 1871, pg 28 (1871 Sept 27), Pueblo Lodge No. 17, Pueblo
  Proceedings 1872, pg 31 (1872 Sept 24), Pueblo Lodge No. 17, Pueblo
  Proceedings 1873, pg 47 (1873 Oct 1), Pueblo Lodge No. 17, Pueblo

Leroy, A R
 Proceedings 1874, pg 223 (1874 Sept 30), Laramie Lodge No. 18, Laramie City

Lessert, Louis B
 Proceedings 1872, pg 32 (1872 Sept 24), Collins Lodge No. 19, Fort Collins
 Proceedings 1873, pg 49 (1873 Oct 1), Collins Lodge No. 19, Fort Collins
 Proceedings 1874, pg 224 (1874 Sept 30), Collins Lodge No. 19, Fort Collins, Larimer County

Lester, J H
 Proceedings 1872, pg 29 (1872 Sept 24), Mount Moriah Lodge No. 15, Canon City

Lester, J W
 Proceedings 1861-1869, pg 148 (1865 Nov 7), Nevada Lodge No. 4, Nevadaville
 Proceedings 1861-1869, pg 166 (1866 Oct 2), Nevada Lodge No. 4, Nevadaville, dimitted
 Proceedings 1873, pg 45 (1873 Oct 1), Mount Moriah Lodge No. 15, Canon City
 Proceedings 1874, pg 220 (1874 Sept 30), Mount Moriah Lodge No. 15, Canon City
 Proceedings 1875, pg 84 (1875 Sept 22), Mount Moriah Lodge No. 15, Canon City
 Proceedings 1876, pg 38 (1876 Sept 20), Mount Moriah Lodge No. 15, Canon City

LeTourrette, J A M
 Proceedings 1876, pg 45 (1876 Sept 20), King Solomon Lodge U D, West Las Animas

Levison, Henry
 Proceedings 1861-1869, pg 305 (1869 Sept 29) Denver Lodge No. 5, Fellowcraft
 Proceedings 1875, pg 75 (1875 Sept 22) Denver Lodge No. 5
 Proceedings 1876, pg 31 (1876 Sept 20) Denver Lodge No. 5

Levy, Alex
 Proceedings 1875, pg 85 (1875 Sept 22) Pueblo Lodge No. 17

Levy, Alexander
 Proceedings 1873, pg 47 (1873 Oct 1), Pueblo Lodge No. 17, Pueblo
 Proceedings 1874, pg 222 (1874 Sept 30), Pueblo Lodge No. 17, Pueblo, Pueblo County
 Proceedings 1876, pg 39 (1876 Sept 20) Pueblo Lodge No. 17
 Proceedings 1876, pg 43 (1876 Sept 20), Huerfano Lodge No. 27, Walsenburg

Levy, Isaac
 Proceedings 1875, pg 90 (1875 Sept 22), Huerfano Lodge U D, Walsenburg
 Proceedings 1876, pg 44 (1876 Sept 20), Las Animas Lodge No. 28, Trinidad
 Proceedings 1876, pg 48 (1876 Sept 20), Huerfano Lodge No. 27, Walsenburg, 1875 Nov 6

Lew, Zadock
 Proceedings 1870, pg 77 (1824 Jan 5) African Lodge at Boston

Lewis, A S
 Proceedings 1861-1869, pg 230 (1868 Oct 7), Valmont Lodge U D, Valmont, Apprentice
 Proceedings 1861-1869, pg 311 (1869 Sept 29), Columbia Lodge No. 14, Boulder City, Fellowcraft

Lewis, Allen
 Proceedings 1861-1869, pg 147 (1865 Nov 7) Golden City Lodge No. 1, Apprentice
 Proceedings 1861-1869, pg 165 (1866 Oct 2) Golden City Lodge No. 1, Apprentice
 Proceedings 1861-1869, pg 191 (1867 Oct 8) Golden City Lodge No. 1, Apprentice
 Proceedings 1861-1869, pg 221 (1868 Oct 7) Golden City Lodge No. 1, Apprentice
 Proceedings 1861-1869, pg 303 (1869 Sept 29) Golden City Lodge No. 1, Apprentice

Lewis, Augustus
 Proceedings 1873, pg 44 (1873 Oct 1), Columbia Lodge No. 14, Boulder, Fellowcraft
 Proceedings 1874, pg 219 (1874 Sept 30), Columbia Lodge No. 14, Boulder, Boulder County, Fellowcraft
 Proceedings 1875, pg 83 (1875 Sept 22), Columbia Lodge No. 14, Boulder, Fellowcraft
 Proceedings 1876, pg 37 (1876 Sept 20), Columbia Lodge No. 14, Boulder, Fellow Craft

Lewis, Augustus J
 Proceedings 1872, pg 28 (1872 Sept 24), Columbia Lodge No. 14, Boulder, Fellowcraft

Lewis, Augustus S
 Proceedings 1870, pg 28 (1870 Sept 28), Columbia Lodge No. 14, Boulder City, Fellowcraft
 Proceedings 1871, pg 26 (1871 Sept 27), Columbia Lodge No. 14, Boulder City, Fellowcraft

Lewis, Charles E
 Proceedings 1876, pg 31 (1876 Sept 20) Denver Lodge No. 5

Lewis, F E
 Proceedings 1861-1869, pg 42 (1861 Dec 10), Summit Lodge No. 2, Parkville
 Proceedings 1861-1869, pg 76 (1862 Nov 4), Summit Lodge No. 2, Parkville
 Proceedings 1861-1869, pg 111 (1863 Nov 3), Summit Lodge No. 2, Parkville, dimitted

Lewis, J F
 Proceedings 1876, pg 42 (1876 Sept 20), Doric Lodge No. 25, Fairplay

Lewis, J H
 Proceedings 1876, pg 45 (1876 Sept 20), King Solomon Lodge U D, West Las Animas

Lewis, J L
 Proceedings 1861-1869, pg 110 (1863 Nov 3), Summit Lodge No. 2, Parkville

Lewis, J R
    Proceedings 1874, pg 211 (1874 Sept 30), Denver Lodge No. 5, Denver
    Proceedings 1875, pg 75 (1875 Sept 22) Denver Lodge No. 5
    Proceedings 1876, pg 31 (1876 Sept 20) Denver Lodge No. 5

Lewis, J S
    Proceedings 1861-1869, pg 152 (1865 Nov 7), Montana Lodge U D, Virginia City, Montana Territory

Lewis, James
    Proceedings 1875, pg 83 (1875 Sept 22), Columbia Lodge No. 14, Boulder
    Proceedings 1876, pg 9 (1876 Sept 2), Doric Lodge No. 25, Fairplay
    Proceedings 1876, pg 37 (1876 Sept 20), Columbia Lodge No. 14, Boulder
    Proceedings 1876, pg 42 (1876 Sept 20), Doric Lodge No. 25, Fairplay, Apprentice

Lewis, John L
    Proceedings 1861-1869, pg 42 (1861 Dec 10), Summit Lodge No. 2, Parkville

Lewis, John S
    Proceedings 1861-1869, pg 76 (1862 Nov 4), Summit Lodge No. 2, Parkville
    Proceedings 1861-1869, pg 132 (1864 Nov 8) Golden City Lodge No. 1

Lewis, L W
    Proceedings 1875, pg 89 (1875 Sept 22), Doric Lodge No. 25, Fairplay
    Proceedings 1876, pg 42 (1876 Sept 20), Doric Lodge No. 25, Fairplay

Lewis, Martin
    Proceedings 1872, pg 19 (1872 Sept 24), Nevada Lodge No. 4, Bald Mountain
    Proceedings 1873, pg 36 (1873 Oct 1), Nevada Lodge No. 4, Nevada
    Proceedings 1874, pg 210 (1874 Sept 30), Nevada Lodge No. 4, Bald Mountain, Gilpin County
    Proceedings 1875, pg 74 (1875 Sept 22), Nevada Lodge No. 4, Nevada
    Proceedings 1876, pg 30 (1876 Sept 20) Nevada Lodge No. 4

Lewis, Morgan
    Proceedings 1874, pg 63 (1874 Sept 30), Major General, U S Army

Lewis, Oscar
    Proceedings 1861-1869, pg 194 (1867 Oct 8), Chivington Lodge No. 6, Central City
    Proceedings 1861-1869, pg 224 (1868 Oct 7), Chivington Lodge No. 6, Central City
    Proceedings 1861-1869, pg 306 (1869 Sept 29), Central Lodge No. 6, Central City
    Proceedings 1870, pg 22 (1870 Sept 28), Central Lodge No. 6, Central City
    Proceedings 1871, pg 20 (1871 Sept 27), Central Lodge No. 6, Central
    Proceedings 1872, pg 21 (1872 Sept 24), Denver Lodge No. 5, Denver
    Proceedings 1873, pg 38 (1873 Oct 1), Central Lodge No. 6, Central City
    Proceedings 1874, pg 213 (1874 Sept 30), Central Lodge No. 6, Central
    Proceedings 1875, pg 76 (1875 Sept 22), Central Lodge No. 6, Central City
    Proceedings 1876, pg 31 (1876 Sept 20), Central Lodge No. 6, Central City

Lewis, S W
    Proceedings 1874, pg 228 (1874 Sept 30), Doric Lodge U D, Fairplay

Lewis, W J
    Proceedings 1875, pg 37 (1875 Sept 22) per diem

Lewis, William G
    Proceedings 1870, pg 88 (1869 Oct 11) Grand Lodge of Missouri, deceased

Lewis, William J
    Proceedings 1874, pg 210 (1874 Sept 30), Nevada Lodge No. 4, Bald Mountain, Gilpin County

Lewis, William R
    Proceedings 1874, pg 217 (1874 Sept 30), Washington Lodge No. 12, Georgetown
    Proceedings 1876, pg 35 (1876 Sept 20), Washington Lodge No. 12, Georgetown

Lewis, Winslow
    Proceedings 1861-1869, pg 260 (1868 Sept 11) Grand Lodge of Massachusetts
    Proceedings 1872, pg 68 (1872 Sept 24) Grand Lodge of Massachusetts
    Proceedings 1874, pg 81 (1874 Sept 30) Grand Lodge of Massachusetts

Lewis, Wm J
    Proceedings 1875, pg 16 (1875 Sept 21) Nevada Lodge No. 4
    Proceedings 1875, pg 74 (1875 Sept 22), Nevada Lodge No. 4, Nevada
    Proceedings 1876, pg 30 (1876 Sept 20) Nevada Lodge No. 4

Lewis, Wm R
    Proceedings 1875, pg 81 (1875 Sept 22), Washington Lodge No. 12, Georgetown
    Proceedings 1876, pg 50 (1876 Sept 20), Washington Lodge No. 12, Georgetown

Leyner, Peter A
    Proceedings 1861-1869, pg 223 (1868 Oct 7) Denver Lodge No. 5, Apprentice
    Proceedings 1861-1869, pg 310 (1869 Sept 29), Columbia Lodge No. 14, Boulder City
    Proceedings 1870, pg 27 (1870 Sept 28), Columbia Lodge No. 14, Boulder City
    Proceedings 1871, pg 25 (1871 Sept 27), Columbia Lodge No. 14, Boulder City
    Proceedings 1872, pg 28 (1872 Sept 24), Columbia Lodge No. 14, Boulder

Proceedings 1875, pg 83 (1875 Sept 22), Columbia Lodge No. 14, Boulder

Proceedings 1876, pg 37 (1876 Sept 20), Columbia Lodge No. 14, Boulder

Libby, Henry

Proceedings 1876, pg 34 (1876 Sept 20) Black Hawk Lodge No. 11

Lietzman, Charles

Proceedings 1875, pg 80 (1875 Sept 22) Black Hawk Lodge No. 11

Light, E A

Proceedings 1861-1869, pg 349 (1868 Sept 17) Grand Master, Grand Lodge of Washington Territory

Limbach, H

Proceedings 1876, pg 36 (1876 Sept 20), El Paso Lodge No. 13, Colorado City

Lincoln, A C

Proceedings 1876, pg 36 (1876 Sept 20), El Paso Lodge No. 13, Colorado City

Lincoln, A G

Proceedings 1861-1869, pg 196 (1867 Oct 8), El Paso Lodge U D, Colorado City

Proceedings 1861-1869, pg 228 (1868 Oct 7), El Paso Lodge No. 13, Colorado City

Proceedings 1861-1869, pg 310 (1869 Sept 29), El Paso Lodge No. 13, Colorado City

Proceedings 1870, pg 27 (1870 Sept 28), El Paso Lodge No. 13, Colorado City

Proceedings 1873, pg 43 (1873 Oct 1), El Paso Lodge No. 13, Colorado City

Proceedings 1874, pg 218 (1874 Sept 30), El Paso Lodge No. 13, Colorado Springs

Proceedings 1875, pg 82 (1875 Sept 22), El Paso Lodge No. 13, Colorado Springs

Lincoln, Andrew G

Proceedings 1871, pg 25 (1871 Sept 27), El Paso Lodge No. 13, Colorado City

Proceedings 1872, pg 27 (1872 Sept 24), El Paso Lodge No. 13, Colorado City

Lindenmeier, William

Proceedings 1872, pg 29 (1872 Sept 24), Cheyenne Lodge No. 16, Cheyenne, Wyoming Territory

Proceedings 1871, pg 27 (1871 Sept 27), Cheyenne Lodge No. 16, Cheyenne, Wyoming Territory

Lindenmier, Wm

Proceedings 1870, pg 29 (1870 Sept 28), Cheyenne Lodge No. 16, Cheyenne, Wyoming Territory

Proceedings 1873, pg 46 (1873 Oct 1), Cheyenne Lodge No. 16, Cheyenne, Wyoming Territory

Lindunmeier, William

Proceedings 1874, pg 221 (1874 Sept 30), Cheyenne Lodge No. 16, Cheyenne, Wyoming Territory

Linton

Proceedings 1873, pg 32 (1873 Oct 1) Grand Tiler

Linton, Th

Proceedings 1876, pg 30 (1876 Sept 20) Denver Lodge No. 5

Linton, Thomas

Proceedings 1871, pg 19 (1871 Sept 27) Denver Lodge No. 5

Proceedings 1872, pg 20 (1872 Sept 24), Denver Lodge No. 5, Denver

Proceedings 1873, pg 3 (1873 Sept 30) Grand Tyler

Proceedings 1873, pg 17 (1873 Oct 1) Grand Tiler

Proceedings 1874, pg 32 (1874 Sept 30) Grand Tyler, Denver

Proceedings 1874, pg 211 (1874 Sept 30), Denver Lodge No. 5, Denver

Proceedings 1874, pg 213 (1874 Sept 30), Union Lodge No. 7, Denver

Proceedings 1875, pg 15 (1875 Sept 21) Grand Tyler

Proceedings 1875, pg 31 (1875 Sept 22) Grand Tyler

Proceedings 1875, pg 33 (1875 Sept 22) Grand Tyler, Denver

Proceedings 1875, pg 36 (1875 Sept 22) Grand Tyler

Proceedings 1875, pg 75 (1875 Sept 22) Denver Lodge No. 5

Proceedings 1875, pg 78 (1875 Sept 22), Union Lodge No. 7, Denver

Proceedings 1876, pg cover (1876 Sept 20) Grand Tiler, Denver

Proceedings 1876, pg 3 (1876 Sept 19) Grand Tiler

Proceedings 1876, pg 25 (1876 Sept 20) Grand Tiler

Proceedings 1876, pg 32 (1876 Sept 20), Union Lodge No. 7, Denver, Not a member

Linton, Thos

Proceedings 1873, pg 37 (1873 Oct 1), Denver Lodge No. 5, Denver

Proceedings 1874, pg 3 (1874 Sept 29) Grand Tiler

Proceedings 1875, pg cover (1875 Sept 22) Grand Tyler, Denver

Lionberger, D C

Proceedings 1874, pg 214 (1874 Sept 30), Union Lodge No. 7, Denver

Proceedings 1875, pg 78 (1875 Sept 22), Union Lodge No. 7, Denver

Proceedings 1876, pg 48 (1876 Sept 20), Union Lodge No. 7, Denver, 1876 Aug 12

Lissert, Louis B

Proceedings 1875, pg 86 (1875 Sept 22), Collins Lodge No. 19, Fort Collins

Proceedings 1876, pg 39 (1876 Sept 20), Collins Lodge No. 19, Fort Collins

Liston, Martin

Proceedings 1872, pg 20 (1872 Sept 24), Denver Lodge No. 5, Denver, Apprentice

Proceedings 1873, pg 37 (1873 Oct 1), Denver Lodge No. 5, Denver

Proceedings 1874, pg 211 (1874 Sept 30), Denver Lodge No. 5, Denver

Proceedings 1875, pg 75 (1875 Sept 22) Denver Lodge No. 5

Colorado's Territorial Masons

Liston, Martin, cont.
   Proceedings 1876, pg 31 (1876 Sept 20) Denver Lodge No. 5

Little, George
   Proceedings 1873, pg 48 (1873 Oct 1), Laramie Lodge No. 18, Laramie, Wyoming Territory, Apprentice
   Proceedings 1874, pg 224 (1874 Sept 30), Laramie Lodge No. 18, Laramie City, Apprentice

Littrel, J Cal
   Proceedings 1876, pg 43 (1876 Sept 20), Huerfano Lodge No. 27, Walsenburg

Litus, Chas H
   Proceedings 1872, pg 68 (1872 Sept 24) Grand Lodge of Massachusetts

Livermore, P P
   Proceedings 1874, pg 211 (1874 Sept 30), Denver Lodge No. 5, Denver
   Proceedings 1875, pg 75 (1875 Sept 22) Denver Lodge No. 5
   Proceedings 1876, pg 31 (1876 Sept 20) Denver Lodge No. 5

Livingston
   Proceedings 1874, pg 99 (1874 Sept 30) Grand Lodge of Nebraska

Livingston, R R
   Proceedings 1874, pg 98 (1874 Sept 30) Grand Lodge of Nebraska

Lloyd, Richard
   Proceedings 1874, pg 220 (1874 Sept 30), Mount Moriah Lodge No. 15, Canon City
   Proceedings 1875, pg 84 (1875 Sept 22), Mount Moriah Lodge No. 15, Canon City
   Proceedings 1876, pg 38 (1876 Sept 20), Mount Moriah Lodge No. 15, Canon City

Loar, Apollos
   Proceedings 1876, pg 31 (1876 Sept 20) Denver Lodge No. 5

Lobach, Ed
   Proceedings 1875, pg 84 (1875 Sept 22), Mount Moriah Lodge No. 15, Canon City

Lobach, Edward
   Proceedings 1874, pg 220 (1874 Sept 30), Mount Moriah Lodge No. 15, Canon City

Lobach, Edwin
   Proceedings 1876, pg 38 (1876 Sept 20), Mount Moriah Lodge No. 15, Canon City

Lockwood
   Proceedings 1872, pg 79 (1872 Sept 24) Grand Lodge of Nevada

Lockwood, Luke A
   Proceedings 1861-1869, pg 242 (1867 May 8) Grand Lodge of Connecticut
   Proceedings 1872, pg 43 (1872 Sept 24) Greenwich, Grand Lodge of Connecticut
   Proceedings 1873, pg 60 (1873 Oct 1) Grand Lodge of Connecticut, Greenwich
   Proceedings 1874, pg 50 (1874 Sept 30) Grand Lodge of Connecticut

Loeb, Bernard
   Proceedings 1875, pg 91 (1875 Sept 22), Las Animas Lodge U D, Trinidad
   Proceedings 1876, pg 43 (1876 Sept 20), Las Animas Lodge No. 28, Trinidad

Loeb, D
   Proceedings 1861-1869, pg 113 (1863 Nov 3), Chivington Lodge No. 6, Central City
   Proceedings 1861-1869, pg 150 (1865 Nov 7), Chivington Lodge No. 6, Central City
   Proceedings 1861-1869, pg 168 (1866 Oct 2), Chivington Lodge No. 6, Central City

Loeb, David
   Proceedings 1861-1869, pg 78 (1862 Nov 4), Chivington Lodge No. 6, Central City
   Proceedings 1861-1869, pg 134 (1864 Nov 8), Chivington Lodge No. 6, Central City
   Proceedings 1861-1869, pg 194 (1867 Oct 8), Chivington Lodge No. 6, Central City, Dimitted

Loeb, Louis
   Proceedings 1872, pg 29 (1872 Sept 24), Cheyenne Lodge No. 16, Cheyenne, Wyoming Territory
   Proceedings 1873, pg 46 (1873 Oct 1), Cheyenne Lodge No. 16, Cheyenne, Wyoming Territory
   Proceedings 1874, pg 221 (1874 Sept 30), Cheyenne Lodge No. 16, Cheyenne, Wyoming Territory

Logan, Hill
   Proceedings 1870, pg 29 (1870 Sept 28), Cheyenne Lodge No. 16, Cheyenne, Wyoming Territory
   Proceedings 1871, pg 27 (1871 Sept 27), Cheyenne Lodge No. 16, Cheyenne, Wyoming Territory
   Proceedings 1872, pg 29 (1872 Sept 24), Cheyenne Lodge No. 16, Cheyenne, Wyoming Territory
   Proceedings 1873, pg 46 (1873 Oct 1), Cheyenne Lodge No. 16, Cheyenne, Wyoming Territory
   Proceedings 1874, pg 221 (1874 Sept 30), Cheyenne Lodge No. 16, Cheyenne, Wyoming Territory

Logan, Taylor
   Proceedings 1876, pg 45 (1876 Sept 20), King Solomon Lodge U D, West Las Animas, Fellow Craft

Logan, Thomas H
   Proceedings 1861-1869, pg 316 (1869 Sept 29) Grand Lodge of West Virginia
   Proceedings 1861-1869, pg 349 (1868 Nov 10) Grand Secretary, Grand Lodge of West Virginia
   Proceedings 1870, pg 34 (1870 Sept 28) Grand Secretary, Grand Lodge of West Virginia
   Proceedings 1870, pg 105 (1869 Nov 9) Grand Secretary, Grand Lodge of West Virginia
   Proceedings 1874, pg 133 (1874 Sept 30) Grand Lodge of West Virginia
   Proceedings 1874, pg 205 (1874 Sept 30) Grand Lodge of West Virginia, Wheeling

Logan, Thos H
　Proceedings 1872, pg 44 (1872 Sept 24) Wheeling, Grand Lodge of West Virginia
　Proceedings 1873, pg 61 (1873 Oct 1) Grand Lodge of West Virginia, Wheeling

Loker, Wm N
　Proceedings 1870, pg 11 (1870 Apr 20) Grant Treasurer, Grand Lodge of Missouri
　Proceedings 1872, pg 41 (1872 Sept 24), of St Louis, Representative of the Grand Lodge of Missouri
　Proceedings 1873, pg 59 (1873 Oct 1), of St Louis, Grand Representative to the Grand Lodge of Missouri
　Proceedings 1874, pg 207 (1874 Sept 30) Grand Lodge of Missouri, St Louis
　Proceedings 1875, pg 95 (1875 Sept 22) Grand Lodge of Missouri, Georgetown, CO
　Proceedings 1876, pg 53 (1876 Sept 20) Grand Lodge of Missouri, of St Louis, MO

Lombard, B E
　Proceedings 1870, pg 107 (1869 Sept 16) Grand Master, Grand Lodge of Washington Territory

Lombard, F P
　Proceedings 1876, pg 36 (1876 Sept 20), El Paso Lodge No. 13, Colorado City

Lonbard, Benj E
　Proceedings 1861-1869, pg 349 (1868 Sept 17) Grand Master, Grand Lodge of Washington Territory

Londoner, Julias
　Proceedings 1861-1869, pg 307 (1869 Sept 29), Union Lodge No. 7, Denver
　Proceedings 1861-1869, pg 225 (1868 Oct 7), Union Lodge No. 7, Denver
　Proceedings 1870, pg 23 (1870 Sept 28), Union Lodge No. 7, Denver
　Proceedings 1871, pg 22 (1871 Sept 27), Union Lodge No. 7, Denver
　Proceedings 1872, pg 22 (1872 Sept 24), Union Lodge No. 7, Denver
　Proceedings 1873, pg 40 (1873 Oct 1), Union Lodge No. 7, Denver
　Proceedings 1874, pg 214 (1874 Sept 30), Union Lodge No. 7, Denver
　Proceedings 1875, pg 17 (1875 Sept 21), Union Lodge No. 7, Denver
　Proceedings 1875, pg 78 (1875 Sept 22), Union Lodge No. 7, Denver
　Proceedings 1876, pg 33 (1876 Sept 20), Union Lodge No. 7, Denver

Londoner, W
　Proceedings 1861-1869, pg 223 (1868 Oct 7) Denver Lodge No. 5
　Proceedings 1861-1869, pg 304 (1869 Sept 29) Denver Lodge No. 5

Londoner, Wolf
　Proceedings 1861-1869, pg 192 (1867 Oct 8) Denver Lodge No. 5
　Proceedings 1870, pg 21 (1870 Sept 28), Denver Lodge No. 5, Denver
　Proceedings 1871, pg 19 (1871 Sept 27) Denver Lodge No. 5
　Proceedings 1872, pg 20 (1872 Sept 24), Denver Lodge No. 5, Denver
　Proceedings 1873, pg 37 (1873 Oct 1), Denver Lodge No. 5, Denver
　Proceedings 1874, pg 211 (1874 Sept 30), Denver Lodge No. 5, Denver
　Proceedings 1875, pg 75 (1875 Sept 22) Denver Lodge No. 5
　Proceedings 1876, pg 31 (1876 Sept 20) Denver Lodge No. 5

Long, John R
　Proceedings 1871, pg 30 (1871 Sept 27), Occidental Lodge U D, Greeley

Long, O S
　Proceedings 1871, pg 35 (1871 Sept 27) Grand Secretary, Grand Lodge of West Virginia
　Proceedings 1872, pg 93 (1872 Sept 24) Grand Lodge of West Virginia
　Proceedings 1874, pg 133 (1874 Sept 30) Grand Lodge of West Virginia
　Proceedings 1874, pg 134 (1874 Sept 30) Grand Lodge of West Virginia

Long, Odell L
　Proceedings 1875, pg 96 (1875 Sept 22) Grand Lodge of West Virginia, Wheeling
　Proceedings 1876, pg 54 (1876 Sept 20) Grand Lodge of West Virginia, Wheeling

Long, Odell S
　Proceedings 1872, pg 44 (1872 Sept 24) Wheeling, Grand Lodge of West Virginia
　Proceedings 1873, pg 61 (1873 Oct 1) Grand Lodge of West Virginia, Wheeling
　Proceedings 1874, pg 205 (1874 Sept 30) Grand Lodge of West Virginia, Wheeling

Longan, J B
　Proceedings 1861-1869, pg 191 (1867 Oct 8) Golden City Lodge No. 1
　Proceedings 1876, pg 29 (1876 Sept 20) Golden City Lodge No. 1

Longan, Jesse
　Proceedings 1870, pg 19 (1870 Sept 28), Golden City Lodge No. 1, Golden City
　Proceedings 1871, pg 17 (1871 Sept 27), Golden City Lodge No. 1, Golden City
　Proceedings 1872, pg 17 (1872 Sept 24), Golden City Lodge No. 1, Golden City
　Proceedings 1873, pg 35 (1873 Oct 1), Golden City Lodge No. 1, Golden City
　Proceedings 1874, pg 209 (1874 Sept 30), Golden City Lodge No. 1, Golden City

Longdon, J B
　Proceedings 1861-1869, pg 147 (1865 Nov 7) Golden City Lodge No. 1

Colorado's Territorial Masons

Longdon, J B, cont.
Proceedings 1861-1869, pg 165 (1866 Oct 2) Golden City Lodge No. 1

Longon, Jessie
Proceedings 1875, pg 73 (1875 Sept 22) Golden City Lodge No. 1

Loomis, Abner
Proceedings 1870, pg 31 (1870 Sept 28), Collins Lodge No. 19, Fort Collins
Proceedings 1871, pg 30 (1871 Sept 27), Collins Lodge No. 19, Fort Collins
Proceedings 1872, pg 33 (1872 Sept 24), Collins Lodge No. 19, Fort Collins
Proceedings 1873, pg 49 (1873 Oct 1), Collins Lodge No. 19, Fort Collins
Proceedings 1874, pg 224 (1874 Sept 30), Collins Lodge No. 19, Fort Collins, Larimer County
Proceedings 1875, pg 86 (1875 Sept 22), Collins Lodge No. 19, Fort Collins
Proceedings 1876, pg 39 (1876 Sept 20), Collins Lodge No. 19, Fort Collins

Loomis, W H
Proceedings 1875, pg 89 (1875 Sept 22), Doric Lodge No. 25, Fairplay, Suspended

Loomis, William H
Proceedings 1876, pg 42 (1876 Sept 20), Doric Lodge No. 25, Fairplay

Loomis, Wm H
Proceedings 1874, pg 228 (1874 Sept 30), Doric Lodge U D, Fairplay
Proceedings 1876, pg 51 (1876 Sept 20), Doric Lodge No. 25, Fairplay, 1875 Dec 18

Looner, Charles
Proceedings 1861-1869, pg 170 (1866 Oct 2), El Paso U D, Colorado City

Lorah, S I
Proceedings 1861-1869, pg 134 (1864 Nov 8), Chivington Lodge No. 6, Central City, Apprentice
Proceedings 1861-1869, pg 150 (1865 Nov 7), Chivington Lodge No. 6, Central City
Proceedings 1861-1869, pg 168 (1866 Oct 2), Chivington Lodge No. 6, Central City
Proceedings 1861-1869, pg 193 (1867 Oct 8), Chivington Lodge No. 6, Central City
Proceedings 1861-1869, pg 217 (1868 Oct 7), Chivington Lodge No. 6, Central City, Secretary
Proceedings 1861-1869, pg 218 (1868 Oct 7), Chivington Lodge No. 6, Central City, Secretary
Proceedings 1861-1869, pg 224 (1868 Oct 7), Chivington Lodge No. 6, Central City
Proceedings 1870, pg 22 (1870 Sept 28), Central Lodge No. 6, Central City
Proceedings 1872, pg cover (1872 Sept 24), Central City Commandery No. 2, Central
Proceedings 1872, pg cover (1872 Sept 24), Central City Chapter No. 1, Central
Proceedings 1873, pg cover (1873 Oct 1), Central City Commandery No. 2, Central
Proceedings 1873, pg cover (1873 Oct 1), Central City Chapter No. 1, Central
Proceedings 1873, pg cover (1873 Oct 1), Central City Council, No 54 (Illinois) Central

Lorah, Sam'l I
Proceedings 1871, pg 20 (1871 Sept 27), Central Lodge No. 6, Central
Proceedings 1872, pg 5 (1872 Sept 24), Central Lodge No. 6, Central
Proceedings 1876, pg 31 (1876 Sept 20), Central Lodge No. 6, Central City

Lorah, Samuel I
Proceedings 1861-1869, pg 306 (1869 Sept 29), Central Lodge No. 6, Central City
Proceedings 1872, pg 21 (1872 Sept 24), Denver Lodge No. 5, Denver
Proceedings 1873, pg 38 (1873 Oct 1), Central Lodge No. 6, Central City
Proceedings 1874, pg 212 (1874 Sept 30), Central Lodge No. 6, Central
Proceedings 1875, pg 76 (1875 Sept 22), Central Lodge No. 6, Central City

Lord, James A
Proceedings 1872, pg 22 (1872 Sept 24), Union Lodge No. 7, Denver
Proceedings 1873, pg 40 (1873 Oct 1), Union Lodge No. 7, Denver
Proceedings 1874, pg 214 (1874 Sept 30), Union Lodge No. 7, Denver
Proceedings 1875, pg 78 (1875 Sept 22), Union Lodge No. 7, Denver
Proceedings 1876, pg 33 (1876 Sept 20), Union Lodge No. 7, Denver

Lord, W A (Rev)
Colorado University Cornerstone Laying, pg 14 (1875 Sept 20) gave an address

Lore, John W
Proceedings 1861-1869, pg 196 (1867 Oct 8), El Paso Lodge U D, Colorado City

Lore, Jos A
Proceedings 1870, pg 24 (1870 Sept 28), Empire Lodge No. 8, Empire

Lore, Joseph
Proceedings 1874, pg 228 (1874 Sept 30), Doric Lodge U D, Fairplay

Lore, Joseph A
Proceedings 1872, pg 23 (1872 Sept 24), Empire Lodge No. 8, Empire
Proceedings 1873, pg 40 (1873 Oct 1), Empire Lodge No. 8, Empire

Loughran, James
Proceedings 1861-1869, pg 227 (1868 Oct 7), Black Hawk Lodge No. 11, Black Hawk

Louis, Isaac
Proceedings 1861-1869, pg 134 (1864 Nov 8), Chivington Lodge No. 6, Central City, dimitted

Proceedings 1861-1869, pg 149 (1865 Nov 7), Nevada Lodge No. 4, Nevadaville

Proceedings 1861-1869, pg 167 (1866 Oct 2) Denver Lodge No. 5, dimitted

Lounsbury, Geo E

Proceedings 1876, pg 17 (1876 Sept 19) Grand Lodge of Illinois, Grand Master, visiting

Love, Edwin Y

Proceedings 1871, pg 25 (1871 Sept 27), El Paso Lodge No. 13, Colorado City, Apprentice

Proceedings 1872, pg 27 (1872 Sept 24), El Paso Lodge No. 13, Colorado City, Apprentice

Proceedings 1873, pg 44 (1873 Oct 1), El Paso Lodge No. 13, Colorado City, Fellowcraft

Proceedings 1874, pg 218 (1874 Sept 30), El Paso Lodge No. 13, Colorado Springs

Proceedings 1875, pg 82 (1875 Sept 22), El Paso Lodge No. 13, Colorado Springs

Proceedings 1876, pg 36 (1876 Sept 20), El Paso Lodge No. 13, Colorado City

Love, J A

Proceedings 1861-1869, pg 151 (1865 Nov 7), Empire Lodge U D, Empire City

Love, J W

Proceedings 1872, pg 26 (1872 Sept 24), El Paso Lodge No. 13, Colorado City

Proceedings 1873, pg 43 (1873 Oct 1), El Paso Lodge No. 13, Colorado City

Love, John

Proceedings 1861-1869, pg 228 (1868 Oct 7), El Paso Lodge No. 13, Colorado City

Love, John W

Proceedings 1861-1869, pg 310 (1869 Sept 29), El Paso Lodge No. 13, Colorado City

Proceedings 1870, pg 26 (1870 Sept 28), El Paso Lodge No. 13, Colorado City

Proceedings 1871, pg 24 (1871 Sept 27), El Paso Lodge No. 13, Colorado City

Proceedings 1874, pg 218 (1874 Sept 30), El Paso Lodge No. 13, Colorado Springs

Proceedings 1875, pg 82 (1875 Sept 22), El Paso Lodge No. 13, Colorado Springs

Proceedings 1876, pg 49 (1876 Sept 20), El Paso Lodge No. 13, Colorado City, 1876 July 22

Love, Jos A

Proceedings 1861-1869, pg 170 (1866 Oct 2), Empire Lodge No. 8, Empire City

Proceedings 1873, pg 6 (1873 Sept 30), Empire Lodge No. 8, Empire

Love, Joseph

Proceedings 1875, pg 89 (1875 Sept 22), Doric Lodge No. 25, Fairplay

Proceedings 1876, pg 42 (1876 Sept 20), Doric Lodge No. 25, Fairplay

Love, Joseph A

Proceedings 1861-1869, pg 195 (1867 Oct 8), Empire Lodge No. 8, Empire City

Proceedings 1861-1869, pg 226 (1868 Oct 7), Empire Lodge No. 8, Empire City

Proceedings 1861-1869, pg 308 (1869 Sept 29), Empire Lodge No. 8, Empire City

Proceedings 1874, pg 215 (1874 Sept 30), Empire Lodge No. 8, Empire

Loveland, H A W

Proceedings 1861-1869, pg 147 (1865 Nov 7) Golden City Lodge No. 1

Loveland, Revillo

Proceedings 1872, pg 32 (1872 Sept 24), Collins Lodge No. 19, Fort Collins

Proceedings 1873, pg 49 (1873 Oct 1), Collins Lodge No. 19, Fort Collins

Proceedings 1874, pg 224 (1874 Sept 30), Collins Lodge No. 19, Fort Collins, Larimer County

Proceedings 1875, pg 86 (1875 Sept 22), Collins Lodge No. 19, Fort Collins

Proceedings 1876, pg 39 (1876 Sept 20), Collins Lodge No. 19, Fort Collins

Loveland, Revilo

Proceedings 1871, pg 30 (1871 Sept 27), Collins Lodge No. 19, Fort Collins, Apprentice

Loveland, W A H

Proceedings 1861-1869, pg 110 (1863 Nov 3) Golden City Lodge No. 1

Proceedings 1861-1869, pg 123 (1864 Nov 8) Golden City Lodge No. 1, Grand Marshal

Proceedings 1861-1869, pg 131 (1864 Nov 8) Golden City Lodge No. 1

Proceedings 1861-1869, pg 191 (1867 Oct 8) Golden City Lodge No. 1

Proceedings 1861-1869, pg 221 (1868 Oct 7) Golden City Lodge No. 1

Proceedings 1861-1869, pg 303 (1869 Sept 29) Golden City Lodge No. 1

Proceedings 1870, pg 19 (1870 Sept 28), Golden City Lodge No. 1, Golden City

Proceedings 1871, pg 17 (1871 Sept 27), Golden City Lodge No. 1, Golden City

Proceedings 1874, pg 209 (1874 Sept 30), Golden City Lodge No. 1, Golden City

Loveland, Wm A H

Proceedings 1872, pg 17 (1872 Sept 24), Golden City Lodge No. 1, Golden City

Proceedings 1875, pg 73 (1875 Sept 22) Golden City Lodge No. 1

Proceedings 1876, pg 29 (1876 Sept 20) Golden City Lodge No. 1

Proceedings 1873, pg 35 (1873 Oct 1), Golden City Lodge No. 1, Golden City

Low, E A

Proceedings 1876, pg 36 (1876 Sept 20), El Paso Lodge No. 13, Colorado City, Fellow Craft

Lowe, G N

Proceedings 1861-1869, pg 305 (1869 Sept 29) Denver Lodge No. 5, Apprentice

Lowe, G W
   Proceedings 1861-1869, pg 112 (1863 Nov 3) Denver Lodge No. 5, Apprentice
   Proceedings 1861-1869, pg 149 (1865 Nov 7), Nevada Lodge No. 4, Nevadaville, Apprentice
   Proceedings 1861-1869, pg 167 (1866 Oct 2) Denver Lodge No. 5, Apprentice

Lowe, Geo N
   Proceedings 1861-1869, pg 223 (1868 Oct 7) Denver Lodge No. 5, Apprentice

Lowe, Geo W
   Proceedings 1861-1869, pg 133 (1864 Nov 8) Denver Lodge No. 5, Apprentice

Lowe, George N
   Proceedings 1861-1869, pg 193 (1867 Oct 8) Denver Lodge No. 5, Apprentice

Luesley, R C
   Proceedings 1876, pg 35 (1876 Sept 20), El Paso Lodge No. 13, Colorado City

Lykins, D J
   Proceedings 1873, pg 51 (1873 Oct 1), St Vrain Lodge No. 23, Longmont
   Proceedings 1874, pg 227 (1874 Sept 30), St Vrain No. 23, Longmont
   Proceedings 1876, pg 41 (1876 Sept 20), St Vrain Lodge No. 23, Longmont

Lykins, David
   Proceedings 1872, pg 35 (1872 Sept 24), St Vrain Lodge No. 23, Longmont

Lykins, David J
   Proceedings 1861-1869, pg 311 (1869 Sept 29), Columbia Lodge No. 14, Boulder City
   Proceedings 1870, pg 27 (1870 Sept 28), Columbia Lodge No. 14, Boulder City
   Proceedings 1871, pg 25 (1871 Sept 27), Columbia Lodge No. 14, Boulder City
   Proceedings 1872, pg 28 (1872 Sept 24), Columbia Lodge No. 14, Boulder
   Proceedings 1873, pg 45 (1873 Oct 1), Columbia Lodge No. 14, Boulder, Dimitted

Lynch, H N
   Proceedings 1861-1869, pg 194 (1867 Oct 8), Chivington Lodge No. 6, Central City

Lynch, H N
   Proceedings 1861-1869, pg 224 (1868 Oct 7), Chivington Lodge No. 6, Central City
   Proceedings 1861-1869, pg 306 (1869 Sept 29), Central Lodge No. 6, Central City
   Proceedings 1870, pg 22 (1870 Sept 28), Central Lodge No. 6, Central City
   Proceedings 1871, pg 20 (1871 Sept 27), Central Lodge No. 6, Central

Lynch, Henry N
   Proceedings 1872, pg 22 (1872 Sept 24), Denver Lodge No. 5, Denver

Lynde
   Proceedings 1874, pg 116 (1874 Sept 30) Grand Lodge of Maine

Lynde, John H
   Proceedings 1861-1869, pg 332 (1869 May 4) Grand Master, Grand Lodge of Maine
   Proceedings 1870, pg 64 (1870 May 3) Grand Master, Grand Lodge of Maine
   Proceedings 1872, pg 70 (1872 Sept 24) Grand Lodge of Maine

Lyner [Leyner], Peter A
   Proceedings 1873, pg 44 (1873 Oct 1), Columbia Lodge No. 14, Boulder
   Proceedings 1874, pg 219 (1874 Sept 30), Columbia Lodge No. 14, Boulder, Boulder County

Lyon, Alvah H
   Proceedings 1873, pg 43 (1873 Oct 1), Washington Lodge No. 12, Georgetown
   Proceedings 1874, pg 217 (1874 Sept 30), Washington Lodge No. 12, Georgetown
   Proceedings 1875, pg 81 (1875 Sept 22), Washington Lodge No. 12, Georgetown
   Proceedings 1876, pg 35 (1876 Sept 20), Washington Lodge No. 12, Georgetown
   Proceedings 1876, pg 50 (1876 Sept 20), Washington Lodge No. 12, Georgetown

Lyon, C A
   Proceedings 1861-1869, pg 304 (1869 Sept 29), Nevada Lodge No. 4, Nevadaville
   Proceedings 1875, pg 74 (1875 Sept 22), Nevada Lodge No. 4, Nevada

Lyon, Cyron A
   Proceedings 1871, pg 18 (1871 Sept 27), Nevada Lodge No. 4, Bald Mountain

Lyon, Cyrus A
   Proceedings 1861-1869, pg 192 (1867 Oct 8), Nevada Lodge No. 4, Nevadaville
   Proceedings 1861-1869, pg 222 (1868 Oct 7), Nevada Lodge No. 4, Nevadaville
   Proceedings 1870, pg 20 (1870 Sept 28), Nevada Lodge No. 4, Nevadaville
   Proceedings 1872, pg 18 (1872 Sept 24), Nevada Lodge No. 4, Bald Mountain
   Proceedings 1873, pg 36 (1873 Oct 1), Nevada Lodge No. 4, Nevada
   Proceedings 1874, pg 210 (1874 Sept 30), Nevada Lodge No. 4, Bald Mountain, Gilpin County
   Proceedings 1876, pg 30 (1876 Sept 20) Nevada Lodge No. 4
   Proceedings 1876, pg 50 (1876 Sept 20) Nevada Lodge No. 4

Lytle, George
   Proceedings 1871, pg 23 (1871 Sept 27), Black Hawk Lodge No. 11, Black Hawk
   Proceedings 1872, pg 25 (1872 Sept 24), Black Hawk Lodge No. 11, Black Hawk
   Proceedings 1873, pg 42 (1873 Oct 1), Black Hawk Lodge No. 11, Black Hawk

Proceedings 1874, pg 216 (1874 Sept 30), Black Hawk Lodge No. 11, Black Hawk, Demitted

Proceedings 1874, pg 219 (1874 Sept 30), Columbia Lodge No. 14, Boulder, Boulder County

Proceedings 1875, pg 83 (1875 Sept 22), Columbia Lodge No. 14, Boulder

Proceedings 1876, pg 37 (1876 Sept 20), Columbia Lodge No. 14, Boulder

Lytle, R T
Proceedings 1875, pg 85 (1875 Sept 22) Pueblo Lodge No. 17

Lytle, Robert F
Proceedings 1873, pg 47 (1873 Oct 1), Pueblo Lodge No. 17, Pueblo

Proceedings 1874, pg 222 (1874 Sept 30), Pueblo Lodge No. 17, Pueblo, Pueblo County

Proceedings 1876, pg 39 (1876 Sept 20) Pueblo Lodge No. 17

M

Mabee, G J W Jr
Proceedings 1861-1869, pg 306 (1869 Sept 29), Central Lodge No. 6, Central City

Proceedings 1870, pg 22 (1870 Sept 28), Central Lodge No. 6, Central City

Mabee, Geo J W
Proceedings 1872, pg 21 (1872 Sept 24), Denver Lodge No. 5, Denver

Mabee, Geo W
Proceedings 1871, pg 20 (1871 Sept 27), Central Lodge No. 6, Central

Proceedings 1873, pg 38 (1873 Oct 1), Central Lodge No. 6, Central City

Proceedings 1874, pg 212 (1874 Sept 30), Central Lodge No. 6, Central

Proceedings 1875, pg 17 (1875 Sept 21) Central Lodge No. 6

Mabee, George W
Proceedings 1875, pg 76 (1875 Sept 22), Central Lodge No. 6, Central City

Proceedings 1876, pg 32 (1876 Sept 20), Central Lodge No. 6, Central City

MacAdams, J G
Proceedings 1870, pg 29 (1870 Sept 28), Cheyenne Lodge No. 16, Cheyenne, Wyoming Territory

MacBroom, John
Proceedings 1874, pg 226 (1874 Sept 30), Weston Lodge No. 22, Littleton

Macdonald, Charles J
Proceedings 1861-1869, pg 316 (1869 Sept 29) Grand Lodge of Nova Scotia

Macdonnell, Chas H
Proceedings 1874, pg 204 (1874 Sept 30) Grand Lodge of Canada, Montreal

Mack, J
Proceedings 1861-1869, pg 113 (1863 Nov 3), Chivington Lodge No. 6, Central City

Proceedings 1861-1869, pg 168 (1866 Oct 2), Chivington Lodge No. 6, Central City

Mack, Jacob
Proceedings 1861-1869, pg 78 (1862 Nov 4), Chivington Lodge No. 6, Central City

Proceedings 1861-1869, pg 134 (1864 Nov 8), Chivington Lodge No. 6, Central City

Proceedings 1861-1869, pg 150 (1865 Nov 7), Chivington Lodge No. 6, Central City

Proceedings 1861-1869, pg 194 (1867 Oct 8), Chivington Lodge No. 6, Central City

Proceedings 1861-1869, pg 224 (1868 Oct 7), Chivington Lodge No. 6, Central City

Proceedings 1861-1869, pg 306 (1869 Sept 29), Central Lodge No. 6, Central City

Proceedings 1870, pg 22 (1870 Sept 28), Central Lodge No. 6, Central City

Proceedings 1871, pg 20 (1871 Sept 27), Central Lodge No. 6, Central

Proceedings 1872, pg 21 (1872 Sept 24), Denver Lodge No. 5, Denver

Proceedings 1873, pg 38 (1873 Oct 1), Central Lodge No. 6, Central City

Proceedings 1874, pg 213 (1874 Sept 30), Central Lodge No. 6, Central

Proceedings 1875, pg 77 (1875 Sept 22), Central Lodge No. 6, Central City

Proceedings 1876, pg 32 (1876 Sept 20), Central Lodge No. 6, Central City

Mack, Wm
Proceedings 1861-1869, pg 131 (1864 Nov 8) Golden City Lodge No. 1

Mackay
Proceedings 1861-1869, pg 87 (1863 Apr 17) Mackey's Jurisprudence

Proceedings 1861-1869, pg 90 (1863 Apr 17) Mackey's Jurisprudence

Mackay, Walter
Proceedings 1861-1869, pg 312 (1869 Sept 29), Cheyenne Lodge No. 16, Cheyenne

Proceedings 1870, pg 29 (1870 Sept 28), Cheyenne Lodge No. 16, Cheyenne, Wyoming Territory

Proceedings 1871, pg 27 (1871 Sept 27), Cheyenne Lodge No. 16, Cheyenne, Wyoming Territory

Proceedings 1872, pg 29 (1872 Sept 24), Cheyenne Lodge No. 16, Cheyenne, Wyoming Territory

Proceedings 1873, pg 46 (1873 Oct 1), Cheyenne Lodge No. 16, Cheyenne, Wyoming Territory

Mackey
Proceedings 1872, pg 79 (1872 Sept 24) Grand Lodge of Nevada

Mackey, A G
Proceedings 1861-1869, pg 280 (1867 Nov 19) Grand Lodge of North Carolina

Colorado's Territorial Masons

Macomb, W R
　Proceedings 1875, pg 85 (1875 Sept 22) Pueblo Lodge No. 17, Apprentice
　Proceedings 1876, pg 39 (1876 Sept 20) Pueblo Lodge No. 17, Fellow Craft

Macomb, William R
　Proceedings 1873, pg 47 (1873 Oct 1), Pueblo Lodge No. 17, Pueblo, Apprentice
　Proceedings 1874, pg 222 (1874 Sept 30), Pueblo Lodge No. 17, Pueblo, Pueblo County, Apprentice

Mahany, J G
　Proceedings 1861-1869, pg 134 (1864 Nov 8), Chivington Lodge No. 6, Central City, Fellowcraft
　Proceedings 1861-1869, pg 150 (1865 Nov 7), Chivington Lodge No. 6, Central City
　Proceedings 1861-1869, pg 168 (1866 Oct 2), Chivington Lodge No. 6, Central City
　Proceedings 1861-1869, pg 194 (1867 Oct 8), Chivington Lodge No. 6, Central City
　Proceedings 1861-1869, pg 224 (1868 Oct 7), Chivington Lodge No. 6, Central City
　Proceedings 1861-1869, pg 306 (1869 Sept 29), Central Lodge No. 6, Central City
　Proceedings 1870, pg 22 (1870 Sept 28), Central Lodge No. 6, Central City
　Proceedings 1871, pg 20 (1871 Sept 27), Central Lodge No. 6, Central

Mahany, Jerry G
　Proceedings 1872, pg 21 (1872 Sept 24), Denver Lodge No. 5, Denver
　Proceedings 1873, pg 38 (1873 Oct 1), Central Lodge No. 6, Central City
　Proceedings 1874, pg 213 (1874 Sept 30), Central Lodge No. 6, Central
　Proceedings 1875, pg 77 (1875 Sept 22), Central Lodge No. 6, Central City
　Proceedings 1876, pg 32 (1876 Sept 20), Central Lodge No. 6, Central City

Mahar, C J
　Proceedings 1861-1869, pg 195 (1867 Oct 8), Union Lodge No. 7, Denver
　Proceedings 1861-1869, pg 225 (1868 Oct 7), Union Lodge No. 7, Denver

Mahar, Con J
　Proceedings 1861-1869, pg 307 (1869 Sept 29), Union Lodge No. 7, Denver
　Proceedings 1870, pg 23 (1870 Sept 28), Union Lodge No. 7, Denver
　Proceedings 1871, pg 22 (1871 Sept 27), Union Lodge No. 7, Denver
　Proceedings 1872, pg 23 (1872 Sept 24), Union Lodge No. 7, Denver
　Proceedings 1873, pg 40 (1873 Oct 1), Union Lodge No. 7, Denver
　Proceedings 1874, pg 214 (1874 Sept 30), Union Lodge No. 7, Denver
　Proceedings 1875, pg 78 (1875 Sept 22), Union Lodge No. 7, Denver
　Proceedings 1876, pg 33 (1876 Sept 20), Union Lodge No. 7, Denver

Mahar, H S
　Proceedings 1872, pg 78 (1872 Sept 24) Grand Lodge of Nevada

Maher, Martin
　Proceedings 1861-1869, pg 313 (1869 Sept 29), Pueblo Lodge No. 17, Pueblo, Dimitted

Maine, W H
　Proceedings 1871, pg 22 (1871 Sept 27), Union Lodge No. 7, Denver
　Proceedings 1873, pg 39 (1873 Oct 1), Union Lodge No. 7, Denver
　Proceedings 1874, pg 214 (1874 Sept 30), Union Lodge No. 7, Denver
　Proceedings 1875, pg 79 (1875 Sept 22), Union Lodge No. 7, Denver, Stricken from the rolls

Maine, William H
　Proceedings 1872, pg 22 (1872 Sept 24), Union Lodge No. 7, Denver

Maldonado, Jose
　Proceedings 1870, pg 34 (1870 Sept 28) Grand Secretary, Grand Lodge of Chile

Mallet, Leon
　Proceedings 1861-1869, pg 221 (1868 Oct 7) Golden City Lodge No. 1, Apprentice
　Proceedings 1861-1869, pg 303 (1869 Sept 29) Golden City Lodge No. 1, Apprentice

Mallett, Lewis
　Proceedings 1861-1869, pg 147 (1865 Nov 7) Golden City Lodge No. 1, Apprentice
　Proceedings 1861-1869, pg 165 (1866 Oct 2) Golden City Lodge No. 1, Apprentice

Mallory, Fred W
　Proceedings 1876, pg 45 (1876 Sept 20) South Pueblo Lodge U D

Maltbie, Noah
　Proceedings 1874, pg 225 (1874 Sept 30), Occidental Lodge No. 20, Greeley
　Proceedings 1875, pg 87 (1875 Sept 22), Occidental Lodge No. 20, Greeley

Maltby, Noah
　Proceedings 1876, pg 48 (1876 Sept 20), Occidental Lodge No. 20, Greeley, 1876 Feb 11

Maltby, O
　Proceedings 1874, pg 228 (1874 Sept 30), Evanston Lodge U D, Evanston, Uintah County, Wyoming Territory, Apprentice

Manasse, William
　Proceedings 1874, pg 223 (1874 Sept 30), Laramie Lodge No. 18, Laramie City
　Proceedings 1873, pg 48 (1873 Oct 1), Laramie Lodge No. 18, Laramie, Wyoming Territory

Manhart, C
Proceedings 1873, pg 51 (1873 Oct 1), Weston Lodge No. 22, Littleton
Proceedings 1875, pg 88 (1875 Sept 22), Weston Lodge No. 22, Littleton
Proceedings 1876, pg 41 (1876 Sept 20), Weston Lodge No. 22, Littleton

Manhart, Christian
Proceedings 1872, pg 35 (1872 Sept 24), Weston Lodge No. 22, Littleton, Apprentice

Manhert, Cris
Proceedings 1874, pg 226 (1874 Sept 30), Weston Lodge No. 22, Littleton

Mann
Proceedings 1873, pg 19 (1873 Oct 1) resolution

Mann, Geo W
Proceedings 1875, pg 82 (1875 Sept 22), El Paso Lodge No. 13, Colorado Springs, died
Proceedings 1875, pg 94 (1875 Sept 22), El Paso Lodge No. 13, Colorado Springs

Mann, George W
Proceedings 1874, pg 218 (1874 Sept 30), El Paso Lodge No. 13, Colorado Springs

Mann, Jos
Proceedings 1873, pg 5 (1873 Sept 30), Golden City Lodge No. 1, Golden City

Mann, Joseph
Proceedings 1872, pg 17 (1872 Sept 24), Golden City Lodge No. 1, Golden City
Proceedings 1873, pg 35 (1873 Oct 1), Golden City Lodge No. 1, Golden City
Proceedings 1874, pg 209 (1874 Sept 30), Golden City Lodge No. 1, Golden City
Proceedings 1875, pg 73 (1875 Sept 22) Golden City Lodge No. 1
Proceedings 1876, pg 29 (1876 Sept 20) Golden City Lodge No. 1

Manners, H
Proceedings 1872, pg 35 (1872 Sept 24), St Vrain Lodge No. 23, Longmont
Proceedings 1873, pg 51 (1873 Oct 1), St Vrain Lodge No. 23, Longmont
Proceedings 1874, pg 227 (1874 Sept 30), St Vrain No. 23, Longmont
Proceedings 1876, pg 41 (1876 Sept 20), St Vrain Lodge No. 23, Longmont

Mansbach, Abe
Proceedings 1875, pg 91 (1875 Sept 22), Las Animas Lodge U D, Trinidad, Apprentice

Mansboch, Abraham
Proceedings 1876, pg 43 (1876 Sept 20), Las Animas Lodge No. 28, Trinidad

Manville, J S D
Proceedings 1870, pg 22 (1870 Sept 28), Central Lodge No. 6, Central City
Proceedings 1871, pg 20 (1871 Sept 27), Central Lodge No. 6, Central

Manville, Jno S D
Proceedings 1872, pg 21 (1872 Sept 24), Denver Lodge No. 5, Denver
Proceedings 1873, pg 38 (1873 Oct 1), Central Lodge No. 6, Central City
Proceedings 1874, pg 213 (1874 Sept 30), Central Lodge No. 6, Central

Manville, John S D
Proceedings 1861-1869, pg 306 (1869 Sept 29), Central Lodge No. 6, Central City
Proceedings 1876, pg 32 (1876 Sept 20), Central Lodge No. 6, Central City

Manville, John S S
Proceedings 1875, pg 77 (1875 Sept 22), Central Lodge No. 6, Central City

Marfell, Hiram
Proceedings 1874, pg 227 (1874 Sept 30), St Vrain No. 23, Longmont, Fellowcraft
Proceedings 1876, pg 41 (1876 Sept 20), St Vrain Lodge No. 23, Longmont

Marix, M Mayer
Proceedings 1872, pg 20 (1872 Sept 24), Denver Lodge No. 5, Denver, Apprentice

Markley, W G
Proceedings 1876, pg 44 (1876 Sept 20), Las Animas Lodge No. 28, Trinidad

Marrant, John
Proceedings 1870, pg 76 (1789 Nov 9) Grand Master, African Lodge of Boston

Marsh, Charles
Proceedings 1861-1869, pg 324 (1868 Oct 18) Grand Master, Grand Lodge of California
Proceedings 1870, pg 45 (1869 Oct 12) Grand Master, Grand Lodge of California

Marsh, H H
Proceedings 1861-1869, pg 229 (1868 Oct 7), Canon Lodge U D, Canon City
Proceedings 1861-1869, pg 311 (1869 Sept 29), Mount Moriah Lodge No. 15, Canon City, died

Marshall, Geo
Proceedings 1861-1869, pg 148 (1865 Nov 7), Nevada Lodge No. 4, Nevadaville
Proceedings 1861-1869, pg 166 (1866 Oct 2), Nevada Lodge No. 4, Nevadaville
Proceedings 1861-1869, pg 222 (1868 Oct 7), Nevada Lodge No. 4, Nevadaville
Proceedings 1871, pg 18 (1871 Sept 27), Nevada Lodge No. 4, Bald Mountain
Proceedings 1874, pg 211 (1874 Sept 30), Nevada Lodge No. 4, Bald Mountain, Gilpin County, Stricken from the rolls

Marshall, George
Proceedings 1861-1869, pg 111 (1863 Nov 3), Nevada Lodge No. 4, Nevadaville

Colorado's Territorial Masons

Marshall, George, cont.
Proceedings 1861-1869, pg 132 (1864 Nov 8), Nevada Lodge No. 4, Nevadaville
Proceedings 1861-1869, pg 192 (1867 Oct 8), Nevada Lodge No. 4, Nevadaville
Proceedings 1861-1869, pg 304 (1869 Sept 29), Nevada Lodge No. 4, Nevadaville
Proceedings 1870, pg 20 (1870 Sept 28), Nevada Lodge No. 4, Nevadaville
Proceedings 1872, pg 19 (1872 Sept 24), Nevada Lodge No. 4, Bald Mountain
Proceedings 1873, pg 36 (1873 Oct 1), Nevada Lodge No. 4, Nevada

Marshall, Henry
Proceedings 1871, pg 30 (1871 Sept 27), Occidental Lodge U D, Greeley

Mart, Julius
Proceedings 1874, pg 225 (1874 Sept 30), Occidental Lodge No. 20, Greeley

Marti, James W
Proceedings 1872, pg 23 (1872 Sept 24), Empire Lodge No. 8, Empire

Martin, Benjamin F
Proceedings 1870, pg 106 (1869 Nov 9) Grand Master, Grand Lodge of West Virginia

Martin, Charles H
Proceedings 1874, pg 217 (1874 Sept 30), Washington Lodge No. 12, Georgetown
Proceedings 1876, pg 35 (1876 Sept 20), Washington Lodge No. 12, Georgetown

Martin, Chas H
Proceedings 1873, pg 42 (1873 Oct 1), Washington Lodge No. 12, Georgetown
Proceedings 1875, pg 81 (1875 Sept 22), Washington Lodge No. 12, Georgetown

Martin, D J
Proceedings 1861-1869, pg 150 (1865 Nov 7), Chivington Lodge No. 6, Central City
Proceedings 1861-1869, pg 168 (1866 Oct 2), Chivington Lodge No. 6, Central City
Proceedings 1861-1869, pg 194 (1867 Oct 8), Chivington Lodge No. 6, Central City
Proceedings 1861-1869, pg 225 (1868 Oct 7), Chivington Lodge No. 6, Central City, Dimitted
Proceedings 1874, pg 214 (1874 Sept 30), Union Lodge No. 7, Denver
Proceedings 1875, pg 79 (1875 Sept 22), Union Lodge No. 7, Denver, Demitted

Martin, David J
Proceedings 1861-1869, pg 134 (1864 Nov 8), Chivington Lodge No. 6, Central City

Martin, F L
Proceedings 1875, pg 82 (1875 Sept 22), El Paso Lodge No. 13, Colorado Springs
Proceedings 1876, pg 36 (1876 Sept 20), El Paso Lodge No. 13, Colorado City

Proceedings 1876, pg 43 (1876 Sept 20), Huerfano Lodge No. 27, Walsenburg

Martin, J H
Proceedings 1876, pg 33 (1876 Sept 20), Union Lodge No. 7, Denver

Martin, J W
Proceedings 1861-1869, pg 111 (1863 Nov 3), Nevada Lodge No. 4, Nevadaville
Proceedings 1861-1869, pg 132 (1864 Nov 8), Nevada Lodge No. 4, Nevadaville
Proceedings 1861-1869, pg 148 (1865 Nov 7), Nevada Lodge No. 4, Nevadaville
Proceedings 1861-1869, pg 151 (1865 Nov 7), Empire Lodge U D, Empire City
Proceedings 1861-1869, pg 166 (1866 Oct 2), Nevada Lodge No. 4, Nevadaville, dimitted
Proceedings 1861-1869, pg 170 (1866 Oct 2), Empire Lodge No. 8, Empire City
Proceedings 1870, pg 24 (1870 Sept 28), Empire Lodge No. 8, Empire

Martin, James W
Proceedings 1861-1869, pg 195 (1867 Oct 8), Empire Lodge No. 8, Empire City
Proceedings 1861-1869, pg 308 (1869 Sept 29), Empire Lodge No. 8, Empire City
Proceedings 1874, pg 215 (1874 Sept 30), Empire Lodge No. 8, Empire

Martin, Jas W
Proceedings 1861-1869, pg 226 (1868 Oct 7), Empire Lodge No. 8, Empire City
Proceedings 1873, pg 41 (1873 Oct 1), Empire Lodge No. 8, Empire

Martin, Jno H
Proceedings 1871, pg 22 (1871 Sept 27), Union Lodge No. 7, Denver

Martin, John H
Proceedings 1861-1869, pg 225 (1868 Oct 7), Union Lodge No. 7, Denver
Proceedings 1861-1869, pg 307 (1869 Sept 29), Union Lodge No. 7, Denver
Proceedings 1870, pg 23 (1870 Sept 28), Union Lodge No. 7, Denver
Proceedings 1872, pg 23 (1872 Sept 24), Union Lodge No. 7, Denver
Proceedings 1873, pg 40 (1873 Oct 1), Union Lodge No. 7, Denver, Stricken from the rolls
Proceedings 1874, pg 214 (1874 Sept 30), Union Lodge No. 7, Denver, Reinstated
Proceedings 1874, pg 214 (1874 Sept 30), Union Lodge No. 7, Denver
Proceedings 1875, pg 78 (1875 Sept 22), Union Lodge No. 7, Denver

Martin, Jonathan
Proceedings 1874, pg 213 (1874 Sept 30), Central Lodge No. 6, Central, Apprentice
Proceedings 1875, pg 77 (1875 Sept 22), Central Lodge No. 6, Central City

Proceedings 1876, pg 32 (1876 Sept 20), Central Lodge No. 6, Central City

Martin, L F
Proceedings 1875, pg 90 (1875 Sept 22), Huerfano Lodge U D, Walsenburg

Martin, P M
Proceedings 1861-1869, pg 168 (1866 Oct 2), Chivington Lodge No. 6, Central City
Proceedings 1861-1869, pg 194 (1867 Oct 8), Chivington Lodge No. 6, Central City
Proceedings 1861-1869, pg 224 (1868 Oct 7), Chivington Lodge No. 6, Central City
Proceedings 1870, pg 22 (1870 Sept 28), Central Lodge No. 6, Central City
Proceedings 1871, pg 20 (1871 Sept 27), Central Lodge No. 6, Central

Martin, Peter
Proceedings 1874, pg 209 (1874 Sept 30), Golden City Lodge No. 1, Golden City
Proceedings 1875, pg 73 (1875 Sept 22) Golden City Lodge No. 1
Proceedings 1876, pg 29 (1876 Sept 20) Golden City Lodge No. 1
Proceedings 1876, pg 50 (1876 Sept 20) Golden City Lodge No. 1

Martin, Phil M
Proceedings 1861-1869, pg 306 (1869 Sept 29), Central Lodge No. 6, Central City

Martin, Philip M
Proceedings 1872, pg 22 (1872 Sept 24), Denver Lodge No. 5, Denver

Martin, T J
Proceedings 1875, pg 91 (1875 Sept 22), Las Animas Lodge U D, Trinidad

Martin, Thomas I
Proceedings 1876, pg 44 (1876 Sept 20), Las Animas Lodge No. 28, Trinidad
Proceedings 1876, pg 50 (1876 Sept 20), Las Animas Lodge No. 28, Trinidad

Martin, William
Proceedings 1871, pg 23 (1871 Sept 27), Black Hawk Lodge No. 11, Black Hawk
Proceedings 1872, pg 25 (1872 Sept 24), Black Hawk Lodge No. 11, Black Hawk
Proceedings 1873, pg 42 (1873 Oct 1), Black Hawk Lodge No. 11, Black Hawk
Proceedings 1874, pg 216 (1874 Sept 30), Black Hawk Lodge No. 11, Black Hawk
Proceedings 1875, pg 80 (1875 Sept 22) Black Hawk Lodge No. 11
Proceedings 1876, pg 34 (1876 Sept 20) Black Hawk Lodge No. 11

Marx, Julius
Proceedings 1872, pg 33 (1872 Sept 24), Occidental Lodge No. 20, Greeley
Proceedings 1873, pg 49 (1873 Oct 1), Occidental Lodge No. 20, Greeley
Proceedings 1875, pg 87 (1875 Sept 22), Occidental Lodge No. 20, Greeley
Proceedings 1876, pg 40 (1876 Sept 20), Occidental Lodge No. 20, Greeley

Marx, Sigismund
Proceedings 1875, pg 87 (1875 Sept 22), Occidental Lodge No. 20, Greeley, Demitted

Maserve, F
Proceedings 1861-1869, pg 149 (1865 Nov 7), Nevada Lodge No. 4, Nevadaville

Mason
Proceedings 1861-1869, pg 117 (1864 Nov 7) motion
Proceedings 1861-1869, pg 127 (1864 Nov 8) motion
Proceedings 1861-1869, pg 127 (1864 Nov 8) donated per diem to the Grand Lodge
Proceedings 1861-1869, pg 161 (1866 Oct 2) motion
Proceedings 1861-1869, pg 163 (1866 Oct 2) resolution
Proceedings 1861-1869, pg 177 (1867 Oct 7) committee
Proceedings 1861-1869, pg 185 (1867 Oct 7) committee
Proceedings 1861-1869, pg 190 (1867 Oct 8) committee
Proceedings 1861-1869, pg 202 (1868 Oct 6) committee
Proceedings 1861-1869, pg 220 (1868 Oct 7) Past Grand Master
Proceedings 1861-1869, pg 236 (1867 Nov 4) Grand Lodge of Arkansas
Proceedings 1861-1869, pg 288 (1869 Sept 28) committee
Proceedings 1861-1869, pg 289 (1869 Sept 28) committee
Proceedings 1861-1869, pg 296 (1869 Sept 28) committee
Proceedings 1861-1869, pg 297 (1869 Sept 28) committee
Proceedings 1861-1869, pg 299 (1869 Sept 29) Past Grand Master
Proceedings 1861-1869, pg 302 (1869 Sept 29) committee
Proceedings 1861-1869, pg 302 (1869 Sept 29) resolution
Proceedings 1870, pg 4 (1870 Sept 27) Past Grand Master
Proceedings 1870, pg 5 (1870 Sept 27) Past Grand Master
Proceedings 1870, pg 14 (1870 Sept 27) Past Grand Master
Proceedings 1870, pg 14 (1870 Sept 27) Grand Marshal
Proceedings 1870, pg 15 (1870 Sept 28) resolution
Proceedings 1871, pg 6 (1861 Dec 10) Past Grand Master
Proceedings 1872, pg 79 (1872 Sept 24) Grand Lodge of Nevada

Mason, A
Proceedings 1861-1869, pg 33 (1861 Dec 10) committee
Proceedings 1861-1869, pg 34 (1861 Dec 10) committee
Proceedings 1861-1869, pg 34 (1861 Dec 10) committee
Proceedings 1861-1869, pg 51 (1862 Nov 4) Grand Marshal
Proceedings 1861-1869, pg 54 (1862 Nov 4) committee
Proceedings 1861-1869, pg 95 (1863 Apr 17) Past Deputy Grand Master
Proceedings 1861-1869, pg 132 (1864 Nov 8), Nevada Lodge No. 4, Nevadaville
Proceedings 1861-1869, pg 138 (1865 Nov 6) committee
Proceedings 1861-1869, pg 151 (1865 Nov 7), Empire Lodge U D, Empire City
Proceedings 1861-1869, pg 163 (1866 Oct 2) committee
Proceedings 1861-1869, pg 166 (1866 Oct 2), Nevada Lodge No. 4, Nevadaville, dimitted

Colorado's Territorial Masons

Mason, A, cont.
    Proceedings 1861-1869, pg 182 (1867 Oct 7) warrant paid
    Proceedings 1861-1869, pg 186 (1867 Oct 8) Past Grand Master
    Proceedings 1861-1869, pg 195 (1867 Oct 8), Empire Lodge No. 8, Empire City
    Proceedings 1861-1869, pg 201 (1868 Oct 6) Past Grand Master
    Proceedings 1861-1869, pg 202 (1868 Oct 6) Past Grand Master
    Proceedings 1861-1869, pg 212 (1868 Oct 6) warrant paid
    Proceedings 1861-1869, pg 216 (1868 Oct 6) committee
    Proceedings 1861-1869, pg 219 (1868 Oct 7) mileage allowed
    Proceedings 1861-1869, pg 220 (1868 Oct 7) committee
    Proceedings 1861-1869, pg 220 (1868 Oct 7) committee
    Proceedings 1861-1869, pg 226 (1868 Oct 7), Empire Lodge No. 8, Empire City
    Proceedings 1861-1869, pg 288 (1869 Sept 28) Past Grand Master
    Proceedings 1870, pg 4 (1870 Sept 27) Past Grand Master
    Proceedings 1870, pg 14 (1870 Sept 27) committee

Mason, Aaron
    Proceedings 1861-1869, pg 228 (1868 Oct 7), El Paso Lodge No. 13, Colorado City
    Proceedings 1861-1869, pg 310 (1869 Sept 29), El Paso Lodge No. 13, Colorado City
    Proceedings 1870, pg 27 (1870 Sept 28), El Paso Lodge No. 13, Colorado City
    Proceedings 1871, pg 25 (1871 Sept 27), El Paso Lodge No. 13, Colorado City
    Proceedings 1872, pg 27 (1872 Sept 24), El Paso Lodge No. 13, Colorado City
    Proceedings 1873, pg 43 (1873 Oct 1), El Paso Lodge No. 13, Colorado City
    Proceedings 1874, pg 218 (1874 Sept 30), El Paso Lodge No. 13, Colorado Springs
    Proceedings 1875, pg 82 (1875 Sept 22), El Paso Lodge No. 13, Colorado Springs, Stricken from the rolls

Mason, Andrew
    Proceedings 1861-1869, pg 33 (1861 Dec 10), Nevada Lodge No. 4, Nevadaville
    Proceedings 1861-1869, pg 36 (1861 Dec 12) Deputy Grand Master
    Proceedings 1861-1869, pg 44 (1862 Nov 3) Deputy Grand Master
    Proceedings 1861-1869, pg 47 (1862 Nov 3) Grand Master
    Proceedings 1861-1869, pg 49 (1862 Nov 3) committee
    Proceedings 1861-1869, pg 77 (1862 Nov 4), Nevada Lodge No. 4, Nevadaville
    Proceedings 1861-1869, pg 79 (1863 May 6) Permanent Member
    Proceedings 1861-1869, pg 80 (1863 May 6) Past Deputy Grand Master
    Proceedings 1861-1869, pg 94 (1863 Apr 17) Past Deputy Grand Master
    Proceedings 1861-1869, pg 111 (1863 Nov 3), Nevada Lodge No. 4, Nevadaville
    Proceedings 1861-1869, pg 115 (1864 Nov 7) Past Deputy Grand Master
    Proceedings 1861-1869, pg 116 (1864 Nov 7) Past Deputy Grand Master
    Proceedings 1861-1869, pg 123 (1864 Nov 8) Grand Marshal
    Proceedings 1861-1869, pg 124 (1864 Nov 8) committee
    Proceedings 1861-1869, pg 126 (1864 Nov 8) Past Deputy Grand Master
    Proceedings 1861-1869, pg 127 (1864 Nov 8) committee
    Proceedings 1861-1869, pg 136 (1865 Nov 6) Past Deputy Grand Master
    Proceedings 1861-1869, pg 137 (1865 Nov 6) Past Deputy Grand Master
    Proceedings 1861-1869, pg 140 (1865 Nov 6) motion
    Proceedings 1861-1869, pg 140 (1865 Nov 6), Empire Lodge No. 8, Empire City
    Proceedings 1861-1869, pg 141 (1865 Nov 7), Empire Lodge No. 8, Empire City
    Proceedings 1861-1869, pg 144 (1865 Nov 7), Empire Lodge No. 8, Empire City
    Proceedings 1861-1869, pg 144 (1865 Nov 7) Grand Master
    Proceedings 1861-1869, pg 148 (1865 Nov 7), Nevada Lodge No. 4, Nevadaville
    Proceedings 1861-1869, pg 153 (1866 Oct 1) Grand Master
    Proceedings 1861-1869, pg 154 (1866 Oct 1) Grand Master
    Proceedings 1861-1869, pg 155 (1866 Oct 1) Grand Master
    Proceedings 1861-1869, pg 159 (1866 Oct 1) warrant
    Proceedings 1861-1869, pg 160 (1866 Oct 2) Grand Master
    Proceedings 1861-1869, pg 162 (1866 Oct 2) Grand Master
    Proceedings 1861-1869, pg 163 (1866 Oct 2) Past Grand Master
    Proceedings 1861-1869, pg 170 (1866 Oct 2), Empire Lodge No. 8, Empire City
    Proceedings 1861-1869, pg 175 (1867 Oct 7) Past Grand Master
    Proceedings 1861-1869, pg 176 (1867 Oct 7) Past Grand Master
    Proceedings 1861-1869, pg 179 (1867 Oct 7), Washington Lodge No. 12, Georgetown
    Proceedings 1861-1869, pg 186 (1867 Oct 8) committee
    Proceedings 1861-1869, pg 202 (1868 Oct 6) committee
    Proceedings 1861-1869, pg 203 (1868 Oct 6) committee
    Proceedings 1861-1869, pg 215 (1868 Oct 6) committee
    Proceedings 1861-1869, pg 227 (1868 Oct 7), Washington Lodge No. 12, Georgetown, Dimitted
    Proceedings 1861-1869, pg 287 (1869 Sept 28) Past Grand Master
    Proceedings 1861-1869, pg 288 (1869 Sept 28) committee
    Proceedings 1861-1869, pg 288 (1869 Sept 28), Empire Lodge No. 8, Empire City
    Proceedings 1861-1869, pg 289 (1869 Sept 28) committee
    Proceedings 1861-1869, pg 299 (1869 Sept 29) committee
    Proceedings 1861-1869, pg 300 (1869 Sept 29) committee
    Proceedings 1861-1869, pg 300 (1869 Sept 29) Past Grand Master
    Proceedings 1861-1869, pg 302 (1869 Sept 29) committee
    Proceedings 1861-1869, pg 308 (1869 Sept 29), Empire Lodge No. 8, Empire City

Mason, Andrew, cont.
- Proceedings 1861-1869, pg 315 (1869 Sept 29) Deputy Grand Master, December 1861
- Proceedings 1861-1869, pg 315 (1869 Sept 29) Grand Master, 1865
- Proceedings 1870, pg cover (1870 Sept 28) Past Grand Master, Empire
- Proceedings 1870, pg 3 (1870 Sept 27) Past Grand Master
- Proceedings 1870, pg 4 (1870 Sept 27) committee
- Proceedings 1870, pg 12 (1870 Sept 27) committee
- Proceedings 1870, pg 16 (1870 Sept 28) Past Grand Master
- Proceedings 1870, pg 24 (1870 Sept 28), Empire Lodge No. 8, Empire
- Proceedings 1870, pg 32 (1870 Sept 28) Grand Master, 1865
- Proceedings 1870, pg 32 (1870 Sept 28) Deputy Grand Master, December 1861
- Proceedings 1871, pg 6 (1861 Dec 10) Deputy Grand Master
- Proceedings 1871, pg 34 (1871 Sept 27) Grand Master, 1865
- Proceedings 1871, pg 34 (1871 Sept 27) Deputy Grand Master, Dec 1861
- Proceedings 1872, pg 23 (1872 Sept 24), Empire Lodge No. 8, Empire
- Proceedings 1872, pg 42 (1872 Sept 24) Deputy Grand Master, December 1861
- Proceedings 1872, pg 42 (1872 Sept 24) Grand Master, 1865
- Proceedings 1873, pg 40 (1873 Oct 1), Empire Lodge No. 8, Empire
- Proceedings 1873, pg 58 (1873 Oct 1) Grand Master, 1865
- Proceedings 1873, pg 58 (1873 Oct 1) Deputy Grand Master, Dec 1861
- Proceedings 1874, pg 206 (1874 Sept 30) Deputy Grand Master, Dec 1861
- Proceedings 1874, pg 206 (1874 Sept 30) Grand Master, 1865
- Proceedings 1874, pg 215 (1874 Sept 30), Empire Lodge No. 8, Empire
- Proceedings 1875, pg 93 (1875 Sept 22) Grand Master, 1865
- Proceedings 1875, pg 93 (1875 Sept 22) Deputy Grand Master, Dec 1861

Mason, E F
- Proceedings 1861-1869, pg 228 (1868 Oct 7), Columbia Lodge No. 14, Columbia City, Died

Mason, Horatio S
- Proceedings 1874, pg 13 (1874 Feb 6) Grand Lodge of Nevada
- Proceedings 1874, pg 204 (1874 Sept 30) Grand Lodge of Nevada, Carson City

Mason, J J
- Proceedings 1874, pg 204 (1874 Sept 30) Grand Lodge of Canada, Hamilton

Mason, John Edwin
- Proceedings 1874, pg 101 (1874 Sept 30) Grand Lodge of the District of Columbia

Mason, John H
- Proceedings 1876, pg 54 (1876 Sept 20) Grand Lodge of Canada, Hamilton, Ontario

Mason, John J
- Proceedings 1875, pg 96 (1875 Sept 22) Grand Lodge of Canada, Hamilton

Mason, Jos
- Proceedings 1874, pg 3 (1874 Sept 29) Junior Grand Steward

Mason, Joseph
- Proceedings 1871, pg 30 (1871 Sept 27), Collins Lodge No. 19, Fort Collins, Apprentice
- Proceedings 1872, pg 33 (1872 Sept 24), Collins Lodge No. 19, Fort Collins, Apprentice
- Proceedings 1873, pg 49 (1873 Oct 1), Collins Lodge No. 19, Fort Collins, Apprentice
- Proceedings 1874, pg 224 (1874 Sept 30), Collins Lodge No. 19, Fort Collins, Larimer County
- Proceedings 1875, pg 86 (1875 Sept 22), Collins Lodge No. 19, Fort Collins
- Proceedings 1876, pg 39 (1876 Sept 20), Collins Lodge No. 19, Fort Collins

Mason, Solon
- Proceedings 1861-1869, pg 196 (1867 Oct 8), El Paso Lodge U D, Colorado City
- Proceedings 1861-1869, pg 228 (1868 Oct 7), El Paso Lodge No. 13, Colorado City
- Proceedings 1861-1869, pg 310 (1869 Sept 29), El Paso Lodge No. 13, Colorado City
- Proceedings 1870, pg 26 (1870 Sept 28), El Paso Lodge No. 13, Colorado City
- Proceedings 1871, pg 25 (1871 Sept 27), El Paso Lodge No. 13, Colorado City
- Proceedings 1872, pg 26 (1872 Sept 24), El Paso Lodge No. 13, Colorado City
- Proceedings 1873, pg 43 (1873 Oct 1), El Paso Lodge No. 13, Colorado City
- Proceedings 1874, pg 218 (1874 Sept 30), El Paso Lodge No. 13, Colorado Springs
- Proceedings 1875, pg 82 (1875 Sept 22), El Paso Lodge No. 13, Colorado Springs
- Proceedings 1876, pg 35 (1876 Sept 20), El Paso Lodge No. 13, Colorado City

Masonic Advocate
- Proceedings 1871, pg 10 (1871 Sept 26) masonic magazine
- Proceedings 1872, pg 11 (1872 Sept 24), published at Indianapolis, IN
- Proceedings 1873, pg 15 (1873 Oct 1), published at Indianapolis, IN
- Proceedings 1874, pg 19 (1874 Sept 29), published at Indianapolis, IN
- Proceedings 1875, pg 23 (1875 Sept 21), published at Indianapolis, IN
- Proceedings 1876, pg 11 (1876 Sept 19), published at Indianapolis, IN

Masonic Board of Relief
    Proceedings 1861-1869, pg 240 (1867 Oct 8), in San Francisco, proposed to create a general charity fund to assist Masons arriving at their port
    Proceedings 1873, pg 15 (1873 Oct 1), Chicago, IL
    Proceedings 1874, pg 74 (1874 Sept 30) supported by the Grand Lodge of Louisiana

Masonic Chronicle
    Proceedings 1875, pg 23 (1875 Sept 21) published at NY
    Proceedings 1876, pg 12 (1876 Sept 19) published at New York City

Masonic Code of Alabama
    Proceedings 1861-1869, pg 238 (1867 Dec 2) received

Masonic Jewel
    Proceedings 1871, pg 10 (1871 Sept 26) masonic magazine
    Proceedings 1872, pg 10 (1872 Sept 24), published at Memphis, TN
    Proceedings 1875, pg 23 (1875 Sept 21), published at Memphis, TN
    Proceedings 1876, pg 11 (1876 Sept 19), published at Memphis, TN
    Proceedings 1872, pg 87 (1872 Sept 24) published at Memphis
    Proceedings 1873, pg 15 (1873 Oct 1), published at Memphis, TN
    Proceedings 1874, pg 19 (1874 Sept 29), published at Memphis, TN

Masonic Life Insurance Company
    Proceedings 1861-1869, pg 238 (1867 Dec 2) proposal to form

Masonic Mirror
    Proceedings 1870, pg 11 (1870 Sept 27), San Francisco, CA
    Proceedings 1871, pg 10 (1871 Sept 26) masonic magazine

Masonic Monthly
    Proceedings 1861-1869, pg 291 (1869 Sept 28) of Boston
    Proceedings 1870, pg 11 (1870 Sept 27), Boston, MA
    The Masonic Token
    Proceedings 1870, pg 11 (1870 Sept 27), Portland, ME

Masonic Publishing Company of New York
    Proceedings 1871, pg 10 (1871 Sept 26) Law and Practice of Masonic Trials

Masonic Review
    Proceedings 1872, pg 11 (1872 Sept 24), published weekly at San Francisco, CA

Masonic Tablet
    Proceedings 1872, pg 11 (1872 Sept 24), published at Jackson, MS
    Proceedings 1873, pg 15 (1873 Oct 1), published at Jackson, MS

Masonic Token
    Proceedings 1871, pg 10 (1871 Sept 26) masonic magazine
    Proceedings 1872, pg 11 (1872 Sept 24), published at Portland, ME
    Proceedings 1873, pg 15 (1873 Oct 1), published at Portland, ME
    Proceedings 1874, pg 19 (1874 Sept 29), published at Portland, ME
    Proceedings 1875, pg 23 (1875 Sept 21), published at Portland, ME
    Proceedings 1876, pg 11 (1876 Sept 19), published at Portland, ME

Masonic Travel
    Proceedings 1871, pg 10 (1871 Sept 26) masonic magazine

Masonic Trestle Board and Constitution of Massachusetts
    Proceedings 1876, pg 11 (1876 Sept 19) received for the Grand Library

Masonic Trowel
    Proceedings 1872, pg 10 (1872 Sept 24), published at Springfield, IL

Masonic Widows and Orphans Home
    Proceedings 1874, pg 73 (1874 Sept 30) supported by the Grand Lodge of Kentucky

Masons' Home Book
    Proceedings 1861-1869, pg 291 (1869 Sept 28) of Philadelphia
    Proceedings 1870, pg 11 (1870 Sept 27), Philadelphia, PA

Massard, C
    Proceedings 1861-1869, pg 112 (1863 Nov 3) Denver Lodge No. 5, dimitted

Massard, Charles
    Proceedings 1861-1869, pg 150 (1865 Nov 7), Chivington Lodge No. 6, Central City, dimitted
    Proceedings 1861-1869, pg 150 (1865 Nov 7), Chivington Lodge No. 6, Central City

Massard, Chas
    Proceedings 1861-1869, pg 77 (1862 Nov 4) Denver Lodge No. 5

Masters, T J
    Proceedings 1871, pg 28 (1871 Sept 27), Cheyenne Lodge No. 16, Cheyenne, Wyoming Territory, Apprentice
    Proceedings 1872, pg 49 (1872 Sept 24), Cheyenne Lodge No. 16, Cheyenne, Wyoming Territory

Maston
    Proceedings 1861-1869, pg 122 (1864 Nov 8) committee

Matchell, Charles G
    Proceedings 1872, pg 84 (1872 Sept 24) Grand Lodge of Ohio

Matheny, James H
    Proceedings 1861-1869, pg 246 (1867 Nov 7) Grand Lodge of Illinois

Matheson, Alexander
    Proceedings 1875, pg 81 (1875 Sept 22), Washington Lodge No. 12, Georgetown
    Proceedings 1876, pg 35 (1876 Sept 20), Washington Lodge No. 12, Georgetown

Mathew, E G
    Proceedings 1861-1869, pg 195 (1867 Oct 8), Union Lodge No. 7, Denver

Mathews, E C
Proceedings 1861-1869, pg 307 (1869 Sept 29), Union Lodge No. 7, Denver

Mathews, E G
Proceedings 1876, pg 33 (1876 Sept 20), Union Lodge No. 7, Denver

Mathews, Elias G
Proceedings 1870, pg 23 (1870 Sept 28), Union Lodge No. 7, Denver

Mathews, John C
Proceedings 1870, pg 31 (1870 Sept 28), Collins Lodge No. 19, Fort Collins, Apprentice

Matthews, E G
Proceedings 1861-1869, pg 225 (1868 Oct 7), Union Lodge No. 7, Denver
Proceedings 1871, pg 21 (1871 Sept 27), Union Lodge No. 7, Denver
Proceedings 1873, pg 40 (1873 Oct 1), Union Lodge No. 7, Denver
Proceedings 1874, pg 214 (1874 Sept 30), Union Lodge No. 7, Denver
Proceedings 1875, pg 78 (1875 Sept 22), Union Lodge No. 7, Denver

Matthews, Elias G
Proceedings 1872, pg 23 (1872 Sept 24), Union Lodge No. 7, Denver

Matthews, Howard
Proceedings 1861-1869, pg 343 (1868 Oct 20) Grand Master, Grand Lodge of Ohio
Proceedings 1870, pg 58 (1870 May 24), Honorary Member, Grand Lodge of Indiana, deceased

Matthews, J C
Proceedings 1871, pg 29 (1871 Sept 27), Collins Lodge No. 19, Fort Collins

Matthews, John C
Proceedings 1872, pg 33 (1872 Sept 24), Collins Lodge No. 19, Fort Collins
Proceedings 1873, pg 49 (1873 Oct 1), Collins Lodge No. 19, Fort Collins
Proceedings 1874, pg 224 (1874 Sept 30), Collins Lodge No. 19, Fort Collins, Larimer County
Proceedings 1875, pg 86 (1875 Sept 22), Collins Lodge No. 19, Fort Collins
Proceedings 1876, pg 39 (1876 Sept 20), Collins Lodge No. 19, Fort Collins

Matzdorf, Herman
Proceedings 1870, pg 30 (1870 Sept 28), Pueblo Lodge No. 17, Pueblo
Proceedings 1871, pg 28 (1871 Sept 27), Pueblo Lodge No. 17, Pueblo
Proceedings 1872, pg 31 (1872 Sept 24), Pueblo Lodge No. 17, Pueblo
Proceedings 1873, pg 47 (1873 Oct 1), Pueblo Lodge No. 17, Pueblo

Matzdorff, H
Proceedings 1861-1869, pg 229 (1868 Oct 7), Pueblo Lodge U D, Pueblo, Apprentice
Proceedings 1861-1869, pg 312 (1869 Sept 29), Pueblo Lodge No. 17, Pueblo

Maulding, James R
Proceedings 1875, pg 76 (1875 Sept 22) Denver Lodge No. 5
Proceedings 1876, pg 48 (1876 Sept 20) Denver Lodge No. 5, 1876 Jan 15

Maxey, John J
Proceedings 1875, pg 79 (1875 Sept 22), Union Lodge No. 7, Denver, Apprentice
Proceedings 1876, pg 33 (1876 Sept 20), Union Lodge No. 7, Denver, Apprentice

Maxon, Leroy
Proceedings 1876, pg 38 (1876 Sept 20), Mount Moriah Lodge No. 15, Canon City, Apprentice

Maxwell, J P
Proceedings 1876, pg 4 (1876 Sept 19) committee
Proceedings 1876, pg 5 (1876 Sept 19), Columbia Lodge No. 14, Boulder
Proceedings 1876, pg 5 (1876 Sept 19) committee
Proceedings 1876, pg 22 (1876 Sept 20), Columbia Lodge No. 14, Boulder

Maxwell, James P
Proceedings 1871, pg 26 (1871 Sept 27), Columbia Lodge No. 14, Boulder City
Proceedings 1872, pg 27 (1872 Sept 24), Columbia Lodge No. 14, Boulder
Proceedings 1873, pg 6 (1873 Sept 30), Columbia Lodge No. 14, Boulder
Proceedings 1873, pg 44 (1873 Oct 1), Columbia Lodge No. 14, Boulder
Proceedings 1874, pg 219 (1874 Sept 30), Columbia Lodge No. 14, Boulder, Boulder County
Proceedings 1875, pg 83 (1875 Sept 22), Columbia Lodge No. 14, Boulder
Proceedings 1876, pg cover (1876 Sept 20) Senior Grand Deacon, Boulder
Proceedings 1876, pg 36 (1876 Sept 20), Columbia Lodge No. 14, Boulder

Maxwell, Jas P
Proceedings 1861-1869, pg 311 (1869 Sept 29), Columbia Lodge No. 14, Boulder City, Fellowcraft
Proceedings 1870, pg 27 (1870 Sept 28), Columbia Lodge No. 14, Boulder City

May, J H
Proceedings 1871, pg 31 (1871 Sept 27), Occidental Lodge U D, Greeley

May, William M
Proceedings 1876, pg 43 (1876 Sept 20), Huerfano Lodge No. 27, Walsenburg

May, Wm M
Proceedings 1875, pg 90 (1875 Sept 22), Huerfano Lodge U D, Walsenburg

Colorado's Territorial Masons

Maynad, J S
Proceedings 1861-1869, pg 147 (1865 Nov 7) Golden City Lodge No. 1
Proceedings 1861-1869, pg 131 (1864 Nov 8) Golden City Lodge No. 1
Proceedings 1861-1869, pg 191 (1867 Oct 8) Golden City Lodge No. 1
Proceedings 1861-1869, pg 221 (1868 Oct 7) Golden City Lodge No. 1
Proceedings 1861-1869, pg 303 (1869 Sept 29) Golden City Lodge No. 1
Proceedings 1870, pg 19 (1870 Sept 28), Golden City Lodge No. 1, Golden City
Proceedings 1871, pg 17 (1871 Sept 27), Golden City Lodge No. 1, Golden City
Proceedings 1872, pg 17 (1872 Sept 24), Golden City Lodge No. 1, Golden City
Proceedings 1873, pg 35 (1873 Oct 1), Golden City Lodge No. 1, Golden City
Proceedings 1874, pg 209 (1874 Sept 30), Golden City Lodge No. 1, Golden City
Proceedings 1875, pg 73 (1875 Sept 22) Golden City Lodge No. 1
Proceedings 1876, pg 29 (1876 Sept 20) Golden City Lodge No. 1
Proceedings 1876, pg 50 (1876 Sept 20) Golden City Lodge No. 1

Maynard, Joseph W
Proceedings 1861-1869, pg 110 (1863 Nov 3) Golden City Lodge No. 1

Maysmith, William
Proceedings 1870, pg 30 (1870 Sept 28), Laramie Lodge No. 18, Laramie, Wyoming Territory

McAdams, J G
Proceedings 1861-1869, pg 312 (1869 Sept 29), Cheyenne Lodge No. 16, Cheyenne
Proceedings 1871, pg 28 (1871 Sept 27), Cheyenne Lodge No. 16, Cheyenne, Wyoming Territory, Apprentice

McAfee, Joseph
Proceedings 1871, pg 24 (1871 Sept 27), Washington Lodge No. 12, Georgetown, Apprentice
Proceedings 1872, pg 26 (1872 Sept 24), Washington Lodge No. 12, Georgetown, Apprentice
Proceedings 1873, pg 43 (1873 Oct 1), Washington Lodge No. 12, Georgetown, Apprentice
Proceedings 1874, pg 217 (1874 Sept 30), Washington Lodge No. 12, Georgetown, Apprentice
Proceedings 1875, pg 81 (1875 Sept 22), Washington Lodge No. 12, Georgetown, Apprentice
Proceedings 1876, pg 35 (1876 Sept 20), Washington Lodge No. 12, Georgetown, Apprentice
Proceedings 1870, pg 26 (1870 Sept 28), Washington Lodge No. 12, Georgetown, Apprentice

McAvoy, J P
Proceedings 1861-1869, pg 194 (1867 Oct 8), Chivington Lodge No. 6, Central City
Proceedings 1861-1869, pg 224 (1868 Oct 7), Chivington Lodge No. 6, Central City
Proceedings 1861-1869, pg 306 (1869 Sept 29), Central Lodge No. 6, Central City
Proceedings 1870, pg 22 (1870 Sept 28), Central Lodge No. 6, Central City
Proceedings 1871, pg 20 (1871 Sept 27), Central Lodge No. 6, Central
Proceedings 1872, pg 22 (1872 Sept 24), Denver Lodge No. 5, Denver

McBaum, H
Proceedings 1874, pg 224 (1874 Sept 30), Laramie Lodge No. 18, Laramie City, Demitted

McBride, Preistly H
Proceedings 1870, pg 88 (1869 Oct 11) Grand Lodge of Missouri, deceased

McBride, Sam
Proceedings 1873, pg 47 (1873 Oct 1), Pueblo Lodge No. 17, Pueblo
Proceedings 1874, pg 6 (1874 Sept 29), Pueblo Lodge No. 17, Pueblo
Proceedings 1875, pg 85 (1875 Sept 22) Pueblo Lodge No. 17
Proceedings 1876, pg 50 (1876 Sept 20) Pueblo Lodge No. 17

McBride, Samuel
Proceedings 1871, pg 28 (1871 Sept 27), Pueblo Lodge No. 17, Pueblo
Proceedings 1872, pg 31 (1872 Sept 24), Pueblo Lodge No. 17, Pueblo
Proceedings 1874, pg 222 (1874 Sept 30), Pueblo Lodge No. 17, Pueblo, Pueblo County
Proceedings 1876, pg 39 (1876 Sept 20) Pueblo Lodge No. 17

McBride, Samuel H
Proceedings 1861-1869, pg 312 (1869 Sept 29), Pueblo Lodge No. 17, Pueblo
Proceedings 1870, pg 30 (1870 Sept 28), Pueblo Lodge No. 17, Pueblo

McBroom, John
Proceedings 1873, pg 51 (1873 Oct 1), Weston Lodge No. 22, Littleton
Proceedings 1875, pg 88 (1875 Sept 22), Weston Lodge No. 22, Littleton
Proceedings 1876, pg 41 (1876 Sept 20), Weston Lodge No. 22, Littleton

McBrown, John
Proceedings 1872, pg 35 (1872 Sept 24), Weston Lodge No. 22, Littleton, Apprentice

McCabe, J C
Proceedings 1872, pg 58 (1872 Sept 24) Grand Lodge of Delaware
Proceedings 1874, pg 51 (1874 Sept 30) Grand Lodge of Delaware

McCabe, John C
Proceedings 1872, pg 43 (1872 Sept 24) Middleton, Grand Lodge of Delaware
Proceedings 1873, pg 60 (1873 Oct 1) Grand Lodge of Delaware, Middleton

McCall, N H
- Proceedings 1861-1869, pg 194 (1867 Oct 8), Chivington Lodge No. 6, Central City
- Proceedings 1861-1869, pg 224 (1868 Oct 7), Chivington Lodge No. 6, Central City
- Proceedings 1861-1869, pg 306 (1869 Sept 29), Central Lodge No. 6, Central City
- Proceedings 1870, pg 22 (1870 Sept 28), Central Lodge No. 6, Central City
- Proceedings 1871, pg 4 (1871 Sept 26), Central Lodge No. 6, Central City
- Proceedings 1871, pg 14 (1871 Sept 27) Senior Grand Steward
- Proceedings 1875, pg cover (1875 Sept 22) Senior Grand Deacon, Central
- Proceedings 1875, pg 17 (1875 Sept 21) committee
- Proceedings 1875, pg 17 (1875 Sept 21) Central Lodge No. 6
- Proceedings 1875, pg 30 (1875 Sept 21) motion
- Proceedings 1875, pg 38 (1875 Sept 22) per diem

McCall, Nathaniel H
- Proceedings 1872, pg 21 (1872 Sept 24), Denver Lodge No. 5, Denver
- Proceedings 1873, pg 38 (1873 Oct 1), Central Lodge No. 6, Central City
- Proceedings 1874, pg 212 (1874 Sept 30), Central Lodge No. 6, Central
- Proceedings 1875, pg 33 (1875 Sept 22) Senior Grand Deacon, Central
- Proceedings 1875, pg 38 (1875 Sept 22) committee
- Proceedings 1875, pg 76 (1875 Sept 22), Central Lodge No. 6, Central City
- Proceedings 1876, pg 31 (1876 Sept 20), Central Lodge No. 6, Central City

McCall, Nat'l H
- Proceedings 1871, pg cover (1871 Sept 27) Senior Grand Steward, Central
- Proceedings 1871, pg 20 (1871 Sept 27), Central Lodge No. 6, Central

McCameron, Hugh C
- Proceedings 1872, pg 25 (1872 Sept 24), Black Hawk Lodge No. 11, Black Hawk

McCammon, Hugh C
- Proceedings 1871, pg 23 (1871 Sept 27), Black Hawk Lodge No. 11, Black Hawk
- Proceedings 1873, pg 42 (1873 Oct 1), Black Hawk Lodge No. 11, Black Hawk
- Proceedings 1874, pg 216 (1874 Sept 30), Black Hawk Lodge No. 11, Black Hawk
- Proceedings 1875, pg 80 (1875 Sept 22) Black Hawk Lodge No. 11

McCamon, H C
- Proceedings 1876, pg 34 (1876 Sept 20) Black Hawk Lodge No. 11

McCandles, J A
- Proceedings 1871, pg 12 (1871 Sept 26), Mount Moriah Lodge No. 15, Canon City, expelled

McCanlas, J A
- Proceedings 1861-1869, pg 311 (1869 Sept 29), Mount Moriah Lodge No. 15, Canon City, Fellowcraft

McCanlas, Jas A
- Proceedings 1861-1869, pg 229 (1868 Oct 7), Canon Lodge U D, Canon City, Apprentice

McCartney, William
- Proceedings 1861-1869, pg 111 (1863 Nov 3), Summit Lodge No. 2, Parkville
- Proceedings 1861-1869, pg 132 (1864 Nov 8) Golden City Lodge No. 1

McCarty, A J
- Proceedings 1873, pg 40 (1873 Oct 1), Union Lodge No. 7, Denver
- Proceedings 1874, pg 214 (1874 Sept 30), Union Lodge No. 7, Denver
- Proceedings 1875, pg 78 (1875 Sept 22), Union Lodge No. 7, Denver
- Proceedings 1876, pg 33 (1876 Sept 20), Union Lodge No. 7, Denver

McCarty, L
- Proceedings 1861-1869, pg 305 (1869 Sept 29) Denver Lodge No. 5
- Proceedings 1870, pg 20 (1870 Sept 28), Denver Lodge No. 5, Denver
- Proceedings 1871, pg 19 (1871 Sept 27) Denver Lodge No. 5
- Proceedings 1876, pg 49 (1876 Sept 20) Denver Lodge No. 5, 1876 Aug 19

McCarty, Leander
- Proceedings 1872, pg 19 (1872 Sept 24), Denver Lodge No. 5, Denver
- Proceedings 1873, pg 37 (1873 Oct 1), Denver Lodge No. 5, Denver
- Proceedings 1874, pg 212 (1874 Sept 30), Denver Lodge No. 5, Denver
- Proceedings 1875, pg 76 (1875 Sept 22) Denver Lodge No. 5

McCarty, M
- Proceedings 1874, pg 222 (1874 Sept 30), Pueblo Lodge No. 17, Pueblo, Pueblo County
- Proceedings 1875, pg 85 (1875 Sept 22) Pueblo Lodge No. 17
- Proceedings 1876, pg 39 (1876 Sept 20) Pueblo Lodge No. 17

McCarty, Michael
- Proceedings 1873, pg 47 (1873 Oct 1), Pueblo Lodge No. 17, Pueblo

McCaskill, John
- Proceedings 1861-1869, pg 111 (1863 Nov 3), Summit Lodge No. 2, Parkville
- Proceedings 1861-1869, pg 132 (1864 Nov 8) Golden City Lodge No. 1

McCaslin, M L
- Proceedings 1861-1869, pg 311 (1869 Sept 29), Columbia Lodge No. 14, Boulder City, Fellowcraft

Colorado's Territorial Masons

McCaslin, M L, cont.
Proceedings 1870, pg 27 (1870 Sept 28), Columbia Lodge No. 14, Boulder City
Proceedings 1871, pg 26 (1871 Sept 27), Columbia Lodge No. 14, Boulder City
Proceedings 1872, pg 14 (1872 Sept 24), St Vrain Lodge No. 23, Longmont
Proceedings 1872, pg 28 (1872 Sept 24), Columbia Lodge No. 14, Boulder
Proceedings 1873, pg 44 (1873 Oct 1), Columbia Lodge No. 14, Boulder
Proceedings 1874, pg 219 (1874 Sept 30), Columbia Lodge No. 14, Boulder, Boulder County
Proceedings 1875, pg 83 (1875 Sept 22), Columbia Lodge No. 14, Boulder
Proceedings 1876, pg 37 (1876 Sept 20), Columbia Lodge No. 14, Boulder

McCaudles, J A
Proceedings 1871, pg 27 (1871 Sept 27), Mount Moriah Lodge No. 15, Canon City, Expelled

McClanahan, Perry D
Proceedings 1871, pg 30 (1871 Sept 27), Collins Lodge No. 19, Fort Collins
Proceedings 1872, pg 33 (1872 Sept 24), Collins Lodge No. 19, Fort Collins
Proceedings 1873, pg 49 (1873 Oct 1), Collins Lodge No. 19, Fort Collins, Dimitted

McClary, Daniel
Proceedings 1861-1869, pg 221 (1868 Oct 7) Golden City Lodge No. 1
Proceedings 1861-1869, pg 303 (1869 Sept 29) Golden City Lodge No. 1

McCleary, Daniel
Proceedings 1861-1869, pg 110 (1863 Nov 3) Golden City Lodge No. 1

McCleary, T
Proceedings 1861-1869, pg 228 (1868 Oct 7), Columbia Lodge No. 14, Columbia City, Dimitted

McCleary, Troy
Proceedings 1861-1869, pg 197 (1867 Oct 8), Columbia Lodge U D, Boulder

McCleery, D
Proceedings 1861-1869, pg 165 (1866 Oct 2) Golden City Lodge No. 1

McCleery, Daniel
Proceedings 1861-1869, pg 42 (1861 Dec 10) Golden City Lodge No. 1
Proceedings 1861-1869, pg 131 (1864 Nov 8) Golden City Lodge No. 1
Proceedings 1861-1869, pg 147 (1865 Nov 7) Golden City Lodge No. 1
Proceedings 1861-1869, pg 191 (1867 Oct 8) Golden City Lodge No. 1

McClellan, J C
Proceedings 1861-1869, pg 113 (1863 Nov 3), Chivington Lodge No. 6, Central City
Proceedings 1861-1869, pg 150 (1865 Nov 7), Chivington Lodge No. 6, Central City
Proceedings 1861-1869, pg 168 (1866 Oct 2), Chivington Lodge No. 6, Central City
Proceedings 1861-1869, pg 194 (1867 Oct 8), Chivington Lodge No. 6, Central City
Proceedings 1861-1869, pg 225 (1868 Oct 7), Chivington Lodge No. 6, Central City, Dimitted

McClellan, Job C
Proceedings 1861-1869, pg 78 (1862 Nov 4), Chivington Lodge No. 6, Central City
Proceedings 1861-1869, pg 134 (1864 Nov 8), Chivington Lodge No. 6, Central City

McClellan, S
Proceedings 1861-1869, pg 223 (1868 Oct 7) Denver Lodge No. 5, Apprentice
Proceedings 1861-1869, pg 305 (1869 Sept 29) Denver Lodge No. 5, Apprentice

McClellan, Samuel
Proceedings 1861-1869, pg 133 (1864 Nov 8) Denver Lodge No. 5, Apprentice

McClelland, S
Proceedings 1861-1869, pg 149 (1865 Nov 7), Nevada Lodge No. 4, Nevadaville, Apprentice

McClintock, Daniel
Proceedings 1861-1869, pg 244 (1867 June 27), Grand Master, Grand Lodge of Delaware
Proceedings 1861-1869, pg 326 (1868 June 27) Grand Master, Grand Lodge of Delaware

McCluer, Timothy J
Proceedings 1875, pg 90 (1875 Sept 22), Huerfano Lodge U D, Walsenburg, Apprentice

McClure, E P
Proceedings 1861-1869, pg 197 (1867 Oct 8), Columbia Lodge U D, Boulder, Fellowcraft
Proceedings 1874, pg 219 (1874 Sept 30), Columbia Lodge No. 14, Boulder, Boulder County
Proceedings 1861-1869, pg 228 (1868 Oct 7), Columbia Lodge No. 14, Columbia City

McClure, Ed P
Proceedings 1875, pg 83 (1875 Sept 22), Columbia Lodge No. 14, Boulder, Stricken from the rolls

McClure, Edmond P
Proceedings 1861-1869, pg 311 (1869 Sept 29), Columbia Lodge No. 14, Boulder City

McClure, Edmund P
Proceedings 1871, pg 26 (1871 Sept 27), Columbia Lodge No. 14, Boulder City
Proceedings 1872, pg 28 (1872 Sept 24), Columbia Lodge No. 14, Boulder
Proceedings 1873, pg 44 (1873 Oct 1), Columbia Lodge No. 14, Boulder

McClure, Edward P
Proceedings 1870, pg 27 (1870 Sept 28), Columbia Lodge No. 14, Boulder City

McClure, Timothy J
  Proceedings 1876, pg 43 (1876 Sept 20), Huerfano Lodge No. 27, Walsenburg, Apprentice

McClure, W H
  Proceedings 1861-1869, pg 196 (1867 Oct 8), El Paso Lodge U D, Colorado City
  Proceedings 1861-1869, pg 228 (1868 Oct 7), El Paso Lodge No. 13, Colorado City, Dimitted
  Proceedings 1861-1869, pg 229 (1868 Oct 7), Canon Lodge U D, Canon City
  Proceedings 1861-1869, pg 311 (1869 Sept 29), Mount Moriah Lodge No. 15, Canon City
  Proceedings 1870, pg 28 (1870 Sept 28), Mount Moriah Lodge No. 15, Canon City
  Proceedings 1871, pg 26 (1871 Sept 27), Mount Moriah Lodge No. 15, Canon City
  Proceedings 1872, pg 28 (1872 Sept 24), Mount Moriah Lodge No. 15, Canon City
  Proceedings 1873, pg 45 (1873 Oct 1), Mount Moriah Lodge No. 15, Canon City
  Proceedings 1874, pg 220 (1874 Sept 30), Mount Moriah Lodge No. 15, Canon City
  Proceedings 1875, pg 84 (1875 Sept 22), Mount Moriah Lodge No. 15, Canon City
  Proceedings 1876, pg 38 (1876 Sept 20), Mount Moriah Lodge No. 15, Canon City

McConnell, Wm
  Proceedings 1861-1869, pg 31 (1861 Dec 10) Grand Tyler
  Proceedings 1861-1869, pg 38 (1861 Dec 12) Grand Pursuivants
  Proceedings 1861-1869, pg 53 (1862 Nov 4) Tyler

McCorkle
  Proceedings 1870, pg 62 (1869 Oct 18) Grand Lodge of Kentucky

McCorkle, J M S
  Proceedings 1861-1869, pg 331 (1868 Oct 19) Grand Secretary, Grand Lodge of Kentucky
  Proceedings 1870, pg 61 (1869 Oct 18) Grand Secretary, Grand Lodge of Kentucky
  Proceedings 1872, pg 43 (1872 Sept 24) Louisville, Grand Lodge of Kentucky
  Proceedings 1873, pg 60 (1873 Oct 1) Grand Lodge of Kentucky, Louisville

McCorkle, John M S
  Proceedings 1861-1869, pg 316 (1869 Sept 29) Grand Lodge of Kentucky
  Proceedings 1870, pg 34 (1870 Sept 28) Grand Secretary, Grand Lodge of Kentucky
  Proceedings 1874, pg 73 (1874 Sept 30) Grand Lodge of Kentucky
  Proceedings 1874, pg 204 (1874 Sept 30) Grand Lodge of Kentucky, Louisville

McCormick, Alexander
  Proceedings 1861-1869, pg 245 (1867 Nov 7) contemporary of George Washington

McCory, V W
  Proceedings 1861-1869, pg 168 (1866 Oct 2), Chivington Lodge No. 6, Central City
  Proceedings 1861-1869, pg 194 (1867 Oct 8), Chivington Lodge No. 6, Central City
  Proceedings 1861-1869, pg 224 (1868 Oct 7), Chivington Lodge No. 6, Central City
  Proceedings 1861-1869, pg 306 (1869 Sept 29), Central Lodge No. 6, Central City
  Proceedings 1870, pg 22 (1870 Sept 28), Central Lodge No. 6, Central City
  Proceedings 1871, pg 20 (1871 Sept 27), Central Lodge No. 6, Central

McCory, Van W
  Proceedings 1872, pg 22 (1872 Sept 24), Denver Lodge No. 5, Denver

McCrimmon, M
  Proceedings 1875, pg 81 (1875 Sept 22), Washington Lodge No. 12, Georgetown, Demitted

McCrimmon, Malcomb
  Proceedings 1873, pg 42 (1873 Oct 1), Washington Lodge No. 12, Georgetown
  Proceedings 1874, pg 217 (1874 Sept 30), Washington Lodge No. 12, Georgetown

McCundlos, J A
  Proceedings 1870, pg 28 (1870 Sept 28), Mount Moriah Lodge No. 15, Canon City, Apprentice

McCune, A
  Proceedings 1861-1869, pg 77 (1862 Nov 4) Denver Lodge No. 5
  Proceedings 1861-1869, pg 112 (1863 Nov 3) Denver Lodge No. 5, Fellowcraft
  Proceedings 1861-1869, pg 133 (1864 Nov 8) Denver Lodge No. 5
  Proceedings 1861-1869, pg 137 (1865 Nov 6) Denver Lodge No. 5
  Proceedings 1861-1869, pg 154 (1866 Oct 1) Denver Lodge No. 5
  Proceedings 1861-1869, pg 166 (1866 Oct 2) Denver Lodge No. 5
  Proceedings 1861-1869, pg 305 (1869 Sept 29) Denver Lodge No. 5

McCune, Alvin
  Proceedings 1861-1869, pg 148 (1865 Nov 7), Nevada Lodge No. 4, Nevadaville
  Proceedings 1861-1869, pg 176 (1867 Oct 7) Denver Lodge No. 5
  Proceedings 1861-1869, pg 192 (1867 Oct 8) Denver Lodge No. 5
  Proceedings 1861-1869, pg 223 (1868 Oct 7) Denver Lodge No. 5
  Proceedings 1870, pg 21 (1870 Sept 28), Denver Lodge No. 5, Denver
  Proceedings 1871, pg 19 (1871 Sept 27) Denver Lodge No. 5
  Proceedings 1872, pg 20 (1872 Sept 24), Denver Lodge No. 5, Denver
  Proceedings 1873, pg 37 (1873 Oct 1), Denver Lodge No. 5, Denver
  Proceedings 1874, pg 212 (1874 Sept 30), Denver Lodge No. 5, Denver

Colorado's Territorial Masons

McCune, Alvin, cont.
Proceedings 1875, pg 76 (1875 Sept 22) Denver Lodge No. 5
Proceedings 1876, pg 31 (1876 Sept 20) Denver Lodge No. 5

McCurdy, Hugh
Proceedings 1873, pg 60 (1873 Oct 1) Grand Lodge of Michigan, Corunna
Proceedings 1874, pg 83 (1874 Sept 30) Grand Lodge of Michigan

McDivit, Clyde J
Proceedings 1872, pg 33 (1872 Sept 24), Collins Lodge No. 19, Fort Collins

McDivitt, C J
Proceedings 1871, pg 29 (1871 Sept 27), Collins Lodge No. 19, Fort Collins

McDivitt, Clyde J
Proceedings 1870, pg 31 (1870 Sept 28), Collins Lodge No. 19, Fort Collins
Proceedings 1873, pg 49 (1873 Oct 1), Collins Lodge No. 19, Fort Collins, Dimitted

McDonald, Charles J
Proceedings 1861-1869, pg 157 (1866 Oct 1), Grand Secretary, Grand Lodge of Nova Scotia

McDonald, Daniel
Proceedings 1874, pg 65 (1874 Sept 30) Grand Lodge of Indiana
Proceedings 1874, pg 204 (1874 Sept 30) Grand Lodge of Indiana, Plymouth

McDonald, F A
Proceedings 1861-1869, pg 149 (1865 Nov 7), Nevada Lodge No. 4, Nevadaville
Proceedings 1861-1869, pg 167 (1866 Oct 2) Denver Lodge No. 5
Proceedings 1861-1869, pg 192 (1867 Oct 8) Denver Lodge No. 5
Proceedings 1861-1869, pg 223 (1868 Oct 7) Denver Lodge No. 5
Proceedings 1861-1869, pg 305 (1869 Sept 29) Denver Lodge No. 5
Proceedings 1870, pg 21 (1870 Sept 28), Denver Lodge No. 5, Denver
Proceedings 1871, pg 19 (1871 Sept 27) Denver Lodge No. 5
Proceedings 1872, pg 20 (1872 Sept 24), Denver Lodge No. 5, Denver
Proceedings 1873, pg 38 (1873 Oct 1), Denver Lodge No. 5, Denver, died

McDougal, Thomas
Proceedings 1870, pg 39 (1869 Dec 6) Grand Lodge of Alabama, deceased

McDowell, J A
Proceedings 1872, pg 36 (1872 Sept 24), Ashlar Lodge U D, Colorado Springs

McDowell, J W
Proceedings 1870, pg 31 (1870 Sept 28), Laramie Lodge No. 18, Laramie, Wyoming Territory, Fellowcraft
Proceedings 1871, pg 29 (1871 Sept 27), Laramie Lodge No. 18, Laramie, Wyoming Territory
Proceedings 1872, pg 32 (1872 Sept 24), Laramie Lodge No. 18, Laramie, Wyoming Territory
Proceedings 1873, pg 48 (1873 Oct 1), Laramie Lodge No. 18, Laramie, Wyoming Territory
Proceedings 1874, pg 223 (1874 Sept 30), Laramie Lodge No. 18, Laramie City

McDowell, John M
Proceedings 1876, pg 37 (1876 Sept 20), Columbia Lodge No. 14, Boulder

McElroy, William S
Proceedings 1876, pg 40 (1876 Sept 20), Occidental Lodge No. 20, Greeley, Apprentice

McFadden, J
Proceedings 1861-1869, pg 151 (1865 Nov 7), Chivington Lodge No. 6, Central City, Fellowcraft
Proceedings 1876, pg 33 (1876 Sept 20), Union Lodge No. 7, Denver

McFadden, J A
Proceedings 1861-1869, pg 225 (1868 Oct 7), Union Lodge No. 7, Denver

McFadden, J H
Proceedings 1861-1869, pg 195 (1867 Oct 8), Union Lodge No. 7, Denver

McFadden, James
Proceedings 1873, pg 40 (1873 Oct 1), Union Lodge No. 7, Denver
Proceedings 1874, pg 214 (1874 Sept 30), Union Lodge No. 7, Denver
Proceedings 1875, pg 78 (1875 Sept 22), Union Lodge No. 7, Denver

McFadden, James A
Proceedings 1861-1869, pg 169 (1866 Oct 2), Union Lodge No. 7, Denver
Proceedings 1861-1869, pg 307 (1869 Sept 29), Union Lodge No. 7, Denver
Proceedings 1870, pg 23 (1870 Sept 28), Union Lodge No. 7, Denver
Proceedings 1872, pg 23 (1872 Sept 24), Union Lodge No. 7, Denver

McFadden, Jas A
Proceedings 1871, pg 22 (1871 Sept 27), Union Lodge No. 7, Denver

McFarland, James
Proceedings 1874, pg 212 (1874 Sept 30), Denver Lodge No. 5, Denver
Proceedings 1875, pg 76 (1875 Sept 22) Denver Lodge No. 5
Proceedings 1876, pg 31 (1876 Sept 20) Denver Lodge No. 5

McFarren, I H B
　Proceedings 1875, pg 82 (1875 Sept 22), El Paso Lodge No. 13, Colorado Springs

McFee, H
　Proceedings 1861-1869, pg 152 (1865 Nov 7), Helena City Lodge U D, Helena City, Montana Territory

McFeeter, Wm
　Proceedings 1861-1869, pg 166 (1866 Oct 2), Nevada Lodge No. 4, Nevadaville, Apprentice

McFeeters, Wm
　Proceedings 1861-1869, pg 112 (1863 Nov 3), Nevada Lodge No. 4, Nevadaville, Apprentice
　Proceedings 1861-1869, pg 132 (1864 Nov 8), Nevada Lodge No. 4, Nevadaville, Apprentice
　Proceedings 1861-1869, pg 148 (1865 Nov 7), Nevada Lodge No. 4, Nevadaville, Apprentice
　Proceedings 1861-1869, pg 192 (1867 Oct 8), Nevada Lodge No. 4, Nevadaville, Apprentice
　Proceedings 1861-1869, pg 222 (1868 Oct 7), Nevada Lodge No. 4, Nevadaville, Apprentice

McFerran, J H B
　Proceedings 1876, pg 36 (1876 Sept 20), El Paso Lodge No. 13, Colorado City

McGarr, C P
　Proceedings 1861-1869, pg 77 (1862 Nov 4), Nevada Lodge No. 4, Nevadaville
　Proceedings 1861-1869, pg 111 (1863 Nov 3), Nevada Lodge No. 4, Nevadaville, deceased

McGeath, A C
　Proceedings 1861-1869, pg 148 (1865 Nov 7), Nevada Lodge No. 4, Nevadaville
　Proceedings 1861-1869, pg 192 (1867 Oct 8), Nevada Lodge No. 4, Nevadaville
　Proceedings 1861-1869, pg 222 (1868 Oct 7), Nevada Lodge No. 4, Nevadaville
　Proceedings 1861-1869, pg 304 (1869 Sept 29), Nevada Lodge No. 4, Nevadaville, died

McGee, James
　Proceedings 1861-1869, pg 196 (1867 Oct 8), El Paso Lodge U D, Colorado City
　Proceedings 1861-1869, pg 228 (1868 Oct 7), El Paso Lodge No. 13, Colorado City
　Proceedings 1861-1869, pg 310 (1869 Sept 29), El Paso Lodge No. 13, Colorado City, Dimitted

McGibbon, James
　Proceedings 1870, pg 30 (1870 Sept 28), Laramie Lodge No. 18, Laramie, Wyoming Territory
　Proceedings 1871, pg 29 (1871 Sept 27), Laramie Lodge No. 18, Laramie, Wyoming Territory
　Proceedings 1872, pg 32 (1872 Sept 24), Laramie Lodge No. 18, Laramie, Wyoming Territory
　Proceedings 1873, pg 48 (1873 Oct 1), Laramie Lodge No. 18, Laramie, Wyoming Territory
　Proceedings 1874, pg 223 (1874 Sept 30), Laramie Lodge No. 18, Laramie City

McGill, P J
　Proceedings 1875, pg 78 (1875 Sept 22), Union Lodge No. 7, Denver
　Proceedings 1876, pg 33 (1876 Sept 20), Union Lodge No. 7, Denver

McGowan, William
　Proceedings 1875, pg 82 (1875 Sept 22), El Paso Lodge No. 13, Colorado Springs, Demitted

McGran, P
　Proceedings 1861-1869, pg 168 (1866 Oct 2), Chivington Lodge No. 6, Central City

McGran, Philip
　Proceedings 1861-1869, pg 194 (1867 Oct 8), Chivington Lodge No. 6, Central City

McGran, Phillip
　Proceedings 1861-1869, pg 134 (1864 Nov 8), Chivington Lodge No. 6, Central City

McGraw, P
　Proceedings 1861-1869, pg 150 (1865 Nov 7), Chivington Lodge No. 6, Central City

McGreggor, A G
　Proceedings 1870, pg 29 (1870 Sept 28), Cheyenne Lodge No. 16, Cheyenne, Wyoming Territory, Fellowcraft

McGregor, A G
　Proceedings 1871, pg 27 (1871 Sept 27), Cheyenne Lodge No. 16, Cheyenne, Wyoming Territory
　Proceedings 1872, pg 29 (1872 Sept 24), Cheyenne Lodge No. 16, Cheyenne, Wyoming Territory
　Proceedings 1873, pg 46 (1873 Oct 1), Cheyenne Lodge No. 16, Cheyenne, Wyoming Territory
　Proceedings 1874, pg 220 (1874 Sept 30), Cheyenne Lodge No. 16, Cheyenne, Wyoming Territory

McGregor, Alex
　Proceedings 1871, pg 19 (1871 Sept 27) Denver Lodge No. 5
　Proceedings 1872, pg 19 (1872 Sept 24), Denver Lodge No. 5, Denver
　Proceedings 1873, pg 37 (1873 Oct 1), Denver Lodge No. 5, Denver
　Proceedings 1874, pg 212 (1874 Sept 30), Denver Lodge No. 5, Denver
　Proceedings 1875, pg 76 (1875 Sept 22) Denver Lodge No. 5, Demitted

McGren, Philip
　Proceedings 1861-1869, pg 224 (1868 Oct 7), Chivington Lodge No. 6, Central City
　Proceedings 1861-1869, pg 306 (1869 Sept 29), Central Lodge No. 6, Central City
　Proceedings 1870, pg 23 (1870 Sept 28), Central Lodge No. 6, Central City, Dimitted

McGuire, M C
　Proceedings 1861-1869, pg 305 (1869 Sept 29) Denver Lodge No. 5, Apprentice

Colorado's Territorial Masons

McHaffey, A J
Proceedings 1874, pg 224 (1874 Sept 30), Laramie Lodge No. 18, Laramie City, Fellowcraft

McHoffey, J A
Proceedings 1873, pg 48 (1873 Oct 1), Laramie Lodge No. 18, Laramie, Wyoming Territory, Apprentice

McIntire, H A
Proceedings 1873, pg 13 (1873 Sept 30), Ashlar Lodge U D, Colorado Springs
Proceedings 1874, pg 218 (1874 Sept 30), El Paso Lodge No. 13, Colorado Springs
Proceedings 1875, pg 82 (1875 Sept 22), El Paso Lodge No. 13, Colorado Springs
Proceedings 1876, pg 36 (1876 Sept 20), El Paso Lodge No. 13, Colorado City

McIntosh, L
Proceedings 1861-1869, pg 197 (1867 Oct 8), Columbia Lodge U D, Boulder, Apprentice
Proceedings 1861-1869, pg 228 (1868 Oct 7), Columbia Lodge No. 14, Columbia City

McIntosh, Lemuel
Proceedings 1861-1869, pg 311 (1869 Sept 29), Columbia Lodge No. 14, Boulder City
Proceedings 1870, pg 27 (1870 Sept 28), Columbia Lodge No. 14, Boulder City
Proceedings 1871, pg 26 (1871 Sept 27), Columbia Lodge No. 14, Boulder City
Proceedings 1873, pg 44 (1873 Oct 1), Columbia Lodge No. 14, Boulder
Proceedings 1874, pg 219 (1874 Sept 30), Columbia Lodge No. 14, Boulder, Boulder County
Proceedings 1875, pg 83 (1875 Sept 22), Columbia Lodge No. 14, Boulder
Proceedings 1876, pg 37 (1876 Sept 20), Columbia Lodge No. 14, Boulder

McIntosh, Samuel
Proceedings 1872, pg 28 (1872 Sept 24), Columbia Lodge No. 14, Boulder

McIntyre, H A
Proceedings 1873, pg 52 (1873 Oct 1), Ashlar Lodge U D, Colorado Springs

McKay, Walter
Proceedings 1874, pg 221 (1874 Sept 30), Cheyenne Lodge No. 16, Cheyenne, Wyoming Territory

McKee, G
Proceedings 1861-1869, pg 195 (1867 Oct 8), Union Lodge No. 7, Denver, Apprentice
Proceedings 1861-1869, pg 226 (1868 Oct 7), Union Lodge No. 7, Denver, Apprentice

McKee, Geo
Proceedings 1872, pg 23 (1872 Sept 24), Union Lodge No. 7, Denver, Apprentice

McKee, George
Proceedings 1861-1869, pg 308 (1869 Sept 29), Union Lodge No. 7, Denver, Apprentice
Proceedings 1870, pg 24 (1870 Sept 28), Union Lodge No. 7, Denver, Apprentice
Proceedings 1871, pg 22 (1871 Sept 27), Union Lodge No. 7, Denver, Apprentice
Proceedings 1873, pg 40 (1873 Oct 1), Union Lodge No. 7, Denver, Apprentice
Proceedings 1874, pg 214 (1874 Sept 30), Union Lodge No. 7, Denver, Apprentice
Proceedings 1875, pg 79 (1875 Sept 22), Union Lodge No. 7, Denver, Apprentice
Proceedings 1876, pg 33 (1876 Sept 20), Union Lodge No. 7, Denver, Apprentice

McKenna, T D
Proceedings 1871, pg 31 (1871 Sept 27), Argenta Lodge U D, Salt Lake City, Utah

McKensie [McKenzie], Niel D
Proceedings 1871, pg 23 (1871 Sept 27), Black Hawk Lodge No. 11, Black Hawk

McKenzie, Neil D
Proceedings 1870, pg 25 (1870 Sept 28), Black Hawk Lodge No. 11, Black Hawk
Proceedings 1872, pg 25 (1872 Sept 24), Black Hawk Lodge No. 11, Black Hawk
Proceedings 1873, pg 42 (1873 Oct 1), Black Hawk Lodge No. 11, Black Hawk
Proceedings 1874, pg 216 (1874 Sept 30), Black Hawk Lodge No. 11, Black Hawk

McKinzee, N D
Proceedings 1876, pg 34 (1876 Sept 20) Black Hawk Lodge No. 11

McKinzie, Niel [Neil] D
Proceedings 1875, pg 80 (1875 Sept 22) Black Hawk Lodge No. 11

McKissick, John
Proceedings 1874, pg 226 (1874 Sept 30), Occidental Lodge No. 20, Greeley, Apprentice
Proceedings 1875, pg 87 (1875 Sept 22), Occidental Lodge No. 20, Greeley, Apprentice
Proceedings 1876, pg 40 (1876 Sept 20), Occidental Lodge No. 20, Greeley, Apprentice

McKnight, H
Proceedings 1872, pg 33 (1872 Sept 24), Occidental Lodge No. 20, Greeley

McKnight, Henderson
Proceedings 1871, pg 30 (1871 Sept 27), Occidental Lodge U D, Greeley
Proceedings 1873, pg 50 (1873 Oct 1), Occidental Lodge No. 20, Greeley
Proceedings 1874, pg 226 (1874 Sept 30), Occidental Lodge No. 20, Greeley, Demitted

McLain, J S
Proceedings 1861-1869, pg 168 (1866 Oct 2), Chivington Lodge No. 6, Central City
Proceedings 1861-1869, pg 194 (1867 Oct 8), Chivington Lodge No. 6, Central City

McLain, L B
Proceedings 1861-1869, pg 149 (1865 Nov 7), Nevada Lodge No. 4, Nevadaville
Proceedings 1861-1869, pg 167 (1866 Oct 2) Denver Lodge No. 5, deceased

McLane, J S
Proceedings 1861-1869, pg 150 (1865 Nov 7), Chivington Lodge No. 6, Central City
Proceedings 1861-1869, pg 225 (1868 Oct 7), Chivington Lodge No. 6, Central City, Dimitted

McLaughin, Hiram C
Proceedings 1876, pg 40 (1876 Sept 20), Occidental Lodge No. 20, Greeley

McLaughlin, H C
Proceedings 1875, pg 87 (1875 Sept 22), Occidental Lodge No. 20, Greeley

McLaughlin, Hiram C
Proceedings 1874, pg 225 (1874 Sept 30), Occidental Lodge No. 20, Greeley

McLaughlin, W M
Proceedings 1861-1869, pg 170 (1866 Oct 2), Black Hawk Lodge U D, Black Hawk

McLaughlin, William
Proceedings 1871, pg 23 (1871 Sept 27), Black Hawk Lodge No. 11, Black Hawk
Proceedings 1874, pg 216 (1874 Sept 30), Black Hawk Lodge No. 11, Black Hawk
Proceedings 1876, pg 51 (1876 Sept 20) Black Hawk Lodge No. 11, 1875 Dec 23

McLaughlin, Wm
Proceedings 1861-1869, pg 195 (1867 Oct 8), Black Hawk Lodge No. 11, Black Hawk
Proceedings 1861-1869, pg 227 (1868 Oct 7), Black Hawk Lodge No. 11, Black Hawk
Proceedings 1861-1869, pg 309 (1869 Sept 29), Black Hawk Lodge No. 11, Black Hawk
Proceedings 1870, pg 25 (1870 Sept 28), Black Hawk Lodge No. 11, Black Hawk
Proceedings 1872, pg 25 (1872 Sept 24), Black Hawk Lodge No. 11, Black Hawk
Proceedings 1873, pg 42 (1873 Oct 1), Black Hawk Lodge No. 11, Black Hawk
Proceedings 1875, pg 80 (1875 Sept 22) Black Hawk Lodge No. 11

McLellan, Samuel
Proceedings 1861-1869, pg 193 (1867 Oct 8) Denver Lodge No. 5, Apprentice
Proceedings 1861-1869, pg 167 (1866 Oct 2) Denver Lodge No. 5, Apprentice
Proceedings 1861-1869, pg 78 (1862 Nov 4) Denver Lodge No. 5, Apprentice

McLemore, C C
Proceedings 1861-1869, pg 307 (1869 Sept 29), Union Lodge No. 7, Denver

McLemore, Chris C
Proceedings 1870, pg 24 (1870 Sept 28), Union Lodge No. 7, Denver, Dimitted

McLenore, C C
Proceedings 1861-1869, pg 225 (1868 Oct 7), Union Lodge No. 7, Denver

McLeod, John W
Proceedings 1871, pg 22 (1871 Sept 27), Union Lodge No. 7, Denver
Proceedings 1872, pg 22 (1872 Sept 24), Union Lodge No. 7, Denver
Proceedings 1873, pg 40 (1873 Oct 1), Union Lodge No. 7, Denver
Proceedings 1874, pg 214 (1874 Sept 30), Union Lodge No. 7, Denver
Proceedings 1875, pg 79 (1875 Sept 22), Union Lodge No. 7, Denver, Expelled

McMaster, ____
Proceedings 1871, pg 30 (1871 Sept 27), Occidental Lodge U D, Greeley

McMaster, Alex G
Proceedings 1874, pg 225 (1874 Sept 30), Occidental Lodge No. 20, Greeley
Proceedings 1875, pg 87 (1875 Sept 22), Occidental Lodge No. 20, Greeley

McMasters, Alex G
Proceedings 1876, pg 40 (1876 Sept 20), Occidental Lodge No. 20, Greeley

McMasters, S Y
Proceedings 1861-1869, pg 263 (1868 Oct 22), Grand Chaplain, Grand Lodge of Minnesota

McMinn, J H
Proceedings 1861-1869, pg 312 (1869 Sept 29), Cheyenne Lodge No. 16, Cheyenne
Proceedings 1870, pg 29 (1870 Sept 28), Cheyenne Lodge No. 16, Cheyenne, Wyoming Territory
Proceedings 1871, pg 27 (1871 Sept 27), Cheyenne Lodge No. 16, Cheyenne, Wyoming Territory
Proceedings 1872, pg 30 (1872 Sept 24), Cheyenne Lodge No. 16, Cheyenne, Wyoming Territory, Dimitted

McMurtie, John A
Proceedings 1873, pg 47 (1873 Oct 1), Pueblo Lodge No. 17, Pueblo

McMurtrie, J A
Proceedings 1874, pg 222 (1874 Sept 30), Pueblo Lodge No. 17, Pueblo, Pueblo County
Proceedings 1875, pg 85 (1875 Sept 22) Pueblo Lodge No. 17
Proceedings 1876, pg 39 (1876 Sept 20) Pueblo Lodge No. 17

McNamee, A
Proceedings 1861-1869, pg 134 (1864 Nov 8), Chivington Lodge No. 6, Central City, Apprentice
Proceedings 1861-1869, pg 150 (1865 Nov 7), Chivington Lodge No. 6, Central City, Fellowcraft

Colorado's Territorial Masons

McNamee, A, cont.
Proceedings 1861-1869, pg 169 (1866 Oct 2), Chivington Lodge No. 6, Central City, Apprentice
Proceedings 1861-1869, pg 194 (1867 Oct 8), Chivington Lodge No. 6, Central City
Proceedings 1861-1869, pg 224 (1868 Oct 7), Chivington Lodge No. 6, Central City
Proceedings 1861-1869, pg 306 (1869 Sept 29), Central Lodge No. 6, Central City
Proceedings 1870, pg 22 (1870 Sept 28), Central Lodge No. 6, Central City
Proceedings 1871, pg 20 (1871 Sept 27), Central Lodge No. 6, Central
Proceedings 1872, pg 21 (1872 Sept 24), Denver Lodge No. 5, Denver
Proceedings 1873, pg 38 (1873 Oct 1), Central Lodge No. 6, Central City
Proceedings 1874, pg 213 (1874 Sept 30), Central Lodge No. 6, Central
Proceedings 1875, pg 77 (1875 Sept 22), Central Lodge No. 6, Central City

McNamee, Allen
Proceedings 1871, pg 11 (1871 Sept 26), Central Lodge No. 6, Central City, living in Denver
Proceedings 1876, pg 32 (1876 Sept 20), Central Lodge No. 6, Central City

McNassar, James
Proceedings 1861-1869, pg 112 (1863 Nov 3) Denver Lodge No. 5
Proceedings 1861-1869, pg 167 (1866 Oct 2) Denver Lodge No. 5
Proceedings 1870, pg 21 (1870 Sept 28), Denver Lodge No. 5, Denver
Proceedings 1871, pg 19 (1871 Sept 27) Denver Lodge No. 5
Proceedings 1872, pg 20 (1872 Sept 24), Denver Lodge No. 5, Denver
Proceedings 1876, pg 31 (1876 Sept 20) Denver Lodge No. 5

McNassar, James Sr
Proceedings 1861-1869, pg 192 (1867 Oct 8) Denver Lodge No. 5

McNassar, Jas
Proceedings 1861-1869, pg 149 (1865 Nov 7), Nevada Lodge No. 4, Nevadaville

McNassar, Jas Sr
Proceedings 1861-1869, pg 223 (1868 Oct 7) Denver Lodge No. 5

McNasser, James
Proceedings 1861-1869, pg 77 (1862 Nov 4) Denver Lodge No. 5
Proceedings 1861-1869, pg 305 (1869 Sept 29) Denver Lodge No. 5
Proceedings 1873, pg 37 (1873 Oct 1), Denver Lodge No. 5, Denver
Proceedings 1874, pg 211 (1874 Sept 30), Denver Lodge No. 5, Denver
Proceedings 1875, pg 75 (1875 Sept 22) Denver Lodge No. 5

McNasser, Jas
Proceedings 1861-1869, pg 133 (1864 Nov 8) Denver Lodge No. 5

McNeal, C W
Proceedings 1875, pg 89 (1875 Sept 22), Doric Lodge No. 25, Fairplay

McNeal, Chas W
Proceedings 1876, pg 42 (1876 Sept 20), Doric Lodge No. 25, Fairplay

McNeil, C W
Proceedings 1874, pg 228 (1874 Sept 30), Doric Lodge U D, Fairplay

McPatten, T F
Proceedings 1872, pg 44 (1872 Sept 24) Salem, Grand Lodge of Oregon

McPheeters, W
Proceedings 1871, pg 18 (1871 Sept 27), Nevada Lodge No. 4, Bald Mountain, Apprentice

McPheeters, Wm
Proceedings 1872, pg 19 (1872 Sept 24), Nevada Lodge No. 4, Bald Mountain, Apprentice

McPherson, Jacob R
Proceedings 1874, pg 225 (1874 Sept 30), Occidental Lodge No. 20, Greeley
Proceedings 1875, pg 87 (1875 Sept 22), Occidental Lodge No. 20, Greeley
Proceedings 1876, pg 40 (1876 Sept 20), Occidental Lodge No. 20, Greeley

McPheters, W
Proceedings 1873, pg 36 (1873 Oct 1), Nevada Lodge No. 4, Nevada, Apprentice
Proceedings 1874, pg 210 (1874 Sept 30), Nevada Lodge No. 4, Bald Mountain, Gilpin County, Apprentice
Proceedings 1875, pg 75 (1875 Sept 22), Nevada Lodge No. 4, Nevada, Apprentice

McPheters, William
Proceedings 1876, pg 30 (1876 Sept 20) Nevada Lodge No. 4, Apprentice

McShane, D
Proceedings 1876, pg 36 (1876 Sept 20), El Paso Lodge No. 13, Colorado City

McShane, David
Proceedings 1861-1869, pg 100 (1863 Aug 13), Summit Lodge No. 2, Parkville
Proceedings 1861-1869, pg 111 (1863 Nov 3), Summit Lodge No. 2, Parkville, dimitted
Proceedings 1861-1869, pg 310 (1869 Sept 29), El Paso Lodge No. 13, Colorado City
Proceedings 1870, pg 27 (1870 Sept 28), El Paso Lodge No. 13, Colorado City
Proceedings 1871, pg 25 (1871 Sept 27), El Paso Lodge No. 13, Colorado City

Proceedings 1872, pg 27 (1872 Sept 24), El Paso Lodge No. 13, Colorado City

Proceedings 1873, pg 43 (1873 Oct 1), El Paso Lodge No. 13, Colorado City

Proceedings 1874, pg 218 (1874 Sept 30), El Paso Lodge No. 13, Colorado Springs

Proceedings 1875, pg 82 (1875 Sept 22), El Paso Lodge No. 13, Colorado Springs

Mead, Marcus S
Proceedings 1876, pg 37 (1876 Sept 20), Columbia Lodge No. 14, Boulder

Medairy
Proceedings 1870, pg 66 (1869 Nov 15) Grand Secretary, Grand Lodge of Maryland

Medairy, J H
Proceedings 1870, pg 65 (1869 Nov 15) Grand Secretary, Grand Lodge of Maryland

Proceedings 1872, pg 69 (1872 Sept 24) Grand Lodge of Maryland

Medairy, Jacob H
Proceedings 1861-1869, pg 261 (1868 Oct 7), Grand Secretary, Grand Lodge of Maryland

Proceedings 1861-1869, pg 316 (1869 Sept 29) Grand Lodge of Maryland

Proceedings 1870, pg 34 (1870 Sept 28) Grand Secretary, Grand Lodge of Maryland

Proceedings 1871, pg 35 (1871 Sept 27) Grand Secretary, Grand Lodge of Maryland

Proceedings 1872, pg 43 (1872 Sept 24) Baltimore, Grand Lodge of Maryland

Proceedings 1872, pg 70 (1872 Sept 24) Grand Lodge of Maryland

Proceedings 1873, pg 60 (1873 Oct 1) Grand Lodge of Maryland, Baltimore

Proceedings 1874, pg 79 (1874 Sept 30) Grand Lodge of Maryland

Proceedings 1874, pg 204 (1874 Sept 30) Grand Lodge of Maryland, Baltimore

Proceedings 1875, pg 96 (1875 Sept 22) Grand Lodge of Maryland, Baltimore

Proceedings 1876, pg 54 (1876 Sept 20) Grand Lodge of Maryland, Baltimore

Megath, A C
Proceedings 1861-1869, pg 111 (1863 Nov 3), Nevada Lodge No. 4, Nevadaville

Proceedings 1861-1869, pg 77 (1862 Nov 4), Nevada Lodge No. 4, Nevadaville

Proceedings 1861-1869, pg 132 (1864 Nov 8), Nevada Lodge No. 4, Nevadaville

Proceedings 1861-1869, pg 166 (1866 Oct 2), Nevada Lodge No. 4, Nevadaville

Megowan, William
Proceedings 1873, pg 13 (1873 Sept 30), Ashlar Lodge U D, Colorado Springs

Megowen, William
Proceedings 1874, pg 218 (1874 Sept 30), El Paso Lodge No. 13, Colorado Springs

Mellet, Leon
Proceedings 1861-1869, pg 131 (1864 Nov 8) Golden City Lodge No. 1, Apprentice

Proceedings 1861-1869, pg 191 (1867 Oct 8) Golden City Lodge No. 1, Apprentice,

Mellinet
Proceedings 1870, pg 63 (1870 Feb 14) Grand Master, Grand Orient of France

Mellor, Geo
Proceedings 1861-1869, pg 224 (1868 Oct 7), Chivington Lodge No. 6, Central City

Mellor, George
Proceedings 1861-1869, pg 194 (1867 Oct 8), Chivington Lodge No. 6, Central City

Proceedings 1861-1869, pg 306 (1869 Sept 29), Central Lodge No. 6, Central City

Proceedings 1871, pg 20 (1871 Sept 27), Central Lodge No. 6, Central

Proceedings 1872, pg 21 (1872 Sept 24), Denver Lodge No. 5, Denver

Proceedings 1873, pg 38 (1873 Oct 1), Central Lodge No. 6, Central City

Proceedings 1874, pg 213 (1874 Sept 30), Central Lodge No. 6, Central

Proceedings 1875, pg 77 (1875 Sept 22), Central Lodge No. 6, Central City

Proceedings 1876, pg 32 (1876 Sept 20), Central Lodge No. 6, Central City

Mellow, Geo
Proceedings 1870, pg 22 (1870 Sept 28), Central Lodge No. 6, Central City

Melvin, John G
Proceedings 1861-1869, pg 308 (1869 Sept 29), Union Lodge No. 7, Denver, Apprentice

Proceedings 1870, pg 24 (1870 Sept 28), Union Lodge No. 7, Denver, Apprentice

Proceedings 1871, pg 22 (1871 Sept 27), Union Lodge No. 7, Denver, Apprentice

Proceedings 1872, pg 23 (1872 Sept 24), Union Lodge No. 7, Denver, Apprentice

Proceedings 1873, pg 40 (1873 Oct 1), Union Lodge No. 7, Denver, Apprentice

Proceedings 1874, pg 214 (1874 Sept 30), Union Lodge No. 7, Denver, Fellowcraft

Proceedings 1875, pg 79 (1875 Sept 22), Union Lodge No. 7, Denver, Fellowcraft

Proceedings 1876, pg 33 (1876 Sept 20), Union Lodge No. 7, Denver, Fellow Craft,

Memfi Resorta
Proceedings 1875, pg 23 (1875 Sept 21), published at Alexandria, Egypt

Memfi Restora
Proceedings 1876, pg 12 (1876 Sept 19), published at Alexandria, Egypt

Mentzer, John
Proceedings 1861-1869, pg 43 (1861 Dec 10), Summit Lodge No. 2, Parkville

Colorado's Territorial Masons

Mentzer, John, cont.
　Proceedings 1861-1869, pg 76 (1862 Nov 4), Summit Lodge No. 2, Parkville, Deceased

Meper, Ferdinand
　Proceedings 1871, pg 22 (1871 Sept 27), Union Lodge No. 7, Denver

Merchant, L
　Proceedings 1861-1869, pg 113 (1863 Nov 3), Chivington Lodge No. 6, Central City
　Proceedings 1861-1869, pg 134 (1864 Nov 8), Chivington Lodge No. 6, Central City
　Proceedings 1861-1869, pg 150 (1865 Nov 7), Chivington Lodge No. 6, Central City
　Proceedings 1861-1869, pg 168 (1866 Oct 2), Chivington Lodge No. 6, Central City

Merchant, Leonard
　Proceedings 1861-1869, pg 78 (1862 Nov 4), Chivington Lodge No. 6, Central City, Apprentice
　Proceedings 1861-1869, pg 194 (1867 Oct 8), Chivington Lodge No. 6, Central City, Died

Merrand, John
　Proceedings 1870, pg 76 (1789 June 4), a black minister from Beech Town, Nova Scotia

Merrell, C H
　Proceedings 1861-1869, pg 166 (1866 Oct 2), Nevada Lodge No. 4, Nevadaville, Fellowcraft

Merriam, William R
　Proceedings 1870, pg 94 (1870 June 7) Grand Lodge of New York, deceased

Merrick, T D
　Proceedings 1861-1869, pg 157 (1866 Oct 1), deceased, Grand Secretary, Grand Lodge of Arkansas

Merrill, C H
　Proceedings 1861-1869, pg 132 (1864 Nov 8), Nevada Lodge No. 4, Nevadaville, Fellowcraft
　Proceedings 1861-1869, pg 148 (1865 Nov 7), Nevada Lodge No. 4, Nevadaville, Fellowcraft
　Proceedings 1861-1869, pg 192 (1867 Oct 8), Nevada Lodge No. 4, Nevadaville, Fellowcraft
　Proceedings 1861-1869, pg 222 (1868 Oct 7), Nevada Lodge No. 4, Nevadaville, Fellowcraft

Merriman, J F
　Proceedings 1871, pg 22 (1871 Sept 27), Union Lodge No. 7, Denver

Merriman, John F
　Proceedings 1872, pg 23 (1872 Sept 24), Union Lodge No. 7, Denver
　Proceedings 1873, pg 40 (1873 Oct 1), Union Lodge No. 7, Denver
　Proceedings 1874, pg 214 (1874 Sept 30), Union Lodge No. 7, Denver
　Proceedings 1875, pg 79 (1875 Sept 22), Union Lodge No. 7, Denver, died

Merrman, John F
　Proceedings 1875, pg 94 (1875 Sept 22), Union Lodge No. 7, Denver

Meserve, F
　Proceedings 1861-1869, pg 133 (1864 Nov 8) Denver Lodge No. 5
　Proceedings 1861-1869, pg 167 (1866 Oct 2) Denver Lodge No. 5
　Proceedings 1861-1869, pg 192 (1867 Oct 8) Denver Lodge No. 5
　Proceedings 1861-1869, pg 305 (1869 Sept 29) Denver Lodge No. 5
　Proceedings 1870, pg 21 (1870 Sept 28), Denver Lodge No. 5, Denver

Meserve, Foster
　Proceedings 1861-1869, pg 223 (1868 Oct 7) Denver Lodge No. 5
　Proceedings 1873, pg 38 (1873 Oct 1), Denver Lodge No. 5, Denver, Striken from the rolls

Messler, W P
　Proceedings 1872, pg 34 (1872 Sept 24), Occidental Lodge No. 20, Greeley, Dimitted

Metcalf, A T
　Proceedings 1861-1869, pg 332 (1868 Nov 16) Grand Master, Grand Lodge of Maryland
　Proceedings 1861-1869, pg 333 (1869 Jan 13) Grand Master, Grand Lodge of Michigan
　Proceedings 1870, pg 77 (1870 Jan 12) Grand Master, Grand Lodge of Michigan

Metcalf, Eli P
　Proceedings 1873, pg 44 (1873 Oct 1), Columbia Lodge No. 14, Boulder
　Proceedings 1874, pg 219 (1874 Sept 30), Columbia Lodge No. 14, Boulder, Boulder County
　Proceedings 1875, pg 83 (1875 Sept 22), Columbia Lodge No. 14, Boulder
　Proceedings 1876, pg 37 (1876 Sept 20), Columbia Lodge No. 14, Boulder

Meyer, Ferd
　Proceedings 1874, pg 214 (1874 Sept 30), Union Lodge No. 7, Denver

Meyer, Ferdinand
　Proceedings 1861-1869, pg 307 (1869 Sept 29), Union Lodge No. 7, Denver
　Proceedings 1870, pg 23 (1870 Sept 28), Union Lodge No. 7, Denver
　Proceedings 1872, pg 23 (1872 Sept 24), Union Lodge No. 7, Denver
　Proceedings 1873, pg 40 (1873 Oct 1), Union Lodge No. 7, Denver
　Proceedings 1875, pg 78 (1875 Sept 22), Union Lodge No. 7, Denver
　Proceedings 1876, pg 33 (1876 Sept 20), Union Lodge No. 7, Denver

Meyer, Frank
　Proceedings 1861-1869, pg 42 (1861 Dec 10), Summit Lodge No. 2, Parkville

Meyer, John L
　Proceedings 1876, pg 24 (1876 Sept 20), Del Norte Lodge No. 29, Del Norte

Proceedings 1876, pg 44 (1876 Sept 20) Del Norte Lodge U D

Michaut, Theodore
Proceedings 1876, pg 37 (1876 Sept 20), Columbia Lodge No. 14, Boulder, Apprentice,

Michigan Freemason
Proceedings 1870, pg 11 (1870 Sept 27), Kalamazoo, MI
Proceedings 1871, pg 10 (1871 Sept 26) masonic magazine
Proceedings 1872, pg 11 (1872 Sept 24), published at Kalamazoo, MI
Proceedings 1873, pg 15 (1873 Oct 1), published at Kalamazoo, MI
Proceedings 1874, pg 19 (1874 Sept 29), published at Kalamazoo, MI
Proceedings 1875, pg 23 (1875 Sept 21), published at Kalamazoo, MI
Proceedings 1876, pg 11 (1876 Sept 19), published at Kalamazoo, MI

Mickel, Reuben
Proceedings 1861-1869, pg 248 (1867 June 4), Grand Master, Grand Lodge of Iowa
Proceedings 1861-1869, pg 250 (1867 June 4), Grand Master, Grand Lodge of Iowa
Proceedings 1861-1869, pg 330 (1868 June 2) Grand Master, Grand Lodge of Iowa

Miksch, A C
Proceedings 1874, pg 226 (1874 Sept 30), Weston Lodge No. 22, Littleton

Miles, John
Proceedings 1876, pg 44 (1876 Sept 20) Del Norte Lodge U D

Milier, Asa L
Proceedings 1873, pg 19 (1873 Oct 1), Nevada Lodge No. 4, Bald Mountain, has been dead for 3 years

Miliken, Robert
Proceedings 1871, pg 18 (1871 Sept 27), Nevada Lodge No. 4, Bald Mountain

Millar, W L H
Proceedings 1876, pg 31 (1876 Sept 20) Denver Lodge No. 5

Miller, A L
Proceedings 1861-1869, pg 99 (1863 Nov 2), Nevada Lodge No. 4, Nevadaville, Grand Tyler
Proceedings 1861-1869, pg 111 (1863 Nov 3), Nevada Lodge No. 4, Nevadaville
Proceedings 1861-1869, pg 119 (1864 Feb 13) warrant drawn
Proceedings 1861-1869, pg 192 (1867 Oct 8), Nevada Lodge No. 4, Nevadaville
Proceedings 1861-1869, pg 222 (1868 Oct 7), Nevada Lodge No. 4, Nevadaville
Proceedings 1861-1869, pg 304 (1869 Sept 29), Nevada Lodge No. 4, Nevadaville

Miller, Asa L
Proceedings 1861-1869, pg 132 (1864 Nov 8), Nevada Lodge No. 4, Nevadaville
Proceedings 1861-1869, pg 148 (1865 Nov 7), Nevada Lodge No. 4, Nevadaville
Proceedings 1861-1869, pg 166 (1866 Oct 2), Nevada Lodge No. 4, Nevadaville
Proceedings 1870, pg 20 (1870 Sept 28), Nevada Lodge No. 4, Nevadaville
Proceedings 1871, pg 18 (1871 Sept 27), Nevada Lodge No. 4, Bald Mountain
Proceedings 1872, pg 19 (1872 Sept 24), Nevada Lodge No. 4, Bald Mountain
Proceedings 1873, pg 36 (1873 Oct 1), Nevada Lodge No. 4, Nevada
Proceedings 1874, pg 211 (1874 Sept 30), Nevada Lodge No. 4, Bald Mountain, Gilpin County, died

Miller, D W
Proceedings 1874, pg 227 (1874 Sept 30), St Vrain No. 23, Longmont
Proceedings 1876, pg 41 (1876 Sept 20), St Vrain Lodge No. 23, Longmont

Miller, David
Proceedings 1872, pg 35 (1872 Sept 24), St Vrain Lodge No. 23, Longmont

Miller, David W
Proceedings 1870, pg 28 (1870 Sept 28), Columbia Lodge No. 14, Boulder City, Fellowcraft
Proceedings 1871, pg 26 (1871 Sept 27), Columbia Lodge No. 14, Boulder City
Proceedings 1872, pg 28 (1872 Sept 24), Columbia Lodge No. 14, Boulder
Proceedings 1873, pg 45 (1873 Oct 1), Columbia Lodge No. 14, Boulder, Dimitted
Proceedings 1873, pg 51 (1873 Oct 1), St Vrain Lodge No. 23, Longmont

Miller, G W
Proceedings 1861-1869, pg 222 (1868 Oct 7), Nevada Lodge No. 4, Nevadaville, Apprentice

Miller, Geo W
Proceedings 1861-1869, pg 148 (1865 Nov 7), Nevada Lodge No. 4, Nevadaville, Apprentice
Proceedings 1861-1869, pg 166 (1866 Oct 2), Nevada Lodge No. 4, Nevadaville, Apprentice
Proceedings 1861-1869, pg 192 (1867 Oct 8), Nevada Lodge No. 4, Nevadaville, Apprentice

Miller, H H
Proceedings 1861-1869, pg 169 (1866 Oct 2), Chivington Lodge No. 6, Central City, Fellowcraft
Proceedings 1861-1869, pg 194 (1867 Oct 8), Chivington Lodge No. 6, Central City
Proceedings 1861-1869, pg 224 (1868 Oct 7), Chivington Lodge No. 6, Central City
Proceedings 1861-1869, pg 306 (1869 Sept 29), Central Lodge No. 6, Central City
Proceedings 1870, pg 22 (1870 Sept 28), Central Lodge No. 6, Central City
Proceedings 1871, pg 20 (1871 Sept 27), Central Lodge No. 6, Central
Proceedings 1872, pg 21 (1872 Sept 24), Denver Lodge No. 5, Denver

Miller, H J
Proceedings 1874, pg 213 (1874 Sept 30), Union Lodge No. 7, Denver
Proceedings 1875, pg 78 (1875 Sept 22), Union Lodge No. 7, Denver
Proceedings 1876, pg 33 (1876 Sept 20), Union Lodge No. 7, Denver

Miller, Hiram H
Proceedings 1873, pg 38 (1873 Oct 1), Central Lodge No. 6, Central City
Proceedings 1874, pg 213 (1874 Sept 30), Central Lodge No. 6, Central
Proceedings 1875, pg 77 (1875 Sept 22), Central Lodge No. 6, Central City
Proceedings 1876, pg 32 (1876 Sept 20), Central Lodge No. 6, Central City
Proceedings 1876, pg 50 (1876 Sept 20), Central Lodge No. 6, Central City

Miller, J D
Proceedings 1861-1869, pg 229 (1868 Oct 7), Pueblo Lodge U D, Pueblo
Proceedings 1861-1869, pg 312 (1869 Sept 29), Pueblo Lodge No. 17, Pueblo
Proceedings 1870, pg 29 (1870 Sept 28), Pueblo Lodge No. 17, Pueblo
Proceedings 1871, pg 28 (1871 Sept 27), Pueblo Lodge No. 17, Pueblo
Proceedings 1872, pg 30 (1872 Sept 24), Pueblo Lodge No. 17, Pueblo
Proceedings 1874, pg 222 (1874 Sept 30), Pueblo Lodge No. 17, Pueblo, Pueblo County
Proceedings 1875, pg 85 (1875 Sept 22) Pueblo Lodge No. 17
Proceedings 1876, pg 39 (1876 Sept 20) Pueblo Lodge No. 17

Miller, James F
Proceedings 1873, pg 61 (1873 Oct 1) Grand Lodge of Texas, Gonzales
Proceedings 1874, pg 124 (1874 Sept 30) Grand Lodge of Texas

Miller, John D
Proceedings 1873, pg 47 (1873 Oct 1), Pueblo Lodge No. 17, Pueblo

Miller, John H
Proceedings 1861-1869, pg 196 (1867 Oct 8), Black Hawk Lodge No. 11, Black Hawk, Fellowcraft
Proceedings 1861-1869, pg 227 (1868 Oct 7), Black Hawk Lodge No. 11, Black Hawk

Miller, Joshua
Proceedings 1861-1869, pg 5 (1861 Aug 2) Senior Grand Deacon, Parkville
Proceedings 1861-1869, pg 42 (1861 Dec 10), Summit Lodge No. 2, Parkville
Proceedings 1861-1869, pg 76 (1862 Nov 4), Summit Lodge No. 2, Parkville, dimitted

Miller, Loring P
Proceedings 1872, pg 21 (1872 Sept 24), Denver Lodge No. 5, Denver

Proceedings 1873, pg 38 (1873 Oct 1), Central Lodge No. 6, Central City
Proceedings 1874, pg 213 (1874 Sept 30), Central Lodge No. 6, Central
Proceedings 1875, pg 77 (1875 Sept 22), Central Lodge No. 6, Central City
Proceedings 1876, pg 32 (1876 Sept 20), Central Lodge No. 6, Central City

Miller, Louis
Proceedings 1870, pg 30 (1870 Sept 28), Laramie Lodge No. 18, Laramie, Wyoming Territory
Proceedings 1871, pg 29 (1871 Sept 27), Laramie Lodge No. 18, Laramie, Wyoming Territory
Proceedings 1872, pg 31 (1872 Sept 24), Laramie Lodge No. 18, Laramie, Wyoming Territory
Proceedings 1873, pg 48 (1873 Oct 1), Laramie Lodge No. 18, Laramie, Wyoming Territory
Proceedings 1874, pg 223 (1874 Sept 30), Laramie Lodge No. 18, Laramie City

Miller, N C
Proceedings 1861-1869, pg 170 (1866 Oct 2), El Paso U D, Colorado City
Proceedings 1861-1869, pg 196 (1867 Oct 8), El Paso Lodge U D, Colorado City
Proceedings 1870, pg 27 (1870 Sept 28), El Paso Lodge No. 13, Colorado City
Proceedings 1871, pg 25 (1871 Sept 27), El Paso Lodge No. 13, Colorado City
Proceedings 1872, pg 27 (1872 Sept 24), El Paso Lodge No. 13, Colorado City
Proceedings 1873, pg 43 (1873 Oct 1), El Paso Lodge No. 13, Colorado City
Proceedings 1874, pg 218 (1874 Sept 30), El Paso Lodge No. 13, Colorado Springs
Proceedings 1875, pg 82 (1875 Sept 22), El Paso Lodge No. 13, Colorado Springs, Stricken from the rolls

Miller, R A
Proceedings 1874, pg 223 (1874 Sept 30), Laramie Lodge No. 18, Laramie City

Miller, R T
Proceedings 1872, pg 43 (1872 Sept 24) Silver City, Grand Lodge of Idaho

Miller, Robert A
Proceedings 1873, pg 48 (1873 Oct 1), Laramie Lodge No. 18, Laramie, Wyoming Territory, Apprentice

Miller, U U
Proceedings 1876, pg 44 (1876 Sept 20) Del Norte Lodge U D

Miller, W L H
Proceedings 1874, pg 212 (1874 Sept 30), Denver Lodge No. 5, Denver
Proceedings 1875, pg 75 (1875 Sept 22) Denver Lodge No. 5

Millerson, E
Proceedings 1861-1869, pg 151 (1865 Nov 7), Chivington Lodge No. 6, Central City
Proceedings 1875, pg 79 (1875 Sept 22), Union Lodge No. 7, Denver, Stricken from the rolls

Millerson, Elisha
- Proceedings 1861-1869, pg 134 (1864 Nov 8), Union Lodge No. 7, Denver
- Proceedings 1861-1869, pg 169 (1866 Oct 2), Union Lodge No. 7, Denver
- Proceedings 1861-1869, pg 195 (1867 Oct 8), Union Lodge No. 7, Denver
- Proceedings 1870, pg 23 (1870 Sept 28), Union Lodge No. 7, Denver

Milleson, Elisha
- Proceedings 1873, pg 40 (1873 Oct 1), Union Lodge No. 7, Denver

Milliken, Robert
- Proceedings 1861-1869, pg 132 (1864 Nov 8), Nevada Lodge No. 4, Nevadaville
- Proceedings 1861-1869, pg 148 (1865 Nov 7), Nevada Lodge No. 4, Nevadaville
- Proceedings 1861-1869, pg 166 (1866 Oct 2), Nevada Lodge No. 4, Nevadaville
- Proceedings 1870, pg 20 (1870 Sept 28), Nevada Lodge No. 4, Nevadaville
- Proceedings 1872, pg 19 (1872 Sept 24), Nevada Lodge No. 4, Bald Mountain
- Proceedings 1873, pg 36 (1873 Oct 1), Nevada Lodge No. 4, Nevada
- Proceedings 1875, pg 74 (1875 Sept 22), Nevada Lodge No. 4, Nevada
- Proceedings 1876, pg 30 (1876 Sept 20) Nevada Lodge No. 4

Milliken, Robt
- Proceedings 1861-1869, pg 192 (1867 Oct 8), Nevada Lodge No. 4, Nevadaville

Millikin, Robert
- Proceedings 1861-1869, pg 222 (1868 Oct 7), Nevada Lodge No. 4, Nevadaville
- Proceedings 1861-1869, pg 304 (1869 Sept 29), Nevada Lodge No. 4, Nevadaville
- Proceedings 1870, pg 19 (1870 Sept 28), Golden City Lodge No. 1, Golden City, Not a member
- Proceedings 1874, pg 210 (1874 Sept 30), Nevada Lodge No. 4, Bald Mountain, Gilpin County

Millison, Elisha
- Proceedings 1861-1869, pg 225 (1868 Oct 7), Union Lodge No. 7, Denver
- Proceedings 1861-1869, pg 307 (1869 Sept 29), Union Lodge No. 7, Denver
- Proceedings 1871, pg 22 (1871 Sept 27), Union Lodge No. 7, Denver
- Proceedings 1872, pg 23 (1872 Sept 24), Union Lodge No. 7, Denver
- Proceedings 1874, pg 214 (1874 Sept 30), Union Lodge No. 7, Denver

Mills, Abraham
- Proceedings 1876, pg 30 (1876 Sept 20) Nevada Lodge No. 4

Mills, Abram
- Proceedings 1861-1869, pg 196 (1867 Oct 8), Columbia Lodge U D, Boulder
- Proceedings 1861-1869, pg 228 (1868 Oct 7), Columbia Lodge No. 14, Columbia City
- Proceedings 1861-1869, pg 311 (1869 Sept 29), Columbia Lodge No. 14, Boulder City
- Proceedings 1871, pg 26 (1871 Sept 27), Columbia Lodge No. 14, Boulder City
- Proceedings 1872, pg 28 (1872 Sept 24), Columbia Lodge No. 14, Boulder
- Proceedings 1873, pg 44 (1873 Oct 1), Columbia Lodge No. 14, Boulder
- Proceedings 1874, pg 219 (1874 Sept 30), Columbia Lodge No. 14, Boulder, Boulder County
- Proceedings 1875, pg 83 (1875 Sept 22), Columbia Lodge No. 14, Boulder, Stricken from the rolls
- Proceedings 1876, pg 48 (1876 Sept 20), Columbia Lodge No. 14, Boulder, 1875 Dec 3
- Proceedings 1876, pg 51 (1876 Sept 20), Columbia Lodge No. 14, Boulder, 1875 Dec 3

Mills, Abt
- Proceedings 1870, pg 27 (1870 Sept 28), Columbia Lodge No. 14, Boulder City

Mills, G H
- Proceedings 1861-1869, pg 195 (1867 Oct 8), Union Lodge No. 7, Denver
- Proceedings 1861-1869, pg 225 (1868 Oct 7), Union Lodge No. 7, Denver

Mills, Geo A
- Proceedings 1870, pg 23 (1870 Sept 28), Union Lodge No. 7, Denver
- Proceedings 1875, pg 81 (1875 Sept 22), Washington Lodge No. 12, Georgetown

Mills, Geo H
- Proceedings 1861-1869, pg 169 (1866 Oct 2), Union Lodge No. 7, Denver, Apprentice
- Proceedings 1861-1869, pg 307 (1869 Sept 29), Union Lodge No. 7, Denver
- Proceedings 1872, pg 23 (1872 Sept 24), Union Lodge No. 7, Denver
- Proceedings 1875, pg 78 (1875 Sept 22), Union Lodge No. 7, Denver

Mills, George A
- Proceedings 1874, pg 217 (1874 Sept 30), Washington Lodge No. 12, Georgetown
- Proceedings 1876, pg 35 (1876 Sept 20), Washington Lodge No. 12, Georgetown

Mills, George H
- Proceedings 1871, pg 22 (1871 Sept 27), Union Lodge No. 7, Denver
- Proceedings 1873, pg 40 (1873 Oct 1), Union Lodge No. 7, Denver
- Proceedings 1874, pg 214 (1874 Sept 30), Union Lodge No. 7, Denver
- Proceedings 1876, pg 33 (1876 Sept 20), Union Lodge No. 7, Denver

Mills, J H
- Proceedings 1873, pg 61 (1873 Oct 1) Grand Lodge of North Carolina, Raleigh

Colorado's Territorial Masons

Mills, James
    Proceedings 1861-1869, pg 196 (1867 Oct 8), Black Hawk Lodge No. 11, Black Hawk, Apprentice
    Proceedings 1861-1869, pg 227 (1868 Oct 7), Black Hawk Lodge No. 11, Black Hawk
    Proceedings 1861-1869, pg 309 (1869 Sept 29), Black Hawk Lodge No. 11, Black Hawk
    Proceedings 1870, pg 25 (1870 Sept 28), Black Hawk Lodge No. 11, Black Hawk
    Proceedings 1871, pg 23 (1871 Sept 27), Black Hawk Lodge No. 11, Black Hawk
    Proceedings 1872, pg 25 (1872 Sept 24), Black Hawk Lodge No. 11, Black Hawk
    Proceedings 1873, pg 42 (1873 Oct 1), Black Hawk Lodge No. 11, Black Hawk
    Proceedings 1874, pg 216 (1874 Sept 30), Black Hawk Lodge No. 11, Black Hawk
    Proceedings 1875, pg 80 (1875 Sept 22) Black Hawk Lodge No. 11, Stricken from the rolls

Mills, S L
    Proceedings 1874, pg 6 (1874 Sept 29), Laramie Lodge No. 18, Laramie, Wyoming Territory
    Proceedings 1874, pg 223 (1874 Sept 30), Laramie Lodge No. 18, Laramie City

Mills, Sydenham
    Proceedings 1875, pg 89 (1875 Sept 22), Doric Lodge No. 25, Fairplay

Mills, Sydham
    Proceedings 1876, pg 42 (1876 Sept 20), Doric Lodge No. 25, Fairplay

Miner, Orlin H
    Proceedings 1861-1869, pg 328 (1868 Oct 6) Grand Secretary, Grand Lodge of Illinois
    Proceedings 1872, pg 43 (1872 Sept 24) Springfield, Grand Lodge of Illinois
    Proceedings 1872, pg 62 (1872 Sept 24) Grand Lodge of Illinois
    Proceedings 1874, pg 61 (1874 Sept 30) Grand Lodge of Illinois

Miner, William B
    Proceedings 1876, pg 39 (1876 Sept 20), Collins Lodge No. 19, Fort Collins

Minor, Orlin H
    Proceedings 1861-1869, pg 316 (1869 Sept 29) Grand Lodge of Illinois
    Proceedings 1870, pg 34 (1870 Sept 28) Grand Secretary, Grand Lodge of Illinois
    Proceedings 1871, pg 35 (1871 Sept 27) Grand Secretary, Grand Lodge of Illinois

Mirch, A C
    Proceedings 1873, pg 51 (1873 Oct 1), Weston Lodge No. 22, Littleton

Misch, A C
    Proceedings 1875, pg 88 (1875 Sept 22), Weston Lodge No. 22, Littleton
    Proceedings 1876, pg 41 (1876 Sept 20), Weston Lodge No. 22, Littleton

Mischler, Samuel
    Proceedings 1875, pg 80 (1875 Sept 22) Black Hawk Lodge No. 11
    Proceedings 1876, pg 34 (1876 Sept 20) Black Hawk Lodge No. 11

Mishler, Samuel
    Proceedings 1871, pg 23 (1871 Sept 27), Black Hawk Lodge No. 11, Black Hawk
    Proceedings 1873, pg 42 (1873 Oct 1), Black Hawk Lodge No. 11, Black Hawk
    Proceedings 1874, pg 216 (1874 Sept 30), Black Hawk Lodge No. 11, Black Hawk

Mitchell
    Proceedings 1872, pg 79 (1872 Sept 24) Grand Lodge of Nevada

Mitchell, E Cappee
    Proceedings 1874, pg 205 (1874 Sept 30) Grand Lodge of Pennsylvania, Philadelphia

Mitchell, Edward
    Proceedings 1870, pg 49 (1869 July 14) Grand Lodge of Canada
    Proceedings 1872, pg 43 (1872 Sept 24) Hamilton, Grand Lodge of Canada
    Proceedings 1873, pg 60 (1873 Oct 1) Grand Lodge of Canada, Hamilton

Mitchell, Emory F
    Proceedings 1870, pg 92 (1869 Sept 21) Grand Lodge of Nevada, deceased

Mitchell, J H
    Proceedings 1861-1869, pg 148 (1865 Nov 7), Nevada Lodge No. 4, Nevadaville
    Proceedings 1861-1869, pg 166 (1866 Oct 2), Nevada Lodge No. 4, Nevadaville
    Proceedings 1861-1869, pg 192 (1867 Oct 8), Nevada Lodge No. 4, Nevadaville, Dimitted

Mitchell, John H
    Proceedings 1861-1869, pg 132 (1864 Nov 8), Nevada Lodge No. 4, Nevadaville

Mitchell, Julius
    Proceedings 1861-1869, pg 149 (1865 Nov 7), Nevada Lodge No. 4, Nevadaville
    Proceedings 1861-1869, pg 192 (1867 Oct 8) Denver Lodge No. 5
    Proceedings 1861-1869, pg 223 (1868 Oct 7) Denver Lodge No. 5
    Proceedings 1861-1869, pg 230 (1868 Oct 7), Germania Lodge U D, Denver
    Proceedings 1861-1869, pg 305 (1869 Sept 29) Denver Lodge No. 5
    Proceedings 1870, pg 21 (1870 Sept 28), Denver Lodge No. 5, Denver
    Proceedings 1871, pg 19 (1871 Sept 27) Denver Lodge No. 5
    Proceedings 1872, pg 20 (1872 Sept 24) Denver Lodge No. 5, Denver
    Proceedings 1873, pg 37 (1873 Oct 1), Denver Lodge No. 5, Denver

Proceedings 1874, pg 211 (1874 Sept 30), Denver Lodge No. 5, Denver

Proceedings 1875, pg 76 (1875 Sept 22) Denver Lodge No. 5, Stricken from the rolls

Proceedings 1876, pg 31 (1876 Sept 20) Denver Lodge No. 5

Proceedings 1876, pg 51 (1876 Sept 20) Denver Lodge No. 5, 1875 Sept 4

Mitchell, S

Proceedings 1861-1869, pg 176 (1867 Oct 7) Denver Lodge No. 5

Mitchell, Sam'l J

Proceedings 1871, pg 19 (1871 Sept 27) Denver Lodge No. 5

Proceedings 1873, pg 37 (1873 Oct 1), Denver Lodge No. 5, Denver, Dimitted

Mitchell, Samuel

Proceedings 1861-1869, pg 167 (1866 Oct 2) Denver Lodge No. 5

Proceedings 1861-1869, pg 192 (1867 Oct 8) Denver Lodge No. 5

Proceedings 1861-1869, pg 223 (1868 Oct 7) Denver Lodge No. 5

Proceedings 1861-1869, pg 305 (1869 Sept 29) Denver Lodge No. 5

Mitchell, Samuel J

Proceedings 1870, pg 21 (1870 Sept 28), Denver Lodge No. 5, Denver

Proceedings 1872, pg 20 (1872 Sept 24), Denver Lodge No. 5, Denver

Proceedings 1875, pg 77 (1875 Sept 22), Central Lodge No. 6, Central City

Proceedings 1876, pg 48 (1876 Sept 20), Central Lodge No. 6, Central City, 1876 Mar 22

Mitchell, Thomas

Proceedings 1876, pg 45 (1876 Sept 20) South Pueblo Lodge U D

Mittnacht, Henry

Proceedings 1861-1869, pg 77 (1862 Nov 4) Denver Lodge No. 5

Proceedings 1861-1869, pg 92 (1863 Apr 17) Denver Lodge No. 5

Proceedings 1861-1869, pg 112 (1863 Nov 3) Denver Lodge No. 5, dimitted

Mize, George W

Proceedings 1876, pg 42 (1876 Sept 20) Idaho Springs Lodge No. 26

Mize, John

Proceedings 1876, pg 29 (1876 Sept 20) Golden City Lodge No. 1

Mize, Peter

Proceedings 1875, pg 73 (1875 Sept 22) Golden City Lodge No. 1

Mochel, Geo L

Proceedings 1874, pg 214 (1874 Sept 30), Union Lodge No. 7, Denver

Proceedings 1875, pg 78 (1875 Sept 22), Union Lodge No. 7, Denver

Mochel, George L

Proceedings 1876, pg 33 (1876 Sept 20), Union Lodge No. 7, Denver

Moe, L S

Proceedings 1861-1869, pg 312 (1869 Sept 29), Cheyenne Lodge No. 16, Cheyenne

Moffatt, G W

Proceedings 1873, pg 46 (1873 Oct 1), Cheyenne Lodge No. 16, Cheyenne, Wyoming Territory

Proceedings 1874, pg 221 (1874 Sept 30), Cheyenne Lodge No. 16, Cheyenne, Wyoming Territory, Demitted

Moffit, John

Proceedings 1861-1869, pg 152 (1865 Nov 7), Helena City Lodge U D, Helena City, Montana Territory

Mohlsan, J

Proceedings 1861-1869, pg 223 (1868 Oct 7) Denver Lodge No. 5, Apprentice

Molsen, J

Proceedings 1861-1869, pg 193 (1867 Oct 8) Denver Lodge No. 5, Apprentice

Molson, J

Proceedings 1861-1869, pg 305 (1869 Sept 29) Denver Lodge No. 5, Apprentice

Molyneaux, E

Proceedings 1875, pg 81 (1875 Sept 22), Washington Lodge No. 12, Georgetown, Demitted

Monroe, Geo W

Proceedings 1875, pg 81 (1875 Sept 22), Washington Lodge No. 12, Georgetown

Monroe, George W

Proceedings 1874, pg 217 (1874 Sept 30), Washington Lodge No. 12, Georgetown

Proceedings 1876, pg 35 (1876 Sept 20), Washington Lodge No. 12, Georgetown

Montana City Lodge No. 9

Proceedings 1875, pg 79 (1875 Sept 22) Grand Lodge of Montana

Montana Lodge No. 2, Virginia City

Proceedings 1870, pg 24 (1870 Sept 28) under the jurisdiction of the Grand Lodge of Montana

Montana Lodge No. 9

Proceedings 1861-1869, pg 141 (1865 Nov 7) granted charter

Proceedings 1861-1869, pg 155 (1866 Oct 1) communication

Proceedings 1861-1869, pg 181 (1867 Oct 7) charter returned

Proceedings 1861-1869, pg 308 (1869 Sept 29) Under the jurisdiction of the Grand Lodge of Montana

Proceedings 1875, pg 20 (1875 Sept 21) Grand Lodge of Montana

Proceedings 1876, pg 46 (1876 Sept 20), Montana Lodge No. 2, Grand Lodge of Montana

Colorado's Territorial Masons

Montana Lodge No. 9, Virginia City
Proceedings 1871, pg 22 (1871 Sept 27) Grand Lodge of Montana
Proceedings 1872, pg 24 (1872 Sept 24) Grand Lodge of Montana
Proceedings 1873, pg 41 (1873 Oct 1), now Montana Lodge No. 2, Grand Lodge of Montana

Montana Lodge No. 9, Virginia City, Montana Terr
Proceedings 1861-1869, pg 226 (1868 Oct 7) Under the jurisdiction of the Grand Lodge of Montana

Montana Lodge No. 9, Virginia City, Montana Territory
Proceedings 1874, pg 215 (1874 Sept 30), now Montana Lodge No. 2, Grand Lodge of Montana

Montana Lodge U D
Proceedings 1861-1869, pg 139 (1865 Apr 4), Montana Lodge U D, Virginia City, Montana Territory
Proceedings 1861-1869, pg 139 (1865 Apr 4) dispensation
Proceedings 1861-1869, pg 139 (1865 Nov 6) requesting charter
Proceedings 1861-1869, pg 139 (1865 Oct 15) petition for charter

Montezume Lodge No. 209, Santa Fe, New Mexico
Proceedings 1861-1869, pg 178 (1867 Mar 4) communication received

Montgomery, J C
Proceedings 1871, pg 19 (1871 Sept 27) Denver Lodge No. 5
Proceedings 1872, pg 19 (1872 Sept 24), Denver Lodge No. 5, Denver

Montgomery, J G
Proceedings 1876, pg 31 (1876 Sept 20) Denver Lodge No. 5

Montgomery, John G
Proceedings 1870, pg 29 (1870 Sept 28), Cheyenne Lodge No. 16, Cheyenne, Wyoming Territory, permission given to take degrees elsewhere
Proceedings 1873, pg 37 (1873 Oct 1), Denver Lodge No. 5, Denver
Proceedings 1874, pg 212 (1874 Sept 30), Denver Lodge No. 5, Denver
Proceedings 1875, pg 76 (1875 Sept 22) Denver Lodge No. 5

Monti, Joshua
Proceedings 1871, pg 24 (1871 Sept 27), Washington Lodge No. 12, Georgetown
Proceedings 1872, pg 26 (1872 Sept 24), Washington Lodge No. 12, Georgetown
Proceedings 1873, pg 42 (1873 Oct 1), Washington Lodge No. 12, Georgetown
Proceedings 1874, pg 217 (1874 Sept 30), Washington Lodge No. 12, Georgetown
Proceedings 1875, pg 81 (1875 Sept 22), Washington Lodge No. 12, Georgetown
Proceedings 1876, pg 35 (1876 Sept 20), Washington Lodge No. 12, Georgetown

Moodie, Charles A
Proceedings 1876, pg 40 (1876 Sept 20), Occidental Lodge No. 20, Greeley

Moody, G L
Proceedings 1861-1869, pg 149 (1865 Nov 7), Nevada Lodge No. 4, Nevadaville
Proceedings 1861-1869, pg 167 (1866 Oct 2) Denver Lodge No. 5
Proceedings 1861-1869, pg 223 (1868 Oct 7) Denver Lodge No. 5
Proceedings 1861-1869, pg 305 (1869 Sept 29) Denver Lodge No. 5

Moody, Geo L
Proceedings 1870, pg 21 (1870 Sept 28), Denver Lodge No. 5, Denver
Proceedings 1872, pg 20 (1872 Sept 24), Denver Lodge No. 5, Denver, Stricken from the Roll

Moody, Geo Lyman
Proceedings 1861-1869, pg 112 (1863 Nov 3) Denver Lodge No. 5
Proceedings 1861-1869, pg 133 (1864 Nov 8) Denver Lodge No. 5

Moody, George L
Proceedings 1861-1869, pg 192 (1867 Oct 8) Denver Lodge No. 5

Moody, Sampson H
Proceedings 1870, pg 77 (1824 Jan 5) African Lodge at Boston

Moore, B F
Proceedings 1861-1869, pg 229 (1868 Oct 7), Canon Lodge U D, Canon City
Proceedings 1861-1869, pg 311 (1869 Sept 29), Mount Moriah Lodge No. 15, Canon City
Proceedings 1870, pg 28 (1870 Sept 28), Mount Moriah Lodge No. 15, Canon City
Proceedings 1871, pg 26 (1871 Sept 27), Mount Moriah Lodge No. 15, Canon City
Proceedings 1872, pg 29 (1872 Sept 24), Mount Moriah Lodge No. 15, Canon City
Proceedings 1873, pg 45 (1873 Oct 1), Mount Moriah Lodge No. 15, Canon City
Proceedings 1874, pg 220 (1874 Sept 30), Mount Moriah Lodge No. 15, Canon City
Proceedings 1875, pg 84 (1875 Sept 22), Mount Moriah Lodge No. 15, Canon City
Proceedings 1876, pg 38 (1876 Sept 20), Mount Moriah Lodge No. 15, Canon City

Moore, C
Proceedings 1861-1869, pg 290 (1869 Sept 28), Fraternal Publishing Company of Cincinnati, OH

Moore, Charles W
Proceedings 1870, pg 70 (1846) Grand Secretary, Grand Lodge of Massachusetts
Proceedings 1870, pg 75 (1870 May 5) Deputy Grand Master, Grand Lodge of Massachusetts
Proceedings 1873, pg 22 (1873 Oct 1) St John's Lodge [Massachusetts]

Proceedings 1874, pg 81 (1874 Sept 30) Grand Lodge of Massachusetts

Proceedings 1874, pg 82 (1874 Sept 30) Grand Lodge of Massachusetts, died 12 Dec 1873

Moore, H W
Proceedings 1874, pg 221 (1874 Sept 30), Cheyenne Lodge No. 16, Cheyenne, Wyoming Territory

Moore, J A
Proceedings 1861-1869, pg 4 (1861 Aug 2) Golden City Lodge No. 1

Proceedings 1861-1869, pg 5 (1861 Aug 2) Grand Sword Bearer, Golden City

Proceedings 1861-1869, pg 6 (1861 Aug 2) committee

Moore, J K
Proceedings 1861-1869, pg 290 (1869 Sept 28), Secretary, Fraternal Publishing Company of Cincinnati, OH

Proceedings 1861-1869, pg 290 (1869 Sept 28) presented a bill for printing

Moore, John A
Proceedings 1861-1869, pg 42 (1861 Dec 10) Golden City Lodge No. 1

Proceedings 1861-1869, pg 110 (1863 Nov 3) Golden City Lodge No. 1

Proceedings 1861-1869, pg 131 (1864 Nov 8) Golden City Lodge No. 1

Proceedings 1861-1869, pg 147 (1865 Nov 7) Golden City Lodge No. 1

Proceedings 1861-1869, pg 165 (1866 Oct 2) Golden City Lodge No. 1

Proceedings 1861-1869, pg 191 (1867 Oct 8) Golden City Lodge No. 1

Proceedings 1861-1869, pg 221 (1868 Oct 7) Golden City Lodge No. 1

Proceedings 1861-1869, pg 303 (1869 Sept 29) Golden City Lodge No. 1, Dimitted

Moore, Joseph
Proceedings 1875, pg 87 (1875 Sept 22), Occidental Lodge No. 20, Greeley

Proceedings 1876, pg 40 (1876 Sept 20), Occidental Lodge No. 20, Greeley

Moore, Joseph C
Proceedings 1874, pg 221 (1874 Sept 30), Cheyenne Lodge No. 16, Cheyenne, Wyoming Territory

Moore, M A
Proceedings 1861-1869, pg 152 (1865 Nov 7), Helena City Lodge U D, Helena City, Montana Territory

Moore, S
Proceedings 1861-1869, pg 168 (1866 Oct 2), Chivington Lodge No. 6, Central City

Moore, S Grant
Proceedings 1861-1869, pg 312 (1869 Sept 29), Cheyenne Lodge No. 16, Cheyenne

Moore, Sam'l
Proceedings 1870, pg 22 (1870 Sept 28), Central Lodge No. 6, Central City

Proceedings 1871, pg 20 (1871 Sept 27), Central Lodge No. 6, Central

Moore, Samuel
Proceedings 1861-1869, pg 194 (1867 Oct 8), Chivington Lodge No. 6, Central City

Proceedings 1861-1869, pg 224 (1868 Oct 7), Chivington Lodge No. 6, Central City

Proceedings 1861-1869, pg 306 (1869 Sept 29), Central Lodge No. 6, Central City

Proceedings 1872, pg 21 (1872 Sept 24), Denver Lodge No. 5, Denver

Proceedings 1873, pg 38 (1873 Oct 1), Central Lodge No. 6, Central City

Proceedings 1874, pg 213 (1874 Sept 30), Central Lodge No. 6, Central

Proceedings 1875, pg 77 (1875 Sept 22), Central Lodge No. 6, Central City

Proceedings 1876, pg 32 (1876 Sept 20), Central Lodge No. 6, Central City

Moore, William
Proceedings 1861-1869, pg 132 (1864 Nov 8) Golden City Lodge No. 1

Proceedings 1874, pg 222 (1874 Sept 30), Pueblo Lodge No. 17, Pueblo, Pueblo County

Proceedings 1875, pg 85 (1875 Sept 22) Pueblo Lodge No. 17

Proceedings 1876, pg 39 (1876 Sept 20) Pueblo Lodge No. 17

Proceedings 1876, pg 45 (1876 Sept 20) South Pueblo Lodge U D

Moore, Wm
Proceedings 1861-1869, pg 111 (1863 Nov 3), Summit Lodge No. 2, Parkville

Proceedings 1872, pg 36 (1872 Sept 24), Ashlar Lodge U D, Colorado Springs

Moorhead, M D
Proceedings 1876, pg 36 (1876 Sept 20), El Paso Lodge No. 13, Colorado City

Morehead, M D
Proceedings 1874, pg 218 (1874 Sept 30), El Paso Lodge No. 13, Colorado Springs

Proceedings 1875, pg 82 (1875 Sept 22), El Paso Lodge No. 13, Colorado Springs

Morgan, G W
Proceedings 1874, pg 222 (1874 Sept 30), Pueblo Lodge No. 17, Pueblo, Pueblo County

Proceedings 1875, pg 85 (1875 Sept 22) Pueblo Lodge No. 17

Proceedings 1876, pg 39 (1876 Sept 20) Pueblo Lodge No. 17

Morgan, Geo W
Proceedings 1870, pg 30 (1870 Sept 28), Pueblo Lodge No. 17, Pueblo

Proceedings 1872, pg 31 (1872 Sept 24), Pueblo Lodge No. 17, Pueblo

Proceedings 1873, pg 47 (1873 Oct 1), Pueblo Lodge No. 17, Pueblo

Colorado's Territorial Masons

Morgan, George W
Proceedings 1861-1869, pg 312 (1869 Sept 29), Pueblo Lodge No. 17, Pueblo
Proceedings 1871, pg 28 (1871 Sept 27), Pueblo Lodge No. 17, Pueblo

Morgan, J M
Proceedings 1861-1869, pg 149 (1865 Nov 7), Nevada Lodge No. 4, Nevadaville, dimitted

Morgan, Jos
Proceedings 1875, pg 85 (1875 Sept 22) Pueblo Lodge No. 17

Morgan, Joseph
Proceedings 1876, pg 39 (1876 Sept 20) Pueblo Lodge No. 17

Morley, Lucius
Proceedings 1876, pg 36 (1876 Sept 20), El Paso Lodge No. 13, Colorado City

Morriosn, George
Proceedings 1861-1869, pg 165 (1866 Oct 2) Golden City Lodge No. 1

Morris
Proceedings 1872, pg 79 (1872 Sept 24) Grand Lodge of Nevada

Morris, James R
Proceedings 1876, pg 35 (1876 Sept 20), Washington Lodge No. 12, Georgetown

Morris, L A
Proceedings 1876, pg 34 (1876 Sept 20) Black Hawk Lodge No. 11

Morris, R S
Proceedings 1861-1869, pg 42 (1861 Dec 10), Summit Lodge No. 2, Parkville

Morris, Rob
Proceedings 1876, pg 13 (1876 Sept 19) books acquired for Grand Library

Morris, Robert
Proceedings 1861-1869, pg 105 (1863 Nov 3) Masonic Chief Conservator
Proceedings 1874, pg 47 (1874 Sept 30) Grand Lodge of Canada

Morrison, Geo
Proceedings 1861-1869, pg 147 (1865 Nov 7) Golden City Lodge No. 1
Proceedings 1861-1869, pg 191 (1867 Oct 8) Golden City Lodge No. 1
Proceedings 1861-1869, pg 221 (1868 Oct 7) Golden City Lodge No. 1
Proceedings 1861-1869, pg 303 (1869 Sept 29) Golden City Lodge No. 1
Proceedings 1874, pg 209 (1874 Sept 30), Golden City Lodge No. 1, Golden City

Morrison, George
Proceedings 1861-1869, pg 110 (1863 Nov 3) Golden City Lodge No. 1
Proceedings 1861-1869, pg 131 (1864 Nov 8) Golden City Lodge No. 1
Proceedings 1870, pg 19 (1870 Sept 28), Golden City Lodge No. 1, Golden City
Proceedings 1871, pg 17 (1871 Sept 27), Golden City Lodge No. 1, Golden City
Proceedings 1872, pg 17 (1872 Sept 24), Golden City Lodge No. 1, Golden City
Proceedings 1873, pg 35 (1873 Oct 1), Golden City Lodge No. 1, Golden City
Proceedings 1875, pg 73 (1875 Sept 22) Golden City Lodge No. 1
Proceedings 1876, pg 29 (1876 Sept 20) Golden City Lodge No. 1

Morrison, R K
Proceedings 1874, pg 228 (1874 Sept 30), Evanston Lodge U D, Evanston, Uintah County, Wyoming Territory

Morrison, Robert
Proceedings 1873, pg 10 (1873 Sept 30), Evanston Lodge U D, Evanston, Wyoming Territory

Morse, S
Proceedings 1872, pg 35 (1872 Sept 24), St Vrain Lodge No. 23, Longmont
Proceedings 1874, pg 227 (1874 Sept 30), St Vrain No. 23, Longmont

Morse, Sullivan
Proceedings 1873, pg 51 (1873 Oct 1), St Vrain Lodge No. 23, Longmont
Proceedings 1876, pg 41 (1876 Sept 20), St Vrain Lodge No. 23, Longmont

Morton, J G
Proceedings 1875, pg 85 (1875 Sept 22) Pueblo Lodge No. 17
Proceedings 1876, pg 38 (1876 Sept 20) Pueblo Lodge No. 17

Morton, J Gould
Proceedings 1874, pg 222 (1874 Sept 30), Pueblo Lodge No. 17, Pueblo, Pueblo County

Morton, Lloyd
Proceedings 1872, pg 44 (1872 Sept 24) Pawtucket, Grand Lodge of Rhode Island
Proceedings 1873, pg 61 (1873 Oct 1) Grand Lodge of Rhode Island, Pawtucket
Proceedings 1874, pg 121 (1874 Sept 30) Grand Lodge of Rhode Island

Moseley, R W
Proceedings 1870, pg 25 (1870 Sept 28), Black Hawk Lodge No. 11, Black Hawk
Proceedings 1871, pg 23 (1871 Sept 27), Black Hawk Lodge No. 11, Black Hawk

Mosely, R W
Proceedings 1861-1869, pg 196 (1867 Oct 8), Black Hawk Lodge No. 11, Black Hawk, Apprentice
Proceedings 1861-1869, pg 227 (1868 Oct 7), Black Hawk Lodge No. 11, Black Hawk
Proceedings 1872, pg 24 (1872 Sept 24), Black Hawk Lodge No. 11, Black Hawk

Moser, Samuel
Proceedings 1875, pg 89 (1875 Sept 22) Idaho Springs Lodge U D
Proceedings 1876, pg 43 (1876 Sept 20) Idaho Springs Lodge No. 26

Mosher, H D
Proceedings 1861-1869, pg 225 (1868 Oct 7), Union Lodge No. 7, Denver
Proceedings 1872, pg 23 (1872 Sept 24), Union Lodge No. 7, Denver
Proceedings 1873, pg 40 (1873 Oct 1), Union Lodge No. 7, Denver
Proceedings 1874, pg 214 (1874 Sept 30), Union Lodge No. 7, Denver
Proceedings 1876, pg 49 (1876 Sept 20), Union Lodge No. 7, Denver, 1876 Aug 26

Mosher, H Deighton
Proceedings 1871, pg 22 (1871 Sept 27), Union Lodge No. 7, Denver
Proceedings 1870, pg 23 (1870 Sept 28), Union Lodge No. 7, Denver

Moshier, H D
Proceedings 1861-1869, pg 307 (1869 Sept 29), Union Lodge No. 7, Denver
Proceedings 1875, pg 78 (1875 Sept 22), Union Lodge No. 7, Denver

Mosier, H D
Proceedings 1861-1869, pg 195 (1867 Oct 8), Union Lodge No. 7, Denver

Mosier, Samuel
Proceedings 1874, pg 229 (1874 Sept 30), Idaho Springs Lodge U D, Idaho Springs

Mosley, R W
Proceedings 1861-1869, pg 309 (1869 Sept 29), Black Hawk Lodge No. 11, Black Hawk

Mosley, Richard W
Proceedings 1873, pg 41 (1873 Oct 1), Black Hawk Lodge No. 11, Black Hawk
Proceedings 1874, pg 216 (1874 Sept 30), Black Hawk Lodge No. 11, Black Hawk
Proceedings 1875, pg 80 (1875 Sept 22) Black Hawk Lodge No. 11
Proceedings 1876, pg 34 (1876 Sept 20) Black Hawk Lodge No. 11

Mosser, Philip
Proceedings 1872, pg 19 (1872 Sept 24), Denver Lodge No. 5, Denver
Proceedings 1874, pg 212 (1874 Sept 30), Denver Lodge No. 5, Denver, Reinstated
Proceedings 1874, pg 212 (1874 Sept 30), Denver Lodge No. 5, Denver
Proceedings 1875, pg 76 (1875 Sept 22) Denver Lodge No. 5
Proceedings 1876, pg 31 (1876 Sept 20) Denver Lodge No. 5
Proceedings 1871, pg 19 (1871 Sept 27) Denver Lodge No. 5
Proceedings 1873, pg 38 (1873 Oct 1), Denver Lodge No. 5, Denver, Striken from the rolls,

Mother Grand Lodge of England
Proceedings 1872, pg 47 (1872 Sept 24), London, England

Mott, Marcus F
Proceedings 1872, pg 44 (1872 Sept 24) Galveston, Grand Lodge of Texas
Proceedings 1874, pg 205 (1874 Sept 30) Grand Lodge of Texas, Galveston

Moulding, James R
Proceedings 1876, pg 44 (1876 Sept 20), Las Animas Lodge No. 28, Trinidad

Mount Moriah Lodge No. 15
Proceedings 1870, pg 15 (1870 Sept 28) no returns
Proceedings 1871, pg 12 (1871 Sept 26)
Proceedings 1875, pg 92 (1875 Sept 22)
Proceedings 1876, pg 52 (1876 Sept 20)

Mount Moriah Lodge No. 15, Canon City
Proceedings 1861-1869, pg 216 (1868 Oct 7) granted charter
Proceedings 1872, pg 11 (1872 Sept 24) failed to make timely returns
Proceedings 1872, pg 14 (1872 Sept 24) returns not complete
Proceedings 1874, pg 8 (1874 Sept 29) recommended a lodge at Fairplay
Proceedings 1874, pg 208 (1874 Sept 30)
Proceedings 1876, pg 8 (1875 Dec 27) lodge dedicated and officers installed
Proceedings 1876, pg 13 (1875 Sept 22) 1875 dues paid
Proceedings 1876, pg 13 (1876 Sept 19) dues paid

Mount Moriah Lodge U D
Proceedings 1861-1869, pg 268 (1867 Sept 17), of Salt Lake City, denied dispensation from the Grand Lodge of Nevada due to the practice of polygamy

Moyle, John H
Proceedings 1875, pg 89 (1875 Sept 22) Idaho Springs Lodge U D
Proceedings 1876, pg 43 (1876 Sept 20) Idaho Springs Lodge No. 26

Moyn, Daniel
Proceedings 1861-1869, pg 77 (1862 Nov 4) Denver Lodge No. 5
Proceedings 1861-1869, pg 112 (1863 Nov 3) Denver Lodge No. 5
Proceedings 1861-1869, pg 133 (1864 Nov 8) Denver Lodge No. 5, deceased,

Mt Moriah Lodge No. 15
Proceedings 1875, pg 23 (1875 Sept 21) has not made returns or paid dues
Proceedings 1875, pg 23 (1875 Sept 21) has not provided a list of officers
Proceedings 1875, pg 34 (1875 Sept 22) have made no returns

Colorado's Territorial Masons

Mt Moriah Lodge No. 70, Salt Lake City, Utah Territory
Proceedings 1872, pg 89 (1872 Sept 24), chartered by the Grand Lodge of Kansas, 21 Oct 1868

Muir
Proceedings 1861-1869, pg 87 (1863 Apr 17) Golden City Lodge No. 1
Proceedings 1861-1869, pg 88 (1863 Apr 17) Golden City Lodge No. 1
Proceedings 1861-1869, pg 89 (1863 Apr 17) Golden City Lodge No. 1
Proceedings 1861-1869, pg 91 (1863 Apr 17) Golden City Lodge No. 1
Proceedings 1861-1869, pg 92 (1863 Apr 17) Golden City Lodge No. 1
Proceedings 1861-1869, pg 93 (1863 Apr 17) Golden City Lodge No. 1

Muir, W T
Proceedings 1861-1869, pg 101 (1862 Nov 4) refunded to Golden City Lodge
Proceedings 1861-1869, pg 110 (1863 Nov 3) Golden City Lodge No. 1, dimitted

Muir, William Train
Proceedings 1861-1869, pg 85 (1863 Apr 7) Golden City Lodge No. 1
Proceedings 1861-1869, pg 86 (1863 Feb 22), Editor, Colorado Democrat

Muir, Wm D
Proceedings 1870, pg 88 (1869 Oct 11) Grand Master, Grand Lodge of Missouri

Muir, Wm T
Proceedings 1861-1869, pg 31 (1861 Dec 10) committee
Proceedings 1861-1869, pg 45 (1862 Nov 3) appeared

Muir, Wm Train
Proceedings 1861-1869, pg 31 (1861 Dec 10) Grand Treasurer
Proceedings 1861-1869, pg 42 (1861 Dec 10) Golden City Lodge No. 1
Proceedings 1861-1869, pg 93 (1863 Apr 17) Golden City Lodge No. 1
Proceedings 1861-1869, pg 94 (1863 Apr 17) Golden City Lodge No. 1

Mulgrene, John H
Proceedings 1875, pg 83 (1875 Sept 22), Columbia Lodge No. 14, Boulder, Apprentice
Proceedings 1876, pg 37 (1876 Sept 20), Columbia Lodge No. 14, Boulder, Apprentice
Proceedings 1872, pg 28 (1872 Sept 24), Columbia Lodge No. 14, Boulder, Apprentice

Mulgrew, John H
Proceedings 1873, pg 45 (1873 Oct 1), Columbia Lodge No. 14, Boulder, Apprentice
Proceedings 1874, pg 219 (1874 Sept 30), Columbia Lodge No. 14, Boulder, Boulder County, Apprentice

Mullen, J
Proceedings 1861-1869, pg 140 (1865 Nov 6), Empire Lodge No. 8, Empire City

Mullen, Louden
Proceedings 1861-1869, pg 195 (1867 Oct 8), Union Lodge No. 7, Denver
Proceedings 1870, pg 23 (1870 Sept 28), Union Lodge No. 7, Denver
Proceedings 1871, pg 22 (1871 Sept 27), Union Lodge No. 7, Denver
Proceedings 1873, pg 40 (1873 Oct 1), Union Lodge No. 7, Denver
Proceedings 1872, pg 23 (1872 Sept 24), Union Lodge No. 7, Denver
Proceedings 1874, pg 214 (1874 Sept 30), Union Lodge No. 7, Denver

Mullen, T
Proceedings 1861-1869, pg 168 (1866 Oct 2), Chivington Lodge No. 6, Central City

Mullen, Thomas
Proceedings 1861-1869, pg 150 (1865 Nov 7), Chivington Lodge No. 6, Central City
Proceedings 1861-1869, pg 194 (1867 Oct 8), Chivington Lodge No. 6, Central City
Proceedings 1873, pg 38 (1873 Oct 1), Central Lodge No. 6, Central City
Proceedings 1874, pg 213 (1874 Sept 30), Central Lodge No. 6, Central
Proceedings 1875, pg 77 (1875 Sept 22), Central Lodge No. 6, Central City
Proceedings 1876, pg 32 (1876 Sept 20), Central Lodge No. 6, Central City

Mullen, Thos
Proceedings 1861-1869, pg 224 (1868 Oct 7), Chivington Lodge No. 6, Central City
Proceedings 1861-1869, pg 306 (1869 Sept 29), Central Lodge No. 6, Central City
Proceedings 1870, pg 22 (1870 Sept 28), Central Lodge No. 6, Central City
Proceedings 1871, pg 20 (1871 Sept 27), Central Lodge No. 6, Central
Proceedings 1872, pg 21 (1872 Sept 24), Denver Lodge No. 5, Denver

Mullin, F F
Proceedings 1875, pg 78 (1875 Sept 22), Union Lodge No. 7, Denver
Proceedings 1876, pg 33 (1876 Sept 20), Union Lodge No. 7, Denver

Mullin, London
Proceedings 1876, pg 33 (1876 Sept 20), Union Lodge No. 7, Denver

Mullin, Louden
Proceedings 1861-1869, pg 102 (1863 Nov 3) petition for formation of a new lodge in Denver
Proceedings 1861-1869, pg 225 (1868 Oct 7), Union Lodge No. 7, Denver

Mullin, Loudin
Proceedings 1861-1869, pg 169 (1866 Oct 2), Union Lodge No. 7, Denver

Mullin, Loudon
Proceedings 1861-1869, pg 134 (1864 Nov 8), Union Lodge No. 7, Denver
Proceedings 1861-1869, pg 151 (1865 Nov 7), Chivington Lodge No. 6, Central City
Proceedings 1861-1869, pg 307 (1869 Sept 29), Union Lodge No. 7, Denver
Proceedings 1875, pg 78 (1875 Sept 22), Union Lodge No. 7, Denver

Muncie, John
Proceedings 1874, pg 223 (1874 Sept 30), Laramie Lodge No. 18, Laramie City

Mund, H H
Proceedings 1874, pg 214 (1874 Sept 30), Union Lodge No. 7, Denver
Proceedings 1876, pg 33 (1876 Sept 20), Union Lodge No. 7, Denver

Mund, Herman H
Proceedings 1870, pg 23 (1870 Sept 28), Union Lodge No. 7, Denver
Proceedings 1871, pg 22 (1871 Sept 27), Union Lodge No. 7, Denver
Proceedings 1872, pg 22 (1872 Sept 24), Union Lodge No. 7, Denver
Proceedings 1875, pg 78 (1875 Sept 22), Union Lodge No. 7, Denver

Mund, Hiram H
Proceedings 1873, pg 40 (1873 Oct 1), Union Lodge No. 7, Denver

Mundell, James A
Proceedings 1861-1869, pg 312 (1869 Sept 29), Cheyenne Lodge No. 16, Cheyenne
Proceedings 1870, pg 29 (1870 Sept 28), Cheyenne Lodge No. 16, Cheyenne, Wyoming Territory, Dimitted

Munger, George D
Proceedings 1875, pg 91 (1875 Sept 22), Las Animas Lodge U D, Trinidad
Proceedings 1876, pg 44 (1876 Sept 20), Las Animas Lodge No. 28, Trinidad

Munson
Proceedings 1861-1869, pg 202 (1868 Oct 6) committee
Proceedings 1872, pg 12 (1872 Sept 24) resolution

Munson, G C
Proceedings 1861-1869, pg 151 (1865 Nov 7), Empire Lodge U D, Empire City
Proceedings 1861-1869, pg 201 (1868 Oct 6) Senior Grand Deacon
Proceedings 1861-1869, pg 202 (1868 Oct 6), Empire Lodge No. 8, Empire City
Proceedings 1861-1869, pg 219 (1868 Oct 7), Empire Lodge No. 8, Empire City
Proceedings 1861-1869, pg 220 (1868 Oct 7) Junior Grand Deacon
Proceedings 1870, pg 16 (1870 Sept 28), Empire Lodge No. 8, Empire City
Proceedings 1872, pg 4 (1872 Sept 24), Empire Lodge No. 8, Empire
Proceedings 1872, pg 5 (1872 Sept 24) committee
Proceedings 1872, pg 16 (1872 Sept 24), Empire Lodge No. 8, Empire

Munson, Geo C
Proceedings 1861-1869, pg 170 (1866 Oct 2), Empire Lodge No. 8, Empire City
Proceedings 1861-1869, pg 226 (1868 Oct 7), Empire Lodge No. 8, Empire City
Proceedings 1870, pg 4 (1870 Sept 27), Empire Lodge No. 8, Empire City
Proceedings 1870, pg 13 (1870 Sept 27) Junior Grand Deacon
Proceedings 1870, pg 15 (1870 Sept 28) committee
Proceedings 1870, pg 24 (1870 Sept 28), Empire Lodge No. 8, Empire
Proceedings 1872, pg 14 (1872 Sept 24) committee
Proceedings 1872, pg 23 (1872 Sept 24), Empire Lodge No. 8, Empire
Proceedings 1873, pg 39 (1873 Oct 1), Central Lodge No. 6, Central City
Proceedings 1874, pg 5 (1874 Sept 29), Central Lodge No. 6, Central City
Proceedings 1874, pg 212 (1874 Sept 30), Central Lodge No. 6, Central
Proceedings 1875, pg 77 (1875 Sept 22), Central Lodge No. 6, Central City

Munson, George C
Proceedings 1861-1869, pg 176 (1867 Oct 7), Empire Lodge No. 8, Empire City
Proceedings 1861-1869, pg 195 (1867 Oct 8), Empire Lodge No. 8, Empire City
Proceedings 1861-1869, pg 308 (1869 Sept 29), Empire Lodge No. 8, Empire City
Proceedings 1870, pg cover (1870 Sept 28) Junior Grand Deacon, Empire
Proceedings 1873, pg 41 (1873 Oct 1), Empire Lodge No. 8, Empire, Dimitted
Proceedings 1876, pg 32 (1876 Sept 20), Central Lodge No. 6, Central City

Murdock, A G
Proceedings 1875, pg 81 (1875 Sept 22), Washington Lodge No. 12, Georgetown

Murdock, Albert G
Proceedings 1873, pg 42 (1873 Oct 1), Washington Lodge No. 12, Georgetown
Proceedings 1874, pg 217 (1874 Sept 30), Washington Lodge No. 12, Georgetown
Proceedings 1874, pg 217 (1874 Sept 30), Washington Lodge No. 12, Georgetown
Proceedings 1876, pg 34 (1876 Sept 20), Washington Lodge No. 12, Georgetown

Murley, John
Proceedings 1861-1869, pg 227 (1868 Oct 7), Washington Lodge No. 12, Georgetown
Proceedings 1861-1869, pg 309 (1869 Sept 29), Washington Lodge No. 12, Georgetown
Proceedings 1870, pg 26 (1870 Sept 28), Washington Lodge No. 12, Georgetown

Colorado's Territorial Masons

Murley, John, cont.
    Proceedings 1871, pg 24 (1871 Sept 27), Washington Lodge No. 12, Georgetown
    Proceedings 1872, pg 26 (1872 Sept 24), Washington Lodge No. 12, Georgetown
    Proceedings 1873, pg 42 (1873 Oct 1), Washington Lodge No. 12, Georgetown
    Proceedings 1874, pg 217 (1874 Sept 30), Washington Lodge No. 12, Georgetown
    Proceedings 1875, pg 81 (1875 Sept 22), Washington Lodge No. 12, Georgetown, died
    Proceedings 1875, pg 94 (1875 Sept 22), Washington Lodge No. 12, Georgetown

Murphy, John A
    Proceedings 1876, pg 45 (1876 Sept 20), King Solomon Lodge U D, West Las Animas

Murray, Franklin
    Proceedings 1861-1869, pg 312 (1869 Sept 29), Pueblo Lodge No. 17, Pueblo, Fellowcraft
    Proceedings 1870, pg 30 (1870 Sept 28), Pueblo Lodge No. 17, Pueblo, Fellowcraft
    Proceedings 1871, pg 28 (1871 Sept 27), Pueblo Lodge No. 17, Pueblo
    Proceedings 1872, pg 31 (1872 Sept 24), Pueblo Lodge No. 17, Pueblo
    Proceedings 1873, pg 47 (1873 Oct 1), Pueblo Lodge No. 17, Pueblo
    Proceedings 1874, pg 222 (1874 Sept 30), Pueblo Lodge No. 17, Pueblo, Pueblo County
    Proceedings 1875, pg 85 (1875 Sept 22) Pueblo Lodge 17
    Proceedings 1876, pg 39 (1876 Sept 20) Pueblo Lodge 17

Murray, Hobart
    Proceedings 1861-1869, pg 111 (1863 Nov 3), Summit Lodge No. 2, Parkville
    Proceedings 1861-1869, pg 131 (1864 Nov 8) Golden City Lodge No. 1

Murray, Timothy J
    Proceedings 1861-1869, pg 259 (1868 May 5), Grand Master, Grand Lodge of Maine
    Proceedings 1861-1869, pg 331 (1869 May 4) Grand Master, Grand Lodge of Maine
    Proceedings 1870, pg 11 (1870 Apr 22) Grand Lodge of Maine
    Proceedings 1872, pg 41 (1872 Sept 24), of Portland, Representative of the Grand Lodge of Maine
    Proceedings 1873, pg 59 (1873 Oct 1), of Portland, Grand Representative to the Grand Lodge of Maine
    Proceedings 1874, pg 78 (1874 Sept 30), Grand Representative, Grand Lodge of Colorado
    Proceedings 1874, pg 207 (1874 Sept 30) Grand Lodge of Maine, Portland
    Proceedings 1875, pg 95 (1875 Sept 22) Grand Lodge of Maine, Portland, ME
    Proceedings 1876, pg 53 (1876 Sept 20) Grand Lodge of Maine, of Portland, ME

Murrin, Luke
    Proceedings 1872, pg 30 (1872 Sept 24), Cheyenne Lodge No. 16, Cheyenne, Wyoming Territory
    Proceedings 1873, pg 46 (1873 Oct 1), Cheyenne Lodge No. 16, Cheyenne, Wyoming Territory
    Proceedings 1874, pg 221 (1874 Sept 30), Cheyenne Lodge No. 16, Cheyenne, Wyoming Territory

Myer, J L
    Proceedings 1874, pg 212 (1874 Sept 30), Denver Lodge No. 5, Denver
    Proceedings 1875, pg 76 (1875 Sept 22) Denver Lodge No. 5
    Proceedings 1876, pg 31 (1876 Sept 20) Denver Lodge No. 5

Myers, B C
    Proceedings 1861-1869, pg 171 (1866 Oct 2), El Paso U D, Colorado City
    Proceedings 1861-1869, pg 196 (1867 Oct 8), El Paso Lodge U D, Colorado City
    Proceedings 1861-1869, pg 228 (1868 Oct 7), El Paso Lodge No. 13, Colorado City
    Proceedings 1861-1869, pg 310 (1869 Sept 29), El Paso Lodge No. 13, Colorado City, Dimitted
    Proceedings 1870, pg 27 (1870 Sept 28), El Paso Lodge No. 13, Colorado City
    Proceedings 1872, pg 27 (1872 Sept 24), El Paso Lodge No. 13, Colorado City
    Proceedings 1873, pg 43 (1873 Oct 1), El Paso Lodge No. 13, Colorado City
    Proceedings 1874, pg 218 (1874 Sept 30), El Paso Lodge No. 13, Colorado Springs
    Proceedings 1875, pg 82 (1875 Sept 22), El Paso Lodge No. 13, Colorado Springs
    Proceedings 1876, pg 49 (1876 Sept 20), El Paso Lodge No. 13, Colorado City, 1876 July 22

Myers, C W
    Proceedings 1861-1869, pg 196 (1867 Oct 8), El Paso Lodge U D, Colorado City
    Proceedings 1861-1869, pg 228 (1868 Oct 7), El Paso Lodge No. 13, Colorado City
    Proceedings 1861-1869, pg 310 (1869 Sept 29), El Paso Lodge No. 13, Colorado City
    Proceedings 1870, pg 26 (1870 Sept 28), El Paso Lodge No. 13, Colorado City
    Proceedings 1871, pg 4 (1871 Sept 26), El Paso Lodge No. 13, Colorado City
    Proceedings 1871, pg 24 (1871 Sept 27), El Paso Lodge No. 13, Colorado City
    Proceedings 1872, pg 26 (1872 Sept 24), El Paso Lodge No. 13, Colorado City
    Proceedings 1873, pg 43 (1873 Oct 1), El Paso Lodge No. 13, Colorado City
    Proceedings 1874, pg 218 (1874 Sept 30), El Paso Lodge No. 13, Colorado Springs
    Proceedings 1875, pg 82 (1875 Sept 22), El Paso Lodge No. 13, Colorado Springs
    Proceedings 1876, pg 49 (1876 Sept 20), El Paso Lodge No. 13, Colorado City, 1876 July 22

Myers, David
    Proceedings 1876, pg 35 (1876 Sept 20), Washington Lodge No. 12, Georgetown, Fellow Craft

Myers, George
Proceedings 1876, pg 35 (1876 Sept 20), Washington Lodge No. 12, Georgetown, Fellow Craft

Myers, J A
Proceedings 1871, pg 27 (1871 Sept 27), Cheyenne Lodge No. 16, Cheyenne, Wyoming Territory
Proceedings 1872, pg 30 (1872 Sept 24), Cheyenne Lodge No. 16, Cheyenne, Wyoming Territory
Proceedings 1873, pg 46 (1873 Oct 1), Cheyenne Lodge No. 16, Cheyenne, Wyoming Territory
Proceedings 1874, pg 221 (1874 Sept 30), Cheyenne Lodge No. 16, Cheyenne, Wyoming Territory

Myers, John H
Proceedings 1861-1869, pg 221 (1868 Oct 7) Golden City Lodge No. 1, Apprentice
Proceedings 1861-1869, pg 303 (1869 Sept 29) Golden City Lodge No. 1, Apprentice

Myers, Z
Proceedings 1861-1869, pg 150 (1865 Nov 7), Chivington Lodge No. 6, Central City
Proceedings 1861-1869, pg 168 (1866 Oct 2), Chivington Lodge No. 6, Central City
Proceedings 1861-1869, pg 170 (1866 Oct 2), Black Hawk Lodge U D, Black Hawk
Proceedings 1861-1869, pg 194 (1867 Oct 8), Chivington Lodge No. 6, Central City, Dimitted
Proceedings 1861-1869, pg 196 (1867 Oct 8), Black Hawk Lodge No. 11, Black Hawk
Proceedings 1861-1869, pg 227 (1868 Oct 7), Black Hawk Lodge No. 11, Black Hawk
Proceedings 1872, pg 48 (1872 Sept 24), Black Hawk Lodge No. 11, Black Hawk

Myers, Zepha
Proceedings 1870, pg 25 (1870 Sept 28), Black Hawk Lodge No. 11, Black Hawk

Myers, Zephemiah
Proceedings 1873, pg 42 (1873 Oct 1), Black Hawk Lodge No. 11, Black Hawk
Proceedings 1874, pg 216 (1874 Sept 30), Black Hawk Lodge No. 11, Black Hawk

Myers, Zepheniah
Proceedings 1875, pg 80 (1875 Sept 22) Black Hawk Lodge No. 11

Myler, S M
Proceedings 1873, pg 6 (1873 Sept 30), Weston Lodge No. 22, Littleton
Proceedings 1874, pg 226 (1874 Sept 30), Weston Lodge No. 22, Littleton
Proceedings 1875, pg 88 (1875 Sept 22), Weston Lodge No. 22, Littleton
Proceedings 1876, pg 41 (1876 Sept 20), Weston Lodge No. 22, Littleton

Myler, Stephen M
Proceedings 1872, pg 7 (1872 Sept 24), [Weston] Lodge U D, Littleton
Proceedings 1872, pg 34 (1872 Sept 24), Weston Lodge No. 22, Littleton
Proceedings 1873, pg 51 (1873 Oct 1), Weston Lodge No. 22, Littleton

Myrack, H L
Proceedings 1875, pg 86 (1875 Sept 22), Collins Lodge No. 19, Fort Collins
Proceedings 1876, pg 39 (1876 Sept 20), Collins Lodge No. 19, Fort Collins

Myres, Zeph
Proceedings 1861-1869, pg 309 (1869 Sept 29), Black Hawk Lodge No. 11, Black Hawk

Myres, Zepheniah
Proceedings 1871, pg 23 (1871 Sept 27), Black Hawk Lodge No. 11, Black Hawk
Proceedings 1876, pg 34 (1876 Sept 20) Black Hawk Lodge No. 11

Mystic Star
Proceedings 1870, pg 11 (1870 Sept 27), Chicago, IL
Proceedings 1871, pg 10 (1871 Sept 26) masonic magazine
Proceedings 1872, pg 11 (1872 Sept 24), published at Chicago, IL
Proceedings 1873, pg 15 (1873 Oct 1), published at Chicago, IL

Napheys, Ben F
Proceedings 1875, pg 81 (1875 Sept 22), Washington Lodge No. 12, Georgetown

Napheys, Benjamin F
Proceedings 1876, pg 35 (1876 Sept 20), Washington Lodge No. 12, Georgetown

Nash, C W
Proceedings 1861-1869, pg 336 (1869 Jan 12) Grand Master, Grand Lodge of Minnesota
Proceedings 1861-1869, pg 341 (1869 Jan 12) Grand Master, Grand Lodge of Minnesota
Proceedings 1870, pg 79 (1870 Jan 11) Grand Master, Grand Lodge of Minnesota
Proceedings 1872, pg 73 (1872 Sept 24) Grand Lodge of Minnesota

Nash, T D
Proceedings 1861-1869, pg 150 (1865 Nov 7), Chivington Lodge No. 6, Central City
Proceedings 1861-1869, pg 168 (1866 Oct 2), Chivington Lodge No. 6, Central City
Proceedings 1861-1869, pg 194 (1867 Oct 8), Chivington Lodge No. 6, Central City
Proceedings 1861-1869, pg 224 (1868 Oct 7), Chivington Lodge No. 6, Central City
Proceedings 1861-1869, pg 306 (1869 Sept 29), Central Lodge No. 6, Central City
Proceedings 1870, pg 22 (1870 Sept 28), Central Lodge No. 6, Central City
Proceedings 1871, pg 20 (1871 Sept 27), Central Lodge No. 6, Central
Proceedings 1872, pg 21 (1872 Sept 24), Denver Lodge No. 5, Denver

Colorado's Territorial Masons

Nash, T D, cont.
Proceedings 1874, pg 213 (1874 Sept 30), Central Lodge No. 6, Central
Proceedings 1875, pg 77 (1875 Sept 22), Central Lodge No. 6, Central City
Proceedings 1876, pg 32 (1876 Sept 20), Central Lodge No. 6, Central City

Nash, T Delos
Proceedings 1873, pg 39 (1873 Oct 1), Central Lodge No. 6, Central City

National Mutterloge
Proceedings 1872, pg 47 (1872 Sept 24), Berlin, Prussia

Naysmith, William
Proceedings 1871, pg 29 (1871 Sept 27), Laramie Lodge No. 18, Laramie, Wyoming Territory
Proceedings 1873, pg 48 (1873 Oct 1), Laramie Lodge No. 18, Laramie, Wyoming Territory
Proceedings 1874, pg 223 (1874 Sept 30), Laramie Lodge No. 18, Laramie City

Naysmith, Wm
Proceedings 1872, pg 32 (1872 Sept 24), Laramie Lodge No. 18, Laramie, Wyoming Territory

Neal, Thomas J
Proceedings 1874, pg 8 (1874 Aug 27), Huerfano Lodge U D, Walsenburg
Proceedings 1874, pg 229 (1874 Sept 30), Huerfano Lodge U D, Walsenburg
Proceedings 1875, pg 19 (1874 Apr), Huerfano Lodge U D, Walsenburg, deceased
Proceedings 1875, pg 90 (1875 Sept 22), Huerfano Lodge U D, Walsenburg, died
Proceedings 1875, pg 94 (1875 Sept 22), Huerfano Lodge U D, Walsenburg

Neatnery, J B
Proceedings 1874, pg 204 (1874 Sept 30) Grand Lodge of North Carolina, Raleigh

Negowan, Wm
Proceedings 1872, pg 36 (1872 Sept 24), Ashlar Lodge U D, Colorado Springs

Nelson, Charles F
Proceedings 1875, pg 84 (1875 Sept 22), Mount Moriah Lodge No. 15, Canon City
Proceedings 1876, pg 38 (1876 Sept 20), Mount Moriah Lodge No. 15, Canon City

Nelson, Christen
Proceedings 1876, pg 29 (1876 Sept 20) Golden City Lodge No. 1, Fellow Craft

Nelson, Howard E
Proceedings 1875, pg 86 (1875 Sept 22), Collins Lodge No. 19, Fort Collins,, permission granted to apply for degrees in Umatilla Lodge No. 40, Oregon

Nelson, J H
Proceedings 1861-1869, pg 229 (1868 Oct 7), Canon Lodge U D, Canon City
Proceedings 1861-1869, pg 311 (1869 Sept 29), Mount Moriah Lodge No. 15, Canon City
Proceedings 1874, pg 220 (1874 Sept 30), Mount Moriah Lodge No. 15, Canon City
Proceedings 1875, pg 84 (1875 Sept 22), Mount Moriah Lodge No. 15, Canon City
Proceedings 1876, pg 38 (1876 Sept 20), Mount Moriah Lodge No. 15, Canon City

Nelson, James H
Proceedings 1871, pg 26 (1871 Sept 27), Mount Moriah Lodge No. 15, Canon City
Proceedings 1873, pg 45 (1873 Oct 1), Mount Moriah Lodge No. 15, Canon City

Nelson, Jas H
Proceedings 1872, pg 29 (1872 Sept 24), Mount Moriah Lodge No. 15, Canon City

Nelson, R W
Proceedings 1872, pg 17 (1872 Sept 24), Golden City Lodge No. 1, Golden City

Nelson, Sam H
Proceedings 1876, pg 35 (1876 Sept 20), Washington Lodge No. 12, Georgetown, Apprentice

Nelson, Samuel
Proceedings 1871, pg 24 (1871 Sept 27), Washington Lodge No. 12, Georgetown, Apprentice
Proceedings 1872, pg 26 (1872 Sept 24), Washington Lodge No. 12, Georgetown, Apprentice
Proceedings 1873, pg 43 (1873 Oct 1), Washington Lodge No. 12, Georgetown, Apprentice

Nelson, Samuel H
Proceedings 1874, pg 217 (1874 Sept 30), Washington Lodge No. 12, Georgetown, Apprentice
Proceedings 1875, pg 81 (1875 Sept 22), Washington Lodge No. 12, Georgetown, Apprentice

Nelson, W H
Proceedings 1876, pg 42 (1876 Sept 20), Doric Lodge No. 25, Fairplay

Nelson, W R
Proceedings 1861-1869, pg 131 (1864 Nov 8) Golden City Lodge No. 1
Proceedings 1861-1869, pg 147 (1865 Nov 7) Golden City Lodge No. 1
Proceedings 1861-1869, pg 165 (1866 Oct 2) Golden City Lodge No. 1
Proceedings 1861-1869, pg 221 (1868 Oct 7) Golden City Lodge No. 1
Proceedings 1861-1869, pg 303 (1869 Sept 29) Golden City Lodge No. 1
Proceedings 1870, pg 19 (1870 Sept 28), Golden City Lodge No. 1, Golden City
Proceedings 1871, pg 17 (1871 Sept 27), Golden City Lodge No. 1, Golden City
Proceedings 1873, pg 35 (1873 Oct 1), Golden City Lodge No. 1, Golden City
Proceedings 1874, pg 209 (1874 Sept 30), Golden City Lodge No. 1, Golden City
Proceedings 1875, pg 73 (1875 Sept 22) Golden City Lodge No. 1

Nelson, William R
  Proceedings 1876, pg 29 (1876 Sept 20) Golden City Lodge No. 1

Nelson, Wm
  Proceedings 1861-1869, pg 110 (1863 Nov 3) Golden City Lodge No. 1

Nelson, Wm R
  Proceedings 1861-1869, pg 191 (1867 Oct 8) Golden City Lodge No. 1

Nemott, T T
  Proceedings 1872, pg 36 (1872 Sept 24), Ashlar Lodge U D, Colorado Springs

Nesmith
  Proceedings 1861-1869, pg 212 (1868 Oct 6) committee

Nesmith, J W
  Proceedings 1861-1869, pg 159 (1866 Oct 1), Black Hawk Lodge No. 11, Black Hawk
  Proceedings 1861-1869, pg 170 (1866 Oct 2), Black Hawk Lodge U D, Black Hawk
  Proceedings 1861-1869, pg 176 (1867 Oct 7), Black Hawk Lodge U D, Black Hawk
  Proceedings 1861-1869, pg 195 (1867 Oct 8), Black Hawk Lodge No. 11, Black Hawk
  Proceedings 1861-1869, pg 203 (1868 Oct 6) Grand Sword Bearer
  Proceedings 1861-1869, pg 226 (1868 Oct 7), Black Hawk Lodge No. 11, Black Hawk
  Proceedings 1861-1869, pg 287 (1869 Sept 28) Junior Grand Warden
  Proceedings 1861-1869, pg 297 (1869 Sept 28), Black Hawk Lodge No. 11, Black Hawk
  Proceedings 1861-1869, pg 301 (1869 Sept 29), Black Hawk Lodge No. 11, Black Hawk
  Proceedings 1861-1869, pg 309 (1869 Sept 29), Black Hawk Lodge No. 11, Black Hawk
  Proceedings 1870, pg 25 (1870 Sept 28), Black Hawk Lodge No. 11, Black Hawk, Past Master
  Proceedings 1871, pg 23 (1871 Sept 27), Black Hawk Lodge No. 11, Black Hawk
  Proceedings 1872, pg 24 (1872 Sept 24), Black Hawk Lodge No. 11, Black Hawk
  Proceedings 1876, pg 34 (1876 Sept 20) Black Hawk Lodge No. 11

Nesmith, J Wellington
  Proceedings 1861-1869, pg 155 (1866 Oct 1), Black Hawk Lodge U D, Black Hawk
  Proceedings 1873, pg 41 (1873 Oct 1), Black Hawk Lodge No. 11, Black Hawk
  Proceedings 1874, pg 216 (1874 Sept 30), Black Hawk Lodge No. 11, Black Hawk
  Proceedings 1875, pg 80 (1875 Sept 22) Black Hawk Lodge No. 11

Nestel, Lyman W
  Proceedings 1876, pg 36 (1876 Sept 20), El Paso Lodge No. 13, Colorado City

Netterton, T S
  Proceedings 1871, pg 27 (1871 Sept 27), Cheyenne Lodge No. 16, Cheyenne, Wyoming Territory
  Proceedings 1870, pg 29 (1870 Sept 28), Cheyenne Lodge No. 16, Cheyenne, Wyoming Territory
  Proceedings 1872, pg 30 (1872 Sept 24), Cheyenne Lodge No. 16, Cheyenne, Wyoming Territory
  Proceedings 1873, pg 46 (1873 Oct 1), Cheyenne Lodge No. 16, Cheyenne, Wyoming Territory
  Proceedings 1874, pg 214 (1874 Sept 30), Union Lodge No. 7, Denver
  Proceedings 1875, pg 78 (1875 Sept 22), Union Lodge No. 7, Denver
  Proceedings 1876, pg 33 (1876 Sept 20), Union Lodge No. 7, Denver

Nettleton, T W
  Proceedings 1874, pg 221 (1874 Sept 30), Cheyenne Lodge No. 16, Cheyenne, Wyoming Territory, Demitted,

Nevada Lodge
  Proceedings 1871, pg 6 (1861 Fall) Grand Lodge of Kansas

Nevada Lodge No. 36
  Proceedings 1861-1869, pg 33 (1861 Dec 10) chartered under the Grand Lodge of Kansas

Nevada Lodge No. 4
  Proceedings 1861-1869, pg 138 (1864 Dec 14) communication
  Proceedings 1861-1869, pg 139 (1865 Nov 6) dues paid
  Proceedings 1861-1869, pg 158 (1866 Oct 1) dues paid
  Proceedings 1861-1869, pg 178 (1866 Dec 28) special dispensation
  Proceedings 1861-1869, pg 181 (1867 Oct 7) dues paid
  Proceedings 1875, pg 25 (1875 Sept 21) dues paid
  Proceedings 1875, pg 92 (1875 Sept 22)
  Proceedings 1876, pg 12 (1876 Sept 19) returns received only 15 days before annual communication
  Proceedings 1876, pg 52 (1876 Sept 20)

Nevada Lodge No. 4, Nevada
  Proceedings 1874, pg 8 (1874 July 14) recommended a lodge at Idaho Springs
  Proceedings 1874, pg 208 (1874 Sept 30)
  Proceedings 1876, pg 13 (1876 Sept 19) dues paid

New York Courier
  Proceedings 1870, pg 11 (1870 Sept 27)

New York Square
  Proceedings 1876, pg 12 (1876 Sept 19) published at New York City

Newcomb, Alexander H
  Proceedings 1872, pg 84 (1872 Sept 24) Grand Lodge of Ohio

Newett, R B
  Proceedings 1875, pg 89 (1875 Sept 22), Doric Lodge No. 25, Fairplay

Newitt, R B
  Proceedings 1876, pg 42 (1876 Sept 20), Doric Lodge No. 25, Fairplay

Colorado's Territorial Masons

Newlan, Thomas
Proceedings 1861-1869, pg 132 (1864 Nov 8), Nevada Lodge No. 4, Nevadaville

Newland, Thos
Proceedings 1861-1869, pg 111 (1863 Nov 3), Nevada Lodge No. 4, Nevadaville

Newlen, Thos
Proceedings 1861-1869, pg 77 (1862 Nov 4), Nevada Lodge No. 4, Nevadaville

Newlin, H B
Proceedings 1876, pg 34 (1876 Sept 20) Black Hawk Lodge No. 11

Newlin, Henry B
Proceedings 1872, pg 25 (1872 Sept 24), Black Hawk Lodge No. 11, Black Hawk
Proceedings 1873, pg 42 (1873 Oct 1), Black Hawk Lodge No. 11, Black Hawk
Proceedings 1874, pg 216 (1874 Sept 30), Black Hawk Lodge No. 11, Black Hawk
Proceedings 1875, pg 80 (1875 Sept 22) Black Hawk Lodge No. 11

Newlun, Thomas
Proceedings 1861-1869, pg 148 (1865 Nov 7), Nevada Lodge No. 4, Nevadaville
Proceedings 1861-1869, pg 192 (1867 Oct 8), Nevada Lodge No. 4, Nevadaville
Proceedings 1861-1869, pg 222 (1868 Oct 7), Nevada Lodge No. 4, Nevadaville
Proceedings 1861-1869, pg 304 (1869 Sept 29), Nevada Lodge No. 4, Nevadaville
Proceedings 1870, pg 20 (1870 Sept 28), Nevada Lodge No. 4, Nevadaville
Proceedings 1871, pg 18 (1871 Sept 27), Nevada Lodge No. 4, Bald Mountain
Proceedings 1872, pg 19 (1872 Sept 24), Nevada Lodge No. 4, Bald Mountain
Proceedings 1873, pg 36 (1873 Oct 1), Nevada Lodge No. 4, Nevada
Proceedings 1876, pg 51 (1876 Sept 20) Nevada Lodge No. 4, 1875 Dec 11

Newlun, Thos
Proceedings 1861-1869, pg 166 (1866 Oct 2), Nevada Lodge No. 4, Nevadaville
Proceedings 1874, pg 211 (1874 Sept 30), Nevada Lodge No. 4, Bald Mountain, Gilpin County, Stricken from the rolls
Proceedings 1876, pg 30 (1876 Sept 20) Nevada Lodge No. 4

Newman
Proceedings 1861-1869, pg 92 (1863 Apr 17) Denver Lodge No. 5

Newman [Newnam], E B
Proceedings 1861-1869, pg 77 (1862 Nov 4), Nevada Lodge No. 4, Nevadaville
Proceedings 1861-1869, pg 222 (1868 Oct 7), Nevada Lodge No. 4, Nevadaville
Proceedings 1861-1869, pg 304 (1869 Sept 29), Nevada Lodge No. 4, Nevadaville, Dimitted
Proceedings 1861-1869, pg 132 (1864 Nov 8), Nevada Lodge No. 4, Nevadaville
Proceedings 1872, pg 7 (1872 June 22), [St Vrain] Lodge U D, Longmont
Proceedings 1872, pg 35 (1872 Sept 24), St Vrain Lodge No. 23, Longmont
Proceedings 1873, pg 6 (1873 Sept 30), St Vrain Lodge No. 23, Longmont
Proceedings 1873, pg 7 (1873 Sept 30), St Vrain Lodge No. 23, Longmont
Proceedings 1873, pg 32 (1873 Oct 1) mileage and per diem
Proceedings 1873, pg 45 (1873 Oct 1), Columbia Lodge No. 14, Boulder, Dimitted
Proceedings 1873, pg 51 (1873 Oct 1), St Vrain Lodge No. 23, Longmont
Proceedings 1874, pg 6 (1874 Sept 29), St Vrain Lodge No. 23, Longmont
Proceedings 1874, pg 32 (1874 Sept 30) Junior Grand Steward, Longmont
Proceedings 1874, pg 36 (1874 Sept 30) per diem
Proceedings 1874, pg 227 (1874 Sept 30), St Vrain No. 23, Longmont

Newman [Newnam], Edw B
Proceedings 1870, pg 27 (1870 Sept 28), Columbia Lodge No. 14, Boulder City

Newman [Newnam], Edward B
Proceedings 1861-1869, pg 111 (1863 Nov 3), Nevada Lodge No. 4, Nevadaville
Proceedings 1872, pg 28 (1872 Sept 24), Columbia Lodge No. 14, Boulder

Newman, A A
Proceedings 1861-1869, pg 81 (1863 Apr 18) Denver Lodge No. 5

Newman, Charles
Proceedings 1876, pg 44 (1876 Sept 20) Del Norte Lodge U D

Newman, Gus
Proceedings 1861-1869, pg 77 (1862 Nov 4) Denver Lodge No. 5
Proceedings 1861-1869, pg 112 (1863 Nov 3) Denver Lodge No. 5
Proceedings 1861-1869, pg 133 (1864 Nov 8) Denver Lodge No. 5, dimitted

Newman, H
Proceedings 1861-1869, pg 312 (1869 Sept 29), Cheyenne Lodge No. 16, Cheyenne
Proceedings 1870, pg 29 (1870 Sept 28), Cheyenne Lodge No. 16, Cheyenne, Wyoming Territory, Dimitted

Newnam, E B
Proceedings 1861-1869, pg 192 (1867 Oct 8), Nevada Lodge No. 4, Nevadaville
Proceedings 1876, pg 41 (1876 Sept 20), St Vrain Lodge No. 23, Longmont

Newnam, Ew'd B
Proceedings 1871, pg 26 (1871 Sept 27), Columbia Lodge No. 14, Boulder City

Newnum [Newnam], E B
Proceedings 1861-1869, pg 148 (1865 Nov 7), Nevada Lodge No. 4, Nevadaville
Proceedings 1861-1869, pg 166 (1866 Oct 2), Nevada Lodge No. 4, Nevadaville

News Steam Printing House
Proceedings 1873, pg cover (1873 Sept 30), Denver, Col.

Newton, Bogue F
Proceedings 1870, pg 24 (1870 Sept 28), Empire Lodge No. 8, Empire, Apprentice

Newton, Wm
Proceedings 1861-1869, pg 131 (1864 Nov 8) Golden City Lodge No. 1
Proceedings 1861-1869, pg 147 (1865 Nov 7) Golden City Lodge No. 1

Nice, Geo
Proceedings 1875, pg 89 (1875 Sept 22), Doric Lodge No. 25, Fairplay

Nicholl, Thos F
Proceedings 1873, pg 40 (1873 Oct 1), Union Lodge No. 7, Denver
Proceedings 1874, pg 214 (1874 Sept 30), Union Lodge No. 7, Denver
Proceedings 1875, pg 79 (1875 Sept 22), Union Lodge No. 7, Denver, Stricken from the rolls

Nicholls, Andrew
Proceedings 1870, pg 20 (1870 Sept 28), Nevada Lodge No. 4, Nevadaville

Nicholls, John
Proceedings 1876, pg 29 (1876 Sept 20) Golden City Lodge No. 1

Nichols
Proceedings 1873, pg 30 (1873 Oct 1) amendment Nichols
Proceedings 1874, pg 29 (1874 Sept 29) Grand Teller

Nichols, Andrew
Proceedings 1861-1869, pg 111 (1863 Nov 3), Nevada Lodge No. 4, Nevadaville
Proceedings 1861-1869, pg 132 (1864 Nov 8), Nevada Lodge No. 4, Nevadaville
Proceedings 1861-1869, pg 148 (1865 Nov 7), Nevada Lodge No. 4, Nevadaville
Proceedings 1861-1869, pg 166 (1866 Oct 2), Nevada Lodge No. 4, Nevadaville
Proceedings 1861-1869, pg 192 (1867 Oct 8), Nevada Lodge No. 4, Nevadaville
Proceedings 1861-1869, pg 304 (1869 Sept 29), Nevada Lodge No. 4, Nevadaville
Proceedings 1871, pg 18 (1871 Sept 27), Nevada Lodge No. 4, Bald Mountain
Proceedings 1872, pg 19 (1872 Sept 24), Nevada Lodge No. 4, Bald Mountain
Proceedings 1873, pg 36 (1873 Oct 1), Nevada Lodge No. 4, Nevada, died
Proceedings 1873, pg 57 (1873 Oct 1), Nevada Lodge No. 4, Nevada

Nichols, Charles L
Proceedings 1874, pg 219 (1874 Sept 30), Columbia Lodge No. 14, Boulder, Boulder County
Proceedings 1875, pg 83 (1875 Sept 22), Columbia Lodge No. 14, Boulder
Proceedings 1876, pg 37 (1876 Sept 20), Columbia Lodge No. 14, Boulder

Nichols, D H
Proceedings 1861-1869, pg 179 (1867 Oct 7) motion
Proceedings 1872, pg 27 (1872 Sept 24), Columbia Lodge No. 14, Boulder
Proceedings 1874, pg 219 (1874 Sept 30), Columbia Lodge No. 14, Boulder, Boulder County

Nichols, David H
Proceedings 1870, pg 27 (1870 Sept 28), Columbia Lodge No. 14, Boulder City
Proceedings 1871, pg 26 (1871 Sept 27), Columbia Lodge No. 14, Boulder City
Proceedings 1873, pg 44 (1873 Oct 1), Columbia Lodge No. 14, Boulder
Proceedings 1875, pg 83 (1875 Sept 22), Columbia Lodge No. 14, Boulder
Proceedings 1876, pg 37 (1876 Sept 20), Columbia Lodge No. 14, Boulder

Nichols, Ezra H
Proceedings 1873, pg 44 (1873 Oct 1), Columbia Lodge No. 14, Boulder
Proceedings 1874, pg 219 (1874 Sept 30), Columbia Lodge No. 14, Boulder, Boulder County
Proceedings 1875, pg 83 (1875 Sept 22), Columbia Lodge No. 14, Boulder
Proceedings 1876, pg 37 (1876 Sept 20), Columbia Lodge No. 14, Boulder

Nichols, F
Proceedings 1872, pg 4 (1872 Sept 24), Central Lodge No. 6, Central
Proceedings 1873, pg 31 (1873 Oct 1) mileage and per diem
Proceedings 1875, pg 16 (1875 Sept 21) committee

Nichols, Foster
Proceedings 1870, pg 22 (1870 Sept 28), Central Lodge No. 6, Central City
Proceedings 1871, pg 20 (1871 Sept 27), Central Lodge No. 6, Central
Proceedings 1872, pg cover (1872 Sept 24), Central City Council, U D, Central
Proceedings 1872, pg 21 (1872 Sept 24), Denver Lodge No. 5, Denver
Proceedings 1873, pg 6 (1873 Sept 30), Central Lodge No. 6, Central
Proceedings 1873, pg 13 (1873 Sept 30) committee
Proceedings 1873, pg 17 (1873 Oct 1) Senior Grand Steward

Nichols, Foster, cont.
    Proceedings 1873, pg 27 (1873 Oct 1) committee
    Proceedings 1873, pg 38 (1873 Oct 1), Central Lodge No. 6, Central City
    Proceedings 1874, pg cover (1874 Sept 30) committee, Central
    Proceedings 1874, pg 5 (1874 Sept 29), Central Lodge No. 6, Central City
    Proceedings 1874, pg 6 (1874 Sept 29) committee
    Proceedings 1874, pg 32 (1874 Sept 30) Senior Grand Deacon, Central
    Proceedings 1874, pg 35 (1874 Sept 30) committee
    Proceedings 1874, pg 36 (1874 Sept 30) per diem
    Proceedings 1874, pg 36 (1874 Sept 30) committee
    Proceedings 1874, pg 38 (1874 Sept 30) resolution
    Proceedings 1874, pg 212 (1874 Sept 30), Central Lodge No. 6, Central
    Proceedings 1875, pg 15 (1875 Sept 21) Senior Grand Deacon
    Proceedings 1875, pg 17 (1875 Sept 21) Central Lodge No. 6
    Proceedings 1875, pg 17 (1875 Sept 21) committee
    Proceedings 1875, pg 18 (1875 Sept 21) committee
    Proceedings 1875, pg 30 (1875 Sept 21) motion
    Proceedings 1875, pg 30 (1875 Sept 21) committee
    Proceedings 1875, pg 38 (1875 Sept 22) per diem
    Proceedings 1875, pg 76 (1875 Sept 22), Central Lodge No. 6, Central City
    Proceedings 1876, pg 31 (1876 Sept 20), Central Lodge No. 6, Central City

Nichols, J H
    Proceedings 1871, pg 27 (1871 Sept 27), Cheyenne Lodge No. 16, Cheyenne, Wyoming Territory
    Proceedings 1872, pg 30 (1872 Sept 24), Cheyenne Lodge No. 16, Cheyenne, Wyoming Territory
    Proceedings 1873, pg 46 (1873 Oct 1), Cheyenne Lodge No. 16, Cheyenne, Wyoming Territory
    Proceedings 1874, pg 221 (1874 Sept 30), Cheyenne Lodge No. 16, Cheyenne, Wyoming Territory

Nichols, John
    Proceedings 1873, pg 61 (1873 Oct 1) Grand Lodge of North Carolina, Raleigh
    Proceedings 1874, pg 113 (1874 Sept 30) Grand Lodge of North Carolina
    Proceedings 1874, pg 204 (1874 Sept 30) Grand Lodge of North Carolina, Raleigh
    Proceedings 1875, pg 73 (1875 Sept 22) Golden City Lodge No. 1

Nichols, W H
    Proceedings 1861-1869, pg 134 (1864 Nov 8), Chivington Lodge No. 6, Central City, Apprentice
    Proceedings 1861-1869, pg 150 (1865 Nov 7), Chivington Lodge No. 6, Central City, Apprentice
    Proceedings 1861-1869, pg 224 (1868 Oct 7), Chivington Lodge No. 6, Central City
    Proceedings 1861-1869, pg 306 (1869 Sept 29), Central Lodge No. 6, Central City
    Proceedings 1871, pg 20 (1871 Sept 27), Central Lodge No. 6, Central

Nichols, W H J
    Proceedings 1873, pg 37 (1873 Oct 1), Denver Lodge No. 5, Denver
    Proceedings 1874, pg 212 (1874 Sept 30), Denver Lodge No. 5, Denver
    Proceedings 1875, pg 76 (1875 Sept 22) Denver Lodge No. 5
    Proceedings 1876, pg 31 (1876 Sept 20) Denver Lodge No. 5

Nichols, William H
    Proceedings 1873, pg 39 (1873 Oct 1), Central Lodge No. 6, Central City
    Proceedings 1874, pg 213 (1874 Sept 30), Central Lodge No. 6, Central
    Proceedings 1875, pg 77 (1875 Sept 22), Central Lodge No. 6, Central City
    Proceedings 1876, pg 32 (1876 Sept 20), Central Lodge No. 6, Central City

Nichols, Wm H
    Proceedings 1861-1869, pg 168 (1866 Oct 2), Chivington Lodge No. 6, Central City
    Proceedings 1861-1869, pg 194 (1867 Oct 8), Chivington Lodge No. 6, Central City
    Proceedings 1870, pg 22 (1870 Sept 28), Central Lodge No. 6, Central City
    Proceedings 1872, pg 21 (1872 Sept 24), Denver Lodge No. 5, Denver

Nicholson, James
    Proceedings 1873, pg 39 (1873 Oct 1), Central Lodge No. 6, Central City
    Proceedings 1874, pg 212 (1874 Sept 30), Central Lodge No. 6, Central
    Proceedings 1875, pg 76 (1875 Sept 22), Central Lodge No. 6, Central City
    Proceedings 1876, pg 32 (1876 Sept 20), Central Lodge No. 6, Central City

Nicholson, John W
    Proceedings 1876, pg 37 (1876 Sept 20), Columbia Lodge No. 14, Boulder

Nicholson, William
    Proceedings 1876, pg 32 (1876 Sept 20), Central Lodge No. 6, Central City

Nickels [Nichols], David
    Proceedings 1861-1869, pg 230 (1868 Oct 7), Valmont Lodge U D, Valmont

Nickerson, Sereno D
    Proceedings 1872, pg 43 (1872 Sept 24) Boston, Grand Lodge of Massachusetts
    Proceedings 1873, pg 22 (1873 Oct 1) Grand Lodge of Massachusetts
    Proceedings 1873, pg 60 (1873 Oct 1) Grand Lodge of Massachusetts, Boston
    Proceedings 1874, pg 80 (1874 Sept 30) Grand Lodge of Massachusetts
    Proceedings 1874, pg 204 (1874 Sept 30) Grand Lodge of Massachusetts, Boston

Colorado's Territorial Masons

Nickolls, Andrew
Proceedings 1861-1869, pg 222 (1868 Oct 7), Nevada Lodge No. 4, Nevadaville

Niles, J S
Proceedings 1874, pg 209 (1874 Sept 30), Golden City Lodge No. 1, Golden City
Proceedings 1875, pg 73 (1875 Sept 22) Golden City Lodge No. 1
Proceedings 1876, pg 29 (1876 Sept 20) Golden City Lodge No. 1

Nixon, George T A
Proceedings 1876, pg 45 (1876 Sept 20), King Solomon Lodge U D, West Las Animas

Noble, J M
Proceedings 1861-1869, pg 171 (1866 Oct 2), El Paso U D, Colorado City, Apprentice
Proceedings 1861-1869, pg 196 (1867 Oct 8), El Paso Lodge U D, Colorado City
Proceedings 1861-1869, pg 228 (1868 Oct 7), El Paso Lodge No. 13, Colorado City, Dimitted
Proceedings 1861-1869, pg 310 (1869 Sept 29), El Paso Lodge No. 13, Colorado City, Dimitted

Nolan, J J
Proceedings 1872, pg 31 (1872 Sept 24), Pueblo Lodge No. 17, Pueblo, Apprentice
Proceedings 1873, pg 47 (1873 Oct 1), Pueblo Lodge No. 17, Pueblo, Apprentice
Proceedings 1874, pg 222 (1874 Sept 30), Pueblo Lodge No. 17, Pueblo, Pueblo County, Apprentice
Proceedings 1875, pg 85 (1875 Sept 22) Pueblo Lodge No. 17, Apprentice
Proceedings 1876, pg 39 (1876 Sept 20) Pueblo Lodge No. 17, Apprentice

Nolan, James J
Proceedings 1861-1869, pg 229 (1868 Oct 7), Pueblo Lodge U D, Pueblo, Apprentice
Proceedings 1861-1869, pg 313 (1869 Sept 29), Pueblo Lodge No. 17, Pueblo, Apprentice
Proceedings 1871, pg 28 (1871 Sept 27), Pueblo Lodge No. 17, Pueblo, Apprentice

Nolan, Wm
Proceedings 1861-1869, pg 223 (1868 Oct 7) Denver Lodge No. 5, Apprentice
Proceedings 1861-1869, pg 305 (1869 Sept 29) Denver Lodge No. 5, Apprentice

Nolas, James J
Proceedings 1870, pg 30 (1870 Sept 28), Pueblo Lodge No. 17, Pueblo, Apprentice

Nomman, Joseph F
Proceedings 1872, pg 89 (1872 Sept 24) Grand Lodge of Utah

Norris, Geo D
Proceedings 1861-1869, pg 239 (1867 Dec 2) Grand Master of Alabama

Norris, George D
Proceedings 1861-1869, pg 321 (1868 Dec 7) Grand Master, Grand Lodge of Alabama
Proceedings 1870, pg 37 (1869 Dec 6) Grand Master, Grand Lodge of Alabama

Norrish, K M
Proceedings 1872, pg 30 (1872 Sept 24), Cheyenne Lodge No. 16, Cheyenne, Wyoming Territory, Dimitted

Norrish, R M
Proceedings 1870, pg 29 (1870 Sept 28), Cheyenne Lodge No. 16, Cheyenne, Wyoming Territory, Fellowcraft
Proceedings 1871, pg 27 (1871 Sept 27), Cheyenne Lodge No. 16, Cheyenne, Wyoming Territory

North, O
Proceedings 1861-1869, pg 77 (1862 Nov 4), Nevada Lodge No. 4, Nevadaville
Proceedings 1861-1869, pg 111 (1863 Nov 3), Nevada Lodge No. 4, Nevadaville
Proceedings 1861-1869, pg 137 (1865 Nov 6), Nevada Lodge No. 4, Nevadaville
Proceedings 1861-1869, pg 138 (1865 Nov 6) committee

North, Orlando
Proceedings 1861-1869, pg 132 (1864 Nov 8), Nevada Lodge No. 4, Nevadaville
Proceedings 1861-1869, pg 138 (1865 Nov 6) committee
Proceedings 1861-1869, pg 141 (1865 Nov 7) committee
Proceedings 1861-1869, pg 142 (1865 Nov 7) committee
Proceedings 1861-1869, pg 147 (1865 Nov 7), Nevada Lodge No. 4, Nevadaville
Proceedings 1861-1869, pg 166 (1866 Oct 2), Nevada Lodge No. 4, Nevadaville
Proceedings 1861-1869, pg 192 (1867 Oct 8), Nevada Lodge No. 4, Nevadaville
Proceedings 1861-1869, pg 222 (1868 Oct 7), Nevada Lodge No. 4, Nevadaville
Proceedings 1861-1869, pg 229 (1868 Oct 7), Cheyenne Lodge U D, Cheyenne, Dakota Territory
Proceedings 1861-1869, pg 304 (1869 Sept 29), Nevada Lodge No. 4, Nevadaville
Proceedings 1861-1869, pg 312 (1869 Sept 29), Cheyenne Lodge No. 16, Cheyenne
Proceedings 1870, pg 20 (1870 Sept 28), Nevada Lodge No. 4, Nevadaville, Dimitted
Proceedings 1870, pg 29 (1870 Sept 28), Cheyenne Lodge No. 16, Cheyenne, Wyoming Territory
Proceedings 1871, pg 27 (1871 Sept 27), Cheyenne Lodge No. 16, Cheyenne, Wyoming Territory
Proceedings 1872, pg 30 (1872 Sept 24), Cheyenne Lodge No. 16, Cheyenne, Wyoming Territory
Proceedings 1873, pg 10 (1873 Sept 30), Evanston Lodge U D, Evanston, Wyoming Territory
Proceedings 1874, pg 221 (1874 Sept 30), Cheyenne Lodge No. 16, Cheyenne, Wyoming Territory
Proceedings 1874, pg 228 (1874 Sept 30), Evanston Lodge U D, Evanston, Uintah County, Wyoming Territory

North, Orlando O
Proceedings 1873, pg 46 (1873 Oct 1), Cheyenne Lodge No. 16, Cheyenne, Wyoming Territory

Northrup
    Proceedings 1874, pg 48 (1874 Sept 30) Grand Lodge of Mississippi, died at Denver
    Proceedings 1874, pg 48 (1874 Sept 30) widow applied for burial with Masonic Ceremonies
    Proceedings 1874, pg 49 (1874 Sept 30) buried with Masonic Ceremonies

Norton, G G
    Proceedings 1861-1869, pg 113 (1863 Nov 3), Chivington Lodge No. 6, Central City
    Proceedings 1861-1869, pg 134 (1864 Nov 8), Chivington Lodge No. 6, Central City
    Proceedings 1861-1869, pg 150 (1865 Nov 7), Chivington Lodge No. 6, Central City
    Proceedings 1861-1869, pg 168 (1866 Oct 2), Chivington Lodge No. 6, Central City
    Proceedings 1861-1869, pg 194 (1867 Oct 8), Chivington Lodge No. 6, Central City
    Proceedings 1861-1869, pg 224 (1868 Oct 7), Chivington Lodge No. 6, Central City
    Proceedings 1861-1869, pg 306 (1869 Sept 29), Central Lodge No. 6, Central City

Norton, Galen G
    Proceedings 1861-1869, pg 78 (1862 Nov 4), Chivington Lodge No. 6, Central City
    Proceedings 1870, pg 23 (1870 Sept 28), Central Lodge No. 6, Central City, Dimitted

Norwood, Abel J
    Proceedings 1861-1869, pg 254 (1868 Feb 10), Grand Master, Grand Lodge of Louisiana

Norwood, C W
    Proceedings 1870, pg 29 (1870 Sept 28), Cheyenne Lodge No. 16, Cheyenne, Wyoming Territory
    Proceedings 1871, pg 27 (1871 Sept 27), Cheyenne Lodge No. 16, Cheyenne, Wyoming Territory
    Proceedings 1872, pg 30 (1872 Sept 24), Cheyenne Lodge No. 16, Cheyenne, Wyoming Territory, Dimitted,

Nowlan
    Proceedings 1861-1869, pg 82 (1863 Apr 18) Denver Lodge No. 5, Accepted
    Proceedings 1861-1869, pg 83 (1863 May 6) Denver Lodge No. 5
    Proceedings 1861-1869, pg 85 (1863 May 6) Denver Lodge No. 5
    Proceedings 1861-1869, pg 92 (1863 Apr 17) Denver Lodge No. 5

Nowlan, Wm
    Proceedings 1861-1869, pg 81 (1863 Apr 18) Denver Lodge No. 5, Rejected
    Proceedings 1861-1869, pg 112 (1863 Nov 3) Denver Lodge No. 5, Apprentice
    Proceedings 1861-1869, pg 133 (1864 Nov 8) Denver Lodge No. 5, Apprentice
    Proceedings 1861-1869, pg 149 (1865 Nov 7), Nevada Lodge No. 4, Nevadaville, Apprentice
    Proceedings 1861-1869, pg 167 (1866 Oct 2) Denver Lodge No. 5, Apprentice
    Proceedings 1861-1869, pg 193 (1867 Oct 8) Denver Lodge No. 5, Apprentice

Noyes, Michael I
    Proceedings 1861-1869, pg 247 (1867 Nov 7) deceased

Nutt, Henry
    Proceedings 1861-1869, pg 151 (1865 Nov 7), Empire Lodge U D, Empire City
    Proceedings 1861-1869, pg 170 (1866 Oct 2), Empire Lodge No. 8, Empire City
    Proceedings 1861-1869, pg 195 (1867 Oct 8), Empire Lodge No. 8, Empire City
    Proceedings 1861-1869, pg 226 (1868 Oct 7), Empire Lodge No. 8, Empire City
    Proceedings 1861-1869, pg 288 (1869 Sept 28), Empire Lodge No. 8, Empire City
    Proceedings 1861-1869, pg 308 (1869 Sept 29), Empire Lodge No. 8, Empire City
    Proceedings 1870, pg 24 (1870 Sept 28), Empire Lodge No. 8, Empire
    Proceedings 1872, pg 23 (1872 Sept 24), Empire Lodge No. 8, Empire
    Proceedings 1873, pg 41 (1873 Oct 1), Empire Lodge No. 8, Empire
    Proceedings 1874, pg 215 (1874 Sept 30), Empire Lodge No. 8, Empire

Nyce, Geo W
    Proceedings 1871, pg 19 (1871 Sept 27) Denver Lodge No. 5
    Proceedings 1872, pg 19 (1872 Sept 24), Denver Lodge No. 5, Denver
    Proceedings 1873, pg 37 (1873 Oct 1), Denver Lodge No. 5, Denver
    Proceedings 1874, pg 212 (1874 Sept 30), Denver Lodge No. 5, Denver
    Proceedings 1875, pg 76 (1875 Sept 22) Denver Lodge No. 5, Demitted

Nyce, George W
    Proceedings 1876, pg 42 (1876 Sept 20), Doric Lodge No. 25, Fairplay

Nye, Loyal S
    Proceedings 1874, pg 214 (1874 Sept 30), Union Lodge No. 7, Denver
    Proceedings 1874, pg 214 (1874 Sept 30), Union Lodge No. 7, Denver
    Proceedings 1875, pg 78 (1875 Sept 22), Union Lodge No. 7, Denver
    Proceedings 1876, pg 33 (1876 Sept 20), Union Lodge No. 7, Denver

O

Oakes, Daniel C
Proceedings 1871, pg 22 (1871 Sept 27), Union Lodge No. 7, Denver
Proceedings 1872, pg 22 (1872 Sept 24), Union Lodge No. 7, Denver

Oakley, A J
Proceedings 1873, pg 36 (1873 Oct 1), Nevada Lodge No. 4, Nevada, Apprentice
Proceedings 1874, pg 210 (1874 Sept 30), Nevada Lodge No. 4, Bald Mountain, Gilpin County
Proceedings 1875, pg 74 (1875 Sept 22), Nevada Lodge No. 4, Nevada
Proceedings 1876, pg 48 (1876 Sept 20) Nevada Lodge No. 4, 1876 June 10

Oaks, D C
Proceedings 1861-1869, pg 307 (1869 Sept 29), Union Lodge No. 7, Denver
Proceedings 1873, pg 39 (1873 Oct 1), Union Lodge No. 7, Denver
Proceedings 1874, pg 214 (1874 Sept 30), Union Lodge No. 7, Denver
Proceedings 1875, pg 78 (1875 Sept 22), Union Lodge No. 7, Denver
Proceedings 1876, pg 33 (1876 Sept 20), Union Lodge No. 7, Denver

Oaks, Daniel C
Proceedings 1870, pg 23 (1870 Sept 28), Union Lodge No. 7, Denver

Oates, John
Proceedings 1874, pg 229 (1874 Sept 30), Idaho Springs Lodge U D, Idaho Springs

O'Brien, Dennis
Proceedings 1861-1869, pg 222 (1868 Oct 7), Nevada Lodge No. 4, Nevadaville
Proceedings 1861-1869, pg 304 (1869 Sept 29), Nevada Lodge No. 4, Nevadaville
Proceedings 1870, pg 20 (1870 Sept 28), Nevada Lodge No. 4, Nevadaville
Proceedings 1871, pg 18 (1871 Sept 27), Nevada Lodge No. 4, Bald Mountain
Proceedings 1872, pg 19 (1872 Sept 24), Nevada Lodge No. 4, Bald Mountain
Proceedings 1873, pg 36 (1873 Oct 1), Nevada Lodge No. 4, Nevada
Proceedings 1874, pg 210 (1874 Sept 30), Nevada Lodge No. 4, Bald Mountain, Gilpin County
Proceedings 1875, pg 74 (1875 Sept 22), Nevada Lodge No. 4, Nevada
Proceedings 1876, pg 30 (1876 Sept 20) Nevada Lodge No. 4

Occidental Lodge
Proceedings 1871, pg 7 (1870 Nov 29) established in Greeley

Occidental Lodge No. 20
Proceedings 1875, pg 23 (1875 Sept 21) has not provided a list of officers
Proceedings 1875, pg 25 (1875 Sept 21) dues paid
Proceedings 1875, pg 92 (1875 Sept 22)
Proceedings 1876, pg 52 (1876 Sept 20)
Proceedings 1871, pg 12 (1871 Sept 26)

Occidental Lodge No. 20, Greeley
Proceedings 1874, pg 208 (1874 Sept 30)
Proceedings 1875, pg 19 (1875 June 7) communication
Proceedings 1876, pg 12 (1876 Sept 19) returns received only 15 days before annual communication
Proceedings 1876, pg 13 (1876 Mar 20) visited by the Grand Lecturer
Proceedings 1876, pg 13 (1876 Sept 19) dues paid

Occidental Lodge U D, Greeley
Proceedings 1871, pg 10 (1871 Sept 26)
Proceedings 1871, pg 12 (1871 Sept 26)

O'Haller, Granville
Proceedings 1872, pg 44 (1872 Sept 24) Coupeville, Grand Lodge of Washington

Old, R O
Proceedings 1861-1869, pg 192 (1867 Oct 8) Denver Lodge No. 5
Proceedings 1861-1869, pg 223 (1868 Oct 7) Denver Lodge No. 5
Proceedings 1861-1869, pg 300 (1869 Sept 29), Denver Lodge No 5, living in Denver
Proceedings 1861-1869, pg 305 (1869 Sept 29) Denver Lodge No. 5
Proceedings 1870, pg 21 (1870 Sept 28), Denver Lodge No. 5, Denver

Oldham, George
Proceedings 1861-1869, pg 42 (1861 Dec 10), Summit Lodge No. 2, Parkville
Proceedings 1861-1869, pg 76 (1862 Nov 4), Summit Lodge No. 2, Parkville
Proceedings 1876, pg 36 (1876 Sept 20), El Paso Lodge No. 13, Colorado City

Oldroyd, L K
Proceedings 1872, pg 36 (1872 Sept 24), Ashlar Lodge U D, Colorado Springs

Olive Branch Lodge U D
Proceedings 1876, pg 52 (1876 Sept 20)

Olive Branch Lodge U D, Saguache
Proceedings 1876, pg 7 (1876 Mar 15) dispensation granted
Proceedings 1876, pg 12 (1876 Sept 19) returns not received
Proceedings 1876, pg 13 (1876 Aug 20) dispensation fee paid
Proceedings 1876, pg 21 (1876 Sept 20) returns reported

Oliver
Proceedings 1872, pg 79 (1872 Sept 24) Grand Lodge of Nevada

Olmstead, Philip
Proceedings 1872, pg 33 (1872 Sept 24), Occidental Lodge No. 20, Greeley
Proceedings 1875, pg 87 (1875 Sept 22), Occidental Lodge No. 20, Greeley
Proceedings 1876, pg 40 (1876 Sept 20), Occidental Lodge No. 20, Greeley

Olmstead, Phillip
Proceedings 1873, pg 50 (1873 Oct 1), Occidental Lodge No. 20, Greeley
Proceedings 1874, pg 225 (1874 Sept 30), Occidental Lodge No. 20, Greeley

O'Neal, Will C
Proceedings 1876, pg 42 (1876 Sept 20) Idaho Springs Lodge No. 26
Proceedings 1875, pg 89 (1875 Sept 22) Idaho Springs Lodge U D

Ony, Justice
Proceedings 1870, pg 28 (1870 Sept 28), Columbia Lodge No. 14, Boulder City, Apprentice

Opal, Martin
Proceedings 1861-1869, pg 131 (1864 Nov 8) Golden City Lodge No. 1
Proceedings 1861-1869, pg 147 (1865 Nov 7) Golden City Lodge No. 1
Proceedings 1861-1869, pg 221 (1868 Oct 7) Golden City Lodge No. 1
Proceedings 1861-1869, pg 303 (1869 Sept 29) Golden City Lodge No. 1

Opel, Martin
Proceedings 1870, pg 19 (1870 Sept 28), Golden City Lodge No. 1, Golden City
Proceedings 1861-1869, pg 191 (1867 Oct 8) Golden City Lodge No. 1
Proceedings 1871, pg 17 (1871 Sept 27), Golden City Lodge No. 1, Golden City

Oppel, Martin
Proceedings 1872, pg 17 (1872 Sept 24), Golden City Lodge No. 1, Golden City
Proceedings 1873, pg 35 (1873 Oct 1), Golden City Lodge No. 1, Golden City
Proceedings 1874, pg 209 (1874 Sept 30), Golden City Lodge No. 1, Golden City
Proceedings 1875, pg 73 (1875 Sept 22) Golden City Lodge No. 1
Proceedings 1876, pg 29 (1876 Sept 20) Golden City Lodge No. 1

Orahood
Proceedings 1861-1869, pg 177 (1867 Oct 7) committee
Proceedings 1861-1869, pg 185 (1867 Oct 7) Teller
Proceedings 1861-1869, pg 185 (1867 Oct 8) motion
Proceedings 1861-1869, pg 186 (1867 Oct 8) motion
Proceedings 1861-1869, pg 187 (1867 Oct 8) motion
Proceedings 1861-1869, pg 189 (1867 Oct 8) motion
Proceedings 1861-1869, pg 202 (1868 Oct 6) committee
Proceedings 1870, pg 9 (1870 Sept 27) committee
Proceedings 1871, pg 15 (1871 Sept 27) resolution
Proceedings 1872, pg 13 (1872 Sept 24) resolution
Proceedings 1872, pg 15 (1872 Sept 24) correspondence
Proceedings 1873, pg 5 (1873 Sept 30) Senior Grand Warden
Proceedings 1873, pg 9 (1873 Sept 30) report
Proceedings 1873, pg 30 (1873 Oct 1) resolution
Proceedings 1874, pg 29 (1874 Sept 29) motion
Proceedings 1874, pg 30 (1874 Sept 29) resolution
Proceedings 1874, pg 39 (1874 Sept 30) resolution
Proceedings 1876, pg 4 (1876 Sept 19) Deputy Grand Master
Proceedings 1876, pg 17 (1876 Sept 19) motion
Proceedings 1876, pg 17 (1876 Sept 19) motion

Orahood, H M
Proceedings 1861-1869, pg 134 (1864 Nov 8), Chivington Lodge No. 6, Central City
Proceedings 1861-1869, pg 150 (1865 Nov 7), Chivington Lodge No. 6, Central City
Proceedings 1861-1869, pg 168 (1866 Oct 2), Chivington Lodge No. 6, Central City
Proceedings 1861-1869, pg 170 (1866 Oct 2), Black Hawk Lodge U D, Black Hawk
Proceedings 1861-1869, pg 176 (1867 Oct 7), Black Hawk Lodge U D, Black Hawk
Proceedings 1861-1869, pg 186 (1867 Oct 8) per diem
Proceedings 1861-1869, pg 188 (1867 Oct 8) committee
Proceedings 1861-1869, pg 190 (1867 Oct 8) Grand Lecturer
Proceedings 1861-1869, pg 194 (1867 Oct 8), Chivington Lodge No. 6, Central City, Dimitted
Proceedings 1861-1869, pg 195 (1867 Oct 8), Black Hawk Lodge No. 11, Black Hawk
Proceedings 1861-1869, pg 201 (1868 Oct 6) Grand Lecturer
Proceedings 1861-1869, pg 202 (1868 Oct 6), Black Hawk Lodge No. 11, Black Hawk
Proceedings 1861-1869, pg 212 (1868 Oct 6) warrant paid
Proceedings 1861-1869, pg 219 (1868 Oct 7) Grand Lecturer
Proceedings 1861-1869, pg 219 (1868 Oct 7), Black Hawk Lodge No. 11, Black Hawk
Proceedings 1861-1869, pg 226 (1868 Oct 7), Black Hawk Lodge No. 11, Black Hawk
Proceedings 1861-1869, pg 309 (1869 Sept 29), Black Hawk Lodge No. 11, Black Hawk
Proceedings 1870, pg 4 (1870 Sept 27), Black Hawk Lodge No. 11, Black Hawk
Proceedings 1870, pg 14 (1870 Sept 27) committee
Proceedings 1870, pg 16 (1870 Sept 28), Black Hawk Lodge No. 11, Black Hawk
Proceedings 1870, pg 25 (1870 Sept 28), Black Hawk Lodge No. 11, Black Hawk
Proceedings 1870, pg 32 (1870 Sept 28) Senior Grand Warden, 1870
Proceedings 1871, pg 3 (1871 Sept 26) Senior Grand Warden
Proceedings 1871, pg 4 (1871 Sept 26) Senior Grand Warden
Proceedings 1871, pg 4 (1871 Sept 26), Black Hawk Lodge No. 11, Black Hawk

Orahood, H M, cont.
- Proceedings 1871, pg 14 (1871 Sept 27) Senior Grand Warden
- Proceedings 1871, pg 34 (1871 Sept 27) Senior Grand Warden, 1871
- Proceedings 1871, pg 34 (1871 Sept 27) Senior Grand Warden, 1870
- Proceedings 1872, pg 4 (1872 Sept 24) Senior Grand Warden
- Proceedings 1872, pg 4 (1872 Sept 24), Black Hawk Lodge No. 11, Black Hawk
- Proceedings 1872, pg 5 (1872 Sept 24) committee
- Proceedings 1872, pg 5 (1872 Sept 24) committee
- Proceedings 1872, pg 15 (1872 Sept 24) committee
- Proceedings 1872, pg 16 (1872 Sept 24) Senior Grand Warden
- Proceedings 1872, pg 42 (1872 Sept 24) Senior Grand Warden, 1870
- Proceedings 1872, pg 42 (1872 Sept 24) Senior Grand Warden, 1871-1872
- Proceedings 1873, pg 5 (1873 Sept 30) Senior Grand Warden
- Proceedings 1873, pg 6 (1873 Sept 30) committee
- Proceedings 1873, pg 6 (1873 Sept 30), Black Hawk Lodge No. 11, Black Hawk
- Proceedings 1873, pg 32 (1873 Oct 1) mileage and per diem
- Proceedings 1873, pg 58 (1873 Oct 1) Senior Grand Warden, 1871-1872
- Proceedings 1873, pg 58 (1873 Oct 1) Senior Grand Warden, 1870
- Proceedings 1874, pg 5 (1874 Sept 29), Black Hawk Lodge No. 11, Black Hawk
- Proceedings 1874, pg 5 (1874 Sept 29) Deputy Grand Master
- Proceedings 1874, pg 21 (1874 Sept 29) committee
- Proceedings 1874, pg 29 (1874 Sept 29) committee
- Proceedings 1874, pg 32 (1874 Sept 30) Grand Lecturer, Central
- Proceedings 1874, pg 36 (1874 Sept 30) per diem
- Proceedings 1875, pg 16 (1875 Sept 21) Past Deputy Grand Master
- Proceedings 1875, pg 17 (1875 Sept 21) committee
- Proceedings 1875, pg 24 (1875 Sept 21) donation to the library fund
- Proceedings 1875, pg 28 (1875 Sept 21) committee
- Proceedings 1875, pg 31 (1875 Sept 22) case of Wm H Dickinson
- Proceedings 1875, pg 35 (1875 Sept 22) motion
- Proceedings 1875, pg 36 (1875 Sept 22) resolution
- Proceedings 1875, pg 37 (1875 Sept 22) per diem
- Proceedings 1875, pg 38 (1875 Sept 22) motion
- Proceedings 1876, pg 4 (1876 Sept 19) Deputy Grand Master
- Proceedings 1876, pg 6 (1876 Sept 19) committee
- Proceedings 1876, pg 22 (1876 Sept 20) Deputy Grand Master

Orahood, Harper M
- Colorado University Cornerstone Laying, pg 3 (1875 Sept 20) Grand Lecturer
- Proceedings 1861-1869, pg 155 (1866 Oct 1), Black Hawk Lodge U D, Black Hawk
- Proceedings 1861-1869, pg 159 (1866 Oct 1), Black Hawk Lodge No. 11, Black Hawk
- Proceedings 1861-1869, pg 187 (1867 Oct 8) committee
- Proceedings 1861-1869, pg 211 (1868 Oct 6) Grand Lecturer
- Proceedings 1870, pg cover (1870 Sept 28) Senior Grand Warden, Blackhawk
- Proceedings 1870, pg 3 (1870 Sept 27) Senior Grand Warden
- Proceedings 1870, pg 13 (1870 Sept 27) Senior Grand Warden
- Proceedings 1871, pg cover (1871 Sept 27) Senior Grand Warden, Black Hawk
- Proceedings 1871, pg 13 (1871 Sept 26) Senior Grand Warden
- Proceedings 1871, pg 23 (1871 Sept 27), Black Hawk Lodge No. 11, Black Hawk
- Proceedings 1872, pg cover (1872 Sept 24) Senior Grand Warden, Black Hawk
- Proceedings 1872, pg 3 (1872 Sept 24) Senior Grand Warden
- Proceedings 1872, pg 12 (1872 Sept 24) Senior Grand Warden
- Proceedings 1872, pg 24 (1872 Sept 24), Black Hawk Lodge No. 11, Black Hawk
- Proceedings 1873, pg cover (1873 Oct 1) Deputy Grand Master, Black Hawk
- Proceedings 1873, pg 3 (1873 Sept 30) Senior Grand Warden
- Proceedings 1873, pg 14 (1873 Sept 30) Deputy Grand Master
- Proceedings 1873, pg 41 (1873 Oct 1), Black Hawk Lodge No. 11, Black Hawk
- Proceedings 1873, pg 59 (1873 Oct 1) Deputy Grand Master, 1873
- Proceedings 1874, pg 4 (1874 Sept 29) Deputy Grand Master
- Proceedings 1874, pg 206 (1874 Sept 30) Senior Grand Warden, 1872
- Proceedings 1874, pg 206 (1874 Sept 30) Deputy Grand Master, 1873
- Proceedings 1874, pg 206 (1874 Sept 30) Senior Grand Warden, 1871
- Proceedings 1874, pg 206 (1874 Sept 30) Senior Grand Warden, 1870
- Proceedings 1874, pg 216 (1874 Sept 30), Black Hawk Lodge No. 11, Black Hawk
- Proceedings 1875, pg cover (1875 Sept 22) Deputy Grand Master, Central
- Proceedings 1875, pg 15 (1875 Sept 21) Grand Lecturer
- Proceedings 1875, pg 30 (1875 Sept 21) Deputy Grand Master
- Proceedings 1875, pg 80 (1875 Sept 22) Black Hawk Lodge No. 11

Orahood, Harper M, cont.
    Proceedings 1875, pg 93 (1875 Sept 22) Senior Grand Warden, 1872
    Proceedings 1875, pg 93 (1875 Sept 22) Senior Grand Warden, 1871
    Proceedings 1875, pg 93 (1875 Sept 22) Deputy Grand Master, 1873
    Proceedings 1875, pg 93 (1875 Sept 22) Senior Grand Warden, 1870
    Proceedings 1875, pg 93 (1875 Sept 22) Deputy Grand Master, 1875
    Proceedings 1876, pg cover (1876 Sept 20) Grand Master, Central
    Proceedings 1876, pg 3 (1876 Sept 19) Deputy Grand Master
    Proceedings 1876, pg 7 (1875 Sept 28) dispensation to dedicate Idaho Springs Lodge No. 26
    Proceedings 1876, pg 18 (1876 Sept 19) Grand Master
    Proceedings 1876, pg 21 (1876 Sept 20) Grand Lodge of West Virginia, Grand Representative
    Proceedings 1876, pg 34 (1876 Sept 20) Black Hawk Lodge No. 11
    Proceedings 1876, pg 53 (1876 Sept 20) Grand Lodge of West Virginia, of Central, CO,

Organ, C P
    Proceedings 1870, pg 29 (1870 Sept 28), Cheyenne Lodge No. 16, Cheyenne, Wyoming Territory, Apprentice
    Proceedings 1871, pg 27 (1871 Sept 27), Cheyenne Lodge No. 16, Cheyenne, Wyoming Territory
    Proceedings 1872, pg 29 (1872 Sept 24), Cheyenne Lodge No. 16, Cheyenne, Wyoming Territory
    Proceedings 1873, pg 46 (1873 Oct 1), Cheyenne Lodge No. 16, Cheyenne, Wyoming Territory
    Proceedings 1874, pg 221 (1874 Sept 30), Cheyenne Lodge No. 16, Cheyenne, Wyoming Territory

Orleans, Louis P
    Proceedings 1871, pg 30 (1871 Sept 27), Collins Lodge No. 19, Fort Collins, Fellowcraft
    Proceedings 1872, pg 33 (1872 Sept 24), Collins Lodge No. 19, Fort Collins
    Proceedings 1873, pg 49 (1873 Oct 1), Collins Lodge No. 19, Fort Collins
    Proceedings 1874, pg 224 (1874 Sept 30), Collins Lodge No. 19, Fort Collins, Larimer County
    Proceedings 1875, pg 86 (1875 Sept 22), Collins Lodge No. 19, Fort Collins
    Proceedings 1876, pg 39 (1876 Sept 20), Collins Lodge No. 19, Fort Collins

Orr, E F
    Proceedings 1875, pg 89 (1875 Sept 22), Doric Lodge No. 25, Fairplay
    Proceedings 1876, pg 42 (1876 Sept 20), Doric Lodge No. 25, Fairplay
    Proceedings 1876, pg 50 (1876 Sept 20), Doric Lodge No. 25, Fairplay

Orr, H N
    Proceedings 1873, pg 46 (1873 Oct 1), Cheyenne Lodge No. 16, Cheyenne, Wyoming Territory
    Proceedings 1874, pg 221 (1874 Sept 30), Cheyenne Lodge No. 16, Cheyenne, Wyoming Territory

Orr, J H
    Proceedings 1872, pg 33 (1872 Sept 24), Occidental Lodge No. 20, Greeley

Orr, James H
    Proceedings 1871, pg 30 (1871 Sept 27), Occidental Lodge U D, Greeley
    Proceedings 1873, pg 50 (1873 Oct 1), Occidental Lodge No. 20, Greeley
    Proceedings 1875, pg 87 (1875 Sept 22), Occidental Lodge No. 20, Greeley
    Proceedings 1876, pg 40 (1876 Sept 20), Occidental Lodge No. 20, Greeley

Orr, James L
    Proceedings 1861-1869, pg 280 (1867 Nov 19), Grand Master, Grand Lodge of South Carolina

Ort, James H
    Proceedings 1874, pg 225 (1874 Sept 30), Occidental Lodge No. 20, Greeley

Orton, Elias
    Proceedings 1875, pg 91 (1875 Sept 22), Las Animas Lodge U D, Trinidad
    Proceedings 1876, pg 43 (1876 Sept 20), Las Animas Lodge No. 28, Trinidad

Ory, Justice
    Proceedings 1871, pg 26 (1871 Sept 27), Columbia Lodge No. 14, Boulder City, Apprentice
    Proceedings 1872, pg 28 (1872 Sept 24), Columbia Lodge No. 14, Boulder, Apprentice
    Proceedings 1873, pg 45 (1873 Oct 1), Columbia Lodge No. 14, Boulder, Apprentice
    Proceedings 1874, pg 219 (1874 Sept 30), Columbia Lodge No. 14, Boulder, Boulder County, Apprentice
    Proceedings 1875, pg 83 (1875 Sept 22), Columbia Lodge No. 14, Boulder, Apprentice

Ory, Justus
    Proceedings 1876, pg 37 (1876 Sept 20), Columbia Lodge No. 14, Boulder, Apprentice

Osborn, E T
    Proceedings 1875, pg 73 (1875 Sept 22) Golden City Lodge No. 1

Osborn, Eben T
    Proceedings 1876, pg 29 (1876 Sept 20) Golden City Lodge No. 1

Osborn, James H
    Proceedings 1861-1869, pg 170 (1866 Oct 2), Empire Lodge No. 8, Empire City

Osborn, James H
    Proceedings 1861-1869, pg 195 (1867 Oct 8), Empire Lodge No. 8, Empire City
    Proceedings 1873, pg 40 (1873 Oct 1), Empire Lodge No. 8, Empire
    Proceedings 1874, pg 215 (1874 Sept 30), Empire Lodge No. 8, Empire

Colorado's Territorial Masons

Osborn, Jas H
    Proceedings 1861-1869, pg 226 (1868 Oct 7), Empire Lodge No. 8, Empire City
    Proceedings 1861-1869, pg 308 (1869 Sept 29), Empire Lodge No. 8, Empire City
    Proceedings 1870, pg 24 (1870 Sept 28), Empire Lodge No. 8, Empire

Osborn, Luther W
    Proceedings 1874, pg 98 (1874 Sept 30) Grand Lodge of Nebraska

Osborn, Ralph A
    Proceedings 1876, pg 38 (1876 Sept 20), Mount Moriah Lodge No. 15, Canon City

Osborn, William
    Proceedings 1870, pg 24 (1870 Sept 28), Empire Lodge No. 8, Empire
    Proceedings 1873, pg 41 (1873 Oct 1), Empire Lodge No. 8, Empire
    Proceedings 1874, pg 215 (1874 Sept 30), Empire Lodge No. 8, Empire

Osborn, Wm
    Proceedings 1872, pg 23 (1872 Sept 24), Empire Lodge No. 8, Empire

Osborne, E T
    Proceedings 1874, pg 209 (1874 Sept 30), Golden City Lodge No. 1, Golden City

Osborne, James H
    Proceedings 1872, pg 23 (1872 Sept 24), Empire Lodge No. 8, Empire

O'Sullivan
    Proceedings 1861-1869, pg 265 (1868 Oct 7), Grand Master, Grand Lodge of Missouri, deceased

O'Sullivan, A
    Proceedings 1861-1869, pg 157 (1866 Oct 1), deceased, Grand Secretary, Grand Lodge of Missouri

O'Sullivan, Anthony
    Proceedings 1861-1869, pg 264 (1868 Oct 7), Grand Master, Grand Lodge of Missouri, deceased in the cholera epidemic of 1866

Oswald, Geo
    Proceedings 1861-1869, pg 42 (1861 Dec 10), Summit Lodge No. 2, Parkville
    Proceedings 1861-1869, pg 76 (1862 Nov 4), Summit Lodge No. 2, Parkville
    Proceedings 1861-1869, pg 110 (1863 Nov 3), Summit Lodge No. 2, Parkville

Oswald, George
    Proceedings 1861-1869, pg 132 (1864 Nov 8) Golden City Lodge No. 1

Otis, Oran G
    Proceedings 1872, pg 22 (1872 Sept 24), Union Lodge No. 7, Denver
    Proceedings 1874, pg 214 (1874 Sept 30), Union Lodge No. 7, Denver
    Proceedings 1875, pg 78 (1875 Sept 22), Union Lodge No. 7, Denver
    Proceedings 1876, pg 33 (1876 Sept 20), Union Lodge No. 7, Denver

Otis, Oren G
    Proceedings 1873, pg 39 (1873 Oct 1), Union Lodge No. 7, Denver

Otterbach, W S
    Proceedings 1875, pg 80 (1875 Sept 22) Black Hawk Lodge No. 11

Otterbach, William L
    Proceedings 1876, pg 34 (1876 Sept 20) Black Hawk Lodge No. 11

Otterback, W S
    Proceedings 1873, pg 6 (1873 Sept 30), Black Hawk Lodge No. 11, Black Hawk

Otterback, William L
    Proceedings 1871, pg 23 (1871 Sept 27), Black Hawk Lodge No. 11, Black Hawk
    Proceedings 1874, pg 216 (1874 Sept 30), Black Hawk Lodge No. 11, Black Hawk

Otterback, Wm L
    Proceedings 1873, pg 41 (1873 Oct 1), Black Hawk Lodge No. 11, Black Hawk
    Proceedings 1872, pg 25 (1872 Sept 24), Black Hawk Lodge No. 11, Black Hawk

Overturf, Geo
    Proceedings 1872, pg 31 (1872 Sept 24), Pueblo Lodge No. 17, Pueblo, Fellowcraft
    Proceedings 1875, pg 85 (1875 Sept 22) Pueblo Lodge No. 17, Fellowcraft
    Proceedings 1876, pg 39 (1876 Sept 20) Pueblo Lodge No. 17, Fellow Craft

Overturf, George
    Proceedings 1873, pg 47 (1873 Oct 1), Pueblo Lodge No. 17, Pueblo, Fellowcraft
    Proceedings 1874, pg 222 (1874 Sept 30), Pueblo Lodge No. 17, Pueblo, Pueblo County, Fellowcraft

Owen, N D
    Proceedings 1861-1869, pg 307 (1869 Sept 29), Central Lodge No. 6, Central City, Apprentice
    Proceedings 1870, pg 22 (1870 Sept 28), Central Lodge No. 6, Central City
    Proceedings 1871, pg 20 (1871 Sept 27), Central Lodge No. 6, Central
    Proceedings 1872, pg 21 (1872 Sept 24), Denver Lodge No. 5, Denver

Owen, Newton D
    Proceedings 1873, pg 38 (1873 Oct 1), Central Lodge No. 6, Central City
    Proceedings 1874, pg 212 (1874 Sept 30), Central Lodge No. 6, Central
    Proceedings 1875, pg 77 (1875 Sept 22), Central Lodge No. 6, Central City
    Proceedings 1876, pg 32 (1876 Sept 20), Central Lodge No. 6, Central City

Colorado's Territorial Masons

Owen, P A
Proceedings 1872, pg 30 (1872 Sept 24), Cheyenne Lodge No. 16, Cheyenne, Wyoming Territory, Fellowcraft
Proceedings 1873, pg 46 (1873 Oct 1), Cheyenne Lodge No. 16, Cheyenne, Wyoming Territory

Owen, Thomas M
Proceedings 1872, pg 22 (1872 Sept 24), Union Lodge No. 7, Denver
Proceedings 1874, pg 215 (1874 Sept 30), Union Lodge No. 7, Denver, Stricken from the rolls

Owen, Thos M
Proceedings 1873, pg 39 (1873 Oct 1), Union Lodge No. 7, Denver

Owens
Proceedings 1874, pg 91 (1874 Sept 30) Grand Lodge of Missouri

Owens, P A
Proceedings 1874, pg 221 (1874 Sept 30), Cheyenne Lodge No. 16, Cheyenne, Wyoming Territory

Owens, Samuel H
Proceedings 1873, pg 60 (1873 Oct 1) Grand Lodge of Missouri, California
Proceedings 1874, pg 90 (1874 Sept 30) Grand Lodge of Missouri

Owens, Thomas F
Proceedings 1870, pg 105 (1869 Dec 13) Grand Master, Grand Lodge of Virginia
Proceedings 1872, pg 90 (1872 Sept 24) Grand Lodge of Virginia

P

Page, F H
Proceedings 1861-1869, pg 112 (1863 Nov 3) Denver Lodge No. 5, Fellowcraft
Proceedings 1861-1869, pg 167 (1866 Oct 2) Denver Lodge No. 5, dimitted

Page, Frank H
Proceedings 1861-1869, pg 133 (1864 Nov 8) Denver Lodge No. 5
Proceedings 1861-1869, pg 149 (1865 Nov 7), Nevada Lodge No. 4, Nevadaville

Pain, G M
Proceedings 1861-1869, pg 152 (1865 Nov 7), Helena City Lodge U D, Helena City, Montana Territory

Paine, Mary P
Proceedings 1861-1869, pg 317 (1869 Sept 29) wife of Allyn Weston

Painter, E R
Proceedings 1876, pg 33 (1876 Sept 20), Union Lodge No. 7, Denver

Painter, Edward R
Proceedings 1874, pg 214 (1874 Sept 30), Union Lodge No. 7, Denver
Proceedings 1875, pg 78 (1875 Sept 22), Union Lodge No. 7, Denver

Painter, J K
Proceedings 1871, pg 27 (1871 Sept 27), Cheyenne Lodge No. 16, Cheyenne, Wyoming Territory, Fellowcraft
Proceedings 1872, pg 29 (1872 Sept 24), Cheyenne Lodge No. 16, Cheyenne, Wyoming Territory
Proceedings 1873, pg 46 (1873 Oct 1), Cheyenne Lodge No. 16, Cheyenne, Wyoming Territory
Proceedings 1874, pg 221 (1874 Sept 30), Cheyenne Lodge No. 16, Cheyenne, Wyoming Territory, Demitted
Proceedings 1874, pg 227 (1874 Sept 30), St Vrain No. 23, Longmont
Proceedings 1876, pg 41 (1876 Sept 20), St Vrain Lodge No. 23, Longmont

Palemon, Wiley
Proceedings 1872, pg 24 (1872 Sept 24), Black Hawk Lodge No. 11, Black Hawk
Proceedings 1873, pg 41 (1873 Oct 1), Black Hawk Lodge No. 11, Black Hawk

Palmer, A D
Proceedings 1861-1869, pg 312 (1869 Sept 29), Cheyenne Lodge No. 16, Cheyenne
Proceedings 1870, pg 29 (1870 Sept 28), Cheyenne Lodge No. 16, Cheyenne, Wyoming Territory
Proceedings 1871, pg 27 (1871 Sept 27), Cheyenne Lodge No. 16, Cheyenne, Wyoming Territory
Proceedings 1872, pg 29 (1872 Sept 24), Cheyenne Lodge No. 16, Cheyenne, Wyoming Territory
Proceedings 1873, pg 46 (1873 Oct 1), Cheyenne Lodge No. 16, Cheyenne, Wyoming Territory
Proceedings 1874, pg 221 (1874 Sept 30), Cheyenne Lodge No. 16, Cheyenne, Wyoming Territory

Palmer, Frank
Proceedings 1861-1869, pg 195 (1867 Oct 8), Union Lodge No. 7, Denver
Proceedings 1861-1869, pg 225 (1868 Oct 7), Union Lodge No. 7, Denver
Proceedings 1861-1869, pg 307 (1869 Sept 29), Union Lodge No. 7, Denver
Proceedings 1870, pg 23 (1870 Sept 28), Union Lodge No. 7, Denver
Proceedings 1871, pg 21 (1871 Sept 27), Union Lodge No. 7, Denver
Proceedings 1872, pg 22 (1872 Sept 24), Union Lodge No. 7, Denver
Proceedings 1873, pg 39 (1873 Oct 1), Union Lodge No. 7, Denver
Proceedings 1874, pg 214 (1874 Sept 30), Union Lodge No. 7, Denver
Proceedings 1875, pg 78 (1875 Sept 22), Union Lodge No. 7, Denver
Proceedings 1876, pg 33 (1876 Sept 20), Union Lodge No. 7, Denver

Palmer, H L
Proceedings 1861-1869, pg 284 (1867 June 11) Grand Lodge of Wisconsin

Palmer, Henry I
Proceedings 1872, pg 44 (1872 Sept 24) Milwaukee, Grand Lodge of Wisconsin

Palmer, Henry L
Proceedings 1872, pg 93 (1872 Sept 24) Grand Lodge of Wisconsin

Palmer, L A
Proceedings 1871, pg 30 (1871 Sept 27), Occidental Lodge U D, Greeley

Palmer, Lester
Proceedings 1876, pg 33 (1876 Sept 20), Union Lodge No. 7, Denver, Fellow Craft

Palmer, R L
Proceedings 1861-1869, pg 196 (1867 Oct 8), Black Hawk Lodge No. 11, Black Hawk
Proceedings 1861-1869, pg 227 (1868 Oct 7), Black Hawk Lodge No. 11, Black Hawk, Dimitted
Proceedings 1870, pg 25 (1870 Sept 28), Black Hawk Lodge No. 11, Black Hawk
Proceedings 1872, pg 25 (1872 Sept 24), Black Hawk Lodge No. 11, Black Hawk, Dimitted

Palmer, Rufus L
Proceedings 1871, pg 23 (1871 Sept 27), Black Hawk Lodge No. 11, Black Hawk

Palmer, W T
Proceedings 1861-1869, pg 285 (1867 June 11), Grand Secretary, Grand Lodge of Wisconsin

Palmer, William T
Proceedings 1871, pg 35 (1871 Sept 27) Grand Secretary, Grand Lodge of Wisconsin

Palmer, Wm T
Proceedings 1861-1869, pg 316 (1869 Sept 29) Grand Lodge of Wisconsin
Proceedings 1861-1869, pg 349 (1868 June 9) Grand Secretary, Grand Lodge of Wisconsin
Proceedings 1870, pg 34 (1870 Sept 28) Grand Secretary, Grand Lodge of Wisconsin
Proceedings 1870, pg 106 (1870 June 14) Grand Secretary, Grand Lodge of Wisconsin
Proceedings 1872, pg 44 (1872 Sept 24) Milwaukee, Grand Lodge of Wisconsin

Palmeter, H C
Proceedings 1861-1869, pg 194 (1867 Oct 8), Chivington Lodge No. 6, Central City, Apprentice
Proceedings 1861-1869, pg 225 (1868 Oct 7), Chivington Lodge No. 6, Central City, Apprentice
Proceedings 1861-1869, pg 307 (1869 Sept 29), Central Lodge No. 6, Central City, Apprentice
Proceedings 1870, pg 22 (1870 Sept 28), Central Lodge No. 6, Central City, Apprentice
Proceedings 1871, pg 21 (1871 Sept 27), Central Lodge No. 6, Central, Apprentice
Proceedings 1872, pg 21 (1872 Sept 24), Denver Lodge No. 5, Denver, Apprentice
Proceedings 1873, pg 39 (1873 Oct 1), Central Lodge No. 6, Central City, Apprentice
Proceedings 1874, pg 213 (1874 Sept 30), Central Lodge No. 6, Central, Apprentice
Proceedings 1875, pg 77 (1875 Sept 22), Central Lodge No. 6, Central City, Apprentice
Proceedings 1876, pg 32 (1876 Sept 20), Central Lodge No. 6, Central City, Apprentice

Pape, Wm H
Proceedings 1874, pg 228 (1874 Sept 30), Evanston Lodge U D, Evanston, Uintah County, Wyoming Territory

Parche
Proceedings 1874, pg 96 (1874 Sept 30) Grand Lodge of Montana

Pardue, A B
Proceedings 1876, pg 45 (1876 Sept 20), King Solomon Lodge U D, West Las Animas, Fellow Craft

Parenteau, William
Proceedings 1876, pg 32 (1876 Sept 20), Central Lodge No. 6, Central City
Proceedings 1876, pg 50 (1876 Sept 20), Central Lodge No. 6, Central City

Park, M T
Proceedings 1874, pg 211 (1874 Sept 30), Denver Lodge No. 5, Denver
Proceedings 1875, pg 75 (1875 Sept 22) Denver Lodge No. 5
Proceedings 1876, pg 49 (1876 Sept 20) Denver Lodge No. 5, 1876 Aug 19

Park, R E
Proceedings 1875, pg 89 (1875 Sept 22), Doric Lodge No. 25, Fairplay
Proceedings 1876, pg 42 (1876 Sept 20), Doric Lodge No. 25, Fairplay

Parker, Charles E
Proceedings 1875, pg 75 (1875 Sept 22) Denver Lodge No. 5
Proceedings 1876, pg 31 (1876 Sept 20) Denver Lodge No. 5

Parker, Chas E
Proceedings 1874, pg 211 (1874 Sept 30), Denver Lodge No. 5, Denver

Parker, E P
Proceedings 1861-1869, pg 150 (1865 Nov 7), Chivington Lodge No. 6, Central City
Proceedings 1861-1869, pg 151 (1865 Nov 7), Chivington Lodge No. 6, Central City, dimitted
Proceedings 1861-1869, pg 168 (1866 Oct 2), Chivington Lodge No. 6, Central City, dimitted

Parker, J S
Proceedings 1876, pg 33 (1876 Sept 20), Union Lodge No. 7, Denver

Parker, James S
Proceedings 1873, pg 40 (1873 Oct 1), Union Lodge No. 7, Denver, Apprentice
Proceedings 1874, pg 214 (1874 Sept 30), Union Lodge No. 7, Denver, Fellowcraft

Colorado's Territorial Masons

Parker, James S, cont.
   Proceedings 1875, pg 78 (1875 Sept 22), Union Lodge No. 7, Denver

Parker, M M
   Proceedings 1872, pg 36 (1872 Sept 24), Ashlar Lodge U D, Colorado Springs

Parker, M P
   Proceedings 1861-1869, pg 227 (1868 Oct 7), Washington Lodge No. 12, Georgetown
   Proceedings 1861-1869, pg 309 (1869 Sept 29), Washington Lodge No. 12, Georgetown
   Proceedings 1871, pg 24 (1871 Sept 27), Washington Lodge No. 12, Georgetown
   Proceedings 1875, pg 81 (1875 Sept 22), Washington Lodge No. 12, Georgetown

Parker, Matthew P
   Proceedings 1870, pg 26 (1870 Sept 28), Washington Lodge No. 12, Georgetown
   Proceedings 1872, pg 26 (1872 Sept 24), Washington Lodge No. 12, Georgetown
   Proceedings 1873, pg 42 (1873 Oct 1), Washington Lodge No. 12, Georgetown
   Proceedings 1874, pg 217 (1874 Sept 30), Washington Lodge No. 12, Georgetown

Parker, W H
   Proceedings 1876, pg 8 (1876 June 26), Union Lodge No. 7, Denver
   Proceedings 1876, pg 33 (1876 Sept 20), Union Lodge No. 7, Denver

Parkhurst, C F
   Proceedings 1861-1869, pg 149 (1865 Nov 7), Nevada Lodge No. 4, Nevadaville, Apprentice
   Proceedings 1861-1869, pg 167 (1866 Oct 2) Denver Lodge No. 5, Fellowcraft
   Proceedings 1861-1869, pg 223 (1868 Oct 7) Denver Lodge No. 5, Fellowcraft
   Proceedings 1861-1869, pg 305 (1869 Sept 29) Denver Lodge No. 5, Fellowcraft
   Proceedings 1870, pg 21 (1870 Sept 28), Denver Lodge No. 5, Denver, died

Parkhurst, Charles F
   Proceedings 1861-1869, pg 193 (1867 Oct 8) Denver Lodge No. 5, Fellowcraft

Parkhurst, Chas F
   Proceedings 1861-1869, pg 133 (1864 Nov 8) Denver Lodge No. 5, Apprentice

Parks, James
   Proceedings 1873, pg 48 (1873 Oct 1), Laramie Lodge No. 18, Laramie, Wyoming Territory, Apprentice
   Proceedings 1874, pg 223 (1874 Sept 30), Laramie Lodge No. 18, Laramie City

Parlan [Parlin], David
   Proceedings 1861-1869, pg 311 (1869 Sept 29), Columbia Lodge No. 14, Boulder City
   Proceedings 1870, pg 21 (1870 Sept 28), Denver Lodge No. 5, Denver

Parlen [Parlin], David
   Proceedings 1861-1869, pg 230 (1868 Oct 7), Valmont Lodge U D, Valmont

Parlin, David
   Proceedings 1861-1869, pg 192 (1867 Oct 8) Denver Lodge No. 5
   Proceedings 1861-1869, pg 223 (1868 Oct 7) Denver Lodge No. 5
   Proceedings 1861-1869, pg 305 (1869 Sept 29) Denver Lodge No. 5
   Proceedings 1870, pg 27 (1870 Sept 28), Columbia Lodge No. 14, Boulder City
   Proceedings 1871, pg 26 (1871 Sept 27), Columbia Lodge No. 14, Boulder City
   Proceedings 1873, pg 44 (1873 Oct 1), Columbia Lodge No. 14, Boulder
   Proceedings 1874, pg 219 (1874 Sept 30), Columbia Lodge No. 14, Boulder, Boulder County
   Proceedings 1875, pg 83 (1875 Sept 22), Columbia Lodge No. 14, Boulder, Stricken from the rolls

Parmelee
   Proceedings 1861-1869, pg 184 (1867 Oct 7) Grand Secretary
   Proceedings 1870, pg 15 (1870 Sept 28) resolution
   Proceedings 1871, pg 4 (1871 Sept 26) Committee
   Proceedings 1871, pg 12 (1871 Sept 26) resolution
   Proceedings 1871, pg 13 (1871 Sept 26) Committee
   Proceedings 1871, pg 15 (1871 Sept 27) resolution
   Proceedings 1872, pg 4 (1872 Sept 24) Grand Secretary
   Proceedings 1872, pg 12 (1872 Sept 24) committee
   Proceedings 1874, pg 34 (1874 Sept 30) amendment
   Proceedings 1876, pg 26 (1876 Sept 20) resolution

Parmelee, E C
   Proceedings 1861-1869, pg 150 (1865 Nov 7), Chivington Lodge No. 6, Central City

Parmelee, Ed C
   Colorado University Cornerstone Laying, pg cover (1875 Sept 20) Grand Secretary, Georgetown
   Colorado University Cornerstone Laying, pg 3 (1875 Sept 20) Grand Secretary
   Colorado University Cornerstone Laying, pg 4 (1875 Sept 20) presented the dedication medal
   Colorado University Cornerstone Laying, pg 14 (1875 Sept 20) Grand Secretary
   Proceedings 1861-1869, pg 113 (1863 Nov 3), Chivington Lodge No. 6, Central City
   Proceedings 1861-1869, pg 113 (1863 Nov 3), Montana Lodge U D, Central City
   Proceedings 1861-1869, pg 127 (1864 Nov 8), Chivington Lodge No. 6, Central City
   Proceedings 1861-1869, pg 133 (1864 Nov 8), Chivington Lodge No. 6, Central City
   Proceedings 1861-1869, pg 160 (1866 Oct 2), Chivington Lodge No. 6, Central City
   Proceedings 1861-1869, pg 161 (1866 Oct 2) Grand Secretary
   Proceedings 1861-1869, pg 163 (1866 Oct 2) Grand Secretary

Parmelee, Ed C, cont.
- Proceedings 1861-1869, pg 168 (1866 Oct 2), Chivington Lodge No. 6, Central City
- Proceedings 1861-1869, pg 175 (1867 Oct 7) Grand Secretary
- Proceedings 1861-1869, pg 176 (1867 Oct 7) Grand Secretary
- Proceedings 1861-1869, pg 176 (1867 Oct 7), Chivington Lodge No. 6, Central City
- Proceedings 1861-1869, pg 181 (1867 Oct 7) Grand Secretary
- Proceedings 1861-1869, pg 182 (1867 Oct 7) Grand Secretary
- Proceedings 1861-1869, pg 185 (1867 Oct 7) Grand Secretary
- Proceedings 1861-1869, pg 186 (1867 Oct 8) committee
- Proceedings 1861-1869, pg 186 (1867 Oct 8) Grand Secretary
- Proceedings 1861-1869, pg 190 (1867 Oct 8) Grand Secretary
- Proceedings 1861-1869, pg 193 (1867 Oct 8), Chivington Lodge No. 6, Central City
- Proceedings 1861-1869, pg 201 (1868 Oct 6) Grand Secretary
- Proceedings 1861-1869, pg 202 (1868 Oct 6) Grand Secretary
- Proceedings 1861-1869, pg 212 (1868 Oct 6) warrant paid
- Proceedings 1861-1869, pg 213 (1868 Oct 6) Grand Secretary
- Proceedings 1861-1869, pg 214 (1868 Oct 6) Grand Secretary
- Proceedings 1861-1869, pg 215 (1868 Oct 6) Grand Secretary
- Proceedings 1861-1869, pg 219 (1868 Oct 7) Grand Secretary
- Proceedings 1861-1869, pg 219 (1868 Oct 7) mileage allowed
- Proceedings 1861-1869, pg 220 (1868 Oct 7) Grand Secretary
- Proceedings 1861-1869, pg 224 (1868 Oct 7), Chivington Lodge No. 6, Central City
- Proceedings 1861-1869, pg 287 (1869 Sept 28) Grand Secretary
- Proceedings 1861-1869, pg 288 (1869 Sept 28) Grand Secretary
- Proceedings 1861-1869, pg 291 (1869 Sept 28) Grand Secretary
- Proceedings 1861-1869, pg 292 (1869 Sept 28) presented credentials
- Proceedings 1861-1869, pg 292 (1869 Sept 28) Grand Secretary
- Proceedings 1861-1869, pg 298 (1869 Sept 28) Grand Secretary
- Proceedings 1861-1869, pg 300 (1869 Sept 29) Grand Secretary
- Proceedings 1861-1869, pg 302 (1869 Sept 29) Grand Secretary
- Proceedings 1861-1869, pg 306 (1869 Sept 29), Central Lodge No. 6, Central City
- Proceedings 1861-1869, pg 315 (1869 Sept 29) Grand Secretary, 1868
- Proceedings 1861-1869, pg 315 (1869 Sept 29) Grand Secretary, 1869
- Proceedings 1861-1869, pg 315 (1869 Sept 29) Grand Secretary, 1866
- Proceedings 1861-1869, pg 315 (1869 Sept 29) Grand Secretary, 1867
- Proceedings 1870, pg cover (1870 Sept 28) Grand Secretary, Georgetown
- Proceedings 1870, pg cover (1870 Sept 28) Grand Secretary, Grand Lodge of Colorado
- Proceedings 1870, pg 2 (1870 Sept 27) Grand Secretary
- Proceedings 1870, pg 3 (1870 Sept 27) Grand Secretary
- Proceedings 1870, pg 4 (1870 Sept 27) Grand Secretary
- Proceedings 1870, pg 5 (1870 Sept 27) representing the Grand Lodge of Oregon
- Proceedings 1870, pg 12 (1870 Sept 27) Grand Secretary
- Proceedings 1870, pg 13 (1870 Sept 27) Grand Secretary
- Proceedings 1870, pg 16 (1870 Sept 28) Grand Secretary
- Proceedings 1870, pg 17 (1870 Sept 28) Grand Secretary
- Proceedings 1870, pg 22 (1870 Sept 28), Central Lodge No. 6, Central City
- Proceedings 1870, pg 32 (1870 Sept 28) Grand Secretary, 1867
- Proceedings 1870, pg 32 (1870 Sept 28) Grand Secretary, 1868
- Proceedings 1870, pg 32 (1870 Sept 28) Grand Secretary, 1870
- Proceedings 1870, pg 32 (1870 Sept 28) Grand Secretary, 1869
- Proceedings 1870, pg 32 (1870 Sept 28) Grand Secretary, 1866
- Proceedings 1870, pg 98 (1870 June 20) Grand Lodge of Colorado
- Proceedings 1871, pg cover (1871 Sept 26) Grand Secretary, Georgetown
- Proceedings 1871, pg cover (1871 Sept 27) Grand Secretary
- Proceedings 1871, pg cover (1871 Sept 27) Grand Secretary, Georgetown
- Proceedings 1871, pg cover (1871 Sept 27) committee, Georgetown
- Proceedings 1871, pg 3 (1871 Sept 26) Grand Secretary
- Proceedings 1871, pg 3 (1871 Sept 26) Grand Representative, Missouri and Oregon
- Proceedings 1871, pg 4 (1871 Sept 26) Grand Secretary
- Proceedings 1871, pg 5 (1871 Sept 26) Committee
- Proceedings 1871, pg 5 (1871 Sept 26) Committee
- Proceedings 1871, pg 10 (1871 Sept 26) Grand Secretary
- Proceedings 1871, pg 11 (1871 Sept 26) Grand Secretary
- Proceedings 1871, pg 13 (1871 Sept 26) Grand Secretary
- Proceedings 1871, pg 14 (1871 Sept 27) Grand Secretary
- Proceedings 1871, pg 15 (1871 Sept 27) Grand Secretary
- Proceedings 1871, pg 16 (1871 Sept 27) Grand Secretary
- Proceedings 1871, pg 16 (1871 Sept 27) Committee
- Proceedings 1871, pg 20 (1871 Sept 27), Central Lodge No. 6, Central
- Proceedings 1871, pg 34 (1871 Sept 27) Grand Secretary, 1866

Colorado's Territorial Masons

Parmelee, Ed C, cont.
    Proceedings 1871, pg 34 (1871 Sept 27) Grand Secretary, 1867
    Proceedings 1871, pg 34 (1871 Sept 27) Grand Secretary, 1868
    Proceedings 1871, pg 34 (1871 Sept 27) Grand Secretary, 1869
    Proceedings 1871, pg 34 (1871 Sept 27) Grand Secretary, 1870
    Proceedings 1871, pg 34 (1871 Sept 27) Grand Secretary, 1871
    Proceedings 1872, pg cover (1872 Sept 24) Grand Secretary
    Proceedings 1872, pg cover (1872 Sept 24), Georgetown Chapter U D, Georgetown
    Proceedings 1872, pg cover (1872 Sept 24) Grand Secretary, Georgetown
    Proceedings 1872, pg 1 (1872 Sept 24) Grand Secretary, Georgetown
    Proceedings 1872, pg 3 (1872 Sept 24) Grand Secretary
    Proceedings 1872, pg 4 (1872 Sept 24) Grand Secretary
    Proceedings 1872, pg 4 (1872 Sept 24), Maine, Missouri, Oregon
    Proceedings 1872, pg 5 (1872 Sept 24) committee
    Proceedings 1872, pg 5 (1872 Sept 24) committee
    Proceedings 1872, pg 6 (1872 Sept 24) committee
    Proceedings 1872, pg 11 (1872 Sept 24) Grand Secretary
    Proceedings 1872, pg 12 (1872 Sept 24) Grand Secretary
    Proceedings 1872, pg 14 (1872 Sept 24) Grand Secretary
    Proceedings 1872, pg 16 (1872 Sept 24) Grand Secretary
    Proceedings 1872, pg 16 (1872 Sept 24) Grand Secretary
    Proceedings 1872, pg 21 (1872 Sept 24), Denver Lodge No. 5, Denver
    Proceedings 1872, pg 41 (1872 Sept 24), Representative of the Grand Lodges of Maine, Missouri and Oregon
    Proceedings 1872, pg 42 (1872 Sept 24) Grand Secretary, 1868
    Proceedings 1872, pg 42 (1872 Sept 24) Grand Secretary, 1869
    Proceedings 1872, pg 42 (1872 Sept 24) Grand Secretary, 1867
    Proceedings 1872, pg 42 (1872 Sept 24) Grand Secretary, 1870
    Proceedings 1872, pg 42 (1872 Sept 24) Grand Secretary, 1871-1872
    Proceedings 1872, pg 42 (1872 Sept 24) Grand Secretary, 1866
    Proceedings 1872, pg 125 (1872 Sept 24) Grand Secretary
    Proceedings 1873, pg cover (1873 Oct 1), Georgetown Chapter U D, Georgetown
    Proceedings 1873, pg cover (1873 Oct 1) committee, Georgetown
    Proceedings 1873, pg cover (1873 Oct 1) Grand Secretary, Georgetown
    Proceedings 1873, pg cover (1873 Sept 30) Grand Secretary, Georgetown, Clear Creek County
    Proceedings 1873, pg 3 (1873 Sept 30) Grand Secretary
    Proceedings 1873, pg 4 (1873 Sept 30), Grand Representative, Maine, Missouri, Oregon
    Proceedings 1873, pg 5 (1873 Sept 30) Grand Secretary
    Proceedings 1873, pg 14 (1873 Sept 30) Grand Secretary
    Proceedings 1873, pg 15 (1873 Oct 1) presented account
    Proceedings 1873, pg 16 (1873 Oct 1) Grand Secretary
    Proceedings 1873, pg 29 (1873 Oct 1) Grand Secretary
    Proceedings 1873, pg 32 (1873 Oct 1) committee
    Proceedings 1873, pg 32 (1873 Oct 1) mileage and per diem
    Proceedings 1873, pg 33 (1873 Oct 1) Grand Secretary
    Proceedings 1873, pg 39 (1873 Oct 1), Central Lodge No. 6, Central City
    Proceedings 1873, pg 42 (1873 Oct 1), Black Hawk Lodge No. 11, Black Hawk
    Proceedings 1873, pg 58 (1873 Oct 1) Grand Secretary, 1867
    Proceedings 1873, pg 58 (1873 Oct 1) Grand Secretary, 1870
    Proceedings 1873, pg 58 (1873 Oct 1) Grand Secretary, 1871-1872
    Proceedings 1873, pg 58 (1873 Oct 1) Grand Secretary, 1868
    Proceedings 1873, pg 58 (1873 Oct 1) Grand Secretary, 1866
    Proceedings 1873, pg 58 (1873 Oct 1) Grand Secretary, 1869
    Proceedings 1873, pg 59 (1873 Oct 1) Grand Secretary, 1873
    Proceedings 1873, pg 59 (1873 Oct 1), Grand Representative of Maine, Missouri, Oregon
    Proceedings 1873, pg 60 (1873 Oct 1) Grand Lodge of Colorado, Georgetown
    Proceedings 1874, pg cover (1874 Sept 29) Grand Secretary, Georgetown, Clear Creek County
    Proceedings 1874, pg cover (1874 Sept 30) Grand Secretary, Georgetown
    Proceedings 1874, pg cover (1874 Sept 30) committee, Georgetown
    Proceedings 1874, pg 3 (1874 Sept 29) Grand Secretary
    Proceedings 1874, pg 5 (1874 Sept 29) Grand Secretary
    Proceedings 1874, pg 5 (1874 Sept 29) Grand Secretary
    Proceedings 1874, pg 20 (1874 Sept 29) Grand Secretary
    Proceedings 1874, pg 29 (1874 Sept 29) Grand Secretary
    Proceedings 1874, pg 34 (1874 Sept 30) committee
    Proceedings 1874, pg 36 (1874 Sept 30) committee
    Proceedings 1874, pg 36 (1874 Sept 30) per diem
    Proceedings 1874, pg 39 (1874 Sept 30) Grand Secretary
    Proceedings 1874, pg 57 (1874 Sept 30) Grand Secretary
    Proceedings 1874, pg 134 (1874 Sept 30) Grand Secretary
    Proceedings 1874, pg 204 (1874 Sept 30) Grand Lodge of Colorado, Georgetown
    Proceedings 1874, pg 206 (1874 Sept 30) Grand Secretary, 1867
    Proceedings 1874, pg 206 (1874 Sept 30) Grand Secretary, 1873
    Proceedings 1874, pg 206 (1874 Sept 30) Grand Secretary, 1869
    Proceedings 1874, pg 206 (1874 Sept 30) Grand Secretary, 1872
    Proceedings 1874, pg 206 (1874 Sept 30) Grand Secretary, 1874

Parmelee, Ed C, cont.
- Proceedings 1874, pg 206 (1874 Sept 30) Grand Secretary, 1866
- Proceedings 1874, pg 206 (1874 Sept 30) Grand Secretary, 1871
- Proceedings 1874, pg 206 (1874 Sept 30) Grand Secretary, 1868
- Proceedings 1874, pg 206 (1874 Sept 30) Grand Secretary, 1870
- Proceedings 1874, pg 207 (1874 Sept 30), Grand Lodge of Maine, Grand Lodge of Missouri, Grand Lodge of Oregon, Georgetown
- Proceedings 1874, pg 213 (1874 Sept 30), Central Lodge No. 6, Central
- Proceedings 1875, pg cover (1875 Sept 22) committee, Georgetown
- Proceedings 1875, pg cover (1875 Sept 22) Grand Secretary, Georgetown
- Proceedings 1875, pg 15 (1875 Sept 21) Grand Secretary
- Proceedings 1875, pg 16 (1875 Sept 21) Grand Secretary
- Proceedings 1875, pg 21 (1875 Sept 21) committee
- Proceedings 1875, pg 24 (1875 Sept 21) Grand Secretary
- Proceedings 1875, pg 30 (1875 Sept 21) Grand Secretary
- Proceedings 1875, pg 36 (1875 Sept 22) Grand Secretary
- Proceedings 1875, pg 37 (1875 Sept 22) per diem
- Proceedings 1875, pg 37 (1875 Sept 22) committee, Georgetown
- Proceedings 1875, pg 38 (1875 Sept 22) Grand Secretary
- Proceedings 1875, pg 77 (1875 Sept 22), Central Lodge No. 6, Central City
- Proceedings 1875, pg 93 (1875 Sept 22) Grand Secretary, 1872
- Proceedings 1875, pg 93 (1875 Sept 22) Grand Secretary, 1867
- Proceedings 1875, pg 93 (1875 Sept 22) Grand Secretary, 1868
- Proceedings 1875, pg 93 (1875 Sept 22) Grand Secretary, 1871
- Proceedings 1875, pg 93 (1875 Sept 22) Grand Secretary, 1873
- Proceedings 1875, pg 93 (1875 Sept 22) Grand Secretary, 1866
- Proceedings 1875, pg 93 (1875 Sept 22) Grand Secretary, 1869
- Proceedings 1875, pg 93 (1875 Sept 22) Grand Secretary, 1870
- Proceedings 1875, pg 93 (1875 Sept 22) Grand Secretary, 1874
- Proceedings 1875, pg 93 (1875 Sept 22) Grand Secretary, 1875
- Proceedings 1875, pg 95 (1875 Sept 22) Grand Lodge of Oregon, Georgetown, CO
- Proceedings 1875, pg 95 (1875 Sept 22) Grand Lodge of Nebraska, Georgetown, CO
- Proceedings 1875, pg 95 (1875 Sept 22) Grand Lodge of Missouri, Georgetown, CO
- Proceedings 1875, pg 95 (1875 Sept 22) Grand Lodge of Maine, Georgetown, CO
- Proceedings 1875, pg 96 (1875 Sept 22) Grand Lodge of Colorado, Georgetown
- Proceedings 1876, pg cover (1876 Sept 20) Grand Secretary, Georgetown
- Proceedings 1876, pg 3 (1876 Sept 19) Grand Secretary
- Proceedings 1876, pg 4 (1876 Sept 19) Grand Secretary
- Proceedings 1876, pg 12 (1876 Sept 19) Grand Secretary
- Proceedings 1876, pg 13 (1876 Sept 19) Grand Secretary
- Proceedings 1876, pg 18 (1876 Sept 19) Grand Secretary
- Proceedings 1876, pg 22 (1876 Sept 20) committee
- Proceedings 1876, pg 22 (1876 Sept 20) Grand Secretary
- Proceedings 1876, pg 25 (1876 Sept 20) Grand Secretary
- Proceedings 1876, pg 26 (1876 Sept 20) Grand Secretary
- Proceedings 1876, pg 32 (1876 Sept 20), Central Lodge No. 6, Central City
- Proceedings 1876, pg 53 (1876 Sept 20) Grand Lodge of Maine, of Georgetown, CO
- Proceedings 1876, pg 53 (1876 Sept 20) Grand Lodge of Oregon, of Georgetown, CO
- Proceedings 1876, pg 54 (1876 Sept 20) Grand Lodge of Colorado, Georgetown

Parmelee, Geo S
- Proceedings 1861-1869, pg 227 (1868 Oct 7), Black Hawk Lodge No. 11, Black Hawk
- Proceedings 1861-1869, pg 309 (1869 Sept 29), Black Hawk Lodge No. 11, Black Hawk
- Proceedings 1870, pg 25 (1870 Sept 28), Black Hawk Lodge No. 11, Black Hawk
- Proceedings 1872, pg 24 (1872 Sept 24), Black Hawk Lodge No. 11, Black Hawk

Parmelee, George S
- Proceedings 1861-1869, pg 196 (1867 Oct 8), Black Hawk Lodge No. 11, Black Hawk, Fellowcraft
- Proceedings 1871, pg 23 (1871 Sept 27), Black Hawk Lodge No. 11, Black Hawk
- Proceedings 1874, pg 216 (1874 Sept 30), Black Hawk Lodge No. 11, Black Hawk
- Proceedings 1875, pg 80 (1875 Sept 22) Black Hawk Lodge No. 11, Demitted

Parmellee
- Proceedings 1874, pg 31 (1874 Sept 29) resolution

Parrin, Theodore S
- Proceedings 1872, pg 64 (1872 Sept 24) Grand Lodge of Iowa

Parrot, Joseph
- Proceedings 1861-1869, pg 131 (1864 Nov 8) Golden City Lodge No. 1, Apprentice
- Proceedings 1861-1869, pg 147 (1865 Nov 7) Golden City Lodge No. 1, Apprentice

Parrott, Jos
- Proceedings 1861-1869, pg 165 (1866 Oct 2) Golden City Lodge No. 1, Apprentice

Parrott, Joseph
- Proceedings 1861-1869, pg 110 (1863 Nov 3) Golden City Lodge No. 1, Apprentice
- Proceedings 1861-1869, pg 191 (1867 Oct 8) Golden City Lodge No. 1, Apprentice
- Proceedings 1861-1869, pg 221 (1868 Oct 7) Golden City Lodge No. 1, Apprentice

Colorado's Territorial Masons

Parrott, Joseph, cont.
   Proceedings 1861-1869, pg 303 (1869 Sept 29) Golden City Lodge No. 1, Apprentice

Parshall, A J
   Proceedings 1874, pg 221 (1874 Sept 30), Cheyenne Lodge No. 16, Cheyenne, Wyoming Territory
   Proceedings 1875, pg 28 (1875 Mar 1) Cheyenne Lodge No. 1

Parsons, George I
   Proceedings 1876, pg 7 (1876 Mar 15), Olive Branch Lodge U D, Saguache

Parsons, George S
   Proceedings 1876, pg 46 (1876 Sept 20), Olive Branch Lodge U D, Saguache

Parsons, I H
   Proceedings 1871, pg 23 (1871 Sept 27), Black Hawk Lodge No. 11, Black Hawk

Parsons, I M
   Proceedings 1861-1869, pg 304 (1869 Sept 29), Nevada Lodge No. 4, Nevadaville
   Proceedings 1874, pg 5 (1874 Sept 29), Nevada Lodge No. 4, Nevada
   Proceedings 1874, pg 6 (1874 Sept 29) committee
   Proceedings 1875, pg cover (1875 Sept 22) Grand Steward, Nevada
   Proceedings 1875, pg 16 (1875 Sept 21) Nevada Lodge No. 4

Parsons, Isaac M
   Proceedings 1870, pg 20 (1870 Sept 28), Nevada Lodge No. 4, Nevadaville
   Proceedings 1871, pg 18 (1871 Sept 27), Nevada Lodge No. 4, Bald Mountain
   Proceedings 1872, pg 18 (1872 Sept 24), Nevada Lodge No. 4, Bald Mountain
   Proceedings 1873, pg 36 (1873 Oct 1), Nevada Lodge No. 4, Nevada
   Proceedings 1874, pg 210 (1874 Sept 30), Nevada Lodge No. 4, Bald Mountain, Gilpin County
   Proceedings 1875, pg 33 (1875 Sept 22) Junior Grand Warden, Nevada
   Proceedings 1875, pg 74 (1875 Sept 22), Nevada Lodge No. 4, Nevada
   Proceedings 1876, pg 30 (1876 Sept 20) Nevada Lodge No. 4

Parsons, J H
   Proceedings 1861-1869, pg 170 (1866 Oct 2), Black Hawk Lodge U D, Black Hawk
   Proceedings 1861-1869, pg 196 (1867 Oct 8), Black Hawk Lodge No. 11, Black Hawk
   Proceedings 1861-1869, pg 227 (1868 Oct 7), Black Hawk Lodge No. 11, Black Hawk
   Proceedings 1861-1869, pg 309 (1869 Sept 29), Black Hawk Lodge No. 11, Black Hawk
   Proceedings 1870, pg 25 (1870 Sept 28), Black Hawk Lodge No. 11, Black Hawk
   Proceedings 1872, pg 25 (1872 Sept 24), Black Hawk Lodge No. 11, Black Hawk
   Proceedings 1874, pg 209 (1874 Sept 30), Golden City Lodge No. 1, Golden City

Parsons, J M
   Proceedings 1874, pg 36 (1874 Sept 30) per diem

Parsons, John H
   Proceedings 1873, pg 35 (1873 Oct 1), Golden City Lodge No. 1, Golden City
   Proceedings 1873, pg 42 (1873 Oct 1), Black Hawk Lodge No. 11, Black Hawk, Dimitted
   Proceedings 1875, pg 73 (1875 Sept 22) Golden City Lodge No. 1
   Proceedings 1876, pg 29 (1876 Sept 20) Golden City Lodge No. 1

Parvin
   Proceedings 1861-1869, pg 181 (1867 Oct 7), Grand Secretary, Grand Lodge of Iowa
   Proceedings 1874, pg 70 (1874 Sept 30) Grand Lodge of Iowa

Parvin, T S
   Proceedings 1861-1869, pg 250 (1867 June 4), Grand Secretary, Grand Lodge of Iowa
   Proceedings 1861-1869, pg 330 (1868 June 2) Grand Secretary, Grand Lodge of Iowa
   Proceedings 1870, pg 59 (1870 June 7) Grand Secretary, Grand Lodge of Iowa
   Proceedings 1872, pg 43 (1872 Sept 24) Iowa City, Grand Lodge of Iowa
   Proceedings 1873, pg 60 (1873 Oct 1) Grand Lodge of Iowa, Iowa City
   Proceedings 1874, pg 68 (1874 Sept 30) Grand Lodge of Iowa
   Proceedings 1874, pg 204 (1874 Sept 30) Grand Lodge of Iowa, Iowa City

Parvin, Theo S
   Proceedings 1861-1869, pg 291 (1869 Sept 28), Grand Secretary, Grand Lodge of Iowa
   Proceedings 1861-1869, pg 316 (1869 Sept 29) Grand Lodge of Iowa
   Proceedings 1870, pg 34 (1870 Sept 28) Grand Secretary, Grand Lodge of Iowa
   Proceedings 1871, pg 35 (1871 Sept 27) Grand Secretary, Grand Lodge of Iowa

Parvin, Theodore S
   Proceedings 1874, pg 66 (1874 Sept 30) Grand Lodge of Iowa
   Proceedings 1875, pg 96 (1875 Sept 22) Grand Lodge of Iowa, Iowa City
   Proceedings 1876, pg 54 (1876 Sept 20) Grand Lodge of Iowa, Iowa City

Pasco, Samuel
   Proceedings 1870, pg 52 (1870 Jan 12) Grand Master, Grand Lodge of Florida
   Proceedings 1870, pg 53 (1870 Jan 12) Grand Master, Grand Lodge of Florida
   Proceedings 1872, pg 43 (1872 Sept 24) Monticello, Grand Lodge of Florida

Proceedings 1872, pg 59 (1872 Sept 24) Grand Lodge of Florida

Paslin, David
Proceedings 1872, pg 28 (1872 Sept 24), Columbia Lodge No. 14, Boulder

Passage, E F
Proceedings 1861-1869, pg 312 (1869 Sept 29), Cheyenne Lodge No. 16, Cheyenne
Proceedings 1870, pg 29 (1870 Sept 28), Cheyenne Lodge No. 16, Cheyenne, Wyoming Territory
Proceedings 1871, pg 27 (1871 Sept 27), Cheyenne Lodge No. 16, Cheyenne, Wyoming Territory
Proceedings 1872, pg 29 (1872 Sept 24), Cheyenne Lodge No. 16, Cheyenne, Wyoming Territory
Proceedings 1873, pg 46 (1873 Oct 1), Cheyenne Lodge No. 16, Cheyenne, Wyoming Territory
Proceedings 1874, pg 221 (1874 Sept 30), Cheyenne Lodge No. 16, Cheyenne, Wyoming Territory

Pasters, Adam
Proceedings 1861-1869, pg 196 (1867 Oct 8), El Paso Lodge U D, Colorado City
Proceedings 1861-1869, pg 171 (1866 Oct 2), El Paso U D, Colorado City

Paton, A B
Proceedings 1876, pg 39 (1876 Sept 20) Pueblo Lodge No. 17

Patrick, C B
Proceedings 1875, pg 89 (1875 Sept 22) Idaho Springs Lodge U D
Proceedings 1876, pg 48 (1876 Sept 20) Idaho Springs Lodge No. 26, 1875 Nov 20

Patten, A B
Proceedings 1871, pg 17 (1871 Sept 27), Golden City Lodge No. 1, Golden City, Dimitted
Proceedings 1861-1869, pg 221 (1868 Oct 7) Golden City Lodge No. 1

Patten, F E W
Proceedings 1861-1869, pg 112 (1863 Nov 3) Denver Lodge No. 5, dimitted

Patten, Geo A
Proceedings 1875, pg 89 (1875 Sept 22) Idaho Springs Lodge U D

Patten, George A
Proceedings 1876, pg 43 (1876 Sept 20) Idaho Springs Lodge No. 26

Patterson, E H N
Proceedings 1876, pg 35 (1876 Sept 20), Washington Lodge No. 12, Georgetown

Patterson, G T F
Proceedings 1874, pg 224 (1874 Sept 30), Laramie Lodge No. 18, Laramie City, Apprentice

Patterson, Geo O
Proceedings 1873, pg 37 (1873 Oct 1), Denver Lodge No. 5, Denver
Proceedings 1874, pg 211 (1874 Sept 30), Denver Lodge No. 5, Denver
Proceedings 1875, pg 75 (1875 Sept 22) Denver Lodge No. 5

Patterson, George O
Proceedings 1876, pg 31 (1876 Sept 20) Denver Lodge No. 5

Patterson, J D
Proceedings 1875, pg 90 (1875 Sept 22), Huerfano Lodge U D, Walsenburg, Fellowcraft
Proceedings 1876, pg 43 (1876 Sept 20), Huerfano Lodge No. 27, Walsenburg

Patterson, Samuel
Proceedings 1876, pg 43 (1876 Sept 20), Huerfano Lodge No. 27, Walsenburg

Patterson, Samuel J
Proceedings 1875, pg 85 (1875 Sept 22) Pueblo Lodge No. 17
Proceedings 1876, pg 39 (1876 Sept 20) Pueblo Lodge No. 17

Patterson, Thomas M
Proceedings 1876, pg 33 (1876 Sept 20), Union Lodge No. 7, Denver

Patterson, Thos M
Proceedings 1874, pg 214 (1874 Sept 30), Union Lodge No. 7, Denver

Patterson, Thos M
Proceedings 1875, pg 78 (1875 Sept 22), Union Lodge No. 7, Denver

Patton
Proceedings 1861-1869, pg 82 (1863 Apr 18) Denver Lodge No. 5, Accepted

Patton, A B
Proceedings 1861-1869, pg 165 (1866 Oct 2) Golden City Lodge No. 1, Apprentice
Proceedings 1861-1869, pg 191 (1867 Oct 8) Golden City Lodge No. 1, Fellowcraft
Proceedings 1870, pg 19 (1870 Sept 28), Golden City Lodge No. 1, Golden City
Proceedings 1874, pg 222 (1874 Sept 30), Pueblo Lodge No. 17, Pueblo, Pueblo County
Proceedings 1875, pg 85 (1875 Sept 22) Pueblo Lodge No. 17

Patton, A P
Proceedings 1861-1869, pg 303 (1869 Sept 29) Golden City Lodge No. 1

Patton, F E W
Proceedings 1861-1869, pg 81 (1863 Apr 18) Denver Lodge No. 5, Rejected

Patton, T McF
Proceedings 1873, pg 61 (1873 Oct 1) Grand Lodge of Oregon, Salem
Proceedings 1874, pg 118 (1874 Sept 30) Grand Lodge of Oregon
Proceedings 1874, pg 132 (1874 Sept 30) Grand Lodge of Oregon

Colorado's Territorial Masons

Patton, Thomas H
Proceedings 1876, pg 33 (1876 Sept 20), Union Lodge No. 7, Denver

Patton, Thos H
Proceedings 1874, pg 214 (1874 Sept 30), Union Lodge No. 7, Denver
Proceedings 1875, pg 78 (1875 Sept 22), Union Lodge No. 7, Denver

Paul, Henry
Proceedings 1861-1869, pg 197 (1867 Oct 8), Columbia Lodge U D, Boulder
Proceedings 1861-1869, pg 228 (1868 Oct 7), Columbia Lodge No. 14, Columbia City
Proceedings 1861-1869, pg 310 (1869 Sept 29), Columbia Lodge No. 14, Boulder City
Proceedings 1870, pg 27 (1870 Sept 28), Columbia Lodge No. 14, Boulder City
Proceedings 1871, pg 26 (1871 Sept 27), Columbia Lodge No. 14, Boulder City
Proceedings 1872, pg 28 (1872 Sept 24), Columbia Lodge No. 14, Boulder
Proceedings 1873, pg 44 (1873 Oct 1), Columbia Lodge No. 14, Boulder
Proceedings 1874, pg 219 (1874 Sept 30), Columbia Lodge No. 14, Boulder, Boulder County
Proceedings 1875, pg 83 (1875 Sept 22), Columbia Lodge No. 14, Boulder
Proceedings 1876, pg 37 (1876 Sept 20), Columbia Lodge No. 14, Boulder

Paul, J M
Proceedings 1871, pg 26 (1871 Sept 27), Mount Moriah Lodge No. 15, Canon City, Apprentice
Proceedings 1875, pg 89 (1875 Sept 22), Doric Lodge No. 25, Fairplay
Proceedings 1876, pg 42 (1876 Sept 20), Doric Lodge No. 25, Fairplay

Paul, J Marshal
Proceedings 1874, pg 220 (1874 Sept 30), Mount Moriah Lodge No. 15, Canon City, Demitted
Proceedings 1872, pg 29 (1872 Sept 24), Mount Moriah Lodge No. 15, Canon City, Fellowcraft
Proceedings 1873, pg 45 (1873 Oct 1), Mount Moriah Lodge No. 15, Canon City
Proceedings 1874, pg 35 (1874 Sept 30), Doric Lodge No. 25, Fairplay
Proceedings 1874, pg 228 (1874 Sept 30), Doric Lodge U D, Fairplay

Paul, John W
Proceedings 1861-1869, pg 242 (1867 May 8), Grand Secretary, Grand Lodge of Connecticut

Pauls, C
Proceedings 1861-1869, pg 311 (1869 Sept 29), Mount Moriah Lodge No. 15, Canon City

Pauls, Charles
Proceedings 1861-1869, pg 171 (1866 Oct 2), El Paso U D, Colorado City
Proceedings 1861-1869, pg 196 (1867 Oct 8), El Paso Lodge U D, Colorado City
Proceedings 1861-1869, pg 229 (1868 Oct 7), Canon Lodge U D, Canon City
Proceedings 1871, pg 26 (1871 Sept 27), Mount Moriah Lodge No. 15, Canon City
Proceedings 1874, pg 220 (1874 Sept 30), Mount Moriah Lodge No. 15, Canon City
Proceedings 1875, pg 84 (1875 Sept 22), Mount Moriah Lodge No. 15, Canon City
Proceedings 1876, pg 38 (1876 Sept 20), Mount Moriah Lodge No. 15, Canon City

Pauls, Chas
Proceedings 1861-1869, pg 228 (1868 Oct 7), El Paso Lodge No. 13, Colorado City, Dimitted
Proceedings 1870, pg 28 (1870 Sept 28), Mount Moriah Lodge No. 15, Canon City
Proceedings 1872, pg 28 (1872 Sept 24), Mount Moriah Lodge No. 15, Canon City
Proceedings 1873, pg 45 (1873 Oct 1), Mount Moriah Lodge No. 15, Canon City

Pauls, Ed
Proceedings 1875, pg 84 (1875 Sept 22), Mount Moriah Lodge No. 15, Canon City
Proceedings 1876, pg 38 (1876 Sept 20), Mount Moriah Lodge No. 15, Canon City

Pauls, Edward
Proceedings 1872, pg 29 (1872 Sept 24), Mount Moriah Lodge No. 15, Canon City
Proceedings 1873, pg 45 (1873 Oct 1), Mount Moriah Lodge No. 15, Canon City
Proceedings 1874, pg 220 (1874 Sept 30), Mount Moriah Lodge No. 15, Canon City

Paxton, John W
Proceedings 1872, pg 86 (1872 Sept 24) Grand Lodge of Tennessee

Payne, W W
Proceedings 1873, pg 39 (1873 Oct 1), Union Lodge No. 7, Denver
Proceedings 1874, pg 214 (1874 Sept 30), Union Lodge No. 7, Denver
Proceedings 1875, pg 78 (1875 Sept 22), Union Lodge No. 7, Denver
Proceedings 1876, pg 33 (1876 Sept 20), Union Lodge No. 7, Denver

Payton, I N
Proceedings 1874, pg 211 (1874 Sept 30), Denver Lodge No. 5, Denver
Proceedings 1875, pg 75 (1875 Sept 22) Denver Lodge No. 5

Peabody, L
Proceedings 1861-1869, pg 111 (1863 Nov 3), Summit Lodge No. 2, Parkville
Proceedings 1861-1869, pg 131 (1864 Nov 8) Golden City Lodge No. 1

Colorado's Territorial Masons

Peabody, Lelon
Proceedings 1873, pg 39 (1873 Oct 1), Union Lodge No. 7, Denver
Proceedings 1874, pg 214 (1874 Sept 30), Union Lodge No. 7, Denver
Proceedings 1875, pg 78 (1875 Sept 22), Union Lodge No. 7, Denver
Proceedings 1876, pg 33 (1876 Sept 20), Union Lodge No. 7, Denver

Peabody, William S
Proceedings 1871, pg 22 (1871 Sept 27), Union Lodge No. 7, Denver
Proceedings 1876, pg 33 (1876 Sept 20), Union Lodge No. 7, Denver

Peabody, Wm S
Proceedings 1861-1869, pg 225 (1868 Oct 7), Union Lodge No. 7, Denver
Proceedings 1861-1869, pg 307 (1869 Sept 29), Union Lodge No. 7, Denver
Proceedings 1870, pg 23 (1870 Sept 28), Union Lodge No. 7, Denver
Proceedings 1872, pg 22 (1872 Sept 24), Union Lodge No. 7, Denver
Proceedings 1873, pg 39 (1873 Oct 1), Union Lodge No. 7, Denver
Proceedings 1874, pg 214 (1874 Sept 30), Union Lodge No. 7, Denver
Proceedings 1875, pg 78 (1875 Sept 22), Union Lodge No. 7, Denver

Peacock, James A
Proceedings 1875, pg 91 (1875 Sept 22), Las Animas Lodge U D, Trinidad
Proceedings 1876, pg 44 (1876 Sept 20), Las Animas Lodge No. 28, Trinidad

Pearce, H S
Proceedings 1870, pg 29 (1870 Sept 28), Cheyenne Lodge No. 16, Cheyenne, Wyoming Territory

Pearce, Henry S
Proceedings 1871, pg 28 (1871 Sept 27), Cheyenne Lodge No. 16, Cheyenne, Wyoming Territory, Apprentice

Pears, Oscar
Proceedings 1861-1869, pg 230 (1868 Oct 7), Valmont Lodge U D, Valmont, Apprentice
Pearson
Proceedings 1874, pg 65 (1874 Sept 30) Grand Lodge of Indiana

Pearson, A D
Proceedings 1870, pg 30 (1870 Sept 28), Laramie Lodge No. 18, Laramie, Wyoming Territory
Proceedings 1871, pg 29 (1871 Sept 27), Laramie Lodge No. 18, Laramie, Wyoming Territory
Proceedings 1872, pg 32 (1872 Sept 24), Laramie Lodge No. 18, Laramie, Wyoming Territory
Proceedings 1874, pg 223 (1874 Sept 30), Laramie Lodge No. 18, Laramie City

Pearson, G Fred
Proceedings 1872, pg 36 (1872 Sept 24), Ashlar Lodge U D, Colorado Springs

Pearson, H K
Proceedings 1861-1869, pg 148 (1865 Nov 7), Nevada Lodge No. 4, Nevadaville
Proceedings 1861-1869, pg 166 (1866 Oct 2), Nevada Lodge No. 4, Nevadaville
Proceedings 1861-1869, pg 179 (1867 Oct 7), Washington Lodge No. 12, Georgetown
Proceedings 1861-1869, pg 222 (1868 Oct 7), Nevada Lodge No. 4, Nevadaville, Dimitted
Proceedings 1861-1869, pg 227 (1868 Oct 7), Washington Lodge No. 12, Georgetown
Proceedings 1861-1869, pg 309 (1869 Sept 29), Washington Lodge No. 12, Georgetown
Proceedings 1870, pg 4 (1870 Sept 27), Washington Lodge No. 12, Georgetown
Proceedings 1871, pg 4 (1871 Sept 26), Washington Lodge No. 12, Georgetown
Proceedings 1871, pg 24 (1871 Sept 27), Washington Lodge No. 12, Georgetown
Proceedings 1873, pg 6 (1873 Sept 30), Washington Lodge No. 12, Georgetown
Proceedings 1873, pg 7 (1873 Sept 30) committee
Proceedings 1873, pg 31 (1873 Oct 1) mileage and per diem
Proceedings 1861-1869, pg 76 (1862 Nov 4), Summit Lodge No. 2, Parkville, Apprentice

Pearson, H R
Proceedings 1872, pg 4 (1872 Sept 24), Black Hawk Lodge No. 11, Black Hawk

Pearson, Henry L
Proceedings 1876, pg 44 (1876 Sept 20), Las Animas Lodge No. 28, Trinidad, Fellow Craft

Pearson, Hollis K
Proceedings 1861-1869, pg 192 (1867 Oct 8), Nevada Lodge No. 4, Nevadaville
Proceedings 1872, pg 25 (1872 Sept 24), Washington Lodge No. 12, Georgetown
Proceedings 1873, pg 42 (1873 Oct 1), Washington Lodge No. 12, Georgetown
Proceedings 1874, pg 217 (1874 Sept 30), Washington Lodge No. 12, Georgetown
Proceedings 1875, pg 81 (1875 Sept 22), Washington Lodge No. 12, Georgetown

Pearson, Holly K
Proceedings 1870, pg 26 (1870 Sept 28), Washington Lodge No. 12, Georgetown

Pearson, Samuel
Proceedings 1874, pg 228 (1874 Sept 30), Evanston Lodge U D, Evanston, Uintah County, Wyoming Territory, Apprentice

Pease, B F
Proceedings 1861-1869, pg 111 (1863 Nov 3), Nevada Lodge No. 4, Nevadaville

Colorado's Territorial Masons

Pease, B F, cont.
   Proceedings 1861-1869, pg 132 (1864 Nov 8), Nevada Lodge No. 4, Nevadaville
   Proceedings 1861-1869, pg 148 (1865 Nov 7), Nevada Lodge No. 4, Nevadaville
   Proceedings 1861-1869, pg 166 (1866 Oct 2), Nevada Lodge No. 4, Nevadaville
   Proceedings 1861-1869, pg 192 (1867 Oct 8), Nevada Lodge No. 4, Nevadaville
   Proceedings 1861-1869, pg 222 (1868 Oct 7), Nevada Lodge No. 4, Nevadaville
   Proceedings 1861-1869, pg 304 (1869 Sept 29), Nevada Lodge No. 4, Nevadaville
   Proceedings 1871, pg 18 (1871 Sept 27), Nevada Lodge No. 4, Bald Mountain
   Proceedings 1872, pg 18 (1872 Sept 24), Nevada Lodge No. 4, Bald Mountain
   Proceedings 1873, pg 36 (1873 Oct 1), Nevada Lodge No. 4, Nevada
   Proceedings 1874, pg 210 (1874 Sept 30), Nevada Lodge No. 4, Bald Mountain, Gilpin County
   Proceedings 1875, pg 74 (1875 Sept 22), Nevada Lodge No. 4, Nevada
   Proceedings 1876, pg 30 (1876 Sept 20) Nevada Lodge No. 4

Pease, Benjamin F
   Proceedings 1870, pg 20 (1870 Sept 28), Nevada Lodge No. 4, Nevadaville

Pease, Harlow
   Proceedings 1861-1869, pg 285 (1867 June 11), Grand Master, Grand Lodge of Wisconsin
   Proceedings 1861-1869, pg 349 (1868 June 9) Grand Master, Grand Lodge of Wisconsin

Pease, L D
   Proceedings 1872, pg 32 (1872 Sept 24), Laramie Lodge No. 18, Laramie, Wyoming Territory
   Proceedings 1873, pg 48 (1873 Oct 1), Laramie Lodge No. 18, Laramie, Wyoming Territory
   Proceedings 1874, pg 223 (1874 Sept 30), Laramie Lodge No. 18, Laramie City

Pease, W D
   Proceedings 1861-1869, pg 134 (1864 Nov 8), Union Lodge No. 7, Denver
   Proceedings 1861-1869, pg 151 (1865 Nov 7), Chivington Lodge No. 6, Central City
   Proceedings 1861-1869, pg 169 (1866 Oct 2), Union Lodge No. 7, Denver
   Proceedings 1861-1869, pg 195 (1867 Oct 8), Union Lodge No. 7, Denver
   Proceedings 1861-1869, pg 225 (1868 Oct 7), Union Lodge No. 7, Denver
   Proceedings 1861-1869, pg 230 (1868 Oct 7), Cheyenne Lodge U D, Cheyenne, Dakota Territory
   Proceedings 1861-1869, pg 307 (1869 Sept 29), Union Lodge No. 7, Denver
   Proceedings 1861-1869, pg 312 (1869 Sept 29), Cheyenne Lodge No. 16, Cheyenne
   Proceedings 1870, pg 29 (1870 Sept 28), Cheyenne Lodge No. 16, Cheyenne, Wyoming Territory
   Proceedings 1871, pg 27 (1871 Sept 27), Cheyenne Lodge No. 16, Cheyenne, Wyoming Territory
   Proceedings 1872, pg 29 (1872 Sept 24), Cheyenne Lodge No. 16, Cheyenne, Wyoming Territory
   Proceedings 1873, pg 46 (1873 Oct 1), Cheyenne Lodge No. 16, Cheyenne, Wyoming Territory
   Proceedings 1874, pg 221 (1874 Sept 30), Cheyenne Lodge No. 16, Cheyenne, Wyoming Territory

Pease, Walter D
   Proceedings 1870, pg 24 (1870 Sept 28), Union Lodge No. 7, Denver, Dimitted
   Peck
   Proceedings 1861-1869, pg 248 (1867 June 4), Grand Master, Grand Lodge of Iowa
   Proceedings 1861-1869, pg 249 (1867 June 4) engaged in a debate over whether dispensations should be granted to negro lodges

Peck, Arthur
   Proceedings 1872, pg 36 (1872 Sept 24), Ashlar Lodge U D, Colorado Springs

Peck, Frank L
   Proceedings 1875, pg 89 (1875 Sept 22) Idaho Springs Lodge U D
   Proceedings 1876, pg 42 (1876 Sept 20) Idaho Springs Lodge No. 26

Peck, G C
   Proceedings 1861-1869, pg 303 (1869 Sept 29) Golden City Lodge No. 1, Dimitted

Peck, Geo C
   Proceedings 1861-1869, pg 165 (1866 Oct 2) Golden City Lodge No. 1

Peck, George C
   Proceedings 1861-1869, pg 221 (1868 Oct 7) Golden City Lodge No. 1, Dimitted

Peck, John L
   Proceedings 1861-1869, pg 299 (1869 Sept 29) Grand Orator

Peck, S
   Proceedings 1861-1869, pg 230 (1868 Oct 7), Valmont Lodge U D, Valmont

Pegg, Lewis
   Proceedings 1861-1869, pg 313 (1869 Sept 29), Pueblo Lodge No. 17, Pueblo, Dimitted

Peiffer, J S
   Proceedings 1874, pg 223 (1874 Sept 30), Laramie Lodge No. 18, Laramie City

Peirson, A D
   Proceedings 1873, pg 48 (1873 Oct 1), Laramie Lodge No. 18, Laramie, Wyoming Territory

Pembroke, Wm N
   Proceedings 1874, pg 204 (1874 Sept 30) Grand Lodge of New Jersey, Elizabeth

Pendarias, J S
   Proceedings 1861-1869, pg 152 (1865 Nov 7), Montana Lodge U D, Virginia City, Montana Territory

Penford, R Delos
Proceedings 1873, pg 61 (1873 Oct 1) Grand Lodge of Wisconsin, Mineral Point

Penick
Proceedings 1861-1869, pg 265 (1868 Oct 7) Grand Lodge of Alabama
Proceedings 1861-1869, pg 266 (1868 Oct 7) Grand Lodge of Alabama

Penick, W C
Proceedings 1861-1869, pg 239 (1867 Dec 2) Grand Lodge of Alabama

Penick, Wm C
Proceedings 1870, pg 40 (1869 Dec 6) Grand Lodge of Alabama

Pennisten, C P
Proceedings 1873, pg 51 (1873 Oct 1), St Vrain Lodge No. 23, Longmont
Proceedings 1874, pg 227 (1874 Sept 30), St Vrain No. 23, Longmont
Proceedings 1876, pg 41 (1876 Sept 20), St Vrain Lodge No. 23, Longmont

Pepper, G W
Proceedings 1861-1869, pg 304 (1869 Sept 29), Nevada Lodge No. 4, Nevadaville
Proceedings 1870, pg 30 (1870 Sept 28), Laramie Lodge No. 18, Laramie, Wyoming Territory
Proceedings 1873, pg 36 (1873 Oct 1), Nevada Lodge No. 4, Nevada

Pepper, Geo W
Proceedings 1861-1869, pg 222 (1868 Oct 7), Nevada Lodge No. 4, Nevadaville
Proceedings 1871, pg 18 (1871 Sept 27), Nevada Lodge No. 4, Bald Mountain
Proceedings 1874, pg 210 (1874 Sept 30), Nevada Lodge No. 4, Bald Mountain, Gilpin County
Proceedings 1875, pg 74 (1875 Sept 22), Nevada Lodge No. 4, Nevada

Pepper, George W
Proceedings 1870, pg 20 (1870 Sept 28), Nevada Lodge No. 4, Nevadaville
Proceedings 1872, pg 18 (1872 Sept 24), Nevada Lodge No. 4, Bald Mountain
Proceedings 1876, pg 30 (1876 Sept 20) Nevada Lodge No. 4
Proceedings 1876, pg 50 (1876 Sept 20) Nevada Lodge No. 4

Peralt, Azrad
Proceedings 1874, pg 218 (1874 Sept 30), El Paso Lodge No. 13, Colorado Springs

Peratt, Azrael
Proceedings 1875, pg 82 (1875 Sept 22), El Paso Lodge No. 13, Colorado Springs

Percival Frederick H
Proceedings 1876, pg 40 (1876 Sept 20), Occidental Lodge No. 20, Greeley

Pergam, William T
Proceedings 1874, pg 219 (1874 Sept 30), Columbia Lodge No. 14, Boulder, Boulder County

Perington, R H
Proceedings 1876, pg 44 (1876 Sept 20), Las Animas Lodge No. 28, Trinidad

Perkins, G W
Proceedings 1861-1869, pg 305 (1869 Sept 29) Denver Lodge No. 5, Apprentice
Proceedings 1870, pg 21 (1870 Sept 28), Denver Lodge No. 5, Denver
Proceedings 1870, pg 84 (1870 Jan 17) Grand Lodge of Mississippi, deceased
Proceedings 1871, pg 19 (1871 Sept 27) Denver Lodge No. 5
Proceedings 1871, pg 31 (1871 Sept 27), Occidental Lodge U D, Greeley
Proceedings 1872, pg 19 (1872 Sept 24), Denver Lodge No. 5, Denver
Proceedings 1873, pg 37 (1873 Oct 1), Denver Lodge No. 5, Denver
Proceedings 1874, pg 211 (1874 Sept 30), Denver Lodge No. 5, Denver
Proceedings 1876, pg 31 (1876 Sept 20) Denver Lodge No. 5

Perkins, Geo H
Proceedings 1873, pg 50 (1873 Oct 1), Occidental Lodge No. 20, Greeley

Perkins, Geo W
Proceedings 1872, pg 33 (1872 Sept 24), Occidental Lodge No. 20, Greeley
Proceedings 1875, pg 75 (1875 Sept 22) Denver Lodge No. 5
Proceedings 1875, pg 87 (1875 Sept 22), Occidental Lodge No. 20, Greeley

Perkins, George W
Proceedings 1874, pg 225 (1874 Sept 30), Occidental Lodge No. 20, Greeley
Proceedings 1876, pg 40 (1876 Sept 20), Occidental Lodge No. 20, Greeley

Perkins, S J
Proceedings 1861-1869, pg 152 (1865 Nov 7), Helena City Lodge U D, Helena City, Montana Territory

Perkins, Samuel C
Proceedings 1872, pg 44 (1872 Sept 24), Grand Lodge of Pennsylvania
Proceedings 1873, pg 61 (1873 Oct 1) Grand Lodge of Pennsylvania
Proceedings 1874, pg 119 (1874 Sept 30) Grand Lodge of Pennsylvania

Perkins, W D
Proceedings 1861-1869, pg 111 (1863 Nov 3), Nevada Lodge No. 4, Nevadaville
Proceedings 1861-1869, pg 132 (1864 Nov 8), Nevada Lodge No. 4, Nevadaville
Proceedings 1861-1869, pg 148 (1865 Nov 7), Nevada Lodge No. 4, Nevadaville

Colorado's Territorial Masons

Perkins, W D, cont.
    Proceedings 1861-1869, pg 166 (1866 Oct 2), Nevada Lodge No. 4, Nevadaville
    Proceedings 1861-1869, pg 192 (1867 Oct 8), Nevada Lodge No. 4, Nevadaville
    Proceedings 1871, pg 18 (1871 Sept 27), Nevada Lodge No. 4, Bald Mountain

Perkins, William F
    Proceedings 1876, pg 31 (1876 Sept 20) Denver Lodge No. 5

Perkins, Wm D
    Proceedings 1861-1869, pg 77 (1862 Nov 4), Nevada Lodge No. 4, Nevadaville
    Proceedings 1861-1869, pg 222 (1868 Oct 7), Nevada Lodge No. 4, Nevadaville
    Proceedings 1872, pg 18 (1872 Sept 24), Nevada Lodge No. 4, Bald Mountain
    Proceedings 1873, pg 36 (1873 Oct 1), Nevada Lodge No. 4, Nevada
    Proceedings 1874, pg 211 (1874 Sept 30), Nevada Lodge No. 4, Bald Mountain, Gilpin County, Stricken from the rolls

Perold, Azical
    Proceedings 1873, pg 44 (1873 Oct 1), El Paso Lodge No. 13, Colorado City, Fellowcraft

Perrault, A
    Proceedings 1876, pg 36 (1876 Sept 20), El Paso Lodge No. 13, Colorado City

Perry, C W
    Proceedings 1873, pg 51 (1873 Oct 1), Weston Lodge No. 22, Littleton, Apprentice
    Proceedings 1875, pg 88 (1875 Sept 22), Weston Lodge No. 22, Littleton, Apprentice

Perry, Chas
    Proceedings 1874, pg 226 (1874 Sept 30), Weston Lodge No. 22, Littleton, Apprentice

Persel, A K
    Proceedings 1875, pg 75 (1875 Sept 22) Denver Lodge No. 5
    Proceedings 1874, pg 211 (1874 Sept 30), Denver Lodge No. 5, Denver

Person, G S
    Proceedings 1872, pg 33 (1872 Sept 24), Occidental Lodge No. 20, Greeley
    Proceedings 1873, pg 50 (1873 Oct 1), Occidental Lodge No. 20, Greeley
    Proceedings 1874, pg 225 (1874 Sept 30), Occidental Lodge No. 20, Greeley
    Proceedings 1875, pg 87 (1875 Sept 22), Occidental Lodge No. 20, Greeley

Persons, Gilman S
    Proceedings 1876, pg 40 (1876 Sept 20), Occidental Lodge No. 20, Greeley

Peryam, William T
    Proceedings 1875, pg 83 (1875 Sept 22), Columbia Lodge No. 14, Boulder
    Proceedings 1876, pg 37 (1876 Sept 20), Columbia Lodge No. 14, Boulder

Peryam, Wm T
    Proceedings 1873, pg 44 (1873 Oct 1), Columbia Lodge No. 14, Boulder, Fellowcraft

Pesdirs, John
    Proceedings 1861-1869, pg 310 (1869 Sept 29), El Paso Lodge No. 13, Colorado City

Pesdirz, John
    Proceedings 1873, pg 43 (1873 Oct 1), El Paso Lodge No. 13, Colorado City

Peters, A R
    Proceedings 1861-1869, pg 35 (1861 Sept 7), Summit Lodge No. 2, Parkville
    Proceedings 1861-1869, pg 42 (1861 Dec 10), Summit Lodge No. 2, Parkville

Peters, A W
    Proceedings 1861-1869, pg 228 (1868 Oct 7), Columbia Lodge No. 14, Columbia City, Fellowcraft
    Proceedings 1872, pg 27 (1872 Sept 24), Columbia Lodge No. 14, Boulder
    Proceedings 1874, pg 219 (1874 Sept 30), Columbia Lodge No. 14, Boulder, Boulder County
    Proceedings 1875, pg 83 (1875 Sept 22), Columbia Lodge No. 14, Boulder, Stricken from the rolls

Peters, Anson W
    Proceedings 1861-1869, pg 311 (1869 Sept 29), Columbia Lodge No. 14, Boulder City
    Proceedings 1870, pg 27 (1870 Sept 28), Columbia Lodge No. 14, Boulder City
    Proceedings 1871, pg 26 (1871 Sept 27), Columbia Lodge No. 14, Boulder City
    Proceedings 1873, pg 44 (1873 Oct 1), Columbia Lodge No. 14, Boulder

Peters, B L
    Proceedings 1870, pg 94 (1869 Sept 22) Grand Master, Grand Lodge of New Brunswick

Peters, B Lester
    Proceedings 1861-1869, pg 342 (1868 Sept 23) Grand Master, Grand Lodge of New Brunswick

Peters, E D
    Proceedings 1876, pg 42 (1876 Sept 20), Doric Lodge No. 25, Fairplay, Apprentice

Peters, Edward D Jr
    Proceedings 1874, pg 228 (1874 Sept 30), Doric Lodge U D, Fairplay, Apprentice

Peterson, H C
    Proceedings 1870, pg 6 (1870 May 9), Fidelity Lodge U D, Fort Collins
    Proceedings 1870, pg 31 (1870 Sept 28), Collins Lodge No. 19, Fort Collins
    Proceedings 1871, pg 5 (1871 Sept 26), Collins Lodge No. 19, Fort Collins
    Proceedings 1871, pg 15 (1871 Sept 27), Collins Lodge No. 19, Fort Collins

Proceedings 1871, pg 29 (1871 Sept 27), Collins Lodge No. 19, Fort Collins
Proceedings 1872, pg 4 (1872 Sept 24), Collins Lodge No. 19, Fort Collins
Proceedings 1872, pg 5 (1872 Sept 24) committee
Proceedings 1872, pg 15 (1872 Sept 24) Junior Grand Warden
Proceedings 1872, pg 16 (1872 Sept 24) committee
Proceedings 1872, pg 16 (1872 Sept 24), Collins Lodge No. 19, Fort Collins
Proceedings 1874, pg 12 (1874 Jan 30), Collins Lodge No. 19, Fort Collins
Proceedings 1875, pg cover (1875 Sept 22) Grand Steward, Fort Collins
Proceedings 1875, pg 17 (1875 Sept 21) committee
Proceedings 1875, pg 33 (1875 Sept 22) Senior Grand Steward, Fort Collins
Proceedings 1875, pg 38 (1875 Sept 22) per diem
Proceedings 1875, pg 38 (1875 Sept 22) committee
Proceedings 1876, pg 39 (1876 Sept 20), Collins Lodge No. 19, Fort Collins

Peterson, Henry C
Proceedings 1872, pg 32 (1872 Sept 24), Collins Lodge No. 19, Fort Collins
Proceedings 1873, pg 49 (1873 Oct 1), Collins Lodge No. 19, Fort Collins
Proceedings 1874, pg 224 (1874 Sept 30), Collins Lodge No. 19, Fort Collins, Larimer County
Proceedings 1875, pg 17 (1875 Sept 21), Collins Lodge No. 19, Fort Collins
Proceedings 1875, pg 86 (1875 Sept 22), Collins Lodge No. 19, Fort Collins

Peterson, P H
Proceedings 1876, pg 42 (1876 Sept 20), Doric Lodge No. 25, Fairplay

Peterson, Pierre J
Proceedings 1876, pg 44 (1876 Sept 20) Del Norte Lodge U D

Petty, Z R
Proceedings 1874, pg 220 (1874 Sept 30), Mount Moriah Lodge No. 15, Canon City
Proceedings 1876, pg 48 (1876 Sept 20), Mount Moriah Lodge No. 15, Canon City, 1876 Feb 19

Petty, Z Y
Proceedings 1875, pg 84 (1875 Sept 22), Mount Moriah Lodge No. 15, Canon City

Peyton, I N
Proceedings 1876, pg 31 (1876 Sept 20) Denver Lodge No. 5

Peyton, Isaac N
Proceedings 1876, pg 7 (1876 Mar 15), Olive Branch Lodge U D, Saguache
Proceedings 1876, pg 46 (1876 Sept 20), Olive Branch Lodge U D, Saguache

Peyton, V
Proceedings 1876, pg 46 (1876 Sept 20), Olive Branch Lodge U D, Saguache

Pfeffer, J S
Proceedings 1872, pg 32 (1872 Sept 24), Laramie Lodge No. 18, Laramie, Wyoming Territory
Proceedings 1870, pg 30 (1870 Sept 28), Laramie Lodge No. 18, Laramie, Wyoming Territory
Proceedings 1871, pg 29 (1871 Sept 27), Laramie Lodge No. 18, Laramie, Wyoming Territory
Proceedings 1873, pg 48 (1873 Oct 1), Laramie Lodge No. 18, Laramie, Wyoming Territory

Pfouts
Proceedings 1861-1869, pg 36 (1861 Dec 10) Denver Lodge No. 5
Proceedings 1861-1869, pg 37 (1861 Dec 12) motion
Proceedings 1861-1869, pg 38 (1861 Dec 12) motion
Proceedings 1861-1869, pg 48 (1862 Nov 3) motion
Proceedings 1861-1869, pg 82 (1863 Apr 18) Denver Lodge No. 5
Proceedings 1861-1869, pg 83 (1863 May 6) Denver Lodge No. 5
Proceedings 1861-1869, pg 83 (1863 May 6) Denver Lodge No. 5
Proceedings 1861-1869, pg 85 (1863 May 6) Denver Lodge No. 5
Proceedings 1861-1869, pg 91 (1863 Apr 17) Denver Lodge No. 5
Proceedings 1861-1869, pg 92 (1863 Apr 17) Denver Lodge No. 5
Proceedings 1861-1869, pg 93 (1863 Apr 17) Denver Lodge No. 5
Proceedings 1861-1869, pg 93 (1863 Apr 17) Denver Lodge No. 5

Pfouts, P A
Proceedings 1861-1869, pg 44 (1862 Nov 3) Senior Grand Warden

Pfouts, P S
Proceedings 1861-1869, pg 36 (1861 Dec 12) Senior Grand Warden
Proceedings 1861-1869, pg 45 (1862 Nov 3) committee
Proceedings 1861-1869, pg 50 (1862 Nov 4) committee
Proceedings 1861-1869, pg 77 (1862 Nov 4) Denver Lodge No. 5
Proceedings 1861-1869, pg 81 (1863 Apr 18) Denver Lodge No. 5
Proceedings 1861-1869, pg 315 (1869 Sept 29) Senior Grand Warden, December 1861, Dimitted
Proceedings 1870, pg 32 (1870 Sept 28) Senior Grand Warden, December 1861, Dimitted
Proceedings 1871, pg 34 (1871 Sept 27) Senior Grand Warden, Dec 1861, Dimitted
Proceedings 1872, pg 42 (1872 Sept 24) Senior Grand Warden, December 1861, Dimitted
Proceedings 1873, pg 58 (1873 Oct 1) Senior Grand Warden, Dec 1861, Dimitted

Pfouts, Paris S
Proceedings 1861-1869, pg 112 (1863 Nov 3) Denver Lodge No. 5, dimitted
Proceedings 1874, pg 206 (1874 Sept 30) Senior Grand Warden, Dec 1861, demitted

Pfouts, Paris S, cont.
 Proceedings 1875, pg 93 (1875 Sept 22) Senior Grand Warden, Dec 1861, Demitted

Phelps, Thomas W
 Proceedings 1874, pg 217 (1874 Sept 30), Washington Lodge No. 12, Georgetown
 Proceedings 1876, pg 34 (1876 Sept 20), Washington Lodge No. 12, Georgetown

Phelps, Thos W
 Proceedings 1875, pg 81 (1875 Sept 22), Washington Lodge No. 12, Georgetown

Phhillips, John F
 Proceedings 1871, pg 18 (1871 Sept 27), Nevada Lodge No. 4, Bald Mountain

Philips, J F
 Proceedings 1861-1869, pg 77 (1862 Nov 4), Nevada Lodge No. 4, Nevadaville

Philips, Thos L
 Proceedings 1875, pg 75 (1875 Sept 22) Denver Lodge No. 5

Phillips
 Proceedings 1861-1869, pg 177 (1867 Oct 7) committee
 Proceedings 1861-1869, pg 187 (1867 Oct 8) motion
 Proceedings 1861-1869, pg 189 (1867 Oct 8) motion
 Proceedings 1861-1869, pg 202 (1868 Oct 6) committee
 Proceedings 1861-1869, pg 289 (1869 Sept 28) committee

Phillips, Albert
 Proceedings 1875, pg 90 (1875 Sept 22), Huerfano Lodge U D, Walsenburg
 Proceedings 1876, pg 43 (1876 Sept 20), Huerfano Lodge No. 27, Walsenburg

Phillips, G T
 Proceedings 1861-1869, pg 311 (1869 Sept 29), Mount Moriah Lodge No. 15, Canon City
 Proceedings 1872, pg 29 (1872 Sept 24), Mount Moriah Lodge No. 15, Canon City
 Proceedings 1875, pg 84 (1875 Sept 22), Mount Moriah Lodge No. 15, Canon City

Phillips, G W
 Proceedings 1871, pg 26 (1871 Sept 27), Mount Moriah Lodge No. 15, Canon City

Phillips, Geo
 Proceedings 1872, pg 35 (1872 Sept 24), St Vrain Lodge No. 23, Longmont

Phillips, Geo S
 Proceedings 1873, pg 51 (1873 Oct 1), St Vrain Lodge No. 23, Longmont
 Proceedings 1874, pg 227 (1874 Sept 30), St Vrain No. 23, Longmont
 Proceedings 1876, pg 41 (1876 Sept 20), St Vrain Lodge No. 23, Longmont

Phillips, Geo T
 Proceedings 1861-1869, pg 229 (1868 Oct 7), Canon Lodge U D, Canon City
 Proceedings 1873, pg 45 (1873 Oct 1), Mount Moriah Lodge No. 15, Canon City
 Proceedings 1874, pg 220 (1874 Sept 30), Mount Moriah Lodge No. 15, Canon City

Phillips, Geo W
 Proceedings 1870, pg 28 (1870 Sept 28), Mount Moriah Lodge No. 15, Canon City

Phillips, George T
 Proceedings 1876, pg 37 (1876 Sept 20), Mount Moriah Lodge No. 15, Canon City

Phillips, J F
 Proceedings 1861-1869, pg 111 (1863 Nov 3), Nevada Lodge No. 4, Nevadaville
 Proceedings 1861-1869, pg 132 (1864 Nov 8), Nevada Lodge No. 4, Nevadaville
 Proceedings 1861-1869, pg 137 (1865 Nov 6), Nevada Lodge No. 4, Nevadaville
 Proceedings 1861-1869, pg 138 (1865 Nov 6) committee
 Proceedings 1861-1869, pg 144 (1865 Nov 7), Nevada Lodge No. 4, Nevadaville
 Proceedings 1861-1869, pg 147 (1865 Nov 7), Nevada Lodge No. 4, Nevadaville
 Proceedings 1861-1869, pg 156 (1866 Oct 1), Nevada Lodge No. 4, Nevadaville
 Proceedings 1861-1869, pg 159 (1866 Oct 1) warrant
 Proceedings 1861-1869, pg 160 (1866 Oct 2) Grand Teller
 Proceedings 1861-1869, pg 166 (1866 Oct 2), Nevada Lodge No. 4, Nevadaville
 Proceedings 1861-1869, pg 176 (1867 Oct 7), Nevada Lodge No. 4, Nevadaville
 Proceedings 1861-1869, pg 190 (1867 Oct 8) Senior Grand Steward
 Proceedings 1861-1869, pg 191 (1867 Oct 8), Nevada Lodge No. 4, Nevadaville
 Proceedings 1861-1869, pg 201 (1868 Oct 6) Grand Steward
 Proceedings 1861-1869, pg 202 (1868 Oct 6), Nevada Lodge No. 4, Nevadaville
 Proceedings 1861-1869, pg 219 (1868 Oct 7), Nevada Lodge No. 4, Nevadaville
 Proceedings 1861-1869, pg 219 (1868 Oct 7) committee
 Proceedings 1861-1869, pg 220 (1868 Oct 7) Grand Steward
 Proceedings 1861-1869, pg 287 (1869 Sept 28) Grand Steward
 Proceedings 1861-1869, pg 288 (1869 Sept 28), Nevada Lodge No. 4, Nevadaville
 Proceedings 1861-1869, pg 300 (1869 Sept 29), Nevada Lodge No. 4, Nevadaville
 Proceedings 1861-1869, pg 304 (1869 Sept 29), Nevada Lodge No. 4, Nevadaville
 Proceedings 1876, pg 30 (1876 Sept 20) Nevada Lodge No. 4

Phillips, John F
 Proceedings 1861-1869, pg 222 (1868 Oct 7), Nevada Lodge No. 4, Nevadaville
 Proceedings 1870, pg 20 (1870 Sept 28), Nevada Lodge No. 4, Nevadaville

Proceedings 1871, pg 18 (1871 Sept 27), Nevada Lodge No. 4, Bald Mountain

Proceedings 1872, pg 18 (1872 Sept 24), Nevada Lodge No. 4, Bald Mountain

Proceedings 1873, pg 36 (1873 Oct 1), Nevada Lodge No. 4, Nevada

Phillips, John F

Proceedings 1874, pg 210 (1874 Sept 30), Nevada Lodge No. 4, Bald Mountain, Gilpin County

Proceedings 1875, pg 74 (1875 Sept 22), Nevada Lodge No. 4, Nevada

Phillips, Thomas G

Proceedings 1871, pg 19 (1871 Sept 27) Denver Lodge No. 5, Apprentice

Phillips, Thomas L

Proceedings 1876, pg 31 (1876 Sept 20) Denver Lodge No. 5

Phillips, Thos G

Proceedings 1872, pg 19 (1872 Sept 24), Denver Lodge No. 5, Denver

Proceedings 1873, pg 37 (1873 Oct 1), Denver Lodge No. 5, Denver

Phillips, Thos L

Proceedings 1874, pg 211 (1874 Sept 30), Denver Lodge No. 5, Denver

Phipps, C J

Proceedings 1874, pg 214 (1874 Sept 30), Union Lodge No. 7, Denver

Proceedings 1875, pg 78 (1875 Sept 22), Union Lodge No. 7, Denver

Proceedings 1876, pg 33 (1876 Sept 20), Union Lodge No. 7, Denver

Phisterer, Ernest

Proceedings 1873, pg 37 (1873 Oct 1), Denver Lodge No. 5, Denver, Apprentice

Proceedings 1876, pg 31 (1876 Sept 20) Denver Lodge No. 5

Proceedings 1874, pg 211 (1874 Sept 30), Denver Lodge No. 5, Denver

Proceedings 1875, pg 75 (1875 Sept 22) Denver Lodge No. 5

Pickett, Thos J

Proceedings 1874, pg 204 (1874 Sept 30) Grand Lodge of Kentucky, Paducah

Pierce, John

Proceedings 1861-1869, pg 134 (1864 Nov 8), Union Lodge No. 7, Denver

Proceedings 1861-1869, pg 151 (1865 Nov 7), Chivington Lodge No. 6, Central City

Proceedings 1861-1869, pg 169 (1866 Oct 2), Union Lodge No. 7, Denver

Proceedings 1861-1869, pg 195 (1867 Oct 8), Union Lodge No. 7, Denver

Proceedings 1861-1869, pg 225 (1868 Oct 7), Union Lodge No. 7, Denver

Proceedings 1861-1869, pg 307 (1869 Sept 29), Union Lodge No. 7, Denver

Proceedings 1870, pg 23 (1870 Sept 28), Union Lodge No. 7, Denver

Proceedings 1871, pg 22 (1871 Sept 27), Union Lodge No. 7, Denver

Proceedings 1872, pg 22 (1872 Sept 24), Union Lodge No. 7, Denver

Proceedings 1873, pg 39 (1873 Oct 1), Union Lodge No. 7, Denver

Proceedings 1874, pg 214 (1874 Sept 30), Union Lodge No. 7, Denver

Proceedings 1875, pg 78 (1875 Sept 22), Union Lodge No. 7, Denver

Proceedings 1876, pg 33 (1876 Sept 20), Union Lodge No. 7, Denver

Pierce, L D

Proceedings 1871, pg 28 (1871 Sept 27), Cheyenne Lodge No. 16, Cheyenne, Wyoming Territory, Apprentice

Proceedings 1872, pg 30 (1872 Sept 24), Cheyenne Lodge No. 16, Cheyenne, Wyoming Territory, Apprentice

Proceedings 1873, pg 46 (1873 Oct 1), Cheyenne Lodge No. 16, Cheyenne, Wyoming Territory, Apprentice

Proceedings 1874, pg 221 (1874 Sept 30), Cheyenne Lodge No. 16, Cheyenne, Wyoming Territory

Pierce, Oscar

Proceedings 1861-1869, pg 310 (1869 Sept 29), Columbia Lodge No. 14, Boulder City

Proceedings 1870, pg 27 (1870 Sept 28), Columbia Lodge No. 14, Boulder City

Proceedings 1871, pg 26 (1871 Sept 27), Columbia Lodge No. 14, Boulder City

Proceedings 1872, pg 28 (1872 Sept 24), Columbia Lodge No. 14, Boulder

Proceedings 1873, pg 45 (1873 Oct 1), Columbia Lodge No. 14, Boulder, Dimitted

Piermont, C A

Proceedings 1874, pg 223 (1874 Sept 30), Laramie Lodge No. 18, Laramie City

Pierson

Proceedings 1870, pg 81 (1870 Jan 11) Grand Lodge of Minnesota

Pierson

Proceedings 1874, pg 89 (1874 Sept 30) Grand Lodge of Minnesota

Pierson, A T C

Proceedings 1870, pg 80 (1870 Jan 11) Grand Lodge of Minnesota

Proceedings 1871, pg 10 (1871 May 10) Grand Ldoge of Minnesota

Proceedings 1872, pg 43 (1872 Sept 24) St Paul, Grand Lodge of Minnesota

Proceedings 1873, pg 59 (1873 Oct 1), of St Paul, Grand Representative to the Grand Lodge of Minnesota

Proceedings 1873, pg 60 (1873 Oct 1) Grand Lodge of Minnesota, St Paul

Proceedings 1874, pg 87 (1874 Sept 30) Grand Lodge of Minnesota

Proceedings 1874, pg 204 (1874 Sept 30) Grand Lodge of Minnesota, St Paul

Colorado's Territorial Masons

Pierson, A T C, cont.
    Proceedings 1874, pg 207 (1874 Sept 30) Grand Lodge of Minnesota, St Paul
    Proceedings 1875, pg 95 (1875 Sept 22) Grand Lodge of Minnesota, St Paul, MN
    Proceedings 1876, pg 53 (1876 Sept 20) Grand Lodge of Minnesota, of St Paul, MN
    Proceedings 1876, pg 54 (1876 Sept 20) Grand Lodge of Minnesota, St Paul

Pierson, Hollis K
    Proceedings 1876, pg 35 (1876 Sept 20), Washington Lodge No. 12, Georgetown

Pierson, Robert K
    Proceedings 1875, pg 78 (1875 Sept 22), Union Lodge No. 7, Denver
    Proceedings 1876, pg 32 (1876 Sept 20), Union Lodge No. 7, Denver

Pierson, Robt K
    Proceedings 1874, pg 214 (1874 Sept 30), Union Lodge No. 7, Denver

Pine, Wm E
    Proceedings 1872, pg 44 (1872 Sept 24) Newark, Grand Lodge of New Jersey
    Proceedings 1872, pg 77 (1872 Sept 24) Grand Lodge of New Jersey
    Proceedings 1873, pg 61 (1873 Oct 1) Grand Lodge of New Jersey, Newark
    Proceedings 1874, pg 108 (1874 Sept 30) Grand Lodge of New Jersey

Piner
    Proceedings 1874, pg 113 (1874 Sept 30) Grand Lodge of New York

Pingrey, Solon W
    Proceedings 1876, pg 44 (1876 Sept 20) Del Norte Lodge U D

Pinkerton, J H
    Proceedings 1861-1869, pg 221 (1868 Oct 7) Golden City Lodge No. 1
    Proceedings 1861-1869, pg 303 (1869 Sept 29) Golden City Lodge No. 1, Dimitted

Pinkerton, James H
    Proceedings 1871, pg 30 (1871 Sept 27), Occidental Lodge U D, Greeley

Pinkerton, Wm R
    Proceedings 1861-1869, pg 191 (1867 Oct 8) Golden City Lodge No. 1

Pinkham, Joseph
    Proceedings 1874, pg 61 (1874 Sept 30) Grand Lodge of Idaho
    Proceedings 1874, pg 204 (1874 Sept 30) Grand Lodge of Idaho, Boise City

Pinneo, B F
    Proceedings 1876, pg 40 (1876 Sept 20), Occidental Lodge No. 20, Greeley

Piper, E W
    Proceedings 1870, pg 29 (1870 Sept 28), Cheyenne Lodge No. 16, Cheyenne, Wyoming Territory
    Proceedings 1871, pg 27 (1871 Sept 27), Cheyenne Lodge No. 16, Cheyenne, Wyoming Territory
    Proceedings 1873, pg 46 (1873 Oct 1), Cheyenne Lodge No. 16, Cheyenne, Wyoming Territory
    Proceedings 1874, pg 221 (1874 Sept 30), Cheyenne Lodge No. 16, Cheyenne, Wyoming Territory

Piper, Edgar W
    Proceedings 1872, pg 29 (1872 Sept 24), Cheyenne Lodge No. 16, Cheyenne, Wyoming Territory

Pisderez, John
    Proceedings 1861-1869, pg 196 (1867 Oct 8), El Paso Lodge U D, Colorado City
    Proceedings 1875, pg 82 (1875 Sept 22), El Paso Lodge No. 13, Colorado Springs, died
    Proceedings 1875, pg 94 (1875 Sept 22), El Paso Lodge No. 13, Colorado Springs

Pisderz, John
    Proceedings 1874, pg 218 (1874 Sept 30), El Paso Lodge No. 13, Colorado Springs
    Proceedings 1861-1869, pg 228 (1868 Oct 7), El Paso Lodge No. 13, Colorado City

Pisdirz, John
    Proceedings 1871, pg 25 (1871 Sept 27), El Paso Lodge No. 13, Colorado City

Pitz, John
    Proceedings 1873, pg 37 (1873 Oct 1), Denver Lodge No. 5, Denver, Apprentice

Pitzer, H D
    Proceedings 1861-1869, pg 195 (1867 Oct 8), Union Lodge No. 7, Denver

Pitzer, H L
    Proceedings 1861-1869, pg 169 (1866 Oct 2), Union Lodge No. 7, Denver
    Proceedings 1861-1869, pg 225 (1868 Oct 7), Union Lodge No. 7, Denver
    Proceedings 1861-1869, pg 307 (1869 Sept 29), Union Lodge No. 7, Denver
    Proceedings 1873, pg 39 (1873 Oct 1), Union Lodge No. 7, Denver
    Proceedings 1874, pg 214 (1874 Sept 30), Union Lodge No. 7, Denver
    Proceedings 1876, pg 33 (1876 Sept 20), Union Lodge No. 7, Denver

Pitzer, Henry L
    Proceedings 1870, pg 23 (1870 Sept 28), Union Lodge No. 7, Denver
    Proceedings 1871, pg 22 (1871 Sept 27), Union Lodge No. 7, Denver
    Proceedings 1872, pg 22 (1872 Sept 24), Union Lodge No. 7, Denver
    Proceedings 1875, pg 78 (1875 Sept 22), Union Lodge No. 7, Denver

Pixley, Frank M
Proceedings 1870, pg 46 (1869 Oct 12) Grand Orator, Grand Lodge of California

Pizdeers, John
Proceedings 1872, pg 27 (1872 Sept 24), El Paso Lodge No. 13, Colorado City

Platt, Henry
Proceedings 1871, pg 30 (1871 Sept 27), Occidental Lodge U D, Greeley

Plumb, Ovid
Proceedings 1871, pg 30 (1871 Sept 27), Occidental Lodge U D, Greeley
Proceedings 1874, pg 225 (1874 Sept 30), Occidental Lodge No. 20, Greeley
Proceedings 1875, pg 87 (1875 Sept 22), Occidental Lodge No. 20, Greeley
Proceedings 1876, pg 40 (1876 Sept 20), Occidental Lodge No. 20, Greeley

Plumb, S J
Proceedings 1873, pg 51 (1873 Oct 1), St Vrain Lodge No. 23, Longmont
Proceedings 1874, pg 227 (1874 Sept 30), St Vrain No. 23, Longmont
Proceedings 1876, pg 41 (1876 Sept 20), St Vrain Lodge No. 23, Longmont

Plummer, D C
Proceedings 1875, pg 89 (1875 Sept 22), Doric Lodge No. 25, Fairplay
Proceedings 1876, pg 42 (1876 Sept 20), Doric Lodge No. 25, Fairplay
Proceedings 1876, pg 50 (1876 Sept 20), Doric Lodge No. 25, Fairplay

Plummer, J E
Proceedings 1861-1869, pg 134 (1864 Nov 8), Chivington Lodge No. 6, Central City
Proceedings 1861-1869, pg 150 (1865 Nov 7), Chivington Lodge No. 6, Central City
Proceedings 1861-1869, pg 168 (1866 Oct 2), Chivington Lodge No. 6, Central City

Pochon, Joseph
Proceedings 1876, pg 45 (1876 Sept 20) South Pueblo Lodge U D

Poleher, Adolph
Proceedings 1870, pg 26 (1870 Sept 28), Washington Lodge No. 12, Georgetown
Proceedings 1871, pg 24 (1871 Sept 27), Washington Lodge No. 12, Georgetown
Proceedings 1872, pg 25 (1872 Sept 24), Washington Lodge No. 12, Georgetown

Polglase, Charles
Proceedings 1873, pg 39 (1873 Oct 1), Central Lodge No. 6, Central City
Proceedings 1874, pg 213 (1874 Sept 30), Central Lodge No. 6, Central
Proceedings 1875, pg 77 (1875 Sept 22), Central Lodge No. 6, Central City
Proceedings 1876, pg 32 (1876 Sept 20), Central Lodge No. 6, Central City

Polglase, John
Proceedings 1873, pg 39 (1873 Oct 1), Central Lodge No. 6, Central City
Proceedings 1874, pg 213 (1874 Sept 30), Central Lodge No. 6, Central
Proceedings 1875, pg 77 (1875 Sept 22), Central Lodge No. 6, Central City
Proceedings 1876, pg 32 (1876 Sept 20), Central Lodge No. 6, Central City

Pollack, P P
Proceedings 1861-1869, pg 191 (1867 Oct 8) Golden City Lodge No. 1

Pollard, C W
Proceedings 1861-1869, pg 151 (1865 Nov 7), Chivington Lodge No. 6, Central City, Apprentice
Proceedings 1861-1869, pg 168 (1866 Oct 2), Chivington Lodge No. 6, Central City
Proceedings 1861-1869, pg 193 (1867 Oct 8), Chivington Lodge No. 6, Central City
Proceedings 1861-1869, pg 224 (1868 Oct 7), Chivington Lodge No. 6, Central City
Proceedings 1861-1869, pg 306 (1869 Sept 29), Central Lodge No. 6, Central City

Pollard, Charles W
Proceedings 1871, pg 24 (1871 Sept 27), Washington Lodge No. 12, Georgetown
Proceedings 1874, pg 217 (1874 Sept 30), Washington Lodge No. 12, Georgetown
Proceedings 1876, pg 35 (1876 Sept 20), Washington Lodge No. 12, Georgetown

Pollard, Chas W
Proceedings 1870, pg 23 (1870 Sept 28), Central Lodge No. 6, Central City, Dimitted
Proceedings 1872, pg 25 (1872 Sept 24), Washington Lodge No. 12, Georgetown
Proceedings 1873, pg 42 (1873 Oct 1), Washington Lodge No. 12, Georgetown
Proceedings 1875, pg 81 (1875 Sept 22), Washington Lodge No. 12, Georgetown

Pollard, L
Proceedings 1861-1869, pg 31 (1861 Dec 10) Junior Grand Warden
Proceedings 1861-1869, pg 42 (1861 Dec 10), Summit Lodge No. 2, Parkville
Proceedings 1861-1869, pg 76 (1862 Nov 4), Summit Lodge No. 2, Parkville

Pollock, P P
Proceedings 1871, pg 17 (1871 Sept 27), Golden City Lodge No. 1, Golden City

Pollock, Perry
Proceedings 1861-1869, pg 110 (1863 Nov 3) Golden City Lodge No. 1, Fellowcraft

Pollock, Perry P
Proceedings 1861-1869, pg 221 (1868 Oct 7) Golden City Lodge No. 1

Colorado's Territorial Masons

Pollock, Perry P, cont.
    Proceedings 1861-1869, pg 303 (1869 Sept 29) Golden City Lodge No. 1
    Proceedings 1872, pg 17 (1872 Sept 24), Golden City Lodge No. 1, Golden City
    Proceedings 1873, pg 35 (1873 Oct 1), Golden City Lodge No. 1, Golden City
    Proceedings 1874, pg 209 (1874 Sept 30), Golden City Lodge No. 1, Golden City
    Proceedings 1875, pg 74 (1875 Sept 22) Golden City Lodge No. 1, Stricken from the rolls

Pollock, Thomas
    Proceedings 1876, pg 44 (1876 Sept 20) Del Norte Lodge U D

Pollock, W P
    Proceedings 1861-1869, pg 147 (1865 Nov 7) Golden City Lodge No. 1
    Proceedings 1861-1869, pg 150 (1865 Nov 7), Chivington Lodge No. 6, Central City
    Proceedings 1861-1869, pg 165 (1866 Oct 2) Golden City Lodge No. 1
    Proceedings 1861-1869, pg 168 (1866 Oct 2), Chivington Lodge No. 6, Central City
    Proceedings 1861-1869, pg 193 (1867 Oct 8), Chivington Lodge No. 6, Central City
    Proceedings 1861-1869, pg 306 (1869 Sept 29), Central Lodge No. 6, Central City
    Proceedings 1870, pg 19 (1870 Sept 28), Golden City Lodge No. 1, Golden City
    Proceedings 1870, pg 22 (1870 Sept 28), Central Lodge No. 6, Central City
    Proceedings 1871, pg 20 (1871 Sept 27), Central Lodge No. 6, Central

Pollock, William P
    Proceedings 1872, pg 21 (1872 Sept 24), Denver Lodge No. 5, Denver
    Proceedings 1873, pg 39 (1873 Oct 1), Central Lodge No. 6, Central City
    Proceedings 1874, pg 213 (1874 Sept 30), Central Lodge No. 6, Central
    Proceedings 1875, pg 77 (1875 Sept 22), Central Lodge No. 6, Central City
    Proceedings 1876, pg 32 (1876 Sept 20), Central Lodge No. 6, Central City

Pollock, Wm P
    Proceedings 1861-1869, pg 131 (1864 Nov 8) Golden City Lodge No. 1
    Proceedings 1861-1869, pg 224 (1868 Oct 7), Chivington Lodge No. 6, Central City

Pollok, I J
    Proceedings 1871, pg 24 (1871 Sept 27), Washington Lodge No. 12, Georgetown, Apprentice

Pollok, Irving J
    Proceedings 1872, pg 26 (1872 Sept 24), Washington Lodge No. 12, Georgetown, Apprentice
    Proceedings 1873, pg 43 (1873 Oct 1), Washington Lodge No. 12, Georgetown, Apprentice
    Proceedings 1874, pg 217 (1874 Sept 30), Washington Lodge No. 12, Georgetown, Apprentice
    Proceedings 1876, pg 35 (1876 Sept 20), Washington Lodge No. 12, Georgetown, Apprentice

Pollok, J Irving
    Proceedings 1875, pg 81 (1875 Sept 22), Washington Lodge No. 12, Georgetown, Apprentice

Pomeroy, J W
    Proceedings 1861-1869, pg 197 (1867 Oct 8), Columbia Lodge U D, Boulder

Pomeroy's Democrat
    Proceedings 1870, pg 11 (1870 Sept 27)
    Proceedings 1871, pg 10 (1871 Sept 26) masonic magazine

Poole, John
    Proceedings 1876, pg 44 (1876 Sept 20) Del Norte Lodge U D

Pope, Thomas M
    Proceedings 1861-1869, pg 131 (1864 Nov 8) Golden City Lodge No. 1, dimitted

Pope, W H
    Proceedings 1873, pg 10 (1873 Sept 30), Evanston Lodge U D, Evanston, Wyoming Territory

Popplewell, Wm
    Proceedings 1874, pg 228 (1874 Sept 30), Evanston Lodge U D, Evanston, Uintah County, Wyoming Territory

Porter, Charles
    Proceedings 1861-1869, pg 77 (1862 Nov 4) Denver Lodge No. 5
    Proceedings 1861-1869, pg 112 (1863 Nov 3) Denver Lodge No. 5, dimitted

Porter, D P
    Proceedings 1861-1869, pg 266 (1867 Jan 20), Grand Secretary, Grand Lodge of Mississippi

Porter, E D B
    Proceedings 1873, pg 60 (1873 Oct 1) Grand Lodge of Minnesota, St Paul
    Proceedings 1874, pg 85 (1874 Sept 30) Grand Lodge of Minnesota
    Proceedings 1874, pg 204 (1874 Sept 30) Grand Lodge of Minnesota, St Paul
    Proceedings 1875, pg 96 (1875 Sept 22) Grand Lodge of Minnesota, St Paul

Porter, T C
    Proceedings 1861-1869, pg 149 (1865 Nov 7), Nevada Lodge No. 4, Nevadaville, dimitted

Porter, Thos C
    Proceedings 1861-1869, pg 133 (1864 Nov 8) Denver Lodge No. 5

Porter, William
    Proceedings 1861-1869, pg 149 (1865 Nov 7), Nevada Lodge No. 4, Nevadaville, dimitted

Porter, Wm
    Proceedings 1861-1869, pg 77 (1862 Nov 4) Denver Lodge No. 5

Proceedings 1861-1869, pg 98 (1863 Nov 2) Denver Lodge No. 5

Proceedings 1861-1869, pg 100 (1863 Nov 2) committee

Proceedings 1861-1869, pg 112 (1863 Nov 3) Denver Lodge No. 5

Proceedings 1861-1869, pg 133 (1864 Nov 8) Denver Lodge No. 5

Posey, Oliver P
Proceedings 1876, pg 44 (1876 Sept 20) Del Norte Lodge U D, Apprentice

Post, E J
Proceedings 1875, pg 91 (1875 Sept 22), Las Animas Lodge U D, Trinidad, Apprentice

Post, Ezra I
Proceedings 1876, pg 44 (1876 Sept 20), Las Animas Lodge No. 28, Trinidad

Potter
Proceedings 1861-1869, pg 92 (1863 Apr 17) committee
Proceedings 1861-1869, pg 202 (1868 Oct 6) committee
Proceedings 1861-1869, pg 289 (1869 Sept 28) committee
Proceedings 1861-1869, pg 293 (1869 Sept 28), Columbia Lodge No. 14, Boulder

Potter, Alfred R
Proceedings 1874, pg 205 (1874 Sept 30) Grand Lodge of Pennsylvania

Potter, Aug G
Proceedings 1871, pg 22 (1871 Sept 27), Union Lodge No. 7, Denver, Apprentice
Proceedings 1872, pg 23 (1872 Sept 24), Union Lodge No. 7, Denver, Apprentice
Proceedings 1873, pg 40 (1873 Oct 1), Union Lodge No. 7, Denver, Apprentice
Proceedings 1874, pg 214 (1874 Sept 30), Union Lodge No. 7, Denver, Apprentice
Proceedings 1875, pg 79 (1875 Sept 22), Union Lodge No. 7, Denver, Apprentice

Potter, Augustus G
Proceedings 1870, pg 24 (1870 Sept 28), Union Lodge No. 7, Denver, Apprentice
Proceedings 1876, pg 33 (1876 Sept 20), Union Lodge No. 7, Denver, Apprentice

Potter, J S
Proceedings 1876, pg 31 (1876 Sept 20) Denver Lodge No. 5

Potter, James S
Proceedings 1873, pg 37 (1873 Oct 1), Denver Lodge No. 5, Denver
Proceedings 1874, pg 211 (1874 Sept 30), Denver Lodge No. 5, Denver
Proceedings 1875, pg 75 (1875 Sept 22) Denver Lodge No. 5

Potter, Richard
Proceedings 1870, pg 77 (1824 Jan 5) African Lodge at Boston

Potter, T H
Proceedings 1871, pg 20 (1871 Sept 27), Central Lodge No. 6, Central

Potter, Thomas H
Proceedings 1872, pg 21 (1872 Sept 24), Denver Lodge No. 5, Denver
Proceedings 1874, pg 213 (1874 Sept 30), Central Lodge No. 6, Central
Proceedings 1875, pg 77 (1875 Sept 22), Central Lodge No. 6, Central City
Proceedings 1876, pg 32 (1876 Sept 20), Central Lodge No. 6, Central City

Potter, Thos H
Proceedings 1861-1869, pg 306 (1869 Sept 29), Central Lodge No. 6, Central City
Proceedings 1870, pg 22 (1870 Sept 28), Central Lodge No. 6, Central City
Proceedings 1873, pg 38 (1873 Oct 1), Central Lodge No. 6, Central City

Potter, Thos J
Proceedings 1861-1869, pg 224 (1868 Oct 7), Chivington Lodge No. 6, Central City

Potter, W F [T]
Proceedings 1861-1869, pg 301 (1869 Sept 29) committee

Potter, W T
Proceedings 1861-1869, pg 76 (1862 Nov 4), Nevada Lodge No. 4, Nevadaville
Proceedings 1861-1869, pg 80 (1863 May 6), Nevada Lodge No. 4, Nevadaville
Proceedings 1861-1869, pg 93 (1863 Apr 17) committee
Proceedings 1861-1869, pg 111 (1863 Nov 3), Nevada Lodge No. 4, Nevadaville
Proceedings 1861-1869, pg 132 (1864 Nov 8), Nevada Lodge No. 4, Nevadaville
Proceedings 1861-1869, pg 148 (1865 Nov 7), Nevada Lodge No. 4, Nevadaville, dimitted
Proceedings 1861-1869, pg 189 (1867 Oct 8), Columbia Lodge No. 14, Columbia
Proceedings 1861-1869, pg 197 (1867 Oct 8), Columbia Lodge U D, Boulder
Proceedings 1861-1869, pg 202 (1868 Oct 6), Columbia Lodge No. 14, Columbia
Proceedings 1861-1869, pg 219 (1868 Oct 7), Columbia Lodge No. 14, Boulder
Proceedings 1861-1869, pg 228 (1868 Oct 7), Columbia Lodge No. 14, Columbia City
Proceedings 1861-1869, pg 288 (1869 Sept 28), Columbia Lodge No. 14, Columbia City
Proceedings 1861-1869, pg 301 (1869 Sept 29), Columbia Lodge No. 14, Boulder
Proceedings 1870, pg 27 (1870 Sept 28), Columbia Lodge No. 14, Boulder City
Proceedings 1871, pg 25 (1871 Sept 27), Columbia Lodge No. 14, Boulder City
Proceedings 1872, pg 18 (1872 Sept 24), Nevada Lodge No. 4, Bald Mountain

Colorado's Territorial Masons

Potter, William T
    Proceedings 1875, pg 74 (1875 Sept 22), Nevada Lodge No. 4, Nevada

Potter, Willie T
    Proceedings 1861-1869, pg 310 (1869 Sept 29), Columbia Lodge No. 14, Boulder City
    Proceedings 1872, pg 28 (1872 Sept 24), Columbia Lodge No. 14, Boulder, Dimitted
    Proceedings 1873, pg 36 (1873 Oct 1), Nevada Lodge No. 4, Nevada
    Proceedings 1874, pg 210 (1874 Sept 30), Nevada Lodge No. 4, Bald Mountain, Gilpin County
    Proceedings 1876, pg 30 (1876 Sept 20) Nevada Lodge No. 4

Potts, J A
    Proceedings 1873, pg 48 (1873 Oct 1), Laramie Lodge No. 18, Laramie, Wyoming Territory, Apprentice

Potts, J H
    Proceedings 1871, pg 29 (1871 Sept 27), Laramie Lodge No. 18, Laramie, Wyoming Territory, Apprentice
    Proceedings 1872, pg 32 (1872 Sept 24), Laramie Lodge No. 18, Laramie, Wyoming Territory, Apprentice
    Proceedings 1874, pg 224 (1874 Sept 30), Laramie Lodge No. 18, Laramie City, Apprentice

Powell, A P
    Proceedings 1871, pg 27 (1871 Sept 27), Cheyenne Lodge No. 16, Cheyenne, Wyoming Territory
    Proceedings 1872, pg 29 (1872 Sept 24), Cheyenne Lodge No. 16, Cheyenne, Wyoming Territory

Powell, Israel N
    Proceedings 1872, pg 43 (1872 Sept 24) Victoria, Grand Lodge of British Columbia

Powell, Israel W
    Proceedings 1873, pg 60 (1873 Oct 1) Grand Lodge of British Columbia, Victoria
    Proceedings 1874, pg 204 (1874 Sept 30) Grand Lodge of British Columbia, Victoria

Powell, Israel Wood
    Proceedings 1872, pg 55 (1872 Sept 24) Grand Lodge of British Columbia

Powell, J P
    Proceedings 1873, pg 51 (1873 Oct 1), Weston Lodge No. 22, Littleton

Powell, J S
    Proceedings 1874, pg 226 (1874 Sept 30), Weston Lodge No. 22, Littleton
    Proceedings 1876, pg 51 (1876 Sept 20), Weston Lodge No. 22, Littleton, 1876 June 3

Powell, James S
    Proceedings 1872, pg 34 (1872 Sept 24), Weston Lodge No. 22, Littleton

Powell, Jas S
    Proceedings 1875, pg 88 (1875 Sept 22), Weston Lodge No. 22, Littleton, Stricken from the rolls

Power, J L
    Proceedings 1861-1869, pg 316 (1869 Sept 29) Grand Lodge of Mississippi
    Proceedings 1861-1869, pg 335 (1869 Jan 18) Grand Secretary, Grand Lodge of Mississippi
    Proceedings 1870, pg 34 (1870 Sept 28) Grand Secretary, Grand Lodge of Mississippi
    Proceedings 1870, pg 81 (1870 Jan 17) Grand Secretary, Grand Lodge of Mississippi
    Proceedings 1871, pg 35 (1871 Sept 27) Grand Secretary, Grand Lodge of Mississippi
    Proceedings 1872, pg 43 (1872 Sept 24) Jackson, Grand Lodge of Mississippi
    Proceedings 1872, pg 71 (1872 Sept 24) Grand Lodge of Mississippi
    Proceedings 1873, pg 60 (1873 Oct 1) Grand Lodge of Mississippi, Jackson
    Proceedings 1874, pg 89 (1874 Sept 30) Grand Lodge of Mississippi
    Proceedings 1874, pg 204 (1874 Sept 30) Grand Lodge of Mississippi, Jackson
    Proceedings 1875, pg 96 (1875 Sept 22) Grand Lodge of Mississippi, Jackson
    Proceedings 1876, pg 54 (1876 Sept 20) Grand Lodge of Mississippi, Jackson

Powers, D L
    Proceedings 1876, pg 39 (1876 Sept 20), Collins Lodge No. 19, Fort Collins

Powers, Daniel L
    Proceedings 1872, pg 32 (1872 Sept 24), Collins Lodge No. 19, Fort Collins
    Proceedings 1873, pg 49 (1873 Oct 1), Collins Lodge No. 19, Fort Collins
    Proceedings 1875, pg 86 (1875 Sept 22), Collins Lodge No. 19, Fort Collins

Powers, Dan'l L
    Proceedings 1874, pg 224 (1874 Sept 30), Collins Lodge No. 19, Fort Collins, Larimer County

Powers, J P
    Proceedings 1874, pg 222 (1874 Sept 30), Pueblo Lodge No. 17, Pueblo, Pueblo County

Powers, Jansen P
    Proceedings 1875, pg 85 (1875 Sept 22) Pueblo Lodge No. 17
    Proceedings 1876, pg 39 (1876 Sept 20) Pueblo Lodge No. 17

Powers, Jason P
    Proceedings 1872, pg 31 (1872 Sept 24), Pueblo Lodge No. 17, Pueblo
    Proceedings 1873, pg 47 (1873 Oct 1), Pueblo Lodge No. 17, Pueblo

Poznainski, F
    Proceedings 1861-1869, pg 150 (1865 Nov 7), Chivington Lodge No. 6, Central City

Poznainsky
    Proceedings 1874, pg 96 (1874 Sept 30) Grand Lodge of Montana

Poznanski, F
Proceedings 1861-1869, pg 113 (1863 Nov 3), Chivington Lodge No. 6, Central City
Proceedings 1861-1869, pg 168 (1866 Oct 2), Chivington Lodge No. 6, Central City, dimitted

Poznansky, Felix
Proceedings 1861-1869, pg 134 (1864 Nov 8), Chivington Lodge No. 6, Central City

Pratt
Proceedings 1874, pg 84 (1874 Sept 30) Grand Lodge of Michigan

Pratt, Barney
Proceedings 1861-1869, pg 147 (1865 Nov 7) Golden City Lodge No. 1, Apprentice
Proceedings 1861-1869, pg 165 (1866 Oct 2) Golden City Lodge No. 1, Apprentice
Proceedings 1861-1869, pg 191 (1867 Oct 8) Golden City Lodge No. 1, Apprentice
Proceedings 1861-1869, pg 221 (1868 Oct 7) Golden City Lodge No. 1, Apprentice
Proceedings 1861-1869, pg 303 (1869 Sept 29) Golden City Lodge No. 1, Apprentice

Pratt, Foster
Proceedings 1873, pg 60 (1873 Oct 1) Grand Lodge of Michigan, Kalamazoo
Proceedings 1874, pg 19 (1874 Sept 29), of Kalamazoo, MI
Proceedings 1874, pg 83 (1874 Sept 30) Grand Lodge of Michigan
Proceedings 1874, pg 204 (1874 Sept 30) Grand Lodge of Michigan, Kalamazoo
Proceedings 1875, pg 96 (1875 Sept 22) Grand Lodge of Michigan, Kalamazoo

Pratt, Leonidas E
Proceedings 1870, pg 48 (1869 Oct 12) Grand Master, Grand Lodge of California
Proceedings 1872, pg 43 (1872 Sept 24) San Francisco, Grand Lodge of California
Proceedings 1872, pg 56 (1872 Sept 24) Grand Lodge of California
Proceedings 1873, pg 60 (1873 Oct 1) Grand Lodge of California, San Francisco
Proceedings 1874, pg 46 (1874 Sept 30) Grand Lodge of California

Pratt, M A
Proceedings 1874, pg 222 (1874 Sept 30), Pueblo Lodge No. 17, Pueblo, Pueblo County
Proceedings 1875, pg 85 (1875 Sept 22) Pueblo Lodge No. 17
Proceedings 1876, pg 49 (1876 Sept 20) Pueblo Lodge No. 17, 1876 Mar 23

Pratt, S J
Proceedings 1861-1869, pg 111 (1863 Nov 3), Summit Lodge No. 2, Parkville, Apprentice
Proceedings 1861-1869, pg 132 (1864 Nov 8) Golden City Lodge No. 1, Apprentice
Prescott
Proceedings 1870, pg 44 (1869 Nov 1) Grand Master, Grand Lodge of Minnesota

Presderz, John
Proceedings 1870, pg 27 (1870 Sept 28), El Paso Lodge No. 13, Colorado City

Preson, A D
Proceedings 1872, pg 33 (1872 Sept 24), Occidental Lodge No. 20, Greeley
Proceedings 1873, pg 49 (1873 Oct 1), Occidental Lodge No. 20, Greeley
Proceedings 1874, pg 225 (1874 Sept 30), Occidental Lodge No. 20, Greeley
Proceedings 1875, pg 87 (1875 Sept 22), Occidental Lodge No. 20, Greeley

Preston, A M
Proceedings 1874, pg 227 (1874 Sept 30), St Vrain No. 23, Longmont
Proceedings 1876, pg 41 (1876 Sept 20), St Vrain Lodge No. 23, Longmont

Preston, Alex
Proceedings 1872, pg 35 (1872 Sept 24), St Vrain Lodge No. 23, Longmont

Preston, Alex M
Proceedings 1873, pg 51 (1873 Oct 1), St Vrain Lodge No. 23, Longmont

Preston, Alvah D
Proceedings 1876, pg 40 (1876 Sept 20), Occidental Lodge No. 20, Greeley

Preston, James
Proceedings 1873, pg 50 (1873 Oct 1), Occidental Lodge No. 20, Greeley, Apprentice
Proceedings 1874, pg 226 (1874 Sept 30), Occidental Lodge No. 20, Greeley, Apprentice
Proceedings 1875, pg 87 (1875 Sept 22), Occidental Lodge No. 20, Greeley, Apprentice
Proceedings 1876, pg 40 (1876 Sept 20), Occidental Lodge No. 20, Greeley, Apprentice

Preston, Jas
Proceedings 1872, pg 34 (1872 Sept 24), Occidental Lodge No. 20, Greeley, Apprentice

Preston, Scott
Proceedings 1873, pg 36 (1873 Oct 1), Nevada Lodge No. 4, Nevada, erroneously reported dead in 1869

Price, Albert
Proceedings 1861-1869, pg 192 (1867 Oct 8), Nevada Lodge No. 4, Nevadaville
Proceedings 1861-1869, pg 222 (1868 Oct 7), Nevada Lodge No. 4, Nevadaville
Proceedings 1861-1869, pg 304 (1869 Sept 29), Nevada Lodge No. 4, Nevadaville
Proceedings 1870, pg 20 (1870 Sept 28), Nevada Lodge No. 4, Nevadaville
Proceedings 1871, pg 18 (1871 Sept 27), Nevada Lodge No. 4, Bald Mountain
Proceedings 1872, pg 18 (1872 Sept 24), Nevada Lodge No. 4, Bald Mountain

Price, Albert, cont.
   Proceedings 1873, pg 36 (1873 Oct 1), Nevada Lodge No. 4, Nevada
   Proceedings 1874, pg 211 (1874 Sept 30), Nevada Lodge No. 4, Bald Mountain, Gilpin County, Stricken from the rolls

Price, Henry
   Proceedings 1870, pg 75 (1775) of Boston
   Proceedings 1872, pg 68 (1872 Sept 24) Grand Lodge of Massachusetts
   Proceedings 1872, pg 69 (1872 Sept 24) Grand Lodge of Massachusetts

Price, John M
   Proceedings 1872, pg 43 (1872 Sept 24) Atchison, Grand Lodge of Kansas
   Proceedings 1873, pg 60 (1873 Oct 1) Grand Lodge of Kansas, Atchison
   Proceedings 1874, pg 71 (1874 Sept 30) Grand Lodge of Kansas

Price, M B
   Proceedings 1874, pg 222 (1874 Sept 30), Pueblo Lodge No. 17, Pueblo, Pueblo County
   Proceedings 1875, pg 85 (1875 Sept 22) Pueblo Lodge No. 17
   Proceedings 1876, pg 39 (1876 Sept 20) Pueblo Lodge No. 17

Price, Mark B
   Proceedings 1861-1869, pg 313 (1869 Sept 29), Pueblo Lodge No. 17, Pueblo, Apprentice
   Proceedings 1870, pg 30 (1870 Sept 28), Pueblo Lodge No. 17, Pueblo
   Proceedings 1871, pg 28 (1871 Sept 27), Pueblo Lodge No. 17, Pueblo
   Proceedings 1872, pg 31 (1872 Sept 24), Pueblo Lodge No. 17, Pueblo
   Proceedings 1873, pg 47 (1873 Oct 1), Pueblo Lodge No. 17, Pueblo
   Proceedings 1876, pg 45 (1876 Sept 20), King Solomon Lodge U D, West Las Animas

Prickett, H E
   Proceedings 1870, pg 34 (1870 Sept 28) Grand Secretary, Grand Lodge of Idaho Territory
   Proceedings 1871, pg 35 (1871 Sept 27) Grand Secretary, Grand Ldoge of Idaho Territory

Primeo, B F
   Proceedings 1871, pg 30 (1871 Sept 27), Occidental Lodge U D, Greeley

Prince Frederick
   Proceedings 1861-1869, pg 260 (1868 Sept 11), Grand Master, Grand Lodge of the Netherlands, mason since 1816

Pritchard, J L
   Proceedings 1861-1869, pg 78 (1862 Nov 4), Chivington Lodge No. 6, Central City
   Proceedings 1861-1869, pg 113 (1863 Nov 3), Chivington Lodge No. 6, Central City
   Proceedings 1861-1869, pg 150 (1865 Nov 7), Chivington Lodge No. 6, Central City
   Proceedings 1861-1869, pg 168 (1866 Oct 2), Chivington Lodge No. 6, Central City
   Proceedings 1861-1869, pg 193 (1867 Oct 8), Chivington Lodge No. 6, Central City
   Proceedings 1861-1869, pg 224 (1868 Oct 7), Chivington Lodge No. 6, Central City
   Proceedings 1861-1869, pg 306 (1869 Sept 29), Central Lodge No. 6, Central City
   Proceedings 1870, pg 22 (1870 Sept 28), Central Lodge No. 6, Central City
   Proceedings 1871, pg 20 (1871 Sept 27), Central Lodge No. 6, Central

Pritchard, Jesse L
   Proceedings 1861-1869, pg 134 (1864 Nov 8), Chivington Lodge No. 6, Central City
   Proceedings 1872, pg 22 (1872 Sept 24), Denver Lodge No. 5, Denver

Prugh, W W
   Proceedings 1875, pg 79 (1875 Sept 22), Union Lodge No. 7, Denver, Fellowcraft
   Proceedings 1876, pg 33 (1876 Sept 20), Union Lodge No. 7, Denver

Pueblo Chapter No. 3
   Proceedings 1871, pg cover (1871 Sept 27) Pueblo

Pueblo Lodge No. 17
   Proceedings 1875, pg 23 (1875 Sept 21) has not provided annual returns
   Proceedings 1875, pg 23 (1875 Sept 21) has not provided a list of officers
   Proceedings 1875, pg 25 (1875 Sept 21) dues paid
   Proceedings 1875, pg 92 (1875 Sept 22)
   Proceedings 1876, pg 52 (1876 Sept 20)
   Proceedings 1861-1869, pg 216 (1868 Oct 7) granted charter

Pueblo Lodge No. 17, Pueblo
   Proceedings 1872, pg 11 (1872 Sept 24) failed to make timely returns
   Proceedings 1874, pg 8 (1874 Sept 29) recommended a lodge at Walsenburg
   Proceedings 1874, pg 9 (1874 Feb 18) dispensation denied
   Proceedings 1874, pg 11 (1874 June 24) request for cornerstone laying
   Proceedings 1874, pg 208 (1874 Sept 30)
   Proceedings 1876, pg 13 (1876 Sept 16) dues paid

Pueblo Lodge U D
   Proceedings 1861-1869, pg 211 (1868 Aug) arranged for a visit

Pueblo Lodge U D, Pueblo
   Proceedings 1861-1869, pg 207 (1868 Apr) requesting a lodge
   Proceedings 1861-1869, pg 208 (1868 Apr) not visited because of Indian troubles

Puett, A W
   Proceedings 1875, pg 84 (1875 Sept 22), Mount Moriah Lodge No. 15, Canon City

Proceedings 1876, pg 38 (1876 Sept 20), Mount Moriah Lodge No. 15, Canon City

Pugh
Proceedings 1861-1869, pg 93 (1863 Apr 17) motion
Proceedings 1861-1869, pg 117 (1864 Nov 7) committee

Pugh, G A
Proceedings 1861-1869, pg 150 (1865 Nov 7), Chivington Lodge No. 6, Central City
Proceedings 1861-1869, pg 168 (1866 Oct 2), Chivington Lodge No. 6, Central City
Proceedings 1861-1869, pg 306 (1869 Sept 29), Central Lodge No. 6, Central City
Proceedings 1870, pg 4 (1870 Sept 27), Central Lodge No. 6, Central City

Pugh, Geo A
Proceedings 1861-1869, pg 45 (1862 Nov 3), Chivington Lodge No. 6, Central City
Proceedings 1861-1869, pg 79 (1863 May 6) Junior Grand Warden
Proceedings 1861-1869, pg 80 (1863 May 6), Chivington Lodge No. 6, Central City
Proceedings 1861-1869, pg 100 (1863 Nov 2) committee
Proceedings 1861-1869, pg 106 (1863 Nov 3) committee
Proceedings 1861-1869, pg 113 (1863 Nov 3), Chivington Lodge No. 6, Central City
Proceedings 1861-1869, pg 115 (1864 Nov 7) Grand Treasurer
Proceedings 1861-1869, pg 116 (1864 Nov 7), Chivington Lodge No. 6, Central City
Proceedings 1861-1869, pg 116 (1864 Nov 7) Grand Treasurer
Proceedings 1861-1869, pg 124 (1864 Nov 8) committee
Proceedings 1861-1869, pg 224 (1868 Oct 7), Chivington Lodge No. 6, Central City
Proceedings 1870, pg 22 (1870 Sept 28), Central Lodge No. 6, Central City
Proceedings 1871, pg cover (1871 Sept 27) Grand Tiler, Central
Proceedings 1871, pg 14 (1871 Sept 27) Grand Tiler
Proceedings 1872, pg 3 (1872 Sept 24) Grand Tyler
Proceedings 1872, pg 14 (1872 Sept 24) Grand Tiler
Proceedings 1872, pg 21 (1872 Sept 24), Denver Lodge No. 5, Denver
Proceedings 1873, pg 6 (1873 Sept 30), Central Lodge No. 6, Central
Proceedings 1873, pg 38 (1873 Oct 1), Central Lodge No. 6, Central City
Proceedings 1874, pg 212 (1874 Sept 30), Central Lodge No. 6, Central
Proceedings 1875, pg 76 (1875 Sept 22), Central Lodge No. 6, Central City
Proceedings 1876, pg 4 (1876 Sept 19), Central Lodge No. 6, Central City
Proceedings 1876, pg 22 (1876 Sept 20), Central Lodge No. 6, Central City

Pugh, Geo E
Proceedings 1861-1869, pg 97 (1863 Nov 2) Grand Junior Warden

Pugh, George A
Proceedings 1861-1869, pg 78 (1862 Nov 4), Chivington Lodge No. 6, Central City
Proceedings 1861-1869, pg 98 (1863 Nov 2), Chivington Lodge No. 6, Central City
Proceedings 1861-1869, pg 100 (1863 Nov 3) Grand Junior Warden
Proceedings 1861-1869, pg 133 (1864 Nov 8), Chivington Lodge No. 6, Central City
Proceedings 1861-1869, pg 193 (1867 Oct 8), Chivington Lodge No. 6, Central City
Proceedings 1871, pg 20 (1871 Sept 27), Central Lodge No. 6, Central
Proceedings 1876, pg 31 (1876 Sept 20), Central Lodge No. 6, Central City

Puison, A T C
Proceedings 1872, pg 41 (1872 Sept 24), of St Paul, Representative of the Grand Lodge of Minnesota

Pulver, Calvin
Proceedings 1861-1869, pg 111 (1863 Nov 3), Summit Lodge No. 2, Parkville
Proceedings 1861-1869, pg 132 (1864 Nov 8) Golden City Lodge No. 1

Pulver, Milton
Proceedings 1861-1869, pg 110 (1863 Nov 3), Summit Lodge No. 2, Parkville
Proceedings 1861-1869, pg 131 (1864 Nov 8) Golden City Lodge No. 1
Proceedings 1873, pg 43 (1873 Oct 1), El Paso Lodge No. 13, Colorado City
Proceedings 1874, pg 218 (1874 Sept 30), El Paso Lodge No. 13, Colorado Springs
Proceedings 1875, pg 82 (1875 Sept 22), El Paso Lodge No. 13, Colorado Springs

Pumphrey, A
Proceedings 1874, pg 214 (1874 Sept 30), Union Lodge No. 7, Denver
Proceedings 1876, pg 33 (1876 Sept 20), Union Lodge No. 7, Denver

Pumphrey, Absalom
Proceedings 1870, pg 23 (1870 Sept 28), Union Lodge No. 7, Denver
Proceedings 1871, pg 22 (1871 Sept 27), Union Lodge No. 7, Denver
Proceedings 1875, pg 78 (1875 Sept 22), Union Lodge No. 7, Denver
Proceedings 1873, pg 39 (1873 Oct 1), Union Lodge No. 7, Denver

Pumphy, Absalom
Proceedings 1872, pg 22 (1872 Sept 24), Union Lodge No. 7, Denver

Purdy, O H
Proceedings 1872, pg 66 (1872 Sept 24) Grand Lodge of Idaho
Proceedings 1875, pg 96 (1875 Sept 22) Grand Lodge of Idaho, Silver City

Purdy, O H, cont.
Proceedings 1876, pg 54 (1876 Sept 20) Grand Lodge of Idaho, Silver City

Purkins, Geo W
Proceedings 1872, pg 17 (1872 Sept 24), Golden City Lodge No. 1, Golden City

Purkins, George W
Proceedings 1873, pg 35 (1873 Oct 1), Golden City Lodge No. 1, Golden City, died

Purkins, George W
Proceedings 1873, pg 57 (1873 Oct 1), Golden City Lodge No. 1, Golden City

Purkins, W D
Proceedings 1861-1869, pg 304 (1869 Sept 29), Nevada Lodge No. 4, Nevadaville

Purkins, William D
Proceedings 1870, pg 20 (1870 Sept 28), Nevada Lodge No. 4, Nevadaville

Purrington, R H
Proceedings 1875, pg 91 (1875 Sept 22), Las Animas Lodge U D, Trinidad

Purron, J H
Proceedings 1870, pg 74 (1827 June 18) United Grand Lodge of England

Pursel, A K
Proceedings 1871, pg 19 (1871 Sept 27) Denver Lodge No. 5
Proceedings 1872, pg 19 (1872 Sept 24), Denver Lodge No. 5, Denver

Pursel, John T
Proceedings 1874, pg 216 (1874 Sept 30), Black Hawk Lodge No. 11, Black Hawk
Proceedings 1875, pg 80 (1875 Sept 22) Black Hawk Lodge No. 11

Pursell, A K
Proceedings 1870, pg 21 (1870 Sept 28), Denver Lodge No. 5, Denver
Proceedings 1873, pg 37 (1873 Oct 1), Denver Lodge No. 5, Denver

Pursell, John T
Proceedings 1876, pg 34 (1876 Sept 20) Black Hawk Lodge No. 11

Pusel, A K
Proceedings 1876, pg 49 (1876 Sept 20) Denver Lodge No. 5, 1876 Aug 19

Pyle, John W
Proceedings 1876, pg 39 (1876 Sept 20) Pueblo Lodge No. 17

Pyper, J M
Proceedings 1874, pg 220 (1874 Sept 30), Cheyenne Lodge No. 16, Cheyenne, Wyoming Territory

Queen, William
Proceedings 1873, pg 38 (1873 Oct 1), Central Lodge No. 6, Central City
Proceedings 1874, pg 212 (1874 Sept 30), Central Lodge No. 6, Central
Proceedings 1875, pg 76 (1875 Sept 22), Central Lodge No. 6, Central City
Proceedings 1876, pg 31 (1876 Sept 20), Central Lodge No. 6, Central City

Quiblian, Asbury H
Proceedings 1875, pg 90 (1875 Sept 22), Huerfano Lodge U D, Walsenburg

Quigley, Jeremiah
Proceedings 1872, pg 33 (1872 Sept 24), Occidental Lodge No. 20, Greeley
Proceedings 1873, pg 50 (1873 Oct 1), Occidental Lodge No. 20, Greeley
Proceedings 1875, pg 87 (1875 Sept 22), Occidental Lodge No. 20, Greeley
Proceedings 1876, pg 40 (1876 Sept 20), Occidental Lodge No. 20, Greeley

Quigley, Jerry
Proceedings 1871, pg 30 (1871 Sept 27), Occidental Lodge U D, Greeley

Quigly, Jeremiah
Proceedings 1874, pg 225 (1874 Sept 30), Occidental Lodge No. 20, Greeley

Quillan, Robert A
Proceedings 1875, pg 34 (1875 Sept 22), Huerfano Lodge No. 27, Walsenburg

Quillian, Asbury H
Proceedings 1876, pg 43 (1876 Sept 20), Huerfano Lodge No. 27, Walsenburg

Quillian, Robert A
Proceedings 1874, pg 8 (1874 Aug 27), Huerfano Lodge U D, Walsenburg
Proceedings 1874, pg 229 (1874 Sept 30), Huerfano Lodge U D, Walsenburg
Proceedings 1875, pg 90 (1875 Sept 22), Huerfano Lodge U D, Walsenburg
Proceedings 1876, pg 43 (1876 Sept 20), Huerfano Lodge No. 27, Walsenburg

Quimby, E M
Proceedings 1873, pg 39 (1873 Oct 1), Union Lodge No. 7, Denver
Proceedings 1874, pg 214 (1874 Sept 30), Union Lodge No. 7, Denver

Quimby, Ed M
Proceedings 1870, pg 23 (1870 Sept 28), Union Lodge No. 7, Denver
Proceedings 1872, pg 22 (1872 Sept 24), Union Lodge No. 7, Denver

Colorado's Territorial Masons

Quimby, Ira
Proceedings 1861-1869, pg 42 (1861 Dec 10) Golden City Lodge No. 1
Proceedings 1861-1869, pg 110 (1863 Nov 3) Golden City Lodge No. 1
Proceedings 1861-1869, pg 147 (1865 Nov 7) Golden City Lodge No. 1, dimitted

Quimby, J M
Proceedings 1861-1869, pg 307 (1869 Sept 29), Union Lodge No. 7, Denver

Quinby, E M
Proceedings 1861-1869, pg 195 (1867 Oct 8), Union Lodge No. 7, Denver, Apprentice
Proceedings 1861-1869, pg 225 (1868 Oct 7), Union Lodge No. 7, Denver
Proceedings 1875, pg 78 (1875 Sept 22), Union Lodge No. 7, Denver
Proceedings 1876, pg 33 (1876 Sept 20), Union Lodge No. 7, Denver

Quinby, Ed M
Proceedings 1871, pg 22 (1871 Sept 27), Union Lodge No. 7, Denver

Quinby, Ira
Proceedings 1861-1869, pg 131 (1864 Nov 8) Golden City Lodge No. 1

Quinn, Geo P
Proceedings 1870, pg 22 (1870 Sept 28), Central Lodge No. 6, Central City
Proceedings 1871, pg 20 (1871 Sept 27), Central Lodge No. 6, Central
Proceedings 1872, pg 21 (1872 Sept 24), Denver Lodge No. 5, Denver
Proceedings 1873, pg 38 (1873 Oct 1), Central Lodge No. 6, Central City
Proceedings 1874, pg 213 (1874 Sept 30), Central Lodge No. 6, Central

Quinn, George P
Proceedings 1875, pg 76 (1875 Sept 22), Central Lodge No. 6, Central City
Proceedings 1876, pg 32 (1876 Sept 20), Central Lodge No. 6, Central City
Proceedings 1876, pg 50 (1876 Sept 20), Central Lodge No. 6, Central City

Quintard, E S
Proceedings 1861-1869, pg 241 (1867 May 8) Grand Lodge of Connecticut

R

Rader, Geo
Proceedings 1861-1869, pg 76 (1862 Nov 4), Summit Lodge No. 2, Parkville
Proceedings 1861-1869, pg 110 (1863 Nov 3), Summit Lodge No. 2, Parkville

Rader, George
Proceedings 1861-1869, pg 132 (1864 Nov 8) Golden City Lodge No. 1, dimitted

Rae, Austin B
Proceedings 1861-1869, pg 227 (1868 Oct 7), Washington Lodge No. 12, Georgetown, Fellowcraft

Rafferty, J C
Proceedings 1875, pg 88 (1875 Sept 22), Weston Lodge No. 22, Littleton
Proceedings 1876, pg 48 (1876 Sept 20), Weston Lodge No. 22, Littleton, 1875 Oct 1

Ramadge, J D
Proceedings 1861-1869, pg 149 (1865 Nov 7), Nevada Lodge No. 4, Nevadaville, dimitted

Ramage, J D
Proceedings 1861-1869, pg 133 (1864 Nov 8) Denver Lodge No. 5

Ramer, J R D
Proceedings 1872, pg 36 (1872 Sept 24), Ashlar Lodge U D, Colorado Springs

Ramey, F M
Proceedings 1875, pg 89 (1875 Sept 22), Doric Lodge No. 25, Fairplay
Proceedings 1876, pg 42 (1876 Sept 20), Doric Lodge No. 25, Fairplay

Ramos, A
Proceedings 1861-1869, pg 150 (1865 Nov 7), Chivington Lodge No. 6, Central City
Proceedings 1861-1869, pg 168 (1866 Oct 2), Chivington Lodge No. 6, Central City
Proceedings 1861-1869, pg 306 (1869 Sept 29), Central Lodge No. 6, Central City

Ramos, Antonio
Proceedings 1861-1869, pg 194 (1867 Oct 8), Chivington Lodge No. 6, Central City
Proceedings 1861-1869, pg 224 (1868 Oct 7), Chivington Lodge No. 6, Central City
Proceedings 1870, pg 22 (1870 Sept 28), Central Lodge No. 6, Central City
Proceedings 1871, pg 21 (1871 Sept 27), Central Lodge No. 6, Central
Proceedings 1872, pg 21 (1872 Sept 24), Denver Lodge No. 5, Denver
Proceedings 1873, pg 38 (1873 Oct 1), Central Lodge No. 6, Central City
Proceedings 1874, pg 212 (1874 Sept 30), Central Lodge No. 6, Central

Colorado's Territorial Masons

Ramos, Antonio, cont.
   Proceedings 1875, pg 76 (1875 Sept 22), Central Lodge No. 6, Central City
   Proceedings 1876, pg 32 (1876 Sept 20), Central Lodge No. 6, Central City

Ramsbottom, J
   Proceedings 1871, pg 29 (1871 Sept 27), Laramie Lodge No. 18, Laramie, Wyoming Territory
   Proceedings 1872, pg 32 (1872 Sept 24), Laramie Lodge No. 18, Laramie, Wyoming Territory, Dimitted

Ramsey, Allan
   Proceedings 1874, pg 225 (1874 Sept 30), Occidental Lodge No. 20, Greeley
   Proceedings 1875, pg 87 (1875 Sept 22), Occidental Lodge No. 20, Greeley
   Proceedings 1871, pg 30 (1871 Sept 27), Occidental Lodge U D, Greeley
   Proceedings 1876, pg 40 (1876 Sept 20), Occidental Lodge No. 20, Greeley

Ramsey, D B
   Proceedings 1871, pg 30 (1871 Sept 27), Occidental Lodge U D, Greeley
   Proceedings 1873, pg 50 (1873 Oct 1), Occidental Lodge No. 20, Greeley
   Proceedings 1874, pg 225 (1874 Sept 30), Occidental Lodge No. 20, Greeley

Ramsey, J W
   Proceedings 1875, pg 87 (1875 Sept 22), Occidental Lodge No. 20, Greeley

Ramsey, John W
   Proceedings 1876, pg 40 (1876 Sept 20), Occidental Lodge No. 20, Greeley

Ramsey, Joseph
   Proceedings 1876, pg 40 (1876 Sept 20), Occidental Lodge No. 20, Greeley

Randal, A T
   Proceedings 1872, pg 22 (1872 Sept 24), Union Lodge No. 7, Denver, Not a member,

Randall
   Proceedings 1873, pg 8 (1873 Sept 30) Grand Orator
   Proceedings 1874, pg 71 (1874 Sept 30) Past Grand Master
   Proceedings 1874, pg 111 (1874 Sept 30) Grand Lodge of Colorado, deceased

Randall, A T
   Proceedings 1861-1869, pg 149 (1865 Nov 7), Nevada Lodge No. 4, Nevadaville
   Proceedings 1861-1869, pg 167 (1866 Oct 2) Denver Lodge No. 5, dimitted
   Proceedings 1861-1869, pg 287 (1869 Sept 28) Grand Tyler
   Proceedings 1861-1869, pg 302 (1869 Sept 29) Grand Tyler
   Proceedings 1861-1869, pg 304 (1869 Sept 29) Denver Lodge No. 5
   Proceedings 1861-1869, pg 307 (1869 Sept 29), Union Lodge No. 7, Denver, Not a Member

Randall, D P
   Proceedings 1876, pg 39 (1876 Sept 20) Pueblo Lodge No. 17

Randall, E S
   Proceedings 1861-1869, pg 171 (1866 Oct 2), El Paso U D, Colorado City, Apprentice
   Proceedings 1861-1869, pg 196 (1867 Oct 8), El Paso Lodge U D, Colorado City
   Proceedings 1861-1869, pg 228 (1868 Oct 7), El Paso Lodge No. 13, Colorado City
   Proceedings 1861-1869, pg 310 (1869 Sept 29), El Paso Lodge No. 13, Colorado City
   Proceedings 1870, pg 27 (1870 Sept 28), El Paso Lodge No. 13, Colorado City
   Proceedings 1872, pg 27 (1872 Sept 24), El Paso Lodge No. 13, Colorado City
   Proceedings 1873, pg 43 (1873 Oct 1), El Paso Lodge No. 13, Colorado City

Randall, Edwin S
   Proceedings 1871, pg 25 (1871 Sept 27), El Paso Lodge No. 13, Colorado City
   Proceedings 1874, pg 218 (1874 Sept 30), El Paso Lodge No. 13, Colorado Springs
   Proceedings 1875, pg 82 (1875 Sept 22), El Paso Lodge No. 13, Colorado Springs

Randall, F D
   Proceedings 1861-1869, pg 111 (1863 Nov 3), Nevada Lodge No. 4, Nevadaville

Randall, Geo M
   Proceedings 1872, pg 15 (1872 Sept 24) Grand Orator
   Proceedings 1872, pg 69 (1872 Sept 24) Grand Lodge of Massachusetts, Rev, now of Denver, is the oldest Past Grand Master of Massachusetts now living.

Randall, George M
   Proceedings 1870, pg 7 (1870 June 24), Past Grand Master of Massachusetts, in charge of the cornerstone laying
   Proceedings 1873, pg 4 (1873 Sept 30) Grand Orator, deceased
   Proceedings 1873, pg 7 (1873 Sept 30), Bishop of Colorado, Wyoming and New Mexico, died 28 Sept 1873
   Proceedings 1873, pg 13 (1873 Sept 30), remains escorted to the depot whence forwarded to Boston, MA
   Proceedings 1873, pg 20 (1873 Oct 1) memorialized
   Proceedings 1873, pg 21 (1873 Oct 1), also of the Grand Lodge of Massachusetts, Reverend and Bishop of Colorado
   Proceedings 1873, pg 22 (1873 Oct 1) grandson of the mason George M Randall
   Proceedings 1873, pg 24 (1873 Oct 1) memorialized
   Proceedings 1873, pg 27 (1873 Oct 1) Grand Orator
   Proceedings 1873, pg 28 (1873 Oct 1) memorialized
   Proceedings 1874, pg 80 (1874 Sept 30) Grand Lodge of Massachusetts, Past Grand Master
   Proceedings 1874, pg 81 (1874 Sept 30) Grand Lodge of Massachusetts

Randall, George Maxwell
  Proceedings 1873, pg 55 (1873 Oct 1), born at Warren, R I, 23 Nov 1810, died at Denver, Colorado Territory, 28 Sept 1873

Randall, L D
  Proceedings 1861-1869, pg 132 (1864 Nov 8), Nevada Lodge No. 4, Nevadaville, dimitted

Randall, O P
  Proceedings 1874, pg 222 (1874 Sept 30), Pueblo Lodge No. 17, Pueblo, Pueblo County
  Proceedings 1875, pg 85 (1875 Sept 22) Pueblo Lodge No. 17

Randall, T D
  Proceedings 1861-1869, pg 77 (1862 Nov 4), Nevada Lodge No. 4, Nevadaville

Randle, A T
  Proceedings 1870, pg cover (1870 Sept 28) Grand Tyler, Denver
  Proceedings 1870, pg 13 (1870 Sept 27) Grand Tyler
  Proceedings 1870, pg 20 (1870 Sept 28), Denver Lodge No. 5, Denver, Not a Member
  Proceedings 1871, pg 3 (1871 Sept 26) Grand Tiler
  Proceedings 1871, pg 15 (1871 Sept 27) Grand Tiler
  Proceedings 1871, pg 19 (1871 Sept 27) Denver Lodge No. 5, Not a member
  Proceedings 1871, pg 21 (1871 Sept 27), Union Lodge No. 7, Denver, Not a member

Randle, Aug T
  Proceedings 1870, pg 23 (1870 Sept 28), Union Lodge No. 7, Denver, Not a Member,

Randolph, Calvin
  Proceedings 1876, pg 40 (1876 Sept 20), Occidental Lodge No. 20, Greeley

Raney, Francis M
  Proceedings 1874, pg 228 (1874 Sept 30), Doric Lodge U D, Fairplay

Rank, J M
  Proceedings 1861-1869, pg 150 (1865 Nov 7), Chivington Lodge No. 6, Central City
  Proceedings 1861-1869, pg 168 (1866 Oct 2), Chivington Lodge No. 6, Central City
  Proceedings 1861-1869, pg 194 (1867 Oct 8), Chivington Lodge No. 6, Central City
  Proceedings 1861-1869, pg 306 (1869 Sept 29), Central Lodge No. 6, Central City

Rank, Jno M
  Proceedings 1871, pg 21 (1871 Sept 27), Central Lodge No. 6, Central

Rank, John M
  Proceedings 1861-1869, pg 134 (1864 Nov 8), Chivington Lodge No. 6, Central City
  Proceedings 1861-1869, pg 224 (1868 Oct 7), Chivington Lodge No. 6, Central City
  Proceedings 1873, pg 38 (1873 Oct 1), Central Lodge No. 6, Central City
  Proceedings 1874, pg 212 (1874 Sept 30), Central Lodge No. 6, Central
  Proceedings 1875, pg 77 (1875 Sept 22), Central Lodge No. 6, Central City, Stricken from the rolls

Ranney, D B
  Proceedings 1872, pg 33 (1872 Sept 24), Occidental Lodge No. 20, Greeley
  Proceedings 1875, pg 87 (1875 Sept 22), Occidental Lodge No. 20, Greeley

Ranney, Dan B
  Proceedings 1876, pg 49 (1876 Sept 20), Occidental Lodge No. 20, Greeley, 1875 Nov 1

Ransom, H A
  Proceedings 1872, pg 35 (1872 Sept 24), St Vrain Lodge No. 23, Longmont
  Proceedings 1873, pg 51 (1873 Oct 1), St Vrain Lodge No. 23, Longmont
  Proceedings 1874, pg 227 (1874 Sept 30), St Vrain No. 23, Longmont
  Proceedings 1876, pg 41 (1876 Sept 20), St Vrain Lodge No. 23, Longmont

Rapp, Charles
  Proceedings 1872, pg 35 (1872 Sept 24), Weston Lodge No. 22, Littleton
  Proceedings 1876, pg 41 (1876 Sept 20), Weston Lodge No. 22, Littleton

Rapp, Chas
  Proceedings 1873, pg 51 (1873 Oct 1), Weston Lodge No. 22, Littleton
  Proceedings 1874, pg 226 (1874 Sept 30), Weston Lodge No. 22, Littleton
  Proceedings 1875, pg 88 (1875 Sept 22), Weston Lodge No. 22, Littleton

Rasky, Joseph
  Proceedings 1861-1869, pg 280 (1867 Nov 19) left his entire estate to the Grand Lodge of South Carolina

Ratleff, J W
  Proceedings 1861-1869, pg 51 (1862 Nov 4) Grand Steward

Ratliff
  Proceedings 1861-1869, pg 117 (1864 Nov 7) committee
  Proceedings 1861-1869, pg 123 (1864 Nov 8) motion
  Proceedings 1861-1869, pg 127 (1864 Nov 8) motion
  Proceedings 1861-1869, pg 187 (1867 Oct 8) motion
  Proceedings 1861-1869, pg 189 (1867 Oct 8) motion
  Proceedings 1861-1869, pg 189 (1867 Oct 8) motion

Ratliff, J W
  Proceedings 1861-1869, pg 38 (1861 Dec 12) Grand Tyler
  Proceedings 1861-1869, pg 44 (1862 Nov 3) Grand Tyler
  Proceedings 1861-1869, pg 76 (1862 Nov 4), Nevada Lodge No. 4, Nevadaville
  Proceedings 1861-1869, pg 79 (1863 May 6) Grand Tyler
  Proceedings 1861-1869, pg 94 (1863 Apr 17) Grand Steward
  Proceedings 1861-1869, pg 95 (1863 Apr 17) donated their per diem to the Grand Lodge

Colorado's Territorial Masons

Ratliff, J W, cont.
    Proceedings 1861-1869, pg 97 (1863 Nov 2) Grand Senior Deacon
    Proceedings 1861-1869, pg 98 (1863 Nov 2) Grand Steward
    Proceedings 1861-1869, pg 100 (1863 Nov 3) Grand Senior Deacon
    Proceedings 1861-1869, pg 116 (1864 Nov 7), Nevada Lodge No. 4, Nevadaville
    Proceedings 1861-1869, pg 137 (1865 Nov 6), Nevada Lodge No. 4, Nevadaville
    Proceedings 1861-1869, pg 166 (1866 Oct 2), Nevada Lodge No. 4, Nevadaville
    Proceedings 1861-1869, pg 178 (1867 Feb 11), Nevada Lodge No. 4, Nevadaville
    Proceedings 1861-1869, pg 186 (1867 Oct 8) per diem
    Proceedings 1861-1869, pg 212 (1868 Oct 6) warrant paid
    Proceedings 1861-1869, pg 222 (1868 Oct 7), Nevada Lodge No. 4, Nevadaville
    Proceedings 1861-1869, pg 222 (1868 Oct 7), Nevada Lodge No. 4, Nevadaville
    Proceedings 1861-1869, pg 304 (1869 Sept 29), Nevada Lodge No. 4, Nevadaville
    Proceedings 1871, pg 18 (1871 Sept 27), Nevada Lodge No. 4, Bald Mountain
    Proceedings 1871, pg 18 (1871 Sept 27), Nevada Lodge No. 4, Bald Mountain
    Proceedings 1875, pg 74 (1875 Sept 22), Nevada Lodge No. 4, Nevada

Ratliff, John W
    Proceedings 1861-1869, pg 111 (1863 Nov 3), Nevada Lodge No. 4, Nevadaville
    Proceedings 1861-1869, pg 132 (1864 Nov 8), Nevada Lodge No. 4, Nevadaville
    Proceedings 1861-1869, pg 147 (1865 Nov 7), Nevada Lodge No. 4, Nevadaville
    Proceedings 1861-1869, pg 176 (1867 Oct 7), Nevada Lodge No. 4, Nevadaville
    Proceedings 1861-1869, pg 191 (1867 Oct 8), Nevada Lodge No. 4, Nevadaville
    Proceedings 1870, pg 20 (1870 Sept 28), Nevada Lodge No. 4, Nevadaville
    Proceedings 1872, pg 18 (1872 Sept 24), Nevada Lodge No. 4, Bald Mountain
    Proceedings 1873, pg 36 (1873 Oct 1), Nevada Lodge No. 4, Nevada
    Proceedings 1874, pg 210 (1874 Sept 30), Nevada Lodge No. 4, Bald Mountain, Gilpin County
    Proceedings 1876, pg 30 (1876 Sept 20) Nevada Lodge No. 4

Rauk, Jno M
    Proceedings 1872, pg 21 (1872 Sept 24), Denver Lodge No. 5, Denver

Rauk, John M
    Proceedings 1870, pg 22 (1870 Sept 28), Central Lodge No. 6, Central City

Raymond
    Proceedings 1876, pg 15 (1876 Jan 26) referred to in communication to Ellwood E Thorne

Raymond, Geo H
    Proceedings 1876, pg 14 (1875 Dec 7) sent communication regarding claims of E T Stone

Raymond, George H
    Proceedings 1875, pg 19 (1875 Mar 15) Grand Lodge of New York, Grand Representative
    Proceedings 1875, pg 95 (1875 Sept 22) Grand Lodge of New York, New York, NY
    Proceedings 1876, pg 53 (1876 Sept 20) Grand Lodge of New York, of New York, NY

Raymond, J D
    Proceedings 1872, pg 36 (1872 Sept 24), Ashlar Lodge U D, Colorado Springs

Raynolds, Frederick A
    Proceedings 1876, pg 38 (1876 Sept 20), Mount Moriah Lodge No. 15, Canon City, Apprentice

Raynor, A G
    Proceedings 1861-1869, pg 43 (1861 Dec 10), Rocky Mountain Lodge No. 3, Gold Hill
    Proceedings 1861-1869, pg 78 (1862 Nov 4), Chivington Lodge No. 6, Central City
    Proceedings 1861-1869, pg 113 (1863 Nov 3), Chivington Lodge No. 6, Central City
    Proceedings 1861-1869, pg 134 (1864 Nov 8), Chivington Lodge No. 6, Central City
    Proceedings 1861-1869, pg 150 (1865 Nov 7), Chivington Lodge No. 6, Central City
    Proceedings 1861-1869, pg 168 (1866 Oct 2), Chivington Lodge No. 6, Central City
    Proceedings 1861-1869, pg 193 (1867 Oct 8), Chivington Lodge No. 6, Central City
    Proceedings 1861-1869, pg 224 (1868 Oct 7), Chivington Lodge No. 6, Central City
    Proceedings 1861-1869, pg 306 (1869 Sept 29), Central Lodge No. 6, Central City
    Proceedings 1870, pg 22 (1870 Sept 28), Central Lodge No. 6, Central City
    Proceedings 1871, pg 20 (1871 Sept 27), Central Lodge No. 6, Central
    Proceedings 1872, pg 22 (1872 Sept 24), Denver Lodge No. 5, Denver

Rea, A B
    Proceedings 1871, pg 24 (1871 Sept 27), Washington Lodge No. 12, Georgetown

Rea, Austin B
    Proceedings 1861-1869, pg 309 (1869 Sept 29), Washington Lodge No. 12, Georgetown
    Proceedings 1870, pg 26 (1870 Sept 28), Washington Lodge No. 12, Georgetown
    Proceedings 1872, pg 26 (1872 Sept 24), Washington Lodge No. 12, Georgetown
    Proceedings 1873, pg 42 (1873 Oct 1), Washington Lodge No. 12, Georgetown

Proceedings 1874, pg 218 (1874 Sept 30), Washington Lodge No. 12, Georgetown, Stricken from the rolls,

Reade
Proceedings 1861-1869, pg 277 (1867 Dec 2), Grand Master, Grand Lodge of North Carolina

Reals, C A
Proceedings 1871, pg 29 (1871 Sept 27), Laramie Lodge No. 18, Laramie, Wyoming Territory
Proceedings 1872, pg 32 (1872 Sept 24), Laramie Lodge No. 18, Laramie, Wyoming Territory
Proceedings 1873, pg 48 (1873 Oct 1), Laramie Lodge No. 18, Laramie, Wyoming Territory
Proceedings 1874, pg 223 (1874 Sept 30), Laramie Lodge No. 18, Laramie City

Reaves, Geo W
Proceedings 1861-1869, pg 221 (1868 Oct 7) Golden City Lodge No. 1, Fellowcraft

Rebold, Emanuel
Proceedings 1861-1869, pg 247 (1867 Nov 7), author, A General History of Freemasonry

Redfield, Joseph B
Proceedings 1875, pg 95 (1875 Sept 22) Grand Lodge of Nebraska, Omaha, NE
Proceedings 1876, pg 53 (1876 Sept 20) Grand Lodge of Nebraska, of Omaha, NE

Redfield, Josiah B
Proceedings 1874, pg 11 (1874 May 9), of Omaha, Grand Representative to the Grand East of Nebraska
Proceedings 1874, pg 207 (1874 Sept 30) Grand Lodge of Nebraska, Omaha

Redgway, Phil
Proceedings 1874, pg 226 (1874 Sept 30), Weston Lodge No. 22, Littleton

Reed
Proceedings 1870, pg 42 (1869 Nov 1), of Covington, KY

Reed, Alex
Proceedings 1872, pg 31 (1872 Sept 24), Pueblo Lodge No. 17, Pueblo
Proceedings 1875, pg 85 (1875 Sept 22) Pueblo Lodge No. 17
Proceedings 1876, pg 50 (1876 Sept 20) Pueblo Lodge No. 17

Reed, Alexander
Proceedings 1861-1869, pg 312 (1869 Sept 29), Pueblo Lodge No. 17, Pueblo
Proceedings 1870, pg 30 (1870 Sept 28), Pueblo Lodge No. 17, Pueblo
Proceedings 1871, pg 28 (1871 Sept 27), Pueblo Lodge No. 17, Pueblo
Proceedings 1873, pg 47 (1873 Oct 1), Pueblo Lodge No. 17, Pueblo
Proceedings 1874, pg 222 (1874 Sept 30), Pueblo Lodge No. 17, Pueblo, Pueblo County
Proceedings 1876, pg 39 (1876 Sept 20) Pueblo Lodge No. 17

Reed, G B
Proceedings 1861-1869, pg 134 (1864 Nov 8), Chivington Lodge No. 6, Central City, Apprentice
Proceedings 1861-1869, pg 150 (1865 Nov 7), Chivington Lodge No. 6, Central City, Apprentice
Proceedings 1861-1869, pg 169 (1866 Oct 2), Chivington Lodge No. 6, Central City, Apprentice
Proceedings 1861-1869, pg 194 (1867 Oct 8), Chivington Lodge No. 6, Central City
Proceedings 1861-1869, pg 224 (1868 Oct 7), Chivington Lodge No. 6, Central City
Proceedings 1861-1869, pg 306 (1869 Sept 29), Central Lodge No. 6, Central City
Proceedings 1870, pg 22 (1870 Sept 28), Central Lodge No. 6, Central City
Proceedings 1871, pg 21 (1871 Sept 27), Central Lodge No. 6, Central

Reed, Gilbert B
Proceedings 1872, pg 21 (1872 Sept 24), Denver Lodge No. 5, Denver
Proceedings 1875, pg 76 (1875 Sept 22), Central Lodge No. 6, Central City
Proceedings 1876, pg 32 (1876 Sept 20), Central Lodge No. 6, Central City

Reed, J H
Proceedings 1861-1869, pg 150 (1865 Nov 7), Chivington Lodge No. 6, Central City
Proceedings 1861-1869, pg 168 (1866 Oct 2), Chivington Lodge No. 6, Central City

Reed, James H
Proceedings 1861-1869, pg 194 (1867 Oct 8), Chivington Lodge No. 6, Central City
Proceedings 1861-1869, pg 225 (1868 Oct 7), Chivington Lodge No. 6, Central City, Dimitted

Reed, James W
Proceedings 1876, pg 42 (1876 Sept 20), Doric Lodge No. 25, Fairplay, Fellow Craft

Reed, T M
Proceedings 1872, pg 92 (1872 Sept 24) Grand Lodge of Washington

Reed, Thomas M
Proceedings 1861-1869, pg 316 (1869 Sept 29) Grand Lodge of Washington
Proceedings 1861-1869, pg 349 (1868 Sept 17) Grand Secretary, Grand Lodge of Washington Territory
Proceedings 1870, pg 34 (1870 Sept 28) Grand Secretary, Grand Lodge of Washington
Proceedings 1870, pg 107 (1869 Sept 16) Grand Secretary, Grand Lodge of Washington Territory
Proceedings 1871, pg 35 (1871 Sept 27) Grand Secretary, Grand Lodge of Washington
Proceedings 1872, pg 44 (1872 Sept 24) Olympia, Grand Lodge of Washington
Proceedings 1873, pg 61 (1873 Oct 1) Grand Lodge of Washington, Olympia
Proceedings 1874, pg 131 (1874 Sept 30) Grand Lodge of Washington

Reed, Thomas M, cont.
Proceedings 1874, pg 205 (1874 Sept 30) Grand Lodge of Washington, Olympia

Reed, Thomas R
Proceedings 1874, pg 221 (1874 Sept 30), Cheyenne Lodge No. 16, Cheyenne, Wyoming Territory, Apprentice

Reed, Thos M
Proceedings 1874, pg 132 (1874 Sept 30) Grand Lodge of Washington
Proceedings 1875, pg 96 (1875 Sept 22) Grand Lodge of Washington, Olympia
Proceedings 1876, pg 54 (1876 Sept 20) Grand Lodge of Washington, Olympia

Reed, William
Proceedings 1875, pg 78 (1875 Sept 22), Union Lodge No. 7, Denver
Proceedings 1876, pg 33 (1876 Sept 20), Union Lodge No. 7, Denver

Reed, Wm
Proceedings 1873, pg 40 (1873 Oct 1), Union Lodge No. 7, Denver
Proceedings 1874, pg 214 (1874 Sept 30), Union Lodge No. 7, Denver

Reed, Wm T
Proceedings 1874, pg 51 (1874 Sept 30) Grand Lodge of Delaware, became a master mason on 18 Nov 1815

Reeder, George
Proceedings 1861-1869, pg 42 (1861 Dec 10), Summit Lodge No. 2, Parkville

Reef, Joseph S
Proceedings 1876, pg 44 (1876 Sept 20) Del Norte Lodge U D, Apprentice

Reepe, Albert C
Proceedings 1870, pg 20 (1870 Sept 28), Nevada Lodge No. 4, Nevadaville

Reese, Albert C
Proceedings 1872, pg 18 (1872 Sept 24), Nevada Lodge No. 4, Bald Mountain

Reeves, G W
Proceedings 1861-1869, pg 303 (1869 Sept 29) Golden City Lodge No. 1
Proceedings 1870, pg 19 (1870 Sept 28), Golden City Lodge No. 1, Golden City
Proceedings 1871, pg 17 (1871 Sept 27), Golden City Lodge No. 1, Golden City

Reeves, Geo W
Proceedings 1861-1869, pg 191 (1867 Oct 8) Golden City Lodge No. 1, Apprentice

Reeves, George W
Proceedings 1872, pg 17 (1872 Sept 24), Golden City Lodge No. 1, Golden City
Proceedings 1873, pg 35 (1873 Oct 1), Golden City Lodge No. 1, Golden City
Proceedings 1874, pg 209 (1874 Sept 30), Golden City Lodge No. 1, Golden City
Proceedings 1875, pg 73 (1875 Sept 22) Golden City Lodge No. 1
Proceedings 1876, pg 29 (1876 Sept 20) Golden City Lodge No. 1

Reid, Edward
Proceedings 1871, pg 31 (1871 Sept 27), Argenta Lodge U D, Salt Lake City, Utah

Reid, Gilbert B
Proceedings 1873, pg 38 (1873 Oct 1), Central Lodge No. 6, Central City
Proceedings 1874, pg 212 (1874 Sept 30), Central Lodge No. 6, Central

Reid, Willis
Proceedings 1861-1869, pg 168 (1866 Oct 2), Chivington Lodge No. 6, Central City
Proceedings 1861-1869, pg 194 (1867 Oct 8), Chivington Lodge No. 6, Central City, Dimitted

Reiley, John P
Proceedings 1873, pg 48 (1873 Oct 1), Laramie Lodge No. 18, Laramie, Wyoming Territory, Fellowcraft
Proceedings 1874, pg 223 (1874 Sept 30), Laramie Lodge No. 18, Laramie City

Rembaugh, H S
Proceedings 1861-1869, pg 312 (1869 Sept 29), Cheyenne Lodge No. 16, Cheyenne, Apprentice
Proceedings 1871, pg 28 (1871 Sept 27), Cheyenne Lodge No. 16, Cheyenne, Wyoming Territory, Apprentice

Remington, Charles
Proceedings 1861-1869, pg 131 (1864 Nov 8) Golden City Lodge No. 1
Proceedings 1861-1869, pg 147 (1865 Nov 7) Golden City Lodge No. 1

Remington, J C
Proceedings 1861-1869, pg 110 (1863 Nov 3) Golden City Lodge No. 1
Proceedings 1861-1869, pg 165 (1866 Oct 2) Golden City Lodge No. 1
Proceedings 1861-1869, pg 191 (1867 Oct 8) Golden City Lodge No. 1
Proceedings 1861-1869, pg 221 (1868 Oct 7) Golden City Lodge No. 1
Proceedings 1861-1869, pg 303 (1869 Sept 29) Golden City Lodge No. 1
Proceedings 1870, pg 19 (1870 Sept 28), Golden City Lodge No. 1, Golden City
Proceedings 1871, pg 17 (1871 Sept 27), Golden City Lodge No. 1, Golden City
Proceedings 1875, pg 74 (1875 Sept 22) Golden City Lodge No. 1, Stricken from the rolls

Remington, James C
Proceedings 1872, pg 17 (1872 Sept 24), Golden City Lodge No. 1, Golden City

Remington, Joseph C
Proceedings 1873, pg 35 (1873 Oct 1), Golden City Lodge No. 1, Golden City

Rene, L L
    Proceedings 1861-1869, pg 131 (1864 Nov 8) Golden City Lodge No. 1, Fellowcraft
    Proceedings 1861-1869, pg 147 (1865 Nov 7) Golden City Lodge No. 1
    Proceedings 1861-1869, pg 165 (1866 Oct 2) Golden City Lodge No. 1
    Proceedings 1861-1869, pg 191 (1867 Oct 8) Golden City Lodge No. 1, Dimitted

Retberg, H O
    Proceedings 1871, pg 28 (1871 Sept 27), Pueblo Lodge No. 17, Pueblo, Apprentice
    Proceedings 1872, pg 31 (1872 Sept 24), Pueblo Lodge No. 17, Pueblo, Apprentice

Rettberg, H O
    Proceedings 1861-1869, pg 229 (1868 Oct 7), Pueblo Lodge U D, Pueblo, Apprentice
    Proceedings 1861-1869, pg 313 (1869 Sept 29), Pueblo Lodge No. 17, Pueblo, Apprentice
    Proceedings 1873, pg 47 (1873 Oct 1), Pueblo Lodge No. 17, Pueblo, Apprentice
    Proceedings 1874, pg 222 (1874 Sept 30), Pueblo Lodge No. 17, Pueblo, Pueblo County, Apprentice
    Proceedings 1875, pg 85 (1875 Sept 22) Pueblo Lodge No. 17, Apprentice
    Proceedings 1876, pg 39 (1876 Sept 20) Pueblo Lodge No. 17, Apprentice

Rettberg, Herman O
    Proceedings 1870, pg 30 (1870 Sept 28), Pueblo Lodge No. 17, Pueblo, Apprentice

Reuber, H J
    Proceedings 1861-1869, pg 43 (1861 Dec 10), Rocky Mountain Lodge No. 3, Gold Hill

Reynolds, F W
    Proceedings 1874, pg 228 (1874 Sept 30), Evanston Lodge U D, Evanston, Uintah County, Wyoming Territory

Reynolds, Geo T
    Proceedings 1870, pg 30 (1870 Sept 28), Pueblo Lodge No. 17, Pueblo, Apprentice
    Proceedings 1872, pg 31 (1872 Sept 24), Pueblo Lodge No. 17, Pueblo
    Proceedings 1875, pg 85 (1875 Sept 22) Pueblo Lodge No. 17
    Proceedings 1876, pg 50 (1876 Sept 20) Pueblo Lodge No. 17

Reynolds, George T
    Proceedings 1871, pg 28 (1871 Sept 27), Pueblo Lodge No. 17, Pueblo, Fellowcraft
    Proceedings 1873, pg 47 (1873 Oct 1), Pueblo Lodge No. 17, Pueblo
    Proceedings 1874, pg 222 (1874 Sept 30), Pueblo Lodge No. 17, Pueblo, Pueblo County
    Proceedings 1874, pg 223 (1874 Sept 30), Pueblo Lodge No. 17, Pueblo, Pueblo County, Reinstated
    Proceedings 1876, pg 39 (1876 Sept 20) Pueblo Lodge No. 17

Reynolds, H G
    Proceedings 1861-1869, pg 246 (1867 Nov 7) Grand Lodge of Illinois
    Proceedings 1861-1869, pg 248 (1867 Nov 7), Grand Secretary, Grand Lodge of Illinois

Reynolds, Harmon G
    Proceedings 1861-1869, pg 328 (1868 Oct 6) Grand Master, Grand Lodge of Illinois

Rhoades, A G
    Proceedings 1876, pg 34 (1876 Sept 20) Black Hawk Lodge No. 11

Rhodes, A G
    Proceedings 1870, pg 25 (1870 Sept 28), Black Hawk Lodge No. 11, Black Hawk
    Proceedings 1871, pg 23 (1871 Sept 27), Black Hawk Lodge No. 11, Black Hawk
    Proceedings 1872, pg 24 (1872 Sept 24), Black Hawk Lodge No. 11, Black Hawk
    Proceedings 1873, pg 41 (1873 Oct 1), Black Hawk Lodge No. 11, Black Hawk
    Proceedings 1874, pg 216 (1874 Sept 30), Black Hawk Lodge No. 11, Black Hawk
    Proceedings 1875, pg 80 (1875 Sept 22) Black Hawk Lodge No. 11

Rhodes, Jeff
    Proceedings 1875, pg 78 (1875 Sept 22), Union Lodge No. 7, Denver

Rhodes, Jefferson
    Proceedings 1876, pg 33 (1876 Sept 20), Union Lodge No. 7, Denver

Rice
    Proceedings 1874, pg 58 (1874 Sept 30) Grand Lodge of Indiana

Rice, I B
    Proceedings 1874, pg 222 (1874 Sept 30), Pueblo Lodge No. 17, Pueblo, Pueblo County

Rice, J B
    Proceedings 1875, pg 85 (1875 Sept 22) Pueblo Lodge No. 17
    Proceedings 1876, pg 39 (1876 Sept 20) Pueblo Lodge No. 17

Rice, James
    Proceedings 1861-1869, pg 312 (1869 Sept 29), Pueblo Lodge No. 17, Pueblo
    Proceedings 1870, pg 29 (1870 Sept 28), Pueblo Lodge No. 17, Pueblo
    Proceedings 1871, pg 28 (1871 Sept 27), Pueblo Lodge No. 17, Pueblo
    Proceedings 1872, pg 30 (1872 Sept 24), Pueblo Lodge No. 17, Pueblo
    Proceedings 1873, pg 47 (1873 Oct 1), Pueblo Lodge No. 17, Pueblo
    Proceedings 1874, pg 222 (1874 Sept 30), Pueblo Lodge No. 17, Pueblo, Pueblo County
    Proceedings 1875, pg 85 (1875 Sept 22) Pueblo Lodge No. 17

Rice, James, cont.
    Proceedings 1876, pg 39 (1876 Sept 20) Pueblo Lodge No. 17

Rice, John B
    Proceedings 1861-1869, pg 312 (1869 Sept 29), Pueblo Lodge No. 17, Pueblo
    Proceedings 1870, pg 30 (1870 Sept 28), Pueblo Lodge No. 17, Pueblo
    Proceedings 1871, pg 28 (1871 Sept 27), Pueblo Lodge No. 17, Pueblo
    Proceedings 1872, pg 31 (1872 Sept 24), Pueblo Lodge No. 17, Pueblo
    Proceedings 1873, pg 47 (1873 Oct 1), Pueblo Lodge No. 17, Pueblo

Rice, Martin H
    Proceedings 1861-1869, pg 328 (1869 May 25) Grand Master, Grand Lodge of Indiana
    Proceedings 1861-1869, pg 330 (1869 May 25) Grand Master, Grand Lodge of Indiana
    Proceedings 1870, pg 57 (1870 May 24) Grand Master, Grand Lodge of Indiana
    Proceedings 1872, pg 64 (1872 Sept 24) Grand Lodge of Indiana
    Proceedings 1873, pg 60 (1873 Oct 1) Grand Lodge of Indiana, Indianapolis
    Proceedings 1874, pg 19 (1874 Sept 29), of Indianapolis, IN

Rice, N H
    Proceedings 1861-1869, pg 149 (1865 Nov 7), Nevada Lodge No. 4, Nevadaville
    Proceedings 1861-1869, pg 167 (1866 Oct 2) Denver Lodge No. 5
    Proceedings 1861-1869, pg 193 (1867 Oct 8) Denver Lodge No. 5
    Proceedings 1861-1869, pg 223 (1868 Oct 7) Denver Lodge No. 5
    Proceedings 1861-1869, pg 304 (1869 Sept 29) Denver Lodge No. 5
    Proceedings 1873, pg 37 (1873 Oct 1), Denver Lodge No. 5, Denver
    Proceedings 1875, pg 75 (1875 Sept 22) Denver Lodge No. 5

Rice, Nahum H
    Proceedings 1861-1869, pg 77 (1862 Nov 4) Denver Lodge No. 5
    Proceedings 1861-1869, pg 112 (1863 Nov 3) Denver Lodge No. 5
    Proceedings 1861-1869, pg 133 (1864 Nov 8) Denver Lodge No. 5
    Proceedings 1870, pg 21 (1870 Sept 28), Denver Lodge No. 5, Denver
    Proceedings 1871, pg 19 (1871 Sept 27) Denver Lodge No. 5
    Proceedings 1872, pg 19 (1872 Sept 24), Denver Lodge No. 5, Denver
    Proceedings 1874, pg 211 (1874 Sept 30), Denver Lodge No. 5, Denver
    Proceedings 1876, pg 49 (1876 Sept 20) Denver Lodge No. 5, 1876 Aug 19

Richards, D M
    Proceedings 1861-1869, pg 224 (1868 Oct 7), Chivington Lodge No. 6, Central City
    Proceedings 1861-1869, pg 306 (1869 Sept 29), Central Lodge No. 6, Central City
    Proceedings 1870, pg 22 (1870 Sept 28), Central Lodge No. 6, Central City
    Proceedings 1871, pg 21 (1871 Sept 27), Central Lodge No. 6, Central

Richards, David M
    Proceedings 1872, pg 21 (1872 Sept 24), Denver Lodge No. 5, Denver
    Proceedings 1873, pg 38 (1873 Oct 1), Central Lodge No. 6, Central City
    Proceedings 1874, pg 212 (1874 Sept 30), Central Lodge No. 6, Central
    Proceedings 1875, pg 76 (1875 Sept 22), Central Lodge No. 6, Central City
    Proceedings 1876, pg 32 (1876 Sept 20), Central Lodge No. 6, Central City

Richards, Hugo
    Proceedings 1861-1869, pg 195 (1867 Oct 8), Union Lodge No. 7, Denver
    Proceedings 1861-1869, pg 225 (1868 Oct 7), Union Lodge No. 7, Denver
    Proceedings 1861-1869, pg 307 (1869 Sept 29), Union Lodge No. 7, Denver
    Proceedings 1870, pg 23 (1870 Sept 28), Union Lodge No. 7, Denver
    Proceedings 1871, pg 22 (1871 Sept 27), Union Lodge No. 7, Denver
    Proceedings 1872, pg 22 (1872 Sept 24), Union Lodge No. 7, Denver
    Proceedings 1873, pg 39 (1873 Oct 1), Union Lodge No. 7, Denver
    Proceedings 1874, pg 214 (1874 Sept 30), Union Lodge No. 7, Denver
    Proceedings 1875, pg 78 (1875 Sept 22), Union Lodge No. 7, Denver
    Proceedings 1876, pg 48 (1876 Sept 20), Union Lodge No. 7, Denver, 1875 Sept 11

Richards, J W
    Proceedings 1861-1869, pg 223 (1868 Oct 7) Denver Lodge No. 5, Fellowcraft
    Proceedings 1861-1869, pg 305 (1869 Sept 29) Denver Lodge No. 5
    Proceedings 1870, pg 20 (1870 Sept 28), Denver Lodge No. 5, Denver
    Proceedings 1872, pg 19 (1872 Sept 24), Denver Lodge No. 5, Denver
    Proceedings 1872, pg 48 (1872 Sept 24), Denver Lodge No. 5, Denver
    Proceedings 1873, pg 37 (1873 Oct 1), Denver Lodge No. 5, Denver
    Proceedings 1874, pg 211 (1874 Sept 30), Denver Lodge No. 5, Denver
    Proceedings 1875, pg 75 (1875 Sept 22) Denver Lodge No. 5
    Proceedings 1876, pg 31 (1876 Sept 20) Denver Lodge No. 5

Richards, Jarius
Proceedings 1861-1869, pg 133 (1864 Nov 8) Denver Lodge No. 5

Richards, N P
Proceedings 1876, pg 39 (1876 Sept 20) Pueblo Lodge No. 17

Richards, Norman P
Proceedings 1876, pg 45 (1876 Sept 20) South Pueblo Lodge U D

Richardson, A B
Proceedings 1870, pg 11 (1870 Apr 20) Past Junior Grand Warden, Grand Lodge of Oregon
Proceedings 1872, pg 41 (1872 Sept 24), of Portland, Representative of the Grand Lodge of Oregon
Proceedings 1873, pg 59 (1873 Oct 1), of Portland, Grand Representative to the Grand Lodge of Oregon
Proceedings 1874, pg 207 (1874 Sept 30) Grand Lodge of Oregon, Portland
Proceedings 1875, pg 95 (1875 Sept 22) Grand Lodge of Oregon, Portland, OR
Proceedings 1876, pg 53 (1876 Sept 20) Grand Lodge of Oregon, of Portland, OR
Proceedings 1870, pg 103 (1870 June 13) Grand Lodge of Texas

Richardson, Geo
Proceedings 1861-1869, pg 149 (1865 Nov 7), Nevada Lodge No. 4, Nevadaville, Apprentice
Proceedings 1861-1869, pg 167 (1866 Oct 2) Denver Lodge No. 5, dimitted
Proceedings 1861-1869, pg 170 (1866 Oct 2), Empire Lodge No. 8, Empire City
Proceedings 1861-1869, pg 195 (1867 Oct 8), Empire Lodge No. 8, Empire City
Proceedings 1861-1869, pg 226 (1868 Oct 7), Empire Lodge No. 8, Empire City
Proceedings 1872, pg 23 (1872 Sept 24), Empire Lodge No. 8, Empire

Richardson, George
Proceedings 1861-1869, pg 308 (1869 Sept 29), Empire Lodge No. 8, Empire City
Proceedings 1870, pg 24 (1870 Sept 28), Empire Lodge No. 8, Empire
Proceedings 1873, pg 41 (1873 Oct 1), Empire Lodge No. 8, Empire
Proceedings 1874, pg 215 (1874 Sept 30), Empire Lodge No. 8, Empire

Richardson, J
Proceedings 1861-1869, pg 112 (1863 Nov 3) Denver Lodge No. 5

Richardson, Jared
Proceedings 1861-1869, pg 149 (1865 Nov 7), Nevada Lodge No. 4, Nevadaville, deceased

Richardson, Jas D
Proceedings 1874, pg 205 (1874 Sept 30) Grand Lodge of Tennessee, Murfreesboro

Richardson, John
Proceedings 1861-1869, pg 196 (1867 Oct 8), Columbia Lodge U D, Boulder

Richardson, R C
Proceedings 1875, pg 73 (1875 Sept 22) Golden City Lodge No. 1

Richardson, W H
Proceedings 1861-1869, pg 170 (1866 Oct 2), Black Hawk Lodge U D, Black Hawk
Proceedings 1861-1869, pg 226 (1868 Oct 7), Black Hawk Lodge No. 11, Black Hawk
Proceedings 1861-1869, pg 309 (1869 Sept 29), Black Hawk Lodge No. 11, Black Hawk
Proceedings 1870, pg 25 (1870 Sept 28), Black Hawk Lodge No. 11, Black Hawk
Proceedings 1871, pg 23 (1871 Sept 27), Black Hawk Lodge No. 11, Black Hawk
Proceedings 1872, pg 24 (1872 Sept 24), Black Hawk Lodge No. 11, Black Hawk
Proceedings 1876, pg 34 (1876 Sept 20) Black Hawk Lodge No. 11

Richardson, William H
Proceedings 1874, pg 216 (1874 Sept 30), Black Hawk Lodge No. 11, Black Hawk

Richardson, Wm H
Proceedings 1861-1869, pg 196 (1867 Oct 8), Black Hawk Lodge No. 11, Black Hawk
Proceedings 1873, pg 41 (1873 Oct 1), Black Hawk Lodge No. 11, Black Hawk
Proceedings 1875, pg 80 (1875 Sept 22) Black Hawk Lodge No. 11

Richey, John
Proceedings 1861-1869, pg 311 (1869 Sept 29), Mount Moriah Lodge No. 15, Canon City

Richie, J W
Proceedings 1861-1869, pg 170 (1866 Oct 2), Black Hawk Lodge U D, Black Hawk

Richmond, R C
Proceedings 1876, pg 29 (1876 Sept 20) Golden City Lodge No. 1
Proceedings 1876, pg 29 (1876 Sept 20) Golden City Lodge No. 1

Ridgeway, H
Proceedings 1876, pg 49 (1876 Sept 20), El Paso Lodge No. 13, Colorado City, 1876 July 22

Ridgeway, Henry
Proceedings 1874, pg 218 (1874 Sept 30), El Paso Lodge No. 13, Colorado Springs
Proceedings 1875, pg 82 (1875 Sept 22), El Paso Lodge No. 13, Colorado Springs

Ridgeway, Philip
Proceedings 1875, pg 88 (1875 Sept 22), Weston Lodge No. 22, Littleton
Proceedings 1876, pg 41 (1876 Sept 20), Weston Lodge No. 22, Littleton

Colorado's Territorial Masons

Rigsby, D T
Proceedings 1861-1869, pg 309 (1869 Sept 29), Washington Lodge No. 12, Georgetown
Proceedings 1871, pg 24 (1871 Sept 27), Washington Lodge No. 12, Georgetown

Rigsby, D Thomas
Proceedings 1875, pg 81 (1875 Sept 22), Washington Lodge No. 12, Georgetown
Proceedings 1876, pg 35 (1876 Sept 20), Washington Lodge No. 12, Georgetown

Rigsby, David T
Proceedings 1861-1869, pg 227 (1868 Oct 7), Washington Lodge No. 12, Georgetown
Proceedings 1870, pg 26 (1870 Sept 28), Washington Lodge No. 12, Georgetown
Proceedings 1872, pg 26 (1872 Sept 24), Washington Lodge No. 12, Georgetown
Proceedings 1873, pg 42 (1873 Oct 1), Washington Lodge No. 12, Georgetown
Proceedings 1874, pg 217 (1874 Sept 30), Washington Lodge No. 12, Georgetown

Riley, Charles
Proceedings 1876, pg 42 (1876 Sept 20), Doric Lodge No. 25, Fairplay, Not a member

Riley, J H
Proceedings 1870, pg 25 (1870 Sept 28), Black Hawk Lodge No. 11, Black Hawk

Riley, James
Proceedings 1876, pg 49 (1876 Sept 20) Black Hawk Lodge No. 11, 1875 Oct 14

Riley, James H
Proceedings 1861-1869, pg 196 (1867 Oct 8), Black Hawk Lodge No. 11, Black Hawk
Proceedings 1871, pg 23 (1871 Sept 27), Black Hawk Lodge No. 11, Black Hawk
Proceedings 1872, pg 24 (1872 Sept 24), Black Hawk Lodge No. 11, Black Hawk
Proceedings 1873, pg 41 (1873 Oct 1), Black Hawk Lodge No. 11, Black Hawk
Proceedings 1874, pg 216 (1874 Sept 30), Black Hawk Lodge No. 11, Black Hawk
Proceedings 1875, pg 80 (1875 Sept 22) Black Hawk Lodge No. 11

Riley, Jas H
Proceedings 1861-1869, pg 227 (1868 Oct 7), Black Hawk Lodge No. 11, Black Hawk

Riley, Jno H
Proceedings 1861-1869, pg 309 (1869 Sept 29), Black Hawk Lodge No. 11, Black Hawk

Rime, James
Proceedings 1861-1869, pg 228 (1868 Oct 7), El Paso Lodge No. 13, Colorado City

Ripley, Frank
Proceedings 1872, pg 35 (1872 Sept 24), St Vrain Lodge No. 23, Longmont
Proceedings 1873, pg 51 (1873 Oct 1), St Vrain Lodge No. 23, Longmont
Proceedings 1874, pg 227 (1874 Sept 30), St Vrain No. 23, Longmont, Stricken from the rolls

Ripley, W D
Proceedings 1861-1869, pg 221 (1868 Oct 7) Golden City Lodge No. 1
Proceedings 1861-1869, pg 303 (1869 Sept 29) Golden City Lodge No. 1

Rippey, W D
Proceedings 1861-1869, pg 110 (1863 Nov 3) Golden City Lodge No. 1, Apprentice
Proceedings 1870, pg 19 (1870 Sept 28), Golden City Lodge No. 1, Golden City
Proceedings 1871, pg 17 (1871 Sept 27), Golden City Lodge No. 1, Golden City

Rippey, Wm D
Proceedings 1861-1869, pg 191 (1867 Oct 8) Golden City Lodge No. 1

Rippy, W D
Proceedings 1861-1869, pg 147 (1865 Nov 7) Golden City Lodge No. 1
Proceedings 1861-1869, pg 165 (1866 Oct 2) Golden City Lodge No. 1
Proceedings 1872, pg 18 (1872 Sept 24), Golden City Lodge No. 1, Golden City, Stricken from the Roll

Rippy, Wm D
Proceedings 1861-1869, pg 131 (1864 Nov 8) Golden City Lodge No. 1

Ritchie, J W
Proceedings 1861-1869, pg 196 (1867 Oct 8), Black Hawk Lodge No. 11, Black Hawk
Proceedings 1870, pg 25 (1870 Sept 28), Black Hawk Lodge No. 11, Black Hawk, Dimitted
Proceedings 1875, pg 83 (1875 Sept 22), Columbia Lodge No. 14, Boulder, Stricken from the rolls

Ritchie, John
Proceedings 1861-1869, pg 229 (1868 Oct 7), Canon Lodge U D, Canon City
Proceedings 1870, pg 28 (1870 Sept 28), Mount Moriah Lodge No. 15, Canon City
Proceedings 1871, pg 27 (1871 Sept 27), Mount Moriah Lodge No. 15, Canon City, Dimitted

Ritchie, John W
Proceedings 1861-1869, pg 227 (1868 Oct 7), Black Hawk Lodge No. 11, Black Hawk
Proceedings 1861-1869, pg 230 (1868 Oct 7), Valmont Lodge U D, Valmont
Proceedings 1861-1869, pg 309 (1869 Sept 29), Black Hawk Lodge No. 11, Black Hawk
Proceedings 1861-1869, pg 310 (1869 Sept 29), Columbia Lodge No. 14, Boulder City
Proceedings 1870, pg 27 (1870 Sept 28), Columbia Lodge No. 14, Boulder City
Proceedings 1871, pg 26 (1871 Sept 27), Columbia Lodge No. 14, Boulder City
Proceedings 1872, pg 28 (1872 Sept 24), Columbia Lodge No. 14, Boulder
Proceedings 1873, pg 44 (1873 Oct 1), Columbia Lodge No. 14, Boulder

Proceedings 1874, pg 219 (1874 Sept 30), Columbia Lodge No. 14, Boulder, Boulder County

Ritter, G M
Proceedings 1874, pg 36 (1874 Sept 30) per diem

Ritter, G W
Proceedings 1870, pg 30 (1870 Sept 28), Laramie Lodge No. 18, Laramie, Wyoming Territory
Proceedings 1871, pg 29 (1871 Sept 27), Laramie Lodge No. 18, Laramie, Wyoming Territory
Proceedings 1872, pg 31 (1872 Sept 24), Laramie Lodge No. 18, Laramie, Wyoming Territory
Proceedings 1873, pg 48 (1873 Oct 1), Laramie Lodge No. 18, Laramie, Wyoming Territory
Proceedings 1874, pg 223 (1874 Sept 30), Laramie Lodge No. 18, Laramie City

Ritter, George W
Proceedings 1874, pg 6 (1874 Sept 29), Laramie Lodge No. 18, Laramie, Wyoming Territory

Robbins
Proceedings 1861-1869, pg 36 (1861 Dec 10)
Proceedings 1861-1869, pg 38 (1861 Dec 12) motion

Robbins, Joseph
Proceedings 1872, pg 43 (1872 Sept 24) Quincy, Grand Lodge of Illinois
Proceedings 1872, pg 63 (1872 Sept 24) Grand Lodge of Illinois
Proceedings 1873, pg 60 (1873 Oct 1) Grand Lodge of Illinois, Quincy
Proceedings 1874, pg 62 (1874 Sept 30) Grand Lodge of Illinois
Proceedings 1874, pg 204 (1874 Sept 30) Grand Lodge of Illinois, Quincy

Robbins, S M
Proceedings 1861-1869, pg 3 (1861 Aug 2), Summit Lodge No 7, Parkville
Proceedings 1861-1869, pg 4 (1861 Aug 2), Summit Lodge No 7, Parkville
Proceedings 1861-1869, pg 4 (1861 Aug 2) committee
Proceedings 1861-1869, pg 5 (1861 Aug 2) Deputy Grand Master, Parkville
Proceedings 1861-1869, pg 5 (1861 Aug 2), Summit Lodge No 7, Parkville
Proceedings 1861-1869, pg 6 (1861 Aug 2) committee
Proceedings 1861-1869, pg 31 (1861 Dec 10) Deputy Grand Master
Proceedings 1861-1869, pg 34 (1861 Dec 10) committee
Proceedings 1861-1869, pg 35 (1861 Dec 10) Deputy Grand Master
Proceedings 1861-1869, pg 35 (1861 Dec 10) Deputy Grand Master
Proceedings 1861-1869, pg 42 (1861 Dec 10), Summit Lodge No. 2, Parkville
Proceedings 1861-1869, pg 76 (1862 Nov 4), Summit Lodge No. 2, Parkville, dimitted
Proceedings 1861-1869, pg 315 (1869 Sept 29) Deputy Grand Master, August 1861, Dimitted
Proceedings 1870, pg 32 (1870 Sept 28) Deputy Grand Master, August 1861, Dimitted
Proceedings 1871, pg 6 (1861 Aug 2) Deputy Grand Master
Proceedings 1871, pg 34 (1871 Sept 27) Deputy Grand Master, Aug 1861, Dimitted
Proceedings 1872, pg 42 (1872 Sept 24) Deputy Grand Master, August 1861, Dimitted
Proceedings 1873, pg 58 (1873 Oct 1) Deputy Grand Master, Aug 1861, Dimitted

Robbins, Samuel N
Proceedings 1874, pg 206 (1874 Sept 30) Deputy Grand Master, Aug 1861, demitted
Proceedings 1875, pg 93 (1875 Sept 22) Deputy Grand Master, Aug 1861, Demitted

Robert, Samuel
Proceedings 1872, pg 14 (1872 Sept 24), St Vrain Lodge No. 23, Longmont

Roberts
Proceedings 1861-1869, pg 228 (1868 Oct 7), El Paso Lodge No. 13, Colorado City

Roberts, Daniel
Proceedings 1861-1869, pg 227 (1868 Oct 7), Washington Lodge No. 12, Georgetown
Proceedings 1861-1869, pg 309 (1869 Sept 29), Washington Lodge No. 12, Georgetown
Proceedings 1870, pg 26 (1870 Sept 28), Washington Lodge No. 12, Georgetown
Proceedings 1871, pg 24 (1871 Sept 27), Washington Lodge No. 12, Georgetown
Proceedings 1872, pg 26 (1872 Sept 24), Washington Lodge No. 12, Georgetown
Proceedings 1873, pg 6 (1873 Sept 30), Washington Lodge No. 12, Georgetown
Proceedings 1873, pg 42 (1873 Oct 1), Washington Lodge No. 12, Georgetown
Proceedings 1874, pg 217 (1874 Sept 30), Washington Lodge No. 12, Georgetown
Proceedings 1875, pg 81 (1875 Sept 22), Washington Lodge No. 12, Georgetown
Proceedings 1876, pg 35 (1876 Sept 20), Washington Lodge No. 12, Georgetown

Roberts, Geo C
Proceedings 1875, pg 78 (1875 Sept 22), Union Lodge No. 7, Denver
Proceedings 1873, pg 37 (1873 Oct 1), Denver Lodge No. 5, Denver

Roberts, Geo T
Proceedings 1874, pg 211 (1874 Sept 30), Denver Lodge No. 5, Denver
Proceedings 1875, pg 75 (1875 Sept 22) Denver Lodge No. 5

Roberts, George C
Proceedings 1876, pg 33 (1876 Sept 20), Union Lodge No. 7, Denver

Roberts, George T
Proceedings 1876, pg 31 (1876 Sept 20) Denver Lodge No. 5

Colorado's Territorial Masons

Roberts, I H
    Proceedings 1876, pg 34 (1876 Sept 20) Black Hawk Lodge No. 11

Roberts, James
    Proceedings 1861-1869, pg 196 (1867 Oct 8), El Paso Lodge U D, Colorado City
    Proceedings 1861-1869, pg 310 (1869 Sept 29), El Paso Lodge No. 13, Colorado City
    Proceedings 1870, pg 26 (1870 Sept 28), El Paso Lodge No. 13, Colorado City
    Proceedings 1870, pg 26 (1870 Sept 28), Washington Lodge No. 12, Georgetown, Died
    Proceedings 1871, pg 24 (1871 Sept 27), El Paso Lodge No. 13, Colorado City
    Proceedings 1872, pg 27 (1872 Sept 24), El Paso Lodge No. 13, Colorado City
    Proceedings 1873, pg 43 (1873 Oct 1), El Paso Lodge No. 13, Colorado City
    Proceedings 1874, pg 218 (1874 Sept 30), El Paso Lodge No. 13, Colorado Springs
    Proceedings 1875, pg 82 (1875 Sept 22), El Paso Lodge No. 13, Colorado Springs

Roberts, Jno G
    Proceedings 1871, pg 21 (1871 Sept 27), Central Lodge No. 6, Central
    Proceedings 1872, pg 21 (1872 Sept 24), Denver Lodge No. 5, Denver

Roberts, John
    Proceedings 1874, pg 229 (1874 Sept 30), Idaho Springs Lodge U D, Idaho Springs

Roberts, John G
    Proceedings 1873, pg 38 (1873 Oct 1), Central Lodge No. 6, Central City
    Proceedings 1874, pg 212 (1874 Sept 30), Central Lodge No. 6, Central
    Proceedings 1875, pg 76 (1875 Sept 22), Central Lodge No. 6, Central City
    Proceedings 1876, pg 32 (1876 Sept 20), Central Lodge No. 6, Central City
    Proceedings 1876, pg 43 (1876 Sept 20) Idaho Springs Lodge No. 26

Roberts, John Henry
    Proceedings 1874, pg 216 (1874 Sept 30), Black Hawk Lodge No. 11, Black Hawk
    Proceedings 1875, pg 80 (1875 Sept 22) Black Hawk Lodge No. 11

Roberts, S K
    Proceedings 1861-1869, pg 154 (1866 Jan 27), El Paso Lodge U D, Colorado City
    Proceedings 1861-1869, pg 170 (1866 Oct 2), El Paso U D, Colorado City
    Proceedings 1861-1869, pg 196 (1867 Oct 8), El Paso Lodge U D, Colorado City
    Proceedings 1861-1869, pg 310 (1869 Sept 29), El Paso Lodge No. 13, Colorado City
    Proceedings 1870, pg 27 (1870 Sept 28), El Paso Lodge No. 13, Colorado City
    Proceedings 1873, pg 43 (1873 Oct 1), El Paso Lodge No. 13, Colorado City

Roberts, S R
    Proceedings 1861-1869, pg 228 (1868 Oct 7), El Paso Lodge No. 13, Colorado City

Roberts, Sam'l K
    Proceedings 1874, pg 218 (1874 Sept 30), El Paso Lodge No. 13, Colorado Springs

Roberts, Samuel
    Proceedings 1872, pg 35 (1872 Sept 24), St Vrain Lodge No. 23, Longmont
    Proceedings 1873, pg 51 (1873 Oct 1), St Vrain Lodge No. 23, Longmont
    Proceedings 1874, pg 227 (1874 Sept 30), St Vrain No. 23, Longmont
    Proceedings 1876, pg 41 (1876 Sept 20), St Vrain Lodge No. 23, Longmont

Roberts, Samuel K
    Proceedings 1871, pg 25 (1871 Sept 27), El Paso Lodge No. 13, Colorado City
    Proceedings 1872, pg 27 (1872 Sept 24), El Paso Lodge No. 13, Colorado City
    Proceedings 1875, pg 82 (1875 Sept 22), El Paso Lodge No. 13, Colorado Springs, Stricken from the rolls

Roberts, W I
    Proceedings 1876, pg 34 (1876 Sept 20) Black Hawk Lodge No. 11

Roberts, W W
    Proceedings 1861-1869, pg 195 (1867 Oct 8), Union Lodge No. 7, Denver, Apprentice
    Proceedings 1861-1869, pg 226 (1868 Oct 7), Union Lodge No. 7, Denver, Fellowcraft
    Proceedings 1861-1869, pg 308 (1869 Sept 29), Union Lodge No. 7, Denver, Fellowcraft
    Proceedings 1872, pg 22 (1872 Sept 24), Union Lodge No. 7, Denver
    Proceedings 1873, pg 39 (1873 Oct 1), Union Lodge No. 7, Denver
    Proceedings 1874, pg 214 (1874 Sept 30), Union Lodge No. 7, Denver
    Proceedings 1875, pg 78 (1875 Sept 22), Union Lodge No. 7, Denver
    Proceedings 1876, pg 33 (1876 Sept 20), Union Lodge No. 7, Denver

Roberts, William W
    Proceedings 1871, pg 22 (1871 Sept 27), Union Lodge No. 7, Denver

Roberts, Wm James
    Proceedings 1874, pg 216 (1874 Sept 30), Black Hawk Lodge No. 11, Black Hawk, Apprentice
    Proceedings 1875, pg 80 (1875 Sept 22) Black Hawk Lodge No. 11

Roberts, Wm W
    Proceedings 1870, pg 23 (1870 Sept 28), Union Lodge No. 7, Denver

Robertson, C E
Proceedings 1872, pg 36 (1872 Sept 24), Ashlar Lodge U D, Colorado Springs

Robertson, D A
Proceedings 1873, pg 6 (1873 Sept 30), Columbia Lodge No. 14, Boulder

Robertson, Henry
Proceedings 1874, pg 50 (1874 Sept 30) Grand Lodge of Canada

Robertson, James
Proceedings 1873, pg 48 (1873 Oct 1), Laramie Lodge No. 18, Laramie, Wyoming Territory
Proceedings 1874, pg 223 (1874 Sept 30), Laramie Lodge No. 18, Laramie City

Robertson, N
Proceedings 1871, pg 27 (1871 Sept 27), Cheyenne Lodge No. 16, Cheyenne, Wyoming Territory
Proceedings 1872, pg 29 (1872 Sept 24), Cheyenne Lodge No. 16, Cheyenne, Wyoming Territory
Proceedings 1873, pg 46 (1873 Oct 1), Cheyenne Lodge No. 16, Cheyenne, Wyoming Territory, Dimitted
Proceedings 1874, pg 225 (1874 Sept 30), Occidental Lodge No. 20, Greeley
Proceedings 1875, pg 87 (1875 Sept 22), Occidental Lodge No. 20, Greeley
Proceedings 1876, pg 40 (1876 Sept 20), Occidental Lodge No. 20, Greeley

Robertson, R H
Proceedings 1872, pg 89 (1872 Sept 24) Grand Lodge of Utah
Proceedings 1874, pg 126 (1874 Sept 30) Grand Lodge of Utah

Robertson, Ruben H
Proceedings 1872, pg 44 (1872 Sept 24) Salt Lake, Grand Lodge of Utah
Proceedings 1873, pg 61 (1873 Oct 1) Grand Lodge of Utah, Salt Lake

Robinson, D A
Proceedings 1872, pg 4 (1872 Sept 24), Columbia Lodge No. 14, Boulder City
Proceedings 1872, pg 27 (1872 Sept 24), Columbia Lodge No. 14, Boulder
Proceedings 1874, pg 6 (1874 Sept 29), Columbia Lodge No. 14, Boulder
Proceedings 1874, pg 32 (1874 Sept 30) Grand Marshal, Boulder
Proceedings 1874, pg 36 (1874 Sept 30) per diem
Proceedings 1875, pg 17 (1875 Sept 21) committee
Proceedings 1875, pg 17 (1875 Sept 21), Columbia Lodge No. 14, Boulder
Proceedings 1875, pg 32 (1875 Sept 22) committee
Proceedings 1875, pg 33 (1875 Sept 22) Grand Marshal

Robinson, Daniel A
Colorado University Cornerstone Laying, pg 3 (1875 Sept 20) Grand Marshal
Proceedings 1861-1869, pg 310 (1869 Sept 29), Columbia Lodge No. 14, Boulder City
Proceedings 1870, pg 27 (1870 Sept 28), Columbia Lodge No. 14, Boulder City
Proceedings 1873, pg 44 (1873 Oct 1), Columbia Lodge No. 14, Boulder
Proceedings 1874, pg 219 (1874 Sept 30), Columbia Lodge No. 14, Boulder, Boulder County
Proceedings 1875, pg 15 (1875 Sept 21) Grand Marshal
Proceedings 1875, pg 83 (1875 Sept 22), Columbia Lodge No. 14, Boulder
Proceedings 1876, pg 36 (1876 Sept 20), Columbia Lodge No. 14, Boulder

Robinson, Dan'l A
Proceedings 1871, pg 25 (1871 Sept 27), Columbia Lodge No. 14, Boulder City

Robinson, George
Proceedings 1872, pg 78 (1872 Sept 24) Grand Lodge of Nevada

Robinson, H S
Proceedings 1861-1869, pg 78 (1862 Nov 4), Chivington Lodge No. 6, Central City
Proceedings 1861-1869, pg 80 (1863 May 6), Chivington Lodge No. 6, Central City
Proceedings 1861-1869, pg 92 (1863 Apr 17) committee
Proceedings 1861-1869, pg 94 (1863 Apr 17) committee
Proceedings 1861-1869, pg 94 (1863 Apr 17), Chivington Lodge No. 6, Central City
Proceedings 1861-1869, pg 95 (1863 Apr 17), Chivington Lodge No. 6, Central City
Proceedings 1861-1869, pg 134 (1864 Nov 8), Chivington Lodge No. 6, Central City
Proceedings 1861-1869, pg 150 (1865 Nov 7), Chivington Lodge No. 6, Central City
Proceedings 1861-1869, pg 168 (1866 Oct 2), Chivington Lodge No. 6, Central City, dimitted

Robinson, Henry S
Proceedings 1861-1869, pg 113 (1863 Nov 3), Chivington Lodge No. 6, Central City

Robinson, L A
Proceedings 1875, pg 85 (1875 Sept 22) Pueblo Lodge No. 17, Apprentice
Proceedings 1876, pg 39 (1876 Sept 20) Pueblo Lodge No. 17, Apprentice

Robinson, L D
Proceedings 1870, pg 30 (1870 Sept 28), Pueblo Lodge No. 17, Pueblo, Apprentice
Proceedings 1871, pg 28 (1871 Sept 27), Pueblo Lodge No. 17, Pueblo, Apprentice
Proceedings 1872, pg 31 (1872 Sept 24), Pueblo Lodge No. 17, Pueblo, Apprentice
Proceedings 1873, pg 47 (1873 Oct 1), Pueblo Lodge No. 17, Pueblo, Apprentice
Proceedings 1874, pg 222 (1874 Sept 30), Pueblo Lodge No. 17, Pueblo, Pueblo County, Apprentice

Robinson, Remus
Proceedings 1875, pg 87 (1875 Sept 22), Occidental Lodge No. 20, Greeley
Proceedings 1876, pg 40 (1876 Sept 20), Occidental Lodge No. 20, Greeley

Colorado's Territorial Masons

Robinson, W D
    Proceedings 1861-1869, pg 149 (1865 Nov 7), Nevada Lodge No. 4, Nevadaville
    Proceedings 1861-1869, pg 166 (1866 Oct 2) Denver Lodge No. 5
    Proceedings 1861-1869, pg 193 (1867 Oct 8) Denver Lodge No. 5
    Proceedings 1861-1869, pg 223 (1868 Oct 7) Denver Lodge No. 5
    Proceedings 1861-1869, pg 229 (1868 Oct 7), Cheyenne Lodge U D, Cheyenne, Dakota Territory
    Proceedings 1861-1869, pg 305 (1869 Sept 29) Denver Lodge No. 5, Dimitted
    Proceedings 1861-1869, pg 311 (1869 Sept 29), Cheyenne Lodge No. 16, Cheyenne
    Proceedings 1870, pg 29 (1870 Sept 28), Cheyenne Lodge No. 16, Cheyenne, Wyoming Territory, Dimitted
    Proceedings 1874, pg 211 (1874 Sept 30), Denver Lodge No. 5, Denver
    Proceedings 1875, pg 76 (1875 Sept 22) Denver Lodge No. 5, Stricken from the rolls

Robley, D T
    Proceedings 1861-1869, pg 5 (1861 Aug 2) Grand Tyler, Parkville
    Proceedings 1861-1869, pg 42 (1861 Dec 10), Summit Lodge No. 2, Parkville
    Proceedings 1861-1869, pg 76 (1862 Nov 4), Summit Lodge No. 2, Parkville

Rockafellow, B F
    Proceedings 1861-1869, pg 311 (1869 Sept 29), Mount Moriah Lodge No. 15, Canon City
    Proceedings 1871, pg 26 (1871 Sept 27), Mount Moriah Lodge No. 15, Canon City
    Proceedings 1872, pg 29 (1872 Sept 24), Mount Moriah Lodge No. 15, Canon City
    Proceedings 1873, pg 45 (1873 Oct 1), Mount Moriah Lodge No. 15, Canon City
    Proceedings 1875, pg 84 (1875 Sept 22), Mount Moriah Lodge No. 15, Canon City
    Proceedings 1876, pg 38 (1876 Sept 20), Mount Moriah Lodge No. 15, Canon City

Rockeyfellow, B F
    Proceedings 1870, pg 28 (1870 Sept 28), Mount Moriah Lodge No. 15, Canon City
    Proceedings 1874, pg 220 (1874 Sept 30), Mount Moriah Lodge No. 15, Canon City

Rocky Mountain Lodge No. 3
    Proceedings 1861-1869, pg 6 (1861 Aug 3) Gold Hill
    Proceedings 1861-1869, pg 116 (1864 Nov 7) No representative present
    Proceedings 1861-1869, pg 222 (1868 Oct 7) extinct
    Proceedings 1876, pg 46 (1876 Sept 20) extinct

Rocky Mountain Lodge No. 3, Gold Hill
    Proceedings 1861-1869, pg 304 (1869 Sept 29) extinct
    Proceedings 1870, pg 19 (1870 Sept 28) extinct
    Proceedings 1871, pg 18 (1871 Sept 27) Extinct
    Proceedings 1872, pg 18 (1872 Sept 24) extinct
    Proceedings 1873, pg 36 (1873 Oct 1) extinct
    Proceedings 1875, pg 74 (1875 Sept 22) extinct

Rocky Mountain Lodge No. 3, Gold Hill, Boulder County
    Proceedings 1874, pg 210 (1874 Sept 30) Extinct

Rocky Mountain Lodge No. 8, Gold Hill
    Proceedings 1861-1869, pg 4 (1861 Aug 2) chartered 5 June 1861 by the M W Grand Lodge of Nebraska

Rocky Mountain Lodge of Gold Hill
    Proceedings 1871, pg 6 (1861 June 5) Grand Lodge of Nebraska

Rockyfellow, B F
    Proceedings 1861-1869, pg 229 (1868 Oct 7), Canon Lodge U D, Canon City

Rodgers, Charles D
    Proceedings 1870, pg 31 (1870 Sept 28), Collins Lodge No. 19, Fort Collins, Fellowcraft

Rogers, A N
    Proceedings 1861-1869, pg 194 (1867 Oct 8), Chivington Lodge No. 6, Central City
    Proceedings 1861-1869, pg 224 (1868 Oct 7), Chivington Lodge No. 6, Central City
    Proceedings 1861-1869, pg 306 (1869 Sept 29), Central Lodge No. 6, Central City
    Proceedings 1870, pg 22 (1870 Sept 28), Central Lodge No. 6, Central City
    Proceedings 1871, pg 21 (1871 Sept 27), Central Lodge No. 6, Central

Rogers, Andrews N
    Proceedings 1872, pg 21 (1872 Sept 24), Denver Lodge No. 5, Denver
    Proceedings 1873, pg 38 (1873 Oct 1), Central Lodge No. 6, Central City
    Proceedings 1874, pg 212 (1874 Sept 30), Central Lodge No. 6, Central
    Proceedings 1875, pg 76 (1875 Sept 22), Central Lodge No. 6, Central City
    Proceedings 1876, pg 32 (1876 Sept 20), Central Lodge No. 6, Central City

Rogers, B W
    Proceedings 1861-1869, pg 223 (1868 Oct 7) Denver Lodge No. 5
    Proceedings 1861-1869, pg 296 (1869 Sept 28) Denver Lodge No 5
    Proceedings 1861-1869, pg 304 (1869 Sept 29) Denver Lodge No. 5
    Proceedings 1870, pg 21 (1870 Sept 28), Denver Lodge No. 5, Denver
    Proceedings 1871, pg 19 (1871 Sept 27) Denver Lodge No. 5
    Proceedings 1872, pg 19 (1872 Sept 24), Denver Lodge No. 5, Denver
    Proceedings 1873, pg 37 (1873 Oct 1), Denver Lodge No. 5, Denver
    Proceedings 1874, pg 211 (1874 Sept 30), Denver Lodge No. 5, Denver

Proceedings 1875, pg 75 (1875 Sept 22) Denver Lodge No. 5

Rogers, Charles D
Proceedings 1871, pg 30 (1871 Sept 27), Collins Lodge No. 19, Fort Collins
Proceedings 1872, pg 33 (1872 Sept 24), Collins Lodge No. 19, Fort Collins
Proceedings 1873, pg 49 (1873 Oct 1), Collins Lodge No. 19, Fort Collins
Proceedings 1874, pg 224 (1874 Sept 30), Collins Lodge No. 19, Fort Collins, Larimer County
Proceedings 1875, pg 86 (1875 Sept 22), Collins Lodge No. 19, Fort Collins
Proceedings 1876, pg 39 (1876 Sept 20), Collins Lodge No. 19, Fort Collins

Rogers, H J
Proceedings 1861-1869, pg 149 (1865 Nov 7), Nevada Lodge No. 4, Nevadaville
Proceedings 1861-1869, pg 167 (1866 Oct 2) Denver Lodge No. 5
Proceedings 1861-1869, pg 193 (1867 Oct 8) Denver Lodge No. 5
Proceedings 1861-1869, pg 223 (1868 Oct 7) Denver Lodge No. 5
Proceedings 1861-1869, pg 305 (1869 Sept 29) Denver Lodge No. 5
Proceedings 1871, pg 19 (1871 Sept 27) Denver Lodge No. 5

Rogers, Henry J
Proceedings 1861-1869, pg 133 (1864 Nov 8) Denver Lodge No. 5
Proceedings 1870, pg 21 (1870 Sept 28), Denver Lodge No. 5, Denver
Proceedings 1872, pg 19 (1872 Sept 24), Denver Lodge No. 5, Denver
Proceedings 1873, pg 38 (1873 Oct 1), Denver Lodge No. 5, Denver, Striken from the rolls

Rogers, John W
Proceedings 1872, pg 20 (1872 Sept 24), Denver Lodge No. 5, Denver, Apprentice

Rogers, M A
Proceedings 1861-1869, pg 151 (1865 Nov 7), Chivington Lodge No. 6, Central City
Proceedings 1861-1869, pg 169 (1866 Oct 2), Union Lodge No. 7, Denver
Proceedings 1861-1869, pg 176 (1867 Oct 7), Union Lodge No. 7, Denver
Proceedings 1861-1869, pg 195 (1867 Oct 8), Union Lodge No. 7, Denver
Proceedings 1861-1869, pg 225 (1868 Oct 7), Union Lodge No. 7, Denver
Proceedings 1861-1869, pg 307 (1869 Sept 29), Union Lodge No. 7, Denver
Proceedings 1871, pg 4 (1871 Sept 26), Union Lodge No. 7, Denver
Proceedings 1871, pg 21 (1871 Sept 27), Union Lodge No. 7, Denver
Proceedings 1876, pg 33 (1876 Sept 20), Union Lodge No. 7, Denver

Rogers, Merrick A
Proceedings 1861-1869, pg 139 (1865 Jan 7), Union Lodge No. 7, Denver
Proceedings 1870, pg 23 (1870 Sept 28), Union Lodge No. 7, Denver
Proceedings 1872, pg 22 (1872 Sept 24), Union Lodge No. 7, Denver
Proceedings 1873, pg 39 (1873 Oct 1), Union Lodge No. 7, Denver
Proceedings 1874, pg 214 (1874 Sept 30), Union Lodge No. 7, Denver
Proceedings 1875, pg 78 (1875 Sept 22), Union Lodge No. 7, Denver

Rogers, W C
Proceedings 1874, pg 209 (1874 Sept 30), Golden City Lodge No. 1, Golden City
Proceedings 1874, pg 209 (1874 Sept 30), Golden City Lodge No. 1, Golden City
Proceedings 1875, pg 73 (1875 Sept 22) Golden City Lodge No. 1
Proceedings 1876, pg 29 (1876 Sept 20) Golden City Lodge No. 1
Proceedings 1876, pg 50 (1876 Sept 20) Golden City Lodge No. 1

Rohm, Robert L
Proceedings 1875, pg 77 (1875 Sept 22), Central Lodge No. 6, Central City, Apprentice
Proceedings 1876, pg 32 (1876 Sept 20), Central Lodge No. 6, Central City, Apprentice

Roney, A R
Proceedings 1861-1869, pg 303 (1869 Sept 29) Golden City Lodge No. 1

Rooney, Alex
Proceedings 1871, pg 17 (1871 Sept 27), Golden City Lodge No. 1, Golden City
Proceedings 1872, pg 17 (1872 Sept 24), Golden City Lodge No. 1, Golden City
Proceedings 1873, pg 35 (1873 Oct 1), Golden City Lodge No. 1, Golden City
Proceedings 1874, pg 209 (1874 Sept 30), Golden City Lodge No. 1, Golden City

Rooney, Alexander
Proceedings 1870, pg 19 (1870 Sept 28), Golden City Lodge No. 1, Golden City
Proceedings 1876, pg 29 (1876 Sept 20) Golden City Lodge No. 1
Proceedings 1876, pg 29 (1876 Sept 20) Golden City Lodge No. 1

Rooney, Alix
Proceedings 1875, pg 73 (1875 Sept 22) Golden City Lodge No. 1

Root, Mansel H
Proceedings 1875, pg 77 (1875 Sept 22), Central Lodge No. 6, Central City, Fellowcraft

Root, Mansel H, cont.
    Proceedings 1876, pg 32 (1876 Sept 20), Central Lodge No. 6, Central City

Ropes, E E
    Proceedings 1861-1869, pg 133 (1864 Nov 8) Denver Lodge No. 5
    Proceedings 1861-1869, pg 149 (1865 Nov 7), Nevada Lodge No. 4, Nevadaville
    Proceedings 1861-1869, pg 167 (1866 Oct 2) Denver Lodge No. 5
    Proceedings 1861-1869, pg 193 (1867 Oct 8) Denver Lodge No. 5
    Proceedings 1861-1869, pg 223 (1868 Oct 7) Denver Lodge No. 5
    Proceedings 1861-1869, pg 305 (1869 Sept 29) Denver Lodge No. 5
    Proceedings 1870, pg 21 (1870 Sept 28), Denver Lodge No. 5, Denver

Rose, S
    Proceedings 1861-1869, pg 328 (1868 Oct 27) Grand Secretary, Grand Lodge of Georgia

Rose, Samuel
    Proceedings 1873, pg 37 (1873 Oct 1), Denver Lodge No. 5, Denver
    Proceedings 1874, pg 211 (1874 Sept 30), Denver Lodge No. 5, Denver
    Proceedings 1875, pg 75 (1875 Sept 22) Denver Lodge No. 5
    Proceedings 1876, pg 31 (1876 Sept 20) Denver Lodge No. 5

Rose, Simri
    Proceedings 1861-1869, pg 291 (1869 Sept 28), Grand Secretary, Grand Lodge of Georgia
    Proceedings 1870, pg 55 (1869 Oct 26) Grand Lodge of Georgia, deceased

Rosenfield, W
    Proceedings 1861-1869, pg 150 (1865 Nov 7), Chivington Lodge No. 6, Central City
    Proceedings 1861-1869, pg 168 (1866 Oct 2), Chivington Lodge No. 6, Central City

Rosenfield, William
    Proceedings 1861-1869, pg 78 (1862 Nov 4), Chivington Lodge No. 6, Central City
    Proceedings 1861-1869, pg 134 (1864 Nov 8), Chivington Lodge No. 6, Central City

Rosenfield, Wm
    Proceedings 1861-1869, pg 49 (1862 Nov 3), Chivington Lodge No. 6, Central City
    Proceedings 1861-1869, pg 113 (1863 Nov 3), Chivington Lodge No. 6, Central City
    Proceedings 1861-1869, pg 193 (1867 Oct 8), Chivington Lodge No. 6, Central City
    Proceedings 1861-1869, pg 225 (1868 Oct 7), Chivington Lodge No. 6, Central City, Dimitted

Rosevear, John
    Proceedings 1871, pg 18 (1871 Sept 27), Nevada Lodge No. 4, Bald Mountain, Dimitted

Rosita Lodge U D, Rosita
    Proceedings 1876, pg 7 (1876 Feb 14) dispensation refused

Ross, F W
    Proceedings 1874, pg 225 (1874 Sept 30), Occidental Lodge No. 20, Greeley
    Proceedings 1875, pg 87 (1875 Sept 22), Occidental Lodge No. 20, Greeley

Ross, Frank W
    Proceedings 1876, pg 40 (1876 Sept 20), Occidental Lodge No. 20, Greeley

Ross, Rhoderick
    Proceedings 1874, pg 229 (1874 Sept 30), Idaho Springs Lodge U D, Idaho Springs

Ross, W A
    Proceedings 1874, pg 8 (1874 July 14), Idaho Springs Lodge U D, Idaho Springs
    Proceedings 1874, pg 229 (1874 Sept 30), Idaho Springs Lodge U D, Idaho Springs
    Proceedings 1875, pg 34 (1875 Sept 22) Idaho Springs Lodge No. 26
    Proceedings 1875, pg 89 (1875 Sept 22) Idaho Springs Lodge U D
    Proceedings 1876, pg 42 (1876 Sept 20) Idaho Springs Lodge No. 26

Rosseau, Gen
    Proceedings 1861-1869, pg 260 (1868 June)

Roster, R M
    Proceedings 1861-1869, pg 111 (1863 Nov 3), Nevada Lodge No. 4, Nevadaville

Rothchild, D C H
    Proceedings 1873, pg 61 (1873 Oct 1) Grand Lodge of Washington, Port Townsend

Rothrick, W L
    Proceedings 1861-1869, pg 42 (1861 Dec 10) Golden City Lodge No. 1
    Proceedings 1861-1869, pg 165 (1866 Oct 2) Golden City Lodge No. 1
    Proceedings 1861-1869, pg 191 (1867 Oct 8) Golden City Lodge No. 1, Dimitted

Rothrock, W L
    Proceedings 1861-1869, pg 110 (1863 Nov 3) Golden City Lodge No. 1
    Proceedings 1861-1869, pg 131 (1864 Nov 8) Golden City Lodge No. 1
    Proceedings 1861-1869, pg 147 (1865 Nov 7) Golden City Lodge No. 1

Rothschild, D C H
    Proceedings 1874, pg 205 (1874 Sept 30) Grand Lodge of Washington, Port Townsend

Rouk, D T
    Proceedings 1872, pg 36 (1872 Sept 24), Ashlar Lodge U D, Colorado Springs

Rowe
    Proceedings 1870, pg 69 (1869 Sept 8) Provincial Grand Master, of England

Rowell, John H
 Proceedings 1861-1869, pg 342 (1868 June 10) Grand Master, Grand Lodge of New Hampshire

Rowen, A M
 Proceedings 1873, pg 46 (1873 Oct 1), Cheyenne Lodge No. 16, Cheyenne, Wyoming Territory, Dimitted

Royal Solomon Mother Lodge No. 293
 Proceedings 1874, pg 47 (1874 Sept 30) Jerusalem

Royal York Zur Freundschaft
 Proceedings 1872, pg 47 (1872 Sept 24), Berlin, Prussia

Rucker, Thomas H
 Proceedings 1875, pg 82 (1875 Sept 22), El Paso Lodge No. 13, Colorado Springs

Rudd, A
 Proceedings 1875, pg 84 (1875 Sept 22), Mount Moriah Lodge No. 15, Canon City

Rudd, Anson
 Proceedings 1874, pg 220 (1874 Sept 30), Mount Moriah Lodge No. 15, Canon City
 Proceedings 1876, pg 38 (1876 Sept 20), Mount Moriah Lodge No. 15, Canon City

Rudolph, A E
 Proceedings 1871, pg 20 (1871 Sept 27) Denver Lodge No. 5, Dimitted
 Proceedings 1872, pg 28 (1872 Sept 24), Mount Moriah Lodge No. 15, Canon City
 Proceedings 1873, pg 45 (1873 Oct 1), Mount Moriah Lodge No. 15, Canon City
 Proceedings 1874, pg 220 (1874 Sept 30), Mount Moriah Lodge No. 15, Canon City
 Proceedings 1875, pg 84 (1875 Sept 22), Mount Moriah Lodge No. 15, Canon City
 Proceedings 1876, pg 37 (1876 Sept 20), Mount Moriah Lodge No. 15, Canon City

Rudolph, C G
 Proceedings 1870, pg 25 (1870 Sept 28), Black Hawk Lodge No. 11, Black Hawk
 Proceedings 1871, pg 23 (1871 Sept 27), Black Hawk Lodge No. 11, Black Hawk
 Proceedings 1872, pg 24 (1872 Sept 24), Black Hawk Lodge No. 11, Black Hawk
 Proceedings 1873, pg 42 (1873 Oct 1), Black Hawk Lodge No. 11, Black Hawk, died

Rudolph, C J
 Proceedings 1873, pg 57 (1873 Oct 1), Black Hawk Lodge No. 11, Black Hawk

Rudolph, F A
 Proceedings 1861-1869, pg 170 (1866 Oct 2), Black Hawk Lodge U D, Black Hawk
 Proceedings 1861-1869, pg 196 (1867 Oct 8), Black Hawk Lodge No. 11, Black Hawk
 Proceedings 1861-1869, pg 227 (1868 Oct 7), Black Hawk Lodge No. 11, Black Hawk
 Proceedings 1861-1869, pg 309 (1869 Sept 29), Black Hawk Lodge No. 11, Black Hawk
 Proceedings 1870, pg 25 (1870 Sept 28), Black Hawk Lodge No. 11, Black Hawk
 Proceedings 1871, pg 23 (1871 Sept 27), Black Hawk Lodge No. 11, Black Hawk
 Proceedings 1872, pg 24 (1872 Sept 24), Black Hawk Lodge No. 11, Black Hawk
 Proceedings 1873, pg 41 (1873 Oct 1), Black Hawk Lodge No. 11, Black Hawk
 Proceedings 1874, pg 216 (1874 Sept 30), Black Hawk Lodge No. 11, Black Hawk

Rudolph, Fred A
 Proceedings 1875, pg 80 (1875 Sept 22) Black Hawk Lodge No. 11
 Proceedings 1876, pg 34 (1876 Sept 20) Black Hawk Lodge No. 11

Rumbaugh, H S
 Proceedings 1873, pg 46 (1873 Oct 1), Cheyenne Lodge No. 16, Cheyenne, Wyoming Territory, Apprentice
 Proceedings 1874, pg 221 (1874 Sept 30), Cheyenne Lodge No. 16, Cheyenne, Wyoming Territory, Apprentice

Rumsbottom, J
 Proceedings 1870, pg 31 (1870 Sept 28), Laramie Lodge No. 18, Laramie, Wyoming Territory

Runbaugh, H S
 Proceedings 1870, pg 29 (1870 Sept 28), Cheyenne Lodge No. 16, Cheyenne, Wyoming Territory, permission given to take degrees elsewhere
 Proceedings 1872, pg 30 (1872 Sept 24), Cheyenne Lodge No. 16, Cheyenne, Wyoming Territory, Apprentice

Runington, J C
 Proceedings 1874, pg 209 (1874 Sept 30), Golden City Lodge No. 1, Golden City

Rupe, A C
 Proceedings 1861-1869, pg 192 (1867 Oct 8), Nevada Lodge No. 4, Nevadaville
 Proceedings 1861-1869, pg 222 (1868 Oct 7), Nevada Lodge No. 4, Nevadaville
 Proceedings 1861-1869, pg 304 (1869 Sept 29), Nevada Lodge No. 4, Nevadaville
 Proceedings 1871, pg 18 (1871 Sept 27), Nevada Lodge No. 4, Bald Mountain
 Proceedings 1873, pg 36 (1873 Oct 1), Nevada Lodge No. 4, Nevada
 Proceedings 1874, pg 211 (1874 Sept 30), Nevada Lodge No. 4, Bald Mountain, Gilpin County, Stricken from the rolls

Rusling, Robert
 Proceedings 1870, pg 94 (1870 Jan 19) Grand Master, Grand Lodge of New Jersey

Russell, Albert J
 Proceedings 1873, pg 60 (1873 Oct 1) Grand Lodge of Florida, Jacksonville
 Proceedings 1874, pg 55 (1874 Sept 30) Grand Lodge of Florida
 Proceedings 1874, pg 204 (1874 Sept 30) Grand Lodge of Florida, Jacksonville

Russell, G W
 Proceedings 1874, pg 224 (1874 Sept 30), Laramie Lodge No. 18, Laramie City, Fellowcraft

Russell, H M
　Proceedings 1861-1869, pg 191 (1867 Oct 8) Golden City Lodge No. 1
　Proceedings 1871, pg 17 (1871 Sept 27), Golden City Lodge No. 1, Golden City

Russell, J C
　Proceedings 1861-1869, pg 111 (1863 Nov 3), Nevada Lodge No. 4, Nevadaville
　Proceedings 1861-1869, pg 166 (1866 Oct 2), Nevada Lodge No. 4, Nevadaville
　Proceedings 1861-1869, pg 192 (1867 Oct 8), Nevada Lodge No. 4, Nevadaville

Russell, John C
　Proceedings 1861-1869, pg 76 (1862 Nov 4), Nevada Lodge No. 4, Nevadaville
　Proceedings 1861-1869, pg 132 (1864 Nov 8), Nevada Lodge No. 4, Nevadaville
　Proceedings 1861-1869, pg 222 (1868 Oct 7), Nevada Lodge No. 4, Nevadaville, Dimitted

Russell, Robert
　Proceedings 1861-1869, pg 76 (1862 Nov 4), Nevada Lodge No. 4, Nevadaville
　Proceedings 1861-1869, pg 77 (1862 Nov 4), Nevada Lodge No. 4, Nevadaville, Deceased

Russell, S A
　Proceedings 1876, pg 33 (1876 Sept 20), Union Lodge No. 7, Denver

Ruter, Charles
　Proceedings 1861-1869, pg 134 (1864 Nov 8), Union Lodge No. 7, Denver
　Proceedings 1861-1869, pg 169 (1866 Oct 2), Union Lodge No. 7, Denver
　Proceedings 1861-1869, pg 195 (1867 Oct 8), Union Lodge No. 7, Denver
　Proceedings 1870, pg 23 (1870 Sept 28), Union Lodge No. 7, Denver
　Proceedings 1871, pg 22 (1871 Sept 27), Union Lodge No. 7, Denver
　Proceedings 1872, pg 22 (1872 Sept 24), Union Lodge No. 7, Denver
　Proceedings 1873, pg 40 (1873 Oct 1), Union Lodge No. 7, Denver, Stricken from the rolls

Ruter, Chas
　Proceedings 1861-1869, pg 102 (1863 Nov 3) petition for formation of a new lodge in Denver
　Proceedings 1861-1869, pg 151 (1865 Nov 7), Chivington Lodge No. 6, Central City
　Proceedings 1861-1869, pg 225 (1868 Oct 7), Union Lodge No. 7, Denver
　Proceedings 1861-1869, pg 307 (1869 Sept 29), Union Lodge No. 7, Denver

Rutherford, John
　Proceedings 1861-1869, pg 304 (1869 Sept 29), Nevada Lodge No. 4, Nevadaville
　Proceedings 1870, pg 20 (1870 Sept 28), Nevada Lodge No. 4, Nevadaville
　Proceedings 1871, pg 18 (1871 Sept 27), Nevada Lodge No. 4, Bald Mountain
　Proceedings 1872, pg 19 (1872 Sept 24), Nevada Lodge No. 4, Bald Mountain, Dimitted

Rutherford, Samuel H
　Proceedings 1876, pg 42 (1876 Sept 20), Doric Lodge No. 25, Fairplay, Fellow Craft

Ruthven, E R
　Proceedings 1871, pg 31 (1871 Sept 27), Occidental Lodge U D, Greeley
　Proceedings 1872, pg 34 (1872 Sept 24), Occidental Lodge No. 20, Greeley, Apprentice
　Proceedings 1873, pg 50 (1873 Oct 1), Occidental Lodge No. 20, Greeley, Apprentice
　Proceedings 1874, pg 226 (1874 Sept 30), Occidental Lodge No. 20, Greeley, Apprentice
　Proceedings 1875, pg 87 (1875 Sept 22), Occidental Lodge No. 20, Greeley, Demitted

Rutledge, J K
　Proceedings 1861-1869, pg 77 (1862 Nov 4), Nevada Lodge No. 4, Nevadaville
　Proceedings 1861-1869, pg 77 (1862 Nov 4), Nevada Lodge No. 4, Nevadaville, Admitted
　Proceedings 1861-1869, pg 111 (1863 Nov 3), Nevada Lodge No. 4, Nevadaville
　Proceedings 1861-1869, pg 134 (1864 Nov 8), Chivington Lodge No. 6, Central City
　Proceedings 1861-1869, pg 153 (1866 Oct 1) Grant Tyler
　Proceedings 1861-1869, pg 161 (1866 Oct 2) Tyler
　Proceedings 1861-1869, pg 168 (1866 Oct 2), Chivington Lodge No. 6, Central City
　Proceedings 1861-1869, pg 182 (1867 Oct 7) warrant paid
　Proceedings 1861-1869, pg 193 (1867 Oct 8), Chivington Lodge No. 6, Central City
　Proceedings 1861-1869, pg 225 (1868 Oct 7), Chivington Lodge No. 6, Central City, Died
　Proceedings 1861-1869, pg 132 (1864 Nov 8), Nevada Lodge No. 4, Nevadaville, dimitted

Ruttencutter, Wm C
　Proceedings 1876, pg 35 (1876 Sept 20), Washington Lodge No. 12, Georgetown

Ryalls, Thomas
　Proceedings 1861-1869, pg 197 (1867 Oct 8), Columbia Lodge U D, Boulder
　Proceedings 1861-1869, pg 310 (1869 Sept 29), Columbia Lodge No. 14, Boulder City
　Proceedings 1870, pg 27 (1870 Sept 28), Columbia Lodge No. 14, Boulder City
　Proceedings 1871, pg 26 (1871 Sept 27), Columbia Lodge No. 14, Boulder City
　Proceedings 1872, pg 27 (1872 Sept 24), Columbia Lodge No. 14, Boulder
　Proceedings 1873, pg 44 (1873 Oct 1), Columbia Lodge No. 14, Boulder
　Proceedings 1874, pg 219 (1874 Sept 30), Columbia Lodge No. 14, Boulder, Boulder County
　Proceedings 1875, pg 83 (1875 Sept 22), Columbia Lodge No. 14, Boulder, Stricken from the rolls

S

Sackett, S G
Proceedings 1875, pg 81 (1875 Sept 22), Washington Lodge No. 12, Georgetown

Sackett, Sherman G
Proceedings 1876, pg 35 (1876 Sept 20), Washington Lodge No. 12, Georgetown
Proceedings 1876, pg 50 (1876 Sept 20), Washington Lodge No. 12, Georgetown

Safendorf, A
Proceedings 1861-1869, pg 137 (1865 Nov 6) Senior Grand Warden
Proceedings 1861-1869, pg 141 (1865 Nov 7) motion
Proceedings 1861-1869, pg 144 (1865 Nov 7) Grand Marshal
Proceedings 1861-1869, pg 161 (1866 Oct 2) Deputy Grand Master
Proceedings 1861-1869, pg 163 (1866 Oct 2) committee

Sagendorf
Proceedings 1861-1869, pg 85 (1863 May 6) Denver Lodge No. 5
Proceedings 1861-1869, pg 161 (1866 Oct 2) motion
Proceedings 1861-1869, pg 163 (1866 Oct 2) motion
Proceedings 1861-1869, pg 177 (1867 Oct 7) committee
Proceedings 1861-1869, pg 184 (1867 Oct 7) motion
Proceedings 1861-1869, pg 189 (1867 Oct 8) motion
Proceedings 1861-1869, pg 190 (1867 Oct 8) committee
Proceedings 1861-1869, pg 202 (1868 Oct 6) committee
Proceedings 1861-1869, pg 214 (1868 Oct 6) resolution
Proceedings 1861-1869, pg 217 (1868 Oct 7) motion
Proceedings 1876, pg 25 (1876 Sept 20) resolution

Sagendorf, A
Proceedings 1861-1869, pg 80 (1863 May 6) Denver Lodge No. 5
Proceedings 1861-1869, pg 94 (1863 Apr 17) Denver Lodge No. 5
Proceedings 1861-1869, pg 95 (1863 Apr 17) donated their per diem to the Grand Lodge
Proceedings 1861-1869, pg 112 (1863 Nov 3) Denver Lodge No. 5
Proceedings 1861-1869, pg 133 (1864 Nov 8) Denver Lodge No. 5
Proceedings 1861-1869, pg 144 (1865 Nov 7) Senior Grand Warden
Proceedings 1861-1869, pg 159 (1866 Oct 1) warrant
Proceedings 1861-1869, pg 160 (1866 Oct 2) Denver Lodge No. 5
Proceedings 1861-1869, pg 167 (1866 Oct 2) Denver Lodge No. 5
Proceedings 1861-1869, pg 176 (1867 Oct 7) committee
Proceedings 1861-1869, pg 176 (1867 Oct 7) Deputy Grand Master
Proceedings 1861-1869, pg 176 (1867 Oct 7) committee
Proceedings 1861-1869, pg 180 (1867 Oct 7) committee
Proceedings 1861-1869, pg 186 (1867 Oct 8) Deputy Grand Master
Proceedings 1861-1869, pg 189 (1867 Oct 8) committee
Proceedings 1861-1869, pg 192 (1867 Oct 8) Denver Lodge No. 5
Proceedings 1861-1869, pg 201 (1868 Oct 6) Deputy Grand Master
Proceedings 1861-1869, pg 202 (1868 Oct 6) Denver Lodge No. 5
Proceedings 1861-1869, pg 202 (1868 Oct 6) Past Grand Master
Proceedings 1861-1869, pg 212 (1868 Oct 6) warrant paid
Proceedings 1861-1869, pg 215 (1868 Oct 6) committee
Proceedings 1861-1869, pg 216 (1868 Oct 6) committee
Proceedings 1861-1869, pg 219 (1868 Oct 7) mileage allowed
Proceedings 1861-1869, pg 223 (1868 Oct 7) Denver Lodge No. 5
Proceedings 1861-1869, pg 305 (1869 Sept 29) Denver Lodge No. 5
Proceedings 1861-1869, pg 315 (1869 Sept 29) Deputy Grand Master, 1868
Proceedings 1861-1869, pg 315 (1869 Sept 29) Senior Grand Warden, 1864
Proceedings 1861-1869, pg 315 (1869 Sept 29) Deputy Grand Master, 1866
Proceedings 1870, pg 13 (1870 Sept 27) committee
Proceedings 1870, pg 32 (1870 Sept 28) Deputy Grand Master, 1868
Proceedings 1870, pg 32 (1870 Sept 28) Deputy Grand Master, 1866
Proceedings 1870, pg 32 (1870 Sept 28) Senior Grand Warden, 1864
Proceedings 1871, pg cover (1871 Sept 27) Past Deputy Grand Master, Denver
Proceedings 1871, pg 16 (1871 Sept 27) Committee
Proceedings 1871, pg 19 (1871 Sept 27) Denver Lodge No. 5
Proceedings 1871, pg 34 (1871 Sept 27) Deputy Grand Master, 1868
Proceedings 1871, pg 34 (1871 Sept 27) Deputy Grand Master, 1866
Proceedings 1871, pg 34 (1871 Sept 27) Senior Grand Warden, 1864
Proceedings 1872, pg 16 (1872 Sept 24) committee
Proceedings 1872, pg 19 (1872 Sept 24), Denver Lodge No. 5, Denver
Proceedings 1872, pg 42 (1872 Sept 24) Senior Grand Warden, 1864
Proceedings 1872, pg 42 (1872 Sept 24) Deputy Grand Master, 1866
Proceedings 1872, pg 42 (1872 Sept 24) Deputy Grand Master, 1868
Proceedings 1873, pg 58 (1873 Oct 1) Deputy Grand Master, 1868, Dropped from the Rolls
Proceedings 1873, pg 58 (1873 Oct 1) Senior Grand Warden, 1864, Dropped from the Rolls
Proceedings 1873, pg 58 (1873 Oct 1) Deputy Grand Master, 1866, Dropped from the Rolls

Sagendorf, A J
Proceedings 1861-1869, pg 81 (1863 Apr 18) Denver Lodge No. 5

Colorado's Territorial Masons

Sagendorf, Andrew
- Proceedings 1861-1869, pg 77 (1862 Nov 4) Denver Lodge No. 5
- Proceedings 1861-1869, pg 118 (1864 Nov 8) Denver Lodge No. 5, Senior Grand Warden
- Proceedings 1861-1869, pg 136 (1865 Nov 6) Senior Grand Warden
- Proceedings 1861-1869, pg 140 (1865 Nov 6) motion
- Proceedings 1861-1869, pg 145 (1865 Nov 7) committee
- Proceedings 1861-1869, pg 159 (1866 Oct 1) Grand Marshal
- Proceedings 1861-1869, pg 175 (1867 Oct 7) Deputy Grand Master
- Proceedings 1861-1869, pg 215 (1868 Oct 6) Deputy Grand Master
- Proceedings 1870, pg 21 (1870 Sept 28), Denver Lodge No. 5, Denver
- Proceedings 1872, pg cover (1872 Sept 24) committee, Frankstown
- Proceedings 1873, pg 38 (1873 Oct 1), Denver Lodge No. 5, Denver, Striken from the rolls
- Proceedings 1874, pg 206 (1874 Sept 30) Senior Grand Warden, 1864, Stricken from roll
- Proceedings 1874, pg 206 (1874 Sept 30) Deputy Grand Master, 1868, Stricken from roll
- Proceedings 1874, pg 206 (1874 Sept 30) Deputy Grand Master, 1866, Stricken from roll
- Proceedings 1875, pg 76 (1875 Sept 22) Denver Lodge No. 5, Reinstated
- Proceedings 1875, pg 76 (1875 Sept 22) Denver Lodge No. 5, Demitted
- Proceedings 1875, pg 93 (1875 Sept 22) Senior Grand Warden, 1864, Demitted
- Proceedings 1875, pg 93 (1875 Sept 22) Deputy Grand Master, 1866, Demitted
- Proceedings 1875, pg 93 (1875 Sept 22) Deputy Grand Master, 1868, Demitted
- Proceedings 1876, pg 4 (1876 Sept 19) Past Deputy Grand Master
- Proceedings 1876, pg 4 (1876 Sept 19) Past Deputy Grand Master

Sagui, Jacob
- Proceedings 1861-1869, pg 253 (1867 June 14), Past Grand Master, Grand Lodge of Kansas, deceased on 14 June 1867

Salamon, Fred Z
- Proceedings 1872, pg 22 (1872 Sept 24), Union Lodge No. 7, Denver

Salomon, A Z
- Proceedings 1876, pg 40 (1876 Sept 20), Occidental Lodge No. 20, Greeley

Salomon, F Z
- Proceedings 1861-1869, pg 51 (1862 Nov 4) Grand Pursuivant
- Proceedings 1861-1869, pg 79 (1863 May 6) Grand Pursuivant
- Proceedings 1861-1869, pg 81 (1863 Apr 18) Denver Lodge No. 5
- Proceedings 1861-1869, pg 94 (1863 Apr 17) Grand Pursuivant
- Proceedings 1861-1869, pg 95 (1863 Apr 17) donated their per diem to the Grand Lodge
- Proceedings 1861-1869, pg 151 (1865 Nov 7), Chivington Lodge No. 6, Central City
- Proceedings 1873, pg 40 (1873 Oct 1), Union Lodge No. 7, Denver
- Proceedings 1875, pg 78 (1875 Sept 22), Union Lodge No. 7, Denver
- Proceedings 1876, pg 33 (1876 Sept 20), Union Lodge No. 7, Denver

Salomon, Fred Z
- Proceedings 1861-1869, pg 77 (1862 Nov 4) Denver Lodge No. 5
- Proceedings 1861-1869, pg 112 (1863 Nov 3) Denver Lodge No. 5
- Proceedings 1861-1869, pg 133 (1864 Nov 8) Denver Lodge No. 5
- Proceedings 1861-1869, pg 169 (1866 Oct 2), Union Lodge No. 7, Denver
- Proceedings 1870, pg 23 (1870 Sept 28), Union Lodge No. 7, Denver
- Proceedings 1871, pg 22 (1871 Sept 27), Union Lodge No. 7, Denver

Salomon, H Z
- Proceedings 1861-1869, pg 47 (1862 May 3) Denver Lodge No. 5
- Proceedings 1861-1869, pg 77 (1862 Nov 4) Denver Lodge No. 5
- Proceedings 1861-1869, pg 133 (1864 Nov 8) Denver Lodge No. 5
- Proceedings 1870, pg 21 (1870 Sept 28), Denver Lodge No. 5, Denver
- Proceedings 1871, pg 19 (1871 Sept 27) Denver Lodge No. 5
- Proceedings 1872, pg 20 (1872 Sept 24), Denver Lodge No. 5, Denver
- Proceedings 1873, pg 37 (1873 Oct 1), Denver Lodge No. 5, Denver
- Proceedings 1874, pg 211 (1874 Sept 30), Denver Lodge No. 5, Denver
- Proceedings 1876, pg 31 (1876 Sept 20) Denver Lodge No. 5

Salsbury, James
- Proceedings 1874, pg 121 (1874 Sept 30) Grand Lodge of Rhode Island, deceased

Sampson, A J
- Proceedings 1876, pg 37 (1876 Sept 20), Mount Moriah Lodge No. 15, Canon City

Sanders, Addison
- Proceedings 1871, pg 19 (1871 Sept 27) Denver Lodge No. 5, Apprentice
- Proceedings 1872, pg 20 (1872 Sept 24), Denver Lodge No. 5, Denver, Fellowcraft

Sanders, George
- Proceedings 1874, pg 213 (1874 Sept 30), Central Lodge No. 6, Central

Proceedings 1875, pg 77 (1875 Sept 22), Central Lodge No. 6, Central City

Proceedings 1876, pg 51 (1876 Sept 20), Central Lodge No. 6, Central City, 1876 Mar 14

Sanders, J G
Proceedings 1861-1869, pg 152 (1865 Nov 7), Helena City Lodge U D, Helena City, Montana Territory, Fellowcraft

Sanders, W F
Proceedings 1861-1869, pg 267 (1867 Jan 20), Grand Secretary, Grand Lodge of Montana

Proceedings 1870, pg 88 (1868 Oct 5) Grand Secretary, Grand Lodge of Montana

Proceedings 1870, pg 89 (1868 Oct 5) Grand Master, Grand Lodge of Montana

Proceedings 1870, pg 89 (1869 Oct 4) Grand Master, Grand Lodge of Montana,

Sanderson
Proceedings 1870, pg 76 (1789 Nov 9) African Lodge at Boston, deceased

Sanderson, Thomas
Proceedings 1861-1869, pg 334 (1784 Sept 29) African Lodge No. 459

Proceedings 1870, pg 72 (1784 Sept 29) African Lodge at Boston

Proceedings 1870, pg 73 (1784 Sept 29) African Lodge at Boston

Proceedings 1870, pg 77 (1784 Sept 29)

Sands, Isaac
Proceedings 1861-1869, pg 166 (1866 Oct 2), Nevada Lodge No. 4, Nevadaville

Proceedings 1861-1869, pg 191 (1867 Oct 8), Nevada Lodge No. 4, Nevadaville

Proceedings 1861-1869, pg 222 (1868 Oct 7), Nevada Lodge No. 4, Nevadaville

Proceedings 1861-1869, pg 304 (1869 Sept 29), Nevada Lodge No. 4, Nevadaville

Proceedings 1870, pg 20 (1870 Sept 28), Nevada Lodge No. 4, Nevadaville

Proceedings 1871, pg 18 (1871 Sept 27), Nevada Lodge No. 4, Bald Mountain

Proceedings 1872, pg 18 (1872 Sept 24), Nevada Lodge No. 4, Bald Mountain

Proceedings 1873, pg 36 (1873 Oct 1), Nevada Lodge No. 4, Nevada

Proceedings 1874, pg 211 (1874 Sept 30), Nevada Lodge No. 4, Bald Mountain, Gilpin County, Stricken from the rolls,

Sanford
Proceedings 1870, pg 59 (1870 June 7) Grand Lodge of Iowa

Sanford, B L
Proceedings 1861-1869, pg 36 (1861 Dec 10), Rocky Mountain Lodge No. 3, Gold Hill

Sanford, B N
Proceedings 1861-1869, pg 43 (1861 Dec 10), Rocky Mountain Lodge No. 3, Gold Hill

Sanford, George R
Proceedings 1876, pg 24 (1876 Sept 20), King Solomon Lodge No. 30, West Las Animas

Proceedings 1876, pg 45 (1876 Sept 20), King Solomon Lodge U D, West Las Animas

Sarter, A
Proceedings 1876, pg 38 (1876 Sept 20), Mount Moriah Lodge No. 15, Canon City

Sarton, Augustus
Proceedings 1871, pg 26 (1871 Sept 27), Mount Moriah Lodge No. 15, Canon City

Sartor, A
Proceedings 1861-1869, pg 311 (1869 Sept 29), Mount Moriah Lodge No. 15, Canon City

Proceedings 1870, pg 28 (1870 Sept 28), Mount Moriah Lodge No. 15, Canon City

Sartor, Aug
Proceedings 1861-1869, pg 229 (1868 Oct 7), Canon Lodge U D, Canon City

Sartor, August
Proceedings 1874, pg 220 (1874 Sept 30), Mount Moriah Lodge No. 15, Canon City

Sartor, Augustus
Proceedings 1872, pg 29 (1872 Sept 24), Mount Moriah Lodge No. 15, Canon City

Saunders, Samuel H
Proceedings 1870, pg 87 (1869 Oct 11) Grand Lodge of Missouri

Saville, J J
Proceedings 1861-1869, pg 77 (1862 Nov 4) Denver Lodge No. 5

Proceedings 1861-1869, pg 133 (1864 Nov 8) Denver Lodge No. 5

Proceedings 1861-1869, pg 149 (1865 Nov 7), Nevada Lodge No. 4, Nevadaville

Proceedings 1861-1869, pg 167 (1866 Oct 2) Denver Lodge No. 5

Proceedings 1861-1869, pg 193 (1867 Oct 8) Denver Lodge No. 5

Proceedings 1861-1869, pg 223 (1868 Oct 7) Denver Lodge No. 5

Proceedings 1870, pg 21 (1870 Sept 28), Denver Lodge No. 5, Denver

Sawdy, Edgar
Proceedings 1874, pg 219 (1874 Sept 30), Columbia Lodge No. 14, Boulder, Boulder County

Proceedings 1875, pg 83 (1875 Sept 22), Columbia Lodge No. 14, Boulder

Proceedings 1876, pg 37 (1876 Sept 20), Columbia Lodge No. 14, Boulder

Sawin, F O
Proceedings 1861-1869, pg 165 (1866 Oct 2) Golden City Lodge No. 1

Proceedings 1861-1869, pg 176 (1867 Oct 7) Golden City Lodge No. 1

Proceedings 1861-1869, pg 221 (1868 Oct 7) Golden City Lodge No. 1

Colorado's Territorial Masons

Sawin, F O, cont.
Proceedings 1861-1869, pg 303 (1869 Sept 29) Golden City Lodge No. 1
Proceedings 1870, pg 19 (1870 Sept 28), Golden City Lodge No. 1, Golden City
Proceedings 1871, pg 17 (1871 Sept 27), Golden City Lodge No. 1, Golden City
Proceedings 1872, pg 18 (1872 Sept 24), Golden City Lodge No. 1, Golden City, Stricken from the Roll

Sawin, Frank O
Proceedings 1861-1869, pg 191 (1867 Oct 8) Golden City Lodge No. 1

Sawin, M L
Proceedings 1861-1869, pg 191 (1867 Oct 8) Golden City Lodge No. 1
Proceedings 1861-1869, pg 221 (1868 Oct 7) Golden City Lodge No. 1
Proceedings 1861-1869, pg 303 (1869 Sept 29) Golden City Lodge No. 1
Proceedings 1870, pg 19 (1870 Sept 28), Golden City Lodge No. 1, Golden City
Proceedings 1871, pg 17 (1871 Sept 27), Golden City Lodge No. 1, Golden City
Proceedings 1872, pg 17 (1872 Sept 24), Golden City Lodge No. 1, Golden City
Proceedings 1873, pg 35 (1873 Oct 1), Golden City Lodge No. 1, Golden City
Proceedings 1874, pg 209 (1874 Sept 30), Golden City Lodge No. 1, Golden City
Proceedings 1875, pg 74 (1875 Sept 22) Golden City Lodge No. 1, Stricken from the rolls

Sawtell, W L
Proceedings 1861-1869, pg 111 (1863 Nov 3), Nevada Lodge No. 4, Nevadaville
Proceedings 1861-1869, pg 132 (1864 Nov 8), Nevada Lodge No. 4, Nevadaville
Proceedings 1861-1869, pg 148 (1865 Nov 7), Nevada Lodge No. 4, Nevadaville
Proceedings 1861-1869, pg 151 (1865 Nov 7), Empire Lodge U D, Empire City
Proceedings 1875, pg 88 (1875 Sept 22), Weston Lodge No. 22, Littleton

Sawtell, W S
Proceedings 1861-1869, pg 166 (1866 Oct 2), Nevada Lodge No. 4, Nevadaville, dimitted

Sawtell, William
Proceedings 1873, pg 51 (1873 Oct 1), Weston Lodge No. 22, Littleton
Proceedings 1874, pg 226 (1874 Sept 30), Weston Lodge No. 22, Littleton

Sawtell, William L
Proceedings 1876, pg 41 (1876 Sept 20), Weston Lodge No. 22, Littleton

Sawtell, Wm I
Proceedings 1872, pg 23 (1872 Sept 24), Empire Lodge No. 8, Empire

Sawtell, Wm L
Proceedings 1861-1869, pg 77 (1862 Nov 4), Nevada Lodge No. 4, Nevadaville
Proceedings 1861-1869, pg 170 (1866 Oct 2), Empire Lodge No. 8, Empire City
Proceedings 1861-1869, pg 195 (1867 Oct 8), Empire Lodge No. 8, Empire City
Proceedings 1861-1869, pg 226 (1868 Oct 7), Empire Lodge No. 8, Empire City
Proceedings 1861-1869, pg 308 (1869 Sept 29), Empire Lodge No. 8, Empire City
Proceedings 1870, pg 24 (1870 Sept 28), Empire Lodge No. 8, Empire
Proceedings 1872, pg 34 (1872 Sept 24), Weston Lodge No. 22, Littleton
Proceedings 1873, pg 41 (1873 Oct 1), Empire Lodge No. 8, Empire
Proceedings 1874, pg 215 (1874 Sept 30), Empire Lodge No. 8, Empire, Demitted

Sawyer, H F
Proceedings 1861-1869, pg 168 (1866 Oct 2), Chivington Lodge No. 6, Central City
Proceedings 1861-1869, pg 193 (1867 Oct 8), Chivington Lodge No. 6, Central City
Proceedings 1861-1869, pg 224 (1868 Oct 7), Chivington Lodge No. 6, Central City
Proceedings 1870, pg 22 (1870 Sept 28), Central Lodge No. 6, Central City
Proceedings 1871, pg 21 (1871 Sept 27), Central Lodge No. 6, Central

Sawyer, H T
Proceedings 1861-1869, pg 306 (1869 Sept 29), Central Lodge No. 6, Central City

Sawyer, Hiram F
Proceedings 1872, pg 21 (1872 Sept 24), Denver Lodge No. 5, Denver
Proceedings 1873, pg 38 (1873 Oct 1), Central Lodge No. 6, Central City
Proceedings 1874, pg 213 (1874 Sept 30), Central Lodge No. 6, Central
Proceedings 1875, pg 77 (1875 Sept 22), Central Lodge No. 6, Central City
Proceedings 1876, pg 32 (1876 Sept 20), Central Lodge No. 6, Central City

Sawyer, J E
Proceedings 1861-1869, pg 76 (1862 Nov 4), Summit Lodge No. 2, Parkville
Proceedings 1861-1869, pg 110 (1863 Nov 3), Summit Lodge No. 2, Parkville
Proceedings 1861-1869, pg 132 (1864 Nov 8) Golden City Lodge No. 1

Saxton, John
Proceedings 1861-1869, pg 191 (1867 Oct 8) Golden City Lodge No. 1

Saxton, John M
Proceedings 1861-1869, pg 42 (1861 Dec 10) Golden City Lodge No. 1

Sayer, Alfred
   Proceedings 1861-1869, pg 307 (1869 Sept 29), Union Lodge No. 7, Denver
   Proceedings 1872, pg 22 (1872 Sept 24), Union Lodge No. 7, Denver

Sayer, Daniel
   Proceedings 1875, pg 24 (1875 Sept 21) Grand Lodge of Alabama
   Proceedings 1875, pg 96 (1875 Sept 22) Grand Lodge of Alabama, Montgomery
   Proceedings 1876, pg 54 (1876 Sept 20) Grand Lodge of Alabama, Montgomery,

Sayr
   Proceedings 1861-1869, pg 206 (1868 Oct 6) motion
   Proceedings 1861-1869, pg 214 (1868 Oct 6) resolution
   Proceedings 1861-1869, pg 215 (1868 Oct 6) Teller
   Proceedings 1861-1869, pg 289 (1869 Sept 28) committee
   Proceedings 1861-1869, pg 292 (1869 Sept 28) resolution
   Proceedings 1861-1869, pg 297 (1869 Sept 28) committee
   Proceedings 1861-1869, pg 297 (1869 Sept 28) Teller
   Proceedings 1870, pg 4 (1870 Sept 27) Junior Grand Warden
   Proceedings 1870, pg 9 (1870 Sept 27) committee

Sayr, Hal
   Proceedings 1861-1869, pg 134 (1864 Nov 8), Chivington Lodge No. 6, Central City
   Proceedings 1861-1869, pg 150 (1865 Nov 7), Chivington Lodge No. 6, Central City
   Proceedings 1861-1869, pg 168 (1866 Oct 2), Chivington Lodge No. 6, Central City
   Proceedings 1861-1869, pg 190 (1867 Oct 8) Grand Marshal
   Proceedings 1861-1869, pg 193 (1867 Oct 8), Chivington Lodge No. 6, Central City
   Proceedings 1861-1869, pg 203 (1868 Oct 6) Grand Marshal
   Proceedings 1861-1869, pg 220 (1868 Oct 7) Grand Marshal
   Proceedings 1861-1869, pg 220 (1868 Oct 7) committee
   Proceedings 1861-1869, pg 224 (1868 Oct 7), Chivington Lodge No. 6, Central City
   Proceedings 1861-1869, pg 288 (1869 Sept 28), Central Lodge No. 6, Central City
   Proceedings 1861-1869, pg 298 (1869 Sept 28) Junior Grand Warden
   Proceedings 1861-1869, pg 301 (1869 Sept 29) committee
   Proceedings 1861-1869, pg 301 (1869 Sept 29), Central Lodge No. 6, Central City
   Proceedings 1861-1869, pg 306 (1869 Sept 29), Central Lodge No. 6, Central City
   Proceedings 1861-1869, pg 315 (1869 Sept 29) Junior Grand Warden, 1869
   Proceedings 1861-1869, pg 349 (1869 Sept 29) Committee on Foreign Correspondence
   Proceedings 1870, pg 3 (1870 Sept 27) Junior Grand Warden
   Proceedings 1870, pg 4 (1870 Sept 27) committee
   Proceedings 1870, pg 4 (1870 Sept 27) Junior Grand Warden
   Proceedings 1870, pg 16 (1870 Sept 28) Junior Grand Warden
   Proceedings 1870, pg 17 (1870 Sept 28) committee
   Proceedings 1870, pg 22 (1870 Sept 28), Central Lodge No. 6, Central City
   Proceedings 1870, pg 32 (1870 Sept 28) Junior Grand Warden, 1869
   Proceedings 1871, pg 20 (1871 Sept 27), Central Lodge No. 6, Central
   Proceedings 1871, pg 34 (1871 Sept 27) Junior Grand Warden, 1869
   Proceedings 1872, pg 21 (1872 Sept 24), Denver Lodge No. 5, Denver
   Proceedings 1872, pg 42 (1872 Sept 24) Junior Grand Warden, 1869
   Proceedings 1873, pg 38 (1873 Oct 1), Central Lodge No. 6, Central City
   Proceedings 1873, pg 58 (1873 Oct 1) Junior Grand Warden, 1869
   Proceedings 1874, pg 206 (1874 Sept 30) Junior Grand Warden, 1869
   Proceedings 1874, pg 212 (1874 Sept 30), Central Lodge No. 6, Central
   Proceedings 1875, pg 76 (1875 Sept 22), Central Lodge No. 6, Central City
   Proceedings 1875, pg 93 (1875 Sept 22) Junior Grand Warden, 1869
   Proceedings 1876, pg 31 (1876 Sept 20), Central Lodge No. 6, Central City

Sayre
   Proceedings 1861-1869, pg 213 (1868 Oct 6) Grand Secretary of Alabama

Sayre, Alfred
   Proceedings 1861-1869, pg 151 (1865 Nov 7), Chivington Lodge No. 6, Central City
   Proceedings 1861-1869, pg 169 (1866 Oct 2), Union Lodge No. 7, Denver
   Proceedings 1861-1869, pg 195 (1867 Oct 8), Union Lodge No. 7, Denver
   Proceedings 1861-1869, pg 225 (1868 Oct 7), Union Lodge No. 7, Denver
   Proceedings 1870, pg 23 (1870 Sept 28), Union Lodge No. 7, Denver
   Proceedings 1871, pg 22 (1871 Sept 27), Union Lodge No. 7, Denver
   Proceedings 1873, pg 40 (1873 Oct 1), Union Lodge No. 7, Denver
   Proceedings 1874, pg 214 (1874 Sept 30), Union Lodge No. 7, Denver
   Proceedings 1875, pg 78 (1875 Sept 22), Union Lodge No. 7, Denver
   Proceedings 1876, pg 33 (1876 Sept 20), Union Lodge No. 7, Denver

Sayre, Daniel
   Proceedings 1861-1869, pg 239 (1867 Dec 2) Grand Secretary of Alabama
   Proceedings 1861-1869, pg 316 (1869 Sept 29) Grand Lodge of Alabama

Sayre, Daniel, cont.
  Proceedings 1861-1869, pg 322 (1868 Dec 7) Grand Secretary, Grand Lodge of Alabama
  Proceedings 1870, pg 34 (1870 Sept 28) Grand Secretary, Grand Lodge of Alabama
  Proceedings 1870, pg 37 (1869 Dec 6) Grand Secretary, Grand Lodge of Alabama
  Proceedings 1870, pg 40 (1869 Dec 6) Grand Secretary, Grand Lodge of Alabama
  Proceedings 1871, pg 35 (1871 Sept 27) Grand Secretary, Grand Lodge of Alabama
  Proceedings 1872, pg 43 (1872 Sept 24) Montgomery, Grand Lodge of Alabama
  Proceedings 1872, pg 53 (1872 Sept 24) Grand Lodge of Alabama
  Proceedings 1873, pg 60 (1873 Oct 1) Grand Lodge of Alabama, Montgomery
  Proceedings 1874, pg 43 (1874 Sept 30) Grand Lodge of Alabama
  Proceedings 1874, pg 204 (1874 Sept 30) Grand Lodge of Alabama, Montgomery

Schaffer, B F
  Proceedings 1861-1869, pg 222 (1868 Oct 7), Nevada Lodge No. 4, Nevadaville

Scharnhorst, Charles J
  Proceedings 1874, pg 217 (1874 Sept 30), Washington Lodge No. 12, Georgetown
  Proceedings 1875, pg 81 (1875 Sept 22), Washington Lodge No. 12, Georgetown, Stricken from the rolls

Scharnhorst, Chas J
  Proceedings 1872, pg 26 (1872 Sept 24), Washington Lodge No. 12, Georgetown
  Proceedings 1873, pg 43 (1873 Oct 1), Washington Lodge No. 12, Georgetown

Scheidler, Jacob
  Proceedings 1874, pg 218 (1874 Sept 30), El Paso Lodge No. 13, Colorado Springs

Scheidler, Thomas
  Proceedings 1873, pg 43 (1873 Oct 1), El Paso Lodge No. 13, Colorado City
  Proceedings 1874, pg 218 (1874 Sept 30), El Paso Lodge No. 13, Colorado Springs

Schell, Charles G
  Proceedings 1872, pg 20 (1872 Sept 24), Denver Lodge No. 5, Denver, Dimitted

Schenck, Philip
  Proceedings 1861-1869, pg 152 (1865 Nov 7), Montana Lodge U D, Virginia City, Montana Territory, Apprentice

Schenofscky, Jules C A
  Proceedings 1874, pg 221 (1874 Sept 30), Cheyenne Lodge No. 16, Cheyenne, Wyoming Territory, Apprentice
  Proceedings 1872, pg 30 (1872 Sept 24), Cheyenne Lodge No. 16, Cheyenne, Wyoming Territory, Apprentice
  Proceedings 1873, pg 46 (1873 Oct 1), Cheyenne Lodge No. 16, Cheyenne, Wyoming Territory, Apprentice

Schimer, Fred
  Proceedings 1870, pg 21 (1870 Sept 28), Denver Lodge No. 5, Denver

Schinner, Adolph
  Proceedings 1870, pg 21 (1870 Sept 28), Denver Lodge No. 5, Denver
  Proceedings 1871, pg 19 (1871 Sept 27) Denver Lodge No. 5
  Proceedings 1872, pg 20 (1872 Sept 24), Denver Lodge No. 5, Denver
  Proceedings 1873, pg 37 (1873 Oct 1), Denver Lodge No. 5, Denver
  Proceedings 1874, pg 211 (1874 Sept 30), Denver Lodge No. 5, Denver
  Proceedings 1875, pg 75 (1875 Sept 22) Denver Lodge No. 5
  Proceedings 1876, pg 31 (1876 Sept 20) Denver Lodge No. 5
  Proceedings 1861-1869, pg 193 (1867 Oct 8) Denver Lodge No. 5

Schirmer, F
  Proceedings 1861-1869, pg 230 (1868 Oct 7), Germania Lodge U D, Denver

Schirmer, Fred
  Proceedings 1861-1869, pg 193 (1867 Oct 8) Denver Lodge No. 5
  Proceedings 1861-1869, pg 223 (1868 Oct 7) Denver Lodge No. 5
  Proceedings 1872, pg 20 (1872 Sept 24), Denver Lodge No. 5, Denver

Schirmer, Fred J
  Proceedings 1873, pg 37 (1873 Oct 1), Denver Lodge No. 5, Denver
  Proceedings 1874, pg 211 (1874 Sept 30), Denver Lodge No. 5, Denver

Schirmer, Fred'k
  Proceedings 1871, pg 19 (1871 Sept 27) Denver Lodge No. 5

Schirmer, J F L
  Proceedings 1875, pg 75 (1875 Sept 22) Denver Lodge No. 5
  Proceedings 1876, pg 31 (1876 Sept 20) Denver Lodge No. 5

Schirmer, Jacob F L
  Colorado University Cornerstone Laying, pg 4 (1875 Sept 20) presented the Trade Dollar

Schnider, Charles
  Proceedings 1874, pg 120 (1874 Sept 30) Grand Lodge of Pennsylvania, deceased

Schnofskey, Jules C A
  Proceedings 1870, pg 29 (1870 Sept 28), Cheyenne Lodge No. 16, Cheyenne, Wyoming Territory, Apprentice
  Proceedings 1871, pg 28 (1871 Sept 27), Cheyenne Lodge No. 16, Cheyenne, Wyoming Territory, Apprentice

Schonecker, A
   Proceedings 1861-1869, pg 113 (1863 Nov 3), Chivington Lodge No. 6, Central City, Apprentice
   Proceedings 1861-1869, pg 134 (1864 Nov 8), Chivington Lodge No. 6, Central City, Apprentice
   Proceedings 1861-1869, pg 150 (1865 Nov 7), Chivington Lodge No. 6, Central City, Apprentice
   Proceedings 1861-1869, pg 169 (1866 Oct 2), Chivington Lodge No. 6, Central City, Apprentice
   Proceedings 1861-1869, pg 194 (1867 Oct 8), Chivington Lodge No. 6, Central City, Apprentice
   Proceedings 1861-1869, pg 225 (1868 Oct 7), Chivington Lodge No. 6, Central City, Apprentice
   Proceedings 1861-1869, pg 307 (1869 Sept 29), Central Lodge No. 6, Central City, Apprentice
   Proceedings 1870, pg 22 (1870 Sept 28), Central Lodge No. 6, Central City, Apprentice

Schonecker, Andrew
   Proceedings 1871, pg 21 (1871 Sept 27), Central Lodge No. 6, Central, Apprentice
   Proceedings 1874, pg 213 (1874 Sept 30), Central Lodge No. 6, Central, Apprentice
   Proceedings 1875, pg 77 (1875 Sept 22), Central Lodge No. 6, Central City, died
   Proceedings 1872, pg 21 (1872 Sept 24), Denver Lodge No. 5, Denver, Apprentice
   Proceedings 1874, pg 221 (1874 Sept 30), Cheyenne Lodge No. 16, Cheyenne, Wyoming Territory, Apprentice
   Proceedings 1861-1869, pg 312 (1869 Sept 29), Cheyenne Lodge No. 16, Cheyenne, Apprentice
   Proceedings 1870, pg 29 (1870 Sept 28), Cheyenne Lodge No. 16, Cheyenne, Wyoming Territory, Apprentice
   Proceedings 1871, pg 28 (1871 Sept 27), Cheyenne Lodge No. 16, Cheyenne, Wyoming Territory, Apprentice
   Proceedings 1872, pg 30 (1872 Sept 24), Cheyenne Lodge No. 16, Cheyenne, Wyoming Territory, Apprentice
   Proceedings 1873, pg 46 (1873 Oct 1), Cheyenne Lodge No. 16, Cheyenne, Wyoming Territory, Apprentice

Schornhorst, Charles
   Proceedings 1871, pg 24 (1871 Sept 27), Washington Lodge No. 12, Georgetown

Schornhorst, Chas J
   Proceedings 1870, pg 26 (1870 Sept 28), Washington Lodge No. 12, Georgetown

Schram, G
   Proceedings 1861-1869, pg 168 (1866 Oct 2), Chivington Lodge No. 6, Central City

Schram, Geo
   Proceedings 1861-1869, pg 113 (1863 Nov 3), Chivington Lodge No. 6, Central City
   Proceedings 1861-1869, pg 170 (1866 Oct 2), Black Hawk Lodge U D, Black Hawk
   Proceedings 1861-1869, pg 225 (1868 Oct 7), Chivington Lodge No. 6, Central City, Dimitted

Schram, George
   Proceedings 1861-1869, pg 78 (1862 Nov 4), Chivington Lodge No. 6, Central City
   Proceedings 1861-1869, pg 134 (1864 Nov 8), Chivington Lodge No. 6, Central City
   Proceedings 1861-1869, pg 150 (1865 Nov 7), Chivington Lodge No. 6, Central City
   Proceedings 1861-1869, pg 194 (1867 Oct 8), Chivington Lodge No. 6, Central City

Schriber, A J
   Proceedings 1874, pg 221 (1874 Sept 30), Cheyenne Lodge No. 16, Cheyenne, Wyoming Territory

Schrontz, Silas B
   Proceedings 1876, pg 45 (1876 Sept 20) South Pueblo Lodge U D

Schulze, Henry
   Proceedings 1875, pg 90 (1875 Sept 22), Huerfano Lodge U D, Walsenburg
   Proceedings 1876, pg 43 (1876 Sept 20), Huerfano Lodge No. 27, Walsenburg

Schuyler, Howard
   Proceedings 1870, pg 23 (1870 Sept 28), Union Lodge No. 7, Denver, Fellowcraft
   Proceedings 1871, pg 22 (1871 Sept 27), Union Lodge No. 7, Denver
   Proceedings 1872, pg 23 (1872 Sept 24), Union Lodge No. 7, Denver
   Proceedings 1873, pg 40 (1873 Oct 1), Union Lodge No. 7, Denver

Schwartzenberger, Lipman
   Proceedings 1873, pg 57 (1873 Oct 1), Columbia Lodge No. 14, Boulder

Schwaub, Samuel
   Proceedings 1861-1869, pg 149 (1865 Nov 7), Nevada Lodge No. 4, Nevadaville
   Proceedings 1861-1869, pg 167 (1866 Oct 2) Denver Lodge No. 5, dimitted

Schweder, J H
   Proceedings 1870, pg 22 (1870 Sept 28), Central Lodge No. 6, Central City
   Proceedings 1871, pg 20 (1871 Sept 27), Central Lodge No. 6, Central
   Proceedings 1872, pg 21 (1872 Sept 24), Denver Lodge No. 5, Denver

Schweder, John H
   Proceedings 1861-1869, pg 306 (1869 Sept 29), Central Lodge No. 6, Central City
   Proceedings 1873, pg 38 (1873 Oct 1), Central Lodge No. 6, Central City
   Proceedings 1874, pg 213 (1874 Sept 30), Central Lodge No. 6, Central
   Proceedings 1875, pg 77 (1875 Sept 22), Central Lodge No. 6, Central City
   Proceedings 1876, pg 50 (1876 Sept 20), Central Lodge No. 6, Central City
   Proceedings 1876, pg 32 (1876 Sept 20), Central Lodge No. 6, Central City

Schworzenberger, L
   Proceedings 1872, pg 28 (1872 Sept 24), Columbia Lodge No. 14, Boulder

Colorado's Territorial Masons

Scoot, Captain
Proceedings 1870, pg 76 (1789 June 4)

Scott, F M
Proceedings 1876, pg 33 (1876 Sept 20), Union Lodge No. 7, Denver

Scott, F N B
Proceedings 1875, pg 86 (1875 Sept 22), Collins Lodge No. 19, Fort Collins
Proceedings 1876, pg 39 (1876 Sept 20), Collins Lodge No. 19, Fort Collins

Scott, Francis M
Proceedings 1861-1869, pg 170 (1866 Oct 2), Empire Lodge No. 8, Empire City
Proceedings 1861-1869, pg 195 (1867 Oct 8), Empire Lodge No. 8, Empire City
Proceedings 1861-1869, pg 226 (1868 Oct 7), Empire Lodge No. 8, Empire City, Dimitted

Scott, Geo
Proceedings 1870, pg 25 (1870 Sept 28), Black Hawk Lodge No. 11, Black Hawk
Proceedings 1872, pg 24 (1872 Sept 24), Black Hawk Lodge No. 11, Black Hawk

Scott, George
Proceedings 1861-1869, pg 309 (1869 Sept 29), Black Hawk Lodge No. 11, Black Hawk
Proceedings 1871, pg 23 (1871 Sept 27), Black Hawk Lodge No. 11, Black Hawk
Proceedings 1873, pg 42 (1873 Oct 1), Black Hawk Lodge No. 11, Black Hawk
Proceedings 1874, pg 216 (1874 Sept 30), Black Hawk Lodge No. 11, Black Hawk
Proceedings 1875, pg 80 (1875 Sept 22) Black Hawk Lodge No. 11
Proceedings 1876, pg 34 (1876 Sept 20) Black Hawk Lodge No. 11

Scott, J C Jr
Proceedings 1870, pg 8 (1870 Sept 27), Pride of the West Lodge No. 179, St Louis, MO
Proceedings 1870, pg 12 (1870 Sept 27), Pride of the West Lodge No. 179, St Louis, MO
Proceedings 1870, pg 12 (1870 Sept 27) expelled, Cheyenne Lodge No. 16, Cheyenne
Proceedings 1870, pg 29 (1870 Sept 28), Pride of the West Lodge No. 179, St Louis, MO, expelled

Scott, J S
Proceedings 1861-1869, pg 131 (1864 Nov 8) Golden City Lodge No. 1
Proceedings 1861-1869, pg 165 (1866 Oct 2) Golden City Lodge No. 1
Proceedings 1861-1869, pg 229 (1868 Oct 7), Cheyenne Lodge U D, Cheyenne, Dakota Territory

Scott, James
Proceedings 1861-1869, pg 207 (1868 Apr), Cheyenne Lodge U D, Cheyenne, Dakota Territory, Worshipful Master
Proceedings 1861-1869, pg 216 (1868 Oct 7) removed as Worshipful Master of Cheyenne
Proceedings 1861-1869, pg 288 (1869 Sept 28) Golden City Lodge No. 1
Proceedings 1861-1869, pg 303 (1869 Sept 29) Golden City Lodge No. 1
Proceedings 1870, pg 76 (1789 Nov 9) Captain

Scott, James B
Proceedings 1872, pg 43 (1872 Sept 24) New Orleans, Grand Lodge of Louisiana
Proceedings 1872, pg 68 (1872 Sept 24) Grand Lodge of Louisiana

Scott, James C
Proceedings 1861-1869, pg 191 (1867 Oct 8) Golden City Lodge No. 1
Proceedings 1872, pg 21 (1872 Sept 24), Denver Lodge No. 5, Denver
Proceedings 1873, pg 38 (1873 Oct 1), Central Lodge No. 6, Central City
Proceedings 1874, pg 213 (1874 Sept 30), Central Lodge No. 6, Central
Proceedings 1875, pg 77 (1875 Sept 22), Central Lodge No. 6, Central City
Proceedings 1876, pg 32 (1876 Sept 20), Central Lodge No. 6, Central City

Scott, James S
Proceedings 1861-1869, pg 147 (1865 Nov 7) Golden City Lodge No. 1
Proceedings 1861-1869, pg 221 (1868 Oct 7) Golden City Lodge No. 1
Proceedings 1861-1869, pg 312 (1869 Sept 29), Cheyenne Lodge No. 16, Cheyenne
Proceedings 1870, pg 19 (1870 Sept 28), Golden City Lodge No. 1, Golden City
Proceedings 1871, pg 17 (1871 Sept 27), Golden City Lodge No. 1, Golden City
Proceedings 1871, pg 17 (1871 Sept 27), Golden City Lodge No. 1, Golden City
Proceedings 1872, pg 17 (1872 Sept 24), Golden City Lodge No. 1, Golden City
Proceedings 1876, pg 29 (1876 Sept 20) Golden City Lodge No. 1

Scott, Jas S
Proceedings 1874, pg 209 (1874 Sept 30), Golden City Lodge No. 1, Golden City
Proceedings 1875, pg 73 (1875 Sept 22) Golden City Lodge No. 1

Scott, John
Proceedings 1870, pg 59 (1870 June 7) Grand Master, Grand Lodge of Iowa

Scott, Preston
Proceedings 1861-1869, pg 77 (1862 Nov 4), Nevada Lodge No. 4, Nevadaville
Proceedings 1861-1869, pg 111 (1863 Nov 3), Nevada Lodge No. 4, Nevadaville
Proceedings 1861-1869, pg 132 (1864 Nov 8), Nevada Lodge No. 4, Nevadaville
Proceedings 1861-1869, pg 148 (1865 Nov 7), Nevada Lodge No. 4, Nevadaville

Proceedings 1861-1869, pg 166 (1866 Oct 2), Nevada Lodge No. 4, Nevadaville

Proceedings 1861-1869, pg 192 (1867 Oct 8), Nevada Lodge No. 4, Nevadaville

Proceedings 1861-1869, pg 222 (1868 Oct 7), Nevada Lodge No. 4, Nevadaville

Proceedings 1861-1869, pg 304 (1869 Sept 29), Nevada Lodge No. 4, Nevadaville, died

Scott, Robert W

Proceedings 1873, pg 39 (1873 Oct 1), Central Lodge No. 6, Central City, Apprentice

Proceedings 1874, pg 213 (1874 Sept 30), Central Lodge No. 6, Central, Apprentice

Proceedings 1875, pg 77 (1875 Sept 22), Central Lodge No. 6, Central City, Apprentice

Proceedings 1876, pg 32 (1876 Sept 20), Central Lodge No. 6, Central City, Apprentice

Scott, Samuel

Proceedings 1874, pg 219 (1874 Sept 30), Columbia Lodge No. 14, Boulder, Boulder County

Proceedings 1875, pg 83 (1875 Sept 22), Columbia Lodge No. 14, Boulder

Proceedings 1876, pg 37 (1876 Sept 20), Columbia Lodge No. 14, Boulder

Scott, Walter

Proceedings 1861-1869, pg 192 (1867 Oct 8), Nevada Lodge No. 4, Nevadaville

Proceedings 1861-1869, pg 222 (1868 Oct 7), Nevada Lodge No. 4, Nevadaville

Proceedings 1861-1869, pg 304 (1869 Sept 29), Nevada Lodge No. 4, Nevadaville

Proceedings 1870, pg 20 (1870 Sept 28), Nevada Lodge No. 4, Nevadaville

Proceedings 1871, pg 18 (1871 Sept 27), Nevada Lodge No. 4, Bald Mountain

Proceedings 1872, pg 19 (1872 Sept 24), Nevada Lodge No. 4, Bald Mountain

Proceedings 1873, pg 36 (1873 Oct 1), Nevada Lodge No. 4, Nevada

Proceedings 1874, pg 210 (1874 Sept 30), Nevada Lodge No. 4, Bald Mountain, Gilpin County

Proceedings 1875, pg 74 (1875 Sept 22), Nevada Lodge No. 4, Nevada

Scotte, James S

Proceedings 1871, pg 30 (1871 Sept 27), Occidental Lodge U D, Greeley

Scriber, S J

Proceedings 1861-1869, pg 229 (1868 Oct 7), Cheyenne Lodge U D, Cheyenne, Dakota Territory

Proceedings 1861-1869, pg 312 (1869 Sept 29), Cheyenne Lodge No. 16, Cheyenne

Proceedings 1870, pg 29 (1870 Sept 28), Cheyenne Lodge No. 16, Cheyenne, Wyoming Territory

Proceedings 1871, pg 27 (1871 Sept 27), Cheyenne Lodge No. 16, Cheyenne, Wyoming Territory

Proceedings 1872, pg 29 (1872 Sept 24), Cheyenne Lodge No. 16, Cheyenne, Wyoming Territory

Proceedings 1873, pg 46 (1873 Oct 1), Cheyenne Lodge No. 16, Cheyenne, Wyoming Territory

Scudder, E

Proceedings 1861-1869, pg 305 (1869 Sept 29) Denver Lodge No. 5

Scudder, Edwin

Proceedings 1861-1869, pg 112 (1863 Nov 3) Denver Lodge No. 5, Fellowcraft

Proceedings 1861-1869, pg 133 (1864 Nov 8) Denver Lodge No. 5

Proceedings 1861-1869, pg 149 (1865 Nov 7), Nevada Lodge No. 4, Nevadaville

Proceedings 1861-1869, pg 167 (1866 Oct 2) Denver Lodge No. 5

Proceedings 1861-1869, pg 193 (1867 Oct 8) Denver Lodge No. 5

Proceedings 1861-1869, pg 223 (1868 Oct 7) Denver Lodge No. 5

Proceedings 1870, pg 21 (1870 Sept 28), Denver Lodge No. 5, Denver

Proceedings 1871, pg 19 (1871 Sept 27) Denver Lodge No. 5

Proceedings 1872, pg 20 (1872 Sept 24), Denver Lodge No. 5, Denver, died

Proceedings 1872, pg 39 (1872 Sept 24), Denver Lodge No. 5, Denver

Seabring, A F

Proceedings 1870, pg 28 (1870 Sept 28), Mount Moriah Lodge No. 15, Canon City, Apprentice

Seabring, A I

Proceedings 1861-1869, pg 311 (1869 Sept 29), Mount Moriah Lodge No. 15, Canon City, Fellowcraft

Seabring, A T

Proceedings 1861-1869, pg 229 (1868 Oct 7), Canon Lodge U D, Canon City, Apprentice

Proceedings 1871, pg 27 (1871 Sept 27), Mount Moriah Lodge No. 15, Canon City, Dimitted

Proceedings 1873, pg 47 (1873 Oct 1), Pueblo Lodge No. 17, Pueblo

Proceedings 1874, pg 222 (1874 Sept 30), Pueblo Lodge No. 17, Pueblo, Pueblo County

Proceedings 1875, pg 85 (1875 Sept 22) Pueblo Lodge No. 17

Proceedings 1875, pg 90 (1875 Sept 22), Huerfano Lodge U D, Walsenburg

Proceedings 1876, pg 43 (1876 Sept 20), Huerfano Lodge No. 27, Walsenburg

Proceedings 1876, pg 48 (1876 Sept 20) Pueblo Lodge No. 17, 1876 Feb 11

Seabury, A P

Proceedings 1861-1869, pg 170 (1866 Oct 2), Black Hawk Lodge U D, Black Hawk

Seaman, H C

Proceedings 1873, pg 43 (1873 Oct 1), Washington Lodge No. 12, Georgetown, Fellowcraft

Colorado's Territorial Masons

Seaman, Henry C
Proceedings 1874, pg 217 (1874 Sept 30), Washington Lodge No. 12, Georgetown, Demitted

Seaman, O A
Proceedings 1861-1869, pg 51 (1862 Nov 4) Grand Tyler

Sears, W F
Proceedings 1861-1869, pg 150 (1865 Nov 7), Chivington Lodge No. 6, Central City
Proceedings 1861-1869, pg 168 (1866 Oct 2), Chivington Lodge No. 6, Central City
Proceedings 1861-1869, pg 224 (1868 Oct 7), Chivington Lodge No. 6, Central City
Proceedings 1871, pg 21 (1871 Sept 27), Central Lodge No. 6, Central

Sears, William F
Proceedings 1861-1869, pg 306 (1869 Sept 29), Central Lodge No. 6, Central City
Proceedings 1875, pg 77 (1875 Sept 22), Central Lodge No. 6, Central City, Stricken from the rolls
Proceedings 1875, pg 77 (1875 Sept 22), Central Lodge No. 6, Central City
Proceedings 1875, pg 77 (1875 Sept 22), Central Lodge No. 6, Central City, Reinstated

Sears, Wm F
Proceedings 1861-1869, pg 190 (1867 Oct 8) Grand Tyler
Proceedings 1861-1869, pg 193 (1867 Oct 8), Chivington Lodge No. 6, Central City
Proceedings 1870, pg 22 (1870 Sept 28), Central Lodge No. 6, Central City
Proceedings 1872, pg 21 (1872 Sept 24), Denver Lodge No. 5, Denver
Proceedings 1873, pg 38 (1873 Oct 1), Central Lodge No. 6, Central City
Proceedings 1874, pg 213 (1874 Sept 30), Central Lodge No. 6, Central

Seaton, L R
Proceedings 1861-1869, pg 194 (1867 Oct 8), Chivington Lodge No. 6, Central City, Fellowcraft

Seaton, Lee R
Proceedings 1861-1869, pg 169 (1866 Oct 2), Chivington Lodge No. 6, Central City, Fellowcraft

Seaver, Chas L
Proceedings 1873, pg 46 (1873 Oct 1), Cheyenne Lodge No. 16, Cheyenne, Wyoming Territory

Secor, W W
Proceedings 1872, pg 35 (1872 Sept 24), St Vrain Lodge No. 23, Longmont, Fellowcraft
Proceedings 1874, pg 227 (1874 Sept 30), St Vrain No. 23, Longmont
Proceedings 1876, pg 41 (1876 Sept 20), St Vrain Lodge No. 23, Longmont

Secor, Wm W
Proceedings 1873, pg 51 (1873 Oct 1), St Vrain Lodge No. 23, Longmont

Sedman, Oscar A
Proceedings 1861-1869, pg 77 (1862 Nov 4) Denver Lodge No. 5
Proceedings 1861-1869, pg 112 (1863 Nov 3) Denver Lodge No. 5, dimitted

Seeley, J S
Proceedings 1872, pg 33 (1872 Sept 24), Occidental Lodge No. 20, Greeley
Proceedings 1873, pg 49 (1873 Oct 1), Occidental Lodge No. 20, Greeley

Seeley, Jos S
Proceedings 1874, pg 225 (1874 Sept 30), Occidental Lodge No. 20, Greeley

Seeley, Joseph S
Proceedings 1875, pg 87 (1875 Sept 22), Occidental Lodge No. 20, Greeley
Proceedings 1876, pg 40 (1876 Sept 20), Occidental Lodge No. 20, Greeley

Seely, R P
Proceedings 1861-1869, pg 152 (1865 Nov 7), Helena City Lodge U D, Helena City, Montana Territory

Sefton, H T
Proceedings 1875, pg 90 (1875 Sept 22), Huerfano Lodge U D, Walsenburg, Apprentice
Proceedings 1876, pg 43 (1876 Sept 20), Huerfano Lodge No. 27, Walsenburg, Apprentice

Segmund, Christ
Proceedings 1874, pg 227 (1874 Sept 30), St Vrain No. 23, Longmont

Sehrman, H C
Proceedings 1875, pg 87 (1875 Sept 22), Occidental Lodge No. 20, Greeley, Demitted

Seidell, James M
Proceedings 1874, pg 228 (1874 Sept 30), Doric Lodge U D, Fairplay

Seley, A H
Proceedings 1872, pg 32 (1872 Sept 24), Laramie Lodge No. 18, Laramie, Wyoming Territory
Proceedings 1874, pg 223 (1874 Sept 30), Laramie Lodge No. 18, Laramie City

Seley, A M
Proceedings 1871, pg 29 (1871 Sept 27), Laramie Lodge No. 18, Laramie, Wyoming Territory
Proceedings 1873, pg 48 (1873 Oct 1), Laramie Lodge No. 18, Laramie, Wyoming Territory

Selkirk, E A
Colorado University Cornerstone Laying, pg 5 (1875 Sept 20) presented the sealed envelope

Seville, J J
Proceedings 1861-1869, pg 305 (1869 Sept 29) Denver Lodge No. 5
Proceedings 1873, pg 38 (1873 Oct 1), Denver Lodge No. 5, Denver, Striken from the rolls

Sexton, J
Proceedings 1861-1869, pg 147 (1865 Nov 7) Golden City Lodge No. 1
Proceedings 1861-1869, pg 165 (1866 Oct 2) Golden City Lodge No. 1

Sexton, J M
Proceedings 1861-1869, pg 110 (1863 Nov 3) Golden City Lodge No. 1

Sexton, John
Proceedings 1861-1869, pg 131 (1864 Nov 8) Golden City Lodge No. 1
Proceedings 1861-1869, pg 221 (1868 Oct 7) Golden City Lodge No. 1
Proceedings 1861-1869, pg 303 (1869 Sept 29) Golden City Lodge No. 1

Seymour, James
Proceedings 1872, pg 43 (1872 Sept 24) St Catharines, Grand Lodge of Canada

Shackman, David
Proceedings 1861-1869, pg 230 (1868 Oct 7), Cheyenne Lodge U D, Cheyenne, Dakota Territory
Proceedings 1861-1869, pg 312 (1869 Sept 29), Cheyenne Lodge No. 16, Cheyenne
Proceedings 1870, pg 29 (1870 Sept 28), Cheyenne Lodge No. 16, Cheyenne, Wyoming Territory
Proceedings 1871, pg 27 (1871 Sept 27), Cheyenne Lodge No. 16, Cheyenne, Wyoming Territory
Proceedings 1872, pg 29 (1872 Sept 24), Cheyenne Lodge No. 16, Cheyenne, Wyoming Territory
Proceedings 1873, pg 46 (1873 Oct 1), Cheyenne Lodge No. 16, Cheyenne, Wyoming Territory
Proceedings 1874, pg 221 (1874 Sept 30), Cheyenne Lodge No. 16, Cheyenne, Wyoming Territory

Shaefer, Sam H
Proceedings 1861-1869, pg 191 (1867 Oct 8) Golden City Lodge No. 1

Shafer, B F
Proceedings 1871, pg 26 (1871 Sept 27), Mount Moriah Lodge No. 15, Canon City
Proceedings 1872, pg 6 (1872 Sept 24), Mount Moriah Lodge No. 15, Canon City
Proceedings 1872, pg 16 (1872 Sept 24), Mount Moriah Lodge No. 15, Canon City

Shafer, Sam F
Proceedings 1875, pg 74 (1875 Sept 22) Golden City Lodge No. 1, Stricken from the rolls

Shafer, Samuel F
Proceedings 1861-1869, pg 303 (1869 Sept 29) Golden City Lodge No. 1

Shaffer, B F
Proceedings 1861-1869, pg 77 (1862 Nov 4), Nevada Lodge No. 4, Nevadaville, Apprentice
Proceedings 1861-1869, pg 112 (1863 Nov 3), Nevada Lodge No. 4, Nevadaville, Apprentice
Proceedings 1861-1869, pg 132 (1864 Nov 8), Nevada Lodge No. 4, Nevadaville, Apprentice
Proceedings 1861-1869, pg 148 (1865 Nov 7), Nevada Lodge No. 4, Nevadaville
Proceedings 1861-1869, pg 166 (1866 Oct 2), Nevada Lodge No. 4, Nevadaville
Proceedings 1861-1869, pg 192 (1867 Oct 8), Nevada Lodge No. 4, Nevadaville
Proceedings 1861-1869, pg 304 (1869 Sept 29), Nevada Lodge No. 4, Nevadaville
Proceedings 1871, pg 18 (1871 Sept 27), Nevada Lodge No. 4, Bald Mountain, Dimitted
Proceedings 1872, pg 28 (1872 Sept 24), Mount Moriah Lodge No. 15, Canon City
Proceedings 1873, pg 6 (1873 Sept 30), Mount Moriah Lodge No. 15, Canon City
Proceedings 1873, pg 7 (1873 Sept 30) committee
Proceedings 1873, pg 7 (1873 Sept 30) committee
Proceedings 1873, pg 18 (1873 Oct 1) committee
Proceedings 1873, pg 31 (1873 Oct 1) mileage and per diem
Proceedings 1873, pg 45 (1873 Oct 1), Mount Moriah Lodge No. 15, Canon City
Proceedings 1874, pg 220 (1874 Sept 30), Mount Moriah Lodge No. 15, Canon City
Proceedings 1875, pg 84 (1875 Sept 22), Mount Moriah Lodge No. 15, Canon City
Proceedings 1876, pg 5 (1876 Sept 19) committee
Proceedings 1876, pg 5 (1876 Sept 19), Mount Moriah Lodge No. 15, Canon City
Proceedings 1876, pg 22 (1876 Sept 20), Mount Moriah Lodge No. 15, Canon City

Shaffer, Benjamin F
Proceedings 1870, pg 20 (1870 Sept 28), Nevada Lodge No. 4, Nevadaville
Proceedings 1876, pg cover (1876 Sept 20) Grand Steward, Canon City
Proceedings 1876, pg 37 (1876 Sept 20), Mount Moriah Lodge No. 15, Canon City

Shaffer, S F
Proceedings 1861-1869, pg 147 (1865 Nov 7) Golden City Lodge No. 1
Proceedings 1861-1869, pg 165 (1866 Oct 2) Golden City Lodge No. 1

Shaffer, Sam F
Proceedings 1870, pg 19 (1870 Sept 28), Golden City Lodge No. 1, Golden City
Proceedings 1871, pg 17 (1871 Sept 27), Golden City Lodge No. 1, Golden City
Proceedings 1872, pg 17 (1872 Sept 24), Golden City Lodge No. 1, Golden City

Shaffer, Sam'l F
Proceedings 1874, pg 209 (1874 Sept 30), Golden City Lodge No. 1, Golden City

Shaffer, Samuel F
Proceedings 1861-1869, pg 42 (1861 Dec 10) Golden City Lodge No. 1
Proceedings 1861-1869, pg 110 (1863 Nov 3) Golden City Lodge No. 1

Shaffer, Samuel F, cont.
  Proceedings 1861-1869, pg 131 (1864 Nov 8) Golden City Lodge No. 1
  Proceedings 1861-1869, pg 221 (1868 Oct 7) Golden City Lodge No. 1
  Proceedings 1873, pg 35 (1873 Oct 1), Golden City Lodge No. 1, Golden City

Shakespear, A D
  Proceedings 1861-1869, pg 312 (1869 Sept 29), Cheyenne Lodge No. 16, Cheyenne
  Proceedings 1870, pg 29 (1870 Sept 28), Cheyenne Lodge No. 16, Cheyenne, Wyoming Territory, Dimitted

Shank, J
  Proceedings 1874, pg 209 (1874 Sept 30), Golden City Lodge No. 1, Golden City, Apprentice

Shanley, Patrick
  Proceedings 1876, pg 45 (1876 Sept 20), King Solomon Lodge U D, West Las Animas

Shannon, H N
  Proceedings 1861-1869, pg 305 (1869 Sept 29) Denver Lodge No. 5, Apprentice

Shanstrom, John A
  Proceedings 1870, pg 20 (1870 Sept 28), Nevada Lodge No. 4, Nevadaville
  Proceedings 1871, pg 18 (1871 Sept 27), Nevada Lodge No. 4, Bald Mountain
  Proceedings 1873, pg 36 (1873 Oct 1), Nevada Lodge No. 4, Nevada
  Proceedings 1874, pg 210 (1874 Sept 30), Nevada Lodge No. 4, Bald Mountain, Gilpin County
  Proceedings 1875, pg 74 (1875 Sept 22), Nevada Lodge No. 4, Nevada
  Proceedings 1876, pg 30 (1876 Sept 20) Nevada Lodge No. 4

Shanstrom, P G
  Proceedings 1875, pg 74 (1875 Sept 22), Nevada Lodge No. 4, Nevada

Shanstrom, Peter G
  Proceedings 1870, pg 20 (1870 Sept 28), Nevada Lodge No. 4, Nevadaville
  Proceedings 1871, pg 18 (1871 Sept 27), Nevada Lodge No. 4, Bald Mountain
  Proceedings 1873, pg 36 (1873 Oct 1), Nevada Lodge No. 4, Nevada
  Proceedings 1874, pg 210 (1874 Sept 30), Nevada Lodge No. 4, Bald Mountain, Gilpin County
  Proceedings 1876, pg 30 (1876 Sept 20) Nevada Lodge No. 4

Shanstron, J A
  Proceedings 1861-1869, pg 304 (1869 Sept 29), Nevada Lodge No. 4, Nevadaville

Shanstron, P G
  Proceedings 1861-1869, pg 304 (1869 Sept 29), Nevada Lodge No. 4, Nevadaville

Shanton, James W
  Proceedings 1870, pg 20 (1870 Sept 28), Nevada Lodge No. 4, Nevadaville

Sharp, W T
  Proceedings 1876, pg 43 (1876 Sept 20), Huerfano Lodge No. 27, Walsenburg

Sharplen, S K
  Proceedings 1873, pg 46 (1873 Oct 1), Cheyenne Lodge No. 16, Cheyenne, Wyoming Territory

Sharpless, Seth K
  Proceedings 1872, pg 29 (1872 Sept 24), Cheyenne Lodge No. 16, Cheyenne, Wyoming Territory
  Proceedings 1874, pg 221 (1874 Sept 30), Cheyenne Lodge No. 16, Cheyenne, Wyoming Territory

Shastrom, John A
  Proceedings 1872, pg 18 (1872 Sept 24), Nevada Lodge No. 4, Bald Mountain

Shauk, Jacob
  Proceedings 1872, pg 17 (1872 Sept 24), Golden City Lodge No. 1, Golden City, Apprentice

Shaustrom, Peter G
  Proceedings 1872, pg 18 (1872 Sept 24), Nevada Lodge No. 4, Bald Mountain

Shaw, D J
  Proceedings 1861-1869, pg 312 (1869 Sept 29), Cheyenne Lodge No. 16, Cheyenne, Apprentice
  Proceedings 1870, pg 29 (1870 Sept 28), Cheyenne Lodge No. 16, Cheyenne, Wyoming Territory, Apprentice
  Proceedings 1871, pg 28 (1871 Sept 27), Cheyenne Lodge No. 16, Cheyenne, Wyoming Territory, Apprentice
  Proceedings 1872, pg 30 (1872 Sept 24), Cheyenne Lodge No. 16, Cheyenne, Wyoming Territory, Apprentice
  Proceedings 1873, pg 46 (1873 Oct 1), Cheyenne Lodge No. 16, Cheyenne, Wyoming Territory, Apprentice
  Proceedings 1874, pg 221 (1874 Sept 30), Cheyenne Lodge No. 16, Cheyenne, Wyoming Territory, Apprentice

Shaw, E H
  Proceedings 1871, pg 31 (1871 Sept 27), Argenta Lodge U D, Salt Lake City, Utah

Shaw, Horace
  Proceedings 1861-1869, pg 166 (1866 Oct 2), Nevada Lodge No. 4, Nevadaville
  Proceedings 1861-1869, pg 192 (1867 Oct 8), Nevada Lodge No. 4, Nevadaville
  Proceedings 1861-1869, pg 222 (1868 Oct 7), Nevada Lodge No. 4, Nevadaville
  Proceedings 1861-1869, pg 304 (1869 Sept 29), Nevada Lodge No. 4, Nevadaville
  Proceedings 1870, pg 20 (1870 Sept 28), Nevada Lodge No. 4, Nevadaville
  Proceedings 1871, pg 18 (1871 Sept 27), Nevada Lodge No. 4, Bald Mountain
  Proceedings 1872, pg 18 (1872 Sept 24), Nevada Lodge No. 4, Bald Mountain
  Proceedings 1873, pg 36 (1873 Oct 1), Nevada Lodge No. 4, Nevada

Proceedings 1874, pg 211 (1874 Sept 30), Nevada Lodge No. 4, Bald Mountain, Gilpin County, Stricken from the rolls

Shaw, John H
Proceedings 1876, pg 44 (1876 Sept 20) Del Norte Lodge U D

Shaw, M K
Proceedings 1871, pg 8 (1871 Apr 8), Argenta Lodge U D, Salt Lake City

Shaw, Simon
Proceedings 1876, pg 34 (1876 Sept 20) Black Hawk Lodge No. 11, Fellow Craft

Shaw, Thomas
Proceedings 1870, pg 31 (1870 Sept 28), Laramie Lodge No. 18, Laramie, Wyoming Territory, Apprentice

Shea, Henry
Proceedings 1861-1869, pg 110 (1863 Nov 3) Golden City Lodge No. 1

Shea, W H
Proceedings 1861-1869, pg 131 (1864 Nov 8) Golden City Lodge No. 1

Shedbee, Benjamin F
Proceedings 1871, pg 30 (1871 Sept 27), Collins Lodge No. 19, Fort Collins

Sheets, Daniel
Proceedings 1861-1869, pg 223 (1868 Oct 7) Denver Lodge No. 5
Proceedings 1870, pg 21 (1870 Sept 28), Denver Lodge No. 5, Denver
Proceedings 1871, pg 20 (1871 Sept 27) Denver Lodge No. 5, Dimitted
Proceedings 1874, pg 222 (1874 Sept 30), Pueblo Lodge No. 17, Pueblo, Pueblo County
Proceedings 1875, pg 85 (1875 Sept 22) Pueblo Lodge No. 17
Proceedings 1876, pg 39 (1876 Sept 20) Pueblo Lodge No. 17

Sheidler, Jacob
Proceedings 1870, pg 27 (1870 Sept 28), El Paso Lodge No. 13, Colorado City
Proceedings 1873, pg 43 (1873 Oct 1), El Paso Lodge No. 13, Colorado City
Proceedings 1875, pg 82 (1875 Sept 22), El Paso Lodge No. 13, Colorado Springs

Sheidler, Thomas
Proceedings 1870, pg 27 (1870 Sept 28), El Paso Lodge No. 13, Colorado City
Proceedings 1875, pg 82 (1875 Sept 22), El Paso Lodge No. 13, Colorado Springs

Sheilds, W H
Proceedings 1873, pg 46 (1873 Oct 1), Cheyenne Lodge No. 16, Cheyenne, Wyoming Territory

Shelden, E
Proceedings 1861-1869, pg 77 (1862 Nov 4), Nevada Lodge No. 4, Nevadaville

Shelden, H I
Proceedings 1875, pg 82 (1875 Sept 22), El Paso Lodge No. 13, Colorado Springs

Shelden, H J
Proceedings 1876, pg 49 (1876 Sept 20), El Paso Lodge No. 13, Colorado City, 1876 July 22

Shenden, Thomas
Proceedings 1861-1869, pg 221 (1868 Oct 7) Golden City Lodge No. 1, Apprentice
Proceedings 1861-1869, pg 303 (1869 Sept 29) Golden City Lodge No. 1, Apprentice

Shepherd, Alfred
Proceedings 1876, pg 45 (1876 Sept 20) South Pueblo Lodge U D

Shepherd, Wm
Proceedings 1861-1869, pg 230 (1868 Oct 7), Valmont Lodge U D, Valmont

Sheppard, S A
Proceedings 1876, pg 31 (1876 Sept 20) Denver Lodge No. 5

Sheridan, Thos
Proceedings 1861-1869, pg 147 (1865 Nov 7) Golden City Lodge No. 1, Apprentice
Proceedings 1861-1869, pg 165 (1866 Oct 2) Golden City Lodge No. 1, Apprentice
Proceedings 1861-1869, pg 191 (1867 Oct 8) Golden City Lodge No. 1, Apprentice

Sherman, C D
Proceedings 1861-1869, pg 312 (1869 Sept 29), Cheyenne Lodge No. 16, Cheyenne
Proceedings 1870, pg 28 (1870 Sept 28), Cheyenne Lodge No. 16, Cheyenne, Wyoming Territory
Proceedings 1871, pg 28 (1871 Sept 27), Cheyenne Lodge No. 16, Cheyenne, Wyoming Territory, Apprentice

Sherman, Charles E
Proceedings 1874, pg 213 (1874 Sept 30), Central Lodge No. 6, Central
Proceedings 1875, pg 77 (1875 Sept 22), Central Lodge No. 6, Central City
Proceedings 1876, pg 32 (1876 Sept 20), Central Lodge No. 6, Central City

Sherman, Chas E
Proceedings 1872, pg 21 (1872 Sept 24), Denver Lodge No. 5, Denver
Proceedings 1873, pg 38 (1873 Oct 1), Central Lodge No. 6, Central City
Proceedings 1876, pg 50 (1876 Sept 20), Central Lodge No. 6, Central City

Sherman, F T
Proceedings 1861-1869, pg 132 (1864 Nov 8), Nevada Lodge No. 4, Nevadaville, Apprentice
Proceedings 1861-1869, pg 148 (1865 Nov 7), Nevada Lodge No. 4, Nevadaville
Proceedings 1861-1869, pg 166 (1866 Oct 2), Nevada Lodge No. 4, Nevadaville

Colorado's Territorial Masons

Sherman, F T, cont.
Proceedings 1861-1869, pg 192 (1867 Oct 8), Nevada Lodge No. 4, Nevadaville
Proceedings 1861-1869, pg 222 (1868 Oct 7), Nevada Lodge No. 4, Nevadaville, Dimitted

Sherman, H C
Proceedings 1873, pg 50 (1873 Oct 1), Occidental Lodge No. 20, Greeley
Proceedings 1874, pg 225 (1874 Sept 30), Occidental Lodge No. 20, Greeley

Sherman, Philo B
Proceedings 1875, pg 91 (1875 Sept 22), Las Animas Lodge U D, Trinidad
Proceedings 1876, pg 44 (1876 Sept 20), Las Animas Lodge No. 28, Trinidad

Sherman, W H
Proceedings 1876, pg 34 (1876 Sept 20) Black Hawk Lodge No. 11

Sherman, Wm B
Proceedings 1875, pg 82 (1875 Sept 22), El Paso Lodge No. 13, Colorado Springs

Sherman, Wm H
Proceedings 1873, pg 42 (1873 Oct 1), Black Hawk Lodge No. 11, Black Hawk
Proceedings 1874, pg 216 (1874 Sept 30), Black Hawk Lodge No. 11, Black Hawk
Proceedings 1875, pg 80 (1875 Sept 22) Black Hawk Lodge No. 11
Proceedings 1875, pg 80 (1875 Sept 22) Black Hawk Lodge No. 11

Sherson, S
Proceedings 1873, pg 48 (1873 Oct 1), Laramie Lodge No. 18, Laramie, Wyoming Territory, Apprentice
Proceedings 1874, pg 224 (1874 Sept 30), Laramie Lodge No. 18, Laramie City, Apprentice

Sherwood, C A
Proceedings 1874, pg 219 (1874 Sept 30), Columbia Lodge No. 14, Boulder, Boulder County
Proceedings 1875, pg 83 (1875 Sept 22), Columbia Lodge No. 14, Boulder

Sherwood, Clarence A
Proceedings 1876, pg 37 (1876 Sept 20), Columbia Lodge No. 14, Boulder

Sherwood, Edwin
Proceedings 1861-1869, pg 167 (1866 Oct 2) Denver Lodge No. 5

Sherwood, Fred W
Proceedings 1872, pg 33 (1872 Sept 24), Collins Lodge No. 19, Fort Collins

Sherwood, Frederick W
Proceedings 1871, pg 30 (1871 Sept 27), Collins Lodge No. 19, Fort Collins
Proceedings 1873, pg 49 (1873 Oct 1), Collins Lodge No. 19, Fort Collins
Proceedings 1874, pg 224 (1874 Sept 30), Collins Lodge No. 19, Fort Collins, Larimer County
Proceedings 1875, pg 86 (1875 Sept 22), Collins Lodge No. 19, Fort Collins
Proceedings 1876, pg 39 (1876 Sept 20), Collins Lodge No. 19, Fort Collins

Sherwood, M B
Proceedings 1861-1869, pg 112 (1863 Nov 3) Denver Lodge No. 5
Proceedings 1861-1869, pg 133 (1864 Nov 8) Denver Lodge No. 5
Proceedings 1861-1869, pg 149 (1865 Nov 7), Nevada Lodge No. 4, Nevadaville
Proceedings 1861-1869, pg 167 (1866 Oct 2) Denver Lodge No. 5
Proceedings 1861-1869, pg 193 (1867 Oct 8) Denver Lodge No. 5
Proceedings 1861-1869, pg 223 (1868 Oct 7) Denver Lodge No. 5
Proceedings 1861-1869, pg 305 (1869 Sept 29) Denver Lodge No. 5
Proceedings 1870, pg 21 (1870 Sept 28), Denver Lodge No. 5, Denver
Proceedings 1872, pg 20 (1872 Sept 24), Denver Lodge No. 5, Denver

Shidler, Jacob
Proceedings 1871, pg 25 (1871 Sept 27), El Paso Lodge No. 13, Colorado City
Proceedings 1872, pg 27 (1872 Sept 24), El Paso Lodge No. 13, Colorado City

Shidler, Thomas
Proceedings 1871, pg 25 (1871 Sept 27), El Paso Lodge No. 13, Colorado City
Proceedings 1872, pg 26 (1872 Sept 24), El Paso Lodge No. 13, Colorado City

Shields, W H
Proceedings 1872, pg 30 (1872 Sept 24), Cheyenne Lodge No. 16, Cheyenne, Wyoming Territory, Apprentice
Proceedings 1874, pg 221 (1874 Sept 30), Cheyenne Lodge No. 16, Cheyenne, Wyoming Territory

Shinner, A
Proceedings 1861-1869, pg 223 (1868 Oct 7) Denver Lodge No. 5
Proceedings 1861-1869, pg 305 (1869 Sept 29) Denver Lodge No. 5

Shirmer, F
Proceedings 1861-1869, pg 305 (1869 Sept 29) Denver Lodge No. 5

Shonecker, Andrew
Proceedings 1873, pg 39 (1873 Oct 1), Central Lodge No. 6, Central City, Apprentice
Proceedings 1875, pg 94 (1875 Sept 22), Central Lodge No. 6, Central City

Shortridge, William T
Proceedings 1876, pg 31 (1876 Sept 20) Denver Lodge No. 5

Shortridge, Wm T
Proceedings 1871, pg 19 (1871 Sept 27) Denver Lodge No. 5

Proceedings 1872, pg 20 (1872 Sept 24), Denver Lodge No. 5, Denver

Proceedings 1873, pg 37 (1873 Oct 1), Denver Lodge No. 5, Denver

Proceedings 1874, pg 211 (1874 Sept 30), Denver Lodge No. 5, Denver

Proceedings 1875, pg 75 (1875 Sept 22) Denver Lodge No. 5

Shoup Geo L

Proceedings 1861-1869, pg 133 (1864 Nov 8) Denver Lodge No. 5

Shoup, G L

Proceedings 1861-1869, pg 149 (1865 Nov 7), Nevada Lodge No. 4, Nevadaville

Proceedings 1861-1869, pg 167 (1866 Oct 2) Denver Lodge No. 5

Proceedings 1861-1869, pg 305 (1869 Sept 29) Denver Lodge No. 5

Shoup, Geo L

Proceedings 1861-1869, pg 223 (1868 Oct 7) Denver Lodge No. 5

Proceedings 1870, pg 21 (1870 Sept 28), Denver Lodge No. 5, Denver

Proceedings 1873, pg 37 (1873 Oct 1), Denver Lodge No. 5, Denver, Dimitted

Shoup, George L

Proceedings 1861-1869, pg 193 (1867 Oct 8) Denver Lodge No. 5

Shrock, Frank H

Proceedings 1876, pg 45 (1876 Sept 20) South Pueblo Lodge U D

Shryock, J W

Proceedings 1876, pg 45 (1876 Sept 20), King Solomon Lodge U D, West Las Animas

Shuler, G

Proceedings 1870, pg 30 (1870 Sept 28), Laramie Lodge No. 18, Laramie, Wyoming Territory

Proceedings 1871, pg 29 (1871 Sept 27), Laramie Lodge No. 18, Laramie, Wyoming Territory

Proceedings 1874, pg 223 (1874 Sept 30), Laramie Lodge No. 18, Laramie City

Shuler, Gustave

Proceedings 1872, pg 32 (1872 Sept 24), Laramie Lodge No. 18, Laramie, Wyoming Territory

Proceedings 1873, pg 48 (1873 Oct 1), Laramie Lodge No. 18, Laramie, Wyoming Territory

Shute, G M

Proceedings 1874, pg 225 (1874 Sept 30), Occidental Lodge No. 20, Greeley

Proceedings 1875, pg 87 (1875 Sept 22), Occidental Lodge No. 20, Greeley

Shute, Geo M

Proceedings 1872, pg 34 (1872 Sept 24), Occidental Lodge No. 20, Greeley, Apprentice

Proceedings 1873, pg 50 (1873 Oct 1), Occidental Lodge No. 20, Greeley

Shute, George M

Proceedings 1876, pg 40 (1876 Sept 20), Occidental Lodge No. 20, Greeley

Shuts, Daniel

Proceedings 1861-1869, pg 193 (1867 Oct 8) Denver Lodge No. 5

Proceedings 1861-1869, pg 305 (1869 Sept 29) Denver Lodge No. 5, Dimitted

Shuyler, Howard

Proceedings 1875, pg 79 (1875 Sept 22), Union Lodge No. 7, Denver, Stricken from the rolls

Sibley, N L

Proceedings 1861-1869, pg 113 (1863 Nov 3), Chivington Lodge No. 6, Central City, Apprentice

Proceedings 1861-1869, pg 134 (1864 Nov 8), Chivington Lodge No. 6, Central City, Apprentice

Proceedings 1861-1869, pg 150 (1865 Nov 7), Chivington Lodge No. 6, Central City, Apprentice

Proceedings 1861-1869, pg 169 (1866 Oct 2), Chivington Lodge No. 6, Central City, Apprentice

Proceedings 1861-1869, pg 194 (1867 Oct 8), Chivington Lodge No. 6, Central City, Apprentice

Proceedings 1861-1869, pg 225 (1868 Oct 7), Chivington Lodge No. 6, Central City, Apprentice

Proceedings 1861-1869, pg 307 (1869 Sept 29), Central Lodge No. 6, Central City, Apprentice

Proceedings 1870, pg 22 (1870 Sept 28), Central Lodge No. 6, Central City, Apprentice

Proceedings 1873, pg 39 (1873 Oct 1), Central Lodge No. 6, Central City, Apprentice

Proceedings 1874, pg 213 (1874 Sept 30), Central Lodge No. 6, Central, Apprentice

Proceedings 1875, pg 77 (1875 Sept 22), Central Lodge No. 6, Central City, Apprentice

Proceedings 1876, pg 32 (1876 Sept 20), Central Lodge No. 6, Central City, Apprentice

Sibley, N S

Proceedings 1871, pg 21 (1871 Sept 27), Central Lodge No. 6, Central, Apprentice

Proceedings 1872, pg 21 (1872 Sept 24), Denver Lodge No. 5, Denver, Apprentice

Sidell, G A

Proceedings 1875, pg 89 (1875 Sept 22), Doric Lodge No. 25, Fairplay

Proceedings 1876, pg 42 (1876 Sept 20), Doric Lodge No. 25, Fairplay

Sigmund, Christ

Proceedings 1876, pg 41 (1876 Sept 20), St Vrain Lodge No. 23, Longmont

Proceedings 1876, pg 50 (1876 Sept 20), St Vrain Lodge No. 23, Longmont

Silver, S D

Proceedings 1874, pg 219 (1874 Sept 30), Columbia Lodge No. 14, Boulder, Boulder County

Proceedings 1875, pg 83 (1875 Sept 22), Columbia Lodge No. 14, Boulder

Silver, S D, cont.
Proceedings 1876, pg 37 (1876 Sept 20), Columbia Lodge No. 14, Boulder

Simkins, S H
Proceedings 1873, pg 50 (1873 Oct 1), Occidental Lodge No. 20, Greeley

Simmons, John
Proceedings 1861-1869, pg 227 (1868 Oct 7), Black Hawk Lodge No. 11, Black Hawk
Proceedings 1861-1869, pg 309 (1869 Sept 29), Black Hawk Lodge No. 11, Black Hawk, Dimitted

Simmons, T F
Proceedings 1871, pg 24 (1871 Sept 27), Washington Lodge No. 12, Georgetown

Simmons, Theo F
Proceedings 1861-1869, pg 309 (1869 Sept 29), Washington Lodge No. 12, Georgetown
Proceedings 1870, pg 26 (1870 Sept 28), Washington Lodge No. 12, Georgetown
Proceedings 1873, pg 43 (1873 Oct 1), Washington Lodge No. 12, Georgetown

Simmons, Theodore F
Proceedings 1872, pg 26 (1872 Sept 24), Washington Lodge No. 12, Georgetown
Proceedings 1874, pg 217 (1874 Sept 30), Washington Lodge No. 12, Georgetown
Proceedings 1875, pg 81 (1875 Sept 22), Washington Lodge No. 12, Georgetown
Proceedings 1876, pg 35 (1876 Sept 20), Washington Lodge No. 12, Georgetown

Simons
Proceedings 1872, pg 79 (1872 Sept 24) Grand Lodge of Nevada

Simons, John W
Proceedings 1870, pg 94 (1870 June 7) Grand Lodge of New York
Proceedings 1874, pg 204 (1874 Sept 30) Grand Lodge of New York, New York

Simpson, D J
Proceedings 1874, pg 220 (1874 Sept 30), Mount Moriah Lodge No. 15, Canon City
Proceedings 1875, pg 84 (1875 Sept 22), Mount Moriah Lodge No. 15, Canon City
Proceedings 1876, pg 38 (1876 Sept 20), Mount Moriah Lodge No. 15, Canon City

Simpson, J C
Proceedings 1861-1869, pg 151 (1865 Nov 7), Chivington Lodge No. 6, Central City, dimitted

Simpson, John D
Proceedings 1861-1869, pg 134 (1864 Nov 8), Union Lodge No. 7, Denver

Sinclair, E W
Proceedings 1861-1869, pg 168 (1866 Oct 2), Chivington Lodge No. 6, Central City
Proceedings 1861-1869, pg 194 (1867 Oct 8), Chivington Lodge No. 6, Central City
Proceedings 1861-1869, pg 224 (1868 Oct 7), Chivington Lodge No. 6, Central City
Proceedings 1861-1869, pg 306 (1869 Sept 29), Central Lodge No. 6, Central City
Proceedings 1870, pg 22 (1870 Sept 28), Central Lodge No. 6, Central City
Proceedings 1871, pg 21 (1871 Sept 27), Central Lodge No. 6, Central

Sinclair, Ellis W
Proceedings 1872, pg 21 (1872 Sept 24), Denver Lodge No. 5, Denver
Proceedings 1873, pg 38 (1873 Oct 1), Central Lodge No. 6, Central City
Proceedings 1874, pg 213 (1874 Sept 30), Central Lodge No. 6, Central
Proceedings 1875, pg 77 (1875 Sept 22), Central Lodge No. 6, Central City
Proceedings 1876, pg 32 (1876 Sept 20), Central Lodge No. 6, Central City
Proceedings 1876, pg 50 (1876 Sept 20), Central Lodge No. 6, Central City

Sinclair, Walter
Proceedings 1870, pg 31 (1870 Sept 28), Laramie Lodge No. 18, Laramie, Wyoming Territory
Proceedings 1871, pg 29 (1871 Sept 27), Laramie Lodge No. 18, Laramie, Wyoming Territory
Proceedings 1872, pg 31 (1872 Sept 24), Laramie Lodge No. 18, Laramie, Wyoming Territory
Proceedings 1873, pg 48 (1873 Oct 1), Laramie Lodge No. 18, Laramie, Wyoming Territory
Proceedings 1874, pg 223 (1874 Sept 30), Laramie Lodge No. 18, Laramie City

Singleton
Proceedings 1874, pg 53 (1874 Sept 30) Grand Lodge of the District of Columbia
Proceedings 1874, pg 107 (1874 Sept 30) Grand Lodge of the District of Columbia

Singleton, R W
Proceedings 1872, pg 43 (1872 Sept 24) Washington, Grand Lodge of the District of Columbia
Proceedings 1872, pg 58 (1872 Sept 24) Grand Lodge of the District of Columbia
Proceedings 1873, pg 60 (1873 Oct 1) Grand Lodge of the District of Columbia, Washington
Proceedings 1874, pg 204 (1874 Sept 30) Grand Lodge of the District of Columbia, Washington

Sinkins, S H
Proceedings 1874, pg 226 (1874 Sept 30), Occidental Lodge No. 20, Greeley, Demitted,

Sir Knights of Colorado Commandery No. 1
Colorado University Cornerstone Laying, pg 4 (1875 Sept 20) Denver

Sites, Geo L
Proceedings 1861-1869, pg 227 (1868 Oct 7), Washington Lodge No. 12, Georgetown, Apprentice
Proceedings 1861-1869, pg 309 (1869 Sept 29), Washington Lodge No. 12, Georgetown

Proceedings 1870, pg 26 (1870 Sept 28), Washington Lodge No. 12, Georgetown

Proceedings 1872, pg 26 (1872 Sept 24), Washington Lodge No. 12, Georgetown

Proceedings 1875, pg 81 (1875 Sept 22), Washington Lodge No. 12, Georgetown

Sites, George L

Proceedings 1871, pg 24 (1871 Sept 27), Washington Lodge No. 12, Georgetown

Proceedings 1873, pg 43 (1873 Oct 1), Washington Lodge No. 12, Georgetown

Proceedings 1874, pg 217 (1874 Sept 30), Washington Lodge No. 12, Georgetown

Proceedings 1875, pg 17 (1875 Sept 21), Washington Lodge No. 12, Georgetown

Proceedings 1876, pg 35 (1876 Sept 20), Washington Lodge No. 12, Georgetown

Sitzer, C L

Proceedings 1875, pg 85 (1875 Sept 22) Pueblo Lodge No. 17

Sizer, E W

Proceedings 1875, pg 78 (1875 Sept 22), Union Lodge No. 7, Denver

Proceedings 1876, pg 33 (1876 Sept 20), Union Lodge No. 7, Denver

Sizer, Warren W

Proceedings 1876, pg 45 (1876 Sept 20), King Solomon Lodge U D, West Las Animas

Skelton, Boyington

Proceedings 1870, pg 21 (1870 Sept 28), Denver Lodge No. 5, Denver

Proceedings 1873, pg 38 (1873 Oct 1), Denver Lodge No. 5, Denver, Striken from the rolls

Proceedings 1875, pg 75 (1875 Sept 22) Denver Lodge No. 5

Proceedings 1876, pg 49 (1876 Sept 20) Denver Lodge No. 5, 1876 Aug 19

Skelton, Boynton

Proceedings 1874, pg 211 (1874 Sept 30), Denver Lodge No. 5, Denver

Proceedings 1874, pg 212 (1874 Sept 30), Denver Lodge No. 5, Denver, Reinstated

Skerrett, Thos W

Proceedings 1875, pg 74 (1875 Sept 22), Nevada Lodge No. 4, Nevada

Proceedings 1876, pg 30 (1876 Sept 20) Nevada Lodge No. 4

Slane, A

Proceedings 1861-1869, pg 305 (1869 Sept 29) Denver Lodge No. 5

Slane, Andrew

Proceedings 1861-1869, pg 193 (1867 Oct 8) Denver Lodge No. 5

Proceedings 1870, pg 21 (1870 Sept 28), Denver Lodge No. 5, Denver

Proceedings 1871, pg 19 (1871 Sept 27) Denver Lodge No. 5

Proceedings 1872, pg 20 (1872 Sept 24), Denver Lodge No. 5, Denver

Proceedings 1873, pg 37 (1873 Oct 1), Denver Lodge No. 5, Denver

Proceedings 1874, pg 212 (1874 Sept 30), Denver Lodge No. 5, Denver, Stricken from the rolls

Proceedings 1876, pg 48 (1876 Sept 20) Denver Lodge No. 5, 1876 Feb 5

Proceedings 1876, pg 51 (1876 Sept 20) Denver Lodge No. 5, 1876 Feb 5,

Slater

Proceedings 1870, pg 4 (1870 Sept 27) motion

Proceedings 1870, pg 5 (1870 Sept 27) committee

Proceedings 1870, pg 14 (1870 Sept 27) motion

Slater, A

Proceedings 1861-1869, pg 147 (1865 Nov 7) Golden City Lodge No. 1

Proceedings 1861-1869, pg 165 (1866 Oct 2) Golden City Lodge No. 1

Slater, Abraham

Proceedings 1861-1869, pg 131 (1864 Nov 8) Golden City Lodge No. 1

Proceedings 1873, pg 19 (1873 Oct 1), Golden City Lodge No. 1, Golden City

Proceedings 1875, pg 73 (1875 Sept 22) Golden City Lodge No. 1

Slater, Abram

Proceedings 1861-1869, pg 191 (1867 Oct 8) Golden City Lodge No. 1

Proceedings 1861-1869, pg 221 (1868 Oct 7) Golden City Lodge No. 1

Proceedings 1861-1869, pg 303 (1869 Sept 29) Golden City Lodge No. 1

Proceedings 1870, pg 19 (1870 Sept 28), Golden City Lodge No. 1, Golden City

Proceedings 1871, pg 17 (1871 Sept 27), Golden City Lodge No. 1, Golden City

Proceedings 1872, pg 18 (1872 Sept 24), Golden City Lodge No. 1, Golden City, Stricken from the Roll

Proceedings 1873, pg 35 (1873 Oct 1), Golden City Lodge No. 1, Golden City

Proceedings 1874, pg 209 (1874 Sept 30), Golden City Lodge No. 1, Golden City

Proceedings 1876, pg 29 (1876 Sept 20) Golden City Lodge No. 1

Slater, M H

Proceedings 1861-1869, pg 195 (1867 Oct 8), Union Lodge No. 7, Denver

Proceedings 1870, pg 4 (1870 Sept 27), Union Lodge No. 7, Denver

Proceedings 1870, pg 13 (1870 Sept 27) committee

Proceedings 1870, pg 13 (1870 Sept 27) Grand Teller

Proceedings 1870, pg 16 (1870 Sept 28) committee

Proceedings 1870, pg 16 (1870 Sept 28), Union Lodge No. 7, Denver

Proceedings 1870, pg 17 (1870 Sept 28) committee

Proceedings 1871, pg 3 (1871 Sept 26) Senior Grand Deacon

Slater, M H, cont.
- Proceedings 1874, pg 214 (1874 Sept 30), Union Lodge No. 7, Denver
- Proceedings 1875, pg 78 (1875 Sept 22), Union Lodge No. 7, Denver
- Proceedings 1876, pg 33 (1876 Sept 20), Union Lodge No. 7, Denver

Slater, Milo H
- Proceedings 1861-1869, pg 169 (1866 Oct 2), Union Lodge No. 7, Denver
- Proceedings 1861-1869, pg 225 (1868 Oct 7), Union Lodge No. 7, Denver
- Proceedings 1861-1869, pg 288 (1869 Sept 28), Union Lodge No. 7, Denver
- Proceedings 1861-1869, pg 307 (1869 Sept 29), Union Lodge No. 7, Denver
- Proceedings 1870, pg cover (1870 Sept 28) Senior Grand Deacon, Denver
- Proceedings 1870, pg 13 (1870 Sept 27) Senior Grand Deacon
- Proceedings 1870, pg 23 (1870 Sept 28), Union Lodge No. 7, Denver
- Proceedings 1871, pg 22 (1871 Sept 27), Union Lodge No. 7, Denver
- Proceedings 1872, pg 22 (1872 Sept 24), Union Lodge No. 7, Denver
- Proceedings 1873, pg 40 (1873 Oct 1), Union Lodge No. 7, Denver

Slater, W C
- Proceedings 1861-1869, pg 197 (1867 Oct 8), Columbia Lodge U D, Boulder

Slater, William C
- Proceedings 1861-1869, pg 310 (1869 Sept 29), Columbia Lodge No. 14, Boulder City
- Proceedings 1871, pg 26 (1871 Sept 27), Columbia Lodge No. 14, Boulder City
- Proceedings 1874, pg 219 (1874 Sept 30), Columbia Lodge No. 14, Boulder, Boulder County
- Proceedings 1875, pg 83 (1875 Sept 22), Columbia Lodge No. 14, Boulder, Stricken from the rolls

Slater, Wm C
- Proceedings 1861-1869, pg 228 (1868 Oct 7), Columbia Lodge No. 14, Columbia City
- Proceedings 1870, pg 27 (1870 Sept 28), Columbia Lodge No. 14, Boulder City
- Proceedings 1872, pg 28 (1872 Sept 24), Columbia Lodge No. 14, Boulder
- Proceedings 1873, pg 44 (1873 Oct 1), Columbia Lodge No. 14, Boulder

Slaughter W W
- Proceedings 1861-1869, pg 223 (1868 Oct 7) Denver Lodge No. 5

Slaughter, B F
- Proceedings 1861-1869, pg 228 (1868 Oct 7), Columbia Lodge No. 14, Columbia City, Dimitted

Slaughter, B H
- Proceedings 1875, pg 83 (1875 Sept 22), Columbia Lodge No. 14, Boulder, Terricken from the rolls
- Proceedings 1861-1869, pg 310 (1869 Sept 29), Columbia Lodge No. 14, Boulder City

Slaughter, Benj H
- Proceedings 1870, pg 27 (1870 Sept 28), Columbia Lodge No. 14, Boulder City
- Proceedings 1872, pg 28 (1872 Sept 24), Columbia Lodge No. 14, Boulder

Slaughter, Benjamin H
- Proceedings 1871, pg 26 (1871 Sept 27), Columbia Lodge No. 14, Boulder City
- Proceedings 1873, pg 44 (1873 Oct 1), Columbia Lodge No. 14, Boulder
- Proceedings 1874, pg 219 (1874 Sept 30), Columbia Lodge No. 14, Boulder, Boulder County

Slaughter, J N
- Proceedings 1871, pg 27 (1871 Sept 27), Cheyenne Lodge No. 16, Cheyenne, Wyoming Territory, Fellowcraft
- Proceedings 1872, pg 30 (1872 Sept 24), Cheyenne Lodge No. 16, Cheyenne, Wyoming Territory, Fellowcraft
- Proceedings 1873, pg 46 (1873 Oct 1), Cheyenne Lodge No. 16, Cheyenne, Wyoming Territory, Fellowcraft
- Proceedings 1874, pg 221 (1874 Sept 30), Cheyenne Lodge No. 16, Cheyenne, Wyoming Territory

Slaughter, James N
- Proceedings 1861-1869, pg 312 (1869 Sept 29), Cheyenne Lodge No. 16, Cheyenne, Fellowcraft
- Proceedings 1870, pg 29 (1870 Sept 28), Cheyenne Lodge No. 16, Cheyenne, Wyoming Territory, Fellowcraft

Slaughter, W M
- Proceedings 1861-1869, pg 149 (1865 Nov 7), Nevada Lodge No. 4, Nevadaville
- Proceedings 1861-1869, pg 167 (1866 Oct 2) Denver Lodge No. 5
- Proceedings 1861-1869, pg 300 (1869 Sept 29), Denver Lodge No 5, living in Georgetown
- Proceedings 1861-1869, pg 305 (1869 Sept 29) Denver Lodge No. 5

Slaughter, W W
- Proceedings 1861-1869, pg 149 (1865 Nov 7), Nevada Lodge No. 4, Nevadaville
- Proceedings 1861-1869, pg 167 (1866 Oct 2) Denver Lodge No. 5
- Proceedings 1861-1869, pg 193 (1867 Oct 8) Denver Lodge No. 5
- Proceedings 1861-1869, pg 230 (1868 Oct 7), Cheyenne Lodge U D, Cheyenne, Dakota Territory
- Proceedings 1861-1869, pg 305 (1869 Sept 29) Denver Lodge No. 5
- Proceedings 1861-1869, pg 311 (1869 Sept 29), Cheyenne Lodge No. 16, Cheyenne
- Proceedings 1870, pg 21 (1870 Sept 28), Denver Lodge No. 5, Denver
- Proceedings 1870, pg 29 (1870 Sept 28), Cheyenne Lodge No. 16, Cheyenne, Wyoming Territory
- Proceedings 1871, pg 27 (1871 Sept 27), Cheyenne Lodge No. 16, Cheyenne, Wyoming Territory
- Proceedings 1872, pg 29 (1872 Sept 24), Cheyenne Lodge No. 16, Cheyenne, Wyoming Territory

Proceedings 1873, pg 46 (1873 Oct 1), Cheyenne Lodge No. 16, Cheyenne, Wyoming Territory

Proceedings 1874, pg 221 (1874 Sept 30), Cheyenne Lodge No. 16, Cheyenne, Wyoming Territory

Slaughter, William M

Proceedings 1861-1869, pg 112 (1863 Nov 3) Denver Lodge No. 5

Slaughter, Wm M

Proceedings 1861-1869, pg 77 (1862 Nov 4) Denver Lodge No. 5

Proceedings 1861-1869, pg 133 (1864 Nov 8) Denver Lodge No. 5

Proceedings 1861-1869, pg 193 (1867 Oct 8) Denver Lodge No. 5

Proceedings 1861-1869, pg 223 (1868 Oct 7) Denver Lodge No. 5

Proceedings 1870, pg 21 (1870 Sept 28), Denver Lodge No. 5, Denver

Proceedings 1871, pg 19 (1871 Sept 27) Denver Lodge No. 5

Proceedings 1872, pg 20 (1872 Sept 24), Denver Lodge No. 5, Denver

Proceedings 1873, pg 38 (1873 Oct 1), Denver Lodge No. 5, Denver, Striken from the rolls

Slawson, John

Proceedings 1861-1869, pg 151 (1865 Nov 7), Empire Lodge U D, Empire City

Proceedings 1861-1869, pg 170 (1866 Oct 2), Empire Lodge No. 8, Empire City

Proceedings 1861-1869, pg 195 (1867 Oct 8), Empire Lodge No. 8, Empire City

Proceedings 1861-1869, pg 226 (1868 Oct 7), Empire Lodge No. 8, Empire City

Slifer, E G

Proceedings 1861-1869, pg 230 (1868 Oct 7), Valmont Lodge U D, Valmont

Slifer, E S

Proceedings 1875, pg 83 (1875 Sept 22), Columbia Lodge No. 14, Boulder, Stricken from the rolls

Slifer, Esram G

Proceedings 1870, pg 27 (1870 Sept 28), Columbia Lodge No. 14, Boulder City

Slifer, Esrom G

Proceedings 1861-1869, pg 311 (1869 Sept 29), Columbia Lodge No. 14, Boulder City

Proceedings 1871, pg 26 (1871 Sept 27), Columbia Lodge No. 14, Boulder City

Proceedings 1872, pg 28 (1872 Sept 24), Columbia Lodge No. 14, Boulder

Proceedings 1873, pg 44 (1873 Oct 1), Columbia Lodge No. 14, Boulder

Proceedings 1874, pg 219 (1874 Sept 30), Columbia Lodge No. 14, Boulder, Boulder County

Smail, Charles

Proceedings 1872, pg 25 (1872 Sept 24), Black Hawk Lodge No. 11, Black Hawk

Proceedings 1874, pg 216 (1874 Sept 30), Black Hawk Lodge No. 11, Black Hawk

Proceedings 1875, pg 80 (1875 Sept 22) Black Hawk Lodge No. 11

Smail, Thomas

Proceedings 1871, pg 23 (1871 Sept 27), Black Hawk Lodge No. 11, Black Hawk, Apprentice

Proceedings 1872, pg 25 (1872 Sept 24), Black Hawk Lodge No. 11, Black Hawk

Proceedings 1873, pg 42 (1873 Oct 1), Black Hawk Lodge No. 11, Black Hawk

Proceedings 1874, pg 216 (1874 Sept 30), Black Hawk Lodge No. 11, Black Hawk

Proceedings 1875, pg 80 (1875 Sept 22) Black Hawk Lodge No. 11

Proceedings 1876, pg 34 (1876 Sept 20) Black Hawk Lodge No. 11

Smailes, John D

Proceedings 1872, pg 24 (1872 Sept 24), Black Hawk Lodge No. 11, Black Hawk

Smails, Charles

Proceedings 1876, pg 34 (1876 Sept 20) Black Hawk Lodge No. 11

Smails, J D

Proceedings 1870, pg 25 (1870 Sept 28), Black Hawk Lodge No. 11, Black Hawk

Smails, John D

Proceedings 1861-1869, pg 227 (1868 Oct 7), Black Hawk Lodge No. 11, Black Hawk

Proceedings 1861-1869, pg 309 (1869 Sept 29), Black Hawk Lodge No. 11, Black Hawk

Proceedings 1871, pg 23 (1871 Sept 27), Black Hawk Lodge No. 11, Black Hawk

Proceedings 1873, pg 41 (1873 Oct 1), Black Hawk Lodge No. 11, Black Hawk

Proceedings 1874, pg 216 (1874 Sept 30), Black Hawk Lodge No. 11, Black Hawk

Proceedings 1875, pg 80 (1875 Sept 22) Black Hawk Lodge No. 11, Stricken from the rolls

Small, Jos A

Proceedings 1873, pg 46 (1873 Oct 1), Cheyenne Lodge No. 16, Cheyenne, Wyoming Territory

Small, Joseph A

Proceedings 1874, pg 221 (1874 Sept 30), Cheyenne Lodge No. 16, Cheyenne, Wyoming Territory

Smedley, William

Proceedings 1873, pg 40 (1873 Oct 1), Union Lodge No. 7, Denver

Proceedings 1874, pg 214 (1874 Sept 30), Union Lodge No. 7, Denver

Proceedings 1875, pg 78 (1875 Sept 22), Union Lodge No. 7, Denver

Proceedings 1876, pg 33 (1876 Sept 20), Union Lodge No. 7, Denver

Colorado's Territorial Masons

Smedley, Wm
Proceedings 1872, pg 22 (1872 Sept 24), Union Lodge No. 7, Denver

Smeltzer, George W
Proceedings 1876, pg 35 (1876 Sept 20), Washington Lodge No. 12, Georgetown

Smith
Proceedings 1874, pg 45 (1874 Sept 30) Grand Lodge of Arkansas

Smith & Doll
Proceedings 1874, pg 49 (1874 Sept 30) bill for coffin and hearse

Smith, A
Proceedings 1861-1869, pg 170 (1866 Oct 2), Black Hawk Lodge U D, Black Hawk
Proceedings 1861-1869, pg 176 (1867 Oct 7), Black Hawk Lodge U D, Black Hawk

Smith, A A
Proceedings 1861-1869, pg 345 (1868 June 22) Grand Master, Grand Lodge of Oregon
Proceedings 1874, pg 219 (1874 Sept 30), Columbia Lodge No. 14, Boulder, Boulder County
Proceedings 1875, pg 83 (1875 Sept 22), Columbia Lodge No. 14, Boulder

Smith, Alonzo
Proceedings 1861-1869, pg 195 (1867 Oct 8), Black Hawk Lodge No. 11, Black Hawk
Proceedings 1861-1869, pg 226 (1868 Oct 7), Black Hawk Lodge No. 11, Black Hawk
Proceedings 1861-1869, pg 309 (1869 Sept 29), Black Hawk Lodge No. 11, Black Hawk
Proceedings 1870, pg 25 (1870 Sept 28), Black Hawk Lodge No. 11, Black Hawk
Proceedings 1871, pg 23 (1871 Sept 27), Black Hawk Lodge No. 11, Black Hawk
Proceedings 1872, pg 24 (1872 Sept 24), Black Hawk Lodge No. 11, Black Hawk
Proceedings 1873, pg 41 (1873 Oct 1), Black Hawk Lodge No. 11, Black Hawk
Proceedings 1874, pg 216 (1874 Sept 30), Black Hawk Lodge No. 11, Black Hawk
Proceedings 1875, pg 80 (1875 Sept 22) Black Hawk Lodge No. 11
Proceedings 1876, pg 34 (1876 Sept 20) Black Hawk Lodge No. 11

Smith, Asa
Proceedings 1870, pg 52 (1870 May 11) Grand Master, Grand Lodge of Connecticut
Proceedings 1871, pg 10 (1871 May 17) Grand Lodge of Connecticut
Proceedings 1872, pg 41 (1872 Sept 24), of Newark, Representative of the Grand Lodge of Connecticut
Proceedings 1873, pg 59 (1873 Oct 1), of Newark, Grand Representative to the Grand Lodge of Connecticut
Proceedings 1874, pg 207 (1874 Sept 30) Grand Lodge of Connecticut, Norwalk
Proceedings 1875, pg 95 (1875 Sept 22) Grand Lodge of Connecticut, Norwalk, CT

Smith, Avery A
Proceedings 1861-1869, pg 344 (1868 June 22) Grand Master, Grand Lodge of Oregon
Proceedings 1870, pg 97 (1869 June 21) Grand Master, Grand Lodge of Oregon

Smith, Azron A
Proceedings 1876, pg 37 (1876 Sept 20), Columbia Lodge No. 14, Boulder

Smith, B F
Proceedings 1861-1869, pg 207 (1867 Dec 11) Senior Warden
Proceedings 1861-1869, pg 229 (1868 Oct 7), Canon Lodge U D, Canon City
Proceedings 1861-1869, pg 311 (1869 Sept 29), Mount Moriah Lodge No. 15, Canon City
Proceedings 1870, pg 28 (1870 Sept 28), Mount Moriah Lodge No. 15, Canon City
Proceedings 1871, pg 26 (1871 Sept 27), Mount Moriah Lodge No. 15, Canon City
Proceedings 1872, pg 28 (1872 Sept 24), Mount Moriah Lodge No. 15, Canon City
Proceedings 1873, pg 45 (1873 Oct 1), Mount Moriah Lodge No. 15, Canon City, Dimitted
Proceedings 1874, pg 209 (1874 Sept 30), Golden City Lodge No. 1, Golden City
Proceedings 1875, pg 73 (1875 Sept 22) Golden City Lodge No. 1

Smith, Benjamin F
Proceedings 1876, pg 29 (1876 Sept 20) Golden City Lodge No. 1

Smith, Boston
Proceedings 1861-1869, pg 334 (1784 Sept 29) African Lodge No. 459
Proceedings 1870, pg 72 (1784 Sept 29) African Lodge at Boston
Proceedings 1870, pg 73 (1784 Sept 29) African Lodge at Boston
Proceedings 1870, pg 77 (1784 Sept 29)

Smith, C A
Proceedings 1871, pg 21 (1871 Sept 27), Central Lodge No. 6, Central

Smith, C C
Proceedings 1870, pg 31 (1870 Sept 28), Laramie Lodge No. 18, Laramie, Wyoming Territory
Proceedings 1871, pg 29 (1871 Sept 27), Laramie Lodge No. 18, Laramie, Wyoming Territory
Proceedings 1872, pg 32 (1872 Sept 24), Laramie Lodge No. 18, Laramie, Wyoming Territory
Proceedings 1873, pg 48 (1873 Oct 1), Laramie Lodge No. 18, Laramie, Wyoming Territory, Dimitted

Smith, C J
Proceedings 1874, pg 214 (1874 Sept 30), Union Lodge No. 7, Denver
Proceedings 1875, pg 78 (1875 Sept 22), Union Lodge No. 7, Denver

Proceedings 1876, pg 33 (1876 Sept 20), Union Lodge No. 7, Denver

Smith, C W
Proceedings 1861-1869, pg 5 (1861 Aug 2) Junior Grand Deacon, Gold Hill
Proceedings 1861-1869, pg 38 (1861 Dec 12) Sword Bearer
Proceedings 1861-1869, pg 43 (1861 Dec 10), Rocky Mountain Lodge No. 3, Gold Hill
Proceedings 1861-1869, pg 133 (1864 Nov 8) Denver Lodge No. 5
Proceedings 1861-1869, pg 149 (1865 Nov 7), Nevada Lodge No. 4, Nevadaville
Proceedings 1861-1869, pg 167 (1866 Oct 2) Denver Lodge No. 5, dimitted

Smith, Clark A
Proceedings 1861-1869, pg 168 (1866 Oct 2), Chivington Lodge No. 6, Central City
Proceedings 1861-1869, pg 194 (1867 Oct 8), Chivington Lodge No. 6, Central City
Proceedings 1861-1869, pg 224 (1868 Oct 7), Chivington Lodge No. 6, Central City
Proceedings 1870, pg 22 (1870 Sept 28), Central Lodge No. 6, Central City
Proceedings 1872, pg 21 (1872 Sept 24), Denver Lodge No. 5, Denver
Proceedings 1873, pg 38 (1873 Oct 1), Central Lodge No. 6, Central City
Proceedings 1874, pg 213 (1874 Sept 30), Central Lodge No. 6, Central
Proceedings 1875, pg 77 (1875 Sept 22), Central Lodge No. 6, Central City
Proceedings 1876, pg 32 (1876 Sept 20), Central Lodge No. 6, Central City
Proceedings 1861-1869, pg 306 (1869 Sept 29), Central Lodge No. 6, Central City

Smith, D Thomas
Proceedings 1876, pg 33 (1876 Sept 20), Union Lodge No. 7, Denver

Smith, D Tom
Proceedings 1872, pg 22 (1872 Sept 24), Union Lodge No. 7, Denver
Proceedings 1873, pg 40 (1873 Oct 1), Union Lodge No. 7, Denver
Proceedings 1874, pg 214 (1874 Sept 30), Union Lodge No. 7, Denver
Proceedings 1875, pg 78 (1875 Sept 22), Union Lodge No. 7, Denver

Smith, E A
Proceedings 1861-1869, pg 170 (1866 Oct 2), El Paso U D, Colorado City
Proceedings 1861-1869, pg 196 (1867 Oct 8), El Paso Lodge U D, Colorado City
Proceedings 1861-1869, pg 228 (1868 Oct 7), El Paso Lodge No. 13, Colorado City
Proceedings 1861-1869, pg 310 (1869 Sept 29), El Paso Lodge No. 13, Colorado City
Proceedings 1870, pg 27 (1870 Sept 28), El Paso Lodge No. 13, Colorado City
Proceedings 1871, pg 25 (1871 Sept 27), El Paso Lodge No. 13, Colorado City
Proceedings 1872, pg 27 (1872 Sept 24), El Paso Lodge No. 13, Colorado City
Proceedings 1873, pg 43 (1873 Oct 1), El Paso Lodge No. 13, Colorado City
Proceedings 1874, pg 218 (1874 Sept 30), El Paso Lodge No. 13, Colorado Springs
Proceedings 1875, pg 82 (1875 Sept 22), El Paso Lodge No. 13, Colorado Springs, Stricken from the rolls

Smith, E B
Proceedings 1861-1869, pg 42 (1861 Dec 10) Golden City Lodge No. 1
Proceedings 1861-1869, pg 86 (1863 Feb 22) Golden City Lodge No. 1
Proceedings 1861-1869, pg 110 (1863 Nov 3) Golden City Lodge No. 1
Proceedings 1861-1869, pg 131 (1864 Nov 8) Golden City Lodge No. 1
Proceedings 1861-1869, pg 147 (1865 Nov 7) Golden City Lodge No. 1
Proceedings 1861-1869, pg 165 (1866 Oct 2) Golden City Lodge No. 1
Proceedings 1861-1869, pg 191 (1867 Oct 8) Golden City Lodge No. 1
Proceedings 1861-1869, pg 221 (1868 Oct 7) Golden City Lodge No. 1
Proceedings 1861-1869, pg 303 (1869 Sept 29) Golden City Lodge No. 1
Proceedings 1870, pg 19 (1870 Sept 28), Golden City Lodge No. 1, Golden City
Proceedings 1871, pg 17 (1871 Sept 27), Golden City Lodge No. 1, Golden City
Proceedings 1872, pg 17 (1872 Sept 24), Golden City Lodge No. 1, Golden City
Proceedings 1873, pg 35 (1873 Oct 1), Golden City Lodge No. 1, Golden City
Proceedings 1874, pg 209 (1874 Sept 30), Golden City Lodge No. 1, Golden City
Proceedings 1875, pg 73 (1875 Sept 22) Golden City Lodge No. 1

Smith, Elias
Proceedings 1876, pg 35 (1876 Sept 20), Washington Lodge No. 12, Georgetown

Smith, Ensign B
Proceedings 1876, pg 29 (1876 Sept 20) Golden City Lodge No. 1

Smith, Foot
Proceedings 1870, pg 29 (1870 Sept 28), Cheyenne Lodge No. 16, Cheyenne, Wyoming Territory

Smith, Frank C
Proceedings 1873, pg 47 (1873 Oct 1), Pueblo Lodge No. 17, Pueblo, Apprentice
Proceedings 1874, pg 222 (1874 Sept 30), Pueblo Lodge No. 17, Pueblo, Pueblo County, Apprentice
Proceedings 1875, pg 85 (1875 Sept 22) Pueblo Lodge No. 17, Apprentice

Smith, Frank C, cont.
Proceedings 1876, pg 39 (1876 Sept 20) Pueblo Lodge No. 17, Apprentice
Proceedings 1876, pg 45 (1876 Sept 20), King Solomon Lodge U D, West Las Animas

Smith, Fred
Proceedings 1872, pg 29 (1872 Sept 24), Cheyenne Lodge No. 16, Cheyenne, Wyoming Territory
Proceedings 1873, pg 46 (1873 Oct 1), Cheyenne Lodge No. 16, Cheyenne, Wyoming Territory

Smith, G A
Proceedings 1861-1869, pg 151 (1865 Nov 7), Empire Lodge U D, Empire City, Fellowcraft

Smith, G F
Proceedings 1874, pg 221 (1874 Sept 30), Cheyenne Lodge No. 16, Cheyenne, Wyoming Territory, died

Smith, Geo A
Proceedings 1861-1869, pg 170 (1866 Oct 2), Empire Lodge No. 8, Empire City
Proceedings 1861-1869, pg 226 (1868 Oct 7), Empire Lodge No. 8, Empire City
Proceedings 1870, pg 24 (1870 Sept 28), Empire Lodge No. 8, Empire
Proceedings 1872, pg 23 (1872 Sept 24), Empire Lodge No. 8, Empire

Smith, George A
Proceedings 1861-1869, pg 195 (1867 Oct 8), Empire Lodge No. 8, Empire City
Proceedings 1861-1869, pg 308 (1869 Sept 29), Empire Lodge No. 8, Empire City
Proceedings 1873, pg 41 (1873 Oct 1), Empire Lodge No. 8, Empire
Proceedings 1874, pg 215 (1874 Sept 30), Empire Lodge No. 8, Empire
Proceedings 1875, pg 29 (1875 Sept 21), Empire Lodge No. 8, Empire, an invalid
Proceedings 1875, pg 30 (1875 Sept 21) money appropriated for his care
Proceedings 1876, pg 12 (1876 Sept 19), supported by Washington Lodge No. 12, Georgetown
Proceedings 1876, pg 24 (1876 Sept 20) communication received
Proceedings 1876, pg 25 (1876 Sept 20), cared for by Washington Lodge No. 12, Georgetown

Smith, Henry F
Proceedings 1874, pg 214 (1874 Sept 30), Union Lodge No. 7, Denver
Proceedings 1875, pg 78 (1875 Sept 22), Union Lodge No. 7, Denver
Proceedings 1876, pg 33 (1876 Sept 20), Union Lodge No. 7, Denver

Smith, Irwin A
Proceedings 1873, pg 36 (1873 Oct 1), Nevada Lodge No. 4, Nevada
Proceedings 1874, pg 210 (1874 Sept 30), Nevada Lodge No. 4, Bald Mountain, Gilpin County
Proceedings 1875, pg 74 (1875 Sept 22), Nevada Lodge No. 4, Nevada
Proceedings 1876, pg 48 (1876 Sept 20) Nevada Lodge No. 4, 1876 Jan 22
Proceedings 1876, pg 53 (1876 Sept 20) Grand Lodge of Connecticut, of Norfolk, CT

Smith, J C
Proceedings 1871, pg 31 (1871 Sept 27), Occidental Lodge U D, Greeley
Proceedings 1872, pg 33 (1872 Sept 24), Occidental Lodge No. 20, Greeley
Proceedings 1873, pg 50 (1873 Oct 1), Occidental Lodge No. 20, Greeley
Proceedings 1874, pg 225 (1874 Sept 30), Occidental Lodge No. 20, Greeley
Proceedings 1875, pg 87 (1875 Sept 22), Occidental Lodge No. 20, Greeley
Proceedings 1876, pg 40 (1876 Sept 20), Occidental Lodge No. 20, Greeley

Smith, J E
Proceedings 1872, pg 30 (1872 Sept 24), Pueblo Lodge No. 17, Pueblo
Proceedings 1872, pg 49 (1872 Sept 24), Pueblo Lodge No. 17, Pueblo
Proceedings 1874, pg 222 (1874 Sept 30), Pueblo Lodge No. 17, Pueblo, Pueblo County
Proceedings 1875, pg 85 (1875 Sept 22) Pueblo Lodge No. 17
Proceedings 1876, pg 39 (1876 Sept 20) Pueblo Lodge No. 17

Smith, J L
Proceedings 1861-1869, pg 149 (1865 Nov 7), Nevada Lodge No. 4, Nevadaville, dimitted

Smith, J Lloyd
Proceedings 1861-1869, pg 77 (1862 Nov 4) Denver Lodge No. 5
Proceedings 1861-1869, pg 112 (1863 Nov 3) Denver Lodge No. 5
Proceedings 1861-1869, pg 133 (1864 Nov 8) Denver Lodge No. 5

Smith, J M
Proceedings 1861-1869, pg 111 (1863 Nov 3), Nevada Lodge No. 4, Nevadaville
Proceedings 1861-1869, pg 132 (1864 Nov 8), Nevada Lodge No. 4, Nevadaville
Proceedings 1861-1869, pg 148 (1865 Nov 7), Nevada Lodge No. 4, Nevadaville
Proceedings 1861-1869, pg 151 (1865 Nov 7), Empire Lodge U D, Empire City
Proceedings 1861-1869, pg 166 (1866 Oct 2), Nevada Lodge No. 4, Nevadaville, dimitted
Proceedings 1861-1869, pg 170 (1866 Oct 2), Empire Lodge No. 8, Empire City
Proceedings 1861-1869, pg 195 (1867 Oct 8), Empire Lodge No. 8, Empire City
Proceedings 1861-1869, pg 227 (1868 Oct 7), Washington Lodge No. 12, Georgetown

Proceedings 1870, pg 26 (1870 Sept 28), Washington Lodge No. 12, Georgetown

Proceedings 1871, pg 24 (1871 Sept 27), Washington Lodge No. 12, Georgetown

Proceedings 1872, pg 26 (1872 Sept 24), Washington Lodge No. 12, Georgetown

Smith, J Nelson

Proceedings 1861-1869, pg 78 (1862 Nov 4), Chivington Lodge No. 6, Central City

Proceedings 1861-1869, pg 134 (1864 Nov 8), Chivington Lodge No. 6, Central City, deceased

Smith, J W

Proceedings 1861-1869, pg 113 (1863 Nov 3), Chivington Lodge No. 6, Central City

Smith, James E

Proceedings 1861-1869, pg 313 (1869 Sept 29), Pueblo Lodge No. 17, Pueblo, Apprentice

Proceedings 1870, pg 30 (1870 Sept 28), Pueblo Lodge No. 17, Pueblo

Proceedings 1873, pg 47 (1873 Oct 1), Pueblo Lodge No. 17, Pueblo

Smith, James J

Proceedings 1872, pg 19 (1872 Sept 24), Nevada Lodge No. 4, Bald Mountain

Proceedings 1873, pg 36 (1873 Oct 1), Nevada Lodge No. 4, Nevada

Proceedings 1874, pg 210 (1874 Sept 30), Nevada Lodge No. 4, Bald Mountain, Gilpin County

Proceedings 1876, pg 30 (1876 Sept 20) Nevada Lodge No. 4

Smith, James M

Proceedings 1873, pg 49 (1873 Oct 1), Collins Lodge No. 19, Fort Collins

Proceedings 1874, pg 224 (1874 Sept 30), Collins Lodge No. 19, Fort Collins, Larimer County

Proceedings 1875, pg 86 (1875 Sept 22), Collins Lodge No. 19, Fort Collins

Proceedings 1876, pg 39 (1876 Sept 20), Collins Lodge No. 19, Fort Collins

Smith, James M Jr

Proceedings 1871, pg 30 (1871 Sept 27), Collins Lodge No. 19, Fort Collins

Smith, James M Sr

Proceedings 1871, pg 30 (1871 Sept 27), Collins Lodge No. 19, Fort Collins

Proceedings 1872, pg 33 (1872 Sept 24), Collins Lodge No. 19, Fort Collins, died

Proceedings 1872, pg 39 (1872 Sept 24), Collins Lodge No. 19, Fort Collins

Smith, Jas J

Proceedings 1875, pg 74 (1875 Sept 22), Nevada Lodge No. 4, Nevada

Smith, Jas M

Proceedings 1870, pg 31 (1870 Sept 28), Collins Lodge No. 19, Fort Collins

Smith, Jas M Jr

Proceedings 1872, pg 33 (1872 Sept 24), Collins Lodge No. 19, Fort Collins

Smith, Jas M Sr

Proceedings 1872, pg 33 (1872 Sept 24), Collins Lodge No. 19, Fort Collins

Smith, Johnathan M

Proceedings 1873, pg 43 (1873 Oct 1), Washington Lodge No. 12, Georgetown

Smith, Jotham

Proceedings 1861-1869, pg 309 (1869 Sept 29), Washington Lodge No. 12, Georgetown

Smith, Jotham M

Proceedings 1874, pg 217 (1874 Sept 30), Washington Lodge No. 12, Georgetown

Proceedings 1875, pg 81 (1875 Sept 22), Washington Lodge No. 12, Georgetown

Proceedings 1876, pg 35 (1876 Sept 20), Washington Lodge No. 12, Georgetown

Proceedings 1861-1869, pg 226 (1868 Oct 7), Empire Lodge No. 8, Empire City, Dimitted

Smith, M G

Proceedings 1861-1869, pg 43 (1861 Dec 10), Rocky Mountain Lodge No. 3, Gold Hill

Proceedings 1861-1869, pg 197 (1867 Oct 8), Columbia Lodge U D, Boulder

Proceedings 1861-1869, pg 228 (1868 Oct 7), Columbia Lodge No. 14, Columbia City

Proceedings 1861-1869, pg 310 (1869 Sept 29), Columbia Lodge No. 14, Boulder City

Proceedings 1870, pg 27 (1870 Sept 28), Columbia Lodge No. 14, Boulder City

Proceedings 1872, pg 27 (1872 Sept 24), Columbia Lodge No. 14, Boulder

Proceedings 1873, pg 44 (1873 Oct 1), Columbia Lodge No. 14, Boulder

Proceedings 1874, pg 6 (1874 Sept 29), Columbia Lodge No. 14, Boulder

Proceedings 1874, pg 219 (1874 Sept 30), Columbia Lodge No. 14, Boulder, Boulder County

Smith, M H

Proceedings 1873, pg 50 (1873 Oct 1), Occidental Lodge No. 20, Greeley

Proceedings 1874, pg 225 (1874 Sept 30), Occidental Lodge No. 20, Greeley

Proceedings 1875, pg 87 (1875 Sept 22), Occidental Lodge No. 20, Greeley

Proceedings 1876, pg 40 (1876 Sept 20), Occidental Lodge No. 20, Greeley

Smith, Marinus G

Proceedings 1871, pg 25 (1871 Sept 27), Columbia Lodge No. 14, Boulder City

Proceedings 1871, pg 25 (1871 Sept 27), Columbia Lodge No. 14, Boulder City

Proceedings 1875, pg 83 (1875 Sept 22), Columbia Lodge No. 14, Boulder

Proceedings 1876, pg 36 (1876 Sept 20), Columbia Lodge No. 14, Boulder

Colorado's Territorial Masons

Smith, Marshall B
Proceedings 1874, pg 109 (1874 Sept 30) Grand Lodge of New Jersey

Smith, Milo
Proceedings 1861-1869, pg 131 (1864 Nov 8) Golden City Lodge No. 1, Apprentice
Proceedings 1861-1869, pg 147 (1865 Nov 7) Golden City Lodge No. 1
Proceedings 1861-1869, pg 165 (1866 Oct 2) Golden City Lodge No. 1
Proceedings 1861-1869, pg 191 (1867 Oct 8) Golden City Lodge No. 1, Dimitted

Smith, Nathaniel G
Proceedings 1870, pg 41 (1869 Nov 1) Grand Lodge of Arkansas, deceased
Proceedings 1870, pg 43 (1869 Nov 1) Grand Lodge of Arkansas, deceased

Smith, Obadiah
Proceedings 1874, pg 216 (1874 Sept 30), Black Hawk Lodge No. 11, Black Hawk
Proceedings 1875, pg 80 (1875 Sept 22) Black Hawk Lodge No. 11
Proceedings 1876, pg 34 (1876 Sept 20) Black Hawk Lodge No. 11

Smith, P L
Proceedings 1861-1869, pg 131 (1864 Nov 8) Golden City Lodge No. 1, Apprentice
Proceedings 1861-1869, pg 147 (1865 Nov 7) Golden City Lodge No. 1, Fellowcraft
Proceedings 1861-1869, pg 165 (1866 Oct 2) Golden City Lodge No. 1
Proceedings 1861-1869, pg 191 (1867 Oct 8) Golden City Lodge No. 1
Proceedings 1861-1869, pg 221 (1868 Oct 7) Golden City Lodge No. 1
Proceedings 1870, pg 19 (1870 Sept 28), Golden City Lodge No. 1, Golden City
Proceedings 1871, pg 17 (1871 Sept 27), Golden City Lodge No. 1, Golden City

Smith, Perry L
Proceedings 1861-1869, pg 303 (1869 Sept 29) Golden City Lodge No. 1
Proceedings 1872, pg 17 (1872 Sept 24), Golden City Lodge No. 1, Golden City
Proceedings 1873, pg 19 (1873 Oct 1), Golden City Lodge No. 1, Golden City

Smith, Samuel L
Proceedings 1876, pg 44 (1876 Sept 20), Las Animas Lodge No. 28, Trinidad

Smith, T M
Proceedings 1870, pg 31 (1870 Sept 28), Collins Lodge No. 19, Fort Collins
Proceedings 1873, pg 6 (1873 Sept 30), Collins Lodge No. 19, Fort Collins
Proceedings 1873, pg 31 (1873 Oct 1) mileage and per diem
Proceedings 1874, pg 12 (1874 Jan 30), Collins Lodge No. 19, Fort Collins
Proceedings 1876, pg 39 (1876 Sept 20), Collins Lodge No. 19, Fort Collins

Smith, T R
Proceedings 1861-1869, pg 196 (1867 Oct 8), Black Hawk Lodge No. 11, Black Hawk
Proceedings 1861-1869, pg 227 (1868 Oct 7), Black Hawk Lodge No. 11, Black Hawk, Dimitted

Smith, Thos R
Proceedings 1861-1869, pg 170 (1866 Oct 2), Black Hawk Lodge U D, Black Hawk

Smith, Timothy M
Proceedings 1871, pg 30 (1871 Sept 27), Collins Lodge No. 19, Fort Collins
Proceedings 1872, pg 32 (1872 Sept 24), Collins Lodge No. 19, Fort Collins
Proceedings 1873, pg 49 (1873 Oct 1), Collins Lodge No. 19, Fort Collins
Proceedings 1874, pg 224 (1874 Sept 30), Collins Lodge No. 19, Fort Collins, Larimer County
Proceedings 1875, pg 86 (1875 Sept 22), Collins Lodge No. 19, Fort Collins

Smith, W D
Proceedings 1861-1869, pg 76 (1862 Nov 4), Summit Lodge No. 2, Parkville

Smith, W G
Proceedings 1870, pg 31 (1870 Sept 28), Laramie Lodge No. 18, Laramie, Wyoming Territory
Proceedings 1871, pg 29 (1871 Sept 27), Laramie Lodge No. 18, Laramie, Wyoming Territory
Proceedings 1872, pg 32 (1872 Sept 24), Laramie Lodge No. 18, Laramie, Wyoming Territory
Proceedings 1873, pg 48 (1873 Oct 1), Laramie Lodge No. 18, Laramie, Wyoming Territory
Proceedings 1874, pg 223 (1874 Sept 30), Laramie Lodge No. 18, Laramie City

Smith, W H
Proceedings 1861-1869, pg 197 (1867 Oct 8), Columbia Lodge U D, Boulder, Apprentice
Proceedings 1861-1869, pg 228 (1868 Oct 7), Columbia Lodge No. 14, Columbia City, Fellowcraft
Proceedings 1871, pg 26 (1871 Sept 27), Columbia Lodge No. 14, Boulder City
Proceedings 1872, pg 28 (1872 Sept 24), Columbia Lodge No. 14, Boulder
Proceedings 1874, pg 219 (1874 Sept 30), Columbia Lodge No. 14, Boulder, Boulder County

Smith, Walter H
Proceedings 1861-1869, pg 311 (1869 Sept 29), Columbia Lodge No. 14, Boulder City
Proceedings 1870, pg 27 (1870 Sept 28), Columbia Lodge No. 14, Boulder City
Proceedings 1873, pg 44 (1873 Oct 1), Columbia Lodge No. 14, Boulder
Proceedings 1875, pg 83 (1875 Sept 22), Columbia Lodge No. 14, Boulder
Proceedings 1876, pg 37 (1876 Sept 20), Columbia Lodge No. 14, Boulder

Smith, William D
Proceedings 1861-1869, pg 132 (1864 Nov 8) Golden City Lodge No. 1, dimitted

Smith, William L
Proceedings 1876, pg 29 (1876 Sept 20) Golden City Lodge No. 1

Smith, Winton
Proceedings 1872, pg 35 (1872 Sept 24), St Vrain Lodge No. 23, Longmont, Apprentice
Proceedings 1873, pg 51 (1873 Oct 1), St Vrain Lodge No. 23, Longmont
Proceedings 1874, pg 227 (1874 Sept 30), St Vrain No. 23, Longmont
Proceedings 1876, pg 41 (1876 Sept 20), St Vrain Lodge No. 23, Longmont

Smith, Wm D
Proceedings 1861-1869, pg 110 (1863 Nov 3), Summit Lodge No. 2, Parkville

Smith, Wm L
Proceedings 1875, pg 73 (1875 Sept 22) Golden City Lodge No. 1

Smithers, G T
Proceedings 1872, pg 44 (1872 Sept 24) Halifax, Grand Lodge of Nova Scotia
Proceedings 1873, pg 61 (1873 Oct 1) Grand Lodge of Nova Scotia, Halifax
Proceedings 1874, pg 204 (1874 Sept 30) Grand Lodge of Nova Scotia, Halifax

Smithers, Geo T
Proceedings 1872, pg 77 (1872 Sept 24) Grand Lodge of Nova Scotia

Smithers, George T
Proceedings 1874, pg 117 (1874 Sept 30) Grand Lodge of Nova Scotia

Smithson, W W
Proceedings 1870, pg 30 (1870 Sept 28), Laramie Lodge No. 18, Laramie, Wyoming Territory
Proceedings 1871, pg 29 (1871 Sept 27), Laramie Lodge No. 18, Laramie, Wyoming Territory
Proceedings 1872, pg 32 (1872 Sept 24), Laramie Lodge No. 18, Laramie, Wyoming Territory
Proceedings 1873, pg 48 (1873 Oct 1), Laramie Lodge No. 18, Laramie, Wyoming Territory
Proceedings 1874, pg 223 (1874 Sept 30), Laramie Lodge No. 18, Laramie City

Snider, A J
Proceedings 1861-1869, pg 77 (1862 Nov 4) Denver Lodge No. 5
Proceedings 1861-1869, pg 133 (1864 Nov 8) Denver Lodge No. 5
Proceedings 1870, pg 6 (1870 May 9), Fidelity Lodge U D, Fort Collins
Proceedings 1870, pg 15 (1870 Sept 28) Collins Lodge No. 19

Snider, Fred'k J
Proceedings 1870, pg 31 (1870 Sept 28), Collins Lodge No. 19, Fort Collins

Snow, C L
Proceedings 1871, pg 27 (1871 Sept 27), Cheyenne Lodge No. 16, Cheyenne, Wyoming Territory

Snow, Charles L
Proceedings 1870, pg 29 (1870 Sept 28), Cheyenne Lodge No. 16, Cheyenne, Wyoming Territory
Proceedings 1872, pg 29 (1872 Sept 24), Cheyenne Lodge No. 16, Cheyenne, Wyoming Territory
Proceedings 1874, pg 221 (1874 Sept 30), Cheyenne Lodge No. 16, Cheyenne, Wyoming Territory

Snow, E P
Proceedings 1861-1869, pg 312 (1869 Sept 29), Cheyenne Lodge No. 16, Cheyenne, Fellowcraft
Proceedings 1870, pg 29 (1870 Sept 28), Cheyenne Lodge No. 16, Cheyenne, Wyoming Territory
Proceedings 1871, pg 4 (1871 Sept 26), Cheyenne Lodge No. 16, Cheyenne, Wyoming Territory
Proceedings 1871, pg 27 (1871 Sept 27), Cheyenne Lodge No. 16, Cheyenne, Wyoming Territory
Proceedings 1872, pg 29 (1872 Sept 24), Cheyenne Lodge No. 16, Cheyenne, Wyoming Territory
Proceedings 1873, pg 46 (1873 Oct 1), Cheyenne Lodge No. 16, Cheyenne, Wyoming Territory
Proceedings 1874, pg 221 (1874 Sept 30), Cheyenne Lodge No. 16, Cheyenne, Wyoming Territory

Snow, Edgar P
Proceedings 1875, pg 24 (1875 Sept 21), Wyoming Lodge No. 28, South Pass City, member of Cheyenne Lodge No. 16

Snowden, James
Proceedings 1872, pg 21 (1872 Sept 24), Denver Lodge No. 5, Denver

Snyder, A J
Proceedings 1861-1869, pg 149 (1865 Nov 7), Nevada Lodge No. 4, Nevadaville, dimitted

Snyder, Andy J
Proceedings 1861-1869, pg 112 (1863 Nov 3) Denver Lodge No. 5

Snyder, Hanson
Proceedings 1871, pg 26 (1871 Sept 27), Columbia Lodge No. 14, Boulder City, Apprentice
Proceedings 1872, pg 28 (1872 Sept 24), Columbia Lodge No. 14, Boulder, Apprentice
Proceedings 1874, pg 219 (1874 Sept 30), Columbia Lodge No. 14, Boulder, Boulder County
Proceedings 1875, pg 83 (1875 Sept 22), Columbia Lodge No. 14, Boulder
Proceedings 1876, pg 37 (1876 Sept 20), Columbia Lodge No. 14, Boulder

Snyder, Howard
Proceedings 1874, pg 214 (1874 Sept 30), Union Lodge No. 7, Denver

Snyder, J W O
Proceedings 1861-1869, pg 229 (1868 Oct 7), Pueblo Lodge U D, Pueblo
Proceedings 1861-1869, pg 312 (1869 Sept 29), Pueblo Lodge No. 17, Pueblo

Colorado's Territorial Masons

Snyder, J W O, cont.
Proceedings 1873, pg 47 (1873 Oct 1), Pueblo Lodge No. 17, Pueblo
Proceedings 1874, pg 222 (1874 Sept 30), Pueblo Lodge No. 17, Pueblo, Pueblo County
Proceedings 1875, pg 85 (1875 Sept 22) Pueblo Lodge No. 17
Proceedings 1876, pg 38 (1876 Sept 20) Pueblo Lodge No. 17

Snyder, John W O
Proceedings 1870, pg 30 (1870 Sept 28), Pueblo Lodge No. 17, Pueblo
Proceedings 1871, pg 28 (1871 Sept 27), Pueblo Lodge No. 17, Pueblo
Proceedings 1872, pg 31 (1872 Sept 24), Pueblo Lodge No. 17, Pueblo

Snyder, Lorenzo
Proceedings 1871, pg 30 (1871 Sept 27), Collins Lodge No. 19, Fort Collins, Apprentice
Proceedings 1872, pg 33 (1872 Sept 24), Collins Lodge No. 19, Fort Collins, Fellowcraft
Proceedings 1873, pg 49 (1873 Oct 1), Collins Lodge No. 19, Fort Collins, Fellowcraft
Proceedings 1874, pg 224 (1874 Sept 30), Collins Lodge No. 19, Fort Collins, Larimer County, Fellowcraft
Proceedings 1875, pg 86 (1875 Sept 22), Collins Lodge No. 19, Fort Collins, Fellowcraft
Proceedings 1876, pg 40 (1876 Sept 20), Collins Lodge No. 19, Fort Collins, Fellow Craft

Snyder, S O
Proceedings 1872, pg 20 (1872 Sept 24), Denver Lodge No. 5, Denver, Apprentice
Proceedings 1873, pg 37 (1873 Oct 1), Denver Lodge No. 5, Denver
Proceedings 1874, pg 211 (1874 Sept 30), Denver Lodge No. 5, Denver
Proceedings 1875, pg 75 (1875 Sept 22) Denver Lodge No. 5
Proceedings 1876, pg 30 (1876 Sept 20) Denver Lodge No. 5

Snyder, William
Proceedings 1876, pg 46 (1876 Sept 20), Olive Branch Lodge U D, Saguache

Solamon, H Z
Proceedings 1861-1869, pg 305 (1869 Sept 29) Denver Lodge No. 5

Solomon, A Z
Proceedings 1875, pg 87 (1875 Sept 22), Occidental Lodge No. 20, Greeley, Fellowcraft

Solomon, F Z
Proceedings 1861-1869, pg 195 (1867 Oct 8), Union Lodge No. 7, Denver
Proceedings 1861-1869, pg 225 (1868 Oct 7), Union Lodge No. 7, Denver
Proceedings 1861-1869, pg 307 (1869 Sept 29), Union Lodge No. 7, Denver
Proceedings 1874, pg 214 (1874 Sept 30), Union Lodge No. 7, Denver

Solomon, H Z
Proceedings 1861-1869, pg 149 (1865 Nov 7), Nevada Lodge No. 4, Nevadaville
Proceedings 1861-1869, pg 167 (1866 Oct 2) Denver Lodge No. 5
Proceedings 1861-1869, pg 193 (1867 Oct 8) Denver Lodge No. 5
Proceedings 1861-1869, pg 223 (1868 Oct 7) Denver Lodge No. 5
Proceedings 1875, pg 75 (1875 Sept 22) Denver Lodge No. 5

Solomon, Weil
Proceedings 1870, pg 25 (1870 Sept 28), Black Hawk Lodge No. 11, Black Hawk, Fellowcraft

Sommer, W
Proceedings 1861-1869, pg 228 (1868 Oct 7), Columbia Lodge No. 14, Columbia City

Sommer, Wilhelm
Proceedings 1861-1869, pg 197 (1867 Oct 8), Columbia Lodge U D, Boulder
Proceedings 1861-1869, pg 310 (1869 Sept 29), Columbia Lodge No. 14, Boulder City

Sommers, W
Proceedings 1871, pg 25 (1871 Sept 27), Columbia Lodge No. 14, Boulder City
Proceedings 1872, pg 28 (1872 Sept 24), Columbia Lodge No. 14, Boulder

Sommers, Wilhelm
Proceedings 1870, pg 27 (1870 Sept 28), Columbia Lodge No. 14, Boulder City
Proceedings 1874, pg 219 (1874 Sept 30), Columbia Lodge No. 14, Boulder, Boulder County
Proceedings 1875, pg 83 (1875 Sept 22), Columbia Lodge No. 14, Boulder, Stricken from the rolls
Proceedings 1873, pg 44 (1873 Oct 1), Columbia Lodge No. 14, Boulder

Songar, John
Proceedings 1871, pg 17 (1871 Sept 27), Golden City Lodge No. 1, Golden City, Apprentice

Songer, John
Proceedings 1874, pg 209 (1874 Sept 30), Golden City Lodge No. 1, Golden City, Fellow Craft
Proceedings 1875, pg 73 (1875 Sept 22) Golden City Lodge No. 1
Proceedings 1876, pg 29 (1876 Sept 20) Golden City Lodge No. 1

Sopris
Proceedings 1861-1869, pg 185 (1867 Oct 8) motion
Proceedings 1861-1869, pg 189 (1867 Oct 8) Grand Treasurer
Proceedings 1861-1869, pg 202 (1868 Oct 6) committee
Proceedings 1861-1869, pg 202 (1868 Oct 6) committee
Proceedings 1861-1869, pg 217 (1868 Oct 7) Grand Treasurer
Proceedings 1861-1869, pg 301 (1869 Sept 29) Deputy Grand Master

Proceedings 1870, pg 10 (1870 Sept 27) Past Grand Treasurer

Proceedings 1871, pg 8 (1871 Sept 26) Past Deputy Grand Master

Sopris, R
Proceedings 1861-1869, pg 54 (1862 Nov 4) committee
Proceedings 1861-1869, pg 136 (1865 Nov 6) Grand Treasurer
Proceedings 1861-1869, pg 159 (1866 Oct 1) Grand Treasurer
Proceedings 1861-1869, pg 162 (1866 Oct 2) committee
Proceedings 1861-1869, pg 162 (1866 Oct 2) Grand Treasurer
Proceedings 1861-1869, pg 167 (1866 Oct 2) Denver Lodge No. 5
Proceedings 1861-1869, pg 176 (1867 Oct 7) committee
Proceedings 1861-1869, pg 182 (1867 Oct 7) warrant paid
Proceedings 1861-1869, pg 188 (1867 Oct 8) committee
Proceedings 1861-1869, pg 192 (1867 Oct 8) Denver Lodge No. 5
Proceedings 1861-1869, pg 202 (1868 Oct 6) committee
Proceedings 1861-1869, pg 202 (1868 Oct 6) Grand Treasurer
Proceedings 1861-1869, pg 212 (1868 Oct 6) warrant paid
Proceedings 1861-1869, pg 219 (1868 Oct 7) mileage allowed
Proceedings 1861-1869, pg 223 (1868 Oct 7) Denver Lodge No. 5
Proceedings 1861-1869, pg 225 (1868 Oct 7), Union Lodge No. 7, Denver
Proceedings 1861-1869, pg 230 (1868 Oct 7), Germania Lodge U D, Denver
Proceedings 1861-1869, pg 288 (1869 Sept 28) Grand Treasurer
Proceedings 1861-1869, pg 289 (1869 Sept 28) Grand Treasurer
Proceedings 1861-1869, pg 300 (1869 Sept 29) Grand Treasurer
Proceedings 1861-1869, pg 305 (1869 Sept 29) Denver Lodge No. 5
Proceedings 1873, pg 19 (1873 Oct 1) committee
Proceedings 1873, pg 31 (1873 Oct 1) mileage and per diem
Proceedings 1874, pg 5 (1874 Sept 29) Past Deputy Grand Master
Proceedings 1874, pg 17 (1874 Sept 29) committee
Proceedings 1874, pg 21 (1874 Sept 29) committee
Proceedings 1874, pg 36 (1874 Sept 30) per diem

Sopris, Richard
Colorado University Cornerstone Laying, pg 3 (1875 Sept 20) Past Deputy Grand Master
Proceedings 1861-1869, pg 38 (1861 Dec 12) Grand Orator
Proceedings 1861-1869, pg 46 (1862 Nov 3) Junior Grand Warden
Proceedings 1861-1869, pg 51 (1862 Nov 4) Junior Grand Warden
Proceedings 1861-1869, pg 77 (1862 Nov 4) Denver Lodge No. 5
Proceedings 1861-1869, pg 112 (1863 Nov 3) Denver Lodge No. 5
Proceedings 1861-1869, pg 133 (1864 Nov 8) Denver Lodge No. 5
Proceedings 1861-1869, pg 140 (1865 Nov 6) Grand Marshal
Proceedings 1861-1869, pg 141 (1865 Nov 7) Denver Lodge No. 5
Proceedings 1861-1869, pg 149 (1865 Nov 7), Nevada Lodge No. 4, Nevadaville
Proceedings 1861-1869, pg 153 (1866 Oct 1) Grand Treasurer
Proceedings 1861-1869, pg 154 (1866 Oct 1) Grand Treasurer
Proceedings 1861-1869, pg 154 (1866 Oct 1) committee
Proceedings 1861-1869, pg 154 (1866 Oct 1) committee
Proceedings 1861-1869, pg 155 (1866 Oct 1) committee
Proceedings 1861-1869, pg 159 (1866 Oct 1) Grand Treasurer
Proceedings 1861-1869, pg 160 (1866 Oct 2) Denver Lodge No. 5
Proceedings 1861-1869, pg 161 (1866 Oct 2) Grand Treasurer
Proceedings 1861-1869, pg 175 (1867 Oct 7) Grand Treasurer
Proceedings 1861-1869, pg 176 (1867 Oct 7) Grand Treasurer
Proceedings 1861-1869, pg 182 (1867 Oct 7) Grand Treasurer
Proceedings 1861-1869, pg 185 (1867 Oct 7) Grand Treasurer
Proceedings 1861-1869, pg 201 (1868 Oct 6) Grand Treasurer
Proceedings 1861-1869, pg 211 (1868 Oct 6) Grand Treasurer
Proceedings 1861-1869, pg 215 (1868 Oct 6) Grand Treasurer
Proceedings 1861-1869, pg 287 (1869 Sept 28) Grand Treasurer
Proceedings 1861-1869, pg 298 (1869 Sept 28) Deputy Grand Master
Proceedings 1861-1869, pg 315 (1869 Sept 29) Grand Treasurer, 1865
Proceedings 1861-1869, pg 315 (1869 Sept 29) Deputy Grand Master, 1869
Proceedings 1861-1869, pg 315 (1869 Sept 29) Grand Treasurer, 1869
Proceedings 1861-1869, pg 315 (1869 Sept 29) Grand Treasurer, 1868
Proceedings 1861-1869, pg 315 (1869 Sept 29) Grand Treasurer, 1866
Proceedings 1861-1869, pg 315 (1869 Sept 29) Grand Treasurer, 1867
Proceedings 1861-1869, pg 315 (1869 Sept 29) Junior Grand Warden, 1862
Proceedings 1870, pg 21 (1870 Sept 28), Denver Lodge No. 5, Denver
Proceedings 1870, pg 32 (1870 Sept 28) Grand Treasurer, 1866
Proceedings 1870, pg 32 (1870 Sept 28) Deputy Grand Master, 1869
Proceedings 1870, pg 32 (1870 Sept 28) Grand Treasurer, 1865

Colorado's Territorial Masons

Sopris, Richard, cont.
   Proceedings 1870, pg 32 (1870 Sept 28) Junior Grand Warden, 1862
   Proceedings 1870, pg 32 (1870 Sept 28) Grand Treasurer, 1867
   Proceedings 1870, pg 32 (1870 Sept 28) Grand Treasurer, 1868
   Proceedings 1871, pg 19 (1871 Sept 27) Denver Lodge No. 5
   Proceedings 1871, pg 34 (1871 Sept 27) Grand Treasurer, 1867
   Proceedings 1871, pg 34 (1871 Sept 27) Grand Treasurer, 1868
   Proceedings 1871, pg 34 (1871 Sept 27) Junior Grand Warden, 1862
   Proceedings 1871, pg 34 (1871 Sept 27) Grand Treasurer, 1866
   Proceedings 1871, pg 34 (1871 Sept 27) Deputy Grand Master, 1869
   Proceedings 1871, pg 34 (1871 Sept 27) Grand Treasurer, 1865
   Proceedings 1872, pg 20 (1872 Sept 24), Denver Lodge No. 5, Denver
   Proceedings 1872, pg 42 (1872 Sept 24) Grand Treasurer, 1868
   Proceedings 1872, pg 42 (1872 Sept 24) Grand Treasurer, 1867
   Proceedings 1872, pg 42 (1872 Sept 24) Deputy Grand Master, 1869
   Proceedings 1872, pg 42 (1872 Sept 24) Grand Treasurer, 1866
   Proceedings 1872, pg 42 (1872 Sept 24) Grand Treasurer, 1865
   Proceedings 1872, pg 42 (1872 Sept 24) Junior Grand Warden, 1862
   Proceedings 1873, pg cover (1873 Oct 1) committee, Denver
   Proceedings 1873, pg 4 (1873 Sept 30) Past Deputy Grand Master
   Proceedings 1873, pg 5 (1873 Sept 30) Past Deputy Grand Master
   Proceedings 1873, pg 7 (1873 Sept 30) committee
   Proceedings 1873, pg 32 (1873 Oct 1) committee
   Proceedings 1873, pg 58 (1873 Oct 1) Junior Grand Warden, 1862
   Proceedings 1873, pg 58 (1873 Oct 1) Grand Treasurer, 1868
   Proceedings 1873, pg 58 (1873 Oct 1) Grand Treasurer, 1867
   Proceedings 1873, pg 58 (1873 Oct 1) Deputy Grand Master, 1869
   Proceedings 1873, pg 58 (1873 Oct 1) Grand Treasurer, 1865
   Proceedings 1873, pg 58 (1873 Oct 1) Grand Treasurer, 1866
   Proceedings 1874, pg 3 (1874 Sept 29) Past Deputy Grand Master
   Proceedings 1874, pg 206 (1874 Sept 30) Grand Treasurer, 1866
   Proceedings 1874, pg 206 (1874 Sept 30) Grand Treasurer, 1865
   Proceedings 1874, pg 206 (1874 Sept 30) Junior Grand Warden, 1862
   Proceedings 1874, pg 206 (1874 Sept 30) Grand Treasurer, 1868
   Proceedings 1874, pg 206 (1874 Sept 30) Grand Treasurer, 1867
   Proceedings 1874, pg 206 (1874 Sept 30) Deputy Grand Master, 1869
   Proceedings 1874, pg 211 (1874 Sept 30), Denver Lodge No. 5, Denver
   Proceedings 1875, pg 16 (1875 Sept 21) Past Deputy Grand Master
   Proceedings 1875, pg 75 (1875 Sept 22) Denver Lodge No. 5
   Proceedings 1875, pg 93 (1875 Sept 22) Grand Treasurer, 1865
   Proceedings 1875, pg 93 (1875 Sept 22) Grand Treasurer, 1868
   Proceedings 1875, pg 93 (1875 Sept 22) Grand Treasurer, 1867
   Proceedings 1875, pg 93 (1875 Sept 22) Junior Grand Warden, 1862
   Proceedings 1875, pg 93 (1875 Sept 22) Deputy Grand Master, 1869
   Proceedings 1875, pg 93 (1875 Sept 22) Grand Treasurer, 1866
   Proceedings 1876, pg 31 (1876 Sept 20) Denver Lodge No. 5

Sortor, August
   Proceedings 1875, pg 84 (1875 Sept 22), Mount Moriah Lodge No. 15, Canon City

Sortor, Augustus
   Proceedings 1873, pg 45 (1873 Oct 1), Mount Moriah Lodge No. 15, Canon City

Sougan, John
   Proceedings 1872, pg 17 (1872 Sept 24), Golden City Lodge No. 1, Golden City, Apprentice,

South Pass City
   Proceedings 1861-1869, pg 294 (1869 Sept 28) not granted a dispensation to open a lodge

South Pueblo Lodge No. 31
   Proceedings 1876, pg 52 (1876 Sept 20)

South Pueblo Lodge No. 31, South Pueblo
   Proceedings 1876, pg 24 (1876 Sept 20) charter granted

South Pueblo Lodge U D
   Proceedings 1876, pg 7 (1876 Mar 17) dispensation granted

South Pueblo Lodge U D, South Pueblo
   Proceedings 1876, pg 12 (1876 Sept 19) returns received only 15 days before annual communication
   Proceedings 1876, pg 12 (1876 Sept 19) dues paid and petition for a charter received
   Proceedings 1876, pg 13 (1876 Aug 20) dispensation fee paid

Proceedings 1876, pg 13 (1876 Sept 9) dues paid
Proceedings 1876, pg 24 (1876 Sept 20) returns correct

Southard, D B
Proceedings 1876, pg 33 (1876 Sept 20), Union Lodge No. 7, Denver
Southard, S H
Proceedings 1876, pg 41 (1876 Sept 20), St Vrain Lodge No. 23, Longmont, Apprentice

Southard, Sam'l H
Proceedings 1873, pg 52 (1873 Oct 1), St Vrain Lodge No. 23, Longmont, Apprentice

Southard, Samuel H
Proceedings 1874, pg 227 (1874 Sept 30), St Vrain No. 23, Longmont, Apprentice

Southerland, D E
Proceedings 1872, pg 28 (1872 Sept 24), Columbia Lodge No. 14, Boulder, Dimitted

Southland, Judson
Proceedings 1875, pg 83 (1875 Sept 22), Columbia Lodge No. 14, Boulder
Proceedings 1876, pg 37 (1876 Sept 20), Columbia Lodge No. 14, Boulder

Souver, Charles
Proceedings 1861-1869, pg 196 (1867 Oct 8), El Paso Lodge U D, Colorado City

Sowden, James
Proceedings 1870, pg 22 (1870 Sept 28), Central Lodge No. 6, Central City
Proceedings 1871, pg 21 (1871 Sept 27), Central Lodge No. 6, Central
Proceedings 1873, pg 38 (1873 Oct 1), Central Lodge No. 6, Central City
Proceedings 1874, pg 213 (1874 Sept 30), Central Lodge No. 6, Central
Proceedings 1875, pg 77 (1875 Sept 22), Central Lodge No. 6, Central City
Proceedings 1876, pg 50 (1876 Sept 20), Central Lodge No. 6, Central City
Proceedings 1876, pg 32 (1876 Sept 20), Central Lodge No. 6, Central City

Sparks, D
Proceedings 1861-1869, pg 111 (1863 Nov 3), Summit Lodge No. 2, Parkville, dimitted

Sparks, D P
Proceedings 1861-1869, pg 42 (1861 Dec 10), Summit Lodge No. 2, Parkville
Proceedings 1861-1869, pg 76 (1862 Nov 4), Summit Lodge No. 2, Parkville

Sparks, D T
Proceedings 1861-1869, pg 111 (1863 Nov 3), Nevada Lodge No. 4, Nevadaville

Sparks, O F
Proceedings 1861-1869, pg 132 (1864 Nov 8), Nevada Lodge No. 4, Nevadaville
Proceedings 1861-1869, pg 148 (1865 Nov 7), Nevada Lodge No. 4, Nevadaville

Sparks, O T
Proceedings 1861-1869, pg 154 (1866 Oct 1), Nevada Lodge No. 4, Nevadaville
Proceedings 1861-1869, pg 155 (1866 Oct 1) committee
Proceedings 1861-1869, pg 166 (1866 Oct 2), Nevada Lodge No. 4, Nevadaville
Proceedings 1861-1869, pg 222 (1868 Oct 7), Nevada Lodge No. 4, Nevadaville
Proceedings 1861-1869, pg 304 (1869 Sept 29), Nevada Lodge No. 4, Nevadaville
Proceedings 1871, pg 18 (1871 Sept 27), Nevada Lodge No. 4, Bald Mountain
Proceedings 1874, pg 210 (1874 Sept 30), Nevada Lodge No. 4, Bald Mountain, Gilpin County
Proceedings 1875, pg 74 (1875 Sept 22), Nevada Lodge No. 4, Nevada
Proceedings 1876, pg 30 (1876 Sept 20) Nevada Lodge No. 4

Sparks, Ozias T
Proceedings 1861-1869, pg 191 (1867 Oct 8), Nevada Lodge No. 4, Nevadaville
Proceedings 1870, pg 20 (1870 Sept 28), Nevada Lodge No. 4, Nevadaville
Proceedings 1872, pg 19 (1872 Sept 24), Nevada Lodge No. 4, Bald Mountain
Proceedings 1873, pg 36 (1873 Oct 1), Nevada Lodge No. 4, Nevada

Sparrow, Thomas
Proceedings 1872, pg 84 (1872 Sept 24) Grand Lodge of Ohio, deceased

Spaulding, F C
Proceedings 1872, pg 36 (1872 Sept 24), Ashlar Lodge U D, Colorado Springs
Proceedings 1873, pg 13 (1873 Sept 30), Ashlar Lodge U D, Colorado Springs

Spaulding, J F
Proceedings 1861-1869, pg 166 (1866 Oct 2), Nevada Lodge No. 4, Nevadaville, Fellowcraft
Proceedings 1861-1869, pg 197 (1867 Oct 8), Columbia Lodge U D, Boulder
Proceedings 1861-1869, pg 222 (1868 Oct 7), Nevada Lodge No. 4, Nevadaville, Dimitted

Spaulding, Jared F
Proceedings 1861-1869, pg 192 (1867 Oct 8), Nevada Lodge No. 4, Nevadaville

Spearin, D A
Proceedings 1872, pg 25 (1872 Sept 24), Black Hawk Lodge No. 11, Black Hawk
Proceedings 1876, pg 34 (1876 Sept 20) Black Hawk Lodge No. 11

Spearin, Daniel A
Proceedings 1873, pg 42 (1873 Oct 1), Black Hawk Lodge No. 11, Black Hawk
Proceedings 1874, pg 216 (1874 Sept 30), Black Hawk Lodge No. 11, Black Hawk
Proceedings 1875, pg 80 (1875 Sept 22) Black Hawk Lodge No. 11

Speelman, David
    Proceedings 1870, pg 26 (1870 Sept 28), El Paso Lodge No. 13, Colorado City
    Proceedings 1873, pg 43 (1873 Oct 1), El Paso Lodge No. 13, Colorado City
    Proceedings 1874, pg 218 (1874 Sept 30), El Paso Lodge No. 13, Colorado Springs
    Proceedings 1875, pg 82 (1875 Sept 22), El Paso Lodge No. 13, Colorado Springs

Spencer, John C
    Proceedings 1861-1869, pg 77 (1862 Nov 4) Denver Lodge No. 5
    Proceedings 1861-1869, pg 112 (1863 Nov 3) Denver Lodge No. 5, dimitted
    Proceedings 1861-1869, pg 113 (1863 Nov 3), Montana Lodge U D, Central City

Sperry, L B
    Proceedings 1861-1869, pg 168 (1866 Oct 2), Chivington Lodge No. 6, Central City

Sperry, L P
    Proceedings 1861-1869, pg 150 (1865 Nov 7), Chivington Lodge No. 6, Central City
    Proceedings 1861-1869, pg 194 (1867 Oct 8), Chivington Lodge No. 6, Central City, Dimitted

Spicer, N F
    Proceedings 1861-1869, pg 170 (1866 Oct 2), Black Hawk Lodge U D, Black Hawk, Apprentice
    Proceedings 1861-1869, pg 196 (1867 Oct 8), Black Hawk Lodge No. 11, Black Hawk, Apprentice
    Proceedings 1861-1869, pg 227 (1868 Oct 7), Black Hawk Lodge No. 11, Black Hawk, Apprentice

Spielman, D
    Proceedings 1876, pg 49 (1876 Sept 20), El Paso Lodge No. 13, Colorado City, 1876 July 22

Spielman, David
    Proceedings 1861-1869, pg 310 (1869 Sept 29), El Paso Lodge No. 13, Colorado City
    Proceedings 1871, pg 24 (1871 Sept 27), El Paso Lodge No. 13, Colorado City
    Proceedings 1872, pg 27 (1872 Sept 24), El Paso Lodge No. 13, Colorado City

Spilleke, F
    Proceedings 1861-1869, pg 229 (1868 Oct 7), Pueblo Lodge U D, Pueblo, Apprentice
    Proceedings 1861-1869, pg 313 (1869 Sept 29), Pueblo Lodge No. 17, Pueblo, Apprentice
    Proceedings 1876, pg 39 (1876 Sept 20) Pueblo Lodge No. 17, Apprentice

Spilleke, Ferd
    Proceedings 1871, pg 28 (1871 Sept 27), Pueblo Lodge No. 17, Pueblo, Apprentice
    Proceedings 1872, pg 31 (1872 Sept 24), Pueblo Lodge No. 17, Pueblo, Apprentice

Spilleke, Ferdinand
    Proceedings 1870, pg 30 (1870 Sept 28), Pueblo Lodge No. 17, Pueblo, Apprentice
    Proceedings 1873, pg 47 (1873 Oct 1), Pueblo Lodge No. 17, Pueblo, Apprentice
    Proceedings 1874, pg 222 (1874 Sept 30), Pueblo Lodge No. 17, Pueblo, Pueblo County, Apprentice
    Proceedings 1875, pg 85 (1875 Sept 22) Pueblo Lodge No. 17, Apprentice

Spooner, A
    Proceedings 1870, pg 31 (1870 Sept 28), Laramie Lodge No. 18, Laramie, Wyoming Territory

Sprague, L M
    Proceedings 1875, pg 79 (1875 Sept 22), Union Lodge No. 7, Denver, died
    Proceedings 1875, pg 94 (1875 Sept 22), Union Lodge No. 7, Denver

Sprague, Leander M
    Proceedings 1871, pg 22 (1871 Sept 27), Union Lodge No. 7, Denver
    Proceedings 1872, pg 23 (1872 Sept 24), Union Lodge No. 7, Denver
    Proceedings 1873, pg 40 (1873 Oct 1), Union Lodge No. 7, Denver
    Proceedings 1874, pg 214 (1874 Sept 30), Union Lodge No. 7, Denver
    Proceedings 1870, pg 23 (1870 Sept 28), Union Lodge No. 7, Denver

Sproul, Thomas
    Proceedings 1872, pg 31 (1872 Sept 24), Pueblo Lodge No. 17, Pueblo, Apprentice
    Proceedings 1874, pg 222 (1874 Sept 30), Pueblo Lodge No. 17, Pueblo, Pueblo County, Fellowcraft

Sproule, Thomas
    Proceedings 1873, pg 47 (1873 Oct 1), Pueblo Lodge No. 17, Pueblo, Fellowcraft
    Proceedings 1876, pg 39 (1876 Sept 20) Pueblo Lodge No. 17, Permission granted to take degrees elsewhere

Sproule, Thos
    Proceedings 1875, pg 85 (1875 Sept 22) Pueblo Lodge No. 17, Fellowcraft

Sproull, Thomas
    Proceedings 1875, pg 90 (1875 Sept 22), Huerfano Lodge U D, Walsenburg
    Proceedings 1876, pg 43 (1876 Sept 20), Huerfano Lodge No. 27, Walsenburg

Squires, G C
    Proceedings 1872, pg 28 (1872 Sept 24), Columbia Lodge No. 14, Boulder

Squires, Geo C
    Proceedings 1870, pg 27 (1870 Sept 28), Columbia Lodge No. 14, Boulder City
    Proceedings 1873, pg 44 (1873 Oct 1), Columbia Lodge No. 14, Boulder

Squires, George C
    Proceedings 1861-1869, pg 311 (1869 Sept 29), Columbia Lodge No. 14, Boulder City
    Proceedings 1871, pg 26 (1871 Sept 27), Columbia Lodge No. 14, Boulder City

Proceedings 1874, pg 219 (1874 Sept 30), Columbia Lodge No. 14, Boulder, Boulder County

Proceedings 1875, pg 83 (1875 Sept 22), Columbia Lodge No. 14, Boulder

Proceedings 1876, pg 37 (1876 Sept 20), Columbia Lodge No. 14, Boulder

Squires, W B

Proceedings 1861-1869, pg 150 (1865 Nov 7), Chivington Lodge No. 6, Central City

Proceedings 1861-1869, pg 168 (1866 Oct 2), Chivington Lodge No. 6, Central City

Proceedings 1861-1869, pg 194 (1867 Oct 8), Chivington Lodge No. 6, Central City

Proceedings 1861-1869, pg 306 (1869 Sept 29), Central Lodge No. 6, Central City

Proceedings 1870, pg 22 (1870 Sept 28), Central Lodge No. 6, Central City

Proceedings 1871, pg 21 (1871 Sept 27), Central Lodge No. 6, Central

Proceedings 1872, pg 21 (1872 Sept 24), Denver Lodge No. 5, Denver

Squires, William B

Proceedings 1861-1869, pg 134 (1864 Nov 8), Chivington Lodge No. 6, Central City

Proceedings 1875, pg 77 (1875 Sept 22), Central Lodge No. 6, Central City, Stricken from the rolls

Squires, Wm B

Proceedings 1861-1869, pg 113 (1863 Nov 3), Chivington Lodge No. 6, Central City, Apprentice

Proceedings 1873, pg 38 (1873 Oct 1), Central Lodge No. 6, Central City

Proceedings 1874, pg 212 (1874 Sept 30), Central Lodge No. 6, Central

Proceedings 1861-1869, pg 224 (1868 Oct 7), Chivington Lodge No. 6, Central City

St John's College

Proceedings 1861-1869, pg 235 (1867 Nov 4) founded by the Grand Lodge of Arkansas

St Paul Lodge No. 124, Auburn, NY

Proceedings 1875, pg 36 (1875 Sept 22)

St Vrain Lodge No. 23

Proceedings 1875, pg 20 (1874 May) communication

Proceedings 1875, pg 23 (1875 Sept 21) has not made returns or paid dues

Proceedings 1875, pg 23 (1875 Sept 21) has not provided a list of officers

Proceedings 1875, pg 34 (1875 Sept 22) have made no returns

Proceedings 1875, pg 92 (1875 Sept 22)

Proceedings 1876, pg 12 (1875 Oct 6) dues paid

Proceedings 1876, pg 12 (1876 Jan 20) returns received

Proceedings 1876, pg 52 (1876 Sept 20)

St Vrain Lodge No. 23, Longmont

Proceedings 1872, pg 13 (1872 Sept 24) granted charter

Proceedings 1872, pg 35 (1872 Sept 24) chartered as No. 23 on 22 June 1872

Proceedings 1874, pg 19 (1874 Sept 29) returns late

Proceedings 1874, pg 208 (1874 Sept 30)

Proceedings 1875, pg 88 (1875 Sept 22) no returns

Proceedings 1876, pg 13 (1875 Oct 6) 1875 dues paid

Proceedings 1876, pg 24 (1876 Sept 20) correction to returns

[St Vrain] Lodge U D, Longmont

Proceedings 1872, pg 7 (1872 June 22) dispensation given

St Vrain Lodge U D, Longmont

Proceedings 1872, pg 11 (1872 Sept 24) has made returns

Stafford, Abraham

Proceedings 1861-1869, pg 148 (1865 Nov 7), Nevada Lodge No. 4, Nevadaville, Apprentice

Proceedings 1861-1869, pg 166 (1866 Oct 2), Nevada Lodge No. 4, Nevadaville, Apprentice

Proceedings 1861-1869, pg 192 (1867 Oct 8), Nevada Lodge No. 4, Nevadaville, Apprentice

Stafford, E A

Proceedings 1861-1869, pg 228 (1868 Oct 7), El Paso Lodge No. 13, Colorado City, Dimitted

Stafford, E F

Proceedings 1861-1869, pg 169 (1866 Oct 2), Chivington Lodge No. 6, Central City, Apprentice

Proceedings 1861-1869, pg 196 (1867 Oct 8), El Paso Lodge U D, Colorado City

Proceedings 1861-1869, pg 229 (1868 Oct 7), Pueblo Lodge U D, Pueblo

Standart, W H

Proceedings 1876, pg 36 (1876 Sept 20), El Paso Lodge No. 13, Colorado City, Apprentice

Standiford, James W

Proceedings 1876, pg 44 (1876 Sept 20), Las Animas Lodge No. 28, Trinidad, Fellow Craft

Standley, Jos

Proceedings 1861-1869, pg 148 (1865 Nov 7), Nevada Lodge No. 4, Nevadaville

Proceedings 1861-1869, pg 222 (1868 Oct 7), Nevada Lodge No. 4, Nevadaville

Standley, Joseph

Proceedings 1861-1869, pg 192 (1867 Oct 8), Nevada Lodge No. 4, Nevadaville

Proceedings 1861-1869, pg 304 (1869 Sept 29), Nevada Lodge No. 4, Nevadaville

Proceedings 1872, pg 19 (1872 Sept 24), Nevada Lodge No. 4, Bald Mountain

Proceedings 1873, pg 36 (1873 Oct 1), Nevada Lodge No. 4, Nevada

Proceedings 1874, pg 210 (1874 Sept 30), Nevada Lodge No. 4, Bald Mountain, Gilpin County

Proceedings 1875, pg 74 (1875 Sept 22), Nevada Lodge No. 4, Nevada

Proceedings 1876, pg 30 (1876 Sept 20) Nevada Lodge No. 4

Proceedings 1870, pg 20 (1870 Sept 28), Nevada Lodge No. 4, Nevadaville

Proceedings 1871, pg 18 (1871 Sept 27), Nevada Lodge No. 4, Bald Mountain

Colorado's Territorial Masons

Stanley, Jos
Proceedings 1861-1869, pg 166 (1866 Oct 2), Nevada Lodge No. 4, Nevadaville

Stansbury, C F
Proceedings 1874, pg 52 (1874 Sept 30) Grand Lodge of the District of Columbia

Stansbury, Charles F
Proceedings 1872, pg 58 (1872 Sept 24) Grand Lodge of the District of Columbia

Stansbury, Chas F
Proceedings 1872, pg 43 (1872 Sept 24) Washington, Grand Lodge of the District of Columbia
Proceedings 1873, pg 60 (1873 Oct 1) Grand Lodge of the District of Columbia, Washington
Proceedings 1874, pg 204 (1874 Sept 30) Grand Lodge of the District of Columbia, Washington,

Stanton
Proceedings 1876, pg 17 (1876 Sept 19) motion
Proceedings 1876, pg 20 (1876 Sept 20) motion

Stanton, I W
Proceedings 1875, pg cover (1875 Sept 22) Grand Marshal, Pueblo
Proceedings 1875, pg 17 (1875 Sept 21) committee
Proceedings 1875, pg 17 (1875 Sept 21) Pueblo Lodge No. 17
Proceedings 1875, pg 29 (1875 Sept 21) motion
Proceedings 1875, pg 36 (1875 Sept 22) resolution
Proceedings 1875, pg 38 (1875 Sept 22) committee
Proceedings 1875, pg 38 (1875 Sept 22) per diem
Proceedings 1875, pg 85 (1875 Sept 22) Pueblo Lodge No. 17
Proceedings 1876, pg 4 (1876 Sept 19) committee
Proceedings 1876, pg 5 (1876 Sept 19) committee
Proceedings 1876, pg 5 (1876 Sept 19) Pueblo Lodge No. 17

Stanton, Irving W
Proceedings 1875, pg 33 (1875 Sept 22) Grand Marshal, Pueblo
Proceedings 1876, pg 3 (1876 Sept 19) Junior Grand Warden
Proceedings 1876, pg 38 (1876 Sept 20) Pueblo Lodge No. 17

Stanton, J A
Proceedings 1861-1869, pg 197 (1867 Oct 8), Columbia Lodge U D, Boulder
Proceedings 1861-1869, pg 228 (1868 Oct 7), Columbia Lodge No. 14, Columbia City

Stanton, J W
Proceedings 1861-1869, pg 111 (1863 Nov 3), Nevada Lodge No. 4, Nevadaville
Proceedings 1861-1869, pg 132 (1864 Nov 8), Nevada Lodge No. 4, Nevadaville
Proceedings 1861-1869, pg 148 (1865 Nov 7), Nevada Lodge No. 4, Nevadaville
Proceedings 1861-1869, pg 166 (1866 Oct 2), Nevada Lodge No. 4, Nevadaville
Proceedings 1861-1869, pg 304 (1869 Sept 29), Nevada Lodge No. 4, Nevadaville

Stanton, James W
Proceedings 1861-1869, pg 192 (1867 Oct 8), Nevada Lodge No. 4, Nevadaville

Stanton, Jas W
Proceedings 1861-1869, pg 222 (1868 Oct 7), Nevada Lodge No. 4, Nevadaville
Proceedings 1871, pg 18 (1871 Sept 27), Nevada Lodge No. 4, Bald Mountain, Dimitted

Stanton, John A
Proceedings 1861-1869, pg 311 (1869 Sept 29), Columbia Lodge No. 14, Boulder City
Proceedings 1870, pg 27 (1870 Sept 28), Columbia Lodge No. 14, Boulder City
Proceedings 1871, pg 26 (1871 Sept 27), Columbia Lodge No. 14, Boulder City
Proceedings 1872, pg 28 (1872 Sept 24), Columbia Lodge No. 14, Boulder
Proceedings 1873, pg 44 (1873 Oct 1), Columbia Lodge No. 14, Boulder
Proceedings 1874, pg 219 (1874 Sept 30), Columbia Lodge No. 14, Boulder, Boulder County
Proceedings 1875, pg 83 (1875 Sept 22), Columbia Lodge No. 14, Boulder, Stricken from the rolls

Stapler, D C
Proceedings 1874, pg 224 (1874 Sept 30), Laramie Lodge No. 18, Laramie City, Suspended

Staples, D C
Proceedings 1873, pg 48 (1873 Oct 1), Laramie Lodge No. 18, Laramie, Wyoming Territory

Star, Sol
Proceedings 1861-1869, pg 316 (1869 Sept 29) Grand Lodge of Montana
Proceedings 1870, pg 34 (1870 Sept 28) Grand Secretary, Grand Lodge of Montana
Proceedings 1870, pg 89 (1868 Oct 5) Grand Secretary, Grand Lodge of Montana
Proceedings 1870, pg 89 (1869 Oct 4) Grand Secretary, Grand Lodge of Montana
Proceedings 1874, pg 204 (1874 Sept 30) Grand Lodge of Montana, Helena

Stark, Albert G
Proceedings 1875, pg 19 (1875 Mar 15), Las Animas Lodge U D, Trinidad
Proceedings 1875, pg 34 (1875 Sept 22), Las Animas Lodge No. 28, Trinidad
Proceedings 1875, pg 91 (1875 Sept 22), Las Animas Lodge U D, Trinidad
Proceedings 1876, pg 43 (1876 Sept 20), Las Animas Lodge No. 28, Trinidad

Starkweather, Charles R
Proceedings 1861-1869, pg 247 (1867 Nov 7) deceased

Starr, John O
Proceedings 1875, pg 91 (1875 Sept 22), Las Animas Lodge U D, Trinidad

Proceedings 1876, pg 44 (1876 Sept 20), Las Animas Lodge No. 28, Trinidad

Steart, Thomas
Proceedings 1874, pg 219 (1874 Sept 30), Columbia Lodge No. 14, Boulder, Boulder County

Steel, M F
Proceedings 1870, pg 30 (1870 Sept 28), Pueblo Lodge No. 17, Pueblo, Apprentice
Proceedings 1874, pg 222 (1874 Sept 30), Pueblo Lodge No. 17, Pueblo, Pueblo County
Proceedings 1875, pg 85 (1875 Sept 22) Pueblo Lodge No. 17

Steel, Mathew F
Proceedings 1871, pg 28 (1871 Sept 27), Pueblo Lodge No. 17, Pueblo
Proceedings 1872, pg 31 (1872 Sept 24), Pueblo Lodge No. 17, Pueblo

Steel, T J
Proceedings 1874, pg 222 (1874 Sept 30), Pueblo Lodge No. 17, Pueblo, Pueblo County

Steel, Thos J
Proceedings 1875, pg 85 (1875 Sept 22) Pueblo Lodge No. 17

Steele, H R
Proceedings 1876, pg 39 (1876 Sept 20) Pueblo Lodge No. 17, Apprentice

Steele, M F
Proceedings 1861-1869, pg 313 (1869 Sept 29), Pueblo Lodge No. 17, Pueblo, Apprentice
Proceedings 1876, pg 39 (1876 Sept 20) Pueblo Lodge No. 17

Steele, Matthew F
Proceedings 1873, pg 47 (1873 Oct 1), Pueblo Lodge No. 17, Pueblo

Steele, Thomas J
Proceedings 1873, pg 47 (1873 Oct 1), Pueblo Lodge No. 17, Pueblo, Apprentice
Proceedings 1876, pg 39 (1876 Sept 20) Pueblo Lodge No. 17

Stein, Wilhelm
Proceedings 1876, pg 44 (1876 Sept 20) Del Norte Lodge U D

Steinbach, E
Proceedings 1876, pg 44 (1876 Sept 20) Del Norte Lodge U D

Stephens, Evan
Proceedings 1875, pg 89 (1875 Sept 22) Idaho Springs Lodge U D
Proceedings 1876, pg 43 (1876 Sept 20) Idaho Springs Lodge No. 26

Stephens, Henry
Proceedings 1861-1869, pg 221 (1868 Oct 7) Golden City Lodge No. 1
Proceedings 1861-1869, pg 303 (1869 Sept 29) Golden City Lodge No. 1
Proceedings 1874, pg 209 (1874 Sept 30), Golden City Lodge No. 1, Golden City
Proceedings 1875, pg 73 (1875 Sept 22) Golden City Lodge No. 1

Stephens, Samuel B
Proceedings 1870, pg 52 (1870 Jan 12) Grand Lodge of Florida

Stephens, W L
Proceedings 1876, pg 44 (1876 Sept 20) Del Norte Lodge U D

Stephenson
Proceedings 1861-1869, pg 277 (1867 Dec 2) author of Masonic materials

Stepp, William
Proceedings 1861-1869, pg 133 (1864 Nov 8) Denver Lodge No. 5
Proceedings 1861-1869, pg 149 (1865 Nov 7), Nevada Lodge No. 4, Nevadaville

Stepp, Wm
Proceedings 1861-1869, pg 112 (1863 Nov 3) Denver Lodge No. 5
Proceedings 1861-1869, pg 167 (1866 Oct 2) Denver Lodge No. 5
Proceedings 1861-1869, pg 193 (1867 Oct 8) Denver Lodge No. 5
Proceedings 1861-1869, pg 223 (1868 Oct 7) Denver Lodge No. 5
Proceedings 1861-1869, pg 305 (1869 Sept 29) Denver Lodge No. 5
Proceedings 1870, pg 21 (1870 Sept 28), Denver Lodge No. 5, Denver
Proceedings 1872, pg 20 (1872 Sept 24), Denver Lodge No. 5, Denver

Stetlimes, John L
Proceedings 1874, pg 117 (1874 Sept 30) Grand Lodge of Ohio

Stetzer, C L
Proceedings 1876, pg 39 (1876 Sept 20) Pueblo Lodge No. 17

Stevens Andrew
Proceedings 1875, pg 34 (1875 Sept 22) Idaho Springs Lodge No. 26
Proceedings 1874, pg 229 (1874 Sept 30), Idaho Springs Lodge U D, Idaho Springs
Proceedings 1875, pg 89 (1875 Sept 22) Idaho Springs Lodge U D
Proceedings 1876, pg 42 (1876 Sept 20) Idaho Springs Lodge No. 26

Stevens, Henry
Proceedings 1861-1869, pg 110 (1863 Nov 3) Golden City Lodge No. 1
Proceedings 1861-1869, pg 131 (1864 Nov 8) Golden City Lodge No. 1
Proceedings 1861-1869, pg 147 (1865 Nov 7) Golden City Lodge No. 1
Proceedings 1861-1869, pg 165 (1866 Oct 2) Golden City Lodge No. 1

Stevens, Henry, cont.
    Proceedings 1861-1869, pg 191 (1867 Oct 8) Golden City Lodge No. 1
    Proceedings 1870, pg 19 (1870 Sept 28), Golden City Lodge No. 1, Golden City
    Proceedings 1871, pg 17 (1871 Sept 27), Golden City Lodge No. 1, Golden City
    Proceedings 1872, pg 17 (1872 Sept 24), Golden City Lodge No. 1, Golden City
    Proceedings 1873, pg 35 (1873 Oct 1), Golden City Lodge No. 1, Golden City
    Proceedings 1876, pg 29 (1876 Sept 20) Golden City Lodge No. 1

Stevens, Isaac
    Proceedings 1872, pg 29 (1872 Sept 24), Cheyenne Lodge No. 16, Cheyenne, Wyoming Territory
    Proceedings 1873, pg 46 (1873 Oct 1), Cheyenne Lodge No. 16, Cheyenne, Wyoming Territory
    Proceedings 1874, pg 221 (1874 Sept 30), Cheyenne Lodge No. 16, Cheyenne, Wyoming Territory

Stevens, James
    Proceedings 1861-1869, pg 110 (1863 Nov 3) Golden City Lodge No. 1, Apprentice
    Proceedings 1861-1869, pg 131 (1864 Nov 8) Golden City Lodge No. 1, Apprentice
    Proceedings 1861-1869, pg 147 (1865 Nov 7) Golden City Lodge No. 1, Apprentice
    Proceedings 1861-1869, pg 165 (1866 Oct 2) Golden City Lodge No. 1, Apprentice

Stevenson, A A
    Proceedings 1861-1869, pg 325 (1868 July 8) Grand Master, Grand Lodge of Canada
    Proceedings 1870, pg 48 (1869 July 14) Grand Master, Grand Lodge of Canada

Stevenson, Levi L
    Proceedings 1874, pg 130 (1874 Sept 30) Grand Lodge of Virginia, deceased

Stevenson, R M
    Proceedings 1876, pg 39 (1876 Sept 20) Pueblo Lodge No. 17

Stevenson, Thomas D
    Proceedings 1874, pg 221 (1874 Sept 30), Cheyenne Lodge No. 16, Cheyenne, Wyoming Territory

Stevenson, Thos D
    Proceedings 1873, pg 46 (1873 Oct 1), Cheyenne Lodge No. 16, Cheyenne, Wyoming Territory, Fellowcraft

Stewart, Edward
    Proceedings 1861-1869, pg 272 (1867 Jan 16), Past Grand Master, Grand Lodge of New Jersey, deceased

Stewart, Henry J
    Proceedings 1861-1869, pg 327 (1868 Jan 13) Grand Master, Grand Lodge of Florida

Stewart, J E
    Proceedings 1861-1869, pg 151 (1865 Nov 7), Chivington Lodge No. 6, Central City
    Proceedings 1861-1869, pg 169 (1866 Oct 2), Union Lodge No. 7, Denver
    Proceedings 1861-1869, pg 195 (1867 Oct 8), Union Lodge No. 7, Denver

Stewart, John E
    Proceedings 1861-1869, pg 135 (1864 Nov 8), Union Lodge No. 7, Denver, Apprentice
    Proceedings 1861-1869, pg 139 (1865 Jan 12), Union Lodge No. 7, Denver
    Proceedings 1861-1869, pg 226 (1868 Oct 7), Union Lodge No. 7, Denver, Dimitted

Stewart, Thomas
    Proceedings 1875, pg 83 (1875 Sept 22), Columbia Lodge No. 14, Boulder
    Proceedings 1876, pg 37 (1876 Sept 20), Columbia Lodge No. 14, Boulder

Stiles, H C
    Proceedings 1872, pg 28 (1872 Sept 24), Columbia Lodge No. 14, Boulder
    Proceedings 1872, pg 35 (1872 Sept 24), St Vrain Lodge No. 23, Longmont
    Proceedings 1873, pg 51 (1873 Oct 1), St Vrain Lodge No. 23, Longmont
    Proceedings 1874, pg 227 (1874 Sept 30), St Vrain No. 23, Longmont
    Proceedings 1876, pg 41 (1876 Sept 20), St Vrain Lodge No. 23, Longmont

Stiles, Henry C
    Proceedings 1871, pg 26 (1871 Sept 27), Columbia Lodge No. 14, Boulder City
    Proceedings 1873, pg 45 (1873 Oct 1), Columbia Lodge No. 14, Boulder, Dimitted

Stillings, E B
    Proceedings 1861-1869, pg 150 (1865 Nov 7), Chivington Lodge No. 6, Central City, Fellowcraft
    Proceedings 1861-1869, pg 168 (1866 Oct 2), Chivington Lodge No. 6, Central City
    Proceedings 1861-1869, pg 193 (1867 Oct 8), Chivington Lodge No. 6, Central City
    Proceedings 1861-1869, pg 224 (1868 Oct 7), Chivington Lodge No. 6, Central City
    Proceedings 1861-1869, pg 306 (1869 Sept 29), Central Lodge No. 6, Central City
    Proceedings 1870, pg 22 (1870 Sept 28), Central Lodge No. 6, Central City
    Proceedings 1871, pg 21 (1871 Sept 27), Central Lodge No. 6, Central
    Proceedings 1872, pg 21 (1872 Sept 24), Denver Lodge No. 5, Denver

Stillings, Edw B
    Proceedings 1873, pg 38 (1873 Oct 1), Central Lodge No. 6, Central City
    Proceedings 1874, pg 213 (1874 Sept 30), Central Lodge No. 6, Central

Stillings, Edward B
    Proceedings 1875, pg 77 (1875 Sept 22), Central Lodge No. 6, Central City, Demitted

Colorado's Territorial Masons

Stimpson, G B
Proceedings 1873, pg 46 (1873 Oct 1), Cheyenne Lodge No. 16, Cheyenne, Wyoming Territory

Stimpson, Geo B
Proceedings 1861-1869, pg 225 (1868 Oct 7), Union Lodge No. 7, Denver
Proceedings 1861-1869, pg 307 (1869 Sept 29), Union Lodge No. 7, Denver
Proceedings 1872, pg 29 (1872 Sept 24), Cheyenne Lodge No. 16, Cheyenne, Wyoming Territory

Stimpson, George B
Proceedings 1861-1869, pg 195 (1867 Oct 8), Union Lodge No. 7, Denver
Proceedings 1870, pg 23 (1870 Sept 28), Union Lodge No. 7, Denver
Proceedings 1871, pg 22 (1871 Sept 27), Union Lodge No. 7, Denver, Dimitted
Proceedings 1871, pg 27 (1871 Sept 27), Cheyenne Lodge No. 16, Cheyenne, Wyoming Territory
Proceedings 1874, pg 221 (1874 Sept 30), Cheyenne Lodge No. 16, Cheyenne, Wyoming Territory

Stitlinius, John L
Proceedings 1873, pg 61 (1873 Oct 1) Grand Lodge of Ohio, Cincinnati

Stitzer, C L
Proceedings 1874, pg 222 (1874 Sept 30), Pueblo Lodge No. 17, Pueblo, Pueblo County

Stitzer, Charles L
Proceedings 1870, pg 30 (1870 Sept 28), Pueblo Lodge No. 17, Pueblo
Proceedings 1871, pg 28 (1871 Sept 27), Pueblo Lodge No. 17, Pueblo
Proceedings 1873, pg 13 (1873 Sept 30), Ashlar Lodge U D, Colorado Springs
Proceedings 1873, pg 47 (1873 Oct 1), Pueblo Lodge No. 17, Pueblo

Stitzer, Chas L
Proceedings 1872, pg 31 (1872 Sept 24), Pueblo Lodge No. 17, Pueblo
Proceedings 1872, pg 36 (1872 Sept 24), Ashlar Lodge U D, Colorado Springs

Stoddard, Frank
Proceedings 1873, pg 40 (1873 Oct 1), Union Lodge No. 7, Denver, Apprentice
Proceedings 1874, pg 214 (1874 Sept 30), Union Lodge No. 7, Denver, Fellowcraft
Proceedings 1875, pg 79 (1875 Sept 22), Union Lodge No. 7, Denver, Fellowcraft
Proceedings 1876, pg 33 (1876 Sept 20), Union Lodge No. 7, Denver

Stogsdall, D
Proceedings 1861-1869, pg 43 (1861 Dec 10), Summit Lodge No. 2, Parkville
Proceedings 1861-1869, pg 76 (1862 Nov 4), Summit Lodge No. 2, Parkville
Proceedings 1861-1869, pg 110 (1863 Nov 3), Summit Lodge No. 2, Parkville
Proceedings 1861-1869, pg 132 (1864 Nov 8) Golden City Lodge No. 1

Stoler, Samuel B
Proceedings 1870, pg 24 (1870 Sept 28), Empire Lodge No. 8, Empire
Proceedings 1872, pg 24 (1872 Sept 24), Empire Lodge No. 8, Empire, Dimitted,

Stone
Proceedings 1861-1869, pg 207 (1867 Nov 8) of Canon City
Proceedings 1861-1869, pg 289 (1869 Sept 28) committee
Proceedings 1870, pg 9 (1870 Sept 27) committee
Proceedings 1871, pg 15 (1871 Sept 27) resolution
Proceedings 1872, pg 7 (1872 Sept 24), El Paso Lodge No. 13, Colorado City
Proceedings 1873, pg 5 (1873 Sept 30) Junior Grand Warden
Proceedings 1876, pg 12 (1876 Sept 19) resolution and summons to be served on W H Dickinson

Stone, C H
Proceedings 1872, pg 36 (1872 Sept 24), Ashlar Lodge U D, Colorado Springs

Stone, E T
Proceedings 1861-1869, pg 154 (1866 Jan 27), El Paso Lodge U D, Colorado City
Proceedings 1861-1869, pg 170 (1866 Oct 2), El Paso U D, Colorado City
Proceedings 1861-1869, pg 196 (1867 Oct 8), El Paso Lodge U D, Colorado City
Proceedings 1861-1869, pg 220 (1868 Oct 7) Grand Sword Bearer
Proceedings 1861-1869, pg 228 (1868 Oct 7), El Paso Lodge No. 13, Colorado City
Proceedings 1861-1869, pg 287 (1869 Sept 28) Grand Sword Bearer
Proceedings 1861-1869, pg 288 (1869 Sept 28), El Paso Lodge No. 13, Colorado City
Proceedings 1861-1869, pg 299 (1869 Sept 29) Junior Grand Warden
Proceedings 1861-1869, pg 301 (1869 Sept 29), El Paso Lodge No. 13, Colorado City
Proceedings 1861-1869, pg 310 (1869 Sept 29), El Paso Lodge No. 13, Colorado City
Proceedings 1870, pg 3 (1870 Sept 27) Junior Grand Deacon
Proceedings 1870, pg 4 (1870 Sept 27), El Paso Lodge No. 13, Colorado City
Proceedings 1870, pg 16 (1870 Sept 28), El Paso Lodge No. 13, Colorado City
Proceedings 1870, pg 17 (1870 Sept 28) committee
Proceedings 1870, pg 26 (1870 Sept 28), El Paso Lodge No. 13, Colorado City
Proceedings 1871, pg 3 (1871 Sept 26) Junior Grand Warden
Proceedings 1871, pg 4 (1871 Sept 26) Junior Grand Warden
Proceedings 1871, pg 5 (1871 Sept 26) Committee
Proceedings 1871, pg 14 (1871 Sept 27) Junior Grand Warden

Colorado's Territorial Masons

Stone, E T, cont.
- Proceedings 1871, pg 25 (1871 Sept 27), El Paso Lodge No. 13, Colorado City
- Proceedings 1872, pg 4 (1872 Sept 24) Junior Grand Warden
- Proceedings 1872, pg 5 (1872 Sept 24), El Paso Lodge No. 13, Colorado City
- Proceedings 1872, pg 5 (1872 Sept 24) committee
- Proceedings 1872, pg 16 (1872 Sept 24) Junior Grand Warden
- Proceedings 1872, pg 26 (1872 Sept 24), El Paso Lodge No. 13, Colorado City
- Proceedings 1873, pg 5 (1873 Sept 30) Junior Grand Warden
- Proceedings 1873, pg 6 (1873 Sept 30), El Paso Lodge No. 13, Colorado City
- Proceedings 1873, pg 6 (1873 Sept 30) committee
- Proceedings 1873, pg 32 (1873 Oct 1) mileage and per diem
- Proceedings 1873, pg 43 (1873 Oct 1), El Paso Lodge No. 13, Colorado City
- Proceedings 1874, pg 4 (1874 Sept 29) committee
- Proceedings 1874, pg 5 (1874 Sept 29) Senior Grand Warden
- Proceedings 1874, pg 6 (1874 Sept 29), El Paso Lodge No. 13, Colorado City
- Proceedings 1874, pg 6 (1874 Sept 29) committee
- Proceedings 1874, pg 6 (1874 Sept 29) committee
- Proceedings 1874, pg 21 (1874 Sept 29) committee
- Proceedings 1874, pg 35 (1874 Sept 30) committee
- Proceedings 1874, pg 36 (1874 Sept 30) per diem
- Proceedings 1874, pg 218 (1874 Sept 30), El Paso Lodge No. 13, Colorado Springs
- Proceedings 1875, pg 16 (1875 Sept 21) Deputy Grand Master
- Proceedings 1875, pg 16 (1875 Sept 21) committee
- Proceedings 1875, pg 16 (1875 Sept 21) Deputy Grand Master
- Proceedings 1875, pg 17 (1875 Sept 21) committee
- Proceedings 1875, pg 30 (1875 Sept 21) committee
- Proceedings 1875, pg 31 (1875 Sept 21), to be repaid a sum he lent to a Mason belonging to St Paul Lodge No. 124, New York
- Proceedings 1875, pg 33 (1875 Sept 22), to be repaid a sum he lent to a Mason belonging to St Paul Lodge No. 124, New York
- Proceedings 1875, pg 36 (1875 Sept 22), refunded $200 advanced to a member of St Paul Lodge No. 124, of Auburn, NY
- Proceedings 1875, pg 37 (1875 Sept 22) per diem
- Proceedings 1875, pg 82 (1875 Sept 22), El Paso Lodge No. 13, Colorado Springs
- Proceedings 1876, pg 4 (1876 Sept 19) Past Deputy Grand Master
- Proceedings 1876, pg 5 (1876 Sept 19) committee
- Proceedings 1876, pg 5 (1876 Sept 19), El Paso Lodge No. 13, Colorado Springs
- Proceedings 1876, pg 14 (1874 Oct 6), telegram to Frank J Stupp of Auburn, NY
- Proceedings 1876, pg 14 (1876 Sept 19), claim against St Paul Lodge, Auburn, NY
- Proceedings 1876, pg 22 (1876 Sept 20), El Paso Lodge No. 13, Colorado Springs

Stone, Edmund T
- Colorado University Cornerstone Laying, pg 3 (1875 Sept 20) Deputy Grand Master
- Proceedings 1870, pg cover (1870 Sept 28) Junior Grand Warden, Colorado City
- Proceedings 1870, pg 13 (1870 Sept 27) Junior Grand Warden
- Proceedings 1870, pg 32 (1870 Sept 28) Junior Grand Warden, 1870
- Proceedings 1871, pg cover (1871 Sept 27) Junior Grand Warden, Colorado City
- Proceedings 1871, pg 13 (1871 Sept 26) Junior Grand Warden
- Proceedings 1871, pg 34 (1871 Sept 27) Junior Grand Warden, 1871
- Proceedings 1871, pg 34 (1871 Sept 27) Junior Grand Warden, 1870
- Proceedings 1872, pg cover (1872 Sept 24) Junior Grand Warden, Colorado City
- Proceedings 1872, pg 3 (1872 Sept 24) Junior Grand Warden
- Proceedings 1872, pg 12 (1872 Sept 24) Junior Grand Warden
- Proceedings 1872, pg 42 (1872 Sept 24) Junior Grand Warden, 1870
- Proceedings 1872, pg 42 (1872 Sept 24) Junior Grand Warden, 1871-1872
- Proceedings 1873, pg cover (1873 Oct 1) Senior Grand Warden, Colorado City
- Proceedings 1873, pg 3 (1873 Sept 30) Junior Grand Warden
- Proceedings 1873, pg 14 (1873 Sept 30) Senior Grand Warden
- Proceedings 1873, pg 58 (1873 Oct 1) Junior Grand Warden, 1870
- Proceedings 1873, pg 58 (1873 Oct 1) Junior Grand Warden, 1871-1872
- Proceedings 1873, pg 59 (1873 Oct 1) Senior Grand Warden, 1873
- Proceedings 1874, pg cover (1874 Sept 30) Deputy Grand Master, Colorado Springs
- Proceedings 1874, pg 3 (1874 Sept 29) Senior Grand Warden
- Proceedings 1874, pg 29 (1874 Sept 29) Deputy Grand Master
- Proceedings 1874, pg 206 (1874 Sept 30) Junior Grand Warden, 1870
- Proceedings 1874, pg 206 (1874 Sept 30) Junior Grand Warden, 1871
- Proceedings 1874, pg 206 (1874 Sept 30) Junior Grand Warden, 1872
- Proceedings 1874, pg 206 (1874 Sept 30) Senior Grand Warden, 1873
- Proceedings 1874, pg 206 (1874 Sept 30) Deputy Grand Master, 1874

Stone, Edmund T, cont.
Proceedings 1875, pg 15 (1875 Sept 21) Deputy Grand Master
Proceedings 1875, pg 37 (1875 Sept 22) committee, Colorado Springs
Proceedings 1875, pg 93 (1875 Sept 22) Junior Grand Warden, 1871
Proceedings 1875, pg 93 (1875 Sept 22) Deputy Grand Master, 1874
Proceedings 1875, pg 93 (1875 Sept 22) Junior Grand Warden, 1870
Proceedings 1875, pg 93 (1875 Sept 22) Senior Grand Warden, 1873
Proceedings 1875, pg 93 (1875 Sept 22) Junior Grand Warden, 1872
Proceedings 1876, pg 3 (1876 Sept 19) Senior Grand Deacon
Proceedings 1876, pg 4 (1876 Sept 19) Past Deputy Grand Master
Proceedings 1876, pg 35 (1876 Sept 20), El Paso Lodge No. 13, Colorado City

Stone, R [E] T
Proceedings 1875, pg 18 (1875 Sept 21) committee

Stopdill, Daniel
Proceedings 1875, pg 73 (1875 Sept 22) Golden City Lodge No. 1

Storer, William
Proceedings 1861-1869, pg 242 (1867 May 8), Grand Master, Grand Lodge of Connecticut
Proceedings 1861-1869, pg 325 (1869 May 12) Grand Master, Grand Lodge of Connecticut

Storm, C P
Proceedings 1875, pg 74 (1875 Sept 22), Nevada Lodge No. 4, Nevada

Storm, Charles P
Proceedings 1873, pg 36 (1873 Oct 1), Nevada Lodge No. 4, Nevada
Proceedings 1876, pg 30 (1876 Sept 20) Nevada Lodge No. 4

Storm, Chas P
Proceedings 1872, pg 19 (1872 Sept 24), Nevada Lodge No. 4, Bald Mountain

Story, J R
Proceedings 1875, pg 85 (1875 Sept 22) Pueblo Lodge No. 17
Proceedings 1876, pg 48 (1876 Sept 20) Pueblo Lodge No. 17, 1876 Mar 23

Stotts, Joseph
Proceedings 1876, pg 40 (1876 Sept 20), Collins Lodge No. 19, Fort Collins, Apprentice

Stotts, Joseph L
Proceedings 1872, pg 33 (1872 Sept 24), Collins Lodge No. 19, Fort Collins, Apprentice
Proceedings 1873, pg 49 (1873 Oct 1), Collins Lodge No. 19, Fort Collins, Apprentice
Proceedings 1874, pg 225 (1874 Sept 30), Collins Lodge No. 19, Fort Collins, Larimer County, Apprentice
Proceedings 1875, pg 86 (1875 Sept 22), Collins Lodge No. 19, Fort Collins, Apprentice

Stout, Geo W
Proceedings 1870, pg 30 (1870 Sept 28), Pueblo Lodge No. 17, Pueblo
Proceedings 1872, pg 31 (1872 Sept 24), Pueblo Lodge No. 17, Pueblo

Stout, George W
Proceedings 1861-1869, pg 312 (1869 Sept 29), Pueblo Lodge No. 17, Pueblo
Proceedings 1871, pg 28 (1871 Sept 27), Pueblo Lodge No. 17, Pueblo
Proceedings 1873, pg 47 (1873 Oct 1), Pueblo Lodge No. 17, Pueblo
Proceedings 1874, pg 223 (1874 Sept 30), Pueblo Lodge No. 17, Pueblo, Pueblo County, Stricken from the rolls

Stover, W C
Proceedings 1876, pg 39 (1876 Sept 20), Collins Lodge No. 19, Fort Collins

Stover, William C
Proceedings 1871, pg 30 (1871 Sept 27), Collins Lodge No. 19, Fort Collins
Proceedings 1873, pg 49 (1873 Oct 1), Collins Lodge No. 19, Fort Collins
Proceedings 1874, pg 224 (1874 Sept 30), Collins Lodge No. 19, Fort Collins, Larimer County
Proceedings 1875, pg 86 (1875 Sept 22), Collins Lodge No. 19, Fort Collins

Stover, Wm P
Proceedings 1872, pg 32 (1872 Sept 24), Collins Lodge No. 19, Fort Collins

Strang
Proceedings 1876, pg 20 (1876 Sept 20) committee

Strang, C A
Proceedings 1871, pg 21 (1871 Sept 27), Central Lodge No. 6, Central

Strang, R D
Proceedings 1870, pg 22 (1870 Sept 28), Central Lodge No. 6, Central City
Proceedings 1875, pg 34 (1875 Sept 22) Idaho Springs Lodge No. 26
Proceedings 1876, pg 5 (1876 Sept 19) Idaho Springs Lodge No. 26
Proceedings 1876, pg 22 (1876 Sept 20) Idaho Springs Lodge No. 26
Proceedings 1876, pg 23 (1876 Sept 20) committee

Strang, Romeo D
Proceedings 1861-1869, pg 306 (1869 Sept 29), Central Lodge No. 6, Central City
Proceedings 1872, pg 21 (1872 Sept 24), Denver Lodge No. 5, Denver
Proceedings 1873, pg 38 (1873 Oct 1), Central Lodge No. 6, Central City
Proceedings 1874, pg 213 (1874 Sept 30), Central Lodge No. 6, Central
Proceedings 1874, pg 229 (1874 Sept 30), Idaho Springs Lodge U D, Idaho Springs

Colorado's Territorial Masons

Strang, Romeo D, cont.
    Proceedings 1875, pg 77 (1875 Sept 22), Central Lodge No. 6, Central City
    Proceedings 1875, pg 89 (1875 Sept 22) Idaho Springs Lodge U D
    Proceedings 1876, pg 42 (1876 Sept 20) Idaho Springs Lodge No. 26
    Proceedings 1876, pg 48 (1876 Sept 20), Central Lodge No. 6, Central City, 1875 Sept 22

Stratton, Harris
    Proceedings 1870, pg 31 (1870 Sept 28), Collins Lodge No. 19, Fort Collins
    Proceedings 1873, pg 49 (1873 Oct 1), Collins Lodge No. 19, Fort Collins
    Proceedings 1874, pg 224 (1874 Sept 30), Collins Lodge No. 19, Fort Collins, Larimer County
    Proceedings 1875, pg 86 (1875 Sept 22), Collins Lodge No. 19, Fort Collins
    Proceedings 1876, pg 39 (1876 Sept 20), Collins Lodge No. 19, Fort Collins

Stratton, Harris Jr
    Proceedings 1871, pg 30 (1871 Sept 27), Collins Lodge No. 19, Fort Collins
    Proceedings 1872, pg 33 (1872 Sept 24), Collins Lodge No. 19, Fort Collins

Strickland, O F
    Proceedings 1872, pg 89 (1872 Sept 24) Grand Lodge of Utah

Strickler, J M
    Proceedings 1861-1869, pg 169 (1866 Oct 2), Union Lodge No. 7, Denver
    Proceedings 1861-1869, pg 195 (1867 Oct 8), Union Lodge No. 7, Denver
    Proceedings 1861-1869, pg 225 (1868 Oct 7), Union Lodge No. 7, Denver
    Proceedings 1861-1869, pg 307 (1869 Sept 29), Union Lodge No. 7, Denver
    Proceedings 1872, pg 23 (1872 Sept 24), Union Lodge No. 7, Denver
    Proceedings 1873, pg 40 (1873 Oct 1), Union Lodge No. 7, Denver
    Proceedings 1874, pg 214 (1874 Sept 30), Union Lodge No. 7, Denver
    Proceedings 1875, pg 78 (1875 Sept 22), Union Lodge No. 7, Denver

Strickler, James M
    Proceedings 1870, pg 23 (1870 Sept 28), Union Lodge No. 7, Denver
    Proceedings 1871, pg 22 (1871 Sept 27), Union Lodge No. 7, Denver
    Proceedings 1876, pg 32 (1876 Sept 20), Union Lodge No. 7, Denver

Strickler, W M
    Proceedings 1872, pg 26 (1872 Sept 24), El Paso Lodge No. 13, Colorado City
    Proceedings 1875, pg 82 (1875 Sept 22), El Paso Lodge No. 13, Colorado Springs

Strickler, William M
    Proceedings 1871, pg 25 (1871 Sept 27), El Paso Lodge No. 13, Colorado City
    Proceedings 1874, pg 218 (1874 Sept 30), El Paso Lodge No. 13, Colorado Springs

Strickler, Wm M
    Proceedings 1870, pg 27 (1870 Sept 28), El Paso Lodge No. 13, Colorado City
    Proceedings 1873, pg 43 (1873 Oct 1), El Paso Lodge No. 13, Colorado City
    Proceedings 1876, pg 35 (1876 Sept 20), El Paso Lodge No. 13, Colorado City

Strom, Chas P
    Proceedings 1874, pg 210 (1874 Sept 30), Nevada Lodge No. 4, Bald Mountain, Gilpin County

Strouse, Jno
    Proceedings 1861-1869, pg 131 (1864 Nov 8) Golden City Lodge No. 1

Strouse, John
    Proceedings 1861-1869, pg 147 (1865 Nov 7) Golden City Lodge No. 1
    Proceedings 1861-1869, pg 165 (1866 Oct 2) Golden City Lodge No. 1
    Proceedings 1861-1869, pg 191 (1867 Oct 8) Golden City Lodge No. 1
    Proceedings 1861-1869, pg 221 (1868 Oct 7) Golden City Lodge No. 1
    Proceedings 1861-1869, pg 303 (1869 Sept 29) Golden City Lodge No. 1
    Proceedings 1870, pg 19 (1870 Sept 28), Golden City Lodge No. 1, Golden City
    Proceedings 1871, pg 17 (1871 Sept 27), Golden City Lodge No. 1, Golden City
    Proceedings 1873, pg 19 (1873 Oct 1), Golden City Lodge No. 1, Golden City

Strouse, John A
    Proceedings 1874, pg 209 (1874 Sept 30), Golden City Lodge No. 1, Golden City
    Proceedings 1875, pg 73 (1875 Sept 22) Golden City Lodge No. 1
    Proceedings 1876, pg 29 (1876 Sept 20) Golden City Lodge No. 1

Strousse, John
    Proceedings 1872, pg 17 (1872 Sept 24), Golden City Lodge No. 1, Golden City

Studer, A M
    Proceedings 1861-1869, pg 150 (1865 Nov 7), Chivington Lodge No. 6, Central City
    Proceedings 1861-1869, pg 194 (1867 Oct 8), Chivington Lodge No. 6, Central City
    Proceedings 1861-1869, pg 224 (1868 Oct 7), Chivington Lodge No. 6, Central City
    Proceedings 1861-1869, pg 306 (1869 Sept 29), Central Lodge No. 6, Central City

Studer, Adelbert M
    Proceedings 1870, pg 23 (1870 Sept 28), Central Lodge No. 6, Central City, Dimitted

Studer, W H
　Proceedings 1870, pg 25 (1870 Sept 28), Black Hawk Lodge No. 11, Black Hawk
　Proceedings 1872, pg 25 (1872 Sept 24), Black Hawk Lodge No. 11, Black Hawk, Dimitted

Studer, William H
　Proceedings 1871, pg 23 (1871 Sept 27), Black Hawk Lodge No. 11, Black Hawk

Studer, Wm H
　Proceedings 1861-1869, pg 170 (1866 Oct 2), Black Hawk Lodge U D, Black Hawk
　Proceedings 1861-1869, pg 196 (1867 Oct 8), Black Hawk Lodge No. 11, Black Hawk
　Proceedings 1861-1869, pg 227 (1868 Oct 7), Black Hawk Lodge No. 11, Black Hawk
　Proceedings 1861-1869, pg 309 (1869 Sept 29), Black Hawk Lodge No. 11, Black Hawk

Studor, A M
　Proceedings 1861-1869, pg 168 (1866 Oct 2), Chivington Lodge No. 6, Central City

Stupp, Frank J
　Proceedings 1876, pg 14 (1874 Oct 6) sent telegram from E T Stone

Sullivan, James
　Proceedings 1875, pg 86 (1875 Sept 22), Collins Lodge No. 19, Fort Collins
　Proceedings 1876, pg 39 (1876 Sept 20), Collins Lodge No. 19, Fort Collins

Summers, Geo
　Proceedings 1872, pg 36 (1872 Sept 24), Ashlar Lodge U D, Colorado Springs

Summit Lodge No. 2
　Proceedings 1861-1869, pg 6 (1861 Aug 3) Parkville

Summit Lodge No. 2, Parkville
　Proceedings 1861-1869, pg 40 (1861 Dec 4) 24 original members
　Proceedings 1861-1869, pg 106 (1863 Nov 3) dispensation to suspend work for the winter
　Proceedings 1861-1869, pg 139 (1865 Nov 6) surrendered its charter
　Proceedings 1861-1869, pg 221 (1868 Oct 7) charter surrendered
　Proceedings 1861-1869, pg 303 (1869 Sept 29) charter surrendered
　Proceedings 1870, pg 19 (1870 Sept 28) charter surrendered
　Proceedings 1871, pg 17 (1871 Sept 27) charter surrendered
　Proceedings 1872, pg 11 (1872 Sept 24) sale of the effects the lodge netted $13.85
　Proceedings 1872, pg 18 (1872 Sept 24) charter surrendered
　Proceedings 1873, pg 35 (1873 Oct 1) charter surrendered
　Proceedings 1875, pg 74 (1875 Sept 22) charter surrendered
　Proceedings 1876, pg 13 (1875 Oct 6) dues from members paid
　Proceedings 1876, pg 46 (1876 Sept 20) charter surrendered

Summit Lodge No. 2, Parkville, Summit County
　Proceedings 1874, pg 210 (1874 Sept 30) Charter surrendered

Summit Lodge No. 7, Parkville
　Proceedings 1861-1869, pg 4 (1861 Aug 2) chartered 5 June 1861 by the M W Grand Lodge of Nebraska

Summit Lodge of Parkville
　Proceedings 1871, pg 6 (1861 June 5) Grand Lodge of Nebraska

Sumner, W L
　Proceedings 1872, pg 48 (1872 Sept 24), Denver Lodge No. 5, Denver

Sumner, William L
　Proceedings 1876, pg 31 (1876 Sept 20) Denver Lodge No. 5

Sumner, Wm L
　Proceedings 1870, pg 20 (1870 Sept 28), Denver Lodge No. 5, Denver
　Proceedings 1872, pg 20 (1872 Sept 24), Denver Lodge No. 5, Denver
　Proceedings 1873, pg 37 (1873 Oct 1), Denver Lodge No. 5, Denver
　Proceedings 1874, pg 212 (1874 Sept 30), Denver Lodge No. 5, Denver, Stricken from the rolls
　Proceedings 1875, pg 75 (1875 Sept 22) Denver Lodge No. 5
　Proceedings 1875, pg 76 (1875 Sept 22) Denver Lodge No. 5, Reinstated,

Supreme Council
　Proceedings 1872, pg 47 (1872 Sept 24), Brussels, Belgium

Supreme Grand Council
　Proceedings 1872, pg 47 (1872 Sept 24), Caraccas, Venezuela

Supreme Helvetic Council
　Proceedings 1872, pg 47 (1872 Sept 24), Berne, Switzerland

Surles, Z
　Proceedings 1873, pg 37 (1873 Oct 1), Denver Lodge No. 5, Denver, Not a member

Surles, Ziba
　Proceedings 1874, pg 211 (1874 Sept 30), Denver Lodge No. 5, Denver
　Proceedings 1875, pg 75 (1875 Sept 22) Denver Lodge No. 5
　Proceedings 1876, pg 31 (1876 Sept 20) Denver Lodge No. 5

Sutfin, John H
　Proceedings 1871, pg 19 (1871 Sept 27) Denver Lodge No. 5
　Proceedings 1872, pg 20 (1872 Sept 24), Denver Lodge No. 5, Denver
　Proceedings 1873, pg 37 (1873 Oct 1), Denver Lodge No. 5, Denver

Colorado's Territorial Masons

Sutfin, John H, cont.
Proceedings 1874, pg 211 (1874 Sept 30), Denver Lodge No. 5, Denver
Proceedings 1875, pg 75 (1875 Sept 22) Denver Lodge No. 5
Proceedings 1876, pg 31 (1876 Sept 20) Denver Lodge No. 5
Proceedings 1876, pg 50 (1876 Sept 20) Denver Lodge No. 5

Sutherland
Proceedings 1861-1869, pg 210 (1868 Jan) recommended as W M for Valmont

Sutherland, D E
Proceedings 1861-1869, pg 230 (1868 Oct 7), Valmont Lodge U D, Valmont
Proceedings 1861-1869, pg 310 (1869 Sept 29), Columbia Lodge No. 14, Boulder City
Proceedings 1870, pg 27 (1870 Sept 28), Columbia Lodge No. 14, Boulder City
Proceedings 1871, pg 26 (1871 Sept 27), Columbia Lodge No. 14, Boulder City

Sutherland, Datus E
Proceedings 1861-1869, pg 207 (1868 Jan 13), Valmont Lodge U D, Valmont, Worshipful Master

Sutherland, F F
Proceedings 1872, pg 36 (1872 Sept 24), Ashlar Lodge U D, Colorado Springs

Sutherland, F H
Proceedings 1873, pg 13 (1873 Sept 30), Ashlar Lodge U D, Colorado Springs
Proceedings 1874, pg 218 (1874 Sept 30), El Paso Lodge No. 13, Colorado Springs
Proceedings 1875, pg 82 (1875 Sept 22), El Paso Lodge No. 13, Colorado Springs
Proceedings 1876, pg 35 (1876 Sept 20), El Paso Lodge No. 13, Colorado City

Sutler, Joseph M
Proceedings 1874, pg 216 (1874 Sept 30), Black Hawk Lodge No. 11, Black Hawk

Sutten, I M
Proceedings 1871, pg 23 (1871 Sept 27), Black Hawk Lodge No. 11, Black Hawk

Sutter, J M
Proceedings 1861-1869, pg 309 (1869 Sept 29), Black Hawk Lodge No. 11, Black Hawk
Proceedings 1870, pg 25 (1870 Sept 28), Black Hawk Lodge No. 11, Black Hawk

Sutter, Jos M
Proceedings 1876, pg 34 (1876 Sept 20) Black Hawk Lodge No. 11

Sutter, Joseph M
Proceedings 1872, pg 25 (1872 Sept 24), Black Hawk Lodge No. 11, Black Hawk
Proceedings 1873, pg 42 (1873 Oct 1), Black Hawk Lodge No. 11, Black Hawk
Proceedings 1875, pg 80 (1875 Sept 22) Black Hawk Lodge No. 11

Sutton, H G
Proceedings 1873, pg 48 (1873 Oct 1), Laramie Lodge No. 18, Laramie, Wyoming Territory
Proceedings 1874, pg 223 (1874 Sept 30), Laramie Lodge No. 18, Laramie City

Swallow, George R
Proceedings 1875, pg 19 (1875 Mar 15), Las Animas Lodge U D, Trinidad
Proceedings 1875, pg 34 (1875 Sept 22), Las Animas Lodge No. 28, Trinidad
Proceedings 1875, pg 91 (1875 Sept 22), Las Animas Lodge U D, Trinidad
Proceedings 1876, pg 44 (1876 Sept 20), Las Animas Lodge No. 28, Trinidad

Swasey, H R
Proceedings 1874, pg 73 (1874 Sept 30) Grand Lodge of Louisiana, deceased

Swasey, Henry R
Proceedings 1861-1869, pg 255 (1868 Feb 10), Grand Master, Grand Lodge of Louisiana
Proceedings 1861-1869, pg 331 (1868 Feb 8) Grand Master, Grand Lodge of Louisiana

Sweet, C Wallace
Proceedings 1874, pg 221 (1874 Sept 30), Cheyenne Lodge No. 16, Cheyenne, Wyoming Territory

Sweet, Wallace
Proceedings 1872, pg 30 (1872 Sept 24), Cheyenne Lodge No. 16, Cheyenne, Wyoming Territory, Fellowcraft
Proceedings 1873, pg 46 (1873 Oct 1), Cheyenne Lodge No. 16, Cheyenne, Wyoming Territory

Sweetland, W
Proceedings 1861-1869, pg 196 (1867 Oct 8), El Paso Lodge U D, Colorado City

Sweetland, William
Proceedings 1871, pg 25 (1871 Sept 27), El Paso Lodge No. 13, Colorado City
Proceedings 1874, pg 218 (1874 Sept 30), El Paso Lodge No. 13, Colorado Springs
Proceedings 1875, pg 82 (1875 Sept 22), El Paso Lodge No. 13, Colorado Springs

Sweetland, Wm
Proceedings 1861-1869, pg 228 (1868 Oct 7), El Paso Lodge No. 13, Colorado City
Proceedings 1861-1869, pg 310 (1869 Sept 29), El Paso Lodge No. 13, Colorado City
Proceedings 1870, pg 27 (1870 Sept 28), El Paso Lodge No. 13, Colorado City
Proceedings 1872, pg 27 (1872 Sept 24), El Paso Lodge No. 13, Colorado City
Proceedings 1873, pg 43 (1873 Oct 1), El Paso Lodge No. 13, Colorado City
Proceedings 1876, pg 49 (1876 Sept 20), El Paso Lodge No. 13, Colorado City, 1876 July 22

Colorado's Territorial Masons

Swift, G W
Proceedings 1871, pg 30 (1871 Sept 27), Collins Lodge No. 19, Fort Collins

Swift, Geo W
Proceedings 1870, pg 31 (1870 Sept 28), Collins Lodge No. 19, Fort Collins
Proceedings 1872, pg 33 (1872 Sept 24), Collins Lodge No. 19, Fort Collins

Swift, George W
Proceedings 1873, pg 49 (1873 Oct 1), Collins Lodge No. 19, Fort Collins, Dimitted

Swigart, L D
Proceedings 1873, pg 48 (1873 Oct 1), Laramie Lodge No. 18, Laramie, Wyoming Territory, Fellowcraft

Swigert, L C
Proceedings 1872, pg 32 (1872 Sept 24), Laramie Lodge No. 18, Laramie, Wyoming Territory, Apprentice

Swigert, L D
Proceedings 1874, pg 223 (1874 Sept 30), Laramie Lodge No. 18, Laramie City

Swisher, M D
Proceedings 1873, pg 52 (1873 Oct 1), Ashlar Lodge U D, Colorado Springs, Apprentice

Symonds, M
Proceedings 1861-1869, pg 112 (1863 Nov 3), Nevada Lodge No. 4, Nevadaville, Apprentice
Proceedings 1861-1869, pg 192 (1867 Oct 8), Nevada Lodge No. 4, Nevadaville, Apprentice
Proceedings 1861-1869, pg 222 (1868 Oct 7), Nevada Lodge No. 4, Nevadaville, Apprentice

Symonds, Marine
Proceedings 1861-1869, pg 148 (1865 Nov 7), Nevada Lodge No. 4, Nevadaville, Apprentice
Proceedings 1861-1869, pg 166 (1866 Oct 2), Nevada Lodge No. 4, Nevadaville, Apprentice
Proceedings 1861-1869, pg 132 (1864 Nov 8), Nevada Lodge No. 4, Nevadaville, Apprentice

T

Tabb, Geo E
Proceedings 1870, pg 30 (1870 Sept 28), Pueblo Lodge No. 17, Pueblo, Fellowcraft
Proceedings 1872, pg 31 (1872 Sept 24), Pueblo Lodge No. 17, Pueblo, Fellowcraft
Proceedings 1875, pg 85 (1875 Sept 22) Pueblo Lodge No. 17, Fellowcraft

Tabb, George E
Proceedings 1871, pg 28 (1871 Sept 27), Pueblo Lodge No. 17, Pueblo, Fellowcraft
Proceedings 1873, pg 47 (1873 Oct 1), Pueblo Lodge No. 17, Pueblo, Fellowcraft
Proceedings 1874, pg 222 (1874 Sept 30), Pueblo Lodge No. 17, Pueblo, Pueblo County, Fellowcraft

Taber, George D
Proceedings 1876, pg 44 (1876 Sept 20), Las Animas Lodge No. 28, Trinidad

Taesdale, George
Proceedings 1871, pg 29 (1871 Sept 27), Laramie Lodge No. 18, Laramie, Wyoming Territory

Taggart, C D
Proceedings 1874, pg 213 (1874 Sept 30), Union Lodge No. 7, Denver

Taggart, Charles D
Proceedings 1873, pg 40 (1873 Oct 1), Union Lodge No. 7, Denver
Proceedings 1876, pg 32 (1876 Sept 20), Union Lodge No. 7, Denver

Taggart, Chas D
Proceedings 1875, pg 78 (1875 Sept 22), Union Lodge No. 7, Denver

Taggert, Charles D
Proceedings 1871, pg 22 (1871 Sept 27), Union Lodge No. 7, Denver, Fellowcraft

Taggert, Chas D
Proceedings 1872, pg 23 (1872 Sept 24), Union Lodge No. 7, Denver, Fellowcraft

Tallman, Isaac T
Proceedings 1876, pg 37 (1876 Sept 20), Columbia Lodge No. 14, Boulder

Tallman, J M
Proceedings 1861-1869, pg 193 (1867 Oct 8) Denver Lodge No. 5, Apprentice
Proceedings 1861-1869, pg 223 (1868 Oct 7) Denver Lodge No. 5, Apprentice
Proceedings 1876, pg 31 (1876 Sept 20) Denver Lodge No. 5

Tallman, Jacob
Proceedings 1861-1869, pg 227 (1868 Oct 7), Black Hawk Lodge No. 11, Black Hawk
Proceedings 1861-1869, pg 309 (1869 Sept 29), Black Hawk Lodge No. 11, Black Hawk

Tallman, Jaco, cont.
    Proceedings 1870, pg 25 (1870 Sept 28), Black Hawk Lodge No. 11, Black Hawk, Dimitted
    Proceedings 1871, pg 23 (1871 Sept 27), Black Hawk Lodge No. 11, Black Hawk
    Proceedings 1872, pg 25 (1872 Sept 24), Black Hawk Lodge No. 11, Black Hawk
    Proceedings 1873, pg 42 (1873 Oct 1), Black Hawk Lodge No. 11, Black Hawk
    Proceedings 1874, pg 216 (1874 Sept 30), Black Hawk Lodge No. 11, Black Hawk
    Proceedings 1875, pg 80 (1875 Sept 22) Black Hawk Lodge No. 11
    Proceedings 1876, pg 34 (1876 Sept 20) Black Hawk Lodge No. 11

Tallman, John M
    Proceedings 1875, pg 76 (1875 Sept 22) Denver Lodge No. 5

Talman, J N
    Proceedings 1861-1869, pg 305 (1869 Sept 29) Denver Lodge No. 5, Apprentice

Tankersley, Charles W
    Proceedings 1876, pg 44 (1876 Sept 20) Del Norte Lodge U D

Tanner, S J
    Proceedings 1874, pg 220 (1874 Sept 30), Mount Moriah Lodge No. 15, Canon City
    Proceedings 1875, pg 84 (1875 Sept 22), Mount Moriah Lodge No. 15, Canon City
    Proceedings 1876, pg 38 (1876 Sept 20), Mount Moriah Lodge No. 15, Canon City

Tanner, Virgil
    Proceedings 1874, pg 220 (1874 Sept 30), Mount Moriah Lodge No. 15, Canon City, Apprentice

Tanner, Virgil R
    Proceedings 1875, pg 84 (1875 Sept 22), Mount Moriah Lodge No. 15, Canon City, Apprentice
    Proceedings 1876, pg 38 (1876 Sept 20), Mount Moriah Lodge No. 15, Canon City, Apprentice

Tapan, S F
    Proceedings 1871, pg 21 (1871 Sept 27), Central Lodge No. 6, Central

Tappan, J E
    Proceedings 1861-1869, pg 149 (1865 Nov 7), Nevada Lodge No. 4, Nevadaville
    Proceedings 1861-1869, pg 167 (1866 Oct 2) Denver Lodge No. 5

Tappan, John E
    Proceedings 1861-1869, pg 112 (1863 Nov 3) Denver Lodge No. 5
    Proceedings 1861-1869, pg 133 (1864 Nov 8) Denver Lodge No. 5
    Proceedings 1861-1869, pg 193 (1867 Oct 8) Denver Lodge No. 5, Dimitted

Tappan, S F
    Proceedings 1861-1869, pg 78 (1862 Nov 4), Chivington Lodge No. 6, Central City
    Proceedings 1861-1869, pg 113 (1863 Nov 3), Chivington Lodge No. 6, Central City
    Proceedings 1861-1869, pg 134 (1864 Nov 8), Chivington Lodge No. 6, Central City
    Proceedings 1861-1869, pg 150 (1865 Nov 7), Chivington Lodge No. 6, Central City
    Proceedings 1861-1869, pg 168 (1866 Oct 2), Chivington Lodge No. 6, Central City
    Proceedings 1861-1869, pg 194 (1867 Oct 8), Chivington Lodge No. 6, Central City
    Proceedings 1861-1869, pg 224 (1868 Oct 7), Chivington Lodge No. 6, Central City
    Proceedings 1861-1869, pg 306 (1869 Sept 29), Central Lodge No. 6, Central City
    Proceedings 1870, pg 22 (1870 Sept 28), Central Lodge No. 6, Central City

Tappan, Sam'l F
    Proceedings 1876, pg 48 (1876 Sept 20), Central Lodge No. 6, Central City, 1875 Oct 13

Tappan, Samuel F
    Proceedings 1872, pg 21 (1872 Sept 24), Denver Lodge No. 5, Denver
    Proceedings 1873, pg 38 (1873 Oct 1), Central Lodge No. 6, Central City
    Proceedings 1874, pg 213 (1874 Sept 30), Central Lodge No. 6, Central
    Proceedings 1875, pg 77 (1875 Sept 22), Central Lodge No. 6, Central City

Tarvin, E M
    Proceedings 1876, pg 37 (1876 Sept 20), Columbia Lodge No. 14, Boulder

Tayler
    Proceedings 1874, pg 59 (1874 Sept 30)

Taylor
    Proceedings 1872, pg 79 (1872 Sept 24) Grand Lodge of Nevada

Taylor, A C
    Proceedings 1874, pg 212 (1874 Sept 30), Denver Lodge No. 5, Denver
    Proceedings 1875, pg 75 (1875 Sept 22) Denver Lodge No. 5
    Proceedings 1876, pg 31 (1876 Sept 20) Denver Lodge No. 5

Taylor, C R
    Proceedings 1874, pg 223 (1874 Sept 30), Laramie Lodge No. 18, Laramie City

Taylor, D A
    Proceedings 1873, pg 48 (1873 Oct 1), Laramie Lodge No. 18, Laramie, Wyoming Territory, Fellowcraft
    Proceedings 1874, pg 223 (1874 Sept 30), Laramie Lodge No. 18, Laramie City

Colorado's Territorial Masons

Taylor, Daniel
Proceedings 1871, pg 28 (1871 Sept 27), Pueblo Lodge No. 17, Pueblo
Proceedings 1872, pg 31 (1872 Sept 24), Pueblo Lodge No. 17, Pueblo
Proceedings 1873, pg 47 (1873 Oct 1), Pueblo Lodge No. 17, Pueblo
Proceedings 1874, pg 222 (1874 Sept 30), Pueblo Lodge No. 17, Pueblo, Pueblo County
Proceedings 1875, pg 85 (1875 Sept 22) Pueblo Lodge No. 17
Proceedings 1876, pg 39 (1876 Sept 20) Pueblo Lodge No. 17

Taylor, J S
Proceedings 1861-1869, pg 150 (1865 Nov 7), Chivington Lodge No. 6, Central City
Proceedings 1861-1869, pg 168 (1866 Oct 2), Chivington Lodge No. 6, Central City
Proceedings 1861-1869, pg 170 (1866 Oct 2), Black Hawk Lodge U D, Black Hawk
Proceedings 1861-1869, pg 194 (1867 Oct 8), Chivington Lodge No. 6, Central City, Dimitted
Proceedings 1861-1869, pg 195 (1867 Oct 8), Black Hawk Lodge No. 11, Black Hawk
Proceedings 1861-1869, pg 227 (1868 Oct 7), Black Hawk Lodge No. 11, Black Hawk
Proceedings 1861-1869, pg 309 (1869 Sept 29), Black Hawk Lodge No. 11, Black Hawk
Proceedings 1870, pg 25 (1870 Sept 28), Black Hawk Lodge No. 11, Black Hawk
Proceedings 1871, pg 27 (1871 Sept 27), Cheyenne Lodge No. 16, Cheyenne, Wyoming Territory
Proceedings 1872, pg 30 (1872 Sept 24), Cheyenne Lodge No. 16, Cheyenne, Wyoming Territory
Proceedings 1873, pg 46 (1873 Oct 1), Cheyenne Lodge No. 16, Cheyenne, Wyoming Territory
Proceedings 1874, pg 221 (1874 Sept 30), Cheyenne Lodge No. 16, Cheyenne, Wyoming Territory

Taylor, Jas R
Proceedings 1872, pg 20 (1872 Sept 24), Denver Lodge No. 5, Denver

Taylor, Jos R
Proceedings 1871, pg 19 (1871 Sept 27) Denver Lodge No. 5

Taylor, Joseph R
Proceedings 1873, pg 38 (1873 Oct 1), Denver Lodge No. 5, Denver, Striken from the rolls

Taylor, M S
Proceedings 1876, pg 29 (1876 Sept 20) Golden City Lodge No. 1, Apprentice

Taylor, Matt S
Proceedings 1874, pg 209 (1874 Sept 30), Golden City Lodge No. 1, Golden City, Apprentice
Proceedings 1875, pg 73 (1875 Sept 22) Golden City Lodge No. 1, Apprentice

Taylor, Matthew S
Proceedings 1872, pg 17 (1872 Sept 24), Golden City Lodge No. 1, Golden City, Apprentice

Taylor, R H
Proceedings 1872, pg 78 (1872 Sept 24) Grand Lodge of Nevada
Proceedings 1872, pg 82 (1872 Sept 24) Grand Lodge of Nevada

Taylor, R T
Proceedings 1874, pg 6 (1874 Sept 29), El Paso Lodge No. 13, Colorado City
Proceedings 1874, pg 36 (1874 Sept 30) per diem
Proceedings 1874, pg 218 (1874 Sept 30), El Paso Lodge No. 13, Colorado Springs
Proceedings 1875, pg 82 (1875 Sept 22), El Paso Lodge No. 13, Colorado Springs

Taylor, R W
Proceedings 1861-1869, pg 308 (1869 Sept 29), Empire Lodge No. 8, Empire City
Proceedings 1870, pg 24 (1870 Sept 28), Empire Lodge No. 8, Empire

Taylor, Robert H
Proceedings 1861-1869, pg 226 (1868 Oct 7), Empire Lodge No. 8, Empire City
Proceedings 1870, pg 92 (1869 Sept 21) Grand Orator, Grand Lodge of Nevada
Proceedings 1872, pg 43 (1872 Sept 24) Virginia City, Grand Lodge of Nevada
Proceedings 1873, pg 60 (1873 Oct 1) Grand Lodge of Nevada, Virginia City
Proceedings 1874, pg 100 (1874 Sept 30) Grand Lodge of Nevada

Taylor, Robert W
Proceedings 1872, pg 23 (1872 Sept 24), Empire Lodge No. 8, Empire
Proceedings 1873, pg 41 (1873 Oct 1), Empire Lodge No. 8, Empire

Taylor, Robt H
Proceedings 1874, pg 204 (1874 Sept 30) Grand Lodge of Nevada, Virginia

Taylor, Samuel Jr
Proceedings 1872, pg 26 (1872 Sept 24), Washington Lodge No. 12, Georgetown
Proceedings 1873, pg 43 (1873 Oct 1), Washington Lodge No. 12, Georgetown
Proceedings 1874, pg 217 (1874 Sept 30), Washington Lodge No. 12, Georgetown, Demitted

Taylor, U D
Proceedings 1872, pg 66 (1872 Sept 24) Grand Lodge of Iowa
Proceedings 1872, pg 97 (1872 Sept 24) of Iowa
Proceedings 1872, pg 125 (1872 Sept 24) of Iowa

Taylor, William
Proceedings 1870, pg 31 (1870 Sept 28), Laramie Lodge No. 18, Laramie, Wyoming Territory
Proceedings 1871, pg 29 (1871 Sept 27), Laramie Lodge No. 18, Laramie, Wyoming Territory

Taylor, William, cont.
- Proceedings 1873, pg 48 (1873 Oct 1), Laramie Lodge No. 18, Laramie, Wyoming Territory
- Proceedings 1874, pg 223 (1874 Sept 30), Laramie Lodge No. 18, Laramie City
- Proceedings 1874, pg 223 (1874 Sept 30), Laramie Lodge No. 18, Laramie City

Taylor, Wm
- Proceedings 1872, pg 32 (1872 Sept 24), Laramie Lodge No. 18, Laramie, Wyoming Territory
- Proceedings 1872, pg 77 (1872 Sept 24) Grand Lodge of Nova Scotia

Taylor, Wm M
- Proceedings 1872, pg 88 (1872 Sept 24) Grand Lodge of Texas, deceased

Teal, James
- Proceedings 1875, pg 81 (1875 Sept 22), Washington Lodge No. 12, Georgetown, Apprentice
- Proceedings 1876, pg 35 (1876 Sept 20), Washington Lodge No. 12, Georgetown

Teasdale, Geo
- Proceedings 1872, pg 32 (1872 Sept 24), Laramie Lodge No. 18, Laramie, Wyoming Territory

Teasdale, George
- Proceedings 1870, pg 31 (1870 Sept 28), Laramie Lodge No. 18, Laramie, Wyoming Territory
- Proceedings 1873, pg 48 (1873 Oct 1), Laramie Lodge No. 18, Laramie, Wyoming Territory
- Proceedings 1874, pg 223 (1874 Sept 30), Laramie Lodge No. 18, Laramie City

Teed, Matthew
- Proceedings 1861-1869, pg 77 (1862 Nov 4) Denver Lodge No. 5
- Proceedings 1861-1869, pg 78 (1862 Nov 4) Denver Lodge No. 5, dimitted,

Teller
- Proceedings 1861-1869, pg 51 (1862 Nov 4) motion
- Proceedings 1861-1869, pg 52 (1862 Nov 4) committee
- Proceedings 1861-1869, pg 95 (1863 Apr 17) motion
- Proceedings 1861-1869, pg 123 (1864 Nov 8) Grand Master
- Proceedings 1861-1869, pg 125 (1864 Nov 8) Past Grand Master
- Proceedings 1861-1869, pg 127 (1864 Nov 8) donated per diem to the Grand Lodge
- Proceedings 1861-1869, pg 140 (1865 Nov 6) Grand Marshal
- Proceedings 1861-1869, pg 140 (1865 Nov 6) motion
- Proceedings 1861-1869, pg 142 (1865 Nov 7) motion
- Proceedings 1861-1869, pg 180 (1867 Oct 7) motion
- Proceedings 1861-1869, pg 185 (1867 Oct 7) committee
- Proceedings 1861-1869, pg 187 (1867 Oct 8) motion
- Proceedings 1861-1869, pg 190 (1867 Oct 8) PGM
- Proceedings 1861-1869, pg 289 (1869 Sept 28) Grand Master
- Proceedings 1861-1869, pg 292 (1869 Sept 28) donation
- Proceedings 1861-1869, pg 297 (1869 Sept 28) Grand Master
- Proceedings 1861-1869, pg 298 (1869 Sept 29) Grand Master
- Proceedings 1870, pg 5 (1870 Sept 27) Grand Master
- Proceedings 1870, pg 10 (1870 Sept 27) donation
- Proceedings 1870, pg 13 (1870 Sept 27) Grand Master
- Proceedings 1870, pg 14 (1870 Sept 28) Grand Master
- Proceedings 1870, pg 90 (1869 Oct 4) Grand Lodge of Colorado
- Proceedings 1871, pg 5 (1871 Sept 26) Grand Master
- Proceedings 1871, pg 13 (1871 Sept 26) Grand Master
- Proceedings 1871, pg 13 (1871 Sept 27) Grand Master
- Proceedings 1872, pg 6 (1872 Sept 24) Grand Master
- Proceedings 1872, pg 13 (1872 Sept 24) Grand Master
- Proceedings 1873, pg 7 (1873 Sept 30), Grand Representative, Illinois
- Proceedings 1873, pg 14 (1873 Oct 1) Grand Master
- Proceedings 1873, pg 14 (1873 Sept 30) Grand Master
- Proceedings 1873, pg 17 (1873 Oct 1) Grand Master
- Proceedings 1873, pg 19 (1873 Oct 1) Grand Master
- Proceedings 1873, pg 19 (1873 Oct 1) Grand Master
- Proceedings 1873, pg 20 (1873 Oct 1) Grand Master
- Proceedings 1873, pg 26 (1873 Oct 1) motion
- Proceedings 1873, pg 29 (1873 Oct 1) motion
- Proceedings 1873, pg 29 (1873 Oct 1) motion
- Proceedings 1873, pg 31 (1873 Oct 1) resolution
- Proceedings 1874, pg 8 (1874 Sept 29) Grand Master
- Proceedings 1874, pg 29 (1874 Sept 29) motion
- Proceedings 1874, pg 35 (1874 Sept 30) committee
- Proceedings 1874, pg 38 (1874 Sept 30) resolution
- Proceedings 1874, pg 39 (1874 Sept 30) motion
- Proceedings 1874, pg 73 (1874 Sept 30) Grand Master
- Proceedings 1874, pg 76 (1874 Sept 30) Grand Master
- Proceedings 1874, pg 77 (1874 Sept 30) Grand Master
- Proceedings 1874, pg 87 (1874 Sept 30) Grand Master
- Proceedings 1874, pg 96 (1874 Sept 30) Grand Master
- Proceedings 1874, pg 101 (1874 Sept 30) Grand Master
- Proceedings 1874, pg 107 (1874 Sept 30) Grand Master
- Proceedings 1874, pg 111 (1874 Sept 30) Grand Master
- Proceedings 1874, pg 124 (1874 Sept 30) Grand Master

Teller, H M
- Proceedings 1861-1869, pg 45 (1862 Nov 3) committee
- Proceedings 1861-1869, pg 45 (1862 Nov 3), Chivington Lodge No. 6, Central City
- Proceedings 1861-1869, pg 51 (1862 Nov 4) Grand Orator
- Proceedings 1861-1869, pg 53 (1862 Nov 4) committee
- Proceedings 1861-1869, pg 54 (1862 Nov 4) committee
- Proceedings 1861-1869, pg 54 (1862 Nov 4) committee
- Proceedings 1861-1869, pg 78 (1862 Nov 4), Chivington Lodge No. 6, Central City
- Proceedings 1861-1869, pg 79 (1863 May 6) Grand Orator
- Proceedings 1861-1869, pg 80 (1863 May 6), Chivington Lodge No. 6, Central City
- Proceedings 1861-1869, pg 91 (1863 Apr 17) committee
- Proceedings 1861-1869, pg 93 (1863 Apr 17) committee
- Proceedings 1861-1869, pg 94 (1863 Apr 17), Chivington Lodge No. 6, Central City
- Proceedings 1861-1869, pg 94 (1863 Apr 17) Grand Orator
- Proceedings 1861-1869, pg 95 (1863 Apr 17) donated their per diem to the Grand Lodge

Teller, H M, cont.
  Proceedings 1861-1869, pg 95 (1863 Apr 17) motion
  Proceedings 1861-1869, pg 97 (1863 Nov 2) Grand Senior Warden
  Proceedings 1861-1869, pg 98 (1863 Nov 2) Grand Orator
  Proceedings 1861-1869, pg 98 (1863 Nov 2), Chivington Lodge No. 6, Central City
  Proceedings 1861-1869, pg 99 (1863 Nov 2), Chivington Lodge No. 6, Central City, Grand Master
  Proceedings 1861-1869, pg 100 (1863 Nov 3) Grand Master
  Proceedings 1861-1869, pg 103 (1863 Nov 3), Chivington Lodge No. 6, Central City
  Proceedings 1861-1869, pg 106 (1863 Nov 3) Grand Master
  Proceedings 1861-1869, pg 107 (1863 Nov 3) Grand Master
  Proceedings 1861-1869, pg 112 (1863 Nov 3), Chivington Lodge No. 6, Central City
  Proceedings 1861-1869, pg 119 (1863 Nov 3) warrant drawn
  Proceedings 1861-1869, pg 122 (1864 Nov 8) Grand Master
  Proceedings 1861-1869, pg 126 (1864 Nov 8) Grand Master
  Proceedings 1861-1869, pg 127 (1864 Nov 8) committee
  Proceedings 1861-1869, pg 134 (1864 Nov 8), Chivington Lodge No. 6, Central City
  Proceedings 1861-1869, pg 136 (1865 Nov 6) Past Grand Master
  Proceedings 1861-1869, pg 138 (1865 Nov 6) committee
  Proceedings 1861-1869, pg 138 (1865 Nov 6) committee
  Proceedings 1861-1869, pg 138 (1865 Nov 6) committee
  Proceedings 1861-1869, pg 141 (1865 Nov 7) committee
  Proceedings 1861-1869, pg 142 (1865 Nov 7) committee
  Proceedings 1861-1869, pg 143 (1865 Nov 7) committee
  Proceedings 1861-1869, pg 144 (1865 Nov 7) Past Grand Master
  Proceedings 1861-1869, pg 145 (1865 Nov 7), Chivington Lodge No. 6, Central City, Grand Orator
  Proceedings 1861-1869, pg 150 (1865 Nov 7), Chivington Lodge No. 6, Central City
  Proceedings 1861-1869, pg 157 (1866 Oct 1) absent from the Territory
  Proceedings 1861-1869, pg 159 (1866 Oct 1) warrant
  Proceedings 1861-1869, pg 163 (1866 Oct 2) committee
  Proceedings 1861-1869, pg 168 (1866 Oct 2), Chivington Lodge No. 6, Central City
  Proceedings 1861-1869, pg 176 (1867 Oct 7) Past Grand Master
  Proceedings 1861-1869, pg 186 (1867 Oct 8) Past Grand Master
  Proceedings 1861-1869, pg 194 (1867 Oct 8), Chivington Lodge No. 6, Central City
  Proceedings 1861-1869, pg 202 (1868 Oct 6) Grand Master
  Proceedings 1861-1869, pg 209 (1868 Oct 6) Grand Master
  Proceedings 1861-1869, pg 212 (1868 Oct 6) warrant paid
  Proceedings 1861-1869, pg 219 (1868 Oct 7) mileage allowed
  Proceedings 1861-1869, pg 224 (1868 Oct 7), Chivington Lodge No. 6, Central City
  Proceedings 1861-1869, pg 288 (1869 Sept 28) Grand Master
  Proceedings 1861-1869, pg 296 (1869 Sept 28) Grand Master
  Proceedings 1861-1869, pg 300 (1869 Sept 29) Grand Master
  Proceedings 1861-1869, pg 306 (1869 Sept 29), Central Lodge No. 6, Central City
  Proceedings 1870, pg 4 (1870 Sept 27) Grand Master
  Proceedings 1870, pg 9 (1870 Sept 27) Grand Master
  Proceedings 1870, pg 16 (1870 Sept 28) Grand Master
  Proceedings 1871, pg 3 (1871 Sept 26) Grand Representative, Minnesota
  Proceedings 1871, pg 4 (1871 Sept 26) Grand Master
  Proceedings 1871, pg 10 (1871 Sept 26)
  Proceedings 1871, pg 14 (1871 Sept 27) Grand Master
  Proceedings 1871, pg 20 (1871 Sept 27), Central Lodge No. 6, Central
  Proceedings 1872, pg 4 (1872 Sept 24) Grand Master
  Proceedings 1872, pg 9 (1872 Sept 24) Grand Master
  Proceedings 1872, pg 16 (1872 Sept 24) Grand Master
  Proceedings 1873, pg 12 (1873 Sept 30) Grand Master
  Proceedings 1873, pg 31 (1873 Oct 1) mileage and per diem
  Proceedings 1874, pg 5 (1874 Sept 29) Past Grand Master
  Proceedings 1874, pg 21 (1874 Sept 29) committee
  Proceedings 1874, pg 32 (1874 Sept 30) Past Grand Master
  Proceedings 1874, pg 33 (1874 Sept 30) motion
  Proceedings 1874, pg 34 (1874 Sept 30) committee
  Proceedings 1874, pg 36 (1874 Sept 30) per diem
  Proceedings 1875, pg 16 (1875 Sept 21) Past Grand Master
  Proceedings 1875, pg 17 (1875 Sept 21) committee
  Proceedings 1875, pg 24 (1875 Sept 21) donation to the library fund
  Proceedings 1875, pg 28 (1875 Sept 21) resolution
  Proceedings 1875, pg 31 (1875 Sept 21) resolution
  Proceedings 1875, pg 32 (1875 Sept 22) committee
  Proceedings 1875, pg 35 (1875 Sept 22) resolution
  Proceedings 1875, pg 35 (1875 Sept 22) committee
  Proceedings 1875, pg 37 (1875 Sept 22) per diem
  Proceedings 1875, pg 37 (1875 Sept 22) committee
  Proceedings 1876, pg 12 (1876 Sept 19) donation to the library fund

Teller, Henry M
  Colorado University Cornerstone Laying, pg 3 (1875 Sept 20) Past Grand Master
  Proceedings 1861-1869, pg 115 (1864 Nov 7) Grand Master
  Proceedings 1861-1869, pg 116 (1864 Nov 7) Grand Master
  Proceedings 1861-1869, pg 116 (1864 Nov 7) Grand Master
  Proceedings 1861-1869, pg 125 (1864 Nov 8) committee
  Proceedings 1861-1869, pg 127 (1864 Nov 8) committee
  Proceedings 1861-1869, pg 145 (1865 Nov 7) committee
  Proceedings 1861-1869, pg 160 (1866 Oct 2), Chivington Lodge No. 6, Central City, Grand Orator
  Proceedings 1861-1869, pg 161 (1866 Oct 2) Grand Orator
  Proceedings 1861-1869, pg 175 (1867 Oct 7) Grand Orator
  Proceedings 1861-1869, pg 185 (1867 Oct 7) Grand Master

Colorado's Territorial Masons

Teller, Henry M, cont
- Proceedings 1861-1869, pg 201 (1868 Oct 6) Grand Master
- Proceedings 1861-1869, pg 215 (1868 Oct 6) Grand Master
- Proceedings 1861-1869, pg 287 (1869 Sept 28) Grand Master
- Proceedings 1861-1869, pg 298 (1869 Sept 28) Grand Master
- Proceedings 1861-1869, pg 299 (1869 Sept 29) Grand Master
- Proceedings 1861-1869, pg 315 (1869 Sept 29) Grand Master, 1869
- Proceedings 1861-1869, pg 315 (1869 Sept 29) Grand Master, 1863
- Proceedings 1861-1869, pg 315 (1869 Sept 29) Grand Master, 1868
- Proceedings 1861-1869, pg 315 (1869 Sept 29) Grand Master, 1867
- Proceedings 1870, pg cover (1870 Sept 28) Grand Master, Central City
- Proceedings 1870, pg 2 (1870 Sept 27) Grand Master
- Proceedings 1870, pg 3 (1870 Sept 27) Grand Master
- Proceedings 1870, pg 5 (1870 Sept 27) representing the Grand Lodge of Minnesota
- Proceedings 1870, pg 13 (1870 Sept 27) Grand Master
- Proceedings 1870, pg 14 (1870 Sept 27) Grand Master
- Proceedings 1870, pg 22 (1870 Sept 28), Central Lodge No. 6, Central City
- Proceedings 1870, pg 32 (1870 Sept 28) Grand Master, 1867
- Proceedings 1870, pg 32 (1870 Sept 28) Grand Master, 1868
- Proceedings 1870, pg 32 (1870 Sept 28) Grand Master, 1863
- Proceedings 1870, pg 32 (1870 Sept 28) Grand Master, 1870
- Proceedings 1870, pg 32 (1870 Sept 28) Grand Master, 1869
- Proceedings 1871, pg cover (1871 Sept 26) Grand Master, Central
- Proceedings 1871, pg cover (1871 Sept 27) Grand Master, Central City
- Proceedings 1871, pg 3 (1871 Sept 26) Grand Master
- Proceedings 1871, pg 9 (1871 Sept 26) Grand Master
- Proceedings 1871, pg 13 (1871 Sept 26) Grand Master
- Proceedings 1871, pg 34 (1871 Sept 27) Grand Master, 1867
- Proceedings 1871, pg 34 (1871 Sept 27) Grand Master, 1870
- Proceedings 1871, pg 34 (1871 Sept 27) Grand Master, 1863
- Proceedings 1871, pg 34 (1871 Sept 27) Grand Master, 1871
- Proceedings 1871, pg 34 (1871 Sept 27) Grand Master, 1868
- Proceedings 1871, pg 34 (1871 Sept 27) Grand Master, 1869
- Proceedings 1872, pg cover (1872 Sept 24) Grand Master, Central City
- Proceedings 1872, pg cover (1872 Sept 24), Central City Commandery No. 2, Central
- Proceedings 1872, pg 1 (1872 Sept 24) Grand Master, Central
- Proceedings 1872, pg 3 (1872 Sept 24) Grand Master
- Proceedings 1872, pg 4 (1872 Sept 24) Minnesota
- Proceedings 1872, pg 12 (1872 Sept 24) Grand Master
- Proceedings 1872, pg 21 (1872 Sept 24), Denver Lodge No. 5, Denver
- Proceedings 1872, pg 41 (1872 Sept 24) Representative of the Grand Lodge of Minnesota
- Proceedings 1872, pg 42 (1872 Sept 24) Grand Master, 1867
- Proceedings 1872, pg 42 (1872 Sept 24) Grand Master, 1868
- Proceedings 1872, pg 42 (1872 Sept 24) Grand Master, 1863
- Proceedings 1872, pg 42 (1872 Sept 24) Grand Master, 1869
- Proceedings 1872, pg 42 (1872 Sept 24) Grand Master, 1870
- Proceedings 1872, pg 42 (1872 Sept 24) Grand Master, 1871-1872
- Proceedings 1873, pg cover (1873 Oct 1) committee, Central
- Proceedings 1873, pg cover (1873 Oct 1), Central City Commandery No. 2, Central
- Proceedings 1873, pg 3 (1873 Sept 30) Grand Master
- Proceedings 1873, pg 4 (1873 Sept 30), Grand Representative, Minnesota
- Proceedings 1873, pg 5 (1873 Sept 30) Grand Master
- Proceedings 1873, pg 27 (1873 Oct 1) Grand Master
- Proceedings 1873, pg 32 (1873 Oct 1) committee
- Proceedings 1873, pg 38 (1873 Oct 1), Central Lodge No. 6, Central City
- Proceedings 1873, pg 58 (1873 Oct 1) Grand Master, 1870
- Proceedings 1873, pg 58 (1873 Oct 1) Grand Master, 1871-1872
- Proceedings 1873, pg 58 (1873 Oct 1) Grand Master, 1868
- Proceedings 1873, pg 58 (1873 Oct 1) Grand Master, 1863
- Proceedings 1873, pg 58 (1873 Oct 1) Grand Master, 1867
- Proceedings 1873, pg 58 (1873 Oct 1) Grand Master, 1869
- Proceedings 1873, pg 59 (1873 Oct 1), Grand Representative of Illinois, Minnesota
- Proceedings 1874, pg cover (1874 Sept 30) committee, Central
- Proceedings 1874, pg 4 (1874 Sept 29) Past Grand Master
- Proceedings 1874, pg 36 (1874 Sept 30) committee
- Proceedings 1874, pg 206 (1874 Sept 30) Grand Master, 1867
- Proceedings 1874, pg 206 (1874 Sept 30) Grand Master, 1871
- Proceedings 1874, pg 206 (1874 Sept 30) Grand Master, 1863
- Proceedings 1874, pg 206 (1874 Sept 30) Grand Master, 1872
- Proceedings 1874, pg 206 (1874 Sept 30) Grand Master, 1868
- Proceedings 1874, pg 206 (1874 Sept 30) Grand Master, 1869
- Proceedings 1874, pg 206 (1874 Sept 30) Grand Master, 1870

Colorado's Territorial Masons

Teller, Henry M, cont.
    Proceedings 1874, pg 207 (1874 Sept 30), Grand Lodge of Illinois, Grand Lodge of Minnesota, Grand Lodge of Nebraska, Central
    Proceedings 1874, pg 212 (1874 Sept 30), Central Lodge No. 6, Central
    Proceedings 1875, pg cover (1875 Sept 22) committee, Central
    Proceedings 1875, pg 16 (1875 Sept 21) Past Grand Master
    Proceedings 1875, pg 37 (1875 Sept 22) committee, Central
    Proceedings 1875, pg 76 (1875 Sept 22), Central Lodge No. 6, Central City
    Proceedings 1875, pg 93 (1875 Sept 22) Grand Master, 1869
    Proceedings 1875, pg 93 (1875 Sept 22) Grand Master, 1868
    Proceedings 1875, pg 93 (1875 Sept 22) Grand Master, 1867
    Proceedings 1875, pg 93 (1875 Sept 22) Grand Master, 1863
    Proceedings 1875, pg 93 (1875 Sept 22) Grand Master, 1872
    Proceedings 1875, pg 93 (1875 Sept 22) Grand Master, 1871
    Proceedings 1875, pg 93 (1875 Sept 22) Grand Master, 1870
    Proceedings 1875, pg 95 (1875 Sept 22) Grand Lodge of Minnesota, Central City, CO
    Proceedings 1875, pg 95 (1875 Sept 22) Grand Lodge of Illinois, Central City, CO
    Proceedings 1876, pg cover (1876 Sept 20) committee, Central
    Proceedings 1876, pg 26 (1876 Sept 20) committee
    Proceedings 1876, pg 31 (1876 Sept 20), Central Lodge No. 6, Central City
    Proceedings 1876, pg 53 (1876 Sept 20) Grand Lodge of Minnesota, of Central, CO
    Proceedings 1876, pg 53 (1876 Sept 20) Grand Lodge of Illinois, of Central, CO

Temby, Richard
    Proceedings 1861-1869, pg 306 (1869 Sept 29), Central Lodge No. 6, Central City
    Proceedings 1870, pg 23 (1870 Sept 28), Central Lodge No. 6, Central City, Dimitted

Templeton, James H
    Proceedings 1876, pg 49 (1876 Sept 20), El Paso Lodge No. 13, Colorado City, 1876 July 22

Templeton, James M
    Proceedings 1875, pg 82 (1875 Sept 22), El Paso Lodge No. 13, Colorado Springs

Tennis, William
    Proceedings 1861-1869, pg 306 (1869 Sept 29), Central Lodge No. 6, Central City, Fellowcraft
    Proceedings 1872, pg 21 (1872 Sept 24), Denver Lodge No. 5, Denver
    Proceedings 1874, pg 213 (1874 Sept 30), Central Lodge No. 6, Central
    Proceedings 1875, pg 77 (1875 Sept 22), Central Lodge No. 6, Central City
    Proceedings 1876, pg 32 (1876 Sept 20), Central Lodge No. 6, Central City
    Proceedings 1876, pg 50 (1876 Sept 20), Central Lodge No. 6, Central City

Tennis, Wm
    Proceedings 1870, pg 22 (1870 Sept 28), Central Lodge No. 6, Central City
    Proceedings 1871, pg 21 (1871 Sept 27), Central Lodge No. 6, Central
    Proceedings 1873, pg 38 (1873 Oct 1), Central Lodge No. 6, Central City

Terry, John W
    Proceedings 1875, pg 91 (1875 Sept 22), Las Animas Lodge U D, Trinidad
    Proceedings 1876, pg 44 (1876 Sept 20), Las Animas Lodge No. 28, Trinidad

Terry, Peter G
    Proceedings 1876, pg 39 (1876 Sept 20), Collins Lodge No. 19, Fort Collins

Terry, William
    Proceedings 1861-1869, pg 349 (1868 Dec 14) Grand Master, Grand Lodge of Virginia
    Proceedings 1870, pg 104 (1869 Dec 13) Grand Master, Grand Lodge of Virginia

Teter, Wesley
    Proceedings 1861-1869, pg 147 (1865 Nov 7) Golden City Lodge No. 1, Fellowcraft
    Proceedings 1861-1869, pg 165 (1866 Oct 2) Golden City Lodge No. 1, Fellowcraft
    Proceedings 1861-1869, pg 191 (1867 Oct 8) Golden City Lodge No. 1, Fellowcraft
    Proceedings 1861-1869, pg 221 (1868 Oct 7) Golden City Lodge No. 1, Fellowcraft
    Proceedings 1861-1869, pg 303 (1869 Sept 29) Golden City Lodge No. 1, Fellowcraft,

Texas Masonic Mirror
    Proceedings 1873, pg 15 (1873 Oct 1), published at Houston, TX

Thatcher, H C
    Proceedings 1874, pg 222 (1874 Sept 30), Pueblo Lodge No. 17, Pueblo, Pueblo County
    Proceedings 1875, pg 85 (1875 Sept 22) Pueblo Lodge No. 17
    Proceedings 1876, pg 39 (1876 Sept 20) Pueblo Lodge No. 17

Thatcher, Henry C
    Proceedings 1872, pg 31 (1872 Sept 24), Pueblo Lodge No. 17, Pueblo
    Proceedings 1873, pg 47 (1873 Oct 1), Pueblo Lodge No. 17, Pueblo

Thatcher, J
    Proceedings 1861-1869, pg 32 (1861 Dec 10), Summit Lodge No 7, Parkville
    Proceedings 1861-1869, pg 33 (1861 Dec 10) committee
    Proceedings 1861-1869, pg 40 (1861 Dec 12) chairman

Colorado's Territorial Masons

Thatcher, J, cont.
Proceedings 1861-1869, pg 42 (1861 Dec 10), Summit Lodge No. 2, Parkville

Thatcher, J E
Proceedings 1861-1869, pg 110 (1863 Nov 3), Summit Lodge No. 2, Parkville
Proceedings 1861-1869, pg 132 (1864 Nov 8) Golden City Lodge No. 1, dimitted

Thatcher, Jos E
Proceedings 1861-1869, pg 76 (1862 Nov 4), Summit Lodge No. 2, Parkville

Thatcher, Joseph
Proceedings 1861-1869, pg 38 (1861 Dec 12) Grand Pursuivants

Thatcher, M D
Proceedings 1861-1869, pg 312 (1869 Sept 29), Pueblo Lodge No. 17, Pueblo
Proceedings 1870, pg 29 (1870 Sept 28), Pueblo Lodge No. 17, Pueblo
Proceedings 1872, pg 31 (1872 Sept 24), Pueblo Lodge No. 17, Pueblo
Proceedings 1875, pg 85 (1875 Sept 22) Pueblo Lodge No. 17
Proceedings 1876, pg 39 (1876 Sept 20) Pueblo Lodge No. 17

Thatcher, Mahlon D
Proceedings 1871, pg 28 (1871 Sept 27), Pueblo Lodge No. 17, Pueblo
Proceedings 1873, pg 47 (1873 Oct 1), Pueblo Lodge No. 17, Pueblo
Proceedings 1874, pg 222 (1874 Sept 30), Pueblo Lodge No. 17, Pueblo, Pueblo County

Thayer, I E
Proceedings 1875, pg 84 (1875 Sept 22), Mount Moriah Lodge No. 15, Canon City, died
Proceedings 1875, pg 94 (1875 Sept 22), Mount Moriah Lodge No. 15, Canon City

Thede, N
Proceedings 1861-1869, pg 224 (1868 Oct 7) Denver Lodge No. 5, Dimitted

Thede, Nichoas
Proceedings 1861-1869, pg 133 (1864 Nov 8) Denver Lodge No. 5
Proceedings 1861-1869, pg 35 (1861 Aug 3), Summit Lodge No. 2, Parkville
Proceedings 1861-1869, pg 42 (1861 Dec 10), Summit Lodge No. 2, Parkville
Proceedings 1861-1869, pg 76 (1862 Nov 4), Summit Lodge No. 2, Parkville, dimitted
Proceedings 1861-1869, pg 77 (1862 Nov 4) Denver Lodge No. 5
Proceedings 1861-1869, pg 112 (1863 Nov 3) Denver Lodge No. 5
Proceedings 1861-1869, pg 149 (1865 Nov 7), Nevada Lodge No. 4, Nevadaville
Proceedings 1861-1869, pg 167 (1866 Oct 2) Denver Lodge No. 5
Proceedings 1861-1869, pg 193 (1867 Oct 8) Denver Lodge No. 5

Thenks, Jacob
Proceedings 1875, pg 73 (1875 Sept 22) Golden City Lodge No. 1, Apprentice
Proceedings 1876, pg 29 (1876 Sept 20) Golden City Lodge No. 1, Apprentice,

Thevenot
Proceedings 1870, pg 34 (1870 Sept 28) Grand Secretary, Grand Orient of France

Thomas, H K
Proceedings 1871, pg 29 (1871 Sept 27), Laramie Lodge No. 18, Laramie, Wyoming Territory
Proceedings 1872, pg 32 (1872 Sept 24), Laramie Lodge No. 18, Laramie, Wyoming Territory
Proceedings 1873, pg 48 (1873 Oct 1), Laramie Lodge No. 18, Laramie, Wyoming Territory
Proceedings 1874, pg 223 (1874 Sept 30), Laramie Lodge No. 18, Laramie City

Thomas, H R
Proceedings 1870, pg 30 (1870 Sept 28), Laramie Lodge No. 18, Laramie, Wyoming Territory

Thomas, J D
Proceedings 1861-1869, pg 42 (1861 Dec 10), Summit Lodge No. 2, Parkville
Proceedings 1861-1869, pg 111 (1863 Nov 3), Summit Lodge No. 2, Parkville, dimitted

Thomas, J J
Proceedings 1861-1869, pg 151 (1865 Nov 7), Chivington Lodge No. 6, Central City, Apprentice
Proceedings 1861-1869, pg 229 (1868 Oct 7), Pueblo Lodge U D, Pueblo
Proceedings 1870, pg 29 (1870 Sept 28), Pueblo Lodge No. 17, Pueblo
Proceedings 1871, pg 28 (1871 Sept 27), Pueblo Lodge No. 17, Pueblo
Proceedings 1875, pg 85 (1875 Sept 22) Pueblo Lodge No. 17
Proceedings 1876, pg 39 (1876 Sept 20) Pueblo Lodge No. 17

Thomas, Jno B
Proceedings 1873, pg 46 (1873 Oct 1), Cheyenne Lodge No. 16, Cheyenne, Wyoming Territory

Thomas, John B
Proceedings 1872, pg 30 (1872 Sept 24), Cheyenne Lodge No. 16, Cheyenne, Wyoming Territory
Proceedings 1874, pg 221 (1874 Sept 30), Cheyenne Lodge No. 16, Cheyenne, Wyoming Territory

Thomas, John D
Proceedings 1861-1869, pg 76 (1862 Nov 4), Summit Lodge No. 2, Parkville

Thomas, John J
Proceedings 1861-1869, pg 312 (1869 Sept 29), Pueblo Lodge No. 17, Pueblo
Proceedings 1872, pg 31 (1872 Sept 24), Pueblo Lodge No. 17, Pueblo

Proceedings 1873, pg 47 (1873 Oct 1), Pueblo Lodge No. 17, Pueblo

Proceedings 1874, pg 222 (1874 Sept 30), Pueblo Lodge No. 17, Pueblo, Pueblo County

Proceedings 1876, pg 7 (1876 Mar 17), South Pueblo Lodge U D, South Pueblo

Proceedings 1876, pg 24 (1876 Sept 20), South Pueblo Lodge No. 31, South Pueblo

Proceedings 1876, pg 45 (1876 Sept 20) South Pueblo Lodge U D

Thomas, M

Proceedings 1861-1869, pg 150 (1865 Nov 7), Chivington Lodge No. 6, Central City

Proceedings 1861-1869, pg 168 (1866 Oct 2), Chivington Lodge No. 6, Central City

Proceedings 1861-1869, pg 194 (1867 Oct 8), Chivington Lodge No. 6, Central City

Proceedings 1861-1869, pg 224 (1868 Oct 7), Chivington Lodge No. 6, Central City

Thomas, Morris

Proceedings 1861-1869, pg 306 (1869 Sept 29), Central Lodge No. 6, Central City

Proceedings 1870, pg 22 (1870 Sept 28), Central Lodge No. 6, Central City

Proceedings 1871, pg 21 (1871 Sept 27), Central Lodge No. 6, Central

Proceedings 1872, pg 21 (1872 Sept 24), Denver Lodge No. 5, Denver

Proceedings 1873, pg 38 (1873 Oct 1), Central Lodge No. 6, Central City

Proceedings 1874, pg 213 (1874 Sept 30), Central Lodge No. 6, Central

Proceedings 1875, pg 77 (1875 Sept 22), Central Lodge No. 6, Central City

Proceedings 1876, pg 32 (1876 Sept 20), Central Lodge No. 6, Central City

Thomas, Stephen

Proceedings 1871, pg 24 (1871 Sept 27), Washington Lodge No. 12, Georgetown

Proceedings 1872, pg 26 (1872 Sept 24), Washington Lodge No. 12, Georgetown

Proceedings 1873, pg 43 (1873 Oct 1), Washington Lodge No. 12, Georgetown

Proceedings 1874, pg 217 (1874 Sept 30), Washington Lodge No. 12, Georgetown

Proceedings 1875, pg 81 (1875 Sept 22), Washington Lodge No. 12, Georgetown

Proceedings 1876, pg 48 (1876 Sept 20), Washington Lodge No. 12, Georgetown, 1875 Sept 11

Thombs, P R

Proceedings 1861-1869, pg 229 (1868 Oct 7), Pueblo Lodge U D, Pueblo

Proceedings 1861-1869, pg 312 (1869 Sept 29), Pueblo Lodge No. 17, Pueblo

Proceedings 1870, pg 29 (1870 Sept 28), Pueblo Lodge No. 17, Pueblo

Proceedings 1872, pg 30 (1872 Sept 24), Pueblo Lodge No. 17, Pueblo

Proceedings 1875, pg 85 (1875 Sept 22) Pueblo Lodge No. 17

Thombs, Pembroke R

Proceedings 1873, pg 47 (1873 Oct 1), Pueblo Lodge No. 17, Pueblo

Proceedings 1874, pg 222 (1874 Sept 30), Pueblo Lodge No. 17, Pueblo, Pueblo County

Proceedings 1876, pg 38 (1876 Sept 20) Pueblo Lodge No. 17

Proceedings 1871, pg 28 (1871 Sept 27), Pueblo Lodge No. 17, Pueblo

Thompson, A H

Proceedings 1873, pg 45 (1873 Oct 1), Mount Moriah Lodge No. 15, Canon City

Thompson, Alex

Proceedings 1875, pg 76 (1875 Sept 22) Denver Lodge No. 5

Proceedings 1876, pg 30 (1876 Sept 20) Denver Lodge No. 5

Thompson, J R

Proceedings 1876, pg 31 (1876 Sept 20) Denver Lodge No. 5

Thompson, John

Proceedings 1861-1869, pg 42 (1861 Dec 10), Summit Lodge No. 2, Parkville

Proceedings 1861-1869, pg 76 (1862 Nov 4), Summit Lodge No. 2, Parkville, Suspended

Proceedings 1861-1869, pg 110 (1863 Nov 3), Summit Lodge No. 2, Parkville

Proceedings 1861-1869, pg 132 (1864 Nov 8) Golden City Lodge No. 1

Proceedings 1861-1869, pg 316 (1869 Sept 29) Grand Lodge of Pennsylvania

Proceedings 1861-1869, pg 346 (1868 Dec 2) Grand Secretary, Grand Lodge of Pennsylvania

Proceedings 1870, pg 34 (1870 Sept 28) Grand Secretary, Grand Lodge of Pennsylvania

Proceedings 1874, pg 119 (1874 Sept 30) Grand Lodge of Pennsylvania

Proceedings 1874, pg 205 (1874 Sept 30) Grand Lodge of Pennsylvania, Philadelphia

Thompson, John R

Proceedings 1870, pg 21 (1870 Sept 28), Denver Lodge No. 5, Denver

Proceedings 1871, pg 19 (1871 Sept 27) Denver Lodge No. 5

Proceedings 1872, pg 20 (1872 Sept 24), Denver Lodge No. 5, Denver

Proceedings 1873, pg 37 (1873 Oct 1), Denver Lodge No. 5, Denver

Proceedings 1874, pg 212 (1874 Sept 30), Denver Lodge No. 5, Denver

Proceedings 1875, pg 75 (1875 Sept 22) Denver Lodge No. 5

Thompson, Thomas

Proceedings 1861-1869, pg 149 (1865 Nov 7), Nevada Lodge No. 4, Nevadaville

Thompson, Thos
Proceedings 1861-1869, pg 167 (1866 Oct 2) Denver Lodge No. 5, dimitted

Thompson, W H
Proceedings 1861-1869, pg 229 (1868 Oct 7), Canon Lodge U D, Canon City
Proceedings 1861-1869, pg 311 (1869 Sept 29), Mount Moriah Lodge No. 15, Canon City
Proceedings 1870, pg 28 (1870 Sept 28), Mount Moriah Lodge No. 15, Canon City
Proceedings 1871, pg 26 (1871 Sept 27), Mount Moriah Lodge No. 15, Canon City
Proceedings 1872, pg 29 (1872 Sept 24), Mount Moriah Lodge No. 15, Canon City
Proceedings 1874, pg 220 (1874 Sept 30), Mount Moriah Lodge No. 15, Canon City
Proceedings 1875, pg 84 (1875 Sept 22), Mount Moriah Lodge No. 15, Canon City

Thompson, W J
Proceedings 1861-1869, pg 167 (1866 Oct 2) Denver Lodge No. 5
Proceedings 1861-1869, pg 193 (1867 Oct 8) Denver Lodge No. 5
Proceedings 1861-1869, pg 223 (1868 Oct 7) Denver Lodge No. 5
Proceedings 1861-1869, pg 305 (1869 Sept 29) Denver Lodge No. 5
Proceedings 1870, pg 21 (1870 Sept 28), Denver Lodge No. 5, Denver
Proceedings 1873, pg 37 (1873 Oct 1), Denver Lodge No. 5, Denver, Dimitted
Proceedings 1873, pg 51 (1873 Oct 1), Weston Lodge No. 22, Littleton
Proceedings 1875, pg 88 (1875 Sept 22), Weston Lodge No. 22, Littleton

Thompson, W W
Proceedings 1872, pg 35 (1872 Sept 24), St Vrain Lodge No. 23, Longmont
Proceedings 1873, pg 51 (1873 Oct 1), St Vrain Lodge No. 23, Longmont
Proceedings 1874, pg 212 (1874 Sept 30), Denver Lodge No. 5, Denver
Proceedings 1875, pg 76 (1875 Sept 22) Denver Lodge No. 5, Expelled

Thompson, W Wallace
Proceedings 1874, pg 227 (1874 Sept 30), St Vrain No. 23, Longmont

Thompson, William
Proceedings 1876, pg 48 (1876 Sept 20), Weston Lodge No. 22, Littleton, 1876 Jan 15

Thompson, Wm H
Proceedings 1876, pg 38 (1876 Sept 20), Mount Moriah Lodge No. 15, Canon City

Thomson, John
Proceedings 1870, pg 99 (1869 Dec 27) Grand Secretary, Grand Lodge of Pennsylvania
Proceedings 1871, pg 35 (1871 Sept 27) Grand Secretary, Grand Lodge of Pennsylvania
Proceedings 1872, pg 44 (1872 Sept 24) Philadelphia, Grand Lodge of Pennsylvania
Proceedings 1872, pg 85 (1872 Sept 24) Grand Lodge of Pennsylvania
Proceedings 1873, pg 61 (1873 Oct 1) Grand Lodge of Pennsylvania, Philadelphia
Proceedings 1875, pg 96 (1875 Sept 22) Grand Lodge of Pennsylvania, Philadelphia
Proceedings 1876, pg 54 (1876 Sept 20) Grand Lodge of Pennsylvania, Philadelphia

Thorne, Ellwood E
Proceedings 1874, pg 204 (1874 Sept 30) Grand Lodge of New York, New York
Proceedings 1875, pg 26 (1875 Sept 21) Grand Lodge of New York
Proceedings 1876, pg 15 (1876 Jan 26), Grand Master, Grand Lodge of New York, sent communication regarding the case of E T Stone

Thornton, G E
Proceedings 1861-1869, pg 168 (1866 Oct 2), Chivington Lodge No. 6, Central City
Proceedings 1871, pg 24 (1871 Sept 27), Washington Lodge No. 12, Georgetown

Thornton, Geo E
Proceedings 1861-1869, pg 225 (1868 Oct 7), Chivington Lodge No. 6, Central City, Dimitted
Proceedings 1861-1869, pg 227 (1868 Oct 7), Washington Lodge No. 12, Georgetown
Proceedings 1861-1869, pg 309 (1869 Sept 29), Washington Lodge No. 12, Georgetown
Proceedings 1870, pg 26 (1870 Sept 28), Washington Lodge No. 12, Georgetown
Proceedings 1872, pg 26 (1872 Sept 24), Washington Lodge No. 12, Georgetown
Proceedings 1873, pg 43 (1873 Oct 1), Washington Lodge No. 12, Georgetown, Dimitted

Thornton, George E
Proceedings 1861-1869, pg 194 (1867 Oct 8), Chivington Lodge No. 6, Central City

Thornton, Solon
Proceedings 1861-1869, pg 316 (1869 Sept 29) Grand Lodge of Massachusetts
Proceedings 1861-1869, pg 331 (1868 Dec 9) Grand Secretary, Grand Lodge of Massachusetts
Proceedings 1870, pg 34 (1870 Sept 28) Grand Secretary, Grand Lodge of Massachusetts
Proceedings 1870, pg 67 (1869 Sept 8) Grand Secretary, Grand Lodge of Massachusetts

Thurman, L B
Proceedings 1871, pg 31 (1871 Sept 27), Argenta Lodge U D, Salt Lake City, Utah

Tidland, J A
Proceedings 1861-1869, pg 113 (1863 Nov 3), Chivington Lodge No. 6, Central City, Apprentice

Tilden, Alphonso F
Proceedings 1871, pg 31 (1871 Sept 27), Argenta Lodge U D, Salt Lake City, Utah

Tillett, H R
Proceedings 1873, pg 51 (1873 Oct 1), Weston Lodge No. 22, Littleton
Proceedings 1875, pg 88 (1875 Sept 22), Weston Lodge No. 22, Littleton
Proceedings 1876, pg 41 (1876 Sept 20), Weston Lodge No. 22, Littleton

Tillott, H R
Proceedings 1874, pg 226 (1874 Sept 30), Weston Lodge No. 22, Littleton

Tilney, Robert H
Proceedings 1876, pg 37 (1876 Sept 20), Columbia Lodge No. 14, Boulder

Tilton, D W
Proceedings 1861-1869, pg 113 (1863 Nov 3), Chivington Lodge No. 6, Central City
Proceedings 1861-1869, pg 134 (1864 Nov 8), Chivington Lodge No. 6, Central City
Proceedings 1861-1869, pg 150 (1865 Nov 7), Chivington Lodge No. 6, Central City, dimitted

Tindall, George E
Proceedings 1876, pg 35 (1876 Sept 20), Washington Lodge No. 12, Georgetown

Tisdall, Fitzgerald
Proceedings 1861-1869, pg 275 (1867 June 4), publisher of a Masonic weekly newspaper, expelled for writing libelous articles

Titcomb
Proceedings 1876, pg 17 (1876 Sept 19) motion
Proceedings 1876, pg 18 (1876 Sept 19) Grand Teller

Titcomb, J S
Proceedings 1872, pg 33 (1872 Sept 24), Occidental Lodge No. 20, Greeley
Proceedings 1874, pg 225 (1874 Sept 30), Occidental Lodge No. 20, Greeley

Titcomb, John S
Proceedings 1873, pg 50 (1873 Oct 1), Occidental Lodge No. 20, Greeley
Proceedings 1875, pg 83 (1875 Sept 22), Columbia Lodge No. 14, Boulder
Proceedings 1875, pg 87 (1875 Sept 22), Occidental Lodge No. 20, Greeley, Demitted
Proceedings 1876, pg 5 (1876 Sept 19), Columbia Lodge No. 14, Boulder
Proceedings 1876, pg 36 (1876 Sept 20), Columbia Lodge No. 14, Boulder

Titus, Charles H
Proceedings 1871, pg 35 (1871 Sept 27) Grand Secretary, Grand Lodge of Massachusetts
Proceedings 1874, pg 204 (1874 Sept 30) Grand Lodge of Massachusetts, Boston

Titus, Chas H
Proceedings 1872, pg 43 (1872 Sept 24) Boston, Grand Lodge of Massachusetts
Proceedings 1873, pg 60 (1873 Oct 1) Grand Lodge of Massachusetts, Boston
Proceedings 1874, pg 80 (1874 Sept 30) Grand Lodge of Massachusetts
Proceedings 1875, pg 96 (1875 Sept 22) Grand Lodge of Massachusetts, Boston
Proceedings 1876, pg 54 (1876 Sept 20) Grand Lodge of Massachusetts, Boston

Titus, Isaac S
Proceedings 1874, pg 204 (1874 Sept 30) Grand Lodge of California, Stockton,

Todd
Proceedings 1872, pg 68 (1872 Sept 24) Grand Lodge of Louisiana

Todd, George B
Proceedings 1872, pg 17 (1872 Sept 24), Golden City Lodge No. 1, Golden City, Apprentice

Todd, J W
Proceedings 1861-1869, pg 152 (1865 Nov 7), Montana Lodge U D, Virginia City, Montana Territory

Todd, John M
Proceedings 1875, pg 96 (1875 Sept 22) Grand Lodge of Kentucky, Louisville
Proceedings 1876, pg 54 (1876 Sept 20) Grand Lodge of Kentucky, Louisville

Todd, S M
Proceedings 1870, pg 62 (1870 Feb 14) Grand Master, Grand Lodge of Louisiana

Todd, Samuel
Proceedings 1861-1869, pg 227 (1868 Oct 7), Washington Lodge No. 12, Georgetown
Proceedings 1861-1869, pg 309 (1869 Sept 29), Washington Lodge No. 12, Georgetown
Proceedings 1870, pg 26 (1870 Sept 28), Washington Lodge No. 12, Georgetown
Proceedings 1871, pg 24 (1871 Sept 27), Washington Lodge No. 12, Georgetown
Proceedings 1872, pg 26 (1872 Sept 24), Washington Lodge No. 12, Georgetown
Proceedings 1873, pg 43 (1873 Oct 1), Washington Lodge No. 12, Georgetown
Proceedings 1874, pg 217 (1874 Sept 30), Washington Lodge No. 12, Georgetown
Proceedings 1875, pg 81 (1875 Sept 22), Washington Lodge No. 12, Georgetown
Proceedings 1876, pg 35 (1876 Sept 20), Washington Lodge No. 12, Georgetown

Todd, Samuel M
Proceedings 1861-1869, pg 331 (1868 Feb 8) Grand Master, Grand Lodge of Louisiana
Proceedings 1872, pg 43 (1872 Sept 24) New Orleans, Grand Lodge of Louisiana
Proceedings 1872, pg 67 (1872 Sept 24) Grand Lodge of Louisiana

Colorado's Territorial Masons

Todd, W B
    Proceedings 1874, pg 209 (1874 Sept 30), Golden City Lodge No. 1, Golden City, Apprentice
    Proceedings 1875, pg 73 (1875 Sept 22) Golden City Lodge No. 1, Apprentice
    Proceedings 1876, pg 29 (1876 Sept 20) Golden City Lodge No. 1, Apprentice

Tolles, L C
    Proceedings 1861-1869, pg 194 (1867 Oct 8), Chivington Lodge No. 6, Central City
    Proceedings 1861-1869, pg 224 (1868 Oct 7), Chivington Lodge No. 6, Central City
    Proceedings 1861-1869, pg 306 (1869 Sept 29), Central Lodge No. 6, Central City
    Proceedings 1870, pg 22 (1870 Sept 28), Central Lodge No. 6, Central City
    Proceedings 1871, pg 21 (1871 Sept 27), Central Lodge No. 6, Central

Tolles, Larkin C
    Proceedings 1872, pg 21 (1872 Sept 24), Denver Lodge No. 5, Denver
    Proceedings 1873, pg 38 (1873 Oct 1), Central Lodge No. 6, Central City
    Proceedings 1874, pg 213 (1874 Sept 30), Central Lodge No. 6, Central
    Proceedings 1875, pg 77 (1875 Sept 22), Central Lodge No. 6, Central City
    Proceedings 1876, pg 32 (1876 Sept 20), Central Lodge No. 6, Central City

Tomlin, A B
    Proceedings 1875, pg 86 (1875 Sept 22), Collins Lodge No. 19, Fort Collins, Fellowcraft
    Proceedings 1876, pg 40 (1876 Sept 20), Collins Lodge No. 19, Fort Collins, Fellow Craft

Tomsen, Wm
    Proceedings 1874, pg 226 (1874 Sept 30), Weston Lodge No. 22, Littleton

Toncray, Nelson
    Proceedings 1861-1869, pg 42 (1861 Dec 10), Summit Lodge No. 2, Parkville
    Proceedings 1861-1869, pg 76 (1862 Nov 4), Summit Lodge No. 2, Parkville
    Proceedings 1861-1869, pg 110 (1863 Nov 3), Summit Lodge No. 2, Parkville
    Proceedings 1861-1869, pg 132 (1864 Nov 8) Golden City Lodge No. 1, dimitted

Tooker, D
    Proceedings 1861-1869, pg 113 (1863 Nov 3), Chivington Lodge No. 6, Central City
    Proceedings 1861-1869, pg 150 (1865 Nov 7), Chivington Lodge No. 6, Central City
    Proceedings 1861-1869, pg 168 (1866 Oct 2), Chivington Lodge No. 6, Central City
    Proceedings 1861-1869, pg 194 (1867 Oct 8), Chivington Lodge No. 6, Central City
    Proceedings 1861-1869, pg 225 (1868 Oct 7), Chivington Lodge No. 6, Central City, Dimitted
    Proceedings 1861-1869, pg 227 (1868 Oct 7), Washington Lodge No. 12, Georgetown

Tooker, Dubois
    Proceedings 1861-1869, pg 78 (1862 Nov 4), Chivington Lodge No. 6, Central City, Apprentice
    Proceedings 1861-1869, pg 134 (1864 Nov 8), Chivington Lodge No. 6, Central City
    Proceedings 1861-1869, pg 179 (1867 Oct 7), Washington Lodge No. 12, Georgetown
    Proceedings 1861-1869, pg 309 (1869 Sept 29), Washington Lodge No. 12, Georgetown
    Proceedings 1870, pg 26 (1870 Sept 28), Washington Lodge No. 12, Georgetown
    Proceedings 1871, pg 24 (1871 Sept 27), Washington Lodge No. 12, Georgetown
    Proceedings 1872, pg 26 (1872 Sept 24), Washington Lodge No. 12, Georgetown
    Proceedings 1873, pg 43 (1873 Oct 1), Washington Lodge No. 12, Georgetown
    Proceedings 1874, pg 217 (1874 Sept 30), Washington Lodge No. 12, Georgetown
    Proceedings 1875, pg 81 (1875 Sept 22), Washington Lodge No. 12, Georgetown
    Proceedings 1876, pg 35 (1876 Sept 20), Washington Lodge No. 12, Georgetown

Topping, C S
    Proceedings 1875, pg 89 (1875 Sept 22), Doric Lodge No. 25, Fairplay
    Proceedings 1876, pg 42 (1876 Sept 20), Doric Lodge No. 25, Fairplay

Townsend, George A
    Proceedings 1876, pg 44 (1876 Sept 20) Del Norte Lodge U D, Apprentice

Townsend, Samuel C
    Proceedings 1876, pg 44 (1876 Sept 20) Del Norte Lodge U D

Tracy, G J
    Proceedings 1861-1869, pg 150 (1865 Nov 7), Chivington Lodge No. 6, Central City
    Proceedings 1861-1869, pg 168 (1866 Oct 2), Chivington Lodge No. 6, Central City

Tracy, Geo J
    Proceedings 1861-1869, pg 224 (1868 Oct 7), Chivington Lodge No. 6, Central City
    Proceedings 1861-1869, pg 306 (1869 Sept 29), Central Lodge No. 6, Central City
    Proceedings 1870, pg 22 (1870 Sept 28), Central Lodge No. 6, Central City
    Proceedings 1871, pg 21 (1871 Sept 27), Central Lodge No. 6, Central
    Proceedings 1872, pg 22 (1872 Sept 24), Denver Lodge No. 5, Denver

Tracy, George J
    Proceedings 1861-1869, pg 194 (1867 Oct 8), Chivington Lodge No. 6, Central City

Tracy, Luther W
    Proceedings 1870, pg 107 (1870 June 14) Grand Lodge of Wisconsin, deceased

Colorado's Territorial Masons

Tracy, T F
Proceedings 1872, pg 7 (1872 Sept 24), Argenta Lodge U D, Salt Lake City, Utah

Tracy, Theo F
Proceedings 1871, pg 31 (1871 Sept 27), Argenta Lodge U D, Salt Lake City, Utah

Trank, Hiram
Proceedings 1874, pg 221 (1874 Sept 30), Cheyenne Lodge No. 16, Cheyenne, Wyoming Territory, Demitted

Trapp, Lewis
Proceedings 1870, pg 26 (1870 Sept 28), Washington Lodge No. 12, Georgetown
Proceedings 1871, pg 24 (1871 Sept 27), Washington Lodge No. 12, Georgetown
Proceedings 1872, pg 26 (1872 Sept 24), Washington Lodge No. 12, Georgetown
Proceedings 1873, pg 43 (1873 Oct 1), Washington Lodge No. 12, Georgetown
Proceedings 1874, pg 217 (1874 Sept 30), Washington Lodge No. 12, Georgetown
Proceedings 1875, pg 81 (1875 Sept 22), Washington Lodge No. 12, Georgetown, died
Proceedings 1875, pg 94 (1875 Sept 22), Washington Lodge No. 12, Georgetown

Trary, L W
Proceedings 1872, pg 48 (1872 Sept 24), Montana Lodge No. 9, Virginia City

Travena, Richard
Proceedings 1874, pg 217 (1874 Sept 30), Washington Lodge No. 12, Georgetown
Proceedings 1875, pg 81 (1875 Sept 22), Washington Lodge No. 12, Georgetown

Treadway, J R
Proceedings 1876, pg 33 (1876 Sept 20), Union Lodge No. 7, Denver

Treadway, James R
Proceedings 1873, pg 40 (1873 Oct 1), Union Lodge No. 7, Denver
Proceedings 1874, pg 214 (1874 Sept 30), Union Lodge No. 7, Denver
Proceedings 1875, pg 78 (1875 Sept 22), Union Lodge No. 7, Denver

Treadwell, J T
Proceedings 1876, pg 36 (1876 Sept 20), El Paso Lodge No. 13, Colorado City, Fellow Craft

Treat, S M
Proceedings 1875, pg 75 (1875 Sept 22) Denver Lodge No. 5

Treat, S W
Proceedings 1861-1869, pg 167 (1866 Oct 2) Denver Lodge No. 5
Proceedings 1861-1869, pg 193 (1867 Oct 8) Denver Lodge No. 5
Proceedings 1861-1869, pg 223 (1868 Oct 7) Denver Lodge No. 5
Proceedings 1861-1869, pg 305 (1869 Sept 29) Denver Lodge No. 5
Proceedings 1870, pg 21 (1870 Sept 28), Denver Lodge No. 5, Denver
Proceedings 1871, pg 19 (1871 Sept 27) Denver Lodge No. 5
Proceedings 1872, pg 20 (1872 Sept 24), Denver Lodge No. 5, Denver
Proceedings 1873, pg 37 (1873 Oct 1), Denver Lodge No. 5, Denver
Proceedings 1874, pg 211 (1874 Sept 30), Denver Lodge No. 5, Denver
Proceedings 1876, pg 31 (1876 Sept 20) Denver Lodge No. 5

Trenchard, Charles
Proceedings 1873, pg 35 (1873 Oct 1), Golden City Lodge No. 1, Golden City
Proceedings 1875, pg 74 (1875 Sept 22) Golden City Lodge No. 1, Demitted

Trenchard, Chas
Proceedings 1874, pg 209 (1874 Sept 30), Golden City Lodge No. 1, Golden City

Trenoweth, Charles
Proceedings 1872, pg 25 (1872 Sept 24), Washington Lodge No. 12, Georgetown
Proceedings 1873, pg 42 (1873 Oct 1), Washington Lodge No. 12, Georgetown
Proceedings 1874, pg 217 (1874 Sept 30), Washington Lodge No. 12, Georgetown
Proceedings 1875, pg 81 (1875 Sept 22), Washington Lodge No. 12, Georgetown
Proceedings 1876, pg 35 (1876 Sept 20), Washington Lodge No. 12, Georgetown

Trenton, James
Proceedings 1872, pg 43 (1872 Sept 24) Detroit, Grand Lodge of Michigan

Trevarrow, Wm
Proceedings 1874, pg 229 (1874 Sept 30), Idaho Springs Lodge U D, Idaho Springs
Proceedings 1876, pg 48 (1876 Sept 20) Idaho Springs Lodge No. 26, 1876 Feb 19

Trevena, Richard
Proceedings 1876, pg 35 (1876 Sept 20), Washington Lodge No. 12, Georgetown

Trevorrow, William
Proceedings 1875, pg 89 (1875 Sept 22) Idaho Springs Lodge U D

Treweck, Wm H
Proceedings 1874, pg 228 (1874 Sept 30), Doric Lodge U D, Fairplay

Treweek, W H
Proceedings 1875, pg 89 (1875 Sept 22), Doric Lodge No. 25, Fairplay

Treweek, William H
Proceedings 1876, pg 42 (1876 Sept 20), Doric Lodge No. 25, Fairplay

Trezise, James
　Proceedings 1861-1869, pg 304 (1869 Sept 29), Nevada Lodge No. 4, Nevadaville, Fellowcraft
　Proceedings 1870, pg 20 (1870 Sept 28), Nevada Lodge No. 4, Nevadaville
　Proceedings 1871, pg 18 (1871 Sept 27), Nevada Lodge No. 4, Bald Mountain
　Proceedings 1872, pg 19 (1872 Sept 24), Nevada Lodge No. 4, Bald Mountain, Dimitted,

Tribune Association Printers
　Proceedings 1872, pg 1 (1872 Sept 24) Denver

Trichburn, George
　Proceedings 1874, pg 223 (1874 Sept 30), Laramie Lodge No. 18, Laramie City

Tripp, Layton
　Proceedings 1873, pg 49 (1873 Oct 1), Collins Lodge No. 19, Fort Collins, Apprentice
　Proceedings 1874, pg 225 (1874 Sept 30), Collins Lodge No. 19, Fort Collins, Larimer County, Apprentice
　Proceedings 1875, pg 86 (1875 Sept 22), Collins Lodge No. 19, Fort Collins, Apprentice
　Proceedings 1876, pg 40 (1876 Sept 20), Collins Lodge No. 19, Fort Collins, Apprentice

Tritch, Geo
　Proceedings 1861-1869, pg 112 (1863 Nov 3) Denver Lodge No. 5
　Proceedings 1861-1869, pg 148 (1865 Nov 7), Nevada Lodge No. 4, Nevadaville
　Proceedings 1861-1869, pg 166 (1866 Oct 2) Denver Lodge No. 5
　Proceedings 1861-1869, pg 223 (1868 Oct 7) Denver Lodge No. 5
　Proceedings 1861-1869, pg 304 (1869 Sept 29) Denver Lodge No. 5
　Proceedings 1872, pg 19 (1872 Sept 24), Denver Lodge No. 5, Denver
　Proceedings 1874, pg 211 (1874 Sept 30), Denver Lodge No. 5, Denver

Tritch, George
　Proceedings 1861-1869, pg 77 (1862 Nov 4) Denver Lodge No. 5
　Proceedings 1861-1869, pg 133 (1864 Nov 8) Denver Lodge No. 5
　Proceedings 1861-1869, pg 192 (1867 Oct 8) Denver Lodge No. 5
　Proceedings 1870, pg 20 (1870 Sept 28), Denver Lodge No. 5, Denver
　Proceedings 1871, pg 19 (1871 Sept 27) Denver Lodge No. 5
　Proceedings 1873, pg 37 (1873 Oct 1), Denver Lodge No. 5, Denver
　Proceedings 1875, pg 75 (1875 Sept 22) Denver Lodge No. 5
　Proceedings 1876, pg 30 (1876 Sept 20) Denver Lodge No. 5

Trounstein, P
　Proceedings 1861-1869, pg 223 (1868 Oct 7) Denver Lodge No. 5

Trounstein, Phil
　Proceedings 1870, pg 20 (1870 Sept 28), Denver Lodge No. 5, Denver
　Proceedings 1872, pg 19 (1872 Sept 24), Denver Lodge No. 5, Denver
　Proceedings 1871, pg 19 (1871 Sept 27) Denver Lodge No. 5
　Proceedings 1873, pg 37 (1873 Oct 1), Denver Lodge No. 5, Denver
　Proceedings 1874, pg 212 (1874 Sept 30), Denver Lodge No. 5, Denver
　Proceedings 1875, pg 75 (1875 Sept 22) Denver Lodge No. 5
　Proceedings 1876, pg 31 (1876 Sept 20) Denver Lodge No. 5

Troup, Wm H
　Proceedings 1870, pg 107 (1869 Sept 16) Grand Master, Grand Lodge of Washington Territory

Trout, R M
　Proceedings 1871, pg 27 (1871 Sept 27), Cheyenne Lodge No. 16, Cheyenne, Wyoming Territory
　Proceedings 1861-1869, pg 312 (1869 Sept 29), Cheyenne Lodge No. 16, Cheyenne

Trout, R W
　Proceedings 1870, pg 29 (1870 Sept 28), Cheyenne Lodge No. 16, Cheyenne, Wyoming Territory

Trout, Russel W
　Proceedings 1872, pg 30 (1872 Sept 24), Cheyenne Lodge No. 16, Cheyenne, Wyoming Territory
　Proceedings 1873, pg 46 (1873 Oct 1), Cheyenne Lodge No. 16, Cheyenne, Wyoming Territory
　Proceedings 1874, pg 221 (1874 Sept 30), Cheyenne Lodge No. 16, Cheyenne, Wyoming Territory

Trueman, Edgar
　Proceedings 1873, pg 40 (1873 Oct 1), Empire Lodge No. 8, Empire

Tubbs, O H
　Proceedings 1861-1869, pg 197 (1867 Oct 8), Columbia Lodge U D, Boulder

Tuchbaum, George
　Proceedings 1871, pg 29 (1871 Sept 27), Laramie Lodge No. 18, Laramie, Wyoming Territory, Apprentice
　Proceedings 1873, pg 48 (1873 Oct 1), Laramie Lodge No. 18, Laramie, Wyoming Territory

Tuchburn, Geo
　Proceedings 1872, pg 32 (1872 Sept 24), Laramie Lodge No. 18, Laramie, Wyoming Territory

Tucker, A W
　Proceedings 1861-1869, pg 304 (1869 Sept 29), Nevada Lodge No. 4, Nevadaville
　Proceedings 1873, pg 36 (1873 Oct 1), Nevada Lodge No. 4, Nevada
　Proceedings 1875, pg 74 (1875 Sept 22), Nevada Lodge No. 4, Nevada
　Proceedings 1876, pg 30 (1876 Sept 20) Nevada Lodge No. 4

Tucker, Anthony W
Proceedings 1870, pg 20 (1870 Sept 28), Nevada Lodge No. 4, Nevadaville
Proceedings 1871, pg 18 (1871 Sept 27), Nevada Lodge No. 4, Bald Mountain
Proceedings 1872, pg 18 (1872 Sept 24), Nevada Lodge No. 4, Bald Mountain
Proceedings 1874, pg 210 (1874 Sept 30), Nevada Lodge No. 4, Bald Mountain, Gilpin County

Tucker, Philip C
Proceedings 1861-1869, pg 90 (1863 Apr 17) Masonic Jurist
Proceedings 1861-1869, pg 348 (1869 June 14) Grand Master, Grand Lodge of Texas
Proceedings 1870, pg 102 (1870 June 13) Grand Master, Grand Lodge of Texas

Tucker, Thomas H
Proceedings 1870, pg 20 (1870 Sept 28), Nevada Lodge No. 4, Nevadaville, Fellowcraft

Tucker, Thos H
Proceedings 1871, pg 18 (1871 Sept 27), Nevada Lodge No. 4, Bald Mountain, Dimitted

Tudor, W V
Proceedings 1872, pg 68 (1872 Sept 24) Grand Lodge of Louisiana

Tunnstein, P
Proceedings 1861-1869, pg 304 (1869 Sept 29) Denver Lodge No. 5

Tuppan, J W
Proceedings 1876, pg 31 (1876 Sept 20) Denver Lodge No. 5

Tuppen, J W
Proceedings 1874, pg 212 (1874 Sept 30), Denver Lodge No. 5, Denver
Proceedings 1875, pg 75 (1875 Sept 22) Denver Lodge No. 5

Turner
Proceedings 1872, pg 47 (1872 Sept 24) Grand Lodge of Wisconsin

Turner, B F
Proceedings 1861-1869, pg 111 (1863 Nov 3), Summit Lodge No. 2, Parkville
Proceedings 1861-1869, pg 132 (1864 Nov 8) Golden City Lodge No. 1, dimitted

Turner, Charles
Proceedings 1874, pg 219 (1874 Sept 30), Columbia Lodge No. 14, Boulder, Boulder County
Proceedings 1875, pg 83 (1875 Sept 22), Columbia Lodge No. 14, Boulder
Proceedings 1876, pg 37 (1876 Sept 20), Columbia Lodge No. 14, Boulder

Turner, Edward W
Proceedings 1874, pg 73 (1874 Sept 30) Grand Lodge of Kentucky

Turner, Edwin M
Proceedings 1873, pg 60 (1873 Oct 1) Grand Lodge of Kentucky, Richmond

Turner, J F
Proceedings 1861-1869, pg 100 (1863 Sept 12), Summit Lodge No. 2, Parkville

Turner, John
Proceedings 1872, pg 95 (1872 Sept 24) Grand Lodge of Wisconsin

Turner, W E
Proceedings 1861-1869, pg 167 (1866 Oct 2) Denver Lodge No. 5
Proceedings 1861-1869, pg 192 (1867 Oct 8) Denver Lodge No. 5
Proceedings 1861-1869, pg 223 (1868 Oct 7) Denver Lodge No. 5
Proceedings 1861-1869, pg 305 (1869 Sept 29) Denver Lodge No. 5
Proceedings 1870, pg 21 (1870 Sept 28), Denver Lodge No. 5, Denver
Proceedings 1873, pg 37 (1873 Oct 1), Denver Lodge No. 5, Denver
Proceedings 1874, pg 212 (1874 Sept 30), Denver Lodge No. 5, Denver

Turner, Wm
Proceedings 1861-1869, pg 42 (1861 Dec 10), Summit Lodge No. 2, Parkville
Proceedings 1861-1869, pg 76 (1862 Nov 4), Summit Lodge No. 2, Parkville, dimitted
Proceedings 1861-1869, pg 76 (1862 Nov 4), Summit Lodge No. 2, Parkville

Turner, Wm E
Proceedings 1871, pg 19 (1871 Sept 27) Denver Lodge No. 5
Proceedings 1872, pg 20 (1872 Sept 24), Denver Lodge No. 5, Denver
Proceedings 1875, pg 76 (1875 Sept 22) Denver Lodge No. 5, Stricken from the rolls

Turpin, James H
Proceedings 1876, pg 45 (1876 Sept 20), King Solomon Lodge U D, West Las Animas

Tuttle, F A
Proceedings 1876, pg 38 (1876 Sept 20), Mount Moriah Lodge No. 15, Canon City

Tuttle, Frank A
Proceedings 1875, pg 84 (1875 Sept 22), Mount Moriah Lodge No. 15, Canon City

Tuttle, H B
Proceedings 1861-1869, pg 223 (1868 Oct 7) Denver Lodge No. 5
Proceedings 1861-1869, pg 305 (1869 Sept 29) Denver Lodge No. 5
Proceedings 1870, pg 21 (1870 Sept 28), Denver Lodge No. 5, Denver
Proceedings 1871, pg 30 (1871 Sept 27), Occidental Lodge U D, Greeley

Tuttle, H B, cont.
  Proceedings 1872, pg 33 (1872 Sept 24), Occidental Lodge No. 20, Greeley
  Proceedings 1873, pg 50 (1873 Oct 1), Occidental Lodge No. 20, Greeley, Dimitted
  Proceedings 1874, pg 222 (1874 Sept 30), Pueblo Lodge No. 17, Pueblo, Pueblo County
  Proceedings 1875, pg 85 (1875 Sept 22) Pueblo Lodge No. 17, Demitted
  Proceedings 1876, pg 31 (1876 Sept 20) Denver Lodge No. 5

Twibell, D C
  Proceedings 1861-1869, pg 110 (1863 Nov 3), Summit Lodge No. 2, Parkville
  Proceedings 1861-1869, pg 124 (1864 Nov 8) committee
  Proceedings 1861-1869, pg 124 (1864 Nov 8), Summit Lodge No. 2, Parkville, Grand Steward
  Proceedings 1861-1869, pg 131 (1864 Nov 8) Golden City Lodge No. 1

Twibell, D T
  Proceedings 1861-1869, pg 116 (1864 Nov 7), Summit Lodge No. 2, Parkville

Twiet, R W
  Proceedings 1861-1869, pg 230 (1868 Oct 7), Cheyenne Lodge U D, Cheyenne, Dakota Territory

Twining, H C D
  Proceedings 1870, pg 34 (1870 Sept 28) Grand Secretary, Grand Lodge of Nova Scotia
  Proceedings 1871, pg 35 (1871 Sept 27) Grand Secretary, Grand Lodge of Nova Scotia

Tynon, James
  Proceedings 1873, pg 40 (1873 Oct 1), Union Lodge No. 7, Denver, Fellowcraft
  Proceedings 1874, pg 213 (1874 Sept 30), Union Lodge No. 7, Denver
  Proceedings 1875, pg 78 (1875 Sept 22), Union Lodge No. 7, Denver
  Proceedings 1876, pg 33 (1876 Sept 20), Union Lodge No. 7, Denver

Tyrell, Norman J
  Proceedings 1873, pg 44 (1873 Oct 1), Columbia Lodge No. 14, Boulder
  Proceedings 1874, pg 219 (1874 Sept 30), Columbia Lodge No. 14, Boulder, Boulder County
  Proceedings 1875, pg 83 (1875 Sept 22), Columbia Lodge No. 14, Boulder
  Proceedings 1876, pg 37 (1876 Sept 20), Columbia Lodge No. 14, Boulder

Tyroff, Aug W
  Proceedings 1875, pg 87 (1875 Sept 22), Occidental Lodge No. 20, Greeley

Tyroff, August W
  Proceedings 1874, pg 225 (1874 Sept 30), Occidental Lodge No. 20, Greeley
  Proceedings 1876, pg 40 (1876 Sept 20), Occidental Lodge No. 20, Greeley

Tyson, John H
  Proceedings 1872, pg 43 (1872 Sept 24), Grand Lodge of Maryland

Tyson, John S
  Proceedings 1872, pg 69 (1872 Sept 24) Grand Lodge of Maryland

Unfug, Charles O
  Proceedings 1871, pg 28 (1871 Sept 27), Pueblo Lodge No. 17, Pueblo
  Proceedings 1873, pg 47 (1873 Oct 1), Pueblo Lodge No. 17, Pueblo
  Proceedings 1874, pg 222 (1874 Sept 30), Pueblo Lodge No. 17, Pueblo, Pueblo County
  Proceedings 1875, pg 90 (1875 Sept 22), Huerfano Lodge U D, Walsenburg
  Proceedings 1876, pg 43 (1876 Sept 20), Huerfano Lodge No. 27, Walsenburg

Unfug, Chas
  Proceedings 1872, pg 31 (1872 Sept 24), Pueblo Lodge No. 17, Pueblo

Unfug, Chas O
  Proceedings 1875, pg 85 (1875 Sept 22) Pueblo Lodge No. 17
  Proceedings 1876, pg 5 (1876 Sept 19), Huerfano Lodge No. 27, Walsenburg
  Proceedings 1876, pg 22 (1876 Sept 20), Huerfano Lodge No. 27, Walsenburg
  Proceedings 1876, pg 48 (1876 Sept 20) Pueblo Lodge No. 17, 1876 Feb 11

Union Lodge No. 27, Denver
  Proceedings 1876, pg 8 (1876 June 26), dispensation granted to appear in a public procecession for the centennial celebration on July 4, 1876

Union Lodge No. 7
  Proceedings 1861-1869, pg 139 (1865 Jan 7) communication
  Proceedings 1861-1869, pg 139 (1865 Nov 6) dues paid
  Proceedings 1861-1869, pg 158 (1866 Oct 1) dues paid
  Proceedings 1875, pg 92 (1875 Sept 22)
  Proceedings 1876, pg 52 (1876 Sept 20)

Union Lodge No. 7, Denver
  Proceedings 1861-1869, pg 181 (1867 Oct 7) dues paid
  Proceedings 1874, pg 208 (1874 Sept 30)
  Proceedings 1875, pg 18 (1875 Sept 21) host
  Proceedings 1875, pg 25 (1875 Sept 21) dues paid
  Proceedings 1876, pg 8 (1875 June 26) dispensation granted to confer a degree to W H Parker
  Proceedings 1876, pg 13 (1875 Sept 5) dues paid

Updegraff, J W
  Proceedings 1871, pg 21 (1871 Sept 27), Central Lodge No. 6, Central

Updegraff, Joseph S
Proceedings 1872, pg 21 (1872 Sept 24), Denver Lodge No. 5, Denver
Proceedings 1873, pg 38 (1873 Oct 1), Central Lodge No. 6, Central City
Proceedings 1874, pg 213 (1874 Sept 30), Central Lodge No. 6, Central
Proceedings 1875, pg 77 (1875 Sept 22), Central Lodge No. 6, Central City
Proceedings 1876, pg 32 (1876 Sept 20), Central Lodge No. 6, Central City

Upton, John
Proceedings 1861-1869, pg 78 (1862 Nov 4) Denver Lodge No. 5, Apprentice
Proceedings 1861-1869, pg 133 (1864 Nov 8) Denver Lodge No. 5, Apprentice
Proceedings 1861-1869, pg 193 (1867 Oct 8) Denver Lodge No. 5, Apprentice
Proceedings 1861-1869, pg 223 (1868 Oct 7) Denver Lodge No. 5, Apprentice
Proceedings 1861-1869, pg 305 (1869 Sept 29) Denver Lodge No. 5, Apprentice

Uren, W R
Proceedings 1861-1869, pg 132 (1864 Nov 8), Nevada Lodge No. 4, Nevadaville
Proceedings 1861-1869, pg 147 (1865 Nov 7), Nevada Lodge No. 4, Nevadaville
Proceedings 1861-1869, pg 304 (1869 Sept 29), Nevada Lodge No. 4, Nevadaville, Dimitted

Uren, Wm R
Proceedings 1861-1869, pg 166 (1866 Oct 2), Nevada Lodge No. 4, Nevadaville
Proceedings 1861-1869, pg 192 (1867 Oct 8), Nevada Lodge No. 4, Nevadaville
Proceedings 1861-1869, pg 222 (1868 Oct 7), Nevada Lodge No. 4, Nevadaville

V

Valiton, L F
Proceedings 1861-1869, pg 76 (1862 Nov 4), Summit Lodge No. 2, Parkville
Proceedings 1861-1869, pg 110 (1863 Nov 3), Summit Lodge No. 2, Parkville
Proceedings 1861-1869, pg 132 (1864 Nov 8) Golden City Lodge No. 1

Valiton, Peter
Proceedings 1861-1869, pg 42 (1861 Dec 10), Summit Lodge No. 2, Parkville
Proceedings 1861-1869, pg 76 (1862 Nov 4), Summit Lodge No. 2, Parkville, dimitted,

Valmont Lodge U D
Proceedings 1861-1869, pg 179 (1867 Oct 7) dispensation granted
Proceedings 1861-1869, pg 207 (1868 Jan 13) requesting a lodge
Proceedings 1861-1869, pg 207 (1868 June 27) in working order
Proceedings 1861-1869, pg 208 (1868 Apr) will not be granted a charter if Columbia Lodge No. 14 moves to Boulder City
Proceedings 1861-1869, pg 210 (1868 Jan 22), Visited 'found their lodge room very comfortable and perfectly safe'
Proceedings 1861-1869, pg 211 (1868 July) visited

Van Bokelen, Wm A M
Proceedings 1861-1869, pg 269 (1867 Sept 17), Grand Secretary, Grand Lodge of Nevada
Proceedings 1874, pg 99 (1874 Sept 30) Grand Lodge of Nevada

Van Bokkelen, A M
Proceedings 1861-1869, pg 342 (1868 Sept 15) Grand Secretary, Grand Lodge of Nevada

Van Bokkelen, W A M
Proceedings 1870, pg 34 (1870 Sept 28) Grand Secretary, Grand Lodge of Nevada

Van Bokkelen, William A M
Proceedings 1870, pg 92 (1869 Sept 21) Grand Secretary, Grand Lodge of Nevada

Van Bokkelen, Wm A M
Proceedings 1872, pg 43 (1872 Sept 24) Virginia City, Grand Lodge of Nevada
Proceedings 1873, pg 60 (1873 Oct 1) Grand Lodge of Nevada, Virginia City

Van Clay, M
Proceedings 1873, pg 44 (1873 Oct 1), Columbia Lodge No. 14, Boulder

Van Derem
Proceedings 1861-1869, pg 44 (1862 Nov 3) committee

Van Derem, J M
Proceedings 1861-1869, pg 46 (1862 Nov 3) Teller

Van Deren
Proceedings 1861-1869, pg 80 (1863 May 6) committee
Proceedings 1861-1869, pg 99 (1863 Nov 2) Grand Marshal
Proceedings 1861-1869, pg 99 (1863 Nov 2) teller
Proceedings 1861-1869, pg 106 (1863 Nov 3) resolution
Proceedings 1861-1869, pg 107 (1863 Nov 3) motion
Proceedings 1861-1869, pg 115 (1864 Nov 7) committee
Proceedings 1861-1869, pg 117 (1864 Nov 7) committee
Proceedings 1861-1869, pg 123 (1864 Nov 8) Denver Lodge No. 5
Proceedings 1861-1869, pg 144 (1865 Nov 7) Grand Master
Proceedings 1861-1869, pg 145 (1865 Nov 7) motion
Proceedings 1861-1869, pg 160 (1866 Oct 2) Grand Marshal
Proceedings 1861-1869, pg 161 (1866 Oct 2) motion
Proceedings 1861-1869, pg 162 (1866 Oct 2) motion
Proceedings 1861-1869, pg 162 (1866 Oct 2) motion
Proceedings 1861-1869, pg 163 (1866 Oct 2) motion
Proceedings 1861-1869, pg 178 (1866 Nov 17) Columbia City Lodge U D

Van Deren, cont.
    Proceedings 1861-1869, pg 185 (1867 Oct 8) motion
    Proceedings 1861-1869, pg 187 (1867 Oct 8) motion
    Proceedings 1861-1869, pg 189 (1867 Oct 8) motion
    Proceedings 1861-1869, pg 189 (1867 Oct 8) motion
    Proceedings 1861-1869, pg 190 (1867 Oct 8) PGM
    Proceedings 1861-1869, pg 190 (1867 Oct 8) committee
    Proceedings 1861-1869, pg 202 (1868 Oct 6) committee
    Proceedings 1861-1869, pg 202 (1868 Oct 6) committee
    Proceedings 1861-1869, pg 216 (1868 Oct 7) resolution
    Proceedings 1861-1869, pg 217 (1868 Oct 7) resolution
    Proceedings 1861-1869, pg 219 (1868 Oct 7) resolution
    Proceedings 1861-1869, pg 296 (1869 Sept 28) committee
    Proceedings 1861-1869, pg 301 (1869 Sept 29) Past Grand Master
    Proceedings 1861-1869, pg 302 (1869 Sept 29) committee
    Proceedings 1870, pg 14 (1870 Sept 27) Past Grand Master
    Proceedings 1870, pg 15 (1870 Sept 28) resolution
    Proceedings 1870, pg 17 (1870 Sept 28) committee
    Proceedings 1872, pg 4 (1872 Sept 24) Past Grand Master
    Proceedings 1872, pg 13 (1872 Sept 24) committee
    Proceedings 1872, pg 15 (1872 Sept 24) Past Grand Master
    Proceedings 1873, pg 29 (1873 Oct 1) committee

Van Deren, A J
    Proceedings 1861-1869, pg 44 (1862 Nov 3) Grand Senior Deacon
    Proceedings 1861-1869, pg 45 (1862 Nov 3) committee
    Proceedings 1861-1869, pg 45 (1862 Nov 3), Nevada Lodge No. 4, Nevadaville
    Proceedings 1861-1869, pg 46 (1862 Nov 3) motion
    Proceedings 1861-1869, pg 47 (1862 Nov 3) committee
    Proceedings 1861-1869, pg 48 (1862 Nov 3) amendment
    Proceedings 1861-1869, pg 76 (1862 Nov 4), Nevada Lodge No. 4, Nevadaville
    Proceedings 1861-1869, pg 79 (1863 May 6) Grand Lecturer
    Proceedings 1861-1869, pg 80 (1863 May 6), Nevada Lodge No. 4, Nevadaville
    Proceedings 1861-1869, pg 80 (1863 May 6) committee
    Proceedings 1861-1869, pg 83 (1863 May 6) Grand Lecturer
    Proceedings 1861-1869, pg 85 (1863 May 6) Grand Lecturer
    Proceedings 1861-1869, pg 91 (1863 Apr 17) committee
    Proceedings 1861-1869, pg 93 (1863 Apr 17) committee
    Proceedings 1861-1869, pg 94 (1863 Apr 17) Grand Lecturer
    Proceedings 1861-1869, pg 94 (1863 Apr 17), Nevada Lodge No. 4, Nevadaville
    Proceedings 1861-1869, pg 95 (1863 Apr 17) donated their per diem to the Grand Lodge
    Proceedings 1861-1869, pg 97 (1863 Nov 2) Grand Lecturer
    Proceedings 1861-1869, pg 98 (1863 Nov 2) Grand Lecturer
    Proceedings 1861-1869, pg 98 (1863 Nov 2) motion
    Proceedings 1861-1869, pg 98 (1863 Nov 2) committee
    Proceedings 1861-1869, pg 98 (1863 Nov 2) committee
    Proceedings 1861-1869, pg 98 (1863 Nov 2), Nevada Lodge No. 4, Nevadaville
    Proceedings 1861-1869, pg 99 (1863 Nov 2), Nevada Lodge No. 4, Nevadaville, Deputy Grand Master
    Proceedings 1861-1869, pg 100 (1863 Nov 2) committee
    Proceedings 1861-1869, pg 100 (1863 Nov 3) Deputy Grand Master
    Proceedings 1861-1869, pg 102 (1863 Nov 3) committee
    Proceedings 1861-1869, pg 103 (1863 Nov 3), Nevada Lodge No. 4, Nevadaville
    Proceedings 1861-1869, pg 104 (1863 Nov 3) resolution
    Proceedings 1861-1869, pg 106 (1863 Nov 3) committee
    Proceedings 1861-1869, pg 107 (1863 Nov 3) committee
    Proceedings 1861-1869, pg 111 (1863 Nov 3), Nevada Lodge No. 4, Nevadaville
    Proceedings 1861-1869, pg 115 (1864 Nov 7) Deputy Grand Master
    Proceedings 1861-1869, pg 116 (1864 Nov 7) Deputy Grand Master
    Proceedings 1861-1869, pg 116 (1864 Nov 7) Deputy Grand Master
    Proceedings 1861-1869, pg 116 (1864 Nov 7) committee
    Proceedings 1861-1869, pg 117 (1864 Nov 7) committee
    Proceedings 1861-1869, pg 118 (1864 Nov 8), Chivington Lodge No. 6, Central City, Grand Master
    Proceedings 1861-1869, pg 119 (1863 Nov 3) warrant drawn
    Proceedings 1861-1869, pg 119 (1864 Nov 8) committee
    Proceedings 1861-1869, pg 123 (1864 Nov 8) Grand Master
    Proceedings 1861-1869, pg 123 (1864 Nov 8) committee
    Proceedings 1861-1869, pg 123 (1864 Nov 8) committee
    Proceedings 1861-1869, pg 126 (1864 Nov 8) committee
    Proceedings 1861-1869, pg 126 (1864 Nov 8) Deputy Grand Master
    Proceedings 1861-1869, pg 128 (1864 Nov 8) Grand Master
    Proceedings 1861-1869, pg 132 (1864 Nov 8), Nevada Lodge No. 4, Nevadaville
    Proceedings 1861-1869, pg 136 (1865 Nov 6) Grand Master
    Proceedings 1861-1869, pg 137 (1865 Nov 6) Grand Master
    Proceedings 1861-1869, pg 137 (1865 Nov 6) Grand Master
    Proceedings 1861-1869, pg 139 (1864 Nov 30) library fund
    Proceedings 1861-1869, pg 140 (1865 Nov 6) special dispensation
    Proceedings 1861-1869, pg 144 (1865 Nov 7) Grand Master
    Proceedings 1861-1869, pg 145 (1865 Nov 7) committee
    Proceedings 1861-1869, pg 148 (1865 Nov 7), Nevada Lodge No. 4, Nevadaville
    Proceedings 1861-1869, pg 153 (1866 Oct 1) Deputy Grand Master
    Proceedings 1861-1869, pg 154 (1866 Oct 1) Past Grand Master
    Proceedings 1861-1869, pg 155 (1866 Oct 1) committee
    Proceedings 1861-1869, pg 156 (1866 Oct 1) committee
    Proceedings 1861-1869, pg 156 (1866 Oct 1) motion
    Proceedings 1861-1869, pg 159 (1866 Oct 1) warrant

Van Deren, A J, cont.
- Proceedings 1861-1869, pg 159 (1866 Oct 1) motion
- Proceedings 1861-1869, pg 162 (1866 Oct 2) Past Grand Master
- Proceedings 1861-1869, pg 163 (1866 Oct 2) committee
- Proceedings 1861-1869, pg 166 (1866 Oct 2), Nevada Lodge No. 4, Nevadaville
- Proceedings 1861-1869, pg 175 (1867 Oct 7) Past Grand Master
- Proceedings 1861-1869, pg 176 (1867 Oct 7) committee
- Proceedings 1861-1869, pg 176 (1867 Oct 7) Past Grand Master
- Proceedings 1861-1869, pg 176 (1867 Oct 7) committee
- Proceedings 1861-1869, pg 180 (1867 Oct 7) committee
- Proceedings 1861-1869, pg 182 (1867 Oct 7) warrant paid
- Proceedings 1861-1869, pg 186 (1867 Oct 8) Past Grand Master
- Proceedings 1861-1869, pg 188 (1867 Oct 8) committee
- Proceedings 1861-1869, pg 192 (1867 Oct 8), Nevada Lodge No. 4, Nevadaville
- Proceedings 1861-1869, pg 196 (1867 Oct 8), Columbia Lodge U D, Boulder
- Proceedings 1861-1869, pg 201 (1868 Oct 6) Past Grand Master
- Proceedings 1861-1869, pg 202 (1868 Oct 6) committee
- Proceedings 1861-1869, pg 202 (1868 Oct 6) Past Grand Master
- Proceedings 1861-1869, pg 212 (1868 Oct 6) warrant paid
- Proceedings 1861-1869, pg 215 (1868 Oct 6) committee
- Proceedings 1861-1869, pg 216 (1868 Oct 6) committee
- Proceedings 1861-1869, pg 219 (1868 Oct 7) mileage allowed
- Proceedings 1861-1869, pg 220 (1868 Oct 7) committee
- Proceedings 1861-1869, pg 222 (1868 Oct 7), Nevada Lodge No. 4, Nevadaville
- Proceedings 1861-1869, pg 289 (1869 Sept 28) Past Grand Master
- Proceedings 1861-1869, pg 299 (1869 Sept 29) committee
- Proceedings 1861-1869, pg 300 (1869 Sept 29) Past Grand Master
- Proceedings 1861-1869, pg 302 (1869 Sept 29) committee
- Proceedings 1861-1869, pg 304 (1869 Sept 29), Nevada Lodge No. 4, Nevadaville
- Proceedings 1861-1869, pg 315 (1869 Sept 29) Grand Master, 1864
- Proceedings 1861-1869, pg 315 (1869 Sept 29) Deputy Grand Master, 1863
- Proceedings 1870, pg cover (1870 Sept 28) Past Grand Master, Central
- Proceedings 1870, pg 3 (1870 Sept 27) Past Grand Master
- Proceedings 1870, pg 12 (1870 Sept 27) committee
- Proceedings 1870, pg 14 (1870 Sept 27) committee
- Proceedings 1870, pg 16 (1870 Sept 28) Past Grand Master
- Proceedings 1870, pg 20 (1870 Sept 28), Nevada Lodge No. 4, Nevadaville
- Proceedings 1870, pg 32 (1870 Sept 28) Grand Master, 1864
- Proceedings 1870, pg 32 (1870 Sept 28) Deputy Grand Master, 1863
- Proceedings 1871, pg 18 (1871 Sept 27), Nevada Lodge No. 4, Bald Mountain
- Proceedings 1871, pg 34 (1871 Sept 27) Deputy Grand Master, 1863
- Proceedings 1871, pg 34 (1871 Sept 27) Grand Master, 1864
- Proceedings 1872, pg 3 (1872 Sept 24) Past Grand Master
- Proceedings 1872, pg 4 (1872 Sept 24) Past Grand Master
- Proceedings 1872, pg 5 (1872 Sept 24) committee
- Proceedings 1872, pg 16 (1872 Sept 24) Past Grand Master
- Proceedings 1872, pg 18 (1872 Sept 24), Nevada Lodge No. 4, Bald Mountain
- Proceedings 1872, pg 42 (1872 Sept 24) Deputy Grand Master, 1863
- Proceedings 1872, pg 42 (1872 Sept 24) Grand Master, 1864
- Proceedings 1873, pg cover (1873 Oct 1), Central City Council, No 54 (Illinois) Central
- Proceedings 1873, pg cover (1873 Oct 1) committee, Central
- Proceedings 1873, pg 4 (1873 Sept 30) Past Grand Master
- Proceedings 1873, pg 5 (1873 Sept 30) Past Grand Master
- Proceedings 1873, pg 7 (1873 Sept 30) committee
- Proceedings 1873, pg 14 (1873 Sept 30) committee
- Proceedings 1873, pg 19 (1873 Oct 1) committee
- Proceedings 1873, pg 31 (1873 Oct 1) mileage and per diem
- Proceedings 1873, pg 36 (1873 Oct 1), Nevada Lodge No. 4, Nevada
- Proceedings 1873, pg 58 (1873 Oct 1) Deputy Grand Master, 1863
- Proceedings 1873, pg 58 (1873 Oct 1) Grand Master, 1864
- Proceedings 1874, pg 5 (1874 Sept 29) Past Grand Master
- Proceedings 1874, pg 15 (1874 Sept 29) committee
- Proceedings 1874, pg 17 (1874 Sept 29) committee
- Proceedings 1874, pg 21 (1874 Sept 29) committee
- Proceedings 1874, pg 36 (1874 Sept 30) per diem
- Proceedings 1874, pg 210 (1874 Sept 30), Nevada Lodge No. 4, Bald Mountain, Gilpin County
- Proceedings 1875, pg 74 (1875 Sept 22), Nevada Lodge No. 4, Nevada
- Proceedings 1876, pg 30 (1876 Sept 20) Nevada Lodge No. 4

Van Deren, Archibald J
- Proceedings 1873, pg 32 (1873 Oct 1) committee
- Proceedings 1874, pg 4 (1874 Sept 29) Past Grand Master
- Proceedings 1874, pg 206 (1874 Sept 30) Deputy Grand Master, 1863
- Proceedings 1874, pg 206 (1874 Sept 30) Grand Master, 1864
- Proceedings 1875, pg 93 (1875 Sept 22) Deputy Grand Master, 1863
- Proceedings 1875, pg 93 (1875 Sept 22) Grand Master, 1864

Van Deren, J M
- Proceedings 1861-1869, pg 45 (1862 Nov 3), Nevada Lodge No. 4, Nevadaville
- Proceedings 1861-1869, pg 45 (1862 Nov 3) committee
- Proceedings 1861-1869, pg 46 (1862 Nov 3) Senior Grand Warden

Van Deren, J M, cont.
Proceedings 1861-1869, pg 47 (1862 Nov 3) committee
Proceedings 1861-1869, pg 50 (1862 Nov 4) committee
Proceedings 1861-1869, pg 51 (1862 Nov 4) Senior Grand Warden
Proceedings 1861-1869, pg 54 (1862 Nov 4) committee
Proceedings 1861-1869, pg 54 (1862 Nov 4) installed
Proceedings 1861-1869, pg 76 (1862 Nov 4), Nevada Lodge No. 4, Nevadaville
Proceedings 1861-1869, pg 111 (1863 Nov 3), Nevada Lodge No. 4, Nevadaville
Proceedings 1861-1869, pg 113 (1863 Nov 3), Montana Lodge U D, Central City
Proceedings 1861-1869, pg 132 (1864 Nov 8), Nevada Lodge No. 4, Nevadaville
Proceedings 1861-1869, pg 148 (1865 Nov 7), Nevada Lodge No. 4, Nevadaville, dimitted
Proceedings 1861-1869, pg 315 (1869 Sept 29) Senior Grand Warden, 1862, Dimitted
Proceedings 1870, pg 32 (1870 Sept 28) Senior Grand Warden, 1862, Dimitted
Proceedings 1871, pg 34 (1871 Sept 27) Senior Grand Warden, 1862, Dimitted
Proceedings 1872, pg 42 (1872 Sept 24) Senior Grand Warden, 1862
Proceedings 1873, pg 58 (1873 Oct 1) Senior Grand Warden, 1862, Dropped from the Rolls

Van Deren, John M
Proceedings 1874, pg 206 (1874 Sept 30) Senior Grand Warden, 1862, demitted
Proceedings 1875, pg 93 (1875 Sept 22) Senior Grand Warden, 1862, Demitted

Van Rensallear, Stephen
Proceedings 1874, pg 63 (1874 Sept 30) Grand Lodge of New York, 1830

Van Riper, C
Proceedings 1874, pg 219 (1874 Sept 30), Columbia Lodge No. 14, Boulder, Boulder County

Van Riper, Cornelius
Proceedings 1875, pg 83 (1875 Sept 22), Columbia Lodge No. 14, Boulder
Proceedings 1876, pg 50 (1876 Sept 20), Columbia Lodge No. 14, Boulder

Van Schyock, L
Proceedings 1861-1869, pg 310 (1869 Sept 29), El Paso Lodge No. 13, Colorado City, Fellowcraft

Van Schyock, Levi
Proceedings 1861-1869, pg 228 (1868 Oct 7), El Paso Lodge No. 13, Colorado City, Fellowcraft

Van Shyock, L
Proceedings 1870, pg 27 (1870 Sept 28), El Paso Lodge No. 13, Colorado City, Fellowcraft

Van Shyock, Levi
Proceedings 1871, pg 25 (1871 Sept 27), El Paso Lodge No. 13, Colorado City, Fellowcraft
Proceedings 1872, pg 27 (1872 Sept 24), El Paso Lodge No. 13, Colorado City, Fellowcraft
Proceedings 1873, pg 44 (1873 Oct 1), El Paso Lodge No. 13, Colorado City, Fellowcraft

Van, C M
Proceedings 1874, pg 219 (1874 Sept 30), Columbia Lodge No. 14, Boulder, Boulder County

Van, Clay M
Proceedings 1875, pg 17 (1875 Sept 21), Columbia Lodge No. 14, Boulder
Proceedings 1875, pg 83 (1875 Sept 22), Columbia Lodge No. 14, Boulder
Proceedings 1876, pg 37 (1876 Sept 20), Columbia Lodge No. 14, Boulder
Proceedings 1876, pg 50 (1876 Sept 20), Columbia Lodge No. 14, Boulder

VanBokkelen
Proceedings 1872, pg 82 (1872 Sept 24) Grand Lodge of Nevada

VanBokkelen, A M
Proceedings 1872, pg 78 (1872 Sept 24) Grand Lodge of Nevada
Proceedings 1872, pg 79 (1872 Sept 24) Grand Lodge of Nevada

VanBokkelen, W A M
Proceedings 1861-1869, pg 316 (1869 Sept 29) Grand Lodge of Nevada

Vance, E J
Proceedings 1861-1869, pg 169 (1866 Oct 2), Chivington Lodge No. 6, Central City, Fellowcraft
Proceedings 1861-1869, pg 194 (1867 Oct 8), Chivington Lodge No. 6, Central City
Proceedings 1861-1869, pg 224 (1868 Oct 7), Chivington Lodge No. 6, Central City
Proceedings 1870, pg 22 (1870 Sept 28), Central Lodge No. 6, Central City

Vance, Em J
Proceedings 1861-1869, pg 306 (1869 Sept 29), Central Lodge No. 6, Central City
Proceedings 1871, pg 21 (1871 Sept 27), Central Lodge No. 6, Central

Vance, Emory J
Proceedings 1872, pg 21 (1872 Sept 24), Denver Lodge No. 5, Denver
Proceedings 1873, pg 39 (1873 Oct 1), Central Lodge No. 6, Central City
Proceedings 1874, pg 213 (1874 Sept 30), Central Lodge No. 6, Central
Proceedings 1875, pg 77 (1875 Sept 22), Central Lodge No. 6, Central City, Stricken from the rolls

Vance, Robert B
Proceedings 1861-1869, pg 343 (1868 Dec 7) Grand Master, Grand Lodge of North Carolina
Proceedings 1870, pg 95 (1869 Dec 6) Grand Master, Grand Lodge of North Carolina

Vandewark, Martin
Proceedings 1876, pg 39 (1876 Sept 20), Collins Lodge No. 19, Fort Collins

Proceedings 1861-1869, pg 230 (1868 Oct 7), Germania Lodge U D, Denver, Apprentice

VanGieson, William H
Proceedings 1876, pg 44 (1876 Sept 20) Del Norte Lodge U D

VanLiew, William M
Proceedings 1876, pg 44 (1876 Sept 20) Del Norte Lodge U D

VanRiper, Cornelius
Proceedings 1876, pg 37 (1876 Sept 20), Columbia Lodge No. 14, Boulder

VanSlyck, Nicholas
Proceedings 1874, pg 205 (1874 Sept 30) Grand Lodge of Rhode Island, Providence

Vasquez, Hiram W
Proceedings 1875, pg 90 (1875 Sept 22), Huerfano Lodge U D, Walsenburg
Proceedings 1876, pg 43 (1876 Sept 20), Huerfano Lodge No. 27, Walsenburg

Vasquez, Louis
Proceedings 1876, pg 43 (1876 Sept 20), Huerfano Lodge No. 27, Walsenburg, Fellow Craft

Vaughan, H C
Proceedings 1873, pg 45 (1873 Oct 1), Mount Moriah Lodge No. 15, Canon City
Proceedings 1861-1869, pg 229 (1868 Oct 7), Canon Lodge U D, Canon City
Proceedings 1861-1869, pg 311 (1869 Sept 29), Mount Moriah Lodge No. 15, Canon City
Proceedings 1870, pg 28 (1870 Sept 28), Mount Moriah Lodge No. 15, Canon City
Proceedings 1871, pg 26 (1871 Sept 27), Mount Moriah Lodge No. 15, Canon City
Proceedings 1872, pg 28 (1872 Sept 24), Mount Moriah Lodge No. 15, Canon City
Proceedings 1874, pg 220 (1874 Sept 30), Mount Moriah Lodge No. 15, Canon City
Proceedings 1875, pg 84 (1875 Sept 22), Mount Moriah Lodge No. 15, Canon City
Proceedings 1876, pg 38 (1876 Sept 20), Mount Moriah Lodge No. 15, Canon City

Vaux, Richard
Proceedings 1861-1869, pg 345 (1868 Dec 2) Grand Master, Grand Lodge of Pennsylvania
Proceedings 1861-1869, pg 346 (1868 Dec 2) Grand Master, Grand Lodge of Pennsylvania
Proceedings 1870, pg 99 (1869 Dec 27) Grand Master, Grand Lodge of Pennsylvania

Vawter, J G
Proceedings 1861-1869, pg 102 (1863 Nov 3) petition for formation of a new lodge in Denver

Veach, Elias
Proceedings 1876, pg 39 (1876 Sept 20) Pueblo Lodge No. 17

Veal, Sam'l
Proceedings 1874, pg 210 (1874 Sept 30), Nevada Lodge No. 4, Bald Mountain, Gilpin County

Veal, Samuel
Proceedings 1873, pg 36 (1873 Oct 1), Nevada Lodge No. 4, Nevada, Apprentice
Proceedings 1875, pg 74 (1875 Sept 22), Nevada Lodge No. 4, Nevada
Proceedings 1876, pg 30 (1876 Sept 20) Nevada Lodge No. 4

Veatch, E
Proceedings 1874, pg 222 (1874 Sept 30), Pueblo Lodge No. 17, Pueblo, Pueblo County

Veatch, Elias
Proceedings 1861-1869, pg 312 (1869 Sept 29), Pueblo Lodge No. 17, Pueblo
Proceedings 1871, pg 28 (1871 Sept 27), Pueblo Lodge No. 17, Pueblo
Proceedings 1872, pg 31 (1872 Sept 24), Pueblo Lodge No. 17, Pueblo
Proceedings 1873, pg 47 (1873 Oct 1), Pueblo Lodge No. 17, Pueblo
Proceedings 1875, pg 85 (1875 Sept 22) Pueblo Lodge No. 17

Veath, E
Proceedings 1870, pg 29 (1870 Sept 28), Pueblo Lodge No. 17, Pueblo

Vermillion, J S
Proceedings 1874, pg 223 (1874 Sept 30), Laramie Lodge No. 18, Laramie City

Vernon, W H
Proceedings 1861-1869, pg 309 (1869 Sept 29), Black Hawk Lodge No. 11, Black Hawk
Proceedings 1870, pg 25 (1870 Sept 28), Black Hawk Lodge No. 11, Black Hawk
Proceedings 1871, pg 23 (1871 Sept 27), Black Hawk Lodge No. 11, Black Hawk
Proceedings 1872, pg 25 (1872 Sept 24), Black Hawk Lodge No. 11, Black Hawk
Proceedings 1873, pg 42 (1873 Oct 1), Black Hawk Lodge No. 11, Black Hawk
Proceedings 1874, pg 216 (1874 Sept 30), Black Hawk Lodge No. 11, Black Hawk

Vernon, Wm H
Proceedings 1861-1869, pg 227 (1868 Oct 7), Black Hawk Lodge No. 11, Black Hawk
Proceedings 1875, pg 80 (1875 Sept 22) Black Hawk Lodge No. 11, Stricken from the rolls

Vickers, S I
Proceedings 1876, pg 14 (1874 Nov 6), Secretary, St Paul Lodge No. 124, Auburn, NY, gave account of the runeral of Amsbury,

Vincent
Proceedings 1870, pg 60 (1869 Oct 20) Grand Lodge of Kansas
Proceedings 1870, pg 90 (1869 Oct 4) Grand Lodge of Colorado

Colorado's Territorial Masons

Vincent, Addi
   Proceedings 1861-1869, pg 77 (1862 Nov 4), Nevada Lodge No. 4, Nevadaville
   Proceedings 1861-1869, pg 111 (1863 Nov 3), Nevada Lodge No. 4, Nevadaville
   Proceedings 1861-1869, pg 132 (1864 Nov 8), Nevada Lodge No. 4, Nevadaville
   Proceedings 1861-1869, pg 148 (1865 Nov 7), Nevada Lodge No. 4, Nevadaville
   Proceedings 1861-1869, pg 166 (1866 Oct 2), Nevada Lodge No. 4, Nevadaville, dimitted

Vincent, B P
   Proceedings 1861-1869, pg 201 (1868 Oct 6) Grand Orator

Vincent, B T
   Proceedings 1861-1869, pg 123 (1864 Nov 8), Chivington Lodge No. 6, Central City, Grand Chaplain
   Proceedings 1861-1869, pg 134 (1864 Nov 8), Chivington Lodge No. 6, Central City
   Proceedings 1861-1869, pg 136 (1865 Nov 6) Grand Chaplain
   Proceedings 1861-1869, pg 145 (1865 Nov 7), Chivington Lodge No. 6, Central City, Grand Chaplain
   Proceedings 1861-1869, pg 145 (1865 Nov 7) Grand Chaplain
   Proceedings 1861-1869, pg 150 (1865 Nov 7), Chivington Lodge No. 6, Central City
   Proceedings 1861-1869, pg 168 (1866 Oct 2), Chivington Lodge No. 6, Central City
   Proceedings 1861-1869, pg 190 (1867 Oct 8) Grand Orator
   Proceedings 1861-1869, pg 194 (1867 Oct 8), Chivington Lodge No. 6, Central City
   Proceedings 1861-1869, pg 203 (1868 Oct 6) Grand Orator
   Proceedings 1861-1869, pg 224 (1868 Oct 7), Chivington Lodge No. 6, Central City
   Proceedings 1861-1869, pg 306 (1869 Sept 29), Central Lodge No. 6, Central City
   Proceedings 1870, pg cover (1870 Sept 28) Grand Chaplain, Denver
   Proceedings 1870, pg 13 (1870 Sept 27) Grand Chaplain
   Proceedings 1870, pg 22 (1870 Sept 28), Central Lodge No. 6, Central City
   Proceedings 1871, pg cover (1871 Sept 27) Grand Chaplain, Denver
   Proceedings 1871, pg 14 (1871 Sept 27) Grand Chaplain
   Proceedings 1871, pg 21 (1871 Sept 27), Central Lodge No. 6, Central
   Proceedings 1872, pg 15 (1872 Sept 24) Grand Chaplain

Vincent, Benoni T
   Proceedings 1872, pg 21 (1872 Sept 24), Denver Lodge No. 5, Denver
   Proceedings 1873, pg 39 (1873 Oct 1), Central Lodge No. 6, Central City
   Proceedings 1874, pg 213 (1874 Sept 30), Central Lodge No. 6, Central
   Proceedings 1875, pg 77 (1875 Sept 22), Central Lodge No. 6, Central City, Stricken from the rolls

Vincil, John D
   Proceedings 1861-1869, pg 335 (1868 Oct 12) Grand Master, Grand Lodge of Missouri
   Proceedings 1870, pg 84 (1869 Oct 11) Grand Master, Grand Lodge of Missouri

Visscher, C
   Proceedings 1861-1869, pg 166 (1866 Oct 2), Nevada Lodge No. 4, Nevadaville
   Proceedings 1861-1869, pg 191 (1867 Oct 8), Nevada Lodge No. 4, Nevadaville
   Proceedings 1861-1869, pg 304 (1869 Sept 29), Nevada Lodge No. 4, Nevadaville
   Proceedings 1876, pg 30 (1876 Sept 20) Nevada Lodge No. 4

Visscher, Corneilus [Cornelius]
   Proceedings 1873, pg 36 (1873 Oct 1), Nevada Lodge No. 4, Nevada

Visscher, Cornelius
   Proceedings 1861-1869, pg 222 (1868 Oct 7), Nevada Lodge No. 4, Nevadaville
   Proceedings 1870, pg 20 (1870 Sept 28), Nevada Lodge No. 4, Nevadaville
   Proceedings 1871, pg 18 (1871 Sept 27), Nevada Lodge No. 4, Bald Mountain
   Proceedings 1872, pg 19 (1872 Sept 24), Nevada Lodge No. 4, Bald Mountain
   Proceedings 1874, pg 210 (1874 Sept 30), Nevada Lodge No. 4, Bald Mountain, Gilpin County
   Proceedings 1875, pg 74 (1875 Sept 22), Nevada Lodge No. 4, Nevada

Vivian, Geo G
   Proceedings 1875, pg 89 (1875 Sept 22) Idaho Springs Lodge U D

Vivian, George G
   Proceedings 1876, pg 43 (1876 Sept 20) Idaho Springs Lodge No. 26

Voice of Masonry
   Proceedings 1874, pg 19 (1874 Sept 29), published at Chicago, IL
   Proceedings 1875, pg 23 (1875 Sept 21), published at Chicago, IL
   Proceedings 1876, pg 11 (1876 Sept 19), published at Chicago, IL

Von Gohren, L
   Proceedings 1871, pg 30 (1871 Sept 27), Occidental Lodge U D, Greeley
   Proceedings 1872, pg 33 (1872 Sept 24), Occidental Lodge No. 20, Greeley
   Proceedings 1873, pg 50 (1873 Oct 1), Occidental Lodge No. 20, Greeley
   Proceedings 1875, pg 87 (1875 Sept 22), Occidental Lodge No. 20, Greeley

Von Gohren, Ludwig
   Proceedings 1874, pg 225 (1874 Sept 30), Occidental Lodge No. 20, Greeley

VonGohren, L
   Proceedings 1876, pg 40 (1876 Sept 20), Occidental Lodge No. 20, Greeley

Voorheis, J H
Proceedings 1861-1869, pg 230 (1868 Oct 7), Cheyenne Lodge U D, Cheyenne, Dakota Territory
Proceedings 1861-1869, pg 312 (1869 Sept 29), Cheyenne Lodge No. 16, Cheyenne
Proceedings 1861-1869, pg 167 (1866 Oct 2) Denver Lodge No. 5
Proceedings 1861-1869, pg 224 (1868 Oct 7) Denver Lodge No. 5, Dimitted
Proceedings 1861-1869, pg 133 (1864 Nov 8) Denver Lodge No. 5
Proceedings 1861-1869, pg 193 (1867 Oct 8) Denver Lodge No. 5

Vosburg, N O
Proceedings 1876, pg 33 (1876 Sept 20), Union Lodge No. 7, Denver

Vost, Rufus C
Proceedings 1876, pg 44 (1876 Sept 20), Las Animas Lodge No. 28, Trinidad, Apprentice

Wadman
Proceedings 1870, pg 11 (1870 Sept 27), of Boston, MA,, Editor, The Masonic Monthly

Waggoner, F R
Proceedings 1861-1869, pg 112 (1863 Nov 3), Nevada Lodge No. 4, Nevadaville, Apprentice
Proceedings 1861-1869, pg 193 (1867 Oct 8) Denver Lodge No. 5
Proceedings 1861-1869, pg 305 (1869 Sept 29) Denver Lodge No. 5
Proceedings 1870, pg 21 (1870 Sept 28), Denver Lodge No. 5, Denver
Proceedings 1872, pg 20 (1872 Sept 24), Denver Lodge No. 5, Denver

Wagner, John
Proceedings 1875, pg 89 (1875 Sept 22), Doric Lodge No. 25, Fairplay

Wagner, John B
Proceedings 1874, pg 228 (1874 Sept 30), Doric Lodge U D, Fairplay

Wagoner, F R
Proceedings 1861-1869, pg 132 (1864 Nov 8), Nevada Lodge No. 4, Nevadaville, Apprentice
Proceedings 1861-1869, pg 133 (1864 Nov 8) Denver Lodge No. 5, Fellowcraft
Proceedings 1861-1869, pg 149 (1865 Nov 7), Nevada Lodge No. 4, Nevadaville
Proceedings 1861-1869, pg 167 (1866 Oct 2) Denver Lodge No. 5
Proceedings 1861-1869, pg 223 (1868 Oct 7) Denver Lodge No. 5

Wakefield, C A
Proceedings 1876, pg 38 (1876 Sept 20), Mount Moriah Lodge No. 15, Canon City

Walbrach, Conrad
Proceedings 1861-1869, pg 230 (1868 Oct 7), Germania Lodge U D, Denver

Walf, Hans
Proceedings 1861-1869, pg 42 (1861 Dec 10), Summit Lodge No. 2, Parkville

Walker, F
Proceedings 1874, pg 222 (1874 Sept 30), Pueblo Lodge No. 17, Pueblo, Pueblo County
Proceedings 1875, pg 85 (1875 Sept 22) Pueblo Lodge No. 17

Walker, Frank
Proceedings 1874, pg 212 (1874 Sept 30), Denver Lodge No. 5, Denver
Proceedings 1875, pg 76 (1875 Sept 22) Denver Lodge No. 5
Proceedings 1876, pg 31 (1876 Sept 20) Denver Lodge No. 5

Walker, Franklin
Proceedings 1861-1869, pg 312 (1869 Sept 29), Pueblo Lodge No. 17, Pueblo
Proceedings 1870, pg 30 (1870 Sept 28), Pueblo Lodge No. 17, Pueblo
Proceedings 1871, pg 28 (1871 Sept 27), Pueblo Lodge No. 17, Pueblo
Proceedings 1872, pg 31 (1872 Sept 24), Pueblo Lodge No. 17, Pueblo
Proceedings 1873, pg 47 (1873 Oct 1), Pueblo Lodge No. 17, Pueblo
Proceedings 1876, pg 39 (1876 Sept 20) Pueblo Lodge No. 17

Walker, G B
Proceedings 1861-1869, pg 150 (1865 Nov 7), Chivington Lodge No. 6, Central City
Proceedings 1861-1869, pg 168 (1866 Oct 2), Chivington Lodge No. 6, Central City

Walker, Geo B
Proceedings 1861-1869, pg 224 (1868 Oct 7), Chivington Lodge No. 6, Central City
Proceedings 1861-1869, pg 306 (1869 Sept 29), Central Lodge No. 6, Central City
Proceedings 1870, pg 22 (1870 Sept 28), Central Lodge No. 6, Central City
Proceedings 1871, pg 21 (1871 Sept 27), Central Lodge No. 6, Central
Proceedings 1872, pg 21 (1872 Sept 24), Denver Lodge No. 5, Denver
Proceedings 1873, pg 39 (1873 Oct 1), Central Lodge No. 6, Central City

Walker, George B
Proceedings 1861-1869, pg 194 (1867 Oct 8), Chivington Lodge No. 6, Central City
Proceedings 1874, pg 213 (1874 Sept 30), Central Lodge No. 6, Central, died

Walker, John
Proceedings 1861-1869, pg 307 (1869 Sept 29), Union Lodge No. 7, Denver

Colorado's Territorial Masons

Walker, John, cont.
Proceedings 1870, pg 23 (1870 Sept 28), Union Lodge No. 7, Denver
Proceedings 1871, pg 22 (1871 Sept 27), Union Lodge No. 7, Denver
Proceedings 1872, pg 23 (1872 Sept 24), Union Lodge No. 7, Denver
Proceedings 1873, pg 6 (1873 Sept 30), Denver [Union] Lodge No. 7, Denver
Proceedings 1873, pg 39 (1873 Oct 1), Union Lodge No. 7, Denver
Proceedings 1874, pg 214 (1874 Sept 30), Union Lodge No. 7, Denver
Proceedings 1875, pg 78 (1875 Sept 22), Union Lodge No. 7, Denver
Proceedings 1875, pg 89 (1875 Sept 22), Doric Lodge No. 25, Fairplay
Proceedings 1876, pg 33 (1876 Sept 20), Union Lodge No. 7, Denver

Walker, John Z
Proceedings 1876, pg 42 (1876 Sept 20), Doric Lodge No. 25, Fairplay

Walker, Lewis
Proceedings 1870, pg 77 (1824 Jan 5) African Lodge at Boston

Walker, Thomas C
Proceedings 1874, pg 219 (1874 Sept 30), Columbia Lodge No. 14, Boulder, Boulder County, Apprentice
Proceedings 1875, pg 83 (1875 Sept 22), Columbia Lodge No. 14, Boulder
Proceedings 1876, pg 37 (1876 Sept 20), Columbia Lodge No. 14, Boulder

Walker, Thomas D
Proceedings 1874, pg 219 (1874 Sept 30), Columbia Lodge No. 14, Boulder, Boulder County
Proceedings 1875, pg 83 (1875 Sept 22), Columbia Lodge No. 14, Boulder
Proceedings 1876, pg 37 (1876 Sept 20), Columbia Lodge No. 14, Boulder

Wall, B R
Proceedings 1871, pg 18 (1871 Sept 27), Nevada Lodge No. 4, Bald Mountain, Apprentice
Proceedings 1872, pg 19 (1872 Sept 24), Nevada Lodge No. 4, Bald Mountain, Apprentice
Proceedings 1873, pg 36 (1873 Oct 1), Nevada Lodge No. 4, Nevada, Apprentice
Proceedings 1875, pg 75 (1875 Sept 22), Nevada Lodge No. 4, Nevada, Apprentice

Wall, Beniar R
Proceedings 1876, pg 30 (1876 Sept 20) Nevada Lodge No. 4, Apprentice

Wall, Benias R
Proceedings 1874, pg 210 (1874 Sept 30), Nevada Lodge No. 4, Bald Mountain, Gilpin County, Apprentice

Wallace, Joseph W
Proceedings 1872, pg 21 (1872 Sept 24), Denver Lodge No. 5, Denver
Proceedings 1873, pg 38 (1873 Oct 1), Central Lodge No. 6, Central City
Proceedings 1874, pg 213 (1874 Sept 30), Central Lodge No. 6, Central
Proceedings 1875, pg 77 (1875 Sept 22), Central Lodge No. 6, Central City
Proceedings 1876, pg 32 (1876 Sept 20), Central Lodge No. 6, Central City
Proceedings 1876, pg 50 (1876 Sept 20), Central Lodge No. 6, Central City

Wallace, R B
Proceedings 1872, pg 36 (1872 Sept 24), Ashlar Lodge U D, Colorado Springs

Wallace, William J
Proceedings 1873, pg 44 (1873 Oct 1), Columbia Lodge No. 14, Boulder
Proceedings 1874, pg 219 (1874 Sept 30), Columbia Lodge No. 14, Boulder, Boulder County
Proceedings 1875, pg 83 (1875 Sept 22), Columbia Lodge No. 14, Boulder
Proceedings 1876, pg 37 (1876 Sept 20), Columbia Lodge No. 14, Boulder

Wallace, Wm J
Proceedings 1876, pg 50 (1876 Sept 20), Columbia Lodge No. 14, Boulder

Walley, Stephen
Proceedings 1876, pg 45 (1876 Sept 20) South Pueblo Lodge U D

Wallinford, A M
Proceedings 1861-1869, pg 147 (1865 Nov 7) Golden City Lodge No. 1, Apprentice

Wallingford, A M
Proceedings 1861-1869, pg 131 (1864 Nov 8) Golden City Lodge No. 1, Apprentice
Proceedings 1861-1869, pg 165 (1866 Oct 2) Golden City Lodge No. 1, Apprentice
Proceedings 1861-1869, pg 191 (1867 Oct 8) Golden City Lodge No. 1, Apprentice
Proceedings 1861-1869, pg 221 (1868 Oct 7) Golden City Lodge No. 1, Apprentice
Proceedings 1861-1869, pg 303 (1869 Sept 29) Golden City Lodge No. 1, Apprentice

Walls, B R
Proceedings 1861-1869, pg 192 (1867 Oct 8), Nevada Lodge No. 4, Nevadaville, Apprentice
Proceedings 1861-1869, pg 222 (1868 Oct 7), Nevada Lodge No. 4, Nevadaville, Apprentice

Walls, Benail
Proceedings 1861-1869, pg 112 (1863 Nov 3), Nevada Lodge No. 4, Nevadaville, Apprentice

Walls, Benair
Proceedings 1861-1869, pg 132 (1864 Nov 8), Nevada Lodge No. 4, Nevadaville, Apprentice
Proceedings 1861-1869, pg 148 (1865 Nov 7), Nevada Lodge No. 4, Nevadaville, Apprentice
Proceedings 1861-1869, pg 166 (1866 Oct 2), Nevada Lodge No. 4, Nevadaville, Apprentice

Walsen, Fred
Proceedings 1874, pg 222 (1874 Sept 30), Pueblo Lodge No. 17, Pueblo, Pueblo County
Proceedings 1875, pg 17 (1875 Sept 21) Pueblo Lodge No. 17
Proceedings 1875, pg 19 (1874 Apr), Huerfano Lodge U D, Walsenburg
Proceedings 1875, pg 34 (1875 Sept 22), Huerfano Lodge No. 27, Walsenburg
Proceedings 1875, pg 85 (1875 Sept 22) Pueblo Lodge No. 17
Proceedings 1875, pg 90 (1875 Sept 22), Huerfano Lodge U D, Walsenburg
Proceedings 1876, pg 48 (1876 Sept 20) Pueblo Lodge No. 17, 1876 Feb 10

Walsen, Frederick
Proceedings 1876, pg 43 (1876 Sept 20), Huerfano Lodge No. 27, Walsenburg

Walsh, Lawrence
Proceedings 1870, pg 26 (1870 Sept 28), Washington Lodge No. 12, Georgetown
Proceedings 1871, pg 24 (1871 Sept 27), Washington Lodge No. 12, Georgetown
Proceedings 1872, pg 26 (1872 Sept 24), Washington Lodge No. 12, Georgetown, Dimitted

Walsh, M J
Proceedings 1861-1869, pg 42 (1861 Dec 10), Summit Lodge No. 2, Parkville
Proceedings 1861-1869, pg 111 (1863 Nov 3), Summit Lodge No. 2, Parkville, dimitted

Walsh, Martin J
Proceedings 1861-1869, pg 76 (1862 Nov 4), Summit Lodge No. 2, Parkville

Walshall, Wm T
Proceedings 1874, pg 204 (1874 Sept 30) Grand Lodge of Alabama, Mobile

Walson, Ferd
Proceedings 1871, pg 28 (1871 Sept 27), Pueblo Lodge No. 17, Pueblo, Apprentice

Walter, Scott
Proceedings 1876, pg 48 (1876 Sept 20) Nevada Lodge No. 4, 1876 Jan 8

Walters, A
Proceedings 1861-1869, pg 230 (1868 Oct 7), Cheyenne Lodge U D, Cheyenne, Dakota Territory

Walters, Abraham
Proceedings 1861-1869, pg 312 (1869 Sept 29), Cheyenne Lodge No. 16, Cheyenne
Proceedings 1872, pg 30 (1872 Sept 24), Cheyenne Lodge No. 16, Cheyenne, Wyoming Territory, Dropped from the Rolls

Walters, Richard
Proceedings 1873, pg 42 (1873 Oct 1), Black Hawk Lodge No. 11, Black Hawk
Proceedings 1874, pg 216 (1874 Sept 30), Black Hawk Lodge No. 11, Black Hawk
Proceedings 1875, pg 80 (1875 Sept 22) Black Hawk Lodge No. 11

Walters, William B
Proceedings 1876, pg 35 (1876 Sept 20), Washington Lodge No. 12, Georgetown

Walts, James
Proceedings 1875, pg 84 (1875 Sept 22), Mount Moriah Lodge No. 15, Canon City
Proceedings 1876, pg 38 (1876 Sept 20), Mount Moriah Lodge No. 15, Canon City

Wanlass, Geo F
Proceedings 1861-1869, pg 308 (1869 Sept 29), Union Lodge No. 7, Denver, Apprentice

Wanlass, George F
Proceedings 1870, pg 24 (1870 Sept 28), Union Lodge No. 7, Denver, Apprentice

Wanlass, John
Proceedings 1861-1869, pg 300 (1869 Sept 29), Denver Lodge No 5, living in Laramie
Proceedings 1861-1869, pg 305 (1869 Sept 29) Denver Lodge No. 5
Proceedings 1870, pg 21 (1870 Sept 28), Denver Lodge No. 5, Denver

Wanless, Geo F
Proceedings 1861-1869, pg 226 (1868 Oct 7), Union Lodge No. 7, Denver, Apprentice
Proceedings 1872, pg 23 (1872 Sept 24), Union Lodge No. 7, Denver, Fellowcraft
Proceedings 1873, pg 40 (1873 Oct 1), Union Lodge No. 7, Denver, Fellowcraft
Proceedings 1875, pg 79 (1875 Sept 22), Union Lodge No. 7, Denver, Fellowcraft

Wanless, George F
Proceedings 1871, pg 22 (1871 Sept 27), Union Lodge No. 7, Denver, Apprentice
Proceedings 1874, pg 214 (1874 Sept 30), Union Lodge No. 7, Denver, Fellowcraft
Proceedings 1876, pg 33 (1876 Sept 20), Union Lodge No. 7, Denver, Fellow Craft

Wanless, John
Proceedings 1861-1869, pg 77 (1862 Nov 4) Denver Lodge No. 5
Proceedings 1861-1869, pg 82 (1863 Apr 18) Denver Lodge No. 5
Proceedings 1861-1869, pg 99 (1863 Nov 2) Denver Lodge No. 5, Grand Steward
Proceedings 1861-1869, pg 100 (1863 Nov 3) Grand Steward
Proceedings 1861-1869, pg 112 (1863 Nov 3) Denver Lodge No. 5
Proceedings 1861-1869, pg 116 (1864 Nov 7) Denver Lodge No. 5
Proceedings 1861-1869, pg 123 (1864 Nov 8) Denver Lodge No. 5, Grand Lecturer
Proceedings 1861-1869, pg 123 (1864 Nov 8) Denver Lodge No. 5

Colorado's Territorial Masons

Wanless, John, cont.
   Proceedings 1861-1869, pg 126 (1864 Nov 8) Denver Lodge No. 5
   Proceedings 1861-1869, pg 133 (1864 Nov 8) Denver Lodge No. 5
   Proceedings 1861-1869, pg 140 (1864 Nov 8) warrant
   Proceedings 1861-1869, pg 149 (1865 Nov 7), Nevada Lodge No. 4, Nevadaville
   Proceedings 1861-1869, pg 167 (1866 Oct 2) Denver Lodge No. 5
   Proceedings 1861-1869, pg 193 (1867 Oct 8) Denver Lodge No. 5
   Proceedings 1861-1869, pg 223 (1868 Oct 7) Denver Lodge No. 5
   Proceedings 1871, pg 19 (1871 Sept 27) Denver Lodge No. 5
   Proceedings 1872, pg 20 (1872 Sept 24), Denver Lodge No. 5, Denver
   Proceedings 1873, pg 38 (1873 Oct 1), Denver Lodge No. 5, Denver, Striken from the rolls

Ward, Elijah
   Proceedings 1871, pg 21 (1871 Sept 27), Central Lodge No. 6, Central
   Proceedings 1872, pg 21 (1872 Sept 24), Denver Lodge No. 5, Denver, Dimitted
   Proceedings 1876, pg 35 (1876 Sept 20), Washington Lodge No. 12, Georgetown

Ward, Samuel
   Proceedings 1861-1869, pg 152 (1865 Nov 7), Montana Lodge U D, Virginia City, Montana Territory, Apprentice

Ward, W P
   Proceedings 1874, pg 214 (1874 Sept 30), Union Lodge No. 7, Denver
   Proceedings 1875, pg 78 (1875 Sept 22), Union Lodge No. 7, Denver
   Proceedings 1876, pg 33 (1876 Sept 20), Union Lodge No. 7, Denver
   Proceedings 1876, pg 50 (1876 Sept 20), Union Lodge No. 7, Denver

Warden
   Proceedings 1861-1869, pg 144 (1865 Nov 7) motion

Warden, G S
   Proceedings 1861-1869, pg 105 (1863 Nov 3) motion
   Proceedings 1861-1869, pg 106 (1863 Nov 3) motion failed

Ware
   Proceedings 1861-1869, pg 202 (1868 Oct 6) committee
   Proceedings 1861-1869, pg 210 (1868 Feb 25), Washington Lodge No. 12, Georgetown
   Proceedings 1861-1869, pg 289 (1869 Sept 28) committee
   Proceedings 1870, pg 4 (1870 Sept 27) Grand Treasurer
   Proceedings 1872, pg 4 (1872 Sept 24) Grand Treasurer

Ware, Sampson
   Proceedings 1872, pg 48 (1872 Sept 24), Empire Lodge No. 8, Empire
   Proceedings 1873, pg 41 (1873 Oct 1), Empire Lodge No. 8, Empire, Apprentice
   Proceedings 1874, pg 215 (1874 Sept 30), Empire Lodge No. 8, Empire, Apprentice

Ware, W W
   Proceedings 1861-1869, pg 220 (1868 Oct 7) Grand Steward
   Proceedings 1861-1869, pg 301 (1869 Sept 29), Washington Lodge No. 12, Georgetown
   Proceedings 1861-1869, pg 309 (1869 Sept 29), Washington Lodge No. 12, Georgetown
   Proceedings 1870, pg 4 (1870 Sept 27) Grand Treasurer
   Proceedings 1870, pg 4 (1870 Sept 27) committee
   Proceedings 1870, pg 10 (1870 Sept 27) Grand Treasurer
   Proceedings 1871, pg 4 (1871 Sept 26) Grand Treasurer
   Proceedings 1871, pg 9 (1871 Sept 26) Grand Treasurer
   Proceedings 1871, pg 24 (1871 Sept 27), Washington Lodge No. 12, Georgetown
   Proceedings 1872, pg 5 (1872 Sept 24) committee
   Proceedings 1872, pg 5 (1872 Sept 24) committee
   Proceedings 1872, pg 10 (1872 Sept 24) Grand Treasurer
   Proceedings 1872, pg 15 (1872 Sept 24) committee
   Proceedings 1873, pg 5 (1873 Sept 30) Grand Treasurer
   Proceedings 1873, pg 16 (1873 Oct 1) Grand Treasurer
   Proceedings 1873, pg 32 (1873 Oct 1) mileage and per diem
   Proceedings 1874, pg 5 (1874 Sept 29) Grand Treasurer
   Proceedings 1874, pg 36 (1874 Sept 30) per diem
   Proceedings 1875, pg 15 (1875 Sept 21) Grand Treasurer
   Proceedings 1875, pg 16 (1875 Sept 21) Grand Treasurer
   Proceedings 1875, pg 22 (1875 Sept 21) Grand Treasurer
   Proceedings 1875, pg 24 (1875 Sept 21) donation to the library fund
   Proceedings 1875, pg 37 (1875 Sept 22) per diem
   Proceedings 1876, pg 4 (1876 Sept 19) Grand Treasurer
   Proceedings 1876, pg 11 (1876 Sept 19) Grand Treasurer
   Proceedings 1876, pg 22 (1876 Sept 20) Grand Treasurer

Ware, W Wm
   Proceedings 1861-1869, pg 227 (1868 Oct 7), Washington Lodge No. 12, Georgetown

Ware, William W
   Proceedings 1861-1869, pg 288 (1869 Sept 28), Washington Lodge No. 12, Georgetown
   Proceedings 1871, pg 34 (1871 Sept 27) Grand Treasurer, 1871
   Proceedings 1871, pg 34 (1871 Sept 27) Grand Treasurer, 1870
   Proceedings 1871, pg 34 (1871 Sept 27) Grand Treasurer, 1869
   Proceedings 1872, pg 42 (1872 Sept 24) Grand Treasurer, 1869
   Proceedings 1872, pg 42 (1872 Sept 24) Grand Treasurer, 1870
   Proceedings 1872, pg 42 (1872 Sept 24) Grand Treasurer, 1871-1872
   Proceedings 1873, pg 58 (1873 Oct 1) Grand Treasurer, 1870
   Proceedings 1873, pg 58 (1873 Oct 1) Grand Treasurer, 1871-1872
   Proceedings 1873, pg 58 (1873 Oct 1) Grand Treasurer, 1869

Proceedings 1873, pg 59 (1873 Oct 1) Grand Treasurer, 1873

Proceedings 1874, pg 206 (1874 Sept 30) Grand Treasurer, 1870

Proceedings 1874, pg 206 (1874 Sept 30) Grand Treasurer, 1874

Proceedings 1874, pg 206 (1874 Sept 30) Grand Treasurer, 1869

Proceedings 1874, pg 206 (1874 Sept 30) Grand Treasurer, 1873

Proceedings 1874, pg 206 (1874 Sept 30) Grand Treasurer, 1871

Proceedings 1874, pg 206 (1874 Sept 30) Grand Treasurer, 1872

Proceedings 1875, pg 93 (1875 Sept 22) Grand Treasurer, 1875

Proceedings 1875, pg 93 (1875 Sept 22) Grand Treasurer, 1869

Proceedings 1875, pg 93 (1875 Sept 22) Grand Treasurer, 1872

Proceedings 1875, pg 93 (1875 Sept 22) Grand Treasurer, 1871

Proceedings 1875, pg 93 (1875 Sept 22) Grand Treasurer, 1870

Proceedings 1875, pg 93 (1875 Sept 22) Grand Treasurer, 1873

Proceedings 1875, pg 93 (1875 Sept 22) Grand Treasurer, 1874

Ware, Wm W

Colorado University Cornerstone Laying, pg 3 (1875 Sept 20) Grand Treasurer

Proceedings 1861-1869, pg 179 (1867 Oct 7), Washington Lodge No. 12, Georgetown

Proceedings 1861-1869, pg 202 (1868 Oct 6), Washington Lodge No. 12, Georgetown

Proceedings 1861-1869, pg 287 (1869 Sept 28) Grand Steward

Proceedings 1861-1869, pg 298 (1869 Sept 28) Grand Treasurer

Proceedings 1870, pg cover (1870 Sept 28) Grand Treasurer, Georgetown

Proceedings 1870, pg 3 (1870 Sept 27) Grand Treasurer

Proceedings 1870, pg 13 (1870 Sept 27) Grand Treasurer

Proceedings 1870, pg 16 (1870 Sept 28) Grand Treasurer

Proceedings 1870, pg 26 (1870 Sept 28), Washington Lodge No. 12, Georgetown

Proceedings 1870, pg 32 (1870 Sept 28) Grand Treasurer, 1870

Proceedings 1870, pg 32 (1870 Sept 28) Grand Treasurer, 1869

Proceedings 1871, pg cover (1871 Sept 27) Grand Treasurer, Georgetown

Proceedings 1871, pg 3 (1871 Sept 26) Grand Treasurer

Proceedings 1871, pg 13 (1871 Sept 26) Grand Treasurer

Proceedings 1871, pg 14 (1871 Sept 27) Grand Treasurer

Proceedings 1872, pg cover (1872 Sept 24) Grand Treasurer, Georgetown

Proceedings 1872, pg 3 (1872 Sept 24) Grand Treasurer

Proceedings 1872, pg 4 (1872 Sept 24) Grand Treasurer

Proceedings 1872, pg 16 (1872 Sept 24) Grand Treasurer

Proceedings 1873, pg cover (1873 Oct 1) Grand Treasurer, Georgetown

Proceedings 1873, pg 3 (1873 Sept 30) Grand Treasurer

Proceedings 1873, pg 14 (1873 Sept 30) Grand Treasurer

Proceedings 1874, pg cover (1874 Sept 30) Grand Treasurer, Georgetown

Proceedings 1874, pg 3 (1874 Sept 29) Grand Treasurer

Proceedings 1874, pg 18 (1874 Sept 29) Grand Treasurer

Proceedings 1874, pg 29 (1874 Sept 29) Grand Treasurer

Proceedings 1875, pg cover (1875 Sept 22) Grand Treasurer, Georgetown

Proceedings 1875, pg 30 (1875 Sept 21) Grand Treasurer

Proceedings 1876, pg 3 (1876 Sept 19) Grand Treasurer

Ware, Wm Wallace

Proceedings 1872, pg 12 (1872 Sept 24) Grand Treasurer

Proceedings 1872, pg 25 (1872 Sept 24), Washington Lodge No. 12, Georgetown

Proceedings 1873, pg 42 (1873 Oct 1), Washington Lodge No. 12, Georgetown

Ware, Wm Wallace

Proceedings 1874, pg 217 (1874 Sept 30), Washington Lodge No. 12, Georgetown

Proceedings 1875, pg 81 (1875 Sept 22), Washington Lodge No. 12, Georgetown

Proceedings 1876, pg 35 (1876 Sept 20), Washington Lodge No. 12, Georgetown

Warner, Morgan

Proceedings 1872, pg 30 (1872 Sept 24), Cheyenne Lodge No. 16, Cheyenne, Wyoming Territory, Fellowcraft

Proceedings 1873, pg 46 (1873 Oct 1), Cheyenne Lodge No. 16, Cheyenne, Wyoming Territory

Proceedings 1874, pg 220 (1874 Sept 30), Cheyenne Lodge No. 16, Cheyenne, Wyoming Territory

Warrant, J H

Proceedings 1875, pg 85 (1875 Sept 22) Pueblo Lodge No. 17

Warrant, James H

Proceedings 1861-1869, pg 312 (1869 Sept 29), Pueblo Lodge No. 17, Pueblo, Fellowcraft

Proceedings 1870, pg 30 (1870 Sept 28), Pueblo Lodge No. 17, Pueblo

Proceedings 1871, pg 28 (1871 Sept 27), Pueblo Lodge No. 17, Pueblo

Proceedings 1873, pg 47 (1873 Oct 1), Pueblo Lodge No. 17, Pueblo

Proceedings 1874, pg 223 (1874 Sept 30), Pueblo Lodge No. 17, Pueblo, Pueblo County, Stricken from the rolls

Proceedings 1876, pg 39 (1876 Sept 20) Pueblo Lodge No. 17

Warrant, Jas H

Proceedings 1872, pg 31 (1872 Sept 24), Pueblo Lodge No. 17, Pueblo

Proceedings 1875, pg 85 (1875 Sept 22) Pueblo Lodge No. 17, Reinstated

Warrant, R T

Proceedings 1861-1869, pg 229 (1868 Oct 7), Pueblo Lodge U D, Pueblo

Warrant, R T, cont.
Proceedings 1861-1869, pg 312 (1869 Sept 29), Pueblo Lodge No. 17, Pueblo
Proceedings 1875, pg 85 (1875 Sept 22) Pueblo Lodge No. 17
Proceedings 1876, pg 39 (1876 Sept 20) Pueblo Lodge No. 17

Warrant, Robert T
Proceedings 1870, pg 30 (1870 Sept 28), Pueblo Lodge No. 17, Pueblo
Proceedings 1871, pg 28 (1871 Sept 27), Pueblo Lodge No. 17, Pueblo
Proceedings 1872, pg 31 (1872 Sept 24), Pueblo Lodge No. 17, Pueblo
Proceedings 1873, pg 47 (1873 Oct 1), Pueblo Lodge No. 17, Pueblo
Proceedings 1874, pg 222 (1874 Sept 30), Pueblo Lodge No. 17, Pueblo, Pueblo County

Warren
Proceedings 1870, pg 69 (1869 Sept 8) Provincial Grand Master, of England,

Warren Lodge No. 74 at Ketesville [MO]
Proceedings 1870, pg 85 (1869 Oct 11) refused to conform to the work
Proceedings 1870, pg 86 (1869 Oct 11) charter arrested

Warren, D H
Proceedings 1861-1869, pg 78 (1862 Nov 4), Chivington Lodge No. 6, Central City
Proceedings 1861-1869, pg 113 (1863 Nov 3), Chivington Lodge No. 6, Central City
Proceedings 1861-1869, pg 134 (1864 Nov 8), Chivington Lodge No. 6, Central City
Proceedings 1876, pg 44 (1876 Sept 20), Las Animas Lodge No. 28, Trinidad

Wasatch Lodge No. 8, Salt Lake City
Proceedings 1871, pg 8 (1871 Apr 8) recommended the formation of Argenta Lodge

Wasatch Lodge No. 8, Salt Lake City, Utah Territory
Proceedings 1872, pg 89 (1872 Sept 24), chartered by the Grand Lodge of Montana, 7 Oct 1867

Washburn
Proceedings 1870, pg 42 (1869 Nov 1) Grand Lodge of Arkansas

Washburn, H E
Proceedings 1873, pg 51 (1873 Oct 1), St Vrain Lodge No. 23, Longmont
Proceedings 1874, pg 227 (1874 Sept 30), St Vrain No. 23, Longmont
Proceedings 1876, pg 41 (1876 Sept 20), St Vrain Lodge No. 23, Longmont

Washington Lodge No. 12
Proceedings 1875, pg 25 (1875 Sept 21) dues paid
Proceedings 1875, pg 31 (1875 Sept 21) to pay the expenses of George A Smith
Proceedings 1875, pg 92 (1875 Sept 22)
Proceedings 1876, pg 52 (1876 Sept 20)

Washington Lodge No. 12, Georgetown
Proceedings 1861-1869, pg 206 (1867 Oct 22), Washington Lodge No. 12, Georgetown, dedicated and officers installed
Proceedings 1861-1869, pg 210 (1868 Feb 25) visited
Proceedings 1874, pg 9 (1874 Jan 10) dispensation granted
Proceedings 1874, pg 208 (1874 Sept 30)
Proceedings 1876, pg 12 (1876 Sept 19) warrant paid for money expended for George A Smith
Proceedings 1876, pg 12 (1876 Sept 19) returns received only 15 days before annual communication
Proceedings 1876, pg 13 (1876 Sept 19) dues paid
Proceedings 1876, pg 25 (1876 Sept 20) caring for George A Smith

Washington National Monument
Proceedings 1876, pg 25 (1876 Sept 20) to be given $400

Washington National Monument Association
Proceedings 1876, pg 14 (1876 Sept 19) communication received

Washington National Monument Society
Proceedings 1876, pg 16 (1876 Sept 19), to receive $500 and a 4'x2' block of Colorado granite, inscribed with From Grand Lodge of Masons of Colorado, The Centennial State, A. D. 1876.

Washington, George
Proceedings 1861-1869, pg 245 (1867 Nov 7)

Washman, H E
Proceedings 1872, pg 35 (1872 Sept 24), St Vrain Lodge No. 23, Longmont

Waterman, B C
Proceedings 1861-1869, pg 112 (1863 Nov 3), Nevada Lodge No. 4, Nevadaville, Apprentice
Proceedings 1861-1869, pg 132 (1864 Nov 8), Nevada Lodge No. 4, Nevadaville
Proceedings 1861-1869, pg 148 (1865 Nov 7), Nevada Lodge No. 4, Nevadaville
Proceedings 1861-1869, pg 166 (1866 Oct 2), Nevada Lodge No. 4, Nevadaville
Proceedings 1861-1869, pg 176 (1867 Oct 7), Nevada Lodge No. 4, Nevadaville
Proceedings 1861-1869, pg 191 (1867 Oct 8), Nevada Lodge No. 4, Nevadaville
Proceedings 1861-1869, pg 222 (1868 Oct 7), Nevada Lodge No. 4, Nevadaville
Proceedings 1861-1869, pg 304 (1869 Sept 29), Nevada Lodge No. 4, Nevadaville
Proceedings 1870, pg 20 (1870 Sept 28), Nevada Lodge No. 4, Nevadaville
Proceedings 1871, pg 18 (1871 Sept 27), Nevada Lodge No. 4, Bald Mountain
Proceedings 1872, pg 19 (1872 Sept 24), Nevada Lodge No. 4, Bald Mountain

Waterman, Benoni C
Proceedings 1873, pg 36 (1873 Oct 1), Nevada Lodge No. 4, Nevada, died
Proceedings 1873, pg 57 (1873 Oct 1), Nevada Lodge No. 4, Nevada

Waters, Abraham
Proceedings 1871, pg 27 (1871 Sept 27), Cheyenne Lodge No. 16, Cheyenne, Wyoming Territory

Waters, Abram
Proceedings 1870, pg 29 (1870 Sept 28), Cheyenne Lodge No. 16, Cheyenne, Wyoming Territory

Waters, Ozias P
Proceedings 1872, pg 43 (1872 Sept 24) Muscatine, Grand Lodge of Iowa
Proceedings 1872, pg 64 (1872 Sept 24) Grand Lodge of Iowa
Proceedings 1873, pg 60 (1873 Oct 1) Grand Lodge of Iowa, Muscatine
Proceedings 1874, pg 66 (1874 Sept 30) Grand Lodge of Iowa

Waters, Richard
Proceedings 1871, pg 23 (1871 Sept 27), Black Hawk Lodge No. 11, Black Hawk
Proceedings 1872, pg 25 (1872 Sept 24), Black Hawk Lodge No. 11, Black Hawk

Watkins, Lew
Proceedings 1872, pg 36 (1872 Sept 24), Ashlar Lodge U D, Colorado Springs

Watkins, W L
Proceedings 1873, pg 13 (1873 Sept 30), Ashlar Lodge U D, Colorado Springs
Proceedings 1875, pg 82 (1875 Sept 22), El Paso Lodge No. 13, Colorado Springs

Wats, H C
Proceedings 1873, pg 50 (1873 Oct 1), Occidental Lodge No. 20, Greeley

Watsen, Fred
Proceedings 1873, pg 47 (1873 Oct 1), Pueblo Lodge No. 17, Pueblo

Watson, B F
Proceedings 1876, pg 20 (1876 Sept 20), Past Master of Eureka Lodge No. 39, Springfield, MO

Watson, Ferd
Proceedings 1872, pg 31 (1872 Sept 24), Pueblo Lodge No. 17, Pueblo

Watson, Fred
Proceedings 1872, pg 49 (1872 Sept 24), Pueblo Lodge No. 17, Pueblo

Watson, H C
Proceedings 1872, pg 34 (1872 Sept 24), Occidental Lodge No. 20, Greeley

Watson, Henry C
Proceedings 1874, pg 225 (1874 Sept 30), Occidental Lodge No. 20, Greeley
Proceedings 1875, pg 87 (1875 Sept 22), Occidental Lodge No. 20, Greeley
Proceedings 1876, pg 49 (1876 Sept 20), Occidental Lodge No. 20, Greeley, 1875 Nov 1

Watson, J W
Proceedings 1861-1869, pg 134 (1864 Nov 8), Chivington Lodge No. 6, Central City, Fellowcraft
Proceedings 1861-1869, pg 150 (1865 Nov 7), Chivington Lodge No. 6, Central City
Proceedings 1861-1869, pg 168 (1866 Oct 2), Chivington Lodge No. 6, Central City
Proceedings 1861-1869, pg 179 (1867 Oct 7), Washington Lodge No. 12, Georgetown
Proceedings 1861-1869, pg 194 (1867 Oct 8), Chivington Lodge No. 6, Central City
Proceedings 1861-1869, pg 225 (1868 Oct 7), Chivington Lodge No. 6, Central City, Dimitted
Proceedings 1861-1869, pg 227 (1868 Oct 7), Washington Lodge No. 12, Georgetown

Watson, James H
Proceedings 1876, pg 44 (1876 Sept 20) Del Norte Lodge U D

Watson, William
Proceedings 1861-1869, pg 78 (1862 Nov 4), Chivington Lodge No. 6, Central City
Proceedings 1861-1869, pg 113 (1863 Nov 3), Chivington Lodge No. 6, Central City
Proceedings 1861-1869, pg 134 (1864 Nov 8), Chivington Lodge No. 6, Central City
Proceedings 1872, pg 22 (1872 Sept 24), Denver Lodge No. 5, Denver

Watson, Wm
Proceedings 1861-1869, pg 150 (1865 Nov 7), Chivington Lodge No. 6, Central City
Proceedings 1861-1869, pg 168 (1866 Oct 2), Chivington Lodge No. 6, Central City
Proceedings 1861-1869, pg 194 (1867 Oct 8), Chivington Lodge No. 6, Central City
Proceedings 1861-1869, pg 224 (1868 Oct 7), Chivington Lodge No. 6, Central City
Proceedings 1861-1869, pg 306 (1869 Sept 29), Central Lodge No. 6, Central City
Proceedings 1870, pg 22 (1870 Sept 28), Central Lodge No. 6, Central City
Proceedings 1871, pg 21 (1871 Sept 27), Central Lodge No. 6, Central

Watters, Richard
Proceedings 1876, pg 34 (1876 Sept 20) Black Hawk Lodge No. 11

Waugh, DeWitt C
Proceedings 1861-1869, pg 78 (1862 Nov 4) Denver Lodge No. 5, Apprentice
Proceedings 1861-1869, pg 112 (1863 Nov 3) Denver Lodge No. 5
Proceedings 1861-1869, pg 133 (1864 Nov 8) Denver Lodge No. 5
Proceedings 1861-1869, pg 167 (1866 Oct 2) Denver Lodge No. 5, dimitted

Wearne, John
Proceedings 1874, pg 210 (1874 Sept 30), Nevada Lodge No. 4, Bald Mountain, Gilpin County, Apprentice

Colorado's Territorial Masons

Wearne, John, cont.
Proceedings 1875, pg 75 (1875 Sept 22), Nevada Lodge No. 4, Nevada, Apprentice
Proceedings 1876, pg 30 (1876 Sept 20) Nevada Lodge No. 4, Apprentice

Weaver, J B
Proceedings 1876, pg 45 (1876 Sept 20), King Solomon Lodge U D, West Las Animas

Webb
Proceedings 1870, pg 42 (1869 Nov 1) Grand Lodge of Arkansas

Webb, C O
Proceedings 1874, pg 226 (1874 Sept 30), Weston Lodge No. 22, Littleton
Proceedings 1875, pg 88 (1875 Sept 22), Weston Lodge No. 22, Littleton
Proceedings 1876, pg 41 (1876 Sept 20), Weston Lodge No. 22, Littleton

Webb, H N
Proceedings 1872, pg 28 (1872 Sept 24), Mount Moriah Lodge No. 15, Canon City
Proceedings 1873, pg 45 (1873 Oct 1), Mount Moriah Lodge No. 15, Canon City
Proceedings 1874, pg 220 (1874 Sept 30), Mount Moriah Lodge No. 15, Canon City
Proceedings 1876, pg 38 (1876 Sept 20), Mount Moriah Lodge No. 15, Canon City

Webb, Henry N
Proceedings 1871, pg 26 (1871 Sept 27), Mount Moriah Lodge No. 15, Canon City

Webber, N F
Proceedings 1874, pg 223 (1874 Sept 30), Laramie Lodge No. 18, Laramie City

Webber, N T
Proceedings 1871, pg 29 (1871 Sept 27), Laramie Lodge No. 18, Laramie, Wyoming Territory
Proceedings 1872, pg 32 (1872 Sept 24), Laramie Lodge No. 18, Laramie, Wyoming Territory
Proceedings 1873, pg 48 (1873 Oct 1), Laramie Lodge No. 18, Laramie, Wyoming Territory

Webber, W L
Proceedings 1874, pg 204 (1874 Sept 30) Grand Lodge of Michigan, East Saginaw,

Webster
Proceedings 1873, pg 30 (1873 Oct 1) resolution
Proceedings 1874, pg 29 (1874 Sept 29) Grand Teller

Webster, G W
Proceedings 1861-1869, pg 149 (1865 Nov 7), Nevada Lodge No. 4, Nevadaville, Apprentice
Proceedings 1861-1869, pg 167 (1866 Oct 2) Denver Lodge No. 5
Proceedings 1861-1869, pg 193 (1867 Oct 8) Denver Lodge No. 5
Proceedings 1861-1869, pg 223 (1868 Oct 7) Denver Lodge No. 5
Proceedings 1861-1869, pg 230 (1868 Oct 7), Valmont Lodge U D, Valmont
Proceedings 1861-1869, pg 305 (1869 Sept 29) Denver Lodge No. 5
Proceedings 1870, pg 21 (1870 Sept 28), Denver Lodge No. 5, Denver

Webster, Geo W
Proceedings 1870, pg 27 (1870 Sept 28), Columbia Lodge No. 14, Boulder City
Proceedings 1872, pg 28 (1872 Sept 24), Columbia Lodge No. 14, Boulder
Proceedings 1872, pg 35 (1872 Sept 24), St Vrain Lodge No. 23, Longmont
Proceedings 1873, pg 45 (1873 Oct 1), Columbia Lodge No. 14, Boulder, Dimitted
Proceedings 1873, pg 51 (1873 Oct 1), St Vrain Lodge No. 23, Longmont
Proceedings 1874, pg 227 (1874 Sept 30), St Vrain No. 23, Longmont

Webster, George W
Proceedings 1861-1869, pg 311 (1869 Sept 29), Columbia Lodge No. 14, Boulder City
Proceedings 1871, pg 26 (1871 Sept 27), Columbia Lodge No. 14, Boulder City
Proceedings 1876, pg 41 (1876 Sept 20), St Vrain Lodge No. 23, Longmont

Webster, J W
Proceedings 1861-1869, pg 144 (1865 Nov 7) Tyler
Proceedings 1861-1869, pg 167 (1866 Oct 2) Denver Lodge No. 5
Proceedings 1861-1869, pg 189 (1867 Oct 8) Tyler
Proceedings 1861-1869, pg 190 (1867 Oct 8) Junior Grand Steward
Proceedings 1861-1869, pg 192 (1867 Oct 8) Denver Lodge No. 5
Proceedings 1861-1869, pg 193 (1867 Oct 8) Denver Lodge No. 5
Proceedings 1861-1869, pg 212 (1868 Oct 6) warrant paid
Proceedings 1861-1869, pg 223 (1868 Oct 7) Denver Lodge No. 5
Proceedings 1861-1869, pg 288 (1869 Sept 28) Denver Lodge No 5
Proceedings 1861-1869, pg 304 (1869 Sept 29) Denver Lodge No. 5
Proceedings 1873, pg 6 (1873 Sept 30), Denver Lodge No. 5, Denver
Proceedings 1874, pg 6 (1874 Sept 29) committee
Proceedings 1874, pg 30 (1874 Sept 29) resolution
Proceedings 1874, pg 31 (1874 Sept 29) resolution
Proceedings 1874, pg 34 (1874 Sept 30) committee
Proceedings 1874, pg 34 (1874 Sept 30) resolution
Proceedings 1874, pg 36 (1874 Sept 30) per diem
Proceedings 1876, pg 30 (1876 Sept 20) Denver Lodge No. 5

Webster, John W
Proceedings 1861-1869, pg 175 (1867 Oct 7) Grand Tyler
Proceedings 1870, pg 21 (1870 Sept 28), Denver Lodge No. 5, Denver

Proceedings 1871, pg 19 (1871 Sept 27) Denver Lodge No. 5

Proceedings 1872, pg cover (1872 Sept 24), Denver Chapter No. 2, Denver

Proceedings 1872, pg 20 (1872 Sept 24), Denver Lodge No. 5, Denver

Proceedings 1873, pg cover (1873 Oct 1), Denver Chapter No. 2, Denver

Proceedings 1873, pg 31 (1873 Oct 1) mileage and per diem

Proceedings 1873, pg 37 (1873 Oct 1), Denver Lodge No. 5, Denver

Proceedings 1874, pg cover (1874 Sept 30) committee, Denver

Proceedings 1874, pg 5 (1874 Sept 29), Denver Lodge No. 5, Denver

Proceedings 1874, pg 36 (1874 Sept 30) committee

Proceedings 1874, pg 211 (1874 Sept 30), Denver Lodge No. 5, Denver

Proceedings 1874, pg 211 (1874 Sept 30), Denver Lodge No. 5, Denver

Proceedings 1875, pg 75 (1875 Sept 22) Denver Lodge No. 5

Webster, R C

Proceedings 1874, pg 214 (1874 Sept 30), Union Lodge No. 7, Denver

Proceedings 1875, pg 78 (1875 Sept 22), Union Lodge No. 7, Denver

Proceedings 1876, pg 33 (1876 Sept 20), Union Lodge No. 7, Denver

Webster, S D

Proceedings 1861-1869, pg 229 (1868 Oct 7), Canon Lodge U D, Canon City

Proceedings 1861-1869, pg 288 (1869 Sept 28), Mount Moriah Lodge No. 15, Canon City

Proceedings 1861-1869, pg 311 (1869 Sept 29), Mount Moriah Lodge No. 15, Canon City

Proceedings 1870, pg 28 (1870 Sept 28), Mount Moriah Lodge No. 15, Canon City

Proceedings 1871, pg 26 (1871 Sept 27), Mount Moriah Lodge No. 15, Canon City

Proceedings 1872, pg 28 (1872 Sept 24), Mount Moriah Lodge No. 15, Canon City

Proceedings 1873, pg 45 (1873 Oct 1), Mount Moriah Lodge No. 15, Canon City

Proceedings 1874, pg 220 (1874 Sept 30), Mount Moriah Lodge No. 15, Canon City

Proceedings 1875, pg 84 (1875 Sept 22), Mount Moriah Lodge No. 15, Canon City

Proceedings 1876, pg 38 (1876 Sept 20), Mount Moriah Lodge No. 15, Canon City

Webster, T J

Proceedings 1870, pg 31 (1870 Sept 28), Laramie Lodge No. 18, Laramie, Wyoming Territory, Apprentice

Proceedings 1871, pg 29 (1871 Sept 27), Laramie Lodge No. 18, Laramie, Wyoming Territory

Proceedings 1872, pg 31 (1872 Sept 24), Laramie Lodge No. 18, Laramie, Wyoming Territory

Proceedings 1873, pg 48 (1873 Oct 1), Laramie Lodge No. 18, Laramie, Wyoming Territory

Proceedings 1874, pg 223 (1874 Sept 30), Laramie Lodge No. 18, Laramie City

Wedderburn, Wm

Proceedings 1872, pg 76 (1872 Sept 24) Grand Lodge of New Brunswick

Weed, John

Proceedings 1875, pg 89 (1875 Sept 22), Doric Lodge No. 25, Fairplay

Proceedings 1876, pg 42 (1876 Sept 20), Doric Lodge No. 25, Fairplay

Weeks, N

Proceedings 1873, pg 31 (1873 Oct 1) mileage and per diem

Weeks, Nicholas

Proceedings 1871, pg 28 (1871 Sept 27), Cheyenne Lodge No. 16, Cheyenne, Wyoming Territory, Apprentice

Proceedings 1872, pg 30 (1872 Sept 24), Cheyenne Lodge No. 16, Cheyenne, Wyoming Territory

Proceedings 1873, pg 6 (1873 Sept 30), Cheyenne Lodge No. 16, Cheyenne, Wyoming Territory

Proceedings 1873, pg 46 (1873 Oct 1), Cheyenne Lodge No. 16, Cheyenne, Wyoming Territory

Proceedings 1874, pg 221 (1874 Sept 30), Cheyenne Lodge No. 16, Cheyenne, Wyoming Territory

Weidman, J

Proceedings 1861-1869, pg 150 (1865 Nov 7), Chivington Lodge No. 6, Central City

Proceedings 1861-1869, pg 168 (1866 Oct 2), Chivington Lodge No. 6, Central City

Proceedings 1861-1869, pg 194 (1867 Oct 8), Chivington Lodge No. 6, Central City

Proceedings 1861-1869, pg 224 (1868 Oct 7), Chivington Lodge No. 6, Central City

Weidman, Jacob

Proceedings 1861-1869, pg 113 (1863 Nov 3), Chivington Lodge No. 6, Central City, Apprentice

Proceedings 1861-1869, pg 134 (1864 Nov 8), Chivington Lodge No. 6, Central City

Proceedings 1861-1869, pg 307 (1869 Sept 29), Central Lodge No. 6, Central City, died

Weier, Jerome A

Proceedings 1872, pg 27 (1872 Sept 24), El Paso Lodge No. 13, Colorado City

Weil, H I

Proceedings 1861-1869, pg 306 (1869 Sept 29), Central Lodge No. 6, Central City

Proceedings 1870, pg 25 (1870 Sept 28), Black Hawk Lodge No. 11, Black Hawk

Proceedings 1871, pg 23 (1871 Sept 27), Black Hawk Lodge No. 11, Black Hawk

Weil, H J

Proceedings 1861-1869, pg 224 (1868 Oct 7), Chivington Lodge No. 6, Central City

Weil, Herman I

Proceedings 1872, pg 25 (1872 Sept 24), Black Hawk Lodge No. 11, Black Hawk

Colorado's Territorial Masons

Weil, Herman I, cont.
  Proceedings 1875, pg 77 (1875 Sept 22), Central Lodge No. 6, Central City
  Proceedings 1875, pg 80 (1875 Sept 22) Black Hawk Lodge No. 11, Demitted
  Proceedings 1876, pg 32 (1876 Sept 20), Central Lodge No. 6, Central City

Weil, Hermann J
  Proceedings 1870, pg 23 (1870 Sept 28), Central Lodge No. 6, Central City, Dimitted

Weil, L
  Proceedings 1861-1869, pg 113 (1863 Nov 3), Chivington Lodge No. 6, Central City
  Proceedings 1861-1869, pg 150 (1865 Nov 7), Chivington Lodge No. 6, Central City

Weil, L B
  Proceedings 1861-1869, pg 111 (1863 Nov 3), Nevada Lodge No. 4, Nevadaville, dimitted
  Proceedings 1861-1869, pg 168 (1866 Oct 2), Chivington Lodge No. 6, Central City
  Proceedings 1861-1869, pg 194 (1867 Oct 8), Chivington Lodge No. 6, Central City
  Proceedings 1861-1869, pg 224 (1868 Oct 7), Chivington Lodge No. 6, Central City
  Proceedings 1861-1869, pg 229 (1868 Oct 7), Cheyenne Lodge U D, Cheyenne, Dakota Territory
  Proceedings 1861-1869, pg 300 (1869 Sept 29), Central Lodge No. 6, living in Cheyenne
  Proceedings 1861-1869, pg 306 (1869 Sept 29), Central Lodge No. 6, Central City
  Proceedings 1870, pg 15 (1870 Sept 28) now living at Central City, Cheyenne Lodge No. 16, Cheyenne
  Proceedings 1870, pg 29 (1870 Sept 28), Cheyenne Lodge No. 16, Cheyenne, Wyoming Territory
  Proceedings 1871, pg 28 (1871 Sept 27), Cheyenne Lodge No. 16, Cheyenne, Wyoming Territory, Apprentice

Weil, Leopold
  Proceedings 1861-1869, pg 77 (1862 Nov 4), Nevada Lodge No. 4, Nevadaville

Weil, Leopold B
  Proceedings 1870, pg 23 (1870 Sept 28), Central Lodge No. 6, Central City, Dimitted

Weil, Sol
  Proceedings 1872, pg 25 (1872 Sept 24), Black Hawk Lodge No. 11, Black Hawk, Dimitted

Weil, Solomon
  Proceedings 1871, pg 23 (1871 Sept 27), Black Hawk Lodge No. 11, Black Hawk
  Proceedings 1872, pg 21 (1872 Sept 24), Denver Lodge No. 5, Denver
  Proceedings 1873, pg 39 (1873 Oct 1), Central Lodge No. 6, Central City
  Proceedings 1874, pg 213 (1874 Sept 30), Central Lodge No. 6, Central
  Proceedings 1875, pg 77 (1875 Sept 22), Central Lodge No. 6, Central City
  Proceedings 1876, pg 32 (1876 Sept 20), Central Lodge No. 6, Central City

Weinberger, Nathan
  Proceedings 1875, pg 77 (1875 Sept 22), Central Lodge No. 6, Central City
  Proceedings 1876, pg 32 (1876 Sept 20), Central Lodge No. 6, Central City

Weir, I A
  Proceedings 1875, pg 82 (1875 Sept 22), El Paso Lodge No. 13, Colorado Springs

Weir, J
  Proceedings 1861-1869, pg 196 (1867 Oct 8), El Paso Lodge U D, Colorado City
  Proceedings 1861-1869, pg 228 (1868 Oct 7), El Paso Lodge No. 13, Colorado City

Weir, J A
  Proceedings 1870, pg 27 (1870 Sept 28), El Paso Lodge No. 13, Colorado City
  Proceedings 1873, pg 43 (1873 Oct 1), El Paso Lodge No. 13, Colorado City
  Proceedings 1874, pg 218 (1874 Sept 30), El Paso Lodge No. 13, Colorado Springs

Weir, J B
  Proceedings 1861-1869, pg 310 (1869 Sept 29), El Paso Lodge No. 13, Colorado City

Weir, Jerome A
  Proceedings 1871, pg 25 (1871 Sept 27), El Paso Lodge No. 13, Colorado City

Weis, Robert M
  Proceedings 1870, pg 58 (1870 May 24), Jefferson Lodge No. 104, Grand Lodge of Indiana, murdered on the island of Cuba

Weiss, Henry
  Proceedings 1872, pg 31 (1872 Sept 24), Pueblo Lodge No. 17, Pueblo
  Proceedings 1873, pg 47 (1873 Oct 1), Pueblo Lodge No. 17, Pueblo
  Proceedings 1874, pg 222 (1874 Sept 30), Pueblo Lodge No. 17, Pueblo, Pueblo County
  Proceedings 1875, pg 85 (1875 Sept 22) Pueblo Lodge No. 17
  Proceedings 1876, pg 44 (1876 Sept 20) Del Norte Lodge U D

Weitbrec, B F
  Proceedings 1873, pg 13 (1873 Sept 30), Ashlar Lodge U D, Colorado Springs

Weitbrec, R F
  Proceedings 1873, pg 52 (1873 Oct 1), Ashlar Lodge U D, Colorado Springs
  Proceedings 1874, pg 218 (1874 Sept 30), El Paso Lodge No. 13, Colorado Springs
  Proceedings 1875, pg 82 (1875 Sept 22), El Paso Lodge No. 13, Colorado Springs

Welch, A L
  Proceedings 1872, pg 34 (1872 Sept 24), Occidental Lodge No. 20, Greeley
  Proceedings 1873, pg 50 (1873 Oct 1), Occidental Lodge No. 20, Greeley

Proceedings 1874, pg 225 (1874 Sept 30), Occidental Lodge No. 20, Greeley

Proceedings 1875, pg 87 (1875 Sept 22), Occidental Lodge No. 20, Greeley

Proceedings 1876, pg 40 (1876 Sept 20), Occidental Lodge No. 20, Greeley

Welch, C C

Proceedings 1861-1869, pg 194 (1867 Oct 8), Chivington Lodge No. 6, Central City

Proceedings 1861-1869, pg 224 (1868 Oct 7), Chivington Lodge No. 6, Central City

Proceedings 1861-1869, pg 306 (1869 Sept 29), Central Lodge No. 6, Central City

Proceedings 1870, pg 22 (1870 Sept 28), Central Lodge No. 6, Central City

Proceedings 1871, pg 21 (1871 Sept 27), Central Lodge No. 6, Central

Welch, Charles C

Proceedings 1875, pg 77 (1875 Sept 22), Central Lodge No. 6, Central City

Proceedings 1876, pg 32 (1876 Sept 20), Central Lodge No. 6, Central City

Welch, Chas C

Proceedings 1872, pg 21 (1872 Sept 24), Denver Lodge No. 5, Denver

Proceedings 1873, pg 39 (1873 Oct 1), Central Lodge No. 6, Central City

Proceedings 1874, pg 213 (1874 Sept 30), Central Lodge No. 6, Central

Welch, Frank

Proceedings 1874, pg 204 (1874 Sept 30) Grand Lodge of Nebraska, Norfolk

Welch, William H

Proceedings 1876, pg 38 (1876 Sept 20), Mount Moriah Lodge No. 15, Canon City

Well, Leopold

Proceedings 1861-1869, pg 133 (1864 Nov 8), Chivington Lodge No. 6, Central City

Wellford, B R Jr

Proceedings 1872, pg 44 (1872 Sept 24), Grand Lodge of Virginia

Proceedings 1872, pg 91 (1872 Sept 24) Grand Lodge of Virginia

Proceedings 1873, pg 61 (1873 Oct 1) Grand Lodge of Virginia, Richmond

Proceedings 1874, pg 130 (1874 Sept 30) Grand Lodge of Virginia

Proceedings 1874, pg 205 (1874 Sept 30) Grand Lodge of Virginia, Richmond

Wellman, Luther C

Proceedings 1872, pg 28 (1872 Sept 24), Columbia Lodge No. 14, Boulder

Proceedings 1872, pg 48 (1872 Sept 24), Columbia Lodge No. 14, Boulder

Proceedings 1873, pg 44 (1873 Oct 1), Columbia Lodge No. 14, Boulder

Proceedings 1874, pg 219 (1874 Sept 30), Columbia Lodge No. 14, Boulder, Boulder County

Proceedings 1875, pg 83 (1875 Sept 22), Columbia Lodge No. 14, Boulder

Proceedings 1876, pg 37 (1876 Sept 20), Columbia Lodge No. 14, Boulder

Wellman, S

Proceedings 1874, pg 219 (1874 Sept 30), Columbia Lodge No. 14, Boulder, Boulder County

Wellman, Sylvanus

Proceedings 1870, pg 27 (1870 Sept 28), Columbia Lodge No. 14, Boulder City

Proceedings 1871, pg 26 (1871 Sept 27), Columbia Lodge No. 14, Boulder City

Proceedings 1872, pg 28 (1872 Sept 24), Columbia Lodge No. 14, Boulder

Proceedings 1873, pg 44 (1873 Oct 1), Columbia Lodge No. 14, Boulder

Proceedings 1875, pg 83 (1875 Sept 22), Columbia Lodge No. 14, Boulder

Proceedings 1876, pg 37 (1876 Sept 20), Columbia Lodge No. 14, Boulder

Wells (Collier & Wells)

Proceedings 1861-1869, pg 140 (1864 Nov 8) warrant

Wells, B T

Proceedings 1874, pg 216 (1874 Sept 30), Black Hawk Lodge No. 11, Black Hawk

Proceedings 1875, pg 80 (1875 Sept 22) Black Hawk Lodge No. 11

Proceedings 1876, pg 34 (1876 Sept 20) Black Hawk Lodge No. 11

Wells, F B

Proceedings 1876, pg 34 (1876 Sept 20) Black Hawk Lodge No. 11

Wells, F P

Proceedings 1872, pg 25 (1872 Sept 24), Black Hawk Lodge No. 11, Black Hawk, Apprentice

Wells, Frank B

Proceedings 1873, pg 42 (1873 Oct 1), Black Hawk Lodge No. 11, Black Hawk

Proceedings 1874, pg 216 (1874 Sept 30), Black Hawk Lodge No. 11, Black Hawk

Proceedings 1875, pg 80 (1875 Sept 22) Black Hawk Lodge No. 11

Wells, Geo W

Proceedings 1870, pg 25 (1870 Sept 28), Black Hawk Lodge No. 11, Black Hawk

Proceedings 1871, pg 23 (1871 Sept 27), Black Hawk Lodge No. 11, Black Hawk

Proceedings 1872, pg 25 (1872 Sept 24), Black Hawk Lodge No. 11, Black Hawk

Proceedings 1875, pg 80 (1875 Sept 22) Black Hawk Lodge No. 11

Wells, George W

Proceedings 1873, pg 42 (1873 Oct 1), Black Hawk Lodge No. 11, Black Hawk

Colorado's Territorial Masons

Wells, George W, cont.
   Proceedings 1874, pg 216 (1874 Sept 30), Black Hawk Lodge No. 11, Black Hawk
   Proceedings 1876, pg 34 (1876 Sept 20) Black Hawk Lodge No. 11

Wells, S L
   Proceedings 1873, pg 37 (1873 Oct 1), Denver Lodge No. 5, Denver, Dimitted

Wells, S T
   Proceedings 1861-1869, pg 223 (1868 Oct 7) Denver Lodge No. 5
   Proceedings 1861-1869, pg 305 (1869 Sept 29) Denver Lodge No. 5

Wels, Simon
   Proceedings 1871, pg 19 (1871 Sept 27) Denver Lodge No. 5

Wels, Simon L
   Proceedings 1870, pg 21 (1870 Sept 28), Denver Lodge No. 5, Denver
   Proceedings 1872, pg 20 (1872 Sept 24), Denver Lodge No. 5, Denver

Welton, N W
   Proceedings 1861-1869, pg 151 (1865 Nov 7), Chivington Lodge No. 6, Central City
   Proceedings 1861-1869, pg 169 (1866 Oct 2), Union Lodge No. 7, Denver
   Proceedings 1861-1869, pg 195 (1867 Oct 8), Union Lodge No. 7, Denver
   Proceedings 1861-1869, pg 225 (1868 Oct 7), Union Lodge No. 7, Denver
   Proceedings 1861-1869, pg 307 (1869 Sept 29), Union Lodge No. 7, Denver
   Proceedings 1873, pg 40 (1873 Oct 1), Union Lodge No. 7, Denver, Stricken from the rolls

Welton, Norton W
   Proceedings 1861-1869, pg 134 (1864 Nov 8), Union Lodge No. 7, Denver
   Proceedings 1870, pg 23 (1870 Sept 28), Union Lodge No. 7, Denver
   Proceedings 1871, pg 22 (1871 Sept 27), Union Lodge No. 7, Denver
   Proceedings 1872, pg 23 (1872 Sept 24), Union Lodge No. 7, Denver

Wemott, S S
   Proceedings 1861-1869, pg 43 (1861 Dec 10), Rocky Mountain Lodge No. 3, Gold Hill
   Proceedings 1861-1869, pg 48 (1862 Nov 3), Rocky Mountain Lodge No. 3, Gold Hill

Wendt, Fred
   Proceedings 1874, pg 210 (1874 Sept 30), Nevada Lodge No. 4, Bald Mountain, Gilpin County

Wendt, Frederick
   Proceedings 1875, pg 74 (1875 Sept 22), Nevada Lodge No. 4, Nevada
   Proceedings 1876, pg 30 (1876 Sept 20) Nevada Lodge No. 4

Wentworth, W A
   Proceedings 1870, pg 29 (1870 Sept 28), Cheyenne Lodge No. 16, Cheyenne, Wyoming Territory
   Proceedings 1871, pg 28 (1871 Sept 27), Cheyenne Lodge No. 16, Cheyenne, Wyoming Territory, died
   Proceedings 1871, pg 32 (1871 Sept 27), Cheyenne Lodge No. 16, Cheyenne, Wyoming Territory

Wertzback, J E
   Proceedings 1861-1869, pg 170 (1866 Oct 2), Black Hawk Lodge U D, Black Hawk

Werzebach, J E
   Proceedings 1861-1869, pg 227 (1868 Oct 7), Black Hawk Lodge No. 11, Black Hawk

West
   Proceedings 1874, pg 30 (1874 Sept 29) resolution
   Proceedings 1874, pg 39 (1874 Sept 30) motion
   Proceedings 1875, pg 34 (1875 Sept 22) committee

West, H T
   Proceedings 1871, pg 30 (1871 Sept 27), Occidental Lodge U D, Greeley
   Proceedings 1872, pg 33 (1872 Sept 24), Occidental Lodge No. 20, Greeley
   Proceedings 1874, pg 4 (1874 Sept 29) gave the prayer
   Proceedings 1874, pg 6 (1874 Sept 29), Occidental Lodge No. 20, Greeley
   Proceedings 1874, pg 6 (1874 Sept 29) committee
   Proceedings 1874, pg 29 (1874 Sept 29) committee
   Proceedings 1874, pg 34 (1874 Sept 30) committee
   Proceedings 1874, pg 36 (1874 Sept 30) per diem
   Proceedings 1874, pg 37 (1874 Sept 30) resolution
   Proceedings 1875, pg 28 (1875 Sept 21) committee
   Proceedings 1875, pg 35 (1875 Sept 22) committee
   Proceedings 1875, pg 37 (1875 Sept 22) committee
   Proceedings 1875, pg 87 (1875 Sept 22), Occidental Lodge No. 20, Greeley
   Proceedings 1876, pg 40 (1876 Sept 20), Occidental Lodge No. 20, Greeley

West, Henry T
   Proceedings 1871, pg 15 (1871 Sept 27) Senior Grand Warden
   Proceedings 1873, pg 50 (1873 Oct 1), Occidental Lodge No. 20, Greeley
   Proceedings 1874, pg cover (1874 Sept 30) committee, Greeley
   Proceedings 1874, pg 36 (1874 Sept 30) committee
   Proceedings 1874, pg 225 (1874 Sept 30), Occidental Lodge No. 20, Greeley
   Proceedings 1875, pg cover (1875 Sept 22) committee, Greeley
   Proceedings 1875, pg 38 (1875 Sept 22) per diem

West, S R
   Proceedings 1861-1869, pg 229 (1868 Oct 7), Canon Lodge U D, Canon City
   Proceedings 1861-1869, pg 311 (1869 Sept 29), Mount Moriah Lodge No. 15, Canon City, Dimitted

Westcoat, E C
   Proceedings 1861-1869, pg 151 (1865 Nov 7), Empire Lodge U D, Empire City

Proceedings 1861-1869, pg 170 (1866 Oct 2), Empire Lodge No. 8, Empire City
Proceedings 1861-1869, pg 195 (1867 Oct 8), Empire Lodge No. 8, Empire City
Proceedings 1861-1869, pg 226 (1868 Oct 7), Empire Lodge No. 8, Empire City
Proceedings 1861-1869, pg 308 (1869 Sept 29), Empire Lodge No. 8, Empire City
Proceedings 1870, pg 24 (1870 Sept 28), Empire Lodge No. 8, Empire

Westcoat, Edw C
Proceedings 1873, pg 41 (1873 Oct 1), Empire Lodge No. 8, Empire

Westcoat, Edward C
Proceedings 1872, pg 23 (1872 Sept 24), Empire Lodge No. 8, Empire
Proceedings 1874, pg 215 (1874 Sept 30), Empire Lodge No. 8, Empire

Weston
Proceedings 1861-1869, pg 44 (1862 Nov 3) committee
Proceedings 1861-1869, pg 45 (1862 Nov 3) motion
Proceedings 1861-1869, pg 45 (1862 Nov 3) committee
Proceedings 1861-1869, pg 47 (1862 Nov 3) committee
Proceedings 1861-1869, pg 49 (1862 Nov 3) motion
Proceedings 1861-1869, pg 51 (1862 Nov 4) motion
Proceedings 1861-1869, pg 296 (1869 Sept 28)

Weston Lodge No. 22
Proceedings 1875, pg 23 (1875 Sept 21) has not provided a list of officers
Proceedings 1875, pg 23 (1875 Sept 21) has not made returns
Proceedings 1875, pg 25 (1875 Sept 21) dues paid
Proceedings 1875, pg 34 (1875 Sept 22) have made no returns
Proceedings 1875, pg 92 (1875 Sept 22)
Proceedings 1876, pg 12 (1875 Oct 6) returns received
Proceedings 1876, pg 52 (1876 Sept 20)

Weston Lodge No. 22, Littleton
Proceedings 1872, pg 13 (1872 Sept 24) granted charter
Proceedings 1872, pg 34 (1872 Sept 24) chartered as No. 22 on 1 Mar 1872
Proceedings 1874, pg 208 (1874 Sept 30)
Proceedings 1876, pg 13 (1876 Sept 7) dues paid

[Weston] Lodge U D, Littleton
Proceedings 1872, pg 7 (1872 Sept 24) dispensation given

Weston Lodge U D, Littleton
Proceedings 1872, pg 11 (1872 Sept 24), has made returns, has had 5 initiations
Proceedings 1872, pg 11 (1872 Sept 24) failed to make timely returns

Weston, A
Proceedings 1861-1869, pg 150 (1865 Nov 7), Chivington Lodge No. 6, Central City
Proceedings 1861-1869, pg 194 (1867 Oct 8), Chivington Lodge No. 6, Central City

Weston, Allyn
Proceedings 1861-1869, pg 34 (1861 Dec 10) petition to form a lodge at Central City
Proceedings 1861-1869, pg 38 (1861 Dec 12) Grand Lecturer
Proceedings 1861-1869, pg 44 (1862 Nov 3) Grand Lecturer
Proceedings 1861-1869, pg 45 (1862 Nov 3) committee
Proceedings 1861-1869, pg 46 (1862 Nov 3) Grand Master
Proceedings 1861-1869, pg 49 (1862 Nov 3) committee
Proceedings 1861-1869, pg 50 (1862 Nov 4) committee
Proceedings 1861-1869, pg 51 (1862 Nov 4) Grand Master
Proceedings 1861-1869, pg 55 (1862 Nov 4) Grand Master
Proceedings 1861-1869, pg 78 (1862 Nov 4), Chivington Lodge No. 6, Central City
Proceedings 1861-1869, pg 79 (1863 May 6) Grand Master
Proceedings 1861-1869, pg 80 (1863 May 6) Grand Master
Proceedings 1861-1869, pg 81 (1863 Apr 18) Grand Master
Proceedings 1861-1869, pg 93 (1863 Apr 17) Grand Master
Proceedings 1861-1869, pg 93 (1863 Apr 17) Grand Master
Proceedings 1861-1869, pg 94 (1863 Apr 17) Grand Master
Proceedings 1861-1869, pg 95 (1863 Apr 17) Grand Master
Proceedings 1861-1869, pg 95 (1863 Apr 17) Grand Master
Proceedings 1861-1869, pg 101 (1863 Apr 18) dispensation Montana Lodge
Proceedings 1861-1869, pg 107 (1863 Nov 3) committee
Proceedings 1861-1869, pg 107 (1863 Nov 3) committee
Proceedings 1861-1869, pg 113 (1863 Nov 3), Chivington Lodge No. 6, Central City
Proceedings 1861-1869, pg 134 (1864 Nov 8), Chivington Lodge No. 6, Central City
Proceedings 1861-1869, pg 168 (1866 Oct 2), Chivington Lodge No. 6, Central City
Proceedings 1861-1869, pg 224 (1868 Oct 7), Chivington Lodge No. 6, Central City
Proceedings 1861-1869, pg 295 (1869 Sept 28), Past Grand Master, deceased in Brooklyn, NY on 12 May 1869, buried near his father's home in Massachusetts
Proceedings 1861-1869, pg 299 (1869 Sept 29), Past Grand Master, deceased
Proceedings 1861-1869, pg 307 (1869 Sept 29), Central Lodge No. 6, Central City, died
Proceedings 1861-1869, pg 315 (1869 Sept 29) Grand Master, 1862, deceased
Proceedings 1861-1869, pg 317 (1869 Sept 29) Past Grand Master, 3 Nov 1825-12 May 1869
Proceedings 1861-1869, pg 319 (1869 Sept 29), 3 Nov 1825-12 May 1869, aged 43Y 6M 9D
Proceedings 1870, pg 32 (1870 Sept 28) Grand Master, 1862, deceased
Proceedings 1871, pg 34 (1871 Sept 27) Grand Master, 1862, deceased
Proceedings 1872, pg 42 (1872 Sept 24) Grand Master, 1862, deceased

Colorado's Territorial Masons

Weston, Allyn, cont.
    Proceedings 1873, pg 58 (1873 Oct 1) Grand Master, 1862, deceased
    Proceedings 1874, pg 206 (1874 Sept 30) Grand Master, 1862, deceased
    Proceedings 1875, pg 93 (1875 Sept 22) Grand Master, 1862, Deceased

Weston, F A
    Proceedings 1872, pg 36 (1872 Sept 24), Ashlar Lodge U D, Colorado Springs

Westover, J D
    Proceedings 1861-1869, pg 196 (1867 Oct 8), Black Hawk Lodge No. 11, Black Hawk
    Proceedings 1861-1869, pg 227 (1868 Oct 7), Black Hawk Lodge No. 11, Black Hawk
    Proceedings 1861-1869, pg 309 (1869 Sept 29), Black Hawk Lodge No. 11, Black Hawk
    Proceedings 1870, pg 25 (1870 Sept 28), Black Hawk Lodge No. 11, Black Hawk
    Proceedings 1871, pg 23 (1871 Sept 27), Black Hawk Lodge No. 11, Black Hawk
    Proceedings 1872, pg 25 (1872 Sept 24), Black Hawk Lodge No. 11, Black Hawk
    Proceedings 1876, pg 34 (1876 Sept 20) Black Hawk Lodge No. 11

Westover, Joseph D
    Proceedings 1873, pg 42 (1873 Oct 1), Black Hawk Lodge No. 11, Black Hawk
    Proceedings 1874, pg 216 (1874 Sept 30), Black Hawk Lodge No. 11, Black Hawk
    Proceedings 1875, pg 80 (1875 Sept 22) Black Hawk Lodge No. 11

Whalan, John
    Proceedings 1874, pg 223 (1874 Sept 30), Laramie Lodge No. 18, Laramie City
    Proceedings 1873, pg 48 (1873 Oct 1), Laramie Lodge No. 18, Laramie, Wyoming Territory

Wharton, Joseph J
    Proceedings 1873, pg 44 (1873 Oct 1), Columbia Lodge No. 14, Boulder
    Proceedings 1874, pg 219 (1874 Sept 30), Columbia Lodge No. 14, Boulder, Boulder County
    Proceedings 1875, pg 83 (1875 Sept 22), Columbia Lodge No. 14, Boulder
    Proceedings 1876, pg 37 (1876 Sept 20), Columbia Lodge No. 14, Boulder

Whedbee, Benj T
    Proceedings 1872, pg 33 (1872 Sept 24), Collins Lodge No. 19, Fort Collins

Whedbee, Benjamin T
    Proceedings 1873, pg 49 (1873 Oct 1), Collins Lodge No. 19, Fort Collins
    Proceedings 1874, pg 224 (1874 Sept 30), Collins Lodge No. 19, Fort Collins, Larimer County
    Proceedings 1875, pg 86 (1875 Sept 22), Collins Lodge No. 19, Fort Collins
    Proceedings 1876, pg 39 (1876 Sept 20), Collins Lodge No. 19, Fort Collins

Wheeler
    Proceedings 1874, pg 51 (1874 Sept 30) Grand Lodge of Connecticut

Wheeler, A J
    Proceedings 1874, pg 19 (1874 Sept 29), of Memphis, TN
    Proceedings 1874, pg 73 (1874 Sept 30) Grand Lodge of Kentucky

Wheeler, B A
    Proceedings 1876, pg 5 (1876 Sept 19), Union Lodge No. 7, Denver

Wheeler, Byron A
    Proceedings 1874, pg 214 (1874 Sept 30), Union Lodge No. 7, Denver
    Proceedings 1875, pg 78 (1875 Sept 22), Union Lodge No. 7, Denver
    Proceedings 1876, pg 32 (1876 Sept 20), Union Lodge No. 7, Denver

Wheeler, C S
    Proceedings 1861-1869, pg 305 (1869 Sept 29) Denver Lodge No. 5, Apprentice

Wheeler, Charles B
    Proceedings 1874, pg 11 (1874 Aug 11) Grand Representative to the Grand East of Louisiana
    Proceedings 1874, pg 207 (1874 Sept 30) Grand Lodge of Louisiana, New Orleans
    Proceedings 1875, pg 95 (1875 Sept 22) Grand Lodge of Louisiana, New Orleans, LA
    Proceedings 1876, pg 53 (1876 Sept 20) Grand Lodge of Louisiana, of Bastrop, LA

Wheeler, Chas S
    Proceedings 1861-1869, pg 193 (1867 Oct 8) Denver Lodge No. 5, Apprentice
    Proceedings 1861-1869, pg 223 (1868 Oct 7) Denver Lodge No. 5, Apprentice

Wheeler, J K
    Proceedings 1870, pg 50 (1870 May 11) Grand Secretary, Grand Lodge of Connecticut

Wheeler, Jas K
    Proceedings 1874, pg 204 (1874 Sept 30) Grand Lodge of Connecticut, Hartford

Wheeler, Joseph K
    Proceedings 1861-1869, pg 242 (1867 May 8), Grand Secretary, Grand Lodge of Connecticut
    Proceedings 1861-1869, pg 316 (1869 Sept 29) Grand Lodge of Connecticut
    Proceedings 1861-1869, pg 325 (1869 May 12) Grand Secretary, Grand Lodge of Connecticut
    Proceedings 1870, pg 34 (1870 Sept 28) Grand Secretary, Grand Lodge of Connecticut
    Proceedings 1871, pg 35 (1871 Sept 27) Grand Secretary, Grand Lodge of Connecticut
    Proceedings 1872, pg 57 (1872 Sept 24) Grand Lodge of Connecticut
    Proceedings 1874, pg 50 (1874 Sept 30) Grand Lodge of Connecticut
    Proceedings 1875, pg 96 (1875 Sept 22) Grand Lodge of Connecticut, Hartford

Proceedings 1876, pg 54 (1876 Sept 20) Grand Lodge of Connecticut, Hartford

Wheeler, Joseph R
Proceedings 1872, pg 43 (1872 Sept 24) Hartford, Grand Lodge of Connecticut
Proceedings 1873, pg 60 (1873 Oct 1) Grand Lodge of Connecticut, Hartford

Whidbee, Benj T
Proceedings 1870, pg 31 (1870 Sept 28), Collins Lodge No. 19, Fort Collins

Whipple, L
Proceedings 1872, pg 36 (1872 Sept 24), Ashlar Lodge U D, Colorado Springs
Proceedings 1873, pg 13 (1873 Sept 30), Ashlar Lodge U D, Colorado Springs

Whipple, Lewis
Proceedings 1875, pg 82 (1875 Sept 22), El Paso Lodge No. 13, Colorado Springs

Whipple, Louis
Proceedings 1871, pg 30 (1871 Sept 27), Occidental Lodge U D, Greeley

Whitaker, C J
Proceedings 1861-1869, pg 169 (1866 Oct 2), Chivington Lodge No. 6, Central City, Apprentice
Proceedings 1861-1869, pg 194 (1867 Oct 8), Chivington Lodge No. 6, Central City, Apprentice
Proceedings 1861-1869, pg 225 (1868 Oct 7), Chivington Lodge No. 6, Central City, Apprentice
Proceedings 1861-1869, pg 307 (1869 Sept 29), Central Lodge No. 6, Central City, Apprentice

Whitaker, Clem J
Proceedings 1874, pg 213 (1874 Sept 30), Central Lodge No. 6, Central, Apprentice

Whitaker, Clement J
Proceedings 1871, pg 21 (1871 Sept 27), Central Lodge No. 6, Central, Apprentice
Proceedings 1873, pg 39 (1873 Oct 1), Central Lodge No. 6, Central City, Apprentice
Proceedings 1875, pg 77 (1875 Sept 22), Central Lodge No. 6, Central City, Apprentice
Proceedings 1876, pg 32 (1876 Sept 20), Central Lodge No. 6, Central City, Apprentice

Whitcomb, Edwin W
Proceedings 1871, pg 30 (1871 Sept 27), Collins Lodge No. 19, Fort Collins
Proceedings 1872, pg 33 (1872 Sept 24), Collins Lodge No. 19, Fort Collins
Proceedings 1873, pg 49 (1873 Oct 1), Collins Lodge No. 19, Fort Collins
Proceedings 1874, pg 224 (1874 Sept 30), Collins Lodge No. 19, Fort Collins, Larimer County
Proceedings 1875, pg 86 (1875 Sept 22), Collins Lodge No. 19, Fort Collins
Proceedings 1876, pg 39 (1876 Sept 20), Collins Lodge No. 19, Fort Collins

White
Proceedings 1861-1869, pg 37 (1861 Dec 12) motion
Proceedings 1861-1869, pg 38 (1861 Dec 12) motion
Proceedings 1861-1869, pg 47 (1862 Nov 3) committee
Proceedings 1861-1869, pg 50 (1862 Nov 4) motion
Proceedings 1861-1869, pg 123 (1864 Nov 8) absent
Proceedings 1872, pg 93 (1872 Sept 24) Grand Lodge of West Virginia

White, C M
Proceedings 1861-1869, pg 107 (1863 Nov 3) committee

White, Eben
Proceedings 1873, pg 51 (1873 Oct 1), St Vrain Lodge No. 23, Longmont
Proceedings 1874, pg 227 (1874 Sept 30), St Vrain No. 23, Longmont
Proceedings 1876, pg 41 (1876 Sept 20), St Vrain Lodge No. 23, Longmont

White, G G
Proceedings 1875, pg 73 (1875 Sept 22) Golden City Lodge No. 1

White, George G
Proceedings 1876, pg 29 (1876 Sept 20) Golden City Lodge No. 1

White, Henry
Proceedings 1861-1869, pg 170 (1866 Oct 2), El Paso U D, Colorado City
Proceedings 1861-1869, pg 196 (1867 Oct 8), El Paso Lodge U D, Colorado City
Proceedings 1861-1869, pg 228 (1868 Oct 7), El Paso Lodge No. 13, Colorado City

White, J T
Proceedings 1861-1869, pg 144 (1865 Nov 7), Chivington Lodge No. 6, Central City
Proceedings 1861-1869, pg 150 (1865 Nov 7), Chivington Lodge No. 6, Central City
Proceedings 1861-1869, pg 159 (1866 Oct 1) warrant
Proceedings 1861-1869, pg 168 (1866 Oct 2), Chivington Lodge No. 6, Central City
Proceedings 1861-1869, pg 182 (1867 Oct 7) warrant paid
Proceedings 1861-1869, pg 194 (1867 Oct 8), Chivington Lodge No. 6, Central City
Proceedings 1861-1869, pg 210 (1868 Feb 25), Washington Lodge No. 12, Georgetown
Proceedings 1861-1869, pg 306 (1869 Sept 29), Central Lodge No. 6, Central City
Proceedings 1870, pg 22 (1870 Sept 28), Central Lodge No. 6, Central City

White, James F
Proceedings 1861-1869, pg 137 (1865 Nov 6), Chivington Lodge No. 6, Central City

White, James L
Proceedings 1871, pg 30 (1871 Sept 27), Occidental Lodge U D, Greeley

White, James T
Proceedings 1861-1869, pg 78 (1862 Nov 4), Chivington Lodge No. 6, Central City, Fellowcraft

White, James T, cont.
- Proceedings 1861-1869, pg 99 (1863 Nov 2), Chivington Lodge No. 6, Central City, Grand Senior Deacon
- Proceedings 1861-1869, pg 116 (1864 Nov 7) Senior Grand Deacon
- Proceedings 1861-1869, pg 116 (1864 Nov 7), Chivington Lodge No. 6, Central City
- Proceedings 1861-1869, pg 133 (1864 Nov 8), Chivington Lodge No. 6, Central City
- Proceedings 1861-1869, pg 141 (1865 Nov 7) Teller
- Proceedings 1861-1869, pg 145 (1865 Nov 7), Chivington Lodge No. 6, Central City, Grand Marshal
- Proceedings 1861-1869, pg 162 (1866 Oct 2) Junior Grand Warden
- Proceedings 1871, pg 20 (1871 Sept 27), Central Lodge No. 6, Central
- Proceedings 1871, pg 34 (1871 Sept 27) Junior Grand Warden, 1865
- Proceedings 1872, pg 21 (1872 Sept 24), Denver Lodge No. 5, Denver
- Proceedings 1872, pg 42 (1872 Sept 24) Junior Grand Warden, 1865
- Proceedings 1873, pg 38 (1873 Oct 1), Central Lodge No. 6, Central City
- Proceedings 1873, pg 58 (1873 Oct 1) Junior Grand Warden, 1865
- Proceedings 1874, pg 206 (1874 Sept 30) Junior Grand Warden, 1865
- Proceedings 1874, pg 212 (1874 Sept 30), Central Lodge No. 6, Central
- Proceedings 1875, pg 76 (1875 Sept 22), Central Lodge No. 6, Central City
- Proceedings 1875, pg 93 (1875 Sept 22) Junior Grand Warden, 1865
- Proceedings 1876, pg 31 (1876 Sept 20), Central Lodge No. 6, Central City

White, Jas T
- Proceedings 1861-1869, pg 113 (1863 Nov 3), Chivington Lodge No. 6, Central City
- Proceedings 1861-1869, pg 122 (1864 Nov 8) committee
- Proceedings 1861-1869, pg 125 (1864 Nov 8) committee
- Proceedings 1861-1869, pg 141 (1865 Nov 7), Chivington Lodge No. 6, Central City
- Proceedings 1861-1869, pg 153 (1866 Oct 1) Junior Grand Warden
- Proceedings 1861-1869, pg 154 (1866 Oct 1) committee
- Proceedings 1861-1869, pg 154 (1866 Oct 1) committee
- Proceedings 1861-1869, pg 154 (1866 Oct 1) Junior Grand Warden
- Proceedings 1861-1869, pg 155 (1866 Oct 1) committee
- Proceedings 1861-1869, pg 162 (1866 Oct 2) committee
- Proceedings 1861-1869, pg 224 (1868 Oct 7), Chivington Lodge No. 6, Central City
- Proceedings 1861-1869, pg 315 (1869 Sept 29) Junior Grand Warden, 1865
- Proceedings 1870, pg 32 (1870 Sept 28) Junior Grand Warden, 1865

White, John A
- Proceedings 1876, pg 44 (1876 Sept 20) Del Norte Lodge U D

White, M C
- Proceedings 1861-1869, pg 31 (1861 Dec 10) Senior Grand Warden
- Proceedings 1861-1869, pg 31 (1861 Dec 10) committee
- Proceedings 1861-1869, pg 32 (1861 Dec 10) committee
- Proceedings 1861-1869, pg 32 (1861 Dec 10), Summit Lodge No 7, Parkville
- Proceedings 1861-1869, pg 33 (1861 Dec 10) committee
- Proceedings 1861-1869, pg 36 (1861 Dec 12) Junior Grand Warden
- Proceedings 1861-1869, pg 39 (1861 Dec 12) chairman
- Proceedings 1861-1869, pg 42 (1861 Dec 10), Summit Lodge No. 2, Parkville
- Proceedings 1861-1869, pg 44 (1862 Nov 3) Junior Grand Warden
- Proceedings 1861-1869, pg 45 (1862 Nov 3), Summit Lodge No. 2, Parkville
- Proceedings 1861-1869, pg 46 (1862 Nov 3) Deputy Grand Master
- Proceedings 1861-1869, pg 49 (1862 Nov 3) committee
- Proceedings 1861-1869, pg 50 (1862 Nov 4) committee
- Proceedings 1861-1869, pg 51 (1862 Nov 4) Deputy Grand Master
- Proceedings 1861-1869, pg 54 (1862 Nov 4) installed
- Proceedings 1861-1869, pg 76 (1862 Nov 4), Summit Lodge No. 2, Parkville
- Proceedings 1861-1869, pg 97 (1863 Nov 2) Grand Master
- Proceedings 1861-1869, pg 98 (1863 Nov 2) Deputy Grand Master
- Proceedings 1861-1869, pg 100 (1863 Nov 3) Deputy Grand Master
- Proceedings 1861-1869, pg 100 (1863 Nov 3) Past Grand Master
- Proceedings 1861-1869, pg 101 (1863 Nov 3) Deputy Grand Master
- Proceedings 1861-1869, pg 102 (1863 Nov 3) petition for formation of a new lodge in Denver
- Proceedings 1861-1869, pg 103 (1863 Nov 3) Deputy Grand Master
- Proceedings 1861-1869, pg 107 (1863 Nov 3) motion
- Proceedings 1861-1869, pg 110 (1863 Nov 3), Summit Lodge No. 2, Parkville
- Proceedings 1861-1869, pg 116 (1864 Nov 7), Union Lodge No. 7, Denver
- Proceedings 1861-1869, pg 116 (1864 Nov 7) Past Deputy Grand Master
- Proceedings 1861-1869, pg 117 (1864 Nov 7) committee
- Proceedings 1861-1869, pg 117 (1864 Nov 7) motion
- Proceedings 1861-1869, pg 117 (1864 Nov 7) motion
- Proceedings 1861-1869, pg 118 (1864 Nov 8) Teller
- Proceedings 1861-1869, pg 119 (1863 Nov 3) warrant drawn
- Proceedings 1861-1869, pg 126 (1864 Nov 8) Past Deputy Grand Master
- Proceedings 1861-1869, pg 134 (1864 Nov 8), Union Lodge No. 7, Denver
- Proceedings 1861-1869, pg 140 (1864 Nov 8) warrant
- Proceedings 1861-1869, pg 151 (1865 Nov 7), Chivington Lodge No. 6, Central City, dimitted
- Proceedings 1861-1869, pg 315 (1869 Sept 29) Junior Grand Warden, December 1861, Dimitted

Proceedings 1861-1869, pg 315 (1869 Sept 29) Deputy Grand Master, 1862, Dimitted

Proceedings 1870, pg 32 (1870 Sept 28) Deputy Grand Master, 1862, Dimitted

Proceedings 1870, pg 32 (1870 Sept 28) Junior Grand Warden, December 1861, Dimitted

Proceedings 1871, pg 34 (1871 Sept 27) Deputy Grand Master, 1862, Dimitted

Proceedings 1871, pg 34 (1871 Sept 27) Junior Grand Warden, Dec 1861, Dimitted

Proceedings 1872, pg 42 (1872 Sept 24) Deputy Grand Master, 1862, Dimitted

Proceedings 1872, pg 42 (1872 Sept 24) Junior Grand Warden, December 1861, Dimitted

Proceedings 1873, pg 58 (1873 Oct 1) Junior Grand Warden, Dec 1861, Dimitted

Proceedings 1873, pg 58 (1873 Oct 1) Deputy Grand Master, 1862, Dimitted

White, Marcus C

Proceedings 1874, pg 206 (1874 Sept 30) Deputy Grand Master, 1862, demitted

Proceedings 1874, pg 206 (1874 Sept 30) Junior Grand Warden, Dec 1861, demitted

Proceedings 1875, pg 93 (1875 Sept 22) Deputy Grand Master, 1862, Demitted

Proceedings 1875, pg 93 (1875 Sept 22) Junior Grand Warden, Dec 1861, Demitted

White, Mark C

Proceedings 1861-1869, pg 116 (1864 Nov 7), Union Lodge No. 7, Denver

White, Robert

Proceedings 1870, pg 106 (1869 Nov 9) Senior Grand Warden, Grand Lodge of West Virginia

Proceedings 1872, pg 92 (1872 Sept 24) Grand Lodge of West Virginia

White, William

Proceedings 1876, pg 29 (1876 Sept 20) Golden City Lodge No. 1

White, Wm

Proceedings 1875, pg 73 (1875 Sept 22) Golden City Lodge No. 1, Apprentice,

Whitehead

Proceedings 1861-1869, pg 273 (1867 Jan 16), Grand Master, Grand Lodge of New Jersey

Whitehead, A H

Proceedings 1861-1869, pg 150 (1865 Nov 7), Chivington Lodge No. 6, Central City

Proceedings 1861-1869, pg 168 (1866 Oct 2), Chivington Lodge No. 6, Central City

Proceedings 1861-1869, pg 194 (1867 Oct 8), Chivington Lodge No. 6, Central City

Proceedings 1861-1869, pg 224 (1868 Oct 7), Chivington Lodge No. 6, Central City

Proceedings 1861-1869, pg 306 (1869 Sept 29), Central Lodge No. 6, Central City

Proceedings 1870, pg 22 (1870 Sept 28), Central Lodge No. 6, Central City

Proceedings 1871, pg 21 (1871 Sept 27), Central Lodge No. 6, Central

Proceedings 1872, pg 21 (1872 Sept 24), Denver Lodge No. 5, Denver

Proceedings 1873, pg 39 (1873 Oct 1), Central Lodge No. 6, Central City

Proceedings 1874, pg 213 (1874 Sept 30), Central Lodge No. 6, Central

Proceedings 1875, pg 77 (1875 Sept 22), Central Lodge No. 6, Central City

Proceedings 1876, pg 32 (1876 Sept 20), Central Lodge No. 6, Central City

Proceedings 1876, pg 50 (1876 Sept 20), Central Lodge No. 6, Central City

Whitehead, Aug H

Proceedings 1861-1869, pg 134 (1864 Nov 8), Chivington Lodge No. 6, Central City

Whitehead, Silas

Proceedings 1861-1869, pg 272 (1867 Jan 16), Grand Master, Grand Lodge of New Jersey

Proceedings 1861-1869, pg 274 (1867 Jan 16), Grand Master, Grand Lodge of New Jersey

Whiteley, Simeon

Proceedings 1861-1869, pg 169 (1866 Oct 2), Union Lodge No. 7, Denver, demitted

Proceedings 1861-1869, pg 151 (1865 Nov 7), Chivington Lodge No. 6, Central City

Whitford, B C

Proceedings 1871, pg 30 (1871 Sept 27), Occidental Lodge U D, Greeley

Whitford, Corydon A

Proceedings 1873, pg 43 (1873 Oct 1), Washington Lodge No. 12, Georgetown

Proceedings 1874, pg 217 (1874 Sept 30), Washington Lodge No. 12, Georgetown

Proceedings 1875, pg 81 (1875 Sept 22), Washington Lodge No. 12, Georgetown

Proceedings 1876, pg 35 (1876 Sept 20), Washington Lodge No. 12, Georgetown

Proceedings 1876, pg 50 (1876 Sept 20), Washington Lodge No. 12, Georgetown

Proceedings 1872, pg 26 (1872 Sept 24), Washington Lodge No. 12, Georgetown

Whiting, C G W

Proceedings 1861-1869, pg 76 (1862 Nov 4), Summit Lodge No. 2, Parkville, dimitted

Whiting, D G W

Proceedings 1873, pg 40 (1873 Oct 1), Union Lodge No. 7, Denver

Proceedings 1874, pg 214 (1874 Sept 30), Union Lodge No. 7, Denver

Proceedings 1875, pg 78 (1875 Sept 22), Union Lodge No. 7, Denver

Proceedings 1876, pg 48 (1876 Sept 20), Union Lodge No. 7, Denver, 1876 Aug 26

Colorado's Territorial Masons

Whiting, George C
Proceedings 1861-1869, pg 244 (1867 Sept 4), Grand Master, Grand Lodge of District of Columbia, deceased

Whiting, George Carlyle
Proceedings 1861-1869, pg 264 (1868 Oct 22), Grand Master, Grand Lodge of District of Columbia, deceased

Whitley, Simeon
Proceedings 1861-1869, pg 134 (1864 Nov 8), Union Lodge No. 7, Denver

Whitman, B N
Proceedings 1876, pg 43 (1876 Sept 20), Huerfano Lodge No. 27, Walsenburg

Whitman, George
Proceedings 1874, pg 220 (1874 Sept 30), Mount Moriah Lodge No. 15, Canon City
Proceedings 1875, pg 84 (1875 Sept 22), Mount Moriah Lodge No. 15, Canon City
Proceedings 1876, pg 38 (1876 Sept 20), Mount Moriah Lodge No. 15, Canon City

Whitney, F S
Proceedings 1871, pg 27 (1871 Sept 27), Cheyenne Lodge No. 16, Cheyenne, Wyoming Territory
Proceedings 1874, pg 220 (1874 Sept 30), Cheyenne Lodge No. 16, Cheyenne, Wyoming Territory

Whitney, Frank L
Proceedings 1870, pg 29 (1870 Sept 28), Cheyenne Lodge No. 16, Cheyenne, Wyoming Territory

Whitney, Frank S
Proceedings 1872, pg 30 (1872 Sept 24), Cheyenne Lodge No. 16, Cheyenne, Wyoming Territory

Whitney, H T
Proceedings 1874, pg 229 (1874 Sept 30), Idaho Springs Lodge U D, Idaho Springs

Whittaker, Clement J
Proceedings 1872, pg 21 (1872 Sept 24), Denver Lodge No. 5, Denver, Apprentice

Whittaker, O J
Proceedings 1870, pg 22 (1870 Sept 28), Central Lodge No. 6, Central City, Apprentice

Whittalsey, Charles H
Proceedings 1872, pg 39 (1872 Sept 24), Cheyenne Lodge No. 16, Cheyenne, Wyoming Territory

Whittelsey, C H
Proceedings 1871, pg 27 (1871 Sept 27), Cheyenne Lodge No. 16, Cheyenne, Wyoming Territory

Whittelsey, Charles H
Proceedings 1872, pg 30 (1872 Sept 24), Cheyenne Lodge No. 16, Cheyenne, Wyoming Territory, died

Whittelsey, Chas H
Proceedings 1861-1869, pg 312 (1869 Sept 29), Cheyenne Lodge No. 16, Cheyenne

Whittemore
Proceedings 1861-1869, pg 44 (1862 Nov 3) committee
Proceedings 1861-1869, pg 51 (1862 Nov 4) motion
Proceedings 1861-1869, pg 80 (1863 May 6) committee
Proceedings 1861-1869, pg 93 (1863 Apr 17) motion
Proceedings 1861-1869, pg 106 (1863 Nov 3) resolution
Proceedings 1861-1869, pg 106 (1863 Nov 3) resolution
Proceedings 1861-1869, pg 140 (1865 Nov 6) motion
Proceedings 1861-1869, pg 161 (1866 Oct 2) motion
Proceedings 1861-1869, pg 177 (1866 Nov 17) communication received
Proceedings 1861-1869, pg 182 (1867 Oct 7) committee
Proceedings 1861-1869, pg 184 (1867 Oct 7) committee
Proceedings 1861-1869, pg 217 (1868 Oct 7) resolution
Proceedings 1861-1869, pg 218 (1868 Oct 7) resolution
Proceedings 1861-1869, pg 288 (1869 Sept 28) opened with prayer
Proceedings 1861-1869, pg 288 (1869 Sept 28) committee
Proceedings 1861-1869, pg 289 (1869 Sept 28) committee
Proceedings 1861-1869, pg 290 (1869 Sept 28) resolution
Proceedings 1861-1869, pg 297 (1869 Sept 28) resolution
Proceedings 1861-1869, pg 298 (1869 Sept 28) Past Grand Master
Proceedings 1861-1869, pg 299 (1869 Sept 29) Grand Marshal
Proceedings 1861-1869, pg 301 (1869 Sept 29) resolution
Proceedings 1870, pg 7 (1870 June 24) permission to lay a cornerstone at the Denver Pacific Railway depot at Denver
Proceedings 1871, pg 6 (1861 Aug 2) the only member from the original Grand Lodge still in the Territory
Proceedings 1871, pg 6 (1861 Dec 10) Grand Secretary
Proceedings 1876, pg 25 (1876 Sept 20) motion

Whittemore, B M
Proceedings 1873, pg 37 (1873 Oct 1), Denver Lodge No. 5, Denver
Proceedings 1874, pg 212 (1874 Sept 30), Denver Lodge No. 5, Denver
Proceedings 1875, pg 76 (1875 Sept 22) Denver Lodge No. 5
Proceedings 1876, pg 49 (1876 Sept 20) Denver Lodge No. 5, 1876 Aug 19
Proceedings 1872, pg 20 (1872 Sept 24), Denver Lodge No. 5, Denver

Whittemore, O A
Proceedings 1861-1869, pg 3 (1861 Aug 2), Summit Lodge No 7, Parkville
Proceedings 1861-1869, pg 5 (1861 Aug 2) Grand Secretary, Parkville
Proceedings 1861-1869, pg 5 (1861 Aug 2) Grand Secretary
Proceedings 1861-1869, pg 5 (1861 Aug 2), Summit Lodge No 7, Parkville
Proceedings 1861-1869, pg 7 (1861 Aug 3) Grand Secretary
Proceedings 1861-1869, pg 31 (1861 Dec 10) committee
Proceedings 1861-1869, pg 31 (1861 Dec 10) Grand Secretary
Proceedings 1861-1869, pg 32 (1861 Dec 10) committee
Proceedings 1861-1869, pg 33 (1861 Dec 10) committee
Proceedings 1861-1869, pg 34 (1861 Dec 10) committee
Proceedings 1861-1869, pg 36 (1861 Dec 12) Grand Secretary

Whittemore, O A, cont.
- Proceedings 1861-1869, pg 37 (1861 Dec 12) motion
- Proceedings 1861-1869, pg 41 (1861 Dec 12) Grand Secretary
- Proceedings 1861-1869, pg 41 (1861 Dec 12), Summit Lodge No. 2, Parkville
- Proceedings 1861-1869, pg 42 (1861 Dec 10), Summit Lodge No. 2, Parkville
- Proceedings 1861-1869, pg 44 (1862 Nov 3) Grand Secretary
- Proceedings 1861-1869, pg 45 (1862 Nov 3) committee
- Proceedings 1861-1869, pg 45 (1862 Nov 3) committee
- Proceedings 1861-1869, pg 46 (1862 Nov 3) Grand Secretary
- Proceedings 1861-1869, pg 49 (1862 Nov 3) committee
- Proceedings 1861-1869, pg 50 (1862 Nov 4) committee
- Proceedings 1861-1869, pg 51 (1862 Nov 4) Grand Secretary
- Proceedings 1861-1869, pg 53 (1862 Nov 4) Grand Secretary
- Proceedings 1861-1869, pg 55 (1862 Nov 4) Grand Secretary
- Proceedings 1861-1869, pg 76 (1862 Nov 4), Summit Lodge No. 2, Parkville
- Proceedings 1861-1869, pg 79 (1863 May 6) Grand Secretary
- Proceedings 1861-1869, pg 80 (1863 May 6) committee
- Proceedings 1861-1869, pg 80 (1863 May 6) Grand Secretary
- Proceedings 1861-1869, pg 81 (1863 Apr 18) Grand Secretary
- Proceedings 1861-1869, pg 94 (1863 Apr 17) Grand Secretary
- Proceedings 1861-1869, pg 95 (1863 Apr 17) Grand Secretary
- Proceedings 1861-1869, pg 97 (1863 Nov 2) Grand Secretary
- Proceedings 1861-1869, pg 98 (1863 Nov 2) Grand Secretary
- Proceedings 1861-1869, pg 98 (1863 Nov 2) committee
- Proceedings 1861-1869, pg 99 (1863 Nov 2), Summit Lodge No. 2, Parkville, Grand Secretary
- Proceedings 1861-1869, pg 100 (1863 Nov 2) committee
- Proceedings 1861-1869, pg 100 (1863 Nov 3) Grand Secretary
- Proceedings 1861-1869, pg 101 (1863 Nov 3) Grand Secretary
- Proceedings 1861-1869, pg 101 (1863 Nov 3) Grand Secretary
- Proceedings 1861-1869, pg 102 (1863 Nov 3) petition for formation of a new lodge in Denver
- Proceedings 1861-1869, pg 103 (1863 Nov 3) committee
- Proceedings 1861-1869, pg 103 (1863 Nov 3) Grand Secretary
- Proceedings 1861-1869, pg 103 (1863 Nov 3) committee
- Proceedings 1861-1869, pg 104 (1863 Nov 3) committee
- Proceedings 1861-1869, pg 107 (1863 Nov 3) committee
- Proceedings 1861-1869, pg 107 (1863 Nov 3) Grand Secretary
- Proceedings 1861-1869, pg 110 (1863 Nov 3), Summit Lodge No. 2, Parkville
- Proceedings 1861-1869, pg 115 (1864 Nov 7) Grand Secretary
- Proceedings 1861-1869, pg 116 (1864 Nov 7) Grand Secretary
- Proceedings 1861-1869, pg 116 (1864 Nov 7) Grand Secretary
- Proceedings 1861-1869, pg 118 (1864 Nov 8) Denver Lodge No. 5, Grand Secretary
- Proceedings 1861-1869, pg 119 (1863 Nov 3) warrant drawn
- Proceedings 1861-1869, pg 119 (1863 Nov 3) warrant drawn
- Proceedings 1861-1869, pg 119 (1864 Nov 8) Grand Secretary
- Proceedings 1861-1869, pg 126 (1864 Nov 8) Grand Secretary
- Proceedings 1861-1869, pg 127 (1864 Nov 8) committee
- Proceedings 1861-1869, pg 127 (1864 Nov 8) Grand Secretary
- Proceedings 1861-1869, pg 128 (1864 Nov 8) Grand Secretary
- Proceedings 1861-1869, pg 134 (1864 Nov 8), Union Lodge No. 7, Denver
- Proceedings 1861-1869, pg 136 (1865 Nov 6) Grand Secretary
- Proceedings 1861-1869, pg 137 (1865 Nov 6), Union Lodge No. 7, Denver
- Proceedings 1861-1869, pg 137 (1865 Nov 6) Grand Secretary
- Proceedings 1861-1869, pg 139 (1865 Nov 6) Grand Secretary
- Proceedings 1861-1869, pg 139 (1865 Nov 6) Grand Secretary
- Proceedings 1861-1869, pg 140 (1864 Nov 8) warrant
- Proceedings 1861-1869, pg 141 (1865 Nov 7), Union Lodge No. 7, Denver
- Proceedings 1861-1869, pg 144 (1865 Nov 7) Grand Secretary
- Proceedings 1861-1869, pg 144 (1865 Nov 7) Grand Secretary
- Proceedings 1861-1869, pg 145 (1865 Nov 7) committee
- Proceedings 1861-1869, pg 145 (1865 Nov 7) Grand Secretary
- Proceedings 1861-1869, pg 151 (1865 Nov 7), Chivington Lodge No. 6, Central City
- Proceedings 1861-1869, pg 153 (1866 Oct 1) Grand Secretary
- Proceedings 1861-1869, pg 154 (1866 Oct 1) Grand Secretary
- Proceedings 1861-1869, pg 154 (1866 Oct 1), Union Lodge No. 7, Denver
- Proceedings 1861-1869, pg 157 (1866 Oct 1) committee
- Proceedings 1861-1869, pg 158 (1866 Oct 1) committee
- Proceedings 1861-1869, pg 159 (1866 Oct 1) warrant
- Proceedings 1861-1869, pg 161 (1866 Oct 2) Grand Secretary
- Proceedings 1861-1869, pg 162 (1866 Oct 2) Grand Secretary

Whittemore, O A, cont.
- Proceedings 1861-1869, pg 163 (1866 Oct 2) committee
- Proceedings 1861-1869, pg 163 (1866 Oct 2) Past Grand Secretary
- Proceedings 1861-1869, pg 169 (1866 Oct 2), Union Lodge No. 7, Denver
- Proceedings 1861-1869, pg 182 (1867 Oct 7) warrant paid
- Proceedings 1861-1869, pg 185 (1867 Oct 7) Deputy Grand Master
- Proceedings 1861-1869, pg 195 (1867 Oct 8), Union Lodge No. 7, Denver
- Proceedings 1861-1869, pg 201 (1868 Oct 6) Deputy Grand Master
- Proceedings 1861-1869, pg 202 (1868 Oct 6) Deputy Grand Master
- Proceedings 1861-1869, pg 207 (1867 Dec 17) Denver Lodge No. 5
- Proceedings 1861-1869, pg 219 (1868 Oct 7) mileage allowed
- Proceedings 1861-1869, pg 220 (1868 Oct 7) committee
- Proceedings 1861-1869, pg 225 (1868 Oct 7), Union Lodge No. 7, Denver
- Proceedings 1861-1869, pg 287 (1869 Sept 28) Past Grand Master
- Proceedings 1861-1869, pg 288 (1869 Sept 28) Past Grand Master
- Proceedings 1861-1869, pg 288 (1869 Sept 28) committee
- Proceedings 1861-1869, pg 300 (1869 Sept 29) Past Deputy Grand Master
- Proceedings 1861-1869, pg 300 (1869 Sept 29) committee
- Proceedings 1861-1869, pg 302 (1869 Sept 29) committee
- Proceedings 1861-1869, pg 307 (1869 Sept 29), Union Lodge No. 7, Denver
- Proceedings 1861-1869, pg 315 (1869 Sept 29) Grand Secretary, 1865
- Proceedings 1861-1869, pg 315 (1869 Sept 29) Grand Secretary, 1864
- Proceedings 1861-1869, pg 315 (1869 Sept 29) Grand Secretary, 1863
- Proceedings 1861-1869, pg 315 (1869 Sept 29) Grand Secretary, 1862
- Proceedings 1861-1869, pg 315 (1869 Sept 29) Deputy Grand Master, 1867
- Proceedings 1861-1869, pg 315 (1869 Sept 29) Grand Secretary, August 1861
- Proceedings 1861-1869, pg 315 (1869 Sept 29) Grand Secretary, December 1861
- Proceedings 1870, pg 23 (1870 Sept 28), Union Lodge No. 7, Denver
- Proceedings 1870, pg 32 (1870 Sept 28) Grand Secretary, December 1861
- Proceedings 1870, pg 32 (1870 Sept 28) Grand Secretary, 1865
- Proceedings 1870, pg 32 (1870 Sept 28) Grand Secretary, 1862
- Proceedings 1870, pg 32 (1870 Sept 28) Grand Secretary, 1863
- Proceedings 1870, pg 32 (1870 Sept 28) Grand Secretary, 1864
- Proceedings 1870, pg 32 (1870 Sept 28) Grand Secretary, August 1861
- Proceedings 1870, pg 32 (1870 Sept 28) Deputy Grand Master, 1867
- Proceedings 1871, pg 6 (1861 Aug 2) Grand Secretary
- Proceedings 1871, pg 21 (1871 Sept 27), Union Lodge No. 7, Denver
- Proceedings 1871, pg 34 (1871 Sept 27) Deputy Grand Master, 1867
- Proceedings 1871, pg 34 (1871 Sept 27) Grand Secretary, 1862
- Proceedings 1871, pg 34 (1871 Sept 27) Grand Secretary, Dec 1861
- Proceedings 1871, pg 34 (1871 Sept 27) Grand Secretary, 1865
- Proceedings 1871, pg 34 (1871 Sept 27) Grand Secretary, 1864
- Proceedings 1871, pg 34 (1871 Sept 27) Grand Secretary, 1863
- Proceedings 1871, pg 34 (1871 Sept 27) Grand Secretary, Aug 1861
- Proceedings 1872, pg 22 (1872 Sept 24), Union Lodge No. 7, Denver
- Proceedings 1872, pg 42 (1872 Sept 24) Grand Secretary, August 1861
- Proceedings 1872, pg 42 (1872 Sept 24) Grand Secretary, 1864
- Proceedings 1872, pg 42 (1872 Sept 24) Grand Secretary, 1862
- Proceedings 1872, pg 42 (1872 Sept 24) Deputy Grand Master, 1867
- Proceedings 1872, pg 42 (1872 Sept 24) Grand Secretary, 1863
- Proceedings 1872, pg 42 (1872 Sept 24) Grand Secretary, 1865
- Proceedings 1872, pg 42 (1872 Sept 24) Grand Secretary, December 1861
- Proceedings 1873, pg 39 (1873 Oct 1), Union Lodge No. 7, Denver
- Proceedings 1873, pg 39 (1873 Oct 1), Union Lodge No. 7, Denver
- Proceedings 1873, pg 58 (1873 Oct 1) Deputy Grand Master, 1867
- Proceedings 1873, pg 58 (1873 Oct 1) Grand Secretary, 1862
- Proceedings 1873, pg 58 (1873 Oct 1) Grand Secretary, Aug 1861
- Proceedings 1873, pg 58 (1873 Oct 1) Grand Secretary, Dec 1861
- Proceedings 1873, pg 58 (1873 Oct 1) Grand Secretary, 1864
- Proceedings 1873, pg 58 (1873 Oct 1) Grand Secretary, 1865
- Proceedings 1873, pg 58 (1873 Oct 1) Grand Secretary, 1863
- Proceedings 1874, pg 213 (1874 Sept 30), Union Lodge No. 7, Denver
- Proceedings 1875, pg 16 (1875 Sept 21) Past Deputy Grand Master

Whittemore, O A, cont.
- Proceedings 1875, pg 18 (1875 Sept 21), Union Lodge No. 7, Denver
- Proceedings 1875, pg 37 (1875 Sept 22) per diem
- Proceedings 1875, pg 78 (1875 Sept 22), Union Lodge No. 7, Denver
- Proceedings 1876, pg 6 (1876 Sept 19) committee
- Proceedings 1876, pg 12 (1876 Sept 19) donation to the library fund

Whittemore, Oliver A
- Proceedings 1874, pg 206 (1874 Sept 30) Grand Secretary, 1862
- Proceedings 1874, pg 206 (1874 Sept 30) Deputy Grand Master, 1867
- Proceedings 1874, pg 206 (1874 Sept 30) Grand Secretary, 1864
- Proceedings 1874, pg 206 (1874 Sept 30) Grand Secretary, Aug 1861
- Proceedings 1874, pg 206 (1874 Sept 30) Grand Secretary, 1863
- Proceedings 1874, pg 206 (1874 Sept 30) Grand Secretary, Dec 1861
- Proceedings 1874, pg 206 (1874 Sept 30) Grand Secretary, 1865
- Proceedings 1875, pg 93 (1875 Sept 22) Grand Secretary, Dec 1861
- Proceedings 1875, pg 93 (1875 Sept 22) Grand Secretary, 1862
- Proceedings 1875, pg 93 (1875 Sept 22) Grand Secretary, Aug 1861
- Proceedings 1875, pg 93 (1875 Sept 22) Grand Secretary, 1864
- Proceedings 1875, pg 93 (1875 Sept 22) Deputy Grand Master, 1867
- Proceedings 1875, pg 93 (1875 Sept 22) Grand Secretary, 1863
- Proceedings 1875, pg 93 (1875 Sept 22) Grand Secretary, 1865
- Proceedings 1876, pg 4 (1876 Sept 19) Past Deputy Grand Master
- Proceedings 1876, pg 4 (1876 Sept 19) Past Deputy Grand Master
- Proceedings 1876, pg 32 (1876 Sept 20), Union Lodge No. 7, Denver

Whittier, O H
- Proceedings 1861-1869, pg 151 (1865 Nov 7), Chivington Lodge No. 6, Central City, Fellowcraft
- Proceedings 1861-1869, pg 195 (1867 Oct 8), Union Lodge No. 7, Denver
- Proceedings 1861-1869, pg 225 (1868 Oct 7), Union Lodge No. 7, Denver
- Proceedings 1876, pg 33 (1876 Sept 20), Union Lodge No. 7, Denver
- Proceedings 1876, pg 50 (1876 Sept 20), Union Lodge No. 7, Denver
- Proceedings 1861-1869, pg 135 (1864 Nov 8), Union Lodge No. 7, Denver, Apprentice

Whittier, Oscar H
- Proceedings 1861-1869, pg 169 (1866 Oct 2), Union Lodge No. 7, Denver
- Proceedings 1861-1869, pg 307 (1869 Sept 29), Union Lodge No. 7, Denver
- Proceedings 1870, pg 23 (1870 Sept 28), Union Lodge No. 7, Denver
- Proceedings 1871, pg 22 (1871 Sept 27), Union Lodge No. 7, Denver
- Proceedings 1872, pg 23 (1872 Sept 24), Union Lodge No. 7, Denver
- Proceedings 1873, pg 40 (1873 Oct 1), Union Lodge No. 7, Denver
- Proceedings 1874, pg 214 (1874 Sept 30), Union Lodge No. 7, Denver
- Proceedings 1875, pg 78 (1875 Sept 22), Union Lodge No. 7, Denver

Whittlesey, C H
- Proceedings 1870, pg 28 (1870 Sept 28), Cheyenne Lodge No. 16, Cheyenne, Wyoming Territory

Wibb, H N
- Proceedings 1875, pg 84 (1875 Sept 22), Mount Moriah Lodge No. 15, Canon City

Widderfield, John W
- Proceedings 1876, pg 24 (1876 Sept 20), King Solomon Lodge No. 30, West Las Animas
- Proceedings 1876, pg 45 (1876 Sept 20), King Solomon Lodge U D, West Las Animas

Wiess, Henry
- Proceedings 1876, pg 39 (1876 Sept 20) Pueblo Lodge No. 17

Wigginton, J W
- Proceedings 1861-1869, pg 197 (1867 Oct 8), Columbia Lodge U D, Boulder
- Proceedings 1861-1869, pg 228 (1868 Oct 7), Columbia Lodge No. 14, Columbia City
- Proceedings 1875, pg 83 (1875 Sept 22), Columbia Lodge No. 14, Boulder, Stricken from the rolls

Wigginton, John W
- Proceedings 1861-1869, pg 311 (1869 Sept 29), Columbia Lodge No. 14, Boulder City
- Proceedings 1870, pg 27 (1870 Sept 28), Columbia Lodge No. 14, Boulder City
- Proceedings 1871, pg 26 (1871 Sept 27), Columbia Lodge No. 14, Boulder City
- Proceedings 1872, pg 28 (1872 Sept 24), Columbia Lodge No. 14, Boulder
- Proceedings 1873, pg 44 (1873 Oct 1), Columbia Lodge No. 14, Boulder
- Proceedings 1874, pg 219 (1874 Sept 30), Columbia Lodge No. 14, Boulder, Boulder County

Wightman, James L
- Proceedings 1876, pg 44 (1876 Sept 20) Del Norte Lodge U D

Wilbur, Geo D
- Proceedings 1874, pg 205 (1874 Sept 30) Grand Lodge of Wisconsin, Mineral Point

Colorado's Territorial Masons

Wilcox, A F
    Proceedings 1874, pg 224 (1874 Sept 30), Laramie Lodge No. 18, Laramie City, Apprentice

Wilcox, A T
    Proceedings 1870, pg 31 (1870 Sept 28), Laramie Lodge No. 18, Laramie, Wyoming Territory, Apprentice
    Proceedings 1871, pg 29 (1871 Sept 27), Laramie Lodge No. 18, Laramie, Wyoming Territory, Apprentice
    Proceedings 1872, pg 32 (1872 Sept 24), Laramie Lodge No. 18, Laramie, Wyoming Territory, Apprentice
    Proceedings 1873, pg 48 (1873 Oct 1), Laramie Lodge No. 18, Laramie, Wyoming Territory, Apprentice

Wilcox, Charles
    Proceedings 1872, pg 15 (1872 Sept 24) Grand Tiler
    Proceedings 1873, pg 39 (1873 Oct 1), Union Lodge No. 7, Denver, Not a member

Wilcoxen, I N
    Proceedings 1871, pg 21 (1871 Sept 27), Central Lodge No. 6, Central

Wilcoxen, Isaac N
    Proceedings 1876, pg 32 (1876 Sept 20), Central Lodge No. 6, Central City

Wilcoxin, I N
    Proceedings 1861-1869, pg 168 (1866 Oct 2), Chivington Lodge No. 6, Central City
    Proceedings 1861-1869, pg 194 (1867 Oct 8), Chivington Lodge No. 6, Central City
    Proceedings 1861-1869, pg 224 (1868 Oct 7), Chivington Lodge No. 6, Central City
    Proceedings 1861-1869, pg 306 (1869 Sept 29), Central Lodge No. 6, Central City
    Proceedings 1870, pg 22 (1870 Sept 28), Central Lodge No. 6, Central City
    Proceedings 1876, pg 50 (1876 Sept 20), Central Lodge No. 6, Central City

Wilcoxin, Isaac N
    Proceedings 1872, pg 21 (1872 Sept 24), Denver Lodge No. 5, Denver
    Proceedings 1873, pg 39 (1873 Oct 1), Central Lodge No. 6, Central City
    Proceedings 1874, pg 213 (1874 Sept 30), Central Lodge No. 6, Central
    Proceedings 1875, pg 77 (1875 Sept 22), Central Lodge No. 6, Central City

Wild, Charles R
    Proceedings 1874, pg 224 (1874 Sept 30), Collins Lodge No. 19, Fort Collins, Larimer County
    Proceedings 1875, pg 86 (1875 Sept 22), Collins Lodge No. 19, Fort Collins
    Proceedings 1876, pg 39 (1876 Sept 20), Collins Lodge No. 19, Fort Collins

Wilder, E
    Proceedings 1861-1869, pg 150 (1865 Nov 7), Chivington Lodge No. 6, Central City
    Proceedings 1861-1869, pg 168 (1866 Oct 2), Chivington Lodge No. 6, Central City
    Proceedings 1861-1869, pg 170 (1866 Oct 2), Black Hawk Lodge U D, Black Hawk
    Proceedings 1861-1869, pg 194 (1867 Oct 8), Chivington Lodge No. 6, Central City, Dimitted

Wilder, Eugene
    Proceedings 1861-1869, pg 195 (1867 Oct 8), Black Hawk Lodge No. 11, Black Hawk
    Proceedings 1861-1869, pg 227 (1868 Oct 7), Black Hawk Lodge No. 11, Black Hawk
    Proceedings 1861-1869, pg 309 (1869 Sept 29), Black Hawk Lodge No. 11, Black Hawk
    Proceedings 1870, pg 25 (1870 Sept 28), Black Hawk Lodge No. 11, Black Hawk
    Proceedings 1871, pg 23 (1871 Sept 27), Black Hawk Lodge No. 11, Black Hawk
    Proceedings 1872, pg 25 (1872 Sept 24), Black Hawk Lodge No. 11, Black Hawk
    Proceedings 1873, pg 42 (1873 Oct 1), Black Hawk Lodge No. 11, Black Hawk
    Proceedings 1874, pg 216 (1874 Sept 30), Black Hawk Lodge No. 11, Black Hawk, Demitted
    Proceedings 1874, pg 219 (1874 Sept 30), Columbia Lodge No. 14, Boulder, Boulder County
    Proceedings 1875, pg 83 (1875 Sept 22), Columbia Lodge No. 14, Boulder
    Proceedings 1876, pg 37 (1876 Sept 20), Columbia Lodge No. 14, Boulder

Wilder, Marshall P
    Proceedings 1861-1869, pg 260 (1868 Sept 11) Grand Lodge of Massachusetts

Wiley, P
    Proceedings 1876, pg 34 (1876 Sept 20) Black Hawk Lodge No. 11

Wiley, Paleman
    Proceedings 1871, pg 23 (1871 Sept 27), Black Hawk Lodge No. 11, Black Hawk

Wiley, Palemon
    Proceedings 1861-1869, pg 309 (1869 Sept 29), Black Hawk Lodge No. 11, Black Hawk
    Proceedings 1870, pg 25 (1870 Sept 28), Black Hawk Lodge No. 11, Black Hawk
    Proceedings 1874, pg 216 (1874 Sept 30), Black Hawk Lodge No. 11, Black Hawk
    Proceedings 1875, pg 80 (1875 Sept 22) Black Hawk Lodge No. 11

Wilford, Samuel N
    Proceedings 1873, pg 43 (1873 Oct 1), Washington Lodge No. 12, Georgetown
    Proceedings 1874, pg 218 (1874 Sept 30), Washington Lodge No. 12, Georgetown, died

Wilgus, C H
    Proceedings 1875, pg 84 (1875 Sept 22), Mount Moriah Lodge No. 15, Canon City
    Proceedings 1876, pg 38 (1876 Sept 20), Mount Moriah Lodge No. 15, Canon City
    Proceedings 1876, pg 50 (1876 Sept 20), Mount Moriah Lodge No. 15, Canon City

Wilhite, E S
Proceedings 1861-1869, pg 77 (1862 Nov 4) Denver Lodge No. 5
Proceedings 1861-1869, pg 112 (1863 Nov 3) Denver Lodge No. 5, dimitted

Wilkins, A F
Proceedings 1873, pg 46 (1873 Oct 1), Cheyenne Lodge No. 16, Cheyenne, Wyoming Territory, Fellowcraft
Proceedings 1874, pg 221 (1874 Sept 30), Cheyenne Lodge No. 16, Cheyenne, Wyoming Territory

Wilkins, Corneilus
Proceedings 1873, pg 41 (1873 Oct 1), Empire Lodge No. 8, Empire
Proceedings 1874, pg 215 (1874 Sept 30), Empire Lodge No. 8, Empire
Proceedings 1861-1869, pg 226 (1868 Oct 7), Empire Lodge No. 8, Empire City
Proceedings 1861-1869, pg 308 (1869 Sept 29), Empire Lodge No. 8, Empire City
Proceedings 1870, pg 24 (1870 Sept 28), Empire Lodge No. 8, Empire
Proceedings 1872, pg 23 (1872 Sept 24), Empire Lodge No. 8, Empire
Proceedings 1876, pg 37 (1876 Sept 20), Columbia Lodge No. 14, Boulder

Wilkins, Geo
Proceedings 1873, pg 46 (1873 Oct 1), Cheyenne Lodge No. 16, Cheyenne, Wyoming Territory

Wilkins, George
Proceedings 1874, pg 221 (1874 Sept 30), Cheyenne Lodge No. 16, Cheyenne, Wyoming Territory, Demitted

Willard, L B
Proceedings 1875, pg 87 (1875 Sept 22), Occidental Lodge No. 20, Greeley
Proceedings 1876, pg 40 (1876 Sept 20), Occidental Lodge No. 20, Greeley

Willard, O A
Proceedings 1861-1869, pg 123 (1864 Nov 8), Union Lodge No. 7, Denver, Grand Orator
Proceedings 1861-1869, pg 134 (1864 Nov 8), Union Lodge No. 7, Denver
Proceedings 1861-1869, pg 151 (1865 Nov 7), Chivington Lodge No. 6, Central City, reverend
Proceedings 1861-1869, pg 169 (1866 Oct 2), Union Lodge No. 7, Denver
Proceedings 1861-1869, pg 195 (1867 Oct 8), Union Lodge No. 7, Denver
Proceedings 1861-1869, pg 226 (1868 Oct 7), Union Lodge No. 7, Denver, Dimitted

Willey, D W
Proceedings 1861-1869, pg 110 (1863 Nov 3), Summit Lodge No. 2, Parkville
Proceedings 1861-1869, pg 131 (1864 Nov 8) Golden City Lodge No. 1

Willey, Thomas H
Proceedings 1874, pg 228 (1874 Sept 30), Doric Lodge U D, Fairplay, Fellowcraft

Willey, Thomas T
Proceedings 1876, pg 42 (1876 Sept 20), Doric Lodge No. 25, Fairplay

Willey, Thos T
Proceedings 1875, pg 89 (1875 Sept 22), Doric Lodge No. 25, Fairplay, Fellowcraft

William, Donald
Proceedings 1871, pg 23 (1871 Sept 27), Black Hawk Lodge No. 11, Black Hawk, Apprentice,

Williams
Proceedings 1861-1869, pg 87 (1863 Apr 17) Golden City Lodge No. 1
Proceedings 1861-1869, pg 88 (1863 Apr 17) Golden City Lodge No. 1
Proceedings 1861-1869, pg 89 (1863 Apr 17) Golden City Lodge No. 1
Proceedings 1861-1869, pg 238 (1867 Dec 2) Grand Master of Alabama
Proceedings 1870, pg 44 (1869 Nov 1) Grand Lodge of Arkansas

Williams, A T
Proceedings 1870, pg 31 (1870 Sept 28), Laramie Lodge No. 18, Laramie, Wyoming Territory
Proceedings 1871, pg 29 (1871 Sept 27), Laramie Lodge No. 18, Laramie, Wyoming Territory
Proceedings 1872, pg 32 (1872 Sept 24), Laramie Lodge No. 18, Laramie, Wyoming Territory

Williams, C H
Proceedings 1861-1869, pg 76 (1862 Nov 4), Summit Lodge No. 2, Parkville, dimitted
Proceedings 1872, pg cover (1872 Sept 24), Pueblo Chapter No. 3, Pueblo

Williams, Campion
Proceedings 1874, pg 214 (1874 Sept 30), Union Lodge No. 7, Denver

Williams, Champion
Proceedings 1875, pg 78 (1875 Sept 22), Union Lodge No. 7, Denver
Proceedings 1876, pg 33 (1876 Sept 20), Union Lodge No. 7, Denver

Williams, Charles A
Proceedings 1872, pg 17 (1872 Sept 24), Golden City Lodge No. 1, Golden City
Proceedings 1873, pg 35 (1873 Oct 1), Golden City Lodge No. 1, Golden City, died
Proceedings 1873, pg 57 (1873 Oct 1), Golden City Lodge No. 1, Golden City

Williams, Geo
Proceedings 1861-1869, pg 169 (1866 Oct 2), Union Lodge No. 7, Denver
Proceedings 1861-1869, pg 225 (1868 Oct 7), Union Lodge No. 7, Denver
Proceedings 1861-1869, pg 230 (1868 Oct 7), Cheyenne Lodge U D, Cheyenne, Dakota Territory
Proceedings 1872, pg 23 (1872 Sept 24), Union Lodge No. 7, Denver

Williams, Geo, cont.
    Proceedings 1873, pg 46 (1873 Oct 1), Cheyenne Lodge No. 16, Cheyenne, Wyoming Territory

Williams, George
    Proceedings 1861-1869, pg 195 (1867 Oct 8), Union Lodge No. 7, Denver
    Proceedings 1861-1869, pg 307 (1869 Sept 29), Union Lodge No. 7, Denver
    Proceedings 1861-1869, pg 312 (1869 Sept 29), Cheyenne Lodge No. 16, Cheyenne
    Proceedings 1870, pg 23 (1870 Sept 28), Union Lodge No. 7, Denver
    Proceedings 1870, pg 29 (1870 Sept 28), Cheyenne Lodge No. 16, Cheyenne, Wyoming Territory
    Proceedings 1871, pg 22 (1871 Sept 27), Union Lodge No. 7, Denver
    Proceedings 1871, pg 27 (1871 Sept 27), Cheyenne Lodge No. 16, Cheyenne, Wyoming Territory
    Proceedings 1872, pg 30 (1872 Sept 24), Cheyenne Lodge No. 16, Cheyenne, Wyoming Territory
    Proceedings 1873, pg 40 (1873 Oct 1), Union Lodge No. 7, Denver, Stricken from the rolls
    Proceedings 1874, pg 221 (1874 Sept 30), Cheyenne Lodge No. 16, Cheyenne, Wyoming Territory

Williams, J B
    Proceedings 1872, pg 31 (1872 Sept 24), Pueblo Lodge No. 17, Pueblo, Fellowcraft
    Proceedings 1875, pg 74 (1875 Sept 22) Golden City Lodge No. 1, Stricken from the rolls

Williams, J D
    Proceedings 1861-1869, pg 170 (1866 Oct 2), Black Hawk Lodge U D, Black Hawk
    Proceedings 1861-1869, pg 195 (1867 Oct 8), Black Hawk Lodge No. 11, Black Hawk
    Proceedings 1861-1869, pg 309 (1869 Sept 29), Black Hawk Lodge No. 11, Black Hawk
    Proceedings 1870, pg 25 (1870 Sept 28), Black Hawk Lodge No. 11, Black Hawk
    Proceedings 1871, pg 23 (1871 Sept 27), Black Hawk Lodge No. 11, Black Hawk, Dimitted

Williams, Jno B
    Proceedings 1875, pg 85 (1875 Sept 22) Pueblo Lodge No. 17, Fellowcraft

Williams, John B
    Proceedings 1861-1869, pg 313 (1869 Sept 29), Pueblo Lodge No. 17, Pueblo, Apprentice
    Proceedings 1870, pg 30 (1870 Sept 28), Pueblo Lodge No. 17, Pueblo, Fellowcraft
    Proceedings 1871, pg 28 (1871 Sept 27), Pueblo Lodge No. 17, Pueblo, Fellowcraft
    Proceedings 1873, pg 47 (1873 Oct 1), Pueblo Lodge No. 17, Pueblo, Fellowcraft
    Proceedings 1874, pg 222 (1874 Sept 30), Pueblo Lodge No. 17, Pueblo, Pueblo County, Fellowcraft
    Proceedings 1876, pg 39 (1876 Sept 20) Pueblo Lodge No. 17, Fellow Craft

Williams, Owen
    Proceedings 1861-1869, pg 147 (1865 Nov 7) Golden City Lodge No. 1
    Proceedings 1861-1869, pg 165 (1866 Oct 2) Golden City Lodge No. 1
    Proceedings 1861-1869, pg 191 (1867 Oct 8) Golden City Lodge No. 1
    Proceedings 1861-1869, pg 221 (1868 Oct 7) Golden City Lodge No. 1
    Proceedings 1861-1869, pg 303 (1869 Sept 29) Golden City Lodge No. 1
    Proceedings 1870, pg 19 (1870 Sept 28), Golden City Lodge No. 1, Golden City
    Proceedings 1871, pg 17 (1871 Sept 27), Golden City Lodge No. 1, Golden City
    Proceedings 1872, pg 17 (1872 Sept 24), Golden City Lodge No. 1, Golden City
    Proceedings 1873, pg 35 (1873 Oct 1), Golden City Lodge No. 1, Golden City
    Proceedings 1874, pg 209 (1874 Sept 30), Golden City Lodge No. 1, Golden City
    Proceedings 1875, pg 74 (1875 Sept 22) Golden City Lodge No. 1, Stricken from the rolls

Williams, R H
    Proceedings 1874, pg 227 (1874 Sept 30), St Vrain No. 23, Longmont, Apprentice
    Proceedings 1876, pg 41 (1876 Sept 20), St Vrain Lodge No. 23, Longmont

Williams, S B
    Proceedings 1861-1869, pg 42 (1861 Dec 10) Golden City Lodge No. 1
    Proceedings 1861-1869, pg 80 (1863 May 6) Golden City Lodge No. 1
    Proceedings 1861-1869, pg 94 (1863 Apr 17) Golden City Lodge No. 1
    Proceedings 1861-1869, pg 94 (1863 Apr 17) Golden City Lodge No. 1
    Proceedings 1861-1869, pg 110 (1863 Nov 3) Golden City Lodge No. 1
    Proceedings 1861-1869, pg 131 (1864 Nov 8) Golden City Lodge No. 1
    Proceedings 1861-1869, pg 147 (1865 Nov 7) Golden City Lodge No. 1
    Proceedings 1861-1869, pg 165 (1866 Oct 2) Golden City Lodge No. 1
    Proceedings 1861-1869, pg 191 (1867 Oct 8) Golden City Lodge No. 1
    Proceedings 1861-1869, pg 221 (1868 Oct 7) Golden City Lodge No. 1
    Proceedings 1861-1869, pg 303 (1869 Sept 29) Golden City Lodge No. 1
    Proceedings 1870, pg 19 (1870 Sept 28), Golden City Lodge No. 1, Golden City
    Proceedings 1871, pg 17 (1871 Sept 27), Golden City Lodge No. 1, Golden City
    Proceedings 1872, pg 17 (1872 Sept 24), Golden City Lodge No. 1, Golden City
    Proceedings 1873, pg 35 (1873 Oct 1), Golden City Lodge No. 1, Golden City

Proceedings 1874, pg 209 (1874 Sept 30), Golden City Lodge No. 1, Golden City

Williams, S W
Proceedings 1870, pg 43 (1869 Nov 1) Grand Lodge of Arkansas

Williams, Samuel W
Proceedings 1861-1869, pg 236 (1867 Nov 4) Grand Lodge of Arkansas
Proceedings 1872, pg 43 (1872 Sept 24) Little Rock, Grand Lodge of Arkansas
Proceedings 1872, pg 54 (1872 Sept 24) Grand Lodge of Arkansas

Williams, Thomas P
Proceedings 1876, pg 41 (1876 Sept 20), St Vrain Lodge No. 23, Longmont

Williams, Thos P
Proceedings 1874, pg 227 (1874 Sept 30), St Vrain No. 23, Longmont

Williams, W H
Proceedings 1876, pg 33 (1876 Sept 20), Union Lodge No. 7, Denver

Williams, W O
Proceedings 1874, pg 221 (1874 Sept 30), Cheyenne Lodge No. 16, Cheyenne, Wyoming Territory, Apprentice

Williams, Wilson
Proceedings 1861-1869, pg 236 (1867 Dec 2) Grand Master of Alabama

Williams, Wm H
Proceedings 1875, pg 78 (1875 Sept 22), Union Lodge No. 7, Denver

Williamson, W A
Proceedings 1861-1869, pg 42 (1861 Dec 10), Summit Lodge No. 2, Parkville
Proceedings 1861-1869, pg 76 (1862 Nov 4), Summit Lodge No. 2, Parkville, Fellowcraft

Willis, Joseph R
Proceedings 1870, pg 15 (1870 Sept 28) Senior Warden, Collins Lodge No. 19

Willis, Robert B
Proceedings 1874, pg 8 (1874 Aug 27), Huerfano Lodge U D, Walsenburg
Proceedings 1874, pg 229 (1874 Sept 30), Huerfano Lodge U D, Walsenburg
Proceedings 1875, pg 34 (1875 Sept 22), Huerfano Lodge No. 27, Walsenburg
Proceedings 1875, pg 90 (1875 Sept 22), Huerfano Lodge U D, Walsenburg
Proceedings 1876, pg 43 (1876 Sept 20), Huerfano Lodge No. 27, Walsenburg

Willoughby
Proceedings 1873, pg 30 (1873 Oct 1) resolution

Willoughby, E A
Proceedings 1861-1869, pg 307 (1869 Sept 29), Union Lodge No. 7, Denver
Proceedings 1871, pg 4 (1871 Sept 26), Union Lodge No. 7, Denver
Proceedings 1871, pg 21 (1871 Sept 27), Union Lodge No. 7, Denver
Proceedings 1872, pg 4 (1872 Sept 24), Union Lodge No. 7, Denver
Proceedings 1872, pg 5 (1872 Sept 24) committee
Proceedings 1872, pg 15 (1872 Sept 24) Grand Marshal
Proceedings 1872, pg 16 (1872 Sept 24) committee
Proceedings 1872, pg 16 (1872 Sept 24), Union Lodge No. 7, Denver
Proceedings 1872, pg 22 (1872 Sept 24), Union Lodge No. 7, Denver
Proceedings 1873, pg 6 (1873 Sept 30), Denver [Union] Lodge No. 7, Denver
Proceedings 1873, pg 7 (1873 Sept 30) committee
Proceedings 1873, pg 31 (1873 Oct 1) mileage and per diem
Proceedings 1873, pg 32 (1873 Oct 1) committee
Proceedings 1873, pg 39 (1873 Oct 1), Union Lodge No. 7, Denver
Proceedings 1874, pg 213 (1874 Sept 30), Union Lodge No. 7, Denver
Proceedings 1875, pg 78 (1875 Sept 22), Union Lodge No. 7, Denver
Proceedings 1876, pg 32 (1876 Sept 20), Union Lodge No. 7, Denver

Willoughby, Ed A
Proceedings 1872, pg 3 (1872 Sept 24) Junior Grand Deacon

Willoughby, Edmund A
Proceedings 1873, pg 3 (1873 Sept 30) Grand Marshal
Proceedings 1873, pg 16 (1873 Oct 1) Grand Marshal
Proceedings 1874, pg 4 (1874 Sept 29) Grand Marshal

Willoughby, R A
Proceedings 1870, pg 23 (1870 Sept 28), Union Lodge No. 7, Denver

Wills, J R
Proceedings 1873, pg 6 (1873 Sept 30), Collins Lodge No. 19, Fort Collins

Wills, Joseph R
Proceedings 1870, pg 31 (1870 Sept 28), Collins Lodge No. 19, Fort Collins
Proceedings 1871, pg 29 (1871 Sept 27), Collins Lodge No. 19, Fort Collins
Proceedings 1872, pg 32 (1872 Sept 24), Collins Lodge No. 19, Fort Collins
Proceedings 1873, pg 49 (1873 Oct 1), Collins Lodge No. 19, Fort Collins
Proceedings 1874, pg 224 (1874 Sept 30), Collins Lodge No. 19, Fort Collins, Larimer County
Proceedings 1875, pg 86 (1875 Sept 22), Collins Lodge No. 19, Fort Collins
Proceedings 1876, pg 39 (1876 Sept 20), Collins Lodge No. 19, Fort Collins

Willson, G M
Proceedings 1861-1869, pg 165 (1866 Oct 2) Golden City Lodge No. 1

Colorado's Territorial Masons

Willson, John M
    Proceedings 1873, pg 44 (1873 Oct 1), Columbia Lodge No. 14, Boulder

Wilson, A D
    Proceedings 1876, pg 33 (1876 Sept 20), Union Lodge No. 7, Denver

Wilson, Adair
    Proceedings 1876, pg 7 (1875 Sept 24) Del Norte Lodge U D
    Proceedings 1876, pg 44 (1876 Sept 20) Del Norte Lodge U D
    Proceedings 1876, pg 44 (1876 Sept 20) Del Norte Lodge U D

Wilson, Andrew D
    Proceedings 1870, pg 23 (1870 Sept 28), Union Lodge No. 7, Denver, Fellowcraft
    Proceedings 1871, pg 22 (1871 Sept 27), Union Lodge No. 7, Denver
    Proceedings 1872, pg 23 (1872 Sept 24), Union Lodge No. 7, Denver
    Proceedings 1873, pg 40 (1873 Oct 1), Union Lodge No. 7, Denver
    Proceedings 1874, pg 214 (1874 Sept 30), Union Lodge No. 7, Denver
    Proceedings 1875, pg 78 (1875 Sept 22), Union Lodge No. 7, Denver

Wilson, B F
    Proceedings 1876, pg 37 (1876 Sept 20), Columbia Lodge No. 14, Boulder

Wilson, Christopher
    Proceedings 1876, pg 39 (1876 Sept 20) Pueblo Lodge No. 17
    Proceedings 1876, pg 45 (1876 Sept 20) South Pueblo Lodge U D

Wilson, Cyrus
    Proceedings 1871, pg 24 (1871 Sept 27), Washington Lodge No. 12, Georgetown
    Proceedings 1872, pg 26 (1872 Sept 24), Washington Lodge No. 12, Georgetown
    Proceedings 1873, pg 43 (1873 Oct 1), Washington Lodge No. 12, Georgetown
    Proceedings 1874, pg 217 (1874 Sept 30), Washington Lodge No. 12, Georgetown
    Proceedings 1875, pg 81 (1875 Sept 22), Washington Lodge No. 12, Georgetown
    Proceedings 1876, pg 35 (1876 Sept 20), Washington Lodge No. 12, Georgetown

Wilson, D P
    Proceedings 1861-1869, pg 151 (1865 Nov 7), Chivington Lodge No. 6, Central City, Apprentice
    Proceedings 1861-1869, pg 169 (1866 Oct 2), Union Lodge No. 7, Denver, Apprentice
    Proceedings 1861-1869, pg 195 (1867 Oct 8), Union Lodge No. 7, Denver, Apprentice
    Proceedings 1861-1869, pg 226 (1868 Oct 7), Union Lodge No. 7, Denver, Apprentice
    Proceedings 1861-1869, pg 308 (1869 Sept 29), Union Lodge No. 7, Denver, Apprentice
    Proceedings 1870, pg 24 (1870 Sept 28), Union Lodge No. 7, Denver, Apprentice
    Proceedings 1871, pg 22 (1871 Sept 27), Union Lodge No. 7, Denver, Apprentice
    Proceedings 1872, pg 23 (1872 Sept 24), Union Lodge No. 7, Denver, Apprentice
    Proceedings 1873, pg 40 (1873 Oct 1), Union Lodge No. 7, Denver, Apprentice
    Proceedings 1874, pg 215 (1874 Sept 30), Union Lodge No. 7, Denver, permission to apply for degrees in No. 17

Wilson, G E
    Proceedings 1861-1869, pg 150 (1865 Nov 7), Chivington Lodge No. 6, Central City
    Proceedings 1861-1869, pg 168 (1866 Oct 2), Chivington Lodge No. 6, Central City

Wilson, G M
    Proceedings 1861-1869, pg 86 (1863 Feb 14) Golden City Lodge No. 1
    Proceedings 1861-1869, pg 110 (1863 Nov 3) Golden City Lodge No. 1
    Proceedings 1861-1869, pg 110 (1863 Nov 3) Golden City Lodge No. 1
    Proceedings 1861-1869, pg 131 (1864 Nov 8) Golden City Lodge No. 1
    Proceedings 1861-1869, pg 147 (1865 Nov 7) Golden City Lodge No. 1
    Proceedings 1874, pg 71 (1874 Sept 30) Grand Lodge of Canada

Wilson, Geo E
    Proceedings 1861-1869, pg 224 (1868 Oct 7), Chivington Lodge No. 6, Central City
    Proceedings 1861-1869, pg 306 (1869 Sept 29), Central Lodge No. 6, Central City
    Proceedings 1870, pg 23 (1870 Sept 28), Central Lodge No. 6, Central City, Dimitted

Wilson, Geo M
    Proceedings 1861-1869, pg 191 (1867 Oct 8) Golden City Lodge No. 1, Dimitted

Wilson, Geo W
    Proceedings 1874, pg 227 (1874 Sept 30), St Vrain No. 23, Longmont

Wilson, George E
    Proceedings 1861-1869, pg 134 (1864 Nov 8), Chivington Lodge No. 6, Central City, Apprentice
    Proceedings 1861-1869, pg 194 (1867 Oct 8), Chivington Lodge No. 6, Central City

Wilson, George W
    Proceedings 1876, pg 41 (1876 Sept 20), St Vrain Lodge No. 23, Longmont

Wilson, Isaiah A
    Proceedings 1874, pg 204 (1874 Sept 30) Grand Lodge of Alabama, Union Springs

Wilson, J C
    Proceedings 1872, pg 36 (1872 Sept 24), Ashlar Lodge U D, Colorado Springs

Wilson, J W
Proceedings 1861-1869, pg 134 (1864 Nov 8), Chivington Lodge No. 6, Central City, Apprentice
Proceedings 1861-1869, pg 150 (1865 Nov 7), Chivington Lodge No. 6, Central City, Apprentice
Proceedings 1861-1869, pg 169 (1866 Oct 2), Chivington Lodge No. 6, Central City, Apprentice
Proceedings 1861-1869, pg 194 (1867 Oct 8), Chivington Lodge No. 6, Central City, Apprentice
Proceedings 1861-1869, pg 225 (1868 Oct 7), Chivington Lodge No. 6, Central City, Apprentice
Proceedings 1861-1869, pg 307 (1869 Sept 29), Central Lodge No. 6, Central City, Apprentice

Wilson, J Wentz
Proceedings 1870, pg 22 (1870 Sept 28), Central Lodge No. 6, Central City, Apprentice
Proceedings 1871, pg 21 (1871 Sept 27), Central Lodge No. 6, Central, Apprentice
Proceedings 1872, pg 21 (1872 Sept 24), Denver Lodge No. 5, Denver, Apprentice
Proceedings 1873, pg 39 (1873 Oct 1), Central Lodge No. 6, Central City, Apprentice
Proceedings 1874, pg 213 (1874 Sept 30), Central Lodge No. 6, Central, Apprentice
Proceedings 1875, pg 77 (1875 Sept 22), Central Lodge No. 6, Central City, Apprentice
Proceedings 1876, pg 32 (1876 Sept 20), Central Lodge No. 6, Central City, Apprentice

Wilson, Joel
Proceedings 1861-1869, pg 152 (1865 Nov 7), Helena City Lodge U D, Helena City, Montana Territory

Wilson, John
Proceedings 1876, pg 35 (1876 Sept 20), Washington Lodge No. 12, Georgetown

Wilson, John M
Colorado University Cornerstone Laying, pg 3 (1875 Sept 20) Junior Grand Deacon
Proceedings 1874, pg 6 (1874 Sept 29), Columbia Lodge No. 14, Boulder
Proceedings 1874, pg 219 (1874 Sept 30), Columbia Lodge No. 14, Boulder, Boulder County
Proceedings 1875, pg 17 (1875 Sept 21), Columbia Lodge No. 14, Boulder
Proceedings 1875, pg 38 (1875 Sept 22) per diem
Proceedings 1875, pg 83 (1875 Sept 22), Columbia Lodge No. 14, Boulder
Proceedings 1876, pg 36 (1876 Sept 20), Columbia Lodge No. 14, Boulder

Wilson, Joseph C
Proceedings 1875, pg 82 (1875 Sept 22), El Paso Lodge No. 13, Colorado Springs

Wilson, Luther
Proceedings 1861-1869, pg 135 (1864 Nov 8), Union Lodge No. 7, Denver, Apprentice
Proceedings 1861-1869, pg 151 (1865 Nov 7), Chivington Lodge No. 6, Central City, Apprentice
Proceedings 1861-1869, pg 169 (1866 Oct 2), Union Lodge No. 7, Denver, Apprentice
Proceedings 1861-1869, pg 195 (1867 Oct 8), Union Lodge No. 7, Denver, Apprentice
Proceedings 1861-1869, pg 226 (1868 Oct 7), Union Lodge No. 7, Denver, Apprentice
Proceedings 1861-1869, pg 308 (1869 Sept 29), Union Lodge No. 7, Denver, Apprentice
Proceedings 1870, pg 24 (1870 Sept 28), Union Lodge No. 7, Denver, Apprentice
Proceedings 1871, pg 22 (1871 Sept 27), Union Lodge No. 7, Denver, Apprentice
Proceedings 1872, pg 23 (1872 Sept 24), Union Lodge No. 7, Denver, Apprentice
Proceedings 1873, pg 40 (1873 Oct 1), Union Lodge No. 7, Denver, Apprentice
Proceedings 1874, pg 214 (1874 Sept 30), Union Lodge No. 7, Denver, Apprentice
Proceedings 1875, pg 79 (1875 Sept 22), Union Lodge No. 7, Denver, Apprentice
Proceedings 1876, pg 33 (1876 Sept 20), Union Lodge No. 7, Denver, Apprentice

Wilson, Robert
Proceedings 1871, pg 29 (1871 Sept 27), Laramie Lodge No. 18, Laramie, Wyoming Territory
Proceedings 1872, pg 32 (1872 Sept 24), Laramie Lodge No. 18, Laramie, Wyoming Territory
Proceedings 1873, pg 48 (1873 Oct 1), Laramie Lodge No. 18, Laramie, Wyoming Territory
Proceedings 1874, pg 224 (1874 Sept 30), Laramie Lodge No. 18, Laramie City, Demitted

Wilson, Sidney
Proceedings 1861-1869, pg 152 (1865 Nov 7), Montana Lodge U D, Virginia City, Montana Territory, Apprentice

Wilson, William Mercer
Proceedings 1861-1869, pg 325 (1868 July 8) Grand Master, Grand Lodge of Canada

Wilson, Wm M
Proceedings 1861-1869, pg 243 (1867 July 10), Grand Master, Grand Lodge of Canada
Proceedings 1873, pg 60 (1873 Oct 1) Grand Lodge of Canada, Sincoe
Proceedings 1874, pg 47 (1874 Sept 30) Grand Lodge of Canada
Proceedings 1874, pg 204 (1874 Sept 30) Grand Lodge of Canada, Simcoe

Wilter, D B
Proceedings 1871, pg 30 (1871 Sept 27), Occidental Lodge U D, Greeley

Winbourn, R W
Proceedings 1861-1869, pg 312 (1869 Sept 29), Pueblo Lodge No. 17, Pueblo

Winbourn, Richard
Proceedings 1870, pg 30 (1870 Sept 28), Pueblo Lodge No. 17, Pueblo

Winbourn, Richard T
Proceedings 1872, pg 31 (1872 Sept 24), Pueblo Lodge No. 17, Pueblo, died

Colorado's Territorial Masons

Winbourn, Richard T, cont.
Proceedings 1872, pg 39 (1872 Sept 24), Pueblo Lodge No. 17, Pueblo

Winbourn, Richard W
Proceedings 1871, pg 28 (1871 Sept 27), Pueblo Lodge No. 17, Pueblo

Wingate, John W
Proceedings 1876, pg 44 (1876 Sept 20) Del Norte Lodge U D

Winkler, Clinton M
Proceedings 1870, pg 103 (1870 June 13) Grand Master, Grand Lodge of Texas
Proceedings 1872, pg 88 (1872 Sept 24) Grand Lodge of Texas

Winn, Alexander M
Proceedings 1861-1869, pg 342 (1868 June 10) Grand Master, Grand Lodge of New Hampshire

Winne, Peter
Proceedings 1861-1869, pg 225 (1868 Oct 7), Union Lodge No. 7, Denver
Proceedings 1861-1869, pg 307 (1869 Sept 29), Union Lodge No. 7, Denver
Proceedings 1870, pg 23 (1870 Sept 28), Union Lodge No. 7, Denver
Proceedings 1871, pg 22 (1871 Sept 27), Union Lodge No. 7, Denver
Proceedings 1872, pg 23 (1872 Sept 24), Union Lodge No. 7, Denver
Proceedings 1873, pg 40 (1873 Oct 1), Union Lodge No. 7, Denver
Proceedings 1874, pg 214 (1874 Sept 30), Union Lodge No. 7, Denver
Proceedings 1875, pg 78 (1875 Sept 22), Union Lodge No. 7, Denver
Proceedings 1876, pg 33 (1876 Sept 20), Union Lodge No. 7, Denver

Winneka, Otto
Proceedings 1861-1869, pg 312 (1869 Sept 29), Pueblo Lodge No. 17, Pueblo
Proceedings 1870, pg 30 (1870 Sept 28), Pueblo Lodge No. 17, Pueblo
Proceedings 1871, pg 28 (1871 Sept 27), Pueblo Lodge No. 17, Pueblo
Proceedings 1872, pg 30 (1872 Sept 24), Pueblo Lodge No. 17, Pueblo
Proceedings 1873, pg 47 (1873 Oct 1), Pueblo Lodge No. 17, Pueblo
Proceedings 1875, pg 85 (1875 Sept 22) Pueblo Lodge No. 17
Proceedings 1876, pg 38 (1876 Sept 20) Pueblo Lodge No. 17
Proceedings 1874, pg 222 (1874 Sept 30), Pueblo Lodge No. 17, Pueblo, Pueblo County

Wintz, Andrew G
Proceedings 1871, pg 19 (1871 Sept 27) Denver Lodge No. 5, Fellowcraft
Proceedings 1872, pg 48 (1872 Sept 24), Denver Lodge No. 5, Denver

Wise
Proceedings 1861-1869, pg 268 (1867 June 19) Grand Lodge of Nebraska

Wise, J N
Proceedings 1861-1869, pg 316 (1869 Sept 29) Grand Lodge of Nebraska
Proceedings 1870, pg 90 (1868 June 24) Grand Secretary, Grand Lodge of Nebraska,

Wisebart
Proceedings 1861-1869, pg 182 (1866 Oct 2) per diem
Proceedings 1861-1869, pg 214 (1868 Oct 6) motion
Proceedings 1861-1869, pg 218 (1868 Oct 7), resolution that Germania Lodge combine with Denver Lodge, and that Valmont Lodge combine with Columbia No. 14
Proceedings 1861-1869, pg 218 (1868 Oct 7) motion
Proceedings 1861-1869, pg 288 (1869 Sept 28) committee
Proceedings 1861-1869, pg 292 (1869 Sept 28) donation
Proceedings 1861-1869, pg 297 (1869 Sept 28) motion
Proceedings 1872, pg 12 (1872 Sept 24) motion
Proceedings 1872, pg 13 (1872 Sept 24) motion
Proceedings 1873, pg 13 (1873 Sept 30) absent from the Territory

Wisebart, B W
Proceedings 1861-1869, pg 113 (1863 Nov 3), Chivington Lodge No. 6, Central City
Proceedings 1861-1869, pg 113 (1863 Nov 3), Montana Lodge U D, Central City
Proceedings 1861-1869, pg 136 (1865 Nov 6) Junior Grand Deacon
Proceedings 1861-1869, pg 137 (1865 Nov 6), Chivington Lodge No. 6, Central City
Proceedings 1861-1869, pg 150 (1865 Nov 7), Chivington Lodge No. 6, Central City
Proceedings 1861-1869, pg 153 (1866 Oct 1) Junior Grand Deacon
Proceedings 1861-1869, pg 154 (1866 Oct 1), Chivington Lodge No. 6, Central City
Proceedings 1861-1869, pg 160 (1866 Oct 2), Chivington Lodge No. 6, Central City, Senior Grand Deacon
Proceedings 1861-1869, pg 161 (1866 Oct 2) Senior Grand Deacon
Proceedings 1861-1869, pg 162 (1866 Oct 2), Chivington Lodge No. 6, Central City
Proceedings 1861-1869, pg 168 (1866 Oct 2), Chivington Lodge No. 6, Central City
Proceedings 1861-1869, pg 182 (1867 Oct 7) warrant paid
Proceedings 1861-1869, pg 194 (1867 Oct 8), Chivington Lodge No. 6, Central City
Proceedings 1861-1869, pg 201 (1868 Oct 6) Junior Grand Deacon
Proceedings 1861-1869, pg 202 (1868 Oct 6), Chivington Lodge No. 6, Central City
Proceedings 1861-1869, pg 213 (1868 Oct 6) Grand Secretary of Nebraska

Proceedings 1861-1869, pg 217 (1868 Oct 7), Chivington Lodge No. 6, Central City, Worshipful Master
Proceedings 1861-1869, pg 219 (1868 Oct 7), Central Lodge No. 6, Central City
Proceedings 1861-1869, pg 224 (1868 Oct 7), Chivington Lodge No. 6, Central City
Proceedings 1861-1869, pg 287 (1869 Sept 28) Senior Grand Warden
Proceedings 1861-1869, pg 288 (1869 Sept 28) Senior Grand Warden
Proceedings 1861-1869, pg 300 (1869 Sept 29) Senior Grand Warden
Proceedings 1861-1869, pg 306 (1869 Sept 29), Central Lodge No. 6, Central City
Proceedings 1861-1869, pg 315 (1869 Sept 29) Senior Grand Warden, 1869
Proceedings 1861-1869, pg 315 (1869 Sept 29) Senior Grand Warden, 1868
Proceedings 1870, pg 22 (1870 Sept 28), Central Lodge No. 6, Central City
Proceedings 1870, pg 32 (1870 Sept 28) Senior Grand Warden, 1868
Proceedings 1871, pg 34 (1871 Sept 27) Senior Grand Warden, 1868
Proceedings 1872, pg 4 (1872 Sept 24) visiting
Proceedings 1872, pg 4 (1872 Sept 24), Central Lodge No. 6, Central
Proceedings 1872, pg 5 (1872 Sept 24) committee
Proceedings 1872, pg 16 (1872 Sept 24) committee
Proceedings 1872, pg 16 (1872 Sept 24), Cental Lodge No. 6, Central
Proceedings 1872, pg 42 (1872 Sept 24) Senior Grand Warden, 1868
Proceedings 1873, pg cover (1873 Oct 1), Central City Chapter No. 1, Central
Proceedings 1873, pg 58 (1873 Oct 1) Senior Grand Warden, 1868

Wisebart, Benj F
Proceedings 1861-1869, pg 133 (1864 Nov 8), Chivington Lodge No. 6, Central City

Wisebart, Benj W
Proceedings 1861-1869, pg 215 (1868 Oct 6) Senior Grand Warden
Proceedings 1861-1869, pg 288 (1869 Sept 28) committee
Proceedings 1871, pg 20 (1871 Sept 27), Central Lodge No. 6, Central
Proceedings 1872, pg 21 (1872 Sept 24), Denver Lodge No. 5, Denver
Proceedings 1872, pg 21 (1872 Sept 24), Denver Lodge No. 5, Denver
Proceedings 1875, pg 76 (1875 Sept 22), Central Lodge No. 6, Central City
Proceedings 1876, pg 31 (1876 Sept 20), Central Lodge No. 6, Central City

Wisebart, Benjamin W
Proceedings 1873, pg 38 (1873 Oct 1), Central Lodge No. 6, Central City
Proceedings 1874, pg 206 (1874 Sept 30) Senior Grand Warden, 1868
Proceedings 1874, pg 212 (1874 Sept 30), Central Lodge No. 6, Central
Proceedings 1875, pg 93 (1875 Sept 22) Senior Grand Warden, 1868

Wisebart, G W
Proceedings 1872, pg cover (1872 Sept 24) committee, Central

Wiseman, G C
Proceedings 1875, pg 89 (1875 Sept 22), Doric Lodge No. 25, Fairplay

Wiseman, Geo W
Proceedings 1876, pg 48 (1876 Sept 20), Doric Lodge No. 25, Fairplay, 1876 Jan 1

Witcher, J R
Proceedings 1870, pg 28 (1870 Sept 28), Mount Moriah Lodge No. 15, Canon City
Proceedings 1871, pg 26 (1871 Sept 27), Mount Moriah Lodge No. 15, Canon City
Proceedings 1874, pg 220 (1874 Sept 30), Mount Moriah Lodge No. 15, Canon City
Proceedings 1875, pg 84 (1875 Sept 22), Mount Moriah Lodge No. 15, Canon City

Witcher, John
Proceedings 1861-1869, pg 311 (1869 Sept 29), Mount Moriah Lodge No. 15, Canon City

Witcher, John R
Proceedings 1872, pg 29 (1872 Sept 24), Mount Moriah Lodge No. 15, Canon City
Proceedings 1873, pg 45 (1873 Oct 1), Mount Moriah Lodge No. 15, Canon City
Proceedings 1876, pg 38 (1876 Sept 20), Mount Moriah Lodge No. 15, Canon City

Withers, Robert E
Proceedings 1872, pg 44 (1872 Sept 24) Richmond, Grand Lodge of Virginia
Proceedings 1873, pg 61 (1873 Oct 1) Grand Lodge of Virginia, Richmond
Proceedings 1874, pg 129 (1874 Sept 30) Grand Lodge of Virginia

Withrow
Proceedings 1861-1869, pg 117 (1864 Nov 7) committee
Proceedings 1861-1869, pg 119 (1864 Nov 8) motion
Proceedings 1861-1869, pg 127 (1864 Nov 8) donated per diem to the Grand Lodge
Proceedings 1861-1869, pg 190 (1867 Oct 8) Grand Master
Proceedings 1861-1869, pg 190 (1867 Oct 8) committee
Proceedings 1861-1869, pg 296 (1869 Sept 28) committee
Proceedings 1861-1869, pg 296 (1869 Sept 28) motion
Proceedings 1861-1869, pg 301 (1869 Sept 29) Past Grand Master
Proceedings 1870, pg 9 (1870 Sept 27) committee
Proceedings 1870, pg 17 (1870 Sept 28) committee

Withrow, C
Proceedings 1861-1869, pg 148 (1865 Nov 7), Nevada Lodge No. 4, Nevadaville
Proceedings 1861-1869, pg 182 (1867 Oct 7) warrant paid
Proceedings 1861-1869, pg 212 (1868 Oct 6) warrant paid

Withrow, Chase
- Proceedings 1861-1869, pg 76 (1862 Nov 4), Nevada Lodge No. 4, Nevadaville
- Proceedings 1861-1869, pg 79 (1863 May 6) Senior Grand Warden
- Proceedings 1861-1869, pg 80 (1863 May 6), Nevada Lodge No. 4, Nevadaville
- Proceedings 1861-1869, pg 92 (1863 Apr 17) committee
- Proceedings 1861-1869, pg 94 (1863 Apr 17), Nevada Lodge No. 4, Nevadaville
- Proceedings 1861-1869, pg 94 (1863 Apr 17) committee
- Proceedings 1861-1869, pg 94 (1863 Apr 17), Nevada Lodge No. 4, Nevadaville
- Proceedings 1861-1869, pg 97 (1863 Nov 2) Grand Tyler
- Proceedings 1861-1869, pg 98 (1863 Nov 2), Nevada Lodge No. 4, Nevadaville
- Proceedings 1861-1869, pg 99 (1863 Nov 2), Nevada Lodge No. 4, Nevadaville, Grand Lecturer
- Proceedings 1861-1869, pg 100 (1863 Nov 2) committee
- Proceedings 1861-1869, pg 100 (1863 Nov 3) Grand Lecturer
- Proceedings 1861-1869, pg 103 (1863 Nov 3) committee
- Proceedings 1861-1869, pg 111 (1863 Nov 3), Nevada Lodge No. 4, Nevadaville
- Proceedings 1861-1869, pg 115 (1864 Nov 7) Senior Grand Deacon
- Proceedings 1861-1869, pg 116 (1864 Nov 7) Grand Lecturer
- Proceedings 1861-1869, pg 116 (1864 Nov 7), Nevada Lodge No. 4, Nevadaville
- Proceedings 1861-1869, pg 118 (1864 Nov 8), Nevada Lodge No. 4, Nevadaville, Junior Grand Warden
- Proceedings 1861-1869, pg 118 (1864 Nov 8) Teller
- Proceedings 1861-1869, pg 124 (1864 Nov 8) committee
- Proceedings 1861-1869, pg 126 (1864 Nov 8), Nevada Lodge No. 4, Nevadaville
- Proceedings 1861-1869, pg 132 (1864 Nov 8), Nevada Lodge No. 4, Nevadaville
- Proceedings 1861-1869, pg 136 (1865 Nov 6) Junior Grand Warden
- Proceedings 1861-1869, pg 137 (1865 Nov 6) committee
- Proceedings 1861-1869, pg 137 (1865 Nov 6) committee
- Proceedings 1861-1869, pg 137 (1865 Nov 6) Junior Grand Warden
- Proceedings 1861-1869, pg 138 (1865 Nov 6) committee
- Proceedings 1861-1869, pg 138 (1865 Nov 6) committee
- Proceedings 1861-1869, pg 141 (1865 Nov 7), Nevada Lodge No. 4, Nevadaville
- Proceedings 1861-1869, pg 142 (1865 Nov 7) motion
- Proceedings 1861-1869, pg 143 (1865 Nov 7) committee
- Proceedings 1861-1869, pg 144 (1865 Nov 7) Junior Grand Warden
- Proceedings 1861-1869, pg 144 (1865 Nov 7) committee
- Proceedings 1861-1869, pg 145 (1865 Nov 7) committee
- Proceedings 1861-1869, pg 153 (1866 Oct 1) Senior Grand Warden
- Proceedings 1861-1869, pg 154 (1866 Oct 1) Senior Grand Warden
- Proceedings 1861-1869, pg 154 (1866 Oct 1) committee
- Proceedings 1861-1869, pg 154 (1866 Oct 1) committee
- Proceedings 1861-1869, pg 155 (1866 Oct 1), Black Hawk Lodge U D, Black Hawk
- Proceedings 1861-1869, pg 155 (1866 Oct 1) committee
- Proceedings 1861-1869, pg 156 (1866 Oct 1) committee
- Proceedings 1861-1869, pg 159 (1866 Oct 1) warrant
- Proceedings 1861-1869, pg 159 (1866 Oct 1), Black Hawk Lodge No. 11, Black Hawk
- Proceedings 1861-1869, pg 160 (1866 Oct 2), Black Hawk Lodge No. 11, Black Hawk
- Proceedings 1861-1869, pg 160 (1866 Oct 2) committee
- Proceedings 1861-1869, pg 160 (1866 Oct 2) Grand Master
- Proceedings 1861-1869, pg 161 (1866 Oct 2) Grand Master
- Proceedings 1861-1869, pg 162 (1866 Oct 2) committee
- Proceedings 1861-1869, pg 162 (1866 Oct 2) Senior Grand Warden
- Proceedings 1861-1869, pg 166 (1866 Oct 2), Nevada Lodge No. 4, Nevadaville
- Proceedings 1861-1869, pg 170 (1866 Oct 2), Black Hawk Lodge U D, Black Hawk
- Proceedings 1861-1869, pg 175 (1867 Oct 7) Grand Master
- Proceedings 1861-1869, pg 176 (1867 Oct 7) Grand Master
- Proceedings 1861-1869, pg 179 (1867 Oct 7) Grand Master
- Proceedings 1861-1869, pg 186 (1867 Oct 8) Grand Master
- Proceedings 1861-1869, pg 192 (1867 Oct 8), Nevada Lodge No. 4, Nevadaville, Dimitted
- Proceedings 1861-1869, pg 196 (1867 Oct 8), Black Hawk Lodge No. 11, Black Hawk
- Proceedings 1861-1869, pg 227 (1868 Oct 7), Black Hawk Lodge No. 11, Black Hawk
- Proceedings 1861-1869, pg 289 (1869 Sept 28) Past Grand Master
- Proceedings 1861-1869, pg 299 (1869 Sept 29) committee
- Proceedings 1861-1869, pg 299 (1869 Sept 29) Grand Lecturer
- Proceedings 1861-1869, pg 300 (1869 Sept 29) Past Grand Master
- Proceedings 1861-1869, pg 302 (1869 Sept 29) committee
- Proceedings 1861-1869, pg 309 (1869 Sept 29), Black Hawk Lodge No. 11, Black Hawk
- Proceedings 1861-1869, pg 315 (1869 Sept 29) Senior Grand Warden, 1865
- Proceedings 1861-1869, pg 315 (1869 Sept 29) Junior Grand Warden, 1864
- Proceedings 1861-1869, pg 315 (1869 Sept 29) Grand Master, 1866
- Proceedings 1870, pg cover (1870 Sept 28) Past Grand Master, Central
- Proceedings 1870, pg 25 (1870 Sept 28), Black Hawk Lodge No. 11, Black Hawk, Past Master
- Proceedings 1870, pg 32 (1870 Sept 28) Grand Master, 1866
- Proceedings 1870, pg 32 (1870 Sept 28) Junior Grand Warden, 1864
- Proceedings 1870, pg 32 (1870 Sept 28) Senior Grand Warden, 1865
- Proceedings 1871, pg cover (1871 Sept 27) Past Grand Master, Central
- Proceedings 1871, pg 16 (1871 Sept 27) Committee
- Proceedings 1871, pg 23 (1871 Sept 27), Black Hawk Lodge No. 11, Black Hawk

Withrow, Chase, cont.
    Proceedings 1871, pg 34 (1871 Sept 27) Senior Grand Warden, 1865
    Proceedings 1871, pg 34 (1871 Sept 27) Junior Grand Warden, 1864
    Proceedings 1871, pg 34 (1871 Sept 27) Grand Master, 1866
    Proceedings 1872, pg cover (1872 Sept 24), Central City Chapter No. 1, Central
    Proceedings 1872, pg 24 (1872 Sept 24), Black Hawk Lodge No. 11, Black Hawk
    Proceedings 1872, pg 42 (1872 Sept 24) Grand Master, 1866
    Proceedings 1872, pg 42 (1872 Sept 24) Senior Grand Warden, 1865
    Proceedings 1872, pg 42 (1872 Sept 24) Junior Grand Warden, 1864
    Proceedings 1873, pg 41 (1873 Oct 1), Black Hawk Lodge No. 11, Black Hawk
    Proceedings 1873, pg 58 (1873 Oct 1) Senior Grand Warden, 1865
    Proceedings 1873, pg 58 (1873 Oct 1) Junior Grand Warden, 1864
    Proceedings 1873, pg 58 (1873 Oct 1) Grand Master, 1866
    Proceedings 1874, pg 206 (1874 Sept 30) Junior Grand Warden, 1864
    Proceedings 1874, pg 206 (1874 Sept 30) Senior Grand Warden, 1865
    Proceedings 1874, pg 206 (1874 Sept 30) Grand Master, 1866
    Proceedings 1874, pg 216 (1874 Sept 30), Black Hawk Lodge No. 11, Black Hawk
    Proceedings 1875, pg 18 (1875 Sept 21) Past Grand Master
    Proceedings 1875, pg 37 (1875 Sept 22) per diem
    Proceedings 1875, pg 80 (1875 Sept 22) Black Hawk Lodge No. 11
    Proceedings 1875, pg 93 (1875 Sept 22) Grand Master, 1866
    Proceedings 1875, pg 93 (1875 Sept 22) Senior Grand Warden, 1865
    Proceedings 1875, pg 93 (1875 Sept 22) Junior Grand Warden, 1864
    Proceedings 1876, pg 49 (1876 Sept 20) Black Hawk Lodge No. 11, 1875 Oct 14

Witler, Daniel
    Proceedings 1861-1869, pg 307 (1869 Sept 29), Union Lodge No. 7, Denver

Wittemore
    Proceedings 1870, pg 10 (1870 Sept 27) donation

Witter, D P
    Proceedings 1872, pg 33 (1872 Sept 24), Occidental Lodge No. 20, Greeley
    Proceedings 1875, pg 87 (1875 Sept 22), Occidental Lodge No. 20, Greeley

Witter, Daniel
    Proceedings 1861-1869, pg 135 (1864 Nov 8), Union Lodge No. 7, Denver, Apprentice
    Proceedings 1861-1869, pg 151 (1865 Nov 7), Chivington Lodge No. 6, Central City, Apprentice
    Proceedings 1861-1869, pg 169 (1866 Oct 2), Union Lodge No. 7, Denver, Apprentice
    Proceedings 1861-1869, pg 195 (1867 Oct 8), Union Lodge No. 7, Denver, Apprentice
    Proceedings 1861-1869, pg 225 (1868 Oct 7), Union Lodge No. 7, Denver
    Proceedings 1870, pg 23 (1870 Sept 28), Union Lodge No. 7, Denver
    Proceedings 1871, pg 22 (1871 Sept 27), Union Lodge No. 7, Denver
    Proceedings 1872, pg 23 (1872 Sept 24), Union Lodge No. 7, Denver
    Proceedings 1873, pg 40 (1873 Oct 1), Union Lodge No. 7, Denver
    Proceedings 1874, pg 214 (1874 Sept 30), Union Lodge No. 7, Denver
    Proceedings 1875, pg 78 (1875 Sept 22), Union Lodge No. 7, Denver
    Proceedings 1876, pg 33 (1876 Sept 20), Union Lodge No. 7, Denver

Witter, Daniel P
    Proceedings 1873, pg 50 (1873 Oct 1), Occidental Lodge No. 20, Greeley
    Proceedings 1874, pg 225 (1874 Sept 30), Occidental Lodge No. 20, Greeley
    Proceedings 1876, pg 40 (1876 Sept 20), Occidental Lodge No. 20, Greeley

Wolaver, J M
    Proceedings 1875, pg 87 (1875 Sept 22), Occidental Lodge No. 20, Greeley

Wolaver, Jacob M
    Proceedings 1876, pg 40 (1876 Sept 20), Occidental Lodge No. 20, Greeley

Wolever, J M
    Proceedings 1874, pg 225 (1874 Sept 30), Occidental Lodge No. 20, Greeley, Fellowcraft

Wolf, D T
    Proceedings 1873, pg 51 (1873 Oct 1), Weston Lodge No. 22, Littleton
    Proceedings 1875, pg 88 (1875 Sept 22), Weston Lodge No. 22, Littleton
    Proceedings 1876, pg 41 (1876 Sept 20), Weston Lodge No. 22, Littleton

Wolf, James S
    Proceedings 1875, pg 82 (1875 Sept 22), El Paso Lodge No. 13, Colorado Springs

Wolfe, J S
    Proceedings 1874, pg 218 (1874 Sept 30), El Paso Lodge No. 13, Colorado Springs

Wolfe, James S
    Proceedings 1872, pg 36 (1872 Sept 24), Ashlar Lodge U D, Colorado Springs
    Proceedings 1876, pg 35 (1876 Sept 20), El Paso Lodge No. 13, Colorado City

Colorado's Territorial Masons

Wolfe, William
- Proceedings 1875, pg 76 (1875 Sept 22) Denver Lodge No. 5
- Proceedings 1876, pg 31 (1876 Sept 20) Denver Lodge No. 5

Wood, Gardner P
- Proceedings 1876, pg 24 (1876 Sept 20), Columbia Lodge No. 14, Boulder
- Proceedings 1876, pg 37 (1876 Sept 20), Columbia Lodge No. 14, Boulder

Woodbury
- Proceedings 1861-1869, pg 117 (1864 Nov 7) committee

Woodbury, A
- Proceedings 1871, pg 15 (1871 Sept 27), Occidental Lodge No. 20, Greeley

Woodbury, A J
- Proceedings 1873, pg 40 (1873 Oct 1), Union Lodge No. 7, Denver
- Proceedings 1874, pg 214 (1874 Sept 30), Union Lodge No. 7, Denver
- Proceedings 1875, pg 78 (1875 Sept 22), Union Lodge No. 7, Denver
- Proceedings 1876, pg 32 (1876 Sept 20), Union Lodge No. 7, Denver

Woodbury, B
- Proceedings 1861-1869, pg 170 (1866 Oct 2), Black Hawk Lodge U D, Black Hawk
- Proceedings 1861-1869, pg 196 (1867 Oct 8), Black Hawk Lodge No. 11, Black Hawk

Woodbury, Benj
- Proceedings 1861-1869, pg 227 (1868 Oct 7), Black Hawk Lodge No. 11, Black Hawk
- Proceedings 1861-1869, pg 309 (1869 Sept 29), Black Hawk Lodge No. 11, Black Hawk
- Proceedings 1873, pg 42 (1873 Oct 1), Black Hawk Lodge No. 11, Black Hawk

Woodbury, Benjamin
- Proceedings 1870, pg 25 (1870 Sept 28), Black Hawk Lodge No. 11, Black Hawk
- Proceedings 1871, pg 23 (1871 Sept 27), Black Hawk Lodge No. 11, Black Hawk
- Proceedings 1872, pg 25 (1872 Sept 24), Black Hawk Lodge No. 11, Black Hawk
- Proceedings 1874, pg 216 (1874 Sept 30), Black Hawk Lodge No. 11, Black Hawk
- Proceedings 1875, pg 80 (1875 Sept 22) Black Hawk Lodge No. 11
- Proceedings 1876, pg 34 (1876 Sept 20) Black Hawk Lodge No. 11

Woodbury, I C
- Proceedings 1875, pg 82 (1875 Sept 22), El Paso Lodge No. 13, Colorado Springs

Woodbury, J A
- Proceedings 1871, pg 30 (1871 Sept 27), Occidental Lodge U D, Greeley
- Proceedings 1872, pg 33 (1872 Sept 24), Occidental Lodge No. 20, Greeley
- Proceedings 1873, pg 50 (1873 Oct 1), Occidental Lodge No. 20, Greeley

Woodbury, J C
- Proceedings 1861-1869, pg 196 (1867 Oct 8), El Paso Lodge U D, Colorado City, Fellowcraft
- Proceedings 1861-1869, pg 228 (1868 Oct 7), El Paso Lodge No. 13, Colorado City
- Proceedings 1861-1869, pg 310 (1869 Sept 29), El Paso Lodge No. 13, Colorado City
- Proceedings 1870, pg 27 (1870 Sept 28), El Paso Lodge No. 13, Colorado City
- Proceedings 1871, pg 25 (1871 Sept 27), El Paso Lodge No. 13, Colorado City
- Proceedings 1872, pg 27 (1872 Sept 24), El Paso Lodge No. 13, Colorado City
- Proceedings 1873, pg 43 (1873 Oct 1), El Paso Lodge No. 13, Colorado City
- Proceedings 1874, pg 218 (1874 Sept 30), El Paso Lodge No. 13, Colorado Springs

Woodbury, Joseph A
- Proceedings 1874, pg 225 (1874 Sept 30), Occidental Lodge No. 20, Greeley
- Proceedings 1875, pg 87 (1875 Sept 22), Occidental Lodge No. 20, Greeley
- Proceedings 1876, pg 40 (1876 Sept 20), Occidental Lodge No. 20, Greeley

Woodbury, R W
- Proceedings 1861-1869, pg 307 (1869 Sept 29), Union Lodge No. 7, Denver
- Proceedings 1872, pg 4 (1872 Sept 24), Union Lodge No. 7, Denver
- Proceedings 1872, pg 22 (1872 Sept 24), Union Lodge No. 7, Denver
- Proceedings 1873, pg 6 (1873 Sept 30), Denver [Union] Lodge No. 7, Denver
- Proceedings 1873, pg 7 (1873 Sept 30) committee
- Proceedings 1873, pg 39 (1873 Oct 1), Union Lodge No. 7, Denver
- Proceedings 1874, pg 5 (1874 Sept 29), Union Lodge No. 7, Denver
- Proceedings 1874, pg 6 (1874 Sept 29) committee
- Proceedings 1874, pg 29 (1874 Sept 29) committee
- Proceedings 1874, pg 37 (1874 Sept 30) resolution
- Proceedings 1874, pg 213 (1874 Sept 30), Union Lodge No. 7, Denver
- Proceedings 1875, pg 17 (1875 Sept 21), Union Lodge No. 7, Denver
- Proceedings 1875, pg 28 (1875 Sept 21) committee
- Proceedings 1875, pg 38 (1875 Sept 22) per diem
- Proceedings 1875, pg 78 (1875 Sept 22), Union Lodge No. 7, Denver
- Proceedings 1876, pg cover (1876 Sept 20) Senior Grand Warden, Denver
- Proceedings 1876, pg 5 (1876 Sept 19), Union Lodge No. 7, Denver
- Proceedings 1876, pg 6 (1876 Sept 19) committee
- Proceedings 1876, pg 12 (1876 Sept 19) donation to the library fund

Proceedings 1876, pg 16 (1876 Sept 19) committee
Proceedings 1876, pg 22 (1876 Sept 20) committee
Proceedings 1876, pg 22 (1876 Sept 20), Union Lodge No. 7, Denver
Proceedings 1876, pg 23 (1876 Sept 20) committee
Proceedings 1876, pg 26 (1876 Sept 20) committee

Woodbury, Roger W
Proceedings 1870, pg 23 (1870 Sept 28), Union Lodge No. 7, Denver
Proceedings 1871, pg 22 (1871 Sept 27), Union Lodge No. 7, Denver
Proceedings 1874, pg cover (1874 Sept 30) committee, Denver
Proceedings 1874, pg 6 (1874 Sept 29), Grand Representative, Grand Lodge of Louisiana
Proceedings 1874, pg 36 (1874 Sept 30) committee
Proceedings 1874, pg 207 (1874 Sept 30) Grand Lodge of Louisiana, Denver
Proceedings 1875, pg cover (1875 Sept 22) committee, Denver
Proceedings 1875, pg 37 (1875 Sept 22) committee, Denver
Proceedings 1875, pg 95 (1875 Sept 22) Grand Lodge of Louisiana, Denver, CO
Proceedings 1876, pg 18 (1876 Sept 19) Senior Grand Warden
Proceedings 1876, pg 32 (1876 Sept 20), Union Lodge No. 7, Denver
Proceedings 1876, pg 53 (1876 Sept 20) Grand Lodge of Louisiana, of Denver, CO

Woodbury, S S
Proceedings 1861-1869, pg 76 (1862 Nov 4), Summit Lodge No. 2, Parkville
Proceedings 1861-1869, pg 110 (1863 Nov 3), Summit Lodge No. 2, Parkville
Proceedings 1861-1869, pg 116 (1864 Nov 7), Summit Lodge No. 2, Parkville
Proceedings 1861-1869, pg 122 (1864 Nov 8) committee
Proceedings 1861-1869, pg 125 (1864 Nov 8) committee
Proceedings 1861-1869, pg 126 (1864 Nov 8) committee
Proceedings 1861-1869, pg 126 (1864 Nov 8), Summit Lodge No. 2, Parkville
Proceedings 1861-1869, pg 127 (1864 Nov 8) committee
Proceedings 1861-1869, pg 131 (1864 Nov 8) Golden City Lodge No. 1
Proceedings 1861-1869, pg 140 (1864 Nov 8) warrant
Proceedings 1861-1869, pg 169 (1866 Oct 2), Union Lodge No. 7, Denver
Proceedings 1861-1869, pg 195 (1867 Oct 8), Union Lodge No. 7, Denver
Proceedings 1861-1869, pg 225 (1868 Oct 7), Union Lodge No. 7, Denver
Proceedings 1861-1869, pg 307 (1869 Sept 29), Union Lodge No. 7, Denver
Proceedings 1873, pg 40 (1873 Oct 1), Union Lodge No. 7, Denver
Proceedings 1874, pg 214 (1874 Sept 30), Union Lodge No. 7, Denver
Proceedings 1875, pg 78 (1875 Sept 22), Union Lodge No. 7, Denver
Proceedings 1876, pg 33 (1876 Sept 20), Union Lodge No. 7, Denver

Woodbury, Sam'l S
Proceedings 1871, pg 22 (1871 Sept 27), Union Lodge No. 7, Denver

Woodbury, Samuel S
Proceedings 1870, pg 23 (1870 Sept 28), Union Lodge No. 7, Denver
Proceedings 1872, pg 23 (1872 Sept 24), Union Lodge No. 7, Denver

Woodgate, I H
Proceedings 1875, pg 82 (1875 Sept 22), El Paso Lodge No. 13, Colorado Springs

Woodgate, J H
Proceedings 1874, pg 218 (1874 Sept 30), El Paso Lodge No. 13, Colorado Springs
Proceedings 1876, pg 35 (1876 Sept 20), El Paso Lodge No. 13, Colorado City

Woodhull, John M
Proceedings 1875, pg 96 (1875 Sept 22) Grand Lodge of Wisconsin, Milwaukee

Woodhull, John W
Proceedings 1876, pg 54 (1876 Sept 20) Grand Lodge of Wisconsin, Milwaukee

Woodhull, William S
Proceedings 1871, pg 31 (1871 Sept 27), Argenta Lodge U D, Salt Lake City, Utah

Woodruff, D P
Proceedings 1861-1869, pg 196 (1867 Oct 8), Black Hawk Lodge No. 11, Black Hawk
Proceedings 1861-1869, pg 227 (1868 Oct 7), Black Hawk Lodge No. 11, Black Hawk
Proceedings 1861-1869, pg 309 (1869 Sept 29), Black Hawk Lodge No. 11, Black Hawk, Dimitted

Woods, H A
Proceedings 1861-1869, pg 113 (1863 Nov 3), Chivington Lodge No. 6, Central City
Proceedings 1861-1869, pg 150 (1865 Nov 7), Chivington Lodge No. 6, Central City
Proceedings 1861-1869, pg 168 (1866 Oct 2), Chivington Lodge No. 6, Central City
Proceedings 1861-1869, pg 194 (1867 Oct 8), Chivington Lodge No. 6, Central City
Proceedings 1861-1869, pg 225 (1868 Oct 7), Chivington Lodge No. 6, Central City, Dimitted

Woods, Henry A
Proceedings 1861-1869, pg 78 (1862 Nov 4), Chivington Lodge No. 6, Central City
Proceedings 1861-1869, pg 134 (1864 Nov 8), Chivington Lodge No. 6, Central City

Woods, R
Proceedings 1861-1869, pg 168 (1866 Oct 2), Chivington Lodge No. 6, Central City

Colorado's Territorial Masons

Woods, Robert
Proceedings 1861-1869, pg 194 (1867 Oct 8), Chivington Lodge No. 6, Central City
Proceedings 1861-1869, pg 224 (1868 Oct 7), Chivington Lodge No. 6, Central City
Proceedings 1861-1869, pg 306 (1869 Sept 29), Central Lodge No. 6, Central City
Proceedings 1872, pg 21 (1872 Sept 24), Denver Lodge No. 5, Denver
Proceedings 1873, pg 39 (1873 Oct 1), Central Lodge No. 6, Central City
Proceedings 1874, pg 213 (1874 Sept 30), Central Lodge No. 6, Central
Proceedings 1875, pg 77 (1875 Sept 22), Central Lodge No. 6, Central City
Proceedings 1876, pg 32 (1876 Sept 20), Central Lodge No. 6, Central City

Woods, Robt
Proceedings 1870, pg 22 (1870 Sept 28), Central Lodge No. 6, Central City
Proceedings 1871, pg 21 (1871 Sept 27), Central Lodge No. 6, Central

Woodson, A E
Proceedings 1876, pg 45 (1876 Sept 20), King Solomon Lodge U D, West Las Animas

Woodward, Bruce
Proceedings 1861-1869, pg 110 (1863 Nov 3) Golden City Lodge No. 1, Apprentice
Proceedings 1861-1869, pg 131 (1864 Nov 8) Golden City Lodge No. 1, Apprentice
Proceedings 1861-1869, pg 147 (1865 Nov 7) Golden City Lodge No. 1, Apprentice
Proceedings 1861-1869, pg 165 (1866 Oct 2) Golden City Lodge No. 1, Apprentice
Proceedings 1861-1869, pg 191 (1867 Oct 8) Golden City Lodge No. 1, Apprentice
Proceedings 1861-1869, pg 221 (1868 Oct 7) Golden City Lodge No. 1, Apprentice
Proceedings 1861-1869, pg 303 (1869 Sept 29) Golden City Lodge No. 1, Apprentice

Woodward, Charles A
Proceedings 1872, pg 44 (1872 Sept 24) Steubenville, Grand Lodge of Ohio

Woodward, S
Proceedings 1871, pg 31 (1871 Sept 27), Argenta Lodge U D, Salt Lake City, Utah

Woodward, T
Proceedings 1861-1869, pg 166 (1866 Oct 2), Nevada Lodge No. 4, Nevadaville

Woodward, Thomas
Proceedings 1861-1869, pg 192 (1867 Oct 8), Nevada Lodge No. 4, Nevadaville
Proceedings 1861-1869, pg 222 (1868 Oct 7), Nevada Lodge No. 4, Nevadaville
Proceedings 1870, pg 20 (1870 Sept 28), Nevada Lodge No. 4, Nevadaville
Proceedings 1871, pg 18 (1871 Sept 27), Nevada Lodge No. 4, Bald Mountain
Proceedings 1872, pg 19 (1872 Sept 24), Nevada Lodge No. 4, Bald Mountain
Proceedings 1873, pg 36 (1873 Oct 1), Nevada Lodge No. 4, Nevada
Proceedings 1874, pg 210 (1874 Sept 30), Nevada Lodge No. 4, Bald Mountain, Gilpin County
Proceedings 1875, pg 75 (1875 Sept 22), Nevada Lodge No. 4, Nevada, Demitted
Proceedings 1875, pg 81 (1875 Sept 22), Washington Lodge No. 12, Georgetown
Proceedings 1876, pg 35 (1876 Sept 20), Washington Lodge No. 12, Georgetown

Woodward, Thos
Proceedings 1861-1869, pg 148 (1865 Nov 7), Nevada Lodge No. 4, Nevadaville
Proceedings 1861-1869, pg 304 (1869 Sept 29), Nevada Lodge No. 4, Nevadaville

Woolcos, J E
Proceedings 1874, pg 228 (1874 Sept 30), Evanston Lodge U D, Evanston, Uintah County, Wyoming Territory, Apprentice

Woolf, D T
Proceedings 1872, pg 35 (1872 Sept 24), Weston Lodge No. 22, Littleton, Apprentice

Woolover, J M
Proceedings 1873, pg 50 (1873 Oct 1), Occidental Lodge No. 20, Greeley, Fellowcraft

Work, George H F
Proceedings 1876, pg 39 (1876 Sept 20) Pueblo Lodge No. 17

Worth, Wm J
Proceedings 1873, pg 60 (1873 Oct 1) Grand Lodge of Maryland, Baltimore

Wright, Alpheus
Proceedings 1873, pg 44 (1873 Oct 1), Columbia Lodge No. 14, Boulder
Proceedings 1874, pg 219 (1874 Sept 30), Columbia Lodge No. 14, Boulder, Boulder County
Proceedings 1875, pg 83 (1875 Sept 22), Columbia Lodge No. 14, Boulder
Proceedings 1876, pg 36 (1876 Sept 20), Columbia Lodge No. 14, Boulder

Wright, S H
Proceedings 1861-1869, pg 166 (1866 Oct 2), Nevada Lodge No. 4, Nevadaville, Apprentice

Wright, Sam H
Proceedings 1861-1869, pg 192 (1867 Oct 8), Nevada Lodge No. 4, Nevadaville, Apprentice

Wright, Silas
Proceedings 1871, pg 28 (1871 Sept 27), Pueblo Lodge No. 17, Pueblo, Apprentice
Proceedings 1872, pg 49 (1872 Sept 24), Pueblo Lodge No. 17, Pueblo

Proceedings 1873, pg 47 (1873 Oct 1), Pueblo Lodge No. 17, Pueblo, Apprentice
Proceedings 1874, pg 222 (1874 Sept 30), Pueblo Lodge No. 17, Pueblo, Pueblo County, Apprentice
Proceedings 1875, pg 85 (1875 Sept 22) Pueblo Lodge No. 17, Apprentice
Proceedings 1876, pg 39 (1876 Sept 20) Pueblo Lodge No. 17, Apprentice

Wulfjin, C W
Proceedings 1874, pg 221 (1874 Sept 30), Cheyenne Lodge No. 16, Cheyenne, Wyoming Territory

Wurtele, C A
Proceedings 1872, pg 30 (1872 Sept 24), Cheyenne Lodge No. 16, Cheyenne, Wyoming Territory, Apprentice

Wurtell, C E
Proceedings 1874, pg 228 (1874 Sept 30), Evanston Lodge U D, Evanston, Uintah County, Wyoming Territory

Wurtels, C A
Proceedings 1873, pg 46 (1873 Oct 1), Cheyenne Lodge No. 16, Cheyenne, Wyoming Territory, Apprentice

Wurtzebach, J E
Proceedings 1861-1869, pg 196 (1867 Oct 8), Black Hawk Lodge No. 11, Black Hawk
Proceedings 1861-1869, pg 230 (1868 Oct 7), Germania Lodge U D, Denver
Proceedings 1861-1869, pg 309 (1869 Sept 29), Black Hawk Lodge No. 11, Black Hawk, Dimitted

Wyman, Geo B
Proceedings 1873, pg 50 (1873 Oct 1), Occidental Lodge No. 20, Greeley
Proceedings 1875, pg 87 (1875 Sept 22), Occidental Lodge No. 20, Greeley

Wyman, George B
Proceedings 1874, pg 225 (1874 Sept 30), Occidental Lodge No. 20, Greeley
Proceedings 1876, pg 40 (1876 Sept 20), Occidental Lodge No. 20, Greeley

Wyman, John A
Proceedings 1875, pg 83 (1875 Sept 22), Columbia Lodge No. 14, Boulder

Wymer, John A
Proceedings 1873, pg 44 (1873 Oct 1), Columbia Lodge No. 14, Boulder
Proceedings 1874, pg 219 (1874 Sept 30), Columbia Lodge No. 14, Boulder, Boulder County
Proceedings 1876, pg 36 (1876 Sept 20), Columbia Lodge No. 14, Boulder

Wyoming Lodge No. 28, South Pass City
Proceedings 1875, pg 24 (1875 Sept 21) Grand Lodge of Nebraska

Wythe, J H
Proceedings 1870, pg 98 (1869 June 21) orator, Grand Lodge of Oregon

Wythe, M C
Proceedings 1861-1869, pg 134 (1864 Nov 8), Chivington Lodge No. 6, Central City
Proceedings 1861-1869, pg 150 (1865 Nov 7), Chivington Lodge No. 6, Central City
Proceedings 1861-1869, pg 168 (1866 Oct 2), Chivington Lodge No. 6, Central City
Proceedings 1861-1869, pg 194 (1867 Oct 8), Chivington Lodge No. 6, Central City
Proceedings 1861-1869, pg 224 (1868 Oct 7), Chivington Lodge No. 6, Central City
Proceedings 1861-1869, pg 306 (1869 Sept 29), Central Lodge No. 6, Central City
Proceedings 1870, pg 22 (1870 Sept 28), Central Lodge No. 6, Central City
Proceedings 1871, pg 21 (1871 Sept 27), Central Lodge No. 6, Central

Wythe, Monroe C
Proceedings 1872, pg 21 (1872 Sept 24), Denver Lodge No. 5, Denver, Dimitted
Proceedings 1872, pg 26 (1872 Sept 24), Washington Lodge No. 12, Georgetown
Proceedings 1873, pg 43 (1873 Oct 1), Washington Lodge No. 12, Georgetown
Proceedings 1874, pg 217 (1874 Sept 30), Washington Lodge No. 12, Georgetown
Proceedings 1875, pg 81 (1875 Sept 22), Washington Lodge No. 12, Georgetown
Proceedings 1876, pg 35 (1876 Sept 20), Washington Lodge No. 12, Georgetown

Y

Yates, Daniel F
Proceedings 1874, pg 217 (1874 Sept 30), Washington Lodge No. 12, Georgetown, Apprentice

Yates, L F
Proceedings 1861-1869, pg 310 (1869 Sept 29), Washington Lodge No. 12, Georgetown, Apprentice
Proceedings 1870, pg 26 (1870 Sept 28), Washington Lodge No. 12, Georgetown, Apprentice
Proceedings 1871, pg 24 (1871 Sept 27), Washington Lodge No. 12, Georgetown, Apprentice
Proceedings 1875, pg 81 (1875 Sept 22), Washington Lodge No. 12, Georgetown, Apprentice

Yates, Lemuel
Proceedings 1873, pg 43 (1873 Oct 1), Washington Lodge No. 12, Georgetown, Apprentice

Yates, Lemuel F
Proceedings 1872, pg 26 (1872 Sept 24), Washington Lodge No. 12, Georgetown, Apprentice
Proceedings 1876, pg 35 (1876 Sept 20), Washington Lodge No. 12, Georgetown, Apprentice

Yates, W A
Proceedings 1874, pg 52 (1874 Sept 30) Grand Lodge of the District of Columbia

Colorado's Territorial Masons

Yates, Wm A
    Proceedings 1873, pg 60 (1873 Oct 1) Grand Lodge of the District of Columbia, Washington
    Proceedings 1874, pg 204 (1874 Sept 30) Grand Lodge of the District of Columbia, Washington
    Proceedings 1875, pg 96 (1875 Sept 22) Grand Lodge of District of Columbia, Washington
    Proceedings 1876, pg 54 (1876 Sept 20) Grand Lodge of the District of Columbia, Washington

Yelton, D P
    Proceedings 1876, pg 39 (1876 Sept 20), Collins Lodge No. 19, Fort Collins

Yelton, O P
    Proceedings 1874, pg 6 (1874 Sept 29), Collins Lodge No. 19, Fort Collins
    Proceedings 1874, pg 12 (1874 Jan 30), Collins Lodge No. 19, Fort Collins
    Proceedings 1874, pg 36 (1874 Sept 30) per diem
    Proceedings 1875, pg 86 (1875 Sept 22), Collins Lodge No. 19, Fort Collins

Yelton, Oliver P
    Proceedings 1873, pg 49 (1873 Oct 1), Collins Lodge No. 19, Fort Collins
    Proceedings 1874, pg 224 (1874 Sept 30), Collins Lodge No. 19, Fort Collins, Larimer County

Yonker, J T
    Proceedings 1861-1869, pg 167 (1866 Oct 2) Denver Lodge No. 5
    Proceedings 1861-1869, pg 149 (1865 Nov 7), Nevada Lodge No. 4, Nevadaville
    Proceedings 1861-1869, pg 193 (1867 Oct 8) Denver Lodge No. 5
    Proceedings 1861-1869, pg 223 (1868 Oct 7) Denver Lodge No. 5
    Proceedings 1861-1869, pg 305 (1869 Sept 29) Denver Lodge No. 5
    Proceedings 1870, pg 21 (1870 Sept 28), Denver Lodge No. 5, Denver
    Proceedings 1872, pg 20 (1872 Sept 24), Denver Lodge No. 5, Denver
    Proceedings 1873, pg 37 (1873 Oct 1), Denver Lodge No. 5, Denver
    Proceedings 1875, pg 76 (1875 Sept 22) Denver Lodge No. 5
    Proceedings 1875, pg 76 (1875 Sept 22) Denver Lodge No. 5, Reinstated
    Proceedings 1876, pg 31 (1876 Sept 20) Denver Lodge No. 5

York, Lewis
    Proceedings 1870, pg 74 (1827 June 18) United Grand Lodge of England

York, Noble J
    Proceedings 1873, pg 18 (1873 Oct 1), Occidental Lodge No. 20, Greeley
    Proceedings 1873, pg 50 (1873 Oct 1), Occidental Lodge No. 20, Greeley, Expelled

York, U J
    Proceedings 1871, pg 30 (1871 Sept 27), Occidental Lodge U D, Greeley

Young
    Proceedings 1873, pg 9 (1873 Sept 30), Ashlar Lodge U D, Colorado Springs
    Proceedings 1873, pg 10 (1873 Sept 30), Ashlar Lodge U D, Colorado Springs
    Proceedings 1873, pg 19 (1873 Oct 1), Ashlar Lodge U D, Colorado Springs
    Proceedings 1874, pg 13 (1874 Sept 29), Ashlar Lodge U D, Colorado Springs

Young, E T
    Proceedings 1872, pg 27 (1872 Sept 24), El Paso Lodge No. 13, Colorado City

Young, Frank C
    Proceedings 1872, pg 21 (1872 Sept 24), Denver Lodge No. 5, Denver
    Proceedings 1873, pg 38 (1873 Oct 1), Central Lodge No. 6, Central City
    Proceedings 1874, pg 212 (1874 Sept 30), Central Lodge No. 6, Central
    Proceedings 1875, pg 76 (1875 Sept 22), Central Lodge No. 6, Central City
    Proceedings 1876, pg 31 (1876 Sept 20), Central Lodge No. 6, Central City

Young, Jonathan
    Proceedings 1861-1869, pg 247 (1867 Nov 7) deceased

Young, T T
    Proceedings 1861-1869, pg 196 (1867 Oct 8), El Paso Lodge U D, Colorado City
    Proceedings 1861-1869, pg 228 (1868 Oct 7), El Paso Lodge No. 13, Colorado City
    Proceedings 1861-1869, pg 310 (1869 Sept 29), El Paso Lodge No. 13, Colorado City
    Proceedings 1870, pg 27 (1870 Sept 28), El Paso Lodge No. 13, Colorado City
    Proceedings 1871, pg 25 (1871 Sept 27), El Paso Lodge No. 13, Colorado City
    Proceedings 1874, pg 218 (1874 Sept 30), El Paso Lodge No. 13, Colorado Springs

Young, Trimble T
    Proceedings 1873, pg 43 (1873 Oct 1), El Paso Lodge No. 13, Colorado City
    Proceedings 1875, pg 82 (1875 Sept 22), El Paso Lodge No. 13, Colorado Springs, Stricken from the rolls

Young, W B
    Proceedings 1873, pg 8 (1873 Jan 23), Ashlar Lodge U D, Colorado Springs
    Proceedings 1873, pg 29 (1873 Oct 1), Ashlar Lodge U D, Colorado Springs

Young, William B
    Proceedings 1872, pg 35 (1872 Sept 24), Ashlar Lodge U D, Colorado Springs
    Proceedings 1875, pg 82 (1875 Sept 22), El Paso Lodge No. 13, Colorado Springs

Young, Wm B
Proceedings 1872, pg 13 (1872 Sept 24), Ashlar Lodge U D, Colorado Springs
Proceedings 1874, pg 30 (1874 Sept 29) case dismissed

Youngs
Proceedings 1861-1869, pg 284 (1867 June 11), Grand Master, Grand Lodge of Wisconsin

Younkers, J T
Proceedings 1874, pg 212 (1874 Sept 30), Denver Lodge No. 5, Denver, Stricken from the rolls

Yunker, J T
Proceedings 1871, pg 19 (1871 Sept 27) Denver Lodge No. 5

Zabriskie, E B
Proceedings 1871, pg 31 (1871 Sept 27), Argenta Lodge U D, Salt Lake City, Utah

Zang, Philip
Proceedings 1874, pg 212 (1874 Sept 30), Denver Lodge No. 5, Denver
Proceedings 1875, pg 76 (1875 Sept 22) Denver Lodge No. 5
Proceedings 1876, pg 31 (1876 Sept 20) Denver Lodge No. 5
Proceedings 1873, pg 37 (1873 Oct 1), Denver Lodge No. 5, Denver

Zates, L F
Proceedings 1861-1869, pg 227 (1868 Oct 7), Washington Lodge No. 12, Georgetown, Apprentice

Zehner, P
Proceedings 1861-1869, pg 230 (1868 Oct 7), Germania Lodge U D, Denver

Zehner, Philip
Proceedings 1874, pg 221 (1874 Sept 30), Cheyenne Lodge No. 16, Cheyenne, Wyoming Territory

Zerbe, J B
Proceedings 1861-1869, pg 168 (1866 Oct 2), Chivington Lodge No. 6, Central City
Proceedings 1861-1869, pg 194 (1867 Oct 8), Chivington Lodge No. 6, Central City
Proceedings 1861-1869, pg 224 (1868 Oct 7), Chivington Lodge No. 6, Central City
Proceedings 1861-1869, pg 307 (1869 Sept 29), Central Lodge No. 6, Central City, Dimitted

Zilligan, Joseph
Proceedings 1873, pg 42 (1873 Oct 1), Black Hawk Lodge No. 11, Black Hawk
Proceedings 1874, pg 216 (1874 Sept 30), Black Hawk Lodge No. 11, Black Hawk
Proceedings 1875, pg 80 (1875 Sept 22) Black Hawk Lodge No. 11
Proceedings 1876, pg 34 (1876 Sept 20) Black Hawk Lodge No. 11

Zobriski, Elias
Proceedings 1871, pg 8 (1871 Apr 8), Argenta Lodge U D, Salt Lake City

Zoellar, Philip
Proceedings 1875, pg 85 (1875 Sept 22) Pueblo Lodge No. 17
Proceedings 1874, pg 222 (1874 Sept 30), Pueblo Lodge No. 17, Pueblo, Pueblo County
Proceedings 1876, pg 39 (1876 Sept 20) Pueblo Lodge No. 17
Proceedings 1871, pg 28 (1871 Sept 27), Pueblo Lodge No. 17, Pueblo
Proceedings 1872, pg 31 (1872 Sept 24), Pueblo Lodge No. 17, Pueblo
Proceedings 1873, pg 47 (1873 Oct 1), Pueblo Lodge No. 17, Pueblo

Zulauf, H
Proceedings 1861-1869, pg 81 (1863 Apr 18) Denver Lodge No. 5, Rejected
Proceedings 1861-1869, pg 82 (1863 Apr 18) Denver Lodge No. 5, Rejected

Colorado's Territorial Masons